The Mendelssohn Companion

The Mendelssohn Companion

Edited by **Douglass Seaton**

GREENWOOD PRESS
Westport, Connecticut • London

Library of Congress Cataloging-in-Publication Data

The Mendelssohn companion / edited by Douglass Seaton.
    p. cm.
Includes bibliographical references and index.
ISBN 0–313–28445–8 (alk. paper)
1. Mendelssohn-Bartholdy, Felix, 1809–1847. 2. Composers—Germany—Biography.
I. Seaton, Douglass.
ML410.M5M55 2001
780′.92—dc21   00–033129
[B]

British Library Cataloguing in Publication Data is available.

Library of Congress Catalog Card Number: 00–033129
ISBN: 0–313–28445–8

First published in 2001

Greenwood Press, 88 Post Road West, Westport, CT 06881
An imprint of Greenwood Publishing Group, Inc.
www.greenwood.com

Printed in the United States of America

The paper used in this book complies with the
Permanent Paper Standard issued by the National
Information Standards Organization (Z39.48–1984).

10 9 8 7 6 5 4 3 2 1

Contents

Illustrations

Preface

Felix Mendelssohn Bartholdy (1809–1847), within his own lifetime perhaps more admired than any other composer in history, eventually became the most misunderstood of the major nineteenth-century composers. Beginning almost immediately after his death and continuing up to the middle of the twentieth century, opinion about him divided between idealizing hero-worship, largely in popular literature and especially in the English-speaking world, and vicious denigration by self-conscious progressives who made him their whipping boy and by outright anti-Semitists. Neither extreme encouraged serious, balanced understanding of the composer's life or his music.

Needed source material for the study of Mendelssohn and his works was lacking, as well. The collection of his works published by Breitkopf & Härtel under the editorial direction of Julius Rietz in the 1870s was by no means either complete or a proper critical edition. Many of Mendelssohn's letters were published in the late nineteenth century, some in tacitly expurgated form and in most cases either to contribute to the idealization of the composer or to promote the reputation of his correspondents.

For the most part, then, serious, scholarly work on Mendelssohn has begun in earnest only recently. Much of the music has been located, though a considerable quantity still remains to be published, and the critical editing is proceeding slowly (with the Leipzig Mendelssohn Ausgabe, which languished somewhat under the former German Democratic Republic but has recently been revitalized, and with the extensive editions of choral music by Carus in Stuttgart). Publication of a critical edition of the composer's vast correspondence is still stalled.

In the last few decades, however, a number of scholars have undertaken studies that have helped to bring Mendelssohn and his music into clearer focus and richer context. Study of the music manuscripts has brought to light much previously overlooked music. Compositional process studies have helped us to understand the composer's musical thinking. Reconsideration of the biography has allowed fairer and more realistic portrayal of the man.

The present volume offers overviews of both Mendelssohn's life and his music by a number of leading scholars. Our first three chapters help to place the composer into his intellectual context, discuss his family and social circle, and examine his professional activities, respectively. Later chapters, in turn, take up the major areas of his compositional work, providing new analytical observations, contextual perspectives, and interpretations. In addition to each chapter are provided Historical Views and Documents—a few familiar, some correcting or completing previously known items, and others little known. All are newly translated. Finally, we offer a major bibliographical tool for future research, an updated list of Mendelssohn's works, identifying the autograph manuscripts and the most important published editions.

The Mendelssohn Companion has been a long time in preparation. A word of heartfelt appreciation is certainly due to all the contributors, who labored hard and waited long for this result. Among the scholars who have provided information at various stages, gratitude is especially due to Karl-Heinz Köhler, Richard McNutt, Jeffrey Sposato, and Ralf Wehner. In addition, thanks go to many graduate students and research assistants at The Florida State University, who proofread copy, drafted translations, prepared music examples, tracked bibliographic citations, and probably performed many other now-forgotten tasks to help the book along: Reeves Ely Shulstad, James A. Grymes, Monika Hennemann, Michael Hix, Amy Keyser, Laura Moore, Michael O'Connor, and Lori Seitz.

Finally, I am grateful to the editorial staff at the Greenwood Press over the past several years, all of whom have been constantly patient and unflaggingly helpful, especially Alicia Merritt, Pamela St. Clair, and Nicole Cournoyer.

1

Neoclassicism, Romanticism, and Emancipation: The Origins of Felix Mendelssohn's Aesthetic Outlook

Leon Botstein

I

> In Mendelssohn's time classicism was no longer an inner necessity; it was merely a
> component of higher education and culture, approached from without, as was the art
> of classical antiquity.[1]

Paul Henry Lang wrote this in 1941. In the intervening half century, despite enormous strides in scholarship, little seems to have changed in our fundamental views on musical culture in the early nineteenth century. Lang's view that classicism, or rather neoclassicism, in Mendelssohn's time was out of step with the age, an artifact of social privilege and distant from the dominant "inner" spirit of the times, has persisted and continues to plague our capacity to understand and appreciate the greatness of Felix Mendelssohn.

Mendelssohn has been the subject of recent outstanding research and writing. The work of R. Larry Todd and Greg Vitercik on the young Mendelssohn confirms the composer's profound debt to classical models and his consummate and original command of sonata form. Despite these accomplishments, however, we find ourselves still uncertain about Mendelssohn's relationship to Romanticism and to his times.[2] Even Charles Rosen's magisterial work *The Romantic Generation*, despite its enormous virtues, does not help much in the case of Mendelssohn. Rosen argues that in Op. 7, for example, "the romantic sensibility" was "poorly adapted" to "the continuation of Classical techniques."

In the end, for Rosen, Mendelssohn is, above all, the inventor of "religious kitsch" in music. The decline in Mendelssohn's prestige since the composer's death in 1847 is therefore justified; it is the result of the claim that Mendelssohn excelled at creating "a simple beauty that raises no questions and does not attempt to puzzle us." His later works "charm but they neither provoke nor astonish." In the mature work of Mendelssohn, Rosen argues, religious feeling "dwindled into a simple feeling of awe." Despite "habitual craftsmanship" (Rosen refers here to the C-minor Trio), Mendelssohn's strategic choices (i.e., the use of a simulated drumroll) can be termed "shameless" in contrast to Beethoven. Mendelssohn's legacy is at best audible in works by César Franck and Camille Saint-Saëns.[3]

What is to be done in order to rescue Mendelssohn from such posthumous contempt and condescension? Are we content with the image of either a wunderkind who never fulfilled his early promise or, as Lang implies, a composer who worked "from without" in maintaining his relationship to classicism? Was Mendelssohn acting without the "inner necessity" characteristic of a new Romantic sensibility? Perhaps our grasp of Mendelssohn's place in the history of Romanticism also has changed little, in part because we have not looked more closely at the first three decades of the nineteenth century in German-speaking Europe, particularly in Berlin, and the interrelationship between neoclassicism and Romanticism.[4]

We ought to fashion a different way of hearing Mendelssohn, primarily the works written after 1835, by reconstructing a different notion of "Mendelssohn's time" and his role in it. Lang, like so many subsequent writers, focuses on Mendelssohn's 1829 performance of Bach's *St. Matthew Passion* as Mendelssohn's seminal contribution to the evolution of music in the nineteenth century[5]; it was part of a Romantic literary "search for the German past." Into this picture all of Mendelssohn's subsequent advocacy of Bach, Handel, Haydn, and Beethoven fits, but , in a positive sense, his compositional work does not.

The nearly exclusive focus on Mendelssohn's role in the evolution of nineteenth-century historicism distorts and obscures the culture and philosophical outlook in which Mendelssohn grew up, as well as his own aesthetic ambitions. The effort to reconcile Mendelssohn with early Romanticism, a "new mentality" that sought to come to terms with "classic form," continues to frame the scholarly debate. What happens if one takes an alternative route to understanding not only what Mendelssohn is about but why our traditional expectations seem perpetually disappointed? This chapter undertakes this task.

If one initially turns one's attention away from formal analytic issues tied to the history of early-nineteenth-century music, it becomes clear that classicism, understood as an aesthetic ideal rooted in philosophy and art, played a constructive and essential role in Mendelssohn's evolution as a composer. He came of age intellectually and emotionally in an environment in which classicism was, contrary to Lang, a profoundly powerful movement whose implications extended well beyond education and social class.

Classicism, apart from the arena of compositional procedures, was, for the young Felix Mendelssohn, an "inner necessity." It resulted in the unique defining characteristic of his career and aesthetic outlook.[6] "Classicism," inclusive of the neoclassical movements in architecture and the visual arts, provided the composer in his formative years with criteria for judging works of music and the function of music in society; therefore, neoclassicism as an ideology informed the self-image of a composer. It guided him throughout his life, often in conjunction with the sensibilities of Romanticism. This fact, in turn, separated him more profoundly from many of his contemporaries than otherwise might be apparent. Despite Mendelssohn's distance from contemporaries who have fared better in posterity, his musical achievement, taken on its own terms and not from within a dominant paradigm of Romanticism, turns out to have been greater than the notion of mere aesthetic simplicity suggests.

Mendelssohn's music retains the capacity to provoke and astonish in ways that were lost on successive nineteenth-century generations, particularly those profoundly influenced by Wagner. The aesthetic assumptions that emerged with the advent of modernism during the first half of the twentieth century did little to rehabilitate Mendelssohn's music. If we take Mendelssohn out of the "Romantic generation" and defy the narrow chronology of a music-historical narrative segmented out of cultural and social history and consider Mendelssohn anew, our expectations may change so that we can engage successfully, as Mendelssohn's contemporaries did, the greatness of the entire range of his compositional output.

The argument here seeks to supplement our current understanding of Mendelssohn's early musical training. We know that the young Mendelssohn had a "remarkable reverence for musical tradition."[7] It is also clear that in contrast to views held a century ago, the "great" works of the early years "reveal an extensive and carefully worked-out complex of strategies" reflecting Mendelssohn's profound command of classical style and sonata form. This skill resulted in "a synthesis of the formal principles of classical sonata style and the harmonic, thematic, and organizational characteristics of the romantic language." Whether that language actually can be termed "Romantic" is unclear. It is a fact, however, that Mendelssohn explicitly sought to use a classical heritage to fashion a contemporary equivalent; and therefore his elaborations of sonata style can properly be termed "Romantic" only in the narrow sense of chronology.[8]

Perhaps Mendelssohn's career and work can be more properly understood as the moral equivalents of the career and work of the greatest German architect of the age, Karl Friedrich Schinkel. Like Schinkel, Mendelssohn was a unique figure in the realization of an idealist neoclassicism, quite different from its eighteenth-century French predecessors. Early-nineteenth-century neoclassicism was not only directed against the nascent cultural and political Romanticism that followed Russia's defeat at Jena in 1806 but was designed to enhance a renewed, classically inspired construct of civic and theological humanism for a post-Napoleonic Germany. Like Mendelssohn, Schinkel, particularly in his neo-Gothic structures and his painterly output, bridged overt neoclassicism with a newer Romantic sensibility.

This view is based on the contact between Mendelssohn and four interrelated coincident historical factors:

1. The relationship of Felix Mendelssohn to neoclassicism in painting, architecture, and sculpture in the early decades of the nineteenth century, up to the early 1830s, in Berlin.[9]

2. The impact on the young Mendelssohn of a widespread and general allegiance among the elite of the first and second generations of the nineteenth century (an allegiance that, curiously enough, was sustained throughout German-Jewish history among emancipated and acculturated Jews) to classical antiquity and aesthetic neoclassicism. The high-water marks of neoclassicism in late eighteenth- and early nineteenth-century German art and culture coincided with the first and most promising and optimistic era of religious toleration and Jewish emancipation and assimilation.[10] The decline in the prestige of neoclassicism and the rise of a "new mentality"—inclusive of Romanticism—coincided in the nineteenth century with the emergence of new forms of anti-Semitism. These made their appearance particularly after 1806 and 1819, the year of the Hep Hep riots, which affected Mendelssohn directly, notably in an incident in 1824.[11] Mendelssohn's resistance to much of what we now praise in Romanticism and his struggle to compete with it and adapt it can be connected to this crucial biographical circumstance. Furthermore, this dynamic tension suggests that his achievement in religious music was something more than "kitsch."[12]

3. The influence of the late Goethe on Mendelssohn. This demands another look. If one takes into account Goethe's views on aesthetic matters during the mid-1820s, as witnessed by the conversations with Eckermann, one can see how close the attitudes of Goethe and the mature Mendelssohn were. The cause of this affinity was not only psychological; it does not rest purely on the aura of Goethe's stature and approval and the awe of authority that Goethe must have inspired in the parents of Mendelssohn and in the young Mendelssohn himself, the prize pupil of Goethe's close friend, Zelter. Rather, by the time Mendelssohn met Goethe, he had already developed a philosophical outlook that the prejudices that Goethe held in his later years helped to confirm and deepen.

    The influence of the aging Goethe on any artist or writer born in 1809 has to be deemed conservative. A comparison of Mendelssohn with Schumann makes this point especially clear. Two of Schumann's most decisive literary and philosophical influences were Jean Paul Richter and Wolfgang Menzel, both of whom represented an explicit challenge to Goethe's authority and influence.[13] Goethe offered Mendelssohn a decisive validation of a neoclassical outlook and its potential to serve as the basis of a nonatavistic musical aesthetic. If the result of this particular avenue of inquiry is to inspire us to rehear Mendelssohn's music as parallel to the second part of Goethe's *Faust*, then we will have made considerable progress.

4. Mendelssohn's education and intellectual inheritance. What differentiated Mendelssohn from his contemporaries in the crucial generation of composers born around 1809 and 1810—particularly Robert Schumann—was more than mere "higher education and culture" (from which Schumann also benefited); the difference rested in the specific character of his intellectual formation. The young Felix Mendelssohn's classical education will be considered alongside the considerable legacy of philosophical speculation (defined in the terms set by his grandfather, Moses Mendelssohn) to which he was exposed. The link between grandfather and grandson rests in the transmission of an eighteenth-century philosophical tradition, in which aesthetics are central to a unified philosophical system of ethics and epistemology.[14]

It is probable that elements of Moses Mendelssohn's aesthetics were handed down in the form of informal attitudes regarding works of art, music, and civic culture evident in conversations in Felix's parental home. More to the point, hints of Moses Mendelssohn's influence reappear in Felix Mendelssohn's letters and, above all, his music.[15]   What linked Moses Mendelssohn to Felix were a fundamental conception of art, the determining criteria of aesthetic judgment, and the construct of the moral and civic function of art.

From the perspective of the early nineteenth century, Felix Mendelssohn's philosophical position harked back to Lord Shaftesbury (1671–1713), Jean Baptiste Dubos (1670–1742), and Christian Wolff (1679–1754), not forward to Hegel and Schopenhauer, despite the affinity between Schleiermacher and Felix Mendelssohn concerning the relationship between music and religion. Schleiermacher's views on this matter are not entirely dissimilar from Moses Mendelssohn's. Despite the vast differences in their respective philosophical outlooks, Schleiermacher may have been influenced by Moses Mendelssohn.

The conclusion from an investigation of these four factors is that the particular form that Mendelssohn gave to "classicism" took its inspiration from neoclassicism in the visual arts and late-eighteenth-century philosophy.   These provided Mendelssohn with not only a strategy for composition but emotional and ethical purpose. Mendelssohn's evolution of a neoclassic ideology helps to explain the trajectory, in terms of formal models and internal struggles, of his career after the mid-1830s. It can illuminate the problems that have plagued his posthumous reputation to this day as an early Romantic figure, placed alongside Byron, Novalis, or Schlegel. To put the contrast a different way: as a mature composer, Schumann set Byron's *Manfred* to music; Mendelssohn, in his prime, set new German translations of Sophocles's *Antigone* and *Oedipus at Colonus*.

II

The art historians Ernst Kris and Otto Kurz, in their seminal work on the genesis and meaning of the traditions of artist biographies, noted that a biographical tale of humble origins, chance discovery, and childhood virtuosity is essential to secure a posthumous aura of greatness for an artist.[16] Mendelssohn possessed only one of these, precocity. The wealth of his family, its prominence, and the quality of his education made him the object of envy in his own time (e.g., Schumann and Wagner) and, tragically, forever since. No one can seem to forgive the privilege and apparent domestic tranquillity into which he was born. Mendelssohn's biography will never fit our seemingly oppositional image of the artist; our allegiances to the construct of the artist as outsider and angry rebel, socially obscure but self-made, will never be satisfied by Mendelssohn. His biography supports our expectation that his music somehow is merely affirmative and unproblematic.

Although Mendelssohn's biographers always place stress on the 1829 Bach performance, there are two more significant moments in the 1820s, before the *St. Matthew Passion* revival, that lead us away from the traditional association between Mendelssohn and the Bach revival of mid-nineteenth-century Romanticism.   The first is Mendelssohn's 1826 translation of a comedy by Terence, and the second is Mendelssohn's participation in a celebration of the

300th anniversary of the death of Albrecht Dürer in April 1828.[17]

The fact of the Terence translation is well known. It is cited by all biographers, primarily as a way of indicating the high level of the private tutoring that the young Mendelssohn received, the range of his general education, and the versatility of his talent.[18] The circumstances surrounding the translation are not notable. It was done to fulfill a requirement so that Mendelssohn could enroll in the university. The choice of the play was equally unexceptional. The *Andria* (otherwise known as the *Girl [or Maiden; or Lady] from Andros*) was a favorite vehicle for the teaching of Latin to young people in late-eighteenth- and early-nineteenth-century German-speaking Europe. The *Andria* was edited and translated in Germany more than twice as often as any of the other of the surviving Terence plays.[19] Ten editions of the Latin text of the play came out in the fifty-year period before 1826, as opposed to four for the next two most popular Terence plays, *Adelphoe* and *Eunuchus*.

But the translation itself and its publication are significant and worthy of attention. In her 1988 monograph on the reception of Plautus and Terence in the nineteenth century, Barbara Kes spends considerable time highlighting the originality of the young Mendelssohn's translation.[20] It represented an influential turning point within the world of nineteenth-century classical studies and education. The sixteen-year-old Mendelssohn sought to retain the metric structure of the Latin and the poetic form but avoid archaisms in language and usage. Unlike many eighteenth-century versions, there was no radical attempt to modernize the play or even dispense with its verse form.

Likewise, Mendelssohn resisted the notion of rendering German in such a manner that the play would assume a rhetoric reminiscent of the Latin original. In other words, he attempted to adapt a strict classical model by the explicit deployment of modern language and usage. At the heart of the endeavor was the integration of classical verse proportions and form into common, everyday usage; the translation sought to transform and elevate, through a classical framework, the modern freely, without denying its particularity. As K. L. Heyse, Mendelssohn's tutor, put it in his introduction, Mendelssohn used modern expressions, colloquial German words and usage; he "substituted the new" without allowing "the color of antiquity" to disappear entirely; Mendelssohn achieved a delicate synthesis, not a "total modernization" but a "revision of classical material for the contemporary theater."[21]

The quality of the translation and the elaborate introduction written by Heyse testify to the fact that this was no mere act of vanity nor the result of a tutor's work, pawned off as the offhand effort of the famous scion of a rich and powerful family. The sensibility of the composer is audible throughout the German translation. His musicality and experience in adapting classical models in composition under Zelter's tutelage showed its mark. Mendelssohn's pride in the result is best demonstrated by the fact that he sent one of the first copies to Goethe.[22]

Clearly, Mendelssohn, already an experienced performer and composer with a keen interest in opera, had his eye on the performance possibilities and the theatrical dimensions of the comedy. The effect of the play on the audience was uppermost in his mind. Indeed, the result is elegant. The challenge of achieving an unobtrusive retention of the classical character that almost subconsciously evoked the original without displaying the patina of antiquity, by using metrical devices and structural conventions, was alluring to Mendelssohn as an analogy to the demands of modern musical composition. Here was a test case for the normative formal claims of neoclassicist aesthetics. Could classical models be adapted to modernity, thereby avoiding the trap of historicist aesthetics, in which the demands of each age dictated the creation of new forms (a position more akin to Schumann's own efforts before the early 1840s)?

Mendelssohn came to this Terence play, its language, and the task of translation with a definite affinity. The translation was clearly more than a required exercise, dutifully completed. Apart from the elegant simplicity of the Latin, which helped make Terence an obligatory author in the teaching of Latin, it was also the good-humored, humanistic moralism of the play that appealed to Mendelssohn. Prior to the Renaissance the symmetry between stylistic excellence and moral probity in Terence made him, as opposed to Plautus, the favorite example of a Roman culture compatible with Christian virtue. In the Middle Ages, extracts of Terence's plays became woven into popular theological treatises. Terence was considered a healthy carryover in the classical heritage of pre-Christian antiquity.[23]

During the Renaissance the emphasis of praise shifted to the exemplary formal properties of Terence in terms of dramatic structure,[24] but the legacy of medieval approval was not entirely forgotten. When the extension of literacy and classical education became matters of state policy in Prussia in the late eighteenth century, the humanism of Terence was not overlooked. Unlike much of the classical literary heritage, it was deemed fit (and perhaps even enjoyable) for the young to read, given its spirit of enlightenment and tolerance. For the young Mendelssohn, Terence's moral of the happy reconciliation of warring families, strangers, and foreigners was strikingly appropriate. He had grown up in a family caught between its legendary Jewish heritage and its newfound Protestant identity. During his formative adolescent years he witnessed the first significant, overt tensions between Jews and non-Jews after decades of rapid progress in assimilation and acculturation among the Jewish elite of Berlin.[25]

With a renewed awareness of anti-Semitism around him in the late 1820s threatening the very premises of his own father's strategy in life, it is hard to see how the moral of Terence's comedy could not appeal to Felix. Furthermore, in terms of its ethical significance as a work of theater, translating Terence opened up the opportunity to test, independently of music, a vital aesthetic hypothesis. Would it be possible to utilize effectively a normative form, a classical model, with a modern audience, thereby ensuring the success of the play's ethical substance without entirely violating its aesthetic properties?

Mendelssohn was sixteen when he began to work on the translation. He had already written a substantial amount of music and also had studied and absorbed a great deal from so-called classical musical models. What may have caught his eye in the Terence play, which inclined him to pursue further his study of it and the translation project, was the play's famous prologue. Terence used the prologue to address his critics, who accused him of lack of originality and of unsuccessfully mixing up more than one model from Menander.[26]

In the *Andria* Terence came forward with a truly Mendelssohn-like defense of himself. His purpose, he declared, was to please his audience. In terms of Mendelssohn, this directly fits the aesthetic principles of Dubos, whose 1719 *Critical Reflections on Poetry and Painting* influenced eighteenth-century German aesthetic thought, particularly that of Moses Mendelssohn.[27] In Dubos's work, aesthetics becomes less the province of the study of the work of art alone, divorced from its audience; rather, it begins to look at the consequences of art and the impressions and perceptions of art from the point of view of the spectator. A connection is forged between formal considerations and the normative judgment of the quality and character of an artwork, on the one hand, and the acts of hearing and seeing by the spectator, on the other. For all of Mendelssohn's career, the writing of music remained tied to this dynamic, reciprocal concept of the work of art. The work itself exists, in terms of judgment, in its realization by its audience. Writing and performing music were undertaken with contemporaries in mind as a realizing audience. The aesthetic whole was incomplete without creating what Ernst Cassirer termed the "mirror in which both artist and spectator find themselves reflected."[28]

In the prologue Terence defended himself by making distinctions among "content" (*Inhalt*), "expression" (*Ausdruck*), and "manner" or "style" (*Behandlung*). Terence argued that he took freely from more than one Menander play, as did Plautus and Ennius. Like them, by "freely" combining discrete virtues from different models, he met both the demands of artistic originality and adherence to normative formal criteria. Here Mendelssohn disagreed with Terence's conservative critics of the day ("Tadler dunkler Fehlerlosigkeit," critics of a murky perfection) and defended, as does Terence, with irony, a surface "Regellosigkeit" (freedom from rules).[29] This freedom from rules—the failure to replicate the ancient text—actually becomes a more profound realization of the ideals of neoclassical aesthetics. Innovation within tradition and the seemingly eclectic appropriation of models became the hallmark not only of the Terence translation but of the composition of music (e.g., particularly a decade later in *Paulus*, in which Mendelssohn employed a wide and disparate set of models).

In Terence, Mendelssohn found a classical model of a young, gifted poet who came of age in a self-consciously derivative period. With Menander and Plautus behind him (read, in Mendelssohn's case, Bach and Beethoven), the task for Terence was to generate an elegant and innovative adaptation, designed to reach the contemporary audience. The result in Mendelssohn's case, as in Terence's, of the close study of prior models was a refined style and musical language, a clear reference to formal precedents, and an overt contemporary, didactic, ethical agenda. We shall return to Mendelssohn's attraction to the ethical aspect of art, when the legacy of Moses Mendelssohn is analyzed. Felix's youthful affection for Terence suggests that, like his grandfather, the young composer resisted a philosophical tendency evident in early-nineteenth-century aesthetics to delimit and dispute a clear linkage between art and morality.

III

The second event entirely overshadowed by the 1829 Bach performance was Mendelssohn's participation in a tercentenary celebration of Albrecht Dürer, which took place in Berlin on 18 April 1828. The centerpiece was a lyrical drama in verse by Konrad Levezow, which Mendelssohn set to music. The event took place in the Odeon of the Singakademie. Apart from the presence of an orchestra, chorus, and singers (including the young Devrient) there was, as might well be expected, given the subject matter at hand, a plethora of visual elements. In back of the orchestra were decorations designed and executed by Schinkel, Schadow, and Tieck. There was a new statue of Dürer by Wichmann. In the side rooms were allegorical sculptures representing painting, geometry, perspective, and military design and architecture. Other elements were paintings by H. Daehling and by Schinkel's old friend, the decorative painter Gropius.[30]

A word about these individuals is in order. Karl Friedrich Schinkel (1781–1841) was, of course, the dominant architect of the age, whose work defined nineteenth-century Berlin and Potsdam.[31] In 1828, at the height of his career, he was in the midst of the building of the great Potsdam Schloss Charlottenhof. The Berlin Schauspielhaus was nearly a decade old; so, too, was the famous Schlossbrücke and the Neue Wache. Schinkel's designs transformed Berlin and set the standard for the interior design, stage design, and architecture of his age. His achievements would become the focal point, throughout the nineteenth century, for the opposition to, and the emulation of, German and Austrian architectural historicism. Schinkel remained at the center of the debate, for all sides, during the emergence of modernism in the beginning of this century.

After a brief turn away from neoclassicism (in reaction against the linkage between eighteenth-century France and classicist aesthetics) in search of another source for a new national German architectural aesthetic, in 1825 Schinkel completed the famous painting *A View of Greece in its Prime*, which marked the start of a new, mature phase of neoclassical work. By the late 1820s Schinkel had emerged not only as a proponent of classical aesthetics, in the formalist sense, exemplified by the great 1830 "New" Museum on the Lustgarten (now called *Altes Museum*); he was convinced, as his 1825 canvas suggests, that Greece offered German Europe a model of a civic community. He sought to "ennoble human relationships" through design.[32]

As his remarkably modernist, but less neoclassical-looking, Schloss Tegel from 1824 suggests, the task of the architect was to think of form beyond normative, geometric, ahistorical terms. One could not merely imitate the ancients, since the civic echo in design through its use was a necessary component of architecture. Indeed, the task, as Barry Bergdoll has put it, was, through contemporary art and design, to "effect a synthesis between the daily civic life of the ancients . . . and the spirituality of Christianity" for modern times. Schinkel, like Alexander and Wilhelm von Humboldt, believed that the Greeks were exemplary.[33] Classical antiquity could serve as a model for modernity and for the moral and aesthetic cultivation of an ideal community.[34]

Mendelssohn, as his participation in the Dürer ceremony makes plain, was in contact with the leading philosophical and artistic personalities of Berlin in the 1820s. Furthermore, insofar as music and architecture were understood by contemporaries to be closely related art forms, not only in terms of analogous formal procedures that each employed but in their necessarily dual civic (public) and domestic (private) character, it is probable that Schinkel's conception of architecture, particularly after 1825 in its decidedly neoclassical celebration of the Greek civic ideal, was influential on the young Mendelssohn. The project of a synthesis between the classical humanism of antiquity and modern German spirituality that defined Schinkel's work and the intense political and cultural debate that surrounded it are mirrored in Mendelssohn's tireless engagement with music as a civic, religious, and political enterprise, first in Düsseldorf, then in Leipzig and Berlin in the 1840s. Key to this enterprise was finding, in music, a parallel or moral equivalent to the adaptation of classical models in architecture and their integration with Christian ideals. If the completion of the Cologne Cathedral remains associated with Schumann and the "Rhenish" Symphony, then Schinkel's 1830 Lustgarten Museum and the Nikolaikirche in Potsdam should be linked to Mendelssohn's *Lobgesang* (the Symphony no. 2).

The rest of the painters represented in the Dürer event knew one another through Schinkel and constituted the core of Berlin's neoclassical aesthetic idealists.[35] Johann Gottfried Schadow (1764–1850) was the most famous Berlin sculptor, who, since 1816, had directed the Berlin Academy. Schadow coliaborated with Schinkel on the Neue Wache. His son, Friedrich Wilhelm, also a painter, became a friend of Felix's and drew one of the most famous portraits of the composer. The elder Schadow is most famous for the reliefs on the Branden-burg Gate. Christian Friedrich Tieck (1776–1851), brother of the writer, was also a friend of Schinkel's who collaborated with him, particularly on the 1830 new museum. Tieck was a student of Schadow and David in Paris and remained rooted in Berlin neoclassicism. He worked on the interiors of the new castle at Weimar and made famous busts of Goethe and Alexander von Humboldt. Like Mendelssohn, part of his aesthetic development involved a seminal sojourn in Italy. He also taught at the Berlin Academy.

There were two Wichmanns, Karl Friedrich (1775–1836) and Ludwig Wilhelm (1784–1859). These brothers also studied with Schadow. They worked together and produced sculpture for the Berlin opera, the museum, and Schinkel's Potsdam Nikolaikirche. Karl Wilhelm Gropius (1793–1870) was a painter who opened a theatrical business using the diorama in Berlin. Schinkel lived with Gropius for a time after 1807 and designed illusionistic pictures for him. Gropius also did the decorative painting in Schinkel's Schauspielhaus and was famed as a caricaturist.

At the Dürer festival, in addition to Mendelssohn's musical setting of a Levezow poem, took place a performance of a Mendelssohn symphony and a public oration. Levezow's poem to Dürer and the commentary on it stressed three interrelated, salient points. First, Dürer represented the great ancestor ("Ahne") of German art. Second, he expressed his religious faith not with "the barrenness of systematic sectarianism" but with "poetic spirit and poetic truth." Dürer embodied the "spirit of truth." "Nature" was his only model; "truth" guided him, and he sought the "light of knowledge." Third, as if to bolster further the linkage between Dürer and classical antiquity, Ovid, Praxiteles, and Lysippus were brought to bear as points of comparison.[36] Dürer took over where classical antiquity left off: he transplanted the virtues of classical antiquity onto German soil. The Dürer celebration mirrored Schinkel's agenda of fusing antiquity with German Christianity.

The April 1828 celebration shared attributes with the Terence translation. Among these was the conviction Heyse, Mendelssohn's tutor, expressed in his preface to the translation that "no other living language possesses the capacity that German displays to reproduce, without sacrificing its unique characteristics, the form and expression of classical Latin." No living modern language, Heyse wrote, has "demonstrated its ability" to realize so well the necessary "synthesis of content and form" that exists in an exemplary manner in great classical works of art.[37] Through modern German, the transcendent unity of a poetic work can be communicated so that the "local and habitual" can be relinquished and the reader rendered close to what was once foreign and strange. The translation permitted the reader to appropriate the normative aesthetic essence of the work through his or her own German thought and feeling.

The cultural patriotism of the translation was identical to that of the Dürer celebration. Modern Germany was the heir of antiquity, both Rome and Greece. In Rome, classical Greek culture had been amalgamated and renewed. Likewise, in the contemporary German world, language, spirituality, and culture would continue what Dürer had begun: the extension of classical aesthetic virtues, integrated, with a tolerant Christian faith, into the modernity of Northern Europe.

Beyond this transparent rhetorical mixture of idealism and chauvinism, one needs to consider the visual background to Mendelssohn's music. No doubt, like other privileged, wealthy, assimilated Jewish families in Berlin in the early nineteenth century, the dominant interior and exterior aesthetic taste was neoclassical.[38] The public display in 1828 at the Dürer celebration of a close affinity between visual neoclassicism, as practiced in the 1820s in Berlin, and Mendelssohn's music deserves closer scrutiny, however. We know that Mendelssohn was an admirer of the great neoclassical sculptor Bertel Thorwaldsen (1770–1844), but the linkage to Schinkel, Tieck, and Gropius suggests further that Mendelssohn's judgments regarding beauty and form, even in music, were influenced by his eye. Insofar as they were influenced by the visual, the architecture, design, and painting to which Mendelssohn was attracted took on a powerful neoclassical cast. The idea that Mendelssohn was indeed susceptible to visual models is supported by his own lifelong activity as a visual artist and his evident love of, and fascination with, drawing and painting.[39] The self-conscious mix of adaptation and deviation in the use of classical and Renaissance models in the work of Schadow and Thordwaldsen is suggestive of Mendelssohn's point of view toward his own craft as a musician. This further suggests that for Mendelssohn, in contrast to Schumann or Chopin, the notion of music as a "Romantic" art, in the sense of Wackenroder or Jean Paul and even Caspar David Friedrich, remained somewhat more distant. Music possessed for Mendelssohn its own unique, precise mode of being, but the aesthetics by which it was to be understood shared, by analogy, normative principles governing architecture and painting in the manner defined by Winckelmann in 1755.

IV

This brings us to the influence of Goethe. Mendelssohn visited Goethe and corresponded with him.[40] These encounters doubtless deepened and confirmed many of the young composer's views. Crucial in this regard were the attitudes of the aging Goethe toward contemporary art, music, and poetry.

The young Mendelssohn met a living legend who saw himself as being out of step with his own age. Goethe took exception to Schumann's hero Wolfgang Menzel (1798–1873), the critic and literary historian, with whom he associated the ever-present "deficiency in character" found throughout new literary works. Furthermore, in his attitudes and judgments in his later years, Goethe returned with regularity to his own version of neoclassic aesthetics. In 1805 Goethe wrote his famous essay on Winckelmann. In it Goethe characterized modern man as launching out "into infinity" only to return, "if he is lucky," to a limited point, as opposed to the ancients, who "remain firmly within the pleasant confines of the beautiful world." The ancients represented for Goethe the apogee of healthy creativity, when "all resources are united," when man, functioning as a "totality," feels himself "in the world as in a vast, beautiful, worthy and valued whole." Modern man, however, is isolated, reduced to working on several levels simultaneously but without achieving the potential harmony realized by the ancients. Winckelmann is put forth as a model of how a modern man can elude this fate. Winckelmann vindicated the creative power of neoclassicism; he used his love of antiquity to transcend mere academicism and rigid principles and realized the classical ideal in his life and work in modern terms.[41]

By the 1820s Goethe had drifted closer to a standpoint of cultural pessimism. He complained to Eckermann as early as 1824 that the moderns were too enamored of mere knowledge and abstract concepts. Contemplating an ancient carving, Goethe lamented the absence of the "purely natural, purely naive" motivation, the "grace" befitting the making of great art.[42] The concept of the loss of "grace" comes back in Goethe's discussion of Sophocles. This was not lost on Mendelssohn, whose explicit desire to communicate a love of gracefulness carried with it an ethical purpose. As Goethe lamented in 1826, "In our bad times, where is the need for excellence? Where are the sensory capacities to embrace it?"[43] In Goethe's later conversations, the admonition to take one's inspiration, as Raphael did, from antiquity, recurs over and over.

The crucial dimension of the outlook of the Goethe whom the young Mendelssohn played for, got to know, and corresponded with is best expressed in a passage from a conversation with Eckermann in 1827. Goethe observed, "In order to satisfy the need to find some exemplary model, we must always return to the ancient Greeks, in whose works the beautiful human being is always portrayed. Everything else we must consider as historical, and extract, as far as possible, the good contained within it." In terms of aesthetic form, in the ancient world, form in art achieved its "highest point of development."[44]

Goethe's distinction between the normative and the historical is crucial to understanding the aesthetic development of the young Mendelssohn. Goethe's dichotomy itself was an extension of Winckelmann's famous 1755 contrast between Dutch genre painting and ancient art. The Dutch were content to practice a form of representational realism. The Greeks went beyond the mere imitation of nature and found a way to realize "universal beauty and ideal images."[45] Goethe accepts this premise but extends it further by positing a theory of history that renders each successive era after antiquity as being trapped in its own limited frame of reference. The normative achievement of the Greeks, which was to realize fully the immanent possibilities of art, constituted, in retrospect, a unique suprahistorical truth. It was then the task of modern artists to utilize this exemplary model in their own time and thereby to transcend their own specific but narrow historical context by, in effect, using it against itself.

The use of the term "historical" was not arbitrary. Goethe took a dim view of the culture of his day and took issue with the evolution of early-nineteenth-century historical and empirical aesthetics, which tended to glorify subjectivity and therefore historicize taste and aesthetic judgment. Against the nascent ideology of contingent standards of taste or of a dialectical process of historical unfolding, Goethe maintained that no matter the significance of Shakespeare or Molière, the idea of progress after antiquity was not applicable to the arts. The issue was not only aesthetic but ethical as well; as he argued, "Greek tragedy made the beauty of morality its subject."[46]

Goethe's aesthetic categories and judgments, however, found their limit in the arena of music. In aesthetic theory, insofar as music as an art form remained subordinate to language, as in song, opera, and theater (i.e., incidental music), confronting the issue of music as such could be postponed. It had yet to be fully emancipated from language. With the development of a tradition of pure instrumental music during the eighteenth century, the issue of the place of music in aesthetic theory, particularly neoclassical theory, emerged as a seemingly paradoxical problem. Only later in the nineteenth century, after the death of Mendelssohn and in part due to Mendelssohn's advocacy during his tenure at the Gewandhaus, did Viennese classicism assume a place closely analogous to the normative status that antiquity held in the plastic arts in the eighteenth century.

Music occupied a special place, historically speaking. Curiously, it was an art form with no long history of formalist logic of its own. Despite Goethe's penchant for the music of Haydn's generation, no evident yardstick was at hand. Compared to painting, sculpture, architecture, poetry, or drama—the primary arenas of the neoclassical debate—it was a peculiarly modern art. Therefore, it lent itself to the appropriation by a new generation as the quintessentially "Romantic" art befitting a new age.

The influence of Goethe on Mendelssohn reinforced the impression made by the classicism that Mendelssohn encountered in Berlin. If music was to operate along lines that were rational and yet participate in a normative philosophical, ethical, and civic concept of beauty, it could not be merely an art form tied to its particular ephemeral historical moment. In order to escape being considered just "historical" in Goethe's terms, modern music had to have its own history with its own analogues to the Greeks. It had to find its own suprahistorical formalist center. It was precisely the influence of Goethe's anti-Romantic, neoclassical aesthetics that sustained Mendelssohn's interest in Bach in the late 1820s. By re-creating a normative history for music and by elevating the generations of Bach, Mozart, and Beethoven, a synthesis of normative criteria and contemporaneity, similar to the task of the Terence translation, could be fashioned. Indeed, Mendelssohn's approach to Terence prefigured and mirrored his approach to Bach. Mendelssohn's attention to history constituted an antihistoricist use of history. History was used against itself as a process by which the aesthetic practices of a particular era could be segmented and declared normative for subsequent eras. This became Mendelssohn's ambition, both in his youth and in his maturity.

Goethe lacked a coherent, direct answer to the place of music in aesthetics. For Goethe, music was either analogous to architecture or demonic, impervious to understanding, and endowed with an immediacy that made it difficult to come to terms with. It had magical, but ultimately irrational, properties. Beyond the perception that in music's history models similar to those celebrated by Winckelmann and Goethe had been found, for Mendelssohn there had to be a broader framework into which music could fit, as part of the harmonious totality that so appealed to Goethe in his old age and to Winckelmann, Humboldt, and Schinkel. In order to meet this challenge, Mendelssohn turned to the traditions of his grandfather.

V

The legacy of the comprehensive, eighteenth-century philosophical systematic tradition into which music could fit lay close to home. How much of Moses Mendelssohn's writings the young Felix knew is not certain, but if one judges from his later years, it is more than likely that he read his grandfather's German-language philosophical writings, particularly those on aesthetics. Even if he had not, the ideas in them would not have been foreign, given the high regard in which

Moses Mendelssohn's aesthetics were held and the extent to which they were cited well into the 1820s.

Before connecting Moses Mendelssohn's views on art and music to the development of Felix Mendelssohn's aesthetic credo, it is important to acknowledge the role that neoclassicism played among Jews in the two generations before Felix, those of Moses and Abraham Mendelssohn. Emancipation and recognition of the rights of Jews outside the ghetto coincided with the rise of aesthetic neoclassicism in Germany. Insofar as Napoleon was responsible for a broader-based emancipation of the Jews east of the Rhine, the reaction against neoclassicism and the rise of Romanticism in the early nineteenth century can be linked to the evident synthesis of anti-Semitism and post-1806 German nationalism. France was closely connected to neoclassicism around 1800. It was therefore no accident that the German form of neoclassicism evident in the 1820s in Berlin sought to take on an explicit nationalistic bent, as Heyse's comments and the Dürer celebration make plain.

Prior and subsequent to any nineteenth-century linkage between nationalism and aesthetic taste, however, neoclassicism retained special appeal among emancipated Jews. An attractive symmetry flourished between the revival of the taste for a pre-Christian civilization and the spread of tolerance toward the Jews. In an enlightened context, the Jews assumed the status of an ancient civilization, contemporaneous with Greece and Rome. Antiquity had not been monotheistic but religiously syncretistic. Greece and Rome were held up as cultures that celebrated the rational and the religiously tolerant in an explicitly anti-Catholic manner. Well before the Romantic revival of Catholicism, the links between the rediscovery of antiquity and religious toleration were clear.

Neoclassicism made circumventing the entire Christian era nearly possible in the pursuit of secular *Bildung* among Jews.[47] Moses Mendelssohn, by using Socratic dialogue and other classical forms as literary models, was able to enter the conduct of philosophy without conversion or a fundamental encounter with Christian doctrine. In the plastic arts, in poetry, literature, and philosophy, neoclassicism and the veneration of classical heritage were ideally suited for Jews eager to enter Christian society and letters without abandoning their heritage.

With the collapse of the Enlightenment, the onset of the Terror, and the invasions of Napoleon, all this became less and less plausible in German-speaking Europe. Nationalism brought with it a revivalist construct of a German heritage that centered on a spiritual Christian heritage, both Catholic and Protestant. The conversion of Moses Mendelssohn's children to Catholicism (Dorothea Schegel) and Protestantism (Felix's parents and their children) bears testimony to the difficulties that the nineteenth century brought to the strategy of acculturation and assimilation without a direct acceptance of the heritage of Christianity. Nevertheless, throughout Western European history, in German-speaking lands, the affinity between Jewish intellectuals and artists and classical learning and art forged in the crucible of the 1780s and 1790s never quite vanished. It would reappear most visibly a century after Felix Mendelssohn in the case of Sigmund Freud.[48]

To return to Moses Mendelssohn's aesthetics: the first crucial characteristic was Mendelssohn's conception of human reason as a static category. Moses Mendelssohn saw no conflict between the historical and the rational. All temporal and empirical experience is part of God's unity, which reason alone cannot fully penetrate. Second, aesthetics, much in the sense of Wolff's work, was part of a unified system, in which faith and intuition play a crucial role. Reason alone is not sufficient, even though reason and the divine are not in conflict. Ultimately, Mendelssohn differed from Lessing in the matter of the significance of historical change in aesthetic judgment. Differentiation, particularly through historical change, despite the significance that it held for the individual, was, in the end, a subsidiary phenomenon. Underlying all historical change was the essential unity that mirrored the essence of God.

For Moses Mendelssohn, aesthetic criteria were related to epistemological questions. These became contingent on psychological issues of perception and response and, in turn, were connected to matters of ethics and morals. Drawing on the evolution of aesthetic theory in the eighteenth century beyond the realm of a formalist consideration of the work of art, Mendelssohn turned to the issues of effect and cognition in art; he dealt with the origins and criteria of aesthetic taste and judgment rather than aesthetic properties within the work. Furthermore, in a rational system these needed to be linked to the consequences of art on the beholder. In 1771 he argued that rules of beauty had to possess parallels in psychology. Art for Mendelssohn assumed significance because it connected to a person's unique combination of reason, intuition, and sense perception. Art demanded imagination that went beyond the apperception of representation and realism. Therefore, all the varieties of aesthetic expression were uniquely human phenomena, all reconcilable with divine unity.

Anticipating Schleiermacher and his own grandson Felix, Moses Mendelssohn attributed to the psychological processes of aesthetic perception a capacity to augment and transcend the limits of reason. In this way the individual could come closer to a moral sensibility and to faith. Faith was enhanced by the sensibility generated through aesthetic contemplation, particularly of harmony, perfection, and the infinite. Therefore Mendelssohn accepted a notion of the sublime and integrated, through a psychological approach, notions of the effect of art into what formally constituted a work of great art. The assumption of a normative psychological framework of perception had its mirror image in the criteria that governed aesthetic creations, those that evoked the fullest apperception of the sublime and brought the beholder emotionally closer to ethical truth and the recognition of the divine.[49]

In the eleventh letter of his 1755 treatise on feelings, Mendelssohn offered a précis of his psychological theory on the origins of human pleasure. There were three sources: (1) singularity within complexity, which he termed beauty (following Shaftesbury, Mendelssohn accepted a discrete, but integrated, category of beauty defined as a response to perceived characteristics); (2) unity in complexity, which he termed fulfilled rationality; and (3) the improved condition of our physical being, which Mendelssohn termed sensual desire.[50]

What distinguished Mendelssohn's argument here was that he singled out music as the art form uniquely capable of utilizing all three sources of pleasure and realizing them to the fullest. Mendelssohn's formulation borrows directly from the adoption of mathematical models of reasoning evident in the work of Leibnitz and Boileau-Despréaux. The latter developed the notion of unity in multiplicity. Music possesses a nearly unimaginable practical and psychological power and potential to generate a sense of totality in its hearers through formal complexity.

Therefore, beyond the expected examples of the correspondence between human passion and music and the effect of dissonance, Mendelssohn outlined some particular formal claims for music: the relationship of parts to the whole over time; and the creation of doubt, expectation, and anticipation through the use of harmony (which creates singularity) and then their resolution. The specificity of each well-crafted piece of music is the source of its beauty. Its formal clarity is the source of its rational completeness. The satisfaction gained in the resolution of tension created by diverse elements over the time frame of the musical experience results in the fulfillment of sensual desire.

Mendelssohn proceeded to argue the comparative limits of color, despite Newton's discoveries, in comparison to music. The task in the understanding of the function of color becomes, by analogy, a search for qualities immediately present in music, particularly that of "harmony." Even though each of our senses possesses its own immanent potential, the fulfillment of each is discussed in terms of the model set by music's effect. Therefore, the deaf person must sacrifice more in terms of feeling, well-being, and pleasure than the blind person. The human emotional capacity for feeling is most directly, fully, and unexpectedly elicited by music.[51]

Apart from Moses Mendelssohn's concept of the tripartite elements that constitute pleasure and underlie music's unique power and function, the prestige that he accords it is significant in terms of Felix Mendelssohn's ambitions.[52] For Moses and Felix Mendelssohn, however, the power of music was to be measured in the work itself only as a consequence of its effect on the listener. Great music, therefore, like the language of the Terence play, had to find its mark with its audience. The interplay with contemporary expectations, tastes, and conventions—the common musical language of the era—demanded of the composer that he manipulate them to the greatest effect, with the greatest immediacy.

The classical models in music—the formal examples of the past—provided for Felix the structural schemes in which fulfilling Moses Mendelssohn's tripartite definition of pleasure could be accomplished. But the actual material substance, the content, had to generate in the individual and the audience the full, threefold range of feeling. Felix Mendelssohn then needed to absorb the complex accumulations of tradition and fashion (from Bach to C. M. von Weber), since he did not seek to invest his music with aesthetic properties independent of the listening audience's frame of reference. His civic ambition was not to defy history (by being ahead of one's time or in the Wagnerian sense by creating work for a "future") or to be radically original or oppositional. Rather, it was to use music to permit his contemporaries to encounter, intuitively through the pleasure (defined philosophically, not as mere entertainment) of music, the fullness of beauty, desire, and the recognition of perfection, that is, God.

The possibility that Mendelssohn's music no longer works on audiences quite the same way as it did in his lifetime does not diminish his achievement. It may tell us more about ourselves and our quite contingent philosophical preconceptions and expectations concerning what greatness and originality in art are than about Mendelssohn's music. Felix Mendelssohn vindicated his grandfather's claim, made in the eleventh letter, that because the "aptitude is in our emotions," ways will be found in the future to unlock the fullness of pleasure and "the magical power of harmony" immanent in music. As Moses Mendelssohn put it, "Maybe our grandchildren will be able to enjoy this glorious discovery." His grandson undertook to prove him right.

VI

The connections between these disparate influences and the work of Felix Mendelssohn can be seen best in two excerpts from his letters. The first, written in July 1837, describes the composer's ambition to write a sequel to *St. Paul*. Mendelssohn put the issue to Schubring this way: "My question, then, is whether you think this possible, or at least so far possible that it may become something important and personal for every member of the community?"[53] In the second, the famous letter on the nature of music to Souchay from October 1842, Mendelssohn commented on the capacity of music to "fill the soul" with "a thousand things better than words." Music's power is precisely in its capacity to reconcile unity with particularity, and multiplicity with unity. The same song, Mendelssohn observed, "can arouse the same feelings in one person as in another, a feeling that is not expressed, however, by the same words . . . words have many meanings, but music we could both understand correctly."[54]

Mendelssohn adopted his grandfather's strategy. The unity in the apperception of music derives from a nonlinguistic sense of identity underlying the subjective response. Music goes beyond words and finds in many listeners a commonality not achievable by words. The reason this is possible is the intuitive emotional "aptitude" in human feelings and senses (once again in Moses Mendelssohn's terminology) that music unleashes and satisfies. The particularity is in the unique arrangement of sounds that makes up a specific piece of music. This particularity is enhanced by the specificity of initial expectation in the Songs without Words of a denotative and representational program. The presence of a title deepens the contrast between the weaknesses of language and the power of music.

In order to achieve this effect, the music must possess a wide-ranging capacity to elicit response. Its form and content must reach the audience, unambiguously, in musical terms. A surface that to us might seem lacking in complexity and ambiguity, that does not "puzzle" or "raise questions" arbitrarily or capriciously, is precisely what Mendelssohn sought. Simplicity and beauty that evoke the three aspects of Moses Mendelssohn's sense of the power of music—the intuitive sense of beauty, rational completeness, and fulfilled desire—are the objective. Therefore, the work of music must be organized formally and internally within a normative framework to achieve this result.

Music, therefore, is at the heart of the formation of a community, for it can create that sense of solidarity that the world, through the everyday conduct of life, fails to generate. The "same words," Mendelssohn cautioned, "never mean the same things to different people," but music can achieve this elusive, but noble, goal. In this way music can and must be something "important and personal" for every member of the community. If, for his more "romantic" contemporaries, music was the art of the historical moment and a unique vehicle for the assertion of subjectivity, for Mendelssohn music was equally the most important art form. In Mendelssohn's case, however, the greatness of music lay in its philosophical and humanistic objectivity, not in its potential to express either the infinite or the subjective. Music was precise in human terms but not in a linguistic sense. If later in the century art would become a surrogate for religion, in Mendelssohn art was a component of faith. Through the intuitive grasp of art, the underlying unity of God and his creation could be perceived, overriding all surface realities of difference.

For a devout Protestant, and a convert from Judaism—bearing the most famous Jewish name of the day, living in a world increasingly self-conscious of religious, national, and economic distinctions marked by violence and oppression and rapid change—this conception of music was more than an "inner necessity." This was no "art for art's sake" credo. It rejected a purely formalist internal consideration of the artwork's objective content and structure apart from any perceiver. One's suspicion that greatness resided in the materials of a work of music, in fact, was a consequence of its impact on the audience. Music was a magical, human form of life, whose function could vindicate a vision of the harmonious synthesis of nature, humanity, and the divine, accessible to humans beyond the scope of reason alone. This moral vision was rendered accessible by feelings evoked by art, which supplemented reason in a unified philosophical conception of the human condition. We could do worse than try to find a way in our own time to respond to Mendelssohn's music so that we find commonality in humanity where we frequently see and communicate only difference.

The astonishment and provocation explicit in Mendelssohn's music transcend aesthetics. The staggeringly problematic challenge in Mendelssohn comes to us in the form of its explicit and clear simplicity and beauty. The well-worn and commonplace aversion to Mendelssohn may, only on the surface, signal a sophisticated and subtle taste. That criterion of judgment may turn out to be a convenient and commonplace self- delusion. Perhaps we will come to realize that Mendelssohn's music, of all of the music of his generation, is in its apparent transparency, the most puzzling and problematic because it asks the most of us.

NOTES

1. Paul Henry Lang, *Music in Western Civilization* (New York: Norton, 1941), 802.

2. See R. Larry Todd, *Mendelssohn's Musical Education: A Study and Edition of His Exercises in Composition* (Cambridge: Cambridge University Press, 1983); Greg Vitercik, *The Early Works of Felix Mendelssohn: A Study in Romantic Sonata Style* (Philadelphia: Gordon and Breach, 1992).

3. Charles Rosen, *The Romantic Generation* (Cambridge: Harvard University Press, 1995), esp. Chapter 10; the phrases quoted here may be found on pp. 587, 589, 595, 596. It is curious that Rosen often uses the term "beauty" with reference to Mendelssohn as if it were somehow an insufficient criterion. If one reattaches the notion of beauty to its eighteenth-century meaning, which is not invidious as it is today, perhaps *mere* beauty is precisely what Mendelssohn sought. Therefore, the problem may be our incapacity to respond to it.

4. It should be said also that while considerable progress has been made in unraveling the history and sources of posthumous Mendelssohn reception, much of the later music remains less well appreciated, and Mendelssohn's compositional achievements are still underestimated. See James Webster, "Ambivalenzen um Mendelssohn: Zwischen Werk und Rezeption," in *Felix Mendelssohn Bartholdy: Kongreß-Bericht Berlin 1994*, ed. Christian Martin Schmidt (Wiesbaden: Breitkopf & Härtel, 1997), 257–78; Hans Mayer, "Felix Mendelssohn Bartholdy: Der geschichtliche Augenblick," and Eike Middell, "Der 'Schöne Zwischenfall' oder 'Wie ein Walzer zur Predigt': Das Problem Mendelssohn aus literarhistorischer Sicht," in *Felix Mendelssohn—Mitwelt und Nachwelt: Bericht zum 1. Leipziger Mendelssohn Kolloquium* (Wiesbaden: Breitkopf & Härtel, 1996), 5–14, 117–22.

5. For a newer analysis of this event, see Michael Marissen, "Religious Aims in Mendelssohn's 1829 Berlin-Singakademie Performances of Bach's *St. Matthew Passion*," *The Musical Quarterly* 77/4 (1993), 718–26.

6. I want to thank Douglass Seaton for his support and patience. This chapter is written in the form of speculative historical argument. As a result, the text offers only the basic outline of the argument. The footnote apparatus is designed not only to indicate the sources of the claims made but to direct readers further and to generate a useful bibliography through which the issues might be developed. I am citing only the most essential publications within the standard scholarly literature on Felix Mendelssohn, even when the arguments here differ, in the expectation that readers are already familiar with that material.

In different versions, this chapter was given at Dartmouth College and at Harvard University in the fall of 1996. I wish to thank Karen Painter, Judith Tick, and Reinhold Brinckmann for their suggestions and encouragement.

7. Todd, *Mendelssohn's Musical Education*, 85.

8. Vitercik, *The Early Works of Felix Mendelssohn*, 5, 7, and 307.

9. On the musical context of Berlin, see the volume edited by Carl Dahlhaus, *Studien zur Musikgeschichte Berlins im frühen 19. Jahrhundert* (Regensburg: Bosse, 1980), particularly the essay by Klaus Kropfinger, "Klassik-Rezeption in Berlin (1800–1830)."

10. See David Sorkin, *The Transformation of German Jewry 1780–1840* (New York: Oxford University Press, 1987); Deborah Hertz, *Jewish High Society in Old Regime Berlin* (New Haven, CT: Yale University Press, 1988); the essays by Julius Carlebach, Jacob Toury, and Johanna Philippson in Hans Liebeschütz and Arnold Paucker, eds., *Das Judentum in der deutschen Umwelt: Studien zur Frühgeschichte der Emanzipation* (Tübingen: J.C.B. Mohr, 1977), especially pp. 243–49; see also the essays by Steven M. Lowenstein and Michael A. Meyer in *Jüdische Geschichte in Berlin: Essays und Studien*, ed. Reinhard Rurup (Berlin: Heinrich, 1995); also the essay by this author, "The Aesthetics of Assimilation and

Affirmation: Reconstructing the Career of Felix Mendelssohn," in *Mendelssohn and His World*, ed. R. Larry Todd (Princeton: Princeton University Press, 1991), 5–42.

11. Eric Werner, *Mendelssohn: A New Image of the Composer and His Age* (New York: Free Press of Glencoe, 1963), 40.

12. Rosen, *The Romantic Generation*, 590. Just in case the reader may think that the word "kitsch" is not derogatory, I refer those who may not be familiar with how cruel the term is to Nicolas Slonimsky's apt definition, reprinted in Richard Kostelanetz, ed., *Nicolas Slonimsky: The First Hundred Years* (New York: Schirmer Books, 1994), 347–48.

13. See the discussion of this in Leon Botstein, "History, Rhetoric and the Self: Robert Schumann and Music Making in German-Speaking Europe, 1800–1860," in *Schumann and His World*, ed. R. Larry Todd (Princeton: Princeton University Press, 1994), 3–45.

14. See Ernst Cassirer, *The Philosophy of the Enlightenment* (Boston: Beacon, 1955), 275–360.

15. Felix Mendelssohn clearly was familiar with the writings of his grandfather. This is made explicit in the letter he sent to Joseph Mendelssohn on 20 February 1840. Felix complained about the errors in and incompleteness of the existing Vienna edition of his grandfather's work. When finally a new complete edition came out later in the decade, Joseph wrote back to Felix saying that the new edition existed only because of him. See *Bankiers, Künstler und Gelehrte: Unveröffentlichte Briefe der Familie Mendelssohn aus dem 19. Jahrhundert*, ed. Felix Gilbert (Tübingen: J.C.B. Mohr, 1975), 128–29.

16. See Ernst Kris and Otto Kurz, *Die Legende vom Künstler: Ein geschichtlicher Versuch* (Frankfurt am Main: Suhrkamp, 1934; repr. 1980).

17. This latter event is not discussed in most of the standard biographies, particularly Arnd Richter, *Mendelssohn* (Munich: Piper 1994), and Werner, *A New Image*. Wulf Konold mentions the event (particularly Mendelssohn's election as an honorary member of the Künstlerverein) in his chronology. See *Felix Mendelssohn Bartholdy und seine Zeit* (Regensburg: Laaber, 1984), 22. The music is in autograph form at the Deutsche Staatsbibliothek and is entitled "Grosse Festmusik zum Dürerfest" written for solo voices, chorus, and orchestra.

18. Werner, *A New Image*, 14, 78; Richter, *Mendelssohn*, 56.

19. This can be checked in Giovanni Cupaiuolo, *Bibliografia terenziana (1470–1983)*, Studi e testi dell'antichità 16 (Naples: Società editrice napoletana, 1984). I am indebted to Professor R. J. Tarrant of Harvard University for his help in this regard.

20. Barbara R. Kes, *Die Rezeption der Kömodien des Plautus und Terenz im 19. Jahrhundert: Theorie, Bearbeitung, Bühne* (Amsterdam: Gruner, 1988), 45–49.

21. *Das Mädchen von Andros: Eine Kömodie des Terentius in den Versmassen des Originals übersetzt von F****. Mit Einleitung und Anmerkungen herausgegeben von K.W.L. Heyse* (Berlin: Ferdinand Dummler, 1826), ix.

22. Richter, *Mendelssohn*, 102–3; for a detailed analysis of Mendelssohn's metrical adaptation, see Heyse's extensive explanation in *Das Mädchen von Andros*, 1–20.

23. The *Andria* was the first and only Roman comedy to be translated into English before 1600. On Terence and Roman comedy see R. L. Hunter, *The New Comedy of Greece and Rome* (Cambridge: Cambridge University Press, 1985); George E. Duckworth, *The Nature of Roman Comedy: A Study in Popular Entertainment*, 2d ed., ed. R. Hunter (Norman: University of Oklahoma Press, 1994). See the discussion of Terence through to the end of the Renaissance in R. R. Bolgar, *The Classical Heritage and Its Beneficiaries* (New York: Harper and Row, 1964).

24. See Gian Biagio Conte, *Latin Literature: A History*, trans. Joseph B. Solodow (Baltimore: Johns Hopkins University Press, 1994).

25. Despite the recent revelations by Jeffrey Sposato, the basic view of Mendelssohn's relationship to his Jewish identity seems to be a combination of (1) a keen awareness of anti-Semitism, (2) profound faith in Protestantism, and (3) pride in his familial heritage and therefore a residual, lifelong sense of connection to Jews and Judaism. See Jeffrey S. Sposato, "Creative Writing: The [Self-] Identification of Mendelssohn as a Jew," *The Musical Quarterly* 82/1 (1998), 190–209; also Leon Botstein, "Mendelssohn and the Jews," *The Musical Quarterly* 82/1 (1998), 210–19.

26. For an English translation of the *Andria*, see Palmer Bovie's version in Palmer Bovie, ed., *Terence: The Comedies* (Baltimore: Johns Hopkins University Press, 1992); the Latin and English can be found in J. Sargeaunt, ed., *Terence*, vol. 1, Loeb Classical Library 22 (Cambridge: Harvard University Press, 1912), 3–109.

27. For an excerpt of the Dubos text in English, see Peter le Huray and James Day, eds., *Music and Aesthetics in the Eighteenth and Early-Nineteenth Centuries* (Cambridge: Cambridge University Press, 1981), 17–22. It is possible that Felix Mendelssohn's attraction to the task of translation may have been motivated, in part, by the example of his grandfather, whose translations of the Psalms and the Old Testament were considered among his finest achievements and, in the case of the Psalms, his most poetic and artistic. See David Sorkin, *Moses Mendelssohn and the Religious Enlightenment* (Berkeley: University of California Press, 1996), 46–52.

28. Cassirer, *The Philosophy of the Enlightenment*, 304.

29. Mendelssohn's translation appears on pp. 25 and 26 of *Das Mädchen von Andros*.

30. The text and details of the celebration are contained in the pamphlet *Albrecht Dürer: Lyrische Dichtung zur Gedächtnis-Feier des Kunstlers in Berlin, den 18. April 1828, von Konrad Levezow, in Musik gesetzt von Felix Mendelssohn-Bartholdy* (Berlin: A. W. Hayn, 1828). The indispensable source for this discussion, which includes a full score of the music, is Kent Eugene Hatteberg,"*Gloria* (1822) and *Große Festmusik zum Dürerfest* (1828): Urtext Editions of Two Unpublished Choral-Orchestral Works by Felix Mendelssohn with Background and Commentary," vol. 1 (Ph.D. diss., University of Iowa, 1995). The text and the description of the musical events are included. The assessment of the music is very negative, a view that cannot be taken on faith in the absence of a modern performance. For a positive account of the event, see Sebastian Hensel, *Die Familie Mendelssohn: Nach Briefen und Tagebüchern, 1729–1847*, vol. 2 (Leipzig: Insel, 1924), 203–6.

31. On Schinkel, see Barry Bergdoll, *Karl Friedrich Schinkel: An Architecture for Prussia* (New York: Rizzoli, 1994); Michael Snodin, ed., *Karl Friedrich Schinkel: A Universal Man* (New Haven, CT: Yale University Press, 1991).

32. See David van Zanten, "The Harmony of Landscape, Architecture and Community: Schinkel's Encounter with Huyot, 1826," in *Karl Friedrich Schinkel: The Drama of Architecture*, ed. John Zukowsky (Chicago: Art Institute of Chicago, 1994).

33. See Bergdoll, *Karl Friedrich Schinkel*, 44–-102. Alexander von Humboldt was friendly with the Mendelssohn family, as was his older brother. See Gilbert, *Bankiers, Künstler und Gelehrte*.

34. Bergdoll, *Karl Friedrich Schinkel*.

35. See Max Schmid, *Kunstgeschichte des 19. Jahrhunderts* (Leipzig: G. Seemann, 1904); Anton Springer and Max Osborn, *Handbuch der Kunstgeschichte*, vol. 5, *Das 19. Jahrhundert* (Leipzig: G. Seeman, 1912); Friedrich Haack, *Die Kunst des 19. Jahrhunderts*, 4th ed. (Esslingen: Paul Neff, 1913).

36. *Albrecht Dürer*, 13–14, 18–20.

37. *Das Mädchen von Andros*, iv–v.

38. See the works collected by Jewish banking families in *Along the Royal Road: Berlin and Potsdam in KPM Porcelain and Painting 1815–1848* (New York: Bard Graduate Center for Studies in the Decorative Arts, 1993).

39. See the most complete selection of Mendelssohn's own artwork in the Japanese edition *Oneiros* No. 7, ed. R. Larry Todd (Tokyo: Mujinkin, 1992).

40. Richter, *Mendelssohn*, 95–112.

41. The comments on Menzel can be found in Johann Peter Eckermann, *Gespräche mit Goethe in den letzten Jahren seines Lebens*, ed. Fritz Bergemann (Baden-Baden: Insel, 1981), 150, 475, and 511. The Goethe essay on Winckelmann can be found in English, along with Winckelmann's own seminal essay "Thoughts on the Imitation of the Painting and Sculpture of the Greeks," in *German Aesthetic and Literary Criticism: Winckelmann, Lessing, Hamann, Herder, Schiller, Goethe*, ed. and trans. H. B. Nisbet, (Cambridge: Cambridge University Press, 1985); see pp. 236–37.

42. Eckermann, *Gespräche mit Goethe*, 80.

43. Ibid., 176.

44. Ibid., 212, 249.

45. From Winckelmann's own essay, in Nisbet, *German Aesthetic and Literary Criticism*, 38.

46. Eckermann, *Gespräche mit Goethe*, 571–72.

47. For more on the concept of *Bildung*, see the Historical Views and Documents section following this chapter.

48. It should be noted that Felix Mendelssohn's interest in classical antiquity was sustained through his entire life. He corresponded with Johann Gustav Droysen, and, as mentioned in this chapter, in the 1840s he wrote incidental music to two Sophocles plays. See Michael P. Steinberg, "The Incidental Politics to Mendelssohn's *Antigone*," in *Mendelssohn and His World*, 137–57. The love of the study of the classical world was sustained within the Mendelssohn family well beyond Felix's death. As G. W. Bowersock has noted, the newly discovered notes of Mommsen's lectures of the 1880s on imperial Rome were prepared by the son and grandson of Fanny Mendelssohn. See the review by G. W. Bowersock of Theodor Mommsen, *A History of Rome under the Emperors*, trans. Clare Korjzl (London: Routledge, 1996), in *The New Republic*, 16 December 1996.

49. Sorkin, *Moses Mendelssohn*, 48.

50. Moses Mendelssohn, "Über die Empfindungen, 1755," in *Moses Mendelssohn's Schriften zur Psychologie und Äesthetik*, ed. Moritz Bratsch, vol. 2 (Leipzig: Voss, 1880), 54–55. For a modern edition see Otto F. Best, ed., *Moses Mendelssohn: Ästhetische Schriften in Auswahl* (Darmstadt: Wissenschaftliche Buchgesellschaft, 1971), 66–67.

51. It is significant that Mendelssohn examines the possibilities of a correspondence between color and sound, a concept of harmony applicable to both, potentially realizable, but not in actuality, in the idea of a "Farbenklavier"; Best, ed., *Moses Mendelssohn*, 68.

52. There is, of course, the parallel in the social history of Berlin and Vienna, where Jewish high society played a decisive role in musical life before 1830 and where the level of musical culture in Jewish families was extraordinarily high. See Peter Wollny, "Sara Levy and the Making of Musical Taste in Berlin," *The Musical Quarterly* 77/4 (1993), 651–88; see also Leon Botstein, *Judentum und Modernität* (Vienna: Böhlau, 1991), 44–53.

53. I am using the standard Selden-Goth translation in Felix Mendelssohn, *Letters* (New York: Vienna House, 1973), 269. The German text can be found in Felix Mendelssohn Bartholdy, *Briefe aus den Jahren 1833–1847* (Leipzig: Hermann Mendelssohn, 1863), 148.

54. Mendelssohn, *Letters*, 314; the German text on pp. 337–38 of the edition cited in note 53.

HISTORICAL VIEWS AND DOCUMENTS

ON THE QUESTION: WHAT DOES ENLIGHTENMENT MEAN?[1]

Moses Mendelssohn, translated by Douglass Seaton

[Felix Mendelssohn's understanding of what it meant for an individual to be a cultivated person and likewise what it would mean for society in his time to manifest an enlightened culture reflected the ideas of his grandfather. In this brief essay Moses Mendelssohn offered some definitions and explored some ideas about the still-fresh concepts of culture and enlightenment in the late eighteenth century.—Ed.]

The words "enlightenment," "culture," "*Bildung*"[2] are still newcomers to our language. For the moment they belong only to literary discourse. The general public hardly understands them. Might this be an indication that these things themselves are new among us? I do not believe so. They say there is a certain people that possesses no precise word for virtue, nor one for superstition, although at the same time they may justly describe that people as having no little amount of both of these.

Meanwhile usage, which appears to want to make a distinction between these synonymous terms, has not yet had time to establish their boundaries. *Bildung*, culture, and enlightenment are modifications of social life, effects of humanity's industry and effort to improve its social condition.

The more that the social condition of a people is brought into harmony with the destiny of humanity by means of art and industry, the more that people possesses *Bildung*.

Bildung may be divided into culture and enlightenment. The former appears more to have to do with practical matters: with goods, refinement and beauty in handicrafts, arts, and social customs (objectively), with skill, industry, and aptitude; the latter is applied (subjectively) to inclination, drive, and custom. In the case of any people, the more these express the destiny of humankind, the more it will be said to have culture, just as the more that cultivation and construction are applied to a plot of land, the more that it will be developed by the diligence of humanity, producing useful things for humanity. Enlightenment, by contrast, appears to relate more to the theoretical—to rational perception (objectively) and skill (subjectively) in rational reflection on things of human life, on the degree of its significance and its influence on the destiny of humankind.

I always set the *destiny of humankind as the measure and goal of all aspiration and effort*, as a point toward which we should direct our eyes, if we wish not to lose ourselves.

A language achieves enlightenment by means of the scholarly disciplines [*Wissenschaften*], and achieves culture by means of social intercourse, poetry, and eloquence. By means of the former it becomes more skilled in theoretical applications, but by the latter in practical ones. Combined, these give a language

Bildung.

Externally, culture means refinement. Hail to the nation whose refinement is the effect of culture and enlightenment, whose outward brilliance and polish are based on inner, genuine authenticity!

Enlightenment relates to culture generally as theory does to practice, as knowledge does to ethics, as criticism does to virtuosity. Considered in and of themselves (objectively), they stand in the closest relationship, although at the same time they can often be separated from each other subjectively.

One may say that the Nürnbergers have more culture, the Berliners more enlightenment; the French more culture, the English more enlightenment; the Chinese more culture and less enlightenment. The Greeks had both culture and enlightenment. As a nation, they were *gebildet*, just as their language is *gebildet*. In general, a people's language is the best indicator of their *Bildung*, of culture as well as of enlightenment, in terms of breadth as well as of strength.

Further, human destiny may be divided into *first*, the destiny of the person as [individual] human, and *second*, the destiny of the person considered as citizen [*Bürger*].

In respect to culture, these considerations merge together, since all practical accomplishments have value only in relation to communal life and therefore must express purely and simply the destiny of humankind as a member of society. The person as a person has no need of culture but does need enlightenment.

One's station and vocation in one's civic life determine the duties and rights of each individual member; they require, according to their degree, different aptitudes and skills, different inclinations, drives, social sense and customs, a different culture and refinement. The more that these correspond with their vocations in all social stations, that is, with their respective destinies as members of society, so much more will the nation possess culture.

They require, however, from each individual, according to the degree of his [or her] station and vocation, different theoretical insights and different skills to achieve the same thing, another level of enlightenment. The enlightenment that interests the person as a person is general, without distinction as to station; the enlightenment of the person considered as a citizen adapts itself according to station and vocation. Human destiny, however, sets the measure and goal of its aspiration here.

According to this, the enlightenment of a nation would depend on: *first*, the degree of its knowledge; *second*, its significance, that is, its relationship to the destiny (1) of the person and (2) of the citizen; *third*, its dissemination through all stations; *fourth*, the degree of its vocation. Thus, the level of the people's enlightenment would be determined by a relationship compounded at least fourfold, whose component parts in their turn are compounded out of simpler component relations.

Personal enlightenment can come into conflict with citizen enlightenment. Certain truths that are useful to the person as a person can sometimes work against the person as a citizen. Here the following is to be taken into consideration. The collision can arise between *first*, essential or *second*, accidental destinies of the person, with *third*, essential or *fourth*, nonessential accidental destinies of the citizen.

Without the essential destinies of the person, an individual declines into a dumb animal; without the nonessential, he [or she] cannot become such a good, noble creature. Without the essential destinies of the person as a citizen, the composition of the state ceases to exist; without the nonessential, it loses the distinctive quality of its various incidental relationships.

Unhappy is the state that must admit that in it the essential destiny of the person does not harmonize with the essential destiny of the citizen, that the enlightenment that is indispensable to humanity cannot be disseminated across all stations of the kingdom without placing its constitution in danger of collapsing. Here philosophy can have nothing to say![3] Necessity may prescribe laws here or even forge shackles, which are to be applied to humanity in order to humiliate it and constantly keep it suppressed.

But when the nonessential destinies of the person come into conflict with the essential or nonessential ones of the citizen, then rules must be established, according to which exceptions may be made and the cases of collision may be resolved.

If by some misfortune the essential destinies of the person are brought into disagreement with his [or her] nonessential destinies, if one may not disseminate certain useful and ornamental truths for the person without tearing apart the principles of religion and morality that are now inherent in him [or her], then the virtue-loving enlightened person will manage with prudence and caution and rather endure prejudice than banish the truth that is so woven into him [or her]. To be sure, this maxim has from time immemorial become the bulwark of hypocrisy, and we have this to thank for so many centuries of barbarism and superstition. As often as one wishes to grasp the offense, it escapes into the sanctuary. Only for the downtrodden will the humanitarian, even in the most enlightened times, nevertheless always have to make allowances. It is difficult, but not impossible, to find the boundary that separates use from abuse here.

The nobler a thing in its perfection, says a Hebrew writer, the uglier in its decay. A rotten stick of wood is not so revolting as a decayed flower, this not so loathsome as a rotten animal, and this not as hideous as a decaying human being. Likewise with culture and enlightenment—the nobler in their blooming, the more horrible in their decay and corruption.

Misuse of enlightenment weakens moral feeling, leads to hardheartedness, egoism, irreligion, and anarchy. Misuse of culture produces arrogance, hypocrisy, weakness, superstition, and slavery.

Where enlightenment and culture proceed side by side, they are for each other the best means of preventing corruption. Each one is directly opposed to the corruption of the other.

The *Bilding* of a nation, which according to the previous explanation of terms is compounded out of culture and enlightenment, will thus be far less subject to corruption.

A *gebildete* nation knows no other danger than the excess of national happiness, which, like the most complete health of the human body, can be called a disease in and of itself. A nation that has arrived at the highest peak of national happiness is, on that very account, in danger of falling, because it cannot ascend any higher. But this leads too far from the question before us!

NOTES

1. First published in the *Berlinische Monatsschrift* 4 (September 1784). An essay by Immanuel Kant on the same question appeared in November of the same year. The present translation is based on the text as found in Moses Mendelssohn, *Ästhetische Schriften in Auswahl*, ed. Otto F. Best, Texte zur Forschung 14 (Darmstadt: Wissenschlaftliche Buchgesellschaft, 1974), 266–69. The essay's actual title is "Auf die Frage: Was heisst afklären?" that is, "On the Question: What Does Enlighten Mean?," but this reads awkwardly in English, and Mendelssohn does not, in fact, consider the verb "auklären" but the noun "Aufklärung"; thus the title here is adapted accordingly.

2. English has no adequate translation for the German term *Bildung* or the participial adjective *gebildet*, also used here. As applied to individuals, it includes personal development, broad and balanced education, the acquisition of culture. Mendelssohn is equally, if not more, inclined to apply it here to the nation. The essay itself explains the meaning of the term about as well as possible.

3. Literally, "philosophy lays its hand over its mouth."

2

"For art has the same place in your heart as mine": Family, Friendship, and Community in the Life of Felix Mendelssohn

Marian Wilson Kimber

While the reputations of most nineteenth-century composers have suffered to some degree from bad biography, Felix Mendelssohn's has been subjected to wide extremes since the first biography of him was published shortly after his death.[1] The expurgated editions of Mendelssohn's letters published in the nineteenth century and the portrayal of his life as one of "moral purity" cut short by a premature death combined to elevate the composer to a position nearing artistic sainthood. Twentieth-century attempts to remedy past over-glorification and render Mendelssohn somewhat more human have frequently erred in the opposite direction. Both extremes of biography ultimately fail to convince their reader of Mendelssohn's status as a Romantic Hero, the common paradigm for composers' biographies; he is lost behind hagiography in the former and leads too happy, too bourgeois a life in the latter. Nonetheless, the various memoirs and letters published by Mendelssohn's friends after his death have frequently served only to confirm events in standard biographical narratives; the individuals who played crucial roles in the composer's life are often mere walk-on characters in the story of the Great Man. The only notable exception to this is the Mendelssohn family, who have always figured prominently in the composer's biography.

Examination of the influences of Mendelssohn's family and his relationships with his close friends can reveal much about the composer's personality. During most of his brief life Mendelssohn traveled widely and knew many of the foremost political, musical, artistic, and intellectual figures of his time. The composer's personal and musical influence was widespread during the 1830s and 1840s. As his musical stature in Europe grew, so did the circumference of his social and professional circles, and so did his correspondence, which became voluminous. A chapter of this scope cannot claim to offer a comprehensive discussion of all of the individuals who played important roles in the composer's life. It can, however, demonstrate that the composer's consciousness of a musical and social community, which had its roots in his family life, was essential to both his personal well-being and his creative life. The support that Mendelssohn found in this community, this web of friendships, encouraged and sustained him through his artistic struggles.

FAMILY

Mendelssohn's immediate family formed the nucleus for his life and greatly influenced his personality, temperament, and artistic outlook. Sebastian Hensel's hope that his history of the Mendelssohn family would be read "as the chronicle of a good middle class family in Germany"[2] can only strike the reader as an understatement in view of the outstanding place of the family in German cultural life.

Felix Mendelssohn's grandfather Moses Mendelssohn (1729–86) was a Jewish Enlightenment philosopher whose writings stressed religious tolerance and the integration of the Jews into German society. His eldest son, Joseph, founded a successful bank, in which Felix's father, Abraham, made his fortune. One of Moses' daughters, Dorothea Mendelssohn Veit, was an influential figure in Berlin salon life at the end of the eighteenth century. Through her association with the writer Friedrich Schlegel, whom she eventually married, she became one of the circle of early German Romantics who congregated at Jena.

Lea Salomon, Mendelssohn's mother, came from the Itzig family, one of the wealthiest families in Berlin.[3] Lea's mother, Bella Salomon, and several of her aunts were well known for their leadership in salon culture. Lea's aunt Sara Levy (1762–1854) had been associated with both Wilhelm Friedemann Bach and Carl Philipp Emanuel Bach, and she donated a large collection of J. S. Bach's manuscripts to the Singakademie in Berlin, the organization that was to revive the *St. Matthew Passion* in 1829 under the direction of Felix Mendelssohn. Fanny von Arnstein (1758–1818) and Caecilie von Eskeles (1759–1818), Felix's maternal great-aunts, married court bankers in Vienna and were active in musical life there.[4] Lea spoke four languages and was sufficiently well educated to read Homer in the original Greek. With her musical background, she was the moving force behind her children's musical education.

Felix Mendelssohn's family background thus combined wealth and a rich intellectual and cultural life. The Mendelssohns might serve as a model family in these regards, but they were by no means merely "a good middle class family."

Both the substance and the style of the education that Abraham and Lea Mendelssohn provided for their children had a lasting influence on Felix's life. Education was paramount to the Mendelssohns; in this they adhered to the prevailing concept of *Bildung*, the self-development of an individual's potential, which stressed his "capacity to become a free, creative, autonomous person, living in harmony with like-minded men, in a spirit of tolerance, solidarity and friendship."[5] Moses Mendelssohn himself had asserted that "every single human being is meant to develop his talents and abilities, hence become increasingly perfect."[6] *Bildung* was also seen as the means by which Jews would achieve integration into German society and eventual complete political emancipation. Thus, the Mendelssohns' stress on education had a practical as well as a philosophical basis; although the family's wealth put them in a strong economic position, education was viewed as the primary means by which they maintained their social status. Their children's future station in life was clearly an important factor in Abraham and Lea's decision to convert their offspring to Christianity in 1816. In this, they were part of a wave of upper-class Jewish families in Berlin who converted in the first two decades of the nineteenth century.[7]

In their children's upbringing, the Mendelssohns emphasized the Enlightenment values stressed in the writings of contemporary Jewish thinkers, as well as in Lutheran sermons of the preceding three decades, especially "industry, family, and the purposeful use of time."[8] David Sorkin has linked these values to Jewish regeneration, writing that "the sanctification of work went along with occupational restructuring; the family and the use of time, with *Bildung*."[9] On a more personal level, a strong work ethic shaped the daily life of Felix Mendelssohn's childhood, and the family that encouraged it figured prominently in his life for many years to come.

Young Felix's extensive education included instruction in French, German, Latin, Greek, arithmetic, geometry, geography, literature, music theory, violin, and drawing.[10] Not only was their education broad in scope, but for the Mendelssohn children, no time was to be wasted. In an 1820 letter, the eleven-year-old Felix wrote, "My work schedule is so organized, that I always prepare tasks in the evening which I have received in the morning."[11] Both parents enforced the discipline necessary for accomplishment. Eduard Devrient recalled Lea's chiding the young boy, "Felix, are you doing nothing?" and sending him back to his studies.[12] Abraham, too, could be especially stern with his children. Julius Schubring recalled that if young Felix "ever gave his father cause for dissatisfaction, he was spared neither the reproving look, nor the serious, but invariably calm, rebuke."[13]

Education was not merely the task of the private tutors hired for the children but an ongoing concern of the entire family. Parental responses to their children's letters typically not only included critical commentary on the content of the offering but also pointed out errors and critiqued the general literary style. Abraham's letters to his children are especially pedantic in tone, full of instructions as to what they are to do and how they are to live. The children themselves came to imitate this tone: Fanny in writing to her younger brother Felix, and Felix in his letters to his younger brother Paul and, in his adult years, to his own children and his nephew Sebastian.[14]

Clearly, Abraham and Lea were aware of their children's remarkable gifts. Yet they were extremely careful in the manner in which they encouraged their progress, avoiding overindulgent flattery at all costs. After Johann Nepomuk Hummel's visit to Berlin in 1821, during which he instructed both Felix and his sister Fanny, Lea wrote that "he was very stingy with praise, which pleased me greatly."[15] The Mendelssohns' choice of Karl Friedrich Zelter (1758–1832) as Felix's composition teacher was no accident. Serious, strict, and crusty in temperament, Zelter kept a close eye on his charge. While Zelter was willing to show off his young prodigy to the great poet Goethe when the boy was only twelve, the official proclamation that Felix was now a professional, a member of the "guild" of composers, did not come until he was fifteen and the composer of numerous works in large forms.[16]

Part of the parents' reticence to praise their son apparently came from their own doubts about Felix's musical future. Ignaz Moscheles described the parents' attitude during his Berlin visit of 1824:

[T]hey are far removed from being proud of their children; they are anxious about Felix's future, whether he has a talent sufficient to achieve true greatness, whether he will not, like so many talented children, suddenly founder. I could not assert enough, how I am convinced of his future mastery, have not the least doubt of his genius; but I had to repeat this often before they believed me.[17]

Abraham in particular worried about his son's professional future. Marx recounted that Abraham suggested "secure" careers in business to his artistically inclined son,[18] a notion that was supported by Lea's brother, Jacob Bartholdy.[19] While music was viewed as a worthwhile pursuit in private settings, it was not considered a legitimate career, like business or law, in part because it was unreliable as a source of income but more because of the dubious social standing of musicians. Felix eventually managed to overcome his father's doubts. In 1828 Abraham wrote to Moscheles, "He is a musician, and wants to remain a musician."[20]

The Mendelssohn children were not entirely denied encouragement. Abraham admitted in a letter to his daughter Fanny, "The more sparing I am with my praise, the more deliberately do I grant it when I find cause for it."[21] Although their parents may have been more cautious than was actually warranted, the Mendelssohn children's rigorous education clearly produced remarkable results. At least one family member found Abraham's expectations of his children too severe, however. Abraham's sister Henrietta Mendelssohn wrote to him from Paris that "one should merely guide, not force, the extraordinary talent of your children. Papa Abraham, however, is insatiable; for him the best is only just good enough."[22] As they matured, Felix and his siblings were able to see through Abraham's sometimes gruff exterior. Writing from Rome at age 21, Felix recommended that his sisters humor their father: "Perhaps you have forgotten a little bit that here and there you must indulge and not provoke, that father considers himself older and more ill-tempered than he really is, thank God, and that it is up to all of us to give in to him once in a while, even if right is on our side, as he has often done."[23] According to Fanny, Abraham's withholding of praise did have a significant effect on Felix and the other siblings. She wrote to him,

You know how it always upset you when our parents concealed their satisfaction from you. Father continues to upset us in the same way, in that he acts so indifferent and stoic, and then we'll catch him reading your letters three or four times, and, like everyone, we know and can clearly see how happy he is about you and everything you encounter. We are the only ones who are not supposed to know it. But we do know it.[24]

Abraham's and Lea's approach to raising their children had a lasting impact on the characters of the younger Mendelssohn generation. The demanding regimen of Mendelssohn's childhood ingrained in the composer the need to be always at work, and his friends' recollections report his ceaseless activity. In later years this unrelenting exertion resulted from his professional situations; as a well-known musical figure Mendelssohn was sought out as conductor, composer, teacher, consultant, and concert organizer. A letter to his mother from 1841 describes the demands placed on him; he had written thirty-five letters in three days and was flooded with scores to review, texts to set, aspiring musicians to advise.[25] Beyond his professional obligations, however, the need to work was an essential part of the composer's character. The same year he wrote to a friend that "the only possible human consolation is to be found in ceaseless, continued work."[26] Felix held himself to exacting standards in his professional life and, more significantly, in his compositions. The expectations of his parents were internalized; as an adult he articulated the position that the artist "must always demonstrate that he is productive"[27] and believed that the artist is led in this by a moral obligation. To Ferdinand Hiller he wrote, "I believe that a man with splendid capabilities has the obligation to become something good, that one can call it his own fault if he does not develop himself fully in accordance with the means given him,"[28] a statement in which one can hear the echo of the composer's grandfather, transmitted through the intervening generation.

More importantly, Felix grew up with strongly self-critical inclinations, continually referring to his abilities and his compositions in a self-deprecatory fashion. His comments to Moscheles in 1834 were not untypical: "You know how I so often suffer from terrible doubts and can do nothing right, and if I then become anxious, I think that the whole world must see it even more clearly than I and even turn its eyes from my work."[29] The often-repeated notion that the extensive musical training of Mendelssohn's childhood rendered him "too facile" as a composer and that composition came too easily to him cannot be verified in Mendelssohn's correspondence or in his surviving musical manuscripts. Obsessed by what he called "the revisions devil," Mendelssohn took his works through numerous drafts, withheld a large portion of his output from publication, and even requested that publishers re-engrave plates with his last-minute changes.[30] His manuscripts reveal that for Felix Mendelssohn, as for his father, the best often appeared only just good enough.

Until his death in 1835, Abraham Mendelssohn continued to have a strong influence in his son's life. Abraham accompanied Felix to England and to the Lower Rhine Music Festival in Düsseldorf in 1833, where he was gratified to experience firsthand the level of his son's professional success. Although their close relationship was transformed into one between independent adults, Felix still valued his father's counsel highly. Both Felix and his sister Fanny remarked that their father, although he had no technical training, had a surprising amount of musical understanding and taste.[31] Felix grieved deeply after Abraham's death, writing to his friend and spiritual counselor Pastor Bauer that he had lost his "instructor in art and in life."[32] For Mendelssohn, his father's death confirmed the end of his youth; he wrote to Schubring that "a new life must now begin for me, or all is finished; the former existence is now severed."[33]

Although the family history written by Hensel concentrates on Abraham as the patriarch of the Mendelssohn clan, the power and influence of Lea over the lives of her children should not be underestimated, especially in regard to encouraging Felix's musical future in his early years. The depth of her involvement with Felix's career is revealed by her negotiations with the publisher Schlesinger regarding several of her son's compositions during the years 1823 to 1834, that is, beginning when Felix was a teenager and lasting into his adulthood.[34] After her husband's death, Lea seems to have assumed the role of family head, which might have been expected to fall to Felix, and she maintained an active involvement in her adult children's personal lives. Felix asked her permission before proposing marriage to Cécile Jeanrenaud in 1836, thus acknowledging her position, although at age twenty-seven he was certainly in a situation to act independently. In his letters to his mother, Mendelssohn was capable of accurately describing his great successes, such as his appearances in England, without lapsing into self-deprecation quite as frequently as he did to his circle in general. He recognized her role in his life along with Abraham's, writing as he recovered after Lea's death, "In the past few weeks I have felt vividly again, what a heavenly calling Art truly is. For this again I have only my parents to thank!"[35]

FANNY MENDELSSOHN HENSEL

The most important musical confidante in Felix Mendelssohn's life was his talented sister Fanny (1805–47). He turned to her for musical advice, and he trusted her opinion above that of all others. Born with what her mother described as "Bach fugue fingers," Fanny received musical training similar to that of her younger brother and early on showed similar remarkable musical abilities. Sebastian Hensel's summarizing description of his mother's character could be applied equally to his uncle. Both siblings had decided opinions, little patience with persons or things that were dull or shallow, and a need for "intercourse with cultured and intelligent people in a small circle, and the pleasures of art."[36]

Throughout their lives music functioned as a personal second language for the siblings. Felix regularly sent his sister compositions on important occasions such as birthdays; he was less successful on more momentous occasions, as his attempts to compose an organ piece for her wedding and a song in honor of the birth of her son Sebastian came to naught.[37] As a youth, Felix affectionately called his older sister "the cantor," and her early letters to him are maternal in their tone. In 1822 she described the immense influence she had in his musical life: "Up to the present moment . . . I possess his unlimited trust. I have seen his talent develop, step by step, and I have contributed to his development to a certain extent myself. He has no musical advisor other than me, also he never puts a thought on paper without first having submitted it to me for examination."[38] As Felix reached adulthood, Fanny commented to Klingemann on his growing independence and maturity:

His direction becomes more and more established, and he steadily advances towards the aim he has set himself, of which he is clearly conscious, but which I would not know how to describe in words, perhaps because in general an idea in art cannot be clothed well in words—otherwise poetry would be the only art—perhaps also because I can follow his steps with loving eyes, more than precede him on wings of the soul and perceive his aim."[39]

During his twenties, Fanny Hensel served, in Marcia Citron's words, as a "mail-order critic" for her brother.[40] She provided extensive comments on *St. Paul*, Op. 36, and the *Melusine* overture, Op. 32. She also assisted with the Berlin Singakademie's performance of the former work in 1838.[41] Felix said that his *Die erste Walpurgisnacht* owed its birth to her Sunday musicales, as he considered what music he could send her for it.[42]

During the period preceding her wedding to the Berlin court painter Wilhelm Hensel (1794–1861), Fanny's letters to Felix were filled with an exaggerated adoration: "[I] get up from the piano, stand in front of your picture, and kiss it, and immerse myself so completely in your presence that I—must now write you. But I am infinitely well, and you are infinitely dear to me. Infinitely dear."[43] Felix, too, took part in this Romantic charade, for example, comparing Fanny favorably to Delphine Schauroth (1813–1887), the young pianist with whom he was flirting in Munich in the summer of 1830. He described how her brother

sits here now in a nice little room, and has your green velvet book with the portraits before him, and writes by the open window. Listen, I want you to be very happy and merry this moment, because I am just thinking of you; and if you were so every moment I think of you, you would never become vexed or out of sorts. But you are a perfect dear, that is for sure, and know a lot about music. . . . and if you need a greater admirer than me, then you can paint him or let him paint you.[44]

The exaggeratedly Romantic tone of the correspondence from around 1828–1829 stemmed from the siblings' involvement with the Romantic literature of the period. As an adult, rereading letters from Felix's European travels ten years later, Fanny commented that "it amused me that all of us expressed ourselves like Jean Paul around the time you left here."[45] Although the Romantic role-playing should not be taken too literally, the emotional intensity of the relationship is undeniable. In the period preceding her marriage to Hensel, Fanny had to come to the realization that the changes in her life that marriage would inevitably bring need not include the loss of her beloved brother.

As they grew into adulthood, the youthful exuberance of the siblings became somewhat tempered, and Fanny commented in 1835, "You know, I find that we now write each other very respectable letters; perhaps not as merry as when Beckchen and I sat together and each kept grabbing the quill out of the other's hand in foolish nonsense, but they're sensible and concern ordinary matters."[46] Felix's and Fanny's relationship underwent stress during Mendelssohn's courtship and marriage, largely due to the composer's failure to bring his new bride home to meet his family. Fanny felt hurt and neglected; she complained about her brother's lack of interest in her and her family.[47] Felix, blissfully honeymooning, assured his family, "trust that I will love you so all my life, that I am so closely connected with you that I cannot do anything else."[48]

During the last ten years of his life, as his professional success increased and as his personal obligations centered more on his own growing family, Mendelssohn's reliance on his sister lessened somewhat, as did hers on him. When Mendelssohn became director of the Gewandhaus Orchestra, he found in Leipzig a larger group of more sophisticated musicians with whom to share his latest compositions than he had in Düsseldorf, and so he needed his sister's critical commentary less. In her letters Fanny sometimes comments that new works by her brother are published of which she knows nothing, in sharp contrast to their youth, when she "knew your things by heart even before you wrote them down."[49] After her trip to Italy in 1840, which fulfilled a lifelong dream, Fanny seems to have arrived at a more peaceful state both in her own life and in her relationship with her brother, in spite of continual complaints that they did not see one another enough. In Italy Fanny met Charles Gounod, who much admired her musical abilities, and back in Berlin, Robert von Keudell commented on her compositions; thus, Fanny was in less need of Felix's musical reassurances. In a particularly reflective moment over their past together and the happy state of their lives, she wrote to him, "One must thank God when people who actually belong together stick together and don't part from each other unless separated by death. And, if I remember correctly, it is this then I actually want to mention—and to tell you again once more how your life and activities please me, and how happy I am that we happen to be siblings."[50]

Fanny Hensel's gender and socioeconomic status meant that her musical endeavors would remain those of a nonprofessional rather than a career performer or composer. In the early nineteenth century it would have been unlikely that a woman of her upper-class status would risk "compromising" her position by accepting money for performing or composing. Even half a century later, an article about Fanny in *The Musical Times* found it laudable that she did not undertake a "descent" into the arena of publishing.[51] As an adult she continued the Sunday soirées established by her mother, performing and conducting her own compositions and those of Felix and others. Although several of her songs had been published, including some Lieder that appeared along with Felix's in his Opp. 8 and 9, Fanny Hensel began serious attempts to publish only at the age of forty in 1846.[52]

As Fanny Hensel's life and achievements have emerged from the shadow of those of her brother, Felix Mendelssohn has received a certain amount of blame for Fanny's inability to bring herself to publish her compositions. Sarah Rothenberg writes, "The temptation to surrender to obstacles in the way of creation was intensified for Fanny not just by the norms of her era and proscribed roles for women, but by the constant competitive alter ego of her brother."[53] Mendelssohn's demurral at his mother's request in 1837 that he encourage Fanny to publish is commonly presented as a repressive action on his part. Rothenberg and other writers have suggested that fear of competition from his sister motivated Felix Mendelssohn, though there is certainly no documentary evidence to support this notion, and such professional jealousy played no part in the composer's character or actions.[54] Mendelssohn's actual letter stresses, however, both that it is not his place to give his sister advice on this subject and that he would support her in whatever she endeavored.[55] When she did finally announce her intention to publish, Felix's response was an official welcome to the guild, acknowledging her new professional status, an echo of Zelter's earlier acknowledgment of Felix's status.[56] Although Mendelssohn's belief that Fanny Hensel's priorities should be her roles as wife and mother reveals that he held a typical nineteenth-century German bourgeois attitude, Fanny Hensel's musical frustrations hardly represented a desire to transform the gender roles of her time. Even when she did resolve to publish, she declared herself "no femme libre."[57] More important, however, was Mendelssohn's feeling that publishing was merely a necessary evil for a composer, requiring a continuous production of musical works, even if not always of the highest caliber, rather than their sporadic appearance.[58] Even when she did decide to undertake it, Fanny Hensel did not view publication in this light but rather saw it as an experiment that she could give up if it did not meet with success.[59] A long-unpublished portion of Felix's letter to his mother about Fanny suggests that his response was partially motivated by his concern over the potential strain such activities might have on his sister's health, a concern that stemmed, in part, from his own frequent illnesses and that seems not at all unfounded in light of Fanny's recent miscarriage and her eventual premature death at age 41.[60]

Rather than blame Fanny Hensel's personal insecurity on her brother, it would be more accurate to view it as not unlike his own well-documented self-doubt. Their similar educations also led to similar emotional development. While Mendelssohn's continual doubts were tempered by his public success and international recognition, it was far more difficult for Fanny to fulfill her need for support of her musical efforts. The role of her supportive husband, who encouraged both the Sunday concerts and publication of her music, is frequently overlooked in the rush to judgment of her brother.

In his respect for her playing ability, Felix ranked his sister above all the virtuosos of the day: "She really plays all of the little fellows such as Döhler into the ground."[61] Gender did not color Felix's evaluation of his sister's or of any woman's compositions.[62] Some of Mendelssohn's highest praise is reserved for his sister's compositions: "But truly there is music which seems to have distilled the very quintessence of music, as if it were the soul of music itself—such as these songs. By Jesus! I know of nothing better."[63] In calming his sister's doubts, he wrote, "But you know how I love all your things and especially those that have grown so close to my heart."[64] After her death Felix arranged to have some of Fanny's compositions published, thus carrying out her wishes.[65]

Felix's reaction to his sister's untimely death was utter devastation, revealing the place of utmost importance that she held in his life, a place intimately connected to music. To Charlotte Moscheles he wrote, "You can well imagine, however, how it is for me—to whom she was present at all times, in every piece of music, and in everything that I could experience, good or evil—and so it is for all of us."[66] To represent this relationship as merely that of a female composer hampered by her more successful male sibling is not only to distort the truth but to ignore the love and great respect that these two artists had for one another.

REBECCA AND PAUL MENDELSSOHN BARTHOLDY

While much attention has been paid to Mendelssohn's relationship with his sister Fanny due to their musical connection, his younger sister Rebecca (1811–1858) also played a large part in his life. Sharp-tongued and quick-witted, Rebecca was a source of family entertainment. Married to a mathematician, Peter LeJeune-Dirichlet, Rebecca remained in Berlin and close to her sister Fanny. Felix referred to the two of them affectionately as the "fish-otters."[67] The somewhat pedantic tone of Fanny's letters to Felix is found less often in Rebecca's. While Fanny was the recipient of Mendelssohn's musical observations, it was to Rebecca that he felt free to confide personal details of all sorts. To Rebecca he confessed having drunk "two hundred and twelve glasses of punch fortissimo" at a party, singing the duet from *Faust* in the street, and his hangover the following day; but then he added, "But this part needs to be cut off before you send the letter to Rome [where Fanny was]; one can trust a younger sister in such as this, but an older, pontifical one,—not on your life!"[68] Mendelssohn's joke indicates the differences in the nature of the two relationships, differences that were based in reality, however. His relationship with Rebecca was more carefree and thus in some ways more intimate. It was to Rebecca that Felix first confided such life-changing events as his newfound love for Cécile Jeanrenaud in the summer of 1836.

Rebecca was conscious of the musical dominance of her brother and sister. She joked, "My older siblings stole my artistic fame. In any other family, I would have been much praised as a musician and perhaps even have directed a small circle. But next to Felix and Fanny, I could not have succeeded in attaining any recognition."[69] Of her siblings she wrote, "You fortunate musicians can turn such a mood and environment into songs without words for mankind's pleasure, while I must write horrid prose *with* words."[70] In spite of her familiarity with the same literary and musical world as her siblings, Rebecca's outlook was decidedly less idealistically Romantic. Felix's letters from Italy were later published, almost like the travel reports stemming from Goethe's *Italienreise*, and Fanny's trip to Italy was the most-longed-for and spiritually and artistically fulfilling experience of her life. Fanny rapturously compared one of her Italian outings to a day found in a novel or a poem, which occurs once in a lifetime.[71] In contrast, when Rebecca made the obligatory family pilgrimage to Italy in 1843–1844, she wrote home realistic accounts of the dirt, the foul odors, and the beggars. Rebecca was not immune to Italy's scenery, art, and history. She wrote of her astonishment "that I am in Sicily, in the land of Homer, the Saracens, the Hohenstaufens, and where God created the world," but she could not resist adding, "If only he had not created so many fleas in the process."[72]

Felix Mendelssohn was also quite close to his younger brother Paul (1812–1874). Like the other members of the Mendelssohn family, Paul was thoroughly familiar with his brother's music. Fanny mentions their arguing about tempos after a performance of *St. Paul* at her home in 1836,[73] and in 1843 Felix requested that his brother, as well as his sister, critique *Die erste Walpurgisnacht*.[74] Although Paul followed in the family business of banking, he was also a cellist, for whom his brother composed his second Cello Sonata, Op. 58. Mendelssohn's respect for his brother's musical abilities is apparent in a letter of 1838:

I hope to be able to speak to you soon, to see you, make music with you, go walking—that is better than a letter. But I must thank you for your most recent one, in which you enlightened ignorant me a little bit about paper management. What can I do about the fact that you are so musical, and I can never return the favor in kind?[75]

Four years younger than Felix, Paul looked up to, and admired, his older brother. In a letter to Felix, Fanny reflected that "what I've always valued about Paul . . . is that he has no trace of envy but rather only love for you, although he is well aware that you are both talented in different ways."[76] To Paul's compliments about his music, Felix responded with his usual self-deprecating remarks: "only to deserve the good that you think of it, it first must become very much better."[77] Paul's pride in his older brother's activities was not limited to his professional accomplishments. Fanny described his delight at Felix's engagement: "he's proud of your love to a certain extent—as if he had found love himself."[78]

When Mendelssohn sought refuge from his ever-increasing professional demands in the 1840s, his brother was his desired companion. Felix and Cécile Mendelssohn vacationed in Switzerland with Paul and his wife, Albertine, in 1842 and 1847. Felix called his brother's home "the only hotel in Berlin that I like."[79] The composer trusted his brother sufficiently to rely on him for everything from procuring red wine,[80] to assisting with the negotiations regarding his court position in Berlin. It is clear that Paul's motivation in the latter case was to facilitate Felix's return to Berlin so that he could be reunited with his brother and the rest of his family. Paul served as Felix's sounding board for his numerous frustrations during the extended negotiations. The episode demonstrates how Mendelssohn turned to his brother with his most pressing concerns.

Felix's letters published by Paul and the composer's son Karl largely do not reflect the intimacy of his relationship with his brother.[81] Both volumes were heavily edited, in part to remove Mendelssohn's negative commentary about persons still living when they were published in the 1860s and in part to preserve family privacy, and many scholars have lamented the resulting limitations and inaccuracies. The first collection is designed mainly as travel reminiscences, featuring Mendelssohn's descriptions of his travels in Italy and Switzerland. Although the second book contains a more general selection from the composer's correspondence, the volume has been shaped to create recognizable themes: the debacles surrounding the composer's position in Berlin, Mendelssohn's views on the education of young composers, his concern for the future of German music, his belief in the importance of moral character and the duty of hard work, his sense of the fleeting nature of public popularity, how he dealt with his own fame, and finally his exhaustion from overwork. In general, the selection and editing of the letters portray Mendelssohn in the public sphere, revealing his private face much less frequently. It is clear that Paul saw the letters less as a means of depicting his brother's personality accurately than as a potential moral force, and he was clearly attracted to the writings in which his brother's tone is most reminiscent of the pedantic tone of the letters of their father Abraham. About a month after his brother's death, he wrote to Karl Klingemann,

The work alone could become, in my opinion, a guiding star for many, many people. . . . When I read and reread those [letters] which I possess, I feel elevated and believe myself to be improved. Now I think it would have to be the same for many other people, and a great part of the letters is of general interest,—thoroughly without personal qualities, purely of an objective nature.[82]

In one sense, the volume's heavy concentration on Mendelssohn's proclamations of his artistic opinions and aesthetic beliefs demonstrates that the composer's brother was most inclined to represent his discoursing about the one thing that was most important to him, music. Felix Mendelssohn, however, who wrote that "I have always made it an inviolable rule, never to write on subjects connected with music in public papers,"[83] might have been somewhat dismayed at his brother's contribution to his historical image.

LEIPZIGERSTRASSE 3

According to historian Deborah Hertz, the sparkling salons of Berlin led by women such as Rahel Levin and Henriette Herz declined in the first decade of the nineteenth century with the rise of anti-French sentiment and anti-Semitism.[84] Although she had no literary aspirations and did not cultivate as conspicuously public a persona as her better-known predecessors, Lea Mendelssohn fostered a social life inspired by their salons at Leipzigerstraße 3, the palatial home of the Mendelssohn family beginning in 1835. Lea's 1842 obituary recalled that "she was the center of a select, animated, both intimate and brilliant social life."[85] The Mendelssohn home was frequented by the foremost intellectual and cultural figures in Berlin, though it was more likely to feature a musical, rather than a purely literary, atmosphere, centering around the well-attended Sunday concerts or *Sonntagsmusiken*, at which Felix could try out his compositions. Julius Schubring recalled the atmosphere in which Felix and his siblings lived:

It was seldom, that they were found quite alone; they either had a number of young people who were on a friendly footing with them, or else their circle was filled up with another class of visitors. But it was seldom that there was what is called a regular party. Whoever felt so inclined went, and whoever took a pleasure in going was welcome. Science, Art and Literature were equally represented . . . . Celebrated and uncelebrated people, travellers of all kinds, and especially musicians, though not to the exclusion of other artists, found their efforts judiciously appreciated. The conversation was always animated and spirited.[86]

As he was growing up, Mendelssohn was never without someone with whom to discuss whatever he had recently read or to whom to show his latest composition. Not only was interchange with his equally educated and musically inclined siblings always possible, but the foremost intellectuals of the time who frequented Leipzigerstraße 3 exposed the young musician to a wide cultural realm. Felix might find the naturalist Alexander von Humboldt undertaking magnetism experiments in a hut in the garden or the philosopher Hegel playing cards in the drawing room. Mendelssohn and his siblings shared not only regular music-making but an interest in the writings of Goethe, Jean Paul, and Shakespeare, and the plays of the latter were produced in amateur family productions. In 1842, when Shakespeare's *A Midsummer Night's Dream* was produced in Berlin with Felix's music, Fanny commented on

what an important part the "Midsummer-night's Dream" has always played in our house, how we had at different ages read all of the parts from Peaseblossom to Hermia and Helena, "and how now we have finally brought it to such glory." But we really were brought up entirely on "Midsummer-night's Dream," and Felix especially has made it his own.[87]

The cultural world that sprang from the ongoing social life at Leipzigerstraße 3 shaped the artist whom Mendelssohn became.

Wilhelm Hensel's drawing "Das Rad" (The Wheel), made in 1829, depicts Felix at its center, surrounded by his siblings and the members of his social circle; as his sister Fanny described it, "the entire fine company revolves around him and dances to his piping."[88] Parts of her description of the people, relationships, and events depicted in the allegorical drawing would be unintelligible to anyone outside the Mendelssohns' social circle, but the placement of Felix at the wheel's center clearly demonstrates the important place he had in the lives of his family and friends during their youth. Eric Werner described the wheel as "tightly closed, inaccessible to the outside world, relying only on itself," and he erroneously interpreted it as a visual symbol of Mendelssohn's inability to form relationships with men outside his immediate circle.[89] While it is certainly true that many of Mendelssohn's closest friendships, such as those with Karl Klingemann, Eduard Devrient, Julius Schubring, and Johann Gustav Droysen, dated from his youth, the world of the household at Leipzigerstraße 3 should not be viewed as a closed circle. Writing to his father in 1830, Mendelssohn criticized the very sort of social cliquishness of which Werner accuses him, and in doing so he described the social life of his youth:

Only I cannot quite understand what you say to me about coteries . . . for I know that I, and all of us, hated and feared with all our hearts, what one usually calls that, a self-contained, empty, social life which clings to peculiarities. It is quite natural, however, that among persons who see each other daily, without changing their interests, for their participation in public life must also be lacking, . . . probably in this case, they form among themselves a merry, cheerful, and private manner of talking about things, perhaps also generating unique language; but this still cannot constitute a coterie, and I am convinced that I will never belong to a coterie.[90]

"Das Rad" is, instead, emblematic of young Felix's role in a community, the community that extended from and surrounded his immediate family and that supported him in his musical endeavors. Mendelssohn's lifelong need for a community of individuals who shared his interests, especially his musical interests, stemmed from his early family life and his youth at Leipzigerstraße 3.

As an adult, Mendelssohn maintained a life independent of his family, while still maintaining close ties. The Mendelssohn siblings' correspondence reveals a nostalgic longing for the intercourse of their idyllic youth. The desire to live together, to return somehow to the kind of existence that adult personal and professional obligations made impossible, was a recurring theme. Strong familial ties colored Mendelssohn's decision to accept the court position in Berlin in 1841 and made his decision to return to Leipzig, against the wishes of his mother, especially painful. Felix's longing for reunification with his brother and sister intensified in his grief over the loss of Fanny in 1847.[91] The deaths of Felix and Fanny completed the remaining Mendelssohn siblings' realization that their past togetherness was finally and permanently irretrievable. After hosting a performance of her brother's *Die Heimkehr aus der Fremde* in Göttingen in 1853, Rebecca wrote, "Yes, yes! We are feeding the people with crumbs from our former glory."[92]

CÉCILE JEANRENAUD MENDELSSOHN

In many biographies Mendelssohn is portrayed as sexually repressed, bound by Victorian social conventions, and passionless in romantic relationships. From all available indications, however, Mendelssohn had a healthy heterosexual interest in women, and his excellent social skills allowed for much successful flirtation. When he lived in Düsseldorf, he complained, "and then there are far too few pretty girls here; one doesn't want to be composing fugues and chorales all day long."[93] In his youth nothing much came of his romantic relationships, perhaps because, as his friend Mary Alexander put it, "Bach and Beethoven would always be dearer to you than any beauty."[94]

In 1836, while directing the Cäcilienverein in Frankfurt am Main, Mendelssohn fell in love with Cécile Charlotte Sophia Jeanrenaud (1817–1853), the daughter of the widow of a Reformed minister.[95] Felix and Cécile shared a love of art and spent time drawing together early in their courtship. The couple became engaged in September and were married in March of the following year. Fanny

Hensel described her new sister-in-law as "such an amiable, childishly innocent, freshly refreshing, always even-tempered and cheerful creature that I can only happily praise Felix for having found her. . . . Her presence has something of the effect of a fresh breeze, she is so light, bright and natural."[96] Mendelssohn's friends and relatives agreed that Cécile's calm and quiet nature provided a good balance to the composer's volatile personality.

Mendelssohn's choice of a life companion and his marriage have been much maligned by biographers. Cécile's reserved temperament is absurdly exaggerated; Heinrich Eduard Jacob's comment "You scarcely even noticed she was in the room"[97] can hardly be taken seriously in view of her striking beauty in the portrait by Eduard Magnus. Eric Werner, in particular, found Cécile the symbol of a conventional domestic life and blamed her for a supposed musical conventionality and decline in "masterpieces" in Mendelssohn's output, writing that "the wish to please and impress Cécile weakened his artistic integrity."[98] There is no evidence to support the notion that Mendelssohn's wife, who had no musical training and was described by the composer himself as not at all musical,[99] had any influence of the sort. Moreover, it was not in the composer's character to compromise his musical tastes, and he firmly believed the artist should remain true to himself. In 1843 he wrote to Devrient, "Ever since I began to compose, I have remained true to the fundamental idea: not to write a page because the greatest public or the prettiest girl wanted it to be thus or thus; but only to write as I myself thought right."[100]

Because Mendelssohn's courtship and marriage lacked the drama and turbulence found in the romantic relationships of his musical contemporaries, such as Berlioz, Schumann, Chopin, Liszt, or Wagner, it falls outside widely held myths regarding the role of suffering and irrational passion as the primary inspirational forces in the creation of great art. That Mendelssohn did not suffer for love and had genuine happiness in his marriage and from his children has left biographers at a loss, and Werner and others misrepresent the case when they suggest that such happiness resulted in artistic failure. Mendelssohn's creativity and his compositional output were in no way affected by his marriage, and Cécile was not a false muse who tempted him to an artistic decline. His happy marriage and his five children were a great source of joy in his life and, in difficult times, a source of much comfort. Mendelssohn's personal life demonstrates the compatibility of domesticity and creative output, and biographers' criticisms of what was, by all accounts, a happy marriage reveal their inability to see beyond stereotypes of the alienated Romantic genius and to place Mendelssohn in the context of the familial community that he established for himself as a mature adult.

MENDELSSOHN'S FRIENDS

Besides the members of his immediate family, Mendelssohn's closest friends were those he knew from his childhood. Mendelssohn had a strong sense of fidelity to the acquaintances of his youth and maintained correspondence with old friends, even if their paths rarely crossed during his travels or if his letters often opened with an apology for the long delay separating them from the previous ones. If he and a friend had a falling-out, however, Mendelssohn could be strong-willed and temperamental, and he was quite capable of holding a grudge. He was true to what he believed, particularly regarding musical matters, even at the expense of ruined friendships. The two major friendships of Mendelssohn's that came to an end, those with Adolf Bernhard Marx and Ferdinand Hiller, both ended over musical disputes. Mendelssohn's close friendship with Marx ended, in part, due to his misgivings over Marx's poor compositions; the precipitous event was Mendelssohn's refusal to perform Marx's oratorio *Moses*.[101] Hiller's relationship with Mendelssohn came under strain, and their correspondence ended, after the 1843–1844 concert season in Leipzig, when Hiller substituted for Mendelssohn as director of the Gewandhaus Orchestra. Mendelssohn seems to have believed that Hiller was taking advantage of his position to feature his own wife, an Italian singer, as soloist with his orchestra too often.[102]

Many of Mendelssohn's closest friends were significantly older than he was. Eduard Devrient was eight years older than the composer, Karl Klingemann eleven years, Adolf Bernhard Marx fourteen, and Ignaz Moscheles fifteen, for example. All of these individuals knew the composer from his childhood, and, with the exception of Marx, the friendships lasted until Mendelssohn's death. Young Mendelssohn must have demonstrated a certain precociousness in social skills as well as in intellect and musical ability to establish and maintain these friendships with older individuals. It is possible that the portrait of Mendelssohn that has been transmitted through contemporary accounts into modern biographies has been influenced by these age differences.[103] A natural curiosity about the nature of a child prodigy, combined with the fact that many of Mendelssohn's closest contemporaries recounted memories of his boyhood, has led to the inaccurate notion that "he never matured emotionally to a sufficient extent to sustain, still less to consolidate, his adolescent genius."[104] In fact, Mendelssohn reached emotional maturity very early, which was essential to his forming in childhood and early youth these relationships, remarkably equal ones, with adults. The numerous accounts of Mendelssohn the remarkable child and exuberant teenager have gained precedence over evidence of the mature adult and professional that Mendelssohn clearly became. The tendency of some of Mendelssohn's contemporaries, particularly Devrient and Marx, to stress their own influence on the youth in their accounts of him further enhances the suggestion that Mendelssohn's talent remained undeveloped and that the composer was somehow unable to function without his friends' guidance.

Not surprisingly, Mendelssohn's closest friends were musicians or individuals who had some knowledge and understanding of music. The cultural surroundings of the composer's upbringing, however, meant that a variety of individuals, particularly those inclined toward artistic, literary, or other intellectual interests, attracted him. Two important examples were the historian Johann Gustav Droysen (1808–1884), who had been his tutor, and the pastor Julius Schubring

(1806–1889), who assisted with the texts of Mendelssohn's oratorios and with whom Mendelssohn could discuss issues surrounding sacred music. In Leipzig he became close friends with the attorney Heinrich Konrad Schleinitz (1802–1881), who was one of the directors of the Gewandhaus concerts and thus also had strong musical interests.

Mendelssohn, who demonstrated talent in drawing, also had many artist friends, including Wilhelm Schadow (1788–1862), Eduard Bendemann (1811–89), and Eduard Magnus (1799–1872). The composer's attraction to artists was partly due to his own artistic inclinations and partly to the fact that art was part of the cultural life of his family—most evidently embodied in the person of his brother-in-law Wilhelm Hensel. A great deal of Mendelssohn's social intercourse with artists took place during his trip to Italy and during his years in Düsseldorf. Writing to his friends about life in Düsseldorf, Mendelssohn complained of the "philistines" there, "so I really associate only with painters here, and they are amiable fellows."[105] However agreeable he found artists as companions, in general Mendelssohn preferred the company of other musicians. Mendelssohn's letters from Italy describe numerous acquaintances and social activities, yet he complains of loneliness and of having no one to whom to show his new compositions: "I have no one here to whom I could very openly communicate everything, who could read my music as I write it and make it doubly dear to me, with whom I could relax completely and be at ease, and from whom I could honestly learn."[106] Friends with whom he could share music were essential to his well-being and helped to stimulate his creativity. Not just any musician could fulfill the composer's needs. Not only was the group of individuals from whom the composer might learn naturally somewhat select, but beyond that, Mendelssohn required someone with similar artistic inclinations and musical tastes. For example, although he knew them professionally, such nineteenth-century musical luminaries as Hector Berlioz and Franz Liszt were not destined to become Mendelssohn's close friends. While differences in personal temperament were clearly a factor in both cases, musical differences were equally or more important. Of Berlioz, Mendelssohn wrote that "he makes me regularly sad, because he is a truly educated, pleasant man and composes so inconceivably badly."[107] In spite of his respect for Liszt's pianistic virtuosity, Mendelssohn found that he lacked "a true talent for composition, really original ideas."[108] William Little's assertion that "Mendelssohn and Liszt were separated by aesthetic, moral, cultural, and artistic differences which were ultimately irreconcilable,"[109] holds equally for Berlioz and, more importantly, describes the spheres in which Mendelssohn's friendships were defined.

EDUARD DEVRIENT

Actor, singer, librettist, director, and theater historian Eduard Devrient (1801–1877) was a member of the Mendelssohns' circle from 1822; he and his wife Thérèse lived in the Mendelssohn family's garden house during the years 1829–1830. Devrient's *Recollections* are an important primary source of information about the composer: his youth, the famous revival of J. S. Bach's *St. Matthew Passion*, and his unsuccessful search for a suitable opera libretto.[110] Devrient vividly depicts Mendelssohn's childhood and adolescence, thus offering an overall portrait of the composer that tends to make him seem somewhat childlike. Devrient himself is the hero of his own book, rather than Mendelssohn, always managing to turn up at crucial moments and offer advice to his younger friend, who seems to need such assistance. For example, in Devrient's account of the decision to perform the *St. Matthew Passion* it is he who is tormented by a desire for the performance,[111] who must drag Felix from a deep slumber to convince him, and who makes the bulk of the arguments necessary to convince a resistant Zelter, while Felix hovers "pale and hurt" by the door, ready to make a rapid escape.[112] Rather than an active participant in the event, Mendelssohn is presented as, at best, a passive observer and, at worst, restrained by timidity, by most accounts not an aspect of his character. Published almost forty years after the event, the entire passage has a fictitious quality about it, complete with actual dialogue. This is not to deny Devrient's place in Mendelssohn's life or even to question the veracity of his accounts. Yet in general his *Recollections* are somewhat self-serving, frequently at the expense of his portrayal of Mendelssohn. His introduction to the volume concludes by stating that the composer was "a noble man, even in his weaknesses and shortcomings," [113] and his emphasis is frequently on the latter qualities.

An ongoing theme in Devrient's *Recollections* is Mendelssohn's approaching death, a death that supposedly stems, in part, from the composer's own musical genius. Devrient writes that Mendelssohn's gifts "aroused frequent doubts in me, as to whether the nervous energy of a brain could sustain such unreasonable demands through the length of an ordinary life."[114] Mendelssohn thus becomes a victim of his own nature, and his musical talent a dangerous force that weakens his health. While Mendelssohn's documented poor health may well have caused his friend concern, linking the composer's physical ailments to his genius, however Romantic, seems, in a more modern light, to be blaming the victim.[115]

Devrient frequently takes a condescending tone toward Mendelssohn's music, as well. As a singer, actor, and librettist, Devrient naturally emphasized Mendelssohn's vocal music or music with obvious extramusical influences, for example, overlooking the Octet in favor of *A Midsummer Night's Dream*.[116] Because Devrient believed that Mendelssohn's true vocation was "dramatic composition,"[117] the composer's inability to produce a mature opera dooms him to professional failure in his friend's eyes. Among the operatic topics Mendelssohn had rejected were numerous suggestions by Devrient, including his libretto *Hans Heiling*, later set by Heinrich Marschner with much success. Even before Mendelssohn's death, Devrient had become associated with Richard Wagner in Dresden; it is likely that by the time the *Recollections* was published in 1869, its author was influenced by both the ideas of his colleague and the changing tenor of the musical aesthetics of the period.[118]

Devrient also complained that late in his life Mendelssohn began to "repeat himself in his composition" and suggested to his friend that by composing less he would be able to create more original works.[119] In his criticism of Mendelssohn's obsessive work habits, Devrient betrays a fundamental lack of understanding of his compositional technique, stemming from Romantic notions about the supposedly spontaneous nature of creativity. Mendelssohn's ideas about the relationship of inspiration and craftsmanship were articulated in a letter to Ferdinand Hiller in 1837. The composer wrote, "There is nothing more offensive to me than finding fault with someone's nature or talent," the very thing that Devrient did years later; "one cannot add a yard to one's stature,—all striving and toiling are useless there, so one must keep silent about it,—God has to have responsibility for it."[120] The composer is, according to Mendelssohn, entirely responsible for the development [*Entwicklung* or *Ausführung*] of the musical ideas that come from inspiration: "I know perfectly well that no musician can make his thoughts [*Gedanken*] or his talents different from what Heaven gives him, but I also know just as well that if Heaven has given him good ones, he must also be able to develop them well."[121]

Devrient found himself unable to reconcile his skewed interpretation of Mendelssohn's belief in a composer's lack of control over his basic musical ideas, that "the first involuntary thought would be the right one even if it is not striking or new," with Mendelssohn's criticism of his finished compositions and his tendency toward extensive revision. Devrient wrote, "I thought he confused his urge to work with the urge to create."[122] Devrient criticized not only Mendelssohn's initial musical ideas but the very aspect of composition over which Mendelssohn believed he had some control, the working out of musical ideas, the process that Devrient deprecatingly described as his "critical fastidiousness." Devrient's wish that the composer not just "work" but hold back in order to "create" not only was entirely against Mendelssohn's nature but is clearly incongruous. Devrient further suggested that Mendelssohn's self-critical nature "doomed his brightest powers to inactivity"[123] and that it was what prevented Mendelssohn from achieving Devrient's goal for him, the composition of an opera. In actuality, Mendelssohn's obsessive revisions to his compositions inevitably improved them—the composer believed that revision brought a work *closer* to its original conception[124]—but this approach was irreconcilable with Devrient's rather naive notion that inspiration is more important than compositional technique and his inability to recognize that a work's originality may be found in the composer's development of musical ideas.

Near the end of the *Recollections*, the themes of premature death and operatic failure are combined in an overly dramatic fashion: "There is a truly Hamletlike tragedy about Mendelssohn's operatic destiny. . . . when at last he overcomes himself to devote himself to the work, even with a questionable poem [*Die Lorelei*], he sinks with the fragment of his toils into the grave."[125]

It is clear that Devrient's most critical remarks are colored by time and influenced by later nineteenth-century aesthetics, and his association with Wagner may be reflected here, as well. Mendelssohn's letters reveal that the friends were able to laugh about the differences between their natures; he teased Devrient about his tendency to be "self-satisfied," and Devrient and his wife jokingly referred to Felix as a disgruntled "Polish count."[126] In spite of the attitudes revealed in his *Recollections*, Devrient's friendship obviously meant a great deal to Mendelssohn during his lifetime, and he was one of the individuals with whom Mendelssohn felt he was in accord: "For art has the same place in your heart as mine, and we have always had a perfect understanding in all the things about which one will never come to an understanding with other people."[127]

FERDINAND HILLER

Ferdinand Hiller (1811–1885) and Mendelssohn met when both were still children, but their friendship began to flourish only in their young adult lives. They had a great deal in common: both were child prodigies who began composing at an early age, and both had careers as pianists and composers. They shared a Jewish heritage as well as an interest in older composers such as Bach and Beethoven.

Hiller's *Letters and Recollections*, published in 1874, though sometimes highly sentimental in tone, has none of the problems of Devrient's. If Hiller strays from his narrative to discuss his own music or an incident in his life, such as his precarious return from a boating excursion with Mendelssohn in 1827, his tone is frequently apologetic, and the anecdote is told purely for amusement, not for self-aggrandizement. Hiller's asides are more often about other contemporaries of Mendelssohn than about himself, and they contribute much to our understanding of cultural context. In his preface the author claims that he hesitated to publish such a book, because he did not wish to be perceived as capitalizing on his friend's fame, and his approach throughout the volume makes one tend to believe him.

The most vivid portions of Hiller's book are those that describe the times he and Mendelssohn spent together in Paris in 1831–1832, mischievously accosting Kalkbrenner on the street with the assistance of their colleagues Liszt and Chopin, indulging in French pastries, and, at Mendelssohn's insistence, practicing their jumps late at night on a deserted Paris street, with all the exuberance of youth.[128] In general, though, Hiller focuses more on Mendelssohn the adult, in particular in a long passage describing his extended visit to Leipzig in 1839, on an invitation from Mendelssohn, who hoped to distract his grieving friend after his mother's death. In his detailed description of Mendelssohn's personal and musical life in Leipzig, his composition habits, and his massive professional obligations, Hiller does not overlook the composer's depression and exhaustion.[129] The leaping youth has, without losing his sense of humor, become a thoughtful adult, capable of conversing with his friend about such philosophical matters as whether he believes in the progress of humanity.[130] Through Hiller we can also get a glimpse of the mature Mendelssohn's superb social skills, for example, during the Lower Rhine Music Festival of 1836, when "Mendelssohn was in every way the center of the Festival, not only as a composer, conductor, and pianist, but also, I want to say, as a cheerful, obliging host, mediating acquaintances, bringing together those who belong together, bestowing kindness wherever he could."[131]

Though prolific as a composer, Hiller was well aware that his compositional abilities could not compare with his friend's, and he was not embarrassed to print Mendelssohn's encouragements and on some occasions, criticisms. Mendelssohn wrote to him, "I believe that you, with your talent, are inferior to no present musician, but I know hardly any piece of yours which is properly worked out."[132] Mendelssohn's appraisals of Hiller's music were tactful and carefully softened with praise. He clearly believed their friendship could sustain his comments, writing, "but how many musicians are there who would permit it from another?"[133]

It is apparent from Mendelssohn's half of the correspondence that Hiller could sometimes be quite self-deprecatory,[134] a tendency in which Mendelssohn must have recognized his own attitudes. One suspects that in his attempts to reassure Hiller, he is in some sense trying to deal with himself. Too much satisfaction with one's accomplishments is bound to lead to stagnation, and so Hiller's—and by association his own—anxiety is justified: "If such a mood leads to cheerful complacency and a person's works always remain the same, then I believe he is a genuine Philistine and that he never does anything decent all his entire life, so I don't complain about your desponding words."[135] Mendelssohn's position was clearly that it is acceptable to be critical of one's own work, even when that work is good (as some of Hiller's work certainly was); indeed, this is far preferable to being satisfied with poor work, as self-satisfaction will inevitably lead to poor results.

In spite of his criticisms, Mendelssohn's optimism about his friend's abilities was genuine. After one of Hiller's improvisations, Mendelssohn told him, "I can't comprehend how you can for an instant ever doubt your musical gifts."[136] The most magnanimous reflection of Mendelssohn's encouragement was his letter to Simrock asking that he publish Hiller's music, accompanied by vehement exhortations that his efforts remain a secret from his friend.[137]

Mendelssohn found Hiller's musical tastes far too influenced by Parisian fashions to suit him, and Hiller acknowledged that they had major differences about both French and Italian music.[138] To Ignaz Moscheles, Mendelssohn confessed, "I have recently seen some etudes by Hiller, which I also did not like; and I am sorry for that, because I am fond of him, and believe he has talent. But Paris is undoubtedly bad soil."[139] One of the recurring themes of Mendelssohn's letters is his questioning Hiller as to whether he will ever leave Paris or Italy and return to take a position in Germany.[140] Mendelssohn may have desired to lure Hiller away from corrupting musical influences or may merely have wanted his friend in closer proximity. In either case, his letters to Hiller reveal him to be intent on maintaining the closeness of the friendship and occasionally contain the kind of nostalgic longing for them to be reunited that he more often expressed to members of his immediate family:

I have quite an unusual pleasure in writing to you today, and chatting with you; I was thinking of how I used to lie on your sofa and complain and make you play the piano for me

... and then I thought how good it would be if we could see one another again soon and really live together, and then I thought how far off that must be.[141]

In the end, what cemented Hiller's and Mendelssohn's relationship is not available to us, that is, the musical interchanges that took place between them at the piano. Hiller writes, "The hours which I spent with Mendelssohn at the piano, in the exchange of our musical perceptions of compositions of various kinds, our own and those of others, were, in a certain sense, the best that I was allowed to pass with him."[142]

While Hiller's concluding chapter sometimes lapses into the sort of flowery Mendelssohn worship that is anathema to modern biographers, it realistically addresses the greatest problem that still lingers in modern Mendelssohn mythology—the notion that the composer's many advantages, wealth, family support, and education, in some way hindered his becoming a great composer and the idea that the fact that he did not suffer enough in his life resulted in a shallowness in his art. Hiller puts the issue to rest:

The struggle for the ordinary necessities of life may well be a difficult one, but in itself it has no particular merit. . . . Therefore, when an artist like Mendelssohn gathered his entire strength together to give to the smallest song which flowed from him the perfection which he continuously had in mind as ideal, when he strained his full abilities and knowledge to further all that is best in his art on every side, he surely deserves no less acknowledgment because he has been granted a position free from all material cares, than if he were forced to wait for compensation for his work in order to satisfy his creditors.[143]

The disagreement that ended their friendship was no longer significant decades later, and Hiller comes to an eloquent defense of Mendelssohn's personal and professional reputation.

IGNAZ MOSCHELES

When Ignaz Moscheles (1794–1870) first encountered Mendelssohn in Berlin in 1824, it was ostensibly to give the prodigy piano lessons. From the beginning and throughout their relationship, however, Moscheles acknowledged Mendelssohn's genius, and he came to realize that his friend was the better composer. Over the years, their friendship changed from that of a child and an adult to that of two adults and progressed from formality to intimacy.

When Moscheles and Mendelssohn first met, the former was a pianist with an international career. Moscheles settled in London in 1826, where he conducted the Royal Philharmonic Society and taught. Mendelssohn's 1829 letters to Moscheles began with restrained politeness, asking for advice and assistance as he began to plan his grand tour. The older artist resolved to help his young acquaintance gain entry into London's musical society and eased Felix's way by renting him rooms and making introductions. Moscheles and his wife were still grieving the recent death of their young son and found Mendelssohn sensitive to their loss. Moscheles wrote in his diary that "he knows how to heal our wounded spirits and seems to have made it his mission to bring us compensation for our sufferings."[144] Mendelssohn's relationship with Moscheles flourished after his 1832 visit to England, a period in which the two men saw one another almost daily and to which Moscheles referred as "glorious days."[145] The Moscheleses came to function as a second family for Felix, and it was to them he turned upon hearing of the death of his teacher Zelter.[146]

Like his letters to Hiller, Mendelssohn's and Moscheles's correspondence is full of talk of their trade, including critiques of the music of Herz, Kalkbrenner, Thalberg, and Chopin and complaints about the insipid nature of much of the virtuosic music of the time. The two pianists took great delight in playing together, both publicly and privately, and engaged in joint improvisations, each including portions of the other's compositions.[147] After Moscheles had improvised with Johann Nepomuk Hummel at Weimar in 1832, he noted in his diary that Hummel, "however, I felt, was no Felix." When the friends were reunited in 1840, Moscheles's wife, Charlotte, commented that it had been worth her seven-year wait to hear them play together.[148] What Mendelssohn looked forward to most about their meetings was the inevitable musical interchange: "We shall make music that's admirable again together. I, at least, am hungrier and thirstier for it than ever."[149] When planning a musical evening for Moscheles in 1846, Mendelssohn wrote, "for a Moscheles . . . we make good music, but not for everybody."[150]

On his first visit to England Mendelssohn continued to treat Moscheles as his superior. Moscheles wrote "that in him I recognized my own master and was enraptured when he expected to be sharply criticized," clearly an expectation that had its origins in Mendelssohn's upbringing. Moscheles continued, "however, he is and remains a subordinate pupil to me, no matter how I try to give him a more correct position relative to me."[151] Although these dynamics changed as Mendelssohn became professionally successful, Moscheles continued to be one of the persons to whom he sometimes turned for comments on his works. If Moscheles's published letters and diaries are any indication, he seems to have served more as a cheering section for his friend than as a critic. Moscheles continually tried to counter Mendelssohn's modesty and self-deprecating manner and attempted to convince him not to undersell his compositions when offering them for publication.[152] Mendelssohn frequently protested that Moscheles was too generous, too indulgent in his praise; nonetheless, he must have found it comforting that a person he held in such high esteem approved of his efforts, and Moscheles undoubtedly helped to reassure Mendelssohn's endless self-doubts.

Yet Mendelssohn's relationship with Moscheles, though founded in their mutual musical interests and tastes, was much deeper than this. Moscheles wrote that he would like to call Mendelssohn a brother or a son,[153] and the intimacy that developed between them is confirmed in Moscheles's report of their 1840 trip to Berlin, in which they discussed their respective courtships and choice of wives.[154] Already by 1839 Mendelssohn could look back somewhat nostalgically on the long years of their friendship, noting that both were now fathers of children.[155] Indeed,

Mendelssohn's affection for Moscheles extended to his entire family. While Ignaz worked to further Felix's musical opportunities in England, his wife, Charlotte, fussed over him somewhat maternally and good-humoredly. Their letters reveal a long running joke about the nature of their friendship: with mock humility, Felix submits to Charlotte's efforts to reform him for his own social betterment, though he confesses that there is little hope of his ever making any improvement. For example, exasperated that after all her efforts Felix was still unable to pin his cravat properly, Charlotte sent him a pre-tied cravat with the assertion that it would allow further time for him to compose, and the cravat problem became the center of numerous jokes.[156]

Mendelssohn's comfort in the circle of the Moscheles family allows us to see him at his funniest and most charming, in contrast to the formal reserve reflected in the letters of the busy professional in Leipzig. His correspondence with Ignaz and Charlotte contains much humor, including Mendelssohn's amusing, cartoonlike drawings recalling their music or major life events, such as the drums and trumpets he penned in 1833 upon the birth of his godson Felix Moscheles. Mendelssohn seems to have inspired Moscheles to humor, as well, and the atmosphere surrounding them was sometimes nothing short of uproarious. Charlotte Moscheles recalled an incident from 1840 when Moscheles and Mendelssohn were traveling by mail coach with the critic Henry Chorley:

Unfortunately the coach has a fourth place, and the trio of friends is disturbed by an uninvited person. "He sleeps well," says one, "let's think about what we shall do with him when he wakes up." "Kill him, that's the only way," says another. At that moment the sleeper stirs; naturally the speakers are alarmed on account of their evil wit, and Moscheles, with his own quick wittedness, breaks in with the words in English, "And then she said she would never marry that man," a sentence which from then on became a proverb among them. Mendelssohn breaks into a Homeric laugh that infects the two others.[157]

Mendelssohn's love of children is quite apparent in his correspondence with Moscheles, as their respective children are frequent topics in their letters. Mendelssohn participated in "games and romps" with his godson Felix Moscheles, as well as an occasional snowball fight.[158] Mendelssohn's correspondence describes the flowers that he would be presenting Moscheles's daughters, were he able to visit in person, rather than by letter. When Moscheles visited the Mendelssohn household, young Karl Mendelssohn delighted in hearing "Uncle" Moscheles play the piano with his fists in a style that his own father could never imitate successfully.[159]

Moscheles's relationship with Mendelssohn, both musical and personal, brought the former to Leipzig after over twenty years in England. In creating the Leipzig Conservatory, Mendelssohn was able both to pursue artistic aims and to enhance his personal community, as well, surrounding himself with musicians with whom he felt personally and artistically at home: Moscheles, Hiller, Ferdinand David, and Robert Schumann, among others. Moscheles was attracted to the artistic community in Leipzig, a community that had Mendelssohn at its center.

Moscheles loved Mendelssohn deeply. Although music was the greatest part of the tie between them, Moscheles's feeling for his friend was not awestruck worship of the brilliant artist but a regard for Mendelssohn the complete human being: "Besides my dearest family ties, he lays claim to my entire self. He appears to me alternately as a brother, son, affectionate friend, but mostly as a burning enthusiast for music, who hardly seems to suspect to what a height he has already ascended."[160]

KARL KLINGEMANN

Although many of Mendelssohn's closest friends were professional musicians, one of his most intimate friends was not. Karl Klingemann (1798–1862) was a Hanoverian diplomat and a member of the Mendelssohn family circle in Berlin. He was a good friend of Fanny Mendelssohn, and in general the family thought highly of the young man, claiming him as one of their own. After he was stationed in London in 1827, he wrote wildly humorous letters describing his new life in a foreign land, but underneath the witty surface it was clear that Klingemann missed the Mendelssohns: "Berlin appears to me a perfect Eldorado, and a Sunday at the Mendelssohns' like a chapter from a fairy tale."[161] According to Fanny, the family reciprocated his feelings, and she chronicled their response to his letters in the same exaggerated scenarios with which she depicted the arrival of her brother's letters:

Each one of us considered the magnificent general letter as his or her own special possession. . . . The longer you made us wait for your letter, the more we enjoyed it when it finally arrived (but do not take this as a rule for the future; for then it will be the opposite case), and we would have been like real Bacchantes tearing at it (we really devoured it) between us, if our parents had not generously resigned themselves and allowed us the first reading.[162]

Klingemann spent the rest of his career in England, and in spite of the long distance between them he became a lifelong friend of Felix Mendelssohn, as well. Although Klingemann's musical position was that of an amateur, he came from the same cultural world as Felix Mendelssohn, and they shared literary as well as musical tastes. When Mendelssohn made his first trip to England in 1829, he and Klingemann were, in spite of the lighthearted tone of their correspondence, still using the formal "Sie." The age difference between the two may account for this, as during this period Klingemann was already in his mid-twenties, while Mendelssohn grew from a teenager into a young man. Even after the friendship had deepened, Felix affectionately called Karl "old Klingemann," though this may not reflect the age difference so much as a parallel to the British upper-class usage by which male friends called each other "old man."

The walking tour of England and Scotland that they undertook together not only provided the young composer with significant musical inspiration but also solidified their friendship. Of their grand adventure in Scotland, Felix wrote,

It is no wonder that the Highlands have been called melancholy. But if two comrades ever went merrily through them, laughed at every opportunity, wrote and sketched together, growled at one another and at the world when they were annoyed or did not find anything to eat, devoured everything edible, and slept twelve hours—this would be the two of us, and we will not forget it as long as we live.[163]

Not only did Felix and Karl face the uncertainties of weather and travel together, but they wrote joint letters about their escapades to Mendelssohn's family in Berlin and maintained a sketchbook, in which Felix drew memorable views, and Klingemann composed poems to go with his friend's drawings. After such a trip, Felix found the separation from his friend particularly lonely:

The night I wrote the last letter, Klingemann had packed his things and gotten ready, and I accompanied him to the post office; he climbed up on the coach, we exchanged a few German words up and down, then the guard sounded the trumpet miserably, the stage clattered away, and London seemed to me so much like home that I might have been born there; I returned alone through the rain to my empty room, and lay down to sleep in the room with two beds; it had all seemed so different just a quarter of an hour before—in short picture for yourselves the worst evening imaginable and you won't even come close to the truth.[164]

Klingemann's dedication to his friend is revealed in the manner in which he took care of Felix during his recuperation from the leg injury he received in a carriage accident. Their mutual friend Friedrich Rosen described this in his letter reassuring the Mendelssohn family back in Berlin:

I cannot leave you without expressing my warmest praise for the faithfulness and care with which Klingemann hardly left the side of our Felix during the entire time of his suffering. With unending love he cared for him and carried out all the little duties which a mother could not have fulfilled more affectionately for her suffering child.[165]

Mendelssohn especially missed his friend while in Italy in 1830, describing Klingemann, "who is so unusual, and so fresh and strange, and at the same time possesses a gentle soul."[166]

Mendelssohn particularly valued Klingemann's dry wit and humorous stories—often exaggerated versions of real events—and was entertained by the amusing plays on words in his friend's letters. Klingemann's hyperbolic tales were legendary among the Mendelssohn family; Felix could protest in his letters home that his recounting of his own escapades "was all true, not Klingemannesque storytelling."[167] Klingemann's sense of humor is demonstrated in his list of the English customs of which Felix needed to be aware, written before his first trip to England, from how to say "No, thank you" to how to avoid knocking on the door like a servant; the most ironic of these is number 7: "Be somewhat musical—they like that here,"[168]—this instruction to the master musician who was about to meet with tremendous success in England.

Klingemann served as Mendelssohn's main personal contact in England, and the composer's letters to him are full of lists of people to greet and numerous inquiries about his English friends. Klingemann the professional diplomat kept Mendelssohn abreast of political events in England. Mendelssohn also relied on Klingemann in many of his dealings with English publishers.[169] Klingemann, in turn, kept Felix generally informed about performances of his compositions in Britain, both good and bad. In 1830 he turned his description of a bad performance of the Overture to *A Midsummer Night's Dream* into a means of expressing how much he missed his friend: "Personality, it is clear to me, predominates here. I've never seen that so clearly as in your case,—it is as if the person of the artist were a bridge to his works. . . . And your works and your friends therefore call: Come soon!"[170]

Because the composer's letters to Klingemann were published in 1909 without the heavy editing found in the family correspondence, they sometimes show glimpses of a Mendelssohn whose discourse with his friends clashes with the widely disseminated image of a perfect Victorian gentleman, as in this passage: "Your crazy joint letter has just arrived. Mother read it to me up to the place in line 8: 'Rosen sat on his a--'—then I took it out of her hand and expressed the opinion that it would probably get even worse."[171]

As a composer, Mendelssohn found it natural to take advantage of his friend's literary abilities. Ten of Mendelssohn's Lieder are settings of Klingemann's poetry, and the text of the Liederspiel *Die Heimkehr aus der Fremde*, for Abraham and Lea Mendelssohn's 1829 silver wedding anniversary, was also Klingemann's creation. Mendelssohn respected his friend's talents and praised Klingemann's libretto as eminently singable: "it was not difficult to compose it, the words are already music, and if I think about the fact that I shall sometime receive worse ones, I do not know how I shall do it. I spoke your words so long until I sang them; then it's easy indeed."[172] Klingemann assisted in translating the texts of Handel's *Solomon* and of *Elijah*. In regard to his help with the latter, the composer described his friend as one "who understands both languages thoroughly, and who understands my music better than both languages."[173]

The link between Mendelssohn and Klingemann was ultimately not literary but musical, like that in all his other important friendships: Mendelssohn and Klingemann saw themselves, as they were on their Scottish trip, as artistic collaborators. Unhappy in Paris and unable to compose, Mendelssohn turned to his friend for help:

My entire letter has spleen, and I also have it entirely and completely; that doesn't come from Paris, however, but because I haven't composed anything in a long time. Can't you help me out and send me a small Lied text? It may be whatever it will, as long as it is pretty. And by you. I would like very much to compose a beautiful song.[174]

In a letter to the composer describing a successful performance of his "Italian" Symphony, Klingemann manifests a similar attitude to that of the composer's parents in refusing to indulge him. At the same time, however, he acknowledges

Felix's musical importance to him personally: "do not expect me to praise you very much today: other people are spoiling my Music Director with their applause, and I will refrain from doing so for a time."[175] Mendelssohn's response to his friend reveals that their relationship was similar to that with Moscheles, in that the friendship helped provide the emotional support for his creative efforts: "I do not believe that any praise will ever spoil me, let alone yours—rather it spurs me onwards, if it comes from you."[176]

Though the friends' plan to collaborate on an opera based on Kotzebue's *Pervonte* dominated their 1834 letters, the project eventually came to naught. Mendelssohn's letters to his librettist friend reveal obsessive attempts to control what Klingemann produced, from the overall plot, to even such details as word order and names of characters. The composer was not especially tactful in his criticisms of Klingemann's attempts, at one point blithely refusing even to consider the third act, before the second met his standards. Mendelssohn's directions became voluminous, so much so that one's sympathies lie with Klingemann in the interchange. Klingemann must have felt as if he could do no right, and it is a testimony both to him and to the strength of the friendship that it survived this extremely trying episode.

The friendship lasted the composer's entire life, and among his many relationships Mendelssohn considered his bond with Klingemann to be unique, even though he often downplayed his expressions of love for his friend with humor. To Karl he wrote,

You're the only person with whom it feels completely to me as though we were together, and as often as I have read your letter again, I was in London and with you, that is, happy. You always paint for me with two words the country and weather and every little feature. I do not know at all whether you deserve it, but I know we belong together. Therefore write to me; I need it very much.[177]

Mendelssohn wrote to his brother, "It is a wonderful thing to have such a friend, something one finds only once in life."[178] To Klingemann himself the composer wrote, "A person can have only one friend says Montaigne, says Vult, it says in *Flegeljahre*. And this I repeated with all my heart when I received your letter, you, one friend."[179] In 1841, during his frustrating deliberations regarding his position in Berlin, Mendelssohn wrote to Klingemann,

You believe that I am asking you for advice, and afterwards do not want to act accordingly. Truthfully, if I were to ask you about this and everything else, if I were to say something to you, to do the opposite, I would say and do it for no other reason than out of instinct. I must speak about or discuss with you something which is important to me, which concerns me deeply—that cannot be otherwise—and that occurs so little on account of the tiresome request for advice, that I am convinced, had you not answered at all, and had we spoken to one another again after ten years, I would put to you the same questions, awaited your answer just as eagerly, would have as happily received it, as now.[180]

Felix took his friend for granted, and while this seems occasionally to have met with some irritation from Klingemann, it also reveals how deeply Mendelssohn relied on him. He came to see Klingemann as a permanent fixture in his life, regardless of disagreements, and regardless of time and distance.

After the composer's early death, Klingemann, with typical self-abnegation, expressed his gratitude for Mendelssohn to his widow; though couched in his Romantic literary style, the passage reveals the pivotal place that Mendelssohn held in Klingemann's life, as well:

It is now a miracle to me, that such a fortune has been mine. I feel truly in deepest humility how undeserved it was, and how little I was to him and could give to him, for all the abundance of the best and most beautiful that he scattered over my past life. But I thank the kind heaven over and over, which granted me such rich blessing. I will take it with me into my old age as my best fortune, and will be revived by it again and again. . . . to be comforted by his music, I will only come to that later, but always I will be edified by the transfiguration in which all spring and all youth, the entire past belongs only to him and with him has been brought to an end.[181]

IN LONDON: THE ALEXANDERS, HORSLEYS, FRIEDRICH ROSEN

Mendelssohn's deep affection for England was due not only to his numerous professional successes during his ten trips there but also to his encounters with a community of individuals who understood him and his music, both professional musicians such as Moscheles, Charles Horsley, Thomas Attwood, and Sir George Smart and personal friends such as Karl Klingemann and Friedrich Rosen. Mendelssohn wrote that "I have become used to this in London" and that he could not expect to find anywhere else a group of friends like those he had in England.[182] Through the help of friends such as Klingemann and Moscheles, Mendelssohn was introduced into communities of English friends with whom he felt at home. English families such as the Horsleys and the Alexanders not only had much in common with the values of the Mendelssohns but they also featured attractive and well-educated daughters, interested both in things German and in music. Welcomed into their homes, Mendelssohn found a comfortable social life in a familial atmosphere, and in these private settings he frequently performed for his friends, trying out new compositions or works in progress. Begun in his young adulthood, Mendelssohn's English friendships were maintained through correspondence and lasted throughout his life, and he took great pleasure in renewing them upon return trips to England.

Because his friendships with women outside his family had no immediately discernible impact on Mendelssohn's career, traditional biographies of the composer have tended to overlook them. Victorian social strictures regarding gender meant that Mendelssohn's friendships with the Alexander or Horsley sisters would necessarily differ from those he established with the men who moved in his professional sphere. When one examines these ties more closely, however, the dichotomy of male/public and female/private commonly used to describe the social structures of the period sometimes seems more of a theoretical construct than a historical reality, which has created a somewhat one-sided picture of the composer's social interactions.

The three Alexander sisters endeared themselves to Felix during his 1833 trip to London, when his father became incapacitated by a fall, and they descended upon the elderly gentleman with food and flowers. Wealthy, fashionable, and well-connected in aristocratic social circles, the sisters were desirable friends who shared many of Mendelssohn's interests. Boyd Alexander has suggested that the sisters' Scottish origins may also have intrigued the composer, who used Scottish subject matter as the inspiration for several works.[183] Margaret Alexander both drew and collected art, and the sisters also helped the Mendelssohns gain access to private art collections.[184] Joanna played the piano and cultivated social occasions at her home, at which Mendelssohn, Moscheles, and violinist Ferdinand David performed. Mary also played the piano and studied German, corresponding with Abraham about which German literature she should undertake.[185] Closer in age to Felix than were her two older sisters, Mary seems to have formed a sentimental, romantic attachment to the composer, which was rekindled by the composer's reappearance in England in 1844 and exacerbated by her own unhappy marriage of convenience.[186]

During his later visits to London, the social demands that the Alexanders placed on the composer and their requests for tickets for the best seats at his concerts took unfair advantage of him, as he ran exhausted from one social or musical engagement to the next.[187] Yet he always remembered them fondly, particularly because of their concern for his father. In a letter to his sister Fanny in 1840 he described visiting the Alexanders, "where in the most elegant rococo drawing room, among all the most fashionable new objects, I again found my father's portrait, by Hensel, in its old favorite place, standing on its own little table."[188] After Fanny's death, when he was deeply depressed, Felix wrote to Joanna,

Yet I want to write to you, and to tell you that I feel grateful and from all my heart indebted to you, and that this feeling remains with me on good and bad days, and shall not leave me. I want to thank you for the kindness you showed to my father and to myself since many years, and now last month again—but you know all this.[189]

Mendelssohn valued the Alexanders' long friendship and their role in the extended community that radiated outward from his immediate family.

The letters of Fanny Horsley (1815–1844) and her younger sister Sophie (1819–1894), published without the bowdlerization of many nineteenth-century editions, provide an uncensored depiction of the composer and his English circle between 1833 and 1836.[190] The two young women were the daughters of organist and composer William Horsley (1774–1858), one of the founders of the Philharmonic Society. The other members of the Horsley family included an attractive older sister, Mary, and two brothers, John and Charles, who subsequently studied at the Leipzig Conservatory. Sophie in particular, the most musically inclined of the sisters, became a lifelong friend of the Mendelssohns, visiting Felix and his family in Leipzig in 1834 and corresponding with Cécile Mendelssohn after her husband's death.[191]

The two teenaged girls took their friend Felix's status as a musical genius entirely for granted. In his absence they maintained great pride in Karl Klingemann's reports of his increasing professional success in Germany. They were as likely, however, to dwell on Felix's entertaining antics and his romps in their garden and were equally pleased with Klingemann's "anecdotes of his oddities and waywardness."[192] Fanny described the instance in which Felix "was very funny and pretended to cry, and imitated a drunk person for my edification with great success."[193] Neither sister was in awe of the composer, and neither was afraid to complain about his less attractive personality traits, from his dreadful moodiness, to his unkempt appearance. Fanny noted, "Mendelssohn is a generous, high-minded creature, but, to descend from these heights, he was dressed very badly, and looked in sad want of the piece of soap and the nailbrush which I have so often threatened to offer him."[194] Sophie recounted an incident brought on by Charlotte Moscheles's complaint that the "cross and sulky" composer, buried in the score of an oratorio that he disliked, took no notice of his infant godchild Felix Moscheles:

upon which he turned round and made a horrid noise at it, partaking of the nose as well as the throat, which frightened the poor thing so that unless Mary [Horsley] had not tossed it up nearly to the ceiling for the following five minutes we should have had a regular squall from Felix Junior, for which Felix Senior would richly have deserved, not to be hung, but to be well reproved, as it would have been entirely his fault.[195]

Fanny Horsley, too, encountered Felix's hyperactivity and fluctuating disposition but appears to have taken them in stride:

Felix was very lachrimose and rushed four times in and out of the room in a very phrenzied [sic] manner. I gazed at him for some time in such deep amaze [sic] that I am sure at last he perceived it. What an odd tempered creature he is. But most geniuses are the same they say, and at any rate he is always delightful for he is always original.[196]

She found him delightful, "even in his bad humour, which is a good deal to say of anyone."[197] The girls' contemporary descriptions of an all-too-human musician are in stark contrast to the published recollection of their brother Charles, who wrote that "In all relations of life . . ., he was humanly speaking perfect."[198] Such a remark, written almost forty years after his sisters' letter, is representative of the English Mendelssohn-worship that lasted for decades following the composer's death.

As Mendelssohn struggled to establish himself in Düsseldorf, the Horsleys found him delinquent as a correspondent and suspected that they were victims of the truism, "out of sight, out of mind." Hurt by his failure to send them the promised piano arrangement of his Overture to *Die schöne Melusine*, Fanny wrote,

I do not have in my heart any such bad opinion of him, but one thing I do begin to suspect, that here is more love on our side than on his. Dr. Rosen in apology said that he was quite distracted by business and pleasure, for being head lion, as well as Director of Düsseldorf, as due share of both fell upon him. I can only say that if he were Emperor of Russia he ought all the same to remember his friends over the water.[199]

In spite of his negligence, Mendelssohn's feelings for his English friends ran deep. As described by Fanny, his departure from the Horsleys in 1833 was an emotional one: "He turned quite as pale as death though he had been fresh as a great damask rose all the walk, and his eyes filled with tears . . . . His last words to us were, 'Oh pray, Mrs. Horsley, pray let me find no changes, let all be the same as ever'—but that is not in our controul [*sic*]."[200]   With this family Mendelssohn found friendship, entertainment, and people who understood music, and he sentimentally wished that the community that he found in England would remain the same in spite of time and distance.

The sisters had plenty with which to occupy themselves in the composer's absence, however, as the object of their deepest affection and admiration was not Mendelssohn but his friend Friedrich Rosen (1805–1837), also a member of their circle.   Shy and retiring, Rosen was Professor of Oriental Languages at the University College of London, a Sanskrit scholar and the translator of numerous works. He taught languages to the Horsley girls, and the two sisters affectionately referred to him as "Sanskrit" in their letters. Rosen had known Mendelssohn in Berlin, beginning in 1824, but he lived in London beginning in 1828. Mendelssohn had a profound regard for both his scholarship and his personality. Fanny Horsley reported that

Mendelssohn talked to me the other night about Dr. Rosen in such affectionate terms that he was quite touching. The tears came to his eyes as he said that he was not only great but good, and that though still so young no one knows him without revering and respecting him. It was difficult which most to admire, the praised or the praiser.[201]

Rosen's sudden illness and death during the first performance of *St. Paul* in England in 1837 deeply saddened Mendelssohn. The activities of the famous composer, interactions with his professional acquaintances, and even the triumph of his oratorio seemed somewhat hollow under the circumstances:

Tuesday, while Rosen was ill, was a day that I will never forget. It was really one of those days in the world, with its mysterious incomprehensible ways. A thousand different people crossed my path and I had to associate with them, and no one was concerned with what was affecting me, and no one cared whether I was sad or happy, and Rosen became worse and worse; no one cared whether he lived or died and yet they all meant so well. . . . Klingemann stayed with him, while I had to go to the performance of my oratorio, which began at seven, and from which, on account of all the uproar in the papers, I could not absent myself. I heard my oratorio for the first time, and on another day that would in itself have thrilled me, while on this particular day I noticed hardly any of it.[202]

MENDELSSOHN AND THE MYTH OF THE ROMANTIC ARTIST

Mendelssohn's friendships took place within the context of larger communities: those of his family and of the artistic and intellectual circles in which he traveled in England and Germany. Mendelssohn's need for intercourse with persons with whom he had something in common stems from his youth at Leipzigerstraße 3, where he was surrounded by musicians and other cultured individuals. The experiences of his youth colored his life; in letters to those closest to him, longing for a more permanent reunion was a frequent theme. Although he clearly realized such a thing was impossible, Mendelssohn believed that family members and like-minded individuals should all be together, if not in actual physical proximity, then in intellectual and artistic communion.

Viewed through the eyes of those closest to him, Mendelssohn emerges not as "humanly speaking perfect" but as a human being capable of moodiness and depression. The upbringing supervised by Abraham and Lea Mendelssohn instilled in the composer an almost obsessive need to work and a strongly self-critical nature. In spite of much self-doubt regarding his own music, Mendelssohn was true to decided opinions about art and behavior, even if these ideals led to fallings-out with friends such as Marx or Hiller. While the picture of Mendelssohn as a sort of saint is obviously a by-product of nineteenth-century overglorification, the image of Mendelssohn the immature underachiever constrained by bourgeois social norms is equally false. That Mendelssohn maintained long-term friendships and functioned successfully within a community of individuals with whom he could share what mattered most to him, music, demonstrates his adult maturity.

Mendelssohn was a Romantic composer, yet his life belies the stereotype of the Romantic artist.[203] The Romantic artist is commonly viewed as alienated from the world in which he lives, dedicated to artistic ideals unknown to average persons, and doomed by his genius to lead a life that will never be happy, or at least never happy in the socially conventional way. The myth that surrounds the artist's relationship to the rest of society is commonly presented as a dichotomy between life and work. In "Psychology and Literature" Carl Jung wrote that an artist's life "cannot be otherwise than full of conflicts, for two forces are at war within him: on the one hand the justified longing of the ordinary man for happiness, satisfaction, and security, and on the other a ruthless passion for creation which may go so far as to override every personal desire."[204] Jung's statements further support the common assumption that an artist cannot be successful in both life and art.

The Romantic notion that artists suffer from the abuse or misunderstanding of the world around them has been transformed into the notion that artists must experience personal alienation in their lives in order to create great art. If Romantic art comes only from the personal expression of the inner soul of the artists, then artists must experience some kind of turbulent upheaval in their souls in order to be able to produce. This upheaval is, in this view, likely to be the result of a life that is in some way radically unconventional.[205] This leads biographers, as Jacques Barzun put it, to "run the risk of taking fame itself as a sure sign of moral and mental turpitude."[206] Indeed, many nineteenth-century composers did conduct their lives in a fashion that was unconventional by current social standards. It is all too easy to accept that such a life should be the norm and that an unconventional lifestyle resulting in social alienation is a requirement for a Romantic artist. Barzun writes,

> What we call a "romantic life" in the vulgar sense is all too often a reflection of the mental confusion fostered by bad biography. . . . What confirms me in this belief is the frequency with which the biographer who has studied a particular romanticist discovers a character differing from what he expected. The critic thereupon asks us to modify the meaning of romantic in that one instance while he continues to use it vulgarly in other contexts.[207]

Barzun could easily cite Mendelssohn in the list of examples that follows, for he is an example of a Romantic artist who does not fit the model of the "Romantic life" that has become widely accepted and is criticized for having had too easy and too happy a life. Felix's role as a member of the Mendelssohn family, both during his youth and as an adult, his happiness as husband and father, and his central place in a larger musical community contradict the Romantic stereotype of the struggling, lone genius. It is all too easy for biographers to assume that Mendelssohn's success in life prevented musical achievement. A recent survey of Romantic music continues the myth of the suffering artist in its consideration of Mendelssohn:

> [T]he question of his character and personality cannot be excluded from consideration. On the surface, his advantages were obvious. He was well educated and widely traveled . . . he was successful in his own country, had a happy marriage and strong family support. A little knowledge of psychology might prompt the reflection that it was all too good to be true. . . . he never matured emotionally to a sufficient extent to sustain, still less to consolidate his adolescent genius.[208]

The irony of this last claim reveals the fallacy in this viewpoint, for one would hardly wish to claim that the presumably "model" Romantics were more "emotionally mature" than Mendelssohn. Mendelssohn is criticized not for actual faults in his music, but for the very aspects of his life that enabled him to be a great musician: education, support from family, artistic interchange with friends across Europe. The Romantic cult of the individual genius prevents a more accurate picture of the artist in his community, the community that provides the personal and artistic support that makes such creativity possible. Mendelssohn valued his family and his friends, and it was through them that he was able to overcome his tormenting self-doubts. Hiller recalled,

> Once when I spoke of the happiness which lies in the conviction of so many people whom one highly esteems being favorably inclined towards one, he agreed with overflowing warmth, and said, "It is certainly the best that one has. When I am sometimes thoroughly dissatisfied with myself, I think of this or that person who has been kind to me, and say to myself, 'Things must not be so bad for you, however, if such men love you.'"[209]

Next to music itself, the affection of his friends was, for Mendelssohn, "the best that one has." Rather than weaken Mendelssohn's place as a significant creative artist, the composer's relationship to a larger community must lead us to reevaluate the myth of the Romantic artist itself.

NOTES

1. W. A. Lampadius, *Felix Mendelssohn-Bartholdy: Ein Denkmal für seine Freunde* (Leipzig: J. C. Hinrich, 1848).

2. Sebastian Hensel, *Die Familie Mendelssohn 1729–1847, nach Briefen und Tagebüchern*, 15th ed. (Berlin: Behr, 1908), 1: ix: "als Chronik einer guter deutschen Bürgerfamilie." The translation "middle-class family" for "Bürgerfamilie" is generally regarded as somewhat misleading.

3. See Steven M. Lowenstein, "Jewish Upper Crust and Berlin Jewish Enlightenment: The Family of Daniel Itzig," in *From East and West: Jews in a Changing Europe, 1750–1870*, ed. Frances Malino and David Sorkin (Oxford: Basil Blackwell, 1990), 182–201.

4. Nancy B. Reich, "The Power of Class: Fanny Hensel," in *Mendelssohn and His World*, ed. R. Larry Todd (Princeton: Princeton University Press, 1991), 89–90.

5. Shulamit Volkov, "The Ambivalence of *Bildung*: Jews and Other Germans," in *The German-Jewish Dialogue Reconsidered: A Symposium in Honor of George L. Mosse*, ed. Klaus L. Berghahn, German Life and Civilization 20 (New York: Peter Lang, 1996), 81.

6. Letter to August Hennings, 25 June 1782 in Moses Mendelssohn, *Briefwechsel*, ed. Alexander Altman, vol. 13 of *Gesammelte Schriften: Jubiläumsausgabe* (Stuttgart: Friedrich Frommann, 1977), 3: 65: "Jeder einzelne Mensch soll seine Anlagen und Fähigkeiten entwickeln, und dadurch immer vollkommener werden."

7. See Steven M. Lowenstein, *The Berlin Jewish Community: Enlightenment, Family, and Crisis, 1770–1830* (New York: Oxford University Press, 1994), esp. 120–33.

8. David Sorkin, *The Transformation of German Jewry, 1780–1840* (New York: Oxford University Press, 1987), 89–90.

9. Ibid., 90.

10. See R. Larry Todd, *Mendelssohn's Musical Education: A Study and Edition of His Exercises in Composition* (Cambridge: Cambridge University Press, 1983), 15.

11. Ibid.

12. Eduard Devrient, *Meine Erinnerungen an Felix Mendelssohn-Bartholdy und seine Briefe an mich* (Leipzig: J. J. Weber, 1869), 6: "Felix, thust du nichts?"

13. Julius Schubring, "Reminiscences of Felix Mendelssohn-Bartholdy. On His 57th Birthday, February 3rd, 1866," *Musical World* 31 (12, 19 May 1866); reprinted in *Mendelssohn and His World*, 222–23.

14. See, for example, his letter of 7 February 1839 to Sebastian Hensel in *Felix Mendelssohn: A Life in Letters*, ed. Rudolf Elvers, trans. Craig Tomlinson (New York: Fromm, 1986), 242. For an example of fifteen-year-old Felix humorously parodying the style, see his letter of 7 July 1824 to Paul, 23–24.

15. 6 May 1821; unpublished, quoted in Albert James Filosa, "The Early Symphonies and Chamber Music of Felix Mendelssohn Bartholdy" (Ph.D. diss., Yale University, 1970), 36.

16. Hensel, *Die Familie Mendelssohn*, 1: 166.

17. Charlotte Moscheles, ed., *Aus Moscheles' Leben: Nach Briefen und Tagebüchern*, 2 vols. (Leipzig: Duncker & Humblot, 1872), 1: 93:

denn sie sind weit entfernt, auf ihre Kinder stolz zu sein; sie machen sich Sorge wegen Felix' Zukunft, ob er wohl ausreichende Begabung habe, um Tüchtiges, wahrhaft Grosses zu leisten? ob er nicht, wie so viele talentvolle Kindern, plötzlich wieder untergehen werde? Ich konnte ihnen nicht genug betheuern wie ich, von seiner dereinstigen Meisterschaft überzeugt, nicht den mindesten Zweifel in sein Genie setze; doch musste ich das oft wiederholen, ehe sie es mir glaubten.

18. Adolf Bernhard Marx, *Erinnerungen aus meinem Leben* (Berlin: O. Janke, 1865), vol. 1, portions reprinted as "From the Memoirs of Adolf Bernhard Marx," trans. Susan Gillespie in *Mendelssohn and His World*, 208.

19. Hensel, *Die Familie Mendelssohn*, 1: 19.

20. 12 December 1828, in *Briefe von Felix Mendelssohn-Bartholdy an Ignaz und Charlotte Moscheles*, ed. Felix Moscheles (Leipzig: Duncker & Humblot, 1888; repr. Walluf-Nendeln: Sändig, 1976), 5: "Er ist Musikus, will Musikus bleiben."

21. 2 July 1819, in Hensel, *Die Familie Mendelssohn*, 1: 109: "Je sparsamer ich mit meinem Lobe bin, desto gewissenhafter erteile ich es, wenn ich Veranlassung dazu finde."

22. Hensel, *Die Familie Mendelssohn*, 1: 124: "sollte das außerordentliche Talent Ihre Kinder bloß leiten, nicht treiben. Papa Abraham ist aber ungenügsam, das Beste ist ihm eben gut genug."

23. 22 November 1830, in *A Life in Letters*, 143.

24. 8 July 1829, in *The Letters of Fanny Hensel to Felix Mendelssohn*, ed. and trans. Marcia Citron (New York: Pendragon, 1987), 67, translation modified; German original, 414:

Du weißt, wie es Dich immer verdroß, wenn die Eltern Dir ihre Zufriedenheit verbargen, denselben Verdruß setzt uns Vater fort, indem er gleichgültig u. stoisch thut, u. wir ihn dann drüber ertappen, wie der Deine Briefe zu drei-viermal liest, u. wie alle Leute wissen u. sehn, wie er sich über Dich u. Alles was dir begegnet, freut, nur wir sollen es nicht wissen. Wir wissen es aber doch.

25. 25 January 1841, in Felix Mendelssohn Bartholdy, *Briefe aus den Jahren 1833 bis 1847*, ed. Paul Mendelssohn Bartholdy and Carl Mendelssohn Bartholdy (Leipzig: Hermann Mendelssohn, 1870), 438.

26. Letter to Woldemar Frege, 28 August 1841, in *A Life in Letters*, 255.

27. Quoted by Johann Christian Lobe, *Fliegende Blätter für die Musik* 1/5 (1855); trans. Susan Gillespie as "Conversations with Felix Mendelssohn" in *Mendelssohn and His World*, 191.

28. 24 January 1843, in Ferdinand Hiller, *Mendelssohn: Briefe und Erinnerungen*, 2d ed. (Cologne: Dumont Schauberg, 1878), 72–73: "ich glaube, daß ein Mensch mit herrlichen Anlagen die Verpflichtung hat, was Gutes zu werden, daß man es seine Schuld nennen kann, wenn er sich nicht ganz so entwickelt, wie ihm die Mittel dazu gegeben sind."

29. End of April 1834, in *Briefe an Ignaz und Charlotte Moscheles*, 82–83: "Du weißt ja, wie ich so oft an bösen Zweifeln laborire, und mir nichts recht machen kann, und wenn mir dann so bange wird, so meine ich, die ganze Welt müßte es noch viel deutlicher sehen als ich, und gar über meine Sachen wegsehen."

30. See, for example, his letters to Breitkopf & Härtel from 6 September 1834 concerning the *Rondo brillant*, Op. 29, and from 16 December 1838 concerning the *Serenade and Allegro giojoso*, Op. 43, in Felix Mendelssohn Bartholdy, *Briefe an deutsche Verleger*, ed. Rudolf Elvers and H. Herzfeld (Berlin: de Gruyter, 1968), 38–39 and 222, respectively. Both letters suggest the possible necessity of engraving new plates due to the

composer's last-minute alterations.

31. Hensel, *Die Familie Mendelssohn*, 2: 2.

32. 9 December 1835, in *Briefe 1833–1847*, 337: "mein Lehrer in der Kunst und im Leben."

33. 6 December 1835; ibid., 335: "es muß für mich eine neues Leben anfangen oder alles aufhören,—das alte ist nun abgeschnitten."

34. See Rudolf Elvers, "Acht Briefe von Lea Mendelssohn an den Verlag Schlesinger in Berlin," in *Das Problem Mendelssohn*, ed. Carl Dahlhaus, Studien zur Musikgeschichte des 19. Jahrhunderts 41 (Regensburg, Bosse, 1974), 47–53.

35. Letter to Karl Klingemann, 17 January 1843, in *Felix Mendelssohn-Bartholdys Briefwechsel mit Legationsrat Karl Klingemann in London*, ed. Karl Klingemann Jr. (Essen: Baedecker, 1909), 279: "seit einigen Wochen habe ich recht lebhaft wieder empfunden, welch himmlischer Beruf eigentlich die Kunst ist. Verdanke ich den doch auch wieder nur den Eltern."

36. Hensel, *Die Familie Mendelssohn*, 2: 447: "wohl aber Umgang mit gebildeten klugen Menschen, im kleinen Kreis, und Kunst genüsse."

37. Mendelssohn's organ piece for Fanny's wedding eventually became the first movement of his Organ Sonata Op. 65 no. 3.

38. Hensel, *Die Familie Mendelssohn*, 1: 161:

Bis zu dem jetzigen Zeitpunkt . . . besitze ich sein uneingeschränktes Vertrauen. Ich habe sein Talent sich Schritt vor Schritt entwickeln sehen und selbst gewissermaßen zu seiner Ausbildung beigetragen. Er hat keinen musikalischen Ratgeber als mich, auch sendet er nie einen Gedanken auf's Papier, ohne ihm mir vorher zur Prüfung vorgelegt zu haben.

39. 8 December 1828, in Hensel, *Die Familie Mendelssohn*, 1: 222:

Seine Richtung befestigt sich immer mehr und er geht bestimmt einem selbst gesteckten, ihm klar bewußten Ziel entgegen welches ich mit Worten nicht deutlich zu bezeichnen wüßte, vielleicht weil sich überhaupt eine Kunstidee nicht wohl in Worte kleiden läßt, denn sonst würde Wortpoesie die einzige Kunst sein, vielleicht auch weil ich mehr mit Augen der Liebe seinen Schritten folge, also auf Flügeln des Geistes ihm vorangehen und sein Ziel ersehen kann.

40. Marcia Citron, "Fanny Hensel's Letters to Felix Mendelssohn in the Green-Books Collection at Oxford," in *Mendelssohn and Schumann: Essays on Their Music and Its Content*, ed. Jon Finson and R. Larry Todd (Durham, NC: Duke University, 1984), 102.

41. Ibid., 103–4.

42. Hensel, *Die Familie Mendelssohn*, 1: 276–77.

43. 29 June 1829, in *The Letters of Fanny Hensel to Felix Mendelssohn*, 57, translation modified; German original, 407: "[Ich] stehe vom Clavier auf, trete vor deine Bild u. küsse es, u. vertiefe mich so ganz in Deine Gegenwart, daß ich—Dir nun schreiben muß. Aber mir ist unendlich wohl, u. ich habe Dich unendlich lieb. Unendlich lieb."

44. 11 June 1830, in Hensel, *Die Familie Mendelssohn*, 1: 353–54:

sitzt jetzt hier in einem netten Stübchen und hat Euer grünes Sammetbuch mit den Porträts vor sich und schreibt am offenen Fenster. Hör' mal, ich wollte, Du wärest recht froh und heiter in diesem Augenblick, weil ich gerade an Dich denke, und so wärest Du es in jedem Moment, wo ich an Dich dächte: da solltest Du nie verdrießlich und unwohl werden. Aber ein ganzer Kerl bist du, das muß wahr sein, und hast einige Musik los. . . . und wenn Du einen größern Anbeter brauchst als mich, so kannst Du ihn malen oder Dich von ihm malen lassen.

The reference at the end is to Wilhelm Hensel.

45. 28 September 1840, in *The Letters of Fanny Hensel to Felix Mendelssohn*, 296; German original, 574: "es mich amüsirt hat, daß wir Alle, um die Zeit Deiner Abreise von hier, Jeanpaulisirten."

46. 17 February 1835, in *The Letters of Fanny Hensel to Felix Mendelssohn*, 174, translation modified; German original, 490: "Weißt du, daß ich finde, wir schreiben uns jetzt sehr ordentliche Briefe; vielleicht nicht ganz so lustig, als da ich mit Beckchen zusammensaß, u. eine der andern immer zu tollerm Zeuge die Feder aus der Hand nahm, aber vernünftig u. über ordentliche Gegenstände."

47. 2 June 1837, *The Letters of Fanny Hensel to Felix Mendelssohn*, 234; German original, 529. See Peter Ward Jones, Introduction to *The Mendelssohns on Honeymoon: The 1837 Diary of Felix and Cécile Mendelssohn Bartholdy, together with Letters to Their Families*, ed. and trans. Peter Ward Jones (Oxford: Clarendon, 1997), xxv–xxx.

48. Letter to Lea Mendelssohn, 8 June 1837, *The Mendelssohns on Honeymoon*, 165.

49. 2 June 1837, in *The Letters of Fanny Hensel to Felix Mendelssohn*, 234, translation modified; German original, 529: "u. Deine neuen Sachen auswendig wußte, ehe Du sie einmal aufschrieben."

50. 28 September 1840, in *The Letters of Fanny Hensel to Felix Mendelssohn*, 294, translation modified; German original, 572:

Man muß Gott danken, wenn nur das zusammen Gehörige auch wirklich zusammen bleibt, u. sich nicht von einander trennt, es scheide denn der Todt. Und darauf habe ich denn, wenn ich mich recht besinne, eigentlich kommen wollen, u. Dir einmal wieder sagen, wie ich mich Deines Lebens u. Webens freue, u. wie gut es mir gefällt, daß wir zufällig Geschwister geworden.

51. "Fanny Mendelssohn," *The Musical Times* 29 (1 June 1888), 341.

52. Camilla Cai has suggested that Fanny was preparing some piano works for publication in late 1837. See her preface to Hensel's *Songs for Pianoforte, 1836–1837*, Recent Researches in the Music of the Nineteenth and Early Twentieth Centuries 22 (Madison, WI: A-R Editions, 1994), viii–ix.

53. Sarah Rothenberg, "'Thus Far, but No Farther': Fanny Mendelssohn-Hensel's Unfinished Journey," *The Musical Quarterly* 77 (1993), 698.

54. See Reich, 92, and Françoise Tillard, *Fanny Mendelssohn*, trans. Camille Naish (Portland, OR: Amadeus Press, 1996), 18. In the preface to *The Letters of Fanny Hensel to Felix Mendelssohn*, xli–xlii, Citron writes, "One might be tempted to infer that Felix senses real competition from his sister if she published and thereby gains a professional foothold, but there is no evidence to support such a claim."

55. 24 June 1837, New York Public Library. See the full text of Mendelssohn's comments about his sister in the Historical Views and Documents accompanying this chapter. This letter has also been published in *The Mendelssohns on Honeymoon*, 165–68.

56. 12 August 1846, in Hensel, *Die Familie Mendelssohn*, 2: 432–33.

57. 9 July 1846, in *The Letters of Fanny Hensel to Felix Mendelssohn*, 349.

58. Quoted by Lobe; see *Mendelssohn and His World*, 191.

59. Letter to Angelica von Woringen, 26 November 1846, quoted in *The Letters of Fanny Hensel to Felix Mendelssohn*, 352f.

60. See Felix's letter of 15 April 1837 to his mother-in-law, Elisabeth Jeanrenaud, describing his concern about Fanny's miscarriage, in *The Mendelssohns on Honeymoon*, 141.

61. 15 May [1837], *The Mendelssohns on Honeymoon*, 156. The more familiar source of this statement, Hensel, mistakenly gave the date as 13 July 1837 and modified the text to avoid giving offense: "Sie spielt wohl alle die kleinen Kerls in den Sack"; Hensel, *Die Familie Mendelssohn*, 2: 43.

62. See, for example, his praise of Josephine Lang's music in a letter dated 6 October 1831, in *Briefe 1833–1847*, 214–15; his critique of a Lied by an unidentified woman in *A Life in Letters*, 273; and his encouragement of young Emily Moscheles's compositions in *Aus Moscheles' Leben*, 2: 54.

63. 25 August 1829, in *A Life in Letters*, 96.

64. 30 January 1836, in *Briefe 1833–1847*, 341: "Wie ich aber alle Deine Sachen lieb habe, und nun gar die, die mir so recht an's Herz gewachsen sind, das weißt Du."

65. Letter to Paul of 24 August 1847, in *A Life in Letters*, 282.

66. 9 June 1847, *Briefe an Ignaz und Charlotte Moscheles*, 280: "Sie können sich aber wohl denken, wie mir es ist, dem sie jede Stunde, bei jedem Musikstück und bei allem, was ich Gutes und Böses erleben könnte, so gegenwärtig war—und so ist es eigentlich uns Allen."

67. This appears to be a reference to an inside joke among the Mendelssohn family circle. The term appears somehow related to Jean Paul Richter's *Flegeljahre*, for Mendelssohn wrote in a letter to Fanny on 12 August 1846, "You are and remain the otters, which I know, among other things, because just now Cécile is suddenly enjoying reading the Flegeljahre, and I see you lying there every day on the table" ["Ihr seid und bleibt die Fischottern, was ich unter anderm daher weiß, weil Cécile jetzt plötzlich die Flegeljahre mit Pläsier liest, und ich Euch da alle Tage auf dem Tisch liegen sehe." Hensel, *Die Familie Mendelssohn*, 2: 434].

The precise meaning of the reference is not at all clear. It may have to do with a statement by Vult, who cites several metaphors for things that would be impossible: "'No,' he said, ' before I would do that, I'd rather drink vinegar out of a copper vessel every day or feed an otter at my breast till it grows up, or read or hear a Kantian Mass, an Easter service,'" ["'Nein,' sagt' er, 'eh ich das täte, lieber wollt' ich täglich Essig aus Kupfer trinken oder eine Fischotter an meiner Brust groß säugen, oder eine kantianische Messe lesen oder hören eine Ostermesse.'"] Jean Paul Richter, *Flegeljahre*, in vol. 4 of *Werke in vier Bänden*, ed. Alfred Brandstetter (Zurich: Stauffacher, 1966), 40. (Thanks to Julie Prandi for locating this passage.)

The two sisters are represented as otters in Wilhelm Hensel's pencil drawing of members of the Mendelssohn circle "The Wheel" ["Das Rad"], where the lower halves of their bodies are intertwined like those of otters at play, evidently a reference to their inseparability. The drawing is reproduced in *The Letters of Fanny Hensel to Felix Mendelssohn*, 72, along with Fanny's letter about it of 15 August 1829, 73–75. No direct connection between the drawing and the novel has yet come to light.

68. 25 March 1845, in *Briefe 1833–1847*, 352.

69. Cited by Reich, in *Mendelssohn and His World*, 87. Quoted from Johanna Kinkel's *Memoiren*, in Konrad Feilchenfeldt, "Karl August Varnhagen von Ense: Sieben Briefe an Rebecka Dirichlet," *Mendelssohn Studien* 3 (1979), 56–57: "Meine älteren Geschwister haben mir meinen Künstlerruhm weggestohlen. In jeder anderen Familie würde ich als Musiker in hoch gepriesen worden sein und vielleicht als Dirigentin einen Kreis beherrscht haben. Neben Felix und Fanny konnte ich zu keiner Anerkennung durchdringen."

70. To Fanny, in Hensel, *Die Familie Mendelssohn*, 2: 384: "Ihr glücklichen Musiker macht aus solcher Stimmung und Umgebung ein Lied ohne Worte, zur Freude der Menschen; ich muß garstige Prosa mit Worten schreiben."

71. 20 May 1840, in Hensel, *Die Familie Mendelssohn*, 2: 150.

72. Hensel, *Die Familie Mendelssohn*, 2: 364: "daß ich in Sizilien bin, im Lande Homers, der Sarazenen, der Hohenstaufen, und wo Gott die Welt erschaffen hat. Hätt' er nur nicht dabei so sehr viel Flöhe erschaffen."

73. 28 June 1836, in *The Letters of Fanny Hensel to Felix Mendelssohn*, 205.

74. 13 January 1843, cited in *The Letters of Fanny Hensel to Felix Mendelssohn*, 315f.

75. 11 February 1838, in *A Life in Letters*, 239.

76. 13 July [1829], in *The Letters of Fanny Hensel to Felix Mendelssohn*, 69, translation modified; German, 415: "Was ich an Paul immer geschätzt habe . . . ist daß er keine Spur von Neid, sondern nur Liebe für Dich hat, obgleich er sehr wohl weiß, daß Ihr verschieden begabt seyd." Gisela Gantzel-Kress has suggested that Paul was secretly frustrated in his musical ambitions and resented his brother's fame, but she bases this largely on one lost letter. See "Noblesse oblige: Ein Beitrag zur Nobilitierung der Mendelssohns," *Mendelssohn Studien* 6 (1986), 168–69.

77. 13 February 1841, in *Briefe 1833–1847*, 441: "damit sie nur allein für sich das Gute verdient, das Du von ihr denkst, dazu müßte sie erst noch viel besser werden."

78. 27 January 1837, in *The Letters of Fanny Hensel to Felix Mendelssohn*, 229; German, 526: "gewißermassen stolz über Deine Liebe, als wenn er die Liebe erfunden hätte."

79. 16 September 1843, in *Briefe 1833–1847*, 514: "dem einzigen Hotel abzusteigen, wo es mir in Berlin gefällt." English, 309.

80. 9 July 1846, *A Life in Letters*, 276.

81. Gisela Gantzel-Kress believes that Karl Mendelssohn Bartholdy's role in the edition of the letters was minimal. See "Karl Mendelssohn Bartholdy, 1838–1897," *Mendelssohn Studien* 8 (1993), 212.

82. 10 December 1847, in Ingeborg Stolzenburg, "Paul Mendelssohn-Bartholdy nach dem Tode seines Brüders Felix," *Mendelssohn Studien* 8 (1993), 184–85:

Allein das Werk könnte meiner Meinung nach ein leitender Stern für viele, viele Menschen werden. . . . Wenn ich diejenigen, welche ich besitze, lese und wieder lese, so fühle ich mich erhoben, und glaube mich gebessert. Nun meine ich, müßte es vielen anderen Menschen ebenso gehen, und ein großer Theil der Briefen ist von allgemeinen Interesse,—durchaus ohne Persönlichkeiten, rein sachlicher Natur.

83. 28 October 1841, i, 466: "Ich habe mir es nämlich zum unverbrüchlichen Gesetz gemacht, niemals etwas Musik betreffendes selbst in öffentliche Blätter zu schreiben."

84. Deborah Hertz, *Jewish High Society in Old Regime Berlin* (New Haven: Yale University Press, 1988), 251–85.

85. Quoted in Hensel, *Die Familie Mendelssohn*, 2: 241. "Sie war der Mittelpunkt einer ausgewählten, belebten, sowohl traulichen als glänzenden Geselligkeit." Hensel believed the obituary was probably written by Karl August Varnhagen von Ense.

86. Excerpted in *Mendelssohn and His World*, 222.

87. To Rebecca, 18 October 1843, in Hensel, *Die Familie Mendelssohn*, 2: 292:

wie *Sommernachtstraum* zu allen Zeiten durch unser Haus gegangen, wie wir in verschiedenen Altern alle verschiedenen Rollen gelesen, von Bohnenblüte bis zu Hermia und Helena, "und wie wir's nun zuletzt so herrlich weit gebracht." Wir sind aber auch wirklich mit dem *Sommernachtstraum* vollkommen verwachsen und namentlich Felix hat sich ganz denselben eigen gemacht.

88. 15 August 1829, in *The Letters of Fanny Hensel to Felix Mendelssohn*, 73–75. The drawing "Das Rad" is reproduced on page 72.

89. Eric Werner, *Mendelssohn: A New Image of the Composer and His Age* (New York: Free Press of Glencoe, 1963), 40.

90. 11 December 1830, in *Eine Reise durch Deutschland, Italien und die Schweiz: Briefe, Tagebuchblätter, Skizzen*, ed. Peter Sutermeister (Tübingen: Heliopolis, 1979), 90:

Nur was Du mir von den Cotterien sagst . . . kann ich nicht recht verstehen; denn ich weiß, daß ich u. wir alle immer das, was man gewöhnlich so nennt, eine abgeschlossene, an Ab-sonderlichkeiten klebende, leere Geselligkeit von Herzen gehaßt u. gefürchtet haben; es ist aber wohl fast natürlich, daß unter Menschen, die sich täglich sehen ohne daß ihr Interesse sich verändert, denn auch die Theilnahme an dem Öffentlichen fehlen muß, ... wohl der Fall ist daß sich bei denen eine lustige, heitere, eigne Art über Dinge zu sprechen, leicht bildet, u. daß so eine besondere, vielleicht auch einförmige Sprache entsteht; aber das kann noch keine Cotterien machen, und ich glaube gewiß, daß ich nie zu einer Cotterie gehören werde.

91. To Rebecca, 20 July 1847, in *Briefe 1833–1847*, 578.

92. Hensel, *Die Familie Mendelssohn*, 2: 457–58: "Ja, ja! Wir füttern die Leute mit Brosamen unserer alten Herrlichkeit."

93. 25 December 1834, in *Briefe an Ignaz und Charlotte Moscheles*, 105: "Und dann gibt es auch wirklich gar zu wenig hübsche Mädchen hier, man will doch nicht den ganzen Tag Fugen und Choräle componiren."

94. Boyd Alexander, "Felix Mendelssohn and Young Women," *Mendelssohn Studien* 2 (1975), 84.

95. See Marian Wilson [Kimber], "Mendelssohn's Wife: Love, Art and Romantic Biography," *Nineteenth Century Studies* 6 (1991), 1–18.

96. Hensel, *Die Familie Mendelssohn*, 2: 49: "Sie ist aber ein so liebenswürdiges, kindhaft unbefangenes, frisch erquickliches, immer gleich und heiter gestimmtes Wesen, daß ich Felix nur glücklich preisen kann, sie gefunden zu haben. . . . Ihre Gegenwart hat etwas von frischer Luft, sie ist so leicht, klar und natürlich."

97. Heinrich Eduard Jacob, *Felix Mendelssohn and His Times*, trans. Richard and Clara Winston (Englewood Cliffs, NJ: Prentice-Hall, 1963), 146. Jacob described Mendelssohn's marriage as "passionless." Although Cécile Mendelssohn destroyed her husband's letters to her, one of them survives in the Green Books in the Bodleian Library at Oxford. Reprinted in the Historical Views and Documents section accompanying this chapter, it attests to Mendelssohn's strong affection for his wife.

98. Werner, *A New Image*, 304.

99. To Rebecca, 6 April 1836, New York Public Library: "musikalisch? Nein, gar nicht."

100. 28 June 1843, Devrient, *Erinnerungen*, 234: "Seit ich mit Componieren anfing, bin ich dem Grundgedanken treu geblieben: nicht eine Seite zu schreiben, weil das größte Publicum oder das hübscheste Mädchen es so und so verlangten, sondern nur so zu schreiben, wie ich es selbst für recht hielt."

101. See Therese Marx, *Adolf Bernhard Marx' Verhältniß zu Felix Mendelssohn-Bartholdy in Bezug auf Eduard Devrient's Darstellung* (Leipzig: Dürr, 1869). Marx reportedly threw Mendelssohn's letters to him in the river, making critical treatment of their relationship difficult for future biographers.

102. Werner, *A New Image*, 392.

103. Charlotte Moscheles in *Recent Music and Musicians*, frequently calls Mendelssohn "childlike," but this is more an indication of her maternal treatment of him than an accurate description of his personality.

104. Arnold Whittall, *Romantic Music: A Concise History from Schubert to Sibelius* (London: Thames and Hudson, 1987), 35.

105. 7 February 1835, *Briefe an Ignaz und Charlotte Moscheles*, 111: "So gehe ich hier eigentlich nur mit Malern um, die nette Leute sind."

106. 7 December 1830, Sutermeister, ed., *Eine Reise*, 80–81: "Ein Mensch fehlt mir hier, dem ich Alles sehr offen mittheilen könnte, der meine Musik im Entstehen läse u. mir doppelt lieb machte, bei dem ich mich so recht vollkommen erholen u. ausruhen u. recht

aufrichting von ihm lernen könnte."

107. 3 January 1831, Sutermeister, ed., *Eine Reise*, 119: "Der macht mich förmlich traurig, weil er ein wirklich gebildeter, angenehmer Mensch ist, und so unbegreiflich schlecht componirt."

108. 21 March 1840, *Briefe an Ignaz und Charlotte Moscheles*, 188: "das rechte Compositionstalent, rechte eigne musikalische Gedanken."

109. Wm. A. Little, "Mendelssohn and Liszt," in *Mendelssohn Studies*, ed. R. Larry Todd (Cambridge: Cambridge University Press, 1992), 125.

110. Eduard Devrient (see note 12). See also J. Rigbie Turner, "Mendelssohn's Letters to Eduard Devrient: Filling in Some Gaps," in *Mendelssohn Studies*, 200–239.

111. Devrient, *Erinnerungen*, 49.

112. Ibid., 57: "blassem und verletztem."

113. Ibid., 6: "edlen Menschen, selbst in seinen Schwächen und Fehlern."

114. Ibid., 69: "erregte mir oft die Sorge, ob die Nervenkraft eines Gehirnes solche Zumuthungen eine gewöhnliche Lebensdauer lang ertragen könne?"

115. Thanks to Peter Ward Jones, personal correspondence, for pointing out Mendelssohn's continuing poor health. While a comprehensive study of the composer's medical history is overdue, available evidence suggests that his hypertension was a hereditary condition.

116. Turner, "Mendelssohn's Letters to Eduard Devrient," 204.

117. Devrient, *Erinnerungen*, 43.

118. Thanks to John Michael Cooper for suggesting the depth of Wagner's influence on Devrient. Wagner wrote a derogatory review of Devrient's *Erinnerungen*, largely criticizing the author's writing style. On 28 January 1869 Cosima Wagner wrote in her diary, "This account is like a confirmation of what Richard wrote about Mendelssohn in his essay," presumably referring to *Das Judentum in der Musik*; *Cosima Wagner's Diaries*, vol. 1, *1869–1877*, ed. Martin Gregor-Dellin and Dietrich Mack, trans. Geoffrey Skelton (New York: Harcourt Brace Jovanovich, 1976), 49.

119. Devrient, *Erinnerungen*, 265: "daß er anfange in seinen Compositionen sich zu wiederholen."

120. 24 January 1837, in Hiller, *Briefe und Erinnerungen*, 72: "Mir ist nichts widerwärtiger, als ein Tadel der Natur oder des Talents eines Menschen; . . . man setzt eben seiner Länge keine Elle zu,—da ist doch alles Streben und Arbeiten umsonst, drum muß man drüber schweigen,—des hat auch Gott zu verantworten."

121. Ibid., 73: "ich weiß recht gut, daß kein Musiker seine Gedanken, sein Talent anders machen kann, als der Himmel sie ihm gibt; daß er aber, wenn der Himmel sie ihm gut gibt, sie auch gut ausführen können muß, das weiß ich ebenfalls."

122. Devrient, *Erinnerungen*, 265–66: "so, sei der unwillkührlich sich bietende Einfall der recht, auch wenn er nicht frappant und neu sei"; "ich meinte: er verwechsle seinen Thätigkeitsdrang mit dem Schöpfungsdrange."

123. Ibid., 282–83: "daß Mendelssohn's wählerische Peinlichkeit seine besten Kräfte zur Thatenlosigkeit verdammt hat."

124. Cf. Mendelssohn's statement to this effect in a letter to Klingemann about his revision of the *Lobgesang*; Klingemann, ed., *Briefwechsel*, 260.

125. Ibid., 283: "Es ist eine wahre Hamletstragik in Mendelssohn's Opernschicksal. . . . als er sich endlich überwindet, an's Werk zu geben, selbst mit einem zweifelhaften Gedichte, sinkt er mit dem Bruchstück der Arbeit in's Grab."

126. Devrient, *Erinnerungen*, 179.

127. Ibid., 234–35: "Denn Dir steht die Kunst auch gerade an solch einem Platz des Herzens wie mir, und wir haben uns immer in all den Dingen verstanden, über die man sich mit allen Anderen nie verstehen wird."

128. Hiller, *Briefe und Erinnerungen*, 21–22, 24.

129. Ibid., 144.

130. Ibid., 148.

131. Ibid., 43: "Mendelssohn bildete in allen Beziehungen den Mittelpunct des Festes, nicht allein als Componist, Dirigent und Clavierspieler, sondern auch als heiterer liebenswürdiger Hausherr möchte ich sagen—Bekanntschaften vermittelnd, Zusammengehörige zusammenbringend, Freundlichkeiten spendend, wo es ihm irgend möglich."

132. 24 January 1837; ibid., 73: "Ich glaube, daß Du, Deinem Talent nach, keinem Musiker jetzt nachstehst, aber ich kenne fast kein Stück von Dir, das ordentlich durchgeführt wäre."

133. Ibid.: "aber wie viele Musiker gibt es, die das einem andern erlauben würden?"

134. 15 April 1839; ibid., 113.

135. 25 March 1843; ibid., 173: "Wenn übringens solche Stimmung der heitern Zufriedenheit mit sich und seinen Werken bei einem Menschen immer dieselbe bleibt, so glaube ich der ist ein echter Philister und macht sein Lebtag nichts Gescheutes und beklage wiederum Deine verdrießlichen Worte nicht."

136. Ibid., 146: "ich begreife nicht, wie Du je an Deiner musicalischen Begabung einen Augenblick zweifeln kannst."

137. 21 September 1842, to N. Simrock, in *Briefe an deutsche Verleger*, 234–36.

138. Ibid., 26.

139. 25 March 1835; *Briefe an Ignaz und Charlotte Moscheles*, 116: "Ich habe neulich Etüden von Hiller gesehen, die mir auch gar nicht gefallen haben, und das thut mir leid, weil ich ihm gut bin und glaube, daß er Talent hat; aber Paris ist gewiß ein schlimmer Boden."

140. See his letters of 14 March 1835 and 20 January 1838; Hiller, *Briefe und Erinnerungen*, 40, 97.

141. 15 April 1839; Hiller, *Briefe und Erinnerungen*, 113: "Heute habe ich ganz aparte Lust, Dir zu schreiben, mit Dir zu plaudern; eben dachte ich so daran, wie ich bei Dir auf dem Sofa lag und klagte und mir Clavier vorspielen ließ . . . und darauf dachte ich, es wäre doch gut, wenn wir uns bald mal wieder sähen und ordentlich zusammen lebten,—und dann dachte ich, wie lange das noch hin sein müßte." See also his letter of 10 December 1837; p. 88.

142. Ibid., xi: "Die Stunden, die ich mit Mendelssohn am Flügel zugebracht, dem Austausche unserer musicalischen Anschauungen Compositionen mannigfacher Art, eigene und fremde, unterlegend, waren in gewissen Sinne die besten, die mir mit ihm zu verleben vergönnt waren."

143. Ibid., 186–87:

Der Kampf um die gemeinen Bedürfnisse des Lebens mag immerhin ein schwerer sein—an und für sich selbst hat er nichts sonderlich Verdienstliches. . . . Wenn nun ein Künstler, wie Mendelssohn, seine ganze Kraft zusammenraffte, um dem kleinsten Liede, welches ihm entströmte, die Vollendung zu geben, die ihm stets als Ideal vorschwebte, wenn er mit Anspannung seines vollen Könnens und Wissens Alles aufbot, um in seiner Kunst nach jeder Seite hin das Beste zu fördern, so verdient dies in der materiel sorgenfreien Stellung, die ihm beschieden war, sicherlich nicht weniger Anerkennung, als wenn er auf den Lohn seiner Arbeit hätte warten müssen um seine Gläubiger zu befriedigen.

144. *Aus Moscheles' Leben*, 1: 206: "weiss er heilsam auf unsere wunden Gemüther zu wirken, und scheint es sich zu Aufgabe gestellt zu haben, uns einigen Ersatz für unsere Leiden zu bringen."

145. Ibid., 1: 246: "herrliche Tage."

146. 15 May 1832, *Briefe an Ignaz und Charlotte Moscheles*, 23.

147. October 1832, *Aus Moscheles' Leben*, 1: 252.

148. Ibid., 2: 54.

149. 8 August 1840, *Briefe an Ignaz und Charlotte Moscheles*, 195: "Da soll wieder was Ehrliches zusammen musicirt werden. Ich wenigstens bin hungriger und durstiger danach als jemals."

150. *Aus Moscheles' Leben*, 2: 163: "Für einen Moscheles . . . macht man gute Musik, aber nicht für Jeden."

151. Ibid., 1: 206: "dass ich meinen Meister in ihm erkannte und da nur hingerissen war, wo er sich eine scharfe Kritik erwartete; er aber ist und bleibt der sich mir untergeordnende Schüler, wie ich es auch versuche ihm eine andere richtigere Stellung mir gegenüber zu geben."

152. Ibid., 2: 114.

153. 26 October 1846; ibid., 2: 159: "den ich Bruder oder Sohn nennen möchte!"

154. Ibid., 2: 59.

155. 30 November 1839; *Briefe an Ignaz und Charlotte Moscheles*, 180.

156. 11 May 1834; ibid., 90.

157. *Aus Moscheles' Leben*, 2: 58:

Leider hat aber der Wagen vier Plätze und ein Ungebetener stört des Freundes-Trio. "Er schläft gut," sagt Einer, "überlegen wir, was wir mit ihm thun, wenn er aufwacht!" "Ihm umbringen, ist das einzige Mittel," sagt ein Andere.—Der Schläfer regt sich im diesem Augeblicke; natürlich erschraken die Sprecher ob ihres schlechten Witzes und Moscheles fällt mit der ihm eigenen Geistesgegenwart (auf englisch) mit den Worten ein: "Und dann sagte sie, nie würde sie diesen Mann heirathen." Ein Satz, der sich von da als Sprichwort unter ihnen erhielt. Mendelssohn bricht in ein homerisches Lachen aus, das die beiden Andern ansteckt.

158. Charlotte Moscheles to relatives, 18 September 1840, *Briefe an Ignaz und Charlotte Moscheles*, 196.

159. Mendelssohn to Charlotte Moscheles, 8 November 1840; ibid., 202.

160. 23 September 1840, *Aus Moscheles' Leben* 2: 55: "und er nimmt neben den theuersten Familienbanden mein ganzes Ich in Anspruch. Er erscheint mir abwechselnd als Bruder, Sohn, Liebhaber, am meisten aber als lodernder Musik-Enthusiast, der es kaum zu ahnen scheint, wie hoch er schon gestiegen ist."

161. 7 December 1827, Hensel, *Die Familie Mendelssohn*, 1: 198: "Berlin kommt mir durchaus vor wie ein Eldorado und ein Mendelssohnscher Sonntag wie ein Kapitel aus einem Zauberroman."

162. 23 December 1827, Hensel, *Die Familie Mendelssohn*, 1: 206:

Ein jeder nämlich von uns betrachtet den prächtigen Generalbrief als sein spezielles Eigentum. . . . Je länger Sie uns auf Ihren Brief warten ließen, je desto mehr hat er uns bei seinem endlichen Erscheinen erfreut (nehmen Sie das aber nicht als Norm für die Zukunft, von jetzt an wird die Sache umgekehrt) und wir würden als wahre Bacchantinnen ihn gewiß zerrissen haben (verschlungen haben wir ihn wirklich), wenn nicht die Eltern großmutig resigniert und uns die erste Lesung überlassen hätten.

163. 13 [not 15, as in early editions of Hensel] August 1829, Hensel, *Die Familie Mendelssohn*, 1: 283:

Es ist kein Wunder, wenn die Hochlande melancholisch genannt sind. Gehen aber zwei Gesellen so lustig durch, lachen, wo's nur Gelegenheit gibt, dichten und zeichnen zusammen, schnauzen einander und die Welt an, wenn sie eben verdrießlich sind, oder nichts zu essen gefunden haben, vertilgen aber alles Eßbare und schlafen zwölf Stunden: so sind das eben wir und vergessen es im Leben nicht.

164. To Abraham Mendelssohn Bartholdy, 25 August 1829; *A Life in Letters*, 91–92.

165. 6 November 1829; Klingemann (see note 35), 63:

Ich kann nicht von Ihnen scheiden, ohne noch mein allerwärmstes Lob über die Treue und Sorgfalt auszusprechen, mit der Klingemann während der ganzen Zeit des Leidens fast nicht von der Seite unseres Felix gewichen ist. Mit unausgesetzter Liebe hat er ihn gepflegt und ihm alle die kleinen Dienste geleistet, die eine Mutter ihrem leidenden Kinde nicht zärtlicher hätte erfüllen können.

166. To Fanny and Rebecca, 22 November 1830; in *A Life in Letters*, 146.

167. To Lea, 11 August 1830; ibid., 129.

168. 12 February 1829; Klingemann, ed., *Briefwechsel*, 50: "Sein Sie etwas musikalisch—man hat es hier gern."

169. Peter Ward Jones, "Mendelssohn and His English Publishers," in *Mendelssohn Studies*, ed. R. Larry Todd (Cambridge: Cambridge University Press, 1992), 241.

170. 30 March 1830; Klingemann, ed., *Briefwechsel*, 76: "die Persönlichkeit, das ist mir klar, wirkt hier überwiegend, ich habe das nie so deutlich gesehen als in Deinem Falle,—es ist als ob die Person des Künstlers eine Brücke zu seinem Werke wäre. . . . Und Deine Werke und Deine Freunde rufen drum: Komm Du bald!"

171. 10 April 1830; ibid., 81: "Euer toller Gesamtbrief ist soeben eingelaufen; Mutter las ihn mir vor bis zur Stelle Zeile 8 'Rosen setzte sich auf seinen A . . .'—Da nahm ich ihn ihr aus der Hand, und meinte es würde wohl noch ärger kommen."

172. 10 February 1830; Klingemann, ed., ibid., 75: "es war nicht schwer es zu komponieren, die Worte sind schon Musik, und wenn ich dran denke, dass ich schlechtere mal bekommen soll, so weiss ich nicht, wie ich's machen werde. Deine Worte sagt' ich mir so lange vor bis ich sie sang; da ist's wohl leicht."

173. To Joseph Moore, 8 May 1864, in F. G. Edwards, *The History of Mendelssohn's Oratorio 'Elijah'* (London: Novello, Ewer & Co., 1896; repr. New York: AMS Press, 1976), 42.

174. 20 December 1831; Klingemann, ed., *Briefwechsel*, 89: "mein ganzer Brief hat den Spleen und ich habe ihn ganz und gar; das kommt aber nicht von Paris, sondern davon, dass ich sehr lange nichts komponiert habe. Kannst Du mir aber dazu verhelfen und einen kleinen Liedertext schicken? Sei er wie er wolle, wenn er nur schön ist. Und von Dir. Ich möchte sehr gern ein wunderschönes Lied komponieren."

175. 3 June 1834, unpublished letter in Green Books, III, 164, Bodleian Library, Oxford, translated in John Michael Cooper, "Felix Mendelssohn Bartholdy and the Italian Symphony: Historical, Musical, and Extramusical Perspectives" (Ph.D. diss., Duke University, 1994), 39; original German on 371: "Also glaube nicht und erwarte nicht daß ich dir heute sehr lob,—die Andren verderben mir meinen Musikdirektor mit ihrem Applaus u. ich halte mal eine Weile ein."

176. 11 June 1834; Klingemann, ed., *Briefwechsel*, 133: "ich glaube nicht, dass mich irgend ein Lob jemals verderben kann, geschweige denn das Deinige—das bringt mich weiter, wenn Du mir's gibst."

177. 25 July 1832; ibid., 96:

Du bist der einzige Mensch, bei dem mir es dann völlig ist, als seien wir zusammen, und so oft ich seitdem Deinen Brief wieder gelesen habe, so war ich in London, und mit Euch, d.h. froh; Du malst mir immer mit zwei Worten Land und Wetter und jeden kleinen Gesichtszug; ich weiss gar nicht, ob das Dein Verdienst ist, aber ich weiss, wir gehören zusammen. Also schreib' mir, ich brauche es sehr.

178. 19 July 1844; *A Life in Letters*, 267.
179. 6 December 1846; Klingemann, ed., *Briefwechsel*, 315: "Nur einen Freund kann der Mensch haben, sagt Montaigne, sagt Vult, steht in den Flegeljahren. Und das sagte ich von ganzem Herzen nach, als ich Deinen Brief bekam, Du einer Freund."
180. 15 July 1841; ibid., 264:

Du glaubst, ich frage über Dich um Rat, und will nachher nicht danach handeln. Wahrhaftig, wenn ich Dich über dies und alles andere frage, wenn ich irgend etwas zu Dir sage, Dir gegenüber tue, sage und tue ich es aus gar keinem anderen Grund, als aus Instinkt. Ich muss über etwas, das mir wichtig ist, das mich nahe angeht, mit Dir sprechen oder verhandeln—das ist mal nicht anders—und das geschieht so wenig wegen des leidigen Ratserholens, dass ich überzeugt bin, hättest Du mir gar nicht geantwortet, und hätten wir uns nach 10 Jahren wieder gesprochen, so würde ich dir dieselben Fragen getan, Deine Antwort ebenso begierig erwartet, so froh erhaltern haben, wie jetzt.

181. 2 December 1847; ibid., 337:

Mir ist es jetzt ein Wunder, dass ein solcher Reichtum mein gewesen ist, ich fühle recht in tiefster Demut, wie unverdient es war, und wie wenig ich Ihm habe sein und geben können für alle die Fülle des Besten und Schönsten, das er über mein vergangenes Leben ausgestreut hat,—aber dem gütigen Himmel danke ich fort und fort, der mir so reichen Segen verliehen hat, ich nehme es wie meinen besten Reichtum mit hinein in meinen alten Tage, und will mich immer und immer wieder daran erquicken! . . . mich an seiner Musik zu trösten, dazu komme ich erst später, aber immer erbaue ich mich an der Verklärung, in der aller Frühling und alle Jugend, die ganze Vergangenheit nur ihm angehört und mit ihm abgeschlossen hat.

182. 25 November 1830; Sutermeister, ed., *Eine Reise*, 75: "ich bin darin in London verwöhnt worden."
183. Alexander, "Felix Mendelssohn and the Alexanders," 95–96.
184. Ibid., 87
185. Boyd Alexander, "Some Unpublished Letters of Abraham Mendelssohn and Fanny Hensel," *Mendelssohn Studien* 3 (1979), 16–17.
186. Boyd Alexander, "Felix Mendelssohn and Young Women," *Mendelssohn Studien* 2 (1975), 77–100.
187. Alexander, "Felix Mendelssohn and the Alexanders," 88.
188. 24 October 1840; *Briefe 1833–1847*, 418: "wo ich im allerelegantesten rococo Visitenzimmer unter den allerfashionabelsten neuen Sachen doch Vater's Portrait von Hensel am alten Lieblingsplatze, auf seinem eigenen Tischchen stehend, wiederfand."
189. Alexander, "Felix Mendelssohn and the Alexanders," 96.
190. Rosamund Brunel Gotch, ed., *Mendelssohn and His Friends in Kensington: Letters from Fanny and Sophy Horsley Written 1833–1836* (London: Oxford University Press, 1934).
191. See Felix Gilbert, "Ein Brief von Cécile Mendelssohn Bartholdy an Sophia Horsley in London aus dem Jahre 1849," *Mendelssohn Studien* 5 (1982), 131–33.
192. Fanny Horsley, 4 November 1834, quoted in Gotch, *Mendelssohn and His Friends in Kensington*, 157.

193. 27 June 1833; ibid., 23.

194. 7 July 1833; ibid., 37.

195. N.d., 1833; ibid., 26–27.

196. 25 July 1833; ibid., 46.

197. 28 August 1833; ibid., 64.

198. Charles Horsley, "Reminiscences of Mendelssohn by His English Pupil," *Dwight's Journal of Music* 32 (1872), 345ff., 353ff., 362ff.; repr. in *Mendelssohn and His World*, 248.

199. 9 January 1834; *Mendelssohn and His Friends in Kensington*, 91.

200. 2 August 1833; ibid., 72.

201. 7 July 1833; ibid., 36–37.

202. Quoted in a letter of Cécile Mendelssohn to Lea Mendelssohn Bartholdy, 21 September 1837, in *The Mendelssohns on Honeymoon*, 192–93.

203. The remainder of this chapter is adapted from my article "Mendelssohn's Wife: Love, Art and Romantic Biography," cited in note 87.

204. Quoted in Jeffrey Meyers, *Married to Genius* (London: London Magazine Edition, 1977), 11.

205. See Neil Kessel, "Genius and Mental Disorder: A History of Ideas Concerning Their Conjunction," in *Genius: The History of an Idea*, ed. Penelope Murray (Oxford: Basil Blackwell, 1989), 196–212.

206. Jacques Barzun, "Truth in Biography: Berlioz," *The University Review: A Journal of the University of Kansas City* 5/4 (Summer 1939), 275.

207. Jacques Barzun, *Classic, Romantic and Modern* (Garden City, NY: Doubleday, 1961), 85.

208. Whittall, *Romantic Music*, 35.

209. Hiller, *Briefe und Erinnerungen*, 147:

Als ich einst von dem Glücke sprach, das in der Ueberzeugung liege, sich so manche Menschen geneigt zu wissen, die man sehr hoch halte, ging er mit überfließender Wärme hierauf ein und sagte: "Es ist sicherlich das Beste, was man hat. Wenn ich zuweilen so recht unzufrieden mit mir bin, denke ich an Diese und Jene, die mir freundschaftlich zugethan sind, und sage mir es muß doch so schlimm nicht mit dir stehen, wenn solche Männer dich lieben."

HISTORICAL VIEWS AND DOCUMENTS

FELIX MENDELSSOHN BARTHOLDY TO LEA MENDELSSOHN BARTHOLDY [EXCERPT]

Translated by Michael Kimber

Frankfurt, 24 June 1837

You write to me about Fanny's new pieces and tell me I ought to persuade her and provide her the opportunity to publish them. You praise her new compositions to me, and that is really not necessary, in that I look forward to them very much, and regard them as beautiful and excellent; for I do know from whom they come. Also I hope I need not say a word [about the fact] that, as soon as she herself decides to publish something, I will, as much as I can, provide the opportunity for this and take all the trouble from her, thereby sparing her from it. But *persuade* her to publish something I cannot, for it is against my view and conviction. We have spoken much about this earlier, and I am still of the same opinion—I consider publication to be something serious (at least it ought to be that) and believe that one should only do it if one wants to present oneself and continue one's whole life as an author. For this a series of works is required, one after the other; one or two alone is only an annoyance to the public, or it becomes a so-called vanity publication [lit., "manuscript for friends"], which I also do not like.

And Fanny, as I know her, has neither desire nor vocation for authorship; in addition, she is too much a wife, as is right, brings up her Sebastian and takes care of her house, and thinks neither of the public nor of the musical world, nor even of music, except when this first vocation is fulfilled. Having [something] printed would only intrude into this, and I just cannot reconcile myself to that. I will not persuade her to do this, forgive me. But don't show these words either to Fanny or to Hensel, who would take it very badly from me or surely misunderstand— better that nothing at all be said of this. If Fanny, on her own initiative, or for Hensel's sake, decides on it, I am, as I said, ready to be as helpful to her as I am able, but to urge [her] on to something that I do not consider right, this I cannot do.

Please write to me again whether these big social gatherings that Fanny gives and the music-making in them do not take their toll on her. I have always become very exhausted by this, and since Fanny, too, often suffers from weak nerves, as I do, I really think she must be very careful of herself in this regard. And will it not do at all for her to go to the seaside resort? It is such a splendid cure, so decisively invigorating, that I would like it very, very much if she did it; and if I could part so soon after marrying Cécile, she can certainly, after many years of marriage, be apart from her husband for a short time.—You write that it is not necessary, but if it did her good and really invigorated and refreshed her, it would indeed be worth the sacrifice. Oh, please advise her to do it, dear Mother, and I will write a few lines to her myself and pester her about it.

FELIX MENDELSSOHN BARTHOLDY TO CÉCILE MENDELSSOHN BARTHOLDY

Translated by Michael Kimber

10 October 1843

Dearest Cécile,

I can only write to you today, and I ought to be speaking to you, kissing you, spending the whole day with you, to delight in your gaze and the festive occasion and my happiness, and to wish you happiness. Good, dear Cécile! It makes me so unhappy, too, not to be able to be with you today. Your kind note, which just arrived, is indeed a great comfort to me, and I thank you for it many thousand times, but how I have read it and read it again, and then again become aware that you are not here; and if we were together and I had kissed you ever so much and kissed you again, then you would have to take notice again and again that I was there; the whole day I would not leave you in peace, with my love and my joy over your birthday; and how happy I would be if I could only spend the few hours remaining in the day with you. You are surely thinking of me, but it is only a surrogate; would that I were there and wished you happiness in person [lit., orally], isn't that right my Cécile?

I want to bring the little hat with me and to follow your instructions as closely as possible. Can you not write to me of any other attire that I can bring to you, as well? I am still waiting for your answer here, but hopefully this is your last letter for this time. I am already so tired of the separation, you don't know how much. In person everything is really twice as good, sounds twice as beautiful. David is coming tomorrow, as he wrote to Paul today; hopefully he will bring me the news that the cold is entirely gone. Ah, what is news! I want to see for myself soon, God willing. And then we will celebrate the birthday late; it seems unlikely to me that you are already at the age when one does not celebrate birthdays anymore.

MY DEAR CARL!
I THANK YOU FOR YOUR LETTER! BE VERY GOOD AND OBEY MAMA COMPLETELY! GREET MARIE AND PAUL AND LITTLE FELIX, AND ALSO GREET A CERTAIN HERR BARON VON FASEL. DO YOU KNOW HIM? GOODBYE, MY DEAR BOY.

YOUR FATHER,
F.M.B.

This evening we will all be at the Falkensteins'; as a matter of fact, I came back from Potsdam again this afternoon, because the Queen suddenly decided to give an opera tonight, so we can't rehearse. Now tomorrow the whole day must be taken up with that. Early, around 8, I will depart with the Souchays (Ady and Charles *inclusive*) and Paul. Apparently in the evening the King will come to the rehearsal already, but today it was still so horribly muddled that it was a disgrace and I almost gave up my earlier bright hopes again. They quarreled about it with one another so terribly that I thought they would finally come to blows, and then they wanted to perform *A Midsummer Night's Dream*. Therefore it was rumored suddenly that the performance would be postponed until Saturday; so you can imagine that my mood was not rosy. Luckily the rumor proved to be unfounded. It appears that it will remain on Thursday, and so I hope to travel Saturday on the first train, and at about 2:30 to be again where I belong, with my dear, good, my only Cécile, with my birthday child. Until we see each other again soon, dear, dear, Cécile.

Yours,
Felix

Love me truly!

RECOLLECTIONS OF FELIX MENDELSSOHN AND HIS FRIENDS[1]

Heinrich Dorn

I was a young man of three-and-twenty, prosecuting my legal studies in Berlin, when I first knew Felix Mendelssohn, then a lad of twelve years old. One winter's experience showed me, that though I could get through my college terms, I should never be able to pass all the necessary law examinations, as I had so much musical business on my hands. At evening-parties I was in constant request, being found very useful, as I was at once a pianoforte-player, an accompanyist, and a solo-singer—a rare combination in one individual, of which I can recall no other instances than Gustav Reichardt and Reissiger. Musical parties in Berlin at that time were at the height of their glory, and attended only by ladies and gentlemen who really loved music and cultivated it as an art, and who were able upon emergency to perform whole operas or oratorios. Tea was handed round before the musical business of the evening began, and we wound up with cold refreshments and quartet-singing.

One Friday, at the "at home" evening of my old countryman Abraham Friedländer, as I was in the midst of the well-known duet of Spohr's between Faust and Röschen, with a talented young singer, a commotion arose in the anteroom, which was most unusual, for a profound silence always prevailed when anything was going on. During the pathetic air, 'Fort von hier auf schönere Auen,' my partner whispered to me, "Felix is come;" and when the duet was finished, I made the acquaintance of Felix Mendelssohn, then a lad of twelve years old, residing with his parents on the Neue Promenade, only a few steps from Friedländer's house. He apologised for having interrupted our song by his entrance, and offered to play the accompaniments for me; "or shall we play them alternately?" he said--a regular Mendelssohn way of putting the question, which, even twenty years later, he made use of to a stranger in a similar position. At that time it would have been difficult to picture a more prepossessing exterior than that of Felix Mendelssohn; though every one made use of the familiar "Du" in addressing him, yet it was very evident that even his most intimate acquaintances set a great value on his presence amongst them. He was rarely allowed to go to such large parties, but when he did do so, the music, and the *con amore* spirit with which it was carried on, seemed to afford him real pleasure, and he, in his turn, contributed largely to the enjoyment. People made a great deal of him, and Johanna Zimmermann, Friedländer's niece, who had lost her husband while bathing in the Tyrol, regularly persecuted the young fellow so that he could scarcely escape from her attentions. Young as he was, he even then accompanied singing in a manner only to be met with amongst the older and more thorough musicians who possessed that especial gift. At Königsberg the orchestral management of the piano was an unknown thing, and even in Berlin I had as yet had no opportunity of admiring this skill and facility in any one. That man was considered a very respectable musician who played from the printed copy *con amore*, and thus helped the singer now and then; but he who was able to enrich the slender pianoforte accompaniment with octave basses and full chords, of course stood in a much higher position. Such a gifted being was Felix even at that time, and in the duet between Florestan and Leonora, which he accompanied, he astonished me in the passage 'Du wieder nun in meinen Armen, o Gott!' by the way in which he represented the violoncello and the contre-basso parts on the piano, playing them two octaves apart. I afterwards asked him why he had chosen this striking way of rendering the passage, and he explained all to me in the kindest manner. How many times since has that duet been sung in Berlin to the pianoforte, but how rarely has it been accompanied in such a manner! In the winter of 1824-25 I was quite at home in the Mendelssohns' house—that is to say, I made my appearance there every Sunday morning at the musical entertainments, and was always invited to their evening parties, as a singer to be reckoned upon, and as one always ready to take a part in the dance. At the *matinées* I became by degrees personally acquainted with all the musicians of importance in Berlin. Men, such as Lanska, who had instructed both Felix and his sister Fanny (Fanny Mendelssohn at this time played more brilliantly than her brother Felix), Wollank (councillor of justice, and the composer of many well-known songs), and Karl Friedrich Zelter, almost alone marked that heavy period of Berlin's musical history, during which time no creative talent of any importance appeared. Simultaneously, however, with the recall of Spontini from Paris, three stars arose, and the whole attention of the musical world was directed to the native genius of Berlin, in the persons of Ludwig Berger, Bernhard Klein, and Felix Mendelssohn, all in the different ages of life.

I very seldom missed one of those interesting gatherings at the Neue Promenade, where, besides the greater compositions, which were henceforth studied under Berger's guidance, the newest works of the wonderful boy Felix were regularly played over—mostly sets of symphonies for stringed instruments with pianoforte accompaniment—by a small number selected from the royal chamber-musicians. Professor Zelter, with whom Felix had studied counterpoint, was his most eager auditor, and at the same time his most severe censor. More than once after the performance, I myself have heard Zelter call out in a loud voice to his pupil that several alterations were necessary, whereupon, without saying a word, Felix would quietly fold up the score, and before the next Sunday he would go over it, and then play the composition with the desired corrections. In these rooms also, before the family removed to Leipziger Strasse, a three-act comic opera was performed, all the characters being apportioned and the dialogue read out at the piano. The *libretto* for 'The Uncle from Boston' was written by a young physician, Dr. Caspar, who afterwards became a famous man. Every one who came in contact with him had something to relate of his wit, and I remember even now Holtei telling me, when I was at Riga, of the sparkling witty farewell speech addressed by Caspar to the Councillor Nernst, on the removal of the latter as Postmaster-General from Berlin to Tilsit. He finished with "Depart, and the peace of Tilsit be with you!"

Although the musical compositions of this 'American Uncle' pleased all the parties connected with it extremely, the subject of it was nevertheless very weak. Dévrient, and his, *fiancée*, Therese Schlesinger, Johanna Zimmermann, the Doctors Andriessen and Dittmar, all took part in this opera. I was also a chorus-singer in it, and from one circumstance this evening will never be forgotten by me. When the opera was finished, there were the regular slices of bread-and-butter, with the usual addition of anchovies, cold meat, cheese, &c. Edward Rietz and myself were enjoying our portion, when Felix, who was going the round of the room to thank all the singers personally, stopped before us to ask how we were faring in the way of refreshments. I showed him my share of the spoil.

"And which do you consider your *dux*?" (the leading, principal subject), he asked; "and which is your *comes*?" (the secondary theme).

"Well, of course, I consider my bread-and-butter my *dux*."

"Oh, no," said he, "a guest must always regard his bread-and-butter as only the *comes*."

Just as he had uttered this little sally, Zelter's voice resounded through the room:

"Felix, come here."

The old gentleman stood in the middle of the room with a brimming glass in his hand, and whilst every one was listening intently, he said: "Felix, you have hitherto only been an apprentice; from today you are an assistant, and now work on till you become a master."

Therewith he gave him a tap on the cheek, as if he were dubbing him a knight, and then the whole party pressed forward to congratulate the affected and astonished parents, as well as Felix, who pressed his old master's hand warmly more than once. This is one of those scenes that can never be effaced from one's memory. It made such a powerful impression on me that I wrote the following day to my guardian to ask if I might become a pupil of Zelter's, and by his help rise to the higher grades. This permission I certainly received, but how different anticipation is to reality! Zelter was a whimsical old fellow, to whom it was all the same whether his pupils were young or old, gifted or without talent, beginners or advanced. All were treated alike, except as in the case of Mendelssohn's private lessons, when he really did instruct. I bore it for half a year, then I could not put up with it any more, and so I went over to Bernhard Klein, and never had reason to repent doing so.

With the removal of the Mendelssohn family from the Neue Promenade to Leipziger Strasse, to the same house where our present Chamber of Deputies hold their sittings, the circle of their acquaintance was much extended, owing in a great measure to Felix' increasing fame. Among the more intimate acquaintances may be reckoned Rietz, Klingemann, Marx, Franck, and Dévrient. Rietz, elder brother of the royal chapel-master at Dresden, was himself a member of the royal orchestra, and Mendelssohn's instructor on the violin. I may safely say that of all Felix' friends no one loved him more enthusiastically than Rietz. He was a grave silent person, of a middle size and spare figure, endowed with a large share of nose between two fiery eyes, and always dressed in a tail-coat. When the two friends were together, the idea was always suggested to me of Faust and Mephistopheles, though there was certainly little enough of the diabolic in either of them. Robert and Bertram might perhaps have been more suitable, but such a connection had not then been proclaimed by Scribe and Meyerbeer. Rietz' artistic career was early cut short by the nerve of his third finger being injured during the performance of "Olympia." He died in 1832. Mendelssohn has dedicated his famous "Octett" to him.

Klingemann, the son of the well-known composer of plays, and manager of the theatre at Brunswick, made the most agreeable impression upon me of all Mendelssohn's more intimate acquaintances. He was attached to the Hanoverian Embassy, and was therefore admitted to the higher circles of society. Both his appearance and demeanour had something unaffectedly aristocratic in them, and in his whole manner to the ladies of the house he was vastly superior to the other visitors. It always appeared to me that Klingemann was most correct in his judgment of Felix. He did not worship him, and it could never have entered into his head to rival him, for he did not compose; he was neither insensible to the great qualities nor blind to the weak points of his young friend; and that he thoroughly knew how to appreciate the strongest side of Mendelssohn's talents is shown in the words which he wrote for Felix to set to music. A great many songs which Mendelssohn has arranged have been quite as well, perhaps even better, set by other musicians, but no one has ever yet succeeded in surpassing a song of Mendelssohn's with Klingemann's words; it was like two hearts beating with one pulsation. The capabilities of the youthful Secretary to the Embassy were certainly not equal to the composition of opera librettos; this was not, however, the field on which Felix ever earned any laurels, even when master of his profession; indeed they never bloomed for him at any time, as is shown by the production of his opera, "The Wedding of Camacho," written in the high tide of his youth. Klingemann was an eager supporter of the Berlin *Musical Times*, which had been started in 1824.

A great contrast in appearance with his colleague was the editor of this paper, A. B. Marx, who, although he had had a more thorough education, both as regards music and his profession as a lawyer, than either of the above-named gentlemen, and far exceeded them in cutting sharpness of intellect, yet, from his lack of polish and manner, his real scientific and dialectic superiority did not have the happy effect on those around that it would otherwise have done. He quickly interested himself about persons and things, and his sympathy once aroused, there could be no warmer nor more skilful advocate than he. He soon gained a great influence over Felix, which was often annoying to the elder Mendelssohn; but he had his own good reasons for not abruptly breaking off the connection. Marx was the editor of the *Musical Times*, at that period the only critical organ, and therefore not to be despised, especially as it was supported by many gifted friends of the Mendelssohns. Moreover, the elder Mendelssohn was very fond of contradicting, and of being contradicted; and in our Abbé (as he was called, after his initials A. B.) he found the right sort of opponent.

Midway between Klingemann and Marx stood Dr. Franck, of Breslau, possessing much of the refinement of the former, with more reserve of manner, and all the liveliness of conversation of the latter, with, however, less solidity. He had a sound judgement in musical matters, and soon discovered the weaknesses in Spontini's "Cortez"; he wrote a stinging article upon that opera in 1826, which was the signal for a complete rupture between Marx and Spontini; he had only armed his party with spectacles, and had overlooked many bright spots in the opera, rejecting the good with the bad. Spontini afterwards led the whole opposition against Mendelssohn; and as previously there had been little affinity between two such different elements, any nearer approach was now rendered impossible.

In 1849 I again met Franck—now, instead of the life-loving, exuberant man that he had been, a complete hypochondriac. He still took an eager interest in literature, and was quite imbued with the Wagner mania, and sent me that composer's "Nibelungen-Tetralogie." What would Mendelssohn have said to this, had he been alive at that time? Franck came to an untimely end soon afterwards in London; but these are painful recollections, and the circle of Felix' friends shall be concluded with the name of Dévrient, to the truth of whose interesting book about Mendelssohn, which has lately appeared, I can vouch. I had frequent opportunities of meeting Mendelssohn at the rooms of Johanna Zimmermann, the young widow previously mentioned, who, although somewhat eccentric, possessed a thoroughly musical nature; so that Felix felt himself completely at his ease in that unconstrained artistic atmosphere. His own home was, of course, much frequented by interesting and celebrated people, but the greater portion of them were not musicians. Foreign musical celebrities were, indeed, always hospitably received, but native talent was very weakly represented. Although Felix was by no means insensible to praise, he was not at all blind as to whether it was given with discrimination or the reverse. Marx and he were at Dehn's rooms on one occasion I remember, and the first part of the evening we employed ourselves in all sorts of fools' tricks, such as cutting out figures with paper and apple-parings, until Felix got up and, unasked, played on the old piano till long after midnight a number of his own and other compositions. This gave him more real satisfaction than on many an occasion at his parents' house, where, with a first-rate Broadwood at his command, he had a large but very mixed audience. I well recollect a lady (Rahel Varnhagen) asking him for the A Minor fugue of Bach's. "If I had played some variations of Czerny's, it would have been all the same to her," he remarked to me afterwards. Such an uncongenial assembly was never to be found at Madame Zimmermann's; there all participated equally, listening and performing; and I have never heard Felix extemporise better than at this house, where he was conscious of being thoroughly understood.

Before I left Berlin in March, 1828, I was present at the first performance of the overture to the "Midsummer Night's Dream," conducted by Mendelssohn himself, with a full orchestra, at his father's house. This work certainly contains the germ and bloom of all Mendelssohn's compositions, and the grand chorus of *St. Paul*, "Mache dir auf, werde Licht," alone deserves to be put by its side.

In May, 1830, Mendelssohn visited me in Leipzig, where I was officiating as director of music, at what was then the Theatre Royal. He had just returned from London, and having attained his one-and-twentieth year, was about to commence his travels through Italy, to which we are indebted for that interesting collection of letters, which afford so deep an insight into a real poetic and musical nature. I invited him with Marschner, who was then busy on his latest work, "The Templar and the Jewess," to come to my house the following evening, and I quickly asked a few other celebrities to meet him; in spite of the party being of the ill-omened number of thirteen, we were most animated, and everything went off admirably until the time arrived for my grand finale. A present I had received some time back of some rare old wine of a celebrated vintage, all covered with cobwebs and dust and dirt of half a century, was to be brought forward on a certain sign from me. The auspicious moment arrived, the maid put fresh glasses on the table and disappeared, and I prepared the minds of my guests for the monstrous sight they were about to see by drawing an exaggerated picture of its horrors. In the midst of my flourishing address, the maid walked in, and placed on the table four brightly-scoured, shining bottles, exactly resembling those containing that agreeable *vin ordinaire* called "Kutscher"; mark, seal, label, all had disappeared, and fallen a sacrifice to the principle, "Cleanliness is next to godliness." My disgust can be well imagined. Fortunately, our palates bore testimony to the excellency of the wine, and so my friend Kistner's honour was retrieved,

On the 2nd of June, 1830, I received the following letter from Mendelssohn, dated from Weimar:—

"Dear Dorn,—Herewith follows my symphony, very punctually, and still in time I hope to be copied out, studied and performed by the day before yesterday. Seriously, however, I am very sorry that I could not fulfil my promise. You always declared you know how it would be, but I can assure you I had quite made up my mind to do it, and the very first day of my arrival here I began the necessary corrections in the score, which soon become so numerous that I had to take away much of the old part, and to add to the last portion. If the copyist recommended to me had kept his promise, you would even then have had the symphony in time, but he put me off from day to day, and here I have been fourteen instead of four days.

It comes at last, you see, and perhaps you will look through it and communicate with Marschner as to the sufficiency of the abbreviations in the last part; when you have had enough of it, which I am afraid will be very soon, will you kindly forward it to Madame Hensel. Perhaps it is as well for some reasons that the performance has been postponed, for it occurred to me afterwards that the choral part and the other Catholicisms would have a strange appearance in a theatre, and that a Reformation song would not sound very well at Whitsuntide. In short, I am an optimist. Remember me very warmly to Marschner, and thank him for his many kindnesses, and for the enjoyment he has afforded me by his beautiful compositions. I mean to write him a long musical letter as soon as I get to Munich. Farewell, and think of me always kindly.—Yours, &c.,

Felix Mendelssohn."

That I have never ceased to do.

On the 13th of September, 1843, Robert Schumann celebrated the birthday of his wife Clara. I appeared as an unexpected guest at the breakfast table, where, besides David and Grützmacher, I met Mendelssohn again after thirteen years. When we had partaken of a bountiful repast, we had a succession of musical enjoyments. Schumann surprised his wife with a new trio, which was instantly tried, and Felix produced as his present "The Spring Song," and played it for the first time. This beautiful piece is the pearl of the fifth book of his "Lieder ohne Worte" which, as is well known, is dedicated to Madame Schumann. The little company was so enraptured with it that the composer had to repeat it twice. It was a worthy conclusion to the celebration of the day.

The next day I dined at Councillor Frege's, and again had the pleasure of meeting Mendelssohn, who even during the dessert placed himself at the piano and gave us some of his beautiful songs, which were sung with full appreciation by Livia Gerhardt, the celebrated singer. My third and last day at Leipzig was devoted to my friend Petschke, who had assembled a little party in honour of Mendelssohn, who seemed to be as much at his ease as he had formerly been as a young man in the house of Johanna Zimmermann. Petschke had asked me to bring some of my own compositions with me, and I found some attentive listeners to my "Schöffen von Paris." Mendelssohn, however, greatly surprised me by declaring he already knew one of the airs I had played, and seating himself at the piano, went through ten or twelve bars, where certainly the harmonies of my air occurred, although I failed to recognise where I had heard them before. "Why, you do not know your own composition again?" said Mendelssohn; "that is the final chorus to 'The Magician and Monster.'" That was a melodrama for which I had written the music, and which Mendelssohn had liked at the time, and of which now, sixteen years later, he could remember chords, that had long since passed from my mind. When I expressed astonishment at his memory, he said, in a very gratifying manner, "It is only good melodies we should endeavour to retain."

I fear that the musical festival at Cologne, which gave rise to so much unpleasantness between the heads of the various musical societies, also caused a coldness between Mendelssohn and myself; I could not, in the interest of my party, approve of all the measures which were carried out, and I fear my conduct was represented to him in a manner calculated to wound. Unfortunately, I had neither time nor opportunity, during his twelve hours' stay, to explain to him the Cologne comedy of "party faction," so I am afraid that he parted from me with resentment in his heart, whilst my admiration for his genius, profound knowledge, noble striving, and great lovableness always remained the same.

On the 9th of November, 1847, five days after Mendelssohn's death, I directed the second winter concert at Cologne, and, amidst the universal sympathy and expression of the deepest grief, the solemn chorus from *St. Paul* was introduced: "Behold, we reckon those happy who have endured; for though the body die, yet will the soul live for ever."

NOTE

1. *Temple Bar* 34 (February 1872), 397–405.

3

Mendelssohn as Performer and Teacher

Donald Mintz

No less great [than his work as a composer] are [Mendelssohn's] services and enormous merits as virtuoso and conductor. That the subscription concerts in this place [Leipzig] have won European fame is unalloyed testimony to this fact. Thoroughly permeated with the spirit of the coryphaei named above [Handel, Bach, Mozart, Haydn, Beethoven, Weber, Schubert], he knew how to incorporate and communicate [in a performance] the most secret intimations and beauties of their works, and while gratitude for having torn the works of Sebastian Bach from oblivion is owed primarily to him, he has also contributed the greatest part to the understanding of Beethoven.[1]

On dit souvent que l'interprétation musicale constitue une tâche fort difficile, mais on ne nous dit que rarement en quoi consiste la difficulté de cette tâche.[2]

TO BEGIN WITH

Mendelssohn's activities as a performer—whether as conductor or as pianist, organist, or violist—have an interest that goes well beyond the immediate activity in question, for they are embedded in a striking and, indeed, fundamental change in the way music is presented and perceived. During Mendelssohn's active years the modern notion that music is to be interpreted came into the general mind, and it is partly due to his activity that the utility and appropriateness of the concept became widely accepted.

We need to begin by trying to understand what this means, for a paradox is involved. Just when performers were being largely stripped of the right to take the text of a piece as a pre-text and were beginning to be required to view it as received and hence sacred, they were also required not merely to present that text but somehow to expound its deeper meaning. The first epigraph above, taken from an obituary notice for Mendelssohn, shows that by the time of his death this idea was easily accepted, at least in some circles, and that (again, at least in some circles) Mendelssohn was viewed as an ideal exponent of this new, hermeneutic art of performance.[3]

Stefan Kunze has remarked that this transformation of attitude came about partly because the music performed was increasingly not of the time of the performer and therefore had aspects that were not (or were no longer) self-evident but also (and in my view largely) because the music's "structure and conception were so constituted as categorically to demand interpretive insight into its structure and content."[4] The difficulty with such a remark, of course, is that while one feels that one understands more or less what is meant, it is very difficult to reduce this understanding to a precise and convincing statement when dealing with a specific piece of music.[5]

Hermann Danuser has tried to clarify the situation this way:

[Leopold] Mozart's formulation [of how to play a piece] presupposes a sort of direct relationship of the (violin) player to the notated musical intention of the composer. The notated piece that the performer is obliged to *render* does not represent the text of a musical work of art in the sense of the romantic theory of art which requires a hermeneutic and performance practice-related *interpretation* in order that its meaning may be revealed.[6]

Though this may still be far from satisfactory as a precise formulation, the practical significance and effect of what a contemporaneous listener perceived as an enlightening interpretation could be enormous. Here is Henry Chorley on hearing Mendelssohn conducting the Leipzig Gewandhaus Orchestra in 1839:

As regarded those works of the Shakspeare of Music [Beethoven's symphonies], I felt, for the first time in my life, in 1839, richly and thoroughly satisfied beyond reserve or question.—There was a breadth and freedom in their outlines, a thorough proportion in all their parts, a poetical development of all their choice and picturesque ideas, which fully compensated for the occasional want of the hyper-brilliancy and the hyper-delicacy, on the possession of which my friends in Paris boast themselves so vain-gloriously. It was not hearing Beethoven played,—it was revelling among his noble creations; and with the most perfect security that nothing would interfere to break the spell, or to call you back from the Master's thought to the medium in which it was given forth. Then those small aggravations of emphasis, those slight retardations of time, neither finically [*sic*] careful, nor fatiguingly numerous,—for which imagination thirsts so eagerly, so rarely to be gratified—were all given; and with such ease and nature, that I felt the gift was no holiday effort, got up for once, but the staple mode of interpretation and execution belonging to the place. Till, indeed, I heard the Leipsic orchestra,—my first love, the Brunswick Festival, not forgotten,—I felt I had no right to say, "Now I am indeed in the musical Germany of which I have so long dreamed."[7]

This contrasts with the tone of a routine review: "Mr. Felix Mendelssohn Bartholdy played Mozart's excellent D-minor Piano Concerto with great taste and solid dexterity, and the melodic Andante was uncommonly tender and simple and was presented with lovely tone."[8]

Clearly, the nature of a review is affected by many factors; one cannot expect a writer faced with dozens of concerts in his hometown and limited space in his hometown journal to adopt the attitude of a pilgrim. Nevertheless, distinct—in some cases drastic—changes of tone are easily noticed, often within the pages of the same journal.

During the 1843–1844 season Mendelssohn was in Berlin, and Ferdinand Hiller became the director of the Gewandhaus concerts. The *Allgemeine musikalische Zeitung* reviewer who was signed "Robert †" or "R. †" undertook to deliver occasional lectures on the nature of interpretation, an entirely new direction for this staid and conservative journal. Reviewing a performance of some music from *Fidelio*, he began with a discussion of the quartet[9] and its relation to the opera's overture, remarked that in the quartet the orchestra had only to support the singers, and continued:

But it is different in the overture. Here the orchestra should and must create the effect alone. For example, in the place from the quartet just mentioned, it must at the least give a clear presentiment, a spiritual vision of the powerful and important moment, since naturally it cannot and should not actually represent it. Accordingly, the coloration of this orchestral section must take on a higher, warmer tone than in the quartet itself, in order to replace insofar as possible what is effectuated in this song and in this action.[10] The orchestra must, so to speak, have spirit and soul; it must permit us to hear from it that the composer's intention has been felt and empathized with. Only a performance of this sort is truly an artistic rendition, for it has spiritual value, and only a performance of this sort can worthily represent the work of art and arouse in the listeners an appropriate, lively comprehension.[11]

This leads to a consideration of the nature of orchestral playing. The reviewer says that the frequently expressed view that the orchestral player has only to play the right notes is not valid. Rather, "every orchestra player must necessarily try to bring his conception of the work into harmony with the conductor's." It follows that the conductor's position is particularly important, "all the more so when he stands at the head of an orchestra that, as is here the case, is inspired by a true artistic spirit and up to now has been led by so highly endowed an artist as Mendelssohn Bartholdy."

Like Hiller, "Robert †" lasted only for a season; the reviews in the *Allgemeine musikalische Zeitung* then reverted to the dry tone of earlier years. His work, however, brought to the *Allgemeine musikalische Zeitung*—if only temporarily—not only a modern notion of the function of interpretation but necessarily also the prerequisite Romantic view of the role and the powers of instrumental music.

Before continuing, it may be useful briefly to consider how Wagner fits into this picture. To begin with, it seems important to recognize that *Über das Dirigieren*[12] is, in the first instance, an anti-Semitic tract and only in the second a treatise about conducting and, more generally, interpretation. Accordingly, Wagner's comments about Mendelssohn's conducting cannot be believed and indeed can often be proved false.[13]

To take a single instance, it is clear that all charges that Mendelssohn cut the Schubert "Great C major" Symphony or that he took all or part of it at unreasonable tempos are untrue. Reports of the premiere of this symphony at the Gewandhaus with Mendelssohn conducting (22 March 1839) give no reason to think cuts were made, and all agree that the running time of the performance was between 55 minutes and an hour. Beyond that, there is complex documentary evidence that has been ably assembled and interpreted by Peter Krause.[14] O. Lorenz's review of the first performance of the symphony[15] says that the "formal breadth" of the third movement could benefit by elimination of the repeats. At this time, eliminating repeats counted as making cuts. It is particularly remarkable that Lorenz suggested cuts of the repeats in the third, rather than the first, movement. Apparently, the scherzo-trio-scherzo structure was thought to maintain its integrity without repeats. Yet, one infers, that the structural integrity of the sonata allegro required the repeat of the exposition. The implications for performance practice and for contemporaneous views of "sonata allegro form" are obvious—and perhaps not what we expect.

We shall need to look again at quarrels and debates about tempo, phrasing, and the like in the context of Mendelssohn's career as a conductor and pianist, for there is a logic to developments in this area that Wagner, in part, elucidated even as he sacrificed historical accuracy to racist polemics.

SPHERES OF INFLUENCE

If we are to assess Mendelssohn's influence as a performer, we need to begin by thinking about the places where he worked and about the influence of the genres in which he was active. It is clear that even at the time of his death opera remained the dominant musical genre for most people in most places. Three examples among many: Ernst Kossack's obituary for Mendelssohn in the *Neue Berliner Musikzeitung* says that at his death Mendelssohn had just begun to work on "the highest art form, the great tragic opera"[16]; during the 1830s and 1840s, the masthead of the *London Times* included the day's events in theater and opera but not in the city's concert halls; correspondents' reports to the musical journals about events in their cities usually begin with discussions of operatic events and devote most of their space to these.

Mendelssohn's influence in operatic matters was negligible. He completed no opera after the comedy *Die Hochzeit des Camacho* (1825), and his career as a conductor of opera was confined to a handful of performances in Düsseldorf.[17] In any case, Düsseldorf was a small place, far better known for its painters than for its musicians. The population was 19,000 in 1800 and 41,000 in 1850.[18] Nevertheless, Mendelssohn's work in Düsseldorf was, in a real sense, a preview of his directorship in Leipzig. Wasielewski wrote that Mendelssohn quickly raised the standards of performance partly by reason of the authority he exuded and partly as a result of his splendid rehearsal technique. He also raised the level of the programming, introducing what was to become his regular approach of combining what we would now call "standard repertory" with carefully selected recent music, while making every effort to avoid music he deemed trivial. According to Wasielewski, Mendelssohn kept up a pretty steady stream of old greats (not all of them necessarily locally familiar): *Messiah, Samson,. Israel in Egypt, Judas Maccabaeus*, music by Bach, Beethoven, Mozart, Haydn, Cherubini. He also kept his own music out as a general rule and had to be urged to program it. What is novel here is not really the blend of old and new; that had been fairly standard in a number of places for some time.[19] The novelty consisted rather in Mendelssohn's diligence in adding neglected works to the repertory of older music and in his continuing efforts—not, however, without occasional compromise—to restrict performances of new music to works that he deemed serious and worthy.

In addition, Mendelssohn was responsible for Düsseldorf's major church music. He was partial to the music of "the old Italians" (meaning Palestrina and his followers, some of them fairly remote *stile antico* followers) and went to considerable lengths to obtain and perform appropriate pieces. He also ended the custom of playing opera overtures in church during Mass.[20]

Leipzig, where Mendelssohn assumed direction of the Gewandhaus concerts in the fall of 1835, while no London or Paris, was a more important place than Düsseldorf. In 1835 Leipzig had about 50,000 people, and the vicinity, about another 20,000.[21] It was the center of the German book trade and a major music-publishing center, home to a significant university, and the site of large fairs whose origins reach back to the Middle Ages. It was also Protestant. Perhaps no less important was what it was not: a *Residenzstadt*, the seat of a churchly or secular ruler. It is clear that Mendelssohn preferred a bourgeois board of directors to the agents of a royal patron and liked the relatively liberal atmosphere of the mercantile city. Moreover, the absence of an opera under royal patronage created an advantage for the symphony concerts, for they, rather than Leipzig's commercial opera, were the center of musical attention and an important part of the city's intellectual life.[22]

The atmosphere of the city and its musical activities toward the end of Mendelssohn's life (and during Hiller's year as music director) were captured—with perhaps more than a bit of hyperbole—by a correspondent of the *Musical World*:

Before all German towns I prefer Leipsic. Berlin is too pompous and formal, Dresden too eclectic, Munich too aristocratic, Prague too Bohemian, Frankfort too motley, Vienna too bustling and Parisian. Leipsic alone has that peculiar aspect which proclaims music to be the dominant passion. The population is so modest that you seem to know everybody; and everybody has an opinion on musical matters. The *table-d'hotes* are the arenas for discussing this engrossing subject. The hour of dinner, half-past one, leaves ample time for relaxation, and no true German will work after the early afternoon. You can imagine nothing more agreeable than the *table-d'hotes*. There you meet such men as David, Gade, Hauptmann, and often even Mendelssohn himself, taking their frugal repast (that is frugal for Germany) and conversing in a tone of animation and hilarity that you have no notion of in your melancholy London dining-rooms. I am no *gourmand*, but I can assure you that at Leipsic, the approach of the dinner-hour makes my pulse beat with anticipations of coming pleasure. Dinner, in short, is the bridge which, passing over a tranquil stream of enjoyment, conducts you from the morning to the evening—it cuts the day in halves, and lays before you clearly the German maxim that eight hours are for business, eight more for pleasure, and the other eight for sleep. Who shall deny the philosophy of this? What is life without relaxation? What are riches without enjoyment? What are honours without leisure? What is ambition without sleep? Let your plodding merchant rail at German life, and dry up the moisture of his being, in a dusty counting-house; for my part, though I do not affect to despise the advantages of wealth, I like to enjoy at least a third of my existence, and eschew the living sepulture of unremitting business-habits—more especially since smoking is out of the question, that being the exclusive prerogative of steam-boats and chimneys.

One of the principal attractions of Leipsic to the lovers of music is to be found in the *Abonnement-Concerts*, held at the *Gewandhaus*. There you have the finest instrumental music executed by an orchestra equal in number and far superior in discipline to that of the London Philharmonic.[23]

Because of its commercial and intellectual importance, Leipzig exerted an influence out of proportion to its size. The fame of the Gewandhaus Orchestra was widely touted not only by people like the anonymous *Musical World* correspondent but also by a figure like Berlioz.

The chronology of Mendelssohn's tenure in Leipzig is complicated by his obligations in Berlin toward the end of his life. It may be useful to summarize that tenure:

1835/1836. He takes over the Leipzig orchestra and conducts regularly until the end of 1840/1841 season. He is then called to Berlin.
1841/1842 and 1842/1843. He conducts in Leipzig as often as possible; Ferdinand David is his *locum tenens*.
1843/1844. He is replaced by Ferdinand Hiller as Musikdirektor.
1844/1845. Hiller is replaced by Niels Gade as Musikdirektor.
1845/1846. Mendelssohn returns as Musikdirektor and remains in the post almost until his death.
1846/1847. Mendelssohn shares the podium with Niels Gade.
1847. He again resigns, but he dies on 4 November 1847.[24]

"London is the most grandiose and complex monster in the world," wrote Mendelssohn on his first arrival in what was then the world city of them all. "Everything swirls around me like a maelstrom and twists and turns and pulls me into it; I haven't seen so many different things and so much contrast in Berlin in the past three years as I have seen here in three days."[25] In 1841 the county population of London was 1,825,714 and that of Greater London 2,235,344, both having roughly doubled since 1801. By contrast, Berlin, where Mendelssohn grew up, had 197,717 inhabitants in 1816 and 431,566 in 1849.[26] Moreover, London was the capital of the Industrial Revolution as well as of the British empire and consequently the source of much technological and organizational innovation. Quiet liberals like Mendelssohn, people who were substantially, if discreetly, unhappy at the politically repressive atmosphere of the German states after the Congress of Vienna, admired the British Constitution even before the Reform Bill of 1832.

Mendelssohn's performing activities in England, as in Leipzig, included piano and organ playing as well as conducting. In England his influence as organist extended beyond repertory and performance practice to the design of the organ. His influence as a conductor had essentially to do with the modernization of regressive English customs with regard to musical organization and control as well as to performance practice. (It seems quite in character for Victorian English musical organizations to have been retrogressive in the face of highly progressive commercial and industrial practices.)

Finally, we need to consider Mendelssohn's activity as occasional director of the Lower Rhine Festival. This work, which on initial inspection may seem secondary at best, in fact has considerable importance because of the extent to which it shaped the standards and the repertory of those festivals of amateur choral groups that were so important to musical life in Germany as well as England during the nineteenth century.[27] Niemöller puts it this way:

> The importance for the musical life of the first half of the nineteenth century of the Lower Rhine Musical Festival, held since 1818 alternately in three cities, Düsseldorf, Cologne, and Aachen, can hardly be exaggerated. Here the members of that layer of the bourgeoisie that carried the musical life of the period came together as both participants and listeners for the cultivation of great works that lay beyond the scope of their individual singing societies and choral groups.[28]

Berlin may be left out of the list of places where Mendelssohn was an influential performer or teacher. His great service to the city in the former capacity was the 1829 performance of the *St. Matthew Passion*, a performance that not only brought the great work to public attention but also helped turn the Singakademie into a group that more or less consistently gave public performances.[29] This event was early in his career, however, and when Karl Friedrich Zelter, the Singakademie's longtime director and one of Mendelssohn's most important teachers, died, Mendelssohn's bid to be his successor was rejected.[30] His later activities as conductor and pianist had some resonance; indeed, it is hard to imagine how they could not have had. Yet no long-term influence emanated from them. Mendelssohn's educational plans were realized not in Berlin, where presumably he was charged with educational reform and development, but in Leipzig, where he was not.[31]

INTERPRETATION

We have already touched a bit on "interpretation" and its nature. Let us now try to be more precise to the limited extent possible. All statements about specific aspects of performance—statements involving tempo, phrasing, dynamics, and the like—are comparative, regardless of their grammatical form. Slow, fast, loud, soft, even legato and staccato have meaning only in reference to some implied baseline, and precise knowledge of that baseline for periods prior to the invention of recording is impossible.[32] Yet while we cannot form a satisfyingly exact and detailed image of what an old performance was like, we can learn enough to develop a tantalizingly vague image. Unhappily, this will have to do.

Given the nature of my topic, it is reasonable for Mendelssohn to be near the center of this relatively general part of the inquiry. Yet we shall not be able to rely much on him as we try to develop this image; his well-known dislike of writing about music was broken in this respect only by occasional comments about details in performances of his works to be conducted by others.

Enlightened interpretation in the first half of the nineteenth century seems to have been based on the idea of the performer as the composer's agent or "advocate," in Erich Leinsdorf's striking term.[33] "Once we argued about your conception of my compositions," wrote Schumann (to Clara) in a diary entry, "But you are not right, Klärchen. The composer, and only he, knows how his pieces are to be represented [*darzustellen*]. No one will object to a few interesting exceptions, provided they are made by important people. It is always better, however, for the virtuoso to give the work of art, not himself."[34] This idea can be found in many places, expressed both positively and negatively. For many, Liszt was the prime example of a performer who gave himself rather than the work of art. A *Musical World* reviewer, for instance, remarked that Liszt's playing "draws attention from the composer to the player."[35]

Another reviewer for the *Musical World* expressed the idea of agency or advocacy this way: "He [the conductor] is, or ought to be, the master-spirit of the band over which he presides—an impersonation of the mind of the composer." He continued: "The Conductor should evince not only the imaginative glow of the poet, but also display a thorough acquaintance with the minutest details of the work entrusted to his superintending care. . . . He should exhibit a warm sympathy with the intentions of his author, and a perfect familiarity with the machinery by which they are to be developed."[36]

In a discussion about what constitutes an adequate review of a musical performance—discussion in itself symptomatic of the increasing interest in "interpretation"—a writer for the *Signale für die Musikalische Welt* said, "After all, musical performance is nothing other than turning outwards the interior of a piece of music so that the layman can sense [*empfinden*] and the connoisseur understand it."[37]

Technical accuracy in performance is a prerequisite for an interpretation but, it appears, not really a constituent of this revelation of the "interior of a piece of music." These constituents, insofar as they can be named or inferred, have to do primarily with tempo and dynamics; of course, matters like "verve," "fire," and so on remain important—as well as ineffable or, in any case, inaccessible to precise verbal description.

The importance and relative rarity of finely shaded dynamics in performance (and of unanimity about their application in the orchestra) were nicely caught by Wilhelm Adolf Lampadius as he looked back on Mendelssohn's first appearance at the Gewandhaus: "of that nice shading, that exact adaptation of each instrument, that perfect harmony of all instruments, attained under Mendelssohn's direction, there had been no conception [under Matthäi, Mendelssohn's predecessor]," though "there had been no lack of excellence in former days, when the concert-master and the first violin had the direction of Beethoven's symphonies."[38]

Franz Brendel made a similar comment toward the end of Mendelssohn's tenure at the Gewandhaus: "the exact and delicate shading in piano and forte of the individual instruments as they play together, and their lively integration such that the orchestra presents itself as a *single* entity and as a virtuoso [are to be] praised." Brendel added that these qualities were not easily to be found elsewhere.[39]

Ignaz Moscheles stressed the importance of dynamic differentiation in a letter to Mendelssohn about a rehearsal of the *Melusine* overture in London:

The contrasting storms went as if Neptune held the sceptre; but when the voices of the Sirens were to disarm that boisterous ruler, I had to call for *piano, piano! piano!* at the top of my voice, bending down to the ground *à la* Beethoven, and in vain trying to restrain the ferocious violins and basses . . . I hope to bring out the lights and shades still better at the performance.[40]

Yet there may well have been disagreement about what finely nuanced playing really was. Mendelssohn's close friend Karl Klingemann had his doubts about Moscheles's conducting of the piece, at least in its earlier rehearsal stages. In a letter to Mendelssohn of 7 February 1834 Klingemann wrote:

I wish I knew if I were right in my view of the overture, that is that the one section must be as still and blissful as the other wild. If I were sure, I would urge this on Moscheles even more strongly than I already did yesterday. I mean that it seems to me that he does not envision this conception clearly enough, for otherwise he could easily have explained this to the orchestra in a few words, and thereby vastly furthered the whole thing.[41]

Did Klingemann demand more than Moscheles was prepared to supply? Or, given the chronology of the letters—Klingemann's comes first—did Moscheles bring his conducting in line with Klingemann's views, views that the full text of the letter seems to suggest were conditioned by Mendelssohn's piano rendition of the score?

The same standards were applied to older music as well. Lampadius wrote,

It is to be said about the performance of the symphonies of Haydn and Mozart that for all his piety toward these old masters of the tonal art, Mendelssohn, through his spirited conception and occasionally somewhat accelerated tempos, and the subtlest nuancing by means of Piano, Decrescendo and Crescendo understood how to reconcile these works with modern demands and taste in the most apt way [*auf das sinnigste*].[42]

The remark raises many questions. Lampadius implies that Mendelssohn broke with an older performance tradition, a tradition that Lampadius presumably knew firsthand, and that this breach adapted the works in question to modern taste without, however, making any alterations in the actual texts. One may speculate that the older tradition was simply straightforward playing without "interpretation" and that the stated "reconciliation" consisted in nothing more nor less than introducing "interpretation." At the simplest level, this means careful observation of dynamic and articulation markings, balancing of climaxes against one another, and similar matters that today are too routine to be consciously expected. At higher levels, of course, it implies those less tangible qualities of fire and commitment and, in the last analysis, communion with the composer.[43]

Questions of tempo divide neatly into two related areas: the absolute (or average) speed of a movement or piece and the degree of variance from the average speed considered allowable.

With regard to the former and its importance for the understanding and rendition of the fundamental character of a work, let us listen for a moment to "J. B." of *Signale für die Musikalische Welt*. If the introduction to the *Wasserträger* (i.e., Cherubini, *Les deux journées*) overture is taken too slowly, he says, its pathos is lost. "Instead, however careful the performance may be with regard to Forte and Piano, the expression of the mysterious takes on more the character of the adventurous than of the edifying." He then turned to a performance of the Schumann B♭ symphony:

We must make the same remarks about the Introduction to Robert Schumann's Symphony (no. 1, B♭ major) and the Andante of the same work. The tempo chosen in the former was almost 3 to 5. No wonder that the Introduction lost a strength and a freshness that could not be replaced by the pathos forced on it by the tempo. On the other hand, while the somewhat too slow tempo of the Andante did not take away its deep tenderness [*Innigkeit*], it did deprive it of that lovely warmth that [otherwise] pervades it.[44]

Detailed information about deviation from the underlying tempo of a movement is harder to come by. Certainly, the general view was that there, indeed, was such a thing as an underlying tempo. Extreme tempo variations within a movement, probably introduced by Wagner, were not a part of the performance practice of the first half of the century.[45] (The Wagnerian approach can be heard, for instance, in the Richard Strauss performance of Beethoven's Fifth that occasionally turns up in historical recordings series.) There is every indication that moderate flexibility like that described by Chorley was the desideratum prior to Wagner's ascent.[46]

Certainly, it is clear that Mendelssohn was a devotee of "strict meter,"[47] that is to say, adherence to a basic, underlying pulse but not to metronomic precision. It is also certain that he liked things fast; comments (and complaints) about his rapid tempos occur far more frequently than remarks that he took this or that piece too slowly. In these ways as in others, he belonged to a musical generation earlier than Wagner's and was bound to have come under Wagnerian attack even had he not had the poor taste to have been born into a Jewish family. Bülow regretted that Mendelssohn had founded no school of conducting, oddly (but perhaps with political tact) attributing this not to the ascendancy of Wagner and the changes in tastes and attitudes signalized by the Revolution of 1848 but rather to the inadequacies of Mendelssohn's "disciples." Bülow was born in 1830; his experiences of Mendelssohn were therefore youthful, and the accuracy of his later memories may be open to question. For present purposes, however, accuracy of recollection is not at issue; what counts is Bülow's ideal of conducting, which he professed to have found in Mendelssohn's work—or in his recollections of it. This ideal was incorporated in the "elastic sensitivity [*Feinfühligkeit*]" and "ingenious shadings of the motion [*Bewegungsschattirungen*]" in Mendelssohn's conducting of the Schubert "Great C major."[48] (For all this, Felix Weingartner did not include Wagner among the "Tempo-Rubato-Dirigenten," of whom, he claimed, Bülow was the main representative![49] Such discrepancies and disagreements are an admonition to caution in dealing with these difficult matters.)

Bülow was not alone in criticizing what he took to be excessive tempo variations (and presumably also excessively heightened expression) within a movement. Galkin reports on Berlioz's strictures against Chopin and César Cui's against Wagner in this regard, and the reverse, Wagner's criticism of what he took to be Berlioz's rigidity.[50]

MENDELSSOHN THE CONDUCTOR

Some of what has been said about interpretation may serve as an introduction to Mendelssohn's activities as a conductor, but a great deal remains to be added. I begin with the question of baton conducting of all music. This form of control was not an absolute novelty when Mendelssohn took over at the Leipzig Gewandhaus in the fall of 1835. Johannes Forner has pointed out that it had been introduced by Ignaz Franz Mosel in Vienna in 1812, by Weber in Dresden in 1817, and also by Reichardt in Berlin and Spohr in Kassel and London.[51] The Moscheles letter cited earlier[52] and many other sources indicate that Beethoven, too, had been a baton conductor. Nevertheless, the Leipzig custom had been otherwise. Friedrich Schmidt summarizes the situation:

Right in this first concert (4 October 1835) Mendelssohn introduced a most useful innovation. Up to this time, the concertmaster, sometimes beating time, sometimes playing, directed instrumental works from his desk. But as soon as singing occurred, the music director beat time. Now Mendelssohn directed all instrumental performances [and vocal performances with the baton] and also conducted all the rehearsals.[53]

Contemporaneous accounts confirm Schmidt's report.

Schumann was not entirely convinced of the value of the novelty. "For myself," wrote "Eusebius,"

the baton was disturbing in the overture as well as in the symphony, and I agreed with Florestan who said that in a symphony the orchestra must be like a republic that recognizes nothing higher than itself. But it was a pleasure to watch F. Meritis [Mendelssohn] and to see the way he anticipated [*vorausnuancierte*] with his eyes all the nuances of the piece from the most delicate to the strongest, and like one overjoyed swam ahead of the generality, instead of behaving like some of the Capellmeister one comes across who threaten to beat the score, the orchestra, and the public with the scepter.[54]

Apparently, Schumann retained some of his reservations. Julius Eckardt quotes a curious letter from him, apparently written sometime in 1841, that seems to suggest to Ferdinand David that he should act as a violin bow conductor in a performance of Schumann's B♭ symphony.[55]

Some resistance to the techniques of baton conducting continued in Leipzig. More than a year after Mendelssohn's debut, the *Neue Zeitschrift für Musik* carried a remarkable anticonductor piece, "Vom Dirigiren und insbesondere von der Manie des Dirigirens." "A good orchestra," said the writer, "and that is what we are talking about here, needs to be conducted only at the beginning and where tempo changes occur when playing symphonies, overtures, etc. At other times, the conductor can stand quietly at his desk, reading the score and listening to hear when his commands are once again necessary." The writer suggested that constant beating may be useful in slow movements, where it is more difficult to keep things together. He opposed what he called "affected, caricature-like conducting, which beats fortes strongly and pianos less so or pulls a face at players when they make mistakes. All that belongs in the rehearsal, not at the concert." Nevertheless, he was in favor of "interpretation," calling for the spirit of the composition to be revealed. But this occurs, he believed, when every player "attaches himself to that spirit." The essay emphasizes that it is not "the play of forte and piano that gives forth the spirit of the composition but its *comprehension and rendition as a work of art*"[56]—in short, a demand for a modern interpretation achieved through traditional—not to say old-fashioned—means.

One must not be misled by all this talk about the baton and its virtues and defects into considering the means of orchestral control to have been paramount in the minds of musicians at this time. The general run of contemporaneous journalism makes it quite clear that what was really at issue on the continent was the question of orchestral control as such, rather than the means by which it was attained. Chorley's comments quoted earlier[57] give full marks to "my friends in Paris" for technical finish; the reference is quite clearly to François-Antoine Habeneck, who presided with the violin bow over the orchestra universally conceded to be the most brilliant in Europe.[58]

The seemingly endless British combat about orchestral control had essentially to do not with violin bow versus baton but with divided versus unified control, the means by which the unified control might be exercised being distinctly secondary. Mendelssohn's role in this was peripheral, and this is not the place to rehearse these entertaining battles beyond remarking that in his series of concerts with the Philharmonic Society in 1844, Mendelssohn effectively ended the debate by demonstrating once and for all the value of consistent leadership by a single musician endowed with full authority over the proceedings.

But what did Mendelssohn do with his baton? We begin with a difficulty. Galkin accepts Ferdinand Hiller's statement that "Mendelssohn turned his right side to the orchestra."[59] Why, after all, would one challenge Hiller in a matter like this? But the full sentence with the material that precedes it reads: "His [Mendelssohn's] movements were short and decided [*bestimmt*] and generally hardly visible, for he turned his right side to the orchestra."[60] Given the position in question and the matter at hand, it must surely have been the orchestra, or at least much of that portion of it seated stage left, rather than the audience, that Hiller was commenting about. It is true, of course, that members of the audience seated audience right would not have got much visual entertainment from the conductor. Indeed, Hiller's comment makes a good deal less sense on examination than on hasty reading.

Wasielewski, whose opportunities to observe Mendelssohn were, if anything, greater than Hiller's, says:

Mendelssohn's fiery eye surveyed and dominated the entire orchestra. And the reverse: every glance clung to the tip of his baton. He was therefore able to move the mass just as he wished at any moment and with sovereign freedom. Whenever during a performance he allowed himself to make occasional small alterations in tempo by means of improvised ritardandos or accelerandos, these were realized in such a way that one would have believed they had been prepared during rehearsal.[61]

It is hard to imagine how such a performance could have been controlled by gestures that were "hardly visible." Hans Erdmann and Hans Rentzow have published a letter from Mendelssohn to Julius Stocks of 22 March 1840 giving details of a platform to be erected for performances of St. Paul and The Creation in Schwerin.[62] Mendelssohn wanted his forces arrayed in a wedge in such a way that he could make eye contact with every member of the enormous mass customary at festival performances. Perhaps in Leipzig, Mendelssohn, obedient to his time's conceptions of politeness, began a performance without fully turning his back to the audience, but gradually—or perhaps not so gradually—moved to the modern position.

Details about baton technique are hard to come by.[63] It seems reasonably clear that Mendelssohn did, in fact, mostly conduct as opposed to merely starting things off and intervening only for tempo changes and disasters (or impending disasters). I am not impressed by speculations about his beat patterns; the information on which these are based is both sparse and shaky.

It is possible to interpret a passage in Ferdinand Simon Gassner's little book as suggesting not only uniform bowing, but uniform string fingering as well.[64] A passage in Wasielewski indicates that David may have indicated uniform bowing and possibly even uniform fingerings for Mendelssohn in Leipzig.[65]

It is interesting to observe that Gassner, who gets fairly short shrift from Galkin, disdains the measure-for-nothing, recommends a modern preparatory beat, and discusses pickups in some detail.[66] There is no evidence that this has anything to do with Mendelssohn, however. Whatever his baton technique may have been, it was adequate to control not only an orchestra but also the enormous masses of singers and players at affairs like the Lower Rhine Festivals.[67] All reports about these performances agree that Mendelssohn achieved remarkable levels of precision of ensemble and variety of dynamics.[68]

Those reports that deal mostly with Mendelssohn's choral conducting, whether in Birmingham, Leipzig, or Berlin, likewise agree that his extraordinary control was achieved partly by dint of enormous personal magnetism (and patience, too) and partly by such sensible, if tiring, measures as conducting as many choral rehearsals himself as possible. For example:

Since the composer himself took all the choral, piano, and orchestral rehearsals with the large groups as well as conducted the performance, one can imagine how complete a rendition and effect resulted. The multifarious tonal pictures, from the thundering fortissimo of the united choral and orchestral forces through all nuances to the dying breath of the most gentle pianissimo, imprinted themselves with purity and sharpness on the deeply moved hearts of the listeners, whose great numbers the large church could scarcely encompass.[69]

Programming is an important aspect of conducting, and though the Leipzig *Directorium* had an overall supervisory role, Mendelssohn seems to have been largely free to express both his personal taste and his sense of duty in arranging the programs for the Gewandhaus. In 1824 a writer for the *Berliner allgemeine musikalische Zeitung* went to war against exactly the sort of program that Mendelssohn, too, was subsequently to be against and outlined the alternative that Mendelssohn was to adopt:

Putting together a mass of pieces of various genres and by various masters, a process by which a botched piece may well slip in, and the arbitrary cutting up that a large and honorable work is often subjected to in order to make room for this or that bravura aria necessarily also cuts up the listener's perceptions [*Innere*]. What is left behind with him is something like those retinal images [*Glanzfiguren*] that jump around in our fantasy after we have seen fireworks. A clever concert-giver, or one with honorable intentions, must therefore be very careful in choosing the pieces and arranging the order in which they will be performed. The more the form and content of individual pieces come together to make up a whole, the more lasting will be the listeners' impressions; both the concert-giver and the listener will gain thereby.[70]

It is curious that even as late as 1837 the old way of doing things had supporters. Carl Borromäus von Miltitz wrote about what he considered the right way to program a concert in the *Allgemeine musikalische Zeitung* for 22 February 1837.[71] A concert should begin, he maintained, with a powerful overture or the first movement of a symphony. A vocal number, solo or ensemble, should follow. Lieder and light songs, however, are not appropriate. In other words, the vocal number should be a concert aria or ensemble or taken from an opera, presumably of appropriate seriousness. The second part of the concert should begin with two of the remaining movements of the symphony or an ensemble for wind and strings like Beethoven's, Hummel's, Winter's, and Kalkbrenner's septets and sextets. The concert should end with the final movement of the symphony. It is curious that this scheme leaves no place for the instrumental virtuoso.

Mendelssohn, I need hardly say, did nothing of the kind. But he did stay with the happy kind of mixture that today is economically impossible except, of course, in radio concerts based on commercial recordings. Here, for instance, is the program for the fourteenth subscription concert of the 1835/1836 season: Part I:

La Vestale overture by Spontini; clarinet variations by Bärmann (Friedrich Hummel from Innsbruck); "Wie nahte mir der Schlummer" from *Der Freischütz* (Henriette Grabau); Mozart D-minor Piano Concerto (Mendelssohn at the piano). Part II: Friedrich Schneider Symphony in B minor; Finale from Boieldieu's *Johann von Paris* (aka *Jean de Paris*).[72] A singer was always on the orchestra's roster during these years and was as much a part of the organization as any of the instrumental players.

One can easily get an idea of the balance over a longer course from a summary article in the *Allgemeine Wiener Musik-Zeitung* for 26 November 1846.[73] The orchestral works played during a six-concert period, Mendelssohn and Niels Gade sharing the conducting, are listed—Overtures: Cherubini's *Wasserträger*, Spohr's Concert Overture, Op. 126, Weber's *Preziosa*, Hiller's Concert Overture no. 1, Lachner's *Vier Menschenalter*, Beethoven's C major, Op. 115, Cherubini's *Faniska*, Weber's *Euryanthe*, Rossini's *William Tell*, and Bennett's *Waldnymphe*; Symphonies: Beethoven's Sixth, Schubert's "Great C major," Haydn's "Fifth" (Hob. I:95 in C minor?), Mozart's *Jupiter*, Schumann's Second (new, from manuscript), and Beethoven's *Eroica*. Soloists were Louise Dulcken (pianist from London), "the young" Joseph Joachim (violin), Clara Schumann-Wieck (piano), the clarinetist Landgraf (a member of the orchestra), and the concertmaster, Ferdinand David (violin). The vocal ensemble pieces performed were the finale from the second act of Weber's *Euryanthe* and the finale of the second act of Rossini's *William Tell*. What this summary does not show is that many of the solo offerings, particularly the pianists', of course, might well have been unaccompanied solos.

Schumann looked over an entire season's offerings in "Rückblick auf das Leipziger Musikleben im Winter 1837/38."[74] Mozart was the most frequently played composer with seventeen appearances; Beethoven with fifteen, Weber with seven, and Haydn with five followed. Cherubini, Spohr, Mendelssohn, and Rossini were represented by three to five pieces each. Handel, Bach, Vogler, Cimarosa, Méhul, Onslow, and Moscheles each had two works played. Naumann, Salieri, Righini, Feska (i.e., Fesca—presumably Friedrich Ernst is meant), Hummel, Spontini, Marschner, "and many others" had one work each on the programs. "The newest composers," Thomas Täglichsbeck, Norbert Bergmüller, and Wenzel Gährich, were also represented by one work each.[75]

The larger modern works for that season are singularly obscure from our point of view. Yet Mendelssohn's record with regard to modern music, as his premieres of Schumann's orchestral music suggest, was better than the 1837/1838 season indicates. He did, for instance, conduct the *Tannhäuser* overture, though there is no reason to believe he was fond of it. On the other hand, in his overview of the 1839/1840 concert season, Schumann complained about the absence of anything by Berlioz,[76] and indeed, Berlioz's music appeared only when the composer himself appeared as its conductor.[77] Yet in some quarters at least, Mendelssohn counted as a champion of modern music. The Berlin correspondent of *Allgemeine Wiener Musik-Zeitung*, J. P. Schmidt, complained that after Mendelssohn's return to Leipzig the amount of recent music played at the königliche Capelle concerts declined sharply.[78]

At Mendelssohn's death, one of his more fervid admirers gave him credit for almost single-handedly having created a sense of continuity with the music of the past—or more accurately, with the German music of the past:

About twenty years ago . . . the seductive melodies of Rossini and Bellini resounded at their most full-throated throughout all of Germany. Then there came along a young man whose strivings made a stir because they seemed so unusual, who did not inquire about the doings in Paris and Italy—indeed he sometimes even went right past Mozart and Haydn—but he thereby investigated all the more diligently the works of Handel and Bach. He made the old forms of these primevally powerful but inflexible masters lively again by treating them more supplely [*geschmeidigere Anwendung*] and took pains to bring the chaste old seriousness back into a music that had become frivolous.[79]

Clearly, this is more than a bit much; but it quite rightly catches the enthusiasm with which Leipzig greeted Mendelssohn's engagement with the music of 100 years earlier. Susanna Großmann-Vendrey has written brilliantly about both the intellectual background to this engagement and Mendelssohn's practical work on behalf of "early music."[80]

Riehl's observation about more supple treatment of old works makes at least a certain amount of sense in connection with Lampadius's comments quoted earlier.[81] Presumably, Riehl is writing about relatively flexible rhythm and considerable attention to dynamics. One wonders what Mendelssohn actually did. He probably never considered anything like the "sewing machine Bach" so common in the middle of our own century. Most likely he did not "romanticize." He almost certainly played and conducted in what he considered a musical fashion while, as we shall see, paying unprecedented and, in some ways, surprisingly modern attention to the texts of the works he was performing. To put it another way, he simply "interpreted" and thereby "revealed" older music in the same way that he dealt with recent music.

Be that as it may, it is worthwhile to stop to take a look at Mendelssohn's "historical" programs, for from them one can draw fuller inferences about what was in Mendelssohn's mind than one can by considering only his letters on the subject. The first cycle of historical concerts took place in Leipzig during the 1837/1838 season. The programs:[82]

15 February	Bach:	D-major Suite, BWV 1068
		E-major Violin Sonata, BWV 1006
	Handel:	Groß ist der Herr from *Zadok the Priest*
	Gluck:	*Iphigenia in Aulis* Overture
		Introduction and scene from *Iphigenia in Tauris*
	Viotti:	unspecified violin concerto
22 February	Righini:	*Tigranes* Overture
		Aria from *Armida*
	Cimarosa:	*Il matrimonio segreto* Overture

	Haydn:	C-major Piano Trio (unspecified)
		Introduction, Recitative, and finale of first part of
		The Creation
	Naumann:	Quintet and Chorus from *I Pelligrini*
	Haydn:	"Farewell" Symphony
1 March	Mozart:	*Die Zauberflöte* overture
		Aria—"Non più tutto ascoltai"
		Quartet from *Zaïde*
		C-minor Piano Concerto, K. 491
	Salieri:	Quartet and chorus from *Palmira*
	Andreas Romberg:	unspecified overture
	Méhul:	Ensemble from *Uthal*
		Symphony in G minor
8 March	Vogler:	*Samori* Overture
	Weber:	Gebet vor der Schlacht
		Hunters' Chorus from *Euryanthe*
		Der Freischütz Overture
	Beethoven:	Prisoners' chorus from *Fidelio*
		Violin Concerto
		Elegischer Gesang, Op. 118
		Symphony no. 6

For orchestral purposes, the history of music began about a century before these concerts were given. Mendelssohn's interest in the "old Italians" could not be indulged here.[83] Clearly, the Leipzig concerts—Mendelssohn referred to them as the "so-called historical" concerts[84]—were intended to demonstrate the continuity of the tradition. In the letter just cited, he remarks that the concerts coming after the historical series will have "all possible modernities in order to bring the number up to twenty."[85]

It looks very much as though Italian opera of the past was acceptable at the historical concerts if it was connected somehow to Mozart (or if Mozart was connected to it) or could be viewed as somewhat Germanized. (More recent Italian opera, that is, music by Rossini, Bellini, and Donizetti, was fairly well represented on Gewandhaus programs in Mendelssohn's time, and surely one can hear the Italian influence in some of his music, the Widow Scene from *Elijah*, for instance.) As the presence of the Méhul symphony and the excerpt from *Uthal* show, Mendelssohn knew about, and respected, the French symphonic and operatic traditions.[86] Schumann was also enthusiastic about the symphony, which he thought—somewhat oddly, it seems to me—was stylistically not very far from the German tradition.[87]

Schumann's general reaction to these concerts was most favorable. He was fascinated and pleased by the music he heard, though annoyed by comments that he could not avoid hearing made by audience members around him. "It is fortunate," he wrote, "that our forefathers could not put on historical concerts turned around to run forward. Cross my heart, we would have come out of that one badly."[88]

Much of Mendelssohn's activity on behalf of older music in Leipzig and elsewhere concentrated on Handel's oratorios.[89] I have already given some indication of the sizes of the forces involved.[90] We need now to deal with questions of arrangements and cuts and to look a bit more at some of the means of control of these large forces.

At the beginning of his work with Handel, Mendelssohn followed the traditional practice of eliminating the organ and adding wind parts to fill out the harmony. In addition to accepting the authority of general late-eighteenth-century tradition—after all, Mozart had participated in the business of supplying additional wind parts for this music—he may well have modeled his work on Zelter's practice at the Singakademie.[91]

Extensive cutting was part of this practice. For instance, in a letter to Karl Klingemann from Berlin on 15 August 1832, Mendelssohn discussed both a translation of *Solomon* into German that Klingemann was preparing for him and the extensive cuts (and added wind parts) that he had in mind for a performance—appropriately enough—at the Singakademie.[92]

At the Lower Rhine Festival of 1833 in Düsseldorf, Mendelssohn conducted *Israel in Egypt* without organ and with additional wind parts by Ignaz Franz von Mosel. At the same time, however, he began his journey toward philological accuracy and concern with something approximating appropriate performance practice by making corrections in the Arnold edition on the basis of the autograph in the King's Library.[93] At the 1835 festival in Cologne, he won the point about the use of the organ, along with the corollary elimination of inauthentic wind parts.[94] The organ parts used by Mendelssohn—he wrote them out himself, and several are extant—are in no sense figured bass parts in Baroque style. As everyone who has dealt with the topic, from Chrysander in 1867 to the present, has understood, Mendelssohn's organ parts are sonorous reinforcements of Handel's chorus and orchestra and are written in a free style; moreover, Mendelssohn did not feel obliged to abide by the figures at all times.[95] From our point of view, then, Mendelssohn represents a sort of halfway point on the road to "historical performance."

In its own time, however, this halfway point was often taken for the end of the road. Reviewing Mendelssohn's edition of *Israel in Egypt*, the *Musical Herald* wrote,

Israel in Egypt has always been regarded as one of the greatest of Handel's works; and, of all the musicians now living, Mendelssohn is the most thoroughly conversant with the writings, and the most deeply imbued with the spirit of "the mighty master." Both these requisites were demanded for the production of such an edition as the present, which is not merely an accurate reprint of the author's text, but contains many things which could have been done only by an artist of kindred genius.

In the first place, the Oratorio, in full score, has been carefully reprinted from Handel's original manuscript in the Queen's library; her Majesty having been graciously pleased to grant the [Handel] society access to this and the other manuscripts of Handel. The editor has neither allowed himself to deviate from the composer's authority in describing the times of the movements, nor in marking pianos and fortes, nor in figuring the bass: he has merely corrected a few evident inaccuracies in the manuscript. We have thus Handel's own score in its original entireness and purity.

But every musician knows that this score does not furnish a complete guide in the performance of the work. The organ part is merely a line of bass, inperfectly [*sic*] figured, from which Handel himself played, and from which succeeding organists continue to play, filling up the harmony according to the various degrees of their own skill and judgment. Mendelssohn has added a complete organ part, thus putting an end (as far as this Oratorio is concerned) to the loose and arbitrary kind of organ accompaniment hitherto in use. He himself says in his judicious preface: "As for the organ part, I have written it down in the manner in which I would play it were I called upon to do so at the performance of this Oratorio. These works ought, of course, never to be performed without an organ, as is done in Germany, where additional wind instruments are introduced to make up the defect. In England the organist plays usually *ad libitum* from the score, as it seems to have been the custom in Handel's time, whether he played himself, or merely conducted, and had an organist under his control. Now, as the task of placing the chords in the fittest manner to bring out all the points to the greatest advantage; in fact, of introducing, as it were, a new part to compositions like Handel's, is of extreme difficulty, I have thought it useful to write down an organ part expressly for those who might not prefer to play one of their own." What organist will prefer playing one of his own to that which has been placed before him by Mendelssohn?

Besides this organ part, Mendelssohn has also given a separate accompaniment for the pianoforte, which will be of infinite use when the Oratorio (or pieces from it) is performed in private societies. To this pianoforte arrangement he has added the descriptions of movements, metronome marks, pianos and fortes, &c., which (he says) he would introduce had he to conduct the performance of the Oratorio. We must add, that the additional organ part, pianoforte arrangement, and all the marks of time, &c., are written in small notes, and in such a manner as to be kept quite distinct from the composer's original score. We have examined the volume with minute attention, and have not been able to detect the slightest mistake or misprint; it seems to be absolutely immaculate. This magnificent volume, in short, is a model of the manner in which a great musical classic ought to be edited.[96]

The edition, while as accurate as Mendelssohn could make it, also represents, as he says, his ideas about how the work should be done. It thus brings us as close as we can get to a performance conducted by Mendelssohn.

It is important to understand that for Mendelssohn the ultimate goal of this sort of editorial work was, in any case, not the production of philologically accurate scores. Such scores were not an end but the means by which the music could best be brought to the public, and there is a clear implication that the public was thereby to become more enlightened.[97]

It followed for Mendelssohn—though it does not for his successors in scholarly performance—that concessions in the form of arrangements of works deemed inaccessible in the original were not scorned. The *Allgemeine musikalische Zeitung* for 19 February 1840[98] reported on one of Ferdinand David's "quartet evenings," at which Mendelssohn, as a pianist, was involved in performances of the Bach Chaconne from the D-minor Partita, BWV 1004, and the Prelude from the E-major Partita, BWV 1006:

Herr Dr. Mendelssohn-Bartholdy accompanied both pieces on the piano with a harmonic realization in free contrapuntal form. These Bach solo pieces were originally written for violin alone without bass or figures and were printed, too, in that manner. This is surely adequate for artists who as such are in a position to recognize and to judge the harmonic progress and its artful working out. But the public needs help to do this, a sort of commentary as it were, that makes the whole thing more clear and makes understanding easier. Accordingly, we advise any violinist to take these remarks into consideration in the event of a public performance of such pieces. An accompaniment of this sort is certainly difficult and demands deep artistic understanding [on the part of its writer]. But without it, a considerable part of the effect [of the piece] and perhaps the most interesting part [of that effect] is lost—and certainly so for the public—because the art works of earlier times, and particularly of Bach's time, rest mostly on a harmonic and contrapuntal basis.

MENDELSSOHN THE PIANIST

The discussion of Mendelssohn's accompaniment to the Bach Chaconne leads us to a wider discussion of his pianism. Throughout his career, he appeared publicly not only in his own music but in a fairly limited repertory—fairly limited by today's standards, that is—of solo keyboard music, chamber music, and works with orchestra.[99]

The tone of reactions to his playing was set at the beginning of his career; as time went by, that tone deepened, and the admiration became more profound— indeed often more marveling—but its essence did not change. Here is an early example, the Stettin correspondent of the *Berliner allgemeine musikalische Zeitung* reporting on Mendelssohn's playing in that city in February 1827:

[Mendelssohn displayed] an astonishing dexterity, lightness, and elegance in his playing, so that the public, which from old and praiseworthy tradition up to now has refrained from applauding at these concerts (because they are supported and sustained by the most disinterested and sacrificing love of art on the part of the more highly placed dilettantes of both sexes), broke out into thunderous applause in order to demonstrate its gratitude toward the artist.

In private soirées in our city that were held during his presence here, he revealed almost even greater [talents] than those we have already mentioned. Moreover, since in the course of intellectual conversation he disclosed in a most charming way a most universal cultivation, [it is not surprising that] he also revealed that culture in his conception of the works of all the great masters who have written for the piano, almost all of which he played from memory. Let me mention to you only Beethoven's colossal B♭ Sonata, op. 106, with the nocturnal F#-minor Adagio and the almost unplayable concluding fugue, which he mastered in a mighty way and at a dashing tempo, Hummel's F♯-minor Sonata, Weber's grand sonatas, etc. . . . .

The second part of the concert was taken up by Beethoven's very recent great D-minor Symphony, in which Mr. Mendelssohn participated as a combatant in the first violin section and compelled his neighbors' admiration.[100]

The attributes of his playing suggested in this excerpt are repeated over and over in review after review, recollection after recollection: enormous dexterity, great accuracy, a feeling of fire, and passionate involvement.

More important than all this is the sense Mendelssohn's listeners got that the music they were hearing was being revealed in the spirit—indeed, almost by the spirit—of the composer, sometimes in cooperation, as it were, with Mendelssohn's own spirit. For instance: "In order to assess the great effectiveness [of his playing], one must see and hear him one's self, the way he sits at the instrument, makes the spirit of the composition live, gives it new pinions and wings through his own genius."[101]

Putting it more generally, the impression was essentially one of music taking precedence over piano playing. Here, for example, is a discussion of an occasion on which Mendelssohn played his G-minor Piano Concerto and several Songs without Words, and then improvised.

The greatest—indeed a truly inspiring—effect was achieved through his piano playing by Mendelssohn, who was enthusiastically greeted upon his appearance. No one plays like him, with such accomplishment and mastery in every respect. None of the most famous virtuosos can follow him with comparable effect. It is not the most outstanding virtuosity alone that compels applause and often urges admiration; rather, the artistic spirit that animates everything Mendelssohn does sweeps every listener involuntarily along, embeds itself deeply and lastingly in heart and spirit, while other brilliant and one-sided virtuoso performances celebrate noisy and fleeting triumphs on empty ground. After *Mendelssohn* had played several of his beautiful Songs without Words and the applause would not end, he reseated himself at the instrument and improvised on one of his Songs and the main theme from the *Euryanthe* overture that had just been played, as well as on the aria from *Oberon*. We well know that to improvise as he does is certainly no less the doing of Heaven than of the artist. Only a few at any time have been so richly endowed as he, and he to whom much is given must himself give much. Yet when we on the one hand admire the brilliant conception, and highly praise its working out, so we must on the other hand be astounded at the technical dexterity that with the most unfailing sureness and mastery overcomes difficulties that have just been created and themselves grow during the performance and often seem designed as if to be the objects of long and difficult study for the most important virtuosos. *Mendelssohn* tosses out all of that as if it must and could only be like that. No effort or strain is visible or audible; the whole great artistic offering flows naturally, freshly, and ceaselessly, without any anxious grasping at effect, confident of its victory, a victory that never fails to materialize whenever nature and art go hand in hand. We have never seen our circumspect Gewandhaus audience in such a state of enthusiasm as after this gleaming Mendelssohn improvisation. Just as this lively participation honors the spirit and cultivation of our audience, so may it at the same time be a sign to Mendelssohn that his artistic effectiveness has fallen on fertile soil and borne rich fruit here.[102]

The last sentence and perhaps other parts of this tribute, too, are barbed. Mendelssohn was appearing as a guest soloist; Hiller had taken over as music director and was having a most difficult time as Mendelssohn's successor. As who would not.

Improvisation in the context of Mendelssohn's time and place included two different sorts of activities. The first, creating a composition from preexisting theme(s) or an original theme of the moment, is largely covered by the preceding review. Only one aspect of Mendelssohn's improvisation of that sort is not directly mentioned there: his contrapuntal dexterity, whether in free counterpoint or fugue. But there is ample testimony to it. For instance:

He took the subjects of her melodies [pieces sung earlier at the private gathering in question by Maria Malibran] one after the other, and as his thoughts thickened, and the capabilities of each developed in the working of them, he contrived, before he finished, to bring three of the subjects together. It was like a tornado. He appeared to require four pair of hands to answer the throng of ideas that were struggling for development. The countenances of his audience were a curiosity during this exhibition.[103]

Or in much fancier terms and with the ever so slightly hidden intention of assuring us that counterpoint need not be obscure or daunting:

His last performance, on a subject given him at the moment, was the most extraordinary of his efforts. The theme was followed with an intenseness and ardour surpassing belief, but in the eagerness of pursuit was never deprived of its dignity or importance. There were no wild eccentricities, no excursive digressions, no ineffective displays of erudition: it was as if whilst anxiously untwisting the subtleties of counterpoint,—
    Something within would still be shadowing out
    All possibilities: with thoughts unsought
    His mind held dalliance, to which his hand
    Gave substance and reality.
    The enthusiasm, the fire and energy, with which the whole was carried on, was perfectly marvellous; he sat at the keys as one inspired, casting forth one gorgeous jewel after the other, sparking in all the radiance of light—throwing out a succession of bright passages, any one of which would have made the reputation of an ordinary performer. His invention never failed him for a moment; there was no return to any phrases or expressions used at an earlier part of his performance, and his genius appeared less unwearied and more boundless than during the first half hour.[104]

The other activity was the improvisation of cadenzas during performances of concertos. Mendelssohn's extraordinary abilities in this line were universally acknowledged. Two testimonies among many:

The two improvised cadenzas at the close of the first and last movements [of the Beethoven G-major Concerto] were true masterpieces. The main motives of the composition developed as if out of a seed, and inspired by the Beethoven spirit, they steadily broadened themselves out, and thundered and billowed together in the most ingenious combinations and the most varied contrapuntal intertwinings. It was the most intimate and at the same time, the most interesting amalgamation of Beethovenian and Mendelssohnian ideas.[105]

An article in *The Musical Times* written in commemoration of the fiftieth anniversary of Mendelssohn's death recalled a performance of the same concerto in 1844:

He played the Pianoforte Concerto in G—"my old *cheval de bataille*" as he called it—at the Philharmonic in 1844 and 1847. On the first occasion he had not seen the music for two or three years and failed to obtain a copy to look it over in time for the Saturday rehearsal; but he played it from memory. At the rehearsal he introduced *three* different cadenzas in the first movement, each time extempore, to the astonishment of the many musicians who were present. But still more wonderful, he played an entirely different one—a fourth—at the concert on the following Monday night.[106]

A number of discussions of Mendelssohn's cadenzas emphasize that he worked with the themes of the movement in question. From the tone of them, one gathers that virtuoso display without much reference to the thematic material of the movements in which they were inserted was not uncommon in the cadenzas of the 1830s and 1840s.[107]

As noted earlier, Mendelssohn's public repertory was limited by our standards. He played a number of Mozart concertos, the Beethoven fourth and fifth concertos, some Bach, and, of course, his own music. As a chamber music player and occasional soloist without orchestra, he specialized in Bach and Beethoven, occasionally playing even a late Beethoven sonata in public. Franz Brendel, writing in the *Neue Zeitschrift für Musik*, was not entirely happy with a performance of Op. 111, finding that in the first movement "the touch [was] too light and fleeting" and complaining that "the monumental character, the painful inner strife of the work" had not been adequately set forth and that "a milder, lighter character" had been forced on it.[108]

In private, however, Mendelssohn ranged much more widely. Sir George Grove reported that Hiller offered the following (among other material) when asked for his recollections of Mendelssohn: "The music of other composers [than Bach, Mozart, Beethoven, himself] he knew, but could not produce as he did theirs. I do not think, for instance, that his execution of Chopin was at all to be compared to his execution of the masters just mentioned; he did not care particularly for it, though when alone he played everything good with interest."[109] I conclude from this remark that Mendelssohn's technique must have been more advanced (speaking chronologically, of course) than one might assume solely on the basis of his music. There is, however, no evidence that he dealt as a pianist with music like Liszt's.

The most detailed descriptions of Mendelssohn's piano playing tend to come from recollections long after the fact—caution is always advised in such cases—and the most comprehensive collection of these memories was assembled by Grove for the article cited in note 109. Much of what is described in this easily accessible source has already been touched on through more contemporaneous material and may thus be considered as at least partly verified. Grove quotes Otto Goldschmidt as saying that Mendelssohn's "mechanism was extremely subtle, and developed with the lightest of wrists (never from the arm); he therefore never strained the instrument or hammered."[110] Clara Schumann mentioned Mendelssohn's quick tempos but said that these were "never to the prejudice of the music. It never occurred to me to compare him with virtuosi," she continued, "Of mere effects of performance he knew nothing—he was always the great musician, and in hearing him one forgot the player, and only revelled in the full enjoyment of the music."[111]

Joseph Joachim said that "his staccato was the most extraordinary thing possible for life and crispness."[112]

Grove also assembled a number of testimonies (from Sir George Macfarren, Konrad Schleinitz, and Hector Berlioz) to Mendelssohn's ability to turn the piano into a representative of the orchestra when playing orchestral music on it.[113]

Let us also turn to the effusive Henry Fothergill Chorley for a comparison of Mendelssohn and other leading pianists. Here he describes—again after the fact, though he may well have had old notes—Mendelssohn's playing at the Brunswick Festival of 1839:

The piano-forte playing, then, was the chief treat. It is rarely that I have been so delighted without novelty or surprise having some share in the delight. The exact fulfilment of any anticipation is generally more or less blanking, though vanity and self-deceit refuse to allow it. It would have been absurd to expect much *pianism*, as distinct from music, in the performance of one writing so straightforwardly, and without the coquetries of embroidery, as Mendelssohn. Accordingly, his performance has none of the exquisite *finesses* of Moscheles, on the score of which it has been elsewhere said that "there is wit in his playing;"—none of the delicate and plaintive and spiritual seductions of Chopin, who sweeps the keys with so insinuating and gossamer a touch, that the crudest and most chromatic harmonies of his music float away under his hand, indistinct yet not unpleasing, like the wild and softened discords of the Æolian harp;—none of the brilliant extravagancies of Liszt, by which he illuminates every composition he undertakes, with a living but lightening fire; and imparts to it a soul of passion, or a dazzling vivacity, the interpretation never contradicting the author's intention, but more poignant, more intense, more glowing than ever the author dreamed of. And yet, no one that has heard Mendelssohn's piano-forte playing can find it dry—can fail to be excited and fascinated by it, despite of its want of all the caprices and colourings of his contemporaries. Solidity in which the organ touch is given to the piano without the organ ponderosity—spirit (witness his execution to the *finale* of the D minor concerto) animating, but never intoxicating the ear—expression which, making every tone sink deep, requires not the garnishing of trills and *appoggiaturii*, or the aid of changes of time,—are among its outward and salient characteristics; but, within and beyond all these, though hard to be conveyed in words, there is felt to be a mind clear and deep, an appreciation of character and form which refers to the inner spirit rather than the outward details: the same which gives so exquisitely southern a character to the barcarole and the gondola tune in Mendelssohn's "Lieder ohne Worte," and its fresh, Ossianic, sea-wildness to his overture to the "Hebriden" ("Isles of Fingal");—the same which enabled him, when little more than a boy, in the happiest piece of descriptive music of our time, to illustrate Shakespeare's exquisite faëry scenes neither feebly nor unworthily. Execution without grimace—fancy cheerful and excursive but never morbid—and feeling under the control of a serene, not sluggish spirit;—I can come no nearer pleasing myself in a character, than by these words, which are still far from doing justice to their subject. One word more, which is perhaps a half-definition.—Mendelssohn's is eminently manly music; and loses effect, beyond that of almost any other of his contemporaries, when attempted by female hands.[114]

Hans von Bülow's *Ausgewählte Schriften* reprints the introductions to his editions of a number of Mendelssohn's piano works. Bülow says, for instance, that the "recurring melismas" in the *Capriccio brilliant* —presumably the introductory

Andante is meant—should be played smoothly and in tempo. Played in this way, he says, they will sound "far nobler and more pleasant" than if played with

passionately aroused rubato. The master believed in strict observance of the meter above all. He categorically forbade any ritardando not prescribed by the score and wanted those delays that were prescribed to be held to the minimum. Moreover, he hated all arbitrary arpeggiation—he never wrote chords *à la* Schumann that could not be taken in the hand's span and thus must be arpeggiated except when he wanted successive attack.

Bülow goes on to say that Mendelssohn viewed the use of the damper pedal as a special effect. In his own music, it follows, the pedal is to be used only when called for.[115]   Of course, modern players must make allowance for the considerable difference between their instrument and Mendelssohn's.

In his later years, the Érard was Mendelssohn's piano of choice.[116] Apparently, he preferred to match his delicate touch to a fuller-toned instrument than the Graf or Pleyel pianos one might have associated with him.   Parkins's description of the Metropolitan Museum Érard explains this:

The sustaining power [of this piano], especially of the strong but clear bass notes, is surprising in contrast to earlier pianos but does not match that of, say, a modern Steinway grand. The treble still retains some of that articulate, almost percussive, clarity of earlier pianos.   The repetition action is quite rapid, and the touch seems relatively light (in comparison to that of most modern grands), although perhaps not as light as a good contemporary Viennese piano with its shallow keyfall. The key action itself is very much like the mechanism of about 1832 described and illustrated by Pierre Érard.[117] . . . By the late 1830s the refined double-escapement action had opened the door for new musical and technical possibilities.[118]

MENDELSSOHN THE ORGANIST

Mendelssohn's activity as organist was in no sense secondary (or tertiary) to his conducting and piano playing. As Susanna Großmann-Vendrey has pointed out, he was concerned with the organ all his life and was indeed one of "the first great organ virtuosos of the nineteenth century."[119]

According to Mathias Pape, organ concerts (as events independent of church services) had been given in Leipzig since the 1830s, and Bach's music had appeared on them. But Mendelssohn was apparently the first to give an all-Bach program[120]—all-Bach in a manner of speaking, that is, since Mendelssohn also improvised. The program of this concert, designed to raise money for a memorial to Bach, is worth examining.[121] Mendelssohn began not with a piece by Bach but with an improvisation that served as a prelude to the great fugue BWV 552 ("St. Anne"). There followed the "fantasy" on "Schmücke dich" BWV 759 and the A-minor Prelude and Fugue BWV 543. After an intermission, Mendelssohn played the C-minor Passacaglia and Fugue BWV 582, the F-major Pastorale BWV 590, and the D-minor Toccata (and Fugue?) BWV 565.[122] He closed with another improvisation "in which," says Schumann, "he showed himself in his full artist's glory. [The improvisation] was based on a chorale, if I am not mistaken, on the text 'O Haupt voll Blut und Wunden,' into which he later wove the name B-A-C-H as a fugal movement and rounded it to so clear and masterful a whole that if printed, it would be a finished work of art."[123]

In 1837 the *Musical World* ran a long article about Mendelssohn's organ playing (and about a "ridiculous accident"):

As a pianist, M. Mendelssohn has been listened to with mingled emotions of delight and astonishment; as a composer he occupies a position of such acknowledged excellence as challenges and almost defies competition; the pupil of Zelter, the worshipper of Sebastian Bach, as an organist, becomes therefore an object of great and absorbing interest. During the present week he has twice touched the organ; on Sunday afternoon at St. Paul's Cathedral, and on Tuesday morning at Christchurch, Newgate Street. On both occasions the large auditories who assembled to listen to his efforts, testified how high they held in estimation the composer of the oratorio of "St. Paul." . . . Genius, however mighty, is ever modest, and even the mind of a Mendelssohn does not instantaneously escape from the scene: hence his opening movements are distinguished for seriousness and solemnity: The perfect purity of his harmonies, the natural manner in which they follow each other, the rigid exclusion of every note not exclusively belonging to them, and their perfect unity one with the other, however, proclaim the refined and accomplished scholar, with whom art has become second nature; and as his thoughts thicken and the spirit retires to commune within itself, the themes break forth one by one, and a warmth and energy, a freedom and fluency, diffuse a life, and spread a charm over his performance, that at once rivet the undivided attention of his auditors.[124] Such was his first voluntary at St. Paul's; but his performance was interrupted ere he could give those memorable instances of his extraordinary abilities by a ridiculous accident. He had played extemporaneously for some time, and had commenced the noble fugue in A minor,[125] the first of the six grand pedal fugues of Sebastian Bach, when the gentlemen who walk about in bombazeen gowns and plated sticks, became annoyed at the want of respect displayed by the audience to their energetic injunctions. "Service is over," had been universally announced, followed by the command "you must go out, Sir."

This attempt to force evacuation of the premises was not successful, so the vergers got the bellows blower to stop work, "and just as Mendelssohn had executed a storm of pedal passages with transcendant skill and energy, the blower was seduced from his post and a further supply of wind forbidden, and the composer was left to exhibit the glorious ideas of Bach in all the dignity of dumb action." Because of this fiasco, arrangements were made for Mendelssohn to play again, this time at Christchurch, Newgate Street. The writer continued:

M. Mendelssohn performed six extempore fantasias, and the pedal fugue he was not allowed to go through with at St. Paul's. Those who know the wide range of passages for the pedals with which this fugue abounds, may conceive how perfectly cool and collected must have been the organist who could on a sudden emergency transpose them to suit the scale of an ordinary English pedal board. His mind has become so assimilated to Bach's compositions, that at one point in the prelude, either by accident or design, he amplified and extended the idea of the author, in a manner so in keeping and natural, that those unacquainted with its details could not by any possibility have discovered the departure from the text. His execution of Bach's music is transcendently great, and so easy, that we presume he has every feature of this author engraven in his memory. His touch is so even and firm, so delicate and volant, that no difficulties, however appalling, either impede or disturb his equanimity.[126]

The reference to the "English pedal board" and its unsuitability to the music of Bach raises the entire question of English organ design and Mendelssohn's influence on it. The complexities of the history of that design have been thoroughly studied by Nicholas Thistlethwaite, and as the quotation from the *Musical World* makes clear, the absence of a proper pedal board in the German sense was one of the impediments to an adequate account of Bach on the English organs of the first part of the nineteenth century.[127] It would take us too far afield to attempt to summarize Thistlethwaite's elaborate discussion of the characteristics of the English organ of Mendelssohn's time and the almost equally elaborate contemporaneous debates about it. With regard to Mendelssohn's influence, Thistlethwaite says,

One contemporary remarked on Mendelssohn's "wiry, crisp, energetic character of delivery" and contrasted this with the technique of one of the leading English players of the previous generation, Benjamin Jacob (1778-1827), who "played in the *legato* manner, and therefore never satisfied us in Bach's organ music." The writer concluded with the reflection that "freedom of touch is an essential requisite to a tale-telling enunciation of Bach's outline, counterpoints, episodes, and countless modes of diversifying his *motifs*."[128]

Comments suggest Mendelssohn's relative infrequency of register changes within the sections of a piece. He seems to have been more conservative in this regard in Bach's music than in his own. Only a very few details are recorded.

The *Musical World* also had this to say:

Mendelssohn introduced Bach to the English, as an organ composer. Our native artists had known and appreciated him, as a writer for the clavichord, the forty-eight *studios* [*sic*] had developed his genius, as a profound adept in the strict school of composition; but we had yet to venerate him as the inventor of a set of totally new effects upon the organ. It was not that [Samuel] Wesley was unacquainted with his Fantasias, Passacaglias, Preludes, and *Codas* [*sic*], that he did not introduce them to the English: but never having heard a German organ, with its ponderous pedale, he could not realise the inventions of the author; and he was too cautious, and too prudent, to risk the reputation of his favourite, by the performance of passages which on the squalling organ (which in his day prevailed in our churches) must have sounded absurd and ridiculous.[129]

As an organist, Mendelssohn easily paralleled his English successes as composer, conductor, and pianist, both in London and at the Birmingham Festivals. Not uncharacteristically, he wrote about one of these occasions in a context of physical and emotional discomfort: "a few days later [i.e., after another Christchurch, Newgate, appearance], when I had to play for 3,000 people in Exeter Hall who shouted Hurrah at me and waved their handkerchiefs and stamped their feet until the hall roared, I didn't immediately notice any ill effects, but the next morning I felt confused and worn out in my head."[130]

"Confused and worn out" on this occasion or not, there can be no doubt that Mendelssohn's organ playing, like his piano playing, was remarkable for its clarity and accuracy as well as for its force. In a long passage in *Music and Manners in France and Germany*, Chorley attributed these traits in his pianism to his also being an organist.[131] Bülow, on the other hand, said that these qualities in his organ playing were attributable to his being a pianist.[132]

Clearly, so far as England is concerned, Mendelssohn's influence on taste and repertory, on the one hand, and on organ construction and playing technique, on the other, necessarily went hand in hand. I turn finally to Thistlethwaite's summary:

By the late-1830s, . . . a few English organists, stimulated by the discovery of Bach's organ music and inspired by Mendelssohn, had acquired a more thoroughgoing appreciation of the continental organs, and it was their influence which led to the rapid emergence during the 1840s of the C-compass organ, with its Pedal division, fully-developed choruses and tonal novelties, and the consequent disappearance . . . of the English long-compass organ.[133]

MENDELSSOHN THE STRING PLAYER

During 1838 Schumann put on a number of "quartet mornings" in his house. The number of listeners was naturally very limited, and I infer from the undertone of a passing remark he makes about his "editorial cockiness" [*Redakteurübermut*] that Schumann justified this aristocratic (or high bourgeois) behavior to himself by his position as editor of the *Neue Zeitschrift für Musik*. In the course of his discussion of the second of these "mornings," that "editorial cockiness" brought him to remark about what seemed to him the ideal group of quartet players (presumably as opposed to the unnamed players he actually had): "[Pierre] Baillot . . . as first, and [Karl] Lipinsky as second violin, Mendelssohn on viola (his main instrument, organ and piano excepted), and Max Bohrer or Fritz Kummer on cello."[134] To place Mendelssohn in this group is simply astounding—unless there is somehow an odd joke buried under the obvious one—and it gives us the idea that Mendelssohn was a very good violist indeed. There seems to be no evidence that he practiced viola (or anything else) to any great extent; such evidence as there is about the matter suggests rather the opposite: that he behaved in this regard like a modern studio musician who, having once acquired a technique, keeps in shape by playing rather than by practicing.[135]

Mendelssohn's public string playing was of two sorts. First, he occasionally sat in with the orchestra when someone else was conducting. For instance, Erdmann and Rentzow report about Mendelssohn's "modestly playing in the viola section" at the Schwerin Festival of 1840,[136] and I have already cited a report of his playing violin in the orchestra at the beginning of his career.[137] Wasielewski remarks that Mendelssohn played viola in the Gewandhaus Orchestra during an appearance by Jenny Lind, Gade conducting, in 1845.[138] The Schwerin orchestra was partly amateur, but the Gewandhaus Orchestra was, of course, one of the Europe's leading ensembles.

Second, he occasionally appeared publicly as a viola player in chamber music. The *Allgemeine musikalische Zeitung* tells us about a concert at which Mendelssohn appeared as both pianist and violist. On 7 March 1840 he played viola in a performance of the Octet—Johann Wenzel Kalliwoda was the other violist—and he joined Ferdinand Hiller in several piano four-hand pieces by Mozart.[139] The *Musical Times* obituary has stories about Mendelssohn's playing bass drum at a concert conducted by Moscheles and singing tenor in choruses on various occasions![140]

A remarkable memory—indeed what seems to have been total recall or something quite close to it—aided all these activities, the more so since playing and conducting without score or music was relatively uncommon in Mendelssohn's time. The following quotation from the *Musical World* implicitly makes this clear:

He has so cultivated his memory, as to have given it a strength and power scarcely to be imagined. He not only played publicly from memory the most difficult compositions by Bach, Beethoven, Hummel, &c., but recollects so perfectly all the great masterpieces of his art, such as the operas of Gluck, Mozart, Beethoven, and Weber, as to be enabled to accompany them with the piano-forte entirely from memory, and indeed has not hesitated to do so publicly upon occasions when the slightest error would certainly not have escaped detection. At one time he knew, literally the *whole score* of Beethoven's "Fidelio" by heart; and we shall never forget hearing him play (from memory) the whole of the first scene to the 2nd act; indicating as he went on, the prominent effects of the different instruments.[141]

A *Musical Times* commemorative article already cited contains a similar story about Mendelssohn's memory,[142] and Dörffel reports that in public he generally played the piano without music.[143]

We may give Wasielewski the last word about Mendelssohn as a performer, his words about Mendelssohn as a conductor having general validity beyond the specifically conductorial:

Mendelssohn raised the Gewandhaus concerts to a point where they were normative for the musical world not only because the orchestral performance he secured attained the importance of a model, but also because creative and performing musicians found occasion there to appear before the public under highly favorable conditions that were not so easy to find elsewhere. Mendelssohn's effectiveness was distinguished not only by his preeminent talent as a conductor but by the great spiritual weight of his winning personality. All participants felt this man's dedicated seriousness and devotion to duty; moreover, everyone willingly and gladly subordinated himself to Mendelssohn so that exemplary discipline reigned in the Gewandhaus orchestra. Everyone made it a point of honor to work on behalf of the good of the whole. Each individual not only did his duty but did it with love and with pleasure in the undertaking.[144]

MENDELSSOHN THE TEACHER

Mendelssohn's activity as teacher has several aspects. First, there is what one might call his theoretical view of musical education: what it should be, how it should be organized, and so on. There is no doubt that he held his views strongly;

he put considerable time and effort into seeing that an institution was established along lines he considered proper. Second, there is his actual practical activity as a teacher. This, in turn, subdivides into two distinct areas, one having to do with formal instruction and the other with informal guidance of the student and would-be musician.

Mendelssohn's theoretical approach had two main thrusts (aside, of course, from insistence on technical competence). The first was toward restricting higher musical education to those who had already acquired a degree of musical and intellectual sophistication in addition to digital dexterity. Not for him the sort of institution that accepts children and carries them through the entire course of a musical education or that teaches music solely as a craft. "The complete course," says his *Pro memoria* for Berlin, "should last three years." The document also says that "a teacher of aesthetics and the history of music, etc., is necessary beyond doubt."[145]

Nothing came of the Berlin proposal. Mendelssohn's ideas about what a conservatory should be were realized in Leipzig, where the conservatory, with Mendelssohn as de facto though not de jure director—that is as leading spirit—was officially opened on 2 April 1843.[146] A few months after its opening, the Conservatory ran an advertisement in the *Allgemeine musikalische Zeitung* seeking students for the "zweites Halbjahr 1843-44" beginning on 1 November 1843, with auditions being held between 22 and 28 October. The advertisement said,

The Conservatory's main goal is *higher education in music*; instruction extends theoretically and practically over all branches of music, viewed as an art and as a scholarly discipline, and comprises harmony and composition, instruments (piano, violin, organ in solo playing, score reading, and quartet and orchestral playing, etc.) and singing (solo and choral). In order to assure comprehensive education of the pupils, there will be lectures about music literature, aesthetics, and other aspects of musical scholarship, as well as instruction in the Italian language where appropriate.[147]

The prospectus issued by the Conservatory in September 1843 gives an uncommonly interesting view of its goals and procedures and also casts sidelights on the social organization and attitudes of its time. Here is a point-by-point summary (for a full translation see the Historical Views and Documents section following this chapter):

§1. "The Conservatory established in Leipzig with royal permission is dedicated to higher education in music; the instruction it will give comprises all practical and theoretical branches of music viewed both as an art and as a scholarly discipline."

§2. Outlines the division of the three-year course of instruction into a number of "disciplines" and "classes"[148] and points out that the academic year begins at Easter, at which time a new cycle of courses begins. These are:

"a. Harmony divided into three classes: Class III in the first year—harmony and voice leading; Class II in the second year—continuation of harmony, counterpoint; Class I in the third year—continuation of harmony, double counterpoint, fugue.

"b. Instruction in form and composition—given in lectures treating of the following: the various forms of vocal and instrumental works and how to handle them; analysis of classical musical works; knowledge of instruments and orchestration.

"c. Playing from score, knowledge of conducting.

"d. Italian language for those dedicated to the higher forms of singing.

"In addition, lectures about musical subjects, changing annually, are part of theoretical instruction. Examples of these lectures: the history of music in ancient and modern times, esthetics of music, acoustics (including experiments), etc.

"A special class in harmony has been established to meet the needs of female pupils who will complete their course in two years."

§3. Explains that practical instruction is organized into singing (two classes), piano (three classes), organ (two classes), violin (three classes). Instruction in the other instruments (cello, bass, wind instruments) will be offered for a modest additional fee.[149]

§4. Tells about the musical events of the city that are available to the pupils (e.g., Gewandhaus Orchestra rehearsals) and says that pupils may also take courses at the University.

§5. Says that pupils interested in orchestral playing will be given opportunities to perform and that opportunities for solo appearances will be available to singers. Advanced pupils will be allowed to sit in with the Gewandhaus Orchestra. [But see "A Postscript about the Statues of the Leipzig Conservatory" in the "Historical Views and Documents" section following this chapter, p. 135.]

§6. Says that the institute is run by a board of directors serving without pay and that the names of those authorized to give instruction appear at the end of the pamphlet. The Inspector's position is defined as essentially disciplinary. (He is a sort of dean of students.)

§7. "The instruction of female pupils is entirely separate from the instruction of male pupils."

§8. Points out that the theory course lasts three years and can be shortened only under special circumstances. The length of the practical instruction can be determined only for each individual and depends on the talent and diligence of the student. No one will be accepted for less than one year, and refunds for those attending less than a year will be made only in case of illness.

§9. Explains that new pupils are taken in only at Easter of each year. Pupils from a great distance may also be accepted at Michaelmas term,[150] provided their theoretical knowledge is sufficient to enable them to enter at a level above the beginning one.

§10. Deals with admission requirements. Pupils must be sufficiently well educated to be able to follow a "systematically organized lecture." Foreign pupils must have enough German to follow lectures and where necessary must arrange for private instruction in the language. Prospective pupils must also have real talent and knowledge of the techniques of music extending to "knowledge of notes and time signatures, adequate preparation on the piano, or the violin, or in singing." Foreign pupils are to bring references from their teachers. Pupils who are still minors must submit their parents' or guardians' permission form found at the end of the pamphlet (on p. 9). Point f. reads: "Every pupil must be able to present a credible document from his parents or an earlier teacher testifying to his good moral behavior. Foreign pupils must have a passport or similar papers. Pupils wishing to leave must notify the Directorate a quarter-year in advance."

§11. Says that each prospective pupil must appear before an entrance committee, which will decide whether he has sufficient talent and prior knowledge of music to be admitted. Pieces must be prepared for performance before this committee. Pupils in composition must send a portfolio in advance or produce it before the committee.

§12. Says that each pupil must submit to the disciplinary regulations of the institution: (1) No pupil may miss a lesson or a class without adequate reason. (2) Each pupil must absolutely obey orders of the Directorate and his teacher. (3) Every pupil regardless of instrument must have regular instruction in figured bass, piano, and voice unless specially excused. (4) Instruction in solo song is given only to those who wish to be solo singers and who are qualified in the view of the instructors. (5) Students may not appear in public performance without special permission (this prohibition appears to apply beyond the boundaries of Leipzig as well as within them). (6) Pupils will behave with due regard for the institution's reputation. (7) "Improper behavior and other violations of the above rules will be taken seriously by the Directors; a ruling that offences have been repeated will result in a punishment of dismissal from the institution."

§13. Lays out the academic calendar. Instruction is given the entire year, with the following vacation periods: at Easter, eight days from Maundy Thursday to the Wednesday after Easter; at Pentecost all of the week; four weeks in July and August, the precise dates to be determined each year; eight days at Michaelmas from 1 to 7 October; eight days at Christmas from 25 December to 1 January. Pupils who do not use these periods for travel will be given special assignments by their teachers for these periods.

§14. Sets half-yearly juries around Easter and Michaelmas. Friends of the institution will be invited to these juries, and student compositions will be performed at all of them. [But see "A Postscript about the Statues of the Leipzig Conservatory" in the "Historical Views and Documents" section following this chapter, p. 135.]

§15. Says that appropriate certificates will be given to students completing the course or honorably discharged prior to completion. "No one lacking such certificate will be legally recognized as an alumnus of the institution."

§16. Sets the tuition charges.

§17. Calls attention to scholarships available to citizens of Saxony.

§18. Requires each pupil to provide his own instrument and to buy his own music and says that pianos are available for rental.

An appended paragraph of special remarks discusses the cost of living in Leipzig and living arrangements for pupils.[151]

Of course, Mendelssohn probably did not write these statutes, but they reflect his influence, particularly with regard to the view of music as an aspect of intellectual life.[152]

Throughout these early years, there was little or no instruction in wind instruments, and as a result orchestral performances at the juries were done with the missing parts played on the piano. For instance, the *Allgemeine Wiener Musik-Zeitung* reports about such a performance, saying that this arrangement makes it possible to hear the "violins"—meaning the strings except for the double basses—more clearly! *Fingal's Cave* was among the pieces performed this way.[153] According to Forner, wind classes were not established until 1882.[154] The reasons for this are not stated in any published Conservatory document I know about, though there must have been some discussion and perhaps some written communication about the matter. They appear to lie in the simple, but remarkable, fact that until the next to the last decade of the nineteenth century, Leipzig produced wind players through traditional apprenticeships to members of the Stadtpfeifferei. It looks very much as though the Conservatory did not want or was unable to invade that territory.[155]

Mendelssohn's own view of himself as a teacher in a formal sense is succinctly conveyed in a letter of 19 September 1839 to Professor Naumann, in which he apparently refused to undertake the musical education of a gifted youngster:

I would ill serve your confidence in me if I did not communicate honestly to you the many and important considerations which prevent me from *directly* taking it on. First, I have convinced myself through repeated experience that, whether from taking too little pleasure in the matter or from too little patience, I completely lack the talent to be a proper formal teacher who gives regular and progressive instruction. In short, I don't succeed at it. Young people have sometimes stayed with me, but whenever this was useful to them, that usefulness arose from joint music making, free intercourse, occasional exchanges of opposing opinions—even arguments. But all this does not comport well with regular instruction. And for so tender a youth is not continual, unceasing, and strict regular instruction better than anything else?[156]

We need to be cautious. Clearly, Mendelssohn is here protecting himself against having someone else's child in the house—surely the "directly" is politesse and not a suggestion that he may change his mind—and under the circumstances he is likely to display his own deficiencies in the harshest possible light. Nevertheless, there may well be something to this self-judgment, despite all the pious statements to the contrary to be found in the sometimes hagiographic memoirs that appeared after Mendelssohn's death. The fact is that it accords well with his often moody (and sometimes tormented) and impatient character, whereas the hagiography often seeks to manufacture a perfect Victorian gentleman.

"My godmother had left Ireland," writes Sir Charles Villiers Stanford, "and my next teacher was a curious, clever and somewhat eccentrically clothed lady, Miss Flynn by name. She also had been a pupil of Moscheles at Leipzig, and had studied, but with many tears, under Mendelssohn, who was a most impatient teacher."[157]

Mendelssohn also seems to have been able to act as a general mentor rather than as a systematic teacher to William Horsley's son Charles:

According to the advice in your letter I try to direct his attention more to execution than to composition, and find it the more necessary as it is evident that his own inclination induces him already not to neglect his talent for composition and will never allow him to become careless as to his progress in that department of his art. I am sure you will be happy to see how perfectly he has developed his talent for composition in Mr. Hauptmann's school, how completely he has fulfilled the object you had in view when you sent him to this master. . . . I think it the more indispensable to induce him to cultivate also those other branches of art to which he seems not driven by his natural inclination, I mean execution, and particularly his playing the Pianoforte. It is indeed very important to his future career, and he plays too well not to play better than he does. It was therefore to this that I particularly directed his attention; I found his fingers a little stiff, and not independent enough; he used to go over difficult passages in great haste in order to arrive sooner in smooth water, in short it was the playing of a young composer who had hardly any thought of anything but counterpoint, harmony, and fugues in the last year. This is not to be changed in the course of a few months, there is hardly anything to be done in the limited time of his residence but a beginning; but yet I think some progress may already be remarked in his touch, which was rather hard, as well as in the independence of his fingers. On the organ he has not been able to practise; our churches are so very cold that a very plain chorale is all that our best organists can perform during service, and ornaments are out of the question.[158]

On the other hand, the view of Mendelssohn as a perfect teacher also has currency—and here we have moved from advice and assistance to formal instruction. Perhaps the best known is contained in William S. Rockstro's *Mendelssohn.*[159] On 3 January 1846, according to Rockstro, Mendelssohn took "sole command" of two piano classes[160] and one composition class. Rockstro particularly remembered Mendelssohn's insistence on full sonority of full chords, the example being the beginning of the Hummel D-minor Septet. As one might expect, Mendelssohn insisted on fidelity to the printed score and insisted, too, on precision of playing and thinking.

"Upon questions of simple technique he rarely touched," wrote Rockstro, "except—as in the case of our first precious lesson upon the chord of D minor—with regard to the rendering of certain passages." These more mundane matters were dealt with by other members of the faculty. In short, Mendelssohn was coaching or giving master classes; he was not giving piano lessons in the narrow sense of the phrase. The Conservatory roster lists him as teaching singing; obviously here, too, what he was doing was coaching. Rockstro also discussed Mendelssohn's method of teaching counterpoint on a cantus firmus; it seems quite traditional. The observations about the way in which Mendelssohn coached improvisation are perhaps more interesting.[161]

Lampadius was no less enthusiastic than Rockstro. Mendelssohn, he wrote, had

an enormous talent for musical pedagogy. His students [*Schüler und Schülerinen*] cannot praise too highly or with more gratitude the instructiveness of his suggestions as he looked through compositions, [and] how stimulating his lessons in piano and voice were. Whenever he was in Leipzig, he undertook the private jurying of the individual classes as well as the semiannual main [i.e., public] juries [*Hauptprüfungen*] with the greatest diligence.[162]

Lampadius also reported that on at least one occasion Mendelssohn sat up "half the night" in order to contrive fully adequate descriptions of the progress and state of knowledge of the several students.[163]

On consideration, the contradictions seem to lessen; indeed, they may disappear. It is clear that Mendelssohn was more accustomed to informal guidance than to formal teaching. It is likewise clear that he was a man of highly uneven temperament, though also of enormous, though not quite perfect, self-control. Moreover, the hidden (or not so hidden) assumption that reducing an occasional student to tears (or reducing all students to occasional tears) is incompatible with good teaching is surely more a modern (and possibly American) prejudice than a dictum valid for all times and all places.

I need to turn briefly to the article by Bruno Hake cited earlier.[164] Despite its title, "Mendelssohn als Lehrer," it does not deal primarily with Mendelssohn as teacher, but rather with Mendelssohn in the role of corresponding adviser to a distant dilettante who persisted in sending him compositions for evaluation. Mendelssohn's patience in this role is remarkable. It is useful to consider also that a cultural conviction as well as personal selflessness were operating here. It is a question of *Bildung*. The pursuit of art is good for the individual; the pursuit of art by many individuals is good for society. The matter is not entirely simple, however, because the production of inferior, would-be works of art is obviously not an unalloyed good. Schumann weighs this dilemma in his usual sensitive fashion in "Zweiter Quartett-morgen."[165] Because of the didactic nature of his journalism, the underlying cultural assumptions are relatively close to the surface.

IN CONCLUSION

There is still much that needs to be done. I have not been able to consult the daily newspapers, The *Times* of London excepted. These were at least as important—indeed probably more important in tracing day-to-day activity—as the musical journals that have supplied so large a part of my story. The problem, of course, is one of accessibility. One may doubt that much would be changed by a close reading of the dailies, but the tale would surely become richer.

Beyond that, some archival work remains undone. For instance, the Deneke Collection at the Bodleian Library of Oxford contains material relevant to the inquiry: correspondence about the Handel editions and drafts of concert programs, to take two examples.[166] Doubtless, there is evidence still lurking in archives in Leipzig and Berlin. Again one may doubt that the picture will change materially, but it would no doubt be significantly enriched, particularly by a deeper understanding of the ways in which social, cultural, and political conditions affected Mendelssohn's views and works.

It might be well to summarize now. Mendelssohn was a significant performer as conductor, organist, and pianist not simply because he was good or influential but also because of his important participation in changing the very nature of musical performance. By the end of his relatively brief career the idea of "interpretation" was established, as were high standards of accuracy and the necessity of nuance. In a curious way, too, some of his activities really mark the beginning of ideas of "historical performance." Small wonder that his obituary in the *Signale für die musikalische Welt* said that his accomplishments as a performer were not less significant than his accomplishments as a composer.[167]

NOTES

Preparation of this chapter was assisted by a grant of six hours of released time by Montclair State University.

1. *Signale für die Musikalische Welt* (hereafter, *Signale*) 5/46 (9 November 1847), 362. Unless otherwise stated, all translations are mine.

2. René Leibowitz, "Notes pour une éthique de l'interprétation musicale," in his *Le compositeur et son double: Essais sur l'interprétation musicale* (Paris: Gallimard, 1971), 24.

3. Much of the literature fails to take this new attitude into account. For instance, there are no entries for "interpret" or "interpretation" in the index to Elliott Galkin's magisterial *A History of Orchestral Conducting in Theory and Practice* (New York: Pendragon, 1988). "Phrasing" seems to be the closest one can get. Galkin quotes Berlioz's distinction between a conductor and a director but does not pick up on its implications (pp. 274–76).

4. Stefan Kunze, Theodor Schmid, Andreas Traub and Gerda Burkhard, eds., *Ludwig van Beethoven, die Werke im Spiegel seiner Zeit: Gesammelte Konzertberichte und Rezensionen bis 1830* (Laaber: Laaber-Verlag, 1987), ix.

5. A convenient discussion of the growth of the theory of interpretation can be found in the editor's "Vortragslehre und Interpretationstheorie," constituting the first part of chapter 4 of *Musikalische Interpretation*, ed. Hermann Danuser, Neues Handbuch der Musikwissenschaft 11 (Laaber: Laaber-Verlag, [1992]), 271–320. Danuser points out that the vocabulary used to discuss "interpretation" during the nineteenth century needs investigation. In German, though many words are involved, the issue is encapsulated in the growing distinction between "Aufführung" and "Vortrag," the latter gradually taking on something like the modern meaning of "interpretation." In English, "interpret" in the sense of "to bring out the meaning of (a dramatic or musical composition, a landscape, etc.) by artistic representation or performance" (*Oxford English Dictionary*, 1989 edition) is a fairly

recent usage. The 1989 *OED* first finds it (and also "interpretation" in this sense) in 1880, but it was, in fact, common by the 1840s. However that may be, there is no doubt that by Mendelssohn's time the notion was pretty well established that while insightful expounding of the inner meaning of a musical text was, in principle, the duty of the performing musician, only a few actually were summoned to so high a calling. There is also no doubt that there was considerable resistance to the idea of interpretation, a resistance perhaps more often expressed by ignoring than by openly opposing it. An example: a report from Berlin by J. P. Schmidt, dated 10 May 1845 (*Allgemeine Wiener Musik-Zeitung* [hereafter, *AWMZ*] 5/69, 275), discusses the *königliche Capelle* season just ended. Schmidt reported that Henning and Taubert, successors to Möser and Mendelssohn as concertmaster and conductor, respectively, were attempting to maintain the high standard set by their predecessors. Schmidt wrote about programming—he found the post-Mendelssohn programs short on new music—and about adequate rehearsal, but he did not mention interpretation.

6. "'. . . als habe er es selbst komponiert': Streiflichter zur musikalischen Interpretation," in *Aspekte der musikalischen Interpretation: Sava Savoff zum 70. Geburtstag*, ed. Hermann Danuser and Christoph Keller (Hamburg: Verlag der Musikalienhandlung Karl Dieter Wagner, 1980), 33. Danuser makes a great deal of the identity or close relationship of composer and performer in the eighteenth century, a point that seems to me to be substantially weakened by such factors as Breitkopf's distribution of manuscript copies of all sorts of music and the activities of Parisian music publishers, among other factors. Couperin's note, "Voyés ma Méthode pour la maniere de doigter cet endroit, page 46," in "La Milordine" in the *Premier Ordre* of 1713 hardly argues for a close relation of performer and composer! Admittedly, there is an important distinction between public and private performance.

7. Henry Fothergill Chorley, *Modern German Music* (London: Smith, Elder, 1854; repr. with a new introduction and index by Hans Lenneberg, 2 vols., New York: Da Capo, 1973), 2: 32-33. Chorley (1808–1863) was music critic of the London journal *Athenaeum* from 1831 to 1868. Obviously, he is here writing some years after the fact; but since he is recollecting a general impression, not a specific detail, the chances of accuracy are greatly enhanced. A description of the Brunswick Festival of 1839 can be found in his *Music and Manners in France and Germany: A Series of Traveling Sketches of Art and Society*, 3 vols. (London: Longman, Brown, Green, and Longmans, 1844), 1: 209–301.

8. *Allgemeine musikalische Zeitung* (hereafter, *AMZ*) 34/48 (28 November 1832), col. 802.

9. Not "Mir ist so wunderbar." See note 10.

10. The reviewer is presumably referring to the trumpet call at the end of the third scene of the second act in the final version and—perhaps more important given the point he is making—the following "Ach! du bist gerettet."

11. *AMZ* 45/46 (15 November 1843), col. 833–34. "Robert †" was clearly unhappy with Hiller's work, and the characterization of the required interpretation and the compliments to the orchestra lead to an expression of dissatisfaction with his direction. Hiller got a lot of bad press during the season. It is impossible to overestimate the importance of the idea that a performance of instrumental music should have "spiritual value." In this connection, see particularly Carl Dahlhaus, *The Idea of Absolute Music*, trans. Roger Lustig (Chicago: University of Chicago Press, 1989).

12. Many editions. I have used the text in *Richard Wagners Gesammelte Schriften*, ed. Julius Kapp (Leipzig: Hesse & Becker, 1914), 9: 153–229. The most easily accessible English text is *On Conducting*, trans. Edward Dannreuther (London: William, Reeves, 1887; repr. New York: Dover, 1989). Dannreuther reduces somewhat the severity of the worst of the racist remarks. In *Three Wagner Essays* (London: Eulenburg Books, 1979), Robert L.

Jacobs offers an abridged translation containing only the musical portions of the work. He thus takes these out of context and misses the main point.

13. Recent studies of Wagner's anti-Semitism have been made by historians of ideas, who apparently avoid *Über das Dirigieren* since it appears to be a technical writing outside their competence. See Paul Lawrence Rose, *Wagner: Race and Revolution* (New Haven, CT: Yale University Press, 1992); L. J. Rather, *Reading Wagner: A Study in the History of Ideas* (Baton Rouge: Louisiana State University Press, 1990); Jacob Katz, *The Darker Side of Genius: Richard Wagner's Anti-Semitism* (Hanover, NH: University Press of New England for Brandeis University Press, 1986). Marc A. Weiner's *Richard Wagner and the Anti-Semitic Imagination* (Lincoln, NE: University of Nebraska Press, 1995) appeared too late to be taken into consideration.

14. See his "Unbekannte Dokumente zur Uraufführung von Franz Schuberts großer C-Dur-Sinfonie durch Felix Mendelssohn Bartholdy," *Beiträge zur Musikwissenschaft* 29/3 (1987), 240–50. Mendelssohn and this symphony are also discussed by Hans von Bülow in his "Lohengrin in Bologna: Kein Leitartikel, sondern ein vertrauliches Gespräch (im australischen Style) durch diplomatische Indiscretion in die Öffentlichkeit gebracht," in his *Ausgewählte Schriften 1850–1892*, 2d expanded ed., 2 vols. in 1 (Leipzig: Breitkopf & Härtel, 1911), 2: 130; originally in *Signale* 30/2 (January 1872), 17–27. Further evidence that there can be no question of Mendelssohn's having made cuts can be found in Otto Erich Deutsch, "The Discovery of Schubert's Great C Major Symphony: A Story in Fifteen Letters," *The Musical Quarterly* 38/4 (October 1952), 528-32. Deutsch quotes a letter to the Philharmonic Society in London in which Mendelssohn recommended eliminating the repeats in the first and third movements.

15. *Neue Zeitschrift für Musik* (hereafter, *NZfM*) 10/34 (26 April 1839): 136.

16. See my "1848, Anti-Semitism, and the Mendelssohn Reception," *Mendelssohn Studies*, ed. R. Larry Todd (Cambridge: Cambridge University Press, 1992), 126–48.

17. The most detailed contemporaneous assessment of Mendelssohn's work in Düsseldorf that I know is [Wilhelm Joseph] v[on] W[asielewski], "Felix Mendelssohn-Bartholdy in Düsseldorf in den Jahren 1833–35," *Neue Berliner Musikzeitung* 1/48 (24 November 1847), 389–92. Mendelssohn relinquished his connection with the opera after some six months of his two-year stint in Düsseldorf; consequently, he conducted relatively few operas. Wasielewski particularly remembers his performances of Weber's *Euryanthe* and Cherubini's *Ali Baba*. Some of Mendelssohn's operatic adventures are vividly described in his letters of 28 December 1833 and 28 March 1834. See Felix Mendelssohn Bartholdy, *Briefe aus den Jahren 1833-1847*, ed. Paul and Dr. Carl Mendelssohn Bartholdy (Leipzig: Hermann Mendelssohn, 1863), 17-23, 30-35.

18. The figures are taken from Reinhold Schmitt-Thomas, *Die Entwicklung der deutschen Konzertkritik im Spiegel der Leipziger Allgemeinen musikalischen Zeitung (1798–1848)*, Kultur im Zeitbild 1 (Frankfurt/M: Kettenhof, 1969), 158.

19. The idea of a "musical canon"—not, of course, called that—seems already to have developed before Mendelssohn's time in both Leipzig and Berlin, where Haydn, Mozart, and Beethoven were accepted repertory staples. The basic idea evolved first in England. See William Weber, "The Intellectual Origins of Musical Canon in Eighteenth-Century England," *Journal of the American Musicological Society* 47/3 (Fall 1994), 488–520.

20. Wasielewski, "Felix Mendelssohn Bartholdy," 391. The article also contains a useful description of the administrative structure of musical life in Düsseldorf and of the duties with which Mendelssohn was formally charged. See also the letter cited of 26 October 1833, *Briefe 1833–1847*, 10–16.

21. Julius Eckardt, *Ferdinand David und die Familie Mendelssohn-Bartholdy: Aus hinterlassenen Briefschaften zusammengestellt* (Leipzig: Duncker & Humblot, 1888), 58. In fact, the book includes considerable narrative by Eckardt; it is not only a collection of letters.

22. For details about musical life in Leipzig and its social and economic background, see particularly Friedrich Schmidt, *Das Musikleben der bürgerlichen Gesellschaft Leipzigs im Vormärz (1815–1848)*, Musikalisches Magazin 47 (Langensalza: Hermann Beyer & Söhne, 1912); Gunter Hempel, "Die bürgerliche Musikkultur Leipzigs im Vormärz," *Beiträge zur Musikwissenschaft*, 1964, 1: 2–14. Schmidt is particularly strong on the relative importance of the several musical institutions. The Marxist scholars of the former German Democratic Republic have contributed very significantly to our understanding of the social, political, and economic climate in which the musicians of the Vormärz worked. For Mendelssohn's activity on behalf of the economic well being of his musicians, see Felix Mendelssohn Bartholdy, *Briefe aus Leipziger Archiven*, ed. Hans-Joachim Rothe and Reinhard Szeskus (Leipzig: VEB Deutscher Verlag für Musik, 1972). See also "Erstes Abonnementconcert im Saale des Gewandhauses zu Leipzig (Sonntag, den 3. October 1847)," *Signale* 5/41 (October 1847), 321–22, where the reviewer says that the opening of the Gewandhaus season is to Leipzig what the opening of the opera season is to an Italian city.

23. *Musical World* 21/50 (1846), 633. The statement that the Gewandhausorchester was as large as the Philharmonic is not correct.

24. After Schmidt, *Das Musikleben*, 99–102.

25. Sebastian Hensel, *Die Familie Mendelssohn 1729 bis 1847: Nach Briefen und Tagebüchern*, 16th ed. (Berlin: Georg Reimer, 1918), 1: 241–42. Letter of 15 April 1829.

26. The figures are from the 11th edition of the *Encyclopaedia Britannica*.

27. On the Festival see particularly Cecilia Hopkins Porter, "The New Public and the Reordering of the Musical Establishment: The Lower Rhine Music Festivals, 1818–67," *19th-Century Music* 3/3 (March 1980), 211–24; idem, "The Reign of the *Dilettanti*: Düsseldorf from Mendelssohn to Schumann," *The Musical Quarterly* 73/4 (Fall 1989): 476–512; and Klaus Wolfgang Niemöller, "Felix Mendelssohn-Bartholdy und das Niederrheinische Musikfest 1835 in Köln," in *Studien zur Musikgeschichte des Rheinlandes III*, ed. Ursula Eckart-Bäcker, Beiträge zur rheinischen Musikgeschichte 62 (Cologne: Arno Volk, 1965), 46–64.

28. Niemöller, "Felix Mendelssohn-Bartholdy," 46.

29. For a detailed study of this performance, its background, and its consequences, see Martin Geck, *Die Wiederentdeckung der Matthäuspassion im 19. Jahrhundert: Die zeitgenössischen Dokumente und ihre ideengeschichtliche Deutung*, Studien zur Musikgeschichte des 19. Jahrhunderts 9 (Regensburg: Bosse, 1967). An earlier public performance, of *Judas Maccabeus* under Zelter, took place on 9 February 1828 and is reported in the *Berliner allgemeine musikalische Zeitung* 5/7,8 (13, 20 February 1828), 54–55, 61–64. See also Wm. A. Little, "Mendelssohn and the Berlin Singakademie: The Composer at the Crossroads," in *Mendelssohn and His World*, ed. R. Larry Todd (Princeton: Princeton University Press, 1991), 65–85.

30. For an account of the affair, see Eric Werner, *Mendelssohn: A New Image of the Composer and His Age*, trans. Dika Newlin (New York: Free Press of Glencoe, 1963), 227–31.

31. For modern discussions of musical conditions in Berlin in Mendelssohn's time, see Eberhard Rudolph, "Mendelssohns Beziehungen zu Berlin," *Beiträge zur Musikwissenschaft* 14/3 (1972), 205–14; Jürgen Rehm, *Zur Musikrezeption im vormärzlichen Berlin: Die Presentation bürgerlichen Selbstverständnißes und biedermeierlicher Kunstanschauung in*

den Musikkritiken Ludwig Rellstab, Studien zur Musikwissenschaft 2 (Hildesheim: Olms, 1983). Rehm is singularly insightful on the relations between political views, on the one hand, and artistic and esthetic ideas, on the other, in the liberal bourgeois mind during the Vormärz. For a fascinating contemporaneous view of musical life in Berlin, see the anonymous "Correspondenz" from Berlin in *NZfM* 1/34 (28 July 1834), 134–36. In his review of the sixth Gewandhaus subscription concert of the season, given on 12 November 1842 (*NZfM* 17/42 [22 November 1842], 174), Wilhelm von Zuccalmaglio noted Mendelssohn's impending departure for Berlin and spent most of his review delivering himself of highly deprecatory (but also highly accurate) remarks about musical life in Berlin and its relation to the court. Zuccalmaglio accurately predicted Mendelssohn's return to Leipzig. There is a substantial literature about the Singakademie; see particularly Martin Blumner, *Geschichte der Sing-Akademie zu Berlin* (Berlin: Horn und Raasch, 1891); Werner Bollert, ed., *Sing-Akademie zu Berlin: Festschrift zum 175-jährigen Bestehen* (Berlin: Rembrandt, 1966).

32. Tempo might perhaps be an exception, if one could find more or less exact timings for particular performances of particular pieces, but these are very rare. The running time of Mendelssohn's performance of the Schubert "Great" C major symphony was between 55 minutes and 1 hour (see note 14). This is useful, but it is not sufficient to establish a true baseline.

33. See Leinsdorf's *The Composer's Advocate: A Radical Orthodoxy for Musicians* (New Haven, CT: Yale University Press, 1981).

34. Quoted without attribution by Klaus Wolfgang Niemöller in his "Die Musik und ihre Interpretation," in *Sequenzen: Frau Prof. Dr. Maria Elisabeth Brockhoff zum 2.4.1982*, ed. Georg Berkemeier and Isolde Maria Weineck (Münster: Westfälischen Wilhelms-Universität, 1982), 258. It is important to remain keenly aware of the rather large loophole. Of course, it is not clear how the performer was to arrive at a knowledge of the composer's intention in situations where personal contact was not possible. Schumann, as a keen observer of the contemporary scene and as a reviewer of great masses of printed music, must surely have been aware that contact between performer and composer was increasingly rare. This nostalgic view seems to arise from one of Schumann's curious conservative streaks.

35. 13/220 (11 June 1840), 363.

36. 8/109 (2 April 1838), 241–42. Because of the divided control characteristic of English orchestral performance even at this late date, fundamental discussions of what conductors ought to do are more common in England than on the continent, where undivided control of performance by a conductor, whether wielding a baton or a violin bow, was completely established. See Galkin, *A History*, Chapter. 9. Dual control is particularly well explained by George Hogarth in his *The Philharmonic Society of London, from Its Foundation, 1813, to Its Fiftieth Year*, 1862 (London: Bradbury & Evans and Addison, Hollier, & Lucas, 1862):

For each concert two individuals were appointed by the Directors; the one to occupy the place of principal violin, with the title of "Leader of the Orchestra," and the other to "preside at the pianoforte." The duty of the leader was not only to execute his own part with exemplary accuracy and firmness, but to attend to all the other performers, who were to look to him for the time of the movements, and to be governed by his beat. His coadjutor, at the pianoforte, and with the full score before him, was to watch the performance and to be ready to correct any mistake. This method, borrowed from the usages (far from uniform) of foreign theatrical and other orchestras, was liable to serious objections. . . . In . . . 1820, the individual who presided at the pianoforte was, for the first time, in the programmes denominated "Conductor." And, in the following year, the pianoforte was removed, and the conductor stationed, as at present, in a desk in front of the orchestra. The title of leader, nevertheless, was still bestowed upon the principal violin; and this continued to be the case till the appointment of Mr. Costa to the office of conductor in the year 1846; though long before that time the title of leader had become merely nominal. (pp. 7–8; 26–27)

37. *Signale* 2/6 (February 1844), 47.
38. *Life of Felix Mendelssohn Bartholdy*—from the German with supplementary sketches by Julius Benedict, Henry F. Chorley, Ludwig Rellstab, Bayard Taylor, R. S. Willis, and J. S. Dwight, trans. William Leonhard Gage (New York and Philadelphia: Frederick Leypoldt, 1865), 44.
39. "Leipziger Musikleben," *NZfM* 23/47 (12 December 1845), 190–92. These remarks are to be taken all the more seriously since Brendel, succeeding Schumann as editor, turned the *NZfM* into an organ of the "progressive" forces around Wagner and Liszt and printed Wagner's notorious and coyly anonymous "Über das Judenthum in der Musik" for the first time. See my essay cited in note 16.
40. *Letters of Felix Mendelssohn to Ignaz and Charlotte Moscheles*, ed. Felix Moscheles (Boston: Ticknor, 1888), 93. The letter is dated 12 February 1834.
41. *Felix Mendelssohn Bartholdys Briefwechsel mit Legationsrat Karl Klingemann in London*, ed. Karl Klingemann (Jr.) (Essen: Baedecker, 1909), 123. See also my *"Melusine: A Mendelssohn Draft," The Musical Quarterly* 42/4 (October 1957), 480–99.
42. Wilhelm Adolf Lampadius, *Felix Mendelssohn Bartholdy: Ein Denkmal für seine Freunde* (Leipzig: Hinrichs, 1848), 51–52.
43. My colleague Roland Hutchinson points out a delightful paradox in this connection. No early music performer would venture a thoughtless, "straight through it" performance of, say, a Mozart symphony (and, indeed, as a result of long training and of unvoiced assumptions might be quite literally incapable of such a performance). Surely no one would want to hear such a performance were it possible. Yet it seems highly likely that interpretive performances of music before Beethoven are profoundly anachronistic.
44. "Fünftes Abonnementconcert im Saale des Gewandhauses zu Leipzig (Den 7. November 1844.)," *Signale* 2/46 (November 1844), 361. Niels Gade was the conductor. The 3:5 presumably refers to the tempo of a former performance, most likely Mendelssohn's, in relation to the Gade performance under review. It is hard to imagine that we ought to take seriously this great display of precision.
45. For an exceptionally fine study of this and similar questions, see Warren Arthur Bebbington, "The Orchestral Conducting Practice of Richard Wagner" (Ph.D. diss., City University of New York, 1984). For the interesting views of a participant, see Felix Weingartner, *Über das Dirigieren*, 3d ed. (Leipzig: Breitkopf & Härtel, 1905).
46. See above, p. 88.
47. See, for instance, his letter of 23 May 1834, in which he criticizes Chopin's and Hiller's playing for excessive metrical irregularity and somewhat unbridled emotionalism but does so in a generally favorable context; *Briefe 1833–1847*, 40–41. The excerpt in Werner, *Mendelssohn*, 244, omits the favorable context and translates "Tact" (i.e., *Takt*) as "tact" rather than as "beat," or more freely but perhaps more accurately, "meter."
48. Bülow, *Ausgewählte Schriften*, 2: 130. It is interesting that the discovery and performance of this symphony seem to have been a symbolic as well as purely musical event, and the symbol, one on which different realities could be hung.
49. Weingartner, *Über das Dirigieren*, 28.
50. Galkin, *A History*, 559–61.
51. Johannes Forner et al., *Die Gewandhauskonzerte zu Leipzig 1781–1981* (Leipzig: VEB Deutscher Verlag für Musik, 1981), 67–68. See also Galkin, *A History*, Chapter 9.
52. p. 95.

53. Schmidt, *Das Musikleben*, 100.

54. "Schwärmbriefe." Eusebius an Chiara," *NZfM* 3/32 (20 October 1835), 127; repr. in his *Gesammelte Schriften über Musik und Musiker*, ed. Martin Kreisig (Leipzig: Breitkopf & Härtel, 1914; repr. Westmead, Farnborough, Hants.: Gregg International, 1969), 1: 118.

55. *Ferdinand David und die Familie Mendelssohn-Bartholdy*, 131–32.

56. *NZfM* 4/31 (15 April 1836), 129–30.

57. See above, p. 88.

58. On Habeneck, see Galkin, *A History*, 469–79. Chorley is among the many Galkin quotes in praise of Habeneck. See also D. Kern Holoman, "The Emergence of the Orchestral Conductor in Paris in the 1830s," and Jean-Michel Nectoux, "Trois orchestres parisiens en 1830: L'Académie royale de musique, le Théâtre-italien et la Société des concerts du conservatoire," both in Peter Bloom, ed., *Music in Paris in the Eighteen-Thirties/La Musique à Paris dans les années mil huit cent trente*, Musical Life in 19th-Century France/La Vie musicale en France aux XIXe siècle 4 (Stuyvesant, NY: Pendragon, 1987), 387–429 and 471–505 respectively. Nectoux also makes considerable use of Chorley.

59. *A History*, 510. Daniel J. Koury agrees. See his *Orchestral Performance Practices in the Nineteenth Century: Size, Proportions, and Seating* (Ann Arbor, MI: UMI Research Press, 1986), 79–80.

60. Ferdinand Hiller, *Mendelssohn: Letters and Recollections*, trans. M. E. von Glehn (London: Macmillan, 1874), 158.

61. Wilhelm Joseph von Wasielewski, *Aus siebzig Jahren: Lebenserinnerungen* (Stuttgart: Deutsche Verlags-Anstalt, 1897), 59. The orchestra thus surveyed had about 40 members. See Koury, *Orchestral Performance Practices*, 149; a seating plan is given on p. 207.

62. "Mendelssohns Oratorien-Praxis: Ein bisher unbekannte Brief des Meisters vom Jahre 1840," *Musica* (Kassel) 6 (September 1952), 352–55.

63. See Galkin, *A History*, Chapter 5 for much of the scant information available.

64. Ferdinand Simon Gassner, *Dirigent und Ripienist für angehende Musikdirigenten, Musiker und Musikfreunde* (Karlsruhe: Groos, 1844), 23, 51. The book, which precedes the Berlioz treatise by more than a decade, is a curious mixture of the old-fashioned and the modern. As the title suggests, it is not directed entirely to the professional; indeed, it is the amateur conductor (or would-be conductor) who is mostly addressed.

65. Wasielewski, *Aus siebzig Jahren*, 67. On the other hand, a note in the *Musical World* 20/9 (27 February 1847), 99–100 (reprinted from the *Athenaeum*) discusses uniform bowing as a discipline peculiar to Habeneck. The writer would have had ample opportunity to see Mendelssohn at work during the season of 1844.

66. Gassner, *Dirigent*, 108–9.

67. See the literature cited in note 27 for detailed information. See also Arntrud Kurzhals-Reuter, *Die Oratorien Felix Mendelssohn Bartholdys: Untersuchung zur Quellenlage, Enstehung, Gestaltung, und Überlieferung* (Tutzing: Schneider, 1978). For a performance of *St. Paul* in 1840, Mendelssohn recommended double winds and strings 15, 15, 15, 14, 7 to go with a chorus of 200 to 250. According to *Eutonia* 9/1 (1835), 89–90, the 1833 Lower Rhine Festival in Düsseldorf employed 83 sopranos, 43 altos, 51 tenors, 88 basses, 62 violins, 19 violas, 18 cellos, 13 double basses, 4 flutes, 4 oboes, 5 clarinets, 4 bassoons, 4 horns, 4 trumpets, 4 trombones, 1 timpanist. Total, they say, 419 (actually 407). There can be no thought that Mendelssohn considered the balance ideal. These were amateur festivals, and his idea was that people who showed up should be given their chance to perform; see the discussion by "v. W." cited in note 17. By 1838 almost 700 players and singers were involved; see "Niederrheinisches Musikfest in Köln," *AmZ* 40/27 (4 July 1838),

cols. 438–39. However, Niemöller maintains that some of Mendelssohn's extraordinary dynamic effects were obtained by the gradual addition of extra players; see his "Felix Mendelssohn-Bartholdy," 62.

68. A few among many: *AmZ* 39/13 (29 March 1837), cols. 209–10 (about *St. Paul* in Leipzig); *AmZ* 49/16 (21 April 1847), col. 264 (about *St. Paul* in Leipzig); *Musical World* 9/120 (new series 2/26) (27 June 1838), 141–43 (about Handel's *Joshua* at the Lower Rhine Festival).

69. From a review of *St. Paul* performed on Good Friday of 1847 in the Pauliner Kirche in Leipzig; *AmZ* 49/16 (21 April 1847), col. 264.

70. "Korrespondenz. Berlin, den 2. April," *Berliner allgemeine musikalische Zeitung* 1/15 (14 April 1824), 137–38.

71. 39/8, col. 126.

72. *AmZ* 38/7 (17 February 1836), cols. 104–5.

73. 6/142 (26 November 1846), 579.

74. *NZfM* 8/27, 28, 29 (3, 6, 10 April 1838), 107–8, 111, 115–16; repr. *Gesammelte Schriften*, 1: 373–80.

75. Repertory lists but few actual programs may be found in Alfred Dörffel, *Die Gewandhausconcerte zu Leipzig: Festschrift zur hundertjährigen Jubelfeier der Einweihung des Concertsaales im Gewandhause zu Leipzig*, 2 vols. (Leipzig: n.p., 1884). This book and its modern reprints are a bibliographic nightmare. There seem to have been two versions bearing the same title and imprint. The second volume's statistics and program lists are more detailed in one version than the other. There are a number of modern reprints in various formats; most reproduce the less detailed second volume.

76. *NZfM* 12/35, 36, 38, 39 40 (28 April, 1, 8, 12, 15 May 1840), 139–40, 143–44, 151–52, 154–55, 159–60. The complaint is on p. 152.

77. Berlioz's marvelously detailed and amusing story of his Leipzig appearance in 1843 is told in his "A M. Stephan Heller," in *Voyage musical en Allemagne et en Italie* (Paris: Labitte, 1844; repr. Westmead, Farnborough, Hants.: Gregg, 1970), 2: 71–90. Despite his dislike of Berlioz's music, Mendelssohn put the orchestra at Berlioz's disposal, took over the preparation of the chorus for Berlioz's concert, and generally made himself useful to his French colleague.

78. 5/69 (10 June 1845), 275. The report is dated 10 May. Schumann remarked on Mendelssohn's general as well as musical interest in the world: "He knew everything that was going on in the world; you couldn't bring him any news"; quoted from Schumann's *Erinnerungen an Felix Mendelssohn Bartholdy* in *Briefe aus Leipziger Archiven*, 15.

79. From Heinrich Riehl's necrology; quoted in Martin Wehnert, "Mendelssohns Traditionsbewußtsein und dessen Widerschein im Werk," *Deutsches Jahrbuch der Musikwissenschaft* 16 (1971), [5]–45.

80. See her "Mendelssohn und die Vergangenheit," in *Die Ausbreitung der Historismus über die Musik*, ed. Walter Wiora, Studien zur Musikgeschichte des 19. Jahrhunderts 14 (Regensburg: Bosse, 1969), 73–84, and her monograph *Felix Mendelssohn Bartholdy und die Musik der Vergangenheit*, Studien zur Musikgeschichte des 19. Jahrhunderts 17 (Regensburg: Bosse, 1969).

81. See pp. 94–95.

82. These programs can be found in many sources, including contemporaneous periodicals and Dörffel, *Geschichte der Gewandhausconcerte*. I give them with slight modification after Großmann-Vendrey, *Felix Mendelssohn Bartholdy*, 161.

83. On the way this interest worked itself out in Düsseldorf, where Mendelssohn was in charge of church music, see Großmann-Vendrey, *Felix Mendelssohn Bartholdy*, 58–61.

84. Letter of 24 February 1838; quoted in ibid., 161.

85. See note 84. Getting up to twenty refers to the fact that there were twenty subscription concerts each season. The number of extra concerts was very great; accordingly, Mendelssohn and the orchestra would have had very full schedules even if they had had no other duties—but they all did. The didactic elements in the historical concerts are obvious. Lampadius remarks (*Ein Denkmal*, 79–80) that Mendelssohn thought that a chronological exposition of the history of music would heighten audience enjoyment: "[Mendelssohn] understood how to increase . . . the pleasure given by these musical pleasures in a new way to make clear to the public the stepwise development of music through historical concerts."

86. The Méhul Symphony no. 1 in G minor from 1808—the first movement has a "backward" recapitulation, and its second theme sounds like the second themes in some of Mendelssohn's early string symphonies—was reprinted in 1985 in an edition by David Charlton, Recent Researches in the Music of the Nineteenth and Early Twentieth Centuries 6 (Madison, WI: A-R Editions).

87. *NZfM* 8/28 (6 April 1838), 111; repr. *Gesammelte Schriften* 1: 375–76. He found the essentially superficial resemblances to Beethoven quite striking.

88. *NZfM* 8/27 (3 April 1838), 108; repr. *Gesammelte Schriften*, 1: 375.

89. See especially the sections on the Lower Rhine Festival and on Mendelssohn as an editor of older music in Großmann-Vendrey, *Felix Mendelssohn Bartholdy*, 67–125, 192–96; Wilgard Lange, "Mendelssohns Händel-Bearbeitungen," in *Georg Friedrich Händel im Verständnis des 19. Jahrhunderts*, Bericht über die wissenschaftliche Konferenz zu den 32. Händelfestspielen der DDR am 13. und 14. Juni 1983 in Halle (Saale), ed. Walther Siegmund-Schultze (Halle/Saale: Martin-Luther-Universität, 1984), 70–77. Lange's work supersedes earlier writings reaching back to Chrysander.

90. See note 67.

91. See Werner Bollert, "Die Händelpflege der Berliner Sing-Akademie unter Zelter und Rungenhagen," in his *Sing-Akademie zu Berlin*, 69–79.

92. Karl Klingemann (Jr.), ed., 98–99.

93. Großmann-Vendrey, *Felix Mendelssohn Bartholdy*, 72.

94. Niemöller, "Felix Mendelssohn-Bartholdy," 52. A footnote contains a most interesting list of the Handel editions with added wind parts then available.

95. See particularly the essay by Lange cited in note 89.

96. *The Musical Herald: A Journal of Music and Musical Literature* 1/21 (for the week ending 26 September 1846), 47.

97. For instance, Lampadius, who does not discuss Mendelssohn's editorial activity, stresses the didactic goal of the historical concerts; *Ein Denkmal*, 79-80; see note 85. Given his time, place, class, and upbringing, it would be surprising if *Bildung* had not been of immense importance to Mendelssohn.

98. 42/8, cols. 162-63. For more on this subject, see Georg Feder, "Geschichte der Bearbeitungen von Bachs Chaconne," in *Bach-Interpretationen: Walter Blankenburg zum 65. Geburtstag*, ed. Martin Geck (Göttingen: Vandenhoeck und Ruprecht, 1969), 168–89. Feder discusses the nature of Mendelssohn's accompaniment in considerable detail. Wilhelm Ressel also wrote an accompaniment for the Chaconne, and Schumann wrote one for the entire partita; see Adolf Nowack, "Bachs Werke für die Violine allein--ihre Rezeption durch Aufführung, Theorie und Komposition," in *Rezeptionsästhetik und Rezeptionsgeschichte in der Musikwissenschaft*, ed. Hermann Danuser and Friedhelm Krummacher, Publikationen der Hochschule für Musik und Theater Hanover 3 ([Laaber:] Laaber-Verlag, 1991), 223–37.

99. A list of everything Mendelssohn played as a pianist under Gewandhaus auspices, chamber music included, can be found in Dörffel, *Geschichte der Gewandhausconcerte*, 121–23.

100. 4/11 (14 March 1827), 84. It is useful to remember that when this was written, Beethoven still had about a month to live, and the late sonatas, like the late quartets, were viewed as the most dangerous of dangerous modern music. Yet even in a relatively minor city like Stettin, the Ninth had its hearings. In later years at the height of his fame, Mendelssohn often continued the practice of sitting in with the orchestra during a performance at which he had had pianistic or conductorial duties. In those years, however, he generally played viola.

101. *AmZ* 43/5 (3 February 1841), col. 124. The piece that drew this effusion was the Beethoven G-major Concerto, one of the works that Mendelssohn played most often in public.

102. *AmZ* 45/41 (11 October 1843), cols. 741–42.

103. *Musical World* 4 (1836), ix (prefatory matter to the volume).

104. *Musical World* 7/79 (15 September 1837), 10. The writer is discussing an organ recital at Christchurch, Newgate, but the discussion of Mendelssohn's contrapuntal dexterity is equally applicable to his piano playing.

105. Wilhelm von Zuccalmaglio in *NZfM* 15/47 (10 December 1841), 188.

106. "Felix Mendelssohn Bartholdy. Died November 4, 1847." *The Musical Times* 38 (1 November 1897), 729-33. Of course, the usual cautions about recollections put down well after the fact apply. But it is the general impression, rather than the details, that concerns us here. Moreover, the article was probably written by Frederick George Edwards, a well-known Mendelssohnian. Edwards was probably in touch with one of Mendelssohn's daughters. See Percy Scholes, *The Mirror of Music 1844–1944: A Century of Musical Life in Britain as Reflected in the pages of the "Musical Times"* (London: Novello & Co., Oxford University Press, 1947), 2: 757. On the contact with Mrs. Benecke, the daughter in question, see *The Musical Times* (1 June 1897), 370.

107. For a relatively early example, see *The Harmonicon* for 11 June 1833, p. 135, where a performance of the Mozart D-minor Concerto given on 13 May is highly praised. In the cadenza to the first movement, Mendelssohn "*adverted* with great address to the subjects of the concerto."

108. 24/8 (25 January 1846), 31–32.

109. Sir George Grove, "Mendelssohn," in his *Beethoven, Schubert, Mendelssohn* (London: Macmillan, 1951), 375. The three essays in this volume are reprinted from the first edition of Grove's *Dictionary of Music and Musicians*.

110. Ibid., 376.

111. Ibid., 374.

112. Ibid., 375.

113. Ibid., 376.

114. Chorley, *Music and Manners*, 1: 274–77.

115. 2: 206–9. In the reprint of this introduction, Bülow does not say whether the melody notes in that part of the Andante where the tune is accompanied by arpeggiated chords should be played right on the beat or at the conclusion of each arpeggio.

116. Robert Parkins, "Mendelssohn and the Erard Piano," *Piano Quarterly* 32/125 (Spring 1984), 53–58. Parkins says that an instrument in the Metropolitan Museum of Art in New York, previously thought to have been built about 1828, contains a brass "harmonic bar" patented in 1838; the piano has thus now been dated ca. 1840. Though it is very fancy and was clearly made as elegant furniture, the mechanism is very like the one in Mendelssohn's piano. All parts are original and the instrument is very well preserved.

117. A footnote refers to Rosamond E. M. Harding's discussion of the Érard action in her *The Piano-forte: Its History Traced to the Great Exhibition of 1851* (Cambridge: Cambridge University Press, 1933; repr. New York: Da Capo, 1973), 156–62.

118. Parkins, 57.

119. See the chapter "Mendelssohn als Organist" in her *Felix Mendelssohn Bartholdy*. The chapter is based in part on still-unpublished letters in the New York Public Library, and the phrase quoted is on p. 179. Her 1965 Vienna dissertation, "Die Orgelwerke von Felix Mendelssohn Bartholdy," was not available.

120. *Mendelssohns Leipziger Orgelkonzert 1840: Ein Beitrag zur Bach-Pflege im 19. Jahrhundert*, Jahresgabe 1987 der Internationalen Bach-Gesellschaft Schaffhausen (Wiesbaden: Breitkopf & Härtel, 1988), 15–16.

121. Reproduced by Pape on p. 20 of his study.

122. Schumann's famous review, *Gesammelte Schriften* 1: 492–93, says A-minor, but Pape has ingeniously worked out the correction. The review is also printed in Großmann-Vendrey, *Felix Mendelssohn Bartholdy*, p. 187, with the A-minor error retained. Großmann-Vendrey identifies the "Schmücke dich" setting as the less familiar BWV 759. Friedhold Bötel's analysis of Mendelssohn's repertory shows that he played BWV 654 quite frequently; see his *Mendelssohns Bach rezeption und ihre Konsequenzen, dargestellt an den Präludien und Fugen für Orgel, Op. 37*, Beiträge zur Musikforschung 14 (Munich: Katzbichler, 1984), 37–41, 43. Bötel also demonstrates that Mendelssohn preferred the "modern" organ built on Vogler's principles to a Baroque-style instrument (see pp. 27–31). See also Wolfgang Metzler, *Romantischer Orgelbau in Deutschland* (Ludwigsburg: E. F. Walcker, [1962]).

123. See note 122.

124. The remark about beginning solemnly and not escaping from the scene probably refers to the fact that this improvisation followed a service.

125. Presumably BWV 543.

126. *Musical World* 7/79 (15 September 1837), 8-10. The passage continues with the description of Mendelssohn's improvisation quoted above, p. 108 (note 104). These passages can also be found in Großmann-Vendrey, *Felix Mendelssohn Bartholdy*, 184–85.

127. *The Making of the Victorian Organ* (Cambridge: Cambridge University Press, 1990).

128. Thistlethwaite, 165–66. The quotations are from the *Musical World* 9 (1838), 210. The "wiry" and "crisp" characterization of Mendelssohn's playing of the organ music of others is supported by the articulation marks in his own music. For a study of these, see Carolyn Schott Haury, "Slur Markings in Mendelssohn's Organ Sonatas, Op. 65: A Study of the Earliest Prints and Manuscripts" (DMA thesis, University of Cincinnati, 1984).

129. *Musical World* 8 (1838), 101–2, quoted in Thistlethwaite, 167.

130. Letter of 21 June 1842; *Briefe 1833–1847*, 317.

131. Chorley, 1: 275; see above p. 110.

132. In his "Alexander Winterberger und das moderne Orgelspiel," *NZfM* 45/1 (1 July 1856), 1–3; repr. in *Ausgewählte Schriften* 1: 187–91.

133. Thistlethwaite, 181.

134. *Gesammelte Schriften*, 1: 339. It is probably no accident that the organ comes before the piano in this formulation.

135. Clara Schumann to Sir George Grove—about Mendelssohn as pianist, to be sure: "In his early days he had acquired perfection of technique; but latterly, as he often told me, he hardly ever practised, and yet he surpassed every one." Grove, *Beethoven, Schubert, Mendelssohn*, 374.

136. "Mendelssohns Oratorien-Praxis," 352.

137. See above, p. 106 and note 100.

138. *Aus siebzig Jahren*, 99–100.

139. 42/12 (18 March 1840), col. 241.

140. 38 (1 November 1897), 732.

141. 4 (1836), viii.

142. See above, p. 108–9, note 106.

143. *Geschichte der Gewandhausconcerte*, 85–86.

144. *Aus siebzig Jahren*, 58.

145. This document was presented to the Prussian government and is dated May 1841. I use the translation in Leonard Milton Phillips Jr., "The Leipzig Conservatory: 1843–1881" (Ph.D., diss. Indiana University, 1979), 81–82. The entire document is well worth reading. A portion is quoted in Bruno Hake, "Mendelssohn als Lehrer: mit bisher ungedruckten Briefen Mendelssohns an Wilhelm v. Boguslawski," *Deutscher Rundschau* 140 (July-September 1909), 453–70. There is a translation of the Hake article by Susan Gillespie in *Mendelssohn and His World*, ed. R. Larry Todd (Princeton: Princeton University Press, 1991), 310–37. Mendelssohn makes a strong statement against "the dominant positivistic, technical-material direction of the present time" in a famous letter about the Conservatory of 8 April 1840 to Johann Paul von Falkenstein; *Briefe 1833–1847*, 227–31.

146. Because of his duties in Berlin, Mendelssohn's residence in Leipzig was sporadic; at best he would have been hard pressed to function as de jure Director even if he had been willing to assume the official role.

147. 45/34 (25 August 1843), col. 624. Italian-language instruction was intended for singers. Of course, the apparent requirement for organists to participate in "quartet playing" arises from careless wording. The absence of instruction in orchestral instruments will be discussed in due course. The *AmZ* 46/45 (6 November 1844), col. 754, claimed that all instruments were taught, but this was either wholly untrue or true only to a very limited extent. In an essay in *Hochschule für Musik Leipzig gegründet als Conservatorium der Musik*, ed. Martin Wehnert, Johannes Forner, and Hansachim Schiller (Leipzig: n.p., [1968]), 13, Wehnert says,

> The goal of instruction was clearly set forth: There was to be no teaching of elementary material and skills, no gratification of the desire for merely pleasant playing for amusement or as an aspect of one's social standing, no tolerance for a mindless and one-sidedly artistic limitation on studies, but rather a musically universal, theoretical and practical, course of instruction with strict discipline and high artistic aims.

This book also offers the clearest available explanation of the financial and legal considerations involved in the conservatory's founding. See also Emil Kneschke, *Das Conservatorium der Musik in Leipzig: Seine Geschichte, seine Lehrer und Zöglinge. Festgabe zum 25jährigen Jubiläum am 2. April 1868* (Leipzig: Breitkopf & Härtel, 1868); *Das königliche Konservatorium der Musik zu Leipzig 1843–1918: Festschrift zum 75-jährigen Bestehen des Königl. Konservatoriums der Musik zu Leipzig am 2. April 1918* (Leipzig: Siegel, 1918); and, above all, a pamphlet issued by the Conservatory's Directorate in 1843, *Das Conservatorium der Musik in Leipzig*, Preface signed Leipzig, zu Michael [i.e., 29 September] 1843, Das Directorium des Conservatoriums der Musik (Leipzig: Breitkopf & Härtel, 1843). This last item is the Conservatory's official prospectus.

148. Strictly speaking, a "class" in this terminology is a level of attainment rather than a unit of a strictly time-bound progression; however, movement through the classes is normally at the rate of one class a year.

149. This is secondary instruction; the Conservatory did not train people who were primarily wind or double bass players at this time, and even the cello was not ranked with violin, piano, organ, and voice.

150. Michaelmas falls on 29 September.

151. After *Das Conservatorium der Musik*, as cited in note 147. Phillips, pp. 94–100, offers a complete translation of the text as taken from the *NZfM* 19/51 (25 December 1843), 201–4.

152. For more about this and for a discussion of the founding faculty members, see Johannes Forner, "Mendelssohns Mitstreiter am Leipziger Conservatorium," *Beiträge zur Musikwissenschaft* 14/3 (1972), 185–204.

153. 4/130 (29 October 1844), 519.

154. "Traditionen im Wandel der Zeit," in *Hochschule für Musik Leipzig*, 68.

155. See Arnold Schering, "Das öffentliche Musikbildungswesen in Deutschland bis zur Gründing des Leipziger Conservatories," *Festschrift zum 75-jährigen Bestehen*, 61–80; Martin Wolschke, *Von der Stadtpfeiferei zu Lehrlingskapelle und Sinfonieorchester: Wandlungen im 19. Jahrhundert*, Studien zur Musikgeschichte des 19. Jahrhunderts 59 (Regensburg: Bosse, 1981).

156. *Briefe 1833–1847*, 208–9.

157. *Pages from an Unwritten Diary* (London: Edward Arnold, 1914), 74. A footnote, same page, reads, "The Bishop of Limerick told me that in the course of a walk at Interlaken in 1847 Felix confided in him his deep regret at this failing."

158. Karl Mendelssohn, *Goethe and Mendelssohn*, trans. M. E. von Glehn, 2d ed. (London: Macmillan, 1874; repr. New York: Haskell House, 1970), 127–29. The letter is said to be dated "Leipzig, 15 March 1841" and was presumably written in English. Hauptmann did not come to Leipzig until 1842; something, then, is wrong. Nevertheless, a certain point is made, and that is what counts in the present context.

159. London: S. Low, Marston, 1895; it is extensively quoted in Phillips, pp. 110–13, from which I take my quotations.

160. "Classes" means just that. It appears that individual lessons were not given.

161. Quotations are taken from Phillips; see note 160. Phillips, 113–14, expresses justified reservations about "the views of a student overawed by admission to the Mendelssohn circle."

162. Lampadius, *Ein Denkmal*, 143. Lampadius also discusses the firmness and conscientiousness with which Mendelssohn dealt with questions of student behavior.

163. Ibid., *Ein Denkmal*, 144.

164. See note 145.

165. *Gesammelte Schriften*, 1: 336–37.

166. See Margaret Crum, *Catalogue of the Mendelssohn Papers in the Bodleian Library, Oxford*, vol. 1, *Correspondence of Felix Mendelssohn Bartholdy and Others* (Tutzing: Hans Schneider, 1980).

167. See the first epigraph.

HISTORICAL VIEWS AND DOCUMENTS

THE REGULATIONS OF THE LEIPZIG CONSERVATORY[1]

Translated by Leonard M. Phillips

¶1. The Conservatory of Music of Leipzig is dedicated to higher education in music and offers practical and theoretical instruction in all branches of music as a science and as an art.

¶2. The theoretical instruction consists of a complete course in the theory and composition of music, which may be completed in *three* years and comprises three levels. With the beginning of each new year, at Easter, a new course will be started so that students may enroll.

Those students who are qualified by possessing an already adequate theoretical knowledge may enroll in the upper levels and thus shorten the study of theory to less than three years. They may be obliged to audit the lower levels in order to understand the structure and method of the entire course.

The theoretical instruction consists of the following subjects:

a) harmony (in three levels);

Level III in the first year: harmony and voice-leading;

Level II in the second year: continuation of harmony with the addition of counterpoint;

Level I in the third year: continuation of harmony, study of double counterpoint and fugue;

b) form and composition are given in lectures which treat the following subjects: songs and instrumental works in the various forms and techniques; analysis of classical musical works; knowledge of instruments and instrumentation;

c) score-reading and conducting techniques;

d) The Italian language for those whose study is dedicated to singing.

In addition to the theoretical studies, there will be lectures on other musical subjects, e.g., the history of music (old and new periods), aesthetics, and acoustics (with experiments), etc.

For women there will be special classes in harmony designed to meet their needs. Completion of the study of harmony may be expected in the course of two years for women.

¶3. The practical instruction consists of training in mechanical dexterity on one of more of the following instruments or in singing, which will be offered on several levels and will comprise the following areas:

a) instruction in singing (solo and choral) in 2 levels;

b) instruction in instrumental playing:

1) pianoforte, in 3 levels;

2) organ, in 2 levels;

3) violin (solo, quartet, and orchestral playing), in three levels.

Also, there will be offered, under the auspices of the Directorium, instruction in the remaining instruments (violoncello, contrabass, and all wind instruments) for payment of a modest fee for those who desire such instruction.

¶4. In addition to the outlined instruction, the student is encouraged to take advantage of the following extracurricular opportunities:

a) attendance at rehearsal of the famous Gewandhaus Concerts, which consist of 20 programs during the winter season;

b) attendance at the quartet rehearsals and performances which take place every winter;

c) attendance at the famous choir of the Thomaskirche, which performs each Saturday and Sunday;

d) attendance at the performances at the Stadttheater.

In addition to these opportunities, the University and its various educational departments offer the student an opportunity to pursue a broad scientific education in all subjects.

¶5. For students interested in orchestral playing, opportunity will be given to perform overtures, symphonies, and accompaniments to large choral compositions in concerts. Those who prepare themselves as concert singers or players will be given the opportunity to appear publicly under the supervision of their individual teachers.

¶6. The instruction is entrusted to the thirteen teachers whose names and subjects are found at the end of this publication. The Inspector of the Institute is also named. His duty is to insure that all ordinances of the Directorium and the Faculty are carried out, that the classes are regularly attended, and above all, that the affairs of the Institute are conducted in the best possible manner.

¶7. The instruction of men and women is completely separate.

¶8. The complete course of music theory lasts, as is indicated in ¶2, for three years and can be shortened only under the specific terms. For instruction in singing or instruments, no specific time period is given, since that depends upon the greater or lesser development and talent of the individual student.

No student may be admitted for less than one year, and those who leave earlier, except when illness is the cause, are obligated to pay the stated tuition for the whole year, which is binding upon the parents or guardian at the time of enrollment. (See the attached enrollment form below.)

¶9. According to the rules, new students may enter the Conservatory only at Easter of each year, at which time the lower levels of a new course begin. The date for enrollment as well as dates for the required entrance examinations will be announced in local and foreign newspapers and musical journals. Foreign students may enter also at Michaelmas [late September] provided they have considerable theoretical knowledge and can conform to the aforementioned rules.

¶10. The following are prerequisites for the admittance of foreign students.

a) They must possess a general school education and must be acquainted with normal classroom procedures.

b) They must be adept enough in the German language to understand lectures. If this is not the case, they must acquire this ability in German through private instruction at their own expense.

c) They must possess true talent and, upon enrollment, demonstrable musical knowledge (of notation, rhythm, adequate ability on the keyboard, the violin, or in singing). Moreover, foreign students must have the specific recommendations of former teachers.

d) Those who wish to dedicate themselves to the study of singing must possess good and teachable voices. Those of doubtful health or those entering during the period of change of voice must obtain permission for vocal activity from the school physician.

e) No student will be admitted without the signed permission of his or her parent or guardian. (See attached enrollment form.)

f) Each student must be able to prove his moral upbringing through creditable testimony of his parents and earlier teachers.

g) Foreign students must have the necessary passport or permit valid for the duration of residency.

¶11. Every prospective student of the Conservatory must take an examination before a special committee prior to enrollment. At that time it will be determined if the student possesses enough talent and musical knowledge to be admitted. In order that practical performance may be judged, each applicant must bring a well-practiced piece of music (for pianoforte, organ, violin, or voice), which will be performed by the student before the committee prior to enrollment. Those who have already engaged in the writing of music and have produced their own compositions should send these, postage paid, to the Directorium before enrollment or submit them prior to the time of the examination.

¶12. Every enrolled student must abide by the following Disciplinary Rules and pledge the fulfillment of the same by the shaking of hands to confirm the vows indicated by his personal signature.

a) No student of the Conservatory may miss a class without a satisfactory excuse.

b) Each student is subject to instruction of his or her teacher.

c) Every student, without regard to the instrument to which he wishes to dedicate his study, must take the regular classes in thoroughbass, keyboard, and choral singing. Only the faculty can suspend this rule in individual cases.

d) Instruction in solo singing is open only to those who wish to become singers, and the judgment of the individual teacher will determine who qualifies for a particular level.

e) No student is permitted, so long as he is enrolled in a department of the Conservatory and has not graduated, to appear on his own initiative in a public place as a member of an orchestra, a soloist, or a singer. Only the Directorium may suspend this rule in individual cases at the special wish of the student's teacher.

f) The success of the aims of the Conservatory is dependent upon the moral conduct of the students, and the Directorium maintains that it is the duty of the individual student not to lose sight of these aims outside the Institution. Immoral conduct and other infringements of the contract will be treated with severity by the Directorium, and the judgment in cases of repetition will result in dismissal from the Conservatory.

¶13. Instruction is given throughout the year with the exception of Sundays and Fridays and the following holidays and vacations:

a) Easter—eight days from Maundy Thursday through Wednesday after Easter;

b) Pentecost—eight days, viz. the complete Pentecost week;

c) summer vacation—four weeks in July and August; the beginning will be determined each year;

d) Michaelmas—eight days, October 1–7;

e) Christmas—eight days, from December 25 to January 1.

Those students who do not travel during the vacations should take advantage of the time for study and submit lessons to the individual teacher, which they have prepared during the vacation times.

¶14. At the end of each Quarter, at Easter, St. John's Day, Michaelmas, and Christmas, a general examination will take place in the presence of the Directorium and the Faculty. The progress of the individual student will be judged, and recommendations will be made. Industry will be praised and laziness will be reprimanded. At Easter and Michaelmas the chief examinations [*Hauptprüfungen*] will include invitations to friends of the Conservatory who are knowledgeable in music. At the examinations only the work of exceptional students will be presented.

¶15. Upon leaving the Conservatory each student will receive a certificate [*Lehrer-Zeugniss*] from the Directorium, on which the duration and success of study will be recorded and the level of education attained will be indicated.

¶16. The tuition for the complete course of study, with the exception of ¶3 (the study of orchestral instruments other than the violin), is 80 thalers per year, which is payable quarterly at 20 thalers at the office of the Conservatory. Also, each student must pay a 3-thaler admission fee to the library (once) and 1 thaler yearly for maintenance of the building.

¶17. There exist six scholarships for native Saxons, given by His Majesty the King, which are awarded each year; they are available to mature and promising students and may be renewed for two or three years. The scholarship students, who must have special certification of their need, receive the complete instruction without payment and have only to pay the 3-thaler library fee and the 1-thaler annual maintenance fee.

The scholarship students are equal in all things to the other students.

¶18. Each student must provide his own instrument and music for practice as well as the necessary text books required by the teachers for instruction at the Institutions. In the case of pianofortes, such instruments may be rented from local concerns.

Special Remarks

The cost of living in Leipzig is on a par with other cities of like size and depends upon the demands of the individual. In addition to the yearly 84 thalers need for tuition and fees, the student needs an additional 200 to 300 thalers. A dwelling—a small room with necessary furnishings—costs 15 to 25 thalers yearly; a room and a bedroom costs 20 to 50 thalers; a bed, if not included in the price, adds around 10 thalers. For midday meals, one pays 3 to 7 neugroschen daily.

Many students, especially women students, find that it is more convenient and economical to live with a family, where they will be treated as family members and pay 10 [*sic*] to 250 thalers annually for room, furniture, meals, laundry, etc. The Directorium is ready to recommend upstanding families who accept students. Such requests should be made at least four weeks prior to arrival in Leipzig.

The normal monthly rental price for an upright pianoforte is from 1 to 2½ thalers; for a grand piano from 1½ to 3⅔ thalers, according to the condition of the instrument. If one should prefer to purchase an instrument for the duration of his studies and find that he cannot afford a new instrument, advertisements appear daily in the local newspapers for the sale of used instruments at more modest prices. Oftentimes the instrument may be sold for a small profit later.

There are local music stores which give the student the opportunity to become acquainted with old and new compositions of every type, which may be purchased by the student.

Questions and written applications should be directed in post-paid letters to the Directorium of the Conservatory of Music at Leipzig.

* *

Application Form

I, the undersigned, declare herewith,

1) that my son (daughter) *Name* . . . . . . seeks to enter the Conservatory of Music at Leipzig with my permission;

2) that I will pay the stated tuition quarterly and that the complete tuition for the first complete year, even in the case that my son (daughter) leaves the institution during this time for any reason other than illness, will be paid;

3) that I will provide necessary support for my son (daughter) for the academic year, as well as for the procurement of an instrument and the necessary music and text books.

. . . ., on . . . . 184 . .

Signature . . . .

* *

Directorium, Faculty, and Other Persons Employed
by the Conservatory
Directorium

v. Falkenstein   Dr. Keil, chairman   Dr. Seeburg

Fr. Kistner   Conr. Schleinitz

Physician of the Institute: Herr Professor Dr. Wendler,
Royal District Physician

Ordentliche Lehrer und Lehrerin[2]

Mad. Bünau-Grabau: Voice Instruction for Women.

Herr Organist Carl F. Becker: Organ Playing and Lectures on Musical
   Subjects

Herr Concertmaster Ferdinand David: Violin Playing.

Herr Musikdirektor Moritz Hauptmann: Harmony and Composition.

Herr Musikdirektor Ferdinand Hiller: Exercises in Composition, in
   Instrumental Playing and Solo Singing, and Analysis of Classical
   Literature.[3]

Herr Dr. Robert Schumann: Pianoforte Playing, Exercises in Composition and
   Score-Reading.

Ausserordentliche Lehrer

Herr Ferdinand Böhme: Voice Instruction for Men.

Herr Giovanni Battista Ghezzi: Italian Language and Diction.

Herr Moritz Klengel: Violin Playing.

Herr Musikdirektor Ernst Ferdinand Richter: Harmony.

Herr Rudolph Sachse: Violin Playing.

Herr Ernst Ferdinand Wenzel: Piano Playing.

Inspector: Herr Carl Grenser.

Institutional Janitor: Johann Gottfried Quasdorf.[4]

A POSTSCRIPT ABOUT THE STATUTES OF THE LEIPZIG CONSERVATORY

Donald Mintz

Leonard Phillips's translation of the Leipzig Conservatory statutes is based on
a text that appeared in Schumann's *Neue Zeitschrift für Musik* for 25 December
1843. A footnote informs us that the text follows "the statutes just issued by the
Directorium."[5]

The New York Public Library has a copy of these statutes in brochure form
(shelf mark Drexel 683), which deserves a full citation: "*Das Conservatorium der
Musik in Leipzig.* 14 + [4] pp. On p. [16]: 'Druck von Breitkopf und Härtel in
Leipzig.' Foreword (p. 4) dated and signed: 'Leipzig, zu Michael 1843. Das
Directorium des Conservatoriums der Musik.'" Though the paper has become
brittle, the copy is otherwise pristine and includes a coupon for parents to sign,
permitting their minor child to register at the conservatory, guaranteeing payment,
and so on.

One might reasonably expect that the *NZfM* text would follow (and presumably
be identical with) the text of this brochure. Not so. There are a number of
differences, some—indeed most—of apparently little consequence, but a few
suggesting interesting changes in the life of the young institution.

Clearly, there is a *terminus ad quem* for the *NZfM* version. But when did the
New York Public Library brochure actually appear? Is, as one may begin to
suspect, the date on the introductory statement erroneously carried over from earlier

versions? The way to answer the question may be found by comparing the faculty list in the brochure with the lists appearing from time to time in the *Ankündigungen* coming at the end of many issues of the *Allgemeine musikalische Zeitung* and also with the known facts of the life of one of the most prominent faculty members.

The first date on which the brochure and *AmZ* lists agree is 26 August 1846 (Jg. 48, No. 34, cols. 583-84), and the key figure is the pianist and composer Ignaz Moscheles (1794-1870). Moscheles appears here for the first time; his name is missing from the list published a bit earlier in the *Ankündigungen* of 18 February of the same year (Jg. 48, No. 7, cols. 127-28). Moscheles arrived in Leipzig on 21 October 1846;[6] his firm engagement necessarily preceded that date by some months.[7] It thus becomes clear that the *NZfM* version translated by Phillips, while not necessarily the very first one, antedates the New York Public Library version by some years, initial appearances to the contrary (including, of course, the date at its beginning) notwithstanding.

Now a brief look at some of the more significant differences between the two versions.

§ 4 a) of the *NZfM* version announces that among the educational opportunities available to students beyond the Conservatory is "Theilnahme an den Proben" of the Gewandhaus Orchestra. "Theilnahme" is a bit ambiguous; conceivably, it could refer to sitting in. The next paragraph, offering "Theilnahme" in "Quartett-Proben und Aufführungen," makes clear that admittance, not participation, is what is meant. Nevertheless, in the later version "Theilnahme" disappears. But so do the rehearsals. A simple listing of the major musical events of a Leipzig season (not including the Euterpe concerts) is all that is left. One may speculate about the reasons for the change.

§ 5 of the *NZfM* version promises students who are preparing for solo careers the opportunity to appear in public. The later revision says merely that such students will be prepared for public concerts. One would hope so.

§ 14 of the *NZfM* version announces quarterly public juries. The later version makes them semiannual. Modern music department faculty members will no doubt prepare their own commentaries about this change. The early version of § 14 also stated that student compositions would be performed on these occasions; the later text drops this commitment.

Other changes are administrative and have the collective effect of creating tighter discipline. They offer a brief and discreet peep through the keyhole.

It remains to be added that instruction on orchestral instruments was not given at the Leipzig Conservatory for some time after the period we are concerned with, though it was available at similar institutions elsewhere, in Prague and Paris, for example. It appears that in Leipzig such instruction was controlled by the guilds until well into the second half of the century. One may assume that the Directorium of the Conservatory did not want to take on that power structure—or perhaps was willing to continue to view these instruments and their practitioners as outside the world of real, first-class modern musicians. Or perhaps a bit of each.

NOTES

1. The following text is translated from the *Neue Zeitschrift für Musik* 19/51 (25 December 1843), 201–4. For further observations about the continuing history of these statutes, see the Postscript by Donald Mintz at the conclusion of this translation.

2. The terms *ordentlich* and *asserordentlich*, borrowed from the university parlance of the time, were used to distinguish faculty rank. The former, being the higher, denoted the privilege of a vote in the administration of the university, whereas the latter had no such privilege. See Friedrich Paulsen, *The German University: Past and Present* (New York: Charles Scribner's Sons, 1909), 79.

3. Ferdinand Hiller assumed Mendelssohn's place on the faculty with his appointment as interim director of the Gewandhaus Concerts.

4. Johann Gottfried Quasdorf, former servant of Heinrich Blümner, became a beloved figure at the Conservatory. Affectionately known as "old Quasdorf," his death was reported in *Dwight's Journal of Music* 34 (1875), 407. His son, Richard Paul Quasdorf, enrolled in the Conservatory in 1864 and joined the faculty in 1883. See Karl Whistling, *Statistik des Königlichen Conservatorium der Musik zu Leipzig: 1843–1883* (Leipzig: Breitkopf & Härtel, [1883]), vi, 21.

5. "Mittheilung aus den so eben vom Directorium veröffentlichten Statuten."

6. Felix Mendelssohn Bartholdy, *Letters of Felix Mendelssohn to Ignaz and Charlotte Moscheles*, trans. Felix Moscheles (Boston: Ticknor and Co., 1888), 282.

7. "Hurrah! your decision is taken, you are coming! Let every one of these lines rejoice," writes Mendelssohn on 11 February. Ibid., 265. [The German version actually reads: "Lieber Freund! Diese Zeilen sollen nichts tun, als jubeln über den Brief, der uns den Entschluß Deines Kommens brachte." Felix Mendelssohn Bartholdy, *Briefe von Felix Mendelssohn-Bartholdy an Ignaz und Charlotte Moscheles*, ed. Felix Moscheles (Leipzig: Duncker & Humblot, 1888), 256.—Ed.]

4

Mendelssohn's Dramatic Music

Douglass Seaton

Mendelssohn's success as a composer certainly did not depend on his compositions for the stage.[1] Yet throughout most of his career he wrote dramatic works or was planning such works. From the earliest period of his composing comes a little dramatic scene in French, "Quel bonheur pour mon coeur," left incomplete; from the last months of 1847 stem the few pieces on which he was working for the unfinished opera *Die Lorelei*. Between the two came a series of domestic dramas composed for his family home in Berlin, his one public production of an opera, a few bits of incidental music for plays in Düsseldorf and Leipzig, any number of attempts to identify a suitable opera libretto, and incidental music for four major productions in the royal theater in Potsdam and subsequently the public theater in Berlin.

Throughout Mendelssohn's activity as a stage composer three threads run. The first is the weaving of his stage works through his life in both personal and professional spheres. Second is the question of his abilities and the suitability of his musical style to these genres. Third is the problem of the values involved in his worldview and the effect they had on his stage-composing career.

Although the composer's career was not built on his stage works, one might nevertheless argue that these works, together with his generally limited output and success in stage genres, hold a determining place in his career. The early, domestic dramas not only represent an important phase and spirit in his biography but also functioned as a testing ground for one aspect of his talent. *Die Hochzeit des Camacho* marked a crucial moment in his maturation and partly conditioned his attitudes toward opera and the direction of his own career and style. His compulsive, but problematic, search for a libretto reveals much about his artistic and cultural values. The incidental music holds a special place in his oeuvre, as a genre closely suited to his principles, talents, and limitations.

EARLIEST DRAMATIC WORKS

The young Felix Mendelssohn first tried his hand at dramatic composition in the music notebook that included many of his earliest independent compositions.[2] The pieces in this volume belong to his student years, but they include works that cannot be regarded as mere studies. The fragmentary scene "Quel bonheur pour mon coeur," apparently his first attempt at a dramatic musical style, dates from 7 March 1820, shortly after Felix's eleventh birthday. It begins with a passage in recitative style but without words. There follows an aria on a text that extols the joys of an amorous life, set in 3/8 meter in the key of G major. The singer is identified as "Vermeille." A second character, "Lubin," is also called for. This is succeeded by a series of brief numbers in operatic style, again without text, but despite this considerable amount of work the experiment was quickly abandoned.

Another early dramatic endeavor was a *Posse* (burlesque or farce) that Lea Mendelssohn, Felix's mother, translated and adapted from the French *L'homme automate*. Lea reported to her cousin Henriette von Pereira-Arnstein that Felix had created an overture for this amusing diversion, a pastiche of popular folk songs.[3] No music can be identified for this overture. It even seems possible, since Lea employed the verb "gemacht" (rather than, e.g., "componiert" or "geschrieben"), that he simply improvised it.

The boy composer's next written dramatic music, dating from mid-1820, consisted of a "Lustspiel" intended to be in three scenes.[4] Given the conditions under which Mendelssohn's later dramatic works were first performed, this may have been planned as an entertainment for a birthday party or some similar event.[5] It remained unfinished, however, with only the first scene complete, the second begun but crossed out, and the third apparently never composed. The Mendelssohn family banking house forms the drama's setting. In the first number, a duet for tenor and bass, the proprietors, explicitly Felix's uncle and father, introduce themselves ("Ich J. Mendelssohn—Ich A. Mendelssohn") in a simple duet that celebrates family ties in an up-tempo section and then turns to a slow, lyric style as the brothers swear eternal friendship. They have hardly made this pledge before an argument erupts over their musical tastes—specifically, about their conflicting opinions of Spontini's *Olympie*.[6] No sooner has this argument passed than a tenor enters, looking for backers for a concert. The brothers reject his solicitation and throw him out, whereupon he sings a fantastic—not to say parodistic—version of a stock "rage" aria, with a text beginning "Götter, welche Schande" ("Ye gods, what a disgrace"). The second scene, still in the bank, begins with a scene in which a good-for-nothing office employee arouses the fury of an entire chorus of clerks.

These early and fragmentary efforts demonstrate, first of all, that Mendelssohn's interest and ability in dramatic music started at the very outset of his career.[7] Moreover, their clear attachment to his own family and home situation represents the context in which his first completed stage works were soon to arise. There is nothing particularly original within the musical style itself; nevertheless, the youthful composer here worked through elements of the dramatic idiom:

recitative and aria styles, expressive types for lyrical and virtuosic singing, duets of both agreement and disagreement, choral scenes, and the dramatic overture.

THE DOMESTIC SINGSPIELE

Die Soldatenliebschaft

Between late 1820 and the middle of 1822 the young Mendelssohn composed three complete stage works on librettos prepared for him by a family friend, the young doctor Johann Ludwig Casper (1796–1814). A native of Berlin, Casper completed his medical degree in Halle in 1819 and then returned to his native city. He later earned a considerable reputation as a pioneer in forensic pathology.[8] In a letter to Henrietta von Pereira-Arnstein, Lea Mendelssohn referred to Casper as the family's "Hausdichter."[9] Besides his avocation as a writer Casper had some ability as an actor and singer, for he participated as performer in some of Mendelssohn's productions.

Casper's first efforts, at least, were simply translations of popular French vaudevilles, a genre with which he had become familiar during his travels in France. The model for the earliest, Die Soldatenliebschaft, remains unknown, but Felix clearly identified it as a translation in a letter to Casper dated 2 August 1820: "How grateful I am to you for the lovely operetta! I will do my best to compose it so as to do credit to the translation. I already have the scheme in my head."[10] The plot, though laid in Spain during the French occupation in the early nineteenth century, depends on a situation distantly reminiscent of Mozart's Die Entführung aus dem Serail; here the French officer Felix (tenor) loves a young Spanish duchess named Elvire (coloratura soprano), who is protected by Tonio (baritone). Both Tonio and the French soldier Victor (tenor) are enamored of Elvire's maid Zerbine (lyric soprano). The characters obviously come from the stock for comic opera, and the plot, which naturally resolves the different romantic troubles, relies on common devices of the genre as well, including a tryst scene for Felix and Elvire observed by Victor hiding in a tree.

Mendelssohn's music demonstrates that he already had a firm grasp of the conventions of this sort of Singspiel.[11] His musical characterizations, though they do not create especially three-dimensional figures, succeed in identifying the types to which the characters belong. Tonio has a "rondo" (no. 4)[12] that—although dramatically he functions more like Osmin—sets him in the same comic, unsophisticated tradition as Papageno. Zerbine, as she is represented by her "Ariette" (no. 6) with cello obbligato, belongs to the type of maid represented by Susanna in Le nozze di Figaro.[13] Elvire's more noble and romantic spirit is expressed in her cavatina "Still und freundlich ist die Nacht" (no. 10), in which the atmosphere of the woods at night as she awaits her lover is well conveyed by the orchestration for strings and echoing woodwinds (see Example 4.1). The boy composer obviously enjoyed writing military music for the hussar Victor, as well.

Example 4.1
Die Soldatenliebschaft, **no. 10, mm. 1–12**

Beyond portraying the individual characters, Mendelssohn also had the opportunity to tackle the problems of composing music for the contrasting emotions of characters within ensemble numbers. The task confronted him immediately in the first vocal piece, a duet for Felix and Tonio. He wrote to Casper, "Of the first duet I can say: 'C'est tout fait, il n'y a qu'à l'écrire.' ['It is all done, nothing is left but to write it down.'] For I have worked it all out in my head already. I am especially pleased with Tonio's 'Ha, ha, I don't believe it' [Hä, hä, glaub's nicht], for example, how he doesn't believe that he is crazy."[14] At the end of the opera there comes an effective contrast trio for Felix and Elvire, with Victor in the tree.

The first performance of *Die Soldatenliebschaft* took place in 1820, on Abraham Mendelssohn's birthday, 11 December, entering into a continuing family tradition. This performance had accompaniment by piano only, but for Felix's next birthday, his twelfth, on 3 February 1821, it was performed with full orchestra.[15]

Die beiden Pädagogen

Casper's second collaboration with Felix Mendelssohn came hard on the heels of the first and apparently arose from Abraham's encouragement. Felix wrote in a letter, "At one of the rehearsals [of *Die Soldatenliebschaft*] Father went into the adjoining room with Dr. Casper, who translated both texts freely from the French, and in a little while they called me in, and Father said that Dr. Casper would set the second for me, and that I should have it ready for mother's birthday, 15 March."[16] The subject, quite possibly Abraham's own choice, came from a satirical comedy by Eugène Scribe, *Les deux précepteurs, ou Asinus asinum fricat*, which had first been performed in Paris in 1817.[17] The title became *Die beiden Pädagogen*, and the German names of the principal characters were transliterated from their French counterparts (i.e., Elise remained unchanged, Roberville became Robert, Charles became Carl, Jeannette became Hannchen), except for those of the two pedants: the genuine, but old-fashioned, Kinderschreck and the impostor Luftig. The pedagogical models whose theories were contrasted in Scribe's original plot were Rousseau and Voltaire; for the Casper-Mendelssohn work they became the North German educational reformer Johann Bernhard Basedow (1723–1790) and the Swiss educator Johann Heinrich Pestalozzi (1746–1827).

The twelve-year-old Felix Mendelssohn was thus already aware of current education theories and pedagogical methods, while other children of his age would merely have been their unconscious subjects or beneficiaries. Basedow took an essentially pragmatic approach to education, emphasizing the cultivation of practical skills for the business of daily life. He stressed study from nature, physical education, manual training, and the use of games as practical applications for educational precepts. Pestalozzi also espoused the idea that learning should be intellectual, moral, and physical and that students should study the "concrete arts." In addition, he worked toward learning based on developing children's individual talents and teaching them to think for themselves. It seems not unlikely that such ideas were discussed in the Mendelssohn household, given the parents' self-conscious devotion to the education of Felix and his sisters and brother. Indeed, we might easily imagine that Felix would have noted a parallelism between Abraham's pragmatic attitudes and those of Basedow, Lea's cultivation of creativity and that of Pestalozzi.

Mendelssohn began composing *Die beiden Pädagogen* on or about 24 January 1821 and completed it on 14 March[18] in order to have it ready for performance on his mother's birthday. It was sung through on the following day, as Felix reported in a letter of 22 March.[19] Devrient describes another performance, in early 1822, in which he played Kinderschreck; his wife, Therese, sang the role of the servant girl Hannchen; and Dr. Casper took the part of the feigned pedagogue Luftig.[20]

Die beiden Pädagogen shows some clear advances in Mendelssohn's theatrical skills over *Die Soldatenliebschaft*. In the arias, first of all, the characters no longer seem to belong merely to stock traditions but take on more individual and appealingly subtle personalities. In all cases they come across in their music as more likable than cardboard characters would be. In her aria no. 1 Hannchen sings that love loves freedom, but she does not seem to belong to the amoral type of servant-girl character represented by Despina in Mozart's *Così fan tutte*; that is, her song never approaches the risqué, due to the sentimental lyricism in its melody and harmony. The backward and self-important pedagogue Kinderschreck, in his aria no. 4, appears pompous as he promotes the application of the switch as the best method to get pupils to work, but he is not mean; the rhythm blusters, and the vocal line refers to the smack of the rod, but the listener probably believes that he would only slap a desk for attention rather than beat a child. Luftig's first ariette (no. 6) portrays him as carefree and flighty; his line hardly appears concerned to make a coherent melody, and the responding interludes from the woodwind choir seem to symbolize the way that he manipulates his environment. Later, in his aria no. 9, he laughs at himself, and his good nature is reflected in the jolly melody and rhythm in diatonic major context.

The ensembles suggest that Mendelssohn had learned something from Mozart's practices. No. 2 is a contrast ensemble for the pair of lovers Elise and Carl, who sing in a lyrical, amorous style, and Hannchen, who comments comically on their naiveté (see Example 4.2). A few turns to minor harmonies give a sentimental shading that warms and rounds the protagonists. Another contrast ensemble is the duet no. 5 for Kinderschreck and Hannchen; as the teacher finds his ambitions frustrated, he indulges in increasing bluster, while his niece Hannchen laughs at him with the audience.

In the trio no. 7 Mendelssohn took another step. This is not just a contrast ensemble but an action ensemble, in which Hannchen finally gets Luftig to join in her melodic material as he admits their earlier relationship; at the end of their exchange comes a striking harmonic surprise, the deceptive resolution from the dominant to the flat submediant (V/B$\flat$→G$\flat$) with the whole orchestra *forte* in unison, as Robert enters and discovers them.

Example 4.2
Die beiden Pädagogen, no. 2, mm. 40–46

Another action ensemble is the penultimate quartet and chorus, in which the young people hold a party while Robert and Kinderschreck are absent. In the course of the number they conscript (actually blackmail) Luftig to play the violin for their dancing.

In the most discussed ensemble in *Die beiden Pädagogen*, no. 8, Luftig, the feigned tutor, begins by trying to bluff his way through a conversation about pedagogical methods. When he pretends to have forgotten the name of a famous author, Carl suggests the name of Basedow, and Luftig latches onto it single-mindedly, while Kinderschreck insists on favoring Pestalozzi. Their bickering leads to the conventional comic device of turning words into nonsense syllables by repetition at fast tempo (at mm. 57–58 Kinderschreck has "Pest-, Pest-, Pest-," the play on the syllable serving as well in German as in English). This reaches its most effective point when Luftig's long "Ba—" is contrasted to Kinderschreck's rapid-fire repetitions of "Pestalozzi" at the number's end. Devrient and Casper greatly enjoyed playing these roles.[21]

The finale is a chorus in which all the characters agree to let bygones be bygones and resolve on a happy ending. For this, curiously, Mendelssohn adopted not a typical buffo style but instead a sort of celebratory hymn style with moments of ecclesiastical-sounding fugato (see Example 4.3). The rhythm broadens from quarter notes to majestic half and whole notes at the end. The violins, meanwhile, keep up a running perpetual motion in eighth notes. The whole concludes with a brief, fanfarelike postlude in the orchestra.

Die wandernden Komödianten

The third effort of Casper and Mendelssohn came with *Die wandernden Komödianten*, composed during the autumn of 1821.[22] A decisive event in Mendelssohn's music-theatrical experience occurred between *Die beiden Pädagogen* and *Die wandernden Komödianten*, the premiere in Berlin on 18 June 1821 of Carl Maria von Weber's *Der Freischütz*. The young Mendelssohn's enthusiasm for Weber's music is reported by Weber's pupil Julius Benedict, whom Mendelssohn met and pumped for advance examples of music from the opera.[23] Heinrich Eduard Jacob recounts the story of the twelve-year-old composer's shyness and refusal to share a carriage with the creator of the great "German Romantic opera" (Weber's classification) but racing home on foot to greet him.[24] More practical recognition of Weber's greatness was the influence that his music gradually came to exert on Mendelssohn's style thereafter.

The score of *Die wandernden Komödianten* bears a title page formally acknowledging the librettist. The spoken text, as with the earlier Singspiele, survives in the Bodleian Library, Oxford.[25]

The plot of *Die wandernden Komödianten* depends on several standard devices, including unpayable debts and legal shenanigans, disguises and mistaken identities, a play-within-the-play (and in this case the action of the outer play wanders into the interior performance), and a happy ending worked out by what amounts to more or less a deus ex machina maneuver. The situations are entirely comic, with no real occasion for romantic or even sentimental expression.

The overture, a standard comic-opera curtain-raiser, is kicked off by a triadic "rocket" arpeggio. The main contrast of material takes place between the strings, which play energetically chugging eighth notes, and the winds, which respond with soft, scalar phrases.

Example 4.3
Die beiden Pädagogen, **Finale, mm. 1–17, chorus**

Mendelssohn's skill at characterization in ensembles found a perfect vehicle in the trio that introduces three members of the traveling theater troupe, the jolly Fröhlich, the timid Hasenfuß, and the overly dramatic poet Fixfinger. Fixfinger opens the ensemble by praising his own newly written verses, which turn out to be of a rather overblown, Sturm und Drang type; Fröhlich sings drunken praises of women, dice, and wine; and Hasenfuß tries to get Fixfinger to be quiet (see

Example 4.3, continued

Example 4.4). By contrast, in no. 3, when the three connive not to pay their bar bill, Mendelssohn gave them an imitative passage, in which each insists on being allowed to treat the others, with the result that none pays (see Example 4.5).

Mendelssohn's comic sense produced not only clever music to set the humorous text but also jokes with musical styles and genres themselves. Especially effective is the scene in which the villains of the piece, the judges Schwarzauge and Holzbein, both intending to capture the stage director Flink, blunder about in the darkness and arrest each other. Here Mendelssohn employed a *parlando* style within a *tempo giusto* to suggest the tiptoeing of the two in the dark. When the two judges are frustrated, their parts turn into comic anger, expressed in a parody of florid "rage" style. Mendelssohn's sense for humorous parody is also revealed in the little overture that he provided for the play within the play, which opens with written-out, violin-tuning fifths.

Critical reaction to *Die wandernden Komödianten* has been mixed, but favorable or unfavorable, it focuses on the constantly comic tone of the piece. For Georg Schünemann, in his extended article "Mendelssohns Jugendopern" of 1922–1923, this work was distinguished by its consistency and by the fact that the story accommodated the twelve-year-old composer's talents, which were not well suited to romantic lyricism but excellent for comedy.[26] For John Warrack, however, it lacks variety: almost all the roles are for men, only two arias contrast with the several ensembles, and the music employs almost entirely duple meters and major keys.[27] Thomas Krettenauer mentions the near absence of cantabile singing in favor of comic *parlando*.[28] All, however, agree that in regard to animated action and stage effect *Die wandernden Komödianten* shows that Mendelssohn had developed a remarkable ability in theatrical music.

Example 4.4
Die wandernden Komödianten, no. 1, mm. 17–41, Vocal Parts

Die beiden Neffen

The last Singspiel on which Mendelssohn and Casper worked together was *Die beiden Neffen*.[29]   *Die beiden Neffen* has broader dimensions than its three forerunners, being laid out in three acts. Unfortunately, the libretto (of which only the first two acts seem to have survived[30]) does not really contain three acts' worth of interest. A work of such scope may have exceeded Casper's capabilities. The

Example 4.5
Die wandernden Komödianten, **no. 3, mm. 8–14, Vocal Parts**

usual criticism of the libretto is that the significant action is compressed into the first act (and particularly into a single dialogue scene),[31] leaving too little dramatic action for the second and third acts.

Despite the book's weaknesses, however, the music shows that the composer had developed new strengths. He undertook to raise his style from that of the conventional comic Singspiel to one more genuinely operatic. That he took much longer over his work and approached the composition more self-consciously than in his earlier efforts is clearly shown by his careful dating of the various numbers as they were composed:

Act 1	No. 1	1 May 1822
	Nos. 2-3	21 June 1822
	No. 4	Darmstadt, 24 June 1822
	No. 5	Schaffhausen, 29 July—Lausanne, 11 September 1822
Act 2	No. 6	12 November–14 December 1822
	end	Berlin, 4 March 1823

Act 3   12 March–6 November 1823
Overture   25 October 1823

Mendelssohn's increasing skill as an opera composer is evident in his greater control over the dramatic progress of action ensembles. In no. 2 Carl (tenor) returns from Boston and hides with Fanny and her maid Lisette (sopranos); the music proceeds convincingly from the pleasure of their meeting through their panic as Carl's pursuers approach and the women hide him in a chest. No. 4, a quartet in which Colonel Felsig (bass), abetted by his officer Lauber (bass), interrogates Fanny about Carl's whereabouts, while Lisette mocks the men, builds to an effective climax with four characters clearly delineated. Similarly successful is the quintet in which Carl and his brother Theodor (tenor), plotting with Fanny and Lisette, are discovered by Lauber. The young women express consternation, Lauber gloats, and Carl and Theodor try to get rid of him.

Even more significant than the progress that Mendelssohn made in constructing ensembles is a new and more operatic quality in the melodic material. Whereas in *Die Soldatenliebschaft, Die beiden Pädagogen*, and *Die wandernden Komödianten* the predominant styles had been buffo *parlando* and sentimental song, in *Die beiden Neffen* Mendelssohn composed a vocal style that genuinely belongs to Romantic opera. One hears in these pieces the influence of both Mozart (in Tamino's and Pamina's arias from *Die Zauberflöte*) and Weber (in *Der Freischütz*). Carl's aria no. 3 opens in a romantic-tenor style and develops into a conventional bravura solo. More lyrical, cantabile melodies than any Mendelssohn had managed in earlier works occur in no. 1, a duet for the two women, and in Fanny's third-act aria.

Die beiden Neffen had its first performance on Felix's fifteenth birthday, 3 February 1824, at the Mendelssohn home.[32] It was on this occasion that his mentor Zelter proclaimed him no longer an apprentice but a member of the fraternity of composers "in the name of Mozart, in the name of Haydn, and in the name of old Bach."[33] This recognition meant a great deal, certainly more than that Mendelssohn had reached a defining age or demonstrated mastery of compositional technique. Rather, it acknowledged that he had attained a style of his own and belonged to the new era of Romanticism, a style beyond what could be learned of harmony and counterpoint and an era beyond the ken of Zelter.

Among Mendelssohn's music to this point the dramatic pieces hold a special place. Keyboard, chamber, and orchestral pieces, as well as vocal works such as chorales and compositions in church style, all grew more or less directly from his study pieces.[34] The dramatic works appear to have been conceived and carried out independently; Zelter did not have experience in this genre and certainly did not try to train his protégé in it. The one-act Singspiele stemmed not from his teacher's direction but from Felix's desire to compose for his own self-fulfillment and for his audience's pleasure. These works did not attempt to master compositional problems but served for practical occasions within the musical life of his family and social situation. In them, more than in his other works of these years, he acted decisively as a composer rather than as a music student.

This is not to say that Mendelssohn did not learn from these dramatic works. He clearly grew as a composer for the musical theater over the five years from his earliest attempts to *Die beiden Neffen*. In taking on a three-act libretto after his earlier one-acts, he must have been conscious of moving forward to a full-size project. Despite the inadequacy of the libretto, he achieved much in that effort. Not without reason he seems to have believed, as Zelter must have believed, that he was ready to attempt a major operatic production in a public venue.

DIE HOCHZEIT DES CAMACHO

Having thus composed two early fragments (possibly three, if the *Posse* mentioned by Lea Mendelssohn represents an actual composition) and four complete domestic Singspiele, the not-yet-fifteen-year-old Mendelssohn undertook a more ambitious project, the composing of a full-length opera for the public stage. The subject was an episode drawn from Cervantes's *Don Quixote*.

The identification of the librettist has been problematic from the beginning. It now seems clear that he was Friedrich Voigts of Hanover, to whom Mendelssohn wrote on 16 January 1824 in response to the receipt of a draft of the libretto.[35] The announcement of the first performance did not identify the librettist, though it names in addition to the composer the stage director and ballet master.[36] The review of the first performance in the *Allgemeine musikalische Zeitung* already referred to the "unknown poet."[37] Devrient seems to have thought the text was by Klingemann,[38] but it is not clear whether by this he meant Mendelssohn's close friend Karl Klingemann or Karl's father, August.[39] Just why such confusion should have continued is not clear. Mendelssohn's correspondence with Voigts appeared in print as early as 1860,[40] Karl Goedeke's 1884 *Grundriß zur Geschichte der deutschen Dichtung aus den Quellen* correctly listed Voigts as the librettist,[41] and in a letter published in 1921 Julius Rietz reported that he had seen and made a copy of a manuscript catalog of Mendelssohn's works of 1820–1830, compiled by Fanny Hensel, which contains the entry "1824. die Hochzeit des Camacho 1ster Akt. Text von Friedrich Voigt [*sic*] in Hannover. . . . 1825. Die Hochzeit des Camacho 2ter Akt."[42] In any case, as the original review reported, the text was thoroughly rewritten for the performance, even after the music was complete. This task presumably fell to the stage director Baron Carl von Lichtenstein.[43]

The actual compositional work occupied Mendelssohn until August 1825. There ensued a long period of negotiation in order to arrange the performance. Mendelssohn gained the support of Count Brühl, the Intendant (general director) of the Royal Theater. Progress was blocked, however, by the opposition of Gaspare Spontini (1774–1851), Friedrich Wilhelm III's royal music director. Eventually, the older composer summoned the ambitious youth and led him through the score in a detailed and withering critique. In the course of this interview Spontini directed Mendelssohn to the window of the Schauspielhaus, pointed to the

French Church adjacent, and said, "Mon ami, il vous faut des idées grandes, grandes comme cette cupole."[44]   One can easily imagine how offended Mendelssohn must have been; in addition to a condemnation of his thoughts as trivial, the image must have seemed to convey Spontini's prejudice against Mendelssohn as both German and Jewish.

The first performance took place on 29 April 1827 at the royal Schauspielhaus. The situation was a mixed one. Mendelssohn's supportive relations and friends occupied much of the theater. At the same time, a large portion of the audience must have been skeptical and prepared to insist on exceptional standards from the still-prodigy composer. The quality of the performance surely did not meet Mendelssohn's expectations. While the *Allgemeine musikalische Zeitung* reviewer praised the orchestra, he complained of faulty intonation in the chorus, which was apparently inadequately prepared.[45]

The music itself is certainly skillfully composed. As the review of the first performance indicates, the composer's models were Mozart, Beethoven, and Weber. It is not obvious what Beethoven contributed to the style, but Mozart and Weber are much in evidence.

The overture opens with the brass playing a heraldic fanfare rhythm that later becomes the signature of Don Quixote (see Example 4.6). The principal theme

Example 4.6
Die Hochzeit des Camacho, **Overture, mm. 1–8, Brass**

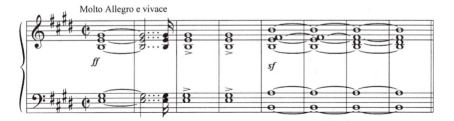

adopts a rollicking, Weberisch style (see Example 4.7). The secondary theme begins with a contrasting motive, introduced by the woodwinds (see Example 4.8), that approaches the lighter style of Mendelssohn's Overture to *A Midsummer Night's Dream*, which would follow *Die Hochzeit des Camacho* by two years; the opera overture's key, too, is E major, that of the *Midsummer Night's Dream*. After extensive and imaginative development and reprise, the brass fanfare returns just before the final measures. In the end, the overture develops into a fine curtain-raiser.

The first vocal number is a duet for the lovers Quiteria and Basilio, the style of which the first reviewer described as "natural and melodic."[46] Basilio attempts to cheer Quiteria, who frets that the joys of youthful love inevitably lead to disappointment. The design of the duet thus permits a sentimental ambivalence as

Example 4.7
Die Hochzeit des Camacho, Overture, mm. 8–16, Violin 1

Example 4.8
Die Hochzeit des Camacho, Overture, mm. 58–65, Flute 1 and Violin 1

to major and minor harmonies and chromatic touches in the melodies. The contrasting ideas of the two characters give way to a parallel duet at the end, where both characters agree that their love and fidelity will see them through their trials.

The lovers are discovered by Quiteria's father, Carrasco, who has set his sights higher than Basilio for his daughter's marriage and who blusters in buffo style at the lovers as they, in turn, protest their long-standing true love. They are outraged by Carrasco's insistence that Quiteria wed the wealthy, but otherwise thoroughly undesirable, Camacho. A shift from D minor to D major in the middle of the trio makes it clear that the situation cannot be taken too seriously. Carrasco's insistent repetition of the dominant in the second half of the number might well lead one to anticipate that his phrases will at any moment break into those of the trio of Basilio, Bartolo, and Marcellina in the second-act finale of *Le nozze di Figaro*. This number forms a model contrast ensemble in the opera buffa tradition of Mozart and Rossini, a type that, as we have seen, Mendelssohn had explored in his early operatic works.

In the aria no. 3 Basilio, left alone, proclaims his belief that Quiteria will remain faithful in her love for him and expresses his confidence that with his sword

and guitar he will be able to win her in the end. This aria derives from the
Singspiel heroic ingenue tenor style of Weber and anticipates the later work of Otto
Nicolai.

No. 4 brings the comic couple Lucinda and Vivaldo. He has returned home,
and she flirtatiously expresses her fear that, like all students and soldiers, he has let
his affections wander while he was away. He points out that poets (he does not
admit to being merely a student) and soldiers are lovers by nature (see Example
4.9). The two agree, at the end, that once lovers have settled down, they are

Example 4.9
Die Hochzeit des Camacho, **no. 4, mm. 5–13, Strings and Voices**

content to find the whole world in their little cottage. The style of this stands
somewhere between that of *Così fan tutte* and that of Papagena and Papageno in
Die Zauberflöte.

Example 4.9, continued

Vivaldo, in the aria no. 5 (actually a strophic Lied in two stanzas), claims to be able to conquer any obstacle to love. He boldly proclaims that by his wits he can manage to win both Lucinda for himself and Quiteria for Basilio. Fermatas at the cadences of the two stanzas (before the la-la-la refrain) demand brief, but bold, cadenzas. The number gradually works its way to the top of the tenor staff and settles in the range between e^1 and b^1. The role thus combines comic bravado in the text with genuinely gutsy vocal demands.

A wedding march in D major (no. 6) in praise of wealth and beauty—that is, the virtues of Camacho and Quiteria—follows, begun by a small wind band on the stage (see Example 4.10) and joined by the chorus and pit orchestra. Between

Example 4.10
Die Hochzeit des Camacho, **no. 6, mm. 1–4**

choral acclamations Carrasco, who says that he will not be denied a grandson in the form of Camacho Jr., brings in the reluctant Quiteria, insisting that she be governed by sense and behave reasonably. Carrasco's style resumes the same buffo that he employed in no. 2. In his first letter to Voigts, Mendelssohn expressed concern about this number, suggesting that Carrasco should not be made entirely to lack a sense of decorum, bullying his daughter in public in a low style.[47] Although this number seems to run such a risk, Carrasco's lines are scored quite separately from the celebration music, and it is possible that the staging can avoid placing the father and daughter directly in view of the celebrating chorus, so that his remonstrances may be understood to be private.

No. 7 is a major ensemble with chorus. Quiteria begins in tragic style in A minor, lamenting her situation and pleading for help from Basilio. Vivaldo tries to convince Basilio that only by deception can he achieve his aim, but the idealistic Basilio will hear nothing of trickery. As Basilio and Quiteria start to indulge in tender promises, Lucinda and Vivaldo warn them of the approach of Carrasco and Camacho with their relatives. Just as the chorus, now in F♯ minor, threatens to do violence to Basilio—with music that anticipates Mendelssohn's chase music of *Die erste Walpurgisnacht*—they are interrupted by the sudden appearance of Sancho Panza, who stops them and, in D major, announces the arrival of Don Quixote, to the annoyance of the chorus and the relief of the lovers. Peculiarly, Sancho sings ("Fühlt ihr nicht ein Beingezitter") to music unmistakably similar to Carrasco's ("folge deines Vaters Lehren" and "lass' dich nicht von ihm bethören") in no. 2. The chorus, momentarily distracted from attacking Basilio, welcomes Quixote to the wedding feast. This is a fine example of the action type of ensemble, with styles and tonal centers continuously changing to accommodate the forward-moving dramatic situations.

No. 8 starts with a reprise of the wedding march in E♭, Sancho Panza now comically joining in. As the onstage band departs, Basilio reemerges from his house, dressed for travel. Accompanied by woodwinds, he sings a brief recitative and reprise in B♭ of his earlier aria, in which he regrets that he must depart but expresses his faith in Quiteria's constancy as he, too, leaves the stage.

Quiteria reappears to sing a full-scale *scena*. It begins as a sentimental ballad with flute echoes. The sad song of parted lovers that makes up the opening F-minor cavatina, in the key and general style of Elvire's cavatina "Still und freundlich ist die Nacht" in *Die Soldatenliebschaft*, reflects her own loss of Basilio. A short *tempo di mezzo* section—recitative and arioso—leads to a breathless *Agitato e presto* cabaletta, in which she resolves to follow Basilio and discover whether he is still alive or has killed himself and, in the latter case, will sing her mournful ballad, which she quotes again at the conclusion of the number.

In no. 10 the relations of Camacho and Carrasco come looking for Basilio at night but find only each other, creating a marvelous scene of mass confusion, an expanded treatment of the situation that Mendelssohn had already tackled with the two judges in *Die wandernden Komödianten*. Meanwhile, Vivaldo has hinted to Camacho that Basilio has found a fabulous fortune in the cave of the giant Montesinos, and Carrasco has changed his mind about who should become Quiteria's husband. Just as the two factions are ready to attack each other, it comes out that Vivaldo has duped them. Now, however, they discover that they cannot locate Quiteria and assume that Basilio has abducted her. Banding together, they set out into the woods after the lovers.

No. 11 is the finale of the first act, an extended action finale that the reviewer for the *Allgemeine musikalische Zeitung* found "especially successful." [48] Basilio appears alone in the woods at night, introduced by sufficiently mysterious and atmospheric music, hinting at the *Midsummer Night's Dream*. He sings, in Romanze style, what is really a self-contained piece, pleading with the mournful cypresses to turn to roses. The florid word-painting on "trauender Kranz" seems perhaps somewhat excessive (possibly even a sort of pun on the image of "flowery"), but it was alert of Mendelssohn to appeal to those words in Voigts's text for a decorative touch in the sentimental aria. Quiteria sings from offstage, calling Basilio's name. In agitated accompanied recitative the always excessively noble Basilio resolves not to flee with her surreptitiously but to find a way to claim her love publicly; he removes himself to a distance, singing echoes of his earlier aria from the end of no. 8. Quiteria continues to pursue him. At this moment Don Quixote finally makes his first appearance, heralded by the blast of brass that marks each of his entrances, thoroughly frightening Quiteria. Characteristically mistaking Quiteria for his Dulcinea del Toboso, Quixote attempts to "rescue" her. She runs away, and Basilio moves to intercept Quixote, who believes Basilio's reflection in the water to be the giant Montesinos and attacks it. Basilio, seeing that Quiteria has escaped, leaves the scene himself. The chorus enters in pursuit of the lovers, singing a continuation of their music from the preceding number. Quixote stops them and hears their explanation that they are chasing the abductor of Camacho's daughter. Vivaldo, singing in the distance and supported by a pair of horns, distracts them all. Quiteria enters, accompanied by Vivaldo. Camacho, seeing her "recaptured," grants Vivaldo his legacy; Vivaldo and Lucinda can now be together. The chorus praises knight-errantry. Basilio abruptly appears, disguised as a ghostly apparition and singing incantations that might seem to be a tenor imitation of Caspar's in the Wolf's Glen scene from Weber's *Der Freischütz*, to threaten Camacho if he should touch Quiteria before she says "I do" in the wedding ceremony, a ban that Don Quixote vows to enforce (see Example 4.11). Lucinda and Vivaldo let Quiteria in on Basilio's trick, Camacho starts to have second thoughts about his marriage, and Carrasco grows enraged at the frustration of his plans. Amid the full ensemble Carrasco's anger, Sancho's growing hunger pangs, and Camacho's fretting eventually form a brief fugato. With this mixture of emotions the act ends in noisy buffo style.

Act 2 opens with wedding preparations, as the chorus cooks the feast. The orchestral figuration depicts the motion of the stirring of pots—according to the *Allgemeine musikalische Zeitung* review "too realistically." [49] Led by the aroma of victuals, Sancho Panza approaches and asks to sample the food.

There follows a strophic drinking song (no. 13) for Sancho Panza in folk-song style, related to the present occasion by its claim that the finest bride in the world, dressed in a wooden dress and iron bands, is muscatel. The first reviewer complained that the five stanzas (the last repeated by the chorus) amounted to three

Example 4.11
Die Hochzeit des Camacho, no. 11, mm. 355–67

too many. Mendelssohn may have considered that his caution to Voigts about the excessive use of strophic texts did not quite apply to this case, since the form is inherent in the genre to which the number alludes. The idea was to create an increase of intensity over the course of the piece—as Mendelssohn put it, "one peasant after another gathers around him until a chorus is formed, which suddenly bursts out fortissimo."[50] The increasing density of the orchestration, the "poco più mosso" of Sancho's last verse, and then the tutti fortissimo and "più allegro should combine with the staging to make the desired effect. The cooking and stirring music returns at the end of the number, to be interrupted by a trumpet fanfare.

The leads to no. 14, a chorus and ballet staged for the wedding celebration. The scene derives from the pantomime entertainment described in Cervantes's romance. An introductory march, suggestion the dance scene in act 3 of *Le nozze di Figaro*, and an explanatory chorus introduce the allegorical action. The choral melody here quotes the second phrase of the secondary theme of the overture, now making its tender character explicit as a representation of the power of love (see Example 4.12) Two enemy forces, representing Love and Wealth, enter to a

Example 4.11 continued

Example 4.12
Die Hochzeit des Camacho, no. 14, mm. 66–70, Soprano

bolero in E minor and a fandango in A major, in turn. Mendelssohn made a stab
at evoking Spanish local color here by calling for triangle, tambourine, cymbals,

and bass drum. There is a brief interlude taken from Basilio's act 1 aria. The two parties battle for the prize, a beautiful maiden, attempting to bind each other with rose garlands and golden chains, respectively, the bolero and fandango music alternating as first one group and the other gains the upper hand. At the climax of the action, in E major and based on the music of the overture, the forces of Love shoot arrows, and those of Wealth throw golden balls at the castle that imprisons the maiden, and its walls collapse. At this moment Don Quixote enters (with his fanfare) and, mistaking the allegorical battle for a real one, "rescues" the maiden (whom he takes for Dulcinea) himself. The marchlike music and love motive of the number's opening then return with the chorus's moral, that, after all, no theatrical staging can decide whom a bride should choose. Love conquers all, but wealth is always prepared to challenge it. Nevertheless, they sing (probably referring to the bride), "Seht hier Alles sich vereinen, was nur Lieb' und Reichthum beut" (Behold everything that brings together love and riches is united here).

No. 15 finds Quiteria lamenting her hopeless condition in a tragic, passionate aria. Lucinda attempts to console her without revealing Basilio's plot, according to which he will feign madness and suicide, make a "dying" wish for Quiteria to marry him—leaving Camacho and Carrasco to plan that she will marry Camacho as soon as she is widowed—and then have a miraculous "resuscitation." Sancho provides a comic foil for this scene, as he begs the two not to spoil his eating with mourning and weeping. As the women appeal to the Queen of Heaven, Sancho assures them that there exists a solution to every problem.

A chorus of bridesmaids appears (no. 16). This piece, which inevitably recalled the bridesmaids' chorus in Weber's *Freischütz*, seemed to the *Allgemeine musikalische Zeitung* reviewer to have risked comparison with its predecessor and fallen short.[51] In fact, except that both pieces are strophic songs for women's chorus, they are not much alike. Where Weber's represents a folk ballad in duple, marchlike rhythm, with stanzas sung by soloists and a refrain for the chorus, Mendelssohn's consists of a lilting, $\frac{6}{8}$-meter prayer for the couple's happiness, sung by the entire ensemble throughout (see Example 4.13).

In the following ensemble (no. 17) Basilio appears in the midst of the wedding ceremonies, sending the entire gathering into confusion. As the relations of Camacho and Carrasco threaten to kill him, Basilio feigns his suicide. The plan succeeds, of course, and in the *finale ultimo* (no. 18) the young people make a stand to defend themselves against the outrage of the others. Don Quixote steps in to prevent any violence and determines that, however it has come about, the marriage of Basilio and Quiteria must be valid, and he will defend it. The alcaide (who sings here for the first time) lends his support, as well.[52] The aggrieved parties resign themselves to the authority of the alcaide and the woeful knight. Camacho decides, in fact, that Quiteria is hardly a desirable match after all, but he agrees not to let his wedding preparations go to waste and to allow the feast to serve as celebration for the marriage of Basilio and Quiteria. The lovers share a tender duet, Sancho reprises his drinking song and the chorus the wedding march, and Don Quixote, his mission accomplished, takes his leave.

Example 4.13
Die Hochzeit des Camacho, no. 16, mm. 10–17, Voices

As has been noted, *Die Hochzeit des Camacho* looks back to important models in the operatic literature, particularly the works of Mozart and Weber. At the same time, it anticipates some of Mendelssohn's future works, including the overture and incidental music for *A Midsummer Night's Dream* in the hints that it gives of the atmospheric music of those works and in the rustic, onstage band. The choral chase scene also anticipates the much more interesting treatment of such a situation in *Die erste Walpurgisnacht*. It is easy to see that, had he continued to work in the genre, there were ideas in *Die Hochzeit des Camacho* that Mendelssohn might have followed up. Such an idea might be Sancho's drinking song. Although he did not do so himself, the type later had a memorable recurrence in Falstaff's song in Nicolai's *Die lustige Weiber von Windsor*. While it would be an exaggeration to agree with Sir George Grove[53] that the recurring trombone motive for Don Quixote's entrances represents the invention of the Leitmotiv by Mendelssohn—it does not qualify as a Leitmotiv in the Wagnerian sense, nor was such a recurring reminiscence motive Mendelssohn's invention—it would have been interesting to see whether Mendelssohn would have followed up on this dramatic device.

The upshot of the performance constituted an important moment in Mendelssohn's career. He had certainly set enormous store by the hoped-for éclat that would launch a public career. The lukewarm reception given to much of the opera disappointed the inexperienced and nervous composer tremendously, and he could not even bear to stay to the end. The Don Quixote, Heinrich Blume, fell ill the next day, making it impossible to repeat the opera.[54] The work was not staged again until a performance in Boston in 1885.[55] This was particularly regrettable, for as the *Allgemeine musikalische Zeitung* reviewer suggested, the success of any opera should depend not only on its opening night but on successive performances.[56] True "completion" of an opera hangs on the minor adjustments made in the course of a run—an opportunity that, ironically, Mendelssohn had in the limited repetitions of his earlier Singspiele at home but not in the theater.[57] By further performances, too, the chorus might have shaped up.[58]

Mendelssohn did retain some commitment to, and affection for, his *Camacho* music. Almost as a stubborn refusal to capitulate to its lack of success in performance, he had a piano-vocal score published as his Op. 10 in a lavish edition in 1828 by Laue. Twelve years after the ill-fated Berlin premiere, the bridal chorus was staged in a tableau vivant in Frankfurt in July 1839; the composer reported to his mother that the scene was represented as a Spanish peasant wedding, with three dancing couples and the mournful knight Don Quixote posed in the background.[59]

Mendelssohn's disappointment seems to have made him intensely cautious about attempting another opera, and indeed he did not seriously undertake one until much later. The fact that Voigts's libretto, rather than Mendelssohn's music, came in for the most serious criticism in the *Allgemeine musikalische Zeitung* review undoubtedly made him especially critical of all the librettos that he considered.

DIE HEIMKEHR AUS DER FREMDE

Following his disappointment with *Die Hochzeit des Camacho*, Mendelssohn did not compose another stage work for two and a half years. In 1829, when the Mendelssohn children began to plan for their parents' silver wedding anniversary, which would occur on 28 December, an occasion arose for such a project. Because Felix was in England—this was the journey that included his walking tour of Scotland with Karl Klingemann—the planning is recorded in correspondence between Berlin and London. The correspondence became even more extensive than it might have been, because Felix injured his leg in a carriage accident and could not return home until nearly the last moment. In fact, he was busily writing the music for his new piece during his journey home.[60]

What finally materialized was a plan for a gala musical-theatrical evening in the Mendelssohn home on the night of 26 December 1829.[61] The performance included a Festspiel by Fanny (who had married Wilhelm Hensel on 3 October) and Felix's new one-act Liederspiel, entitled *Die Heimkehr aus der Fremde*.[62]

The text of *Die Heimkehr aus der Fremde* was written by Klingemann, following a scenario very much controlled by Mendelssohn. The action takes place in a typical German village. Drawing on conventions of the popular comic tradition but also conceived as topical for the occasion, the plot involves the prosperous village mayor and his wife, who are about to celebrate the mayor's fiftieth year in office, their long-lost military recruiting-officer son, the love between the son and the mayor's ward, the intrigues of an unscrupulous, but not very bright, interloper, disguises, and mistaken identities. Mendelssohn apparently had a clear idea of his textual needs, which Klingemann supplied and revised as the two friends took advantage of the enforced opportunity to work closely together.

The shape of the little drama is neatly planned. Directly following the overture comes a romance sung by the mayor's wife as she pines for her absent son, which launches a series of expository numbers introducing the main characters. Since its text tells a story of a family in the same situation as the family in the main action, this romance serves a dramatic function, rather than merely delaying the action to allow for an evocative introduction, as was common with such numbers.[63] The ingenue, Lisbeth, ward of the mayor and his wife, is introduced in a duet with the sorrowful mother, attempting to cheer her up, then sings a Lied that shows her own more sentimental side. The succeeding two numbers present, respectively, the villain of the piece, the comic-bass merchant Kauz, and the returning son, Hermann, who has disguised himself as a traveling musician. The exposition complete, the emphasis shifts to ensembles, bringing the characters into conflict. A dramatic phase of rising tension develops in the next two pieces, trios of the contrast and conflict type, in which Kauz tries first to interfere between Lisbeth and Hermann and then to bamboozle the mayor and his wife. The climax of the action arrives in a nighttime scene, beginning with a Lied sung by Hermann as a serenade to Lisbeth, which Kauz, disguised as the night watchman, keeps interrupting. Kauz then sings a traditional watchman's song, but he is unmasked and terrified by Hermann. An orchestral interlude depicting the passing of the night and the break of day sets up the dénouement. Lisbeth has an aubadelike Lied that balances Hermann's serenade, and the chorus sings in honor of the mayor and his wife on the festive occasion. In the finale the couple recover their son—though only after Kauz has claimed to be he and been stymied at last by the real Hermann. The piece closes in general rejoicing.

Given such a plan, Mendelssohn could construct his score primarily of Lieder in a variety of styles to portray the characters and their moods. The overture establishes the work's chamber-sized orchestra of paired woodwinds, horns, trumpets, timpani, and strings. The mother's opening Romanze combines the conventions that evoke the folk ballad with orchestral interludes immediately recognizable as those of a spinning song (see Example 4.14). Lisbeth's Lieder both represent the sentimental, early Romantic type. Kauz's expository song, by contrast, parodies the typical gestures of comic bass arias in Italian opera buffa, indicating the pretentious, empty bombast of the character in patter and growling low notes (see Example 4.15).[64] Hermann's first Lied shows both his musician's disguise in a lyrical vein, accompanied by the sound effect of the evening bells, and his soldierly nature in an evocation of the military life with trumpet calls (see Example 4.16).

Equally, Mendelssohn combined and contrasted styles to create highly effective ensembles. The duet between Lisbeth and the mother neatly sets the cheerful girl against the morose older woman. The first trio (no. 6) allows for contrast between the two young lovers, who have just recognized each other, and the annoying Kauz. The next piece is particularly striking, combining the highly

Example 4.14
Die Heimkehr aus der Fremde, no. 1, mm. 1–9

Example 4.15
Die Heimkehr aus der Fremde, no. 4

a. mm. 1–8

Ich   bin ein viel-ge-rei-ster Mann, der al-ler Län-der Tän-ze kann,
Ich   bin al-lein der rech-te Mann, der das Con-fu-se lö-sen kann,

ja,   der al-ler Län-der Tän-ze kann.   Von Po-len bis zum
ja,   der das Con-fu-se lö-sen kann.   So'n Bau-er weiss nicht

Schot-ten-land bin ich ge-reist und wohl-be-kannt, und   wohl-be - kannt.
aus noch ein, und stol-pert ü-ber's eig'-ne Bein, über's eig'-ne   Bein.

b. mm. 24–32

sammt Ca-stag-nett', das Stey-ri-sche und I-ri-sche, den Bai-er-tanz und
ist die Cou-rant', die Me-nu-ett ihr nicht ver-steht, und Al-le-mand' macht

Ei-er-tanz,   und Du-del-sack und wel-schen Takt, die   Me-nu-ett sammt'
ihr zu Schand', den Hopp-ser-schritt ca-pirt ihr nit, euch un-be-kannt ist

Ca-stag-nett', das Stey-ri-sche und I-ri-sche, den Bai-er-tanz und Ei-er-tanz.
die Cou-rant', die Me-nu-ett ihr nicht versteht, und Al-le-mand' macht ihr zu Schand';

dramatic phrases that express the anger of the mayor's wife, the bothersome merchant in wildly leaping melodic material, and the stolid figure of the mayor, who sings entirely on a monotone f. This last part was composed for Mendelssohn's brother-in-law Wilhelm Hensel, a complete nonsinger. The climactic confrontation between Kauz and Hermann, both disguised as night

Example 4.16
Die Heimkehr aus der Fremde, no. 5

a. mm. 1–8

watchmen, makes a fine example of an argument duet. Finally, the closing number, rather than a conventional strophic ensemble in which each character sings the same music, turns out to present each one in a different mood, after which, everything finally resolved, all join (with chorus) in a happy closing passage.[65]

What is most important for the understanding of *Die Heimkehr aus der Fremde* is a clear sense of the genre conventions with which it operates. Unlike *Die Hochzeit des Camacho*, the new work was no Romantic opera for the public theater; rather, the composer specifically identified it as a Liederspiel and intended it for a domestic performance, like the earlier Singspiele.[66] It was meant to be performed specifically for and by the composer's family and friends. The overture served not just as a curtain-raiser and a mood-setting introduction but as the composer's devoted gesture of presentation of the work to his parents.[67] At the first performance the role of the mayor's wife was sung by Fanny Hensel; that of

Example 4.16, continued

b. mm. 24–32

the monotone mayor, as mentioned earlier, by Wilhelm Hensel; and the ingenue Lisbeth, by Rebecca Mendelssohn (though she found the part uncomfortably high and handed it over for later performances to Therese Devrient, who had sung in the chorus for the silver anniversary celebration).[68] The obbligato cello part featured in Lisbeth's Lied no. 3 was designed for the youngest Mendelssohn sibling, Paul. The two leading men's parts were assigned to family friends who were excellent performers: the tenor role of Hermann went to the talented student Eduard Mantius (to whom on New Year's Eve Mendelssohn gave an autograph copy of his Lied no. 5[69]); as noted earlier, that of the baritone Kauz, with its many awkward vocal leaps and wide range, was intended for the composer's very dear friend the actor/singer Eduard Devrient.

If regarded as a full-scale opera with public and Romantic pretensions, *Die Heimkehr aus der Fremde* will certainly come across as modest, seemingly a retreat from the ambitious scope of *Die Hochzeit des Camacho*.[70] Considered as a Liederspiel, however, it comes off as strikingly original and Romantic in style. Historically the genre had originally consisted of plays designed around preexisting songs. Liederspiele were unpretentious, suited particularly to the tastes and values of the rising German *Bürgertum* of the mid-eighteenth century. By Mendelssohn's time the genre had already declined, as the increasingly cultivated German public turned to the more popular imported Italian opera and to French and German early Romanticism. To some extent, then, *Die Heimkehr aus der Fremde* represents a late apotheosis of the Liederspiel. It addressed very precisely a particular German *bürgerlich* audience—not the newly and modestly cultured urban commercial class of the eighteenth century, however, but the ideal enlightened *Hochbürgerlichkeit* that the Mendelssohn family represented.[71] The music, ostensibly made up of Lieder (for six of the thirteen vocal numbers are called Lied in the score, not including the opening romance), does not evoke the *volkstümlich* Lied of an earlier era but calls on the more Romantic style that Mendelssohn explored in his contemporaneous songs of Opp. 8 and 9, accompanied by his imaginatively colored orchestrations. At the same time, dramatic depiction stretches the music beyond traditional boundaries. We have already noticed the reference to the Italian buffo style within a so-called Lied to portray the pompous Kauz. In Hermann's Lied no. 8 dramatic realism turns the solo into a semiduet, as Kauz inserts his rude interruptions. In addition, the ensembles bring to the Liederspiel several num bers exemplifying the genuine dramatic types of fully developed opera. The contrast ensemble is best represented in no. 2, as the young girl attempts to cheer the melancholy mood of the older woman, and in no. 6, where the young lovers are set against the interfering Kauz. Nos. 7 and 10 serve as action ensembles.

The orchestral interlude that follows the dramatic climax exemplifies pure Mendelssohnian Romanticism, a perfect example of his style of "characteristic" music, depicting night and sunrise in much the same way that the *Calm Sea and Prosperous Voyage* Overture illustrates the shift from breezeless calm to the coming of the wind or that the overture to *Die erste Walpurgisnacht* represents the transition from winter to spring weather (see Example 4.17). This interlude anticipates the use of entr'acte music, particularly the Nocturne, for *A Midsummer Night's Dream*, composed fourteen years later. At its end, as Lisbeth enters, it quotes the beginning of the overture, bringing the overture into the drama itself.

From this perspective, what surprises about *Die Heimkehr aus der Fremde* is not its modest scope or stylistic conservatism. On the contrary, the most remark-able aspect of this work is that, while it still maintains a close connection to the genre's traditions, it raises the limited genre of the Liederspiel to a level of sophistication so far beyond its conventions. In this way it might have modeled the ideal to which the *bürgerlich* domestic entertainment could have aspired. As it happened, however, the situation was unique: on one hand, no other "good middle-class family in Germany" was equipped to realize such a model; on the other hand, the urban culture of the early industrial age looked outside the home to the public theater for dramatic entertainment.

Example 4.17
Die Heimkehr aus der Fremde, no. 11, mm. 1–38

Example 4.17, continued

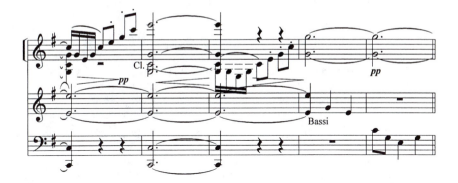

MENDELSSOHN'S SEARCH FOR AN OPERA LIBRETTO

Mendelssohn will never find operatic material that satisfies him; he is much too intelligent for that.

—Karl von Holtei[72]

I will not undertake to say what was the particular dread which possessed him; but that it was *fear*, and nothing else, that influenced his conduct, I am thoroughly convinced. He yearned to compose for the stage—to add his name to those of his great countrymen, Gluck, Mozart, Beethoven, Weber, and Meyerbeer; but invariably shrunk from the effort the moment an opportunity presented itself.

—James Robinson Planché[73]

These judgments by two of Mendelssohn's would-be librettists suggest two different types of explanation for Mendelssohn's failure, after *Die Heimkehr aus der Fremde*, ever to complete another operatic work. The first assigns the blame to Mendelssohn's excessive fastidiousness in his expectations of a libretto. The second attributes his failure to his inner self-doubt. His own statements demonstrate how demanding his judgments were. Whether these masked a deep-seated unwillingness to subject himself again to the disappointment that he had experienced with *Die Hochzeit des Camacho* is more difficult to determine.

Mendelssohn certainly kept operatic projects in mind throughout the rest of his life. He corresponded continuously with potential librettists, searching for a suitable text and sought-after as a composer.[74] To Devrient he expressed his sense that he really ought to compose an opera:

But as you say, above all I would like to compose an opera; and I often long to do so very much. The day before your letter came, I had written to a friend that I often reproach myself on this account, especially when (as here this winter) I hear new German and foreign operas; then I feel as if I were obligated, also, to get involved and cast my vote in score.[75]

Enterprising writers steadily bombarded the composer with offers of librettos for his consideration. Many of these came unsolicited. Almost invariably, he returned these with polite compliments and often with the claim that his other obligations made it impossible to undertake the project. In addition, however, he worked more extensively with several writers on scenarios and libretto drafts that reached various stages before being rejected. It seems obvious that he sincerely wanted to find a suitable opera text but equally clear that he was impossible to please.

Mendelssohn's correspondence and the reports of his conversations with his presumptive librettists give some insights into his reasons for rejecting so many of these many opera librettos. These documents certainly support Holtei's idea that Mendelssohn was simply too critical ever to be satisfied with a libretto. One would, in any case, hardly expect a direct statement from the composer that would support Planché's conviction that he had a deep-seated fear of composing any opera. Whatever his underlying psychological motivations for turning down operatic projects, the rationales he offered show him as a perceptive, thoughtful reader with very high standards.

Three Fruitless Commissions

At various times Mendelssohn received actual opera commissions, but these failed to come to fruition. In fact, these plans generally engendered disappointment with, and sometimes even ill will toward, the composer.

In November 1831 Baron Poissl offered Mendelssohn a commission for an opera to be staged in Munich. Mendelssohn promised that he would soon find a libretto and for some months entertained the idea of setting one by the Düsseldorf writer Karl Immermann based on Shakespeare's *The Tempest*, but in the end this project—to be called *Der Zaubermantel in Calibans Händen*—came to nothing.[76] According to Devrient, the libretto "had no operatic form at all, departed from musically valuable motifs of the original, brought in its own, less promising inventions in their place, and in the end the plot was even more scattered than that of the original."[77] By 27 July 1832 Mendelssohn had given up the project; he wrote to Immermann and suggested that the libretto should perhaps be forwarded to another composer.

The London publisher William Chappell in 1838 commissioned a libretto from the dramatist James Robinson Planché (1796–1880), to be composed by Mendelssohn. Planché had written the librettos for Weber's *Oberon* and for works by Henry Bishop, and he had translated and adapted for the English stage works of Mozart, Auber, Rossini, and Weber. There thus seemed every reason to hope for success. Planché conceived a story to take place during the siege of Calais by Edward III early in the Hundred Years' War (1346). The correspondence surrounding the failure of this project covers two years. Mendelssohn at first felt enthusiastic, but he staunchly maintained his criticisms of the libretto (see below), becoming more and more negative, until he finally abandoned the work altogether.[78]

The Opéra in Paris approached Mendelssohn in 1841 to inquire whether he would consider composing an opera to a libretto by the prominent French librettist Eugène Scribe, but Mendelssohn declined.[79] He did, however, politely express to Scribe his hope that someday the two of them would collaborate. In fact, another opportunity arose in 1846, when Benjamin Lumley, the director of Her Majesty's Theatre in London, commissioned Mendelssohn to compose music for an opera that would feature Jenny Lind, on a libretto by Scribe based on Shakespeare's *The Tempest*.[80] Mendelssohn was not satisfied with the libretto, but Lumley went so far as actually to announce the opera, which annoyed Mendelssohn considerably. By March 1847 he had withdrawn from the commission.[81]

Topics

The topics that Mendelssohn considered represent the gamut of subject matter for Romantic opera. Among them were folk legends and fairy tales, romances, comedies, historical plots, and Shakespeare plays. Among the last-named group *The Tempest* came up on several occasions, as well as *Hamlet, King Lear*, and *The Winter's Tale*.[82]

All sorts of proposals turn up in Mendelssohn's letters. Just to give some idea of the extent of the quantity and variety of subjects, he corresponded with Herrmann Neumann and Gottfried Kinkel in 1843[83] about historical dramatic compositions to be titled *Der Sängerkrieg, Barbarossa in Suza*, and *Otto und Adelheid*. With Charlotte Birch-Pfeiffer he considered a variety of historical and legendary topics: *Der Truchsess von Waldburg, Genoveva* (versions by both Tieck and Hebbel), *Die Kronenwächter* by de la Motte Fouqué, *Consuelo*, Joan of Arc, *Faust, Die Lorelei*, and the *Nibelungenlied*.[84]   Devrient continually plied the composer with opera topics, including ones taken from history, legend, and fairy tales. Among these were episodes from Tasso's *Gerusalemme liberata*, Hans Heiling, Atterbom's *Die Insel der Glückseligkeit*, Bluebeard, "King Thrushbeard" (Drosselbart), "The Musk Apple" (Bisamsapfel), the Loreley, "a plot of my own, of two friends, whose estrangement and reconciliation was to unfold itself in Germany, in the Italian Carnival, and in the Swiss Alps," Kohlhaas, *Andreas Hofer* (from the play by Immermann), and an episode of the Peasants' War.[85]

It is clear from Mendelssohn's responses to this variety of subjects that no particular kind of story failed to interest him per se, if he found the libretto dramatic and expressive. He wrote to Alfred Julius Becher about the possibility of obtaining a libretto from Becher or from Otto Prechtler:

neither *The Tempest* nor *The Steadfast Prince*, which I once thought a lot about, are of the sort that I now envisage. I want such a truly passionate, human, natural, universally moving, original one! Either with no love interest in it or just as well with love that drives one crazy; I want something that everyone has already felt and that no one has yet composed. In a word, the most beautiful of all! But, all joking aside, if Prechtler or you do not have such a subject or another one in your sights, then it is to be taken for granted that I would rather receive and read *The Tempest* than anything.[86]

A similar statement comes in a letter of 18 November 1844 to Griepenkerl:

To Shakespeare's "Tempest," as an Opera, I have, I confess, little inclination; nor does the destruction of Jerusalem—at least as I have hitherto seen it treated—appear to be fit for the Theatre. But the fact is that the whole matter depends more on the *how* than the *what*, and that no subject can be either accepted or rejected unconditionally.[87]

Quite remarkably, Mendelssohn rejected subjects and even entire librettos that other composers would later adopt. In 1827 he turned down Devrient's libretto for *Hans Heiling*, set successfully by Marschner in 1833. Eugène Scribe's 1846 libretto for Mendelssohn based on *The Tempest* (the commission from Lumley for Her Majesty's Theater mentioned earlier), which Mendelssohn could not accept, did not go to waste, for once again what Mendelssohn rejected another composer deemed suitable; the opera became Halévy's *La tempesta* in an Italian translation by Pietro Giannone and was performed at Her Majesty's Theatre in London in 1850 and at Théâtre-Italien Paris in 1851.[88] Mendelssohn never actually had a libretto on the legend of St. Genoveva, on which Schumann composed his only opera in 1850, but he was approached with the topic by Adolf Böttger in 1841,[89] and it was among the ideas that he later considered with the writer Charlotte Birch-Pfeiffer for an opera intended for Jenny Lind.[90]

At several points Mendelssohn considered the *Nibelungenlied*, in 1840 exchanging letters on the subject with his sister Fanny.[91] She certainly recognized in the topic, as Wagner later would realize, the potential for political statements. In her case, though, the result was that this correspondence eventually declined into tongue-in-cheek banter, as Fanny wrote, "should you be uneasy over the success of the opera, I would suggest that you let a double chorus of Huns and Nibelungs, as a *captatio benevolentiae*, sing "sie sollen ihn nicht haben" to the melody of *Ei du lieber Augustin*."[92]

Pervonte: Mendelssohn's Abortive Opera Topic

In one case Mendelssohn not only suggested but also campaigned aggressively for a topic, for which he hoped to get a libretto from his close friend and sometime traveling companion Karl Klingemann. As early as 6 January 1834 Mendelssohn proposed an opera to be based on Kotzebue's dramatization, based, in turn, on C. M. Wieland's verse tale (*epos*), *Pervonte*.[93] Klingemann had written the libretto for *Die Heimkehr aus der Fremde* and continued as one of Mendelssohn's favorite poets for the lyrics of his Lieder, so it is not surprising that he wanted to work with him on a new operatic project. The composer at first became quite excited about the project, writing, "I have recently run across an opera by Kotzebue, *Pervonte*, that not a soul knows; shall I send you the better part of it, or the whole thing, or would such a thing annoy you? Please let me know; I am very much in the mood to compose again now."[94] Again, less than three weeks later, "Shall I send you Kotzebue's *Pervonte*?"[95] and four weeks later still, "But you aren't writing me anything about *Pervonte*! Shall I send you Kotzebue's opera??"[96] By late April 1834 Mendelssohn had commenced work on the scenario himself; on 25 April he sent a complete synopsis and his comments to his friend in London, pointing out scenes that seemed dramatically effective and expressing his preference for Wieland's original ending over Kotzebue's more naive *lieto fine*.[97] Within less than three weeks, however, he had reconceived the scenario and sent Klingemann a new version.[98] Another month thereafter he urged Klingemann just to get started working on act 1, and he continued to prod and encourage his friend, asking him to send along just any bits that he had done.[99] Klingemann finally did send a libretto draft for act 1 on 22 July 1834.[100]

At this point the perhaps foreseeable problems began. Mendelssohn's reply already criticized the act 1 draft and suggested that the two might make a successful libretto by sitting down to work together. He explained that he already had their next opera project in mind.[101] He then sent a detailed response to Klingemann's proposals for act 2.[102] By the end of September it was Klingemann's turn to criticize, as he expressed himself totally perplexed by some of Mendelssohn's ideas.[103]

The situation gradually became more difficult. On 30 November 1834 Mendelssohn wrote to Klingemann that the subject presented more problems than he had thought,[104] and in the following January he sent Klingemann a complete new scenario (see the Historical Views and Documents for this chapter).[105] By this time both men had run out of patience with the subject and with each other, the only time in their relationship that their friendship was strained. They eventually resumed their cordial correspondence, but they never again attempted to collaborate on an operatic project.

It is not easy to explain why the *Pervonte* topic interested the composer so intently. The story is merely a fairy tale, combining the plots of two conventional formulas: the willful princess whose hand is to be gained by the least prepossessing of prospective suitors, and the rustic who is to learn wisdom by discovering the inadequacies of magic wishes. As it turns out, the story hangs more on the magic wishes than on action or even determination by the human characters. The personalities themselves do not become particularly sympathetic. The ending and the moral, if one exists at all, seem confused.

The aspects of *Pervonte* that suggest that it might be effective seem mostly superficial ones. The dramatis personae are purely stock characters, but they are at least distinctive and might be convincingly characterized in music: Pervonte, the uncouth bumpkin; Vastola, the selfish and willful princess; Vastola's father, the pompous monarch; the sycophantic seneschal. Opportunities arise for pageantry and lively musical numbers in the first-act appearance at court of colorful foreign suitors, in the second-act festival scene, and in the storm that concludes that act. Spectacular staging effects include Pervonte's flying fagot, the setting asea of the charmed princess and her rustic suitor in a cask, and the magic production of a palace on the shore where they wash up.

In the final analysis, one finds it difficult to regret the abandonment of *Pervonte*. Mendelssohn might have composed delightful music for it. Its plot, however, seems unlikely to have been salvageable, and the topic's apparent lack of conceptual or moral clarity—or even real interest—probably doomed it from the outset.

Mendelssohn's Desiderata and Criteria for a Libretto

Among Mendelssohn's concerns in considering librettos one thing that does not seem to have been a requirement for him was that it have "beautiful verses."[106] This was not because he did not wish to have well-written lines but rather because he did not find poetic elegance difficult to come by. To Devrient he insisted that "I could get hold of good verses, or even compose bad ones; that is not the problem."[107] He often turned down librettos while complimenting the beauty of the lines. In a typical case, declining William Bartholomew's 1841 libretto for an opera titled *A Christmas Night's Dream*, Mendelssohn wrote,

But the delightful details in which it abounds have so thoroughly fascinated me, that I hope and trust I shall one day have the good luck of writing my music to your beautiful words. The duet of Puck and Amor, when the first asks him all sorts of questions, the delightful opening scene of the second act with the bird's language, the fairies' song with the lovers' duet after it, Eudora's waking afterward, are true gems which it is impossible to read without emotion, without thinking of music, and without thanking the poet who invented them. I do not know whether you will think of altering this libretto, for it would not only be a very difficult task, but the question also is whether my impression is not only a personal one, and whether others would not judge it in quite a different way. At all events, let me hope, as I said before, that I may once be happy enough to find a libretto which unites the dramatic development which I have in my idea to so extraordinary poetical beauties, so musical verses, and such a fine and noble feeling as that which pervades your whole work, and accept my best and sincerest thanks for it.[108]

Equally, Mendelssohn refused to cater to the public taste. In his letter to Devrient of 28 June 1843 he proclaimed his determination to regard the opera as equally worthy of serious treatment as concert music:

Ever since I started composing I have been true to the fundamental principle: not to write a single page just because the great public or a pretty girl wanted it so and so, but only to write in the way the I believed was right and that pleased me. I may not stray from this principle in the case of opera, either. That makes it so difficult, however, because most people, even most poets, do not think of opera as anything more than a popular piece. I know well enough that popularity is externally more important and more pleasant here than in symphonies, oratorios, piano pieces, and the like, although even in these cases it takes some time before one is secure enough so that no distractions make one turn aside, and on that account I still hope to write an opera that I can write with good conscience and with joy in the fact that I have not abandoned my fundamental principles.[109]

Again in 1846 he criticized Devrient's use of historical or local color in the libretto draft of the opera set in the period of the Peasants' War, titled *Knight and Peasant*, which he seems to have felt was more an appeal to popularity than genuinely dramatic in effect:

Precisely the thing that someone else would find attractive in it makes this coloring undesirable to me: I mean the temporary importance that it has just now on the stage and in literature. Where that coloring is *necessary*, why not? There, there should be no hesitation; but where it is not necessary, then for God's sake, not, for then it is the worst kind of striving for effect, flirting with the masses.[110]

After his early works Mendelssohn had clear ideas about the dramatic styles and genres in which he might compose during his mature career. His experience had given him well-formed ideas about the music-dramatic functions of various styles. In withdrawing from the project to compose Immermann's libretto of *The Tempest*, he cited problems in suiting musical styles to the text, writing to Immermann that, for him, the lyric, dramatic, and recitative elements seemed not clearly enough distinguished and suggesting that the librettist should perhaps forward the text to another composer.[111]

Likewise Mendelssohn had no interest in composing another Singspiel—that is, a work with spoken dialogue—but insisted on a through-composed opera. In 1843 Devrient sent Mendelssohn a libretto by a friend, which the composer returned with this criticism:

I am giving the opera text back to you. There was much in it that pleased me, especially the verses, which are always musical and very singable, but also the motif of the love-charm, which in my view would make possible a beautiful, serious effect. But as a whole it is not suitable for me at the outset, because the form of a five-act opera with spoken dialogue runs counter to my inclinations. Actually I would not like to compose an opera with dialogue such as this, and would like to see it disappear even from those with fewer acts; but in the case of a five-act work continuous music seems absolutely necessary to me.[112]

Similarly, in July 1847, while Mendelssohn was already fairly committed to Geibel's *Die Lorelei*, he rejected a libretto to be supplied by Helmina von Chézy on the grounds that he could not accept the separation of dialogue and singing.[113]

Mendelssohn was deeply concerned that any opera he would set should project positive moral values. He made this abundantly clear in a letter of 19 December 1831 to his father, who had written to him in Paris, urging him to find a French author who might provide a libretto for the commissioned opera for Munich. Among Mendelssohn's objections to this idea was his observation of the immorality produced by French librettists' pandering to the audience's taste for shock value:

Any of the new texts here, if brought to the stage for the first time in Germany, would in my opinion not have the slightest success.[114] In addition, the main feature of all of them is one that, even though the times demand it and I can see clearly enough that in general one must go with the times rather than *against* them, one ought to take a stand against: it is that of immorality. When in *Robert le Diable* the nuns come one after another to seduce the hero, till finally the abbess succeeds; when the same hero comes by means of a magic spell to his beloved's bedroom and throws her to the floor in a heap, which the public applauds and perhaps will afterward applaud throughout Germany; and when she then begs him for mercy in an aria; when in another opera the maiden disrobes while singing a song about how tomorrow at this time she will be married:—this makes a great effect, but I have no music for it. For it is low-class stuff, and if today the times wish for it and find it necessary, then I would rather write church music.[115]

Although concerned about the moral position of the opera, Mendelssohn did not wish his libretto to be obviously polemical. He raised this issue clearly in his response to Devrient's 1846 sketch for *Knight and Peasant*. For one thing, Mendelssohn found too much of what he called "historical ballast" that needed to be jettisoned. This seems to have included a certain amount of preaching about sociopolitical issues:

if what you call historical ballast *can* be *less*, if a considerable amount of this local color *can* fall by the wayside, then I know nothing to criticize in the whole thing. For this is all that does not satisfy me in its overall impression—the mass of motives having to do with conditions of freedom, bondage, and society throughout the whole piece. But can these be reduced?

Later in the same letter,

the only thing that disturbs me in the second act is that towards the end the countess becomes a little too modern, too didactic, for me—or were you just suggesting motives there, which would be stated in a few words in the performance? For, at such a time, in such agitation, she must not and cannot give so much weight to the mésalliance.[116]

In fact, Mendelssohn's and Devrient's political positions had begun to diverge, as Devrient's later discussion makes clear.[117] It is possible that Devrient, living at the time in Dresden, had come under the influence of the political radicalism to which Wagner subscribed. Mendelssohn, though he avidly maintained an Enlightenment belief in the social and cultural betterment of the populace, was far from being a revolutionary, and he clearly resisted explicit polemicism in an opera libretto.

The fiasco of the commission by the London publishers Chappell for an opera to a libretto by Planché produced a series of letters in which Mendelssohn articulated some criteria for an opera libretto. Although Planché's report of this unfortunate episode does not reflect the composer in a favorable light, his extensive quotations of Mendelssohn's letters are extremely helpful in understanding the composer's critical approach to a libretto.

One of the most thorough documents in which Mendelssohn laid out criteria for an opera libretto is his letter to Planché, written on 12 February 1838, before any work had begun (see the Historical Views and Documents for this chapter). His list of criteria is strikingly detailed: an opera in three (or two) acts—each act leading effectively to its own finale, on a historical subject, full of adventure but not tragic, with a variety of character types, and with a chorus that represents the entire range of social classes and that acts as a character in its own right. Although he wanted the opera to be original, he suggested as models the two most successful works of the "rescue opera" genre, Cherubini's *Les deux journées* for general character and Beethoven's *Fidelio* for intensity of personal drama. He wanted the story to have a moral position, in that it should celebrate some great human feeling or motivation leading to a noble, virtuous action. This should be a feeling, moreover, with which listeners would identify personally and find applicable to their own lives.[118]

When Planché's first sketch of the subject arrived, Mendelssohn critiqued it carefully and on a number of grounds. He particularly approved of the portrayal of patriotism and of the strong contrasts. He worried, however, about the inability of the situation to sustain interest in the first act and about lack of clarity in the characters' motivations in the third.[119]

Planché's complete version of the first two acts earned Mendelssohn's praise for several individual numbers and for the musicality of the verses. He commended the "occasion for the display of different passions in music" that they offered. On the other hand, he had reservations, partly about some unidentified aspects of the first act and partly about the "great quantity of serious characters and music." The latter problem, he suggested, could be ameliorated by raising the profile of the character Marrant.[120] His letters to William Chappell indicate that this continued to be a concern.[121]

In later correspondence, after he had already attempted to disassociate himself from the project, he framed this criticism a bit differently:

the real objection I had in view was the want of what I may call *characteristic* scenes, a full display of one or different lively and living characters. . . . The leading characters of the opera, excepting Gaultier, seemed to me to act as men more bound by the necessity of the poem, of the plot, than by their own human feeling, as real living people do. . . . I see only the stage and its necessities in the whole of the proceeding. . . . Perhaps you will say that the plot, "la marche de la pièce," is nothing to the composer; but you will *not* say so, knowing better than I do how important it is that no verses, no music, can make up for a want of strength in that quarter.[122]

Mendelssohn's critique of William Bartholomew's libretto for *A Christmas Night's Dream* likewise shows his concern for genuinely dramatic, human situations. While Klingemann seems to have pronounced the libretto "monotonous" and objected to the idea of the fairies, Mendelssohn went into detail about how the libretto lacked unity and real human drama:

In the course of the first act, Earth is spoken of as a contrast to the fairy region; Amor is several times warned of the cares of mortals, of their misery, their wants, etc.; yet these are not brought forward in the subsequent action, for the separation which he must endure in the beginning of the third act is not what we imagine alone when we hear those words in the first act, and besides, we see immediately that the separation is only a whim of Oberon, which has no necessity in itself, and comes too late in the course of the drama to excite real fear or compassion. Also, the fairies I think would come out much better if a real earthly life would have been opposed to their fanciful one. The beautiful verses themselves, and the imaginative songs they sing, seem to demand such a contrast, and can only produce the impression which they ought when combined with those earthly elements. Bottom and his company are certainly essential to the fanciful impression produced by the "Midsummer Night's Dream," and they are not only the first but the second contrast to the fairies, Theseus and the lovers forming the first. Something like this is what I want in your libretto, and the only thing I want in it. Without such a contrast I doubt that I could form a truly effective Opera, at least I do not think myself equal to it.[123]

In a similar vein the composer's response two months later to the proposal from Adolf Böttger that he take on the Legend of St. Genoveva indicates his desire for a strong and active main character:

I have frequently thought over the subject of the Legend of St. Genoveva, which you propose, but have always been deterred from it by a certain passiveness in the character or at least in the action of the chief personage. By which I mean that our interest in Genoveva arises more from what she suffers and the way in which she suffers it, than from what she does, or from any dramatic business or action on her part. . . . I can hardly believe that even under the liveliest treatment any really active dramatic life could be thrown into the principal personage, or a really original and characteristic development given to the subordinate personages in the piece.[124]

Devrient reports that someone had recommended Atterbom's *Insel der Glückseligkeit* to him in 1843 as a possible subject for an opera, and he had, in turn, suggested that Mendelssohn read it in this light.[125] Mendelssohn's reply again points out the absolute necessity for real human experience, rejecting the characters in the poem as mere anthropomorphs:

The nymphs of poetry, of music, of architecture, etc., the god of the zephyr, the mother of the winds, magic spells, miraculous fountains, etc., etc.—all that, in my opinion, does not make something operatic, and the purely human, noble, completely living, which do make it so, of these I have not found much in it, however many beautiful poetic details there are.[126]

What bothered Mendelssohn about Prechtler's idea for *Die Kronenwächter* may have been a similar lack of dramatic, human reality. He expressed himself unable to get over the "soft, dreamy element" of the material.[127]

In his letter to Devrient about *Knight and Peasant* on 9 May 1846, Mendelssohn criticized details that reflect his sharp judgment about character and motivation: that "the countess's brother [is] a much too disagreeable fellow"; that "there is too little motivation for throwing Conrad into the tower"; that the main character's behavior in persuading the peasants to revolt seemed "much too unsympathetic"; that the character distinction between knight and peasant was not handled effectively.[128]

As Mendelssohn came to realize, his primary criterion for an opera libretto was a compelling plot. After about 1840 he increasingly asked not for libretto drafts but simply for scenarios, arguing that a tightly worked-out and convincing plot was the necessary and sufficient condition for him.

Mendelssohn's letter to Julius Fürst, written just shortly after the end of his correspondence with Planché, on 4 January 1840, shows that he had become increasingly concerned with the plot content and design of potential opera subjects rather than details. He specifically mentioned the problems with the Planché libretto in this regard, and his suggestion that he had resolved not to let a librettist become too far committed before the plot was satisfactorily worked out indicates that he had learned a valuable lesson from that episode. He now insisted on previewing the scenario before allowing a librettist to proceed with the text:

what can prevent me from composing a text and to this point has always prevented me, has never been the verses, the individual words, nor the expression of the plot (whatever you want to call it), but always the whole action, the dramatic essence, the incidents,—the *scenarium*. If I do not regard that as good and secure in itself, then it is my firm conviction that the music will not be so either.[129]

He continued by recognizing that not everyone might regard this as a necessary factor in operas, particularly not the public, but he claimed it as a matter of conscience for himself.

In 1845 he wrote to Devrient, raising the difficulty of finding a compelling plot but also insisting that if the dramatic outline convinced him, the composition itself would be no problem:

I apparently do not have the talent to put together a scenario for myself; . . . . since I have been here I have used my free hours every day to read and tried to construct scenic material out of it. All of Zschokke, all sorts of historical works, etc., I have plowed through in my mind—nothing helps me; I do not have the ability to do it. I wanted to write this to you for three weeks, and add a sigh of frustration and say to you, if only you would finally help me! I have faith that you can do it, and I think that with your present perspective on the *répertoire*, coming from your daily involvement and direction of it, a mass of subjects, old and new, must always be running through your mind! If in the course of this you would once think, "Wait! this would make a good opera"—and if you would write out the material for me on two pages of a letter, then you would have fulfilled my wish! More than the topic and the roughest scenario, that is, the breakdown of what would happen in each of three acts, more I do not want; I would not even like more than this, I tell you this again. If I have this, then I have the opera; for I can recognize it on this basis; but I cannot make it myself. How happy I would be if you wanted to help me do it! I know no local poets, and to make the acquaintance of one with this in mind is impossible and would not help; my experiences with this have been too unpleasant, and I will not and may not set a bad libretto (i.e., subject). See whether you know some advice to give me or create for me. The *working* of the text, as I said, I will have done for me, or do it myself; but the basic outline! that's the thing! It must be *German*, and *noble*, and *optimistic*; it might be a Rhenish folk tale, or some other truly national event or fairy tale, or a strong fundamental *character* (as in *Fidelio*). It is *not* Kohlhas and not *Bluebeard*, or *Andreas Hofer*, or the *Lorelei*—but something of all these could be in it! Can you make me a verse out of all this? But I do not mean a verse; I mean a scenario.[130]

Shortly thereafter he repeated this point:

I have again been feeling these days as if in a couple of months I would have written an actual opera score, and as if fresh, patriotic choruses, and all sorts of fiery and quiet ones, and sweet arias and solo songs must contrast to each other in it. But then it occurred to me that the best thing was still lacking; the thread on which they must be strung.[131]

Mendelssohn's trouble with Scribe's 1846 libretto for *The Tempest* again depended on the weakness of the plot. Lumley reports that Mendelssohn could not accept the second part of the opera. According to Lumley, Mendelssohn's judgment was "more strictly logical and analytical" than Scribe's "facile imagination . . . , however fertile in scenic resources," and Mendelssohn insisted on "rigidity of sequence" for the drama.[132]

Die Lorelei

Paradoxically, the question of what led to Mendelssohn's difficulties in composing an opera is only complicated by consideration of the one on which he finally did work. It is difficult to make a convincing case that he began the composition because its libretto was, in fact, superior to those he had rejected, and at the same time his failure to complete the work had not to do with artistic difficulties but only with his death.

The subject of the legend of the Lorelei had been presented to Mendelssohn by the Berlin writer Johann Baptist Rousseau in 1844, and Mendelssohn also discussed the subject with Devrient at the end of that year.[133] The composer later corresponded about this topic for a libretto with Charlotte Birch-Pfeiffer.[134] Emanuel Geibel (with Devrient's help), however, ultimately became the librettist for the opera.

Geibel and Mendelssohn apparently first discussed the requirements for a successful libretto in 1845 in Berlin.[135] In the winter of 1845–1846 the two exchanged ideas and achieved the general outline, but Mendelssohn became increasingly disillusioned with its dramatic problems and called on Devrient to assist in the shaping of the libretto. The work on the libretto and its attendant uncertainties and disagreements continued through the first half of 1847.[136] The composition of the music apparently began in earnest in the summer, even though Mendelssohn remained less than entirely satisfied with the libretto, and ended with his fatal illness.[137]

Mendelssohn wrote a substantial portion of the music for act 1 of *Die Lorelei*. Three numbers were published posthumously: the "Ave Maria" for chorus and soprano solo from scene 3; the vintagers' chorus from scene 4; and the finale, scene 8.[138] In addition, the composer's 1847 manuscript book[139] includes, for scene 2, a thirty-measure sketch of a duet for the two leading characters; for scene 7, thirty-five pages of music, including the complete score of a march for orchestra and chorus, as well as a fully scored revision score for a contrast quartet with chorus, and an incomplete score draft for a festive chorus and soloists. (There are also a couple of rejected, incomplete score fragments for the act 1 finale.)[140]

What finally precipitated Mendelssohn's decision to begin work on an opera cannot be established with certainty. Geibel had little experience as an operatic or even theatrical writer, and commentators generally agree that the libretto is not a very strong one. It has been described, for example, as "Das in seinem innersten

Kern undramatische, . . . Libretto" and an "all-too-lyrical and undramatic text."[141] As already noted, Mendelssohn had his own doubts and hesitations about it.[142]

We should thus probably look to biographical, rather than artistic, forces to explain the composition of this music. Mendelssohn surely must have begun to feel that after so many years of frustration in the search for the ideal libretto, going to work on the best one available was preferable to further dawdling. Eric Werner has advanced the interesting theory that Mendelssohn regarded *Die Lorelei* as a preparatory exercise, after which four or five further attempts might lead to something really good.[143] The death of Mendelssohn's sister Fanny in May 1847 led the composer to a period of attempted sublimation of his grief in intensive work, and the discipline of facing his compositional nemesis, the opera, may be tied in with this. One of his greatest motivations, no doubt, was to compose an opera for his dear friend Jenny Lind, and the Lorelei story was an obvious choice to feature a soprano. The confluence of a number of factors, in any case, provided the necessary and sufficient conditions to bring Mendelssohn to the point that up to this time he had failed to reach.

What can we learn from the music Mendelssohn left for this opera? In some sense it is difficult to critique the surviving music itself, because it clearly does not represent finished work. Eric Werner, though making a qualitative judgment comparing Mendelssohn's *Die Lorelei* to Wagner's music, also stated the historical situation and critical problem quite accurately when he wrote, "Mendelssohn's effort has the effect of a pencil sketch beside a fully executed fresco."[144]

Some critics have found the existing music too lyrical and lacking in drama, just as is the libretto. Treatments of the act 1 finale, for example, include the following:

the master would have found it difficult to make the desired operatic success [from this libretto]. For even the great beauty of the finished finale succeeds much more forcefully in the concert hall than in the occasional staged performances.[145]

The finale of the first act opens with great fire and excitement, but with the entry of Leonora [*sic*], the heroine, the music seems somehow to lose its character, and the effect of the last section is somewhat spoilt by the rather pedestrian rhythm of its main theme.[146]

Mendelssohn was not able to instill his music with dramatic breadth and sensual power. Indeed the half-finished [*sic*] Finale of the first act . . . is no operatic finale.[147]

Observing the pieces that appear in the opera's music, we may note a variety of types. The "Ave Maria," the vintagers' chorus, and the orchestral-choral march constitute closed set pieces in the manner of Mendelssohn's other choral music or the numbers within his incidental music. The sketched duet for Lenore and Otto in scene 2 belongs to the type of operatic duet that expresses the characters' personalities and moods. The revision score of the quartet (with chorus) for Otto, Bertha, Hubert, and Reinald, in which they react in their various ways to Lenore's collapse upon learning that Otto has betrayed her, is a contrast ensemble, based on a static situation but portraying the diverse emotions of the characters.[148] Each of these types is handled quite competently.

The finale raises the question of the actual nature of this opera. Thinking in terms of Mozart's operas, in particular, those on the Da Ponte librettos, criticism might take as normative or ideal the action ensemble, which brings leading characters into direct conflict. *Die Lorelei* has another sort of finale, one that involves a single character, and while she participates in dialogue with the spirits of the Rhine, there is no real conflict between her and them. The finale functions instead to bring the central character to the moment of no return, rather in the manner, for example, of the Wolf's Glen scene in Weber's *Der Freischütz*. Geibel and Mendelssohn's opera thus belongs to the genre of Romantic folktale opera, in which such a scene becomes the crucial one for the progress of the drama.

As we have seen, one of Mendelssohn's recurring concerns about opera librettos was always the presence of real human drama in their plots. While this was a characteristic of the Enlightenment opera buffa—fulfilled most impressively in the Da Ponte/Mozart operas—it is not necessarily the case in Romantic fairy-tale opera. Instead, these operas depend on moments of local color, expression of personal feeling, evocation of the supernatural. Mendelssohn was, in fact, highly qualified to compose such numbers, yet at the same time he apparently felt uncomfortable with this fundamental premise of the genre. His dramatic-critical judgment seems at odds with the opera that, probably due to biographical reasons, he eventually undertook. Such an ambivalent combination of factors, particularly in the absence of a completed *Lorelei*, means that the composer's undertaking, finally, does not help to elucidate the causes of his failure to establish a place for himself in the history of opera.

Mendelssohn's Opera Problem Reconsidered

In the end, then, Mendelssohn's failure to complete an opera in his mature years stems both from inner doubts and from hypercritical judgments of the librettos or topics that he considered, so that both Planché and Holtei saw part of the truth. That he might have composed an effective opera, too, is suggested by the skill demonstrated in his early Singspiele and by the later successes of both his oratorios and his incidental music.

One cannot overlook the fact that Mendelssohn had been severely disappointed in his first and only publicly staged opera, *Die Hochzeit des Camacho*, when he was still very young. Much of the blame went to the libretto. He became gun-shy after that, as he himself admitted to Devrient, and so excessively critical of every idea and libretto that came along that one might argue that he paralyzed himself. In fact, on two occasions—with Klingemann and with Planché—he got into extended correspondence, with detailed scenario drafts, and made a great many very specific suggestions, but they eventually came to nothing and even created quite serious hard feelings. It might seem as though all his criticisms and suggestions were really intended (perhaps subconsciously) to sabotage the projects. To prove this, however, is surely impossible.

One cannot argue that Mendelssohn never encountered a potentially workable opera subject or libretto. Several of the librettists with whom he considered working had highly successful careers in their field, including even Eugène Scribe, undoubtedly one of the most important librettists of the period. Topics that Mendelssohn rejected, including Genoveva and the Nibelungenlied, formed the material for operas by Schumann and Wagner. Actual librettos that Mendelssohn turned down made operas by Marschner and Halévy. In the end, the matter can be only a personal one; as Mendelssohn himself wrote, "The only thing is whether it corresponds with my being, musical and otherwise."[149]

Mendelssohn's ability to compose music for dramatic texts is abundantly demonstrated by the fact that he did write brilliant pieces for oratorios and plays. One might argue that a fundamental aesthetic difference obtains between the musical/dramaturgical principles of the genres and that this made it possible to compose successful oratorios and incidental music for plays but not operas. Just how to define the difference(s) is not so clear, however. It is not obvious why a chorus of heathens in *Elijah* should be different from, say, a secular chorus of rioting peasants in an opera based on the sixteenth-century Peasants' Revolt in Germany, just because the former is biblical, and the latter is not. The Baal chorus in Elijah is also clearly developed from the Bacchic chorus in the incidental music to *Antigone*, so on the face of it the sacred/secular distinction cannot make a decisive difference. Likewise, the ability to express sincere personal emotion in an oratorio aria suggests that the composer could do the same in an opera.[150]

Eric Werner offered the suggestion that Mendelssohn was incapable of composing *Die Lorelei* because he could not get past his own moral position. Werner expressed what he regarded as Mendelssohn's dilemma by quoting Kierkegaard's dictum that "one either has to live esthetically or one has to live ethically."[151] In Werner's view, Mendelssohn could not create the passionate character of Lenore, nor perhaps of any other effective operatic character, because the composer's own morality made him incapable of empathizing with the strong feelings of the morally conflicted characters necessary to a successful opera. Such simplistic psychoartistic solutions inevitably remain intellectually unverifiable. In this case, Werner's hypothesis plays into the old, conventionalized image of Mendelssohn as too "Biedermeier" or too "Victorian" (even too Jewish in, e.g., Wagner's formulation) to produce profound Romantic works. To be sure, Mendelssohn was not a moral or musical Romantic in the manner of Berlioz (whose reputation also does not depend on his operas, however), but both in his life and in his music he did experience and express deep and intense feeling. Werner's argument does not, in the end, constitute a convincing explanation of Mendelssohn's lack of an operatic career.

The historian or critic cannot give a simple, single explanation why Mendelssohn never composed operas during his maturity. Neither musical nor moral hypotheses prove viable, but such hypotheses are really not necessary. The off-putting experience of *Die Hochzeit des Camacho*, Mendelssohn's sharp critical judgment of librettos and scenarios, the fact that he found more than sufficient other projects in his career to occupy him, and, of course, his early death all militated against his becoming an opera composer.

It is worth reconsidering why the absence of mature operas by Mendelssohn should have become an issue at all. Though some of his contemporaries, certainly Mendelssohn's father, still regarded operatic success as a certifying accomplishment for any aspiring master composer, this was no longer so much the case as it once had been. Among Mendelssohn's leading contemporaries, the careers of neither Berlioz nor Liszt nor Schumann nor Chopin were validated by opera. It became an issue for Mendelssohn, in part, because he was bombarded with subjects, scenarios, and librettos, and this came about precisely because he was already regarded as the leading composer of his time. Mendelssohn's "failure" to write an opera does not amount to a sign of psychological or artistic weakness. Ultimately, it is merely a biographical fact.

INCIDENTAL MUSIC

Düsseldorf

At several stages of his life Mendelssohn had occasion to compose music to accompany stage dramas. During his years at Düsseldorf (1832–1835) he wrote movements for productions of plays by the resident dramatist Karl Immermann (1796–1840). The first such piece was a short song, the "Todeslied der Bojaren," for men's chorus in unison, supported by an ensemble of paired woodwind instruments, composed in 1832 for Immermann's tragedy *Alexis*.[152] It was later published as a solo song with piano accompaniment. The most extensive project in the Düsseldorf years was music for Immermann's adaptation of Pedro Calderón de la Barca's (1600–1681) play *The Steadfast Prince (Der standhafte Prinz)* for a performance in April 1833. The music consisted of two men's choruses for a group of Portuguese held captive by Arabs, music to represent a battle (which actually takes place offstage), and two solemn marches.[153] At the end of the same year Mendelssohn contributed to a production of Immermann's *Andreas Hofer* a "Schnadahüpferl" for two tenors, arranged from a popular Tyrolese melody, and a French march.[154]

Leipzig

In Leipzig Mendelssohn wrote the overture and a song for two-part women's chorus for a performance of Victor Hugo's *Ruy Blas*. Approached for both of these pieces, he at first agreed only to write the song, apparently demurring in regard to the overture on the grounds that he did not have enough time. When the representatives of the Theatrical Pension Fund, for whose benefit the play would be performed, suggested that perhaps he could compose an overture for them on some other occasion, when he had more time, Mendelssohn took it as a challenge. He dashed off the overture in three days.[155]

Mendelssohn thought Hugo's play "detestable" and "utterly beneath contempt." The overture consequently is unrelated to the drama but essentially a stock piece, serving as a suitably generic curtain-raiser. Mendelssohn acknowledged this when he wrote that he would later present the work on a concert not as the Overture to *Ruy Blas* but as the Overture to the Theatrical Pension Fund. Despite his antipathy to the play, he obviously enjoyed the accomplishment and the rollicking music itself.

The song is a simple, strophic love song in the key of A major, comparing the beloved to the charms of nature. Mendelssohn scored it for pizzicato strings; it was later published in its piano arrangement in the posthumous set of three duets Op. 77. Its "characteristic" features come from momentary shifts of mode, both to the parallel minor and to the mediant, where the harmonic minor form of the scale produces a distinctive augmented second in the melody.

Berlin

In 1840 the Prussian king Friedrich Wilhelm III died, and his son, who became Friedrich Wilhelm IV, succeeded him. The new king believed deeply that his authority derived from the will of God, and he consequently regarded it as a part of his responsibility to suit himself for the work divinely entrusted to him by surrounding himself with some of the leading intellectuals of Germany in his time and the finest works of culture from both ancient and modern periods. Among his projects proceeding from this principle he sponsored the revival of great works of drama.

One of the most important of the literary figures whom Friedrich Wilhelm IV gathered to Berlin was the author and philosopher Ludwig Tieck. Tieck, renowned for his magnificent public readings, became the king's resident reader.[156] His interpretations of great classical dramas inspired the idea of restaging some of the most important works of the historic theater. One of Tieck's interests was the historical playing spaces of both the Greek and Shakespearean dramas. Tieck became the mastermind of these productions, serving as dramaturge, guiding the staging, and rehearsing the actors. To compose incidental music for these plays, the king looked to Wilhelm Taubert, Giacomo Meyerbeer,[157] and Mendelssohn.

According to the plan devised by the king and his advisers, the plays were first staged in the private royal theater in the New Palace at Sans Souci in Potsdam for the king and his guests. Those invited included the Prussian royal household, government officials, intellectuals, and social and financial leaders of Berlin.[158] Each production was then to be moved to the public theater in the city of Berlin, so that the entire populace could benefit from exposure to these masterpieces.

The plays produced under this plan included mainly those of the Greeks: of Sophocles there was the complete Theban trilogy; of Euripedes, *Medea*[159] and *Hippolytus*. The two non-Greek plays were by Shakespeare and Racine, in both cases composed by Mendelssohn. A number of other plays came under consideration; in addition to the ones he did compose, Mendelssohn turned down requests for music for Aeschylus's *Eumenides* (as did Meyerbeer) and

Shakespeare's *As You Like It*, and there were at one time or another plans for him to compose *Oedipus the King* and *The Tempest*.[160] The ones he actually composed were in 1841, Sophocles's *Antigone*, chosen especially by Tieck as the first to appear in the series; in 1843, Shakespeare's *A Midsummer Night's Dream*, a natural choice considering the success of Mendelssohn's overture of seventeen years earlier; in 1845, both Sophocles's *Oedipus in Colonus*, which stands in the Theban cycle after *Oedipus the King* and before *Antigone*, and Racine's *Athalie*.

Antigone and *Oedipus in Colonus*

Sophocles stood in very high regard among the thinkers of the early nineteenth century, and especially so in the intellectual community surrounding Mendelssohn. Hegel, whose lectures Mendelssohn had heard at the University of Berlin, both Friedrich and August Wilhelm Schlegel, and the classicist August Böckh, who lived for a time in the Mendelssohn mansion at Leipzigerstraße 3, had much to say about Sophocles's plays. *Antigone* in particular resonated with late-Enlightenment/early-Romantic concerns. Its conflict between Antigone's subjective need to fulfill personal, familial, and spiritual obligations and Creon's insistence on the need for civic regulation presented a timely parallel to the modern tension between the rise of the Romantic value of individualism and feeling and the establishment of modern nations and the bourgeois social order.[161]

Mendelssohn himself could well have identified with the two Sophocles plays for which he composed the music. Michael Steinberg has suggested how Mendelssohn's own position in regard to his family heritage and the idea of Jewish assimilation into the larger European bourgeois culture paralleled Antigone's situation.[162] Another parallel might be suggested, as well, for Mendelssohn may have felt a special affinity for both the author and the protagonist of *Oedipus in Colonus*. The descriptions of Sophocles published in August Wilhelm von Schlegel's *Lectures on Dramatic Art and Literature*, which had been published by 1809 and which Mendelssohn therefore probably knew, could equally apply to Mendelssohn himself:

Descended from rich and honourable parents, and born a free citizen of the most enlightened state of [his nation]:—there were birth, necessary condition, and foundation. Beauty of person and of mind, and the uninterrupted enjoyment of both in the utmost perfection . . . ; a most choice and finished education in gymnastics and the musical arts, . . . the possession of and unbroken enjoyment of poetry and art, and the exercise of serene wisdom; love and respect among his fellow citizens, renown abroad, and the countenance and favour of the gods.[163]

Further, Mendelssohn knew that Sophocles had set the story of Oedipus's passing in his own natal town, near Athens. The composer had been recalled by the new king to Berlin, the city in which he had spent his youth and that still represented his family home. Moreover, like Oedipus going to Colonus on the arm of his daughter Antigone, Mendelssohn went to Berlin and was cared for there by his family. All this might well have resonated in Mendelssohn's mind as he approached the composition.

In addition, the drama's plot reflects some aspects of Mendelssohn's personal situation. Like Oedipus's family, he found himself a member of a cursed race, once rejected and exiled from his hometown. After lengthy negotiations, he had gone to Berlin anxious to be reconciled to the city through the king's support, despite misgivings about the king's commitment and the vagueness of his duties. The play's account of Oedipus's going to Colonus and appealing to Theseus, king of Athens, for protection and peace certainly must have seemed apropos to Mendelssohn.[164]

The composition of the Sophoclean plays presented Mendelssohn some special challenges. Since the intention of the production was to re-create the originals as nearly as could be done, an antiquarian approach was applied wherever possible.

The texts were translated but not abridged or adapted. The German used was the metrical translation of Johann Jakob Christian Donner, though somewhat altered in several places by the philologist Böckh and by Mendelssohn himself in order to render awkward passages more grateful for singing.

The Prussian staging for *Antigone* and *Oedipus in Colonus* was modeled on the style of antiquity, as far as it was understood by the archaeology of the time. The stage area in the Sans Souci theater was completely rebuilt based on the theories of the architect Hans Christian Genelli (d. 1823), a friend of Tieck. The front of the stage became circular (actually semicircular) in the manner of the *orchestra* of the Greek theaters, so that it would be visible to all the spectators. In the middle of the orchestra stood the *thymele* or altar (which now served, in thoroughly inauthentic fashion, to hide a prompter). Following Greek practice, the chorus, which would sing the music, consisted of fifteen men—two half choruses of seven singers each and the leader or *coryphaeus*—and remained in the orchestra.[165] At the rear the actors occupied a platform elevated about five feet above the orchestra level. (According to more modern researchers, such a design was not characteristic of the classic, Sophoclean stage but of the later, Hellenistic period.) Actors and chorus entered from the side, an inevitable consequence of the Greek theater design. There was no curtain, and, although Aristotle reports that Sophocles invented scene painting, there was no scenic set or backdrop but merely a back wall in neoclassic architectural style.

Mendelssohn's task here differed considerably from that faced by most composers of dramatic music at the time. He not only had no opportunity for dialogue with the author, as an opera composer might with a librettist, but the idea of "authentic" performance meant that he could hardly argue, as a composer might in other circumstances (and as his dealings with opera texts and scenarios certainly suggest he would have done), for any significant adjustments to the text of the drama.

The general musical structure of the Sophoclean tragedy consists of a standard sequence of actions and set pieces (anticipatory reference to the left-hand columns of Tables 4.1 and 4.2 may be helpful to the reader at this point). The actors are responsible for the *prologos* or exposition. The chorus, led by the aulos player, then enters the orchestra, singing the *parodos*—which, to be effective, must be motivated by the plot. There follows a series of scenes (numbering usually from two to four) for the actors, each called *epeisodion*, and each leading to a choral lyric, the *stasimon* or *ode*, sung by the chorus in the orchestra. The term

Table 4.1
Design of *Antigone*

Dramatic unit	Musical number	Text content	Tonal plan
	Introduction		c (→V)
Parodos	No. 1	Praise of Thebes and arrival of Creon	C
Stasimon No. 2		The wonder of humanity	A
	No. 2a	Arrival of Ismene	
Stasimon No. 3		The curse on the family of Labdacos	F/f
Stasimon/ Kommos	No. 4	The power of Eros	G
		Dialogue with Antigone about her fate	→g
Stasimon No. 5		Cases of the effect of *dike*	
Stasimon No. 6		Appeal to Bacchus	D
Exodos/ exodion	No. 7		c

"stasimon" refers to the static nature of the ode, in two senses: first, the chorus remains within the orchestra; second, the form of the number is particularly stable, as it consists of strophe and antistrophe, possibly two of each, and an *epode* or conclusion. In addition to the stasima, the chorus may participate in passages of dialogue with the actors on the stage, called *kommos*. The last epeisodion leads to the *exodos*, in which the final catastrophe occurs and in which the chorus sings the *exodion* as it exits from the orchestra. The actors may remain to provide the epilogue before their final exit.

The plan for *Antigone* included a truncated overture, which Mendelssohn called "Introduction," followed by seven numbered pieces representing the major choral sections of the drama: parodos, stasima (including one that continues as kommos), and exodos (see Table 4.1). The structure of *Oedipus in Colonus* was similar. Mendelssohn wrote a much briefer orchestral introduction, and there are only three stasima, but the addition of several musical kommoi or dialogues between actors and chorus produced additional musical numbers (see Table 4.2).

Table 4.2
Design of *Oedipus in Colonus*

Dramatic unit	Musical number	Text content	Tonal plan
	Introduction		d (→V)
Prologos		Oedipus and Antigone arrive in Colonus	
Parodos	No. 1	Chorus enters, searching for the intruder	a (→A)
Epeisodion	No. 1a	Decision to appeal to Theseus Ismene arrives	D
Kommos	No. 2	Chorus interrogates Oedipus Theseus promisesprotection to Oedipus	d (→F)
Stasimon No. 3		Praise of Colonus	F
Epeisodion		Creon confronts Oedipus	
Kommos	No. 4	Creon's abduction of Antigone and Ismene	B♭
Stasimon No. 5		Battle to rescue Antigone and Ismene	d→D
Epeisodion		Antigone returns Theseus reports arrival of Polynices	
Stasimon No. 6		Meditation on age	g→G
Exodos		Oedipus meets and curses Polynices	
Kommos	No. 7	Thunderstorm as Furies call Oedipus away	c
Exodion	No. 8	Prayer for Oedipus at his passing	A♭
	No. 9	epilogue	d (→D)

The extant repertoire of Greek music provided, of course, no historical model for an instrumental overture to precede the play. For *Antigone* Mendelssohn composed a substantial orchestral introduction (101 measures) that gives the impression of a slow introduction and fast sonata-form movement but remains open-ended on the dominant. *Oedipus in Colonus* has only a thirteen-measure slow introduction, also ending on the dominant, during which Oedipus and Antigone enter.

In composing the choral movements, Mendelssohn first had to make some general decisions about the style to be used. The distribution of the choral music in the vocal ensemble manifests considerable variety and ingenuity. The fifteen-member chorus offered a variety of possibilities: two combined choruses; two separate choruses, usually exchanging strophe and antistrophe; unison or up to four parts (TTBB) in each or both choruses; passages for solo singers from the chorus (as distinct from the coryphaeus).

Another major concern was the problem of instrumental scoring. Early in his thinking about *Antigone* Mendelssohn apparently took note of—though he did not consider as realistic—the possibility of approximating the instrumentarium of the Greeks: flutes for the aulos, harps for the lyre or kithara, and tubas for the salpinx or keras.[166] He sensibly set aside this hopelessly naive idea and composed the music for a full-sized Romantic orchestra, with the addition of harp. One striking aspect of the scorings in the Sophocles plays is the use of orchestral combinations as rather static blocks, not unlike organ registrations, changing according to structural sections of the choruses. This becomes an important means for articulating strophe from antistrophe, on the one hand, as well as for providing contrasts between sections in which the vocal parts are more or less direct repetitions (for one example of this approach, see the outline of the parodos of *Antigone*, Table 4.3).

Table 4.3
Antigone, No. 1, Scoring

Strophe 1	Antistrophe 1	Strophe 2	Antistrophe 2	Epode
Chorus 1 (unis./div.)	Chorus 2 (unis./div.)	Full chorus (div./recit.)	Full chorus (div.)	Recit. (leader chorus)
2 ob 2 cl 2 bsn 2 hn 2 tpt 3 tbn	2 fl hp str	2 cl, timp, str (with full ww and br punctuation); later full ww, str	ww and hp alternating with full orch	str

While the chorus sang its part, the actors spoke their lines, even in the sections of dialogue between stage and orchestra. In these kommoi the actors' lines received orchestral underscoring—that is, as melodrama. Generally, the actors spoke in free rhythm, the words simply written into the score with fermatas in the orchestral music as necessary. Mendelssohn did experiment briefly with rhythmic speech, as shown in Example 4.18. He intended here that the speech should

Example 4.18
Antigone, no. 4, mm. 110–18

proceed in natural rhythms, the instrumentalists accommodating the notated rhythm to the actor's declamation (see the composer's detailed instructions to George Macfarren for the English performance of *Antigone* in the Historical Views and Documents section of this chapter).

The prosody of the text was a matter of considerable importance. Mendelssohn's contemporaries, as well as the composer himself, had great faith in the intrinsic value of the poetic structure. Wilhelm von Humboldt argued that something of the cultural spirit of the original would be embodied in the translation of ancient works, if the meter were preserved.[167] August Böckh, describing Mendelssohn's approach to the music, suggested that adherence to the original rhythms would carry over to affect the music more broadly: "If the composer subjects himself to the admittedly difficult constraint of the given rhythm, then this will lead him near to the ancient melos, since the two elements must agree."[168]

In a letter to his friend the historian Johann Gustav Droysen, Mendelssohn indicated that he identified with this idea in composing *Antigone*: "the moods and the prosody are so genuinely musical throughout that one does not have to think about the individual words and only needs to compose those moods and the rhythms; then the chorus is finished."[169] In fact, Mendelssohn here suggests his general aesthetic of text setting. He believed that in texted music the words should appear as response to a feeling that was embodied in music. The composer's task thus was to read the text and perceive the feeling that should lie behind it, a feeling that for a musician is coextensive with music. He seems to have agreed with the conception, implicit in the statements by Humboldt and Böckh quoted earlier, that the prosody of the original Greek text—the only extant part of the ancient music—embodied, at least in part, that pretextual feeling.   Submitting to Sophocles's rhythms, therefore, would presumably be a requirement for the composer who wished to reproduce the feeling of the drama.

Mendelssohn's education had uniquely prepared him for the problem of setting classical metrical text. As a boy he had studied classical languages under his family tutor, Karl Wilhelm Ludwig Heyse, and he had marked the completion of his general education at the age of sixteen by publishing a metrical translation of the Latin poet Terence's *Andria*. The Donner translation of Sophocles, from which Mendelssohn worked, included as an appendix metrical tables to clarify for Germans, whose poetry (like English) depends on stress accents, the quantitative prosody of the Greek text.[170]

Some of Mendelssohn's work on the prosody for *Antigone* appears to be preserved on two pages of the autograph miscellany that forms volume 19 of his musical Nachlaß. Across the bottom staves of a bifolio of rejected score staff pages for the fourth movement of the Symphony in A minor, on which Mendelssohn was working at the same time as on *Antigone*, appear three staves of rhythmic notations (see Example 4.19). Each seems to constitute one poetic verse,

Example 4.19
Rhythm Sketches (for *Antigone*?), Staatsbibliothek zu Berlin—Preußischer Kulturbesitz, Mus. ms. autogr. Mendelssohn 19, p. 59, Staff 16

and one includes accent marks. These rhythms do not occur in the final version of *Antigone* (nor *Oedipus in Colonus*), but some resemble the ones that eventually did appear in the music.[171]

To demonstrate how Mendelssohn actually solved the problem of antiquarian rhythm, we can turn to the beautiful choral lyric that Sophocles wrote in praise of his hometown, Colonus. Example 4.20 shows the text of the first strophe, over each line of which are placed the original metrical pattern that governed it and the actual rhythm of the music in Mendelssohn's setting. Mendelssohn faced the task of achieving something that would both reflect the durational rhythm of the Greek poetry and accommodate the stress-based diction of the German language. The essential feature of these lines is the appearance of a central choriamb (long-short-short-long). Mendelssohn mostly set the choriambs similarly, in a durational transcription treating the long syllables as quarter or half notes, and the short ones as a dotted eighth and sixteenth notes on the second or fourth beat of the measure.

This careful reconstruction of the classical prosody creates a style very different from that of other music of the time. The rhythm has a distinctive repetitiveness, but the phrase lengths become somewhat irregular. Consequently, the style differs from Romantic vocal lyricism in its lack of small-scale rhythmic flexibility, while at the same time this rhythmic repetition stands quite apart from the rhythmic repetition associated with dance music, because the phrasing is notably asymmetrical. In the end, the text and the prosodic style thus really do generate a musical language quite unlike that of the rest of Mendelssohn's oeuvre or the music of his contemporaries.

That the composer found both rhythms and melos, as Böckh put it, or prosody and mood, in Mendelssohn's formulation, is demonstrated by other sketches that appear on the two folios immediately framing the prosody sketches mentioned earlier. These range from very brief thematic sketches, to drafts for substantial parts of movements. Their musical content includes not only the characteristic rhythmic/melodic material of each movement but also harmony, usually indications of figuration, and sometimes specification of dynamics and scoring (see Examples 4.21a–b). In some cases the underscoring for passages of melodrama appears here, as well (see Example 4.22). Though these are preliminary notations, they already suggest very clearly the particular moods of the final version of each movement.

Mendelssohn felt sincerely committed to his music for the Sophoclean dramas. As with all his vocal music, the basis for the composition had to be his sense of finding music that embodied the mood from which the words arise, and he felt he had done so effectively in his Sophocles choruses. He wrote from Berlin to Ferdinand David in Leipzig on 21 October 1841, just before the first performance of *Antigone*, "The task was a noble one in its own right, and I worked at it with sincere joy. It was remarkable to me how in art there is so much that remains constant; the moods of all these choruses are just as genuinely musical today, and again so diverse among themselves, that one could not wish for anything more beautiful to compose."[172]

Example 4.20
Prosody and Musical Rhythm in *Antigone*, no. 1

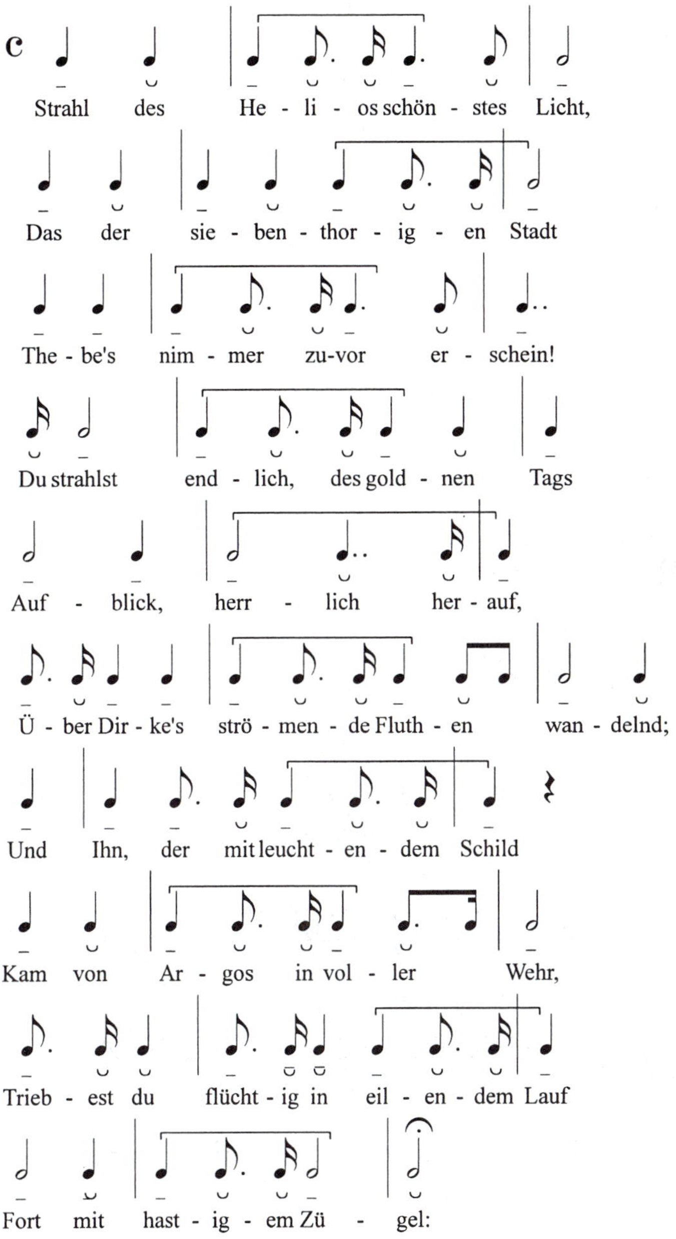

Example 4.21a
**Sketch for *Antigone*, no. 6, Staatsbibliothek zu Berlin—Preußischer Kulturbesitz, Mus.
ms. autogr. Mendelssohn 19, p. 55, Staves 1–2**

Example 4.21b
**Sketch for *Antigone*, no. 3, Staatsbibliothek zu Berlin—Preußischer Kulturbesitz, Mus.
ms. autogr. Mendelssohn 19, p. 55, Staves 5–16**

Example 4.21b, continued

Example 4.22
Sketch for *Antigone*, no. 5, Staatsbibliothek zu Berlin—Preußischer Kulturbesitz, Mus.
ms. autogr. Mendelssohn 19, p. 57, Staves 13–14

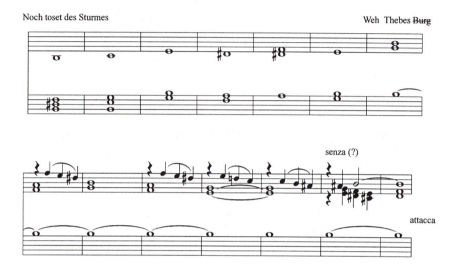

A Midsummer Night's Dream

Mendelssohn faced an altogether different task in composing the music for *A Midsummer Night's Dream*.[173] Taken as a whole, the play offered much more freedom and flexibility for the composer. Shakespeare's play requires songs and dances, to be sure, but Mendelssohn's conception included a good deal more music, including the entr'actes, which have become part of the standard concert repertoire, and underscoring for part of the dialogue.

In terms of style there was no impetus to attempt to capture a historical period. Unlike Sophocles's plays, Shakespeare's action, which takes place in Athens and a neighboring wood, demanded no inherent connection to the playwright's style and period. To set the Tudor play to pseudoantique music or the Greek pastoral action to faked-up Elizabethan music would be equally pointless. Rather, Mendelssohn had to find means within his own Romantic idiom to represent the play's magical and elfin, sylvan, and comic aspects.

It was only natural to begin by borrowing the 1826 concert overture based on the play, Op. 21. Originally intended neither to preface a production of the play nor as a programmatic working-out of the action, the overture consisted of a full-scale, sonata-form, concert work, intended to stand alone. In it Mendelssohn had already solved the problem of capturing in characteristic music the leading groups of characters—Oberon's magic, Puck and the other fairies, Theseus and his court, the lovers, and the rustics—as well as some of the moods of the play.

In addition to the overture, the performance of the play allowed for additional pieces of characteristic music in the entr'actes. That between acts 1 and 2, the Scherzo, introduces the first appearance of the fairies. It is one of Mendelssohn's trademark "elfin scherzos," thoroughly in the spirit of the principal-key theme of the overture, though entirely newly composed. The so-called Intermezzo between acts 2 and 3 begins with an evocation of Hermia's frantic search for Lysander in the forest at night, in breathless fragments exchanged among the orchestral instruments. It ends with the arrival in act 3, scene 1 of the rustics (later in the scene Puck observes them and comments, "What hempen homespuns have we swaggering here"), composed as a bumptious country dance with bagpipe-like drones. The entr'acte after act 3 (known as "Nocturne") sets the background for the sleeping mortals after Puck has reanointed Lysander's eyes with magic flower juice. The horn (and bassoon) theme establishes the sylvan scene, while soft dynamics and slow tempo create the somnolent mood. The interlude before the final act leads into the nuptial festivities of Theseus and Hippolyta, Hermia and Lysander, and Helena and Demetrius with the well-known wedding march.

Performance of *A Midsummer Night's Dream* also calls, of course, for a number of instances of onstage music. Shakespeare specified songs and dances, as well as briefer flourishes.

Most obvious in this category and most extensive is the song "You spotted snakes," sung by the fairies for Titania in act 2, scene 2 to lull her to sleep in the forest. The effect here is more oriented toward the magical mood of the fairy world than toward the lulling of the sleeper. The snakes, hedgehogs, newts and blindworms, spiders, beetles, worms, or snails that might disturb the queen are charmed away by solo singers (Mendelssohn took the liberty of assigning two different singers to the stanzas designated by Shakespeare for the First Fairy) in the minor key and with an accompaniment of humming trills in the orchestra. The chorus sings the refrain in A major and with an elfin/sylvan setting.

Act 4, scene 1 requires quite a few brief passages of music. Mendelssohn did not actually provide music at one point where Shakespeare called for it (lines 80–83):

Oberon: Titania, music call, and strike more dead
        than common sleep of all these five the sense.
Titania: Music, ho! Music, such as charmeth sleep!

instead eliding this command with Oberon's two lines later:

Oberon: Sound, music! Come my queen, take hands with me,
        And rock the ground whereon these sleepers be.

where the music of Nocturne entr'acte returns. The rocking of the ground, in Mendelssohn's interpretation here, feels less like the tremors of a wild dance than like the rocking of a cradle. The arrival of the morning brings the entrance of Theseus and his train, and Shakespeare gives the cue "Wind horn." For this Mendelssohn borrowed the horn calls from measures 70ff. of the overture. These return again as Theseus orders the lovers awakened (line 137): "Go bid the huntsmen wake them with their horns."

Another place where Shakespeare requires music comes at the end of the rustics' ridiculous play within the play, when Theseus declines to hear the epilogue but opts rather for a bergomask. The dance music naturally derives from the rustic music and braying motives of the overture (mm. 195ff. etc.).

Finally, as the fairies close the play, Oberon and Titania order the fairies to sing and dance once more (act 5, lines 386–95):

Oberon: Through the house give glimmering light,
              By the dead and drowsy fire;
          Every elf and fairy sprite
             Hop as light as bird from brier;
          And this ditty, after me,
          Sing, and dance it trippingly.
Titania: First, rehearse your song by rote,
          To each word a warbling note.
          Hand in hand, with fairy grace,
             Will we sing, and bless this place.

Underscoring these speeches, the orchestra sounds the four opening chords of the overture. Shakespeare provided no additional words for the fairy chorus, so Mendelssohn simply reset these ten lines. Emerging out of the opening chords, the orchestral accompaniment is the pianissimo rushing theme of the overture.

In addition to the onstage music called for by Shakespeare, Mendelssohn provided a couple of extra items for the Berlin production. At the performance of the rustics' play there are two brief pieces of incidental music. The first is the flourish of trumpets, not indicated by Shakespeare but called for in some editions of the play, that introduces Peter Quince's Prologue. The joke here is that the timpani enter a measure behind the trumpets and continue to play one measure behind, ending the fanfare by themselves (see Example 4.23). The second piece of incidental music for the play within the play is a funeral march for clarinet, bassoon, and timpani. The march mocks the clichés of the entire genre of funeral pieces for band that derived from the era of the French Revolution.[174] Following the bergomask the mortals exit, and fairies enter, and for this, again though Shakespeare did not suggest it, Mendelssohn supplied a bit of transitional music. The departure of the now-happy couples naturally called up the wedding march, and this diminuendos into the rushing principal theme of the overture.

Mendelssohn supplied underscoring for the play's dialogue in most of the scenes of the fairies. This music falls into two different categories: that which evokes the fairies' movement and that which symbolizes magic spells.

The first example of the former appears at Puck's entrance in act 2, scene 1. It immediately follows and actually continues the "Scherzo" entr'acte, which itself

Example 4.23
A Midsummer Night's Dream, **Op. 61, no. 10, mm. 1–9**

depicts the fairies running or fluttering, and it underscores Puck's own description of his activity (see Example 4.24):

Over hill, over dale,
  Thorough bush, thorough brier,
Over park, over pale,
  Thorough flood, thorough fire;
I do wander everywhere,
Swifter than the moon's sphere . . .

This number continues with a new theme for fairy movement later in the scene, as Oberon and Titania enter (see Example 4.25).

Underscoring music associated with magic spells first appears in act 2, scene 2, as Oberon applies the magic flower potion to Titania's eyes, and then Puck does the same to Lysander (mistakenly for Demetrius). Here it consists of a slow solo line in half notes of two minor seconds separated by an augmented second. In each case the music of the spell slips into rushing eighth notes as Oberon and Puck exit (see Example 4.26).

Both types of fairy underscoring return several times in act 3. When Puck comes upon the "hempen homespuns" and places the ass's head on Bottom, tremolos in the violins (later also violas) depict his fairy movement, while slow solos in the woodwinds indicate the magic (see Example 4.27). A curious passage comes as Bottom enters the fairy world. As Titania wakes and sees Bottom, the

Example 4.24
A Midsummer Night's Dream, Op. 61, no. 2, mm. 1–17

orchestra plays a bizarre variant of the opening chords of the overture, here the tonic E major, a chord[175] voiced g#[1], d#[2], f♮[2], b[3] (replacing the dominant B major), the minor subdominant (as in the overture), and a diminished seventh chord on C# (instead of the tonic). Titania's four attendant fairies then enter and greet Bottom with a new, heraldic sort of fairy-movement music (see Example 4.28). The scene ends as Titania directs the fairies to take Bottom to her bower, accompanied by a return to the soporific music of the overture's coda.

When Puck enters in act 3, scene 2, as well as at his exit ("I go, I go, look how I go"), and as he leads Lysander and Demetrius apart in the forest, yet more fairy-movement music accompanies him.[176] Oberon's application of potion to Demetrius naturally uses magic-spell style.

Example 4.24, continued

In act 4, scene 1 Oberon, relenting from his persecution of Titania, removes the love-spell. The music inverts the music that accompanied the spell when it was imposed (see Example 4.29).

The end of the play (Oberon's last speech and Puck's epilogue) is underscored almost literally by the close of the overture. It thus returns to magic slumber music and the final magic chords.

Example 4.24, continued

Athalie

The story of Joash (or Jehoash), the child king of Judah, recounted in 2 Kings 11, is not generally well known. It represents one of the many instances in the Old Testament in which the Jewish nation was recalled to the true faith. The period is that of the generations shortly following the reigns of Ahab and Jezebel in Israel and of the prophet Elijah. The old queen Athaliah, grandmother of the infant Joash, had seized power and attempted to kill her son's entire family, but Joash was saved and hidden for six years. He was then revealed by the priest Jehoiada (Joad),

Example 4.25
A Midsummer Night's Dream, **Op. 61, no. 2, mm. 37–44**

and Athaliah was executed. The people of Judah rejected the worship of Baal, and Joash went on to repair the temple in Jerusalem (2 Kings 12 and 2 Chronicles 24: 1–14).

The immediate significance of the story of Racine's play, therefore, could be regarded as an example for the seventeenth-century French or, in Mendelssohn's situation, the Prussian king and nation. It does not seem likely that the monarchs in whose reign either the play or the incidental music was written should be directly viewed as in danger of committing the sins of Athaliah, of course. Intended, rather,must be the positive model of Joash, a king who would direct an important spiritual and cultural renewal in his nation. The model applies somewhat more

Example 4.25, continued

obviously to Louis XIV, who became king while still a child, than to Friedrich Wilhelm IV, already middle-aged when he assumed the throne.

The continuation of the story, not pursued within Racine's play, nevertheless contains an implicit warning to the king. Joash's reign did not continue in the direction in which it began. After the death of Jehoiada, the court of Judah turned away from God and began to worship the Asherim and idols, finally stoning to death Jehoiada's son. As punishment the country suffered defeat in war, and Joash was assassinated. The implication of a parallel between Joash and a modern monarch would be that simply to begin on the right path is not enough; one must stay the course. There seems to be no direct evidence as to whether either Louis XIV or Friedrich Wilhelm IV knew the story beyond the end of the play well enough to pick up on this possible message in the subsequent career of Joash.

Unlike its contemporary *Oedipus in Colonus*, Racine's *Athalie* received a substantial overture in Mendelssohn's setting. This begins with a hymnlike slow introduction in F major, followed by a rather free sonata-form movement in D minor, ending in D major. It is therefore less self-contained than the overture of *A Midsummer Night's Dream*, yet not as open-ended as that of *Antigone*.

In *Athalie* Racine followed the strictures of the Académie for the seventeenth-century theater, modeling his play on the ancient Greek drama as interpreted by French Rationalism. As such, it used a chorus, though, in fact, in a somewhat different way from that of Sophocles. Racine specified particular assignments of

Example 4.26
A Midsummer Night's Dream, **Op. 61, no. 4**

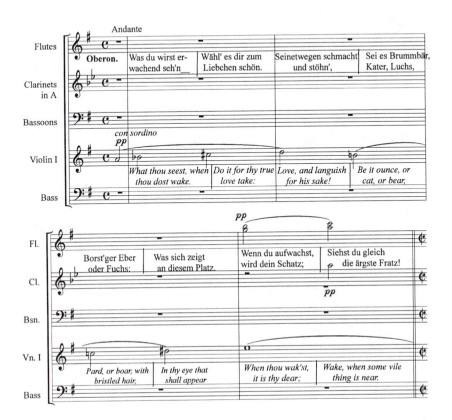

lines to solo singers, which Mendelssohn partly followed, yielding much more solo material than in the Sophocles incidental music, as well as duets and trios. In addition, the text does not stand in large blocks (as in Sophocles, with two strophes and their antistrophes in each stasimon) but in shorter alternations between solo singers and the full chorus or between the solo singers. The vocal numbers consequently give more sense of personal feeling and much more variety of feelings than the comparatively austere and monumental choruses of *Antigone* and *Oedipus in Colonus*.

As with *A Midsummer Night's Dream*, Mendelssohn had no reason to try to re-create a historical musical style, either that of ancient Judah or of France in the late period of the *Roi soleil*. The music invokes a "religious" spirit within the broader Romantic style. Indeed, the general spirit of the work resembles that of *Elijah*, its close contemporary.

Example 4.26, continued

Example 4.27
A Midsummer Night's Dream, Op. 61, no. 6, mm. 1-16

The major factor in controlling the archaizing tone of the choruses in the Sophocles plays had been the Greek poetic meter. In setting the text of *Athalie*, Mendelssohn had to work instead with French alexandrines. (He did, in fact, work from the French text, of which the German was a metrical translation.) The rhythms are thus at the same time more regular than those of the choruses of *Antigone* and *Oedipus in Colonus* and more naturally suited to accommodation to the Classic/Romantic structural model of symmetrical phrasing than those of the Greek dramas. In addition, however, the composer had much less cause to follow the meter so strictly, and this, combined with the more soloistic scorings, allowed

Example 4.27, continued

the vocal melodies of *Athalie* to take on a Romantic lyricism that is nowhere to be found in the Greek plays' choruses.

One way in which Mendelssohn invoked the religious in *Athalie* was through what might be regarded as a *stylus ecclesiasticus* for his period, a hymnlike style. An Enlightenment hymn style appears at the beginning of the first chorus, "Tout l'univers est plein de sa magnificence" (see Example 4.30). The models for this type are the oratorio choruses of Haydn (e.g., "The heavens are telling" from *The Creation*). The chorus no. 2 employs both cantus firmus texture and cantional style, using melodic material that seems to be intended to evoke the Calvinist Psalter melodies of the sixteenth century (see Example 4.31).[177]

Example 4.27, continued

Among the most striking movements is the melodrama for the prophecy of the high priest Jehoiada. The first part evokes the downfall of Jerusalem, under its corrupt kings and worship of heathen gods, by forte outbursts and plaintive, soft, descending phrases. The second part predicts the coming of the new Jerusalem and the infant savior, and here Mendelssohn evoked the Incarnation by quoting Example the Christmas chorale "Vom Himmel hoch, da komm ich her," scored high in the orchestra in a recognizable *Weihnachtsstil* (see Example 4.32).[178]

Example 4.27, continued

The conflation of a story from ancient Jewish history with reformed Christian musical materials and references could certainly strike listeners as a clash of traditions. Mendelssohn gave serious thought to the inclusion of chorales in his oratorios, ultimately deciding to use them in *St. Paul* and not to do so in *Elijah*. The allusion to the Psalter for the psalmlike text of no. 2 and the quotation of the Christmas chorale for the prophecy of the coming of the Messiah clearly have specific symbolic value. More than that, they symbolize Mendelssohn's own

Example 4.28
A Midsummer Night's Dream, Op. 61, no. 6, mm 39–49

position in the assimilation of the German Jews to post-Enlightenment Christianity, integrating the two religious traditions within the musicodramatic work.

The most familiar number in *Athalie* during the remainder of the nineteenth century and through a good part of the twentieth was the "War March of the Priests." In a concert tradition that still admitted brief, characteristic pieces in

Example 4.28, continued

straightforward forms, such a piece (like the entr'actes of *A Midsummer Night's Dream*) held an important place in the repertoire. In the play the march occurs before act 4. At the end of act 3 Jehoiada sends the Levites to arm themselves with

Example 4.28, continued

the arms of King David, which had been kept in the temple, and in act 4 he brings Joash before them, and they swear their loyalty to him (see 2 Kings 11: 10–12). Mendelssohn clearly conceived this march dramatically as a counterpart to its

Example 4.29
A Midsummer Night's Dream, Op. 61, no. 8, mm. 1–10

predecessor in *A Midsummer Night's Dream*, though in this case marking the beginning of the play's climax rather than the denouement. The march has clear stylistic echoes of the Wedding March, too, in particular the triadic rising fanfare from C that forms the introduction and the f♯ diminished seventh chord (vii°⁷/ii in F) in first inversion at the beginning of the second measure of the march proper, which echoes the similarly voiced f♯ half-diminished chord (vii°⁷ of V in C) on the first note of the Wedding March. While the march in *Athalie* is perhaps a bit more severe in quality, the overall tone of the two pieces is surprisingly alike. This probably reflects the fact that even the march for Racine's play, which might have been more military, is instead primarily conceived as ceremonial.

Example 4.30
Athalie, no. 1, mm. 6–13

The incidental music for *Athalie* stands between that for the Sophocles plays, on the one hand, and that for the *A Midsummer Night's Dream*, on the other. While it does not at all approach the fantastic character of Mendelssohn's Shakespeare music, it does not require the austere, archaizing approach of the Greek works. It clearly profits from both. In addition, as a biblical story with a recognizably sacred tone, it also connects the incidental music to the oratorios, particularly *Elijah*, which would follow it shortly.

The Incidental Music in Mendelssohn's Life and Oeuvre

Though it did not occupy Mendelssohn through his entire career as did his operatic endeavors, the incidental music occupies an important place in the composer's musical biography, his artistic development, and the understanding of his cultural values. He entered this field thoroughly naturally in the course of his work, and there was never any question as to its being an aesthetically sympathetic one for him.

Example 4.30, continued

Mendelssohn did not produce incidental music in his earliest period in Berlin, as he did Lieder- and Singspiele and the opera *Die Hochzeit des Camacho*. In each of the German cities in which he held professional positions, however, Mendelssohn had occasion to write music for stage plays. In Düsseldorf this music was related to his interaction with the theater under the direction of Karl Immermann. Particularly in Leipzig, Mendelssohn's output of incidental music was very limited, for his activity there centered around the concert hall and later the founding of the conservatory rather than the stage. In Berlin, though, incidental music constituted his most important contribution to the city's artistic life since the revival of the *St. Matthew Passion*.

From the point of view of Mendelssohn's musical proclivities, incidental music offered a field well suited to the composer. Standing beside opera, with its more lavish staging and its obligation to appeal to the secular public, and the oratorio, intended for the festival stage or concert hall and based on religious topics, music for the stage took advantage of Mendelssohn's skill at capturing the emotional content of the dramatic moment. At the same time, it did not demand music that catered to the needs of diva virtuosity or the titillation of the opera

Example 4.31
Athalie, **no. 1, mm. 6–13**

audience, nor did it enforce on Mendelssohn's style the new radicalism of the
Wagnerian solution that emerged in the "music drama" shortly after Mendelssohn's
death. The Prussian royal project, guided by Tieck's ideas of historical drama-

Example 4.31, continued

turgy, well suited a composer of Mendelssohn's sophisticated education. Each play's author, too, offered the composer distinctive challenges and opportunities, allowing the exploration of different problems: the restriction of the music to the choruses and meters of the Greek tragedies of Sophocles; the quasi-religious tone

Example 4.31, continued

of the Rationalist French Academy in the case of Racine; and the Romantic evocations inspired by the nineteenth century's adopted favorite, Shakespeare.

Example 4.32
Athalie, no. 3, mm. 46–59

The late incidental music for Berlin under Friedrich Wilhelm IV also served as a sympathetic medium for Mendelssohn's cultural and moral values. The plays for which he composed, different as they were from each other, represented some of the greatest dramatists from the history of the theater. Mendelssohn surely found the works of Sophocles, Racine, and Shakespeare much more sympathetic

Example 4.32, continued

than contemporary librettos that appealed to public taste. Especially in the case of Sophocles, the plays embodied the sort of noble cultural values that the composer and his family, since the time of his grandfather, had idealized for the German Bürgertum of their day. Had Mendelssohn been more prescient when he wrote to his father in 1831,[179] he might well have added a phrase to his comment about the

Example 4.32, continued

trashy libretti he deplored: "it is low-class stuff, and if today the times wish for it
and find it necessary, then I would rather write church music—*or incidental music
for the plays of the great historical dramatists.*"

NOTES

1. The literature on Mendelssohn's dramatic works is still quite limited and oriented to individual works. For a concise survey of the operas, see John Warrack, "Mendelssohn's Operas," in *Music and Theatre: Essays in Honour of Winton Dean*, ed. Nigel Fortune (Cambridge: Cambridge University Press, 1987), 263–97.

2. Staatsbibliothek zu Berlin—Preußischer Kulturbesitz, Mus. ms. autogr. Mendelssohn 1 (MN 1).

3. A copy of the letter is preserved in the Bodleian Library in Oxford as MS. M. Deneke Mendelssohn c. 29. Lea wrote, "Felix hatte dazu eine Ouvertüre gemacht, worin nach französischer Art, bekannte Volkslieder verwebt waren."

4. The music appears in the volume cited in note 2.

5. This was suggested by Georg Schünemann in one of the earliest and still most substantial studies of Mendelssohn's early operatic endeavors, "Mendelssohns Jugendopern," *Zeitschrift für Musikwissenschaft* 5 (1922–1923), 507. The music written in MN 1 began on 7 March 1820. This Lustspiel appears somewhat late in the volume, but if it was written very shortly thereafter, it might have been ready for Lea Mendelssohn's birthday on 26(?) March. Otherwise, the birthdays of immediate family members who were apparently old enough to appreciate the piece would not have come around until the late autumn of the year; Fanny was born on 14 November 1805, and Abraham's birthday was 11 December. It is remotely conceivable that the piece might have been intended for Rebecca's ninth birthday on 11 April. Paul was born on 30 October 1813, and thus his birthday seems an unlikely candidate. These dates are taken from Sebastian Hensel, *Die Familie Mendelssohn 1729 bis 1847 nach Briefen und Tagebüchern* (16th ed., Berlin: Georg Reimer, 1918), 1: 85, 102, 103; English version, *The Mendelssohn Family (1729–1847): From Letters and Journals*, trans. Carl Klingemann and an American collaborator (New York: Harper, 1882; repr. New York: Haskell House, 1969), 1: 61, 73, 74. There is some confusion about the date of Lea Mendelssohn's birthday; see note 19.

6. The opera had been first performed in Paris in 1819 and was to have the premiere of its revised version in Berlin in 1821, in a translation by E.T.A. Hoffmann. Abraham Mendelssohn probably saw the first version while in Paris, for he visited that city at the time on business that kept him there for more than a year.

7. See Karl-Heinz Köhler, "Das dramatische Jugendwerk Felix Mendelssohn Bartholdys—Basis seiner Stil- und Persönlichkeitsentwicklung," *International Musicological Society: Report of the Eleventh Congress, Copenhagen 1972*, 2: 495–99.

8. For biographical material on Casper, see *Allgemeine Deutsche Biographie* (Leipzig: Duncker & Humblot, 1875–1912), 4: 58-59.

9. Letter of May 1821, quoted in Thomas Krettenauer, *Felix Mendelssohn Bartholdys "Heimkehr aus der Fremde": Untersuchungen und Dokumente zum Liederspiel op. 89*, Collectanea musicologica 5 (Augsburg: Bernd Wißner, 1994), 55. A copy of the original letter is preserved in the source cited in note 3.

10. *Felix Mendelssohn Bartholdy: Briefe,* ed. Rudolf Elvers (Frankfurt am Main: Fischer Taschenbuch, 1984), 18; published in English as *Felix Mendelssohn: A Life in Letters*, trans. Craig Tomlinson (New York: Fromm, 1986), 3.

11. The music is preserved in the Staatsbibliothek zu Berlin—Preußischer Kulturbesitz as Mus. ms. autogr. Mendelssohn 7. The text, mostly in Casper's hand but partly in the hand of Lea Mendelssohn, is in the M. Deneke Mendelssohn collection in the Bodleian Library, Oxford, where it is cataloged as MS e. 12. See Margaret Crum, *Catalogue of the Mendelssohn Papers in the Bodleian Library, Oxford*, vol. 2, *Music and Papers* (Tutzing: Hans Schneider, 1983), 106.

12. There are two sets of numbers on several of the pieces in the manuscript score of *Die Soldatenliebschaft*. I follow the later (pencil) numbering, in which the first vocal piece, not the overture, is counted as no. 1, as in Mendelssohn's letter to Casper of 2 August 1820 (see note 10).

13. According to Krettenauer, the cello obbligato in this aria was first performed by Paul Mendelssohn, who would have been seven years old at the time. Krettenauer, *Felix Mendelssohn Bartholdys "Heimkehr aus der Fremde,"* 83.

14. Elvers, *A Life in Letters*, 3.

15. The instrumentation of the two performances is specified in the copy of a letter from Lea to Henrietta von Pereira-Arnstein cited in note 3 (quoted in Krettenauer, *Felix Mendelssohn Bartholdys "Heimkehr aus der Fremde,"* 53). See also the letter from Felix to an unknown recipient, which alludes to these performances, though without naming the work in question. This letter is quoted in Krettenauer, *Felix Mendelssohn Bartholdys "Heimkehr aus der Fremde,"* 52, and reproduced in facsimile and translated in R. Larry Todd, *Mendelssohn's Musical Education: A Study and Edition of His Exercises in Composition, Oxford, Bodleian MS Margaret Deneke Mendelssohn C. 48* (Cambridge: Cambridge University Press, 1983), 13–15. Todd, however, following a later pencil annotation on the manuscript, dated the letter to 22 March 1820, with the result (as Krettenauer has also noted) that he was misled regarding the identity of the work in question.

16. Todd, *Mendelssohn's Musical Education*, 14 (my translation); see note 15.

17. Like the text for *Die Soldatenliebschaft*, that for *Die beiden Pädagogen*, one fascicle in Casper's manuscript and additional pages mostly by Fanny Mendelssohn (later Hensel), is in the M. Deneke Mendelssohn collection in the Bodleian Library, Oxford, where it is cataloged as MS e. 13/1 and 2. See Crum, *Catalogue*, 106.

18. The autograph manuscript of the first aria (the complete music is in the Staatsbibliothek zu Berlin—Preußischer Kulturbesitz, catalogued as Mus. ms. autogr. Mendelssohn 8) bears the date 24 January 1821 at the beginning of no. 1, an aria for Hannchen, together with the abbreviation "H. G." (Hilf, Gott). This invocation of divine aid at the start of Mendelssohn's composition manuscripts soon became standardized in the form "L. e. g. G." (Lass es gelingen, Gott) and later more commonly "H. d. m." (Hilf du mir).

19. Todd, *Mendelssohn's Musical Education*, 14; see note 15. The letter is confusing about the date of the birthday performance. Sebastian Hensel places Lea's birthday on 26 March (see note 5). The German reads "ich solle sie zu Mutters Geburtstag dem 15ten März fertig machen." Todd translates this statement as "I should have the piece ready for Mother's birthday on March 15." It might also mean that the score was to be ready on 15 March, in anticipation of a performance to be held on Lea's birthday shortly after that. In a letter to Felix of 2 March 1841, Fanny Hensel seems to imply that Lea's birthday was on 16 March; see *Letters of Fanny Hensel to Felix Mendelssohn*, ed. and trans. Marcia J. Citron (Pendragon Press, 1987), 581 (German text) and 307 (English translation). A letter from Lea herself to her cousin Henriette von Pereira-Arnstein (cited in note 3) suggests 18 March as her birth date, and Thomas Krettenauer also places Lea's birthday on 18 March in reference to its celebration in 1826; see Krettenauer, *Felix Mendelssohn Bartholdys "Heimkehr aus der Fremde,"* 55, 56.

20. Eduard Devrient, *Meine Erinnerungen an Felix Mendelssohn-Bartholdy und seine Briefe an mich* (Leipzig: J. J. Weber, 1869), 10, 12; English version, *My Recollections of Felix Mendelssohn-Bartholdy and His Letters to Me*, trans. Natalia Macfarren (London: Richard Bentley, 1869; repr. New York: Vienna House, 1972), 3–5.

21. Ibid.

22. The overture, probably composed last, is dated 9 December 1821. Schünemann argued that since the finale bears the notation "Zu Leipzig im Hotel de Rome [*sic*]" the work was probably completed on the Mendelssohn family journey to Switzerland in 1822; see Schünemann, "Mendelssohns Jugendopern," 525. In fact, the notation appears not in the finale but in the preceding number (no. 11, p. 89 [=122]), and the name looks more like "Hotel der Russie"; it is quite possible that it had nothing directly to do with the composition of the music at all, as other such notations, apparently simple memoranda of addresses, sometimes occur on pages of Mendelssohn's music manuscripts. Devrient certainly claims that the first performance took place in January 1822—that is, before the Mendelssohns departed from Berlin—he himself singing the bass role and Mendelssohn conducting; see note 20.

23. F. G. Edwards, "Reminiscences of Mendelssohn," *The Musical Times* 33 (1892), 465.

24. Heinrich Eduard Jacob, *Felix Mendelssohn and His Times*, trans. Richard and Clara Winston (Englewood Cliffs, NJ: Prentice-Hall, 1963), 14. Jacob cites F. Garnett, "Great Musicians of Yesterday," *Musical Times* (1892).

25. Like the texts of the earlier Casper-Mendelssohn collaborations, it is found in the papers in the Bodleian Library's M. Deneke Mendelssohn collection, where it is cataloged as MS e. 14. See Crum, *Catalogue*, 106.

26. Schünemann, "Mendelssohns Jugendopern," 532.

27. John Warrack, "Mendelssohn's Operas," 283.

28. Krettenauer, *Felix Mendelssohn Bartholdys "Heimkehr aus der Fremde,"* 89.

29. This title is given on the cover of the manuscript score. The overture is headed "Der Onkel aus Boston."

30. The two surviving acts, like the previously mentioned manuscript librettos, are in the M. Deneke Mendelssohn collection in the Bodleian Library, Oxford, where they are cataloged as MS e. 15/1 and 15/2. See Crum, *Catalogue*, 106.

31. See Warrack, "Mendelssohn's Operas," 285.

32. Exactly how the work was performed is not entirely clear. Devrient refers to "performances of the music, the dialogue being read between the pieces," suggesting that there was no real staging. Whether this refers to the performance of 3 February 1824 remains vague. See Devrient, *Meine Erinnerungen*, 21; *My Recollections*, 15.

33. Sebastian Hensel, *Die Familie Mendelssohn*, 1: 166: "im Namen Mozarts, im Namen Haydns, und im Namen des alten Bach."

34. See Todd, *Mendelssohn's Musical Education*, for a thorough discussion of Mendelssohn's composition training and the music he composed in the course of it.

35. Rudolf Elvers, *"Nichts ist so schwer gut zu componieren als Strophen": Zur Entstehungsgeschichte des Librettos von Felix Mendelssohns Oper "Die Hochzeit des Camacho"* (Berlin and Basel: Mendelssohn-Gesellschaft, 1976). For one of Mendelssohn's letters to Voigts (13 March 1824), see also Felix Mendelssohn Bartholdy, *Briefe*, ed. Elvers, 31–32, and the English translation in *Felix Mendelssohn: A Life in Letters*, 19–21.

36. *Allgemeine musikalische Zeitung* [hereafter, *AmZ*] 29/22 (May 1827), col. 373. See the Historical Views and Documents section following this chapter.

37. *AmZ* 29/24 (June 1827), col. 411. See the Historical Views and Documents section following this chapter.

38. Devrient, *Meine Erinnerungen*, 24; *My Recollections*, 20.

39. Warrack, "Mendelssohn's Operas," 287.

40. See *Dwight's Journal of Music* 17/2 (7 April 1860), 12. The composer's letter of 13 March 1824 is printed there in translation, with the annotation that it had been provided to the London *Musical World* by Mendelssohn's fellow-student and friend Dr. Ferdinand

Rahles.

41. (Dresden: L. Ehlermann, 1884), 3, 2: 1104.

42. See Paul Alfred Merbach, "Briefwechsel zwischen Eduard Devrient und Julius Rietz: Ein Beitrag zur Geschichte des deutschen Theaters um die Mitte des 19. Jahrhunderts," *Archiv für Musikwissenschaft* 3 (1921), 352.

43. Presumably for this reason Alfred Loewenberg, *Annals of Opera 1597–1940*, 3d ed. (Totowa, NJ: Rowman and Littlefield, 1978), col. 707, lists Lichtenstein as author.

44. "My friend, you need great ideas—great like that cupola." Devrient, *Meine Erinnerungen*, 28; *My Recollections*, 24.

45. *AmZ* 29/24 (June 1827), col. 412.

46. Ibid.

47. Elvers, *"Nichts ist so schwer gut zu componieren als Strophen,"* 8:

Er könnte ja mit der trauernden Tochter aus der Thüre kommen, um der Caravane entgegen zu gehn, und ihr nun alle ihre Pflichten vorhalten. Schon die väterliche Eitelkeit erlaubt ihm nicht dies vor so vielen Leuten zu thun. Überhaupt bin ich nicht dafür, des Carrasco Partie ganz niedrig komisch zu halten, er bleibt doch immer Vater der Quiteria, und als solcher darf er dem Publicum nicht verächtlich gemacht werden.

48. *AmZ* 29/24 (June 1827), col. 412, where, however, it is referred to as no. 12.

49. Ibid.

50. Elvers, *"Nichts ist so schwer gut zu componieren als Strophen,"* 10: "ein Bauer nach dem andren um ihn versammelt, bis ein Chor gebildet ist, der plötzlich fortissime losbrüllt."

51. *AmZ* 29/24 (June 1827), col. 412. See the Historical Views and Documents section following this chapter.

52. The alcaide is the mayor or head magistrate of a Spanish town. In Cervantes's original the character here was a priest, but Mendelssohn expressed himself hesitant to represent an ecclesiastical authority on the opera stage. See Elvers, *"Nichts ist so schwer gut zu componieren als Strophen,"* 10.

53. Sir George Grove, "Mendelssohn," in *A Dictionary of Music and Musicians* (Philadelphia: Theodore Presser, [1895]), 1, 2: 259. See also Philip Radcliffe, *Mendelssohn* (London: Dent, 1954), 145; Radcliffe points out Weber's *Euryanthe* as an earlier example of something like the application of Leitmotiv technique.

54. *AmZ* 29/24 (June 1827), col. 412.

55. Loewenberg, *Annals of Opera*, col. 707.

56. *AmZ* 29/24 (June 1827), col. 412.

57. See Krettenauer, *Felix Mendelssohn Bartholdys "Heimkehr aus der Fremde,"* 104.

58. There were later performances in the nineteenth century, after Mendelssohn's death. These include concert performances in Frankfurt in 1860 and Berlin in 1886, as well as in Chicago in 1875. The 1885 Boston performance (in English) was apparently the first actual staging after 1827. Loewenberg, *Annals of Opera*, col. 707.

59. See Mendelssohn's letter to his mother of 3 July 1839; Felix Mendelssohn Bartholdy, *Briefe aus den Jahren 1833 bis 1847* (Leipzig: Hermann Mendelssohn, 1875), 197; *Letters of Felix Mendelssohn Bartholdy from 1833 to 1847*, ed. Paul and Carl Mendelssohn Bartholdy, trans. Lady Wallace (London: Longmans, Green, and Co., 1890), 165.

60. See Mendelssohn's letter from Brussels to his London circle of 1 December 1829; Karl Klingemann, Jr., ed., *Felix Mendelssohn-Bartholdys Briefwechsel mit Legationsrat Karl Klingemann* (Essen: Baedeker, 1909), 65.

61. The plan is outlined in Felix's letter to Wilhelm Hensel of 10–11 September 1829; see Rudolf Elvers, ed., *Briefe*, 91–94; *A Life in Letters*, 97–100. Although the evening was originally intended to include *Die Soldatenliebschaft*, that work was ultimately dropped from the program.

62. For a comprehensive study, see Thomas Krettenauer, *Felix Mendelssohn Bartholdys "Heimkehr aus der Fremde."* For a descriptive discussion of *Die Heimkehr aus der Fremde* in the context of the genre of the Liederspiel, see Susanne Johns, *Das szenische Liederspiel zwischen 1800 und 1830: Ein Beitrag zur Berliner Theatergeschichte*, Quellen und Studien zur Musikgeschichte von der Antike bis in die Gegenwart 20 (Frankfurt am Main: Peter Lang, 1988), 1: 269–95.

63. Krettenauer, *Felix Mendelssohn Bartholdys "Heimkehr aus der Fremde,"* 153.

64. The extremes of range in this role were designed by Mendelssohn to tease his friend Eduard Devrient, who sang it in the original performance. See Devrient, *Meine Erinnerungen*, 95; *My Recollections*, 93.

65. Krettenauer, *Felix Mendelssohn Bartholdys "Heimkehr aus der Fremde,"* 210.

66. Mendelssohn actually declined to allow the work to be performed in public, both because of its scope and because of its personal nature; Eduard Devrient, *Meine Erinnerungen*, 94–95; *My Recollections*, 92–93.

The nature of domestic performance here has to be understood in context. According to Lea's letter to Klingemann of 30 December 1829, the theater constructed at the Mendelssohn home for this purpose admitted 120 people, most of whom could be seated. See Klingemann, ed., *Briefwechsel*, 70. For the occasion the libretto was privately printed in a limited edition by J. G. Brüschke of Berlin; its title page is reproduced in the appendix to Krettenauer, *Felix Mendelssohn Bartholdys "Heimkehr aus der Fremde,"* 352.

67. Eduard Devrient, *Meine Erinnerungen*, 95; *My Recollections*, 93.

68. Therese Devrient, *Jugenderinnerungen* (Stuttgart: C. Krabbe, 1906), 320, recounts having sung Lisbeth's music a number of times in the Mendelssohn circle. One performance, presumably unstaged, took place on Felix's birthday in 1830; see Klingemann, ed., *Briefwechsel*, 75.

69. This manuscript is now held in the New York Public Library.

70. Devrient reworked the libretto for public performance in 1851; for a discussion of the revisions, with examples, see Krettenauer, *Felix Mendelssohn Bartholdys "Heimkehr aus der Fremde,"* 147–50. The work also found some success in England in a translation by Henry Chorley with the title *Son and Stranger*; see Krettenauer, *Felix Mendelssohn Bartholdys "Heimkehr aus der Fremde,"* 276–77. Krettenauer lists a number of further performances running up to the centenary year 1909, including translations into French, Swedish, and Hungarian (278–88).

71. This is the image of the Mendelssohn family—"a good middle-class family [*sic*, for Bürgerfamilie] in Germany"—explicitly espoused in Sebastian Hensel's documentary history. See *Die Familie Mendelssohn*, 1: ix; *The Mendelssohn Family*, 1: vii.

72. Devrient, *Meine Erinnerungen*, 96: "Mendelssohn wird niemals einen Opernstoff finden, der ihm genügt; er ist viel zu gescheidt dazu." Cf. Devrient, *My Recollections*, 94.

73. James Robinson Planché, *The Recollections and Reflections of J. R. Planché, (Somerset Herald): A Professional Autobiography* (London: Tinsley Brothers, 1872), 314–15.

74. For a table listing Mendelssohn's potential librettists and subjects, see R. Larry Todd, "On Mendelssohn's Operatic Destiny: *Die Lorelei* Reconsidered," in *Felix Mendelssohn Bartholdy: Kongreß-Bericht Berlin 1994*, ed. Christian Martin Schmidt (Wiesbaden: Breitkopf & Härtel, 1997), 138–39. See also the forthcoming dissertation by Monika Hennemann, "Felix Mendelssohns Opernprojekte" (University of Mainz).

75. Letter to Devrient of 26 April 1845; Devrient, *Meine Erinnrungen*, 250. See Devrient, *My Recollections*, 258–61.

76. See Felix Mendelssohn, *Reisebriefe aus den Jahren 1830 bis 1832*, ed. Paul Mendelssohn Bartholdy (9th ed., Leipzig: Hermann Mendelssohn, 1882), 300ff.; *Letters from Italy and Switzerland*, trans. Lady Wallace (2d ed., London: Longman, Green, Longmen, Roberts, and Green, 1862), 300ff.; Ludwig Nohl, *Musiker Briefe* (Leipzig: Duncker und Humblot, 1873), 308–9; Karl Immermann, *Briefe*, ed. Peter Hasubek (Munich: Hanser, 1978), 1: 1004–5; Robert Schumann, *Erinnerungen an Felix Mendelssohn Bartholdy*, ed. Georg Eismann (Zwickau: Predella, 1948), 68. The project remained alive through the spring of 1832, as a letter from Mendelssohn to his father of 21 February 1832 shows, for Mendelssohn expressed his plan to return from Paris to Germany to compose his *Sturm*; *Reisebriefe*, 349; *Letters from Italy and Switzerland*, 340. The plan was sufficiently concrete for Mendelssohn to have thought of a specific singer, his friend Franz Hauser, for the role of Caliban; see Eduard Hanslick, *Suite: Aufsätze über Musik und Musiker* (Vienna: Teschen, 1884), 27.

77. Devrient, *Meine Erinnerungen*, 142; see *My Recollections*, 143.

78. See James Robinson Planché, *Recollections and Reflections*, 1: 279–316. Planché's recounting of the episode is extremely bitter and depicts Mendelssohn in a quite unsympathetic light. Mendelssohn's actual views on Planché's libretto are discussed later in this chapter. The libretto rejected by Mendelssohn was later given to Sir Henry Thomas Smart (1813–1879), who, however, did not finish composing it due to trouble with his eyes. Planché, 315.

79. See the letters from Mendelssohn to the director of the Opéra dated 14 January 1841 and to Scribe dated 14 January 1842, in Julien Tiersot, ed., *Lettres de musiciens écrites en français du XVe au XXe siècle* (Paris: Félix Alcan, 1925, 1936), 333–34.

80. See Benjamin Lumley, *Reminiscences of the Opera* (London: Hurst and Blackett, 1864, repr. New York: Da Capo, 1976), 166–68.

81. See Mendelssohn's letter of 10 March 1847 to William Bartholomew in Elise Polko, *Reminiscences of Felix Mendelssohn-Bartholdy: A Social and Artistic Biography*, trans. Lady Wallace (New York: Leypoldt & Holt, 1869; repr. Macomb, IL: Glenbridge, 1987), 199–200.

82. For some of the references to *The Tempest*, see the following discussion. Mendelssohn suggested *King Lear* to Devrient in a letter of 28 June 1843; see Devrient *Meine Erinnerungen*, 235; *My Recollections*, 242. Henry Chorley reports the proposal for *The Winter's Tale* in his note "The Last Days of Mendelssohn," written for Wilhelm Lampadius, *The Life of Felix Mendelssohn-Bartholdy*, trans. W. L. Gage (Boston: Ditson, 1865), 229.

83. Mendelssohn wrote to Herrmann Neumann on 20 February 1843; letter listed in Hellmut Meyer & Ernst auction catalog no. 35, item 165 (9 October 1933). See also the letter from Gottfried Kinkel enclosing part of play of *Otto und Adelheid* in the Bodleian Library's M. Deneke Mendelssohn collection as d. 43 nos. 302–3.

84. Mme Birch-Pfeiffer, who tutored Jenny Lind in German and remained a close friend of the singer, was a Berlin *littérateuse* with experience and understanding of the stage, and she thus seemed a plausible candidate for librettist. Meyerbeer's judgment of her talents was that though she did not write composable verses, her "talent [was] for elaboration of a plot." See Henry Scott Holland and W. S. Rockstro, *Memoir of Madame Jenny Lind-Goldschmidt: Her Early Art-Life and Dramatic Career, 1820–1851* (London: J. Murray, 1891), 1: 390–94.

85. Devrient, *Meine Erinnerungen, My Recollections, passim.* Some of Mendelssohn's ideas that emerge from the correspondence about the opera based on the Peasants' War are discussed later in this chapter.

86. Letter from Mendelssohn to Julius Becher, 13 October 1841, transcribed in Renate Federhofer-Königs, "Der unveröffentliche Briefwechsel Alfred Julius Becher (1803–1848) Felix Mendelssohn Bartholdy (1809–1847)," in *Studien zur Musikwissenschaft, Beihefte der Denkmäler der Tonkunst in Österreich 41,* ed. Othmar Wessely (Tutzing: Hans Schneider, 1992), 61:

weder der <u>Sturm</u> noch der <u>standhafte Prinz</u> [underlining *sic*], an die ich früher viel dachte, sind der Art, wie ich mir jetzt eins in meinen Wünschen ausmale. So ein recht Leidenschaftliches, Menschliches, Natürliches, alle Leute gleich Berührendes, Ursprüngliches möcht' ich haben! Entweder gar keine Liebe darin oder gleich Liebe zum Tollwerden; so was, was jeder schon einmal empfunden, und noch keiner componirt hat, möcht' ich. Mit einem Wort das Allerschönste! Aber ohne Spas, hat *Prechtler* oder haben sie kein solches oder kein andres Sujet auf dem Korn, so versteht sich, daß ich den Sturm über alles gern hieher bekäme u. läse.

87. Carl Mendelssohn Bartholdy, *Goethe and Mendelssohn (1821–1831),* trans. M. E. von Glehn (London: Macmillan 1872), 159.

88. Loewenberg, *Annals of Opera,* col. 882.

89. See Mendelssohn's letter to Böttger of 10 December 1841 in Carl Mendelssohn Bartholdy, *Goethe und Mendelssohn,* 156–58.

90. Holland and Rockstro, *Memoir of Madame Jenny Lind-Goldschmidt,* 1: 393–94.

91. Fanny's letter suggesting the *Nibelungenlied* does not seem to be extant. Felix referred to it in his letter to her of 14 November 1840 (her thirty-fifth birthday); see Felix Mendelssohn Bartholdy, *Letters 1833–1847,* 194–98. Fanny responded to his request for details in a letter of 5 December; see Sebastian Hensel, *Die Familie Mendelssohn,* 2: 212; *The Mendelssohn Family,* 2: 159. Before he received her letter, Felix had already written again to urge her to tell him more about what she saw as the possibilities in the topic; see *Letters of Fanny Hensel to Felix Mendelssohn,* 300n.

92. Letter from Fanny to Felix, 9 December 1840, quoted in *Letters of Fanny Hensel to Felix Mendelssohn,* 299. The joking tone of her letter may have discouraged her brother from further serious consideration of the topic.

93. See Mendelssohn's letter to Klingemann of 6 January 1834, in which he asks his friend to send him "wenigstens den Plan zu einen Plan"; Klingemann, ed., *Briefwechsel,* 120–21. Mendelssohn may have found Kotzebue's play text in the *Opernalmanach* published in Leipzig in 1815 and 1817. I am grateful to Monika Hennemann for this observation.

94. Letter to Klingemann, 18 January 1834; Klingemann, ed., *Briefwechsel,* 122: "Ich habe dieser Tage eine Oper von Kotzebue 'Pervonte' aufgetrieben, die kein Mensch kennt; soll ich Dir das Bessere daraus schicken, oder das Ganze, oder stört Dich so was? Bitt' um Antwort, ich bin jetzt wieder bei grosser Komponierlaune."

95. Letter of 7 February 1834; ibid., 123.

96. Letter of 3 March 1834; ibid., 124.

97. See Mendelssohn's letter to Klingemann of 25 April 1834; ibid., 127–30.

98. See the letter of 11 May 1834; ibid., 131–33.

99. Ibid., 135.

100. The entire libretto draft is published in Klingemann, ed., *Briefwechsel,* 136–46.

101. Ibid., 147.

102. Ibid., 148–51.

103. Ibid., 153.

104. Ibid., 155.

105. Ibid., 162–66.

106. Eric Werner, however, argues that "the antinomy between theatre and poetry" may account at one level for Mendelssohn's failure to pursue certain operas; Eric Werner, *Mendelssohn: A New Image of the Composer and His Age* (New York: Free Press of Glencoe, 1963), 339–41.

107. Letter to Devrient of 26 April 1845; Devrient, *Meine Erinnerungen*, 250; *My Recollections*, 259.

108. Polko, *Reminiscences of Felix Mendelssohn-Bartholdy*, 179–80.

109. Devrient, *Meine Erinnerungen*, 234; see *My Recollections*, 241–42.

110. Letter to Devrient of 9 May 1846; Devrient, *Meine Erinnerungen*, 269; see *My Recollections*, 279.

111. Letter from Mendelssohn to Immermann, 27 July 1832, in D-Dühi, cited in Todd, "On Mendelssohn's Operatic Destiny," 117.

112. Letter of 28 June 1843; Devrient, *Meine Erinnerungen*, 233. See *My Recollections*, 240.

113. See Todd, "On Mendelssohn's Operatic Destiny," 121.

114. The point here is that Germans fawn over whatever is new from Paris, despite their own cultural antipathy to the content of the work.

115. Mendelssohn, *Reisebriefe*, 302–3; *Letters from Italy and Switzerland*, 303. In the English translation by Lady Wallace the final phrase seems to have been affected by her knowledge of Mendelssohn's later career, for it there reads "then I will write oratorios." In fact, he wrote, "so will ich Kirchenmusik schrieben," that is, "then I want to write church music." Church music, of course, was not in the nineteenth century a genre in which a composer could hope to achieve an important international career, so more is meant here than simply a choice between genres. In fact, Mendelssohn's point is that if prospering in his vocation should depend on his acquiescing to popular (French-dominated) taste and morality, he would rather abandon the hope of success.

It is not clear what opera Mendelssohn was referring to in which the young woman disrobes, but he may have actually been thinking of *Robert le Diable* itself; in act 4, scene 1, the main character disrobes while the chorus (not she herself) sings about her forthcoming wedding.

116. See Mendelssohn's letter to Devrient of 9 May 1846; Devrient, *Meine Erinnerungen*, 267–71, esp. 269, 271. See *My Recollections*, 277–82, esp. 278–79, 281.

117. Devrient, *Meine Erinnerungen*, 276–77; see *My Recollections*, 287–88.

118. Planché, *Recollections and Reflections*, 281–83.

119. See Mendelssohn's letter of 18 April 1838; ibid., 284–86.

120. See Mendelssohn's letter of 12 August 1838; ibid., 286–87.

121. Letter of 10 December 1838: "I suppose you are fully acquainted with it, and may tell me whether an opera so thoroughly serious, without any comical or even lighter character in it, would do for an English audience." Ibid., 288.

Letter of 29 December 1838, as a memorandum of a conversation between Mendelssohn and Chappell in Leipzig:

I expressed a doubt whether a poem so entirely consisting of *serious* personages, without a more lively character in it (or a characteristic, romantic, comical, &c., &c., one), would be able to give sufficient interest to the English public as they now are in the theatres.... When Mr. Planché first proposed the story, I was pleased to find it one of the Middle Ages, because had it been earlier (Roman, for instance), anything like characteristic occupation, or parts (like soldiers, boatmen, &c.), could not have been introduced to *vary as much as possible* the incident and style throughout.

I thought, when I only had the two first acts, that for instance Marrant was to be a character which could be considered as forming a contrast to the nobler ones, which are so beautifully drawn, that he would give occasion to a brighter, more characteristic, perhaps more comical style, at least to a more contrasted one. I missed something which gave an insight into the time and customs of that time, not only in the heroical sphere.

As it is, he (Marrant) gradually disappears from the action; and I do not know if the uniformity of sentiment which now pervades the whole, necessary as it may be, would be able to produce that animation amongst the hearers, which they always seem to feel when a series of different and equally striking characters is developed before them. I admired the concerted pieces, and the poetry throughout, and think it most beautiful. It suggested to me in several places musical deas [sic], which I noted down while reading, and found then how adapted to music these flowing and expressive verses are. The only wish I had was the one I uttered before; some character or other that might bring more stirring passions into action, create a greater contrast, and also a greater suspense, till it is brought to issue. (Ibid., 289–90.)

Letter of 23 April 1839: "I . . . begin to fear that we may both be right. That the subject is treated by Mr. Planché as it ought to be; but that in itself it does not afford me those advantages which I consider as essential to the success of a dramatic piece—that variety of human character—of situations—of feelings." Ibid., 292.

122. Ibid., 300–302.

123. Letter to Bartholomew of 4 October 1841, in Polko *Reminiscences of Felix Mendelssohn-Bartholdy*, 179–80.

124. Letter to Böttger of 10 December 1841, in Carl Mendelssohn Bartholdy, *Goethe and Mendelssohn*, 156–58. The version of the Genoveva plot that Mendelssohn states was recently staged in Berlin is not known, but an opera by L. Huth called *Golo und Genoveva* had been performed in Neustrelitz in 1838; see Margaret Ross Griffel, *Operas in German: A Dictionary* (New York: Greenwood, 1990), 95.

Mendelssohn's suggestion that Böttger should reconceive the action of the story stands in contrast to his later request to Charlotte Birch-Pfeiffer that in handling the same subject she should not depart from the traditional legend in order to create either opportunities for stage effects or a "poetical death" for the title character. See Polko, *Reminiscences of Felix Mendelssohn-Bartholdy*, 115–16.

125. Devrient, *Meine Erinnerungen*, 233n; *My Recollections*, 241n.

126. See J. Rigbie Turner, "Mendelssohn's Letters to Eduard Devrient: Filling in Some Gaps," in *Mendelssohn Studies*, ed. R. Larry Todd (Cambridge: Cambridge University Press, 1992), 231.

127. Letter from Mendelssohn to Prechtler of 20 February 1843. The original refers to the "weiche, träumerische Element." I am grateful for Monika Hennemann for providing a transcription of this letter.

128. Devrient, *Meine Erinnerungen*, 270–71; see *My Recollections*, 280.

129. Letter to Fürst, 4 January 1840, in Mendelssohn, *Briefe 1833–1847, 218–19; Letters 1833–1847*, 177.

130. Letter to Devrient of 26 April 1845; Devrient, *Meine Erinnerungen*, 250–51. See *My Recollections*, 258–61.

131. Letter to Devrient of 2 July 1845; Devrient, *Meine Erinnerungen*, 252–53. See *My Recollections*, 261–62.

132. Lumley, *Reminiscences of the Opera*, 168.

133. For Rousseau's scenario, see Bodleian Library, Oxford, Margaret Deneke Mendelssohn Mendelssohn collection, d. 45, No. 162 and c. 27, fols. 74–75. Devrient reports his having proposed the subject to Mendelssohn in his *Erinnerungen*, 247–48; see *My Recollections*, 256.

134. Holland and Rockstro, *Memoir of Madame Jenny Lind-Goldschmidt*, 1: 393–94.

135. Polko, *Reminiscences of Felix Mendelssohn-Bartholdy*, 115–16.

136. The most detailed and helpful discussion of the project's history is that by R. Larry Todd, "On Mendelssohn's Operatic Destiny" (see note 74), 113–40. On the development of the libretto, see pp. 123–24.

For drafts of the libretto, see GB-Ob MDM c.27 (October 1845), fols. 77–90, and Green Books 27, no. 97 (June 1847); and US-Wc.

137. See Devrient, *Erinnerungen*, 282–84; *My Recollections*, 293–95.

138. The three published pieces have been given the opus number 98, but they did not appear all at the same time or in their dramatic order. The finale appeared first through Breitkopf & Härtel in 1852 as Op. 98. The "Ave Maria" and the "Winzer-Chor" were published in 1868 as Op. 98 nos. 2 and 3 by J. Rieter-Biedermann.

139. Mendelssohn Nachlaß vol. 44, presently in the possession of Biblioteka Jagiellońska, Kraków.

140. This large amount of music sufficed to convince Lampadius, who put together a biographical "Denkmal" of the composer immediately after his death, that the first act was completed; Lampadius, *Felix Mendelssohn Bartholdy: Ein Denkmal für seine Freunde* (Leipzig: J. C. Hinrichs, 1848), 189. Lampadius later corrected this to say (still slightly misleadingly) that the surviving music included "[a] beautiful Ave Maria chorus, with solo; then an extremely dramatic finale, in which Lorelei is deceived by her lover and is surrendered to the water sprites who should avenge her, and who declare her to be the bride of the Rhine. In addition, there are also a grand march with chorus and the beginnings of three other pieces"; Lampadius, *The Life of Felix Mendelssohn Bartholdy*, 312–13. Ernst Wolff's biography of Mendelssohn listed the music as consisting of the finale, the Ave Maria, and the vintagers' chorus, as well as a march and the openings of three other pieces; Ernst Wolff, *Felix Mendelssohn Bartholdy* (Berlin: "Harmonie" Verlagsgesellschaft für Literatur und Kunst, 1909), 179. Most biographers discuss the published numbers and fail even to mention the existence of the remaining music, thus underrepresenting the extent of Mendelssohn's work.

141. Wolff, *Felix Mendelssohn Bartholdy*, 179; Werner, *A New Image*, 499.

142. The libretto's weaknesses were not so serious as to put off later composers. The text was published in 1861; a setting of it composed by Max Bruch reached the stage in Mannheim in 1863, and another by the Finnish composer Fredrik Pacius was performed in Helsinki in 1887. See Loewenberg, *Annals of Opera*, cols. 763, 962, 1129.

143. "*Loreley*, die er aber als eine 'Vorübung' ansah, denn er meinte, nach vier oder fünf Versuchen könnte er etwas 'wirkliches Gutes' leisten"; Eric Werner, *Mendelssohn: Leben und Werk in neuer Sicht* (Zurich: Atlantis, 1980), 512. This suggestion does not appear in the earlier, English version of Werner's biography, and it does not appear to be supported by any direct evidence.

144. Werner, *A New Image*, 499.

145. Wolff, *Felix Mendelssohn Bartholdy*, 179.

146. Philip Radcliffe, *Mendelssohn* (London: Dent, 1954), 149.

147. Werner, *A New Image*, 499.

148. A comparable number of slightly later date would be that at the end of act 2, scene 1 of Verdi's *La Traviata*, in which the soloists and chorus respond to Alfredo's outrage toward Violetta.

149. Mendelssohn, *Briefe 1833–1847*, 220; see *Letters 1833–1847*, 178.

150. Eric Werner finally argues that Mendelssohn simply was unable to accommodate his aesthetic *daemon* (in Kierkegaard's sense) to the theater. He attributes this to Mendelssohn's Jewish and Reformed Protestant background, which prevented the composer from regarding the theater as a "serious" form of expression. See Eric Werner, *A New*

Image, 341–42 and 344 n. 79.

151. Ibid., 499–500. The quotation from Kierkegaard is cited from *Either/Or: A Fragment of Life*, trans. Walter Lowrie (Princeton: Princeton University Press, 1946), 2: 141.

152. The song was actually first published with the play; Karl Immermann, *Alexis* (Düsseldorf: Schaub, 1832).

153. The music remains unpublished; the manuscript is included in Mus. ms. autogr. 56 in the Staatsbibliothek zu Berlin—Preussischer Kulturbesitz. For a more detailed description, see Joseph Esser, "Felix Mendelssohn-Bartholdy und die Rheinlande" (Ph. D. diss., Univeristy of Bonn, 1923), 80–83.

154. See Mendelssohn's letter to his father of 28 December 1833; Felix Mendelssohn Bartholdy, *Briefe 1833–1847*, 21, and *Letters 1833–1847*, 19. The song was published with the play the following year; see Karl Immermann, *Andreas Hofer* (Düsseldorf: Schaub, 1834).

155. The story of the composition is recounted in Mendelssohn's letter to his mother of 18 March 1839. See Mendelssohn, *Briefe 1833–1847*, 189–90; *Letters 1833–1847*, 151.

156. For a brief discussion of Tieck's position in the king's theatrical projects, see Roger Paulin, *Ludwig Tieck: A Literary Biography* (Oxford: Clarendon, 1985), Chapter 13, esp. 332–41.

157. In fact Meyerbeer did not actually compose incidental music for any of the plays in this historical series. His music for the play *Struensee* by his brother, Michael Beer, performed in 1846, does not belong to this group. See Lo Kai-Ming, "Giacomo Meyerbeer's Struensee: Zur Schauspielmusik eines Opernkomponisten," in *Studien zur Musikgeschichte: Eine Festschrift für Ludwig Finscher*, ed. Annegrit Laubenthal with Kara Kusan-Windweh (Kassel: Bärenreiter, 1995), 504–10.

158. According to the foreword to the booklet published about *Antigone* (August Böckh, E. H. Toelken, and Friedrich Förster, *Über die Antigone des Sophokles und ihre Darstellung auf dem königl. Schloßtheater im neuen Palais bei Sanssouci: Drei Abhandlungen* [Berlin: E. H. Schroeder, 1842], iii):

Der König, die Prinzen und Prinzessinnen des Königlichen Hauses, der kunstsinnige Großherzog von Mecklenburg-Strelitz, der Prinz Friedrich der Niederlande, der Kronprinz von Württemberg, der Erbgroßherzog von Mecklenburg-Strelitz, hatten sämmtlich auf den amphiteatralisch erhöhten Sitzen im Parterre Platz genommen. Unmittelbar dahinter so wie auf den Gallerien ersten und zweiten Ranges hatten in buntem Gemisch die, auf Befehl Seiner Majestät geladenen Generale, Professoren, Minister, Dichter, Geheimeräthe, Theater-Direktoren, Gesandte, Prediger, Künstler, Kammerherrn, Bischöfe, Zeitungs-Redactoren, Gymnasial-Directoren, Mitglieder der Akademie der Künste und Wissenschaften u.s.w. ihre Plätze eingenommen. Nur einen Mangel theilte die heutige Versammlung mit einem griechischen Theater: Frauen waren nur in sehr spärlicher Anzahl gegenwärtig.

159. The incidental music for *Medea* was composed by Taubert. It was performed on 7 August 1843. See Paulin, *Ludwig Tieck*, 338.

160. Devrient, *Meine Erinnerungen*, 230; see *My Recollections*, 237.

161. For a discussion of these and related ideas, see Michael Steinberg, "The Incidental Politics to Mendelssohn's *Antigone*," in *Mendelssohn and His World*, ed. R. Larry Todd (Princeton: Princeton University Press, 1991), 137–57.

162. Ibid.

163. August Wilhelm Schlegel, *Kritische Schriften und Briefe*, vol 5. *Vorlesungen über dramatische Kunst und Literatur*, part 1, ed. Edgar Lohner (Stuttgart: W. Kohlhammer, 1966), 88:

Von wohlhabenden und ausgesehenen Eltern, als freien Bürger des gebildetsten Staates von Griechenland geboren zu sein, dies waren nur der ersten Voraussetzungen dazu. Schönheit des Leibes wie der Seele, und ungestörter Gebrauch von beider Kräften in vollkommener Gesundheit . . ., eine Erziehung in der gewähltesten Fülle der Gymnastik und Musik . . . ; der Besitz und ununterbrochene Genuß der Poesie und Kunst, und die Ausübung heiterer Weisheit; Liebe und Achtung unter den Mitbürgern, Ruhm im Auslande, und das Wohlgefallen und die Gnade der Götter.

(Published in English as *A Course of Lectures on Dramatic Art and Literature*, trans. John Black, revised by A.J.W. Morrison [London: Henry G. Bohn, 1846; repr. New York: AMS Press, 1973], 96.)

164. Unfortunately, there is no evidence that the king appreciated such an allusion to their respective positions. Friedrich Wilhelm eventually gave Mendelssohn the title Generalmusikdirektor, but from the beginning it was apparent that the king wanted the composer at Berlin primarily as a status symbol, and the Prussian bureaucrats were unwilling to support his plans for the founding of a conservatory there. Mendelssohn twice requested that his considerable salary be pared down, because in good conscience he did not feel that he was in a position to earn the money. He ultimately returned to Leipzig, where he had the Gewandhaus Orchestra and his new conservatory to occupy him.

165. In a letter to his friend and Leipzig concertmaster Ferdinand David, Mendelssohn actually says that the chorus had sixteen members; see the letter of 21 October 1841 in Felix Mendelssohn Bartholdy, *Briefe aus Leipziger Archiven*, ed. Hans-Joachim Rothe and Reinhard Szeskus (Leipzig: VEB Deutscher Verlag für Musik, 1972), 169. Böckh gives the number in the chorus as fifteen, clearly describing them as arrayed at times in three rows of five; see Böckh et al., *Über die Anti‚one*, 92.

166. See Devrient, *Meine Erinnerungen*, 218–19; *My Recollections*, 224.

167. Wilhelm von Humboldt, introduction to *Agamemnon*, in *Gesammelte Schriften* (Berlin: Behr, 1903; repr. Berlin: Walter de Gruyter, 1968), 1, 8: 119–46.

168. Böckh, "Über die Darstellung der Antigone," in Böckh et al., *Über die Antigone*, 95. The German reads, "Unterwirft sich der komponist dem freilich harten Zwang eines gegebenem Rhythmus, so dürfte ihn dieser in einige Nähe auch des alten Melos führen, da beide Elemente übereinstimmen müssen."

169. Johann Gustav Droysen, *Ein tief gegründet Herz: Der Briefwechsel Felix Mendelssohn-Bartholdys mit Johann Gustav Droysen*, ed. Carl Wehmer (Heidelberg: Lambert Schneider, 1959), 72: "die Stimmung und die Versrhythmen sind überall so echt musikalisch, daß man die einzelnen Worte nicht zu denken und nur jene Stimmungen und Rhythmen zu komponieren braucht, dann ist der Chor fertig."

170. For a more detailed discussion of the development of the text and the musical treatment of the prosody, see Andraschke, "Felix Mendelssohns *Antigone*," 141–66. An extensive and helpful analysis of the musical structures of Sophocles's plays is William C. Scott, *Musical Design in Sophoclean Theater* (Hanover, NH: University Press of New England, 1996); for *Oedipus in Colonus*, see pp. 218-53.

171. Staatsbibliothek zu Berlin—Preussischer Kulturbesitz, Mus. ms. autogr. Mendelssohn 19, pages 59, 62. (These pages form the outer side of a bifolio, later bound into the volume so that the continuity between them is not immediately clear.)

172. Letter to David, 21 October 1841 (see note 20): "Die Aufgabe an sich war herrlich, und ich habe mit herzlicher Freude gearbeitet. Mir war's merkwürdig, wie es so viel Unveränderliches in der Kunst giebt; die Stimmungen aller dieser Chöre sind noch heut so ächt musikalisch, und wieder so verschieden unter sich, daß sichs kein Mensch schöner wünschen könnte zur Composition."

173. *A Midsummer Night's Dream* was, of course, an obvious play for Mendelssohn to compose, since he had demonstrated his Romantic sense of the play already in the overture. Already in 1834 Eduard Devrient had proposed a production of the play with music by Mendelssohn; Eduard Devrient, *Meine Erinnerungen*, 169n, and *My Recollections*, 171n.

174. American music history students of a certain age will recognize the style from Gossec's *Marche lugubre*, the example chosen for the first two editions of the *Norton Anthology of Western Music*, ed. Claude Palisca (New York: Norton, 1980; 2d ed., 1988).

175. This is a version of what we have come to think of as a "Tristan" chord, using, in fact, the same pitch classes as at its appearance in the Prelude to *Tristan und Isolde*.

176. The high-register repeated notes and slur in the woodwinds strikes a noticeable echo with a similar figure in Berlioz's "Songe d'une nuit du sabbat" in the *Symphonie fantastique* (mm. 7–9). One need not, of course, regard this as a deliberate reference.

177. Though the idiom of the melody is clear enough, the actual tune seems to be of Mendelssohn's own devising. It does not appear, for example, in the index of Psalter melodies in Pierre Pidoux, *Le Psautier huguenot du XVIe siècle: Mélodies et documents*, vol. 1, *Les Mélodies* (Basel: Bärenreiter, 1962) or among the hymn tunes in Katherine Smith Diehl, *Hymns and Tunes: An Index* (New York: Scarecrow, 1966). Its opening (using the restatements in mm. 245ff. or 283ff. rather than the truncated first phrase in mm. 236ff.) resembles the beginning of a 1524 tune for Luther's chorale "Ach Gott vom Himmel, sieh darein," based on Psalm 11; see Johannes Zahn, *Die Melodien der deutschen evangelischen Kirchenlieder* (repr. Hildesheim: Olms, 1963), 3: 71, item 4431. The last phrase, mm. 272–76, with its characteristic repeated supertonic as the antepenultimate and penultimate notes, sounds most strikingly like a Calvinist psalm melody.

178. The sound may also be heard in the first movement of his Christmas cantata on "Vom Himmel hoch" of 1831.

179. See note 114.

HISTORICAL VIEWS AND DOCUMENTS

ANNOUNCEMENT AND REVIEW OF *DIE HOCHZEIT DES CAMACHO: BERLIN, 1827*

Translated by Douglass Seaton

Announcement[1]

Berlin. On 29 April the royal theater presented a new production: *Die Hochzeit des Gamacho, comic opera in two parts, with ballet; adapted from Cervantes's romance Don Quixote de la Mancha, set to music by Felix Mendelssohn-Bartholdy, arranged and staged for the royal theater by the director Herr Baron v. Lichtenstein, the ballet by the royal ballet master Herr Telle.* This correspondent will be satisfied today to report the long title; more detail in a following report.

Review[2]

Berlin. On 29 April, as was announced in passing in the last report, the first comic opera by the very promising young musician Felix Mendelssohn-Bartholdy, endowed by nature with talent, discernment, and diligence, *Die Hochzeit des Gamacho*, was performed in the royal Schauspielhaus to tempestuous acclaim, but at the close there was some opposition to the exaggerated demonstrations of endless applause and curtain calls for the composer. As an eleven-year-old boy Herr F. Mendelssohn already distinguished himself by the most polished, particularly fiery, and energetic piano-playing and polished score-reading. At first he mostly worked on school exercises in double counterpoint with his worthy teacher, Herr Professor Zelter, and to this end he wrote symphonies in Bach style for string instruments only, which were previously performed in the home of his highly cultured parents. The fiery spirit of the boy soon turned to compositions for his own instrument, however—sonatas, concertos, trios, and quartets—and he finally also attempted operettas, which displayed much lightness of sentiment and natural melody. Grown into a youth, F. Mendelssohn inclined by preference, nevertheless, toward deep, thoughtful seriousness in his instrumental compositions; for that reason his first public debut with a comic opera was striking and appeared to announce a new, formerly unknown side of this genius. Yet concerns were raised by the inadequacy of the chosen libretto, which, after the composition was already finished, had to undergo a complete reworking for the purpose of the performance. *Don Quixote* itself would have offered excellent material for a comic opera, yet the unknown poet satisfied himself with an episode from the Cervantes romance—Camacho's wedding—that does not entirely come to life, no matter how much personnel and scenery are employed. The composer grasped the style of the opera very cleverly but almost too grandly, and he revealed especially a striving for effect that the ingenuous youthful spirit ought to have avoided. Particularly in the ensembles there was no lack of strokes of genius; the arias, to some extent, lack melodic flow, and instrumentation appears too much the main concern. Likewise, the overture, although it is very fiery, is too tumultuous for the romantic-idyllic material. Don Quixote always enters with trombone accompaniment, which certainly indicates effectively the pathetic side of the knight of the woeful countenance but is not suited to the irony of his appearance, in that the music sounds spectral. The first duet is natural and melodic. Less grateful than Vivaldo's cheerfully sustained tenor part is Basilio's elegiac one, which also does not really suit Herr Bader. Especially successful were the chorus no. 12 and the song "Im Walde bei Nacht" and so on. The first chorus of the second act depicts cooking and stirring too realistically. Sancho's Lied is appropriately kept parlando within an old-fashioned style, but it has three verses too many. The allegorical, excessively lengthy ballet would be more interesting if its content was clarified by a program. The chorus of bridal attendants—a dangerous reminiscence—displeased at the first performance because of impure intonation. On the whole the young composer, whose models appear to be Mozart, Beethoven, and C. M. von Weber, has presented with this first opera a decisive test-piece, even if not a masterpiece, of his outstanding talent, which is cultivated in such a well-rounded fashion that it will certainly bear beautiful fruits, if the incense of praise and pride does not raise the young man of wealthy parents too soon to a dizzying height, from which the return to level ground is very difficult. We especially warn him not to try too hard to be original. Further performances (which have so far had to be suspended due to the illness of Herr Blume) will determine the continuing success of the opera, whose presentation is supported on all sides by the best intentions and most enthusiastic efforts. The very busy orchestra, under the direction of Kapellmeister Schneider,[3] particularly distinguished itself.

REVIEW OF *DIE HOCHZEIT DES CAMACHO*: FRANKFURT, 1861[4]

Translated by Douglass Seaton

Frankfurt am Main. Last 30 December, in the large and acoustically effective hall of our sports center, the Opera Singing Union of Messrs. Lichtenstein and Schmidt performed Mendelssohn's *Hochzeit des Camacho* in concert form. This two-act comic opera from the pen of a barely eighteen-year-old youth exerted a peculiar charm on the assembly on that account alone. The hall was packed full, despite the snowstorm that shrouded it on this evening, and attended by numerous professional musicians. A unique interest in this performance, touching in itself, however, must have been aroused by the presence of Mendelssohn's relatives and his younger daughter, who attended here. Though to our knowledge it is impossible to obtain a complete piano score of this opera in music stores, the directors of the Union nonetheless found a way to acquire one privately, which made it possible to present to us a work that, despite its stylistic variety and much long-windedness, into which exuberant youth commonly likes to wander, nevertheless already bears in itself all the seeds that proclaim the developing master. The choruses and ensembles in particular supply the most important element of this opera, which consists of eighteen numbers, and this was probably the main consideration that led the Union to determine to present its production. If one makes use of the text book (which the directors had printed according to the piano version), one will first of all not comprehend how the composer, who later became so choosy in the matter of texts, could accept such a libretto and second, how he could find any more or less logical basis for his melodies out of such a mass of claptrap (a few lyrical verses excepted). In any case, however, this choice gives evidence of having followed from an irresistible impulse, the resplendent banner of the opera, and if worst came to worst this in itself would have elevated even the prose of a restaurant menu into poetry. What struck us is that in the diverse directions of the style—we were reminded of Haydn, Mozart, Weber, and even here and there of the oratorio—that aside from the inspired resiliency and spirituality of this composition, one fails to see the individually characteristic, the original type of the Mendelssohnian elegiac sentimental modulations, which emerged so sharply, but so distinctively, almost simultaneously with this opera in his *Midsummer Night's Dream* and then often in his later works and specifically in his Lieder. Whether it is the case, as word of mouth has it, the truth of which we would not dispute, that Mendelssohn wished for this work to sink into the Lethe, or whether this is not so (aside from a production of *Camacho* in Berlin in the summer of 1827, to our knowledge nothing has been reported of a later performance), the directors of this Union deserve the gratitude of the musical world, because they also knew to produce *this* relic, thereby affording the researcher a glimpse into the history of Mendelssohn's intellectual development, and have added in such a practical way to our knowledge of his output.

REVIEW OF *DIE HEIMKEHR AUS DER FREMDE* IN LEIPZIG, 1851[5]

Translated by Douglass Seaton

On last Friday, 10 April, in the city theater here, for the benefit of the theater pension fund, the first performances of two new operas took place: *Die Heimkehr aus der Fremde*, Liederspiel in one act by Felix Mendelssohn Bartholdy, and *An Adventure of Carl II*, opera in one act by Hoven. Between the two was presented, also for the first time, a new one-act Lustspiel by Benedix: *Die Eifersüchtigen*. The house was crowded to capacity, as was certainly to be expected. The Mendelssohn Liederspiel, *Die Heimkehr aus der Fremde*, probably drew the better part of the public there, although, despite the loud applause, it must be questioned whether the majority valued its full significance. The deceased master wrote the work in his twentieth year, 1829, and never made it public himself, for it was intended specifically and exclusively for performance on his parents' twenty-fifth wedding anniversary and presented by friends and members of the family circle. Nevertheless, the gentlemen who took charge of the public performance of the work deserve the greatest thanks, for in it there emerge more sharply the traits of Mendelssohn's personality that otherwise seldom come into play in his creations;

we have in mind his jovial humor and his masterful dramatic individualization: both characteristics of the master as of any person of consequence. The witty text was provided for him by his friend Karl Klingemann (for many years attaché at the Hanoverian delegation in London), who knew firsthand the personal relationships and the private circumstances of the Mendelssohn family. The musical standpoint of each separate role succeeds masterfully: the burlesque figure of the lying merchant Kauz; the worthy, loving mother; the lovely Lisbeth; the son returning from the war; and the old Schulze (who always sings just a single pitch, for the role was originally intended for a nonsinger, who could be taught to execute only one note). Every scene is finely, deeply, and sincerely realized, with humor down to the smallest details; we have the piano score in front of us, and it recalls to us the impressions we had received. The overture depicts a patriarchal peace, rural comfort, and then joyful quickness. Wind-instrument effects and timpani are dispensed with; the latter first accompany the humorous song of the charlatan Kauz. The mother's spinning song, in ballad style, is charming and touching, without the slightest reminiscence of so many other spinning songs. In the night watchmen scene the lover's pleasant serenade is sharply interrupted by the watchman's night call, which is genially interwoven with the troubadour's love-sighs, since the latter will not allow himself to be disrupted. A warm pulse-beat and a fresh, intimate spirit animate the whole—its structure and economy indicate the master. If Mozart with his first operas comes to mind for us here, it is not in order to compare the two composers, for on the basis of their most innermost nature they have already taken their separate directions: Mozart's nature is predominantly dramatic; Mendelssohn's, thoroughly lyrical. Nevertheless, though, a parallel between, on one hand, the *Entführung aus dem Serail* and the Requiem and, on the other hand, the aforementioned Liederspiel and the larger oratorios *St. Paul* and *Elijah* suggests itself: into the two comic operas drifts a genial youthful spirit—in the sacred works, the seriousness and sublimeness of the perfected genius.

The Hoven opera, *An Adventure of Carl II*, is likewise a welcome offering; if it is not to be compared to the one just discussed in terms of depth and genial treatment, still it flows along smoothly and agreeably and furnishes much interest by means of manifold scenes and situations and by the objectively true standpoint of its music.

The presentation of the two operas succeeded well. Madame Günther-Bachmann developed all the charm of her dramatic vivacity as well in the role of Lisbeth as she did in the part of the tenant farmer woman, and our tenor Widemann and the baritone Behr through their performances proved their worthiness as favorites of the public.—ΔΔ.

MENDELSSOHN'S SCENARIO FOR *PERVONTE*: LETTER TO KARL KLINGEMANN[6]

Translated by Douglass Seaton

Düsseldorf, 11 January 1835

Dear Klingemann,

1. Herewith finally the worked-out plan; I thank you for your letters but most of all for the one of the 15th *ult.*

Let us proceed with the plan as follows: if something in it pleases you, then go ahead and invent situations for it (for mine should be only tentative suggestions, and especially very tentative toward the end), work out the plan and the individual *situations* further, and when you have gotten it so far that you can begin everything in detail, then send me your plan back, so that I can jot down and suggest the musical pieces, which I will then send back to you, after which you then are in charge of the execution and completion. In this way it will work out well.

Mainly there is more to invent for it: a more attractive wish formula than the double wishes; on this subject I wondered whether he could not always turn the words around, as, for example, "nur fort, fort nur" and the like. But that is not the right thing, and I can't hit on it; perhaps something sensible will occur to you. If necessary it will be all right with the repeated wish. Then it is also necessary to invent a distinctive costume for the whole thing, specific people and so on, a distinctive character for the prince, another name and office for the commonplace seneschal, if possible another name for Vastola, which I can't stand, and finally some beautiful things for the closing at the very end, which I wrote down in this way out of expediency—but the couple cannot separate again—it is too undramatic. Beyond that in my opinion, in all the situations, even if I have given them in quite a bit of detail, you must invent and write something—that is, without regard to the *words*, strengthen, expand, give more detail to the situations according to your views. Then send it back to me for the musical pieces and then the text is done. . . .

Pervonte. Act 1.

Scene 1.

In the forest, behind an arbor.

Three fairies. After bathing in the fairies' fountain, weary of the mortal world. Each one tells what trouble and work she has had in the day on earth. They fall asleep under an arbor.

Scene 2.

At the court of Salerno.

Chorus. Resentment over the prudishness of the princess.

The seneschal comes in, asks for silence, then reports cautiously (in a romance of three strophes) in the first two a couple of main points about Vastola's prudishness, in the last about the revenge of the fairies; the chorus agrees, derides and curses Vastola.

Scene 3.

The prince; all at once (dialogue) the whole atmosphere changes, they are afraid of having given themselves away, the prince must be foolishly enamored of, and concerned for, his daughter, wants to grant her every wish; the seneschal speaks in the deepest humility of the wishes of the country. This can be the fourth stanza (but entirely parodied) of the preceding romance (but if that one were to close with the sense that the princess cannot catch any man, then this one has to close by saying that none is good enough for her). The chorus agrees. The prince at first takes the entreaty badly, then becomes convinced to enforce their wish that today she should choose one of the new noblemen.

Scene 4.

Vastola with the entire chorus of women, dressed for hunting; they want to leave. Short song, the prince opposes her, she should stay, not hunt again, that is his wish. She wonders what this is all about, since up to now he has always permitted and praised it; today is a great day, she wants to go out. *Duet.* The prince begins and forbids it point-blank; she pouts and is defiant and finally gets around him. *Dialogue. The Prince.* It would not actually be the hunt that he wanted to forbid her, but—but—beats around the bush and is afraid, Vastola is emboldened by that, asks more and more, the seneschal with the chorus puts forward the country's wish, is interrupted by loud laughter from Vastola, who now makes plain in an aria how in fact no man is good enough for her, how she certainly wants none of them, etc. etc. Then it turns into a hunting chorus for the maidens; the prince warns, the seneschal grumbles with the men's chorus, the maidens storm out.

Scene 5.

In the forest.

Pervonte is not ugly, but only coarsely rustic and dull, not frightening.

Dialogue. The mother drags Pervonte in by the arm, he is supposed to stay here and gather sticks, he is sullen and lazy, doesn't want to do it, she wishes he would get married, he says no girl would be good enough for him, etc. etc. She has a bundle of wood together, he has nothing, she takes it on her back and threatens him that he must follow her in an hour or there will be nothing to eat. She leaves. Pervonte alone. He slowly gathers wood, finds the fairies. Aria. Beginning entirely softly and awkwardly, until he has finished it. Dialogue, because the fairies awaken, he is afraid of them at first, as a reward he should ask them three wishes, doesn't know [what to wish], wishes his bundle of sticks tied up, then a kiss, they refuse him, but now he wants nothing else. Music. They grant him the gift of wishing, one of them cautions him about it, and they disappear. He sits on his fagot in astonishment. (Dialogue.) He is surprised etc., until he wishes that the fagot could carry him. The bundle starts to move and finally carries him into the background. Finale. Vastola turns up there, the maidens hurrying after her, they encounter the fagot. Pervonte cries stop, stop! Now a great deal of mutual teasing, the maidens start out and pick on him, then the reverse (he could bring up in the course of this that he doesn't want to get married either, that no one is good enough for him). Vastola doesn't take offense at this, orders that they should tear apart his fagot, the maidens want to seize it, he holds them off them with an ax, until he finally (this must be motivated by the preceding dialogue) wishes that she would fall madly in love with him (throughout the whole scene he must already have liked her); then she restrains the maidens, who want to punish him for this and who don't understand her at all; everything is confused, and in the midst of this he rides off. The maidens and Vastola remain alone, she wants to sing the hunting chorus, but it doesn't work; she becomes more and more confused and finally falls in a swoon into the arms of the maidens. Group.

2nd act. Scene 1. The palace.

The maidens sad, the hunt is long over; curious about the reason, the seneschal comes then and tells them it is on account of love. They hear her coming, and the others withdraw into the background. Brief scene for her; already half regretful on account of her earlier foolish behavior toward her father and all the others, she feels bewitched and mad since that encounter in the forest; the others hear it, the seneschal triumphs, the prince breaks in and sends them all away, including the seneschal. Short dialogue between father and daughter, in which he tells her to her face that she is in love, and she cannot deny it. *Duet.* She must name the one, whoever he is; she cannot and may not; she must slip over again into the enchanted, bewitched tone. She finally breaks loose and leaves.

Scene 2.

The seneschal comes forward and promises that he will soon get it out of her. The prince, in his joy, swears that whoever it is, he shall have his daughter; the seneschal now proposes a festival to which the entire populace will be invited, at which the man will certainly be among them—the prince takes this badly—and it is settled, he wants the princess so closely watched the whole time that no expression should escape him, and if she blushes, then they will know who he is. Here a comic aria for the seneschal, how he will read him from her face, how he cannot fail (perhaps he could even secretly think he could be the one himself).

Scene 3 in Pervonte's hut.

He alone, bored; how long ago the episode with the bundle already was; now everything is so boring; the princess has not come out hunting even once again, and he liked her so well. (Trumpets outside.) He is too lazy to get up to see what it's all about. The mother comes in from outside, has heard all about the festival, tells him to go to it, to bring back a sausage, cleans him up; he has to go; he thinks he should marry the princess himself, the mother scolds him for such ideas, goes with him.

Scene 4. Open square, the festival. Finale.

In the background everything already in full swing and merriment. The prince comes with the princess, the seneschal watches her constantly. She may say only a few words to herself; otherwise, she is silent and introspective. Tournament. She does not watch. Peasants' dance. The seneschal could sing a love song in Italian style to the zither and watch the effect of that, notices in the end that it has no effect. General dance. The weather turns bad—umbrella. The prince wants to call a halt; Pervonte comes with his mother in the background. Vastola sees him, keeps her composure; the seneschal observes everything, becomes angrier and angrier; finally she falls at Pervonte's feet (or into his arms). Great dismay. She now very wild; this is the man whom she met, this is the beloved; Pervonte is completely satisfied and wants to have her immediately; the prince wilder and wilder; Vastola reminds him of his oath to unite her forever to the one she chose—the prince beside himself: yes, [he says] but not alive—in the sea, shut up in the cask. Pervonte laments and wails, calls on the fairies (but not in the correct way); she remains calm, the storm comes, they are sealed up, and the cask goes off. Storm and thunder.

3rd Act. Scene 1. Desolate beach.

The cask comes ashore. They get out of the cask. Angry dialogue; she perceives his stupidity; her smartness is of no use to him; the whole island is desolate. She finally asks how it happened that several days ago in the forest she felt so drawn to him—he, oh just because I wished it, but now I would wish 1,000 times that I were away from here, and yet it doesn't happen—she, ah, and many have already wished that I loved them, and it hasn't happened—he tries once again to wish himself away—everything remains silent and cold—if only there were a fire here—the fire appears—they are both amazed—Vastola finally figures out that he must repeat his wish—he should try as an experiment to wish twice for a gondola—the gondola appears—he doesn't care much for the power of wishes; she cares more. Duet. She pesters him to wish her a palace and her playmates; at first he will not and says no; finally she wins him over; the palace appears during a musical piece; the maidens are heard singing the earlier hunting chorus; Vastola calls to them; joy at reunion; she presents Pervonte to them, whom in the process she calls boorish and stupid, at the same time she wants to demonstrate to the maidens his wishing power and wishes for a fountain of wine etc.

Scene 2.

All the maidens in the palace; Pervonte, alone, wishes his old mother there; she comes; he tells her about the power of wishes, and she advises him to wish for a little understanding about all things; he does so and changes visibly; the maidens want to go to Salerno, Vastola also; he notices that the gift of wishing gives him a lot to do, but he is no longer afraid of anyone; they all get into the gondola and float away (or wish themselves away).

Scene 3.
In the palace at Salerno.

Seneschal and courtiers, completely exhausted chorus, with reminiscence of the very beginning; the princess with all her moodiness would be better than this tedious life since she disappeared and then the maidens, too. Dialogue. The prince then comes and complains how much he misses his daughter, but that son-in-law would have been altogether too base; the seneschal agrees with him; rather than having such a son-in-law, he would give her up to the waves a thousand times. But it would have been better if she were still there and hunted, and one could still hear her merry hunting song—they hear the hunting chorus in the distance—someone goes out to see how that can be—the prince goes out "and just as they saw her go out of that gate attired for hunting in the morning"—she comes out attired for the hunt—great rejoicing of the prince and Vastola, who finally asks her how she got out of the cask with the shameless peasant; she wants to protect him; the prince to hear nothing about him; the bodyguards are not to let him in—he stands his ground and wants to be recognized as Vastola's husband; the prince calls his guards—now Pervonte also becomes furious, throws the whole guard as well as the prince to their knees, demolishes the palace (or sets it aflame); Vastola tries to reason with him; he immobilizes her, makes horns grow out of the seneschal's cap; the maidens are all struck dumb, and now he sits raving among them and asks whether they will acknowledge him? The old mother comes in, and he comes to himself; she reproaches the whole gift of wishing, which has brought him no happiness, which he now sees; she urges him more and more; he becomes moved, thinks he will now also lose his princess. The mother: then it would have nothing to do with her love for him, if it only depended on his fairy gift. He: now then you good fairies, hear my last wish, take everything back, but leave me Vastola.

Last scene.

The three fairies wish him luck with his decision to give back the magic power of wishing, prophesy good fortune for him and the princess (they could perhaps give him presents). Everything at the court is as it was before—the whole court faded into the background—closing chorus.

MENDELSSOHN'S CRITERIA FOR AN OPERA TEXT: LETTER TO JAMES ROBINSON PLANCHÉ[7]

12 February 1838

Dear Sir,

I was very happy to receive the information in your letter of the 31st (l. m.) that you had kindly consented to write the opera which I am going to compose for the English stage. A good, truly poetical libretto which inspires me at once was, since long, the great object of my wishes, and I may now look forward to its speedy realization, as *you* have undertaken it. I dislike the five acts as you do: it should be three or two. I prefer three acts, but think there could be a subject which would require to be divided into two; and then I should have no objection. I wish it, as you already know, to be a kind of historical opera; serious, but not *tragical*—at least not with the tragical end but as for dangers, fears, and all sorts of passions, I cannot have too much of them. I should also like to have some persons, if not comical, yet of *a gay and lively* character in it; and last, not least, I wish for as *many choruses*, and as active ones, as you may possibly bring in. I should like to have a whole people, or the most different classes of society and of feelings, to express in my choruses, and to have them as a kind of principal persons opposed to the solo singers. Could such a subject be found? Before all, I wish the subject had no likeness whatever to any of the now-popular operas: they have something so exhausted in them which I dislike. As you ask me to name a model, I should say a subject between "Fidelio" and "Les Deux Journées," of Cherubini would suit me most—more like the first with regard to the internal plot—to the development of passion; and like the second in the historical basis—the activity of the choruses and the serene atmosphere which breathes throughout the whole, notwithstanding all the perils and the narrow escapes which occur in it. In short, could you find me a subject in which some virtuous, heroical deed was celebrated (as it is in "Fidelio"), which (as "Fidelio" is the triumph of faithful love) represented the triumph of some noble, striving feeling, equally known to every one of the hearers who knows at all any feeling, and who could then see his own internal life on the stage, but more concentrated—in short, translated into poetry (of course, it ought not to be a common or base feeling, as they have now so often in the opera-house—for of this every one has quite enough at home, and should not find it elsewhere, at least not in art); and if that same story happened in a country, or time, and a people which could give a lively background to the whole (be it dark or not), which, in reminding us of history, could in the same time *remind us of our present time* (as, for instance, the dark figure of Cardinal Mazarin forms a background in the "Deux Journées"; but it could be more prominent still), and if every act of the opera had its own effect, its own poetical point which comes to issue in the finale (as also in "Les Deux Journées," at least in the first and second acts). If you could find such a subject, that would be the one I wish for; and if ever I can succeed, I should be sure to do it with such a subject. Query, can it be found?—and to this question I most anxiously expect your answer.

Excuse my confused description—I would hardly be able to give a good one in my own language; till now, it is more a matter of feeling than of knowing with me; but of this I am sure, if such a subject as I think of should be found, it would force me at once to compose the music. I could not do otherwise; and that, I think would be the best and most promising way of beginning my task. Your assistance, I trust, will lead to the realisation of this long-felt wish of mine; and thanking you for your kindness, and hoping to receive a speedy answer, I am, my dear Sir,

Very truly yours,

Félix Mendelssohn Bartholdy

I have to add that I should be at liberty to begin the music about the end of summer. Whether I shall be able to bring it to England myself is very uncertain, as I have never an idea in what time I shall finish a work; and whether my engagements will then allow me an absence from my country,—I hope so, however.

MENDELSSOHN'S INSTRUCTIONS FOR THE PERFORMANCE OF *ANTIGONE*: LETTER TO GEORGE MACFARREN[8]

Frankfurt, 8th December 1844

My dear Sir,

Your letter came two days before my departure from Berlin, and immediately after it I received the news of the very very sore illness of my youngest child, which called me in great haste back to this place, where I had left my family. The child continues very ill, and the physicians give us but a very faint hope; they say that if it recovers it can only be very slowly, and may last many months, so I need not beg your pardon for not having answered punctually, although the object of your letter was of great musical importance to me. But I say the same words as you do at the end of your letter; and although I love my art, more from my heart than words can say, there are other things before which even that love must vanish and be silent. Do not let me add another word. . . .

Have many thanks for the interest you take in bringing out my music to the Antigone-Choruses; I am very glad it is in your hands, because it wants a musician like you to make it go as intended—quite as a subordinate part of the whole, as a mere link in the chain of the poem, and yet perfectly clear and independent in itself. I am glad you have so many Chorus-singers; I think they will be necessary in your large Theatre. I hope you will also have them placed not on the stage but in the place where usually the Orchestra is, viz. Before the stage, so as it was in Berlin, Dresden, &c., and I believe also at Paris. It enhances the effects of the voices, the distinctness of the words, and the beauty of the scenery most wonderfully. Pray let them pronounce the words as distinctly as possible, so as to make the notes *less* prominent and the words *more* so, than they usually are in Opera-Choruses. Then let the succession of Dialogue and Music be as rapid as possible, indeed quite without the least interruption or pause; for instance when the curtain rises and Antigone has appeared, has called her sister and brought her forward from the background, it must be the last bar but one of the Overture, so that immediately after the last chord of the wind instruments (G ♮) Antigone begins to speak *while* the chord is still kept. Again the first Chorus must begin as soon as Antigone has gone down the steps (not immediately after Ismene's last words of course), and Kreon must be seen immediately when the C major chord, *fortissimo*, comes down before the Recitative of the Choruses, and Kreon must again begin to speak while the chord E flat is hardly given, and it must be kept during the first words—and so on throughout the whole. I wish the effect of the whole music to be very lively and yet not too fast, and very majestic and yet not slow. This applies also particularly to the Chorus-*Recitatives*, which if sung by a whole mass of voices are of a good effect, but they must not drag them, they must not sing them in time, nor waver in their way of delivering them; it must be as if they all did speak the words and understand the meaning now faster now slower as the meaning requires it and never in a dragging and tiresome way; for instance the Recitative at the end of the 2nd Chorus it must be delivered with great energy, and as fast as a single singer would sing the same words—and so all of them. If you have but one of your Solo singers who sings Recitatives well and in a *truly dramatic* way, you will easily make the whole Chorus follow him, and after a few Rehearsals they will do it altogether and by themselves. In the Melodramas, where the words must go together with the notes (with Flutes and Clarinets, &c.), do not let the actress take the tempo of your music (as I heard them do lately at Dresden), but let the flutes accompany *her* tempo of speaking, which is also not difficult if the flutes will follow *you* and *her*.

When the Chorus answers the speaker in the Melodramas again there must not be the least interruption or pause, and their singing must come in immediately after the last word spoken, while the preceding chord of the Orchestra must already have been heard during the last phrase. Then there is the *acting* of the choruses, which is still important. They must but very seldom (as for instance during the Solo in Quartet in G) be *quite* without motion, and then also they must stand in *groups, not* in the usual theatrical *rows*; but this I hope will have been well managed in France, from where you have the direction I believe. For example, at the beginning of Chorus 1, the singers must not be seen before the 1st chord, then they must come two by two, while they sing the beginning and must wander quickly round the altar during the whole of the 4-4, but when the 2-4 begins they must be in their places; and the singers of the 2d chorus must also not be seen, but after the end of this 2-4, when they come in quite the same way and do the same as the others &c. &c. The acting of the Chorus to Bacchus in D must be very lively towards the end, when those who sing "Hear us, Bacchus" must always wave their sticks and even go up the steps of the altar the last time, while the others who continue with the other words may stand in a row in front (in the background) until their turn comes to sing "Hear us, Bacchus," when the order is reversed, until it ends with a very animated group round the Altar, which is disturbed by the messenger &c. &c.

Pray excuse this long analysis; but you would have it! And as for Israel and the other copy of the works, do you not think you could find an opportunity for sending them to me at this place! I intend to stay here till next Autumn, if all goes as I wish it; and there are so many of your countrymen, who visit this part of Germany! I also hope to send you the King of Saxony's name as a Subscriber to the Society very shortly, but I must have a prospectus first, and could not get one at Dresden. Pray send me one, and I hope to arrange the matter directly and easily. Did your negociations [*sic*] with Messrs. Breitkopf and Härtel about the Handel Society lead to no result?

But enough. Believe me always yours,

Felix Mendelssohn Bartholdy

NOTES

1. *Allgemeine musikalische Zeitung* 29/22 (May 1827), col. 373.

2. *Allgemeine musikalische Zeitung* 29/24 (June 1827), cols. 410–12.

3. Georg Abraham Schneider (1770–1839), since 1820 director of the Prussian Royal Theater.

4. *Neue Zeitschrift für Musik* 54 (January–June 1861), 47–48. The author signs the report "Erasmus."

5. "Aus Leipzig vom 14. April," *Rheinische Musikzeitung* 43 (1851): 342.

6. Karl Klingemann Jr., ed., *Felix Mendelssohn-Bartholdys Briefwechsel mit Legationsrat Karl Klingemann in London* (Essen: Baedeker, 1909), 162–66.

7. James Robinson Planché, *The Recollections and Reflections of J. R. Planché* (London: Tinsley Brothers, 1872), 281–83.

8. Karl Mendelssohn Bartholdy, *Goethe and Mendelssohn*, trans. M. E. von Glehn (London: Macmillan, 1872), 128–32.

5

On Felix Mendelssohn Bartholdy's Sacred Music

Georg Feder; translated by Monika Hennemann

MORAL AND ARTISTIC MAXIM

The letters L.e.g.G. (Laß es gelingen, Gott/Let this be successful, God) or H.D.m. (Hilf Du mir/Help thou me), which Mendelssohn put at the top of his manuscript scores in the manner of Bach or Haydn, were added not simply out of habit but as an encoded expression of his devoutness, which formed an inseparable, though inconspicuous, constituent of his harmonic personality and which can be traced throughout in his numerous extant letters, though it was explicitly expressed only on very rare occasions.[1]   Nor are the accounts of his contemporaries always revealing in this regard. At least we find out from Hector Berlioz that he ridiculed Mendelssohn because of his faith,[2] and others, such as the illustrator and writer Johann Peter Lyser[3] and Mendelssohn's first biographer, W. A. Lampadius,[4] give witness of his charity; this does not suffice, however, to form a clear picture of the practical aspect of Mendelssohn's Christianity or of the positive essence of his faith.

Ostensibly, his religious ideas were influenced by Schleiermacher, Hegel, and David Friedrich Strauß.[5] This remains to be investigated more closely. For us it is not so much his devoutness per se that emerges as the morality that is closely connected with it and that permeated his life and works, that which Robert Schumann called the "highest moral and artistic maxim" and observed to guide his friend and colleague.[6]

Doubtless the two aspects of this maxim were somewhat connected with each other. The "sense of truth and earnestness," the "earnestness of art," the "principles of sincerity and veracity" played a central role in Mendelssohn's work. Only "that which flows in deepest earnestness from the inmost part of the soul" had validity for him artistically; everything else he called "falsehood."[7] "Res severa verum gaudium'[8]—if one understands this motto of the Leipzig Gewandhaussaal, the place of Mendelssohn's happiest activity, as an invitation to the kind of earnestness that truly reflects the inner, more pious, noble, and beautiful self, it could function as a summary of Mendelssohn's whole artistic activity.

When applied to Mendelssohn, this motto also includes responsibility for, and faithfulness to, one's principles, self-criticism and striving for perfection, and the belief in the high value of proficiency, no matter to which field it is applied.[9] Though the catch-phrase "Protestant work ethic"[10] does not fully encompass these virtues, it is not inapt. Mendelssohn's virtues might also have included a fair portion of Jewish tradition, especially the Enlightenment philosophy of his grandfather Moses Mendelssohn, in whose doctrines the "continuous development to higher degrees of perfection" plays a central role.[11]

The striving for perfection in particular is manifest in Mendelssohn's work or, more precisely, in his compositional process. However effortlessly the brilliant improvisor conceived and wrote down a work, the self-critical composer struggled painstakingly with the changes he often found necessary (e.g., for *St. Paul*, the *Lobgesang* [*Hymn of Praise*], *Lauda Sion*, and *Elijah*), until the final form met his demands. Many works, among them several sacred compositions, never reached this stage and remained unpublished during his lifetime or even until the present. Thus, one should always make a distinction in ranking between the works published during his lifetime and those published posthumously or never published.[12]

MENDELSSOHN AND MEYERBEER

The same ethos determined his attitude toward the work of others. Occasionally, he showed a moral sensibility, which may have been influenced by his apprenticeship in the Berlin Singakademie,[13] such as when he judged libretti like Meyerbeer's *Robert le Diable*: "It made quite an effect, but I do not have music for it. For it is vulgar, and if such be the demand of the present time, and found necessary, then I want to write church music."[14] Nothing upset Mendelssohn more than "slovenliness." Remembering the uplifting impression of Gluck's *Armide*, he confessed: "This is music; people have talked and felt like that, and thus it will stay forever. I hate the present-day sloppiness wholeheartedly."[15]

Mendelssohn's moral disgust at *Robert le Diable* is set into context, however, when one reads that he would not have composed even such a text as that for Mozart's *Don Giovanni*: "All my nature refuses to make concessions to the vice of immorality . . . , and when I search my heart, I must ask myself whether with this attitude I will ever be successful in creating an effective opera."[16] In fact, Mendelssohn found something to object to in every opera project and libretto that he was offered. Only in the form of the oratorio did he ultimately succeed in providing compositions that suited his nature, that could stand in contrast to contemporary opera production, the "depraved new Parisian tone," which he believed was found even in the late Cherubini.[17] The bon mot that *Elijah* became Mendelssohn's opera is not without validity.[18]

Mendelssohn's highly musically gifted and intelligent sister Fanny certainly agreed with her brother when, in 1836, she formulated the symptomatic opposition of Mendelssohn and Meyerbeer in a "prize question": "How can one talk about the general direction of a time in which *St. Paul* and *The Huguenots* appear simultaneously, and each finds its audience!"[19] Stylistic pluralism, which seems to have almost disappeared during the historical period of Viennese high Classicism (though perhaps not quite justly so), had found its way again in fundamentally different manifestations. Beethoven's last string quartets (1825–1826), Mendelssohn's overture to *A Midsummer Night's Dream* (1826), Paganini's virtuoso playing, which bewitched Germany from 1828, and Bach's rediscovered *St. Matthew Passion* (1829) all appeared in quick succession; influential new developments arose, and all of them existed simultaneously and continued to succeed.

Meyerbeer's grand opera likewise held its ground against Mendelssohn's oratorio, as well. While in 1837 Robert Schumann had emphasized the contrast in a review of *Les Huguenots* and *St. Paul*,[20] Lyser in 1838 declared Schumann's partisanship for Mendelssohn biased[21] and tried in 1842 to define the objective content of the antithesis as follows:

Just as the opponents of Master Giacomo accuse him of seizing every possible opportunity of creating an effect, particularly in his latest large work (the *Huguenots*), Meyerbeer's supporters would be as justified in accusing Master Felix of anxiously avoiding any effects, specifically in his *St. Paul*. In my view both reproaches are unjust, since Meyerbeer cannot compose any differently than he does due to his peculiarity, just as Felix Mendelssohn cannot renounce his peculiarity.[22]

A SECOND ELIJAH

Yet Mendelssohn's "peculiarity" had not come about by chance but was largely influenced by the spirit of classicism, which he felt he must defend and enforce against the errors of the present. His meetings with Chopin in Aachen in 1834 and in Leipzig in 1835 serve as examples. At their first meeting Mendelssohn set Chopin's "Parisian mania for despair and search for passion" in opposition to his own manner, which he characterized as "tact and calmness and the genuinely musical."[23] Shortly afterward, he found some new mazurkas and other pieces by Chopin "so mannered that one can hardly stand it."[24] At his second encounter he praised Chopin as "a truly perfect virtuoso," whom he distinguished from the "semi-virtuosos and semi-classicists," "who would like to unite 'les honneurs de la vertu et les plaisirs du vice' [the honors of virtue with the pleasures of vice] in music," and apparently viewed himself as the perfect classicist. Mendelssohn continues: "The Sunday evening was really odd, when I had to play my oratorio [*St. Paul*, which at this point had not yet been performed] for him, . . . and how between the first and the second part he raced through his new etudes and a new concerto for the astonished Leipzig audience, and then I proceeded with my *St. Paul*, as if an Iroquois and a Kaffir had met and conversed."[25]

With his sense of perfection, however, Mendelssohn could not deny his respect for a perfect virtuoso in his own field, such as the pianist Sigismond Thalberg, and his admiration for Franz Liszt was spoiled only by the fact that he found him unimaginative as a composer ("at least to this point," 1840).[26] He regarded his own vocation as conductor, pianist, and organist, however, as following a different direction. He wanted to provide a counterbalance to sheer virtuosity and obsession with pleasure and to familiarize the public with masterpieces, especially those by Beethoven, Handel, and Bach. In particular, Mendelssohn's importance as a pianist has long been recognized in that "he was the first who declared war on narcissistic virtuosity and placed the most perfect technical abilities exclusively at the service of the objective presentation of important works of art."[27]

Mendelssohn likewise devoted his activities as "Gewandhauskapellmeister" to the goal of raising the audience's taste to a higher level, of inclining it toward the classical in art, as Lyser saw in retrospect.[28] The "Mustervorstellungen" (model performances) of operas, which Mendelssohn presented in collaboration with Immermann in Düsseldorf in 1833–1834, already pointed in that direction. The founding of the Leipzig Conservatory, which owes its existence mainly to Mendelssohn, institutionalized this formation of taste.

Mendelssohn could interpret it as a full recognition of his activities when the British prince consort Albert, after a London performance of *Elijah* on 24 April 1847, wrote the following into a libretto of the oratorio: "To the noble artist, who, surrounded by Baal's services of a false art, has succeeded through genius and study in preserving the service of true art, like a second Elijah."[29] Mendelssohn was deeply touched by these words.

Yet was Mendelssohn the true prophet? Did his music point into the future? Or was he fighting for a lost cause? Mendelssohn's nature belonged to the "Goetheian art period,"[30] as Heinrich Heine called it.[31] As a musician Mendelssohn treasured the ideals of truth, beauty, and goodness (which Moses Mendelssohn was among the first to introduce to the world of the Enlightenment[32]). This, however, did not prevent, and perhaps even promoted, the approval of Mendelssohn's works by a broad audience, while also setting him in opposition not only to the exponents of grand opera and the composing instrumental virtuosos but also to some of the cultural currents of his time.

He realized this gap with increasing pain, without being willing to change his view of the world. This tragic tendency has been noted on different occasions, if also explained and interpreted in various ways. Georg Knepler sees in it the expression of a discontent with the rise of the political radicalism of the Republicans.[33] Like Knepler, Eric Werner finds in Mendelssohn a change from liberalism to conservatism.[34] Norbert Miller speaks generally of Mendelssohn's lagging behind the developments of his time,[35] Susanna Großmann-Vendrey of the irreconcilability of humanism and historical education, on the one hand, and Europe's political and social problems, on the other.[36] Friedhelm Krummacher characterizes Mendelssohn's development as an "increasingly conscious [to him] threat to an artistic existence within rapidly changing surroundings."[37]

The fact that Mendelssohn did not follow new trends in his compositions and was frequently oriented toward the past drew criticism. Friedrich Nietzsche expressed this critique most mildly: "Felix Mendelssohn's music is the music of good taste for everything good that has existed: it always points backward."[38] Berlioz in 1843 stamped Mendelssohn with the macabre epithet: "He is always a little too fond of the dead."[39] Other contemporary and later critics were less gentle with him. Their critical probe was launched particularly against his sacred work as its most sensitive part, on which the judgment of the composer settled. Their most prominent spokesman was Heinrich Heine.

IMPASSIONED INDIFFERENCE?

Making a curious contrast to both Prince Albert's judgment stated earlier and Mendelssohn's self-evaluation, Heine, in his criticism of Mendelssohn (in 1842 and 1844), did not deny the earnestness, but the truthfulness, of his art: "Mendelssohn always gives us an opportunity to reflect upon the highest problems of aesthetics. Namely he always reminds us of the great question: what is the difference between art and a lie?"[40] He also contrasted what he "almost would have liked to call impassioned indifference" in Mendelssohn to the "power of the genius" in Berlioz's music.[41] Mendelssohn would possess "a great, strict, very earnest seriousness" but also a "total lack of naiveté," and Rossini's *Stabat Mater* would be more Christian than Mendelssohn's *St. Paul*, "which is praised by Rossini's opponents as a model of Christianity."[42]

The accusation of passionlessness and lack of mystical depth was later raised even by such pious critics and thorough experts as George Grove, Rudolf Werner, and Eric Werner. But Heine's term "impassioned indifference" already implies that this was not merely a deficiency. Walter Dahms praised Mendelssohn particularly in this regard:

And truly, if we listen closely to Mendelssohn's music and approach him ardently, then we feel in him, as with all great spirits, the tremendous intensity of passion, which flows through the tones and brings them to life. It does not reveal itself in powerful convulsions or overwhelming explosions of emotion, but in the infinitely eloquent, vivid articulation, which fills the smallest detail with unlimited content and makes our emotions tremble and empathize at their very depths.[43]

To be sure, such sympathetic understanding is rare in writings on Mendelssohn. Judgments of Mendelssohn's expressive abilities usually reflect a reproach that was raised very early, namely the accusation of sentimentality.[44] Among Mendelssohn's sacred pieces, objects of such criticism might perhaps be a few works with nonbiblical and nonliturgical texts, which he composed expressly for London, with a predominating solo voice.[45] Even in such works, however, it becomes difficult to demonstrate the existence of sentimentality in its pejorative sense as a tasteless means of expression.

Nevertheless, can we not often find in writings on Mendelssohn a hint of the anti-Semitism to which Wagner intensified Heine's polemics? Out of the "impassioned indifference" there arose in Wagner's judgment an inability to provide more than the "charm of changing colors and forms of the kaleidoscope," whenever it was not a matter of the "expression of soft and melancholic resignation" caused by this very inability. In order to create deeper emotions, Mendelssohn had to seize "openly upon every single formal detail" that belonged to his chosen stylistic models. To expand upon the term "Christentümlichkeit" (Christianliness) that Heine invented, Wagner coined the term "Gebildetheit" (educatedness) in place of genuine German "Bildung" (education); and he denied Mendelssohn true artistic status on the basis of his Jewish heritage.[46] (Given this attitude, it is almost to be taken for granted that Wagner defamed Heine in a similar manner.)

SLAVISH IMITATION?

Besides the accusation of weakness in expression, Heine also raised more generally the accusation of stylistic dependence. Thus, in reference to Mendelssohn's *St. Paul*, Heine spoke of Mendelssohn's "almost obtrusive imitation of classical patterns" and also indirectly accused Mendelssohn of "slavishly copying Handel or Sebastian Bach."[47] This accusation is used by other critics mainly against certain stylistic means that Mendelssohn supposedly employed in the manner of theatrical props for creating a spiritual mood. One thinks of the Protestant chorale in the Reformation Symphony, which Mendelssohn composed in the winter of 1829–1830 on the occasion of the tercentenary of the Augsburg Confession on 25 June 1830,[48] or the chorale quotations in the instrumental part of the *Lobgesang*, but primarily of the chorale settings in *St. Paul*,[49] inserted in the manner of Bach's *St. Matthew Passion*,[50] and of the chorale melodies in the incidental music to Racine's *Athalie* (composed for the Prussian king in 1843–1845). Such criticism leads to suspicion of artificiality everywhere. To Richard Wagner, for example, the whole *Lobgesang* was nothing but a superficial imitation of Beethoven's Ninth Symphony and a "stupid naïveté."[51]

Mendelssohn undoubtedly selected from the depth of his knowledge of the great sacred repertoire—from Palestrina, through Bach and Handel, to Beethoven and Cherubini—means that seemed appropriate to him, for example, the antiphonal or responsorial psalm singing, with which he had become familiar in Rome.[52] He did this not in the sense of a deliberate collage but as an assimilation of what came to him naturally. In order to evaluate Mendelssohn's methods, one must consider that there was no longer a firmly established obligatory tradition in the Protestant church of his time and that contemporary theorists of liturgy and church music continuously produced new thoughts about how "true church music" could be realized in the most "sensible," "useful," and "uplifting" manner.[53]

It may be doubted, however, whether the parallel between Mendelssohn and Overbeck (the head of the "Nazarene" painters in Rome with their backward-looking religious longing), also suggested by Heine, is valid.[54] The association is suggested purely by the fact that the most familiar work of the "Nazarenes," the frescoes in the Casa Bartholdy in Rome, is in the house of one of Felix's maternal uncles, Jacob Bartholdy (Salomon). Mendelssohn, however, dissociated himself explicitly from the "adornment" and "affectation" of the "German Romanticists in Rome."[55] Nevertheless, he called the paintings of his cousin Philipp Veit, who also qualifies as a Nazarene, "so simply beautiful and pious."[56]

This issue deserves an investigation that considers aspects of both art history and musicology. Even if such an investigation should yield a positive result, it could reveal only a partial similarity of orientation, since Mendelssohn's religious output and, even more so, his complete oeuvre do not follow one single line. It is simply not the case that Mendelssohn was a specialist in imitating old Italian a cappella music, a historicizing epigone like his Berlin contemporary August Eduard Grell.

Despite certain "archaizing" tendencies—for example, in *Tu es Petrus* (1827), *Aus tiefer Not* (Op. 23 no. 1, 1830), *Vespergesang* (Op. 121, 1833)— Mendelssohn's modernity is unmistakable. In his large sacred works he continued predominantly in the immediate tradition of the vocal-orchestral oratorio style and church music of the Viennese Classicists, although under the modifying influence of his familiarity with Bach and Handel. The a cappella style had its influence mainly on his smaller sacred compositions. Thus, Mendelssohn's most personal contribution to sacred vocal music is a modern form: the prayerlike arioso, such as "Doch der Herr vergißt der Seinen nicht" (But the Lord Is Mindful of His Own) from *St. Paul* or "Dann werden die Gerechten leuchten" (Then Shall the Righteous Shine Forth) from *Elijah*. Even when imitating or reviving older forms, however, Mendelssohn went decisively beyond traditionalism, historicism, and eclecticism, namely, by the animation that corresponded to his work ethic. This individual trait has recently been pointed out in the style of his organ sonatas.[57] Personal emotion was always the decisive point for Mendelssohn, as he once put it in reference to some of his sacred works:

That I have just now written a number of sacred works was an inner necessity for me, just as one feels sometimes driven to read a specific book, the Bible or something else, which is the only way to make oneself feel good. If it shows similarities to Seb. Bach, I once more cannot help it, since I wrote it according to my mood, and if I felt just like the old Bach when reading the words, so much the better for me. Because you will not think that I copy his forms, without content; if so, I could not finish a single piece due to disgust and emptiness.[58]

In Mendelssohn's understanding of history, no viewpoint would be rejected solely on the basis of its age. For him, progress could also include falling back on older means. As a matter of fact, the "amalgamation of two stylistic periods," which Rudolf Werner regarded as a "characteristic of Mendelssohn's church music in general,"[59] was an almost inevitable heritage of all church music since its split in the early seventeenth century into a *prima* and *seconda prattica*, a *stylus antiquus* and a *stylus modernus*. This polarization was suddenly more striking than before, however, a situation that was to no little extent due to the fact that the *prima prattica*, the strict style, was identified with long-distant past, whose heritage was not so much to be continued as a tradition as to be explored in a historical-critical manner.

The use of the Protestant chorale represented such a recourse to old times and was reminiscent of Bach's *St. Matthew Passion* or Graun's *Der Tod Jesu*, the latter still regularly performed in nineteenth-century Berlin. The chorale was still a living religious symbol, but as such its legitimate place was almost exclusively restricted to congregational singing. That it was problematic to make the chorale an important part of sacred art music, as Mendelssohn did, is indicated by the chorale's becoming "obligatory" on the opera stage at this time, where, as Mendelssohn joked bitterly in a letter to Ferdinand Hiller,[60] it thus did not serve as an inner confession but as an externally effective presentation, as a religious accessory. Mendelssohn might have been thinking of Meyerbeer's *Les Huguenots* (1836), in which the chorale "Ein feste Burg" played an important role, just as it had done already in Mendelssohn's Reformation Symphony.[61] It is possible that this ambivalence was the direct cause of Mendelssohn's doubts about his Reformation Symphony. The use of the chorale in his vocal works is quite different, however. For Mendelssohn the chorale was an indispensable expression of the Christian congregation, and it did not seem anachronistic to him to include chorales even in Old Testament contexts, since in this regard he did not think historically but as a Protestant. For this reason Mendelssohn did not completely dispense with the chorale in his *Elijah*, though he did not use it in its original form but rather invented new melodies in the manner of chorales and had them sung to psalm verses.[62] This precaution saved his *Elijah* from the harshest criticism.

THE PATH TO MASTERSHIP OF SACRED MUSIC

Heine did Mendelssohn a complete injustice when he claimed that Mendelssohn had to "construct the spirit of Christianity scientifically," and he also believed incorrectly that Mendelssohn had been baptized in his thirteenth year.[63] Mendelssohn's Christianity was much more deeply rooted, much more "naive" than Heine supposed, who, in his own situation as a late and purely opportunistic convert, obviously did not understand that Mendelssohn was not a conscious convert and did not "Christianize,"[64] which Heine hated so much, but expressed his true inner self even in his sacred music.

The father, Abraham Mendelssohn, a banker[65] and Berlin city councillor, had a liberal attitude toward the rules and external forms of religion, apparently more liberal than his son did later, yet he found it right to have his children educated in Christian faith as the religion of the time[66] (and he himself and his wife, Lea, née Salomon, converted to Christianity in 1822). This conversion was symptomatic of the Restoration period, which, not only in Prussia, ended certain freedoms granted to the Jews by Napoleon.[67] Abraham Mendelssohn, however, did not simply follow the Romantic current and lead his children and later himself along with his wife to Catholicism, to which his older sister Dorothea, with her second husband, Friedrich

Schlegel, had converted (after earlier changing from Jewish to Protestant faith), but rather turned to the Protestant Reformed faith.

Thus, Felix was a Protestant Christian from 21 March 1816, when he was seven years old, through baptism in the Neue Kirche in Berlin (when he was given the additional first names Jacob Ludwig).[68] His confirmation confession attests that he was completely familiar with the doctrines of the Reformed Church as taught to him by the Berlin pastor Wilmsen.[69] Mendelssohn was also married in the Reformed Church, specifically, the French Reformed Church (Eglise Wallon) in Frankfurt am Main, to Cécile Jeanrenaud, daughter of the previously deceased pastor of this church. At Mendelssohn's funeral service on 7 November 1847 in the Pauliner Kirche in Leipzig, the preacher of the local Reformed congregation, Pastor Howard, officiated.[70]

Felix Mendelssohn, who rarely referred to his origins, appeared to people more familiar with him than was Heine to be a truly Christian personality. A Jewish hue can at most be seen in his strong family bonds and in his nearly absolute obedience to his father. This trait has justly been called a "Jewish patriarchal family spirit."[71] His music rarely shows a hint of Jewish tradition, however; only in the melody of the chorus "Der Herr ging vorüber" (Behold! God the Lord passed by!) from *Elijah* has a reminiscence of synagogue music been established.[72] In addition, Mendelssohn's intimate knowledge of the Bible was of a different kind from that of Heinrich Heine, who mainly concentrated on the Old Testament and was also familiar with postbiblical Jewish literature; Mendelssohn rather took the approach of a good Protestant who saw the Old Testament in relation to the New and, in the tradition of Luther, associated the New Testament with Protestant chorales.

It is apparently not known what songs young Felix sang in the Reformed services. The practical foundation for Mendelssohn's sacred music was laid at first less by the active experience of liturgical music, which at that time had virtually disappeared in post-Enlightenment Berlin, than by his participation in rehearsals and concerts of the Berlin Singakademie under his composition teacher Karl Friedrich Zelter and in Zelter's Friday music meetings.

According to its statutes, the Singakademie was an "art society for holy and serious music, particularly for music in learned style" (1816) and had as its goal the "conservation and revival of thorough artistic connoisseurship through practical exercises of church or sacred music and the most closely related serious vocal music, especially of songs in learned style" (1821).[73] In the ten years that Felix participated in Zelter's rehearsals (1819–1829) as a singer (alto) and piano accompanist, he became familiar not only with works of Bach and Handel, as well as old Italian church music, but also with the imitations of the a cappella style, such as those written by the founder of the Singakademie, Karl Fasch. Besides these, works in the Viennese Classic style, as well as contemporary sacred music, such as Romberg's Psalm settings, Himmel's Masses, sacred works by Fesca, Seyfried, and Neukomm, and oratorios by Friedrich Schneider, were also rehearsed.[74] The culmination and final event of this phase was Mendelssohn's epoch-making performance in 1829 of Bach's *St. Matthew Passion*, which had by that time practically disappeared.

During his numerous trips, Mendelssohn also came into contact with church music. No later than 1825 he became familiar with Cherubini's, Lesueur's, and Hummel's church music in Paris; in 1829, with old English church music through Thomas Attwood, London church organist (and former student of Mozart); in Rome in 1830, at the home of the Prussian Minister Christian Karl Josias Bunsen, with many works by Palestrina. Mendelssohn's "incredible memory" (attested to by Robert Schumann[75]) passionately absorbed all these inspirations.[76]

It is also characteristic for Mendelssohn that his public positions were closely connected to sacred music. The first position on which he set his sight, though unsuccessfully, was that of Zelter's successor as director of the Berlin Sing-akademie. Between 1833 and 1835, as city music director in Düsseldorf, his obligation was "particularly the direction of [Catholic] church music"[77] (at St. Lambertus and St. Maximilian). To be sure, in 1836 he turned down the leadership of the Frankfurt Cäcilienverein,[78] an institution similar to the Berlin Singakademie, as he also declined the Leipzig Thomaskantorat in 1842 (he recommended Moritz Hauptmann).[79] As "Gewandhauskapellmeister" in Leipzig, however, he often performed sacred works, among them his large orchestrated psalm settings,[80] and was additionally required to organize two annual church concerts. On 22 November 1842 he was appointed "General-Musik-Director" by the Prussian king Friedrich Wilhelm IV, as was his antipode Meyerbeer on 11 June of the same year, and his duty was the "supervision and direction of church and sacred music"[81] (while Meyerbeer became Spontini's successor as director of the opera house). In addition, Mendelssohn conducted music festivals, especially the Lower Rhine Music Festivals, which took place during Pentecost and had a partly religious character, and performances of oratorios and other sacred works in England. In Germany, as well as in England, he successfully appeared as an organist, especially preferring works by Bach.

Talent and education enabled Mendelssohn to produce an almost universal output strongly connected to the classics (thus, often called "classicist"), in which sacred music had an incontestable place. That the inclusion of sacred music in a leading composer's oeuvre could no longer be taken for granted becomes immediately obvious by a comparison of Mendelssohn to his contemporary Schumann, for whom sacred music played an entirely subordinate role but who, on the other hand, estimated Mendelssohn's important role in that genre so highly that he wrote about the latter's 42nd Psalm that it stood "on the highest level . . . recent church music has generally reached."[82] Even many of Mendelssohn's secular Lieder and choral songs have a religious, in some cases a specifically Protestant, tinge.[83] Narrow dogmatic limits were unknown to him, so that he was able to write for other confessions as well, if the texts suited his emotions. Luther's translation of the Bible and Protestant chorales remained the center, however. While Protestant church music in general had declined and was almost exclusively left to minor cantors, organists, and schoolteachers, it temporarily regained its dignity through Mendelssohn.

The historian Johann Gustav Droysen clearly recognized Mendelssohn's importance for Protestant church music when in 1842 he wrote to the composer about the rehearsals for a performance of *St. Paul* in Kiel:

It is truly unique how your music is received here especially by the earnest Protestant audience . . . . And it is a major achievement for you that you comply with a certain movement of the time in such an unambivalent manner and take the lead. There is something about the fact that Protestant music, which has lain dormant since J. S. Bach . . . , is finally coming back to life.[84]

It is no coincidence that Mendelssohn's brother-in-law, the painter Wilhelm Hensel, presented the prematurely deceased in a posthumous portrait of 1853 as a master of sacred music: in front of an organ, leaning on the score of *St. Paul*.[85]

OCCASIONS AND PURPOSES FOR HIS SACRED WORKS

Some of the early sacred works may be judged to be mere compositional exercises, such as the lost Kyrie for five voices and orchestra, which Mendelssohn had to compose in 1825 in Paris for Cherubini as proof of his talent.[86] Almost all Mendelssohn's other sacred works had practical purposes or found a practical use. Beginning with his thirteenth year in 1821, his sacred choral songs were performed at the Berlin Singakademie and, from 1822, in the Frankfurt Cäcilienverein; in the same year a motet by the adolescent composer was performed at the Thomaskirche in Leipzig.

The relation to practical use becomes particularly obvious when Mendelssohn had a specific performer in mind. In 1828 he wrote an *Ave maris stella* for the renowned singer Anna Milder-Hauptmann, who performed in a concert at the Berlin Marienkirche. He had in mind the Berlin concert and opera tenor Eduard Mantius and his high A when composing the tenor solo in the eight-voice *Ave Maria*.[87] When at this same time he wrote the chorale cantata *O Haupt voll Blut und Wunden*, he provided an aria for his friend Eduard Devrient.[88] The soprano part in his *Elijah* was supposedly created to fit the voice of the Swedish Nightingale Jenny Lind, whose f♯² enchanted him.[89]

A practical occasion is connected even with the Romantic genesis of the Three Motets for female voices and organ. In December 1830 Mendelssohn had heard the beautiful voices of the two concealed, singing French nuns in the Trinità de' Monti church in Rome. He found the music bad, and he wrote something for their voices that he wanted to send them anonymously and then listen to secretly. (This music later appeared in a different version as Op. 39.)

A performance that must seem odd to the modern reader took place at a private gathering in honor of Mendelssohn in Frankfurt am Main in 1839, where ten of his compositions were performed, the content of each being presented in a *tableau vivant*, among them four sacred pieces. Here Mendelssohn heard and saw what he had wished for in the Trinità de' Monti church: " a chapel with a marvelous Gothic (fake) organ, in front of which a nun sat; two others stood and sang from printed sheet music 'Beati omnes' [Op. 39 no. 2b]; the choir answered from behind the scene."[90]

Was this (Biedermeier?) virtual reality the actual reality of Mendelssohn's sacred music? Some hasty critics would most eagerly say so; but reality was much more complex.

There was not only a private but also a continuous public demand for Mendelssohn's sacred works, both for the church and for the concert hall. The oratorio *St. Paul* was originally a commissioned work for the Frankfurt Cäcilienverein, led by Johann Nepomuk Schelble. The symphony-cantata *Lobgesang* was written in 1840 at the request of the Leipzig city council for the quadricentennial festival that took place throughout Germany (with the exception of Prussia and Austria[91]) in commemoration of the invention of printing from movable type and was first performed on 25 June in the Thomaskirche. The Neue Tempelverein in Hamburg, the liberal synagogue occasionally apostrophized by Heinrich Heine, approached Mendelssohn in 1843 with the request for a musical setting of the 100th Psalm. The completion of the oratorio *Elijah* in 1845–1846, nine years after the first draft of the text,[92] was the result of an 1845 invitation from the Birmingham Music Festival. The *Lauda Sion*, a musical setting of the Corpus Christi sequence of St. Thomas Aquinas, came into existence in 1845–1846 for the Catholic Church of Saint-Martin in Liège on occasion of the 600-year celebration of the introduction of the festival of Corpus Christi.[93] For the French Reformed Church in Frankfurt am Main he composed a Psalm in four voices in 1846. Before Mendelssohn could write music for the consecration of the cathedral in Cologne, death had taken the pen from his hand. Mendelssohn liked such commissions for compositions[94] and may have even interpreted them as a confirmation of the usefulness of his activities.

Only the commissions from Friedrich Wilhelm IV of Prussia, who was an adherent of the old Italian a cappella style[95] and founded the Berlin cathedral choir in connection with Mendelssohn's appointment in Berlin, were not always fulfilled enthusiastically by the composer. His Berlin duties were for him "one of the sourest apples one can bite into."[96] A commissioned setting of Luther's *German Te Deum* in 1843 for the millenary of the German Reich was the "most tedious task" he had ever taken up;[97] it was brought to performance by Mendelssohn in the Berlin Hof- und Domkirche with choir and orchestra (on 6 August), while, according to an old custom, 101 cannon shots were fired in the court square. Similarly, the chorales he composed in 1843 at the command of the king for the Berlin cathedral with "trombones etc." seem to have given him no real pleasure, as he could not acquire a taste for the ambiguous endeavors of the "Romantic on the king's throne" to enrich with music the Prussian unified liturgy established in 1817.

Recent critics ascribe outstanding liturgical value to the Three Psalms (Op. 78), the *Sechs deutsche Sprüche* (known in English as Six Choral Anthems) (Op. 79),[98] and the *Deutsche Liturgie*, composed for the Berlin cathedral choir between 1843 and 1846, mostly scored for eight-voice a cappella choir. Fanny Hensel also found the 2nd Psalm, dated December 1843 (Op. 78 no. 1), "very beautiful, very

Gregorian and Sistine" but added immediately that "Felix would rather compose for orchestra."[99] It is true that Mendelssohn had been familiar with the a cappella style from his early years and had composed many choral works for voices only or for voices with organ or continuo accompaniment (e.g., Three Church Pieces, Op. 23, or Three Motets, Op. 39).[100] He saw his strength, however, mainly in orchestrally accompanied sacred music, of which the most characteristic works (besides his oratorios) are the large-scale Psalms *Non nobis, Domine* (Op. 31, as early as 1830), *Wie der Hirsch schreit* (Op. 42), *Kommt, laßt uns anbeten* (Op. 46), and *Da Israel aus Ägypten zog* (Op. 51), all composed 1837–1839. The return to unaccompanied vocal music seems to have been problematic for him, at least under the conditions that were imposed on him in Berlin. Thus, the cathedral clergy criticized his 98th Psalm (op. 91), composed for New Year's Day 1844, which begins a cappella but in which the composer—in agreement with the words of the Psalm ("Lobet den Herrn mit Harfen"/"Praise the Lord with harps")—called for the use of harps, timpani, and trumpets, in addition to the complete orchestra. The harp, the clergy said, was the most profane musical instrument[101] (presumably because, as a beggar's harp, it had fallen into a low social status).

In contrast to that, inspiration and occasion seem to have been in agreement in the case of his a cappella eight-voice Psalm *Denn er hat seinen Engeln befohlen* (For He Shall Give His Angels Charge over Thee). In its original form the Psalm became part of the Berlin cathedral choir's repertoire; in altered form, Mendelssohn incorporated it into *Elijah*. This choral setting was composed in the summer of 1844, after Mendelssohn had heard of the attempted assassination of Friedrich Wilhelm IV by Mayor Tschech. In the apparently unpublished letter from Bad Soden that Mendelssohn sent with the motet to the king on 15 August 1844, he wrote:

Since I have received this news on my trip to the music festival in Zweibrücken, some verses have been on my mind, which I could not forget, which I have thought over and over, and as soon as I found a quiet moment here again, I had to put them to music. So here they are, and I dare to lay them at the feet of Your Majesty as an expression of my best wishes.[102]

One is reminded of the homage compositions of composers in earlier times. The association is not completely apt, however. Mendelssohn did not write this work as a commission and did not use a prescribed text. It rather shows once more his basic assumption that whatever he undertook as a composer had to be in agreement with his personality, his emotions. He truly felt sympathy for the king (as little as he could stand certain court people), and with perfect tact he chose a Bible verse that both suited the given occasion and could exist equally well without this specific context.

CHURCH OR CONCERT HALL?

All later criticism cannot obscure the fact that Mendelssohn's subjectively genuine expression of his devoutness was, for the most part, also objectively real at his time, at least in Germany and England. A contemporary reported on the premiere of *St. Paul* during Pentecost of 1836 at the "Rittersaal" in Düsseldorf at the Eighteenth Lower Rhine Music Festival that "the effect and enthusiasm among performers and audience in the packed hall caused by the performance of the large work under the encouraging direction of Mendelssohn was indescribable."[103] Almost fifty performances in various European cities and even in the United States are recorded up to the fall of 1838.[104] When Mendelssohn was invited to Buckingham Palace in 1842 and started to play the chorus "Wie lieblich sind die Boten" (How lovely are the messengers) from *St. Paul*, Queen Victoria and Prince Albert could sing along.[105]

The *Lobgesang* was similarly successful at first. At its performance in the completely filled Town Hall in Birmingham in 1840, the audience stood up in response to the chorale "Nun danket alle Gott," a reaction that had previously occurred only at the "Hallelujah" of Handel's *Messiah*.[106] When the *Lobgesang* was performed at the Lower Rhine Music Festival in Düsseldorf in 1842, and the "trombones resounded the first theme into the hall, general rejoicing broke out, even before the choir came in, and Mendelssohn had to start over."[107]

Elijah, which has outlived the other two works, although today its popularity has mostly faded again, was also a success from the very beginning. At the premiere in Birmingham on 26 August 1846 with an audience of 2,000 people, four choruses and four arias had to be repeated.[108] In England—as George Grove observed in 1896[109]—*Elijah* achieved almost the same status as *Messiah* in the nineteenth century.

Richard Wagner wrote about the performance of Mendelssohn's *St. Paul* in Dresden on a Palm Sunday concert in 1843 in terms that are remarkable in their contrast to his later invective:

It is only regrettable that such an oratorio cannot be completely incorporated into our Protestant church worship, since only through that could its true significance be transmitted to the hearts of all the faithful, while without this foundation, and especially in a concert hall, it confronts us more or less only as a serious piece of art, and its real religious effect cannot come to the fore nearly as much as would be the case in the circumstances under which Sebastian Bach introduced his oratorios to the congregation. At least its impact in the concert hall is also moving and uplifting.[110]

The only regret expressed in this statement is that the Protestant service did not allow the performance of such a work. The blame for this is not sought with the composer but with the "Protestant church worship." This is quite reasonable, too, since the Reformed Protestant worship service always had little liturgy and did not provide room for church music, while the Lutheran worship service included less and less liturgy as time went by and expelled concerted church music after the middle of the eighteenth century.

Even such an authority on Mendelssohn's sacred music as Rudolf Werner, therefore, had to conclude that it consisted of "independent works of art with religious content, which could only find their place in church as a sacred decoration."[111] He does not seem to see the cause or fault merely in the historically developed order for the worship services, however. Eric Werner even claims that Mendelssohn lacked a feeling for purely liturgical music.[112] The question of different possible definitions of the term "liturgy"—i.e., whether it can be applied in an absolute sense or rather to a specific denomination or period in time—does not even arise.

Eric Werner's global statement is already sufficiently contradicted by Mendelssohn's Catholic *Lauda Sion* for solo voices, choir, and orchestra, a work that in its time was so liturgical that Mendelssohn doubted it could have any effect outside of the liturgy.[113] Mendelssohn did not have an aversion to purely liturgical music, but rather to purely ceremonial music, in the sense of a liturgical piece that does not allow for any individual expression or emotional animation on the part of the composer.[114] This constitutes an important difference, especially from a Protestant viewpoint, as is illustrated in Mendelssohn's description of the liturgy of Holy Week in the Sistine Chapel. For him the endless Gregorian psalmody partly meant singing "completely without regard for words and meaning."[115] How could an early nineteenth-century Protestant identify himself fully with this alien tradition? (He did, however, find the formal principle of antiphonal singing very convincing.)

Scholars like to point out that Mendelssohn did not see any opportunity to integrate church music organically into the Protestant worship service. This can supposedly be seen in a letter of 12 January 1835 to Pastor Bauer, which reads as follows:

Until now I do not know—even disregarding the Prussian liturgy, which rules out any such things . . .—how music could be made an integral part of our worship services, and not simply a concert that inspires devotion more or less. The Bach Passion was like that;—it was sung in church as an independent piece of music for the sake of edification;—of genuine church music, or better, worship music, I know only the old Italian things for the papal chapel, in which the music only accompanies, however, and subordinates itself to function, and provides support, like the candles, the incense, etc.[116]

Contrary to Wagner, Mendelssohn thus assumed that his own works had the same concert character as Bach's *St. Matthew Passion*. He projected the music actually intended for use in the worship service into a more distant past—just as generally everybody who talks about sacred music shows the tendency to acknowledge its existence only in an illumined past. In the same breath, however, Mendelssohn denied genuine worship music its artistic character by calling it purely functional, being on one level with candles and incense.

He thus appealed to the impossibility of uniting music with autonomous artistic claims and functional liturgical music. This impossibility already existed even during the time of the "old Italian things for the papal chapel," for otherwise there would have been no need for the church music reforms of the Council of Trent. The dilemma is an ancient one, and many solutions that have been praised by some have been condemned by others, as the history of the Protestant church cantata, culminating in Bach's works, demonstrates. Whatever solutions were proposed or established, they could never be dogmatic but only pragmatic in accordance with contemporary tradition and historical context.

IMAGINARY CHURCH MUSIC?

Even Mendelssohn had to develop a practical concept of church music based on the customs of his time and environment. His attitude in this regard was as far removed from the narrowness of doctrine as from all-encompassing tolerance.

Mendelssohn counted his organ fugues in Op. 37 among his "works in church style."[117] This shows that he held to the traditional idea of fugue style as church style. Additionally, Mendelssohn seems to have been influenced by the early Romantic conception of the "dignity" of true church music (Klopstock, Herder, Reichardt), for the sacred works of Haydn, Cherubini, and Hummel were often not serious enough for him; his judgment of a "scandalously funny"[118] Haydn Mass already anticipates the viewpoint of Caecilianism. He did not adopt the narrow Romantic church-music ideal of a pure a cappella style (Thibaut, Winterfeld), although his attention was repeatedly drawn to a cappella music through the influence of Berlin Singakademie, the Frankfurt Cäcilienverein, his visit with Thibaut in Heidelberg, and his stay in Rome, and he even cultivated this style in some of his own smaller works. As an artist Mendelssohn could not agree with the third contemporary main current of church music aesthetics, the genuine Enlightenment movement represented by figures such as Doles and Lobe, which would have banned all high artistic intention from church music and accepted only what was immediately understandable to the churchgoers. At most the inner honesty that was inherent in the goals of the Enlightenment found its parallel in him, namely, in the directness, immediacy, and absolute certainty of his artistic testimony.

To categorize this testimony neatly into "religious," "sacred," and "ecclesiastical" would be a difficult undertaking with Mendelssohn—as with many other historical figures. Historical reality cannot remotely be bound to such idealized classifications.

More important than the question of what is performable and what will be well received during the worship service is, especially with regard to Protestant church music, the question of its inner spiritual qualities. Does what Liszt said in 1882 about oratorios in general apply to Mendelssohn? "These works do not refer to the cult, as they used to, but to art, and they appeal more to our fantasy than to our faith. They poeticize objects without presenting them for us to worship; they elevate our feelings, as do all works of art, without raising this edification to devotion or to true prayer—*oratio*, worship."[119]

This might be true for some pieces, but certainly not for all. Probably the most profound reason for the insertion of chorales in *St. Paul* and the *Lobgesang* or of choralelike passages in *Elijah* was to raise feeling to the level of devotion. Why would Mendelssohn compose his many prayerlike ariosi, if not to stimulate real prayer? If one could talk about "imaginary church music"[120] in this context, then it would be a term that probably would be applicable to a large portion of the church music of preceding centuries. When deciding whether or not musical artworks are church music in their essence, not simply in their function, the question will be, especially from a Protestant perspective, whether they can transform their audience into a spiritual congregation, and this certainly has been the case often enough with Mendelssohn's works.

NOTES

This chapter was originally published as "Zu Felix Mendelssohn Bartholdys geistlicher Musik," in *Religiöse Musik in nicht-liturgischen Werken von Beethoven bis Reger*, ed. Walter Wiora with Günther Massenkeil and Klaus Wolfgang Niemöller, Studien zur Musikgeschichte des 19. Jahrhunderts 51 (Regensburg: Bosse, 1978), 97–117.

1. For example, at the death of his sister Fanny; see Sebastian Hensel, *Die Familie Mendelssohn 1729 bis 1847, nach Briefen und Tagebüchern*, new edition by Friedrich Brandes, 2 vols. (Leipzig: Hesse & Becker, [1929]), 2: 361.

2. "Il croit fermement à sa religion luthérienne, et je le scandalisais quelquefois beaucoup en riant de la Bible"; Hector Berlioz, *Correspondance inédite*, 6 May 1831, quoted in Ernst Wolff, *Felix Mendelssohn Bartholdy* (Berlin: Verlagsgesellschaft für Literatur und Kunst, 1906), 95. In his memoirs Berlioz speaks of Mendelssohn's "opinion toute religieuse et orthodoxe"; *Mémoires de Hector Berlioz*, 2nde série (Paris: Michel Levy frères, 1878), 50.

3. [Max F. Schneider], "Ein unbekanntes Mendelssohn-Bildnis von Johann Peter Lyser," in *Weihnachts- und Neujahrsgabe der Internationalen Felix-Mendelssohn-Gesellschaft* (Basel: Internationale Felix-Mendelssohn-Gesellschaft, 1958), 55ff.

4. Wilhelm Adolf Lampadius, *Felix Mendelssohn Bartholdy: Ein Gesammtbild seines Lebens und Wirkens* (Leipzig: F.E.C. Leuckart, 1886), 367.

5. Eric Werner, "Mendelssohn—Wagner: Eine alte Kontroverse in neuer Sicht," in *Musicae scientiae collectanea: Festschrift K. G. Fellerer zum 70. Geburtstag*, ed. Heinrich Hüschen (Cologne: Arno-Volk-Verlag, 1973), 652.

6. Robert Schumann, *Erinnerungen an Felix Mendelssohn Bartholdy: Nachgelassene Aufzeichnungen*, ed. Georg Eismann (Zwickau: Städtisches Museum, 1948), 77.

7. Letter of 8 April 1840 to Falkenstein in Dresden, in Felix Mendelssohn Bartholdy, *Briefe aus den Jahren 1833 bis 1847*, ed. Paul and Carl Mendelssohn Bartholdy, 4th ed. (Leipzig: Hermann Mendelssohn, 1864), 228; letter of thanks to the director of the Leipzig University for the honorary doctorate granted to him in 1836, in Willi Reich, *Felix Mendelssohn im Spiegel eigener Aussagen und zeitgenössischer Dokumente* (Zurich: Manesse, 1970), 283; letter of 4 May 1844 to Bunsen, in Mendelssohn, *Briefe 1833–1847*, 407–8; letter to Zelter of 18 December 1830, in Felix Mendelssohn Bartholdy, *Reisebriefe von Felix Mendelssohn Bartholdy aus den Jahren 1830 bis 1832*, ed. Paul Mendelssohn Bartholdy, 7th ed. (Leipzig: Hermann Mendelssohn, 1865), 97; see also his letter from 15 July 1831 to Eduard Devrient, ibid., 213; further, the letter of July 1831 to Frau von Pereira, ibid., 205: "Ich nehme es mit der Musik gern sehr ernsthaft, und halte es für unerlaubt, etwas zu komponieren, daß ich eben nicht ganz durch und durch fühle. Es ist als sollte ich eine Lüge sagen, denn die Noten haben doch einen ebenso bestimmten Sinn, wie die Worte,—vielleicht einen noch bestimmteren" (I like to take music very seriously, and I consider it impermissible to compose anything I do not feel through and through. It is as if I told a lie, for notes have just as specific a meaning as words—maybe even more specific).

8. After Seneca, Ep. 23: "Disce gaudere . . . . Mihi crede, res severa est verum gaudium" (Learn to rejoice. . . . Believe me, true joy is a serious matter); Georg Büchmann, *Geflügelte Worte* (Berlin: Haude & Spener, 1964), 546. A related passage is found in Mendelssohn's letter of 22 June 1830 to Zelter: "Since then I always only play what gives me pleasure, be it as serious as it will"; Mendelssohn, *Reisebriefe*, 19.

9. One of the many passages in letters referring to the subject (4 April 1831 to his family): "Und davor habe ich Ehrfurcht, wie überhaupt vor jeder wirklichen Vollkommenheit . . . mir ist es genug, wie gesagt, daß in irgend einer Sphäre etwas mit Treue und Gewissenhaftigkeit, nach Kräften vollkommen ausgeführt werde, um Respekt davor zu haben, und um mich daran zu freuen" (And this strikes me with awe, as does any genuine perfection . . . it is enough for me that in any sphere something is accomplished faithfully and conscientiously, to the limit of one's ability, in order for me to respect and enjoy it); ibid., 139. A similar passage is found in his letter of 13 June 1847 to his nephew Sebastian, in Mendelssohn, *Briefe 1833–1847*, 484–85. A clear differentiation between "pietistic" devoutness and an emphasis on professional and private perfection can be found in his often-quoted letter to Schirmer of 21 November 1838: "Ich soll ein Frommer geworden sein!" (They say I have become a devotee!); ibid., 184–85.

10. Susanna Großmann-Vendrey, "Mendelssohn und die Vergangenheit," in *Die Ausbreitung des Historismus über die Musik: Aufsätze und Diskussionen*, Studien zur Musikgeschichte des 19. Jahrhunderts 14 (Regensburg: Bosse, 1969), 74–75.

11. See Alexander Altmann, "Das Menschenbild und die Bildung des Menschen nach Moses Mendelssohn," *Mendelssohn-Studien: Beiträge zur neueren deutschen Kultur- und Wirtschaftsgeschichte* 1, ed. Cecile Lowenthal-Hensel (Berlin: Duncker & Humblot, 1972), 11ff.

12. See Friedhelm Krummacher, "Über Autographe Mendelssohns und seine Kompositionsweise," in *Bericht über den Internationalen Musikwissenschaftlichen Kongreß Bonn 1970* (Kassel: Bärenreiter, 1971), 484.

13. On the philosophy of the Singakademie, see Karl Rehberg, "Ausstrahlungen der Sing-Akademie auf die Musikerziehung," in *Sing-Akademie zu Berlin: Festschrift zum 175-jährigen Bestehen*, ed. Werner Bollert (Berlin: Rembrandt, 1966), 106ff. At the performance of Haydn's *Seasons*, the "Weinchor," "Spinnerlied," and "Romanze" were cut as being indecent; see Rehberg, 107, 30.

14. Letter of 19 December 1831 from Paris to his father; Mendelssohn, *Reisebriefe*, 303–4): "Es hat Effekt gemacht, aber ich habe keine Musik dafür. Denn es ist gemein, und wenn das heut die Zeit verlangte, und notwendig fände, so will ich Kirchenmusik schreiben."

15. Letter of 14 July 1833 to his family; Mendelssohn, *Reisebriefe*, 208.

16. Letter to Lyser (before 1836): "Meine ganze Natur sträubt sich dawider, dem Laster der Unsittlichkeit irgendein Zugeständnis zu machen . . . . und wenn ich mich prüfe: frage ich mich selbst, ob es bei dieser Ansicht mir glücken wird, jemals eine wirksame Oper zu schaffen"; see Schneider, "Ein unbekanntes Mendelssohn-Bildnis," 54.

17. Letter of 25 December 1834 to Moscheles; Felix Mendelssohn Bartholdy, *Briefe von Felix Mendelssohn Bartholdy an Ignaz und Charlotte Moscheles*, ed. Felix Moscheles (Leipzig: Duncker & Humblot, 1888), 103.

18. See Arno Forchert, "Textanlage und Darstellungsprinzip in Mendelssohns *Elias*," in *Das Problem Mendelssohn*, ed. Carl Dahlhaus, Studien zur Musikgeschichte des 19. Jahrhunderts 41 (Regensburg: Bosse, 1974), 63.

19. Hensel, *Die Familie Mendelssohn*, 2: 15: "Wie kann man von der Richtung einer Zeit im allgemeinen sprechen, wenn gleichzeitig der Paulus und die Hugenotten auftreten und jeder sein Publikum findet!"

20. "Fragmente aus Leipzig, Nr. IV and V," in Robert Schumann, *Gesammelte Schriften über Musik und Musiker* (Leipzig: G. Wiegand, 1875), 1: 323ff.

21. Schneider, "Ein unbekanntes Mendelssohn-Bildnis," 31.

22. Ibid., 38:

Wie die Gegner des Meisters Giacomo demselben den Vorwurf machen, er biete alles auf um zu effektuieren, namentlich in seinem letzten größeren Werke (den *Hugenotten*), so könnten Meyerbeer's Freunde wohl dem Meister Felix mit ebenso gutem Grunde vorwerfen: 'er vermeide es ängstlich: zu effektuieren'; namentlich in seinem *Paulus*. Meiner Ansicht nach sind beide Vorwürfe ungerecht, denn Meyerbeer kann seiner Eigentümlichkeit zufolge ebenso wenig anders komponieren als er komponiert, als Felix Mendelssohn es vermag seine Eigentümlichkeit zu verleugnen.

23. Letter of 23 May 1834 to his mother; Mendelssohn, *Briefe 1833–1847*, 41.

24. Letter of 7 February 1834 to Ignaz and Charlotte Moscheles; Mendelssohn, *Briefe an Ignaz und Charlotte Moscheles*, 112.

25. Letter of 6 October 1835 to his family: "Der Abend des Sonntags war wirklich kurios, wo ich ihm mein Oratorium vorspielen mußte, . . . und wie er zwischen dem ersten und zweiten Teile seine neuen Etüden und ein neues Konzert den erstaunten Leipzigern vorraste, und ich dann wieder in meinem 'Paulus' fortfuhr, als ob ein Irokese und ein Kaffer zusammenkämen und konversierten"; Mendelssohn, *Briefe 1833–1847*, 100.

26. Letter of 30 March 1840 to his mother; Mendelssohn, *Briefe 1833–1847*, 224–25.

27. Wolff, *Felix Mendelssohn Bartholdy*, 124–25.

28. Schneider, "Ein unbekanntes Mendelssohn-Bildnis," 50.

29. Mendelssohn, *Briefe 1833–1847*, 460: "Dem edlen Künstler, der, umgeben von dem Baalsdienst einer falschen Kunst, durch Genius und Studium vermocht hat, den Dienst der wahren Kunst, wie ein anderer Elias treu zu bewahren."

30. Georg Knepler sees Mendelssohn's position in intellectual history in a similar way; see his *Musikgeschichte des 19. Jahrhunderts* (Berlin: Henschelverlag, 1961), 2: 759.

31. Heinrich Heine, *Die romantische Schule*, in his *Sämtliche Werke*, ed. O. Walzel (Leipzig: Insel, 1910), 7/1: 5.

32. Altmann, "Das Menschenbild und die Bildung des Menschen," 26.

33. Knepler, *Musikgeschichte des 19. Jahrhunderts*, 758ff.

34. Eric Werner, Mendelssohn—Wagner: Eine alte Kontroverse in neuer Sicht, 647.

35. Norbert Miller, "Felix Mendelssohn Bartholdys italienische Reise," in *Das Problem Mendelssohn*, 33–34.

36. Großmann-Vendrey, "Mendelssohn und die Vergangenheit," 82.

37. Krummacher, "Über Autographe Mendelssohns und seine Kompositionsweise," 484.

38. "Felix Mendelssohns Musik ist die Musik des guten Geschmacks an allem Guten, was dagewesen ist: sie weist immer hinter sich"; quoted in Walter Dahms, *Mendelssohn* (Berlin: Schuster & Loeffler, 1922), 16.

39. "Seulement il aime toujours un peu trop les morts"; Berlioz, *Mémoires*, 52.

40. *Lutezia* 9 (Supplement: Musical Season of 1844), 400: "Mendelssohn bietet uns immer Gelegenheit, über die höchsten Probleme der Ästhetik nachzudenken. Namentlich werden wir bei ihm immer an die große Frage erinnert: was ist der Unterschied zwischen Kunst und Lüge?"

41. Ibid., 401, 399.

42. *Lutezia* 43 (Paris, middle of April 1842), 227, 224. For ideas Heine took from Parisian music reviews, see Michael Mann, "Heinrich Heines Musikkritiken," in *Heine-Studien*, ed. Manfred Windfuhr (Hamburg: Hoffmann und Campe, 1971), esp. 121–22.

43. Dahms, *Mendelssohn*, 191:

Und wahrlich, wenn wir uns in Mendelssohns Musik hineinhören, und uns ihm mit Inbrunst nahen, dann fühlen wir auch bei ihm wie bei allen Großen die ungeheure Intensität der Leidenschaft, die die Töne durchströmt und mit Leben erfüllt. Sie offenbart sich nicht in gewaltigen Erschütterungen, umwerfenden Gefühlsexplosionen, sondern in der unendlich sprachvollen, lebendigen Artikulation, die auch das Kleinste noch mit grenzenlosem Inhalt erfüllt und unser Empfinden bis ins Tiefste erbeben und miterleben läßt.

44. See Hellmuth Christian Wolff, "Das Mendelssohn-Bild in Vergangenheit und Gegenwart," in *Musa-Mens-Musici: Im Gedenken an Walther Vetter*, ed. Heinz Wegener (Leipzig: Deutscher Verlag für Musik, 1971), 321, who cites Adolf Bernhard Marx. Eduard Krüger's judgment in 1850 is similar to Marx's; see Rudolf Werner, "Felix Mendelssohn Bartholdy als Kirchenmusiker" (Ph.D diss., University of Frankfurt am Main, 1930), 163.

45. Such as the anthem "Why, O Lord"/"Laß o Herr" (*Drei geistliche Lieder*) for alto solo, choir, and organ, composed in 1840 for an English music lover; or the hymn "Hear My Prayer"/"Hör mein Bitten" for soprano solo, choir, and organ, written in 1844 for a London concert.

46. Richard Wagner, "Das Judentum in der Musik" (published first in 1850 under a pseudonym), in *Gesammelte Schriften und Dichtungen* (Leipzig: E. W. Fritzsch, 1898), 5: 66–85; see also "Aufklärungen über das Judentum in der Musik," ibid., 8: 238–60; "Über das Dirigieren," ibid., 8: 261–337; "Über das Dichten und Komponieren," ibid., 10: 137–51.

47. *Lutezia* 43 (1842), 227, 224–25.

48. Mendelssohn later distanced himself from this symphony—it was more interesting for what it stood for than for what it was in itself; see his letter of 23 April 1841 to Julius Rietz, in Mendelssohn, *Briefe 1833–1847*, 282. It was first printed posthumously as Op. 107.

49. Adolf Bernhard Marx had already strongly advised him against the chorales; see Mendelssohn's letters to Julius Schubring of 6 and 14 September 1833 in *Briefwechsel zwischen Felix Mendelssohn Bartholdy and Julius Schubring, zugleich ein Beitrag zur Geschichte und Theorie des Oratoriums* (Leipzig: Duncker & Humblot 1892, repr. Walluf bei Wiesbaden: M. Sandig, 1973), 41, 44.

50. See Mendelssohn's letter of 22 December 1832 to Schubring, where he refers explicitly to Bach as model; Schubring, *Briefwechsel*, 22.

51. "blöde Unbefangenheit"; see Eric Werner, "Mendelssohn, Felix," in *Die Musik in Geschichte und Gegenwart*, ed. Friedrich Blume (Kassel: Bärenreiter, 1961), 9: col. 87.

52. In a letter to Zelter of 16 June 1831 Mendelssohn described the Psalm-singing in the Sistine Chapel and added, "Beiläufig ist diese Einteilung der Psalmverse, und daß sie vom Chor und Gegenchor abgesungen werden, eine der Einrichtungen, die Bunsen für die evangelische Kirche hier gemacht hat" (By the way, the division of the Psalm verses [into two sections, a and b], and that they are sung by choir and opposing choir, is one of the arrangements which Bunsen has made for the Protestant church here); Mendelssohn, *Reisebriefe*, 181–82.

53. See Georg Feder, "Verfall und Restauration," in *Geschichte der evangelischen Kirchenmusik*, ed. Friedrich Blume (Kassel: Bärenreiter, 1965), 221ff., 259ff.

54. *Lutezia* 43 (1842), 223–24.

55. Letter of 15 February 1832 to Zelter; Mendelssohn, *Reisebriefe*, 340.

56. Ibid.

57. Susanna Großmann-Vendrey, "Stilprobleme in Mendelssohns Orgelsonaten op. 65," in *Das Problem Mendelssohn*, 185–94.

58. Letter of 13 July 1831 to Devrient; Eduard Devrient, *Meine Erinnerungen an Felix Mendelssohn-Bartholdy und seine Briefe an mich* [Leipzig: J. J. Weber, 1869], 115 :

Und daß ich grade jetzt mehrere geistliche Musiken geschrieben habe, das ist mir ebenso Bedürfnis gewesen, wie's einen manchmal treibt, grade ein bestimmtes Buch, die Bibel oder sonst was, zu lesen, und wie es einem nur dabei recht wohl wird. Hat es Ähnlichkeit mit Seb. Bach, so kann ich wieder nichts dafür, denn ich habe es geschrieben, wie es mir zu Mute war, und wenn mir einmal bei den Worten so zu Mute geworden ist, wie dem alten Bach, so soll es mir um so lieber sein. Denn Du wirst nicht meinen, daß ich seine Formen kopiere, ohne Inhalt, da könnte ich vor Widerwillen und Leerheit kein Stück zu Ende schreiben.

59. Rudolf Werner, *Mendelssohn als Kirchenmusiker*, 120.

60. Letter of 18 July 1838; Mendelssohn, *Briefe 1833–1847*, 171.

61. Some years later Otto Nicolai used this chorale for an orchestral work, namely, his *Kirchliche Festouvertüre*, Op. 31, written for the bicentennial of the Königsberg University in 1844. Joachim Raff also wrote an overture on "Ein feste Burg" (1867). Richard Wagner quoted the first lines of this chorale in his *Kaisermarsch* (1871). Carl Maria von Weber set the precedent for this sort of orchestral works with his *Jubelouvertüre*, Op. 59 (1818), written for the fiftieth anniversary of the reign of King Friedrich August of Saxony, in which he used the Saxon national anthem "Heil Dir im Rautenkranz," a contrafactum of the English national anthem.

62. See Mendelssohn's letter of 30 December 1846 in Frederick G. Edwards, *The History of Mendelssohn's Oratorio "Elijah"* (London: Novello, Ewer and Co., 1896), 106–7. Only in no. 15 does the melody clearly resemble the chorale originally intended ("O Gott, du frommer Gott").

63. *Lutezia* 43 (1842), 224.

64. See Heine's letter of 11 February 1846 to Ferdinand Lasalle: "Ich habe Malice auf ihn [Felix Mendelssohn] wegen seines Christelns, ich kann diesem . . . unabhängigen Menschen nicht verzeihen, den Pietisten mit seinem großen, ungeheuren Talent zu dienen . . . . Wenn ich das Glück hätte ein Enkel von Moses Mendelssohn zu sein, so würde ich wahrscheinlich mein Talent nicht dazu hergeben" (I am angry with him [Felix Mendelssohn] because of his 'christianizing,' I cannot forgive this . . . independent person for serving the pietists with his great, incredible talent . . . . If I were lucky enough to be a grandson of Moses Mendelssohn, I would certainly not lend my talent to such a thing); quoted in Ludwig Rosenthal, *Heinrich Heine als Jude* (Frankfurt am Main: Ullstein, 1973), 234. Heine also mocked Mendelssohn's baptism in his poetry (*Deutschland, Ein Wintermärchen*, Chapter 16):

Der Abraham hatte mit Lea erzeugt	Abraham begot with Lea
Ein Bübchen, Felix heißt er,	A little boy, Felix is his name,
Der brachte es weit im Christentum,	He got far in Christianity,
Ist schon Kapellenmeister.	He is already Kapellmeister.

See also Heinrich Heine, *Atta Troll*, Chapter 9:

Hört es, hört, ich bin ein Bär,	Hear it, hear, I am a bear,
Nimmer schäm ich mich des Ursprungs,	Never ashamed of my origins,
Und bin stolz darauf, als stammt ich	And I am proud of them, as if I descended
Ab von Moses Mendelssohn.	from Moses Mendelssohn.

65. Until 1821; then he left the business to his brother Joseph; see Wilhelm Treue, "Das Bankhaus Mendelssohn als Beispiel einer Privatbank im 19. und 20. Jahrhundert," *Mendelssohn-Studien* 1, 36. The banking company Mendelssohn & Co. in Berlin was liquidated in 1938 due to the anti-Semitic politics of the Third Reich and taken over by the Deutsche Bank; ibid., 69–70.

66. See his letter to his daughter Fanny in 1820 on the occasion of her confirmation; Hensel, *Die Familie Mendelssohn*, 1: 99–100.

67. See Rosenthal, *Heinrich Heine als Jude*, 218–19.

68. See also Max F. Schneider, "Felix Mendelssohn Bartholdy: Herkommen und Jugendzeit in Berlin," *Jahrbuch Preußischer Kulturbesitz 1963*, 157ff.

69. See Karl Klingemann Jr., ed., *Felix Mendelssohn Bartholdys Briefwechsel mit Legationsrat Karl Klingemann in London* (Essen: Baedeker, 1909), 358ff.

70. George Grove, "Mendelssohn," *Grove's Dictionary of Music and Musicians*, 2d ed., ed. John A. Fuller Maitland (London: Macmillan, 1907), 3: 154; see also Klingemann, *Briefwechsel*, 334–35.

71. Großmann-Vendrey, "Mendelssohn und die Vergangenheit," 73.

72. Eric Werner, *Mendelssohn: A New Image of the Composer and His Age* (New York: Free Press of Glencoe, 1963), 470–71.

73. Quoted, for example, in *Sing-Akademie zu Berlin*, 53, 56; facsimile on page 5.

74. See August Reissmann, *Felix Mendelssohn Bartholdy: Sein Leben und seine Werke* (Leipzig: List & Francke, 1893), 19–20.

75. Schumann, *Erinnerungen an Felix Mendelssohn Bartholdy*, 55.

76. See Susanna Großmann-Vendrey, *Felix Mendelssohn Bartholdy und die Musik der Vergangenheit*, Studien zur Musikgeschichte des 19. Jahrhunderts 17 (Regensburg: Bosse, 1969).

77. Ibid., 54.

78. See his letter to his mother of 18 February 1836; Mendelssohn, *Briefe 1833–1847*, 121–22.

79. Großmann-Vendrey, *Felix Mendelssohn Bartholdy und die Musik der Vergangenheit*, 188–89.

80. Examples include the performances of the 42nd Psalm in the New Year's concert of 1838 and on 21 March 1839 and of the "Prayer" (as Mendelssohn explicitly wanted it to be called) "Verleih uns Frieden gnädiglich" (Grant Us Thy Peace) on the eve of Reformation Day 1839; see Felix Mendelssohn Bartholdy, *Briefe an deutsche Verleger*, ed. Rudolf Elvers (Berlin: de Gruyter, 1968), 94. Additional instances would be the performances of the *Lobgesang* on 3 and 16 December 1840 and of the 114th Psalm on New Year's Day 1840 and 9 March 1843, and others.

81. See Mendelssohn, *Briefe 1833–1847*, 353–54.

82. Robert Schumann, "Rückblick auf das Leipziger Musikleben im Winter 1837–38," in *Gesammelte Schriften* (1875), 2: 49.

83. See, for example, the Lieder Op. 8 no. 4, *Erntelied* ("Es ist ein Schnitter, der heißt Tod"); Op. 8 no. 5, *Pilgerspruch* ("Laß dich nur nichts nicht dauern"); Op. 8 no. 9, *Abendlied* ("Das Tagewerk ist abgetan"); Op. 9 no. 11, *Entsagung* ("Herr, zu Dir will ich mich retten"); Op. 47 no. 4, *Volkslied* ("Es ist bestimmt Gottes Rat"); Op. 71 no. 6, *Nachtlied* ("Vergangen ist der lichte Tag"); Op. 71 no. 1, *Tröstung* ("Werde heiter mein Gemüte"); Op. 86 no. 2, *Morgenlied* ("Erwacht in neuer Stärke").

84. Felix Mendelssohn Bartholdy and Johann Gustav Droysen, *Ein tief gegründetes Herz: Der Briefwechsel Felix Mendelssohn Bartholdys mit Johann Gustav Droysen*, ed. Carl Wehmer (Heidelberg: Lambert Schneider, 1959), 77: "Es ist ganz einzig, wie Deine Musik gerade hier bei dem sehr protestantisch ernsten Publikum rechten Eingang findet . . . . Und

das ist eine große Errungenschaft für Dich, daß Du einer bestimmten Bewegung in der Zeit auf so unzweideutige Weise entsprichst und an ihre Spitze trittst. Es ist etwas damit, daß die protestantische Musik, die seit J. S. Bach still gelegen . . . , endlich wieder lebendig wird."

85. Reproduced in Herbert Kupferberg, *Die Mendelssohns* (Tübingen: Wunderlich, 1972), plate V, between pages 80 and 81. This portrait may be the one Friedrich Wilhelm IV commissioned from Hensel after Mendelssohn's death, according to Reissmann. The order "pour le mérite," which Mendelssohn is wearing, suggests this.

86. It was most likely performed with only piano accompaniment at his parents' house in Berlin in the fall of 1825; see Großmann-Vendrey, *Felix Mendelssohn Bartholdy und die Musik der Vergangenheit*, 22.

87. See Mendelssohn's letter to his family of 30 November 1830; Mendelssohn, *Reisebriefe*, 70.

88. Letter of 5 September 1830 to Devrient; ibid., 107.

89. See Edwards, *The History of Mendelssohn's Oratorio "Elijah,"* 35–36.

90. Letter of 3 July 1839 to his mother; Mendelssohn, *Briefe 1833–1847*, 197: "eine Kapelle mit einer allerliebsten gotischen (Schein-) Orgel, vor der eine Nonne saß; zwei andere standen und sangen nach den gedruckten Notenblättern: Beati omnes; der Chor antwortete hinter der Szene."

91. See Hensel, *Die Familie Mendelssohn*, 2: 160.

92. See Klingemann, *Briefwechsel*, 27.

93. Albert van der Linden, "Un Fragment inédit du "Lauda Sion" de F. Mendelssohn," *Acta musicologica* 26 (1954), 48–64.

94. Klingemann, *Briefwechsel*, 254.

95. Alfred von Reumont, *Aus König Friedrich Wilhelms IV. gesunden und kranken Tagen* (Leipzig: Duncker & Humblot, 1885), 211–12.

96. Letter of 15 July 1841 to Klingemann; Klingemann, *Briefwechsel*, 264: "einer der sauersten Äpfel, in die man beißen kann."

97. Letter of 21 July 1843 to Paul Mendelssohn; Mendelssohn, *Briefe 1833–1847*, 382.

98. It seems odd that Mendelssohn withdrew after a month the manuscript of the *Sechs Deutsche Sprüche*, which he had sent to the publisher Bote & Bock on 17 October 1846; see Mendelssohn, *Briefe an deutsche Verleger*, 342. The work appeared posthumously as Op. 79.

99. Hensel, *Die Familie Mendelssohn*, 2: 263.

100. See Rudolf Werner, *Mendelssohn als Kirchenmusiker, passim*.

101. Reissmann, *Felix Mendelssohn Bartholdy*, 289–90.

102. "Seit ich nämlich auf der Reise zum Musikfest in Zweibrücken jene Nachricht erfuhr, schwebten mir einige Verse vor, die ich nicht wieder aus dem Sinn verlieren, an die ich immer von neuem denken mußte, und sobald ich hier wieder zur Ruhe kam, mußte ich sie in Musik setzen. Die sind es nun, die ich als meinen Glückwunsch zu den Füßen Ew. Majestät hiebei zu legen wage." Autograph in the Deutsches Zentralarchiv Merseburg, Rep. 122 VI ad Nr. 9, a copy of which was provided by courtesy of Dr. Rudolf Elvers, Staatsbibliothek Preußischer Kulturbesitz, Berlin.

103. "Die Wirkung und Begeisterung, welche die Aufführung des großen Werkes unter der anfeuernden Direktion Mendelsohns bei Mitwirkenden und Zuhörenden in dem gedrängt vollen Saale hervorrief, war unbeschreiblich." Quoted from Ernst Wolff, *Felix Mendelssohn Bartholdy*, 128.

104. Friedrich Schmidt, *Das Musikleben in der bürgerlichen Gesellschaft Leipzigs im Vormärz (1815–1848)* (Ph.D. diss. University of Leipzig, 1912; pub. Langensalza: H. Beyer, 1912), 37.

105. Hensel, *Die Familie Mendelssohn*, 2: 185.

106. See Charlotte Moscheles, ed., *Life of Moscheles with Selections from His Diaries and Correspondence, by His Wife*, trans. Arthur D. Coleridge (London: Hurst and Blackett, 1873), 2: 70: "one of the chorales" (There is only one chorale, however. Might she have meant "one of the choruses"?).

107. Account of a contemporary; quoted in Großmann-Vendrey, *Felix Mendelssohn Bartholdy und die Musik der Vergangenheit*, 112.

108. See Mendelssohn's letter of 26 August 1846 to his brother Paul Mendelssohn; Mendelssohn, *Briefe 1833–1847*, 458–59.

109. In the preface to Edwards, *The History of Mendelssohn's Oratorio "Elijah,"* iii.

110. "Richard Wagner über Mendelssohn's 'Paulus,' Gelegentlich der Aufführung des Werkes in Dresden im Jahre 1843," *Musikalisches Wochenblatt* 30/12 (16 March 1899), 173–74:

Zu bedauern ist einzig, daß ein solches Oratorium nicht völlig unserem protestantischen Kirchencultus einverleibt werden kann, weil dadurch erst seine wahre Bedeutung in aller Gläubigen Herzen Übergehen würde, während ohne diese Grundlage und zumal im Concertsaal es uns mehr oder weniger nur als ein Kunstwerk ernster Gattung entgegentritt, und seine eigentliche religiöse Wirksamkeit bei weitem nicht so hervortreten kann, wie dies unter den Verhältnissen der Fall sein würde, unter denen Sebastian Bach seine Oratorien der Gemeinde vorführte. Immerhin ist aber auch die Wirkung im Concertsaale rührend und erhebend.

111. Rudolf Werner, *Mendelssohn als Kirchenmusiker*, 163.

112. Eric Werner, *Mendelssohn: A New Image of the Composer and His Age*, 177, 208.

113. Klingemann, *Briefwechsel*, 319.

114. See the statement in Felix's confirmation confession: "Die Anbetung Gottes im Geist und in der Wahrheit fordert das Christentum von uns, und verwirft leeren Zeremoniendienst und Heuchelei dagegen" (Christianity demands that we worship God in spirit and in truth, and rejects empty service of ceremonies and hypocrisy); see Klingemann, *Briefwechsel*, 360.

115. Letter of 16 June 1831 to Zelter; Mendelssohn, *Reisebriefe*, 184.

116. Mendelssohn, *Briefe 1833–1847*, 75–76:

Bis jetzt weiß ich nicht,—auch wenn ich von der Preussischen Liturgie absehe, die alles Derartige abschneidet . . . —, wie es zu machen sein sollte, daß bei uns die Musik ein integrierender Teil des Gottesdienstes, und nicht bloß ein Konzert werde, das mehr oder weniger zur Andacht anrege. So ist die Bachsche Passion gewesen;—sie ist als ein selbständiges Musikstück zur Erbauung der Kirche gesungen worden;—von eigentlich kirchlicher, oder wenn Du willst gottesdienstlicher Musik kenne ich nur die alt-italienischen Sachen für die päpstliche Kapelle, wo aber wieder die Musik nur begleitend ist, und sich der Funktion unterordnet und mitwirkt wie die Kerzen, der Weihrauch usw.

117. See his letter of 11 March 1837 to Breitkopf & Härtel; in Mendelssohn, *Briefe an deutsche Verleger*, 58.

118. Letter of 26 October 1833 to his sister Rebecka; Mendelssohn, *Briefe 1833–1847*, 10.

119. "Diese Werke beziehen sich nicht auf den Kultus, wie früher, sondern auf die Kunst und wenden sich mehr an unsere Phantasie als an unseren Glauben. Sie poetisieren die Gegenstände, ohne sie unserer Anbetung darzubieten; sie erheben wie alle Kunstwerke unser Gefühl, ohne diese Erhebung bis zur Andacht zu steigern und zum wirklichen Gebet—oratio, Gottesdienst—zu stimmen"; quoted from Carl Dahlhaus, "Zur Problematik der musikalischen Gattungen im 19. Jahrhundert," in *Gattungen der Musik in Einzeldarstellungen: Gedenkschrift Leo Schrade*, vol. 1 (Bern and Munich: Francke, 1973), 886.

120. Carl Dahlhaus, "Mendelssohn und die musikalischen Gattungstraditionen," in *Das Problem Mendelssohn*, 58.

HISTORICAL VIEWS AND DOCUMENTS

REVIEW OF FELIX MENDELSSOHN BARTHOLDY, THREE PSALMS(2, 43, 22), OP. 78—NUMBER 6 OF THE POSTHUMOUS WORKS (LEIPZIG: BREITKOPF & HÄRTEL)

Eduard Krüger[1]; translated by Douglass Seaton

[The exchange that follows, based on some admittedly minor pieces in Mendelssohn's oeuvre, places his sacred music into a context that has to do both with views of religious experience and with the relation of musical style and taste to that experience. Except for one passing reference, Mendelssohn's Jewish heritage is not directly at issue; in fact, it is more the decline of Christianity in post-Enlightenment Berlin that Krüger attacks. Krüger here adopts a conservative, orthodox Christian position, to which Wilhelm Wauer opposes a more progressive, flexible one.—Ed.]

The appearance of the scores under consideration here fills us with sadness for the departed singer from whose legacy works the indefatigable publisher has brought them to light: sadness on account of the one who died young, one who to many was the brightest light in the art of this era. He was not that for us: we believe that there have been contemporaries more gifted not only in natural creative power but also in the correct evaluation of their powers for the progress of our art. The choice of a mistaken direction is an error that does not plague, and still more rarely overcomes, the true genius as it does the seeking, wandering talent. If even Mozart and Beethoven erroneously ventured into the field of sacred music, to which their nature and talent did not belong, they either did not persist in this error—they only touched on, but did not expand into, the foreign territory—or in their error their sparks kindled other lights.

It is quite otherwise in Mendelssohn's case. His whole ecclesiastical career is misdirected. Why should we not say openly that Berlin Christianity is unable to find any blossoms on the tree of life, as is demonstrated every day? If one who has become great in the hustle and bustle of the world, lacerated by criticism, long estranged from heavenly simplicity, pauses in unaccustomed fashion on a quiet day and feels the futility of the blasé court city, and if the emptiness and lifelessness of the stillborn forms of this age anger him—and he feels an unfamiliar ardor, a gentle, mild glow of other worlds and bodies, where there are no criticism and learned stupidity . . . now all that is certainly praiseworthy and moving and certainly essential as *preparation* for a new holy life. But is all that then directly developed creatively, artistically, into the primevally powerful beauty of the new joy of life? No! It is hardly the entrance to the entrance. Quietly self-forgetting tears of conversion form only the first step for one who actually desires and will succeed in creating sacred art.

Not every one of these words *directly* applies to Mendelssohn; to some extent, however, they do apply to him, grown great among the crowds of prominent figures of the age, whom he attempted to cast away; still, one feels the chains rattle, even if more softly than in the case of less refined spirits. We must concede that his gently pious songs at least come closer to more a lofty construction than do other contemporary, nonecclesiastical creations. Even where we perceive something externally more powerful or artistically purer and richer creations—for power old *Fr. Schneider* stands at the forefront; for melodic richness, the much misunderstood *Loewe*[2]—they, nevertheless, stand no closer to that which Mendelssohn also sought. They represented perhaps a higher artistic devotion but did not produce ecclesiastical, but at the most only spiritual, poetry.

The devout can say from personal experience what differentiates the ecclesiastical from the spiritual, and we cannot demonstrate this to others, as people have long attempted to do. One could be content if the true inner satisfaction of the soul arose from worship of the black order of priests instead of the body of the Lord. Anyone who can be satisfied with that could also tolerate the Rossini *Stabat Mater*, suitably tricked out and performed in sacred places with every Parisian beauty mark of good delivery. We are compelled to declare this whole era incapable of the representation of sacred forms; with difficulty Cornelius or Albert Knapp might be in a position to teach the contrary. Only in the north does such simplicity still dwell, the mother of all truth and greatness: there a renewed art may be able to develop independently, freely, and joyfully in the manner of Thorwaldsen's apostles.

Already in Handel's time we observe the intermingling of the secular and the sacred, which moved the nobility at the time but also expressed itself clearly and strikingly to weaker minds. At least that which the mild-mannered *Graun*[3] sang was more closely related to the sacred; he did not stand as one *outside* the temple gates pleading for sanctuary, although, to be sure, he also did not penetrate into the holy of holies. How the age became more and more estranged from the sacred but was then driven rushing back again in longing, and now praying and seeking, and yet was not eager to practice the full and uplifting sacred art: this is demonstrated by the ecclesiastical attempts of Haydn and his contemporaries.

It is not possible to recover the sacred until our life is reformed and has restored itself out of the foaming waves of criticism. To return into the peace of the eternal current of transcendent creation requires more than the doubly reflected reflection of speculative scholasticism, to which we indeed owe the fact that things are *organized*—but we owe it not a single life form. Christianity certainly rescued itself from mere intellect about twenty years ago, but this negation still leaves it far from achieving newly creative affirmation. If we are freed by criticism and history from uncritical and unhistorical deism, if purified scientific method has created clarity for us in the darker Christian as well as artistic regions: this is certainly an achievement of which we should not be ashamed, one that we may keep as a trophy of the time. Yet such times are not suited to encourage holy simplicity, without which every work of art remains a clanging bell.

And because this joyful, holy peace is not granted to the present era, it also lacks any technique that cannot be considered and condemned as mere dexterity. Eccard,[4] Handel, and Bach had this technique in their blood. Indeed, they had to learn it manfully and sweated blood to master by youthful effort fugal composition and all that it involves; but this technique became a part of them, like melody in the case of Mozart, like rhythm in the case of Beethoven. Anyone who turns to that technique today regards it only as technique and learns the skill only for its usefulness—at least this is the case with all that which desires to appear as sacred.

Or might it be, as some of the most modern would like to make us believe, that a new period of Christendom is near, and therefore a new art is in the works? Make no mistake! Christendom will be renewed as it has renewed itself in all centuries, precisely by means of the ever-renewed return to the primordial, original truth, original beauty. And in this way a new church can someday construct itself—but not in the atrophying creation of this age!—which the inspired seers of the future call the *johannine*. But this, *when* it does appear (it does not exist yet! and until it appears, it will not motivate any flowering of art!) will then manifest its reconstructive force not by leveling, but rather by deepening. This is what Winterfeld[5] proclaims to the present age in a powerful, warning voice and what is so often misunderstood: only by means of *revival* of the beauty of happier times will the path be found on which we may approach the sacred shrine. It is not a matter of imitation, repetition, retesting, and reconstruction; rather, it is a matter of self-renewal through truth, of immersion into the true, bright depth of the stream of living water, which today we only hear rushing in the distance. Perhaps a fulfilled, light-surrounded time is in store for our grandchildren, where from the blessed simplicity of Eccard and the proud nobility of Handel and the thundering depth of Sebastian something new will be born that celebrates the newborn johannine church. This, however, will certainly be neither *St. Paul* nor *Elijah* nor Berlin penitential Psalms, but rather a shining, new word from primal springs, before which false, sick humility pales and slick vanity melts weeping away.

We have already often tried to describe how every high path was entirely denied to the soft, lovely, maidenly temperament of our Mendelssohn, and the broad fullness of heroic forms remained inachievable. *St. Paul* and *Elijah* proved this; their fame lasted an hour, their value was limited to the admirable singers who were *currently* active and died with them. That is, indeed, a bitter truth. But it has not just to do with him but also with the time, which he could not escape. If we put aside his oratorios and sacred things in exchange for the lovely, delicate beauty of his youthful songs, for the visionary Romanticism of his wonderful overtures, then we encounter his most inward being, as he himself recognized it in peaceful hours. In talent and ideas he stands approximately on the same level as Emanuel Geibel.[6] Within these limits he is beautiful and good, even powerful like Geibel in the pretty miniature painting of our day; what lies beyond that he could long for painfully but not grasp in tangible reality.

The three Psalms under consideration here, admirably worked out from the external point of view and conveniently supplied with an easy piano arrangement of the vocal score, are written in eight parts without accompaniment. The multiplicity of voices is happily employed, mostly in antiphonal double choruses. But the same could also have been expressed with four voices, perhaps even more richly. We hardly need to remember the Amen from Handel's *Messiah* or the *genuine* eight-voice scoring in Bach's motets.

The treatment of the text is *declamatory*, like in *Elijah* and *St. Paul*, but gentler. If this (Op. 78) was really written late, then it shows no progress as compared to those always ambitious works. One hears the words more than the notes and is immediately turned off at the beginning, when it says (Ps. 2):

Wa-rum to-ben die Hei - den, und re-den die Leu-te so ver-geb - lich

Several dense, brilliant passages with full chords at "Aber der im Himmel wohnet" bring new life; then follow steps in seconds in a well-known style; thereafter a fourfold trio with choir:

The words "Aber ich habe meinen König eingesetzt auf meinem heiligen Berge Zion; ich will von einer solchen Weise predigen" and so on, in trippingly declamatory style, could just as well be sung in an opera or to a didactic epigram. There are a couple more similarly declaimed phrases in seconds, then it says darkly and quietly, but unmelodically:

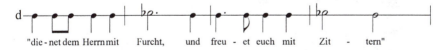

"die - net dem Herrn mit   Furcht,   und   freu - et euch mit   Zit - tern"

Into this the sweet closing section the following breaks as if out of a damp cloud:

"Küsset den Sohn, dass er nicht zürne, und ihr umkommet auf dem Wege." A superfluous closing is appended, based on words not from the Psalm: "Ehre sei dem Vater, Amen," the latter slightly fugal, a gentle ending, closely related in tone to the rest.

The second Psalm (Ps. 43) has its own effects of light, effective miniature painting by the opposition of high and low voices—for which the text offers no compelling basis: (I) "richte mich, Gott, und führe meine Sache wider das unheilige Volk"; (II) "und errette mich" etc., which latter words (II) are sung by a four-part female chorus against the four-part male chorus (I); the men sit like a pedal point on A and later on C, while the remaining words of the first movement are declaimed in unison:

This unison section is immediately thereafter reinterpreted in $\frac{3}{8}$, to the words "dass ich hinein gehe zum Altar Gottes"—otherwise constructed in the same manner, sounding naive and weak, not high and lofty . . . . and now even the words

der mei - ne Freu - de und Won - ne ist.

likewise in unison! The same sort of thing later; there even the melodious women's voices have to sing in unison in rabbinically didactic style to the sweet words

Was be - trübst du dich mei - ne See - le und bist so un - ruh - ig in mir

into which the men then sprinkle a certain harmonic seasoning! What we called naive earlier is described as such in *Berlin* usage; elsewhere it is called careless, sloppy, as, for example, the tone in Willibald Alexis's Brandenburg chronicles[7] and Th. Mundt's scholarly descriptions of the proletariat.[8] In this Psalm only the closing is warm and lively, but unfortunately it flies by too quickly, just where one thinks it is getting on track: "Harre auf Gott! Ich werde ihm noch danken"—a passage somewhat reminiscent of *St. Paul.*

In the third of the Psalms considered here (Ps. 22) we observe somewhat more art and effort; the expression is more carefully chosen. Noticeable, however, is the thoroughly dull rhythm that appears in all Mendelssohnian works, which reminds one undeniably of the naïveté of rabbinic recitation

and similar things, which already struck us earlier in the *Walpurgisnacht*. Such didactic asceticism

in a somber tone, not glowing with color—prosaic, not prophetic—does not lead into the sacred word but out of it.

The effect of this treatment is not encouraging. We regret having had to linger over such negatives. But it is the duty of criticism and history precisely to search for a verdict on a great departed one and to tell the truth for the sake of his reputation.

If we have thereby torn any tender heart away from the new Berlin religion, then we are sorry for the heart, not for the religion; for what sick sophistication has hidden in it must be culled out from it, and only then is newly renewed yet primeval beauty possible, which resounds and flows and kindles an eternal fire like the old prophets. As long as the warm lifeblood is squeezed out and distilled under the vacuum pump of self-righteous intellectual vanity, it produces no vital beauty. Some time ago a sensitive, devout man—no Berliner—personally reproached me with great sincerity for having picked apart *Elijah* so critically. These words are addressed to him most of all, though perhaps they will surprise him: These differences of opinion come not from any pleasure in contradiction, but rather with the prospect of final and infinite affirmation.

Emden, 21 December 1849.

FELIX MENDELSSOHN AND DR. EDUARD KRÜGER

Wilhelm Wauer[9]; translated by Douglass Seaton

Kommt her zum Frühlingswald, ihr Glaubenslosen,
Das ist ein Dom, drin pred'gen tausend Zungen—

. . .

Und dann sprecht: Nein! Es ist ein hohl Getriebe,
Ein Uhrwerk ist's, wir kennen jeden Faden—

. . .

Ihr könnt es nicht. Und thätet ihr's verwehen
In's Nichts würd' eure Läst'rung sonder Spuren
Und keinem Ohr vernommen untergehen
Im tausendfalt'gen "Ja" der Creaturen.

[Come out to the spring forest, faithless ones,
This is a cathedral, in it a thousand tongues preach—
. . .

And then say: No! It is an empty mechanism,
It is clockwork, we know every thread—
. . .

You could not say so. And if you would blaspheme,
It would dissipate into nothing without a trace,
And, heard by no ear, be annihilated
In the thousandfold "Yes" of the creatures.]

Emanuel Geibel

Having only just returned from a trip—prolonged three days by the sudden postponement of the concert and the interruption of the trains due to the winter storms—to Dresden, where we were enticed by a brilliant performance of Robert Schumann's *Paradies und die Peri* under the direction of the composer himself, on which occasion all the praise and all the blame assigned by Dr. Krüger to this work, full of highly poetic beauties and remarkable weaknesses, hovered vividly before our mind, we find in no. 1 of this journal a detailed review from the pen of the aforementioned critic on the three Psalms by Mendelssohn Bartholdy recently published as Opus 78. It is certainly no longer necessary for journal articles to rescue Mendelssohn's sacred music from the critical knife of even such a learned reviewer as Dr. K is. In any case we would rather have left it to someone else to elucidate closely the ideas expressed in that essay about artistic direction and the quality of the deceased master's devout creations, if the close of the article, which had to do with me personally, had not provoked me to oppose Mr. K publicly with special regard to his views on Mendelssohn.

The letter sent to him had as its purpose to encourage the gifted editor to undertake a thoroughgoing discussion of *Elijah*, in which I hoped that he would speak out strongly against the reckless and unworthy reviews of this work that were published here and there without examples and that bore witness to insolent heartlessness. At that time I did not yet know his own article on *Elijah* in the *Neue Zeitschrift für Musik* and therefore had no inkling that I had appealed to an opponent to be an advocate. Mr. K.'s statement is therefore not accurate; at least it might be a question of a reproach for a deed of which I still knew nothing. It seems to us necessary to clarify this so as to avoid general misunderstanding.

It is in any case gratifying that Dr. K. for once speaks out seriously and sets forth his views publicly. In this manner it may become easier for those who hold a different opinion to get a firm footing from which to carry on the battle. As K. very correctly observes, it is, in fact, a matter of the greatest significance that the world gradually become clearer about the whole essence of a great person who is departed, and therefore a feeble champion ought to be allowed—one who otherwise, as Mr. K. can already gather from the introduction of this article, is not a one-sided, exclusive Mendelssohnian—to enter the lists in the expectation that better troops stand ready to pursue the battle with greater force, if he himself has to withdraw with bleeding wounds.

We have not yet gotten to know the new Psalms discussed by Mr. K., so we will leave aside for the moment all the specific things said about them and focus only on the critic's general considerations. K. starts from the viewpoint that the present era absolutely cannot produce any genuinely ecclesiastical works of music, but least of all anyone who came to greatness in the circles of the capital city of Berlin. On this premise Mendelssohn's sacred works cannot possess the true spirit of the church. They constitute only a superficial imitation of the sacred tones of the good old days, not actually tones springing from a holy heart and life. It is a strange thing in the first place to attribute such impotence to a whole period. One must from the outset be cautious with prejudices that affect a certain circle. Thus, it is doubly wretched to deny that in such a confused and diverse time there might happen to be any individual souls in whom Christianity, the substance of a human life reaching beyond the secular, has taken root firmly and broadly enough to find in itself sufficient nourishment and energy not to be misled by the raving, confused cry of the masses. Every period must produce such appearances, and they are precisely the core of a more beautiful general renewal for the future. What is to prevent us from believing that our dear master was such a one? He certainly lived in and with the world, he surely did not draw back timidly in the face of contact with the flood of humanity around him, but Mr. K. does not wish to deny that he preserved his own nature devout and innocent. This writer did not personally know the inner suffering of the noble deceased, but what he has heard and read about him can only confirm him in his belief. Now if one grants all this, then it would remain for Mr. K. to show in what properties of Mendelssohn's sacred works the unecclesiastical, the unhealthiness reside. Eccard, Bach, Handel appear to be the only representatives of church music for Mr. K., as Mr. K. finds them to be orthodox, the only ones who understood how to reproduce the true, genuine churchdom of their day, as of all times. Of Eccard as a man and a Christian, we admit, little or nothing is known. Sebastian Bach certainly lived as a faithful servant of his church, but by his whole direction he belonged to the so-called pietists, and his immortal works do not have much at all to do with the spirit of the church that had faded out at that time but rather are the outpouring of his subjectively Christian, ardent heart and, moreover in a form and style of expression over which one would rightly shake one's head if a modern Christian composer would offer such things now. Bach was not so rooted in his own period, either, that it would not remain for the more recent period to take him to its heart more firmly again. But, indeed, Herr Dr. Krüger, the form is not the main thing; it is the spirit that dwells within it. But only to a minority may it be granted these days (and not only not to mere weaklings) to immerse themselves in those secret depths, in order triumphantly to dredge out the rich prizes of the spirit. We therefore want from our masters new treasures, not antiquarian ones, old wine in new wineskins—the same heart filled with God, but with prayers in a new version. Handel turned to the province of oratorio only when he could no longer support himself in the field of opera, primarily from ambition. He took a fortunate step; here he built great things. One hardly knows whether to say he himself was an ardent Christian; one judges this only on the basis of his works. We shall let that stand; but like Bach, Handel did not live in a time that was pervaded in a lively fashion by Christianity, or, at the very least, the bare, cold literalism of their period was a powerful enemy of the spiritual life and of Christian ardor, and yet we regard their works as the most genuine ecclesiastical tones. What, therefore, gives us grounds to assume that Mendelssohn, because of the fault of his time, could not have been capable of creating something ecclesiastical, truly devout? Rather, it is clear that he wrote from the personal impulse of his heart, he who nevertheless must have known well that the very inclination of the present was not directed toward such creations. And yet he dedicated his best powers to this genre and still intended something sublime to be the capstone of his artistic career. Where, then, are the lack of devotion, the superficiality in the works of our master? Are they lacking in seriousness, loftiness, dignity, inner richness? Nothing more is needed to prove the case, is it, Dr. Krüger? It is bad enough for anyone whose feeling, comprehension, negation are balanced by the feeling, comprehension, affirmation of thousands. A composer who chooses elfin whisperings, love songs, Romantic overtures, Greek tragedies for his tones is perhaps inherently incapable of creating ecclesiastical forms? One or the other! No one can serve two masters! Where can Mr. K. point out in Mendelssohn's sacred things anything undignified, common, frivolous, anything like Rossini's *Stabat mater* in the representation of Christian elements? Where is seriousness absent in what should be serious, loftiness in what should be lofty, sublimity in what should be sublime, gentleness in what should be gentle, or the soft without softness? Where does Mendelssohn depict repentance, contrition, the sorrow of death with tones of earthly pain? Power and richness of melody, beautiful, pure, rich formations: where is there any lack of these? Will Dr. K., in spite of his assertions to the contrary, not see majesty, greatness where it confronts him? Is it a sin in sacred works, too (oratorios are not *church* works), not to suppress the gentle, sweet-scented breath of Romanticism, which K. so admires in our master's songs and overtures, to represent in poetic versions the serious, the disturbing? Are there not just for that reason moments in *St. Paul, Elijah,* the *Lobgesang,* and the three large Psalms, just as there are in the works of the immortals whom Mr. K. honors exclusively, that no human eye can discover? Are not particularly the motets Op. 69 the outpouring of the purest, childlike devoutness that can be imagined? Must, then, Christianity and the godly in general be extended to people only in the strictest forms, and does it cease to be Christian and godly when form is abandoned? Is not the student out for a pleasant walk in Halle, wearing a velvet coat, as he receives instruction about Christian wisdom from the lips of a Tholuck,[10] just as dear to us as the priest in his gown? If one accepts Mendelssohn's oratorios and psalms as what they want to be, not just for churches and holy places (where Handel's creations do not belong either), one accepts them as devotion and ardent faith carried forth with dedication into the world, as missionary sermons in free, appealing form, glowing through with God and ringing out with God. Then, what use is it always and only to evoke the old—the old that is brought closer to us by the new master more comprehensibly and movingly and yet without denying the pure springs from which he drew strength in his youth, the old with which the world estranged from God will be reconciled again precisely by means of this new, and that without the new mediator would already long have become distant and foreign to the present, except for a predestined few? The rest, then, we wish to leave in peace for the future; but if Mr. K. believes that the reputation of *St. Paul* and *Elijah* has died with their creator, then we really don't know with what spectacles he is looking at the world. It may therefore be that Mendelssohn was gentler and softer than Bach and Handel, and so he is not the Bach or Handel of the eighteenth century; rather, he takes over their place for the nineteenth century, just as a founder of a future johannine church will be no St. Paul nor Luther but a man who can accomplish similar things in his own way.

It is further interesting to see which masters of our day Mr. K. places before our Mendelssohn in many regards. Fr. Scheider, Loewe, Hiller, Chopin, Schumann, Gade.[11] We can hardly believe that all these significant men, the venerable creator of *Das Weltgericht*[12] at their head, would applaud Mr. K. for this recognition; they would probably find it difficult to believe such renown themselves.

Even Schumann and Gade, two highly gifted sons of art, two shining stars in the firmament of musical poetry, should still bide their time and work quietly, so that they might truly earn this status. Their most recent works show no progress. Gade's Octet appears to suffer from many defects; Schumann's *Adventlied*, on a poem by Rückert, is, aside from great beauties of detail, a tedious work, not exactly marked by fluidity and swing, with prohibited "steps of seconds." We would still like to hold on to the noble works of their past years.

In the end, that which should be said first and foremost ought to be uncontroversial: this short essay is surely not complete and exhaustive. Let this important topic be discussed from many points of view, seriously and probing into the essence of the matter.

Among the works from Mendelssohn's legacy that have been published so far, *Athalie* and the *Lauda Sion* are by far the most significant and full of content, both beautiful, complete works of art. Whether it was worthwhile to have published the six Sprüche for eight-voice choir, Op. 79, we leave unresolved. They are simple, unpretentious vocal pieces, with no great significance. In the first of these the main theme of *Athalie* is reused, though indeed not to the same words, as is the case with a passage from the second of the three Psalms that Mr. K. reviewed at the words "Was betrübst du dich, meine Seele etc." (see the master's 42nd Psalm). The departed probably did not intend all these things for general circulation, and so we are not sure whether it is a good thing to bring to light such *posthuma*, at least not without careful consideration. There are art lovers who do not possess enough piety not to condemn the composer of such occasional compositions, despite the legion of his truly imperishable masterpieces.

We close now with the conviction that for the moment we will have convinced Dr. Krüger of our viewpoint as little as he has convinced us of his, but we hope, as stated earlier, that our attempt might provide the impetus for further expansion of the vault of apologetics, as long as it should remain necessary in the face of destructive criticism to build such a thing over Mendelssohn's green vernal wood.

Herrnhut, 10 January 1850.

ON THE CRITICISM OF MENDELSSOHN[13]

Dr. Eduard Krüger; translated by Douglass Seaton

On the occasion of the unfavorable judgment of Mendelssohn that appeared a short while ago in these pages, a variety of letters has come to hand. First of all, an anonymous one from Leipzig, which begins with the presupposition that I "disparaged" Mendelssohn only *in order* to make myself and "my compositions popular with the public"! No response is possible to such remarkable naïveté, even if the letter had been written openly and candidly with a full signature. A second fundamental idea of the same letter relies on a trite statement: "It is easier to find fault than to make something better," and advises me in a friendly way to set down a similar work and to achieve comparable approbation in Leipzig before I condemn Mendelssohn. That is to say: no one may say where the shoe pinches except the shoemaker; and no one may call Geibel a mediocre poet unless he himself is a Goethe. Enough of this childish attempt at an apologia, to which the sainted Mendelssohn, if he were to hear it, could only smile: "Lord, preserve me from my friends!"

Then a public letter appeared in no. 4 of this publication on 23 January 1850. Scholarly criticism desires such opponents, ones who are not only honorable and faithful but also get to the root of the matter itself with a certain insight. Mr. Wauer will perhaps permit me first to take up his objections in detail[14] and then to confront his "apologetics" with some general statements.

The atmosphere of Berlin is not favorable to the quiet submersion of the spirit, the childlike, solemn blessedness of innocence. It is undeniable that individual gifted people may live and work outside the stream of superficial secularism; it could even be that more truly devout people live in Berlin than in Herrnhut and Emden combined. Admittedly, we cannot calculate that. The effect of that general Berlin atmosphere is, however, nevertheless evident in many details. This should not be taken to mean that a Sodom and Gomorrah has sprung up on the Spree; but probably few can entirely resist its influence, least of all those who have spent their childhood and youth there and have lived thoroughly in the public eye. A very strong, powerful personality is able to resist it; M.'s characteristic nature was more maidenly than manly, gentle rather than strong.

All these assertions, however, should not prevent our recognizing the opposite and admitting our error, if that which truly is appropriate to the church should actually appear in M.'s works. Many attempts have already been made to lay out the difference between ecclesiastical, spiritual, devout, elegiac-serious. Such things cannot be added up mathematically and can never be proved in merely intellectual terms. If one wished to put it something like this: "The *ecclesiastical* (in art) is the beauty of manifest truth come to life in plastic form; the *spiritual*, a reflection of that, a dark-colored suppression of those bright forms of light; *devoutness* is the sentiment of the divine in the heart, apart from external form; *seriousness* is the opposite of frivolousness and is the outer form of the striving for truth" . . . it would be difficult to gain anything from such definitions. Even those who are of like mind would achieve practical results for art criticism only if they resolved to submit to their friends completely for a brief time and to that end to contemplate quietly and honestly their inmost selves, that is, without negation, reaction, vanity, errors of understanding, and so on, simply to awaken what arises from the heart.

For the *truly subjective* is also *objective*. For anyone who doubts this great truth, the greatest achievement of a philosophical century, all efforts toward truth, criticism, and so on in general must appear completely dubious and futile, and nothing remains for such a person but eternally blasé doubt, first of the world, then of himself. That this statement flows from the manifest teaching of God should be asserted only in opposition to absolute philosophy. But if anyone among the followers of abstract knowledge should fear that all the foolishness of the dark little ego might be consecrated by this statement—indeed Schlegelian Romanticism once erred to this extent!—then let him not forget that an incorruptible guide also dwells in one's own heart, which does not lie, even when the mouth lies outwardly.

It is natural that here our opponent also thinks about *personality*. Mendelssohn accomplished more by his personal amiability than by the depth of his works. I assert this without ever having met him personally, any more than my opponent has. Personal effectiveness finds its expression just as mysteriously as any higher spiritual sort. No one sees the innermost part of the person but oneself and God. So it is, too, with *devoutness*. No one can see this, no one prove it, but only sense it, feel it, represent it. One can see *artworks* and from them conclude what their source is. Naturally, all human judgment is subject to error. For that reason, if Leipzig and Berlin idolize Mendelssohn as the spiritual prophet, Meyerbeer as the secular one, then that is just as subject to error as if some individual claims the opposite. Truth will not be brought out by a large number of voices. Decisive judgment cannot be founded on personal or on any other external motives, but only through the profound contemplation of the work and honest devotion of the heart.

It is well known that Eccard and Bach were devout men. If we did not know it from their biographies, their works would show it inwardly.

Here I must correct one conspicuous error of my respected opponent, since it has to do with Bach and, to some degree, calls into question the whole greatness of the master. "How words toy with people!" a philosopher once said. "*Pietism?*" What does the word mean? Something entirely different today from 100 years ago;

the sense has changed even more than that of the word "*judgment*," which is known to have had a completely different meaning for Luther than it had 100 years later and has now. Nowadays the term "pietist" means something very vague. In common life and among the so-called cultivated it sometimes means the orthodox, sometimes the fanatic, sometimes the dreamer (quietist), sometimes an indeterminate dread and horror compounded of all of the preceding together, with no other unifying characteristic than the enemy's hatred. In this way, then, an amazing variety of people are tossed into the same pot of hatred, such as Hengstenberg, Göschel, Gerlach, Krummacher, Dräseke![15] The urchins of Berlin noticed that vagueness and at once produced a translation into the *lingua vulgaris*: to them anyone is a pietist who goes to church on Sunday in wedding clothes, in order to get edification from the "stultifying clergy." In this they agree with their counterparts in Paris: for the Parisian urchin, too, makes fun of all those "devout ones" who do not believe in the religion of Eugenius Suis or George Sand, Dumas, and their consorts. To be sure, we other Germans do not allow our usage to be prescribed from Berlin, as the French do from Paris; thus, those of us out in the country neither believed in the Berlin "freedom," as it was proclaimed in the fall of 1848 with speeches, banners, and nails, nor do we generally recognize the same meaning for "pietism" that a certain class of Berlin litterati do.

Now what about Bach's time? Today pietism is an epithet, but at the time it was nearly a title of honor. Today the so-called folk throw it with disgust in the face of the so-called court flunkeys; at that time the folk loved those who applied pietism by means of works of love, in order to fulfill the doctrine of eternal truth; today—incorrectly—the *orthodox* is called by that name, but at that time the *pietists were the opponents of the orthodox*! All those who were not followers of Paul and Apollos but were only disposed to be biblical and simply Christian, all who placed the life of love, bliss, and holiness above dogmatic academic squabbles: those were called pietists. Their name arose from the "Collegia Pietatis"—gatherings for the common practice of piety, which were at that time a source of edification and uplift and were able to represent love in works such as the orphanage in Halle. The Freilinghausen Gesangbuch, from which Bach set many songs to music, was written in this sense of pietism.[16] Of Bach's specific persuasion we know only that he was a Lutheran and nevertheless recognized the depth of the Catholic faith, as is evident in his musical works.

This therefore proves nothing one way or the other. I did not call Bach *exclusively ecclesiastical*. What I did say (in no. 1 of these pages) was that out of Eccard's holiness and Bach's profundity at some future time a new third style would come, which does not yet exist.

But all these individual questions get us no closer to the goal. For that reason let us set aside for the moment all Mr. Wauer's specific questions—"where then does Mendelssohn lack seriousness, strength, melody, and so on and whether there is only one form of Christian poetry"—so that perhaps they can be dealt with in a general way. Thus, I may cite those of Mr. Wauer's points that support my view; among other things (p. 27 par. 1), that M.'s sacred songs are to be compared to missionary sermons; that to publish Op. 79 might not be entirely worthwhile, because it has no special significance; that Mr. W. does not yet know these Psalms Op. 78 [*sic*] (p. 26, par. 1), and so on.

Much that is unprovable becomes clear by means of analogies. In Germany there is a variety of churches. One may be a lofty cathedral, soaring on columns, with resounding vaults, thrusting into distant eternity and intimately close to God. On the contrary, another may consist of a flat oblong in the form of a double cube, straight lines, confined resonance, built with care for acoustics but nevertheless breaking up the sound, blinkered, cold-hearted. In the cathedral everything that has breath resounds with overwhelming heavenly power; the long waves of tone wind through the vaults, entwine around the pillars, lose themselves in the floral scent of the distant capitals. There one hears the effect of that which is not calculated for effect but simply born in the church. How these heavenly hosts of tones flow, how the vault roars and never overflows!

> —The Holy Spirit came from heaven
> Filled up the whole house with roaring.—

How clearly and deeply, how brightly shimmering and yet mysteriously these sound images swim, veritable images of the eternal! These crush the concert hall or the oblong prayer hall. Certainly, many have experienced, without knowing why, the fact that Bach's tones—and even more those of Handel, Eccard, Palestrina—behave so strangely in the flat, four-walled boxes and seem to mumble and run together, even almost to burst those right-angled lines of the doctrinaire auditorium! On the contrary one *enthusiastic friend* of Mendelssohn once asked me in confidence why it was that his wonderful church songs sounded better in more limited spaces and became blurred in the cathedral?

Now anyone who calls a prayer hall a church, who takes the Berlin *Werdersche*[17] for a Gothic church, will never recognize the difference between the ecclesiastical and the spiritual, and we will not attempt to prove to him that love and life are eternally unprovable. Yet they resound in every simple heart. And these hearts, who can rightly differentiate a great breath and strong arm from short-windedness, know what our era lacks—without therefore weakening it, for every time is God's time. Even Bach had *temporal* traces, which make him sometimes seem foreign to us. For that reason it is misguided to have him speak directly in our language—as, for example, Schumann in the *Peri* and Second Symphony did through his vigorous prolepses. Whoever wants to carry over *the whole Bach manner directly* into our time lapses into the rococo, the death of all poetry. Who, then, is so foolish among those of goodwill that he wishes for *nothing more* than to reconstruct just any antiquarian point of view, *only* to honor the old times that have passed away? No one believes the opposition capable of such foolishness.

If, on the other hand, one points back to those eternal models of the past, then it will not be just because they are past but because they bear something eternal in themselves. That which is eternal will nourish us, raise us up, someday make us capable of such deeds, when the time comes. All that is temporal is only an image![18] For that reason these examples, too (we chose only the most familiar) are not cited as unique or normative but only in order to indicate what the ecclesiastical should be, what our era lacks, perhaps how its infirmities and errors may be remedied.

As far as the approbation and the permanence of the work of art are concerned, the decision here is not to be determined by means of external grounds of proof. With regard to the significance of a work's approbation and even more with regard to its *effectiveness*, there are various opinions. The attempt is often made to set certain viewpoints in stone. On the whole it remains, to the great sorrow of criticism, usually a matter of the vicissitudes of current opinion, and only after years does a secure core of recognized judgment come to be established. This is natural and certainly not surprising; when Mozart lived, there were opponents like Nägeli[19]; after his death a firmer judgment was formed, and anyone who repudiates Mozart today must recognize the direction of his judgment in general. But where to obtain the verdict on *success*—since journalese is such a difficult (and ambiguous) language? Once again only from lively, deeply sensitive subjectivity, not from the reports of successful and applauded performances. How was it in past years? All the papers rejoiced over *Antigone* and its acceptance by the enlightened public in Berlin, while a few crackpots whispered that the thing was damnedly tedious. One went back to reconsider. . . . A few years later they, too, said it openly. The censorship that the trivial opinion of the press imposes is as obvious here as elsewhere. Around the year 1841 a sharp critical review of M.'s *Walpurgisnacht* could not be printed, since several editors rejected it; it therefore took itself off to the literary papers in Hamburg and gained recognition even from enthusiastic admirers of Mendelssohn.

Finally—permanence? Certainly! every true artist works in order to be understood in the present, but he hopes also to serve the future, if he wants to be immortal. This *judgment* by the *future* is often the only one (though, of course, whatever is human is *also* subject to error!) that is decisive. One can only say this, that truth is eternal. It is arrogant to play the philosopher. I may philosophize only for our brief present—if we actually live a generation—and if time contradicts me, publicly recant: Mendelssohn's church works will fade away after one generation. Beethoven has been dead for a generation, Mozart for two—no one calls them out of date; they change along with us. Of the gentle, maidenly Felix the sweet youthful songs will remain; they are immortal; aside from them, probably some magnificent instrumentations, not all; of the so-called church things, little or nothing.

Let us leave the final word to time! I am sorry to be *polemical* is such a fashion, but it appears necessary. Mr. W. will recognize from this response my respect for him personally as well as for the direction that he has championed and that I must oppose.

Emden, 5 February 1850

NOTES

1. *Neue Berliner Musikzeitung* 4/1 (2 January 1850), 3–5. Eduard Krüger (1807–1885) was a writer and conductor. From 1833 to 1851 he taught at the Gymnasium at Emden. He later became Professor at Göttingen.

2. Friedrich Schneider (1786–1853); Carl Loewe (1796–1869).

3. Carl Heinrich Graun (1703/1704–1759). Graun's *Der Tod Jesu* (1757) was immensely popular in German throughout the latter part of the eighteenth century and into the nineteenth, holding approximately the status that Handel's *Messiah* had in English-speaking countries.

4. Johannes Eccard (1553–1611) was regarded in the nineteenth century as the German counterpart of Palestrina in the classic polyphony of the sixteenth century.

5. The music historian Carl Georg Vivigens von Winterfeld (1784–1852) regarded Eccard as the model for church music (as opposed to merely sacred music) because of his use of the chorale as the foundation for his compositions.

6. Geibel (1815–1884) was a leading poet and dramatist, author of several texts Mendelssohn set as songs and of the libretto for the incomplete opera *Die Lorelei*.

7. Willibald Alexis was the pseudonym of the novelist Georg Wilhelm Heinrich Häring (1798–1871).

8. Theodor Mundt (1808–1861) was a member of the Junges Deutschland movement during the Vormärz.

9. 1827–1902. Wauer's response to Krüger's critique comes from the *Neue Berliner Musikzeitung* 4/4 (23 January 1850), 25–27.

10. The German divine Friedrich August Gottreu Tholuck (1799–1877) was known for his interest in, and support of, divinity students and lower opinion of the clerical establishment. He was fond of holding discussions with students during walks in Halle, where he was Professor of Theology.

11. The last four of these composers are not mentioned by Krüger in the present discussion. Wauer must be referring to references to them in other contexts.

12. *The Last Judgement*, oratorio by Schneider.

13. "Zur Kritik Mendelssohn's," *Neue Berliner Musikzeitung* 4/11 (13 March 1850), 81–83.

14. Some specific personal considerations I shall not answer, for example, that I (now for the first time?) "for once speak out openly." [Krüger's note.]

15. Ernst Wilhelm Hengstenberg (1802–1869) was a theologian and biblical scholar who championed orthodox Lutheranism against the contemporary move toward rationalism. Karl Friedrich Göschel (1784–1861) was a jurist and philosopher who espoused a reconciliation of Christianity and modern culture based on the thinking of Hegel and the poetry of Goethe. In referring to Gerlach, Krüger may have in mind either the jurist, politician, and writer Ludwig von Gerlach (1795–1877) or his younger brother the theologian Otto von Gerlach (1801–1849). The Krummacher referred to here is the Berlin theologian Friedrich Wilhelm Krummacher (1796–1868), who demonstrated a new and less rigidly formal preaching style than had previously been the norm. At the time of the present exchange Krummacher was appointed to the Dreifaltigkeitskirche in Berlin. His study of Elijah, *Elias der Thisbiter* (1826), governed the understanding of the prophet in the years preceding Mendelssohn's oratorio. Johann Heinrich Bernhard Draeseke (1774–1849) had served as bishop of Saxony; he was known for his patriotic and political sermons in a popular style that reached all social classes.

16. Pietist hymnbooks assembled by J. A. Freylinghausen included the *Geistreiches Gesangbuch* (Halle, 1704) and *Neues Geist-reiches Gesang-Buch* (Halle, 1714).

17. The Werdersche Kirche in Berlin was an early (1821–1830) example of Gothic Revival style, designed by the architect Karl Friedrich Schinkel.

18. "Alles Vergängliche ist nur ein Gleichnis." From the *Chorus mysticus* that concludes Goethe's *Faust.*

19. Hans Georg Nägeli (1773–1836), Swiss composer and publisher.

6
Art—History—Religion: On Mendelssohn's Oratorios *St. Paul* and *Elijah*

Friedhelm Krummacher

"*St. Paul* is a work of the purest kind, a work of peace and love." Thus did Robert Schumann formulate it in 1837 in a review that had programmatic consequence for him. In it he took a position on the "two most significant compositions of the time": Meyerbeer's *Huguenots* and Mendelssohn's *St. Paul*.[1] The two works certainly represent different genres, but their religious content creates a common denominator. Schumann's comparative critique proceeds from the problematic relationship between the religious subject and the artistic content. To be sure, in the *Huguenots* it also had to do with musical qualities that "only hatred could deny," but his verdict is grounded in moral argument directed against the handling of the religious material on the opera stage. In contrast to that, it is the reconciliation of art and religion that determines the status of *St. Paul*. Schumann was neither blind nor uncritical: "one sees that objections, and valid ones, may arise."

On the other hand, however, one should set them against that which no one can take away from the oratorio—aside from the inner essence of deeply religious sentiment that emerges everywhere, one should consider all the musical mastery that hits the mark, permeating this noble hymn, this wedding of word with tone . . ., the grace that breathes over the whole work, this freshness, this indelible coloration in the instrumentation, the fully developed style, not to mention the masterful play of all forms of composition.[2]

Such emphatic praise might seem odd, applied to a work whose historical significance has hardly been denied but that at the same time has long been a rarity in musical life. Undoubtedly, *St. Paul* not only signified Mendelssohn's breakthrough to European fame but also a marked turning point in the history of the oratorio. Both are documented in the contemporary approval, as well as the theoretical debate, that the work aroused. It serves as a model for the problematic nature of religious art, toward which Schumann's argumentation was aimed. Just as much as it stood for a significant part of the musical culture of the nineteenth century, however, it was forced into the background of musical awareness. Not only did it suffer according to the changing fortunes of Mendelssohn, as of Romanticism generally, but even today it remains in the shadow of the later *Elijah*.

"In the end, one must remember that Beethoven wrote a *Christus am Ölberge* and also a *Missa solemnis*, and we believe that as Mendelssohn has written an oratorio as a youth, as a man he will also complete one." With this premonition Schumann closed his review of *St. Paul*. In the publication of his *Gesammelte Schriften* in 1854 he attached a footnote to it: "Mendelssohn fulfilled the prophecy (*Elijah*)."[3] That Schumann saw his early prognosis fulfilled gives the later work an even greater significance. For one thing, Schumann had also remarked as a warning, in spite of all his approval of *St. Paul*, that the music "was so clear and popular," as if the composer "had been thinking how to make an impression on the public," but such a viewpoint could, "however, rob future compositions of some of that power and inspiration," could surrender to its "grand material without due consideration, without purpose or restraint." For another, though, the ambivalent reference to Beethoven indicates almost a burden, for as different as his far too little known oratorio of the year 1803 is from the late *Missa solemnis*, so Mendelssohn's two oratorios seem to stand side by side. A comparison with the *Missa solemnis* would establish an expectation that could hardly be met by *Elijah*, which from the very beginning had difficulty in competing with the already widely celebrated *St. Paul*.

Just what was the significance of that prophecy, then, that Schumann found fulfilled in *Elijah*? How does his view appear in relation to that of his contemporaries, and how does it relate to the often discussed differences or similarities of the two oratorios? How, ultimately, it is possible to speak of *Elijah* as a "late work" of a musician who died so early? An answer to such questions presupposes a sketch of the compositional path that, so to speak, marks out the inner biography of Mendelssohn. It requires not only familiarity with the work, with its textual basis and the history of its creation, but also an understanding of Mendelssohn's oeuvre as a whole and his sacred music in particular. It is thus necessary to begin with the history of the creation and reception of both oratorios in order to refer to a couple of reasons for their significance and their suppression. In relation to the genre and its norms, one must sketch out the conflicting relation of religious and aesthetic categories if one wants to judge the contradictory impulses of the works themselves, for only by recognizing the difficulties that had to be resolved in this regard can one reach an understanding that will then permit a more precise judgment.

CONCEPTION AND COMPOSITION OF *ST. PAUL*

St. Paul (1833–1835) was first performed on 22 May 1836 in Düsseldorf, at the Eighteenth Lower Rhine Music Festival. Before that event came a lengthy process of development, the details of which have not yet been entirely clarified but which extends over more than four years in all.

More was achieved with the first revival of Bach's *St. Matthew Passion* on 11 March 1829 than merely the decisive step in the new Bach reception. At the same time Mendelssohn's early development within his parents' upper-class bourgeois home in Berlin reached its closure. Shortly thereafter followed his first foreign journey, with his overwhelming success in England, a journey on which he became acquainted in London with the autographs of Handel's oratorios. From that point dates his lifelong concern with the active cultivation of the works of both masters in increasingly authentic form. At the same time began the uninterrupted attempts at a creative engagement with Bach and Handel. The next great journey—the European educational tour par excellence—led in 1830–1832 by way of Weimar and Vienna to Italy, France, and back to England; it brought not only stimulation and recognition but also conflicts and disturbing impressions. In Vienna and again in Italy Mendelssohn fell back on the composition of church music in the spirit of Bach, even when his friends urged him to seek success with an opera. Therefrom arose the plan for an oratorio of his own that would reflect his familiarity with the Bach Passions as well as the Handel oratorios.

The first more specific evidence is a letter from Paris on 10 March 1832 to Devrient: "I am supposed to create an oratorio for the Cäcilienverein. . . . The topic is supposed to be the Apostle Paul."[4] The impetus came from Johann Nepomuk Schelble, whose Cäcilienverein had undertaken the second performance of the *St. Matthew Passion* in May 1829. Mendelssohn had known him since 1822 and during his years of travel met him in the autumn of 1831 in Frankfurt. The letter to Devrient already sketches out the most important phases of *St. Paul* (although divided into three, rather than two, parts): "the stoning of Stephen and the persecution," "his conversion," "his Christian life and preaching, and either his martyrdom or his farewell to the faithful." Also clear is a further decision: "I would like to take the words mainly from the Bible and the hymnbook, and in addition have some free ones." Devrient, however, declined the request to compile such a text. As a result Mendelssohn consulted another friend from his youth, Adolf Bernhard Marx, who was serving as professor at the University of Berlin and whose composition textbook later made him one of the most important theorists of the time. While Mendelssohn drafted an oratorio text for *Moses* for Marx, the hoped-for reciprocal gift of *St. Paul* was not forthcoming. Only then did the composer turn to his friend the Dessau pastor Julius Schubring, who had earlier been a tutor at the Schleiermachers' home in Berlin. Mendelssohn's correspondence with him is the main source for information about the genesis of the work. It was published in 1892 with the ambitious, but significant, subtitle "An Essay on the History and Theory of the Oratorio."[5] The first communication dates from 25 August 1832: "Toward wintertime I am thinking of composing an oratorio, namely on St. Paul." On 22 December 1832 there followed Mendelssohn's first text draft, which still differed considerably from the final form. Between them lies an extensive correspondence, which reveals the extent of detailed reflection as well as Mendelssohn's own participation.[6]   The collaboration extended to the compositional phase, and the composer asked the theologian again and again to name suitable Bible verses. Just as often such suggestions were rejected, however, and it is especially indicative that this had little to do with the historical truth and completeness of the narrative. More important were the symbolic relevance of the biblical story for the present day, on one hand, and the free arrangement of the text in the interest of musical shaping, on the other hand. All this served the goal of portraying characteristic scenes and poetic situations that were suitable for a compositional interpretation.   The precedence of aesthetic intentions thus powerfully influenced the adaptation of the text, extending to the combination of various Bible passages with free additions in many movements.

Just as complex as the work on the text was the creation of the composition, which extended for more than two years through a process of intense self-criticism. It occurred principally in the period of Mendelssohn's activity in Düsseldorf (1833–1835), even though the work was already begun in Berlin and only completed in Leipzig. Besides a series of meager sketches, there exist broadly developed drafts for nine movements that were eliminated during the working process. Recently, Ralf Wehner not only pursued the compositional history but also investigated in detail the extant sources and closely compared the versions of individual movements.[7] In the course of that investigation it became clear that not only the recitative, with its subtleties of declamation and vocal inflection, was thoroughly revised after the first performance. Even such a self-contained movement as the aria "Vertilge sie, Herr Zebaoth" (no. 12) subsequently experienced yet another thoroughgoing reworking.   All such divergences demonstrate once again how little the composer relied on mere routine or convention and how much more the work was conditioned by critical reflection and subtle planning. In addition, the encounter with Bach, which included fascination as well as distancing, was a determining factor for the decision to exclude a series of further chorales from the definitive version. Thus, even after the original performance, finishing touches were still put on the musical text, right up to the time that the piano score and full score went to the press at the beginning of 1837. Beyond that, two solo movements that were abandoned in the final version appeared in 1868 as Op. 112. The composition of the work cannot be pursued further here, but the indications point in two directions. Just as little as the text depended on the literal authority of the biblical text, likewise the compositional construction did not depend on momentary inspiration. *St. Paul* is through and through an instance of lively consciousness and artistic reflection.

ST. PAUL IN RELATION TO HISTORICAL AND RELIGIOUS MUSIC

The oratorio marks a critical point in Mendelssohn's oeuvre.[8] From the time of his early instruction under Zelter, the boy had confidence in the stages of historical tradition. The works of his youth already centered around the adoption of it. The series of almost 100 works by an eleven- to fifteen-year-old boy is astonishing enough, aside from the fact that it covers almost all genres, from the Lied to the opera and from the concerto to the motet. It is hardly surprising that melodic turns of phrase or figurations from Mozart or Haydn and from Beethoven and Weber echo in it. It is noteworthy, though, that from early on—say in the twelve string sinfonias—unmistakable tones of Bach resonate. It appears almost as if within this series of works a segment of music history is systematically worked out, from Bach, through his sons, to the early Classic period, and to Beethoven. Even more striking, though, are whole movements or parts of movements that unmistakably show an almost proto-Romantic imprint. To the fundamentals of Classic composition belongs the principle of "discontinuity," according to which, in the small-scale frame of measure groups, alternating rhythmic-metric or melodic impulses abut one another in order to unfold the process of a movement. In contrast to that, in the early works of Mendelssohn one already encounters whole phases that are characterized by continuous sound, insistent rhythmic style, or melody that extends itself in waves. With no acquaintance with Schubert's contemporary initial steps, precedents for a new kind of composition appear here, which later come to fruition in the successful early works, especially in the Double Concertos for Two Pianos and the three Piano Quartets Opp. 1-3. The decisive high point is certainly marked in 1825 by the sixteen-year-old's overwhelmingly masterful Octet, Op. 20, whose first movement displays the soaring melodic style in both of its characteristic thematic areas, while the scherzo demonstrates the tension between worked-out and fleeting sounds, cited later in the finale in a fashion that seems just as surprising as it is inevitable.

In the following years, however, comes simultaneously the equally provocative and fertile encounter that involved both the conscious reception of Bach and the early reaction to Beethoven's late works. This is a unique constellation in the history of music, in that the esoteric late work of Beethoven and the oeuvre of the then little-known Bach stand side by side as obligatory models. Long-unknown letters lay out eloquent testimony of the intriguing fascination with Beethoven's late quartets; from them it emerges clearly that for the young Mendelssohn the problem of building motivic unity, not only in a movement but also across a cyclic composition, stemmed from these works. It revolves around the "relationship" of all movements and parts, "so that from the very outset one . . . already knows the secret."[9] Evidence of this critical encounter are, above all, the String Quartets opp. 13 (1827) and 12 (1829), which in varying ways take up cantabile melodies, redefine traditional movement forms, and by extremely complex strategies allow the finale to flow back cyclically to the beginning. Just slightly earlier, however, came the *Charakterstücke* for piano, Op. 7, which unmistakably recall the suite movements, preludes, and fugues of Bach, reinterpreting them in a Romantic transformation. The simultaneous surrender to both great masters—during the period leading up to the involvement with the *St. Matthew Passion*—finally had as consequence repercussions that later, in conjunction with the years of travel and their contradictory experiences, led to a genuine compositional crisis.

The boy had already had to bear several anti-Semitic attacks, the expectations placed on the prodigy soon grew burdensome, and his instruction under Karl Friedrich Zelter came at the price of a difficult relinquishing of the standards of a schooling as strict as it was traditional. As the early period culminated in the undertaking of the revival of the *St. Matthew Passion* in 1829, the years-long Grand Tour included not only a wealth of impressions but also upsetting events and experiences. Among these were not only the loss of his teacher Zelter, his mentor Goethe, and his friend Eduard Rietz but equally the encounter with the antithetical genius of Berlioz and the disturbing musical establishment of Paris. A veritable crisis then came with the miscarriage of the competition to succeed his teacher as leader of the Berlin Singakademie, in which anti-Semitic forces again played a part. During the Grand Tour important works were sketched, but for a long time they were left incomplete: besides the rejected Reformation Symphony, the Scottish and Italian Symphonies, as well as the *Erste Walpurgisnacht*. The letters of 1832 record a phase of distressing unproductivity and uncertain attempts, but an even clearer testimony than this series of statements is the fact that major works were begun and then put aside without being able to find their conclusion.[10]

In this particular phase, however, there appear clear signs of a new orientation. The youth had already written a not inconsiderable number of pieces of church music, and in addition to conventional fugues and motets there were already pretentious Mass movements, a rapturous *Salve Regina*, and a *Jube Domine* for double choir, which already heralded the idiom of later sacred works.[11] Alongside the quartets indebted to Beethoven, however, and further during the years of travel, there appeared the series of seven chorale cantatas, in which Bach was reflected within his own field.[12] Despite their considerable qualities, Mendelssohn published none of these works, which, as they increasingly depart from Bach's models, already find a very individual tone. These interests had further effect, since beginning in 1832 the oeuvre concentrated on historically determined instrumental forms and further on vocal, primarily sacred music. In addition to intimate songs there also developed, to be sure, the most personal type of song, which thereafter accompanied him throughout his life, like a musical diary in concentrated miniatures.[13] Except for the *Schöne Melusine* overture, for more than eight years the chamber and orchestral music eschewed the Classic formal canon. One has to realize what it means that a composer of this period maintained such a great distance from the standard genres of the time. At the center, besides a first psalm cantata, Op. 31, the preludes and fugues for piano and for organ Opp. 35 and 37 took their place, and between them *St. Paul*, Op. 36. For the first time since the eighteenth century, therefore, a composer worked systematically on the pairing of prelude and fugue, to bring the traditional form up to date, and from them came the point of departure for the Organ Sonatas Op. 65, completed ten years later. The focal point, however, is formed by *St. Paul*, a work with which Mendelssohn immersed himself in the tricky task of redefining for the present what was probably the most representative genre of the past. *St. Paul* simultaneously mediated between the diversity of the early works and the strict concentration of the later major works.

After *The Creation* and *The Seasons*—the exceptional works of the elderly Haydn—there were, in fact, quite a few oratorios written in the first third of the century, for example, by Friedrich Schneider, Louis Spohr, or Carl Loewe, but no tradition took shape as in the Baroque period.[14] The more Handel's oratorios and Bach's Passions became better known, the more their demands weighed upon a new oratorio. Such a standard was almost unavoidable for comparative criticism, for in *St. Paul* a biblical oratorio, with narrative recitatives and reflective arias, choruses of the people and even chorales, unexpectedly came to hand, a type that was unusual at the time. This inevitably brought Bach to mind, as later the Old Testament-based *Elijah* recalled Handel. The strictly biblical oratorios were so surprising for the time that one spontaneously associated them with older models, but these were still hardly familiar enough that they would also draw attention to the marked differences that Mendelssohn's music presented. The dichotomy conditioned the critical reaction, which varied from skeptical distance to emphatic approval.[15]

The problems to which Mendelssohn sought solutions can be outlined according to compositional and aesthetic concerns. It was not just that from early on older music became a personal experience for him as for no other musician before him.[16] As it had not become accessible as art, however, it took on an obligatory position: historical music could not be experienced as art if it did not make normative claims. The expressive power and declamatory plasticity of Bach's music did not stand in opposition only to the older vocal polyphony, with its strict linearity, however. Rather, the canon of Classic genres for its part depended for its construction on periodic organization based on motivic-thematic contrasts, whose differentiated treatment had to conform to the discontinuous process of construction. In contrast to this, the Songs without Words quite plainly formed a Romantic prototype, defined by the continuity of the cantabile melodic style combined with the regularity of the accompaniment, and thereby the aesthetic ideal of poetic unity was fulfilled. But if historical music of such varied sorts all occupies an equally normative position, then the problem arises of how the divergent principles are to be combined compositionally. Around this question revolve the works of Mendelssohn's crisis, up to *St. Paul*. Hardly ever again did contradictory models collide with each other as they did here: from sonata movement with chorale quotation in the overture, to the vocal chorale motets; from the expressive arioso, to the large da capo aria; from songlike recitative, to complex choral fugue. In this way the work reflects the problems of its time.

Such plurality might today arouse the accusation of eclecticism. Yet the work was perceived by its contemporaries as a stylistic unity, as Schumann's review shows. The history of its reception at first appears to witness few compositional difficulties. The work had a success that was thoroughly exceptional in the nineteenth century. In the year of the premiere it was performed in Birmingham and Liverpool, in the following year all over Germany, a little later in Boston, Moscow, Paris, and Vienna, and soon fifty performances had been achieved.[17] The work's success lasted—at least in Germany—until about the First World War. The

situation was different in England, where *Elijah* quickly found greater understanding. That hardly had anything to do with the compositional material, but
instead with the English version, with which this commissioned work was planned
from the outset. In Germany, by contrast, Mendelssohn's music, on the one hand,
was worn out by its extraordinary popularity. On the other hand, there arose that
antagonism that expressed itself vehemently already in 1850 in Wagner's
pseudonymous libel "Das Judentum in der Musik." What ended in the fascist ban
of Mendelssohn had far-reaching precedents and long-lasting consequences.
Among the circumstances belongs the widespread anti-Semitism that first made
possible the effect of the condemnation in the Nazi era. Among the consequences
was a generation that grew up without close acquaintance with Mendelssohn's art.
To this must be added the deep antipathy to Romanticism, particularly its church
music, that arose out of the reform movement of youth and church music but also
from musicology after 1918. All this makes it possible to comprehend the
difficulties that a work such as *St. Paul* had to cope with for so long. Whereas in
spite of every rupture *Elijah* could support itself on an Anglo-Saxon tradition, such
foundations did not exist for *St. Paul*. Such difficulties are based not only in the
reception history but also in the work itself. They have their roots in aesthetic
problems that encumber the relationship of music as art to religion in the nineteenth
century.

AESTHETIC PROBLEMS FOR RELIGIOUS MUSIC IN THE NINETEENTH CENTURY

Choral music with orchestra, in particular the oratorio, had an esteem in the
nineteenth century that one cannot easily imagine today. In it, a final connection
seemed to be possible between professional art and the choral song of bourgeois
amateurs, where neither opera nor symphonic music found a permanent place.
After the Napoleonic era, in the period of the Restoration, the great music festivals
also had a thoroughly political significance. The great supply of oratorios was
displaced to the extent that municipal theaters and orchestras were established.
With them the social assumptions of such choral music, which manifested the ideal
of aesthetic participation by the bourgeois in current art, faded. Martin Geck's
source index for the period from 1800 to 1840 gives a conception of the great
production of oratorios.[18] Granted, hardly any of these works are available, even
to the specialist; even Friedrich Schneider's *Weltgericht* (1820) and Spohr's *Die
letzten Dinge* (1826) are as good as lost. The fact that after Haydn's oratorios
those of Mendelssohn are the first to have survived already gives some idea of their
historical significance. The oratorio was attractive to composers, however, because
it offered an opportunity for performance where otherwise hardly any regular large
works could be heard. Of course, this depended on pleasing the public, and it was
not by accident that Schumann coupled his recognition of *St. Paul* with a warning
against its popularization. Moreover, in the oratorio the avoidance of scenic

production meant not only more ease of production than the opera. Because the oratorio managed without the direct reality of the stage, it correspondingly seemed to achieve an inner concentration on an ideal content. Where it employed religious material and actual biblical texts, it could reduce the difficulty of finding suitable libretti, because it relied for these on the authority of the Christian tradition.

Such factors help to clarify the actual situation of the genre in the nineteenth century and, correspondingly, a danger to the artistic claims that were linked to the principles of the new aesthetic of idealism. First among these was the change of aesthetic paradigms since the Enlightenment. As the precedence of vocal music was challenged, instrumental music now appeared as the embodiment of what music could do by means of its own force. As vocal music was bound to texts, it was also burdened with the flaw of being heteronomous. By contrast, instrumental music, which freed itself from texts and functions, posed new questions of understanding and of judgment.[19]

The rise of music aesthetics was associated with the fact that the connection of works and genres to specific functions came to be no longer taken for granted. If in Bach's time it was still self-evident that music primarily had to fulfill social or ecclesiastical functions, its liberation from purposes and pressures now became a sign of its artistic rank. That art in general became an object of philosophy could be justified only insofar as it formed a special domain, separated from other objects and experiences. Its rank as an art was then measured by the degree of its noninterchangeable independence. The individual arts, too, were more precisely definable as their particular possibilities were emphasized. For music this meant nothing other than that it was defined as art by the organization of its materials. The criterion for the artistic position of music is its own system of laws, its autonomy. This becomes threatened when music is bound to tasks in the service of extra-aesthetic purposes. Numbered among these is not only its misuse for entertainment and as background music. Even ecclesiastical appropriation or theatrical application threatens the artistic position of music, if it leads to loss of autonomy. Even the connection to texts and their flow can constitute a danger, in cases when music is too closely bound to the model of the words. Insofar as in language vocal music accommodates another medium, it will hardly meet the challenge; music has to prove itself as art only on its own terms.

The social-historical precedent that led to the liberation of music from functions, therefore, corresponds to the aesthetic concept of the idea of autonomy. Both achieved tangible significance for the history of composition, for the idea of the autonomous work requires that a listener follow music for its own sake. That means nothing less than that composers claims that their work has to satisfy the hearer in itself. The composition demands undivided attention, for it has no other purpose. Such extreme demands bring with them corresponding expectations. From art that deals in such claims innovation and originality are demanded, to reward complete attentiveness. This demand for originality and innovation applies to each artist, as it does—to put it emphatically—afresh for every single work. This, however, makes it possible to understand something of the difficulties that, from this point on, every artist in the nineteenth century had to bear as consequence of the aesthetic of autonomy.

The aesthetic of autonomy arose in the first place as an ontological designation from criteria for art. This question posed itself from the time of Kant, who sought an answer in the analysis of judgment as a subjective capacity between will and perception (1790). The debate then shifted with Hegel and Schelling to take up the character of art itself as object, thereby gaining a further dimension. The idea of autonomy became overlaid by the notion of the absolute content of art. It not only signified the liberation from external purposes but connected to the concept of the absolute spirit. Kant saw art's greatest opportunity as the possibility of opening a perspective on the realm of the ideas of the supersensual that are otherwise closed to us: "Art as symbol of morality" implies a metaphysical horizon.[20] Hegel apprehended the ideas in the notion of "Kunstreligion" (1807), already encountered in Schleiermacher's lectures *On Religion* (1799).[21] For Hegel it indicated that moment in history when the absolute spirit had appeared in the cult of art. In antique sculpture the statue was both art object and cultic symbol: God appeared in the artwork. This elevated status is, of course, denied to the art of modern times, which have granted it to philosophy. In order to be art, however, it is directed to evoking metaphysical ideas. Still more radically, for Schelling (1802) art became the unique path and implement of metaphysics, and principally music is thereafter the "singular and eternal revelation of the absolute." Similarly, K. W. Solger conceived "the actual existence" of music as "always the religious" (1829).[22] In the "idea of absolute music," as Carl Dahlhaus outlines it, the congruence between art and metaphysics became the leading conviction of the time[23]: all art that deserved the name tends toward religion.

To be sure, it was primarily instrumental music that was thought of in this context. It alone realized most purely what music could do. Thus, even vocal music with religious content had only to a limited extent the same value as art. Hegel himself gave preference to "accompanying" music, that is, vocal music, since by means of language it indicated its content more precisely.[24] Nevertheless, music had to pursue its path toward "self-sufficient," absolute music in order to become fully art—though at the risk of becoming difficult to understand. Just as surely, too, for Schopenhauer in 1818 music "is a self-sufficient art," "so certainly it does not need the words of song."[25] Chr. H. Weisse formulated it still more radically in 1830—vocal music was no less than the "ruin of instrumental music," since the connection to language and the physicality of the voice took away its artistic character.[26] This danger of unconcealed naturalism made a high degree of craftsmanship necessary in order to salvage the aesthetic position of vocal music.

It should now be clearer what this aesthetic thinking means for the composition of vocal music, including religious music.[27] As all music that deserves the name of art has metaphysical content, specifically religious music actually becomes superfluous. This is even true for instrumental music that intends to be religious, for if all instrumental music is religious anyhow, then religious instrumental music can achieve its identity only by reference to such prerequisites as the chorale. For sacred vocal music the identity of true art with metaphysics becomes even more precarious. Such music, as a separate area, is unnecessary, if all music, regardless of position, implies religion. Where all art is religious, religious art becomes a tautology. If music must articulate its own religiosity in words, then it tends toward exaggeration. Not only does the connection to text threaten its autonomy, but religious texts express what music should be able to do. Based on the premises of this aesthetic, religious music becomes impossible, since it is unnecessary.

The era of idealism was at the same time a period of thoroughgoing secularization. The rise of the aesthetic of autonomy and the decline of ecclesiastical authority in the aftermath of the Enlightenment were two facets of one process. Thus, the attachment to traditional Bible or chorale texts only became trickier for sacred music. Such texts were necessary less because of their dogmatic than because of their historical authority. Even a narrative like that of *St. Paul* was hardly accepted as a truth of faith but rather was validated by its symbolic content. Unconcerned with such problems, sacred music was still written in this time, and aesthetic theory did not weary of debating its opportunities and the limits of its metaphysical content. Such discussions tried only to clarify what remained possible for absolute instrumental music. Concomitantly, however, for intermediate works the question of their artistic requirements hardly arose.[28]

All this deepened the dilemma involved in the project of writing a biblical oratorio that would then become an exemplary work of art, for there was no longer any strictly ecclesiastical sacred music, and there could not be any. In the concert hall sacred music could rely on the interest of a secularized public, but Bible texts themselves were excluded from aesthetic criticism. While religious music could no longer be taken as a given, however, imitation of models of ecclesiastical music is possible, which would have historical authority in its own right. Reference to Bach or Palestrina becomes tempting, in order to articulate a religious idiom. This tendency is strengthened at the same time because it expresses a further consequence of the aesthetic, for, as a result of the heightened concept of art, historical art achieves a new position. One feature of the concept of true art is the durability factor: nothing would be entirely art if it could easily be forgotten, since the position of art is demonstrated directly by its ability to last through changing times. From this point on, therefore, historical works were assembled into a canon of exemplary patterns, which, as historical models, thus also validate normative demands. The more closely composers cling to historical patterns, the more the freedom of movement for their originality narrows: tradition and innovation become a dichotomy as two facets of the concept of art.

AESTHETIC VALUES IN *ST. PAUL*

The dialectic of the aesthetic of autonomy allows some estimation of the difficulties that Mendelssohn faced in the intention in *St. Paul* to reconstruct the historical oratorio in a contemporary way,[29] for the aesthetic categories did not, by any means, remain an abstract construction; rather, they had their effect in the most concrete manner. Mediated by music theory and criticism, they continued indirectly to color public and private meaning. Even an artist who wanted to escape from public criticism, as Mendelssohn so often stressed, still had to deal with it, however. He was deeply impressed by the theology of Schleiermacher, in whose thought on art and religion he had great confidence. He also heard Hegel's lectures on aesthetics, as a transcript proves. The letters repeatedly reflect Hegel's dark prognosis, according to which present-day art would be threatened in its very substance. The answer that Mendelssohn gave to the question of the meaning of the Songs without Words may be read directly as a catechism of the aesthetics of autonomy.[30] As opposed to the complaint that "music is so ambiguous," for him words, rather, are "so vague, so easily misunderstood." Music has "not thoughts that are too vague to be put into words but too precise." If music is a much more precise language than the word, however, that makes the addition of texts questionable. Reflections on history as a burden and a benefit likewise run through the letters. "If it has similarities with Sebastian Bach, I cannot do anything about it, for I have written it just as I had it in my heart," as he put it in 1831.[31] Further: "For you would not mean that I should copy his forms without content; in that case, from sheer repugnance I could not . . . write a single piece to its end." Against the danger "of giving in to an imitation," "only that which comes in deepest seriousness from the inmost soul" can serve as "the single, unalterable standard." "Certainly no one can forbid me, . . . from continuing to work on that which the great masters have left for me, for probably no one should start over from the beginning; but it should also be a further working according to one's powers, not a lifeless repetition of what already exists."[32] In this context the concern before the first performance of St. Paul is instructive; the repertoire to which it would be juxtaposed should be contemporary, "so that my oratorio will not come into altogether too direct comparison with that [i.e., historical] music."[33]

All this makes it understandable why St. Paul came to be so important to the theory of the oratorio—for the aestheticians Ferdinand Hand or F. T. Vischer as for historians up to Riemann and Schering.[34] The typology of the oratorio is oriented principally toward Bach and Handel; Bach's historiae for the divine service were set against the Handel oratorio, which was intended for the bourgeois public in Enlightenment England. Dramatic works such as Samson or Jephtha were to be distinguished from the epic type of Israel in Egypt or the symbolic type of Messiah; in contrast, the later idyllic or lyrical oratorio, such as Haydn's The Creation and The Seasons, appeared as a later special case. But how, then, was St. Paul to be classified? A New Testament narrative as with Bach, but neither Passion nor liturgical music; complete dramatic plot as with Handel but saturated by lyrical moments; primarily Bible text without free poetry but full of text compilations and chorale citations; and, in its stock of forms and textures, generally based on historical models, from which, however, the music differs, when it is given careful consideration. The broad theoretical debate reflects the confusion that arises from a work that falls between all the categories. That, though, also reveals the subtle artistic understanding by which Mendelssohn knew how to solve the difficulties of the genre in a new way.

The story of *St. Paul* is well enough known that it should be unnecessary to rehearse it here. The organization became difficult from the outset because of the obstacles that arose out of artistic motives. Ferdinand Hand held the opinion that this "greatest work of our day" lacked "unity and suitable organization."[35] The misgivings that arose again and again by unanimous agreement were initially directed to the text and only thereafter to the music. They were first summarized by Schumann, who saw through them clearly and sought to refute them. They had to do with "the resumption of the chorale," "the division of the chorus and the individuals into acting and reflecting masses and persons," as well as to "the character of these details themselves."[36] Upon a closer look it appears, however, that the construction is not at all unclear but rather follows the biblical report (see Table 6.1). The introduction (nos. 1-3), which takes place in stages, is followed

Table 6.1
Structure of *St. Paul* (italics indicate the arias, choruses, and chorales that are not directly involved in the action)

Part	Action	Musical numbers
Part I	1. Opening	1. *Overture* (with *chorale*)
		2. *Chorus*
		3. *Chorale*
	2. Stoning of Stephen	4. Recitative
		5. Chorus
		6. Recitative, Chorus
		7. *Aria*
		8. Recitative—Chorus
		9. Recitative—*Chorale*
		10. Recitative
		11. *Chorus*
	3. Conversion of Paul	12. Recitative—Aria
		13. Recitative—*Arioso*
		14. Recitative
		15. *Chorus*
		16. *Chorale*
		17. Recitative
		18. Aria
		19. Recitative
		20. Aria—*Chorus*
		21. Recitative
		22. *Chorus*

Table 6.1, continued

Part	Action	Musical numbers
Part II	4.a Commissioning of the apostle	23. *Chorale*
		24. Recitative
		25. *Duettino*
		26. *Chorale*
		27. Recitative—*Arioso*
	4.b Opposition of the Jews	28. Recitative—*Chorale*
		29. Chorus—*Chorale*
		30. Recitative
		31. Duet
	5.a Mission to Lystra	32. Recitative
		33. Chorus
		34. Recitative
		35. Chorus
		36. Recitative—*Chorus* (with *Chorale*)
	5.b Persecution and farewell	37. Recitative
		38. Chorus
		39. Recitative
		40. *Cavatina*
		41. Recitative
		42. Chorus—Recitative
	6. Conclusion	43. *Chorale*
		44. Recitative
		45. Chorale

immediately by the connected scenes with the stoning of Stephen (nos. 4-10), before Paul and his conversion take center stage (nos. 12-21). In the middle stands chorus no. 11, while chorus no. 22 closes the first part. The second part has a number of sections, because it takes up Paul's career. After the introductory chorus (no. 23) the following blocks have to do with the apostle's commissioning and the opposition of the Jews (nos. 24-27, 28-31). The story continues with the mission to the Gentiles, which leads into the scenes that tell of Paul's persecution and farewell (nos. 32-36, 37-42). After a summary chorus (no. 43) the two last movements form the conclusion (nos. 44-45). The overview in Table 6.1 does not only show how sparingly, on the whole, chorales appear. Other movements that have reflective or symbolic functions are also introduced only in a quite limited number. Between the parts and sections stand intermediate movements that have retrospective and introductory functions. In addition, the changing combinations of movement reveal how little the layout follows a schema.

The chorales were discussed most vehemently (to which *Elijah* reacted by rejecting chorales). For one thing, people criticized "the extraordinary decoration" with which they were surrounded. Schumann already responded: "as if the art work did not have to satisfy any other demands than that of a singing congregation."[37] For another, people saw in the chorales—without which Handel's oratorios seemed to manage—a dependence on Bach's liturgical Passions. That objection, however, proceeds from the tradition of the divine service and at the same time fails to understand that only an aesthetic function remained to the chorale as a symbol. It was true for the chorales, as it was for all the choruses, that in them the function of the performing vocal groups changed. This can be confusing at first for the listener. Yet in Bach, too, the choruses alternated between different *turbae* and reflective function, extending to the response of the congregation in the corporately performed chorale. In the same manner Handel's choruses, too, had to portray diverse peoples—Jews as well as Gentiles—and these were coupled with the reflective proverb texts or downright choralelike intonations. Thus, the criticism that found fault with the lack of clarity in *St. Paul* fails to recognize the freedom of imagination that distinguishes the oratorio as a genre. In this way it reverses the criteria of opera and oratorio. Since the setting in the oratorio is only imagined and not real, it appeals instead to the imagination of the alert listener to take advantage of the opportunities of the genre. Nothing is less appropriate than the attempt to evaluate the text and development of the oratorio by the criteria of the opera, from which it differs in its rejection of real logic and dramatic strictness. This freedom of the oratorio, which Mendelssohn worked through, would certainly hardly be recognized as long as one oriented oneself by Handel's oratorios, which were also stamped with the experiences of an opera composer. The objection to the imprecise characterization of the protagonists also arose from this misunderstanding. It is true of them, as of the chorus, that the voices in the oratorio—in Bach as in Handel—can change their position. This was Mendelssohn's intention, where he even had the direct words of the narrator sung, thereby ruling out operatic realism. The tenor, for example, sings the roles of Stephen and Ananias, the soprano serves for both narration and reflection; only the character of Paul is reserved for the bass.

Further reservations, following Schumann, had to do with the circumstance that the "main impulses of the whole thing" were already encountered in the first part, that Stephen, as a secondary character, has too much prominence and therefore diminishes the interest in Paul, that Paul himself has more the effect of "proselyte than preacher." This way of looking at it, though, is directed toward a listener who would perceive the thread of continuity from the first scene, for in the Bible the martyrdom of Stephen is linked to the conversion of Saul, and his fate serves as an example to predict that of Paul. Precisely this, however, is reflected in the work. The criticism of the fact that the Lord appears to Saul in a women's chorus is on the same level. Schumann[38] was amazed here at Mendelssohn's "poetic grasp" in "one of his most beautiful inventions," for instead of dramatic directness it had to do with the distance of the unreal—in the choral sonority as well as in the stasis of the number. Unearthly beauty represented—according to Schumann—an unearthly reality. As clearly as he saw the distance from Mendelssohn's historical models, Schumann saw just as clearly that it was not a matter of creating realistic truth but of aesthetically transcending it. He even defined concisely the processes of this distancing: the "most noble song," the "marriage of the word with the tone," the "shading" of the instrumentation, and, above all, "the masterful play of all the forms of compositional technique." Here the criteria are named by which Mendelssohn achieved both distance from his historical models and the solution to the problems of the oratorio. These standards must be identified and demonstrated in specific terms.[39]

ST. PAUL AND THE MODEL OF BACH

As a matter of fact, the Baroque models—both solos and choruses—are given a songlike coloring in their linearity and plasticity. They are, so to speak, put through the filter of the Romantic song. In this one might at first perceive only a simplification. Only in a close hearing does the refinement that gives this contradictory relationship its fascination reveal itself. Second, however, word and tone are not linked in such a way that the music serves the text; rather, the reverse—the texts are laid out in such a way that they accommodate themselves to closed sections. If they are not interpreted particularly graphically, they do follow the plan of permitting motivic development processes. Third, connected with this is the extent of the instrumental part—astonishing for a vocal work—that does not just color the structure but attains an almost symphonic preeminence. Altogether, this yields the "masterful play" with traditions, which Schumann emphasized for good reasons, as a couple of examples will make clear. The overture, first of all, is not—as it initially appears—primarily defined by the chorale "Wachet auf, ruft uns die Stimme." It joins this citation with the fugal model in order to link the two in a symphonic process. If one hears the slow introduction only from the perspective of the first chorale quotation, then the symbolic content seems almost pasted on. The quotation is only one of the premises, however; the fugue subject in the sad, minor-key character that is set up after it is the other. The point is that in the course of the movement both planes are increasingly superimposed, despite their contrasts. This course does not lead, however, to contrapuntal compression; rather, the fugue is replaced by motivic work (Example 6.1), and in that way it provides the background for tying in the chorale in the symphonic conclusion. Thus, the overture presents the idea of the work in two fashions: it unites impulses of historical and present-day music, and thereby it alludes to the actuality of faith over the threats to it. The same also applies to other chorale movements. The chorale "O Jesu Christe, wahres Licht" (no. 28b) at first seems out of place in relation to the chorus directed against Paul, "Ist das nicht, der zu Jerusalem zerstörte," with its cries of "weg mit ihm." It forms, however, the internalized meditation on the incident, which acts as an appeal to the listener. The movement appears to be, in the first place, a reduction of Bachian models, especially in the pairing of the homophonic choral movement with instrumental interludes. These interludes are certainly arranged in less linear and more chordal fashion than in the

Example 6.1
St. Paul, **Overture,**

a. mm. 90–94

b. mm 139–43

case of Bach. In the soloistic sound of the woodwinds, however, cantabile lines unfold that do not function as counterpoints but as subjective commentaries on the chorale (Example 6.2). The increasing superimposition of instrumental and vocal parts brings to fruition a development that was not possible in the Baroque but only in the nineteenth century. In addition, the motet "Aber unser Gott ist im Himmel" (no. 35b) is not just a conventional contrapuntal movement, as it appeared to its contemporaries. It stands at the close of a complex led by a recitative and Paul's aria. There three layers combine: the solo part as a point of departure, the choral *Spruchmotette*, and the chorale "Wir glauben all an einen Gott." These layers proceed, however, in fluid $\frac{3}{2}$ meter, which, nevertheless, sounds less historicizing than songlike. The movement thus develops by the assimilation of its disparate levels.

Example 6.2a
St. Paul, no. 28b, "O Jesu Christe, wahres Licht," mm. 3–5, 17–18

Example 6.2b
St. Paul, no. 35b, "Aber unser Gott ist im Himmel"

mm. 1–9

mm. 80–91

Given all this, it will not be denied that to a listener who approaches the work from the point of view of Bach's music, it will at first seem to be a simplification of the models. The apparent simplification is, however, at the same time an aesthetic complication in that it combines opposing relationships. Anyone who fails to recognize this will overlook the newness of this point of departure and forget that presumably only in this way could the path be cleared for the understanding of Bach. Such a judgment would also be aesthetically hasty, however, because it does not incorporate the specific attraction of that intersection that places the Bachian models into the Romantic setting. This immediately becomes clear in the recitatives, which differ from Baroque practice by their continuous instrumentation. As the *accompagnato* becomes the rule rather than the exception, one may perceive it as a misuse or superfluity. Instead of paying attention only to the expression of the words, however, one ought to hear how Mendelssohn combines the words and sentences into songlike lines. The recitative style with its formulas is not rejected, but it forms only the point of departure for its cantabile transformation. At the same time it is colored by the intensive sonorousness in the orchestral part, which does not primarily emphasize individual words but expresses subjective feelings in the content of the narrative. Accordingly, neutral reportage and personal expression intermingle, in order to convey a poetic situation instead of dramatic detail. This becomes clearest in the testimony of Stephen (no. 5) and in the conversion of Paul (no. 13), where suggestive harmonies and timbres push the formulaic recitative into the background. The expressivity that applies to the recitative has an even greater impact on the arioso solos and especially the choruses as the center of the work.

The soloistic arias and ariosos today run up against a certain skepticism. If they are not histrionically emotional (as are many parts of *St. Paul*), they immediately encounter the accusation that they are weak, sweet, or thoroughly sentimental. Nevertheless, they form a core of the works, and Schumann received them accurately when he stresses the "noble song." Not only do the solos distance themselves most sharply from the Baroque formal model of the da capo aria, the further they develop their lyric diction. Rather, they achieve a subjectivity in their songlike style whereby the significance of the biblical history is communicated to the bewildered listener. The very resistance to the tone of these pieces finally substantiates their high level of originality. Admittedly, they are not all of the same quality, and many an aria hardly retains the melodic magic that people used to hear in it. But one also should not judge in isolation such difficult movements as the arioso "Doch der Herr vergißt die Seinen nicht" (no. 12) or the duettino "So sind wir nun Botschafter" (no. 24). In their context—as resting places along the way, so to speak—they have their function, which becomes evident only when one follows the work as a whole. On the other hand, the large movements of *St. Paul* distinguish themselves by unusually free form and melodic nuance. This is clearest in the prayer "Gott, sei mir gnädig" (no. 17; see Example 6.3), which stands between the radiant choruses "Mache dich auf" (no. 14) and "O, welche eine Tiefe" (no. 21). It is not just that the combination of verses from Psalm 51 is

Example 6.3
St. Paul, no. 17, "Gott, sei mir gnädig"

a. mm. 5–9

b. mm. 23–26

c. mm. 49-60

carefully thought out. Formally, to be sure, the piece is reminiscent of a da capo aria. The slow first part returns at the end; in the middle comes a faster, contrasting part. But the closing part is no repetition but rather a contraction of the beginning, and with all the contrast one principle unites the parts. The vocal part in the inner Allegro is marked "quasi Recitativo," but it tends more and more away from recitative toward the formation of closed melodic arches. By contrast, the Adagio departs from its cantabile head motive, whose conduct, however, devolves more and more into declamatory phrases. This relationship between song and recitative, dissolution and development, gives the course of the movement color and interest but also both intensity and intimacy. The aria "Jerusalem, die du tötest die Propheten" (no. 6) grew to be a favorite piece of the time. If one proceeds only from the words of the text, one might miss the expression of the lament. After the death of Stephen, however, the aria recalls the prophetic words of Jesus (Matt. 23: 27). Its lyrical quietness, nevertheless, directs it into a sphere of the imaginary and unreal; this comes from the steady triplets in the orchestra, out of which the melody line arises first in the clarinet, then in the soprano. To this are added the words, which are hardly declaimed in a terse fashion. In the transparent sonority, however, the nuances of the melodic and harmonic style achieve suggestive expression—especially at the end in the reprise of the beginning of the aria.

The short choruses of Jews and Christians in *St. Paul* are certainly not as concise and artful as the *turbae* in the Bach Passions. If they were, they would seem intrusive in the context of the whole. Nonetheless, it is characteristic that all the choruses of the Jews are in minor keys, marked by fast tempo, syllabic declamation, and repeated notes, as well as colored by sudden harmonic accents (as in nos. 5, 6, 8 but also 28 and 29). The terse declamation, however, also corresponds to a short, motivic style, which, moreover, can be worked out contrapuntally (as in nos. 5, 8, and especially 29). In contrast, the choruses of the pagans—just as in *Elijah*—are marked by a degree of simplicity that has a striking effect (nos. 33 and 35). This not only suggests the primitiveness of the pagan cult, however, but at the same time recalls in stylized tones a cultic ring dance. More important than artificial construction, apparently, is the dramatic presentation of the pagan choruses, which, of course, like the other choruses of people, recede behind the position of the great reflective choruses.

For the most part, the outer movements of praise are immediately reminiscent of Handel's festive choruses. They differ from them, however, not only by their rich harmonic style or their orchestral brilliance.[40] In place of the succession of text segments Mendelssohn is much more inclined to construct his process of combinatory development. Compared with Bachian choral movements, the primarily obbligato function of the instrumental part and the linearity of the voice leading fall away. In *St. Paul* all this has to become subordinate to the development of the movement in the coherence of the work. The orchestra does not present—as in Bach—the thematic material, onto which the choral movement is then fitted. It rather prepares the choral entry, just as the piano prepares that of the singer, and by means of rhythmic figures and tonal accents it adopts changing relationships to the choral movement. As little as the vocal parts are strictly contrapuntal, so much do they maintain a cantabile style—even in inner parts—which is notable even in the primarily chordal setting. In place of traditional counterpoint comes the skill of sketching cantabile voices into the harmonic structure. In this the choruses mark their distance from Handel and from Bach. As opposed to the blocklike intensification of Handelian choruses, Bach's movements are distinguished by the continuity of vocal and instrumental voices in the polyphonic web. Mendelssohn's choruses are certainly less lapidary than

Handel's and less concentrated than Bach's. They attain their character, however, first of all in their development.

Certainly, there are also choruses in which segments of different profiles alternate without producing contrasts (such as the lyrical movements no. 1, "Siehe, wir preisen selig," or no. 42, "Sehet, welch eine Liebe"). In other movements the intensifying alternation of the parts is balanced only by means of the process of motivic separation (as in no. 14, "Mache dich auf," or no. 21, "O welch eine Tiefe"). Other examples are more indicative, however. Nothing would be more erroneous than to hear the apparently fugal choruses from the point of view of Bach's and, as a result, to dismiss Mendelssohn as merely epigonal. The fugue is only a means for him to introduce a process that then departs from the conventional fugue. It has often been observed that such choruses begin as fugues but then insert contrasting parts and give up the fugal style. Meanwhile, it is frankly a rule for Mendelssohn's choral technique that alternating parts and themes appear separately at first in order to be combined thereafter. They hardly form strict double fugues, in which, after their own development, they are set against each other contrapuntally. This applies most to the concluding chorus "Lobe den Herrn, meine Seele," in which the double fugue is certainly complemented by motivic work. Determinative is rather the intention to bridge the changes of text phrases, in which themes and texts are gradually connected. Together with this come artful combinations and thoughtful text references, and the themes should not be heard as isolated but rather as parts of an ongoing development. On one hand, the primacy of the music is thereby maintained, which does not merely submit itself to the flow of the text. On the other hand, the principle of the sonata operates to relate the various themes and parts of a process to each other. As in Mendelssohn's instrumental music, the procedure is carried out primarily in reprises and coda sections of the choruses, and this process is most evident in the departure from Baroque models. Only two more examples for this may be identified. The second part is opened by a choral complex in which the introduction "Der Erdkreis ist nun des Herrn" is followed by a fugato: "Denn alle Heiden" (no. 22). A further section then begins again in fugal style: "denn deine Herrlichkeit ist offenbar geworden." At the end, however, the two passages are united (Example 6.4). The sense of the textual relationship is obvious. It is

Example 6.4
St. Paul, no. 22, Chorus

a. mm. 24–28

Example 6.4, continued

b. mm. 75–80

Denn dei-ne Herr - lich-keit   ist of - fen - bar   ge - wor - den

c. mm. 160–64

denn dei-ne Herr - lich-keit   ist of - fen - bar

denn   al - le Hei-den, al-le Hei - den   wer-den kom - men

especially reinforced by hidden relationships between the two themes in melodic range and rhythmic flow. This means is still more forcibly employed in no. 19. After Paul's solo ("Ich danke dir, Gott") the choir answers, "Der Herr wird die Tränen abwischen." The homophonic middle part complementarily introduces "Denn der Herr hat es gesagt." Promise and encouragement finally complement each other in a thematic combination, whose more masterful expression resides specifically in the fact that it does not have the effect of artifice but rather appears as self-evident (Example 6.5).

Example 6.5
St. Paul, **no. 19, Aria with Chorus**

a. mm. 48–52

Denn Herr wird die Trä - nen von al-len An - ge - sich-tern ab - wi - schen

Example 6.5 continued

b. mm. 89–91

c. mm. 120–23

To paraphrase Schumann: doubts about *St. Paul* are entirely possible, even well-founded ones. Certainly, the work is less dramatically gripping than *Elijah*, it is sometimes long-winded, and its lyrical lines may have a precarious effect today. Anyone who measures it by Bach will unquestionably be disappointed, for history weighs down *St. Paul* more than it does *Elijah*. In *St. Paul* the encounter with Bach was, for the first time, played out productively for a work in this genre. Simultaneously, the problem that arose from the tension between art and religion in a secular time was solved here in the oratorio. This solution had consequences that continued up to the movement complexes in Brahms's *Deutsches Requiem*. The encounter with Bach led Mendelssohn to return to the particular possibilities of the lyrical song movement. After that had been accomplished, a greater breadth could be achieved in *Elijah*.

FROM *ST. PAUL* TO NEW APPROACHES IN *ELIJAH*

Following the first performance of *St. Paul*, Mendelssohn wrote on 12 August to the friend of his youth, Karl Klingemann, in London, "Now that the piece is finished, I am actually only happy to get beyond it and to go on to the future, wherever it leads me." That is followed by the request to send him "the thoughts that you have for your old man, rather about an Elijah, or Peter, or for all I care, Og of Bashan." In February 1837 he then wrote, "I would prefer that you chose Elijah ... with choruses and arias, which you would write yourself either in prose or in verse, or assemble from the Psalms and the prophets, but with really compact, strong, full choruses."[41] From the beginning, therefore, there was the assumption that he would reach a new goal in his own way. The choice, however, inclined toward the material of Elijah, and large choruses took precedence from the outset. As open as the question was of whether the text would be chosen from the Bible or written in poetry, it remained at first equally uncertain whether the plan should be "dramatic" or "epic." The remark about additional passages from the prophets and the Psalms is connected to the conviction that "Elijah and the ascension to heaven at the end would be the most beautiful thing." This idea is expressed in a letter of uncertain date from Ferdinand Hiller,[42] who found Mendelssohn in Leipzig, "the Bible open before him. 'Listen up,' said he. And he read out the passage to me with a soft, impassioned voice . . . 'Und siehe, der Herr ging vorüber.' 'Would that not be magnificent for an oratorio?' he cried." The early decision in favor of this material was thus led by the fascination for the closing with the ascension of Elijah to heaven; this was also accompanied by the desire for large choral movements and characteristic scenes.

The collaboration with Klingemann did not begin immediately, but it led, in the late summer of 1837, during Mendelssohn's visit to London, to the establishment of a scenario, which then remained the basic outline for the further planning. As Klingemann was unable to flesh out the draft more fully in the following year, however, Mendelssohn turned to the Dessau pastor Julius Schubring. He had already been consulted earlier for the text of *St. Paul*, and in the interim the plan for a St. Peter oratorio had been discussed with him. As he had done before, Schubring answered in his letters of autumn 1838 with detailed text suggestions, but he was unable to suppress his skepticism toward the Old Testament material. As a result, he wanted supplementary text from the New Testament in *Elijah* and Christ himself to enter at the end.[43] In view of such differences, the work stalled, being broken off first around 1839. The commission to write a new work for the festival in Birmingham in August 1846 dates only from 11 June 1845. Now the composer again requested Schubring's counsel with reference to the earlier plan. The correspondence with him stretched on into the summer of 1846. In spite of Schubring's numerous suggestions, it has since become evident that Mendelssohn himself determined, largely independently, not only the overall plan but also the details of the wording. Martin Staehelin has identified as a further source the collection of sermons "Elias der Thisbiter" by the Berlin theologian Friedrich Wilhelm Krummacher, which, with seven printings between 1828 and 1903, was the most widely circulated book on the prophet.[44] Indeed, its author mentioned in his 1851 preface that these texts had provided a stimulus to Mendelssohn, and, in fact, there are astonishing correspondences in the layout of the text; instead of a direct inspiration, however, one ought rather to think in terms of mediation by Schubring, especially since both theologians shared the Reformed faith.

Between June 1845 and August 1846 not much time remained for the composition of *Elijah*, and as a result the first version, which was premiered on 26 August 1846 in Birmingham, differed considerably from the second version, which was then performed on 16 April 1847 in London. The extant sources reveal the changes introduced in the engraving stage, which have less to do with the large choruses than with the dialogue and recitative, as well as the arioso parts. It is also not out of the question that the composer could have referred to even earlier sketches from the preceding years. The autograph score, which belonged to Mendelssohn's Nachlaß in the Deutsche Staatsbibliothek in Berlin, is today located in the Biblioteka Jagiellonska in Kraków, but for a long time it was unavailable, and it still could not be evaluated by Arntrud Kurzhals-Reuter in 1978. While in 1961 Donald Mintz investigated the sketches remaining in Berlin, already in 1882 Joseph Bennett, on the basis of a copy of the first version owned by the publisher Novello, had thoroughly described the marked differences from the final version, with numerous musical examples, though without drawing comprehensive conclusions.[45] Instead of detailed examinations of individual examples, here one can only summarize the general tendencies that become clear in the comparison of the two versions. First of all, the reworking dealt to the greatest extent with the recitative, specifically with the dialogue portions, that is, with the parts of the work that had been least subject to a formal decision beforehand. Even in them, choral interjections remain generally untouched; on the other hand, it turns out that numerous small variants also appear in soloistic ariosos. By contrast, the closed forms of the large arias remain identical, at least in outline, though this does not by any means exclude revision in their inner development. From the outset by far the most untouched in this process were the large choruses, in which, as a rule, the reworking concentrated more on details of voice leading, instrumentation, and sometimes also harmony. Significant cuts involve a tenor recitative, "Es ist Elias gekommen," which originally preceded the aria no. 21, "Höre, Israel"/"Hear ye, Israel," as the opening of the second part, and thereafter a choral movement, "Er wird öffnen die Augen der Blinden" in D major, which stood within the movement complex no. 41 between the chorus "Aber Einer erwacht"/"But the Lord from the North" and the quartet "Wohl an, alle"/"O come ev'ry one." Both abbreviations therefore have to do with the reflective blocks of movement that frame the second part. At the same time, too, the soprano aria no. 21 underwent radical revisions, especially in its middle part, as did the closing chorus no. 42, which not only was preceded by a completely different opening but whose fugue used an entirely different text (Eph. 3: 20–21) with intervallically analogous thematic style. While instead of this the final version refers to Ps. 8: 1, the previously mentioned cancellation of the chorus in no. 41 also discarded a movement that, with the fourfold return of a songlike tune, connected to the tradition of the Protestant chorale arrangement. Also corresponding to this tendency is the replacement of the original chorale text in the quartet no. 15 ("Regard thy servant's pray'r") by Old Testament text in the final version (Ps. 55: 23, 108: 5, 25: 30), a change whereby the use of the melody of the chorale "O Gott, du frommer Gott" as an indirect quotation is sublimely disguised. If, on one hand, the revision had to do with the reflective passages, it had, on the other hand, the goal of focusing the drama. In this regard the large scenes in the first part (nos. 8, 10, and 19) underwent a particularly far-reaching revision; especially the dialogue between Elijah and the widow (no. 8) had a thoroughly different form in the first version. The miracle of the son's revival had to be presented here in a few biblical words in a single movement within a direct conversation, and Mendelssohn accomplished this only in the revision. Accordingly, not only the more recitative-like parts were altered but also the prophet's invocation with its solemn arioso gesture. Yet even in such a movement, whose thematic style and basic outline already existed in the first version, the composer relentlessly polished details, as one can perhaps see in the concentration of theme combinations in several choruses (e.g., in nos. 1, 9, 22, or 42). Even Elijah's once-central movements, such as the invocation no. 14, "Herr Gott Abrahams"/"Lord God of Abraham," or the aria no. 26, "Es ist genug"/"It is enough," in both of which the middle part was radically revised, were not spared this reworking. A special point, finally, is that the famous trio no. 28, "Hebe deine Augen auf"/"Lift thine eyes," appears in the first version as a duet for soprano and alto with orchestra, with almost entirely different thematic style.

Altogether it is clear how complicated the compositional history of the work was but also how relentlessly Mendelssohn worked on it to achieve his goal of balancing drama and reflection. In addition, the textual basis is far more complicated than the published reports make clear. Thus, Mendelssohn did not only without free poetry but also, with few exceptions, without New Testament texts (e.g., from Matt. 10: 22 and 13: 43 in nos. 32 and 39). At its core the libretto follows the story of Elijah according to I Kings, Chapters 17–19, but it is supplemented by perhaps eighty additional texts from the Old Testament, making it into a complicated mixture. Moreover, the Bible text is by no means taken over literally, even in the central narrative, but rearranged or paraphrased according to compositional judgment. The redaction succeeded so cleverly, to be sure, that departures from the literal text are hardly noticeable except by very precise checking in the Bible to document each change. In addition, in the second part, to which this discussion will return, compilation predominates to such a degree that hardly any large movement is based on one single Bible text. Mixture is almost the rule, and it demonstrates—besides the literary skill of the composer—his deep familiarity with the Bible. For this he hardly needed theological advice. What is more, the main features of the first part were already established early on, while for the second part Schubring's suggestion that a visionary conversation among Christ, Elijah, and St. Paul be considered for the closing was steadfastly rejected. The decision was already made early, unlike in *St. Paul*—and also unlike in Bach—against the reporting of events by a *testo*. Decisive was not only the intention to eliminate formulaic recitative as much as possible; much more important was the goal of achieving a highly dramatic structure by the direct sequence of situations. Narrative words are, to be sure, occasionally assigned to ensembles of angels or even to the chorus, but the action is primarily to be understood from the direct speech of the characters, which, granted, is not always simple but is also by no means impossible. The appeal to the attentive listener therefore accords with the composer's dramatic intention. Thus, a clear subdivision stands out, as well, in which the first and the second parts each incorporates four scenes or situations (see Table 6.2).

Table 6.2
Text layout in *Elijah*

Part	Section	Numbers	Content
Part 1	Opening		Rec. Elijah (Curse)—Overture
	Block 1	nos. 1–5	Chorus—Duet, Rec.—Aria, Chorus (Lament, Prayer, Exhortation, Promise)
	Block 2	nos. 6–9	Elijah—Widow: Miracle of revival
	Block 3	nos. 10–16	Miracle of fire
	Block 4	nos. 17–20	Miracle of rain
Part 2	Block 5	nos. 21–22	Solo/Chorus (Warning—Exhortation)
	Block 6	nos. 23–30	Threat (Queen)—Elijah's retreat
	Block 7	nos. 31–38	Appearance of God—Elijah's ascension to Heaven—"Heilig, Heilig"
	Block 8	nos. 39–41	Aria, Rec., Chorus, Quartet (Deliverance—Proclamation)
	Closing	no. 42	Final chorus

After the opening, with the curse in Elijah's brief recitative and the overture, there follow in block 1 (nos. 1–5) the lament of the chorus, the exhortation in the duet, and Obadiah's aria, as well as the choral promise ("und tue Barmherzigkeit"/"And his mercies"). Before the lifting of the curse, however, comes—as a delaying scene in the drama—the miracle of the revival of the child in the second block, with the dialogue between Elijah and the widow (nos. 6–9). In the third block follows the miracle of fire (nos. 10–16), whose centerpiece lies in the threefold call to Baal; the prophet's prayer, after a meditative quartet, then leads into the chorus ("Das Feuer fiel herab"/"The fire descend from heav'n"). Only in the fourth block (nos. 17–20) is the curse lifted with the miracle of rain and the closing response of the chorus "Dank sei dir Gott"/"Thanks be to God." The second part, which opens with the soprano aria "Höre, Israel"/"Hear ye, Israel" and the chorus "Fürchte dich nicht"/"Be not afraid" (nos. 21-22), is not laid out in such closed fashion. The sixth scene encompasses the queen's threat against the prophet and his retreat into the wilderness (nos. 23-30), while block 7 reaches a climax in the appearance of God and Elijah's ascension into heaven (nos. 31-38). The eighth and final block is reserved for reflection (nos. 39-42), as the choral proclamation follows the fervent tenor aria, after which the promise in the quartet is answered by the hymnlike final chorus.

Undeniably, therefore, the framing blocks achieve a more contemplative function, while in the middle scenes tensions are shifted so that the appearance of

God and the ascension attain special scope. Unquestionably, too, it is not only the chorus that has changing assignments, in that it acts as the people of Israel or the heathen and then takes over words of proclamation and promise. Similarly, the soloists also receive different functions, as, for example, the part of the widow and the warning to Israel are assigned to the soprano, or the role of the queen and the invocation of an angel, to the alto. All this does not signify any lack of objective logic or dramaturgical rigor but rather corresponds to the inner freedom that distinguishes the oratorio as a genre. The case is fundamentally no different from the function of the choruses in Handel's oratorios and Bach's Passions, even though in them the connection between personae and their arias partly operates more strictly. On the contrary, in *Elijah* other persons appear only in single scenes, like secondary characters who come back again in order to open changing perspectives on the prophet in the center. Whereas opera, as drama in music, is governed by a closed plot, in which the characters undergo development, the opportunity of the oratorio consists in the freedom from realistic representation on the stage. It can trust such matters to the expectation that the audience has the capacity imaginatively to surmount the single place, time, and action. When judging *Elijah*, therefore, one must also proceed from this freedom as the premise of the oratorio.[46]

The critical discussion in Germany—where the work had its first performance only in Hamburg in October 1847, shortly before Mendelssohn's death—centered around the Old Testament material, the disposition of the text, and the work's relationship to its genre. In England it quickly attained the stature of an undisputed masterpiece, especially since the English version was the first to be performed, whereas *St. Paul* had not already been as widely received as in Germany. Very soon after the composer's death anti-Semitic tones mingled with the discussion in Germany, when, for example, in 1848 Franz Brendel, editor of the *Neue Zeitschrift für Musik*, founded by Schumann, stated the rationale for his dislike of the selection of material with the words "the time is past for this preference for Judaism."[47] Even as well-informed an author as the archaeologist Otto Jahn, to whom we owe the groundbreaking Mozart biography, asserted in his evaluation of *St. Paul*, "[H]ow much less is the interest with which we approach *Elijah!*"[48] Still he tempered this opinion with the provision that one should, "in the interest of art, beware of exaggerating it," and he was perceptive enough to understand the significance of the prophet for the Christian faith. The reviews by Eduard Krüger and Otto Lange, which already appeared in December 1847 in the Leipzig *Neue Zeitschrift* and the *Neue Berliner Musikzeitung*, are representative in this connection.[49] From the outset Krüger found the text "crassly Jewish, narrow-mindedly pious," and, on that account, "without interest"; in the "development of the scenes he saw "apparent arbitrariness in the connection" of the texts. The work lacked "a central point, from which the whole thing proceeds," while the plot could not be followed even on multiple hearings "without a libretto." The exceptionally detailed critique, then, which deals with details of the harmony, melody, and rhythm, has as its purpose throughout the demonstration of the contradictions between text and music and especially the lack of originality in comparison to *St. Paul*. In contrast, Otto Lange observed that Mendelssohn had "generally broadened his view of the oratorio," in that he developed it in the direction of "lyrical subjectivity and dramatic life." Despite a lack of "unity," the development freed itself up "by means of a skillful organization," and the unprecedented admiration of the music led to the insight that, in comparison to *St. Paul*, in *Elijah* Mendelssohn "worked out for himself a far greater independence and freedom." As much, thus, as the reviews contradict each other, they are in agreement about the difficulties caused by the layout of the text. Already a decade earlier the reception of *St. Paul* in the critical press had aroused a general discussion about the principles of the oratorio.[50]   In the center stands the question of whether the oratorio should be defined as "dramatic" in the style of Handel or "epically" narrative with "lyrical" tendencies like Bach's Passions. If the criticism of the chorales in *St. Paul* had sparked conflict, it was now kindled by the relation of dramatic action and symbolic treatment in *Elijah*. Otto Jahn sought a balance with the thesis that the oratorio was not only governed by "the epic element" but "capable of genuinely dramatic construction," which, granted, would not qualify as "scenic" but only as "characteristic."   The oratorio should be particularly dedicated to that end, because for it music possesses "an inexhaustible realm of nuance."[51]

Arno Forchert, who reconstructed the genesis of the text of *Elijah*, returned again in 1974 to the discussion of genre theory that continued up to the time of Liszt and Brahms. Based on the evidence of the letters, he concluded that Mendelssohn's goal of a "historical" representation was frustrated by the insertion of choral movements with "symbolic" function for the sake of choral societies.[52] This compromise, however, had an effect on the "Werkgestalt," in which the symbolic choruses had to conceal the lack of dramatic coherence. Moreover, "dramatic and epic text structures" run into contradictions, "in the course of which the musical as well as the textual logic of the representation suffers." Such criticisms appear to sanction the obstacles that *Elijah* encountered when its unexpected renaissance began in Germany about twenty years ago. In the meantime, however, the work has apparently become so familiar that such difficulties should hardly have validity any longer. Not only have the functions of the characters and scenes, whose succession does not at all constitute an artistic flaw, become intelligible, but it has also become much more understandable that the increasing weight of "symbolic" movement in the second part does not represent an awkward compromise but rather corresponds to an internal consequence of the layout, for the more that the "dramatic" action reaches its conclusion, the more that the need to demonstrate its exemplary significance becomes essential. This can succeed, however, only by means of that reflection that is to be read from the choice of texts for the contemplative structural units. Even the quartet no. 41b, "Wohlan alle, die ihr durstig seid"/"O come, ev'ryone that thirsteth," which often seems to be a mere insertion, is legitimated by the relation of the text to the miracle of rain as the center of the first part. All these movements thus indicate that the story of *Elijah* does not tell of the distant past but has a hortatory meaning for the present-day listener—whether understood as one of a public audience or as a member of a congregation. In the balance between religious content and artistic character, however—not unlike in *St. Paul*—there lies a problem, the solution to which determines the proper rank of the work. It is defined precisely in the departure from the models of Bach as well as Handel, and its significance becomes recognizable only in light of the position of the work in the composer's oeuvre.

EXCURSUS ON MENDELSSOHN'S COMPOSITIONAL DEVELOPMENT

It is no easy matter to speak of Mendelssohn's compositional development, because for a long time only isolated essays on the subject existed, while at the same time tenacious prejudices stood in the way of such an attempt.[53] For a long while the image persisted of a fortunate prodigy who had the advantages of a wealthy home and splendid training but who, after a series of absolutely astounding early works, exhausted himself into formal smoothness. Spoiled by the success of a brilliant career, the composer presumably then fell into mere repetition of his "mannerisms," finally becoming an epigone of himself. The image of the incontrovertibly bright, but not particularly deep, Mendelssohn goes back—as would also be shown in the reception of *Elijah*—to the composer's last years and the decade after his death. It established itself to such a degree, however, that his reputation was overshadowed by historical progress and revised by anti-Semitic tendencies that finally ended in the verdict of fascism. Only more recent research has been able to show how inaccurate this picture is, how very much more his life was attended by deep-seated conflicts. These were expressed, too, in compositional crises, which can at the same time serve as a key to the understanding of the music history of the time.

After the encounter with historical forms was accomplished by their adaptation in *St. Paul*, Mendelssohn could now—as if emancipated—return in 1837 to the long-neglected instrumental genres. From this point there appeared in a continuous stream lasting until 1845 the succession of mature masterpieces, opening with the Op. 44 quartets and the Op. 49 trio but including equally instrumental sonatas as well as solo concertos, the "Scottish" Symphony and the *Lobgesang*, the *Walpurgisnacht*, the Psalm-cantatas, and the incidental music to *A Midsummer Night's Dream* or to *Antigone*. In this ripe harvest the innovations do not show up as clearly as in the earlier chamber music. Instead of rough contrasts and cyclic experiments they adopt a concept of constant mediation between the themes themselves and the later phases of a movement, which has as its goal the thematic undergirding of all the segments of the formal process. The process does not, however, take as its point of departure terse motives as in Classic composition, but rather an expansive melodic style in cantabile settings and in closed timbral areas, a material, in other words, that is actually less appropriate for thematic working out. For a long time people reproached these works—aside from the famous Violin

Concerto or the "Scottish"—for a classicistic slickness of form and lack of emotional conflicts: elegance, grace, or spirit did not suit the taste of German criticism—it rather belonged to music from France. In the process, however, what innovations these works did include were also overlooked, for the standards for resolving the contradiction between Romantic thematic style and the developing course of the movement consist in the progressive variation and combination of the thematic substance with the accompanying elements. This applies to concertos as well as quartets, to symphonies as well as Psalm-cantatas, and it affects wide-ranging sonata movements as well as whirring and intricate scherzos, slow song-movements, or complex finales with rondo tendencies. A small example will demonstrate this. The E-minor quartet Op. 44 no. 2 is the first piece of this series after *St. Paul*.[54] The two themes do not produce any contrasts but rather express themselves largely in cantabile phrasing with similar accompaniment. The requisite oppositions, however, are accomplished by apparently free figurations, which then legitimate themselves in the course of the movement by combination with the themes. Then, at the end of the development and in the coda, the central point is decoded, as it were, when the two themes appear compacted together, demonstrating analogy rather than contrast. Similarly, in the Violin Concerto or the "Scottish" the second theme is introduced in such a way that the main theme sounds as a counterpoint to it—no different than in the theme combinations of the *St. Paul* choruses. It is clear from this how much in *St. Paul* procedures were discovered that drew from instrumental music and now turn back to influence the later instrumental works. Around 1845, nonetheless, this continuous series of works breaks off, and—precisely in a phase in which signs of exhaustion, disappointment, and resignation are growing—indications of the search for a new path increase. They open the prospect on a late style that was hardly able to develop completely in the remaining two years until Mendelssohn's death in 1847, but of which the new individuality of *Elijah* nevertheless gives some indication.

After the fragmentation of his energies among Berlin, London, and Leipzig, Mendelssohn intended to withdraw from the public arena in order to devote himself entirely to composition. This remained only an intention, to be sure, as it happened many times that new works, such as another symphony and a piano concerto, were now abandoned. Even the "Italian" and the Second Quintet, Op. 87, were never definitively brought to completion. The reason lay less in the lack of time than in self-critical reflection, as many statements indicate. Yet there also emerged a group of works, to which belong, in addition to *Elijah*, the Second Trio and the Second Cello Sonata, as well as the organ sonatas and the last quartet, composed in the year of his death. What is new in these works is not so much their formal layout, however individual the design of the organ sonatas seems. Much more surprising are sharpened expressive contrasts within a movement structure that rejects the usual cantabile lines. At the same time the former principle of thematic mediation and combinative development recedes. Again a few examples must suffice to establish the context for *Elijah*.

The Organ Sonatas Op. 65, first of all, should hardly be understood as "montages" in the sense of the modern "collage"—as Susanna Großmann-Vendrey regarded them.[55] Granted, they were assembled in 1844–1845 out of a total of twenty-four separate movements, in the process of which isolated earlier movements were also recovered. It is no accident, however, that they combine tonally into cycles, and the sources reveal that movements that belong together were also drafted together. Certainly, they sometimes have an almost improvisational effect (in which the fantastic tendencies of older toccatas doubtless play a part); their layout not only contradicts the Classic norm of a sonata but also changes strikingly from work to work. All the same, their name does not stem from a dilemma but rather from the desire to create new organ music according to the demands of the sonata. What thus at first can seem to be a strange lack of unity or a stylistic rupture results from the intention to confront movement types and characters head-on, so that they achieve their expression through reciprocal contrasts. The chorale in the first movement of the F-minor Sonata no. 1 hardly becomes fused into the movement, as in earlier times; it stands rather in opposition to the meandering figuration, and the two sides instead intersect by means of their contrast. Likewise, the unexpected Lied at the end of the chorale variations in no. 6, which arrives almost as a rupture, actually thus focuses its quiet expressivity. After the persistent work on the historical chorale partita, the subject comes to itself in the lyrical meditation of the Lied. Nevertheless, in the risk of such ruptures, which distance themselves from the unifying ideal of balanced development, eminently modern tendencies present themselves, as then also these works serve as the foundation for the new genus of organ sonata up to Reger and Hindemith.

In the outer movements of the C-minor Trio, Op. 66, analogous tendencies emerge in the pointed expressivity of the themes. Moreover, the main theme in the opening movement consists of unrelentingly pulsating sound surfaces, which steadily jack themselves up within a narrow melodic contour, only to break off abruptly. The driving impulse of the final theme comes unexpectedly—as also happens in the middle movement of the Cello Sonata Op. 58—to meet a visionary chorale melody, whose function remains puzzling until it at last reveals its power at the end of the coda. Alluding to Bach's formula "Quaerendo invenietis" from the *Musical Offering*, Mendelssohn noted: "Suchet, so werdet ihr finden." The contemporary B-major Quintet, which appeared posthumously as Op. 87, certainly contains a remarkable adagio, whose hymnlike coda fades away resignedly at the end. The outer movements, however, again proceed from circling figures that are only weakly legitimated in a thematic sense. As tricky as the material is for this purpose already in the first movement, for the finale a contrasting episode was considered. Amid the ambivalence between the two concepts, however, Mendelssohn gave up this work, which, according to the report of a friend, he regarded as "not good."[56] Nevertheless, a similar intention was realized incomparably more sharply in the F-minor Quartet, Op. 80, the last cycle to be completed. Both outer movements consist of flickering curves with frantic figurations; the themes interact in harsh contrast, breaking off or dissolving into shivering tremolos and chains of trills. This nearly terrifying work makes clear, above all, what innovations were still to be looked for from Mendelssohn.

Of course, one also cannot generalize from this. Although many of the late Lieder point in the same direction as well, church works such as "Hör mein Bitten" or the last motets, Op. 69, follow the principle of subtle balance of texts and themes throughout. The Psalms for double chorus, Op. 78, however, which were already planned in 1844, practically depend on expressive contrasts in the alternation of choral sound, and the quick chordal declamation rejects not only contrapuntal work but often melodic lines with thematic significance, as well.

MUSICAL STYLE IN *ELIJAH*

All these instances undoubtedly now make it possible to judge what peculiar new tendencies *Elijah* shows, as well. Its contemporaries were already surprised by the fact that here not only chorales but also the usual fugues fell away. The rejection of narrative recitative already belongs to the intention of that "progress" that Mendelssohn had in mind as early as 1837, for this step had as its goal the sharp juxtaposition of movements and characters. The difficulties criticism must confront resulted from these deliberately unmediated contrasts. They also decisively influenced the core of the movements, however, with harsh harmonic caesuras and with almost nonthematic build-ups of sound. Certainly, there is no lack of the technique of thematic combination that distinguished *St. Paul*. In *Elijah*, however, it takes place in an even more complex and sometimes extremely intricate fashion.

The opening recitative ends with the conventional falling fourth on the words "Ich sage es denn"/"but according to my word," which, however, becomes highly memorable because of its extension. It will be quoted many times, not only in the overture but also at significant points in the further course of the work. At the beginning there stands in contrast to it the melodic ascent through the triad, which recurs in the chorus no. 5, "Aber der Herr"/"Yet doth the Lord," and in the recitative no. 10, "So wahr der Herr Zebaoth"/"As God the Lord of Sabaoth." Between these in the first recitative on the words of the curse come two diminished triads, which the chorus no. 5 takes up on the text "Der Fluch ist über uns gekommen"/"His curse hath fallen down upon us." In other words, what appear to be formulas in the first recitative turn out to have motivic function across the broad course of the work. Moreover, the fugue theme of the overture likewise also seems to be a model for the theme of the vocal fugue in the final chorus, no. 42. Of course, the two forms of the theme differ in the motivic fragmentation of the one and the melodic continuity of the other. Upon close examination of their intervallic framework, however, they relate to each other as the minor and major variants of a single germ. Across the wide expanse of the whole work, thus, the two outer movements refer to each other (see Example 6.6).

Example 6.6
Elijah

a. Overture, Fugue Theme

b. no. 42, Final Chorus, Fugue Theme

The quartet no. 15, "Wirf dein Anliegen"/"Cast thy burden," based on three psalm verses, has the effect of a modest vocal movement with short interludes, which can make the line-by-line sectionalization of the biblical prose text surprising. At its root lies the slightly altered chorale tune "O Gott, du frommer Gott," which is so well suited to the Bible text that the chorale quotation is hardly noticeable (see Example 6.7). At the end, however, the theme of the bass aria

Example 6.7

a. *Elijah*, no. 15, Quartet, mm. 1–4

b. *Gesangbuch Meiningen*, 1693

"Herr Gott Abrahams"/"Lord God of Abraham" sounds, referring again to the first recitative. The chorus no. 29, "Siehe der Hüter Israels"/"He, watching over Israel," presents a songlike melodic style at the entrance of the psalm text, to which in the second text segment, "wenn du mitten in Angst"/"Shouldst thou, walking in grief," it contrasts an ascending minor scale as fugato theme (see Example 6.8). Where

Example 6.8
Elijah, **no. 29, Chorus**

a. mm. 2–5

Sie - he, der Hü - ter Is - ra-els schläft noch schlum-mert nicht.
He, watch-ing o - ver Is - ra-el, slum - bers not nor sleeps;

b. mm. 20–22

Wenn du mit - ten in Angst wan - delst, so
Shouldst thou, walk - ing in grief lan - guish, He

c. mm. 44–45

sie - he, der Hü - ter Is - ra - els
He, watch-ing o - ver Is - ra - el,

wenn du mit - ten in Angst wan - delst
shouldst thou, walk - ing in grief, lan - guish

the return to the first part begins, however, the two themes are paired simultaneously, so that their texts refer to each other. A maximum of thematic density is constructed in the chorus no. 32, "Wer bis an das Ende beharrt"/"He that shall endure to the end," which introduces two cantabile melodic lines into the two text sections (see Example 6.9). These two themes, however, each of which

Example 6.9
Elijah, no. 32, Chorus

a. mm. 1–5

b. mm. 17–19

occupies two measures, appear thirty-five times in thirty-seven measures. Almost continuously, therefore, several voices simultaneously have thematic function, and exactly in the middle of the movement the two themes overlap simultaneously. Nevertheless, instead of tiresome contrapuntalism one hears the songlike flow of the voices. As the last solo for Elijah, the arioso no. 37, "Ja, es sollen wohl Berge weichen"/"For the mountains shall depart," is no mere contemplation but rather the prophet's spiritual farewell (see Example 6.10). In the striding $\frac{6}{4}$ meter the

Example 6.10
Elijah, no. 37, Arioso

ascending line of the oboe rises above the repeated notes of the basses; the voice takes up this motive, however, and to the remaining text lines the variational development is achieved out of this motivic cell. Such subtle initiatives do not come to the fore demonstratively, however, but remain an unobtrusive background for the sincere expression of apparently modest movements.

All the more striking, other traits appear throughout, which were still foreign to *St. Paul*. Among them are, first of all, the sharp divisions, which occur less between the scenes than between their individual movements. One should recall perhaps the lyric tenor aria no. 4, "So ihr mich von ganzem Herzen suchet"/"If with all your hearts ye truly seek me," which is followed immediately by a choral outburst: "Aber der Herr sieht es nicht"/"Yet doth the Lord see it not." Similarly, the calm chorus no. 9, "Wohl dem, der den Herren fürchtet"/"Blessed are the men who fear Him," is interrupted by the new onset of the recitative "So wahr der Herr"/"As God the Lord." In the reverse of this process the chain of Baal choruses nos. 11–13 runs into the contemplative invocation "Herr Gott Abrahams"/"Lord God of Israel," while the quartet with chorale no. 15 then contrasts with the chorus "Das Feuer fiel herab"/"The fire descends from heav'n." The counterpart to the fiery aria no. 17, "Ist nicht des Herrn Wort wie ein Feuer"/"Is not His word like a fire," is formed by the lamenting arioso "Weh'ihnen"/"Woe, woe unto them," and the dramatic chorus no. 38 leads to the quiet tenor aria "Dann werden die Gerechten leuchten"/"Then, then shall the righteous shine." The purpose of the layout thus is not by any means always a balance between intensification and relaxation; it rather achieves its tension by means of unexpected changes in the conduct of the form.

Between the movements and also within them, then, harmonic accents become noticeable, which mark the divisions or connecting points in the course of the work. After the chorus no. 9, "Wohl dem"/"Blessed are the men," in G major, the recitative "So wahr der Herr"/"As God the Lord" follows directly in E♭ major, that is, in a third-relation. The opening recitative in no. 12 closes with the words "Rufet lauter"/"Call him louder" on the third D♭–B♭; the call to Baal then begins immediately in F♯, and at the end of the movement appears the doubled shift from F♯ minor by way of D to E♭ major. The recitative lead-in in no. 16 leads analogously into an E♭-minor sonority; the chorus "Das Feuer"/"The fire") starts, however in B major—as far away as imaginable. The closing chorus of the first part, "Dank sei dir, Gott"/"Thanks be to God" (no. 20), provides a striking example. The hymnlike song of thanks already undergoes a declamatory accentuation at the words "die Wasserwogen sind groß"/"The stormy billows are high"; after the appeal "doch der Herr"/"But the Lord," however, follows an extensive chain of harmonic progressions in semitone relationships with harsh dissonances (C/D♭, C♯ minor/D, D/E♭). Such harsh progressions do not emerge so decisively in the somewhat more reflective second part as in the dramatic first part, but they are by no means absent even in the framing units. The opening soprano aria starts out in B minor and changes at the Allegro to B major; the following chorus no. 22,

"Fürchte dich nicht"/"Be not afraid," turns, however, in a third-relationship to G major. Similarly, the chorus no. 41 is in D major; the quartet "Wohlan, alle"/"O come ev'ry one" follows, however, as an insertion in B♭ major; the closing movement reaches D major again. The final fugue, moreover, whose theme harks back to the overture, begins over a pedal point with marked dissonances (which Brahms followed up in the third movement of the German Requiem), and even its closing "Amen" peaks in chromatic coloration instead of a smoothly heightened cadence. Such tendencies do not occur everywhere and equally, to be sure, but as a result they become just that much more noticeable, expanding the resources of the medium.

Nor does *Elijah* lack fugal movements, as they are intrinsic to the oratorio, but among these, sections and whole movements stand out in which contrapuntal work takes a back seat to declamatory sound surfaces, which can even make do without melodic lines. Straightaway in the first chorus, in contrast to the chromatically colored fugato "Die Ernte is vergangen"/"The harvest now is over" comes the harsh declamation: "Will denn der Herr nicht mehr Gott sein"/"Will then the Lord be no more God." In the captivating duet no. 2, "Zion streckt ihre Hände aus"/"Zion spreadeth her hands for aid," the chorus comments in sparse, almost psalmodic diction, "Herr, höre unser Gebet"/"Lord, bow thine ear to our prayer," and the chorus no. 5 culminates at the word "Barmherzigkeit" (in the English text at the statement "His mercies on thousands fall") in a broad unfolding of sound surfaces over a pedal point without any actual thematic contour. The same holds true for the famous double quartet of the angels in no. 7 or the "Heilig"/"Holy, holy, holy," no. 35, for in both cases a hymnlike, soaring melody arises out of chordal declamation in stratified columns of sound without linear counterpoint. More than ever, the dramatic high points are characterized by this sort of choral technique, for example, in no. 16, "Das Feuer fiel herab"/"The fire descends from heav'n," or no. 24, "Wehe ihm"/"Woe to him." This is the case generally with the central sections dealing with the appearance of God in no. 34, where broad timbral areas intervene between the solo intonations "Der Herr ging vorüber"/"Behold, God the Lord passed by." They also have hardly any melodic qualities, even though they are set strictly as canons over long pedal points.

In particular, no. 38, with Elijah's ascension to heaven, consists of vehemently mounting blocks of sound, whose declamation is sharpened here mainly by the marked rhythmic style of the orchestral context.   In the process the harmony becomes unusually expanded, whereas the course of the movement is hardly determined by motivic qualities (see Example 6.11). The movement begins in F minor and ends with a half cadence on E♭, but at the outset it arrives relatively conventionally in m. 27 at the dominant C major, which is reaffirmed several times. The next segment of text ("Und da der Herr"/"And when the Lord") begins already in C major in m. 31, but the harmony turns toward the mediant, A major. From here a first modulation leads to C major (m. 38), a second then further to E♭ major (m. 42). Following this model the continuation of the process would produce a circle of minor thirds that would have to lead by way of G♭ back to A major.

Example 6.11
Elijah, no. 38, Chorus

Harmonic model- circle of ascending minor thirds

While Schubert explored circular harmonic constructions based on whole-tone or minor-third relations, in the outer movements of the late G-major Quartet D. 887, for example, Mendelssohn obviously shied away from the mechanical nature of such a schema. Thus, the next stretch of the movement leads to D♭ major in m. 44. The critical point, G♭ major, which, as a link in the broken chain, was avoided, is marked twice in mm. 45–47, however—once by the single chromatic passing tone in the bass (g–g♭) and then in the next chord but one as the high note g♭² on the ii⁷ chord. Such procedures do, in fact, recall the harmonic style of Schubert; but although Mendelssohn promoted the "Great" C-major Symphony after it was brought to his attention by Schumann, there is no reason to assume therefore that he could have known a work like the G-major Quartet. Nevertheless, it cannot be ruled out that the encounter with the works of Schubert as well as those of Schumann provided an impulse that had an impact on the harmonic differentiation in Mendelssohn's late works.

All these procedures differ from the contrapuntal construction of the choruses of people in *St. Paul*, which next to them appear to be comparatively traditional fugatos. Again, this is certainly not the case for all the levels of *Elijah*, but it clearly marks new intentions that extend the radius of the later major works. In the process, however, they also correspond to characteristic traits of the other late works, which risk timbral eruptions without the security of thematic work. Certainly, one should not speak of ruptures in *Elijah*, yet the multiplicity of means extends so far that to hold it together requires that highly personal idiom that later was often discredited as Mendelssohn's mannerism and in reality indicates only a very individual style. This art of balancing dramatic with lyric tendencies, action with reflection, or focus with differentiation in the medium can be revealed only by representative analysis of selected solo and choral movements.

SOLO MOVEMENTS IN *ELIJAH*

The normative arias for Elijah may be taken as examples for the soloistic movements. The widow scene (no. 8), on the construction of which Mendelssohn worked so ceaselessly, is labeled as "Arie" or "Air," although its chain of sections also includes recitative and arioso parts and leads into a duet. An outline allows an overview of the diverse structure, which is articulated by the participation of the two soloists, the change of tempos and meters, and the disposition of the keys (see Table 6.3).

Table 6.3
Structure of *Elijah*, no. 8 (the widow scene)

Key	Meter	Tempo	Mm.	Character(s)
E minor	$^6_8$	Andante agitato	1-64	Widow (mm. 6–16 recit.)
		recit.	65	Elijah
E major	$^4_4$	Andante sostenuto	66- 83	Elijah
E minor	$^6_8$	Andante con moto	84- 90	Elijah
			91- 98	Widow
			99-104	Elijah
		recit.	105-8	Widow
G major	$^4_4$	recit.	109-13	Elijah
	$^6_8$	a tempo	113-22	Widow
G major	$^4_4$	recit.	123-26	Widow—Elijah
	$^4_4$	Andante	127-33	Widow
			135-38	Elijah
			139-143	duet

While the movement begins in E minor in $^6_8$ meter, it ends as a duet in $^4_4$ in G major. Since the beginning and end differ in this way, and since, moreover, the course of the movement incorporates such different parts, it is reasonable to examine the development that nevertheless allows the movement to appear as a closed aria.   Over the repeated notes in the violins, the prelude introduces a narrow-range melodic germ in the oboe, which is spun out by the strings in contrary motion beginning in m. 4, breaking off at the dominant in m. 6.   The soprano's entrance, at which the orchestra pauses, is marked "Recit."; as it continues, the orchestra part is limited to a few chordal attacks.   In m. 8, however, the voice part takes over the characteristic motivic cell, with the suspension e^2-d$\sharp^2$, which is then expressed by the voice and oboe together at m. 13 (Example 6.12).   The continuing

Example 6.12
Elijah, no. 8, Recitative, Aria, and Duet

development of the whole section draws upon this compromise between aria-like thematic style and recitative diction, which already characterize the opening, as recitative-style tendencies in the vocal lines constantly link up with motivic work in the instrumental part. Whereas strings and voice unite in a homophonic setting at the end of m. 52, the oboe at m. 58 recalls again the motivic germ, which the quasi-recitative closing gestures in the soprano then also take up. As a result, it does not seem strange that the entrance of the bass voice in m. 65 emerges as "Recit.," while it is more striking that at this point the movement shifts to the opposite mode, E major. In this somewhat arioso part an accompanying function falls to the orchestra as in a recitative accompagnato, while the cantabile, periodically designed vocal part takes the lead. This part of the movement turns at its midpoint to the dominant, and at the end it culminates in the melodic ascent of the vocal part in mm. 80ff., which at the same time leads back to the cadence on the tonic. Now, however, it is the bass voice itself by which the return to E minor and $\frac{6}{8}$ meter is accomplished (mm. 84ff.), and as opposed to the cantabile middle segment the diction now becomes more recitativelike than ever, when in the continuation the soprano comes in again, and the oboe again takes up the motivic cell (mm. 91ff.). The prophet's next invocation follows, still in E minor and $\frac{6}{8}$, but this leads to a recitative for the soprano with a half cadence in B minor. Only Elijah's final call connects to the $\frac{4}{4}$ meter and the new tonic G major; but it begins explicitly as "Recit.," and by the reverse procedure the turning point is then marked by the soprano solo at m. 113, which persists in G major but in the process returns for the last time to $\frac{6}{8}$ meter. The synthesis of the two levels is formed by the closing part, in which the recitative-like tendencies recede, and both voices resolve into cantabile diction and unite at the end. Thus, on one hand, the bass entrance in m. 13 recalls the prophet's first recitative, while, on the other hand, with their last words the two voices motivate the beginning of the succeeding chorus, which follows without pause. In its development, therefore, the movement at once becomes a model of dramatic flexibility and subtle concentration.

In the bass aria no. 14 "Herr Gott Abrahams"/"Lord God of Abraham," too, the comparison of the versions, especially of the middle part, makes it possible to trace Mendelssohn's detailed work, which justifies a more detailed investigation of the movement. A prose text (1 Kings 18: 36–37) serves as the basis for this adagio in E♭ major, which comprises only thirty-eight measures in $\frac{4}{4}$ time. The preceding Baal chorus ends in F♯ minor with the falling fourth f²-c² in the soprano; to reach the new tonic of E♭, therefore, requires managing the downward shift of a minor third (see Example 6.13). Thus, the bass voice in the antepenultimate measure of no. 13 introduces D as the submediant, the D-major chord is treated as dominant to G minor, and at the falling fourth of the bass voice the rising wind instruments turn the mediant-relation B♭ into a dominant by means of the seventh as the melodic high point. As the direct connection into m. 1 of the adagio aria, this ascent corresponds with the clarinets' falling eighth-note line, which is taken over in m. 2 by the strings. Only after this opening does the thematic germ of the prelude sound, which seizes on the falling fourth, continues in falling sequences,

Example 6.13
Elijah, no. 13, Recitative and Chorus, m. 84–no. 14, Aria, m. 2

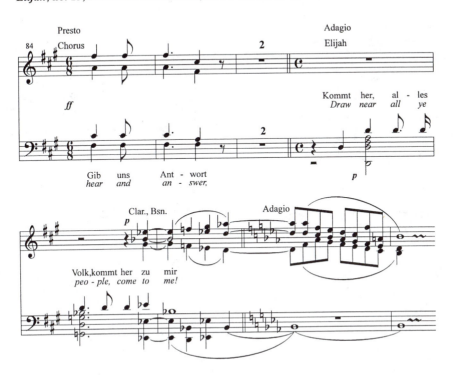

and in its fourth measure reaches its lowest point a tenth below its initial pitch. When it is taken up by the bass entrance in m. 7, the four-measure phrase is extended to a five-measure span, in which, beginning at the lowest note, the ascent does not stop at the tonic but rather leads in steady upward motion through a seventh to the dominant, B♭ (m. 11; see Example 6.14). The restatement of the eginning of the theme in m. 12, with its fermata, at first appears to mark the end of a first section of the form (see Diagram 6.1).

In the formal layout, thus, two components alternate (A and B); in the process Parts A and A' are set out in analogous fashion motivically and textually in the invocation, whereas B and B' correspond only latently, especially as the text also changes here. Starting with the prelude, which (after the opening) includes four measures, the first half (A and B) proceeds in five-measure segments throughout, in contrast to which in the second half (A' and B') there come four-measure units, until the coda returns again to five-measure structure. The B-section from m. 13 contrasts tonally as well as melodically, in that the entrance in G minor with its repeated notes and falling semitone is treated in a sequence of rising thirds (see Example 6.15). The motive does not simply refer back to the repeated notes in the third measure of the main theme (m. 9), however; it is simultaneously made more concentrated by the instrumental parts' imitative entrances at the second in the

Example 6.14
Elijah, no. 14, Aria, mm. 7–11

Diagram 6.1
Form of *Elijah*, no. 14, "Herr Gott Abrahams" ("Lord God of Abraham")

A	B	A'	B'		Coda
mm. 0–12	13–21	22–25	26–29, 30–33		34–38
2+4 5+1	5+5	4	4+4		5
E♭	g–D♭	D♭–B♭	E♭		E♭
Herr Gott . . .	auf daß ich . . .	Herr Gott . . .	daß dies Volk wisse . . .		Herr . . .
Lord God . . .	*O shew to all . . .*	*Lord God . . .*	*and shew this people . . .*		*Lord . . .*

Example 6.15
Elijah, no. 14, Aria, mm. 13–17

und dass ich sol-ches Al-les nach dein-em Wor - te ge-than,   nach deinem Wor-te ge - than.
O shew to all this people that I have done these things   ac-cording to Thy   word!

second halves of the measures (g/a b♭/c d/e♭). By means of the extension of the closing with the following cadence, this formal unit stretches to its fifth measure sustains the high note d♭¹. Whereas up to this point the movement appears to (mm. 13–17), but here the next five-measure unit begins, the upbeat of which modulate by way of G major to C minor, D♭ major is now established as the new tonic, in which the A part enters as a false reprise (m. 22). The fourth restatement of the thematic germ therefore similarly appears at a false pitch level, whereby D♭ major consolidates itself as Neapolitan of C minor with no modulation. Yet the aria began in E♭ major, a semitone higher than the preceding bass introduction in D major—and the consistency of the construction extends even further, for the D♭-major chord is connected to B♭ major by means of the arrival of the seventh (mm. 22–25), so that it produces a minor-third descent, paralleling the major third of the first bass entrance (f♯–D). At the two outer stages, thus, the large harmonic distance is bridged in different ways. In spite of this modulation, the A' part is limited to four measures (mm. 22–25), into which a portion of text from B is inserted ("erhöre mich, Herr"/"O hear me, Lord"). Part B' joins seamlessly, although the text changes again ("Daß dies Volk wisse"/"And shew this people"—see Example 6.16, mm. 26–29). The repeated notes of B are clearly taken up again, but they no longer appear as a rising sequence of falling semitone motions, but rather the reverse—as descending seconds in whole measures (mm. 26ff.). The coda finally brings back the opening prelude—shifted by a half

Example 6.16
Elijah, no. 14, Aria, mm. 26–29

dass dies Volk wis-se, dass du Herr Gott bist, dass du ihr Herz da-nach be-keh - rest,
and shew this peo-ple that thou art Lord God, and let their hearts a-gain be turn - ed.

measure (mm. 33ff. corresponding to mm. 1ff.). The periodic motion is broken in the vocal part by the extension of the first note and then by free declamation. This generally free diction is answered wordlessly in the last measure, however, by the instrumental quotation of the thematic opening. The apparently modest cantabile movement thus reveals itself to be a shifting network full of relationships and variations.

The aria no. 17, "Ist nicht des Herrn Wort"/"Is not His word," appears at first—as do not a few of the movements in *Elijah*—to be a mere counterpart to an earlier model in *St. Paul*, specifically to the aria no. 12, "Vertilge sie, Herr Zebaoth." It is not by any means the mere repetition of a type, however, although the increasing differentiation of the late work becomes clear only upon comparison of the two apparently analogous movements. The formal outline of the aria, which is based on a combination of texts (Is. 23: 29, Ps. 7: 12–13), is presumably clear: after a first part, A (mm. 1–26), there follows the contrasting middle of the movement, B (mm. 27–48), and the reprise closes with the coda (mm. 82–90).

Whereas the comparable aria in *St. Paul* is characterized by the continuous pulsation of the instrumental accompaniment, in the movement from *Elijah* the alternation of textual and formal segments is rhythmically and motivically independent. In the A part the strings are limited, first of all—along with sustained tones in the clarinets—to an accompanying function with static tremolo, and the two-measure introduction, which opens on the dominant, is followed in m. 3 by the vocal entrance on the tonic, which leads back to the dominant in m. 5. In the introduction the horns with their repeated notes and the basses in falling motion mark out a terse rhythmic model of alternating quarter and eighth notes, in which the basses first enter on the second quarter, and their formulation at the same time receives an anacrusic function that extends across m. 2 to reach its goal in m. 3 (see Example 6.17, mm. 1–5, 11–15). In this way the instrumental two-measure unit is

Example 6.17a
***Elijah*, no. 17, Aria**

a. mm. 1–5

b. mm. 11–15

linked to the three-measure vocal part (mm. 1–3, 3–5), and the subsequent variant again corresponds to this five-measure group (mm. 5–7, 7–9). From this process asymmetrical measure groups thus result, which moreover are dovetailed with each other. Only the later bass entrances form regular two-measure units (mm. 8–9, 10–11). Simultaneously, a rising line in eighth notes appears for the first time in the instrumental bass, which joins with the entry of the horns without an upbeat, as before (mm. 11, 13). In the continuation of this line the vocal and instrumental bass are first brought together (mm. 14ff.). Of course, the increasing eighth-note motion already appears in the second vocal entry, which forms a thematic variant due to its syllabic declamation (mm. 7–8, "und wie ein Hammer, der Felsen zerschlägt"/"and like a hammer that breaketh the rock"). In the continuation there are two eighth notes on the second and fourth beat of each measure; the dramatic melisma in m. 14, therefore, does not express the word "Hammer" in isolation but rather is prepared in m. 8. The intensification finally leads into the extensive chromatic ascent of both bass parts in quarter notes (mm. 15–17). Where the coordination of the basses leads to the cadence, the strings for the first time take part in the material in that they take over the melisma from m. 14, which now has motivic status, and dissolve it into sixteenth notes (mm. 19–20). And in the confirmation of the cadential group the bass voices separate from each other in contrary motion, while the clarinets join with the vocal bass line (mm. 20–24). The last two measures in the A part restate the first two of the introduction, forming the bridge to the B part, which starts directly in m. 26.

The middle section contrasts in several ways. First of all, the declamation values become reduced to half and quarter notes, while the accompaniment by all the instruments provides harmonic support in long-held note values; in contradistinction to the rising melodic gestures in the A section, the vocal part tends toward descending lines; and whereas the A section modulated only from the tonic to the dominant, the B section is characterized by harmonic arrangement in falling fifths (F♯–B, B–e, and after a deceptive cadence C–F–B♭ between mm. 26 and 43). Despite all the differences, though, the fundamental relationships to the outer parts must not be overlooked (see Example 6.18, mm. 26–31). At m. 26 and

Example 6.18
Elijah, no. 17, Aria, mm. 26–31

again at m. 32 the instrumental basses take over the tremolo accompaniment of the strings from the A section; it also permeates the violins in mm. 31 and 35, but in these very measures there occurs in the bass the rising line that prepared the characteristic melisma on the word "Hammer" at m. 11. This figure itself appears, however, starting in m. 35, in every other measure in the bass pattern, and already in the B section it prepares the reprise, in that from m. 43—at the bottom of the harmonic descent in B♭ major—the rhythmic germ of the A section appears in quarter and eighth notes in the triadic unit. Because B♭ major functions as Neapolitan in relation to the overall cadential movement toward the tonic A minor, the contrasting sections are connected at the boundaries by harmonic and rhythmic transition. The reprise, for its part, in the A' section is varied in the sense that hardly a single measure from A returns exactly as it was before, with the exception of the beginning (mm. 49–53 corresponding to mm. 3–7). The sequence of the connecting vocal line is accompanied by all the instruments with chordal strokes (mm. 53–56), and the coordination of the layers from A (mm. 19–20) now overlaps in the alternation between winds and strings (mm. 59–61, 63–66, 67–69), before both bass parts are then brought together again (mm. 71–81). In the very last measures before the coda the motivic cell occurs on the dominant, alternating upward and downward in all the instruments; the process thus finds its goal in the coordination of the layers (mm. 78–82). The coda, finally, begins in the vocal part alone, which declaims in even quarter notes, while the instruments come back again only at the cadence, returning in the postlude once more to the structure of the introduction.

If the first section is thus marked primarily by the variants of its rhythmic impulses, the middle section contrasts by means of its motivic and harmonic structure; its disguised rhythmic references connect back to the closing section, whose variants lead to increasing assimilation of the layers. The conventional reference to the aria no. 5 from Handel's *Messiah* ("But who may abide") as a model has little to contribute to the understanding of this structure. In that case there arises from the D-minor Larghetto in $\frac{3}{8}$ meter the fast contrasting section in $\frac{4}{4}$ meter ("For He is like a refiner's fire"), in which the voice is accompanied by the rapid tremolo of the strings. Not only does the form differ in its multiple alternations between sections, however, but in Handel's case the tremolo functions over throbbing eighth notes in the basso continuo as a steady timbral foundation, and aside from sweeping coloratura no comparable development is achieved in the movement. Because of their different presuppositions, therefore, no comparable process exists, and the surface similarities shrink away into a mere topos within an entirely different context. Yet Elijah's aria no. 26, "Es ist genug"/"It is enough," is also not uncommonly understood as an adaptation of Bach's model "Es ist vollbracht" from the *St. John Passion*. The analogy certainly fails, once one gets beyond the falling melodic gesture of the opening motive and the alternation of tempos between the section of the forms. In Bach's case the contrast of the sections is sharpened by the entrance of the trumpet and by the change to the relative major key; in the framing sections, however, which most obviously suggest a comparison, Bach's aria forms a strictly contrapuntal structure, which gains its continuity from the linear function of the voices. In contrast to that, Mendelssohn's aria is marked by the alternating exchange between the voices and their functions, which primarily makes possible the incremental development of the movement's process.

In the aria no. 26, "Es ist genug"/"It is enough" (after Job 7: 16 and I Cor. 19: 4, 10), the sections contrast so much externally that hardly any perceptible relationships still remain to make the form resemble a conventional da capo aria. To the Adagio in $\frac{3}{4}$ meter (mm. 1–45) is contrasted the Allegro vivace in $\frac{4}{4}$ meter (mm. 46–97); the Adagio comes again in the same meter, after which the $\frac{3}{4}$ meter returns (mm. 98–100, 101–18). The transitions between the sections, first of all, establish an equilibrium between the contrasts. The A section is in F♯ minor; in its last measures, however, it remains open on the dominant C♯, and then the middle section begins in F♯ minor. Conversely, the middle section ends on a dominant, after which the last section begins again on the tonic. While the instrumental part in the A section develops from sparse, chordal accompaniment to increasingly dense scoring, in the B section it is conversely reduced from a motivic function to increasingly chordal accompaniment. In the same manner the later relationships between the voices also shift in the course of the movement. Typical for the first section—as in no. 17—is the relationship between the instrumental and vocal bass part, which, however, is modified here into a duet of soloistic partners in the same register. The first measure presents the model of accompaniment with even eighth notes separated by rests on each beat, and over that the solo cello plays in cantabile melodic arches in regular eighth-measure segments (mm. 2–5, 6–9). The bass voice then takes up this line but abbreviates it by tightening up the cadence at seven measures (mm. 10–13, 14–16; see Example 6.19). At the internal division point of the period (mm. 13–14) the cellos bridge the caesura, supplementing the vocal line for the first time with a variant of the opening motive. At m. 17 the partners break up into one-measure units with variants of the opening motive, and when at m. 20 the two voices are combined, the other string parts for the first time depart from the accompaniment function, to take up the cantabile diction of the vocal part. The equality of the solo partners culminates in their parallel motion in thirds, while all the other instruments drop out (mm. 26–29). After the last return of the opening structure in the interlude (mm. 29–34) the vocal part alone dominates, and the instrumental scoring, including the cello, is subordinated to it in even eighth notes. At the same time the vocal melodic style, which from the beginning was determined by syllabic declamation, changes to terse repeated notes, and while the opening motive sounds once more in the bass register (m. 40), it gradually loses the character of the cantabile adagio. The recitative-like character is further supported by the wide-ranging harmony, which extends from F♯ minor through A and D major to the diminished-seventh chord, until it stalls on the Neapolitan in F♯ minor and then remains open-ended on the dominant (mm. 34–45).

Example 6.19
Elijah, no. 26, Aria, mm. 10–16

The contrasting beginning of the middle section is simultaneously linked to the first part by subtle references (see Example 6.20). The terse motive of the

Example 6.20
Elijah, no. 26, Aria, mm. 46–51

violin clearly refers to the main motive of aria no. 17, with the characteristic rhythm of quarter and eighth notes, though in the first measure of the Allegro the bass line marks out the same notes with which the cantabile began (mm. 46f. corresponding to m. 2: c♯' a f♯ e♯). The instrumental opening motive is taken up and pursued in varied form by the bass part from m. 48 on; the following group (mm. 52ff.)

forms a further variant; the rhythmic formula of three anacrusic quarter notes, which was already introduced in m. 46 by the instruments, begins the following phrases as well, however, so that the changing lines of text are linked by rhythmic analogs in the instrumental part. Moreover, the vocal part beginning in m. 61 forms a three-step sequence of two-measure units, which are connected to the upbeat formula in the instrumental part in every other measure. The cadential groups at mm. 68 and 72 are opened in analogous fashion, and this same model controls the continuation up to m. 84. The terse declamation of the words "Und ich bin allein übrig geblieben"/"And I, even I only am left" initiates the closing of the middle section in the expansive triadic pattern, which alludes to the diction of the first recitative from the beginning of the entire work. At the same time the anacrusic figure of three quarter notes in the instrumental scoring is neutralized by the appended repeated notes, but its legato variant, which from m. 91 on permeates the outer instrumental voices in alternating measures, establishes itself concomitantly as an anticipation of the opening motive "Es ist genug"/"It is enough" and thereby prepares the return of the framing section (see Example 6.21). After the aforementioned bridge measures, the structure of the opening is restored in the closing section, though here the canon between instrumental and vocal parts acts as a structural intensification (mm. 101–6). The last measures, finally employ the motivic variant from the transition between the sections (mm. 98ff.), which appears with its dotted form eight times in the alternation of the two solo voices (mm. 110–17). After this dialogue of the two partners, which generated the movement and which returned repeatedly throughout its process, the end returns to it in an intensified concentration.

Elijah's last solo is no. 37, "Ja, es sollen wohl Berge weichen"/"For the mountains shall depart," which is marked in the German score as "Arioso" and in English as "Air." In contrast to the combination of texts in the aria no. 26, the textual basis here is limited to a single Bible verse (Is. 54: 10). That an obbligato solo instrument, specifically the oboe, thoroughly permeates the movement immediately suggests the sound of Bach arias with oboe obbligato and string accompaniment. The highly continuous rhythm, too, might recall Baroque models, but it distances itself considerably from them in its constant melodic flow, which gets along without contrapuntal elaboration in order thereby to bring out the disguised motivic network. The proverb text appears in the Bible as God's promise to the prophet Isaiah ("but my steadfast love shall not depart from you"), but here it is reconstructed by the exchange of personal pronouns into Elijah's prayer ("but Thy kindness shall not depart from me"). The text falls into three sentence segments: after the opening comparison ("Berge weichen und Hügel hinfallen"/"and the hills, the hills be removed") follow assurance ("aber deine Gnade"/"but thy kindness") and certainty ("der Bund deines Friedens"/"the covenant of thy peace"). Nevertheless, the musical setting reveals no conventional partitioning, for the return of the tonic F major at m. 24 arrives with a different melodic structure and no motivic reprise. The last part of the four-measure introduction forms only the elaboration of the tonal goal, which has already been

Example 6.21
Elijah, no. 26, Aria, mm. 91–101

achieved, so that the melodic cell is concentrated in the first three measures. The rhythmic structure in $^6_4$ meter is marked by the fact that the fundamental bass always begins on the downbeat of the measure, while the oboe part follows only on the second beat, so that its opening ascent leads quasi-anacrusically to the first beat of the following measure. The process of the movement is held in suspense throughout by this counterbalance between full-measure and upbeat units. The first melodic ascent of the oboe line in even, legato quarter notes spans a sixth (a'–f²), at its second instance it is compressed to a third (a'–c²), and the third time it plays about the fourth from the tonic note (f'–bb'). What at first suggests a sequence turns out to be a chain of motivic variants. The strings accompany mainly in repeated quarter notes, but within them hidden voice-leadings emerge that interact with the oboe melody and thereby obtain their own motivic quality (Va, mm. 1–2, 2–3, 3 etc.). In the cadential measure itself such inconspicuous melodic gestures permeate almost all the string parts (m. 4). That these must be understood as motivic becomes evident with the entrance of the bass voice (see Example 6.22, mm. 5–10), for the vocal part, starting in unison with the first violin, takes up only the first three notes of the melody (a–b♭–c'). While the first violin extends the line as in the introduction, it is bent out of shape in the bass with the leap of a seventh and a change of octave register (mm. 5–6, c'–d), and the formula of the third starts over sequentially (m. 6, f–g–a). As the relationship of the bass to the violin part thus reveals that the formula of the third is intended as a variant of the melodic cell, it now becomes clear just how thoroughly the entire movement is controlled motivically from measure to measure. In the first place, the harmonic disposition in the introduction and also in the continuation circumscribes only a static expansion of the cadential framework; all the concentration therefore focuses on the melodic variants, which appear in the vocal part as continuous waves between rising and falling segments. The first four-measure vocal phrase at m. 5 extends to m. 9 with the modified cadence; only now is the opening ascent of a sixth taken over in the bass, answered by the oboe (mm. 9–10). That the following two-measure unit relies on a sequence must be perceived from the oboe, while the vocal part reveals a further variant (mm. 11–12). When the cadence in A minor is

Example 6.22
Elijah, **no. 37, Aria, mm. 5–10**

prepared in m. 14, the thematic opening appears once again in the first violin, while its spinning-out in the bass voice returns to static variants (mm. 13–15). The phrase-group in mm. 15–23 would, in any case, be perceived as the inner section ("und der Bund"/"and the covenant"), but instead of motivic contrasts the instrumental scoring is permeated by continuous further variants of the central motive. The syntactic elements of the text thus appear as directly connected, not set apart but rather bound together motivically. The series of variants in the instrumental part permits the compact declamation of the text in the vocal part, which, in turn, is related to the oboe part by free imitation (mm. 16, 18, 21–22). In these measures the harmony also expands, which, after achieving the subdominant B♭ major, leads back to the tonic by way of a chromatic rise in the bass line with secondary dominants (mm. 18–24). Rather than the first text segment, however, the two following ones appear here in a seemingly new melodic version (see Example 6.23, mm. 23–26). Yet in reality still another motivic variant is presented, for in the vocal part the rising sixth emerges again in the melodic continuation (mm. 23–26, e–c'), and it is then answered by the oboe in its original form (mm. 26ff.). In the coda, conversely, the oboe comes back, the vocal part

Example 6.23
Elijah, **no. 37, Aria, mm.23–26**

descends through a sixth (mm. 30–33, g–B) over the repeated pedal notes of the basses, the opening registral shift (mm. 5–6) is expanded to the leap of a tenth upward (m. 33), from there the vocal part descends in a last variant of the formula of the third, and the movement fades away in the last thematic statement of the oboe. Taking the whole together, it is evident that the entire process is produced out of a cell with its variants, which at first covers the interval of a sixth and then contracts to a third. The movement achieves its concentration from the constant exchange of such variants, which along with its highly cantabile continuity makes it a model of variational development.

THE CHORAL MOVEMENTS IN *ELIJAH*

The choral movements in *Elijah* also comprise a multiplicity of compositional structures, which extends considerably beyond the possibilities explored in *St. Paul*. This spectrum cannot be laid out between the poles of choral fugue and homophonic declamation, but in its wealth of solutions it also includes unexpected hybrids and combinations. A surprising heightening of the declamatory and harmonic accents combines, however, with the subtle nuance that was already achieved several times in *St. Paul*. The flexibility in function of these movements corresponds to their changing differentiation in details, as a few examples will demonstrate.

Among the four large movements that frame the two parts as opening and closing, actually only the concluding chorus no. 42 is a fugue in the strict sense. While the multiply staggered introductory chorus devolves into a choral recitative, its counterpart in the second part is linked to the preceding soprano aria, which itself manifests a highly complex layout. By contrast, the chorus no. 20 at the end of the first part initially appears to be rather conventional in that it takes its closing function as the occasion for a festal tutti movement. The text (Ps. 93: 3–4), of course, does not represent a general song of praise but rather simultaneously both takes up the miracle of rain as the last segment of the action and also refers to the prophet's opening curse (see Diagram 6.2).

Immediately characteristic is the dotted rhythm, which in the first measure already stands against the fanfarelike ascent in the strings. The thematic model in the bass responds to that with a falling melodic gesture that contains this same dotted formula four times, and this is promptly taken up by the chordal tutti. The dotted rhythm thereby acquires a central function that determines the entire process. It is a presupposition of the formal design that the two contrasting segments of text ("Dank sei dir Gott"/"Thanks be to God"—"Die Wasserströme erheben sich"/"The waters gather, they rush along") are not restricted to separate parts of the movement but rather are presented from the outset in direct juxtaposition (mm. 1–19, 20–35). To be sure, the rhythm then appears to alter at the second segment of text, as the realistically rushing upward and downward sixteenth-note figures become prominent in the orchestra. The choral setting in chordal declamation is integrated into them, however, constantly recalling the dotted rhythm of the first text segment, and all the more so because the dotted values are accentuated by high pitch and by their metrical position. Moreover, a chain of entries on the same pitch level at m. 28 suggests an emphasis on the principle that was already presented in the beginning in the alternation of bass and tutti and later becomes modified into a compact canon. The first text segment returns again after the second already at m. 35, but it is immediately combined with the second, so that not only the two layers of the text but also the characteristic rhythms of their accompaniments are superimposed (see Example 6.24). Certainly, one can hardly call this a contrapuntal combination, but while the sixteenth notes in the strings are continued, the dotted-rhythm style receives further accentuation by the winds. Instead of a contrapuntal synthesis of themes—as is often the case in *St. Paul*—rhythmic and

Diagram 6.2
Structure of *Elijah*, no. 20, Chorus

Part:	A			B				A'			
Mm.:	1–19	20–35	35–53	54–64	65–73	73–82	82–92	92–100	100–22	123–30	131–40
Text:	1	2a	1+2a	2b	3	1+2b	3	3	1	2a	1
Key:	E♭	E♭	E♭–B♭	B♭–C	C–D♭	D♭–d♭	D♭–d♭	D–E♭	E♭	E♭	E♭

Text 1: Dank sei dir Gott/Thanks be to God

Text 2a–b: Die Wasserströme erheben sich—Die Wasserwogen sind groß/
The waters gather, they rush along—The stormy billows are high

Text 3: Doch der Herr ist noch größer/But the Lord is above them

Example 6.24
Elijah, no. 20, Chorus

a. mm. 6–11

declamatory models thus overlap. In addition, there is a first harmonic expansion by way of secondary dominants (mm. 45 ff.), which admittedly is quickly interrupted by the cadence on the dominant to the first text segment. This open-ended harmony then leads to the second text segment, whose chordal declamation is connected by way of the stepwise sequence from B♭ to C major (mm. 54–64). The literary variants of the text (2a-b in Diagram 6.2) carry little musical weight in this process.

After the double presentation of the first segments of the text, the middle of the movement now opens with an unexpected caesura that corresponds to the appeal in the third text segment, "Doch der Herr ist noch größer in der Höhe"/"But the Lord is above them, and Almighty." After the strongly marked entry of the bass alone the entries of the tenor and alto follow directly a semitone above and then a third higher than that. Over the sustained bass note c' there now sound d♭' and then f'; only with the arrival of the soprano on d♭² does the dissonance resolve with the bass's descending second, out of which the cadence to D♭ emerges. The dissonant layering thus leads the harmony a minor second upward from C to D♭

Example 6.24, continued

b. mm. 22–23

(see Example 6.25) in the briefest space. The first text segments then begin again
in Db major, yet the harmony quickly shifts to Db minor (mm. 73–82).
Throughout, therefore, ten-measure groups result, which are interlocked with each
other. Meanwhile the third text segment ("Doch der Herr") follows once again;
with the same chord progression in harsh dissonance the movement now shifts
from Db to D major, and as the final segment of the chain the progression is
repeated immediately as a shift from D to Eb, whereby the tonic is reached (mm.
82–91 and secured 92–99).

In the third and last section of the movement one would expect a simultaneous
combination of the themes, as occurs many times in *St. Paul* and not uncommonly
in *Elijah*. Because the movement did not take a contrapuntal construction as its
point of departure, however, its outcome cannot produce a linear combination. In

Example 6.24, continued

c. mm. 35–40

conformity with the sense of the whole text, its second segment is incorporated only once, and that in much more limited fashion (mm. 123–28), while the further process is otherwise occupied only with the first segment. After the appeal with the pledge of the middle section, therefore, it is appropriate for the movement to conclude with the song of praise, which is no longer overshadowed by other impulses. Moreover, the entries in the soprano, tenor, and alto resolve on the tonic, in the course of which the soprano and tenor form a canon at the unison (mm. 100–104). Correspondingly, the entries of the upper voices follow on changing scale degrees over a dominant pedal point at one-measure intervals (mm. 114–23), which again produce compact canons. The entire phase of the movement is accompanied by strings in sixteenth notes, as they originally belonged to the second text segment. As its words are only shortly thereafter declaimed on the tonic, the chordal declamation of the first segment of the text in an expanded cadence forms the close of the movement.

Example 6.24c, continued

The movement owes its continuous process of development not only to its declamatory terseness and the unrelenting impulse of the dotted rhythmic style. Just as definitive for this is the metrical linking of the measure groups, which do not proceed in regular periodic fashion, while the well-planned harmonic disposition is accentuated by the abruptly dissonant layering of sound in the middle part. The path from the opening overlapping of the texts to their separation at the end after the contrary intensification in the middle might at first appear to be merely a simplification. In this way this process does not only correspond to the sense of the text; much rather in this case the function of the closing song of praise remains in reserve for the movement's end, without being taken for granted from the beginning. Precisely by that means the tension of the entire event again becomes effective in the closing chorus.

The intimate, songlike choruses, on the other hand—which were always typical of Mendelssohn, though with changing significance—represent a very different character. They found their distinctive stamp already in *St. Paul*, but they achieved a highly differentiated form in *Elijah*. In its definitive version the quartet no. 15, "Wirf dein Anliegen auf den Herrn"/"Cast thy burden upon the Lord," is based—as noted earlier—on a combination of psalm verses (Ps. 55: 22, 108: 5, 25:

Example 6.25
Elijah, no. 20, Chorus, mm. 65-73

3), while the first version still had a chorale stanza as its text. In the final form, the only one heard in Germany, probably only a very well informed listener would recognize that the upper voice is related to the chorale melody "O Gott, du frommer Gott" in a version that goes back to the Meiningen hymnbook of 1693 (see Example 6.7). This fact fades into the background just as much for today's audiences in Germany, however, as it formerly did in the Anglo-Saxon territory. Because of the subtlety with which the melody is introduced, its use becomes an indirect reference. Just as the chorale recedes in *Elijah*, so this procedure corresponds to the hidden chorale citations with which Mendelssohn was familiar from Bach's work. To be sure, the melody was severely altered in the reworking; between its phrases in the cantional setting for the voices there enter, at varying intervals—after line 1, 3, 5, and 7–9—concise interludes, which are limited to ascending triad figures in the violins with chordal support in the orchestra. In the last measure, however, the flute plays—like a reference within the reference—the incipit of the preceding aria, "Herr Gott Abrahams"/"Lord God of Abraham." With that, on the one hand, the ecstatic realm of the chorale movement is concluded, while, on the other hand, by the same means it is integrated into the overall context.

In a completely different way a lyrical inflection marks the choruses nos. 29 and 32; both exhibit contrapuntal phases, but they set them up in opposite ways. While no. 29 evolves from a cantabile beginning into a concise fugue in the center, a contrapuntal intensity, hardly traceable behind the appearance of songlike melody, characterizes no. 32 throughout.

In no. 29, beginning in m. 2, the soprano intones the text "Siehe, der Hüter Israels schläft noch schlummert nicht"/"He, watching over Israel, slumbers not nor sleeps" (Ps. 121:4) above the strings' eighth-note triplets (see Example 6.8). The thematic model is based on an expanded cadence over a tonic pedal point, which is resolved only at its close by the dominant movement in the bass (mm. 1–5). As the constant triplet motion, like the vocal melody, is suited to an expansive tonal range, a unique balance of forces arises (see Example 6.26). This, however, responds precisely to the meaning of the text, whose promise is grounded on the fact that the watcher really does not slumber. At the soprano entrance the fifth of the tonic key is resolved up a second, the added sixth achieves a subdominant function in the next measure, the vocal line soars upward by a sixth, while its cadence is marked by the bass progression. The analogous entrance in the tenor is

Example 6.26
Elijah, no. 29, Chorus, mm. 1–5

complemented by the descending line in the soprano (mm. 6–9); the contracted textual variant in the alto is then set to the melodic inversion of the incipit, which the bass then takes over (mm. 9–13). After a step-by-step filling out of the vocal ensemble, the opening section of the form closes with the first full-voiced presentation of the thematic model, the cadence of which is extended (mm. 14–19). The middle part, "Wenn du mitten in Angst wandelst"/"Shouldst thou, walking in grief, languish" (Ps. 138: 7) begins in F♯ minor. When the triplet motion continues, however, one at first expects that the entrance of the tenor will lead to an analogous structure. The new model, though, which, after a scalar ascent through a sixth, cadences on the fifth, C♯ major, turns out to be the theme of a fugato. The further entrances at first sort themselves out in the regular alternation of *dux* and *comes* (mm. 19–27); after a modulating insertion follow two thematic entrances on B in the outer voices (mm. 29–33); and the last series of entrances is laid out in a rising sequence in alto, soprano, and bass (d, e, f♯, mm. 33–38). The doubled cadence opens in chordal declamation on the dominant, C♯ major (mm. 40–43), and with the succeeding tenor entrance one expects the continuation of the fugato. At that point, however, the motive of the first part of the form appears, and with the overlapping of the two themes the textual layers refer to each other (see Example 6.27, mm. 43–49). The closing phrase group, in which the thematic

Example 6.27
Elijah, no. 29, Chorus, mm. 44–47

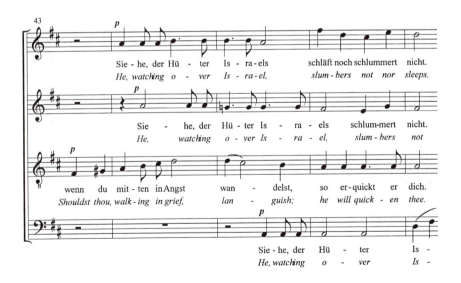

content fades into the background, then forms little more than an extended cadence, but it is characterized by the expansive melodic descent in the upper voice in two phases (mm. 51–59, 59–67). While the cadential area is extended by secondary dominants, the chromatic coloration of the upper voice again hints at the middle part. Between those groups of measures at the end, which are entirely based on a pedal point, the vocal linearity unfolds once again in the chorus a cappella. Furthermore, it is hardly a coincidence that the relation between outer sections in D major and a scalar fugato theme in F♯ minor is also found in the chorus no. 41, "Aber einer erwacht vor Mitternacht"/"But the Lord from the north hath raised one" (Is. 41: 25, 42: 1, 11: 1-2). The text here speaks of the one who "arises," since the Spirit "rests" on him. While the entrance on the fifth of the scale here is extended to the ascending lines, in place of the fugato there appears a concise canonic sequence with the theme falling through a fifth (mm. 13, 34).

The chorus no. 32, "Wer bis an des Ende beharrt"/"He that shall endure to the end" (see Example 6.9), also begins with a similar diction to no. 29 (after Matt. 10: 22 or 24:13, or Mark 13: 13). The two choruses frame the recitative no. 30, in which the prophet's lament replies to an angel's exhortation, the instrumental citation from the middle part of the aria no. 26 referring to the corresponding words ("ich habe geeifert in dem Herrn"/"I have been very jealous for the Lord"). In its reduction the alto aria no. 31, "Sei stille dem Herrn"/"O rest in the Lord" (after Ps. 37: 4-8), prepares the way for movement no. 32, in which the instruments remain *colla parte* with the chorus almost throughout. While the first measure circles around the tonic F major, the second completes the cadence using the primary harmonies. The first two two-measure units (a and b) correspond to the two phrases of the text in a harmonic and metrical analogy. As segment a is characterized by repeated notes and syllabic declamation, segment b stands out by expansion through a fifth with an ascending melisma (see Example 6.28). Already from the beginning, however, the notes of segment b appear in the lower voices of the chordal ensemble (bass f–g–a, tenor c'–b♭), and the delayed bass entrance in m. 3 anticipates the linear dispersal of the chordal construction. The third

Example 6.28
Elijah, no. 32, Chorus, mm. 1–4

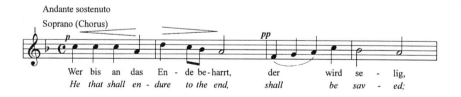

two-measure unit takes up the first in a free voice-exchange (mm. 5–6, segment a in the tenor), but with the first return to b in m. 7 the contrapuntal deployment begins. When motive b in the tenor is answered by its inversion in the alto, the two versions turn out to have equal validity. Motive a is added again at m. 11, which from this point on is continuously linked simultaneously with variants of b. While, on one hand, the periodicity of two-measure units within the individual voices is accepted, on the other hand, the measure groups are overlapped by the staggering of the entrances at measure or half-measure intervals. The result is the impression of a static fluctuation of songlike, cantabile phrases, which constantly intersect each other (see Example 6.29). The expansion of the harmonic radius is created

Example 6.29
Elijah, no. 32, Chorus, mm. 17–22

by extensive sequences, which, for their part, refer back to the songlike core of the movement. Thus, for example, the group at m. 13 starts out from D minor and that at m. 15 from E♭, and the bass entrance on d at m. 14 corresponds to its expanded version a whole tone higher at m. 20. The last series of entrances with segment a in whole- and half-measure intervals links back to the tonic with a series of rising fourths (mm. 24–27, d–g–c–f). The following entrances of segment b assemble the linear statements chordally and form a new sequential group (mm. 28–32, 33–37). At the cadence the incremental narrowing and sinking of the tonal space are coupled; at the same time, the instruments are emancipated for the first time, and their entrance in m. 34 leads motive b upward in a soaring fashion. Here it reaches the third f–a, which is held over the bar line, but it completes the D-minor sonority whose root lies in a low register in the choral unison. In the entire process segment a appears with twelve and b with twenty-two entrances; the thirty-four entrances of the two-measure models would seem to require sixty-eight measures. That the movement nevertheless comprises only thirty-seven measures therefore depends on the compression of the simultaneous working out of the motives. This alone makes clear the linear intensity that is concealed behind the restrained cantabile style.

Even such choruses, which at first seem so simple, thus reveal only upon closer analysis how subtly and sometimes how intricately they are laid out. At the same time, they have their noninterchangeable function, in that they form the contemplative center points in the individual scenes. Still more diverse and hence also more powerful are the great, multiply staged choruses, of which only three will be considered in more depth here: besides the opening chorus, the corresponding movement no. 5 at the end of the first block, as well as the chorus no. 34, which has to solve a particularly tricky problem.

The introductory chorus no. 1 (see Diagram 6.3) combines several Old Testament texts (Jer. 8: 19-20, 1 Kings 17: 7, Lam. 4: 4); it is connected to the

Diagram 6.3
Structure of *Elijah*, no. 1, Chorus

Part:	Prelude	Fugato	Insertion	Combination	Resolution	Choral recit.
Mm.:	1–8/9	10–35	35–41	41–48	49–58	59–60
Text:	1	2+3	4	2+3+4	1, 2, 3	. . .

Text 1:	Hilf, Herr! Willst du uns denn gar vertilgen?/Help , Lord! Wilt thou quite destroy us?
Text 2:	Die Ernte ist vergangen, der Sommer ist dahin,/The harvest now is over, the summer days are gone
Text 3:	und uns ist keine Hilfe gekommen!/And yet no power cometh to help us!
Text 4:	Will denn der Herr nicht mehr Gott sein in Zion?/Will then the Lord be no more God in Zion?

preceding overture and consequently also to the opening recitative. While the overture combines the cadential formula of the first recitative with the fugue theme, it devolves into sixteenth-note figures in the strings, which derive from the spinning out of a split-off segment of the theme; the augmentation of this figure into eighth notes is continued, however, in the first entrance of the chorus with falling and rising triads. The chordal cry "Hilf, Herr"/"Help, Lord" (mm. 1-8) is, of course, derived from only an expanded cadence, and the shift of tonic and dominant is at first colored only by the diminished seventh chord (mm. 1–2, 3–4). Since its third lies in the bass, when it is eliminated, the other notes in m. 5—as constituents of a seventh chord on C—can lead to F major and then to B♭ major. The sonority over the bass note B♭, however, becomes in m. 6 the basis of a secondary dominant seventh chord on E with a flatted fifth (i.e., a French augmented sixth chord), whereby the double tritone (E–B♭, G♯–D) brings about the tension of the double leading tone (B♭–G♯), which then resolves cadentially to the tonic D minor.

With the upbeat to m. 10, the fugato theme begins; its first part, after the leap of a fourth, connects the chromatically filled-in descending third to upward skipping motion across a sixth (b), and its continuation outlines the main harmonic notes in rather recitative-like diction (c). The two themes are again arranged according to the corresponding text segments (b: "Die Ernte ist vergangen"/"The harvest now is over"; c: "und uns ist keine Hilfe gekommen"/"And yet no power cometh to help us"). The first entrance as *dux* in the tenor is answered by the *comes* in the alto (m. 14), but only after the soprano already takes up the continuation separately with segment c (m. 13). As a consequence, from the beginning both segments are connected in such a way that one can hardly decide whether the procedure resembles that of a double fugue or a stretto (see Example 6.30). In the first combination at m. 14 the two segments are still handled quite independently; they continue to be maintained rather distinctly in the course of further concentration from m. 20 (especially in mm. 27–31). The declamatory buildup (c, mm. 32f.; b, mm. 34f.) is followed at m. 35 by a third segment, "Will denn der Herr nicht mehr Gott sein"/"Will then the Lord be no more God." Its entry is not only surprising for its sudden piano; for the first time there appears in the orchestra a characteristic accompaniment in repeated sixteenth notes broken up by rests. The threefold chordal declamation of d (mm. 35–41) nevertheless leads directly to the most intensive combination, in which all three segments are linked (mm. 41–48). While the orchestral accompaniment is retained, the soprano freely extends the last entrance of segment b, which is then complemented note for note by the orchestra and sequenced yet again, so that in the fugato (mm. 45–48) the instrumental part for the first time acquires an obbligato function. Of course, the combination can be clarified if one reduces the thematic segments to elementary gestures such as repeated notes or triads, and the motives are unquestionably designed just so that they can be combined (see Example 6.31). Not only is the flexibility of the pairing astonishing, however, but even more the individual character of the particular thematic segments themselves. For all that, the

Example 6.30
Elijah, no. 1, Chorus, mm. 10–15

combination is not the goal of the process; rather, the coherence of the movement dissolves into single entrances, in which the head of the fugato subject is combined with the drawn-out cries of the opening. Even before the homorhythmic closure of segment c, the music forecasts that diction into which the movement then devolves in the choral recitative, which on its part prepares the succeeding duet with psalmodic interjections by the chorus.

The chorus no. 5, "Aber der Herr sieht es nicht"/"Yet doth the Lord see it not," to a complex combination of texts (Ps. 2: 4; Deut. 28: 22, 2; Exod. 20: 5–6), forms the end of the first block. The movement is in *alla breve* meter throughout, but the opening Allegro vivace in C minor (mm. 1–66) contrasts with the closing part in

Example 6.31
Elijah, no. 1, Chorus, mm. 44–48

C major (mm. 89–138), and mediating between them is a section marked "Grave." The outcry of the beginning, divided between bass and alto, is immediately answered by the homorhythmic tutti (mm. 1–4, 5–6); both segments are repeated on the subdominant, so that the cadence is extended (mm. 7–14). Directly thereafter follows a fugato, which introduces two new motivic ideas: "Der Fluch"/"His curse" (a) and "Er wird uns verfolgen"/"His wrath will pursue us" (b). While the start of the theme is characterized by the interlocking of two falling diminished fifths (f^2–b', c^2–f♯'), the contrasting motive is distinguished by markedly syllabic declamation. The two are at first worked out separately (a: mm. 15–25; b: mm. 25–42), but the movement becomes accentuated throughout by dissonances that refer to the diminished fifth as the framing interval. From m. 43 fugato theme a is incorporated, and in mm. 52–55 both themes are overlapped, though without producing a conventional double fugue (see Example 6.32). The

Example 6.32
Elijah, no. 1, chorus, mm. 52–56

concluding declamation of segment b encounters the repeated tonic pedal point (at m. 59), and at this point the solemn Grave follows as a bridge section. The text recalls the First Commandment, and its intonation evokes the typus of cantional setting. In addition to the melodic increase and reduction come chord progressions, however, that seem to sound from a time long past, because they make one think of modal sonorities (e.g., c–Bb–Eb at m. 74, c–f–Db–f at m. 85). The opening to C major is reached in a half cadence, so that in this key God's promise can be unfolded in majestic columns of sound. The lapidary effect does not depend simply on the harmonic contrast; in the *alla breve* meter, rather, the contrapuntal and declamatory intensity of the first half of the movement is answered by the expansion of the broad tonal areas. By this means in the middle the seventh chord is built up in strata over the pedal point on G by the staggering of the entrances up to the ninth chord (mm. 109–12), an analogous second entry is based on the pedal point on C (at m. 116), before the movement, after a radiant beginning, concludes in relaxed chains of sonority. If the parts of the form contrast by their very different styles, the middle of the movement can be associated with a layer of composition that dates back to the historic past.

The choral movement no. 34 forms the center of the penultimate block in the second part. The narrative of the appearance of the Lord does not depend on a composite text but is based on the story in 1 Kings 19: 11–12. According to Hiller's report, it forms the core of the work, and thus earlier drafts might have gone into its conception. As in no. 5, the layout consists of two parts, which contrast by their use of E minor and E major (mm. 1–114, 115–91). More decisively than in no. 5, however, here fugal or simply contrapuntal impulses recede into the background; determinative, rather, is the multiple layering of powerful sonorous arches. In the A-part one must distinguish the threefold evocation, wherein the "mighty wind" is followed first by the "earthquake" and then by the "fire" (mm. 1–35, 36–71, 71–115). The three-clause text, with its depiction of nature, corresponds to three phases of the movement, which, despite all the analogies that can be drawn among them, exhibit marked differences. At the beginning, as orchestral introduction comes the abrupt expansion of the tonic sonority over a pedal point, into which the main functions are interpolated (see Example 6.33). There then follows the choral cry in unison "Der Herr ging vorüber"/"Behold, God the Lord passed by." The succeeding main phases are also based on a chain of pedal points, until at the end the negative experience is resumed in chordal declamation: "Aber der Herr war nicht"/"But the Lord was not." At the same time between the three phases an internal intensification is completed, in that in the first entry the voice pairs resolve as an apparent two-part canon at the unison without actually forming a four-voice texture. The harmonic filling out of the meager vocal part remains exclusively left to the chords in the orchestra. The second entry then leads in m. 50 to four-voice texture, out of which at m. 53 a genuine four-part canon at the unison results (see Example 6.34). The third entry begins at m. 72 as a chordal tutti, from which a two-part canon in parallel thirds develops at m. 86. The tension is based, first of all, on the contradictory

Example 6.33
Elijah, no. 34, Chorus, mm. 1–11

relationship of contrapuntal canons to the sonorous surfaces of the pedal points.
The differentiation of the three entries is not just the product of their choral closing
parts, which begin a cappella and pianissimo, as opposed to which the end joins its
dynamic intensification with chromatic voice-leading and orchestral accents. On
the contrary, the differentiation of the phases belongs even more to their harmonic
disposition, as well. The first canonic passage is based on E for ten measures,
followed then by six and four measures on D and G. The second phase—after a
six-measure opening on B—across 4+4 measures on B and G♯ and 6+4 on G and
F—reaches its goal in three measures on F♯. In the last phase the harmonic motion
culminates in a constant change of fundamental tones (four measures on C, two
each on B♭, A, G, etc.). At the end a series of falling fifths at the interval of a half
measure results (mm. 99–107), which leads from B to F, the F functioning as
Neapolitan in the cadence to E major. The process of intensification is therefore
based on the compelling chain of variants of analogous models, in the middle of
which stands the canonic compression, while at the end the harmonic progression
is brought to the fore. The B-section apparently works in a much simpler fashion,

Example 6.33, continued

but it is similarly constructed in stages, even though its development is accomplished much less strikingly. After the opening (mm. 115–25), the miracle is intoned three times: "Und in dem Säuseln nahte sich der Herr"/"And in that still voice, onward came the Lord." Precisely this concise text, on the repetition of which the B-part is based, turns out, however, to be an addition to the Old Testament report and owes its presence to the compositional plan. As in the A-part, the model again rests on a pedal point E (mm. 125–34), above which the vocal part circumscribes the lapidary series of cadences. Only at the second entry (mm. 135–42) does it escape from the pedal point, in order to expand the cadential group (mm. 143–51). The third and final entry unfolds in almost imitative fashion (mm. 151–56), then oscillates about the subdominant (mm. 157–64), and flows into the fade-out, which again rests for twenty-one measures on a pedal point (mm. 165–71, 171–91). In this manner the second part, like the first, completes a development that emanates from the movement's phases over a pedal point. It leads on one hand to the escape from this basis, to which on the other hand it returns. Beyond their contrasts, the parts of the movement thus complement one another.

Example 6.34
Eliijah, no. 34, chorus, mm. 53–59

All the contrasts, relationships, and correspondences discussed here raise the question of the extent to which such a detailed plan really corresponded to the intention of the composer. A musician so well versed in literary matters as Mendelssohn certainly did not think in abstract concepts in the act of composing, but rather always in musical categories. The comparison between the versions makes clear the extent of this effort, however, and the final form can be understood as a network that was planned musically but that can be deduced only by means of analytical concepts. If one abandons oneself only to the effect of the music, one runs into the danger of relying on subjective emotion without being able to ground it rationally. If one wants to come to grips with misunderstandings or prejudices, however, then one must depend on intersubjectively valid arguments, which only analysis can mediate. Analytical interpretation can open up that differentiation of the music in which its aesthetic level—including affective content—is grounded.

Given these assumptions, it is difficult to evaluate the significance of the partial movements from the oratorio *Christus* that were published in the collected works after the composer's death. The plans for this work—which cannot be presented in more detail here—reach farther back again; Mendelssohn worked on the composition in 1847 right up to his death; the state of the sources still requires closer investigation. Knowing the detailed work on the two completed oratorios, which can be reconstructed by the comparison of the versions, one will judge only with caution the recitatives and the brief *turbae* that make up the main part of the published fragments from the birth and passion of Christ. For precisely such parts—as indicated earlier—were subjected to the most fundamental revision in *Elijah*.

The larger choral movements, which convey a largely complete impression, thus most easily permit deeper insight. The critical reception of the posthumous edition was determined by the idea that here the composer had to strike out on a new path.[57] Yet this is so much less expected if one remembers that the work on *Elijah* was just finished at this time. In regard to *Christus*, therefore, one should inquire not into entirely new directions but rather into a further differentiation, an inquiry against which, to be sure, the work's fragmentary transmission militates. Nonetheless, a movement such as the chorus "Es wird ein Stern aus Jakob aufgehn" (Num. 24: 17) probably permits some recognition of the way in which the previous experience was to be modified. This choral movement begins in unmistakably cantabile diction, in which the first part takes shape with the succession of entrances. The middle part, however ("der wird zerschmettern Fürsten und Städte"), contrasts with this, on one hand, by its declamatory, dynamic, and harmonic accents, though, on the other hand, the theme of the first part is immediately integrated into it. The technique of mediated contrast thus already enters in the middle of the movement and is not limited to the closing part. The lamenting chorus "Ihr Töchter Zions, weint über euch selbst" (from 2 Sam. 1: 24 and other places) presents another layout. Since instead of contrasting segments the text contains a series of syntactically analogous cries of lamentation, the compositional procedure intensifies up to the middle, to fade away again thereafter by stages. A larger choral movement like the "Kreuzige" is based again on a continuous accompaniment pattern in the strings; the choral cries, however, culminate in a chain of descending sixth chords, to which the upper voice falls through more than an octave. Certainly, the two choral movements that these fragments contain have rather the effect of first drafts, without revealing the traces of a further working over. Yet the evidence probably allows one to judge that in

Christus the composer again sought to continue the procedures of expressive concentration and differentiating mediation.

Mendelssohn wrote *St. Paul* at twenty-six and *Elijah* at thirty-six years of age. It was not without some justification, therefore, that Schumann spoke of works of "the youth" and "the man." Can one, then, talk of the later work—after an interval of only ten years—as a "late work"? Certainly, Mozart and Schubert died younger, and still the Requiem and the *Winterreise* seem to us, if not works of old age, then still "late works." Ten years may not be much, but they can be far more significant in the rich oeuvre of a musician who died so young. *Elijah* is a late work not only in relation to the creative output that preceded it but also in the history of its composition. Between us and this work lies about a century and a half, but only a third of this period belongs to the continuous tradition up to the dissolution of tonality around 1910. In retrospect, this caesura of the modern period, even though it is now separated from us by more than eight decades, shifts the music of the Romantic period into the historic distance—no matter how actively it speaks to us.

If the music of the past was a rarity up to the turn of the century, while music of the time itself was the rule, the reverse is true in modern musical life, in which the power of the past dominates. In the interval the separate steps by which the rapid development between Mendelssohn and Schoenberg took place have gained their own interest and new import. The straight development was not, in the last analysis, grounded upon the concept of unstoppable progress that arose after 1800 with the emphatic idea of the artwork determined by innovation and originality. To the same concept of art also belonged the obligatory value that music acquired from the past, if it were to have genuine artistic status. The opposing claims of progress and tradition are thus two sides of one circumstance that depends on the split between historicism and avant garde. Thus, Mendelssohn was led from the thought of "progress" to the "further" and obligated thereto, but to the same extent he felt himself answerable to tradition as had hardly any musician before him. For the discovery of the past, which was initiated by the performance of the *St. Matthew Passion*, was a new thing for its time and in that way a bit of progress. To this corresponded the conviction that one must "go further on the path . . . or back to the old or correct one (which actually ought to be called forward)."[58] The Berlin critic Otto Lange formulated it perceptively in writing that with Mendelssohn's death "an epoch in art" was certainly not ending, but rather the outlook "on an entirely new phase in dramatic music."[59] Schoenberg also regarded Mendelssohn, who had "exhumed Bach," in the same way: "he was also once new."[60] With the mature works that originated after the crisis of his encounter with Beethoven and Bach, Mendelssohn also counted for Schumann as "the brightest of musicians, who most clearly understood the contradictions of the time and who first reconciled them."[61]

The late work, to which *Elijah* belongs, extends beyond such reconciliation of conflicts. It seems to be late not only in the oeuvre but also in the history of the genre, in that here perhaps for the last time an attempt is made at a narrative biblical oratorio. Its particular quality does not finally come from the tension of the relationship between tradition and the present. To be sure, today one must first make oneself conscious of the new tones discussed earlier, for they are not at all comparable to the radicalism of the *Missa solemnis*, and even the harmonic accents were quickly overshadowed by the discoveries of Schubert and Schumann, as these were for their part soon overtaken by those of Liszt or Wagner. In retrospect it becomes clear, however, what a wealth of possibilities this rich phase in the history of music embraces. This can make today's listeners pause to open their ears to the intermediate tones, to take in the differentiation of this music. This was still difficult when *Elijah* began to return to musical life about twenty years ago. Today one who cares to escape from too-hasty comparisons will hear in *Elijah* not only resonances with better-known works of other musicians but the most independent solution of a difficult *compositional* problem.

NOTES

1. Robert Schumann, "Fragmente aus Leipzig, 4," *Neue Zeitschrift für Musik* 7 (5 September 1837), 73–75; cited according to *Gesammelte Schriften über Musik und Musiker*, 5th ed., ed. M. Kreisig (Leipzig: Breitkopf & Härtel, 1914), 1: 318–24, esp. 322. Schumann began with the words "Today I am like a courageous young soldier, who for the first time takes up his sword in a great cause!" Here he paraphrased a sentence at the beginning of the penultimate chapter of Jean Paul's *Flegeljahre*—the same selection, therefore, that is connected to Schumann's own *Papillons*, Op. 2 (1829–1832); cf. Jean Paul, *Werke*, 3 vols. ed. Norbert Miller (Munich: C. Hanser, 1969), 3: 63: 367: "He was like a hero thirsty for fame, who sets out for his first battle."

2. Schumann, *Gesammelte Schriften*, 1: 323.

3. Ibid., 323n. The following text discussion of *St. Paul* is based on an earlier essay by the author, "Religiosität und Kunstcharakter: über Mendelssons Oratorium 'Paulus,'" in *Geistliche Musik: Studien zu ihrer Geschichte und Funktion im 18. und 19. Jahrhundert*, Hamburger Jahrbuch für Musikwissenschaft 8 (Laaber: Laaber-Verlag, 1985), 97–117.

4. Eduard Devrient, *Meine Erinnerungen an Felix Mendelssohn Bartholdy und seine Briefe an mich*, 2d ed. (Leipzig: J. J. Weber, 1872), 136f. Even before this the planned work was briefly mentioned in letters to his father (November 1831) and to Karl Klingemann (10 December 1831). See Eric Werner, *Mendelssohn: A New Image of the Composer and His Age* (New York: Free Press of Glencoe, 1963), 529; Karl Klingemann Jr., ed., *Felix Mendelssohn-Bartholdys Briefwechsel mit Legationsrat Karl Klingemann in London* (Essen: Baedecker, 1909), 90.

5. Julius Schubring Jr., ed., *Briefwechsel zwischen Felix Mendelssohn und Julius Schubring: Zugleich ein Beitrag zur Geschichte und Theorie des Oratoriums* (Leipzig: Duncker & Humblot, 1892), 20, 22–23; pages 26–31 contain Schubring's first counter-draft of 23 January 1833.

6. Arntrud Kurzhals-Reuter, *Die Oratorien Felix Mendelssohn Bartholdys: Untersuchungen zur Quellenlage, Entstehung, Gestaltung und Überlieferung*, Mainzer Studien zur Musikwissenschaft 12 (Tutzing: H. Schneider, 1978), 45–68 on the selection of the text and 143–49 on the chronology.

7. Ralf Wehner, "Ein anderer Paulus? Bemerkungen zu einer unbekannten Fassung des Mendelssohnschen Oratoriums," in *Lesarten—Spielarten: Internationales Richard-Wagner-Symposion 1993* (forthcoming). On the situation of the sources and the sketches, see Kurzhals-Reuter, *Die Oratorien*, 19ff., 97–114.

8. In regard to the following, see Eric Werner's biography cited in note 4, published in German as *Mendelssohn: Leben und Werk in neuer Sicht* (Zurich and Freiburg i. Br.: Atlantis, 1980), as well as the author's *Mendelssohn—der Komponist: Studien zur Kammermusik für Streicher* (Munich: W. Fink, 1978), 56ff.

9. *Bref till Adolf Fredrik Lindblad från Mendelssohn . . . och andra*, ed. L. Dahlgren (Stockholm: A. Bonnier, 1913), 20. See the author's work cited in note 8, 71f. and 161ff., as well as Wulf Konold, *Felix Mendelssohn Bartholdy und seine Zeit* (Laaber: Laaber-Verlag, 1984), 113–38.

10. Konold, *Felix Mendelssohn Bartholdy*, 138f. and 165f.; cf. the author's "Bach, Berlin und Mendelssohn: über Mendelssohns kompositorische Bach-Rezeption," in *Jahrbuch des Staatlichen Instituts für Musikforschung Preußischer Kulturbesitz 1993*, 44–78, esp. 48–53.

11. Rudolf Werner, *Felix Mendelssohn Bartholdy als Kirchenmusiker* (Frankfurt am Main: Deutschen Musik-Gesellschaft, 1930), 26–30; Ralf Wehner, *Studien zum geistlichen Chorschaffen des jungen Felix Mendelssohn Bartholdy*, Musik und Musikanschauung im 19. Jahrhundert 4 (Sinzig: Studio Verlag Schewe, 1996).

12. Ralf Wehner, *Studien zum geistlichen Chorschaffen*, 44–62; Pietro Zappalà, *Le Choralkantaten di Felix Mendelssohn Bartholdy*, Collezione di tesi Universitarie, IV/2 (Venice: Edizioni Fondazione Levi, 1991); Ulrich Wüster, *Felix Mendelssohn Bartholdys Choralkantaten, Gestalt und Idee: Versuch einer historisch-kritischen Interpretation*, Bonner Schriften zur Musikwissenschaft 1 (Frankfurt am Main: Peter Lang, 1996).

13. Christa Jost, *Mendelssohns Lieder ohne Worte*, Frankfurter Beiträge zur Musikwissenschaft 14 (Tutzing: H. Schneider, 1988). On the preludes and fugues, see Gerda Friedrich née Bertram, "Die Fugenkomposition in Mendelssohns Instrumentalwerk" (diss., University of Bonn, 1969); Friedhold Bötel, *Mendelssohns Bachrezeption und ihre Konsequenzen, dargestellt an den Präludien und Fugen für Orgel op. 37*, Beiträge zur Musikforschung 14 (Munich and Salzburg: E. Katzbichler, 1984).

14. Martin Geck, *Deutsche Oratorien 1800 bis 1840: Verzeichnis der Quellen und Aufführungen*, Quellen-Kataloge zur Musikgeschichte 4 (Wilhelmshaven: Heinrichshofen, 1971).

15. In 1843 Wagner called the work "a testimony to the highest blossoming of art": see Richard Wagner, *Sämtliche Schriften und Dichtungen: Volksausgabe* (Leipzig: Breitkopf & Härtel, 1911), 12: 149f. After the Stuttgart performance Nicolaus Lenau noted on 25 May 1838, "This music has great beauties in the details, but as a whole it seemed to me too limited to move in the established boundaries of Handel's"; *Sämtliche Werke und Briefe*, ed. Walter Dietze (Frankfurt am Main: Insel-Verlag, 1971), 2: 673. For additional documents, see note 34.

16. Susanna Großmann-Vendrey, *Felix Mendelssohn Bartholdy und die Musik der Vergangenheit*, Studien zur Musikgeschichte des 19. Jahrhunderts 17 (Regensburg: Bosse, 1969); Martin Geck, *Die Wiederentdeckung der Matthäuspassion*, Studien zur Musikgeschichte des 19. Jahrhunderts 9 (Regensburg: Bosse, 1967).

17. Kurzhals-Reuter, *Die Oratorien*, 250ff.; 212ff.

18. Geck, *Deutsche Oratorien 1800 bis 1840*. With regard to the sociohistorical context, see Michael Jarczyk, *Die Choralballade im 19. Jahrhundert: Studien zu ihrer Form, Entstehung und Verbreitung*, Berliner musikwissenschaftlicher Arbeiten 16 (Munich and Salzburg: Katzbichler, 1978); Carl Dahlhaus, *Die Musik des 19. Jahrhunderts*, Neues Handbuch der Musikwissenschaft 6 (Wiesbaden: Akademische Verlagsgesellschaft Athenaion, 1980), 132ff., 147ff.

19. Carl Dahlhaus, *Musikästhetik*, Musik-Taschen-Bücher, Theoretica 8 (Cologne: H. Gerig, 1967), 39ff., 71ff.

20. Immanuel Kant, *Kritik des Urteilskraft* (Berlin and Libau: Lagarde und Friederich, 1790), sec. 59.

21. G.W.F. Hegel, *Phänomenologie des Geistes*, vol. 5 of *Sämtliche Werke*, 6th ed., ed. Johannes Hoffmeister, Philosophische Bibliothek 114 (Hamburg: Meiner, 1968), 490ff.; F.D.E. Schleiermacher, *Über die Religion: Reden an die Gebildeten unter ihren Verächtern* (Berlin: Unger, 1799), 168ff. (new ed., ed. C. H. Ratschow, Stuttgart: Reclam, 1969), 112ff.

22. F.W.J. Schelling, *System des transzendentalen Idealismus*, Philosophische Bibliothek 254 (Hamburg: Meiner, 1957), 281ff., 297; K.W.F. Solger, *Vorlesungen über Ästhetik* (Leipzig: Brockhaus, 1829; repr., ed. K.W.L. Heyse, Darmstadt: Wissenschaftliche Buchgesellschaft, 1973), 341ff.

23. Carl Dahlhaus, *Die Idee der absoluten Musik*, dtv Wissenschaftliche Reihe 4310 (Kassel: Bärenreiter, 1978), 91–104.

24. G.W.F. Hegel, *Ästhetik*, ed. Friedrich Bassenge (Berlin: Aufbau, 1965), 2: 306ff., 319ff.

25. Arthur Schopenhauer, *Die Welt als Wille und Vorstellung* (Darmstadt: Wissenschaftliche Buchgesellschaft, 2d ed. 1968), 2: 574; on this point see also Rudolf Odebrecht, ed., *Friedrich Schleiermacher Ästhetik*, Das Literatur-Archiv 4 (Berlin and Leipzig: Walter de Gruyter, 1931), 189, 196f.

26. Christian Hermann Weisse, *System der Ästhetik als Wissenschaft von der Idee des Schönen* (Leipzig: C.H.F. Hartmann, 1830; repr., Hildesheim: Olms, 1966), 2: 63ff., 71ff.

27. See the author's "Kunstreligion und religiöse Musik: Zur ästhetischen Problematik geistlicher Musik im 19. Jahrhundert," in *Die Musikforschung* 32 (1979), 365–93, as well as the collection *Religiöse Musik in nicht-liturgischen Werken von Beethoven bis Reger*, ed. Walter Wiora et al., Studien zur Musikgeschichte des 19. Jahrhunderts 51 (Regensburg: Bosse, 1978). See also the essay by Winfried Kirsch, "Oratorium und Oper: Zu einer gattungsästhetischen Kontroverse in der Oratorientheorie des 19. Jahrhunderts (Materialen zu einer Dramaturgie des Oratoriums)," in *Beiträge zur Geschichte des Oratoriums seit Händel: Festschrift Günther Massenkeil zum 60. Geburtstag*, ed. Rainer Cadenbach and Helmut Loos (Bonn: Voggenreiter, 1986), 221–54.

28. Georg Feder, "Verfall und Restauration," in *Geschichte der evangelischen Kirchenmusik*, ed. Friedrich Blume (Kassel: Bärenreiter, 1965), 215–69; also his "Zu Felix Mendelssohn Bartholdys geistlicher Musik," in *Religiöse Musik* (see note 27), 97–117.

29. Mendelssohn expressed himself skeptically on the outlook for ecclesiastical music: "A genuine sort of church music, i.e., for the Reformed worship service, that would have a place in the sacred ceremony, seems impossible to me." At the same time he considered critically the requirements for the oratorio: "For an oratorio, however, there must be a main plot line, a development of particular persons, otherwise the subject would be too vague" (12 January 1835). His father defined the problem as the "project of uniting old tastes with new means" (10 March 1835). See Felix Mendelssohn Bartholdy, *Briefe aus den Jahren 1833 bis 1847*, 6th ed., ed. Paul and Carl Mendelssohn Bartholdy (Leipzig: Hermann Mendelssohn, 1875), 75ff., 86f.

30. See the letter to Marc André Souchay (15 October 1842), in *Briefe 1833–1847*, 346f.

31. Devrient, *Erinnerungen*, 115 (letter of 13 July 1831).

32. Felix Mendelssohn Bartholdy, *Reisebriefe aus den Jahren 1830 bis 1832*, 8th ed., ed. Paul Mendelssohn Bartholdy (Leipzig: Hermann Mendelssohn, 1869), 97 (letter to Karl Friedrich Zelter of 18 December 1830).

33. See the letter to Otto von Woringen of 12 March 1836, reproduced by Großmann-Vendrey, *Felix Mendelssohn Bartholdy*, 81.

34. On this subject see Erich Reimer, "Kritik und Apologie des Oratoriums im 19. Jahrhundert," in *Religiöse Musik* (see note 27), 247–56. One should cite not only contemporary reviews, such as those by Robert Schumann (see note 1) in *Neue Zeitschrift für Musik* 7 (1837), 73ff., 147ff.; Gottfried Wilhelm Fink in *Allgemeine Musikalische Zeitung* 39 (1837), 497ff., 513ff.; or H. E. Rhese in *Zeitschrift für Deutschlands Musik-Vereine* 1 (1841), 210ff. Attention should also be drawn to the introductions by Theodor Mosewius, *Zur Aufführung des Oratoriums Paulus von Felix Mendelssohn Bartholdy* (Breslau o. J.: Kupfer, 1836) or by Otto Jahn, *Ueber F. Mendelssohn Bartholdys Oratorium Paulus* (Kiel, 1842), also in his *Gesammelte Aufsätze über Musik*, 2d ed. (Leipzig: Breitkopf & Härtel, 1867), 13–39. See also Ferdinand Hand, *Aesthetik der Tonkunst* (Leipzig: C. Hochhausen und Fournes, 1841), 2: 576ff.; F. T. Vischer, *Aesthetik oder Wissenschaft des Schönen* (Stuttgart: Carl Mäcken, 1857), 3/2/4: 1106ff.; Franz Brendel, *Geschichte der Musik in Italien, Deutschland, und Frankreich*, 6th ed. (Leipzig: H. Mathes, 1878), 376ff.; Hermann Kretzschmar, *Führer durch den Konzertsaal*, vol. 2/2, *Oratorium und weltliche Chorwerke*, 2d ed. (Leipzig: Breitkopf & Härtel, 1899), 256–68; Hugo Riemann, *Geschichte der Musik seit Beethoven* (Berlin and Stuttgart: W. Spemann, 1901), 261f.; Arnold Schering, *Geschichte des Oratoriums*, Kleine Handbücher der Musikgeschichte nach Gattungen 3 (Leipzig: Breitkopf & Härtel, 1911).

35. Hand, *Aesthetik*, 2: 576.

36. Schumann, *Gesammelte Schriften*, 322. Regarding the layout, see Erich Reimer, "Textanlage und Szenengestaltung in Mendelssohns 'Paulus,'" *Archiv für Musikwissenschaft* 46 (1989), 42–69; the following overview also relies on Reimer's outline.

37. Schumann, *Gesammelte Schriften*, 323; see also Glenn Stanley, "Bach's *Erbe*: The Chorale in the German Oratorio of the Early Nineteenth Century," *19th-Century Music* 11 (1987), 121–49, esp. 127–32.

38. Schumann, *Gesammelte Schriften*, 322. Regarding the soloistic movements, see Erich Reimer, "Mendelssohns 'edler Gesang': Zur Kompositionsweise der Sologesänge im 'Paulus,'" *Archiv für Musikwissenschaft* 50 (1993), 44–70.

39. On the compositional construction Kurzhals-Reuter's work (see note 6) serves only to give some observations as a point of departure; an analytical investigation of the entire work still remains to be made. The numbering of the movements in the following discussion is that of the *Gesamtausgabe* by Julius Rietz (series 13, no. 85); the overture is unnumbered, and the first chorus is counted as no. 1, whereas the first edition (Bonn: N. Simrock, 1837) begins with the overture as no. 1.

40. On this subject, see Wilgard Lange, "Händel-Rezeption bei Felix Mendelssohn Bartholdy" (diss., Halle-Wittenberg, 1980; typescript), esp. 172–206.

41. Klingemann, *Briefwechsel*, 204, 211. Regarding the letter of 18 February 1837, see F. G. Edwards, *The History of Mendelssohn's Oratorio "Elijah"* (London: Novello, 1896; repr. 1976), 4–11, which contains an English translation of the letters to Klingemann; as well as Jack Werner, *Mendelssohn's "Elijah": A Historical and Analytical Guide to the Oratorio* (London: Chappell, 1965), 1–11; Kurzhals-Reuter, *Die Oratorien*, 150–63.

42. Ferdinand Hiller, *Felix Mendelssohn-Bartholdy: Briefe und Erinnerungen*, 2d ed. (Cologne: M. Dumont Schauberg, 1878), 144; Hiller places his memories of the conversation about *Elijah* in the winter of 1839–1840. See also John Callcott Horsley, *Recollections of a Royal Academician* (London: J. Murray, 1903), 165; according to Horsley's report, Mendelssohn stated in September 1837, "Yes, I have chosen the splendid Bible story of Elijah for my next theme"; on this subject see Jack Werner, *Mendelssohn's "Elijah,"* 2; Kurzhals-Reuter, *Die Oratorien*, 152.

43. See Schubring, *Briefwechsel*, 115f. on Mendelssohn's letter of 12 December 1837 with his hesitant reaction to the suggestions for an oratorio *St. Peter*, 124–47 on the correspondence between October and December 1838, and 204–25 between December 1845 and June 1846. Cf. Edwards, *The History*, 10–27; Kurzhals-Reuter, *Die Oratorien*, 153; Arno Forchert, "Textanlage und Darstellungsprinzipien in Mendelssohns *Elias*," in *Das Problem Mendelssohn*, ed. Carl Dahlhaus, Studien zur Musikgeschichte des 19. Jahrhunderts 41 (Regensburg: Bosse, 1974), 61–77. Regarding the theological implications, see Rüdiger Bartelmus, "Elia(s): Eine Prophetengestalt im Alten Testament und ihre musikalisch-theologische Deutung durch Felix Mendelssohn Bartholdy," *Musik und Kirche* 65 (1995), 182–97.

44. Martin Staehelin, "Elias, Johann Sebastian Bach und der Neue Bund; Zur Arie 'Es ist genug' in Felix Mendelssohn Bartholdys Oratorium *Elias*," in *Beiträge zur Geschichte des Oratoriums*, 283–96; English translation: "Elijah, Johann Sebastian Bach, and the New Covenant: On the Aria 'Es ist genug' in Felix Mendelssohn Bartholdy's Oratorio *Elijah*," in *Mendelssohn and His World*, ed. R. Larry Todd (Princeton: Princeton University Press, 1991), 121–36; Friedrich Wilhelm Krummacher, *Elias der Thisbiter* (Elberfeld: W. Hassel, 1828; 4th ed. 1851), ii.

45. Joseph Bennett, "'Elijah': A Comparison of the Original and Revised Scores," *The Musical Times* 23 (1882) and 24 (1883), *passim*; on the situation of the sources and on the sketches, see Kurzhals-Reuter, *Die Oratorien*, 69–82, 115–41; the overview of the text (pages 83–93) frankly neglects references to the biblical models. See also Edwards, *The History*, 97–113; Jack Werner, *Mendelssohn's "Elijah,"* 76–82. I am grateful to Ralf Wehner of Leipzig for obtaining the literature and for additional information.

46. See Hand, *Aesthetik*, 2: 569–89, esp. 571f. The oratorio is also defined as "lyrical artwork"—in contradistinction to the "dramatic" opera—in Philipp Spitta, "Das Oratorium als Kunstgattung," *Allgemeine Musikalische Zeitung* 3 (1868), 137–39, 145–47, 153–55, 161–64; like the opera, the oratorio also has "plot," but "the artist draws the plot entirely within his own subjectivity and resolves it there" (145).

47. Franz Brendel, "Mendelssohn's *Elias*," *Neue Zeitschrift für Musik* 28 (1848), 89f. Reports in *Signale für die musikalische Welt* 6 (1848), 49–52, 137f., 205f., about performances in Dresden, Weimer, and Leipzig, by contrast, turned out to be uniformly positive.

48. Otto Jahn, "Ueber F. Mendelssohn Bartholdy's Oratorium *Elias*," *Allgemeine Musikalische Zeitung* 50 (1848), cols. 113–22, 137–43 (the quotation is in col. 114); also in his *Gesammelte Aufsätze* (see note 34), 40–63.

49. Eduard Krüger, "Ueber Mendelssohn's *Elias* (Bruchstück aus einem Briefwechsel)," in *Neue Zeitschrift für Musik* 27 (1847), 265–68, 277–82, 289–93, esp. 267f.; Otto Lange, "*Elias*, ein Oratorium nach Worten des alten Testaments componirt von Felix Mendelssohn-Bartholdy," *Neue Berliner Musikzeitung* 1 (1847), 397–400, esp. 397f.

50. See the references cited in note 34; such reservations continued in effect up to the critiques of George Bernard Shaw, *London Music in 1888–89 as Heard by Corno di Bassetto (Later Known as Bernard Shaw)* (London: Constable, 1937; 3d ed. 1950), 221, 251. On this subject, see also the author's "Composition as Accommodation? On Mendelssohn's Music in Relation to England," in *Mendelssohn Studies*, ed. R. Larry Todd (Cambridge: Cambridge University Press, 1992), 80–105. According to Spitta's judgment of *Elijah*, by contrast, "this outstanding work bears the stamp of the bright spirit of art who grasped so completely the nature of the oratorio"; see Spitta, "Das Oratorium als Kunstgattung," 154.

51. Otto Jahn, "Ueber F. Mendelssohn Bartholdy's Oratorium *Elias*," col. 116; also his *Gesammelte Aufsätze*, 44f.

52. Arno Forchert, "Textanlage und Darstellungsprinzipien . . .," 71f.; for the following citations, see also pp. 74, 77. From the reconstruction of the compositional history Forchert was able to conclude (p. 70): "Schubring's total contribution to the final text is decidedly less than it has appeared until now."

53. On this subject see Chapters 15–18 in Eric Werner, *Mendelssohn: A New Image*, as well as the author's *Mendelssohn—der Komponist*, 464–73.

54. On Op. 44 no. 2, see ibid., 277–91; also Chapter 8 in this volume. On the series of Psalm-cantatas, see Wolfgang Dinglinger, *Studien zu den Psalmen mit Orchester von Felix Mendelssohn-Bartholdy*, Berliner Musik Studien 1 (Cologne: Studio, 1993).

55. Susanna Großmann-Vendrey, "Stilprobleme in Mendelssohns Orgelsonaten op. 65," in *Das Problem Mendelssohn*, 185–94, esp. 194.

56. Regarding Opp. 66, 87, and 80, see the author's *Mendelssohn—der Komponist*, 96f. and 325ff., as well as his "Mendelssohn's Late Chamber Music: Some Autograph Sources Recovered," in *Mendelssohn and Schumann: Essays on Their Music and Its Context*, ed. Jon Finson and R. Larry Todd (Durham, NC: Duke University Press, 1984), 71–84.

57. In regard to *Christus*, see Kurzhals-Reuter, 160ff., 197ff. As an example of the lack of understanding in its reception, one may cite the review in the *Süddeutschen Musikzeitung* 2 (1853), 53f. and 57f.; about the middle part of the chorus "Es wird ein Stern aus Jakob aufgehn" it says, "Tilly and Napoleon could agree very well in this wild hatred, for they wrought destruction in just this way. But Christ never wanted to destroy 'Fürsten und Städte' . . . one should rather first learn to understand the significance and the true core of such prophetic words, before one should permit oneself such a distortion."

58. Felix Mendelssohn Bartholdy, *Briefe 1833–1847*, 2 (letter of 4 March 1833): "den Weg weiter gehen . . . oder zum Alten oder Rechten zurück (was man eigentlich vorwärts nennen sollte)."

59. Lange, "*Elias*, ein Oratorium . . .," 400.

60. Arnold Schoenberg, *Harmonielehre* (Vienna: Universal, 1911; 4th ed. 1949), 481.

61. Schumann, *Gesammelte Schriften*, 1: 500f. The person who is capable of reconciling the contradictions must first have dealt with them as Mendelssohn did in his engagement with history and the present.

HISTORICAL VIEWS AND DOCUMENTS

FIRST PERFORMANCES, 1.—MENDELSSOHN'S "ST. PAUL"[1]

F. G. Edwards

"Saint Paul," Mendelssohn's first Oratorio, was given to the world on the evening of Whitsunday, May 22, 1836, when its composer was in his twenty-sixth year. The place was Düsseldorf; the occasion the Lower Rhine Musical Festival. Among the eagerly-expectant audience on the memorable occasion were Carl Klingemann, Ferdinand Hiller, J. W. Davison (not then a journalist), and Sterndale Bennett, then just turned twenty.[2] The first two named have recorded their experiences of the eventful day, so that with the aid of their narratives and those of other contemporary records, there is ample material wherewith to relate the story of the first performance of Mendelssohn's "St. Paul."

First, a word or two as to the Festival itself. In addition to "St. Paul," there were performed Beethoven's Choral Symphony, and his Overtures to "Leonore," No. 1 (then unknown) and No. 3; Mozart's "Davidde penitente"; and a Psalm of Handel's (one of the Chandos anthems). The performance took place in the Rittersaal, "but the room," says Hiller, "was too small for the large audience and orchestra; and in 'Sleepers, wake,' the blast of the trumpets and trombones from the gallery down into the low hall was quite overpowering." The orchestra (led by Ferdinand David[3]) consisted of 172 players; the chorus numbered 364—a total of 536 performers. The chorus were thus distributed: 106 sopranos, 60 altos, 90 tenors, and 108 basses. All the singers, with the exception of the soloists, were amateurs, as were also the greater part of the band. It was this circumstance that gave to the Festival one interesting characteristic. From all the neighbouring towns and the country round, the people gathered together—not to toil at some irksome ill-paid task, but for a great musical field-day, full of soul and song. One venerable chorister, aged seventy-five, sang his tenor part in the chorus with the same enthusiasm with which, in his younger days at Vienna, he had listened to the first performance of Mozart's "Zauberflöte." The love of the art, the good training of the voices, a well-cultivated taste, and a general knowledge of music were here all happily united in the performers. "You felt the life, the pulsation of the music, for their hearts and understandings were in it," says Klingemann. Mendelssohn was the bright particular star of the Festival, not only as a composer, conductor, and pianist, but also as a lively, agreeable host, introducing the visitors to each other and bringing the right people together, with always a kind word for everybody. The preliminary rehearsals having been conducted by Julius Rietz,[4] Mendelssohn on his arrival set to work with his usual energy. Some, at least, of the soloists did not get their parts till within three days of the final rehearsals. An amusing incident is recorded in this connection. Mendelssohn requested F. von W----[5] to sing a recitative that he (Mendelssohn) brought with him just after he had written it down. The words were not very distinctly written, and at the passage "When the heathen heard it they were *glad* (*froh*)," the soloist sang with great vigour "When the heathen heard it they were *saucy* (*frech*)." In spite of the solemn mood of the listeners, this humorous perversion of the text caused roars of continued laughter, in which Mendelssohn heartily joined.[6]

"The performance of the Oratorio," says Klingemann, "was glorious—never did I hear such chorus-singing. What the orchestra missed in minor, delicate details, they made up in striking, general effect." "Mendelssohn," wrote an eye-witness, "is great as a Conductor. No wrong note, no erring performer escapes *him*. He treated these 536 performers as a single instrument, or as a commander would his army, with irresistible authority. He does it most patiently, sparing no one, and cheering them up at the proper moment. The Conductor's place was a sort of pulpit, decorated with a golden lyre. When the performance was over some young ladies showered flowers and garlands upon the composer; they crowned his score; and if they had no more to say, and no further applause to bestow, it was because they had constantly sung and talked of the great work ever since the preparations for the Festival began."

The performance was not quite free from blemish. One of the vocalists in the duet of the "false Witnesses" made a slip. Fanny Hensel, Mendelssohn's gifted sister, who was seated among the contraltos in the chorus, turned pale with anxiety, and bending forward and holding up a sheet of music, she sang the right notes so steadily and firmly that the erring duettist soon got all right again. At the close of the performance Mendelssohn tenderly clasped the hand of his sister-helper in the time of need, and said, with his bright smile, "I am so glad it was one of the *false* witnesses."

We must, however, let Mendelssohn state his own impressions in regard to the performance. He thus writes to his friend Schleinitz,[7] under date July 5, 1836: "You would certainly have been for a long time much amused and delighted with the Musical Festival; and from your taking so friendly an interest in me and my 'St. Paul,' I thought a hundred times, at least, during the rehearsals, what a pity it was that you were not there. You would assuredly have been delighted by the love and goodwill with which the whole affair was carried on, and the marvellous fire with which the chorus and orchestra burst forth; though there were individual passages, especially in the solos, which might have annoyed you. I think I see your face, could you have heard the 'St. Paul's' arias sung in an indifferent, mechanical manner, and I think I hear you uttering abuse on the Apostle of the Gentiles in a dressing-gown; but then I know also how charmed you would have been with 'Rise up, arise,' which went really splendidly. My feelings were singular; during the whole of the rehearsals and the performance I thought little enough about directing, but listened eagerly to the general effect, and whether it went right according to my idea without thinking of anything else. When the people gave me a flourish of trumpets or applauded, it was welcome for a moment, but then my father came back to my mind,[8] and I strove once more to recall my thoughts to my work. Thus, during the entire performance, I was almost in the position of a listener, and I tried to retain an impression of the whole. Many parts caused me much pleasure, others not so; but I learnt a lesson from it all, and hope to succeed better the next time I write an oratorio.—Felix Mendelssohn Bartholdy."

On the third day of the Festival there was, as usual, the so-called Künstler-Concert—chiefly consisting of solo performances by the principals.   The programme for the Concert had to be altered at the last moment owing to the illness of one or more of the solo vocalists. Mendelssohn therefore proposed to Ferdinand David that they should play Beethoven's "Kreutzer" Sonata. Unfortunately the music could not be found, but Mendelssohn said: "We have played it so often together, of course we can play it by heart," and so they did without either music or rehearsal, but with enormous success.[9]

It may be interesting to give the prices of admission to the Concerts. A ticket for both the evening Concerts cost nine shillings, for a single evening six shillings, for the morning Concert three shillings, and for each general rehearsal (of which there were four), one shilling.

Almost immediately after the first performance of "St. Paul" Mendelssohn began his usual conscientious revision and rigorous pruning of the score. "I have an awful reverence for print," he frequently told his friend Devrient, "and I must go on improving my things until I feel sure they are all I can make them." "Mendelssohn rejected no less than fourteen pieces, including two chorales, 'O treuer Heiland' and 'Ein' feste Burg.' One of the choruses evidently belongs to the scene at Lystra. It is a heathen chorus for voices and full orchestra (with big drum), in D, twelve pages long, beginning thus:

Mendelssohn used often to complain in joke that his heathen choruses were more effective than his Christian or Jewish ones."[10] One of the rejected airs, a soprano solo in F minor, "Thou who has doomed man to die," is now published by Messrs Novello, Ewer and Co.

Liverpool is accorded the honour of being the place where "St. Paul" was first performed in England. The work was given at the Liverpool Musical Festival, in St. Peter's Church (now the Cathedral), on Friday morning, October 7, 1836, a little more than four months after its first presentation at Düsseldorf. The revised version of the Oratorio, the form in which we now know the work, was given for the first time on this occasion. Sir George Smart,[11] to whom the English version was dedicated by the publisher, was the Conductor. Malibran, but for her untimely death a fortnight before the Festival, would have sung the principal soprano part.[12] Her place was taken by Madame Caradori-Allen; the other leading vocalists were Mrs. Shaw, Braham, and Henry Phillips.[13] Mr. J. Alfred Novello[14] was doubtless one of the "False Witnesses." Soon after its first performance the copyright of "St. Paul" for England was purchased by Mr. J. Alfred Novello, to the astonishment of the music trade, who probably at that time, though perhaps not subsequently, pitied the purchaser.[15] The earliest announcement of the purchase seems to have appeared in the *Musical World* of August 5, 1836. On the following 18th of November was announced "the pianoforte score of the whole Oratorio, arranged by the author, price 32s.; or, in two parts, 16s. each," *net*, of course. The English translation was made by Mr. William Ball.

"St. Paul" was given in the following year (1837) by the Sacred Harmonic Society (twice), and at the Birmingham Musical Festival, under Mendelssohn's direction. With these initial performances this beautiful work may be said to have been well launched on the flood-tide of artistic success.

ST. PAUL IN DRESDEN, 1843[16]

Richard Wagner; translated by Douglass Seaton

[This favorable review, written during the early part of Wagner's tenure in Dresden, does not yet reflect his later vicious criticism of Mendelssohn. The programming of the concert, with Beethoven's Eighth Symphony following *St. Paul*, would certainly seem curious to modern concertgoers, but Wagner does not suggest that it appeared peculiar in the concert practices of the time.—Ed.]

The last Palm Sunday concert must be acknowledged as one of the most brilliant and left a deep impression on the especially numerous audience. Mendelssohn Bartholdy had been invited to conduct the performance of his oratorio *St. Paul* himself at this concert, and by his willingness to accept this invitation he provided us an unusual kind of satisfaction, that is, an occasion to see a classic work reproduced under the personal direction of its creator. We had already become familiar with this masterpiece through two public performances, which must be said to have succeeded thoroughly, and yet it seemed as though we had just now come to a true understanding, where the direct personal leadership of the master filled every performer with special dedication and inspired them to such a degree that the value of the performance almost attained the level of the work itself. The very strong chorus and orchestra, together with the solo singing of Wüst, Tichatschek, Dettmer,[17] and others, covered themselves with glory in the true sense of the word and thus showed us in complete perfection a work that is evidence of the highest flowering of art and, since it was composed in our day, filled us with rightful pride in the time in which we live. The only thing to be regretted is that such an oratorio cannot be completely incorporated into our Protestant church worship, because by that means its true meaning would most effectively overflow into every faithful heart, while without this foundation, and especially in the concert hall, it affects us more or less only as a work of art and is far from able to bring to the fore its actual religious effectiveness, as was the case with the conditions under which Seb. Bach presented his oratorios to the congregation. Even so, however, the effect in the concert hall is moving and uplifting.—The Beethoven symphony (no. 8 in F major) that followed the oratorio was very well performed by the large number of executants. This is especially noteworthy, since the performance of this particular symphony by such a very large orchestra, given the disadvantage of its presentation in this place, where it cannot be as focused as one would wish, is admittedly difficult. Kapellmeister *Reissiger*[18] conducted it.

ELIJAH IN LEIPZIG, 1848[19]

W. L.; translated by Laura Moore

Elijah by Felix Mendelssohn-Bartholdy.

Performed for the first time in the hall of the Gewandhaus at Leipzig and for the benefit of the orchestra pension funds.

(Thursday, 3 February 1848)[20]

(The solos sung by Mrs. L. Frege, Miss F. Schwarzbach, Miss M. Stark, and Miss S. Schloß, and by Messrs. Behr, Widemann [*sic*], Henry, Vögner, and Zimmermann[21]; the chorus performed by a large host of amateurs in collaboration with the St. Thomas choir.)

It was an evening of tears and joy for Mendelssohn's friends in Leipzig that finally brought them the long-awaited satisfaction of hearing the great, last-completed masterwork of the now immortal musician. Under the motto that he always made so completely his own, *Res severa est verum gaudium*,[22] a medallion in bas-relief of the artist's lifelike portrait surrounded by a garland of fresh evergreen, created by the hand of our gallant Knauer [*sic*][23] on his own accord out of reverence for the deceased, looked down into the hall—the same hall in which he so often stood so full of life, performed his own and others' masterworks to the general delight of eager listeners, and would have been delighted himself, as well, to rehearse and to lead the first performance of this last, perhaps greatest production of his creative muse. Ah, what a short span of time between those happy days, in which he still worked in full strength among us, and this birthday, which we can celebrate only for the deceased! Truly, grounds enough for deep seriousness and bitter mourning and excuse for tears, which, even if not visible everywhere, were certainly wept inwardly by many on this evening. It was our prayer on this occasion that, just as those evergreens symbolized our feeling for the dear departed one, and as the image of his amiable personality will never fade from our hearts, so, too, like this visible picture, the fitting reminder of his extraordinary merit, his influence may continue forever in this place!

But now to the joy. Joy, great joy it was for us to see the Master himself, in effect, spiritually resurrected on his birthday, in a work that one may point to as an entirely new and individual birth of his creative genius. What a splendid and imposing subject is Elijah, this most powerful representative of prophecy in the Old Testament, this keen orator for theocracy in opposition to the kings, this bold advocate for Jehovah against the sensual cult of the servants of idols and the assimilation of the people seduced by them, this strong, even (if one wishes to call him so) obstinate hero of God, who, however, certainly did not escape many truly human stresses, as, for example, in the splendid scene with the widow of Zarepath, the weak despair of the fulfillment of his life's purpose in the desert, and so on, and yet what a highly poetic outcome of it all in the apotheosis, the ascension! Next to Moses (whom the deceased would have taken up, if—as it is said—another person to whom he told the plan did not beat him to it[24]) the artist could not, in fact, have found any more dramatic material in the entire Old Testament, as the continuously rich changes of scene in the oratorio demonstrate. With what skill these scenes, in which the material organizes itself only loosely according to the biblical narrative and finds itself often interrupted by episodes, are connected into an artistic whole; with what refined and, at the same time, deep religious feeling; with what art in writing, what deep understanding of the meaning of prophecy are the related passages chosen from the prophets and the Psalms! That the material is taken from the Old Testament is, in any case, an advantage for the dramatic nature of the oratorio; for the Old Testament, as a complete history of a people, already contains undeniably far more dramatic impulses than the New; and surely no one would wish to place the Old Testament's language, its expressive style, with its pithier and more concentrated force and its richness of poetic images, below that of the New Testament, while we would certainly not disregard the higher moral religious meaning of the New Testament, because of which, however, it certainly does not lend itself to artistic treatment. The whole beauty of a text like *Elijah* can, to be sure, be dealt with only by the worthy individual who himself possesses a certain degree of Bible knowledge, an idea of poetry, particularly folk poetry, and a bit of fantasy. We are not making any accusations against anyone who does not have these qualities, but we ask only that he be somewhat more careful in the judgment of ideas from spheres outside his scope. This much is certain, that the composer chose and arranged this text with complete artistic consciousness and put into his treatment all the fire of his spirit. Should one, however, who witnesses this powerful musical work with an unprejudiced ear not have heard and felt this directly from the composition? It is not a profitable business to want to compare works by the same great master with one another. We remember in this connection a saying of Goethe: "They have quarreled in public for many years about who is greater: Schiller or myself, while they should just be pleased that two men such as he and I exist." Because the question has once come up whether *Elijah* is equal to *St. Paul*, however, whether *Elijah* is a step in the right direction or not, and so on, we permit ourselves to state our opinion that *St. Paul* indeed (on the basis of the material itself) is more churchly; but *Elijah* is greater as a musical work of art on account of its throughgoing originality, its greater richness of invention, its vigorous and more sharply defined presentation of the given situations and characters. That is precisely the reason there is no trace, in our opinion, of a decline in the composer's ability in this composition. For if, as was recently correctly observed from Berlin, the actual productive power of the composer makes itself evident principally in melody, then in which of Mendelssohn's [other] creations is there to be found such a profusion, which impresses itself on any ear that is at all musical, so that it almost never lets go? We remember here as examples the aria of Obadiah "If with all your hearts ye truly seek me," the Baal choruses, the exquisite solo of Elijah with choir "Open the heavens and send us relief," the main theme of the final chorus in the first part, the aria "Hear ye, Israel," the splendid chorus "He, watching over Israel, slumbers not nor sleeps," and so on in the second part. No one would want to claim that the choruses were not forcefully conceived and orchestrated at the appropriate places. They are more than that, however; they are, up until the final fugue of the whole piece "Lord our Creator," very ingenious and new. However, if one regards strength as the ability to express strength, which must concentrate itself particularly here in the person of Elijah, then here, too, we have not found even the smallest thing to be lacking, with the exception of Elijah's aria in the first part: "Is not His word like a fire," which appears to us to conceal a certain lack of inner urgency among lively figurations. But this aria itself would certainly have had greater effect if it were taken at a somewhat slower tempo than it was at our performance. We have to agree wholeheartedly with the singer, who many times in the rehearsals argued for this with the conductor. Likewise, we would have wished for the tempo to be somewhat slower in the scene of the widow with Elijah, so that at the climax, "My son reviveth," the esteemed artist would have been able to open up the greatest strength and warmth of expressive tone. Given the impossibility of going through all the musical beauties of the magnificent musical work individually in these pages, we content ourselves with some hints as to the overall form and understanding of the whole. The two parts into which the work is divided, with all the differences of character, hold the listener in tension throughout. The first part is a thoroughly lively dramatic picture with the finest and most appropriate scenes, which change rapidly by means of the musical treatment. Completely new in form is that at the climax a recitative, which ends in the significant key of D minor and on A major, introduces the prophet himself and at the same time suddenly clarifies to the listener the full force and power of the prophecy. In this manner the tone-poet appears to have had in mind the passage employed later in the oratorio out of

Jesus Sirach: "Then did the prophet Elijah break forth like a fire; his words appeared like burning torches." This, one might say, is the actual overture of the piece, while the overture so named by the composer is actually only an instrumentally constructed transition to the laments of the people and their plea for help, which describes the onset of a dreadful fate for the land in consequence of divine wrath. In the further course of the first part we distinguish three very characteristic main groups of pieces, on which collectively the ideas of the power of prophecy are based: the resuscitation of the son of the widow of Zarepath (Sarepta), the battle and victory of the servants of Jehovah over the priests of Baal, and the reopening of the heavens through the pleading of the prophet. The extraordinarily vivid and dramatic music must lead even the coldest listener by way of the "shaky ladder of sensations" into the midst of the action, whose different situations are not merely of national but of universal human interest. As one of the most beautiful passages of this first part we may point out the passage just cited, "Open the heavens," in the devoutly rapturous A major, within which the words of the boy ring through in the broad intervals of the bright C-major triad like voices of the elements. Here the depictions of the soul and of nature are connected in the most marvelous and moving fashion. The scene with the widow is one of profound tones of feeling, and the one with the priests of Baal is forceful and heroic. Especially magnificent and majestic also is the closing chorus of the first part, where the people give thanks for the rain. The second part contains less real action but is therefore all the more a vivid depiction of states of the soul. It leads step by step into the mystery of the Holy of Holies. The trio of angels, the chorus "Holy, holy," with the luminous trill of the seraph in between, are deep glances into a higher world, which can be opened up only to the eye of the artist inspired by God. Also in this part several sections may again be distinguished: the witness of the prophet against the king and the charge raised against him for that reason by Jezebel, the flight and the sojourn in the desert, the transfiguration on Mount Horeb, and the ascent to heaven.

The Messianic prophecy appended to this appears only as an added attachment, to be sure; nevertheless, it contains still more glorious choruses. Only the final chorus does not entirely equal the otherwise magnificent character of the work. Perhaps the artist would have done better to close with the ascent to heaven, but he did not want to give up the significance of Elijah as a forerunner to Christ.

The instrumentation is majestic throughout; the effect, particularly of the wind instruments, is often genuinely wonderful.

The performance of the oratorio was just what one could expect from the collaboration of our most outstanding musical forces. The orchestra, which appeared to us to be significantly augmented, was, as usual, on the mark. The presentation of the first soprano part completely expressed the intention of an artist[25] who connects the deepest understanding of Mendelssohn's genius with the most magnificent means and called on every resource, as far as it was in her power, in order to produce a perfect presentation of the great work as a worthy tribute to the memory of the universally beloved deceased. Mr. Behr, who sang the difficult and strenuous part of Elijah with as much external perfection as passion of the soul, supported her nobly. Among the other collaborators we should especially note the women, Miss Schloß and Miss Schwarzbach. But indeed the performances of the other ladies and gentlemen all deserve recognition. We would only have wished a little more feeling from the tenor solos. The choruses did not enter precisely enough in the first part, particularly in the two choruses "Yet doth the Lord see it not" and "Woe, woe unto them who forsake him." Indeed, the guilt does not lie in the least with the conductor, Mr. Gade,[26] who, as we all know, made every earthly effort at the rehearsal to eliminate this error and to whom all true music-lovers of Leipzig owe warm thanks for his care and dedication while directing the rehearsals and, finally, the performance. Moreover, the second part went much better than the first and was as fine a testimony to the value of the music as to the enthusiasm of the participants.

The impression of the excellent composition was, as far as we could observe, a powerful, deeply moving, not to say earth-shaking experience for most of the listeners. Fear of an excessively large crowd, the permission to attend the dress rehearsal, and the opportunity to hear the oratorio again in the church prevented many from attending the concert. The approbation of the crowd in attendance remained silent out of regard for the sacred character of the work and for the seriousness of the day. Each person, however, to whom we spoke among our own circle [of acquaintances], was enthralled, uplifted, and moved. Therewith we end our report with the expression of the most complete conviction: every inch a king, every tone a prophet.

NOTES

1. From *The Musical Times* 32 (1891), 137–38.

2. Klingemann was one of Mendelssohn's closest friends (see Chapter 2 in this volume). Hiller (1811–1885) was a pianist, composer, and conductor. Davison (1813–1885) would become a leading English music critic. William Sterndale Bennett (1816–1875) was one of England's most promising young composers.

3. Mendelssohn's longtime friend the violinist David (1810–1873) was concertmaster of the Gewandhaus Orchestra from 1836, later a professor of violin at the Leipzig Conservatory. Mendelssohn consulted his judgment in regard to technical matters in the Violin Concerto in E minor, Op. 64.

4. Rietz (1812–1877), a cellist, had succeeded Mendelssohn in 1835 in the position of city music director for Düsseldorf. He would later prepare the collected edition of Mendelssohn's works.

5. Apparently Felix von Woringen, son of a family who were close friends of Mendelssohn. See Elise Polko, *Reminiscences of Felix Mendelssohn-Bartholdy: A Social and Artistic Biography*, trans. Lady Wallace (New York: Leypoldt & Holt, 1869; repr. Macomb, IL: Glenbridge, 1987), 36.

6. This recitative is probably one of the numbers that Mendelssohn withdrew from the Oratorio after its first performance. [Edwards's note.]

7. Conrad Schleinitz (1805–1881) was a leading figure in Leipzig, one of the board of directors of the Gewandhaus concerts, and later instrumental in the founding of the Leipzig Conservatory.

8. Mendelssohn's father, Abraham Mendelssohn, had died on the previous 19th of November. He had shown a keen interest in the progress of his son's first Oratorio. [Edwards's note.]

9. I owe this to the kindness of Herr Paul David, son of Ferdinand David, and Professor of Music at Uppingham School. [Edwards's note.]

10. Sir George Grove in the Crystal Palace programme of November 30, 1872, and his "Dictionary of Music and Musicians," Vol. II, p. 675. [Edwards's note.]

11. Sir George Smart (1776–1867) was the most important English conductor of his generation. Unlike Mendelssohn, Smart maintained the eighteenth-century practice of leading from the keyboard rather than with a baton from a podium.

12. The great soprano Maria Malibran (1808–1836) had died as the result of injuries from a riding accident. Mendelssohn had composed for her his concert aria "Infelice! . . . Ah, ritorna età dell' oro."

13. Soprano Maria Caradori-Allan (née Munck, 1800–1865), contralto Mary Shaw (née Postons, 1814–1876), tenor John Braham (1774–1856), and bass Henry Phillips (1801–1876) all ranked among the most famous singers in England in the early nineteenth century.

14. Novello (1810–1896), who built his father's music publishing business into one of the leading ones in the world, was also a fine bass singer.

15. See "A Short History of Cheap Music," p. 13 (Novello, Ewer and Co.) [Edwards's note.]

16. From Richard Wagner, *Gesammelte Schriften*, vol. 8, ed. Julius Kapp (Leipzig: Hesse & Becker, 1914), 96–97.

17. Henriette Wüst (1816–1892), soprano; Joseph Tichatschek (1807–1886), tenor; Wilhelm Georg Dettmer (1808–1876), bass. All three singers had participated in the premiere performance of Wagner's *Reinzi* in Dresden in the preceding year.

18. Karl Gottlieb Reissiger (1798–1854) was an important conductor, composer, and teacher.

19. *Signale für die musikalische Welt* 6 (1848), 49–52. The author, "W. L." is presumably Wilhelm Lampadius (1812–1892), Mendelssohn's first biographer.

20. The date would have been Mendelssohn's thirty-ninth birthday.

21. This roster includes some important and some minor local singers. Livia Frege (1818–1891), soprano, was a very dear friend of Mendelssohn. Sophie Schloß (1822–1903) was a leading mezzo-soprano. Soprano Franziska Schwarzbach (1825–1880) sang at the Leipzig Stadttheater. The bass Heinrich Behr (1821–1897), who sang the part of Elijah, would later sing the role of the merchant Kauz in the 1851 Leipzig revival of Mendelssohn's *Heimkehr aus der Fremde*, and in the same performance (Ernst) August Wiedemann (1792–1852) took the tenor part of Hermann. Henry was a bass; August Zimmermann, a tenor. I have not been able to find further information about Miss M. Stark and Mr. Vögner.

22. "True joy is a serious matter."

23. The Leipzig sculptor Imanuel August Hermann Knaur (1811–1872); see *Allgemeine Deutsche Biographie* (Leipzig: Duncker & Humblot, 1882), 270, for a brief biographical sketch.

24. Adolf Bernhard Marx's *Moses* dates from 1841.

25. Livia Frege.

26. The Danish composer Niels Gade (1817–1890) was a protégé of Mendelssohn's in Leipzig and conducted the Gewandhaus Orchestra in Mendelssohn's absence and for a short time after his death.

7

The Orchestral Music

Thomas Grey

THE SYMPHONIES

Mendelssohn's career as symphonist would seem to confirm familiar notions of the composer as a natural-born classicist who adapted only with difficulty to the Romantic temper of his own era or of an early facility tinged with genius that quickly yielded to self-doubt and criticism, further complicated, perhaps, by an impulse to conform to the tastes of a broad, middle-class public. While his overtures did much to establish the composer's reputation, and the concerted works for piano were assured of a positive reception, at least so long as Mendelssohn himself performed them, Mendelssohn's earlier symphonies (nos. 1, 4, and 5 by the traditional reckoning) never managed to take root in the repertoire at the time, and the "Reformation" (no. 5) even met with unaccustomed disapproval or disinterest. It may be that these factors played a part in the composer's increasingly tentative involvement with the genre after the early 1830s. The relative success of the *Lobgesang*, Op. 52, in 1840 and the "Scottish" Symphony, Op. 56 (begun in 1829 but not completed until 1842), was not sufficient to change the course of this decline in symphonic production, at least before the composer's career was cut short by his early death in 1847. This trajectory of early promise and subsequent decline or retrenchment is often projected on Mendelssohn's career as a whole. With regard to specific works, however, this familiar critical model cannot be so neatly maintained, of course, any more for the symphonies than for the overall oeuvre.[1] The "Scottish" Symphony, for example, vies with the "Italian" in critical opinion as Mendelssohn's most significant symphonic achievement; but while they both originated in the same productive period around 1830, much of the "Scottish" (we still cannot say exactly how much) was not completed (or possibly not even conceived) until 1841 and early 1842. Conversely, the "Reformation" Symphony, which continues to be viewed as a somewhat problematic or uneven work, was completed at the time when Mendelssohn was, by consensus, still enjoying the full bloom of his early genius. Whatever their disputed merits or shortcomings, the five canonic symphonies and the baker's dozen of "student" essays for string orchestra (to which we turn next) present a complex, multifaceted portrait of Mendelssohn's development as composer and of the general situation of the symphony in the early nineteenth century. The first major German composer to tackle the symphonic genre after Beethoven, Mendelssohn became in a sense the first (initially unwitting) "victim" of the genre's newly problematic status. Thus, for all its brevity, his symphonic career is also instructive with regard to a variety of stylistic, structural, aesthetic, and cultural issues affecting the nineteenth-century symphony in general.

Prodigious Exercises "in the Old Style": The Early String Symphonies

"His productivity is truly something wonderful," wrote Lea Mendelssohn Bartholdy to one of her Viennese relations in the fall of 1821, reporting with fully justified pride on the accomplishments of her twelve-year-old son, Felix; "in the last year he has composed two operas, [and] the third is almost half finished; besides that, he has also composed a four- and five-part Psalm for the Academy [the Berlin *Singakademie*], including a grand double fugue; [and] six symphonies in the old style, without wind instruments."[2] It is characteristic not only of his rigorous and conservative musical education but also of his ultimate position in musical culture of his time that Felix Mendelssohn's early exercises in composition should pay homage to the past. The six symphonies *nach Art der Alten* (literally, "in the manner of the ancients" or "the old masters") to which Lea Mendelssohn refers are the first of twelve symphonies for strings (an additional movement in C minor is sometimes included to make thirteen) that formed a natural extension of Felix's studies in thoroughbass, chorale, and counterpoint with the noted Berlin musician and pedagogue Karl Friedrich Zelter. Zelter himself was well acquainted with the "ancients," tracing his lineage to J. S. Bach by way of his own teacher, Johann Phillip Kirnberger, one of Bach's foremost pupils and the leading apostle of the Bach heritage across the eighteenth century.[3] Mendelssohn's point of departure in these string symphonies is not so much Bach's music itself, however, as that of his sons and their generation, that is, the early instrumental *sinfonia* as developed in the middle decades of the eighteenth century by the likes of C.P.E and J. C. Bach, Sammartini, Johann Stamitz, and F. X. Richter. The spirit of Haydn and Mozart becomes manifest only in the later group of string symphonies, from the following year. In these string symphonies Mendelssohn took the decisive step beyond prescribed exercises in the realization of figured bass, the harmonization and ornamentation of chorale melodies, and the working out of canons and fugues in two to four voices and moved now to self-guided experiments in "free composition" in the fundamental classical forms. Where the pedagogical precepts of harmony and counterpoint stopped, the creative emulation of classical models took over. The twelve-year-old Felix accomplished this transition with an astounding facility, indeed panache, that can be delightfully observed in the increasing scope and ambition of this group of "student" works, completed as a whole between the first half of 1821 and the autumn of 1823.

Like most of the works of Mendelssohn's prodigious youth, the string symphonies were performed at the famous Sunday musicales hosted by Felix's parents, especially after the family's move in 1825 to the large property in the Leipzigerstraße, which by the end of the decade had become one of Berlin's most significant cultural meeting places. Also like many of the other early works, these symphonies remained unpublished during the composer's lifetime. But while a number of early compositions appeared in print soon after Mendelssohn's death or were incorporated by Julius Rietz into the Breitkopf & Härtel collected edition in the 1860s and 1870s, the string symphonies remained essentially forgotten until their appearance in the first three volumes of the new Leipzig edition of the composer's works between 1965 and 1972. (Since then they have received much attention, especially on recordings.) In accordance with their chronology, these twelve works (or thirteen, counting the additional C minor movement) fall into two fairly distinct stylistic groups, as suggested earlier: while the first six are audibly still apprentice works, we can already glimpse in the second group elements of that astonishingly precocious mastery that would soon manifest itself in such works as the Octet for strings, Op. 20 (1825) and the *Midsummer Night's Dream* Overture (1826). (A list and approximate chronology of the early symphonies are given in Table 7.1.) The first six symphonies resemble each other in their relatively modest

Table 7.1
The Early String Symphonies and Symphony no. 1, Op. 11 (comparative statistics)

Sinfonia I in C major (first half of 1821)
    1. Allegro, 3/4 (C major, 116 mm.)
    2. Andante 3/8 (A minor, 115 mm.)
    3. Allegro 4/4 (C major, 118 mm.)

Sinfonia II in D major (first half of 1821)
    1. Allegro 4/4 (D major, 73 mm.)
    2. Andante 4/4 (B minor, 63 mm.)
    3. Allegro vivace 6/8 (D major, 111 mm.)

Sinfonia III in E minor (first half of 1821)
    1. Allegro di molto 4/4 (E minor, 109 mm.)
    2. Andante 3/8 (G major, 94 mm.)
    3. Allegro 4/4 (E minor, 91 mm.)

Sinfonia IV in C minor (completed 5 September 1821)
    1. Grave 4/4 (C minor, 11 mm.); Allegro 3/4 (C minor, 133 mm.)
    2. Andante 3/8 (C major, 82 mm.)
    3. Allegro vivace 4/4 (C minor, 95 mm.)

Sinfonia V in B-flat major (completed 15 September 1821)
    1. Allegro vivace 4/4 (B♭ major, 120 mm.)
    2. Andante 3/8 (E♭ major, 83 mm.)
    3. Presto 4/4 (B♭ major, 164 mm.)

Sinfonia VI in E-flat major (end of 1821?)
    1. Allegro 4/4 (E♭ major, 113 mm.)
    2. Menuetto 3/4 (E♭ major, 25 mm.)
        Trio (B major, 24+9 mm.); Trio II (B♭ major, 93 mm.)
    3. Prestissimo 2/4 (E♭ major, 262 mm.)

Sinfonia VII in D minor (1821–1822?)
    1. Allegro 4/4 (D minor, 224 mm.)
    2. Andante 3/8 (D major, 145 mm.)
    3. Menuetto 3/4 (D minor, 74 mm.); Trio (B♭ major, 135 mm.)
    4. Allegro molto 6/8 (D minor–D major, 271 mm.)

Sinfonia VIII in D major (6–27 November 1822; arrangement with additional winds, trumpet, and timpani: December 1822)
    1. Grave 3/4 (D minor, 25 mm.); Allegro 4/4 (D major, 255 mm.)
    2. Adagio 3/8 (B minor, 156 mm.)
    3. Menuetto 3/4 (D major, 81 mm.); Trio (D minor, 86+18 mm.)
    4. Allegro molto 4/4 (D major, 559 mm.)

Sinfonia IX in C major (completed 12 March 1823)
    1. Grave 3/4 (C minor, 33 mm.); Allegro 4/4 (C major, 392 mm.)
    2. Andante 2/4 (E major, 169 mm.)
    3. Scherzo 6/8 (C major, 39 mm.); Trio, "La Suisse" (47 mm.)
    4. Allegro vivace 4/4 (C minor–C major, 364 mm.)

Sinfonia X in B minor (13–18 May 1823)
    Adagio 3/4 (B minor, 40 mm.); Allegro 4/4 (B minor, 342 mm.)

Sinfonia XI in f minor (14 June–12 July 1823)
    1. Adagio 4/4 (F major/minor, 36 mm.); Allegro molto 4/4 (F minor, 409 mm.)
    2. Scherzo, "Schweizerlied" 2/4 (D minor, 17 mm.)
    3. Adagio 3/4 (E-flat major, 135 mm.)
    4. Menuetto 6/8 (F minor, 46 mm.); Trio (F major, 25+10 mm.)
    5. Allegro molto 4/4 (F minor, 508 mm.)

Sinfonia XII in G minor (27 August–17 September 1823)
    1. ("Fuga") Grave 4/4 (G minor, 31 mm.); Allegro 4/4 (G minor, 201 mm.)
    2. Andante 6/8 (E♭ major, 85 mm.)
    3. Allegro molto 4/4 (G minor, 435 mm.)

Symphony movement in C minor (dated 29 December [1823?])
    Grave 4/4 (31 mm.); Allegro molto 4/4 (327 mm.)

Symphony no. 1 in C minor, op. 11 (completed 31 March 1824)
   1. Allegro di molto 4/4 (C minor, 487 mm.)
   2. Andante 3/4 (E♭ major, 124 mm.)
   3. Menuetto: Allegro molto 3/4 (C minor, 42 mm.); Trio (A♭ major, 32+43 mm.)
   4. Allegro con fuoco 4/4 (C minor, 284 mm.)

proportions, their adherence to the antiquated, three-movement format (fast–slow–fast) of the pre-Classic *sinfonia,* and their occasionally awkward amalgam of Baroque and galant stylistic traits—onto which are grafted now and then certain whimsical touches that betray the exuberance of the fledgling composer finding his own voice. Mendelssohn himself, in fact, headed the works with the then already archaic designation *Sinfonia,* rather than *Sinfonie* or *Symphonie.*

The first movements of this group are mostly in a simple rounded binary (or "proto"-sonata) form, averaging a little over 100 measures each and lacking any clearly defined thematic articulation of the second key area in the exposition (the new key usually not being firmly established until the end of the section). The modulating passages and modest development sections are largely given over to displays of imitative counterpoint, while nearly every movement opens and closes with a unison statement of the principal theme, contributing to the archaic quality of the style. The internal movements—except for the Menuetto of Sinfonia VI—are all marked andante and are mostly cast in a "galant" $\frac{3}{8}$ meter and simple ternary (ABA) form, of which the central element may consist only in a brief moment of tonal contrast, without independent thematic profile. The finales return to the compact protosonata rounded binary design of the first movements. Here again, Sinfonia VI proves to be the exception, with a finale closer to the jocular, Haydnesque sonata-rondo type.

The most overtly archaizing movement is the B-minor Andante of Sinfonia II, which faithfully transcribes the style and texture of Bach's organ trio sonatas for string quartet. Violas and cellos provide discreet harmonic support to the inter-twining treble lines (see Example 7.1), although the lower instruments also take up the melodic material briefly in the center of the movement. (While the Bach trio sonatas had not yet been published, Mendelssohn may have been introduced to them by Zelter, a well-known hoarder of Bach autographs and manuscript copies, or perhaps by his great-aunt Sara Levy, a highly accomplished musician who had enjoyed significant ties to W. F. and C.P.E. Bach in her youth and who bestowed on Felix the famous gift of the *St. Matthew Passion* score in 1823.) Where this Andante holds consistently to its neo-Baroque matter and method, resulting in a successfully elegant historical pastiche, other movements generate an element of stylistic dissonance, at times, through the juxtaposition of historically disparate elements. Within the opening thematic statement of the Presto finale of Sinfonia V, for instance, an initial rhythmic gesture reminiscent of a Handelian bourrée (i.e., the abrupt cadence in m. 4) is immediately answered by a suave, legato

Example 7.1
Sinfonia II, Andante, mm. 1–5

phrase in a distinctly Classic idiom (see Example 7.2). The central Menuetto of Sinfonia VI contrasts a minuet of a stately Baroque gait (note the antique trilled cadence to the first phrase) with Haydnesque hemiolas in the first of its two trios. In Sinfonia III the explosive, almost Beethovenian gesture that opens the first movement is soon relegated to the status of a busy countersubject to a nondescript fugato subject in half notes. Indeed, Mendelssohn's exercises in ornamented chorale or "chorale prelude" style (*verzierter Gesang*) are everywhere in evidence throughout this early group of symphonies, and it is intriguing to contemplate how all of this practice in restless figurational counterpoint would, within just a few years, be transmuted into the kind of nimble, mercurial filigree that constitutes the distinctively Mendelssohnian trademark of the *Midsummer Night's Dream* Overture, the outer movements of the "Italian" Symphony, the Scherzo of the string Octet, and other chamber works.

In fact, some more distinct anticipations of the "mature" composer who was to emerge by his late teens are evident even in the first six symphonies. Incipient traces of the sentimental, "bourgeois" lyricism of the Songs without Words or the slow movement of the E-minor Violin Concerto, for instance, can be already detected in the andante movements of Sinfonias IV and V. The affecting accompaniment in the C-major Andante of no. IV—a steady triadic arpeggiation in contrary motion between second violins and violas—might put one in mind of

Example 7.2
Sinfonia V, Fourth Movement, mm. 1–8

the first Prelude of the *Well-Tempered Clavier* (while the melodic theme in the first
violins recalls, too, how Gounod and others felt compelled to fill in the "vacuum"
of Bach's beautiful, but unadorned, progressions). The simple subdominant
inflection of the high B♭ in the phrase shown in Example 7.3 from the Andante of
Sinfonia V anticipates a familiar moment in the coda of the *Midsummer Night's
Dream* Overture, the kind of sweetly ingenuous, nostalgic gesture that seems to
typify the image of Mendelssohn as the "classicizing Romantic." The incorpora-

Example 7.3
Sinfonia V, Andante, mm. 38–45

tion of a slow-moving harmonized chorale into the second trio of the minuet
movement in Sinfonia VI offers an early glimpse of the Mendelssohn of the Second
(*Lobgesang*) and Fifth ("Reformation") Symphonies, although what is motivated
there by the explicitly sacred matter of those works remains somewhat enigmatic
in this earlier context.[4] Hints of Mendelssohn's own musical personality are most
audible in the last movement of the last symphony among this first group of six.
Here the ebullient, scampering string idiom of the Op. 20 Octet finale alternates

with a diligent, but lighthearted, fugato that serves as the second subject of a simple, rondolike structure.

In the second group of string symphonies, composed between 1822 and 1823, the proportions of the movements are markedly increased, sometimes to more than two or three times the size of those from the first set (see Table 7.1). In some cases Mendelssohn added a fourth movement (Sinfonias VII, VIII, IX, and XI, the last of these including five movements) and expanded the texture to five voices, with two viola parts (Sinfonias IX, X, and XI, as well as the C-minor movement, "no. XIII"). In the case of Sinfonias VII and VIII, especially, the inclusion of a minuet-and-trio movement as the third of four movements is in keeping with the now more purely high-Classic idiom adopted in these works. The D-major Sinfonia (VIII) is suffused with the spirit of Mozart's "Prague" Symphony and his string quintets, though it cannot lay claim to quite their full measure of musical sophistication. Still, this work represents the most remarkable accomplishment to date by an already astonishingly precocious talent. Indeed, Mendelssohn seems to have registered his own satisfaction with this D-major Sinfonia in choosing to arrange it for full Classic orchestra of strings and winds, almost immediately after the string version. The first movement, like that of the following C-major symphony, is monothematic; but unlike the primitive "monothematicism" of the earlier works (whose expositions lack any distinct formal articulations), these movements adopt the later Classic approach to this technique, whereby the second subject is presented as an independent variant of the first, fully prepared by a lengthy bridge passage and an emphatic moment of textural contrast (the first and second subjects of Sinfonia VIII, movement 1 are shown in Example 7.4a and b), including the Mozartian chromatic anacrusis that introduces the latter. For motivic contrast, a jaunty figure of repeated eighth notes plus a turn-figure introduced in the bridge becomes the faithful contrapuntal companion to these principal subjects throughout the second group, development, and recapitulation. The Adagio, the first of its kind among these string symphonies, breathes a new seriousness, even though it retains the $\frac{3}{8}$ meter favored by the andante movements. A melancholy timbre is imparted by the scoring for violas, divided *a3*, and cello/bass—without violins—and by the slow, repetitive, pulsing gesture that dominates the movement, somewhat reminiscent of such "tragic" slow movements as the Andante of Mozart's Sinfonia Concertante, K. 364, or the Adagio of Beethoven's first String Quartet, Op. 18 no. 1. A purely Haydnesque minuet is paired with a nervously antic trio (presto) that could already suggest the influence of late Beethoven (keeping in mind, however, that Beethoven's "late period" was still in progress at the time). The tutelary genius of the concluding Allegro molto is undoubtedly Mozart's "Jupiter" finale, a presence detectable in a number of the later string symphony movements as well.[5] The movement is a busy *alla breve*—despite the fact that Mendelssohn, for some reason, indicated common time throughout the string symphonies, even where cut time seems clearly understood. This finale generates a seemingly inexhaustible profusion of contrapuntal activity from

Example 7.4
Sinfonia VIII, First Movement

a. mm. 26–38

b. mm. 69–74

combinations of its principal subject and (as in the first movement) a
countersubject introduced in the bridge (see Example 7.5a and b). Only in the

Example 7.5
Sinfonia VIII, Finale

a. mm. 1–11

b. mm. 27–30

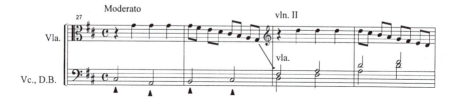

development section is the first subject transformed into a regular and rather
serious fugue. The rest of the movement speaks the language of traditional "florid"
species counterpoint, but from these conventional materials emerges a work of
considerable freshness and verve. Any hint of academic pretension is thoroughly
deflated in two "surprise" codas, the first (m. 513) plunging into a brief passage of
mock-earnest *agitato* in D minor—seemingly quite out of place—and the second
(più presto, m. 531) rushing headlong back to D major in boisterous octaves.

The C-major Sinfonia, no. IX, continues in much the same vein as the
preceding work. In the slow, minor-mode introduction (as in that of Sinfonia VIII)
the young Felix seems to assume a countenance of the utmost adult gravity, as we
are told he did when conducting the little band of musicians who would assemble

at his parents' house for the Sunday afternoon concerts. But this yields to a lighthearted Mozartean Allegro (of ambitious proportions). The E-major Andante of this Sinfonia conducts an interesting formal and timbral experiment. The opening A-section is scored for 4 violins, *divisi*, presenting an angelic tune in sweetly legato homophony. The contrasting B-section is devoted to a ponderous fugato in the lower strings (divided violas with cello/bass). When the A-section returns, the lower strings gradually and unassumingly add their support, with the violas briefly taking up the original melody as the movement draws to a close (a little exercise in Hegelian dialectics, perhaps, or a musical sketch of "Ariel and Caliban"—such were the kinds of themes, after all, that occupied the precocious and receptive student when he was not composing or practicing). The Scherzo approaches the scampering "Mendelssohnian" type that was to be one of the composer's most enduring legacies. Its Trio takes the form of a musical "postcard" of the family's sojourn, in the summer and fall of 1822, in Switzerland, which remained one of Felix's favorite destinations to the end of his life. A simple folkloric tune over a drone bass leads to echoes of the "ranz des vaches," that familiar pastoral tag signifying the rustic sublimities of nature and mountain landscapes for several generations of Romantic composers (see Example 7.6). In the finale Mendelssohn began to approach more contemporary instrumental models (early Beethoven, Schubert, Spohr), and he managed—though not without signs of struggle—to refrain from swamping this attractive and animated movement with extended essays in double counterpoint. The affair culminates, once again, in a pair of brash comic-opera strettos of youthful high spirits.

In some of the remaining string symphonies, however, the impulse for fugal display does predominate, sometimes to a stifling degree. The G-minor Sinfonia (XII) begins with a formal prelude (Grave) and chromatic fugue, accomplished enough but not especially appealing. Its finale also harks back to the Baroque in its materials (including references to the chromatic *soggetto* of the first movement and a strict fugal exposition occupying the position of second group). The movement as a whole suffers from a sense of imbalance and diffuseness, undermining its evident ambitions to synthesize sonata and fugue in the spirit of Mozart.

Much the same might be said about the outer movements of Sinfonia XI (whose finale also sports a fugal second group). The reigning tonality of the work is clearly F minor, despite the oddity of a lengthy slow introduction beginning in F major—though this, too, veers toward the minor as it proceeds. The D-minor tonality of the Scherzo is also peculiar in this F-minor context (while as vi of F major it would, of course, be perfectly normal). Here is another "postcard" from Switzerland, this one an arrangement of a tune known as the "Emmentaler Hochzyt-Tanz" (Emmental wedding dance). Instead of pastoral drone effects, Mendelssohn introduced the "Turkish" colors of drums, cymbals, and triangle in the last part of the movement, evidently in simulation of some other folkloric percussion that he may have witnessed during his travels.

Example 7.6
Sinfonia IX, Third Movement Trio, mm. 39–50

The main Allegro of the preceding one-movement Sinfonia X in B minor has a certain dark, rough-hewn, heavily rhythmic quality to its opening theme that might tempt one to speculate on an ethnic influence of some kind (Slavic or other Central European, even Jewish perhaps?), but the remaining material—second and closing groups—has been thoroughly domesticated to the style of the Biedermeier salon. It is not immediately clear why this work has any greater claims to completeness than the unnumbered movement in C minor (sometimes designated a thirteenth Sinfonia), except that Mendelssohn himself happened to place a Roman numeral at the head of the B-minor movement, as he had done for the preceding nine works (while he did not, for some reason, do so for those now numbered XI and XII). Perhaps some dissatisfaction with the C-minor movement on the composer's part prevented him from adding further movements: it lacks the personal imprint to be found in the Sinfonias VIII through X, for instance, while displaying the same tendency of some of its later companions to dally overlong in stretches of faceless fugato writing.[6] In any event, Zelter's ambitious young pupil had demonstrated clearly enough by this point his capacity for contrapuntal development, as well as his thoroughgoing assimilation of traditional musical languages and formal designs. The later string symphonies as a group convey something of Mendelssohn's eagerness to move beyond compositional exercises in the "old style" and to demonstrate, instead, his rapidly developing ability to speak the language of his own times on a par with the most fluent and accomplished of his contemporaries.

Symphony no. 1 in C minor, Op. 11

In a concert of the London Philharmonic Society of 25 May 1829 Mendelssohn introduced himself to the English public with his first "official" symphony, a work in C minor he had completed five years earlier.[7] After numerous delays, the work eventually became the first of his symphonies to be published, issued as Op. 11 by the Schlesinger firm in Berlin in 1834. Mendelssohn had insisted on the low opus number to indicate the work's earlier origins; but that he persisted with its publication at all and that he had taken some pains to arrange its earlier London performance are evidence that he was not dissatisfied with this early composition. The highly favorable reception that it was accorded by the London audience is not surprising, given its strong stylistic kinship to works that constituted staples of such concerts: Mozart's G-minor Symphony (K. 550), the overtures of Cherubini (especially *Medea*), Weber (especially *Der Freischütz*), and the orchestral works of Louis Spohr, which all belong to the circle of this symphony's elective affinities. That Mendelssohn's C-minor Symphony bears a noticeable resemblance even to works he surely could *not* have known at the time, such as Schubert's Fifth Symphony (B♭), or to works not yet written, such as Marschner's operatic overtures, is a good indication of how comfortably the piece conforms to a kind of *juste milieu* of orchestral writing in the Restoration or early Biedermeier era of about 1815 to 1835. Mendelssohn was fully justified in offering this symphony to the public as proof that the precocious student had graduated to a state of musical adulthood.

In contrast to the string symphonies, Op. 11 shows a deliberate effort to shed all traces of the schoolroom, while demonstrating, instead, a thorough assimilation of various fashionable and tasteful styles (that symphonic *juste milieu* of the time). Not until the finale did Mendelssohn permit himself a passage in strict fugato, at the beginning of the development and coda sections (fourth movement, mm. 102ff., 233ff.). Aside from this, however, the other archaic, Baroque gestures of the student compositions have been abjured altogether. Throughout the symphony Mendelssohn diligently emulated the best contemporary fashions in terms of melodic cut and formal etiquette alike. There is still more Mozart than Beethoven here, but more particularly Mozart as filtered through the well-bred "classicizing" composers of the early nineteenth century. The slow movement, most of all, exudes an air of the late eighteenth century, immediately recognizable, for instance, in the closing phrase of its quasi-sonata form (see Example 7.7). The vigorous but very "tastefully" balanced theme of the finale also echoes a number of Classical minor-mode finale themes, especially that of Mozart's G-minor Symphony (again), while the design of the finale's opening group as a whole is more indebted to Haydn. On the other hand, the scale and overall form of the outer movements, with their emphatic (if not completely convincing) codas, leave no doubt that they belong on the other side of 1800, and even the old-fashioned Menuetto occupying the third-movement position (once again probably modeled on the analogous movement of Mozart's K. 550) is paired with an altogether original Trio.

Example 7.7
Symphony in C Minor, Op. 11, Andante, mm. 47–51

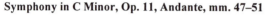

The opening Allegro di molto is conceived very much in the vein of the contemporary overture, particularly that of the German Romantic opera.[8] The principal idea is cut from the same melodic-rhythmic cloth as Cherubini's overture to *Medea*, Weber's to *Der Freischütz*, and Marschner's to *Der Templer und die Jüdin*, to which further examples could doubtless be added (see Example 7.8). Likewise, the complacent lyricism of the second theme (Example 7.9), rocked by alternating tonic and dominant figuration in the second violins, has more in common with the broad "al fresco" idiom of the contemporary overture than with the self-conscious symphonic motivicism of Beethoven or even Schubert. Other theatrical touches include the protracted crescendo (mm. 103–21) leading up to the

Example 7.8

a. Mendelssohn, Symphony no. 1 in C Minor, Op. 11, First Movement, mm. 1–8

b. Cherubini, *Medea*, Overture, mm. 1–8

c. Weber, *Der Freischütz*, mm. 61–69

Example 7.8 continued
d. Marschner, Overture to *Der Templer und die Jüdin*, Main Theme

Allegro con fuoco ed energico

triumphant bluster of the closing theme, dramatized by repeated ♭6 inflections, and
the sudden, portentous cessation of motion that marks the beginning of the coda.[9]
The latter moment, with its eight measures of B♭ sustained pianissimo in the horns,
does suggest Beethoven, but the Beethoven of the *Leonore* overtures rather than
of the symphonies.

The first movement of the Op. 11 symphony reveals already a remarkable
adroitness on the part of the fifteen-year-old composer in the handling of
late-Classic/early-Romantic orchestration and instrumental form. The orchestra
called for is the still-standard one for the day, as found in Haydn's London
symphonies and the earlier Beethoven symphonies: paired woodwinds with

Example 7.9
Mendelssohn, Symphony no. 1 in C Minor, Op. 11, First Movement, mm. 67–74

[Molto allegro e vivace]

clarinets, pairs of horns and trumpets (still of the natural, valveless variety), timpani, and strings, including a separately notated double bass part. The deployment of orchestral textures to articulate the sonata-allegro form also follows the Classic examples of late Haydn (or Mozart) and early Beethoven. The tutti opening group yields to an efficiently modulating bridge section in which the active string parts contrast with the static, harmonic role of the winds, enlivened by a few motivic rhythms. Descending sixth chords in unaccompanied woodwinds (mm. 47–54, 59–66) usher in the lightly scored second group, in which first violin, oboe, and flute engage in a polite melodic dialogue. The previously mentioned crescendo (mm. 103ff.) leading up to the closing theme skillfully reassembles the various orchestral members to join in the boisterous tutti from m. 129 to the end of the section. Just prior to that crescendo a little legato cadence figure in the strings, confirming the new key (E♭), puts a characteristic "Mendelssohnian" imprint on this well-crafted, but otherwise generally derivative, exposition (see Example 7.10)—a figure familiar from the string Octet, among other examples.

The rest of the movement plays out the implications of the exposition material with respect to these stylistic and formal traits, with sufficient ingenuity but without any real surprises. A moderate-size development focuses on the opening gesture of the movement but also incorporates a transformational series on the woodwind chords of the bridge section (mm. 177–200), which is picked up again at the beginning of the coda. Instead of recapitulating the second group in C minor or major, Mendelssohn opted for A♭ major, preserving the "subdominant" relation between tonic recapitulation and original second key (a fifth below or fourth above)

Example 7.10
Symphony in C Minor, Op. 11, First Movement, mm. 87–93

of the traditional major-mode form. The strategy becomes a typical one for the treatment of nontraditional key-areas in Romantic-era sonatas, but a nice touch in this case is the preparation of the second group by V of C (the tonic), which is deftly undercut at the last minute by a D♭–E♭–A♭ motion in the bass line (IV–V–I in A♭), moving up a half step from the previous C. The sizable coda to the movement belongs clearly to a Beethovenian type, effectively working up the movement's principal motive through an extended series of cadential harmonies, following a brief passage of dramatic-rhetorical stasis (mm. 401ff.) that recalls the opening of the development.

In the remaining movements, too, Mendelssohn was often able to transcend the merely competent assimilation of contemporary models, even if such assimilation remains their primary achievement. The Andante is a much more highly crafted movement than any of its counterparts among the string symphonies. The piece is cast in a modified, compact sonata form characterized by consistent recurrences of the cantabile main theme, which also serves as second theme (transferred to woodwinds and restated over string *Rosalien*). Only the presence of a distinct closing idea (the "Mozartean" phrase shown in Example 7.7) and a brief development, based on the transitional B-theme, determine the sonata-like character of the design.

The tranquil A♭ Trio of the Menuetto movement is perhaps the work's most original feature. To identify the slow-moving chordal theme in the clarinets and bassoons (augmented by flutes in the consequent phrases) as a "chorale" would be appropriate but at the same time misleading: this melody has nothing to do with the Lutheran chorale but evokes a more modern, popular (*volkstümlich*) mode of religious-musical expression (one can perhaps imagine it sung by a chorus of nuns in some opera of the period). Mediating between the tranquil lyricism of this Trio and the return to the rugged, syncopated C-minor minuet is a striking, extended transition, which—as others, such as Eric Werner and Wulf Konold, have also noted[10]—must surely have been modeled on the transition between the scherzo and finale in Beethoven's Fifth Symphony. Here, just as in the Fifth, a persistent rhythmic figure (the string accompaniment to the "chorale" theme) spills over the end of the periodic structure, fading to an ominous pianissimo against sustained notes in the strings. Mendelssohn even picks up briefly Beethoven's famous signature rhythm (• • • | •) in the timpani (although this does not congeal into the steady tread of the Beethoven transition), and his transition is also founded on the same neighbor-note motion around the dominant G in the bass (A♭–G–F♯–G). Of course, the musical-expressive contexts are quite dissimilar: where Beethoven's transition breaks through to the glorious triumph of the finale, Mendelssohn is returning to the somewhat dark and turbulent minuet from the oasis of prayerful calm that was the Trio.

The square, classical cut of the finale theme has been mentioned. The movement as a whole, accordingly, unfolds as a fairly regular sonata form, without repeats. Undoubtedly, the most striking feature of the movement is the treatment of the second theme. Its arrival is articulated with the utmost clarity (loud tutti chords on V of E♭, followed by an arpeggiated seventh-chord in solo winds). The first member of the second group, however, consists of nothing but twelve measures of steady, marching chords in pizzicato strings; only in the consequent phrase are these chords supplied with a slightly improvisatory-sounding melody in the solo clarinet (mm. 49–65). This peculiar material returns intact and in place within the recapitulation, the melody doubled by a flute, but otherwise plays no further role in the movement. Only the slightly ponderous four-part fugato of the development section and coda, mentioned earlier, recalls momentarily the world of the early string symphonies. Later in the development this fugato subject is combined simultaneously with two motives from the main theme (mm. 123–36), but in performance the rapid, rocketlike figure of the opening motive tends to be overwhelmed by the rest of the texture here. The loud C-major conclusion to the coda has been justifiably criticized as poorly integrated with the rest of the movement. Apparently, Mendelssohn wanted this triumph to be heard as a consequence of the second bout of fugal exertions that begins the coda, according to that familiar Romantic musical paradigm. Yet even if one were not entirely convinced by the outcome of this local struggle, as enacted in the symphony's closing pages, the work as a whole is convincing evidence of the eminently successful result of the musical exertions represented by those earlier apprentice works. Mendelssohn's first "real" symphony signals a small, but genuine, triumph for its young composer as proof of his convincing mastery of the classical forms. If the string symphonies might be considered Felix's journeyman's papers, the

C-minor Symphony is a fitting validation of old Zelter's solemn induction of his pupil into the guild of musical masters, "in the name of Haydn, Mozart, and old Bach," on his fifteenth birthday, shortly before the completion of this composition.[11]

Symphoniae sacrae: The "Reformation" Symphony and Lobgesang ("Hymn of Praise")

The chronological position of the symphonies now known as nos. 2 and 5 is precisely the inverse of what their numbers indicate, at least with regard to their initial conception. The so-called Fifth Symphony (or the "Reformation," Mendelssohn's own working title for the piece, which he never published) was the second of the full-scale symphonies in order of composition, while the Second Symphony (the Lobgesang, or "Hymn of Praise") was the fifth and last of the symphonies in order of conception, although the Third ("Scottish") Symphony— begun around the same time as the "Reformation"—did not achieve its final form until 1842, two years after the premiere of the Second.[12] The Second and Fifth Symphonies stand somewhat apart from the tradition of an "autonomous" symphonic genre (while at the same time challenging, to some extent, the historical validity of that notion itself), since both were conceived as occasional pieces, intended to accompany the celebration of a civic-religious event. The "Reforma-tion" Symphony was apparently planned for the public ceremonies in Berlin in commemoration of the 300-year anniversary of the Augsburg Confession (the document setting forth the principles of a reformed Christian church, authored by Luther and Melanchthon and presented to Charles V in Augsburg on 25 June 1530). This performance failed to materialize, for a variety of reasons, and the repeated frustrations of faced Mendelssohn's attempts to have the piece performed or published gradually led to a feeling of embittered disaffection toward it. The Lobgesang, on the other hand, was successfully produced for the 1840 celebrations in Leipzig honoring the 400th anniversary of Gutenberg's printing press and quickly became one of Mendelssohn's most widely performed large-scale works in his own day.[13]

Today, both pieces remain distinctly "problematic" cases within the symphonic canon, but problematic in ways that may provoke reflection on a variety of cultural-historical issues and ultimately on the critical status of these works themselves. As a topical work without a poetic text, the "Reformation" Symphony represents an instance of the symphony's controversial new mission—as espoused by A. B. Marx, Mendelssohn's intimate friend and aesthetic adviser-confidant at the time—to embody or represent "ideas," especially grandiose historical and ethical ones of this sort, by means of musical character and form.[14] Its subsequent reception as a marginal example of an ill-defined category of "program music" has tended to misconstrue or simply to ignore the historical-aesthetic context that gave rise to the work, and for that reason, in part, the work has usually been judged harshly. The Lobgesang has met with an equal, if not greater, measure of critical opprobrium since Mendelssohn's time, such that it soon fell—along with most of Mendelssohn's religious music—from the state of grace it had originally enjoyed in *Vormärz* Germany and Victorian England. (The roots of this fall can be located in the backlash against Victorian music and mores instigated by the likes of George Bernard Shaw or Samuel Butler in England, while in Germany it began as early as 1850 with Wagner and other self-styled social and aesthetic "progressives.") Already in Mendelssohn's own day the symphony provoked some unfavorable (if largely irrelevant) comparisons with Beethoven's Ninth and was dismissed as an ill-advised imitation or emulation of Beethoven's "choral symphony." Whether or not the work was intended as such (and it seems unlikely that it was, in any concrete sense), it did represent a still more radical hybridization of the genre than Beethoven's magnum opus, though within an essentially antiradical musical idiom. Both of Mendelssohn's "religious" symphonies, furthermore, are significant documents of what Leon Botstein aptly identifies as a larger project to engage music in the construction of a contemporary bourgeois cultural and moral identity.[15] As sounding monuments to civic pride, to historical and moral self-awareness, these symphonies were meant to contribute, like the oratorios, to a collective aesthetic (and ethical) *Bildung*, a process of communal education and edification.

For Mendelssohn, participation in this project was especially important as a means of affirming his own status as a genuine—and genuinely esteemed—member of a social community to which he and his forebears had only recently gained access. A scion of one of Germany's most prominent Jewish families, Felix Mendelssohn was, like his father and many other relatives, profoundly aware of this heritage, as well as of the complex, volatile, and inescapable issue of Jewish assimilation into middle-class German Protestant society in the early nineteenth century. Felix was baptized in the Lutheran faith at age seven and was consistently encouraged (even admonished) by his father, Abraham, to take seriously the family's act of conversion and the commitment to social assimilation implied by this act. It would be easy to read the significance of Mendelssohn's lifelong engagement with sacred music in various guises (functional liturgical music, large-scale oratorios, as well as these symphonies on religious themes or texts) as dutiful compliance with this directive and as a continually renewed bid for acceptance into the larger social community. But knowing as we do Mendelssohn's staunch refusal to repudiate his family's heritage (as he interpreted his father's demand that he drop entirely the name Mendelssohn in favor of the adopted name Bartholdy) and given the evidence we have of his far from simplistic or opportunistic attitudes toward the issue of assimilation, we ought to accord the sacred works, including these apparently "occasional" symphonies, a more serious, nuanced reading than they usually receive, both as cultural documents and as aesthetic artifacts.

The "Reformation" Symphony: A Musical Offering to the Culture of Assimilation

The earliest recorded reference to plans for a "Reformation" Symphony (already identified by that name) comes from Mendelssohn's first English voyage, in two letters of early September 1829, only about a month after he had received the first impulses for the *Hebrides* Overture and the "Scottish" Symphony.[16] It seems probable that the symphony was planned already with an eye to the upcoming tercentenary celebration of the Augsburg Confession, whether or not Mendelssohn was yet aware of any specific festival agenda in Berlin or elsewhere. As it turned out, he never received any formal commission to contribute to the festivities; instead, Eduard Grell, a fellow Zelter pupil, provided a motet in the "Palestrina style" for ceremonies at the Berlin University (which included an introductory speech in Latin by Hegel and a rendition of "Ein' feste Burg" also—rather inappropriately, it would seem—in Latin) as well as a larger work with chorus and orchestra for the Nikolai-Kirche. Whether Mendelssohn actually made a formal bid to have his symphony performed and whether such a bid was rejected are unclear. With or without a formal guarantee of performance, he went ahead with the composition in the winter of 1829–1830 but did not complete it until 12 May, one day before he embarked on his extended European tour of 1830–1832. By that point, evidently, there was no more question of a Berlin performance. Efforts to have the new symphony performed in Leipzig and Munich, during the first leg of the tour, and later in Paris, near the end of the tour, all came to naught. In the latter case the work got as far as a rehearsal with the Conservatoire orchestra under Habeneck (who had conducted the *Midsummer Night's Dream* Overture to great acclaim). According to one Cuvillon, a violinist in the orchestra, the piece was set aside as being "much too learned, [with] too much *fugato*, too little melody." The pianist-composer Ferdinand Hiller, a close companion during this time in Paris, confirms that this incident "hurt him [Mendelssohn] much." "At the time," Hiller adds, "he was still very fond of it, and the quiet way in which it was shelved certainly pained him. I never referred to the occurrence, and he never spoke of it to me."[17] Mendelssohn did finally secure a public performance back in Berlin that same year (1832), but the work seems not to have made a strong impression then. With no further performances during his lifetime and without the benefit of publication there were no opportunities for critical reappraisal. The bitterness of Mendelssohn's later remarks about the work—as a piece of insignificant juvenilia, a work he could "no longer stand," one that among all his music he would "most gladly burn," and that "should never be published"[18]—certainly reflects an internalization of the repeated frustrations with which the symphony met as much as (or more than) an objective assessment of its value.

This background is perhaps significant for a number of reasons. As Wunderkind and eventually as one of Europe's most celebrated musical talents, Mendelssohn did not cope well with failure. His lifelong resentment over being passed up in favor of the negligible C. F. Rungenhagen as Zelter's successor to direct the Berlin *Singakademie* is a well-known case. The tepid reception of his youthful opera *The Marrriage of Camacho*, though hardly a fiasco, nonetheless seems to have engendered an insurmountable reticence toward the genre almost to the end of his life. (The reverse side of that reticence was an equally tenacious desire to succeed with an opera and thereby expunge the bitterness of that early disappointment.) It seems quite possible that a similar reticence toward the similarly large and "important" genre of the symphony may have resulted from his experience with the "Reformation." The "Italian" Symphony, completed soon after that, was never performed again by the composer after the London premiere and never published. He delayed the completion of the "Scottish" Symphony by over ten years, and the *Lobgesang*—though Mendelssohn did insist on its right to the name "symphony"—moves so far in the direction of the cantata or oratorio that it seems to resist comparison to the rest of the symphonic canon (that with Beethoven's Ninth being presumably unintended by the composer, as I have suggested).

Judith Silber raises the possibility that Mendelssohn's failure to receive a commission to contribute to the celebration of a founding event of the Lutheran Church may have been connected with his Jewish origins, which have traditionally been understood as a factor in the affair of the Singakademie directorship, too.[19] Whether or not this was the case (there is no direct evidence), the fact that Mendelssohn's effort to make a serious musical contribution to this official occasion of national and religious import was not reciprocated, either in Berlin or in Leipzig (as a Catholic center, Munich was a different matter), could be interpreted as a serious blow to that impulse, sketched earlier, to affirm his membership in the German Protestant bourgeoisie and to contribute to the shaping of its collective identity. Whether or not the issue of his Jewishness really did play a part here or in the *Singakademie* affair, it was not, in any case, something that would have been publicly articulated by either party, thus leaving the possibility of anti-Semitic motives forever open in Mendelssohn's own mind, perhaps. (All the same, it should also be recalled that the symphony was not completed until forty-three days before the festivities, and therefore practical matters may well have been involved, too.) Ironically, if the "silencing" of the "Reformation" Symphony in Germany might have been attributable to Mendelssohn's status as a Jew, its rejection in Paris (possibly even in Munich) seems to have been predicated on its appearing either "too German" or "too Lutheran"—too much like "old Bach," at least for Parisian tastes.

What *are*, then, the "Lutheran" or more broadly religious-historical components of the "Reformation" Symphony? What is it in the composition itself that celebrates the "idea" of a reformed Christian church, evokes its history, or portrays its protagonists? The basic referential or topical materials are not hard to find. Most obvious and perhaps inevitable is the chorale, "Ein' feste Burg ist unser Gott," extensively quoted in the finale. This most famous of Lutheran chorales not only is emblematic of Luther as an individual (who composed both melody and text), it also attained the status of something like a national anthem in preimperial nineteenth-century Germany (followed in popular recognition value by "Nun danket Alle Gott," which figures significantly in the *Lobgesang*). The slow introduction to the first movement cites a variety of sacred materials, both directly and by stylistic allusion. The opening four and a half bars build up strettolike entries, steadily ascending, of another familiar nineteenth-century musical sign of the sacred frequently encountered in actual church music—including some of Mendelssohn's own—and generally understood to denote a sense of religious devotion and exaltation (the gesture is often identified as a personal "symbol of the cross" in Liszt's music, for instance). This figure derives from a common intonation formula encountered in Gregorian psalm tones and canticles (such as the Magnificat on the third tone), consisting of a rising major second followed by a minor third; when the third note is resolved downward by a semitone, as it is in most of the voices of these opening bars (see Example 7.11), one can also recognize the incipit of Mozart's "Jupiter" Symphony finale (which also carries vaguely ecclesiastical connotations). Crucial to the "exalted" effect of this introduction, however, is the dissonant overlapping of entries, resolved by suspension, and their systematic ascent—heavenward, as it were. This ascent is crowned by a four-measure phrase in a ceremonial chorale style, scored for woodwinds and brass, including trombones, whose timbre in such contexts was traditionally read as another sign of things solemn and sacred.

Example 7.11
Symphony in D Major, Op. 107, "Reformation," First Movement, mm. 1–5

A further denotative element introduced here is the hortatory, repeated-note gesture variously scored for winds and brass, beginning in m. 23 (but prepared across several measures before that). The ambitus of the figure expands from a third to a fourth and stepwise to a fifth, and the double-dotted rhythm of its tail is further emphasized in a fanfare-like transformation in mm. 31 and 36, surely to be heard as a call to arms for militant reformers. Finally, these climactic calls to arms of the introduction are twice contrasted with beatific, pianissimo statements of the "Dresden Amen" in the strings (now famous as the "Grail" motif from Wagner's *Parsifal*). The hortatory fanfare gesture is transformed again later (opening out to a full fifth) as the principal motif of the following Allegro, while the "Dresden Amen" will effect one more dramatic intercession at the juncture between development and recapitulation of the movement.

Of the explicitly sacred referential materials employed in the symphony, the sense of the Luther chorale, "Ein' feste Burg," is unambiguous, of course, but that of these introductory themes is less so. Wulf Konold suggests that the juxtaposition of the opening contrapuntal expansion of the "psalm-tone" figure with the homophonic choralelike phrase in the winds may be meant to embody the contrasting principles of Catholicism and Protestantism,[20] the antagonistic factions whose struggles are evidently evoked in the ensuing Allegro. (Within the introduction, however, they seem to co-exist peacefully enough.) The hypothesis is a reasonable one, but we must also recall that the revival of a so-called Palestrina style in the nineteenth century was by no means limited to Catholic practitioners, as its presence in Mendelssohn's church music attests. It is equally difficult to attach any specific denominational association to the "Dresden Amen." To the modern listener it signifies, above all, *Parsifal* and Wagner's murky religion of regeneration through art. But what did it mean in 1830? The phrase appears to have originated as a liturgical clausula composed for Catholic services in eighteenth-century Dresden by J. G. Naumann.[21] Mendelssohn employs it not as any concrete, esoteric reference, apparently, but very much as Wagner was to use it, as a sonic icon of some exalted goal, the musical image of a sacred covenant, a promise of salvation. The harmonic motion from tonic to tonicized dominant, with the fifth degree serving as upper voice of each chord, combines with the "ethereal" scoring for widely spaced strings to create an impression of something at once floating and secure, a vision or promise to be fulfilled, invested with divine authority. It scarcely appears as a challenge; rather, it seems to inspire the militant "call to arms" with which it alternates at the end of the introduction. As Konold puts it, the phrase stands apart from its musical context, hovering over it "like a sonorous gloriole."[22]   Other "characteristic" materials that crop up in the symphony—the jaunty wind-band march theme of the second group in the finale or the Beethovenian elements of recitative and *arioso dolente* in the brief Andante movement—are similarly equivocal as to any specific referential meaning, but there can be little doubt that they *are* intended to function as referents, all the same, within the larger musical tableau.

Whatever the Marxian (or, for that matter, Mendelssohnian) "idea" behind the symphony may be, as historical tableau or narrative in tones, it is, of course, not exhausted in the mere enumeration of such characteristic materials or referents. Moreover, the significance, value, and meaning of the "Reformation" Symphony are by no means exhausted in the decoding of its materials to reveal ideas, images, or stories embedded in its forms. The latter point need hardly be stressed today. But since for almost a century critics have felt called upon to redeem works of this sort from the taint of programmatic naiveté and a suspected (concomitant) slackness of formal thought by demonstrating how they are held together through some secret transformation of motivic intervals (inaudible to the naked ear), it might be worthwhile devoting our attention here to some of the ways that Mendelssohn may, indeed, have thought to realize the "idea" of the Reformation in the music of his symphony—not simply by virtue of its thematic materials alone but also through their deployment within its formal processes.

If the music of the slow introduction is possibly meant to convey something Catholic (the chant-based *stile antico* phrases) or a juxtaposition of Catholic and Protestant symbols, the finale obviously leaves no doubt as to the triumphantly Protestant outcome of events, with the opening phrase of Luther's chorale massively hammered out in whole notes by the entire orchestra in its final measures.[23] Even leaving aside the possible role of Catholic symbols (for it would be difficult to locate any concretely Catholic musical agents anywhere in the rest of the symphony), the overarching historical plot is clear enough. The militant musical campaign waged in the first movement—which has been sparked by the religious visions of the introduction and the hortatory voice raised there—is crowned with victory in the finale, signaled not only by the role of Luther's "Ein' feste Burg" chorale, but just as much by the celebrational pomp of the first and second themes themselves, the first theme harking back to the rocket-figures and sweeping *coups d'archet* of the festive eighteenth-century *sinfonia*, and the second cast in the style of a triumphal wind-band march, picked up by the whole orchestra in the recapitulation. The title "Reformation" itself (assuming that Mendelssohn would have sanctioned it, had he ever published the symphony), with its suggestion of spiritual and worldly historical strife, would lead one to infer some such plot type. But even without the title, the bellicose text of Luther's chorale—well matched by the pugnacious melodic incipit of his tune—could also point in this direction.[24] How, or if, the scherzo and slow movement fit into a broad plot of this sort has often been a matter of some puzzlement. The scherzo movement (Allegro vivace) functions as a kind of interlude, presumably, while the arioso-like Andante is clearly treated as a prelude to the finale, which follows it *attacca*. The pattern established by the last two movements of anguished plea (styled as vocal solo) followed by a robust, affirmative "choral" (or indeed, "chorale") response is replicated—or more fully realized—in the later portion of the *Lobgesang*, where the tenor's threefold question "Watchman, is the night soon past?" (set as dramatic recitative) is answered by a jubilant D-major chorus, followed by a setting of the chorale "Nun danket Alle Gott" (first a cappella and then in elaborate "chorale prelude" style).

None of this should imply any naive attempts at concrete historical representation on Mendelssohn's part, and naturally his music has nothing to do with the once-popular genre of battle-pieces represented by Beethoven's *Wellington's Victory*. Rather, he adapts his characteristic or referential materials to movements that, by and large, observe the generic and formal proprieties of the modern "grand symphony." It is interesting to see, nonetheless, how even a critic like Hermann Deiters (a contributor to the resurrected and still conservative *Allgemeine musikalische Zeitung*, best remembered for his contributions to the original edition of Thayer's Beethoven biography) cannot help engaging the implicit narrative of Mendelssohn's symphony—even while he appears to resist it—in his review of the first published score in 1868. (A translation of this review is included among the Historical Views and Documents following this Chapter). Deiters, for example, immediately recognized the role of the portentous recitational and fanfare gestures that emerge within the slow introduction. He notes how the repeated-note recitational figure of mm. 23ff. ("a firm and powerful voice, as if prophesying something yet to come, in a manner reminiscent of old chorale singing") is transformed into the hortatory fanfare gesture at m. 31, described as a "decisive figure suggesting some solemn call or invocation (*Anruf*)." The word *Anruf* here connotes in particular a call to attention, to action, or to arms.

The following Allegro is explicitly read along the lines of the by then already rather overly familiar trope of a spiritual or psychological struggle; this reading duly registers the militant tone of the opening group, the gesture of supplication and hopeful yearning audible in the second theme, and, perhaps most interestingly, the expressive or narrative "idea" conveyed by the particular treatment of the recapitulation. The unexpected return of the "Dresden Amen" to articulate the beginning of the recapitulation is heard as "a gentle admonition, at a point where, amid the raging storm of battle, one has nearly forgotten the true goal." The equally unexpected transformation of the opening group in the recapitulation evidently means something, too, although Deiters declines to hazard any specific guess. This quiet, bleached-out version of the theme, with reduced orchestration, is an eerie, melancholy shadow of the exposition. The transformed theme constitutes an apt aural image for the "reprise" of such struggles, now that the exertions of the battle have taken their toll. (One might even be tempted to hear in it a categorical response—exhausted, pathetic, resigned—to the relentless formal imperative of the recapitulation per se, with its ritual demand for repetition and closure.) The modulations and "restless" eighth-note motion of the strings throughout the center of the development, as Deiters does remark, seem to be driven on by the fanfare-call of the introduction, presiding over the battle like a general or like Luther in the role of warrior-priest. The similar juxtaposition of material heard in the exposition bridge, from which the development derives, is excised from the recapitulation, which consequently maintains its subdued, exhausted aspect throughout.

Deiters attributes the character transformation of the recapitulation to the composer's aim to subject the symphonic form to the purposes of some "idea." The strategy of this subdued recapitulation, however, can be interpreted equally well in formal terms as in those of an extramusical semantics. The abridgment of the recapitulation is a standard procedure of Mendelssohn's sonata forms, as it is with many other composers after Beethoven who chose to devote more space and emphasis to the roles of development and coda. In this case, the energies of the bridge and of the original first group are stored up for a dramatic rerelease within the coda in the form of a large-scale crescendo that climaxes in a tutti statement of the militant main theme in the closing measures (the subdominant chord of the theme's fifth measure now serves as the pre-dominant member of a simple, emphatic cadence).   The appropriate application of the battle scenario is not difficult to discern: the temporarily exhausted soldiers of the Reformation (be they spiritual or temporal, physical soldiers) muster their strength for a final assault; at the height of this final fray the imploring second theme is taken up briefly by the chorus of woodwinds (mm. 507–13). The outcome is apparently decisive (the closing measures of the movement); but it is still too early to celebrate this victory.

The key relation of the inner two movements—in B♭ and G minor, respectively—to the D-minor (and major) tonality of the outer movements is unconventional, as is the key relation of Trio (G major) to Scherzo. There is nothing otherwise formally unusual about the Scherzo, although in rhythmic and melodic character it does not resemble the Beethovenian type especially, and Mendelssohn did not explicitly designate it as Scherzo at all. If anything, it sooner resembles some of the *alla marcia* movements of Beethoven's late sonatas (despite the $\frac{3}{4}$ time signature). Unlike the other movements, there is little about the musical material that would immediately strike one as referential or topical, except perhaps for a certain folkishness, especially in the *Ländler*-like Trio. One peculiar musical detail of the Scherzo is the tiny legato figure that forms an appendix to the rest of the movement (mm. 53–55, see Example 7.12a). This new melodic figure seemingly remains a fragment, cut off by an echo of the main Scherzo theme in flutes and oboes, but it also seems to anticipate the legato, circling melody, also in quarter notes, of the following Trio (Example 7.12b), and hence to form a link between the sections. The sustained flute trills of the Trio are another distinctive feature, possibly conjuring up images of banners or ribbons fluttering in the wind, such as might form the visual background to the kind of popular *Volksfest* evoked by both sections of the movement.[25]

An interesting letter written from Munich not long after the symphony's completion testifies to the kinds of historical images Mendelssohn that had hoped to capture in this movement and the preceding one. "I wish you all could have been with me recently, as I strolled about among the people during the procession," he writes to his family, with reference to a colorful Corpus Christi pageant he had just witnessed in the Bavarian capital:

[I] looked around and was very pleased with myself and the initial movements of my "Church" symphony [*Kirchensymphonie*], for I wouldn't have thought that things today would still correspond so well with the contrasts of the first two movements. But if you had heard how the people recited their prayers so monotonously, with one hoarse priest screeching through it all and another reading off the Gospel, and how all of a sudden military music came blasting right into the middle of things, [or] how the little colorfully painted flags fluttered to and fro, and how the choirboys were draped with golden tassels—then I think you would have praised me, as I did myself, and was pleased.[26]

Although Mendelssohn's symphony does not quite realize the startlingly proto-Mahlerian scenario sketched in this letter (the interruptive march, e.g.), it is not hard to recognize, at least, some of the sound-images he evidently strove to evoke though contrasting elements of his first movement (the hoarsely intoning

Example 7.12
Symphony in D Major, Op. 107, "Reformation," Scherzo

a. mm. 53–60

b. mm. 63–74

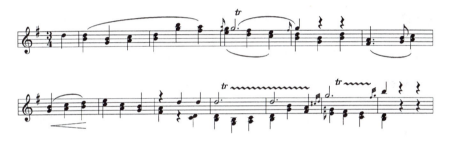

priests), his Scherzo ("military" or festive processional music) and Trio (those "little painted flags fluttering to and fro"?).

The unusual brevity of the following slow movement is explained, in part, by the composer's excision of twenty-eight measures that had originally constituted a concluding section in G major.[27] An examination of these deleted measures leaves little doubt as to the sagacity of the composer's decision to cut them. The passage is essentially transitional, with no thematic relation to the existing movement (although the "liturgical" 1–2–4–3 contour of the first movement introduction is evoked here in a flute recitative that begins the passage); an awkward tonicization of C major in the closing measures is particularly puzzling. The revised, shorter movement is given the aspect of a small ABA¹ form by virtue of a return to its opening gesture alone, briefly echoed but directly followed by new cadential activity. The equally diminutive midsection begins with a modulating melody (G minor to Eb), interrupted by recitative gestures in the first violins. The climax of these expressive gestures in m. 31 resolves (or dissolves), by means of a "recitative" cadence, directly into the fragmentary reprise. The physiognomy of this little tragic-lyrical scene is clearly indebted to the slow movement of

Beethoven's Op. 110 piano sonata, which is likewise directly linked to its ensuing finale. Like the sonata movement (whose melody Beethoven marked as a "song of lament" or *klagende Gesang*), Mendelssohn's Andante evokes gestures of vocal lament (Hermann Kretzschmar heard echoes of Pamina's "Ach, ich fühl's," another G-minor lament), mixing free arioso with elements of a pathetic accompanied recitative. Such a generic-stylistic identification goes some way toward explaining the enigmatic repercussion of the first movement's second theme—that anguished, beseeching figure—in the closing measures of this movement (see Example 7.13).

Example 7.13
Symphony in D Major, Op. 107, "Reformation," Third Movement, mm. 50–54

Those supplications heard amid the din of the first movement have not been extinguished or forgotten. The prayer that rises toward heaven here, like a pair of outstretched hands, is met (after a moment's pause) by the redemptive tones of the chorale "Ein' feste Burg" in the solo flute, introducing the last movement.

Granted, the relation of the first three movements in terms of a linear narrative logic is far from manifest. But in a more abstract sense, one conditioned by the generic requirements of the traditional symphonic cycle, Mendelssohn's musical "picture" of the Reformation establishes its own compelling *telos* of collective historical experience: the rigors of battle (and first-movement form) yield to a moment of relaxation and popular celebration (the Scherzo); but the spiritual need or longing of the people remains and will be fulfilled only by the promise of a new creed, that of the Reformed Protestant Church (the finale). (By using "Ein' feste Burg" as the musical emblem of this historical goal, Mendelssohn inevitably identified that new religious creed, for his nineteenth-century listeners, with that of a new national sovereignty.) Although Mendelssohn himself disdained a flag-waving, chauvinistic brand of nationalism, his finale nevertheless celebrates a new popular national consciousness, just as the occasion for which he conceived it was as much a celebration of national aspirations as of religious history.

Mendelssohn's finale has met with much negative criticism, usually on the grounds of its formal unconventionality—the same grounds on which other composers are generally praised. Eric Werner was bothered by the "brilliant coda" that the composer allowed himself (in which case it is not clear what story he expected Mendelssohn to tell about the Reformation) and by putative reminiscences of Weber's *Freischütz*.[28] Wulf Konold complains of a sense of force or contrivance in the movement's synthesis of chorale-variation and sonata-form elements.[29] Philip Radcliffe, who found the formal design of the movement "interesting and successful," was perhaps closer to the mark in locating its shortcomings in the somewhat bald thematic invention of the movement's sonata-form interior and in what he felt to be a certain unbridgable gulf between "us" and the original musical-cultural aspirations of the movement.[30] It is hard not to suppose that much of the critical discomfort that this movement seems to generate is connected to its extensive parading of the famous chorale tune, which surely strikes some listeners as not being entirely in good symphonic taste. Carl Dahlhaus remarks that the citation of the chorale tune "is more appropriate to an overture than to a symphony, which thereby turns into an oversized overture."[31] That is to say, the incorporation of traditional, popular, or nationalistic material of this sort marks the symphony as an occasional piece rather than a piece of "absolute music." Of course, the genesis of the symphony bears out this association: it was, indeed, conceived as an occasional piece. But at the same time, its subsequent history forces us to reconsider the grounds of this distinction: the "occasion" fell through, yet Mendelssohn still completed the work and tried to perform it on its own merits.

What, finally, was Mendelssohn trying to achieve in this finale and by means of this chorale? "Ein' feste Burg" serves as the subject of an unusual two-part introduction to the movement proper, in the form of a full statement of the chorale tune (harmonized and progressively embellished) followed by a free fantasia upon its opening phrase, in a fast $\frac{6}{8}$. The opening, complete statement of the chorale tune stands as an emblem not only of the Protestant faith but also of congregational singing, itself an emblem of the collective bourgeois social-religious identity that Mendelssohn's symphony celebrates, beyond the specific deeds of Luther and Melanchthon. One is probably more justified in invoking the model of Beethoven's Ninth here than in the case of the *Lobgesang*: just as Beethoven builds up his "Joy" theme as a symbolic accretion of independent voices around a central, "sacral" melody, so Mendelssohn does with "Ein' feste Burg," only in the opposite direction, beginning in the solo flute and working downward. (When the bass trombone undergirds the woodwind choir at m. 11, the timbre of the organ is also evoked, the trombone impersonating the sound of some resonant 16' or 32' pedal stop.) The $\frac{6}{8}$ Allegro vivace passes the head-phrase of the chorale among the instruments—a kind of musical communion, as it were—and generates a new rhythmic momentum that eventually thrusts the listener altogether from the world of sacred ritual into that of civic pomp and circumstance, with the opening of the sonata-form proper (Allegro maestoso, m. 63). The very beginning of the Allegro is really nothing *but* such pomp and circumstance, it might be argued, since it is only the second part of the first group (m. 80; see Example 7.14) that is later recapitulated and that exhibits a more distinct thematic identity than the opening material. The processional, marchlike character of the second theme (m. 121) has already been mentioned. In between comes a typically early-Mendelssohnian fugato bridge, with a busy running accompaniment; the repeated-note fugato

Example 7.14
Symphony in D Major, Op. 107, "Reformation," Finale, mm. 80–83

subject and its subsequent transformations suggest the opening of the chorale-tune, again, without quite citing it. In place of a development Mendelssohn introduced the *central* phrase of the chorale in the bassoon, lightly accompanied by the strings. (Whatever sense of "contrivance" may attach to this synthesizing gesture, it is balanced by the logic of cutting to the middle of the tune at this point.) Full woodwinds and then violins pick up the closing phrase of the chorale and redirect it toward a reprise of the "main" theme from m. 80 (at mm. 199ff.). To justify the introduction of the chorale into the sonata form, Mendelssohn had to play out the consequences of this intrusion, and this he did by superimposing the *opening* phrase over the busy transitional fugato of the strings (mm. 229ff.). If the fugato activity is meant to evoke a sense of diligent striving, as it so often is in the nineteenth century, then Luther's chorale leads it upward and onward here, to the tutti presentation of the "triumphal" second-theme march (m. 246). A beautiful and thoroughly Mendelssohnian effect is produced by the sudden appearance of a series of broad, legato cadential figures, pianissimo, at m. 264, beginning on, and returning to, a first-inversion tonic chord. (The whole passage is strongly reminiscent of portions of the *Meeresstille und glückliche Fahrt* Overture.) The conclusion of that overture is also recalled here in the swelling fanfares that lead into the final apotheosis of "Ein' feste Burg," with which the symphony concludes. Far more than simply representing the triumph of Luther and Protestantism over a dimly demonized group of Catholic opponents, the rather clever synthesis of this chorale into the process of the finale seems to evoke what was, for Mendelssohn, a more significant theme: the merging of spiritual and civic life, ethics, and values ideally represented by the very kind of occasion for which the symphony had been intended. The religion celebrated by Mendelssohn's symphony was that to which the composer willingly subscribed (if also at his father's behest) as a token of his desire to participate in the larger social community of his time and place and to participate in defining the collective identity of that community in terms of its history, culture, and values. With the "Reformation" Symphony he had hoped, it seems, to contribute to the construction of this collective social and cultural identity by offering a musical interpretation of some of the images and stories in which it was grounded.

Lobt den Herrn mit Saitenspiel, lobt Ihn mit eurem Liede: Mendelssohn's "Symphony-Cantata after Words from the Holy Scripture," Op. 52

When Mendelssohn's recently premiered symphonic-vocal hybrid, to which he had given the German title *Lobgesang*, was to be performed as the concluding work to a music festival in Birmingham in September 1840, the composer wrote to his friend Karl Klingemann: "The title 'symphony' must be left out in the English version—but how would one best express the notion of a 'general song of praise' (*allgemeiner Lobgesang*)? Certainly not hymn. Could one say *the song of praise?*"[32] Ironically, despite Mendelssohn's emphatic injunction to the contrary, the work we now know as the Symphony no. 2 has also become universally known, in English, as the "Hymn of Praise." Just why Mendelssohn should have objected particularly to this translation is not immediately clear, nor why he told Klingemann to drop the word "symphony" from its title, when in the very same letter he had just stated quite plainly that "the piece, [written] for the [Gutenberg] festival here, is no oratorio, rather, as I have called it in German, a 'symphony for chorus and orchestra,' under the title *Lobgesang*." There is certainly no reason that the title could not have been translated directly as "Song of Praise," as Mendelssohn suggested. The original generic designation, "symphony for chorus and orchestra," is, in any case, misleading, since the symphonic and choral-vocal portions of the work are quite distinct, more so than in the case of the famous precedent of Beethoven's Ninth. (The fact that Mendelssohn eagerly adopted Klingemann's subsequent suggestion of "symphony-cantata" reinforces the indication in this letter that he came to think it inappropriate to call the work a "symphony" outright.)

Both of these matters—the questions surrounding nomenclature of "song" and "symphony"—may appear to be somewhat trivial, at first. They may, however, be connected and in a way that sheds some light on Mendelssohn's conception of the work and on its awkward generic status. In the same letter to Klingemann, he goes on to describe the contents of the work:

> first three symphonic movements, to which twelve [*sic*] choral and solo movements are appended; the words from the Psalms, and in fact all the movements—vocal and instrumental alike—are composed on the words [*auf die Worte . . . komponiert*]: "All that has breath, praise the Lord!" [*Alles was Odem hat, lobet den Herrn*]; you understand, of course, that first the instruments offer praise in their way, and then the chorus and the individual voices.[33]

This latter observation neatly corresponds to the second line of the work's text, as adapted from the thirty-third Psalm: *Lobt den Herrn mit Saitenspiel, lobt ihn mit eurem Liede* (Praise the Lord with stringed instruments, praise him with your song). Mendelssohn's paraphrase of the psalm text is particularly devised, apparently, to point up the structure of the work as a whole, in which the instrumental "song" of the symphonic movements is supplemented by solo and choral singing (or song proper).[34] The whole work is one large "song" (a kind of "meta-song," so to speak), embracing the high, dignified genres of symphony and oratorio, but without trying to pass for either one or the other, in their pure form.

(As regards the earlier issue of "hymn" versus "song," one can only surmise that, in Mendelssohn's view, there could be songs without words, but not hymns without words.)

The symphony-cantata *Lobgesang* was conceived and at least informally commissioned (by the town council of Leipzig) for a specific public occasion: the 400th anniversary of Gutenberg's invention of printing (both the date and the historical status of this "invention" are rather approximate). This time Mendelssohn clearly was intent on composing a piece that would transcend the mortality of a purely occasional work, as he presumably had been with "Reformation" Symphony. "I am seizing this occasion to write something new," he wrote to Julius Schubring, with whom he had at first discussed the possibility of an oratorio on the subject of St. John for this event, "but I don't mean to compose it [simply] for the occasion."[35] Indeed, the text that Mendelssohn eventually assembled for the cantata portion of the work makes no explicit reference to Gutenberg or to his printing press. (Gutenberg, unlike Luther, would be hard to evoke by musical references alone.) In one sense Gutenberg's emblematic artifact, his printed Bible, provides the point of contact between occasion and composition; the Bible also constitutes a loose link back to Luther, whose translation Mendelssohn paraphrases in his text. But as a "song of praise" drawing on assorted psalm texts, Mendelssohn's symphony-cantata still remains extremely general, autonomous of any particular context—a kind of all-purpose Protestant Te Deum.

The central portion of the text (nos. 6 and 7 of the score, assembled from verses of Ephesians, Isaiah, and Romans) points more directly to the symbolic significance of Gutenberg's achievement, while also forming the dramatic crux of the vocal movements. The imagery of night and darkness yielding to day and light celebrates the universal dissemination of the printed word as an act of enlightenment.[36] With this gesture Mendelssohn paid homage to the legacy of his grandfather, Moses Mendelssohn, and to a tradition of rationalist, universalist ethics that surely must have meant more to Felix, finally, than any details of a specifically Lutheran dogma. If the choice of texts here conceals a potential conflict between the claims of the (scriptural) Word, on one hand, and those of humanistic letters and learning, on the other, as the source of enlightenment, this very conflict is itself of symbolic significance for Mendelssohn's own situation. But then, the actual occasion for this symphony, even more than that for the "Reformation," was an amalgam of secular-civic (even mercantile) ideals and religious worship. It was Mendelssohn's own decision, after all, to write a symphony "after words of the Holy Scripture." Perhaps the very gesture of uniting the genres of symphony and oratorio was imbued with a symbolic import, a symbol of the society's efforts to harmonize religious and worldly values, and of Mendelssohn's own efforts to reconcile his personal allegiance to a Jewish past and a Christian present under the aegis of the Enlightenment.

The symphonic-orchestral portion of the work, to which the following remarks are largely limited, is not, of course, intended as an autonomous, detachable composition in its own right, any more than the first three movements of Beethoven's Ninth Symphony are. It is symptomatic of the power of genre and custom that numerous editions and arrangements since the nineteenth century—at a loss as how to confront this generic hybrid—have offered up the orchestral movements as an incongruous torso, an "unfinished symphony" whose pompously assertive opening movement in B♭ major is thus rounded out by the quiet and distinctly unemphatic conclusion of the D-major Andante religioso (not exactly the kind of formal experiment one would expect from Mendelssohn, after all!).

The principal means of uniting the orchestral "Sinfonia," as Mendelssohn called it, with the vocal cantata is, of course, the prominent motto-theme of the orchestral introduction; this theme later returns to the signature text of the first vocal number, "Alles was Odem hat, lobet den Herrn," and then once again as a brief valedictory statement, after the final Handelian *Schlusschor* with fugue, at the conclusion of the whole work. In the Maestoso introduction to the first (instrumental) movement this motto is already treated in a choral, specifically responsorial manner, pronounced in unison by three sacerdotal trombones, and echoed in full harmony by the rest of the orchestra (see Example 7.15a). The pitch contour of this motto signals the sacred matter of the symphony in combining both the familiar rising second plus minor third psalmodic incipit (transposed to 5–6–8) with the 1–2–4–3 outline of the "Jupiter" finale theme, the tonic pitch B♭ serving as a pivotal joint (see Example 7.15b). The dotted rhythm of the motto imparts a

Example 7.15
Lobgesang

a. no. 1, Sinfonia, mm. 1–5

b. Pitch contour of motto

ceremonial, marchlike atmosphere to the introduction and is carried over into the theme of the ensuing Allegro, most notably in the third and fourth bars (see Example 7.16). Here the ceremonial pomp of the introduction is transformed into a spirit of restless optimism, a propulsive energy that is characteristic of Classic-Romantic symphonic first movements and that one is tempted to associate in this context with the (Judeo-)Protestant work ethic that was so much a part of Mendelssohn's upbringing. (The modulating cast of the otherwise rhythmically relaxed second theme also contributes to this overall character of energetic activity.)

Example 7.16
Lobgesang, **no. Sinfonia, mm. 23–28**

Strictly speaking, of course, there is no representational or even clearly refer-ential impulse to any of these orchestral movements, aside from the introductory motto and the importation of chorale style into the trio of the second movement. Still, Mendelssohn made an effort to weave the motto itself, not only its dotted rhythm, into the entire texture of the first movement, thus linking this movement more strongly to the subsequent texted portion of the work than is the case with the inner movements. One might better say that he wove the motto into the *seams* of the movement, as it figures extensively in the bridge, development, and coda, as well as in the postlude-transition to the following movement, while it is avoided within the principal thematic sections of the form (first, second, and closing groups). In the bridge section (mm. 63–82) and part of the development (mm. 189–209) the motto is played against a busy counterpoint in running sixteenth notes and triplet eighths, respectively, further contributing to the character of unceasing *Tätigkeit* or industry that could be imagined as the latent affect of the movement. The bridge is excised from the recapitulation, corresponding to the composer's usual tendency to abbreviate this section; but in this case the resulting suppression of the motto-theme in the recapitulation provides a nice foil for its grandiose return in the coda, from m. 338, where it is impressively built up in stretto fashion over a dominant pedal (mm. 351–58).

The role of this motto in the first movement brings up a question about the genesis of the symphony that cannot be answered with any certainty. In a number of letters written between 1838 and 1840 Mendelssohn speaks of beginning work on a symphony—in several instances specified as a symphony in B♭—that was never completed, unless perhaps it was incorporated into the *Lobgesang* project.[37] There is certainly some logic to this proposition, given the dates in question and the identification of the key. Furthermore, Mendelssohn was characteristically nonchalant about getting started on his contribution to the Gutenberg festival, and the *Lobgesang* idea seems not to have taken its final shape until sometime in March 1840, just a few months before the performance date. Yet assuming that work on the suppositious "B♭ symphony" of 1838–1839 would have begun with its first movement (as indeed the sketch material seems to indicate), how are we to account for the large role played by the vocally inspired motto in the first movement of the *Lobgesang* symphony? It seems very unlikely that either the motto or introduction as a whole would have taken anything like its present form independently of the choral setting of the psalm verse. It would be intriguing to speculate how much of the present first movement could be conceived of *without* this motto-theme. One might argue that the theme has merely been grafted onto the bridge or development—sewn into the seams. But surely if one were to delete it from these passages, the remaining figurational busywork and thematically ungrounded modulations would sound impossibly empty. Furthermore, other features of the movement, such as the woodwind march-rhythms of the closing group (mm. 121–24, 308–10), seem to derive more directly from the motto than from the Allegro theme itself. In particular, the impressive Beethovenian fragmentation process near the end of the development (mm. 209–26, modeled on mm. 78ff. of the exposition and leading to a surprise "transitional" reprise of theme 2) is unthinkable without the impetus of the motto rhythm. In short, while something of the unfinished B♭ symphony may well have found its way into the "Sinfonia" movements of the *Lobgesang*, that material must have undergone considerable transformation, especially in the first movement.[38]

Whether either of the two interior orchestral movements of Op. 52 may derive from the projected symphony of 1838–1839 also remains an open question. The use of an explicit chorale style within the trio or midsection of the second movement connects it directly with the sacred element of the *Lobgesang*, as does the paraphrase of the motto-theme worked into the texture of that chorale melody; if this movement had existed in some earlier form, it must, like the first movement, have undergone substantial revision. Critics have long been fond of pointing to traces of Mendelssohn's Song-without-Words idiom in the other instrumental works, and this G-minor scherzo movement (headed simply *Allegretto un poco agitato*) is one case where the connection seems justified. The gentle, suave melancholy of the tune, the rocking $\frac{6}{8}$ meter, and the guitarlike accompaniment lead Philip Radcliffe, for instance, to compare it to the barcarolles (or "Gondola Songs") from the Songs without Words.[39] It is perhaps surprising that no one has yet thought to hear allusions to Beethoven's "Nimm sie hin, denn, diese Lieder" in the second phrase of the Allegretto (Example 7.17)—so often connected with

Example 7.17
Lobgesang, no. 1, Allegretto, mm. 16–24

Schumann's Op. 17 Fantasy and Second Symphony—even if there is no reason to suppose Mendelssohn would have intended such an allusion. (On the other hand, the chronological and geographical proximity of the *Lobgesang* to Schumann's Fantasy might be grounds for reflection.) Though not cast in the mold of the classic "Mendelssohn" scherzo, the movement shares the novelty of invention and fluid formal approach of his best scherzo movements, and in its quiet, understated way it constitutes a musical high point of the whole work, or at least of the instrumental "Sinfonia." The "agitato" of the tempo direction is perhaps less audible in the smooth, unruffled melodic surface than in certain irregular details of its construction, for instance, the way the reprise of the opening phrase is slipped into a melodic-harmonic sequence (at m. 49) before it has a chance to resolve itself metrically. Something similar is effected by the metrical overlaps of the little codetta phrase in mm. 64–70. The lilting, insinuating scherzo theme does not even pause for the Trio but continues to murmur on gently throughout it. Or rather, it continues to sound, now in G major, in between the pseudochorale phrases in the woodwinds (see Example 7.18). Built into the "chorale," as mentioned earlier, is a paraphrase of the motto theme, which the oboes must be encouraged to project if it is not to be swallowed up in performance. The Trio is followed by something that is less a *da capo* of the scherzo than a new continuation of it—a logical strategy in view of the continued presence of the scherzo material throughout the Trio section. The movement ends with a characteristic dissolve, familiar from other Mendelssohn scherzos, while the F♮s of the original melody, echoed in the cellos, and the sustained fifth degree on which it comes to rest give the ending a particularly weightless, inconclusive quality.

One cannot help supposing that some "ideal" significance (as the critics were wont to put it at the time) is meant to attach to the chorale theme of the Trio, especially in its dialogue with the major-mode fragments of the Scherzo. It hardly seems far-fetched to imagine an anticipation of the symbolic "light of day" that will be the goal of the ensuing cantata. The chorale theme rings out like a quiet ray of hope in G major, in an organlike scoring for full woodwinds, supported by trombones. (The chorale "Nun danket Alle Gott" will later be sounded in G major in the following cantata.) In any case, Mendelssohn has created an interesting

Example 7.18
Lobgesang, no. 1, Allegretto, mm. 72–81

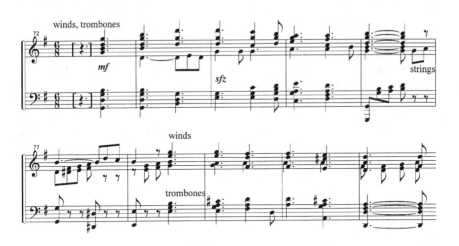

psychological dynamic in the dialogue between these woodwind chorale phrases, as they stride resolutely through their series of major-key cadences and past the snatches of the scherzo material in the strings, which are unable to shake off inflections of minor-mode and diminished harmonies. The reviewer of the published score in the *Neue Zeitschrift*, incidentally, heard this dialogue along the lines suggested here. The Allegretto melody itself is described as "less churchly" than the first movement, expressive of "a restless lament." Alluding to the paraphrase of the motto within the chorale-phrases of the trio, the reviewer adds that "even though a consoling *cantus firmus* (the notes of the principal theme) attempts to interrupt this lament, it is in vain!—[the melody] continues to sound, until the mild, reassuring [*verheissender*] voice of the Adagio [*sic*] is heard, filling the heart with peace and confidence."[40]

The Andante religioso is cast in a version of "slow movement" sonata form, that is, one tending toward a ternary structure with varied reprise and coda. While its structure is not without some sophisticated touches in detail, the overall tone has most contributed to the ineradicable cliché of Mendelssohn as musical incarnation of a blandly sanctimonious Victorian bourgeoisie (what George Bernard Shaw dismissed as Mendelssohn's "Sunday-school music" idiom). At the same time, it is the movement with the least direct ties to the larger conception of the work.[41] Aside from a certain ineffable tone of piety, the movement contains no concretely sacred musical images or references, and one wonders whether the "religioso" appended to the tempo direction might reflect a hope that a sufficiently devotional attitude in performance will bolster the movement's sense of belonging to the rest of the piece.

The question of "belonging," in any case, was a recurrent motif in the early critical reception of the symphony. Whether or not they worried about the alleged resemblance to the unapproachable Ninth Symphony, critics could not help questioning whether the orchestral movements were aesthetically justified as a prelude to the cantata or (perhaps more reasonably) whether the rather extensive cantata could really fulfill the role of a symphonic finale, without entirely overshadowing what precedes it. Not surprisingly, these "big" questions tended to attract more attention than the merits or demerits of the individual movements. It may even be that Mendelssohn's conception of the work as combination of instrumental and vocal "song" on the subject of praise, as expressed in the letter to Klingemann, had somehow come into public circulation, since articles by Gustav Schilling (1841) and A. B. Marx (1847), among others, both claim that the instrumental and vocal sections of the symphony "say the same thing"—a claim that can hardly be based on the musical content of these sections alone.[42] Another common concern was that the cantata-finale seemed to be less convincingly or compellingly prepared by the instrumental symphony than is the case with Beethoven's choral finale. Perhaps better founded was the related concern over the disproportionate length of the cantata: in length and substance it is too extensive to be perceived as a satisfactory "finale" to the instrumental symphony, while, on the other hand, three complete instrumental movements are too much to be heard simply as an "introduction" or overture to a large-scale work for soloists and chorus. (This was also the more common complaint.)

A practical concern regarding the consequences of generic hybridization in the *Lobgesang* is also addressed by more than one critic: the matter of performance venue. Sacred music generally presupposes the resonant acoustic of a high-ceilinged church or cathedral, as well as the presence of an organ (here in nos. 2, 7, 8, and 10), while modern symphonies call for a somewhat more controlled ambience. The *Neue Zeitschrift* reviewer feared that the first movement may be "too complicated in construction" for performance in a church. Presumably, the conjunction of tempo, textures, and harmonic rhythm worried him (though Schumann, in an editorial footnote, takes issue with this reservation).[43] The reviewer in the *Allgemeine musikalische Zeitung* recommended a stronger complement of string instruments for church performances.[44] Mendelssohn conducted the premiere of the *Lobgesang* in Bach's church of St. Thomas in Leipzig—by no means a vast space—and then revived the work in the Gewandhaus concerts at the end of the same year (1840).

Barring the case of some truly cavernous locale, which none of the Leipzig churches would have offered, the issue of church versus concert hall is probably not so significant, finally, but it does serve to underscore larger issues of generic ambivalence raised by the piece, issues not forced in the same way by Beethoven's overtly secular Ninth Symphony. Critics were evidently uncomfortable with the way that Mendelssohn's *Lobgesang* insisted on putting secular symphony and sacred cantata or oratorio on the same footing—under the same roof, as it were. Whereas the *Allgemeine musikalische Zeitung* reviewer approached the piece as sacred music (grouping it with *St. Paul* and the Psalm settings for chorus and orchestra) and found himself largely satisfied on these grounds, a slightly later critic in the *Neue Zeitschrift* was disdainful of what he considered the deleterious effect of the composer's particular religious *Weltanschauung* ("the standpoint of a pious, softly-tuned [*weichgestimmten*] Christian heart, which humbly submits to all sorrow simply as a heaven-sent test of faith") on the whole range of his musical expression, thus already anticipating that familiar strain of post-Victorian criticism.

Despite these critical differences, Mendelssohn's attempted synthesis of symphony and oratorio might also be read as a logical response to the music-festival culture that was becoming such a predominant force, particularly in Germany and England, in the 1830s and 1840s. These musical festivals—typified by, but by no means limited to, the famous Lower Rhine festivals—thrived on precisely the genres of symphony and oratorio, which formed the centerpieces for their celebration of communal music-making. Their orientation was equally civic and religious at once, fostering a sense of nationally shared cultural heritage based on common social and ethical ideals. Mendelssohn's success in addressing just this market is testified by performances of the *Lobgesang* at the 1842 Lower Rhine festival in Düsseldorf, under the composer's direction, at further festivals in Neustadt-Haardt (Rhineland Palatinate) and Lausanne in the same year, and in Rostock and Den Haag in 1843, among many others to follow.[45] One might say that the real "occasion" for which the work had been conceived was this generic one—the early nineteenth-century music festival as such—rather than Leipzig's Gutenberg celebration as a single event. Both the specific occasion and the larger idea of the music festival, in any case, resonate with the central impulse behind this and Mendelssohn's other large-scale compositions: the desire to reconcile the claims of a secular, Enlightenment heritage with the authorities of the modern church and state. In many ways he succeeded brilliantly, of course. But did he try too hard to please, in the end? Was he perhaps too much driven by a desire to conciliate, to conform, to belong? The question of "belonging" raised by the two halves of Mendelssohn's symphony-cantata, the secular and the sacred, thus becomes in a way symbolic of his own situation. Yet, if posterity has tended to judge Mendelssohn rather harshly for responding too readily to this impulse to "belong," perhaps a greater sense of—or historical sensitivity to—the social and aesthetic forces that shaped the music will help to restore an appreciation of what that music is about.

Landscape, History, or *Tableau Vivant*: The "Italian" and "Scottish" Symphonies, Op. 90 and Op. 56

Together with the *Hebrides* Overture, the two symphonies in A minor and A major are principally responsible for Mendelssohn's reputation as a master of the musical "landscape." While the numbering of these symphonies as the Third and Fourth merely reflects, again, the accident of their publication history, precisely the opposite is the case with their familiar titles (the "Scottish" and the "Italian"): neither symphony was published with a descriptive title, yet their genesis and the composer's correspondence leave no doubt as to the particular natural and cultural landscapes that inspired them and that they have generally been understood to evoke.

The genesis and publication history of the two symphonies are intricate and overlapping. The so-called Third Symphony was indeed conceived before the Fourth, during the composer's brief sojourn in Scotland in the summer of 1829. The Fourth Symphony originated about a year and a half later, in the early months of 1831, during Mendelssohn's stay in Rome, where much of it seems at least to have been sketched out. Yet the Fourth was completed, in the version familiar today, by 1833, nine years before the Third was finally finished. (Both works were begun long before the so-called Second.) The Third was published as Op. 56 within a year after its premiere at the Leipzig Gewandhaus in 1842, while the Fourth appeared only posthumously, in 1851, as Op. 90. There is some justification for treating the two symphonies as a pair: both originated during Mendelssohn's youthful travels (while in Rome he was trying to work on both simultaneously, for a time), and both drew directly on impulses received during those travels.[46] The result in both cases was a symphony better identified as "characteristic" than as "programmatic," yet even the matter of specific local color or character was problematized by Mendelssohn in that he ultimately refrained from sanctioning any official title for either work.

In attempting to outline some aspects of character, style, and form in these two works, it will be worthwhile recalling the circumstances that gave rise to them, without losing sight of the critical problems that attend such biographical contextualization. As a background premise to the following remarks, it is worth reconsidering the familiar trope of Mendelssohn the musical "landscape artist" from the perspective of Mendelssohn's immediate cultural background and milieu, as well as from the perspective of symphonic genre as such. Mendelssohn was, of course, an accomplished draftsman who produced a number of highly respectable landscape views in pen and ink and watercolor. But for that very reason, he was also in an unusually good position to appreciate the medial differences between a visual and a musical approach to a landscape or to the "musical" interpretation of images more generally.

What music lacks in denotative power it can make up for in other ways. Music might approach the "feeling," character, and (metaphorically, at least) color of visual images; but more than this, it could also put these abstract values into motion, choreographing them as nuanced and complex action. In this sense, the static landscape could become a kind of *tableau vivant*, to adopt the figure of a popular mode of nineteenth-century cultural sociability as a metaphor for such musical "painting." At the higher end of the cultural spectrum, the prestigious genre of history painting—analogous in status to the symphony as a "large form" with certain academic and classical associations—could be taken as a model for Mendelssohn's ambitions in a work such as the "Scottish" Symphony, where the musical landscape is implicitly populated by historical actors (however shadowy). Where the series of musical *tableaux* in the "Italian" Symphony seem to represent characteristic genre-scenes (of the sort that were turned out in great number by

Mendelssohn's contemporaries studying in Italy), those of the "Scottish" Symphony, it could be argued, are imbued with a greater sense of historical event. In neither case, however, is a story literally "told," of course. Rather, the images or associations evoked by thematic and other modes of musical character are experienced against the background of a more-or-less traditional symphonic mise-en-scène. These images are animated, "brought to life" in musical designs that, without ever attaining any unequivocal discursive meaning, are continuously (if elusively) suggestive of such meanings.

Symphony No. 4 in A Major ("Italian"), Op. 91: The Mendelssohnian "Carnivalesque"?

For what has unquestionably become one of Mendelssohn's best-known works, together with the *Midsummer Night's Dream* Overture and the E-minor Violin Concerto, the "Italian" Symphony led a remarkably obscure existence during the composer's own lifetime and even for some time afterward. Like his other famous "landscapes," the "Scottish" Symphony and the *Hebrides* Overture, the piece was conceived *in situ*, in this case during Felix's Italian sojourn of 1830–1831. Since he remained a much longer time in Italy than he had in Scotland, he was also able to complete much more of the work there, where he also managed to complete a first draft of *The Hebrides* and tried for a time to proceed with the "Scottish" Symphony, until he decided that it was no use trying to sustain the "foggy mood" of that work under the balmy Mediterranean skies. The association of these two symphonies with their places of origin was clearly distinct and important for Mendelssohn. In his correspondence they consistently figure as his "Scottish" and "Italian" Symphonies, even though the A-minor symphony eventually appeared without any descriptive title, and it seems unlikely that the A major—had it reached publication during the composer's lifetime—would have been given a title either (hence, the grounds for Schumann's famous confusion of these two pieces, to which we shall return).

The initial ideas for the A-major Symphony seem to have been worked out in the early months of 1831. By 22 February 1831 Felix was writing from Rome to his sister Fanny that "the Italian symphony is making great progress." "It will be the jolliest piece I've done," he added, "particularly the last movement; I have nothing definite for the Adagio [*sic*] yet, and I think I will save that for Naples."[47] Shortly afterward (1 March) he wrote of saving further work on the symphony as a whole, apparently, for Naples, "for that must play a role in it."[48] It would be interesting to know just how far he had, in fact, progressed with the symphony by this time and, conversely, what role Naples did play in filling out the picture, in Mendelssohn's mind (the letters from Naples mostly complain about the Neapolitan atmosphere of *dolce far niente* and its unconduciveness to sustained thought or work of any sort); it would seem odd if the somber and subdued Andante had really been the only fruit of the Neapolitan experience. Writing to his mother a few weeks after the last letter cited, Mendelssohn mentioned again the "very merry symphony" (*sehr heitere Symphonie*) he was engaged upon, which he also referred to here as the "jolly symphony I am doing" on the country or landscape of Italy (*die lustige Symphonie, die ich auf das Land Italien mache*).[49] All of this leaves no doubt that the composer consciously sought to translate his impressions of Italy's fabled beauties into musical form. In a sense, the "Italian" Symphony seems to have been conceived as a kind of musical counterpart to Goethe's *Italian Journey*, just as Mendelssohn's tour itself was undertaken very much as a cultural pilgrimage in emulation of Goethe's own Italian *Bildungsreise* of fifty years earlier.

The symphony was largely complete, at least in outline, by April 1831, although a full score was not finished until almost two years later (13 March 1833), in response to a commission from the London Philharmonic Society to present a program of new works, which occurred precisely two months afterward (13 May 1833). Mendelssohn's involvement with his A-major symphony did not end there, however. For reasons that must remain unfathomable today (when the "Italian" Symphony is regarded as one of the composer's "perfect" works), Mendelssohn insisted that the first movement should be entirely overhauled, although this plan was never carried out. He did, on the other hand, undertake a number of revisions in the three remaining movements, which nonetheless never found their way into the published score, as Mendelssohn never got so far as producing a complete, authoritative revision of the symphony as a whole.[50] The confidants of these revisions, Ignaz Moscheles and Felix's sister Fanny, were both somewhat perplexed by them and by the composer's insistence on revising the piece in the first place, although Moscheles did encourage him to go through with the revisions, once having begun them. Fanny seems to have sensed a misguided perfectionist impulse behind her brother's unwillingness to leave well enough alone.[51] This excessive scrupulousness afflicted his relationship to the symphonic genre as a whole, as witnessed by the history of the Third, Fourth, and Fifth Symphonies, and may explain in part why, with the exception of the mixed-genre *Lobgesang*, he never began another symphony after his twenty-third year.

The opening measures of Op. 90 announce it right away as a *heitere Symphonie* (in the composer's words). Dispensing with the slow introduction that was, by 1830, the mark of any symphony with even the slightest pretensions to grandeur (i.e., to the status of a *grande symphonie*), this one is set in motion with a single A-major triad strummed by pizzicato strings and sustained by woodwinds with horns in a rapidly pulsing $\frac{6}{8}$. The gay, dancing rhythms of the famous main theme are also distinctly unconventional for a first movement, which was traditionally inclined to the march rather than the dance, or at least to some form of earnest, purposeful jogging motion. (The opening Allegro of Beethoven's Seventh Symphony, with its swinging, giguelike rhythms is an earlier exception, in which one might recognize a faint paternal likeness to Mendelssohn's "Italian," which further extends to the slow movements of these two symphonies.) Thus, the listener is instantly apprised of this symphony's undisguised commitment to pleasure, as if under the institutional dispensation of the Italian carnival. In fact,

Felix was just then experiencing the Roman carnival itself—with mixed feelings—at the very time he seems to have begun sketching his symphony, in the first weeks of February 1831.

To suggest that we might hear the first movement of the A-major symphony as Mendelssohn's "Roman Carnival" is not necessarily to saddle it with one of those long-reviled, condescending, picturesque "programs" by means of which one used to introduce such pieces of classical music to children and other laypersons—or not exactly. Rather, it is to suggest an image or construct (one with real, "factual," historical-biographical points of reference) that might serve as a prism through which to view the character, detail, and design of a symphonic movement, perhaps casting some relevant interpretive light on the other movements, as well. To some extent, the carnival atmosphere of the opening Allegro vivace speaks for itself. The merry main theme is propelled by a heels-in-the-air upbeat figure of a major third that progressively swells, in the consequent phrase, to a fourth, a fifth, and finally a minor seventh (see Example 7.19). The extension of the melodic period to twenty-one measures already signals,

Example 7.19
Symphony in A Major, Op. 90, "Italian," First Movement, mm. 2-23

however unassumingly, a symphonic aspiration transcending the confines of a literal, functional dance form. During the episodic digression that follows (mm. 24–50), preparing the way for a full-scale counterstatement, the "kicking" upbeat motive is singled out and tossed between the woodwinds; now it comes to resemble more a kind of echoing street cry, while the dancing impulse is taken over by the strings in a fleet, scampering figure that substitutes momentarily for the repeated wind chords, up to the energetic tutti counterstatement of the theme at m.

50. These scampering strings (a Mendelssohnian trademark) constitute another characteristic ingredient of this movement and continue to inhabit especially its transitional, episodic, and developmental alleys, as opposed to its more public thematic "piazzas," so to speak. Following upon the delicate and varied textures of the opening thematic statement and interlude and prepared by a swelling contrary motion in the strings, the tutti counterstatement conveys the impression of a crowd in full swing. This counterstatement is extended by a short phrase in which trumpets in D transform the principal upbeat motive into another sort of call or street cry (mm. 66–73), after which the original dancing rhythms lead into a modulatory bridge. Thus, dancing and vocal (calling) gestures, deriving from the same thematic complex, complement one another in creating a general picture of carnivalesque activity.

The second group maintains the same dancing rhythms, while observing the traditional textural and dynamic contrast. Then the main theme reappears in the closing position, in the dominant, as it had in a number of the early string symphonies. In this case it is audibly summoned back by the "calling" transformation of the principal motive (clarinets, mm. 159–66). But rather than directly preparing its own restatement in the tonic (the repeated exposition), as in the early symphonies, the repeat is mediated here by a lengthy transitional first ending. This first ending is worth observing in performance not only because it adds a few extra measures to Mendelssohn's most popular symphony but also for legitimately "structural" reasons: it contains two melodic gestures that will recur in the coda (mm. 531–47), a thematic parallel that would hence be obscured by suppression of this first ending to the exposition.

In the exposition, the carnival spirit remains largely under the control of conventional formal restraints. The development breaks loose from these, although in a manner more playful than threatening or subversive. Just a few bars into the development, the mischievous "scampering" eighth-note patterns encountered in the byways of the exposition surreptitiously smuggle in an entirely new theme in D minor (see Example 7.20), which rapidly multiplies throughout the string section in a hushed fugato. The new theme has an impudent, marchlike air to it, and its sense of impudence increases across the development as it engages in a playful contest with the main theme of the movement, in the winds and brass, from m. 264 on. By m. 274 the new theme has usurped the entire orchestral texture; but soon afterward, this impudent intruder quickly retires from the scene, as if chased off by the upbeat motive of the main theme, which assaults it alternately from above and below (Example 7.21). Across a lengthy retransition the main theme gradually reasserts itself: the upbeat motivic "call" is sent out by oboes, clarinets, and horns, while the steady triplet eighth-note pulse is reawakened in the violins and violas, until the original "dancing" resumes, without fanfare, at the recapitulation (m. 346). The musical scenario of this development is redolent of the commedia dell'arte, with its characters constantly scheming against one another and vying for audience attention, or perhaps of some carnival situation in which uninvited maskers intrude upon a scene of merry-making, only to be driven off again. In one of his letters

Example 7.20
Symphony in A Major, Op. 90, "Italian," First Movement, mm. 199–209

Example 7.21
Symphony in A Major, Op. 90, "Italian," First Movement, mm. 290–97

from Rome Mendelssohn describes how, driving down the Corso in his carriage during the carnival week, he suddenly found himself assaulted by various friends and strangers with a hail of sugar-and-flour *confetti*: "and thus pelting and pelted, with a thousand jests and jeers and amidst the most extravagant masks, the day ended with horse races."[52] Though, to judge by the rest of the letter, he seems at first to have been more nonplussed than amused, Mendelssohn has perhaps transmuted something of the playful antagonisms of the carnival experience into the thematic processes of his unconventional development (as in the routing of this masked thematic intruder, e.g.).

In the recapitulation the festivities are resumed and continue unimpeded, although abridged, in accordance with Mendelssohn's usual recapitulatory procedure. The second theme is newly adorned with arpeggiated triads in the flute and clarinet, like fluttering ribbons (mm. 381–403). Order prevails until the point where the closing group should begin. Here, suddenly (m. 433) the impertinent intruder of the development reappears in A minor (hovering for a few measures in $_4^6$ position) and rapidly invades the whole texture.[53] Development theme and main theme engage in a renewed scuffle, by way of terminal or secondary development, until fanfarelike iterations of the principal motive (mm. 475–487) seize the upper hand, and the coda can continue on its way in undisturbed merriment. The underlying camaraderie of these thematic altercations is revealed at the final tonic arrival in m. 557, where the head-motive of the development theme is allowed to participate in the gesture of closure. Whatever unruly antagonisms are enacted in Mendelssohn's musical carnival, they are easily contained, at last, within the larger social order of the symphonic domain.

"Now it seems everything has changed completely," Mendelssohn wrote home, a week after the letter describing the *confetti* attack in the Corso. "The carnival has been interrupted, people arrested, patrols in the streets—it all bears little resemblance to the carnival and its jesting . . . . There is something very moving about this sudden switch from the wildest merriment to the most bitter gravity."[54] Apparently, social unrest in several cities to the north (Bologna, Ancona) had led to the suppression of carnival celebrations in Rome, out of a fear of political demonstrations. While there is no reason to suppose a direct link between this historical incident and Mendelssohn's symphony, the contrast described here is nonetheless strangely evocative of that between the first and second movements of the "Italian" Symphony. If the first movement is, indeed, conceived in the spirit of carnivalesque abandon (however well contained, in the end), the Andante con moto suddenly sinks into a spirit of sober penitence. Its place among these other pictures of Italian gaiety has long been explained by the notion that this slow movement is meant to evoke a religious processional of some kind, monks or pilgrims slowly filing through the streets of an old Italian city or perhaps threading a path through some harsh, remote mountain landscape. Tovey repeats the story of a religious procession that Mendelssohn is supposed to have witnessed in Naples.[55] But, while there is no concrete evidence of such an experience on Mendelssohn's part (it seems, instead, that his remark about "saving the slow movement for Naples" must have led to the hypothesis), such a procession might well have happened almost anywhere and at any time, as Tovey also admits. Moreover, the image is one that could have been drawn from a repertoire of characteristic, "picturesque" Italian scenes with which Mendelssohn would have been well acquainted through the large colony of German and other foreign painters who flocked to Italy throughout this period. Tovey and others before him have pointed to the litany-like intonation figure (dominant and lowered-sixth neighbor) that stands at the head of the movement in the manner of a motto or heraldic device (as Wulf Konold puts it).[56] The lack of any concrete authorial confirmation of the religious-processional connotations of the music that follows, however, is scarcely sufficient grounds for Konold's and Eric Werner's rejection of this tradition in favor of a supposed resemblance to the melody of Zelter's setting of the Goethe ballad, "Es war ein König in Thule."[57] Certainly, the somber, antique ("Gothic") tone of Mendelssohn's theme (see Example 7.22) might also be appropriate to the Goethe text, although Zelter's tune lacks the explicit modal evocation of Mendelssohn's, with its lowered seventh degree (C natural). More importantly, however, the steady "walking bass" of the Mendelssohn movement was a widely acknowledged sign of both sacred style—the so-called chorale prelude idiom—and a specific gesture of solemn procession (the "armored men" of Mozart's *Magic Flute* and the midsection of the funeral march in the "Eroica" are two well-known examples). To ignore the role of such conventionally understood musical signs in favor of a private, esoteric reference available only to biographers and scholars surely bespeaks a modern prejudice that ought to be questioned.

Example 7.22
Symphony in A Major, Op. 90, "Italian," Second Movement, mm. 1–7

Of course, "conventional" signs were not always universally understood, and the recuperation of their meaning today may depend, after all, on the intervention of biographers and scholars. As early as 1856 A. W. Ambros was questioning the notion—already by then a received one, apparently—that this Andante is meant to evoke a "church style." Instead, he suggests that one might sooner hear it as "speaking of old times in a romantic tone, as if in the style of the chronicles—although from time to time [the A-major episodes] the poet's eye also smiles sadly through."[58] Yet Ambros's train of associations also brings him around to images of "the picturesque fortress towers of Grotta Ferrata, and the old stations of the cross, with their solemn mosaic depictions of saints against a gold background"—that is, he ends up approaching the idea of sacred processional after all (implied by his reference to the stations of the cross).[59] In fact, these associations were already in place by the time of the symphony's first publication in 1851. A reviewer of a performance in Düsseldorf that year, under Robert Schumann's direction, delivers all the now-familiar ingredients: "The second movement introduces us to the deeply religious side of the Italian folk-life; a simple, pious melody is intoned, in the manner of an old church hymn [wie ein altes Kirchenlied]; in our mind's eye we witness a solemn procession passing by."[60] It is not only the persistent "walking bass" pattern of eighth notes throughout the main thematic group and bridge passage (mm. 3–44) that conveys this processional image but also its conjunction with the regular phrasing and deliberate quarter-note pulse of the melodic phrases themselves: the image is one of walking and singing, perfectly apposite to the "pilgrims' march" scenario. The exact, strophic repetition of the eight-measure phrases in the A-section reinforces the sense of a simple, folk-based ritual. Nearly every commentator has praised the beautiful effect of the free melodic counterpoint in the two flutes, added above the second strophes (mm. 12–19, 27–35). The impression that this creates of a "naively" improvised descant also fits well with the image of a pilgrims' march—here, indeed, is one of the few passages in Mendelssohn's output in which he and Berlioz appear as kindred musical spirits. The march feeling is carried over into a brief transitional passage (mm. 35–44, 86–93) that seems consciously to recall the "litany" motto, at the same pitches of a^1 and bb^2.

The contrasting A-major episode of mm. 45–56 (recapitulated in the tonic major, D, at m. 75) is texturally more complex than the main group and more "instrumental," with less resemblance to either simple song or march. (Ambros's observation that the "poet's voice" here interrupts the naive chronicler is an astute one and intriguing, in view of current critical speculations on the possible nature of a musical narrativity.) The reprise of the main group is signaled by the "litany" motto, transposed up a fifth, which brusquely interrupts an extension of the A-major phrase-group at m. 56. This reprise is abridged to two strophes instead of four and is much rewritten. In particular, the transposed theme is inflected with a flatted second degree (bb), marked sforzando (perhaps intended to echo the semitone of the introductory motto), which suffuses the rest of the melodic texture (see Example 7.23). After a return of the major-mode episode (mm. 75–86) in the

Example 7.23
Symphony in A Major, Op. 90, "Italian," Second Movement, mm. 59–63

tonic (D)—this time allowed to complete itself—and a displaced iteration of the bridge material (mm. 86–93), a brief, atmospheric coda rounds out the movement. The "litany" figure is intoned one last time, and fragments of the main tune mingle with the mournful semitone in a gesture that strikingly anticipates the dissolve of the Pilgrims' March in Berlioz's *Harold in Italy*. (Both movements have a common ancestor in the Allegretto of Beethoven's Seventh Symphony.) Out of a few simple materials Mendelssohn has crafted a slow movement whose structure is perfectly transparent and yet completely novel. Yet to ignore its deployment of characteristic, associative gestures, out of a misguided devotion to aesthetic purity or an insistence on strict authorial evidence (that the movement can suggest a "processional" only if Mendelssohn tells us so directly or says so in a letter), is surely to misunderstand Mendelssohn's music and his culture.[61] Failing to recognize the processional gait of the movement's bass line or the explicit sonic retreat toward a "picturesque" horizon in the closing measures would be equivalent to ignoring the referential terms of a literary allegory or the most basic iconographic emblems of a Renaissance or Baroque (or Romantic) painting. One cannot imagine scholarship of any persuasion in those disciplines abdicating such fundamental interpretive responsibilities.

That said, one must admit that there is little representational impulse to be detected in the third movement.[62] Marked simply *Con moto moderato*, it is clearly styled as a minuet. Mendelssohn likewise refrained from labeling the scherzo movements of his other symphonies, perhaps because of their departures from a standard Beethovenian type. Similarly, this movement *recalls* the style of a minuet more than it literally embodies or re-creates it. (Mendelssohn's decision not to spell out what he would rather just suggest could provoke some further reflection on the case of the slow movement, too.) The principal section is all graceful legato elegance: this is no Haydn minuet, in any case, though it might recall that of Mozart's "Jupiter" Symphony. Characteristically Mozartean is the little four-measure appendix added to the otherwise perfectly symmetrical 8+8-measure theme. The design of the whole is quite regular, too, although Mendelssohn omitted the repeat of the larger, second part of the minuet form, as he did again in the Trio.

The Trio yokes two bassoons to the two horns to produce the effect of a quartet of horns. The tradition of hearing this Trio, with its little fanfares for (simulated) horn quartet, as an evocation of the distant *Heimat* of German woods and hills can again be traced back to its earliest commentators. "In the third movement," wrote the reviewer of Schumann's 1851 Düsseldorf performance, "we hear the sounds of a genuine German minuet" (perhaps implying the style of a *Ländler*), "and the gentle melody of the horns in the trio resounds like a greeting from Germany's forests."[63] Ambros seconds this opinion in 1856: "And these *Waldhörner* in the trio, is it not as if [the composer], amidst the paradise of Italy's natural beauties, were suddenly smitten with a true German yearning for the beloved green of his native forests?"[64] This trope of German homesickness amid classical landscapes has scarcely ever been absent from program notes and record liners down to the present day. One might also hear this minuet and trio, however, in the spirit of Schumann's *Papillons* or *Carnaval*, as a pair of carnival masks, embodied in dance form. The "lilting grace" of the minuet would mark it as a feminine mask, in a costume of the *ancien régime*, while the fanfares and chevaleresque dotted rhythms of the trio theme suggest a gallant *gentiluomo* in knightly disguise. After their formal presentation as "solo" dances, these two characters permit themselves a brief embrace in the coda, where knightly fanfare and sweeping scale modestly commingle (see Example 7.24).

Example 7.24
Symphony in A Major, Op. 90, "Italian," Third Movement, mm. 202–6

The finale is another characteristic dance scene, now in wild rustic dress, which Mendelssohn himself designated as a "saltarello." (This is, in fact, the single explicit clue to the "Italian" theme of the symphony provided by the composer, at least in the unpublished form in which he left it.) Until this point the musical image of Italy has been largely an imagined one, with scant reference to any actual repertoire. The situation is consistent with the fact that the *image* of Italy—its traces of classical antiquity, its picturesque landscapes and seascapes, its paintings, frescos, architecture, and sculpture—rather than the *music* of Italy inspired Mendelssohn, just as with Berlioz and many other musical visitors of the time. But by evoking the strains of popular folk dance in the finale, Mendelssohn evokes visual images, too: it is as much the *scene* of the dance as the sound that matters. Peter Rummenhöller suggests a contemporary genre painting by the

Berlin-born artist Franz Ludwig Catel, depicting "Italian folk life near Pozzuoli," as an apt illustration of Mendelssohn's finale: an idealized scene of folk dancing to castanets, tambourine, and mandolin, against a backdrop of ancient, vine-encrusted columns, Italian pines, and the Bay of Naples.[65] A number of Joseph Anton Koch's scenes of country life around Olevano also include such scenes of dancing to tambourines, pipes, and mandolins, as well as being more topographically appropriate to the specific genre of the "saltarello."[66]   It was images of this sort, as supplied by innumerable German painters of the period, that Mendelssohn would have brought with him to Italy in the first place and that he (like they) actively sought out in his travels, in order to experience them firsthand. It is the recollection of such images or scenes that his symphony seeks, in turn, to animate, to bring back to life, to set to music.

The opening of the "saltarello" sets the scene in depicting its characteristic instruments by orchestral means.[67]   The woodwind trills of the first measure followed by a sharp release suggest the rattle and thump of a tambourine flourish. The orchestra announces the signature rhythm of the movement as a whole, as a pure rhythm, like a riff on the castanets. This "castanet" riff subsides to a quiet drone in the violins, on A, while two flutes pipe a repetitive dance tune of narrow range based on the same rhythm. That tune and a second dance tune, again on the same "signature" rhythm, constitute the basis of what starts out as a sonata-form finale (see Example 7.25); yet the persistence of this uniform rhythmic motive naturally works to minimize contrast, as does the minor mode of the second theme.

Example 7.25
Symphony in A Major, Op. 90, "Italian," Finale

a. mm. 6–10

b. mm. 52–54

The development section begins in m. 105 as a modulatory romp with the first dance tune, but this soon gives way to an entirely new episode in hushed perpetual motion, that idiom at which Mendelssohn so excelled. This perpetual-motion subject is provided with a hint of a countersubject worked into its light, chordal accompaniment. The elusiveness of this implied countersubject, which never quite assumes a single, distinct form, is in keeping with the shadowy character of this whole episode. Gradually, the signature dance rhythm mingles with the fragments of the perpetual-motion subject, applied to a lengthy retransition over dominant pedal (E) with timpani ostinato.

The largely independent central episode has already deflected the sonata form toward something more rondolike, but any sense of formal scheme is thrown into further confusion by the reprise (m. 210), which is almost immediately dissipated; only the persistent saltarello-tarantella rhythm preserves some semblance of formal continuity. (Once again here Mendelssohn indulged in the carnival dispensation that lifts restraints governing accepted formal behavior, without forfeiting taste, discretion, and a sense of overall decorum.) It is as if the great momentum built up across the movement and especially the *moto perpetuo* of the preceding episode have virtually swept away the intended return of the dance, as it collapses into a few repeated cadences (mm. 233ff). In the brief coda one hears the receding echoes of these cadences—a favorite means of "bringing to life" imaginary scenes in music, suggesting, in this case, the band of players moving off into the distance. This impression is confirmed (and embellished) by several snatches of the original dance tune played pianissimo in the flutes and clarinets, heard from far away, as it were, or from "offstage." The triplets are whipped up to provide a loud tutti frame in the closing measures—a quick curtain descending on the conclusion of these musical *tableaux vivants* after scenes from Mendelssohn's Italian journey.

Between Epic Narrative and History Painting: Symphony No. 3 in A Minor ("Scottish"), Op. 56

We know from Mendelssohn himself that he received the first impulse for his "Scottish" Symphony from historical images, inspired by a picturesque historical site. He described this in an often-cited letter to his family of 30 July 1829, from Edinburgh:

In the depths of twilight we visited today the palace where Queen Mary lived and loved; there is a little room there, with a spiral staircase near the door; that's where they came up and found Rizzio in that room, and dragged him out, and three rooms further on is a dark corner, where they murdered him. The chapel next door is missing its roof now, much grass and ivy are growing there, and the decrepit altar is where Mary was crowned Queen of Scotland. It's all ruined and crumbling now, and the bright sky shines down into it. I think that there today I've found the beginning of my Scottish symphony.[68]

The latter claim is confirmed by a sketch bearing the same date as this letter and outlining what would become the first sixteen bars of the slow introduction to the

A-minor symphony. Granted, there is no further talk of Mary Stuart or the murder of her musician-secretary, Rizzio, in the correspondence about this symphony; and after some scattered references, over the next year or two, to "mists and melancholy" in conjunction with the mood of the piece, all mention of Scotland itself eventually disappears from the later correspondence, after about 1835.[69] When the symphony finally came to be published in 1843, a year after its premiere in Leipzig, it bore no title, but it had acquired instead a dedication to Queen Victoria and a brief prefatory remark that is revealing with regard to the composer's "intentions" and ambivalences, alike:

> The individual movements of the symphony must follow immediately one upon the other, and are not to be separated by the customary pauses. For the listener, the content of the movements can be indicated on the concert program as follows:
> Introduction and Allegro agitato.—Scherzo assai vivace.—Adagio cantabile.—Allegro guerriero and Finale maestoso.

Mendelssohn had already experimented with the *attacca* performance of individual movements in his two (solo) piano concertos and in the early E-major sonata, among other works, and he came back to it in the E-minor Violin Concerto. (He referred to this idea as a current "hobby-horse" of his in a well-known letter to J. G. Droysen of 11 March 1842.)[70] Perhaps the fact that he felt compelled to stress this in a written directive here reflects a sense that there would be greater resistance to such *attacca* performance in the case of a large symphony than in solo or concerted works, where the soloist could exert greater control over the performance (and the piano, at any rate, would not need to pause for retuning). The movement designations differ slightly from those actually printed in the score before the individual movements: Mendelssohn did not bother to specify there the identity of an "introduction" or "scherzo"; the Adagio is not marked "cantabile"; the finale is marked simply "Allegro vivacissimo," rather than "guerriero" ("warlike"), and the independent A-major coda is headed "Allegro maestoso assai" rather than "Finale maestoso." The slightly more emphatic or pointed headings prescribed for the concert program, together with the directive for continuous performance, are more or less subtle indications of a narrativizing, "historical" subtext to the symphony that Mendelssohn—in the spirit of a Schumannian-Romantic aesthetic—left the individual listener to infer according to personal taste, inclination, imagination, and *Bildung*.

The status of the slow introduction is obvious enough, in terms of formal function. But even at this level it departs from the autonomous classical symphonic introduction by providing the motivic basis for the theme of the following Allegro (see Example 7.26a and b). Like the linking of separate movements without interruption, this is, of course, another symptom of the Romantic drive for cyclic integration. Aside from the motive of formal integration, however, the procedure suggests a desire for the integration of "content," as well. (One might suppose that this is not a term Mendelssohn would have approved of, if he had not himself invoked it in his prefatory note, cited earlier.)

Example 7.26
Symphony in A Minor, Op. 56, "Scottish," First Movement

a. mm. 1–8

b. mm. 64–71

The musical character or gesture of the Andante con moto is also that of an introduction in a literary or poetic sense: it conveys the feeling of a narrative frame, a lens through which the "events" of the following Allegro—or perhaps the symphony as a whole—are to be viewed. A number of writers since the time of the work's premiere have identified a "ballad tone" in this introduction (and we might recall that Scotland's greatest cultural export, along with Ossian and Sir Walter Scott, was the popular folk-ballad). One early reviewer spoke of the "lamenting, choral idiom" of the opening idea; another heard in it a "songlike character . . . which one encounters a number of times in the course of this symphony"; a third spoke of "the first movement, with its delicate, fairy-tale beginning" mounting to the energy of a full-blown storm by the end.[71] The melancholy, reflective, and "singing" character of the introduction seems to speak of something past, a scene or story from history or legend. That Mendelssohn should have felt unable to insist on its Scottishness is understandable, and though Schumann famously mistook the local color for an Italian one (see the Historical Views and Documents following this Chapter), he still responded to a characteristic "coloring" and "folk tone" of the symphony as a whole. A midsection to the introduction begins with rhapsodic, almost recitative-like gestures in the violins (mm. 17ff.); the manner in which the opening motive is woven contrapuntally into these gestures conveys the impression of a remembered scene taking shape and of a mounting excitement that affects the singer of the tale and inspires him or her to perform it for an audience. Although this mounting excitement is suddenly reined in at the end of the midsection—where the music pauses dramatically on the Neapolitan sixth (B♭) before sinking into a brief reprise—the return of the opening idea in A minor is subtly inflected with remnants of the "rhapsodic" gesture. The moment of inspired recollection, in which memory is activated, must yield to a thought-collecting calm before the proper telling of the tale can begin.

The Allegro has a kind of knightly, galloping quality to it, especially due to the role of a little double-sixteenth-note figure used to embellish the transformed theme of the introduction (cf. Example 7.26b). Mendelssohn lets the energy of this material accumulate gradually. The first group maintains a subdued dynamic level, even when the full woodwinds take over the theme from the solo clarinet. This accumulated energy is then unleashed at the beginning of the bridge section (*assai animato*), where the galloping sixteenth-note figure is compounded: the scene or action that had first taken shape in the distance, as it were, comes suddenly tumbling into full view, like some knightly cavalcade rushing past. (However we imagine such a "scene," there can presumably no longer be, by this point, any firm distinction between the "telling" of it—the description of the scene—and the direct experience of it, as reenactment.) The movement's impulse toward thematic unity is enhanced by the unusual procedure of the second group, in which the main theme continues to gallop along, now in E minor, beneath a new countermelody in the clarinet (see Example 7.27). Second group and closing remain in E minor, giving the exposition a particularly dark coloring. A melodically distinct, even songlike closing theme (m. 181) seems to compensate for the lack of an independent second theme.

The opening of the development resembles that of the *Hebrides* Overture (and also the Op. 101 "Trumpet" Overture) in its feeling of a suddenly suspended motion, effected here by sustained chords in the winds (in the *Hebrides* the strings sustain the harmony). In both cases, echoes of the movement's principal motive sound below these sustained harmonies, which gradually migrate downward. This first phase of the development is subsequently connected with the "storm" music of the coda in an interesting way that might easily be overlooked due to the considerable distance separating the two passages. The agitated C-minor crescendo in which this first developmental phase culminates (see Example 7.28) is abruptly truncated, but at the structurally analogous point in the coda (m. 455) the same crescendo leads into an extended passage of unmistakable "storm" music that forms the dynamic climax of the movement. For the time being, in the development, the storm is apparently kept at bay. The rest of the development concerns itself, in dramatic fashion, with complicating the relations among the thematic-motivic characters of the exposition. Specifically, the thematic counterpoint of the second

Example 7.27
Symphony in A Minor, Op. 56, "Scottish," First Movement, mm. 125–33

Example 7.28
Symphony in A Minor, Op. 56, "Scottish," First Movement, mm. 231–37

group is complicated by fragmentary imitations of its constituent motives. A long and clearly directed retransition (such as Mendelssohn often favored) ties smoothly into the recapitulation by virtue of a continuous legato cello line, contributing to the fluid and unobtrusive character of this return. As usual, the recapitulation is abridged, in this case by the excision of the bridge passage, among other things. The second-theme complex is ruffled by an enigmatic gesture of repressed agitation (mm. 355–62), which may constitute another anticipation of the "storm" coda.

The effect of the storm itself cannot be missed. The heaving chromatic scales in string tremolo (mm. 455–76) have often prompted a comparison to the storm music of Wagner's *Der fliegende Holländer*, which they do very much anticipate. Each round of swells is closed off by the "galloping" motive of the main theme, and this motive ushers in a forceful cadential version of the *animato* bridge material, thus making good its absence earlier in the recapitulation. That much makes musical sense, as does the opening of the coda, with its structural analogy to the opening of the development. But why the "storm"?—a purely descriptive event, it would seem, with no legitimate developmental value here. Ambros (who chastised Lampadius and Schumann for imagining the piece as an "Italian" symphony, only to hear it as an "unmistakably German" one, himself) posed the same question, in pondering the hermeneutic enigmas of the Romantic symphony in general:

Then we have Mendelssohn's A-minor symphony. What is meant by the roaring chromatic storm at the end of the first Allegro, or by those gently dreaming [and] solemn march-like phrases in the Adagio—or by the violent battle of the finale?—the *rinforzatos* of the basses sound almost like the roar of a lion, whom some young paladin perhaps has engaged in chivalric contest—or by the appendix [*Anhang*], with its melody in the style of a folk-song and the intensive jubilation [at the end]? And beyond that, the darting elfin play of the Scherzo. We can't help but read a whole fairy-tale into it [*wir dichten uns ein ganzes Märchen hinein*], something thoroughly in the old German manner like Sleeping Beauty, Cinderella, or Snow White.[72]

This indiscriminate invocation of popular tales (the whole canon of Grimm-according-to-Disney) may strike us as a rather inappropriate response to this music. Yet the particular details and character that Ambros detected did incite him to imagine some kind of narrative-historical agglomeration of scenes or images, even if such metaphorical *tableaux vivants* tend toward the cartoonish, in this case. Some kind of landscape is indeed probably projected on the listener's auditory imagination by the melancholic song of the introduction, its "misty," gray-hued scoring, the concluding storm, and any number of details in between. Characteristic of its projection in musical form is not only its elusive, shadowy quality, as representational object, but also its tendency (as "animated" landscape) to become peopled by characters or to become the setting for imaginary actions—whether fictional or historical, natural or phantasmagorical.

At the end of the coda, the scene suddenly fades—in an almost cinematic way—and the slow introduction unexpectedly returns, reinforcing its character as narrative frame. Or one might picture that fading gesture (mm. 501–12) as a kind of curtain that falls for a moment, while a narrator sets the scene for the next tableau. In the same way, then, one can hear a quick curtain rise on the following Vivace non troppo during the eight measures of transition/introduction that precede its theme. This scherzo movement provokes less in the way of interpretive fancy than any of the other movements. Nonetheless, it is full of characteristic verve, and one can easily imagine pictures of some highland romp, especially once alerted to the potentially Scottish folk-character of the theme (Example 7.29). (To call the movement "elfin," as Ambros does, seems rather far-fetched, despite some nice examples of the Mendelssohnian piano-staccato idiom.) It is not only the often-cited pentatonic tendencies of the theme that contribute to its Scottishness but

Example 7.29
Symphony in A Minor, Op. 56, "Scottish," Second Movement, mm. 9–16

also its rhythmic configuration—the conjunction of dotted rhythms and the eighth-plus-quarter trochee (a kind of slow-motion Scottish snap), for instance—and even the initial scoring for solo clarinet, with its connotations of the rustic chalumeau or bagpipe. The form is again novel, but not in any way that would incite extramusical allegory. An a-b-a¹ first group in typical soft-to-loud format is followed by second and closing themes in the dominant (Ambros's "elfin music," probably)—thus a sonata exposition in scherzando guise. A sizable development explores the seemingly naive materials of the "Scottish" tune at some length (mm. 105–51), after which this tune is deftly intertwined with the second main idea (mm. 152–75). A tentative, "false" reprise of the first theme in E♭, in the flute, is bumped up to F major, where it is still not quite recapitulated but played out over a $^6_4$ harmony, with drumrolls, as a buildup to its own imminent return. Instead of the expected return, however, there is a new, rambunctious—and scarcely elfin—setting of the second theme and closing phrases, all shot through with hints of the "Scottish" theme. A quiet coda ensues, newly fashioned from elements of what has gone before. Near the end, the first violins spin the opening motive upward, dissolving into the airy heights. (This closing does bring to mind the scherzos of the Octet or the *Midsummer Night's Dream* music, and to that extent might help to justify Ambros's elves.) As a whole, the movement might also justify Wagner's epithet of a "kaleidoscopic" style in Mendelssohn's music.[73] But what Wagner meant disparagingly and generally—music that is evanescent, spritely, well crafted, but without substance—is embodied here in a sophisticated design that belies Wagner's intended critique.

With the last two movements the symphony returns from the realm of the picturesque (or even "kaleidoscopic") to the epic-historical mode of its first movement. The slow movement and finale, as a pair, are particularly evocative of images from contemporary history painting. Once again, however, the musical realization of such (implicit) images as actively sounding, animated tableaux and the linking of them within the symphonic framework add a temporal dimension that nudges these "images" in the direction of drama or narrative, without, of course, attaining the representational specificity of those discursive modes. Mendelssohn was at pains to convey the underlying image of the finale by attaching the label *guerriero* (martial, warlike) to the "public" version of its heading. He also underscored the unusual formal gesture of his thematically independent coda—or "appendix," as Ambros aptly called it—to the finale by designating it as a "finale" in its own right (*Finale maestoso*): the nomenclature is probably more operatic than symphonic here and clearly draws attention to the role of this major-mode conclusion as a "hymn" of victory and thanks after the battle, that is, as the culminating tableau of the series. (In a letter of 3 March 1842 Mendelssohn authorized Ferdinand David to adjust the instrumentation of the opening measures, if necessary, so that the A-major theme would sound "properly clear and strong, like a men's chorus.")

These fairly unmistakable evocations of the finale as heroic battle followed by hymn of victory cast some light on the possible sound-imagery of the preceding Adagio. The "cantabile" with which Mendelssohn modified the original adagio tempo marking reinforces the kinship of the principal melody with many of his Songs without Words. The expressive-sentimental cast of the melody and the simple, pizzicato chordal accompaniment contribute here to a fairly pure example of the type. Especially characteristic for Mendelssohn is the second half of this melody (Example 7.30), with the sweetly "prayerful" sound of ii^6 and IV^6, and the imploring leap off the diminished chord to the high seventh degree in the fifth and sixth measures. But an orchestral Song without Words, formally unelaborated,

Example 7.30
Symphony in A Minor, Op. 56, "Scottish," Third Movement, mm. 18–20

would not be adequate to the ambitions of a symphony on this scale. Thus, this sweet instrumental song is played off against another, very different complex of ideas, growing from the dark-hued, slightly ominous, marchlike gesture first heard in clarinets, bassoons, and horns (Example 7.31).

It is nearly impossible to overlook the gendered coding of these contrasting materials. Where the A-theme is imbued with images of idealized feminine piety and tender, amorous devotion, the B-theme anticipates the warlike strains of the finale. At its two principal occurrences, the B-theme swells with heroic pride, culminating each time in anxious, unresolved diminished sevenths (m. 48, m. 113)

Example 7.31
Symphony in A Minor, Op. 56, "Scottish," Third Movement, mm. 34–38

that seem to speak of imminent battles and uncertain fate. The movement is clearly enough structured around the alternation of these contrasting elements, but its real interest lies in their musical and expressive interaction. This interaction is foreshadowed already in the introductory-transitional measures (a device this movement shares with the scherzo). Here a beseeching, anguished gesture in the "women's" collective lyrical voice is contrasted with anticipations of the ominous martial rhythms of the "male" chorus of horns and lower woodwinds. This very same material returns after each of these gendered principles or characters has been allotted its proper exposition; in mm. 63–72 the "beseeching" gesture is developed, its anguish amplified by sequential development, but its pleas are broken off by a stern, tutti statement of the martial material, whose expansive motion from D minor to F major gesture seems to counter those anxious pleas with stern words about duty, honor, and glory. Such a scene of the "warrior's farewell" is a classic trope, depicted in countless portrayals of such figures as Aeneas and Rinaldo, and its collective transformation (the "choral" tableau implied here) could surely be found in any number of scenes from grand opera or epic-historical painting from the nineteenth century. In Mendelssohn's movement, the scene remains more tableau than action, but not entirely so. After the brief, climactic interaction just described, the representative positions are taken up again (with musical variations) in a symbolic, choreographic manner, reminding us that music's capacities here lie somewhere between those of the "frozen," painted or sculpted, tableau and the explicitly progressive-temporal teleology of drama or narrative. At the end, only a faint drumbeat (mm. 143–45) recalls the earlier confrontation, perhaps to imply that the troops have already departed and are even now distantly marching toward glorious battle.

That motion implicit at the close of the Adagio becomes immediately audible in the fourth movement, which begins in the style of a quick-march. The rapid quarter-note (quick-march) pulse dominates the whole movement, along with its combination of dotted quarter- and eighth-note rhythms. Whether there is anything distinctively "Scottish" about the marching tunes in this movement would be difficult to say. The scoring of the second theme for oboes and clarinets over a discreet "drone" on the low b of the violins might connote the timbre of bagpipes, as if heard from afar, and the theme itself might be heard to recall the contours of the "ballad" theme of the first movement introduction (see Example 7.32). The rapid tempo and persistent minor mode lend all the themes a sense of determination and untamed ferocity that distinguishes them, in any case, from the regimental parade music of courtly or urban contexts.

Example 7.32
Symphony in A Minor, Op. 56, "Scottish," Finale, mm. 66–74

The main body of the movement, in A minor, pursues an essentially complete sonata form, with no significant deviations until the end. The first theme of the second group (shown in Example 7.32) occurs in the minor dominant, E minor, just as in the first movement, and hence contributes here, as there, to the characteristically somber hue of the movement as a whole. Perhaps the most noticeable feature of the form is the tendency to create thematic groups out of pairs of independent themes. The resulting multiplicity of distinct, independent march tunes could convey an impression of troops assembling from different directions (a "gathering of the clans"?). This is especially the case in the second group, where the first tune, with its muffled "bagpipe" timbre and fifth-degree pedal, suggests something heard from a distance, while the blustery C-major response from all the remaining instruments clearly conveys an immediate presence. The development, the traditional musical "scene of battle," begins simply with reiterations of the first group in different keys. The center of it is devoted to fugato development and recombination of motives from the bridge section, culminating in an energetic tutti restatement of the originally "distant" second-theme march (thus suggesting some element of progressive action).

After a condensed recapitulation there arrives what appears to be the real fray of the battle. This coda-transition, as it might be called—since a second, major-mode coda will follow—substitutes a half-note pulse (derived from a closing figure in the exposition) for the marching quarter notes of the beginning. In the close of the exposition this figure of half-note with quick sixteenth-note upbeat, undergirded by a rising chromatic scale, had served as a braking motion to halt, temporarily, the inexorable march (mm. 135–47). Now in the (first) coda, the rhythm persists for nearly fifty measures (mm. 312–60), and the effect is one of relentless, violent hammer strokes (bringing to mind, perhaps, the clubs, axes, and spears of primitive warfare). Eventually, this tumult fades, and the second ("bagpipe") theme is heard once again "from the distance," this effect of distance now heightened by the widely spaced fifths that the strings sustain for twenty-five measures, while clarinet and bassoon play the march theme in fading counterpoint.

The hymnic quality of the concluding A-major theme is generated, in part, by the psalmodic incipit familiar from the "Reformation" Symphony and the *Lobgesang*, this time in the dominant-to-tonic transposition (Example 7.33); in part, by the scoring for low winds and strings; and, in part, by the simple diatonic conduct of the subsequent melodic line.[74] The $\frac{6}{8}$ meter recalls the first movement and contributes a "folkloric" element that early critics heard both here and there.

Example 7.33
Symphony in A Minor, Op. 56, "Scottish," Finale, mm. 396–403

Allegro maestoso assai

mf   *sfz*   *sfz*

Clar., Bsn., Hn., Vla.

Also hymnlike is the simple strophic structure: the complete melody is stated three times, each time with fuller orchestral texture. (What begins as a *Männerchor*, as Mendelssohn described it, is gradually filled out by alto and treble voices; women and children return to the scene, as it were, to complete this final tableau of victory and rejoicing.) After a brief melodic interlude (mm. 444–63) the melody returns once more, with new cadential extensions, to round out this final "chorus without words" in a tone of earnest, dignified jubilation.

To the extent that the kinds of tableaux sketched here for the movements of the "Italian" and "Scottish" Symphonies—ranging from picturesque landscape and "genre" scenes (Roman carnival or pilgrims' march), to scenes of epic narrative or history painting—are projected (and animated) by the character and formal procedures of the music, the identification of a precise local color may not be essential. Schumann's and Ambros's misapprehensions of the "Scottish" Symphony—as an "Italian" and "German" symphony, respectively—are cases in point. Both critics still understood and admired something of the work's peculiar character, color, and "imagery" (even though Schumann is typically loath to go into detail). In refraining from attaching any official geographical identification to his two "travel" symphonies, Mendelssohn presumably sensed that these more general qualities counted most and that he would have succeeded with these works only if audiences could hear for themselves something of the scenes and scenarios he had tried to evoke, regardless of specific local color. ("Local color" in music, that is, will always be more contingent than expressive gesture as such.) We might also recall something that Schumann said about the program of Berlioz's *Symphonie fantastique*, which he criticized: the program would be discovered and passed along soon enough, without the composer's spelling it out. (In a sense, this is just what happened in Mendelssohn's case.) The remark may reflect Schumann's own particular reticence in such matters. Mendelssohn's reticence about titles, on the other hand, may reflect a somewhat different attitude, a concern for the dignity of the genre. Even Schumann, who had no reservations about attaching suggestive titles to his piano pieces, at least, did not see fit to do so with his symphonies. Both composers shared a sense, perhaps, that putting a descriptive title to a symphony (Beethoven's "Pastoral" notwithstanding) was a breach of generic decorum, an affront to symphonic dignity, *gravitas*, and claims to universality. Decorum and dignity were values that concerned Mendelssohn increasingly with age (excessively, some might say) and may have something to do with what was, all in all, a rather uneasy relationship to the symphonic genre.

By contrast, his approach to the unpedigreed genre of the concert overture was unconstrained and full of a youthful, experimental enthusiasm—indeed, that genre was, to some extent, his own invention. The overtures, as we shall see, are informed by the same impulses of poetic fancy and subtle formal experiment that Mendelssohn had attempted to bring to the symphony. For a brief time during the composer's early career these impulses yielded a few unparalleled successes, in overture and symphony alike.

THE CONCERT OVERTURES (1825–1834)

Writing to his family on 6 October 1830, Mendelssohn informed them: "I am working on my Hebrides overture, which I want to name: *Overture to the Lonesome Isle (Ouvertüre zur einsamen Insel)*. Hopefully it will be finished soon."[75] It is, of course, by the composer's more informal designation here, *The Hebrides*, that we now know the work in question (Op. 26), which was also identified as *Fingal's Cave (Die Fingals-Höhle)*, *Ouverture aux Hébrides*, and *Overture to the Isles of Fingal*, in a variety of original drafts and published editions.[76] Such indecision (which can be a source of some aggravation to scholars and bibliographers) reflects, in part, the fairly protracted genesis of the piece, which was subjected to the same revisionary meticulousness as most of Mendelssohn's major early works. But it also raises certain generic or even ontological questions with regard to traditional nomenclature, questions that are raised by its companion-pieces, as well, such as the overtures *Calm Sea and*

Prosperous Voyage (*Meeresstille und glückliche Fahrt*, Op. 27) and *The Beautiful Melusine* (*Die schöne Melusine*, Op. 32).

What, precisely, are these overtures "to"? What does it mean to compose an overture to an island or to a cave? While "The Lonesome Isle" or "Fingal's Cave" could well be imagined as titles of popular Ossianic dramas or operas of the time, we know perfectly well that this is not the case here. Rather, we understand that these are "concert" overtures, that is, independent compositions in overture form; they are overtures "about" certain figures or themes rather than functional theatrical preambles "to" a specific play or opera. Thus, we understand that the locution "overture to" constitutes, for Mendelssohn and his contemporaries, a holdover from conventional practice, reflecting the habitual power of generic identification. Nonetheless, the peculiarity of the resulting designations might provoke some legitimate reflection on critical and aesthetic issues pertaining to these works. A pair of short poems (Goethe's "Meeresstille" and "Glückliche Fahrt"), a legend-enshrouded site (the so-called "Fingal's Cave" on the Island of Staffa off the western Scottish coast), and a fairy-tale subject without a concrete text (Melusina) are all distinctly different kinds of objects, differing from one another as much as they do from, say, a Shakespeare play (*A Midsummer Night's Dream*), as might constitute a more traditional object for an overture. A consideration of how one might embody such themes in the "form" of the early Romantic overture, of the relation between music and its "object," can tell us a good deal about Mendelssohn's musical-aesthetic sensibilities, about the contemporary status of musical forms and meanings, and about his impact on that status.

Overture to *A Midsummer Night's Dream*, Op. 21

I have had a dream, past the wit of man to say what dream it was. Man is but an ass if he go about to expound this dream.
                    —Bottom (*A Midsummer Night's Dream*, act 4, scene 1)

The composition of the overture to Shakespeare's *A Midsummer Night's Dream* at the age of seventeen remains, among all the prodigious accomplishments of the composer's youth, the quintessential Mendelssohnian miracle. The precocity of this achievement in biographical terms has tended to overshadow its historical precocity, so to speak; for this work, in many ways a paradigm of Romantic musical art, was composed at a time when Beethoven and Schubert were still alive (and Weber, just barely), while it owes almost nothing directly to those composers (or at most something to Weber—but just barely). Ironically, it "became" a traditional, functional dramatic overture only retroactively, when Mendelssohn composed further incidental music for the staging of Shakespeare's comedy at the Prussian court in 1843. When Mendelssohn originally composed the overture in 1826, *A Midsummer Night's Dream* was hardly part of the repertory of German-language theaters; rather, in A. W. Schlegel's still recent translation (as *Ein Sommernachtstraum*) it existed more as a literary artifact. It would be misleading, though, to place too much emphasis on the distinction between the genres of concert and (functional) dramatic overture at this early date. Beethoven's *Coriolan* overture, for instance, had already led a largely independent existence (as a de facto concert overture) up to this time, and other dramatic overtures of Beethoven, Cherubini, and Weber were rapidly becoming mainstays of the concert repertory. But in composing an overture "to" a play that was nonetheless not necessarily, or even primarily, intended to accompany a performance of that play, Mendelssohn was making more pointed claims for the power of the music to convey something essential about the drama, to embody it or characterize it in musical terms. If one were going to listen to an overture "to" a play without subsequently watching the play itself, that overture was evidently assuming a kind of surrogate position with respect to the play, a responsibility not only to "speak of" or preface the play but even to speak *for* it, in a sense.

Bottom's response to his perplexing translation into asinine form ("Man is but an ass if he go about to expound this dream") is an appropriate challenge to anyone undertaking to interpret Mendelssohn's translation of Shakespearean motifs into musical form.   Yet the familiarity of the subject matter, especially to English-speaking audiences, and Mendelssohn's felicitous choice of dramatic elements to "illustrate" it and the deftness of his musical characterizations have together left little doubt about the main outlines of the musical picture. The "elfin" tone devised to evoke the domain of Oberon and Titania and (more particularly) their fairy retainers became a paradigm for the rest of the century.   In the exposition, staccato strings in the treble range dance in rapid, stepwise motion within a narrow ("diminutive") ambitus, supported by repeated eighth notes or pizzicato quarters. In the development section, discreet, hopping gestures in the woodwinds are superimposed, while loud, echoing tones sustained in the horns *con tutta la forza* (as Mendelssohn directs) create a new spatial dimension, filling out the "background" of nocturnal forest scenery to this shimmering fairy foreground. Mendelssohn both maximized and dramatized the musical contrast between fairy and mortal spheres by maintaining the tonic minor for the exposition of the former, while the forceful, deliberate theme that would appear to evoke the pomp of the Athenian court (mm. 62ff.) enters as a sudden, unmediated *tutti* in the tonic major (E).[77] The "hunting horns" sounded at the close of the exposition seem to belong to this same loud, regal human ambience, and the connection is immediately confirmed when the earlier tutti theme returns here, as if in obedient response to the summons of that horn call (see Example 7.34). Two legato themes in a half-note pulse occupy the position of second subject and have traditionally been associated with the two pairs of lovers, although the particular aptness of the dual thematic structure to this purpose seems not to have been remarked (see Example 7.35). A subtle formal detail is Mendelssohn's incorporation of a descending half-note scale from the bridge as the bass line to the first of these themes (bracketed in Example 7.35).

In his memoirs, A. B. Marx took credit for inspiring Mendelssohn to compose Bottom and his fellow "rude mechanicals" into the overture and for sharpening the characteristic detail of the whole exposition, following the E-minor elfin music (the

Example 7.34
A Midsummer Night's Dream Overture, Op. 21, mm. 222–34

surviving sources may bear out something of this claim).[78] No one, in any case, has ever mistaken the import of Bottom's "hee-haws," which are interspersed with a stomping dance that Mendelssohn later used, in the incidental music, for the "Bergomask" that rounds out the rustics' theatrical presentation. (It might be noted, however, that Bottom's famous musical braying is given a certain "naturalistic" variety by employing different intervals—a ninth and a tenth—and different harmonizations across its threefold exposition.) All of these traditional associations happen to be confirmed in an interesting letter from Mendelssohn to his publishers, Breitkopf and Härtel, who apparently contemplated issuing some form of written program for the overture:

I believe it will suffice to remember how the rulers of the elves, Oberon and Titania, constantly appear throughout the play with all their train, now here and now there; then

Example 7.35
A Midsummer Night's Dream **Overture, Op. 21, mm. 130–46**

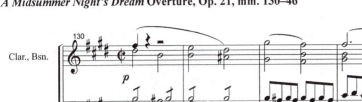

comes Prince Theseus of Athens and joins a hunting party in the forest with his wife; then the two pairs of tender lovers, who lose and find themselves; finally the troop of clumsy, coarse tradesmen, who ply their ponderous amusements; then again the elves, who entice all—and on this the piece is constructed. When at the end all is happily resolved . . . the elves return and bless the house, and disappear as morning arrives. So ends the play, and my overture too.[79]

As we might expect, Mendelssohn's account of his overture attempts to suggest only the inspiration behind the basic thematic elements of his overture, without addressing details of their deployment within the form. His letter to the publishers begins with a disclaimer: "To set forth the ideas for the composition in a program is not possible for me, for this succession of ideas *is* my overture." The points of contact between play and overture consist of certain images, characters, and situations. But the poetic life of the overture resides, finally, in the sum of its musical detail; this can no more be translated into prose than Shakespeare's dramatic verse and prose, as linguistic and semantic structures, could have been translated directly into a musical score in the first place.

Indeed, the achievement of Mendelssohn's overture transcends the mere sum of its characteristic materials, inventive as they are. The development succeeds beautifully in fragmenting and combining these materials, without a trace of mechanical pedantry, in ways that are multiply suggestive while not dependent on the specifics of Shakespeare's text or the actions represented there. The "elfin" music is further enlivened here by a little hopping figure that was first introduced in the second group of the exposition as a discrete, miniature fanfare gesture filling out the consequent extension of the melody of the "wandering lovers" (Example 7.36). In any context the figure might well be described as "puckish." Here, its

Example 7.36
A Midsummer Night's Dream **Overture, mm. 166–68**

interspersion with echoing horn calls that resound through the latter part of the development could certainly be heard as a musical enactment of Puck's mission to lead Demetrius and Lysander astray through the woods until they collapse, exhausted, into sleep. Very likely this is just what Mendelssohn did envision here, for the development itself audibly fades into a reminiscence of the "wandering" second theme, slowed down and brought to a complete stop on the relative minor (C♯ minor) in an unmistakable gesture of exhaustion and repose. In these closing measures of the development (mm. 376–94) Mendelssohn telescoped the consecutive collapses of the four lovers at the end of act 3 into this single musical gesture. The reprise of introductory material (the four woodwind chords) at this juncture between development and recapitulation has respectable precedent in several of Beethoven's works, as a structural device; but at the same time these magic, incantatory chords create a nice musical analogue to Puck's closing speech of act 3 over the sleeping forms of the four lovers ("On the ground / Sleep sound. / I'll apply / To your eye, / Gentle lover, remedy").[80] Even these parallels, however close, do not exhaust the possible connotations of the music, any more than they interfere with the unfolding of a musical design fully satisfying in its own right (as critics ever since Mendelssohn's day have stressed again and again). Those resounding tones of the horns in the development, for example, might equally well conjure up thoughts of Oberon's magic horn, especially for a German audience perhaps more familiar with Wieland and Weber than with Shakespeare (whose Oberon does not actually possess this attribute). Or we might be reminded of the hunting party of Theseus and Hippolyta that enters the forest at daybreak—for, like any narrator, the musician is at liberty to adapt and rearrange temporal events of the "story" (*histoire*) to suit his fancy, and the constructive purposes of his retelling of the tale (*récit*).[81]

A similar artful ambiguity is exemplified by the famous introductory chords. Their incomparable effect is achieved by simple means: an expansion of range and texture from a single major third in the flutes out to a full triad spread over four octaves in horns and winds. Their harmonic magic is equally simple, hinging on the minor inflection of the subdominant chord within the lapidary, "reversed" cadential progression I–V–iv–I. (That note of slight modal instability anticipates, perhaps, the turn to minor in the following theme.) They function, in one very audible sense, as a kind of curtain that slowly opens onto, and draws us into, the fantasy world of the play and of the overture alike. This role as musical curtain is, of course, confirmed by their return at the very end. The recurrence of these chords at the opening of the recapitulation, besides conveying a certain internal structural logic, serves to relate them to the musical image of the sleeping lovers, as mentioned earlier. At the end, they follow upon the celebrated and, again, exquisitely simple transformation of the "court" theme (mm. 663ff.), by which Mendelssohn evokes the sleeping household of the Duke, blessed by Oberon and Titania. In this way, the chords also serve as a musical parallel to the thematization of sleep, dreams, and fantasy throughout Shakespeare's play.[82] In bringing down the "curtain" on the overture, they enunciate Puck's envoi, exhorting the audience to "think but this"—"That you have but slumbered here / While these visions did appear." That the comic edge of Puck's address is softened to a purely "sentimental" expression in Mendelssohn's coda is typical of the composer, perhaps, but it is probably just as typical of a contemporary (sentimentalized) treatment of Shakespeare, more generally. Indeed, the music of the seventeen-year-old Mendelssohn, together with the additional incidental music of 1843, surely did more to determine a collective image of *A Midsummer Night's Dream* for generations to follow than any number of individual stage productions might have done.

Meeresstille und glückliche Fahrt, Op. 27

Mendelssohn's second major concert overture, Op. 27, is part of the legacy of the young composer's friendship with the aging "prince of poets," Johann Wolfgang von Goethe. It may also be, in part, a legacy of his early friendship with the musician and writer Adolf Bernhard Marx. (The friendship with Goethe was cut short by the poet's death in 1832; it was scarcely outlived by the friendship with Marx, which, for a variety of reasons, quickly faded after a period of shared youthful enthusiasm.) Where Goethe had provided the poetic text that would inspire the music, it may well have been Marx who inspired Mendelssohn to dispense with the text itself in creating a purely musical *hommage* to its "poetic ideas." In an aesthetic pamphlet on the subject of musical "tone-painting" (*Ueber Malerei in der Tonkunst*, 1828), published at the very time Mendelssohn was working on his *Meeresstille* overture, Marx alluded to his friend's work-in-progress and its historical significance as an attempt to convey the content or idea of a poem through an independent musical composition.[83]   We do not know whether Mendelssohn was flattered or annoyed by Marx's comparison—to Mendelssohn's advantage—of his efforts with the choral finale in the Ninth Symphony and Beethoven's own vocal setting of the same pair of Goethe poems (as the secular cantata *Meeresstille und glückliche Fahrt*, Op. 112). This praise was as much for the symbolic act of the overture as for its music, which had not even been completed when Marx was writing. It also supports a suspicion that Marx may have had some role in encouraging this act, as it corresponded so well to his notion of a new kind of instrumental music that would draw its inspiration from the world of literature and ideas. In any case, the composition of *Meeresstille und glückliche Fahrt* represents a further, decisive step in the evolution of the "concert overture" as a genre; here, there is no question that we are dealing with an overture "about" Goethe's poems, not "to" them.

The usual English translation of the overture's title, as Tovey remarked, is particularly misleading. "Calm Sea and Prosperous Voyage" reduces the already minimal narrative implied by Goethe's text into a nonnarrative, merely a unitary (lyric) experience of "happy sailing." The poetic model is, in fact, not one but a pair of poems, whose titles ("Meeres Stille," "Glückliche Fahrt") would be better rendered as "Becalmed at Sea" and "Fortunate [or Prosperous] Voyage." As Mendelssohn (and perhaps Marx?) certainly realized, the simple elements of Goethe's miniature, quasi-allegorical lyric pair were especially well suited to musical realization, dominated as they are by dynamic images and corresponding emotional states. If, as Hanslick was to claim, music expresses feelings by imitating their "dynamic" psychological contours, then Goethe's poems were a perfect blueprint for musical expression, since they portray contrasting emotional states by means of dynamic conditions that both cause and reflect those states, at once: a mixture of physical stillness and psychic anxiety corresponding to the ship floating in still, airless waters, followed by the gradual clearing of the air and return of the winds that will enable the vessel to complete its journey. The text of these poems reads as follows:

MEERES STILLE	BECALMED AT SEA
Tiefe Stille herrscht im Wasser,	Deep stillness covers the waters,
Ohne Regung ruht das Meer,	motionless rests the sea,
Und bekümmert sieht der Schiffer	and troubled, the mariner looks
Glatte Fläche rings umher.	at the smooth surface all about him.
Keine Luft von keiner Seite!	Not a breeze from any side!
Todesstille fürchterlich!	Deathly still—dreadfully!
In der ungeheuren Weite	In the terrifying distance
Reget keine Welle sich.	not a wave bestirs itself.

GLÜCKLICHE FAHRT	PROSPEROUS VOYAGE
Die Nebel zerreißen,	The mists now part,
Der Himmel ist helle,	the heavens are clear,
Und Aeolus löset	and Aeolus unfastens
Das ängstliche Band.	the constraining cord.
Es säuseln die Winde,	The winds are rustling,
Es rührt sich der Schiffer.	The mariner arises.
Geschwinde! Geschwinde!	Quickly! Quickly!
Es teilt sich die Welle,	The waves divide,
Es naht sich die Ferne,	The distance approaches,
Schon seh' ich das Land!	Already I see land!

The meter and line lengths of Goethe's verses underscore the dynamic contrast described by the words, progressing from "slow-moving," four-foot iambic lines in "Meeres Stille," to two-foot lines in "Glückliche Fahrt," each line now propelled by an initial dactylic rhythm.[84] A musical setting of the text would naturally translate these contrasts into musical rhythms, but—as Mendelssohn may have wished to demonstrate to the revered, but rather unmusical, poetic master—music alone could accomplish the same and much more in the fields of rhythm, meter, and dynamics.

According to the composer's testimony, the original manuscript score of the *Meeresstille* overture, evidently completed sometime during the summer of 1828, was either stolen or lost in the course of the following year and a half. In writing out a new score of the work, Mendelssohn took the opportunity to introduce substantial revisions, and it would be interesting to know if any of these reflected his first actual experience of the sea, which had occurred during the intervening months, when he traveled to England in 1829. Some surviving pages of an early draft of the exposition do show that a rather conventionally Mendelssohnian theme was later deleted from a passage that now includes one of the score's more "impressionistic" effects (the gradual textural and dynamic crescendo leading into the fanfare-like closing theme (mm. 223–38).[85] It is puzzling to find Fanny Mendelssohn writing in June 1828—at a time when the overture must have been nearly complete—that Felix had cast the piece in two "separate," complementary tableaux instead of a traditional allegro movement with slow introduction.[86] Such a plan would correspond to that of the poetic model, of course, but it is difficult to see how the work in its final form really departs from the traditional introduction and allegro design, apart from a sizable transitional passage in the allegro tempo (mm. 49–98) that evokes the clearing of the mists and meteorological transition from dead calm to cheerful breezes. This transition is, indeed, another one of the more novel passages in the piece, and its emphasis on purely rhythmic and dynamic means is representative of a similar, appropriate emphasis within the overture as a whole. The parting mists and rising breezes are suggested by a prolonged dissonance (vii^{o7}/A over tonic root) that accumulates rhythmic momentum as it presses toward resolution. The dominant prolongation (V/D) that we would expect from such a transition into the main theme is deferred for some measures but then realized at great length (mm. 71–98), as the rhythmic momentum continues to build.

If it is scarcely the independent tableau that Fanny intimated, the adagio introduction ("Meeresstille") is nonetheless substantial, not only in length—48 measures of slow $\frac{4}{4}$—but in musical "substance," as well. It is the most Beethovenian of Mendelssohn's orchestral introductions, in keeping with the similarly Beethovenian qualities that can be detected in the Allegro. In the introduction the broad, hymnic character of the opening measures first brings Beethoven to mind. As the introduction progresses, the permutations of the initial rhythmic motive (see Example 7.37a), as well as an important new expressive tag of a rising minor seventh resolving to a sixth, (Example 7.37b) reinforce the sense of this stylistic heritage. The latter figure evokes the anxieties of Goethe's

Example 7.37
Meeresstille und Glückliche Fahrt **Overture, Op. 27**

a. mm. 1–4

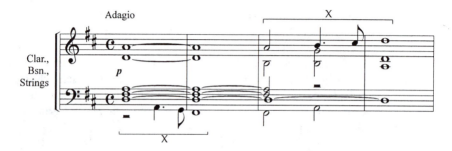

b. mm. 21–26

"troubled mariner" as he surveys the "deadly stillness" all about him, conveyed by a variety of sustained notes and chords, above all, the violins' octave d^2 d^3 in mm. 29–36. Beyond this, the self-consciously "organic" motivicism of Mendelssohn's introduction, later carried over into the Allegro, acknowledges the guiding spirit of Beethoven and Goethe at once, if we choose to read it also as homage to the poet's theories of organic metamorphosis. In the Allegro, the propulsive quarter-half-quarter rhythm of the bridge (mm. 149ff.), as Todd notes,[87] is reminiscent of

Beethoven's Second and Third *Leonore* overtures, as are, perhaps, the trumpet fanfares of the coda. Todd also mentions the "Pastoral" Symphony in connection with a specific tonic-dominant overlap in the transition to the Allegro, but a much more pervasive kinship between the two works might be heard in Mendelssohn's skillful evocation of natural sound patterns (wind and waves, in this case) by means of a varied layering of repeated rhythmic and harmonic figures, often in conjunction with long-sustained harmonic tones. One such instance, the "impressionistic" passage in mm. 223–43, was cited earlier. Another is that leading into the second theme, in which A. W. Ambros explicitly heard the "rustling winds" of Goethe's "Glückliche Fahrt" (mm. 171–88).[88] Perhaps the most striking of the many similar effects to be heard here is the passage serving as a midsection within the first group, where the sweeping melodic line of the violins is sandwiched between quarter-note triplets in the winds and repeated eighth notes in the lower strings (see Example 7.38). Yet another resemblance to the "Pastoral" Symphony

Example 7.38
Meeresstille und Glückliche Fahrt Overture, Op. 27, mm. 115–19

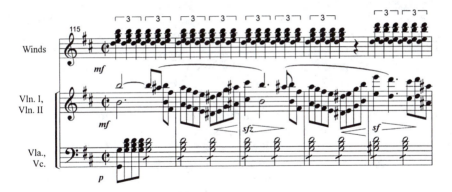

(to the first movement in particular) is the deliberate avoidance or minimizing of traditional developmental techniques such as fragmentation or imitative textural complications in favor of a concentration on gradually shifting dynamics played out over large, slow-moving harmonic blocks. While the relevant natural images are different—sylvan there, maritime here—their related dynamic properties elicit related musical responses.

It is in such quasi-impressionistic detail that Mendelssohn's overture most succeeds, for if there were any "danger" in his poetic program, it would be that this was too simplistic to impart any individuality to its musical execution. After all, almost any Classic or early Romantic introduction-and-allegro pair might serve perfectly well to embody the basic trajectory of Goethe's poems. It is interesting to note that even Mendelssohn felt the need to enliven the rudimentary narrative sequence of the two poems with a few additional episodic details. The smooth sailing of the Allegro, for instance, is momentarily interrupted in the development (as we might well expect) when the "anxious" minor-seventh motive of the introduction is transformed, across mm. 286–334. (Here the gesture is also newly derived, as diminished fifth, from the fanfare-motive of the closing group and related, in turn, to the rhythms of the main theme and introduction.) This passing threat is followed by a reiteration of the second theme, pianissimo, in C major, harmonized in a $^6_4$ position (mm. 335–46), conveying the impression of some safe goal glimpsed from afar—or a goal as yet only promised or imagined. In the coda to his overture, as it has been interpreted since its earliest performances, Mendelssohn further extrapolates from his poetic models by "composing" the eventual safe arrival of the vessel in port, whereas Goethe's second poem ends only with the sighting of land. No less an authority than Mendelssohn's own timpanist in the Gewandhaus orchestra confirmed that the great solo timpani strokes that usher in the coda (Allegro maestoso) were meant to represent "volleys of cannons" greeting the ship's arrival.[89] This is a detail that one might not hit upon unassisted, but few listeners have failed to register the related significance of the trumpet fanfares some measures after that. In addition to fleshing out Goethe's "prosperous voyage" with moments of narrative suspense and a greater degree of incidental, "descriptive" detail, Mendelssohn also felt compelled to provide a stronger narrative closure in place of Goethe's more provisional, anticipatory one ("already I see land").[90] (Here, too, the "anxious" rising seventh is resolved out to an octave in the woodwinds.) Of course, such closure was, in a sense, forced on Mendelssohn by the imperative of Classic tonal forms, which hardly permit the notion of a merely "anticipated" closure. As if to compensate for this enforced modification, Mendelssohn went one step further in the final measures and returned his music to the "calm seas" from which it had proceeded. Although the recurrence of the violin motive from mm. 3–4 of the introduction is buried here (almost inaudibly) in the violas, the placid motion and soothing plagal progression are enough to recall the calm sea of the beginning, now recollected in a new tranquillity—one that is not threatening, like the introduction, but peaceful and confident.[91]

The Hebrides (Fingal's Cave), Op. 26

It is no accident that the *Hebrides* Overture became the paradigmatic Mendelssohnian "landscape" piece. As we know from firsthand evidence—the famous sketch of what became the opening eleven bars of the overture, sent by Felix to his family as a musical memento of his travels—the all-important motivic kernel of the work as well as characteristic elements of scoring, texture, and figuration were all directly inspired by the experience of the rugged, desolate western coast of Scotland, where Mendelssohn jotted down these ideas in the early days of August 1829.[92] Claims that a work such as this might evoke specific natural imagery, even a precise geography and climate, always provoke questions about intersubjective agreement regarding music's effect, character, and "meaning." There is little disagreement, though, that with the simple indication of

Mendelssohn's title (or titles), this music succeeds brilliantly in conveying a host of apposite images by unobtrusive, eminently "musical" means. These means have often been described, especially those deployed at the very outset of the work to suggest an atmosphere of rolling ocean swells, gusts and sea spray, melancholy vistas of rocks and surf, and a palette of varied gray tones worthy of Whistler. The persistence of the famous descending main motive throughout the work, in ever-shifting forms, creates the impression, as Wulf Konold puts it, of something constantly changing in surface detail and yet constantly the same, like the surface of the sea.[93] While the rhythmic-harmonic motion of the Allegro of *Meeresstille und glückliche Fahrt* is strongly directional, in a conventional symphonic-sonata style, *The Hebrides* sounds at first more like an accompaniment without a theme. Indeed, the first real melodic theme surfaces only in the bridge position, at m. 27 (see Example 7.39), and this idea quickly dissolves into mournful echoes of its motivic tail (marked "x" in Example 7.39). The simple device of repeating each

Example 7.39
The Hebrides **Overture, Op. 26, mm. 27–30**

one-measure motivic-harmonic unit of the main idea, almost any time it occurs in the piece, is an inspired example of "imitation" by means of discreet suggestion rather than blatant mimicry; the repetitious action of the waves is continuously suggested, but without falling into an overly literal monotony. The rhythmic layering effects noted in *Meeresstille* are also used to good effect throughout this overture, notably at the end of the first group (mm. 21–25) and across the ensuing bridge section, to convey the interaction of wind, waves, and clouds.

Just as *Meeresstille* supplements the rather sparse outline of Goethe's poems with a variety of "picturesque" musical detail, *The Hebrides* compensates for what it cannot literally depict (on the level of a visual landscape or seascape) by means of other, uniquely musical capacities. The representation of light and shade and their various gradations is, of course, central to landscape painting and drawing, but they are forced to represent these within a static visual field. In creating sonic analogues to such effects of light and shadow, Mendelssohn is also able to deploy these in a more "naturalistic" temporal continuum. The move from a root-position

B-minor chord, to D major, beneath an upper F♯ pedal, in the third and fourth measures, is already a good example of this subtle brand of imitation by suggestion: the somber, "overcast" atmosphere of the opening phrase is inflected by a brief hint of light, just as the subdued calm of that opening phrase is increasingly ruffled by the rhythmic activity in the lower strings during its consequent statement (mm. 9–20), with an effect like mounting breezes or ocean swells. Even if the composer is not able to denote the light, shadow, wind, and the like with infallible specificity (even the visual artist, after all, can portray "wind" only indirectly), he is able to communicate the *experience* of them in time, as changing conditions. With the arrival of the second theme in D major—hailed by Tovey as "quite the greatest melody Mendelssohn ever wrote"—the skies seem to lighten (Example 7.40). The change to the relative major and the emergence of a more lyrical, legato line are largely responsible for this, of course, but the transposition of the accompanying sixteenth-note figuration to the upper strings contributes decisively to the effect, while at the same time maintaining a sense of scenic continuity, a sense that the landscape and seascape have not really changed, but only their lighting.

Because a sustained melodic line is absent from the earlier portion of the movement, there may also be some sense in which the second theme introduces a lyrical, reflecting "subject" into this natural landscape—a lyric voice or "I" who observes and also experiences it. Such hypotheses about the musical projection of a subject or other configurations of human perspective are, of course, usually quite beyond the pale of factual verification or refutation. There is at least a tentative logic to this particular hypothesis, however, that might also be extended to interpret how the "landscape" of the exposition could subsequently be imagined as populated, momentarily, by active beings (or at least fleeting visions of these) in the development. In the closing section of the exposition an energetic transformation of the main motive (in D major) is backed by a distinctly martial figure in the brass (Example 7.41). This martial figure envelops the final measures of the exposition, and echoes of it continue to resound across the opening of the development, mingling with faint wisps of the initial "seascape" motive. These echoes of the closing-group fanfare take on a new character, however, similar to the "call to arms" of the introduction to the "Reformation" Symphony. Passed between different instruments and instrumental groups, at different dynamic levels, the figure takes on the character of a signal or battle cry emitted alternately from different quarters. As if in response to this summons, a little marching motive materializes—entirely new, faintly Scottish sounding, and never to be heard again after these few measures (see Example 7.42). Here the Ossianic associations of the landscape—the island of Staffa and its "Fingal's Cave"—come into play, and it seems as if fleeting visions of Fingal and his legendary exploits are projected onto the scene that might once have framed them. The sense of such a visionary projection is reinforced when this alien music quickly subsides and the second theme (our lyrical "subject") reappears (m. 123)—as if for a brief spell the musical landscape of the exposition resumes its foreground position within that subject's

Example 7.40
The Hebrides Overture, Op. 26, mm. 47–57

mind. In the latter phase of the development, then, landscape (or seascape) and Ossianic visions merge, as the main motive is again transformed, now into the matter of an extended new martial episode of a rather ghostly, disembodied character (mm. 149ff.). These images or visions become louder and more "real," until they suddenly dissolve into a recapitulation of the initial musical landscape (m. 180). A little brass fanfare variant of the main motive (mm. 186–87) adds a

Example 7.41
The Hebrides Overture, Op. 26, mm. 77–80

Example 7.42
The Hebrides Overture, Op. 26, mm. 112–19

nice nuance to this psychological scenario: the heroic visions are not *entirely* suppressed at the point of recapitulation but continue to mingle, fragmentarily, with the scene that inspired them.

When the second theme is recapitulated, almost right away, in B major, it is beautifully transformed as a reminiscence, *molto tranquillo*, in the two clarinets, against chords softly sustained in the strings. In a moment of inward (subjective) reflection or reminiscence, the landscape itself is forgotten for a moment; the omnipresent motive ceases, briefly. Mendelssohn's art of recapitulatory compression is at its zenith here, and after a mere thirty-seven measures of recapitulation a coda sets in (*Animato a tempo*). The landscape image assumes an aspect of legendary grandeur once more; the earlier, fleeting martial transformation of the main motive is sounded again in the brass (m. 234), again in D, and the military trumpet-call of the earlier closing group, over surging strings, now brings the overture to a heroic close. This close is rescued from mere bombast, however, by a device reminiscent of the end of *Meeresstille und glückliche Fahrt*. Out of the loud B-minor cadences the opening motive quietly reemerges, as if—like the wind and waves about Fingal's Cave—it had never really ceased, neither during all of the "imagined" scenes of warlike commotion nor during the moments of subjective introspection, but all the time had been rolling past in the background. Above the echoing motive, a faint reminiscence of the second theme floats away in the flute. With that, our observing "subject" retires from the scene, and so the scenery itself dissolves gently beyond the horizon.

The Tale of the Fair Melusina, Op. 32

"Now I really must be cross. Oh, Fanny, you ask me *which* tale you are to read? How many are there, pray? And how many do I know? And don't you know the story of the 'fair Melusina'? and wouldn't it be better to wrap oneself up in all sorts of instrumental music without titles, when one's own sister (you *Rabenschwester*!) doesn't appreciate such a title?"[94] Mendelsson's half-jocular, half-serious exasperation in this letter to his sister Fanny—who had asked him which version of the "Fair Melusina" fairy tale his overture was "to," or about[95]—is revealing with respect to a dilemma that may have played some part in his subsequent abandonment of this seemingly fertile genre of the concert overture. Indeed, Mendelssohn did essentially go on to "wrap himself in all manner of instrumental music without titles" after this last effort from 1834. There were other factors involved here, too, such as his father's famous and since much-lamented injunction that Felix put behind him all these fairy-tale worlds and concentrate on "more serious things." Abraham's death in 1835 very likely strengthened the force of that injunction for the deeply devoted son, and Felix himself stated quite emphatically that with his father's death his entire outlook on life underwent a radical, sobering change; it was at that moment, he later said, that he at last took full leave of his youth.[96] All the same, Fanny's question clearly alerted Felix to a problem relating to the conception of this overture, in particular, but also to his whole subtle, restrained approach to this "poetic" genre, for which "program music" is far too coarse a designation, as Mendelssohn would surely have insisted. Like the *Midsummer Night's Dream* and *Hebrides* overtures, *Melusina* presupposes a familiarity with certain poetic motifs or images that listeners bring to the music and that inform their "reading" of, or listening to, it. Musical and poetic materials will interact, in the listener's mind, to construct a kind of "poetry" that is freed from the medial restraints of either story or music as "absolute" genres (as Wagner would put it), while partaking of certain capacities of both.

Fanny's question to Felix as to which version of the Melusina story his overture treated probably aggravated him as much for its aptness as for the misconceptions it revealed. It was misconceived, of course, in that the overture was not telling any one distinct (verbal) story, with specific characters, situations, and complications of plot related in accordance with principles of historical probability and causality. Yet, the question *was* apt, nonetheless, because, unlike *A Midsummer Night's Dream*, the Melusina "story" was not widely familiar in any one, authoritative version but remained more a collection of quasi-historical and legendary motifs, scarcely distinguishable from those of other popular Romantic ondine stories (Fouqué's *Undine* being the best known). Some general awareness of the common underlying legendary trope is perhaps sufficient to appreciate the gist of Mendelssohn's overture: a water-nymph or mermaidlike creature takes on human form, is wooed by a mortal prince, betrayed, and condemned to reversion. Fanny was probably familiar, in particular, with Ludwig Tieck's novella, *The Very Marvellous History of Melusina* (*Die sehr wunderbare Geschichte von der Melusina*, 1800), which Schumann also mentioned in his review of the overture (see the translation included in the Historical Views and Documents that follow this Chapter). She was probably perplexed as to how Felix could think to base a musical composition on this self-concious exercise in Romantic-ironic *bizarrerie*, with its imitation of the disjointed, rambling style of medieval chronicle, overflowing with monstrous births, improbable turns of event, and digressive verse interpolations that gradually swamp the narrative itself. Felix, who must also have known the Tieck novella, admitted to Fanny that his overture was inspired (indirectly, at least) by a very different source, a Melusina opera by Conradin Kreutzer that had premiered in Vienna the year before (1833), to a libretto that Franz Grillparzer had originally written for Beethoven. In the letter of 7 April 1834 he continued:

I wrote this overture to an opera by Conradin Kreutzer that I heard last year at this time at the Königstädter theater [in Berlin].—The overture (Kreutzer's, that is) was encored and displeased me thoroughly—as did the rest of the opera, except for Mme. Hähnel, who was quite charming, especially in a scene where she presented herself as a pike and did up her hair. So I got the idea of making an overture of my own, one that people wouldn't encore, perhaps, but that would have more soul to it [*die es mehr inwendig hätte*]; and so I took from this theme [*sujet*] that which pleased me (and that is what also corresponds with the fairy-tale), and in short, my overture was born, and that is its family history.

Grillparzer's libretto thoroughly domesticates Tieck's bizarre *Märchen*, translating the story into the idioms of Viennese *Zauberposse* and Biedermeier romance. Mendelssohn refined the story even further, and his claim that he took only its most general outlines, those (evidently) in which novella and libretto agree, is essentially true, with the exception of a few implicit details suggesting parallels with one particular version or the other, or else invented by the composer.

The fundamental plot elements on which both the Tieck and Grillparzer versions agree are these:

- Melusina is a naiadlike creature whom the count or knight Reymund (or Raimund), while out hunting one day, discovers in the forest with her two sisters by the spring over which they preside as forest spirits;
- despite the protests of other concerned parties, mortal knight and water-sprite enter into a union of marriage;
- separated from her native forest spring, Melusina must devise a means to bathe secretly in her fishlike or serpentine form on a periodic basis;
- one day she is discovered at this activity by Reymund/Raimund, who only then becomes aware of her supernatural condition;
- interpreted on both sides as a fatal breach of faith, this discovery precipitates the separation of the couple and (presumably) Melusina's irrevocable reversion to the spirit world.

Mendelssohn's overture engages this general plot outline at a number of levels in its thematic-formal design, one whose novelty is tempered by an elegance, understatement, and "smoothness" thoroughly characteristic of the composer. The basic thematic material is easily identified with the characters of Melusina and her knightly suitor (see Example 7.43a and b). But their apparent positions invert the

Example 7.43
The Tale of the Fair Melusina **Overture, Op. 32**

a. mm. 1–8

b. mm. 72–79

normal character-relation of first and second themes, the flowing, quiet, major-mode (and explicitly "feminine") material occupying the first-theme position and the aggressive-agitated minor-mode ("masculine") idea that of second theme. The fact that both share the same tonic (F) further undermines the expected formal paradigm, and as the F-minor section progresses, we become aware that it is forging its *own* sonata design based on that modality. A "properly" lyrical second theme emerges in A♭ major, preceded by a chromatic, yearning figure, which (on its second appearance) is interwoven with the aggressive rhythm of the F-minor themes, suggesting an undertone of warning or rebuke (see Example 7.44).

Example 7.44
The Tale of the Fair Melusina **Overture, Op. 32, mm. 124–35**

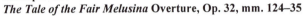

This arrangement of thematic materials and the fact that the overture concludes with a full-scale return of the opening F-major music (suggesting Melusina's return to her native springs) have led some writers to speak of an interior sonata-form embedded within an independent introduction and coda or epilogue.[97] Such a scheme is clearly complicated, however, by the fact that the "introductory" music of Melusina's spring resurfaces throughout the first half of the development section (mm. 161ff.) and is fully recapitulated (mm. 264–88), while the knightly "main" themes are almost completely suppressed. (Because the design of the movement is somewhat unusual and complicated, it has been set out in diagrammatic form in Table 7.2.) In its initial presentation, the opening section in F major is certainly

Table 7.2
Overture, "The Tale of the Fair Melusina," Op. 32 (formal outline)

FIRST THEME-GROUP (or "introduction")

Theme:	a		a'	retransition		a
Key:	F: I		I–V	(V^7)		I
Measures:	1–8		9–15	16–24		25–48
(Comments):	"Melusina" material		trumpet B♭ (♭7) (cf. Schumann)			

SECOND THEME-GROUP (or "sonata" section: main theme group)

Th:	trans.	b1	b2	b1	b2	b3
K:	f: i–V	i	i	i	iv	i
Mm:	49–67	68–74	75–82	83–90	91–99	100–106
(C):	"Knightly" rhythms and themes (Reymund/Raimund)					

THIRD THEME-GROUP (or "sonata section: secondary themes and closing)

Th:	c1	c2	c1	c2	(trans.)	b1–b3
K:	f–V/A♭	A♭	f–V/A♭	A♭		A♭
Mm:	107–14	115–23	124–31	132–38	138–44	144–60
(C):	new "Melusina" themes	b-rhythms			b-rhythms	

DEVELOPMENT (part 1)

	DEVELOPMENT (part 1)	(part 2)		retransition
Th:	a	(a), b1, b2	c1	a
K:				
Mm:	161–99	200–212, 212–28	228–45	245–63
(C):	Develops first theme-group; (original Melusina material, from "intro-ductory period)	b1, b2, and c1 introduced		b-rhythms

Table 7.2, continued

COMPOSITE RECAPITULATION (theme groups 1–3)   Coda
                                                               "Epilogue"

Th:	a	a'	c1	c2	b2 (var.)	b3	a
K:	F: I_4^6	I–V–i	$\flat$VI (D$\flat$)		i	i	I
Mm.	264–71	272–88	289–96	297–318	319–26	327–60	361–406
(C):					b-rhythms	a in accomp.	

self-contained—indeed, symbolically so, as a musical embodiment of Melusina in her original, pure, and untroubled condition, a supernatural icon of the natural world. (It is likely that the image that Mendelssohn thought to suggest with the flowing eighth-note figures was not so much that of "waves," as often assumed, but the welling up of a spring-source, as the rippling flute figure at the end of this section seems to confirm; Mendelssohn was apparently annoyed, afterward, when Schumann mistook his forest-dwelling water-nymph for an oceangoing mermaid.[98]) The ensuing F-minor sonata- exposition is introduced by a passage based on the characteristic "riding" rhythm, a repeating pattern of four eighths followed by a quarter note, in $\frac{6}{4}$ that we are evidently to associate with Melusina's suitor-knight. The passage does not function as a tonal transition, strictly speaking, since it merely involves a modal shift from F major to F minor. It serves more as a transition of mood or character, suggesting the approach of the knight and all the baleful mortal strife that he will introduce into the untroubled, natural world of Melusina. This knightly character and its attendant rhythmic motive remain constant throughout the first group of this internal exposition (themes b1 through b3). The character of the subsidiary theme group within the F-minor exposition was identified with Melusina, by Schumann, on the basis of such attributes as "alluring," "yielding," "delicate," and "caressing" (*lockend, hingebend, zart, anschmiegend*; cf. Historical Views and Documents following this Chapter): this is Melusina in human form, no longer an emblem of untroubled nature but "corrupted" by human desires.

From here through the rest of the overture, until the coda/epilogue, Mendelssohn choreographed this stock of characteristic themes and motives to suggest the interaction of these figures in a manner almost suggestive of an elaborate musical pantomime (or *tableau vivant*?), at the same time integrating a potentially diffuse array of thematic materials. Schumann alluded to this fluid exchange when, after characterizing the "masculine" and "feminine" materials, he added: "it is as if the waves of the stream flooded their embraces, engulfed them, and separated them once more." The chromatic "yearning" theme c1 in the subsidiary group of the interior sonata form (see Table 7.2) literally "embraces" the rhythms of the knightly b-themes in mm. 123–31, as mentioned earlier; these rhythms embrace the entire subsidiary group (c-themes), in turn, when they return as closing material in mm. 138–60. The development returns to the music of the "natural-supernatural" Melusina and her forest spring.

One of the constants of the Melusina story is her periodic retreat to a secret bathing-chamber, where she can resume her amphibious form. It might seem too facile to suggest that the tonal displacement of this introductory material in the development analogizes the displacement of Melusina's spring to the artificial swimming-chamber of her tower. Yet one way or another, there can be little doubt that Mendelssohn had this central episode of the Melusina story in mind here. A new, wistful melodic counterpoint in the oboe (mm. 188–200) seems to express something of the sorrow of her exile from the natural realm or perhaps a foreboding of other sorrows to come. For at this point (mm. 200ff.) the knightly rhythms of the b-themes stealthily sneak onto the scene, pianissimo—an unmistakable musical image of the spying husband, whose suspicious behavior precipitates the catastrophe of the tale. Indeed, a real dramatic-musical encounter now ensues between Reymund's b-themes and Melusina's human, yearning theme $c1$, at first imploring, and gradually defiant or angry.

The recapitulation of the introductory, "natural" material (a) problematizes both musical form and "story" alike. The subtly destabilizing effect of its second-inversion harmonization (over a C-pedal) was to become a favorite device in Romantic sonata forms. Mendelssohn, who regularly condensed his recapitulations, as we have seen, here excised nearly all of the knightly themes, leaving us to ponder which of Melusina's forms, supernatural or human, will prevail (for the c-themes are fully recapitulated). Of Reymund's music only the original closing material (b3) returns, and it is now made to contend with Melusina's fishlike or serpentine figuration in the violins (mm. 327–39). The climax of this musical story comes, as it well might, just before the coda/epilogue. A mournful minor third is isolated from the closing variants of Reymund's themes, as the music of Melusina's spring seems to beckon her to return (F major). Melusina's yearning-human motive (c1) is uttered against this, in recitative-like augmentation, as a last desperate plea for the cause of her human incarnation (mm. 364–67, see Example 7.45). But nature and cyclic closure win out, and the

Example 7.45
The Tale of the Fair Melusina **Overture, Op. 32, mm. 364–69**

overture concludes with the tranquil, rippling sounds of Melusina's spring in the flutes and strings. (A persistent minor-second figure sounded throughout much of the Reymund material, especially in b3, is here resolved to a major 6–5 motion at the final cadence.)

A memorable motif of the Melusina legend is the terrible cry that she is supposed to have emitted upon departing from her husband and the human world. Tieck described her famous cry with full Romantic excess as "a terrifying scream [*Geschrei*] . . . that sounded so strange and unreal [*unerhört*] that it caused to tremble in their bodies the hearts of all who heard it, and they feared nothing so much as to hear that sound again, so shattering and piercing it was, so mournful, as if the whole world were about to end."[99] In Tieck's version the parting Melusina emits this awful sound three times, while circling in the air, "after which nothing more was heard, and she disappeared." Grillparzer describes a much milder departure, with Melusina reaching out to Reymund as she is drawn, Eurydice-like, back into the spirit world by fellow nymphs (a *Geisterchor*). She and Reymund are ultimately united in a kind of *Liebestod*-transfiguration (Tieck's novella brings her back once or twice as a nocturnal shade, after which she is lost from sight among spiraling narrative digressions in prose and verse). Mendelssohn's climax clearly has more in common with the catastrophe as depicted by Grillparzer, though a gentle rendition of her terrible cries might be heard in the falling minor thirds of mm. 355–60. Unlike either the prose tale or the operatic libretto, however, Mendelssohn's overture returns Melusina to her original, natural state. Such a strategy is almost foreordained by the role of this material as both introduction and interpolation into the sonata-form body of the overture. It also accords with Mendelssohn's own musical nature and his stated aim to compose a more "inward" version of the tale. (With regard to the resulting formal hybrid of sonata form and a more "simple, natural" ABA scheme—which here disfigures the normal outline of the sonata when merged with it—it would be tempting to see a musical-formal analogy to Melusina's own hybrid form and the "disfiguring" consequences.)

The *mésalliance* as which Mendelssohn jokingly summed up the "meaning" of his overture, according to Schumann, may have turned out to apply to the composer's own relationship to the genre of the programmatic-characteristic concert overture. This relationship, which had started out as such a promising one, was to be broken off after the *Melusina* overture. Mendelssohn had already approached the composition of this piece with a certain sense of defiance: as a protest against Kreutzer's fleetingly popular, but trivial, overture, he proposed "one that people won't encore, perhaps, but that will have more soul to it."[100] On learning that the London premiere was little more than a *succès d'estime*, Mendelssohn reacted defensively, and he continued to pride himself on the work's "inward" qualities in the face of outward indifference. It is true enough that *Melusine* lacks something of the *Glanz* and immediate musical appeal of the better-known overtures, but it also points up a more fundamental problem that may well have contributed to Mendelssohn's early and seemingly puzzling divorce from this genre. In repeatedly referring here to motifs and images from the background "subject" of the overture, I have sought not so much to prove that it is a programmatic piece in the popularly maligned sense but to suggest how much it really does engage elements of that subject in terms of form, character, and detail. Mendelssohn, as I have also tried to show, composed his own "story"; but to appreciate fully how he went about doing so requires a sensitive ear for musical form, character, and detail, as well as some familiarity with the subject matter to which they allude (as one would need to bring, for instance, to a painting on a historical, sacred, or legendary subject). The fact that even such kindred spirits as Fanny Hensel and Robert Schumann failed, in some respect, to respond to the implicit background images and situations of the overture, as Mendelssohn seems to have envisioned these, must have alerted him to the difficulty of finding a larger audience sufficiently in tune with his own refined, "poetic" sensibilities and education. Perhaps he did come to feel, after all, that the only alternatives left were either to "wrap himself in all manner of instrumental pieces without titles" or to continue his quest for the right opera subject and text.

Overture for Wind Band (*Harmonie-Ouvertüre*), Op. 24, and "Trumpet" Overture, Op. 101

Of course, Mendelssohn was to get no closer to fulfilling his lifelong operatic quest than the sadly uncompleted *Lorelei* of 1847. But in the somewhat miscellaneous group of works we might loosely classify under the rubric of "dramatic" overtures and incidental music we have the traces of his tentative early approaches toward the genre (the "private" Singspiele and the unlucky youthful operatic essay *Die Hochzeit des Camacho*) or else of his involvement with affiliated genres (music for the spoken theater, secular cantata, oratorio) that may, to some extent, have been regarded as substitutes, filling the vacuum left by deferred operatic ambitions.

Before moving on to this next group of orchestral works, however, some mention should be made of the two early concert overtures "without titles" composed during Mendelssohn's student years in Berlin: the overture for wind instruments (or *Harmoniemusik*) published as Op. 24 only in 1839, though originally composed in 1824; and the so-called Trumpet overture of 1826, published posthumously as Op. 101. Both works are in C major, and they share faintly militaristic associations that might lead one to think of them as Mendelssohn's particular contribution to a "Prussian" musical culture, the earlier work having been composed for the woodwind-brass ensemble (or *Harmoniemusik*) typical of the nineteenth-century regimental band or *Kapelle*, and the second work deriving its nickname from the trumpet-fanfare gestures that serve as introductory and recurrent motto. Aside from these superficial "militarisms," however, the works represent, like the contemporaneous C-minor Symphony, the teenage composer's assimilation of current orchestral idioms; stylistically, this music was just as much at home in the Mendelssohns' *haut-bourgeois* Jewish salon (where Op. 101 was performed on several occasions) as it might have been in the context of Prussian court of parade ground—if not more so. The Op. 24 *Harmonie* overture was, in fact, originally composed for performance by the spa-orchestra at Bad Doberan, on the Baltic coast of Mecklenburg, where Felix had journeyed with his father Abraham in July 1824 for a brief vacation; according to Reissmann, it was only afterward scored for full military band.[101] Of the two overtures, the second (Op. 101) is by far the more interesting piece, as the two years' difference during this crucial period in Mendelssohn's musical development would lead one to expect.

Yet the earlier *Harmonie* overture is by no means void of ambition: it is introduced by an *Andante con moto* of no less than 67 measures (which may, however, seem a bit disproportionate to the 159-measure *Allegro vivace* that follows), and the development resuscitates an imposing dotted-rhythm octave motive from the introduction, which serves to punctuate the fugato development of a motive from the second theme, put through a variety of keys. This is spirited and "modern" music that, like the First Symphony, demonstrates Mendelssohn's progress beyond the epigonal idioms of the string symphonies. Yet at the same time it lacks the assurance and jaunty wit of the best of those pieces; only the second theme exhibits some liveliness of character, while the imitations and modulations of the development sound, on the whole, somewhat routine and mechanical (and in that way resemble the reverse side of the string symphonies).

The "Trumpet" overture, on the other hand, begins with rather neutral material—an introduction in the main allegro tempo prolonging the tonic harmony, dominated by a three-note fanfare-motto, and followed by a squarely constructed main theme, enlivened slightly by some internal chromatic passing notes—but it generates an unexpected interest precisely in its development section. The second group contains two separate ideas, a bouncy, rather Mendelssohnian phrase in staccato woodwinds (mm. 71ff.) and a more typical, legato *Gesangsthema* or lyrical second theme (mm. 88ff.) anticipating the manner of Marschner, Lortzing, and the like. The development surprises the listener with a rather clear anticipation of the *Hebrides* Overture: quiet string arpeggios create a wash of sustained harmonic color, against which a triadic motive in half notes and whole notes is sounded through various keys, at first forte and then piano, foreshadowing a similar effect at the beginning of the *Hebrides* development. It must have been this larger procedural parallel that Eduard Devrient was actually thinking of when he claimed that Mendelssohn "made no scruple . . . afterwards to introduce this trumpet-call [*sic*] into his later overture [i.e., *The Hebrides*]."[102] While the actual trumpet-call motives of the two overtures are quite distinct from one another, the broader musical effect of the two developments is close indeed. In Op. 101, furthermore, the simple introductory fanfare itself, built of reiterated half notes, does not figure in this opening phase of the development at all, although it is worked into the latter phase at some length, and the whole introductory "fanfare" period is recapitulated as a coda. One is also surprised to read in Devrient's memoirs that Abraham Mendelssohn "was so fond of this overture, that I have heard him say he would like to hear it in his dying hour." (This is competent music, perhaps, but hardly transcendent.) When we consider that this was the same father who dissuaded Felix from pursuing the path of his *Midsummer Night's Dream*, *Hebrides*, and *Melusina* overtures, we must begin to wonder again about the ultimate soundness of his influence on his gifted son, for all the educational benefits he provided and for all that Felix was wont to compliment his father on his tremendous amateur perspicacity in musical matters. Perhaps, like so many other amateurs (since the beginning), Abraham was easily aroused to enthusiasm by the trumpet's call; perhaps he was moved, too, by a faith in the salubrious influence of "instrumental music without titles."

DRAMATIC OVERTURES AND INCIDENTAL MUSIC

The overtures that Mendelssohn composed specifically to introduce various stage works, oratorios, and other large-scale vocal compositions have never acquired an independent life in the orchestral repertory comparable to that of his concert overtures or to the operatic and dramatic overtures of such composers as Mozart, Beethoven, Weber, Rossini, or Schubert. This situation can be explained partly by the heterogeneous nature of the works in question and partly by Mendelssohn's chosen approach in individual cases. The operatic overtures are early works, all predating even the *Midsummer Night's Dream* overture, and some remain unpublished. Of the later theatrical overtures, only that to Hugo's *Ruy Blas* was published separately, and even that work Mendelssohn regarded as something of a potboiler, although it has maintained a modest presence in the repertory over the years. The overtures to the oratorios and to the "model" productions of classic plays for the Berlin court theater (*Antigone*, *Oedipus at Colonos*, *Athalie*) were generally treated by the composer more as introductions than as independent movements. In the case of the oratorios this seems to reflect a broader nineteenth-century conception of what is appropriate to the genre, while in the case of the plays of Sophocles and Racine Mendelssohn may have looked to the classical model of Gluck (the overtures to *Alceste* or the *Iphigénie* operas, which may have been a model for his overture to Goethe's *Erste Walpurgisnacht*, as well). These orchestral numbers are consequently best heard and understood in the context of the larger works that they introduce, but a brief look at this disparate group of works can also tell us something about the various ways that Mendelssohn conceived the function of the instrumental overture *as* "functional" music (in some cases), as well as provide a glimpse of some of his lesser-known orchestral music. Among the incidental music, on the other hand, the only significant instrumental pieces are those to *A Midsummer Night's Dream*, which, like the overture, have long since detached themselves from their theatrical context to become some of the composer's best-known concert music.

Early Dramatic Overtures (1821–25)

With the exception of the amusing one-act Singspiele, *Die beiden Pädagogen* ("The Two Pedagogues," 1821, after Eugène Scribe's 1817 comedy *Les deux précepteurs, ou asinus asinam fricat*) and *Die Heimkehr aus der Fremde* of 1829 (literally, "The Return from Abroad," but known as "Son and Stranger" since the public premiere of the work in London in 1851), the early stage works that Mendelssohn composed for performance in the context of the family musicales remain unpublished. The overtures to the two most mature of these early comic-dramatic essays—*Die Heimkehr* and the full-scale comic opera *Die Hochzeit des Camacho* (completed August 1825)—can be taken here to represent the young composer's accomplishments in this field prior to his premature abandonment of the operatic genre, as least as regards completed works.

The overture to *Die Hochzeit des Camacho* ("Camacho's Wedding," based on an episode from volume 2 of *Don Quixote*) stands alongside the coeval First Symphony (Op. 11) as an example of Felix's early mastery of contemporary musical idioms. This is music that elicits such critical epithets as "lively and spirited," "skillfully orchestrated," "well crafted," and the like, implying a level of accomplishment that, for a fifteen-year-old, can well count as genius, even if the product is not quite up to the level of similar works by Schubert or Weber, with which it invites comparison. On the other hand, it is probably safe to say that this overture is distinctly superior to analogous works by the likes of such contemporary "adult" composers as Kalliwoda, Lindpainter, Franz Lachner, Kreutzer, or Kittl, which held sway in the concert repertory of the 1820s and 1830s. It was perhaps only the unfortunate circumstances attending the opera's premiere in 1829—after which it dropped from sight—that prevented Mendelssohn's only "real" opera overture from gaining at least a modicum of exposure during this same period. Neither the overture nor the rest of the opera contains much in the way of Spanish local color (aside from a bolero and fandango in the second-act dances, the former surely owing more to the "Spanish dance music" in act 3 of Mozart's *Marriage of Figaro* than to any authentic sources). The same ballet-pantomime in act 2 provides the marchlike second theme of the overture (Example 7.46), which constitutes the principal material of a modest development section. As if to compensate for the slightly exiguous development, both first and second themes are combined and further developed in the course of the recapitulation. In good contemporary operatic style the coda of the overture returns in the opera's final tableau, a patch of E-major rejoicing music consisting mainly of rhythmic and harmonic cadential impulses.

Die Heimkehr aus der Fremde was composed in honor of the silver wedding anniversary of Lea and Abraham in 1829, coinciding with the return of their own son from abroad following the first of his educational-professional tours, this one to England and Scotland between April and November of that year. The plot is slender and unassuming (a small-town comic idyll concerning the unexpected return of a long-absent son), and some of the numbers are still imbued with a retrospective, if genially realized, eighteenth-century spirit. While the overture is

Example 7.46
Overture to *Die Hochzeit des Camacho*, Op. 10, Second Theme

Flute

similarly unassuming, it already exhibits a whole series of traits typical of the mature composer—something we have every reason to expect by this date. A $\frac{6}{8}$ andante introduction sets the idyllic tone of the piece as a whole. This is separated from the main sonata-allegro movement by a brief transition in the new tempo, along the lines of the contemporaneous *Meeresstille und glückliche Fahrt* overture. The brief development, with its low string pedal-points and triadic motivic figuration, also seems to recall that work, and a new rising octave move in dotted rhythm (mm. 190–206)—a kind of gesture of salutation—even suggests a virtual citation from the concert overture. (The allusions to the *Meeresstille und glückliche Fahrt* overture would be appropriate to the occasion of Felix's own return home, certainly, even though the young hero of the Singspiel arrives by land rather than by sea.) The main theme is full of the melodic appoggiaturas that would eventually become a sign of the sentimental-elegant Mendelssohn "manner," while the second theme, alternating between staccato winds and strings (mm. 119–32), evokes his classic bouncy, elfin vein. Still a further personal trademark is the sustained, legato countermelody in violas and cellos played against this theme in its consequent extension (mm. 136ff.). Like its more substantial counterpart, the *Meeresstille* overture, this one also exhibits a few rhythmic-melodic debts to Beethoven's *Leonore* overtures (see the closing of the exposition, for instance), and the jubilant coda—presumably expressive of joyous reunion—recaptures some of the dynamic energy of the coda to Beethoven's *Egmont* overture (the minor-inflected string crescendo into tutti cadential jubilation also recalls a similar idea in the first movement of the Op. 11 C-minor Symphony).

Overture to *Ruy Blas*

Among Mendelssohn's later contributions to the theater, only the overture that he provided for an 1839 Leipzig performance of Victor Hugo's *Ruy Blas* can really be viewed as an independent orchestral work (discounting the earlier *Midsummer Night's Dream* overture, of course, which was incorporated into the incidental music for the production of the play at the Berlin court in 1843). When it was decided to give Hugo's latest play (written in 1838) as a benefit performance for the pension fund of the Leipzig theater, Mendelssohn was approached to contribute a few vocal numbers to the production as a means of boosting public interest. Mendelssohn found the play "utterly wretched and beneath contempt," as he wrote to his mother on 18 March 1839, and could bring himself only to dash off a Romanza for two voices. At the last minute, less than a week before the opening, as he recounts it, the composer relented and decided to slap together an overture, after all, almost as a kind of stunt or self-dare, it seems. Despite a rehearsal and concert at the Gewandhaus that same week, Mendelssohn claims to have managed to write the overture and have the parts copied within six days, in time to rehearse it three times on the morning of the seventh: "That same evening it was performed with the dreadful play (*zu dem infamen Stück*), and I enjoyed it nearly as much as anything I've done. In the next [Gewandhaus] concert we will play it again, by popular demand; though this time I won't call it an 'Overture to *Ruy Blas*,' but instead, 'Overture to the Theater Pension Fund.'"[103] There is no reason to doubt the fidelity of Mendelssohn's account, and indeed, the *Ruy Blas* overture has something of the perfunctory quality of a last-minute commission about it. At the same time, it is possible to detect a note of that gleeful satisfaction described in the composer's letter—satisfaction at having turned out a full-scale overture at such short notice but also, perhaps, at having captured the spirit of Hugo's crass historical cloak-and-dagger melodrama (as Mendelssohn saw it) in a perfectly straight-faced "parody" of a melodramatic overture in the modern Franco-Italian idiom.

The introductory alternation of a set of somber, "fateful" chords in C minor with an accompanied-recitative-like anticipation of the allegro molto main theme (in tempo) suggests the possible influence of Berlioz's early overtures. The lento chordal motto—outlining a half-cadence in C minor—occurs three times within the thirty-one-measure introductory gambit, in two slightly different forms, and twice more within the Allegro itself, marking the juncture between bridge and second theme in both exposition and recapitulation. Even without any knowledge of Hugo's *Ruy Blas*, one might easily hear in this an evocation of those stage curses looming over the action of such operatically familiar dramas as *Le Roi s'amuse* (as *Rigoletto*) and *Hernani* (as *Ernani*). The opening group of the Allegro strikes a note of somewhat generic C-minor agitated pathos not unlike that sounded in the first movement of the Op. 11 C-minor Symphony. A basic rhythmic motive of four eighth notes with upbeat, on the second half of the measure, is implemented to varying musical and expressive ends in the main theme, the bridge theme, and the closing theme (see Example 7.47a–c). Shorn of its upbeat, this rhythmic figure also informs the extension of the second theme in mm. 117–39. The jaunty second theme (mm. 101ff.) begins in a mildly syncopated version for staccato strings, anticipating some of Verdi's "tiptoeing" choruses of conspirators and assassins (in *Rigoletto* or *Macbeth*, e.g.), followed by a lyrical legato variant of the same idea carried by clarinet, bassoon, and cello. (To Tovey the staccato opening version of the theme suggested Hugo's virtuosic and sometimes ludicrous juggling of the classical Alexandrine meter, such as one instance where the twelve-syllable line is

Example 7.47
Overture to *Ruy Blas*

a. mm. 32–44

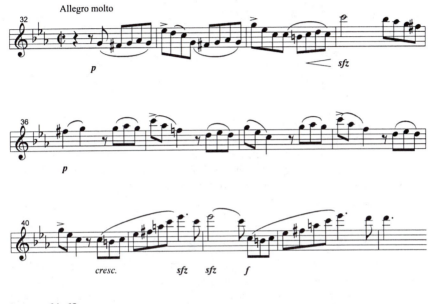

b. mm. 64–68

spread across a six-part exchange between two characters, creating a kind of awkward verbal staccato.[104]) It has been pointed out—by Tovey, among others—that the triumphant coda, following a brief secondary development of the agitated main theme, has no particular motivating point in the drama. This overlooks the fact that most overtures to serious or tragic subjects from this period reserve the right to depict the "moral triumph" or catharsis of the tragic end in terms of a musical affirmation (a point that Tovey recognizes but seems unwilling to accept in this instance) and that many, if not most, full-scale overtures—as opposed to nonautonomous operatic preludes or introductions—regard such an affirmative close as a kind of generic imperative. Nonetheless, there remains the

c. mm. 140–48

possibility that Mendelssohn's triumphant (if scarcely overwhelming) coda entails, like the overture as a whole, an element of parody; perhaps Mendelssohn was no more convinced of Ruy Blas's "moral triumph" than of the triumph evoked in such a relatively routine fashion in his own coda or in dozens of similarly high-spirited *sinfonie* to contemporary operatic melodramas.

Music for the Berlin Court Theater (1841–45)

When the idealistic new Prussian monarch Friedrich Wilhelm IV ascended the throne in 1840, he began almost right away to implement a wide range of political and cultural reforms—perhaps too wide, for it is generally agreed that his laudable ambitions outstripped his practical capacity to carry them all out. The new king's vision of a cultural renaissance in the Prussian capital, that sometime "Athens on the Spree," was not unlike the one masterminded by Ludwig I in Bavaria some twenty years earlier, but it reached beyond civic architecture and the visual arts (the principal areas of Ludwig's patronage) to embrace theater and music as part of a newly established Academy of Arts. Mendelssohn was engaged to oversee the musical component of the new Academy (which, as an instructional institution, was not to materialize during his time, after all) and to contribute to a series of productions classic plays (Sophocles, Racine, Shakespeare) in collaboration with Ludwig Tieck and other literary and dramatic luminaries. The amount of music generated by the Berlin appointment remained relatively insignificant in comparison to the extensive deliberations attendant upon it and to the amount of disruption wrought in Mendelssohn's personal and professional life during the five years that the appointment lasted (Mendelssohn's troubled relationship to his native city was perpetuated here, but not resolved). On the other hand, the commissions for the Berlin court theater were at least responsible for bringing Mendelssohn back to the material of Shakespeare's *Midsummer Night's Dream*, which had elicited the masterpiece of his younger years.

The two Sophocles productions (*Antigone*, 1841, and *Oedipus at Colonos*, 1845) were historicizing affairs, attempting to fit the texts of the original Greek choruses with appropriate music in a contemporary idiom, while faithfully maintaining the Greek meters in German translation, the disposition of strophes and antistrophes, and so on. Within this context there was little room for the songs and entr'actes of conventional incidental music. *Oedipus* uses the orchestra only as accompaniment to the choruses or to lines of text declaimed as melodrama by chorus or by individual characters. The same is true of *Antigone*, the first of the Berlin theatrical projects, with the exception of a quasi-independent orchestral introduction (presumably, Mendelssohn calls it "introduction" rather than "overture" because of its somewhat fragmentary form and because of its open ending, on a half-cadence in C minor). A thirty-bar slow introduction to the "introduction," Andante maestoso, is cast in a–b–a^1 form and unites a variety of ceremonial and sacred figures: chordal fanfares in dotted rhythms, a fugato in vocal style, and a return of the ceremonial fanfare with walking bass in "chorale-prelude" texture. The seventy-one-bar Allegro assai appassionato presents an interesting kind of formal experiment. The new tempo begins unexpectedly on the Neapolitan harmony (D♭), but with what must be taken as the main theme of the allegro. Rather than cadencing back to C minor, the music proceeds to modulate in the direction of E♭ (III of C minor), as if it had cut directly into the middle of a normal sonata exposition—an exposition presented *in medias res*, as it were. Even this (implicit) process of truncated sonata exposition is deflected, as the cadence to E♭ is turned back on the tonic (C minor) and a "reprise" of the main theme at m. 52—paradoxically, heard only now for the first time in the tonic key. One might speak of a displaced or deferred exposition of the tonic, but it represents at the same time a structural reprise, in tonal terms; for when the curtain is raised at this point, the tonic is prolonged throughout the remainder of the introduction, settling on a protracted half cadence (mm. 86–101). Here is yet another example of Mendelssohn's continuing penchant for formal experimentation, which Tovey so often tried to highlight in an effort to explode the entrenched notion of the composer as a timidly polite formalist. Yet, as so often, the formal experiment here is effectively disguised by the *politesse* of the melodic-stylistic surface, in this case the flowing $^{12}_{8}$ melodic contours familiar from many of the Songs without Words, whose genteel passing-note chromaticism seems to speak more of the parlor than of the politics and passions of the Greek tragedy.

As we might expect, the music written for Racine's Old Testament drama *Athalie* (1845) bears a strong kinship to Mendelssohn's oratorios. This time he provided an independent overture, in D minor, with an introduction in F major. It is, however, the choruses and vocal solos that resemble the oratorio music, rather than the overture and the once-popular "War-March of the Priests" preceding the fourth act (which latter happens to be, instead, a surprisingly close cousin to the "Wedding March" from *A Midsummer Night's Dream*). A reviewer of an early concert performance of the overture in Berlin felt "justified in stating that this overture is not among the outstanding works of this great composer." This critical intuition is indeed probably justified, if not exactly for the reasons the reviewer went on to adduce, which have mainly to do with a lack of sufficient formal clarity and "rounding" (*Abrundung*). "It even seems," he continued, "as if a certain confusion among the most heterogenous ideas, a certain lack of clarity, one might say, were actually intended."[105] Repeated hearings might have served to clarify this confused impression; but even as an initial impression such "confusion" was fundamentally unacceptable to this critic, who further complained of what seemed to him a "decided lack of melody" or melodic interest. This is closer to the point, surely, as the overture does tend to suggest the work of some merely competent Mendelssohn imitator, of which there was no shortage by the late 1840s.

The piece incorporates certain prayerful and warlike strains, appropriate to the Old Testament subject matter, but the bulk of it is constituted of a few relatively undistinguished themes of a rather square and repetitive nature. The *Neue Zeitschrift* critic may have been disoriented by, among other things, the proportional metric relation between the introduction (Maestoso con moto, $\frac{4}{4}$) and the Molto Allegro (alla breve), which makes the return of the second idea from the introduction as the second theme of the Allegro (both times accompanied by harps and pizzicato strings) essentially indistinguishable from its earlier appearance in the introduction. Moreover, while this theme is of very regular phrase construction, its precise tonal physiognomy can be elusive (a feature common to a number of second themes in Mendelssohn as well as in Schumann). The model of the introduction (mm. 19ff.) would suggest that the second theme was going to establish C major as the second key area, though, in fact, it turns around to the minor dominant, A minor. The hymnlike opening theme of the introduction (Example 7.48) recurs as an interpolation in F major between the second and closing groups (both centered on A minor), and it continues, in reduced note values, to form the backbone of a perfunctory development section (mm. 239–69).

Example 7.48
Incidental Music to Racine's *Athalie*, Overture, mm. 1–4

The fact that only the second theme is recapitulated (mm. 270ff.) may have further contributed to our critic's confusion. A later and more appreciative critic, reviewing the printed vocal score of the incidental music, spoke of an "interrupted" development, interpreting the secondary development that forms a climax to the recapitulation (mm. 332-70) as a continuation of the original one, interrupted only by the reprise of the second theme.[106] This critic also registered the sense of distinct dramatic climax and decision generated by this secondary development, as it works through an extended chromatic bass motion from A to D, culminating in a "victorious" return of the mottolike "prayer" theme in D major and a coda transposing the second (and second introductory) theme to D. Once again, the formal design has an element of novelty and dramatic efficacy that, as in the *Antigone* introduction, is partially undone by the routine aspects of melodic invention and phrase structure. (The subtonic or IV/IV chords over tonic pedal and extended seventh-degree trill in the violins contribute a certain element of surprise to the end of the coda, though the effect of both is more than a little awkward.)

The "War March of the Priests," which serves as an entr'acte between acts 3 and 4 of the play, was a popular item on symphonic programs around the turn of the century but has since then sunk into oblivion. The flourishes of triplets that introduce it immediately bring to mind those of the famous "Wedding March," and a certain harmonic energy is imparted to the principal tunes of both marches by means of secondary-dominant/diminished-seventh chords. The "War March" is also related to the orchestral marches of contemporary grand opera (we might recall that Spontini ruled over the opera in Berlin during much of Mendelssohn's lifetime, even if the younger composer felt little affinity with him or his music). The main march is neither better nor worse than might be expected. The second Trio (in B♭) is distinguished by a certain refined nobility; but even this passing note of dignity is vitiated by one of those banal cadences that occasionally crop up in Mendelssohn's music and lead one to suspect that, as was perhaps the case here, he was not wholly committed to the work at hand.

The incidental music for *A Midsummer Night's Dream* (produced, like *Antigone* and *Oedipus*, at the court theater of the Neues Palais in Potsdam, while *Athalie* was first given at Charlottenburg) is altogether a different matter, and it has usually been assumed that Mendelssohn's personal attachment to the Shakespeare play and to his own early overture for it are the principal factors involved. This music, rather than that for the classic tragedies, should make us particularly regret Mendelssohn's failure to decide on a truly sympathetic subject for an opera before his early death. The *Midsummer Night's Dream* music differs from that for the other plays not only in a more extensive involvement of music with the stage action, as melodrama and pantomime (though with fewer songs or choruses), but also in the provision of instrumental entr'actes, which are what concern us here.

According to Eduard Devrient, we owe the existence of two of the four new orchestral numbers to a misunderstanding on Mendelssohn's part. Where Mendelssohn had provided instrumental movements to separate the acts of the traditional five-act arrangement, which was preserved in A. W. Schlegel's translation, Tieck had planned a production in three acts, making the second and third of Mendelssohn's entr'actes—the A-minor Intermezzo and the famous E-major Nocturne—technically superfluous. As Devrient recalled the situation,

Some expedient was to be found to bring in these pieces in the course of the act without dropping the curtain. This could be done with the *agitato* in A minor (No. 5), to accompany Hermia's seeking after her lover, especially if filled by the actress with grace and variety; but with the *notturno* in E major (No. 7), the long contemplation of the sleeping lovers was rather a painful effort, and Tieck's escape from the dilemma, by pushing forward some pieces of scenery to screen the lovers, was rather coarse and stagey, and of doubtful effect.[107]

It is not immediately clear why a curtain could not have been lowered at these junctures, even without an intermission or change of scenery. Also puzzling about Devrient's account is the fact that the agitated A-minor Intermezzo, intended to follow the original second act, leads directly into the bumptious A-major music accompanying the entrance of the rustics at the beginning of act 3, as they gather to rehearse in the woods. (Was the entr'acte perhaps rewritten after Mendelssohn was apprised of Tieck's production plans?) As for the Nocturne, the faintly ludicrous spectacle described by Devrient nicely points up the fact that this music evokes, depicts, or otherwise expresses something far more than the presence of four inert bodies—a physical presence that, against this music, could quickly come to seem not merely superfluous but even distracting and discomforting.

Each of Mendelssohn's entr'actes embodies a certain aspect or mood of Shakespeare's play appropriate to the action just past, passing, or to come. To some extent they can be said to add a further dimension to the mood or action of the play; certainly, they do as much to define a particular interpretive image for the play as do the paintings of Fuseli or any other traditional visual illustrations. The "Mendelssohnian" image of the play—with its emphasis on the sentimental and the picturesque elements of Shakespeare's fantasy world—may have met with resistance in our time, after almost a century of hegemonic influence; but to dismiss it as somehow "inauthentic" to Shakespeare would be historically and critically naive. The Scherzo re-creates the "elfin" world of the overture with entirely new musical material, though by similar technical means. The perpetual-motion quality of the overture (the running eighth notes of the first group) is generated in the Scherzo more by motivic insistence than by means of a literal *moto perpetuo* rhythm, and the role of high, divided strings is replaced here by staccato woodwinds, as a kind of signature texture and timbre to which the movement returns with each reprise of the main idea. Both movements, however, rely on a preponderantly diminutive intervallic vocabulary and hushed dynamics. In both cases, too, the desired effect of these "elfin" intervallic and dynamic modes is cannily constructed by setting them in relief against occasional explosions of louder music and larger intervals, projecting a sense that the whole "elfin" sound-world is a fragile, vulnerable, and elusive one, liable to evaporate at any moment. One such contrasting incursion in the Scherzo is a tritone appoggiatura figure that sounds like a modified reminiscence of Bottom's braying from the overture (see Example 7.49). A more striking instance is the crescendo-and-dissolution process heard twice following the first reprise of the main theme (mm. 115ff.). Over a dominant pedal, first in D minor, then in G minor, the motive of the main theme is worked up to a small explosion at the point of harmonic resolution (m. 129, m. 151), followed by a sudden dispersion of energy and texture across several single lines. The gesture suggests some Puckish trick, like those cataloged at the beginning of act 2 (to fragments of the Scherzo, in Mendelssohn's stage music for the scene), such as Puck's impersonation of a "three-foot stool" beneath an earnest,

Example 7.49
Incidental Music to *A Midsummer Night's Dream*, Scherzo, mm. 55–62

tale-spinning aunt ("Then slip I from her bum, down topples she, / And 'tailor' cries, and falls into a cough").

The Scherzo is filled with felicitous details of phrase, form, and instrumentation, combining to create an effect that might, again, be described as "kaleidoscopic." When phrases are repeated or recalled, they are invariably subjected to some subtle instrumental modification, transposed, or otherwise altered. The tripping hemiola phrase of the first bridge section (mm. 41–48, outlined by the trills in the upper melodic voice) is heard in two different scorings in its original exposition, then turned almost invisible when rescored for strings in the recapitulation (mm. 288–94). The "puckish" textural dissolve following the crescendo and miniature explosion, described earlier, is similarly reconstituted instrumentally upon repetition, as is the main theme itself in the principal reprise, newly illuminated by a measured, high string tremolo (c^4, g^3: violin 1, mm. 258–73). The perpetual motion "implicit" throughout the movement is finally realized in the extended flute solo of the coda, dissolving back into the motive of the main theme in the final measures. When the curtain rises at the end of the Scherzo, we are given a cue to imagine, in retrospect, the coda and the Scherzo as a whole in terms of the "wandering spirit" whom Puck now addresses (act 2, scene 2) and of the description of his (or her?) fairy peregrinations in the service of Titania. Devrient's assessment of Mendelssohn's achievement here, as in the overture and in the other incidental music, unwittingly captures the double-edged aspect of the composer's indisputable success (this from 1868): "The originality of his portrayal of fairy life has become typical; all later composers have, in similar subjects, followed in his footsteps."[108]

The second entr'acte, the A-minor Allegro appassionato (Intermezzo), was even more explicitly attached to an imaginary action "between" the acts, as we have seen. As published in the original complete edition, under Julius Rietz, the score of this number specifies the accompanying stage action: "Hermia seeks Lysander, and loses herself in the wood." The movement is characterized by a constant motivic to-and-fro appropriate to the image of Hermia's anxious seeking. As Friedhelm Krummacher points out, this *durchbrochene Arbeit* (the displacement of thematic lines across different instrumental parts) is not limited to thematic development but constitutes the central, continuous texture of the piece, while the resulting feeling of thematic fragility or evanescence is compensated, to some degree, by the binding role of a nearly continuous sixteenth-note tremolo in the middle string register (violin 2, viola, and sometimes cello, without double bass).[109]

This textural-thematic hide-and-seek continues across the faintly articulated B-section (mm. 37ff.), which scarcely leaves the tonic, A minor, except for a brief tonicization of the Neapolitan, B♭, prior to a retransition based on the main motive (mm. 60–73). The formal return of the main idea (m. 74) is embellished with one of Mendelssohn's favorite devices, a new legato countermelody in the tenor register of the cello and bassoon. In this case, the new countermelody takes on the aspect of a "real" main theme in comparison to the nervous, fragmented quality of the original material (see Example 7.50)—as if the actual theme had been suppressed in the original A-section and deferred until the return.

Example 7.50
Incidental Music to *A Midsummer Night's Dream*, Intermezzo, mm. 74–81

In this least known of the entr'actes Mendelssohn most closely approaches the paradigmatic musical Romanticism of a composer like Schumann. With its darting, shadowy motivic play, it is a genuine *Nachtstück* of a more sinister, eerie sort than the lyrical Nocturne that follows. This music might put one in mind of those descriptions by Tieck, Wackenroder, or Hoffmann of music as an elusive world of nocturnal spirits and subconscious fantasy, a world inhabited not only by Oberon's Puck and Titania's amusing train but also by the likes of Goethe's and Schubert's Erlkönig. Also in the spirit of a Schumannian Romanticism is the idea of a secret, hidden melodic line (the cello countermelody) revealed only in the gradual course of things (the countermelody also makes a brief and even slightly menacing reappearance at the beginning of the coda, mm. 111–23, now in the bass register). The entrance music of the rustics, by contrast, belongs to the world of Haydn at his most bucolic and naive; it might easily form the theme of a Haydn variation movement, except perhaps for the clownishly overemphatic reiterations of the opening motive across the closing measures.

Even the Nocturne proper (no. 7), for all the beautiful lyricism of its opening E-major period, is not without its darker, midnight tones. Like many of Chopin's nocturnes, it includes a more agitated, minor-mode developmental mid-section (mm. 39–72), which is not without its effect on the reprise. The quiet susurration of triplet figures in the strings that initiates the middle section of the movement is carried over into the reprise, as is a counterfigure of drooping duplet eighth-note pairs in the flutes; when these figurations are combined at the reprise, they surround the main lyrical subject in the horns and bassoons rather in the way that the four unconscious lovers might lie surrounded by the whispering of leaves and the cooing and whirring of nocturnal birds and insects. If we are tempted to classify this movement as a "song without words" (as any nocturne might be considered), then it combines two types, as Krummacher notes.[110] The opening period belongs to the *Chorlied* type, the combination of two horns and two bassoons—scarcely accompanied—suggesting an a cappella men's chorus or quartet. With the whispering figuration added in the midsection, the song comes to resemble more the traditional solo type, with arpeggiated instrumental accompaniment (although it could just as well be thought of as an accompanied *choral* song, for the melody retains the four-part homophonic texture, in tenor and bass ranges). The scoring of the principal melody (a simple, cavatina-like aa¹bb¹a structure) for horns with bassoons is clearly meant to evoke the forest setting, just as the music evokes the kind of evening song or nighttime serenade that might celebrate such a setting. Given the beauty and tranquillity of the piece as a whole, Mendelssohn chose not to make its ending ironic, as he might well have done, considering that the curtain rises to reveal Titania and the transformed Bottom lying in each other's arms.

The all-too-famous Wedding March is actually one of three instrumental marches provided for the play, whose sharply contrasting styles and proportions reflect the contrasting dramatic levels of the Athenian nobles, the fairy world, and the rustics' parodistic play.[111] The minuscule mock-funeral march in C minor that accompanies Thisbe's discovery of the dead Pyramus is a striking and probably fortuitous adumbration of Mahler's much more highly evolved parodic-funereal tone, as in the third movement of his First Symphony, for example. In Mendelssohn's march, bassoon and timpani intone a three-note dirge motive (c–d–e♭), while the C-clarinet repeats a two-measure "lamenting" melody, with a Lydian (raised) fourth imparting a characteristic, twangy whine. The "elfin march" that accompanies the simultaneous entrance of the warring couple, Oberon and Titania, with their respective entourages in act 2 is another miniature, though much more developed than the "funeral march." Here Mendelssohn returned to the E-minor tonality of the overture, as well as to the diminutive intervals and whirring rhythms that had characterized the elfin world there. Staccato articulations, repressed dynamics, pizzicato, and (in the closing phrase) melodic and harmonic chromaticism all play their part in painting a comical picture of elfin *hauteur* and diminutive pomposity. This music, unfortunately, makes all the more evident (as

Devrient noted) the incongruity of life-size actors impersonating the imaginary elfin population evoked by Shakespeare's fantastical poetic conceits.

The Wedding March, on the other hand, is a fully life-size march, whose affinities of style and structure with the "War March of the Priests" in *Athalie* have already been noted (Tovey dubbed it "gloriously squirearchic").[112] There is no actual scenic requirement for this march, which serves instead to signify the offstage nuptials of Theseus, Hippolyta, and the rest. The immediately distinctive feature of the tune is the unexpected, slightly oblique harmonization of its first two measures: the opening C of the melody is harmonized not as tonic but as a half-diminished seventh of G (first inversion), followed by a fleeting tonicization of E minor, until C major is stabilized in the second half of the phrase. It has occasionally been pointed out how, for all the millions who can recognize the main tune and possibly even put a name to it, scarcely any would be in a position to identify the music of the two internal trios. The melody and harmonization of the second of these, in F major (mm. 52ff.), are given a slight chromatic urgency, underscored by the rhythmic accompaniment, which makes for a nice foil to the ritual pomp of the rest. This second trio is elegantly dovetailed with the return of the main march theme (m. 84), which is amplified by an arpeggiated string accompaniment redolent of Wagner's operas of the 1840s, *Tannhäuser* and—appropriately enough—*Lohengrin* (the source of the "rival" Wedding March, of course). Paradoxically, Mendelssohn's Wedding March constitutes not only the most familiar number of his incidental music but also part of one of the least familiar numbers: the fragmentary reprise of the march (no. 12) designed to accompany the nobles' exit after the end of the festivities of act 5. Here Mendelssohn recomposed the second strain of the march tune as a textural and dynamic decrescendo, and the tonicization of E minor in the first phrase is broken off by an unexpected reminiscence of the E-minor elfin music of the overture, as Puck appears to introduce the fairies' incantations of domestic bliss. With the return of this familiar music here and in the closing chorus, Mendelssohn closes the circle of his own involvement with Shakespeare's comedy by harking back to the inimitable inspiration of his former, seventeen-year-old self. Schumann criticized Mendelssohn's decision, arguing that he had missed a golden opportunity to create something new here (although the solo verses of this finale *are* newly composed, in fact). But the occasion to return to this music of his youth must have afforded Mendelssohn a great personal satisfaction; and as we know from Mendelssohn's own account, cited earlier, the end of his overture was conceived as an evocation of the end of the play, in the first place.

ORATORIOS AND *DIE ERSTE WALPURGISNACHT*

It is probably fair to say that by Mendelssohn's time the fully independent instrumental overture, extractable for the purposes of concert performance, was deemed unsuitable to the genre of the oratorio. The glamorous instrumental solos and cadenzas common to the slow introductions to operatic overtures, the fiery first themes, jaunty second themes, marchlike closing ideas, and brassy, boisterous codas that made many full-length operatic overtures such popular concert fare were naturally suspect in the eyes of a "serious" oratorio composer and scarcely compatible with Mendelssohn's compositional aesthetic, in any case. (His closest approach to the typical opera overture, in *Ruy Blas*, has a hint of parody to it, as we have seen.)

Both of Mendelssohn's sacred oratorios are introduced by sober, minor-mode introductions in something like a neo-Handelian fugal manner. That to the earlier oratorio, *St. Paul* (1836), is considerably more developed and at least nominally independent; it has a sizable slow introduction of 43 measures, based on the familiar chorale tune "Wachet auf, ruft uns die Stimme" (Sleepers, Awake), and it comes to a full close in A major, elaborating the final phrase of the chorale. The main body of the overture (Con moto, A minor–A major, 163 mm.) is a hybrid of fugue and chorale prelude, not unlike what one finds in many of Bach's opening cantata choruses. Such a model would be appropriate to this particular oratorio, with its incorporation of Lutheran chorales and Bach-like choral *turbae* (even if Handel remains the predominant influence in the more massive, direct style of the principal choruses). The A-minor fugue subject of the overture is distinguished by a 1̂-to-5̂ scalar motion and an "affective" falling seventh, resolved in the second half of the subject. After a slightly amplified exposition of this subject and an episodic development of its opening motive, the first phrase of the "Sleepers, awake" chorale is introduced in E minor (m. 90), followed by statements in C major and D minor. A second series of fugal entries begins in D minor, assuming a more developmental character, until chorale (harmonized as V of A minor) and fugue subject combine in a climactic *Steigerung* leading toward the emphatic arrival in A major (m. 156). Here, in a kind of synthetic coda-reprise, the chorale tune is at last heard in its entirety, while it continues to interact with the fugue subject, gradually finding its way back to A. The closing phase of the overture (mm. 178–205), as already mentioned, elaborates the cadential phrase of the chorale in triumphant tones. Though considerably shorter than Mendelssohn's concert overtures and consciously more uniform in character, the piece has sufficient musical interest to be heard for its own sake. The fugue subject signals its affinity with the affective world of the Baroque clearly enough, but it is probably also meant to convey something of the values of ethical and spiritual "striving" often associated with such minor-key fugal work in the nineteenth century. Typically Romantic and un-Baroque is the dramatized movement from A minor to A major toward the end; the effect is underscored by the fact that the first chorale incipits were heard in the "wrong" (minor) mode. This strategy gives added weight to the implicit teleology of the overture, as an embodiment, presumably, of the conversion of Saul: the process of spiritual seeking and sudden "enlightenment." (The conversion is celebrated within the oratorio by a festive setting of the same chorale, following Saul's vision on the road to Damascus and the chorus, "Mache dich auf, werde Licht!"—translated with unintended informality in the C. F. Peters score as "Rise up, arise, rise and shine!")

The overture or introduction to *Elijah* (1846–1847), by contrast, maintains its darker hues throughout, serving specifically to introduce the first chorus ("Help Lord! Wilt thou quite destroy us?") and the plight of the drought-stricken Hebrew people. The material is again informed by Baroque affective gestures (half-step melodic "sigh" figures, a descending chromatic countersubject, falling sevenths and minor sixths, etc.). The modern or Mendelssohnian aspect of the fugal design, in this case, is its layout as a gradual, unrelenting crescendo to the climactic, homophonic statement of the subject at the end. A minimization of any contrasting episodic activity in favor of nearly continuous presentations of the subject or brief developments of it contributes to the overall effect of somber urgency. The listener is prepared for the tone of the instrumental introduction and even for its expressive message by the short recitative that Mendelssohn set *before* it, in which Elijah pronounces God's punishment of his disobedient children.

Mendelssohn's setting of Goethe's dramatic ballad *Die erste Walpurgisnacht* (The First Walpurgis-Night) might best be grouped with the oratorios for our purposes, although the piece is an anomaly in the composer's oeuvre in more ways than one. On the face of it, it might seem more like a kind of antioratorio—not merely secular but explicitly "pagan" in its celebration of the clandestine survival of an enlightened druidic pantheism in opposition to the rise of an oppressive and intolerant Christian hegemony. It is hardly the sort of thing that one expects from the subsequent paragon of stained-glass piety, Bernard Shaw's "oratorio mongerer." It may well be that Mendelssohn would never have set the poem without Goethe's personal urging. (The poet seems to have been eager to have it composed; his friend and Mendelssohn's teacher, Zelter, had demurred many years earlier, and consequently the task was passed on to Felix by way of two of the most influential figures of his youth.) Composed in the course of his European tour of 1830–1832, the work could be regarded as a last testament of his early "Romantic" period, and, indeed, the central choruses elicited some of his most unbridled, diabolical, almost Berliozian music (no accident that Berlioz admired the work and perhaps no less that its composition partially coincided with Mendelssohn's acquaintance with Berlioz in Rome).

On reflection, the piece becomes somewhat less anomalous. As has been pointed out, the poem can and should be read as a paean to Enlightenment reason and tolerance, issues that were at the core of Mendelssohn's ethical upbringing and that he continually sought to reconcile with his adopted religious beliefs.[113] The genre of the musical setting that resulted, although difficult to classify beyond the rather vague category of "secular cantata," is one that became increasingly popular in the course of the nineteenth century. (Mendelssohn's friend and disciple Niels Gade, for instance, composed a number of successful dramatic ballads of this sort for chorus, soloists, and orchestra, and the "secular cantata" was the official genre prescribed for the musical aspirants to the French *Prix de Rome* throughout the century.) It is interesting that when he came to revise and perform his *Erste Walpurgisnacht* in 1842–1843 (creating a parallel to the genesis of the "Scottish" Symphony), Mendelssohn several times spoke of his desire to expand it as a "symphony-cantata," with reference to his designation for the *Lobgesang* of 1840.[114] The composer's correspondence makes it clear that this would have entailed expanding (or replacing) the overture with a series of instrumental pieces. It would be intriguing to know just what kind of pieces Mendelssohn had in mind; one assumes that they would have been much more "descriptive" or programmatic than the symphonic movements of the *Lobgesang*. It would also be possible, perhaps even more plausible, to imagine a series of instrumental movements inserted into the course of the vocal setting at various points, along the lines of Berlioz's "dramatic symphony," *Roméo et Juliette*.

In the end, the revisions of 1842 affected only the vocal numbers of the piece, and the overture remained as Mendelssohn had composed it at the very end of his original work on *Die erste Walpurgisnacht* in early February 1832.[115] As with the introduction to *Elijah*, the overture runs into the first vocal number of the work (tenor solo and chorus, "Es lacht der Mai") and thus serves to prepare a specific situation rather than to convey an overall impression of the poem as a whole. The role of the overture in this case, however, is much more sharply defined than in *Elijah*, and its musical expression is carried out on a more ambitious scale. As Mendelssohn himself indicated in the final score, the opening Allegro con fuoco (A minor, $\frac{3}{4}$, 349 mm.) is intended to represent "bad weather" ("Das schlechte Wetter"), the last blasts of winter, the unpredictable mix of conditions that north Germans sum up as *Aprilwetter*. These storms yield gradually to a sixty-measure transitional passage in A major, representing the arrival of spring ("Der Übergang zum Frühling").

Just as Mendelssohn was later undecided about whether or not to expand his ballad setting into something larger that he could call a "symphony-cantata," so he was initially undecided about how to treat the overture itself. In the summer of 1831, after having finished the setting of Goethe's ballad text as such, Mendelssohn had not yet provided it with an overture, and he was uncertain whether he should write a *große Symphonie* for this purpose or simply "a short spring-like introduction" ("eine kurze Frühlingseinleitung").[116] The decision to include music for the stormy weather prior to the advent of spring was a fortunate one. Not only did the overture become one of his more ambitious instrumental movements, but the turbulence of the A-minor Allegro aptly conveys something of the social-historical strife that figures as the background to the druids' initially bucolic rites of spring. The general conception of instrumental tempest fading into an opening antique-ceremonial chorus might have been suggested, in part, by the example of Gluck's introduction to *Iphigénie en Tauride*. Mendelssohn's music, however, is much closer to Beethoven here than to Gluck—not only the Beethoven of the "Pastoral" Symphony, as we might expect, but also of the "Eroica" first movement. An extended series of syncopations in the violins during the bridge section (mm. 72–81) suggests Beethoven or even passages from Berlioz, while the motivic fragmentations that follow are strongly reminiscent of the "Eroica" in particular. A new, sharply profiled figure in the development, battering down like sheets of rain, is subjected to incessant development that suggests the storm music

Example 7.51
Die erste Walpurgisnacht, Overture, mm. 139–44

of the "Pastoral" (mm. 139ff., see Example 7.51). At the height of this storm, where the figure appears in threefold overlapping entries, a triple-forte chord of F major in the full orchestra suddenly brakes its juggernaut momentum.

In the musical space cleared by this sudden interruption, a triadic call is uttered by bassoons and horns. The mysterious and suggestive quality of this call has something almost Mahlerian about it, especially when, upon repetition, it extends the prevailing meter and reaches up a fifth (c^1 to g^1) at the end (see Example 7.52).

Example 7.52
Die erste Walpurgisnacht, Overture, mm. 193–97

This "voice of nature" is probably meant to be heard here either as a herald of spring or (in retrospect, at least) as a call to gather the druids and their followers to observe their vernal rites. It alternates several times with fragments of the main theme and its blustery accompaniment, before fading out into doleful half steps, as the recapitulation of the main theme in A minor ensues. This recapitulation is modified even more than usual, however. The exposition itself had lacked anything that could be called a "second theme"; now the main theme combines with the "storm" motive (Example 7.51) for a passage of secondary development, leading to a coda-resolution in which both figures are allowed to expend themselves in a gradual decrescendo in A minor. As they do so, the druidic "call" returns, again in F, and is taken up by other wind instruments, while the strings and timpani offer tremolo mutterings such as traditionally depict the sounds of receding storms. The music gradually reaches A major, by way of V of D minor, and the concluding section, marked by Mendelssohn as the "transition to Spring." Against a gently pulsing background are heard anticipations of the melody of the following druidic hymn to the new season ("Es lacht der Mai, der Wald ist frei von Eis und Reifgehänge"). In the course of the transition one also recognizes this new melody (see Example 7.53) as a transformation of the "call" itself, in faster rhythmic

Example 7.53
Die erste Walpurgisnacht, **Overture, mm. 358–63**

values. The derivation of this new theme from the "call" highlights, in turn, a common resemblance to the original "bad weather" theme of the overture.[117] The whole process thus becomes an appropriate musical symbol of the gradual, organic "rebirth" of spring, embodied in a similarly appropriate process of Goethean "metamorphosis" that lends a fundamental, internal, symbolic support to the audible surface processes of harmonic modulation, rhythm, and melody.

CONCERTOS AND CONCERTED WORKS

In the course of his career, Mendelssohn came to represent a principal figure of opposition to the type of modern instrumental virtuoso that had emerged in the first decades of the nineteenth century. The would-be reformer of opera and theater in Düsseldorf, the conductor of the Leipzig Gewandhaus concerts (and the engineer of their influentially high-minded, classically oriented programs), the musical collaborator in the model productions of ancient Greek and neoclassical French tragedy at the Berlin court, the composer of *St. Paul* and *Elijah*—all of these professional personae were diametrically opposed to the kinds of gaudy, exhibitionistic display that seemed to have invaded concert and operatic life by the 1820s and 1830s (an invasion that the more serious-minded elements of the musical press never tired of denouncing). Yet Mendelssohn also produced, in what must de facto be considered his "late" period, a work that has become probably the single most familiar virtuoso vehicle for any instrument: the E-minor Violin Concerto, Op. 64. Similarly paradoxical is the fact that this concerto, by far his most celebrated, was written for an instrument on which Mendelssohn possessed merely functional competence as a performer, while the concertos he wrote for his own instrument—the piano—have maintained only a marginal status in the concert repertoire. A closer look at the composer's involvement with the concerto as a genre may help to explain something (if not everything) of these paradoxes, while also shedding light on some of his lesser-known large-form instrumental works.

Early Concertos

Among Mendelssohn's copious output in his early to mid-teens are several concerted works designed to showcase his prodigious talents as a pianist as well as composer. These works follow the models provided in some abundance by such pianist-composers of the day as J. N. Hummel, Ferdinand Ries, Friedrich Kalkbrenner, John Field, Carl Maria von Weber, and Mendelssohn's own friend and mentor Ignaz Moscheles. The earliest of these works—a still-unpublished concerto for piano and strings in A minor composed probably around 1822—is testimony to Mendelssohn's pianistic prowess at the age of thirteen.[118] The first movement is built around a mildly "pathetic," agitated main idea and a gavottelike, graceful, and Mozartean second theme in the relative major. Exposition and recapitulation are rounded out by the kind of brilliant (somewhat mechanical) etudelike solo passage-work that tends to occupy this position in most concertos of the period. The lengthy development section, by contrast, opens with an extended section of an unusually relaxed nature. The adagio second movement begins with a serene, hymnlike period for strings, vaguely reminiscent of the slow movement of Beethoven's "Emperor" concerto. This is briefly contrasted with a central episode in the character of a dramatic recitative, where freely embellished vocalizing outbursts from the solo piano are framed by quiet, agitated tremolos in the strings; this dramatic-operatic episode is alluded to later, just prior to the tranquil conclusion of the movement. The finale, Allegro ma non troppo, works with the same combination of rondolike themes and sonata-oriented form that will characterize virtually all of the subsequent concerto finales. The principal idea of this finale has a faintly *alla turca* quality, and the opening group as a whole shows a marked tendency to gravitate toward the major mode. As in the first movement, the closing sections of this finale indulge in fleet finger work of a more-or-less mechanical nature. The essential fluency of this full-scale exercise in the contemporary concerto idiom might justly impress as much, if not more, than the performance skills it presupposes. But judged against the best of Mendelssohn's youthful compositions, the A-minor concerto is at times bland and shallow (qualities that it shares with not a few of the contemporary models that Mendelssohn would have encountered in this genre).

A violin concerto in D minor composed in the same year for his close friend and sometime violin teacher, Eduard Rietz (1802–1832), is a considerably tauter work, taking its cue from the classically oriented French school of violin music represented by Viotti, Pierre Rode, Pierre Baillot, and Rodolphe Kreutzer. Even before its publication in the *Neue Leipziger Mendelssohn-Ausgabe*, this early violin concerto was revived and popularized, to some extent, by Yehudi Menuhin in the 1950s. The first movement (Allegro) opens with an imposing unison theme of an almost Baroque aspect. Overall, the opening tutti is a broadly-scaled ABA[1], in which the central modulation to F major, however, does not include the expected preview of the movement's second theme. When the actual second theme does arrive, in the course of the fairly condensed solo exposition, it vacillates poignantly between major and minor. The closing group of the exposition indulges once again in the etudelike passage-work indigenous to this function in most concertos in the "brilliant" manner, yet with an ingenuous forthrightness that is somehow appealing. (In the recapitulation, this passage-work is omitted.) The andante second movement in $\frac{3}{8}$ time (D major) is close kin to the slow movements of some of the contemporaneous string *sinfonie*, fleshed out in this case with a variety of cadenza-like material for the soloist. The smooth course of the movement is interrupted briefly toward the end by ominous, dramatic rumblings in the low strings (compare the similar effect in slow movement of the A-minor piano concerto), yielding to a fragile final statement of the theme in the solo violin. The soloist's sustained final tonic (d^3) provides an *attacca* link to the closing rondo movement, thus anticipating the interconnection of movements that particularly characterizes Mendelssohn's later works in this genre. The theme of the final rondo has an engaging, somewhat gypsylike quality. By virtue of a variety of witty permutations, this principal theme goes on to dominate even the episodic portions of the movement. The playful use of modulation and the coy, extended retransitional gestures are reminiscent of Classic models to an extent that is not encountered again in the later concertos.

The two concertos for two pianos and orchestra composed between 1823 and 1824 bear the same relation to Mendelssohn's earliest essays in the genre as the C-minor Symphony, Op. 11 (also composed in 1824) does to the early string symphonies.   Like the C-minor Symphony, these two concertos represent the young composer's thorough assimilation of the latest musical styles and techniques, shedding any traces of youthful awkwardness or the occasional archaisms of his earliest works. The earlier concerto (in E major) was performed by Felix and Fanny at one of the Mendelssohns' house concerts on the occasion of Fanny's nineteenth birthday (14 November 1824). Felix thought highly enough of the work to revive it for one of his London concerts during the first visit in 1829, when he performed it with Moscheles. The fact that this concert of 13 July (a benefit concert for flood victims in Silesia) also included the *Midsummer Night's Dream* overture suggests that the composer still considered the concerto a thoroughly respectable accomplishment. (The substitution of the orchestrally arranged Scherzo from the Op. 20 Octet for the original minuet movement of the C-minor Symphony in the preceding London concert, as mentioned earlier, is another sign that Mendelssohn made a point of presenting the very best of his early works during this first English sojourn.) On the other hand, he probably also took into account the relatively light weight and fashionable brilliance of the piece as well, calculated to win the approval of his London audience. Another factor would have been the opportunity of performing together with Moscheles, by now a local musical celebrity in London (the two had originally met in Berlin in 1824). We know of only one public performance of the second duo-concerto, in A♭, at a concert in Stettin (20 February 1827) under the direction of Carl Loewe, who also played the second piano part. (As it happens, this program also included the premiere of the *Midsummer Night's Dream* in its full orchestral guise.) Both double concertos disappeared from view after 1830. Despite their large dimensions and skillful craftsmanship, they are manifestly less serious works than the First Symphony or even the early piano quartets, and it is not surprising that after 1830 Mendelssohn chose not to publish them.[119]

While the two duo-piano concertos partake very much of the loquacious *style brilliant* of such composers as Hummel, Czerny, Kalkbrenner, or Moscheles, neither of them exploits the tone of pompous, pseudoheroic pathos that had become standard for grand concertos, particularly in the minor mode, since the 1810s (a tone and attendant broad formal pacing that can probably be traced back to Beethoven's C-minor concerto at the very beginning of the century). These works, on the other hand, both adopt a sunny, easygoing lyricism in their opening movements, reminiscent of Mozart in his "A-major" mood (e.g., the Piano Concerto, K. 488, the Clarinet Concerto, and Clarinet Quintet). The moderate pace of both opening tuttis leaves ample space for exchanges of decorative pianistic embellishment during the extensive solos that follow. Both opening tutti sections contain broadly scaled orchestral expositions in the contemporary, post-Classic manner, including full modulations to the dominant for the second theme groups. The alternation of quiet, cantabile thematic statements of both first and second groups in the orchestral expositions of both concertos with more boisterous bridge and closing material underscores the close kinship of these two first movements, further reinforced by the identical implementation of a quiet reminiscence of the opening theme of each concerto to effect a transition into the first solo (mm. 76–88 in the first Allegro of the E-major Concerto, mm. 87–110 in that of the A♭ Concerto). Both movements, furthermore, make use of piano transitional periods to introduce their respective second themes in orchestral and solo expositions alike.

The first solo of the E-major Concerto begins with a cadenza-like *Eingang* or lead-in, another common feature of the Classic and post-Classic concerto tradition. Up to the second group (or the modulatory introduction to it, mm. 120ff.) the soloists are engaged primarily in scalar passage-work and arpeggios. Here, as in the A♭ Concerto, Mendelssohn observed the Classic concerto conventions of giving the second theme—a lyrical antecedent-consequent period—to the soloists, with minimal accompaniment, following this with an extensive closing group (animated by more scales and arpeggios), and culminating in the typical extended cadential trills to signal the final cadence in the dominant. (In the E-major Concerto, this *Schlußtriller* invades both hands of both parts, to create a full, four-part trilled dominant seventh.) The solo *Eingang* returns to introduce both development and recapitulation, the development being kept relatively brief and ending with a restatement of the second theme on the dominant, by way of retransition. As in the A♭ Concerto, the opening tutti is dispensed with in the recapitulation, except for the original orchestral bridge-phrase, which is brought back in both cases, appropriately reworked, before the solo transition and second group. Both movements, in other words, adopt precisely the same means of integrating tutti and solo recapitulations, which had been a standard procedure, of course, since Mozart's time. Neither concerto includes a formal cadenza in the first movement, which may seem justified by the quantity of "brilliant" writing that already pervades the solo portions.

The first movement of the A♭ Concerto, as suggested earlier, follows the formal outline of its near-twin sibling quite closely. Rather than beginning the solo with a metrically free *Eingang*, however, the first solo begins with a florid, but measured, period of dialogue between the soloists, before the orchestra sets in motion the official modulation (where both orchestral and solo themes are briefly cited). The development is considerably more extended in this movement, beginning with a recollection of the opening florid solo period in the distant key of B major. Arpeggiated figures from the first solo period combine with the animated figurational dialogue of the closing section (originally mm. 212ff.) to fill out the 117 measures of this development (mm. 309–425), concluding with an extended dominant prolongation that is consistently colored by inflections of the tonic minor. Once again, a cadenza-like extension of the closing group substitutes for a free, unaccompanied cadenza.

Both slow movements are in $\frac{6}{8}$ meter, and, despite the Adagio non troppo marking of the first one (in C major), both recall the tone of the slow movements of the early string symphonies, while the unassuming lyrical substance is here, naturally, filled out by extensive solo figuration. The Adagio non troppo of the E-major Concerto adopts a simple ABA[1] structure, with a central section in C minor. The nocturnelike main theme and its embellishment are restricted to the first piano throughout the original A-section. The *minore* central section (B) is then given entirely to the second piano, while the reprise (A[1]) is, logically, shared between them, the first piano picking up the original theme as the second piano continues with the accompaniment figure in sixteenth-note triplets that it had inaugurated in the course of the B-section. The Andante of the A♭ Concerto (in E major, again a third-relation to the key of the first movement) is cast in a variant of "slow-movement" sonata form, a vestigial development being followed almost immediately by a florid variation-reprise of the main theme. Additional allusions to this theme are interpolated into the exposition (m. 40) and the opening of the development (m. 70), giving a refrainlike feeling to the structure.

The finales of the two double concertos are both sonata-form movements with spirited, rondolike themes. The keyboard writing in these movements probably conveys a good idea of the performance style cultivated by the young Mendelssohn: nimble and clean, "brilliant," but in an understated, tasteful way, closer to the style of John Field, perhaps, than to such heavier-hitting virtuosi as Hummel and Kalkbrenner. (Nonetheless, the ideal of the light, "pearling" scale—singly, as well as in thirds or octaves—and the crystalline arpeggio is common to most of this contemporary repertoire, as nearly any page from the concertos of these composers will reveal.) The finale of the E-major Double Concerto is designed as a sonata form without development, although a somewhat extended retransitional passage (mm. 114–36) puts some distance between the exposition's closing and the return of the first group. Despite the rondolike character of the lightly syncopated initial theme and of this retransition into its principal reprise, appearances of the "main" theme remain scarce. Aside from the opening solo and the principal return at m. 136 (in neither case does the implied antecedent phrase receive a matching consequent), the theme is merely alluded to near the beginning of the coda (mm. 256–59). Rather, the contrasting, legato consequent phrase paired with the "main" theme assumes greater prominence (see Example 7.54), returning in the orchestral tuttis of the first group and reprise, as well as forming the basis of the second theme (mm. 73, 199).

Example 7.54
Concerto in E Major for Two Pianos, Finale, mm. 9–14

The finale of the A♭ Concerto again follows the Classic precedent in beginning with a solo period. This is extended, with the discrete participation of strings and timpani, and some transitional passage-work in thirds then leads into the tutti counterstatement and further development of the theme. This theme starts off as a cheerful romp à la Weber, but its most distinctive trait is a surprise drop to the subtonic (G♭ major), when piano II answers with what should be a normal consequent phrase, rebeginning off the tonic (mm. 4–8). (One can imagine that this little *jeu d'esprit* may have been accompanied by looks of feigned surprise and dismay on the faces of Felix and Fanny, performing the piece for the entertainment of the family circle in the Mendelssohns' Berlin home.[120]) This bit of simulated *gaucherie* (which remains an integral part of the theme-group at every recurrence) is quickly rectified by the cooperation of the two pianos and rounded off by a pair of cadential phrases, before the orchestra picks up the whole group. While the general mood of playful insouciance resembles that of the E-major Concerto finale, the solo parts here exhibit markedly contrapuntal tendencies. Indeed, the solo bridge (mm. 63ff.) evolves into a kind of four-part invention on the opening motive of the main theme—a novel stylistic cross-fertilization of Bachian counterpoint and Biedermeier pianism. A felicitous touch is the emergence of the tune that will eventually serve as the "real" solo second theme at first in the woodwinds, quietly and unassumingly superimposed over the continuation of the two pianos' busy transitional contrapuntal exercises (mm. 90ff.). Although the new theme already appears in the dominant, the underlying $^6_4$ harmonization and the persistence of the two pianos in weaving their scalar garlands around motives of the first theme all conspire to underemphasize the presence of the new material, at first. As in the finale of the E-major Concerto, the end of the closing section here is not strongly demarcated but flows (in this case) directly into a real development, running the initial motive of the movement through a variety of keys. A rather strongly prepared (and hence more than usually deceptive) "false recapitulation" in the dominant (m. 180) initiates some further modulation through B and D♭ before the tonic (and thematic) reprise finally arrives in mm. 202–3. The contrapuntal activity of the solo bridge section is considerably amplified in the reprise (mm. 237–68, 278–316), with the orchestra taking part, this time, in a genuine fugato at m. 262. A secondary development reenacts much of the original development (mm. 346ff.), and an additional reprise of the main theme newly extended, from m. 366 onward, gives the movement as a whole a rondolike aspect in keeping with the character of the theme itself. On top of all this Mendelssohn adds a brief coda based on the main theme, sneaking in yet one more time (*più presto*, mm. 417–34) the opening gambit of falling from A♭ to G♭, before a series of exuberant cadences in the tonic finally puts this now old joke firmly to rest.

Solo Piano Concertos, Op. 25 and Op. 40

For all their appealing fluency, the two double concertos in E and A♭ are symptomatic of the condition that was increasingly afflicting the concerto in general through the 1820s and 1830s: a disproportionate relation between ever-expanding dimensions and an often minimal melodic-thematic substance. One of the causal factors here was the tendency to adhere, in first movements, to the Classic "double-exposition" format, even as the dimensions of both orchestral and solo expositions continued to expand, just as they were doing in the contemporary sonata and symphony. In the concerto, however—especially as practiced by the new generation of virtuoso pianist-composers—the quantity of ornamental passage-work and technical display within the solo sections (particularly in bridges, closing groups, and developments) was growing to the point where the form threatened to collapse under its own weight. All three of Mendelssohn's mature solo concertos—the piano concertos in G minor and D minor, and the E-minor Violin Concerto—can be seen, in part, as responses to this dilemma, while all three also exhibit common traces of other compositional preoccupations on the part of their composer—in particular his "hobbyhorse," as he called it, of unifying multimovement instrumental works by means of *attacca* performance, written-out transitions between movements, and elements of incipient "cyclic" thematic return and transformation.

The Piano Concerto in G minor, Op. 25, was completed during Mendelssohn's second visit to Munich, in October 1831, on the return leg of the Italian journey of 1830–1831, en route to the final goal of his extended European tour in Paris. Mendelssohn later remarked to his father that the concerto was a thing of small consequence, tossed off in three days, but it appears that the substance of the work had already been conceived in the course of the preceding winter and spring in Italy. The Munich premiere had to be postponed until the middle of October, after Munich society and its musicians were free from the obligations of the *Oktoberfest*, but was no less successful for that.[121]

In the first movement of the G-minor Concerto the orchestra and piano collaborate in a brief series of dramaticized introductory gestures, before the soloist presents a concise, two-measure idea that will serve as the main "theme" of the movement (mm. 20–21, 22–23). After some few measures of soloistic activity the orchestra picks up and extends this brief figure, but even this apparently principal tutti or orchestral ritornello lasts no more than fourteen measures, at which point the soloist reenters with scalar passages initiating the modulation toward the new key. The *tranquillo* second group in B♭ belongs almost entirely to the soloist. Its sense of tranquil "apartness" is further underscored by a sudden turn to D♭ (as flatted mediant of the "principal" second key, B♭), which turns out to dominate this quintessentially relaxed, lyrical second group. The closing section returns to B♭ (mm. 121ff.), and works in the second theme again, now decorated by arpeggiated chords in the piano. Any central tutti is altogether suppressed, and what little development there is has more the effect of a modulatory extension of the closing group; while the listener is very likely still waiting for a clear resolution of the soloist's closing gestures (a kind of written-out chordal trill, interrupted by a restatement of the second theme in D major), the introductory orchestral crescendo returns to usher in a recapitulation in which the already economical exposition is further telescoped. As in the following D-minor Concerto, no provision is made for an improvised cadenza in any of the movements here. In fact, where the usual cadenza-point would occur, in the course of the tutti rounding off the solo recapitulation, an unexpected event intervenes: in place of an anticipatory $^6_4$ chord, ushering in a solo cadenza, a root-position tonic chord (G minor, m. 246) becomes the initial member of a fanfarelike gesture (see Example 7.55) that is briefly developed as a transition between G minor and the dominant of E (the key of the following movement).

This same figure—which can be loosely related, as a rhythm, to the main themes of the outer movements—will return to effect a transition from slow movement to finale. In both cases, the soloist appears to respond to the orchestra's transitional "cue" (this rhythmic fanfare), completing the transitional impulse—in terms of harmonic progression and modification of rhythmic motion, tempo, and mood—initiated by the orchestra.

Example 7.55
Piano Concerto in G Minor, Op. 25, First Movement, mm. 246–51

The Andante is a straightforward ABA[1] movement, with a rhythmically animated central section (in V), as is commonly encountered in slow movements of Romantic concertos. The thirty-second-note figuration of this central section is carried over to the reprise of the A-section (abbreviated), by way of variation. The original A-section assumes the tone and design of a typical operatic cavatina, an *aaba*[1] phrase group, of which the principal melody recalls somewhat the mood and manner of Mendelssohn's Op. 15 Fantasy on "The Last Rose of Summer." (The B-section, by contrast, is melodically elusive, and before one can grasp hold of anything like a stable theme, it is already returning to the melody and key of the A-section.)

It appears to be the high-spirited finale, Molto allegro e vivace (see Example 7.56), that is mainly responsible for the lasting popularity of this concerto. The introductory approach into the finale in both concertos is strikingly similar. In both movements this approach is made from tonic minor and minor-inflected dominant prolongation to a lively, major-mode staccato theme in the solo piano, and it would seem that in the later concerto (Op. 40) Mendelssohn deliberately attempted to recapture the tone (and popular success) of the earlier finale. In the Op. 25 finale Mendelssohn succeeded particularly in crossing elements of his individual, antic "scherzo" idiom (see, e.g., mm. 9ff. of the first tutti, Molto allegro e vivace) with the quicksilver, unpretentious virtuosity of Weber's keyboard style to create a unique blend, which the Op. 40 finale does not, finally, quite manage to simulate.[122] The move from the first of these styles to the second—that is, from the principal refrain to the first, extended solo episode—involves a formal witticism appropriate to the tone of the movement as a whole. After the central phrases of the opening group have prolonged the dominant for some time (mm. 55–70), we fully expect

Example 7.56
Piano Concerto in G Minor, Op. 25, Finale, mm. 40–45

the tripping main theme to reappear and round out the group. Instead, the piano immediately launches into the extended "Weber-like" episode, a harmonic-figurational *perpetuum mobile*, which continues to turn back on the tonic rather than establish the dominant or any other new, secondary key.

The rest of the movement is primarily structured as a dialogue between these two elements, the main theme returning in I, V, and I, while the episodic *perpetuum mobile* material does, eventually, initiate some harmonic exploration to B, E minor, and elsewhere. Another surprise, for which the tone of the movement does not prepare us, is the unexpected, momentary reappearance of the second theme from the first movement (*espressivo* and *ritardando*, in G minor) at mm. 219–24, concluding with a hesitant fermata on the dominant. The effect is a wholly Romantic one, in the spirit of Schumann or Jean Paul; one is tempted to think of the melancholy countenance of Schumann's Eusebius intruding momentarily within some exuberant essay by Florestan, whether in prose or music (though Schumann's poetic-critical alter egos were still five years from being born at the time of Mendelssohn's concerto). The C♯ diminished chord (vii°⁷/V) that paves the way for this brief, pensive intrusion, together with the melodic B♭ highlighted at this juncture, might be thought to recall the diminished and minor-mode harmonic inflections of the movement's introduction (cf. mm. 24–38 and 216–18). It would also be possible to trace a "new" derivation of this old theme to the fourth and fifth bars of the finale's main theme (which are heard again fourteen measures before this; see Example 7.57). What seems most important here, though, is the rhetorical-expressive gesture, rather than the revelation of some secret motivic nexus. The music pauses to meditate, for a brief moment, on things past, on

Example 7.57
Piano Concerto in G Minor, Op. 25, Finale

a. mm. 204–8

b. mm. 215–24

not-quite-suppressed sorrows, before plunging headlong back into the octaves, arpeggios, and fleet passage-work à la Weber to effect a suitably brilliant close (a gesture reminiscent—in retrospect, at least—of Violetta's attempt to suppress the strains of Alfredo's "Di quell'amor" as she vows to plunge herself recklessly into the "vortex of voluptuous pleasures" that is Paris).

The D-minor Concerto, Op. 40, follows the general model of the earlier concerto in many particulars, as already suggested. There is no reason to suppose that Mendelssohn himself attached any less, or any more, significance to this work than to the G minor concerto. The two works closely resemble one another with respect to the general musical character of their individual movements, the streamlining of the concerto-sonata form in their first movements, the characteristic "bourgeois-religious lyricism" (as we might call it) of their slow movements, the high-spirited filigree of their finales, and even—as we have seen—the specific techniques used to link these movements together. It is difficult to explain, then, the decided critical bias against the Op. 40 concerto that seems to have emerged sometime since the later nineteenth century (original audiences registered no such discrepancy between the artistic merit of these two concertos, so far as one can tell).

The first movement, Allegro appassionato, is only slightly longer than the extremely compact Molto allegro con fuoco of the G-minor Concerto, whose formal outlines it follows very closely. It certainly bears no closer resemblance to the "empty and superficial brilliance" of the "French salon composers Kalkbrenner, Herz, and Thalberg" (as Eric Werner charges[123]) than does the earlier work. Both of them pad out their bridge and closing sections with ample finger-work in the "brilliant" manner, as does nearly every other concerto of this era; but even Mendelssohn's "brilliant" writing remains relatively clean and restrained (if these be virtues, even in the concerto context). Elsewhere in the first movement and throughout the work the composer's personal identity is unmistakable. The reviewer of this concerto in the *Allgemeine musikalische Zeitung* (see the Historical Views and Documents following this Chapter), far from comparing it unfavorably with Op. 25, took the occasion to discourse at length about Mendelssohn's evenhanded treatment of solo and orchestra in the Classic manner of Mozart and Beethoven, a relationship that he conceptualizes through metaphors of both political and domestic economies of power.[124]

As in Op. 25, the soloist enters the Op. 40 concerto almost immediately, following a brief dramatic (and motivic) flourish in the orchestra. The solo episode that precedes—here, as before—the principal tutti resembles the improvisatory, *a piacere* solo entrances or lead-ins characteristic of Hummel's concertos, where, however, they follow upon full-length orchestral expositions of the movements' complete thematic material. In Op. 40 (again, as in Op. 25) Mendelssohn defers the principal opening tutti until after the initial solo statement. The approach to the second group is handled in an ingenious manner, related to that encountered in the first movement of the A♭ Double Concerto. The frantic sixteenth-note energy of the bridge material dissipates only gradually as the Schumannesque, fragmentary and tonally elusive "second theme" emerges, poised between A minor and C major (mm. 91ff.; the melody, accompaniment, and harmony all resemble, to some extent, the opening of Schumann's Op. 17 *Fantasie*). Only when the "proper" second key area (F major, or III of D minor) is reached in m. 103 does the rhythmic energy of the bridge section finally yield to a more tranquil eighth-note motion. This second theme, with its lulling, repetitive, and circular design, is worked into the bravura display of the closing section (just as the second theme of the Op. 25 first movement had been), in alternation with a motive from the first group. In this closing context it figures in the middle of the texture, shared between the right and left hands in a technique that had been recently "patented" by the then-famous Thalberg in the middle of the 1830s. Despite the extended dominant *Schlußtriller* that articulate the close of the movement, there is again no place made for a formal cadenza to the first movement. As in Op. 25, there is a sense that the function of the cadenza has been displaced to the written-out transition between first and slow movements—an impression that is underlined here by fantasia-like hints of the second theme and by the (albeit modest) set of dominant-seventh arpeggios for the soloist that conclude this transition.

The slow movement (Adagio) is another ABA¹ design, this time with a partially independent orchestral frame. The faintly hymnlike closing phrase of this orchestral frame returns to close both the A and A¹ sections of the solo, in V (F) and in I (B♭), respectively. The second time, after this melody is stated in a majestic fortissimo by the piano, it is repeated quietly to woodwind accompaniment and opens out harmonically, before returning to a tonic cadence and brief coda for the soloist.

The finale begins with the longest of the movement-transitions in Mendelssohn's concertos, moving gradually, though with little difficulty, from G minor (relative minor of the preceding B♭ tonality) to V in D major. The whole of this forty-six-measure transition is based on the staccato eighth-note figure that will form the basis of the *leggiero* main theme in D major, first given out (as expected) by the soloist (see Example 7.58). This finale is another novel hybrid of

Example 7.58
Piano Concerto in D Minor, Op. 40, Finale, mm. 47–50

sonata and rondo elements, now tending more in the direction of rondo. A gently rocking lyrical idea—and a quintessentially Mendelssohnian one, *pace* Werner—emerges in the piano in what sounds like the first episode of a rondo structure or a sonata second theme, although it never really leaves the tonic before issuing back into the main theme or rondo "refrain" again (in I) at m. 147. Another solo episode, based on this principal or refrain theme, does establish the dominant for a short while (mm. 173ff.), after which a developmental section puts both refrain and episode themes through a modulatory development. In the reprise, the lyrical episode theme is suppressed, while the second, refrain-based solo episode is restated in the tonic, tipping the formal scales back in the direction of sonata. The underlying strategy of this omission, as it turns out, is to make room for an extended, codalike return of the lyrical idea (both solo and orchestra collaborating, as before) that will bring the movement to a conclusion at once graceful and suitably emphatic. This last movement is supposed to have been a favorite with Mendelssohn's wife, Cécile (née Jeanrenaud). Her preference may reflect happy associations with the piece, which Mendelssohn composed in the course of the honeymoon sojourn in the countryside of southern and central Germany during the summer of 1837 (it had been commissioned for the Birmingham festival held in September of that year). But from the little that one can glean of the personality and temperament of Cécile—who keeps a rather low profile in the surviving documentary literature—the relaxed good spirits of this movement would be well matched to her character.[125] Like much of Mendelssohn's music, this movement and the concerto as a whole seem to embody a kind of bourgeois social and aesthetic ideal that is not to be disdained: sociable, refined, intelligent, tasteful—not finally remarkable, perhaps, but not banal.

Violin Concerto in E minor, Op. 64

The E-minor Violin Concerto has become such a universally familiar commodity among performers and listeners in the century and a half since its premiere (Leipzig, 13 March 1845) that, more than any other of Mendelssohn's works (the "Wedding March" excepted), it seems almost to have dissociated itself from its composer and to lead an autonomous existence, like some product of nature. One scarcely thinks to compare it with the far less familiar piano concertos, although it shares many of those same formal traits discussed earlier. While the Violin Concerto counts among Mendelssohn's relatively few major "late works," it was initially conceived in 1838, about a year after the composition of the D-minor Piano Concerto. In an often-cited letter of 30 July 1838 to his friend Ferdinand David, recently appointed by Mendelssohn as concertmaster of the Gewandhaus Orchestra, he wrote, "I'd like to do a violin concerto for you for next winter [season]; one in E minor is running through my head, and the opening of it will not leave me in peace." As it happened, however, this work would have to spend a considerable time yet running through the composer's head before it would see the full light of day; not until six years later, at the end of a summer vacation in the countryside near Frankfurt in 1844, was the score of the work completed. It is easy to see how the famous, haunting theme with which the soloist opens this concerto would have lodged itself so tenaciously in Mendelssohn's mind at the start. Several surviving sketch leaves for the first movement demonstrate another reason for that situation: a number of false starts in drafting the principal thematic ideas of the movement. As is so often the case with the process of melodic invention, the difficulty lay not so much in shaping the opening of the idea as with its continuation and rounding off.[126] As is also very common in the genesis of now-canonical violin concertos (Beethoven, Brahms, Tchaikovsky, and others), details of the solo part were worked out in consultation with the player for whom the work was intended, in this case, David. Although Mendelssohn had been an accomplished violinist himself since childhood and had produced no small amount of idiomatic writing for solo violin in his numerous chamber works, the E-minor Violin Concerto is the first piece to place considerable technical demands on the performer, in terms of range, rapid arpeggiation, octaves, extensive double stopping, and the like.

As in the two solo piano concertos, an "introductory" solo precedes the first tutti. In the present case, however, the opening solo has a distinctly thematic function, stating the famous main theme (see Example 7.59) at length, across twenty-four measures, before yielding to the kind of introductory flourishes that might more commonly occupy this position. When the full orchestra restates the theme, it is rounded out by a new, orchestrally conceived continuation (mm. 62–71), leading to a distinctive bridge theme (Example 7.60) that will play an important role throughout the movement, particularly in the coda. The second theme arrives eventually in the expected key of the relative major (G major), but approached circuitously by way of G minor and *its* relative major, B♭. At first the soloist merely accompanies this new theme in the most modest and retiring fashion

Example 7.59
Violin Concerto in E Minor, Op. 64, First Movement, mm. 1–12

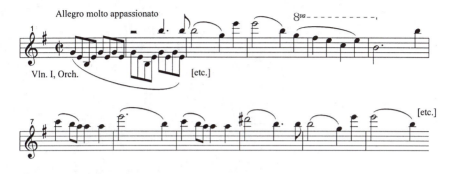

Example 7.60
Violin Concerto in E Minor, Op. 64, First Movement, mm. 73–76

imaginable, holding its low open G string beneath the theme as this is stated—pianissimo and *tranquillo*—by flutes and clarinets. The second theme per se (Example 7.61) also bespeaks modesty and tranquillity, and in this it anticipates something of the character of the slow movement.

The closing of the exposition begins with a restatement of the first theme in G (mm. 168ff.) and culminates in some widely spaced arpeggiations of the G_4^6 chord, which is not finally resolved, however, but leads into a brief, impassioned dialogue between the soloist (main theme) and the orchestra, the latter responding to the soloist with angry-sounding outbursts of *tremolando* chords and trills. The development, after revisiting the bridge idea (marked *agitato* in the solo part), mainly concerns itself with the gradual dismantling of the main theme.

A famous quirk of this movement is the placement of the soloist's cadenza before the recapitulation rather than at the end of it. In this way the cadenza comes to function as a retransition, embellishing the dominant-seventh preparation of the reprise rather than the conventional I_4^6 cadence that articulates the "structural" close of the reprise. Mendelssohn underscores this (re-)transitional function by adapting a device already heard in earlier concertos, overlaying the entrance of a theme (here, the return of the main theme) with figuration carried over, without a break, from the preceding section. In this case the soloist continues with the spiccato arpeggiated chords of the cadenza, which lend a new urgency to the main theme,

Example 7.61
Violin Concerto in E Minor, Op. 64, First Movement, mm. 131–39

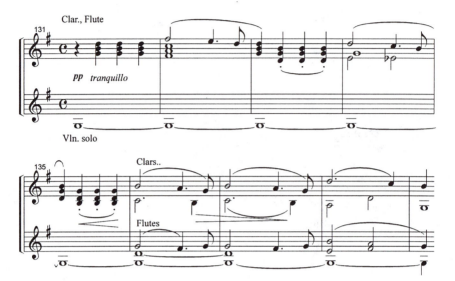

doubling the rhythmic rate of the already rather nervous accompaniment figure (in eighth notes) of the lower orchestral strings. The second theme is quickly arrived at in the recapitulation, now in E major. Instead of a cadenza at the usual juncture (the tonic $^6_4$, here in mm. 453–55), Mendelssohn brings back the "angry" exchange between tutti and solo heard at the analogous point at the close of the exposition. This brief exchange is now followed by a presto coda, based almost entirely on the bridge theme (see Example 7.60), underneath which the incipit of the main theme may be detected by the attentive listener.

While Mendelssohn connected the movements of the Op. 64 Concerto, as he had done in the piano concertos, the first movement comes to a more emphatic conclusion here than it had in the earlier pieces. Here the transition is effected mainly within the new tempo (Andante), picking up from a sustained B in the first bassoon. (Although this B could very easily have been harmonized as the dominant of the initial C pitch and chord of the Andante theme, Mendelssohn chose to create a greater sense of tonal distance between the movements by inserting a four-measure chord progression led by rising half steps.) The familiarity of this Andante might, again, obscure its close structural kinship to the analogous movements of the earlier concertos. As before, a simple—perhaps self-consciously naive—cavatina-like melody in the A-section is contrasted with a rhythmically and harmonically more active middle section. Again, the accompaniment figures (in thirty-second notes) of the central section are carried over into the reprise of the original theme (just the a^1 of the originally aa^1ba^1 group)—although here the accompanimental activity soon fades, as the solo reaches up to the high c^4 that signals the cadence to this group. Unlike the earlier concertos, however, the central contrast in this movement strikes a note of genuine emotional agitation, beyond a mere increase of rhythmic activity.

The brief Allegretto non troppo that serves as a link between slow movement and finale would appear to be designed more as a transition of tempo and mood than simply of key (the dominant of E is reached already in the fourth measure). It also recalls the shape and character of the first movement theme, without literally reproducing it. The finale proper opens with a brief, twofold fanfare in the brass and winds, from which emerges the sprightly, *leggiero* main theme in the solo violin. The combined effect of this mercurial theme and the accompanying staccato chords in upper woodwinds has often elicited comparison with the world of the *Midsummer Night's Dream* music (a resemblance possibly reinforced by the E-major tonality). The shape of the principal thematic period suggests a rondo, but as in the preceding concertos, the movement unfolds in something closer to a traditional sonata form. The second theme is a marchlike figure (more shades of *Midsummer?*) presented by the full orchestra, with fragments of the main theme interspersed. The end of the exposition is scarcely articulated (by now a common phenomenon in Mendelssohn's concerto movements). The development, after working first and second themes through a variety of keys, introduces a discrete new theme, first in the solo (in G) and then in the orchestra (in B), both times in counterpoint to the main theme as it is developed in the other parts. At the point of recapitulation this new, dignified processional theme is stated in the tonic, against the original solo theme in the violin (see Example 7.62).

The recapitulation is dominated by the marchlike second theme up to the cadenza-point at m. 832 (counting continuously across the concerto). One again, Mendelssohn suppressed a full-scale cadenza (the first-movement cadenza remains an exception in his oeuvre of concerted works, not only for its placement but even for its presence at all). A series of violin trills ushers in a brief appearance of the main theme, in its "elfin" scoring of staccato flutes and clarinets, followed by a coda (mm. 855ff.) on the march theme, which is accompanied here by energetic repeated-note figures and double stops in the solo part.

There is, of course, no reason to imagine that Mendelssohn could have regarded this concerto as the last of his orchestral works, as it was to become upon his premature death in 1847. All the same, it seems fitting, if fortuitous, that it should combine one of his most serious and personal orchestral movements (the opening Allegro) with a nostalgic return to the world of *A Midsummer Night's Dream* in the finale—the world of Mendelssohn's "enchanted youth" and the music that, more than any other, epitomizes his contribution to the history of music.

Other Concerted Works

Some mention should be made, finally, of three single-movement concerted works for piano and orchestra composed in the 1830s: a *Capriccio brillant* in B minor, Op. 22 (1832), a *Rondo brillant* in E♭, Op. 29 (1834), and a *Serenade and*

Example 7.62
Violin Concerto in E Minor, Op. 64, Finale, mm. 147–51

Allegro giojoso, Op. 43 (1838). These works have received scant attention in the Mendelssohn literature,[127] and only the first of them (op. 22) has maintained any kind of presence in the concert repertoire through this century. As the appellations "brilliant" and "joyous" in the titles suggest, these are relatively light fare, the kind of piece that the traveling virtuoso of Mendelssohn's day could depend on to secure him or her a favorable reception from most audiences. Yet all three works can be favorably compared to the two solo piano concertos with regard to style and substance, and the *Serenade and Allegro*, in particular, deserves to be better known.

   Like the later *Serenade and Allegro*, the Op. 22 *Capriccio brillant* begins with a cantabile introduction, set at first to a strummed (arpeggiated), "serenade-like" accompaniment. The manner in which the B-major cantabile theme is superimposed over a series of chords first heard unaccompanied and unadorned in the solo piano suggests a kind of improvised prelude, to which the orchestra gradually lends its discreet support. A prolonged dominant lead-in (mm. 24–42) to the main movement, in the new tempo, recalls similar transitional lead-ins to the finales of the G-minor and D-minor Piano Concertos. As in the concerto finales, the principal theme of the Allegro con fuoco is presented by the soloist. The marchlike second theme in D major is the only important idea to be played by the orchestra at all in this work, where Mendelssohn seems to have been at pains to keep demands on the orchestra to a minimum. (Perhaps he sensed that works of this genre were likely to be programmed with little—if any—rehearsal time allotted to the orchestra.) A brief and efficient development alternates and then combines the "brilliant" main theme and marchlike secondary theme before leading back to an abbreviated recapitulation. This time the soloist is given the second theme, as well, now in B major, pianissimo and *leggiero*. This hushed version of the second group provides an effective foil for a new and newly energized closing group (mm. 271ff.) and coda in the "brilliant" style, punctuated throughout by allusions to the march rhythm in the orchestra. Something of a surprise in a work of this style and genre is the minor-mode ending, despite the integration of the (originally major-mode) march theme within the coda.

The *Rondo brillant* in E♭, Op. 29, was dedicated to Mendelssohn's close friend Ignaz Moscheles, who performed it at a Gewandhaus concert in Leipzig in 1835 and again at the Mendelssohn family house in Berlin (with Felix accompanying on a second piano) shortly thereafter. The Rondo is a sprightly affair in ⁶⁄₈, kicked off by a fanfare motive in the horn and woodwinds, followed by flourish on the piano. The refrain includes two ideas, of which the second—a sparkling string of staccato eighth-notes ignited by a swift scalar anacrusis—comes to predominate the piece. Other material includes a legato B-theme in the dominant (B♭) in slower rhythms and a middle or C-section in the relative minor, including some brief fugal development and fragmentary combinations of material from the main (A) themes. Internal recurrences of the second, staccato A-theme involve much rapid scalar writing for the piano, while the flute and other instruments take over the bouncing eighth notes of the theme itself. An extended coda based on both A-themes includes a surprise move from E♭ to C shortly before the conclusion, which is brought back around to the tonic E♭ by circle-of-fifths motion.

The introductory "serenade" of the Op. 43 *Serenade and Allegro giojoso* is based on an attractive, somewhat wistful tune in B minor (see Example 7.63). Its

Example 7.63
Serenade and Allegro giojoso, Op. 43, mm. 1–4

simplicity of tone and the slight modal equivocation in the second part of its opening phrase give it something of the flavor of a pseudoantique *romanza* or *chanson gothique*. This character is enhanced when, after a florid central episode, the tune returns in the solo flute, while the piano continues with its decorative embellishments. The somewhat operatic tone of this opening section—reminiscent of the sentimental ballades and romances of early Romantic *opéra comique*—is reinforced by the dramatic, syncopated agitations of the following transitional material, beginning with a diminished seventh chord in the manner of accompanied recitative or *scena*. These dramatic gestures are ironically belied, however, by the saucy insouciance of the D-major Allegro giojoso, whose opening idea seems to be derived, at some remove, from a prominent cadential motive of the earlier serenade (compare Examples 7.64a and b).

Example 7.64
Serenade and Allegro giojoso, Op. 43

a. Cadential idea of Serenade

b. Main idea of Allegro

The soloist indulges in the usual brilliant-style passagework in the bridge and continues this beneath the legato second theme. A simple and rhythmically vigorous closing idea in the orchestra, however, preempts the brilliant solo figuration that so often figures in this position in other concerted works. If the stylistic signals of the introduction ("serenade") and transition had suggested the operatic domain, the Allegro could be interpreted as responding not with another vocal model but with that of an overture, at least formally. Following the common scheme of the early Romantic Italian operatic *sinfonia*, the Allegro returns almost immediately to the reprise of its main idea, after a merely perfunctory development of its closing theme. The reprise proceeds directly to the vigorous, marchlike closing idea in the tonic, while the second theme is reserved for further treatment in the coda.

The tone of this Allegro is uniformly vivacious, even flippant—close kin to the popular finale of the G-minor Concerto. (The composite effect of melancholy introduction and jolly finale also recalls Weber's influential F-minor *Konzertstück*.) Like the *Rondo brillant*, Op. 43 aspires to nothing more than providing cultivated entertainment. In their jovial directness, both works make a nice foil to the quasi-pathetic rhetorical posturings of some of the other concerted works, such as the first movements of the two solo piano concertos or even the main Allegro of the *Capriccio brillant*. Here we seem to witness the quick-witted, humorous side of the composer so often manifested in the correspondence—a biographical point that likewise serves as an appropriate foil to the familiar, but one-sided, notion of Mendelssohn as a primly decorous exemplar of bourgeois piety. In music like this we hear Mendelssohn conversing musically, as it were, with professional friends such as Moscheles or Hiller, unconcerned, for the moment, with any of those imposing figures from the past or present—Bach or Beethoven, Goethe or Tieck, Friedrich Wilhelm IV of Prussia or Queen Victoria, or his own father, Abraham—with whom Mendelssohn was otherwise so often obliged to contend, both in his life and in his music.

NOTES

1. This familiar trajectory of early genius and subsequent decline is revisited and, to a large extent, revalidated, in Greg Vitercek's recent volume *The Early Works of Felix Mendelssohn: A Study in the Romantic Sonata Style* (Philadelphia: Gordon and Breach, 1992).

2. Letter of 19 October 1821 to Henriette von Pereira-Arnstein, cited by H. C. Wolff in *Leipziger Ausgabe der Werke Felix Mendelssohn Bartholdys*, ser. 1, vol. 1 (Leipzig: Deutscher Verlag für Musik, 1972), v.

3. A large collection of exercises Mendelssohn carried out under Zelter's tutelage between September 1819 and January 1821 (Oxford, Bodleian Library MS Margaret Deneke Mendelssohn C. 43) has been transcribed and analyzed by R. Larry Todd in *Mendelssohn's Musical Education* (Cambridge: Cambridge University Press, 1983).

4. The chorale tune of this trio movement seems not yet to have been identified with any traditional, texted Lutheran chorale. It bears a strong family likeness to two chorale themes that appear in Mendelssohn's student exercises: one is an original, ornamented setting of a text by C. F. Gellert ("Erinnere dich mein Geist"); the other, an untexted chorale tune set in four voices, without embellishment (see the transcriptions of these in Todd, *Mendelssohn's Musical Education*, 141–42, 167).

5. Mendelssohn had begun an arrangement of Mozart's "Jupiter" Symphony (K. 551) for piano duet in 1821, which is preserved in the Mendelssohn Archive of the Staatsbibliothek zu Berlin—Preussischer Kulturbesitz.

6. The manuscript is dated 29 December, but the year has been cut off, leaving the question open as to whether this was the last such work composed (at the end of 1823), or whether it might date from the end of the previous year. H. C. Wolff argues that its position in the bound volume of manuscripts suggests a late date (see *Leipziger Ausgabe* ser. 1, vol. 1, p. vi), and stylistically it does resemble movements from Sinfonias XI and XII—if not necessarily to its advantage.

7. For this performance Mendelssohn substituted an orchestral arrangement of the scherzo from his Octet for strings (Op. 20) in place of the minuet. Mendelssohn himself evidently valued this remarkable movement as highly as have later generations and wished to put his best foot forward on this auspicious occasion. This arrangement of the Octet scherzo still exists and has been transcribed by Wulf Konold in *Die Symphonien Felix Mendelssohn Bartholdys* (Laaber: Laaber-Verlag, 1992), 438–77. Konold has argued, incidentally, that the First Symphony had been previously performed (with its original minuet rather than the scherzo arrangement) not only in Leipzig in 1827—which has been

generally known—but possibly at one of the Mendelssohn family musicales on 14 November 1824 (Fanny Mendelssohn's birthday) and again in an 1825 public concert in Berlin under Louis Maurer (p. 40). In one or both of these earlier cases, however, it is also possible that the orchestral arrangement of the eighth string symphony was the work in question.

8. See also Konold, *Die Symphonien Felix Mendelssohn Bartholdys*, 54–55, 78. While Konold stresses the "operatic" (overture-like) dramatization of the move into the coda of the first movement and the "noisy" theatrical character of the conclusions of the first and fourth movements, his observation could well be extended to describe the thematic material in the first movement as a whole.

9. One might relate the repercussive ♭6–5 motion across this crescendo with what Greg Vitercik identifies as a motivic "cell" of the movement as a whole: g–a♭ (and d♭–c) within the main theme, and the same pitches, reinterpreted as 3–4 of E♭, within the second theme (Vitercik, *The Early Works of Felix Mendelssohn*, 54–55, 60), although it seems to me that these motivic gestures should sooner be attributed to the general stylistic vocabulary on which Mendelssohn is drawing here. It might be noted, on the other hand, that this half-step "cell" does figure audibly in the beginning of the coda, partly at the original g–a♭ pitches, and is introduced as a prominent, expressive "sighing" gesture within the solo clarinet melody of the second theme in the finale (mm. 53–56).

10. Eric Werner, *Mendelssohn: A New Image of the Composer and his Age* (New York: Free Press of Glencoe, 1963), 61; Konold, *Die Symphonien Felix Mendelssohn Bartholdys*, 65. Konold also describes some of the common traits shared by this minuet and that of Mozart's K. 550 (p. 61).

11. See Werner, *Mendelssohn: A New Image*, 26; Todd, *Mendelssohn's Musical Education*, 84.

12. The high opus number of the Fifth Symphony (Op. 107), which might appear to confirm its illusory numbering as the last symphony, is rather a result of its posthumous publication in 1868 (by Simrock in Bonn), seventeen years after the similarly posthumous publication of the Fourth or "Italian" Symphony (Leipzig: Breitkopf and Härtel, 1851).

13. The Leipzig festivities occurred on 24 June, just one day from the date of the Augsburg Confession (recognized as an annual feast day in the Lutheran liturgical calendar) and coinciding also with the feast of St. John, the occasion for the civic musical festivities of Wagner's Nuremberg masters. Midsummer's Day was apparently and understandably perceived as a propitious time for such *völkisch* gatherings. The complicated biographical circumstances surrounding the conception and early fate of the "Reformation" Symphony have been scrutinized in detail by Judith Silber in her article "Mendelssohn and His *Reformation* Symphony," *Journal of the American Musicological Society* 60 (1987), 310–36. Silber argues convincingly that Mendelssohn by no means gave up on the cause of the symphony as readily as has generally been supposed and that his eventual disavowal of the work was the product of an even greater series of personal frustrations and defeats than previously recognized.

14. See Judith Silber Ballan's discussion of Marx and his possible influences on Mendelssohn's works between about 1825 and 1830, "Marxian Programmatic Music: A Stage in Mendelssohn's Musical Development," in *Mendelssohn Studies*, ed. R. Larry Todd (Cambridge: Cambridge University Press, 1992), 149–61.

15. Leon Botstein, "The Aesthetics of Assimilation and Affirmation: Reconstructing the Career of Felix Mendelssohn," in *Mendelssohn and his World*, ed. R. Larry Todd (Princeton: Princeton University Press, 1991), 5–42.

16. Letters of 2 and 10 September 1829 to the Mendelssohn family in Berlin, in Sebastian Hensel, *Die Familie Mendelssohn* (Berlin: Georg Reimer, 1918), 1: 300, 304. See also Silber, "Mendelssohn and His *Reformation* Symphony," 314ff.

17. Ferdinand Hiller, *Mendelssohn: Letters and Recollections*, trans. M. E. von Glehn (London, 1874; repr. New York, 1972), 21–22 (the verdict reported by Cuvillon is cited from Hiller's memoirs, as well).

18. Letter of 1838 to Julius Rietz ("Die Reformations-Symphonie kann ich gar nicht mehr ausstehen, möchte sie lieber verbrennen, als irgend meiner Stücke, soll niemals herauskommen"). Max Friedländer, "Ein Brief Felix Mendelssohns," *Vierteljahrsschrift für Musikwissenschaft* 5 (1889), 484, gives the date as 11 February, and Konold (p. 99) follows him; Eric Werner, however, dates the letter 20 June (*Mendelssohn: A New Image*, 225, n. 33).

19. "Mendelssohn and His *Reformation* Symphony," 322–23. Perhaps more likely is the other thesis offered here, that a full-length instrumental symphony simply had no place in the kind of ceremonial activities arranged for this occasion. Furthermore, Eduard Grell was Mendelssohn's senior by nine years and had official ties to some of the organizations involved in this event.

20. Konold, *Die Symphonien*, 108.

21. Alfred Heuss, "Das 'Dresdner Amen' im ersten Satz von Mendelssohns Reformations-Sinfonie," *Signale für die musikalische Welt* 62 (1904), 281ff. Why Eric Werner asserts that the phrase "would be familiar to all Protestant church musicians"—rather than Catholic ones—is not immediately evident; see *Mendelssohn: Leben und Werk in neuer Sicht* (Zurich: Atlantis, 1980), 243.

22. Konold, *Die Symphonien*, 108.

23. Judith Silber Ballan points out this implicit broad narrative trajectory in discussing the possible role of A. B. Marx on the "programmatic" or characteristic conception of this symphony, among other larger works of the 1826–1830 period ("Marxian Programmatic Music").

24. Hermann Kretzschmar states that the "first movement is devoted to the serious religious side of the Reformation itself, its combative (*streitbaren*) nature, its joyful readiness for the fight, its firmness of faith and trust in God." The fanfare-motive of the introduction, he notes, "resounds through the movement like the secure call of the watchman through the night." See Hermann Kretzschmar, *Führer durch den Konzertsaal* (Leipzig, 1932), 1: 328.

25. Kretzschmar calls the movement an evocation of the Reformation as a historical period, "a musical embodiment of simple, grandfatherly (*altväterisch*), plain and energetic merriment" (ibid., 329). Wulf Konold dismisses this notion as irrelevant and "unwittingly comical," but one suspects that Kretzschmar's stock of historical-musical imagery was more in tune with Mendelssohn's than Konold cares to believe.

26. Unpublished letter of 15 June 1830 to Rebecca Mendelssohn Bartholdy, cited in Silber, "Mendelssohn and His *Reformation* Symphony," 327.

27. The original ending of the Andante is transcribed by Konold in *Die Symphonien*, 365–68.

28. Werner, *Mendelssohn: A New Image*, 218.

29. Wulf Konold, "Opus 11 und Opus 107: Analytische Bemerkungen zu zwei unbekannten [*sic*] Sinfonien Felix Mendelssohn Bartholdys," in *Musik-Konzepte* 14/15, ed. H.-K. Metzger and R. Riehn (Munich: Text + Kritik, 1980), 28.

30. Philip Radcliffe, *Mendelssohn* (London: Dent, 1954; 3d ed., 1976), 105.

31. Carl Dahlhaus, *Nineteenth-Century Music*, trans. J. Bradford Robinson (Berkeley and Los Angeles: University of California Press, 1989), 156.

32. Letter to Karl Klingemann of 21 July 1840, *Felix Mendelssohn Bartholdys Briefwechsel mit Karl Klingemann*, ed. K. Klingemann (Essen: G. D. Baedeker, 1909), 245. (The last phrase of the passage quoted is originally in English.)

33. Ibid. "Composed on the words" is meant here in a general sense, of course. Mendelssohn's response to the title "symphony-cantata" occurs in the letter of 18 November 1840 (p. 251). The reference to twelve vocal numbers here may be puzzling at first, since Mendelssohn later claimed to have *added* "three new pieces" to the work when he revived it for a Leipzig Gewandhaus concert the following December, while this final version contains only *nine* vocal numbers (as published). In fact, Mendelssohn both added to and subtracted from the vocal portion of the work in the course of its composition; the three numbers he "added" to the final version were actually replacements, while the revised *Schlußchor* ("Ihr Völker . . . Alles was Odem hat") was counted as a single number, where it had earlier been divided in two. The crucial element among these later changes was the addition (substitution) of the climactic tenor recitative "Wir riefen in die Finsternis." On the evolution of the autograph score and musical content, see Douglass Seaton, Vorwort to Felix Mendelssohn Bartholdy, *Lobgesang*, op. 52 (Stuttgart: Carus, 1990), vi–vii.

34. A later critic, in discussing generic issues of symphony versus cantata or oratorio with respect to Berlioz's *Roméo et Juliette*, noted precisely this conceptual foundation of Mendelssohn's generic hybrid: "With Mendelssohn [the *Lobgesang* symphony-cantata] the transition from one form into the other is the very *idea itself*. Not merely the instruments alone—the voices of unconscious creation—are meant to sing God's praises, but 'all that has life and breath.'" Wilhelm Wauer, "Die Form der 'dramatischen Symphonie' *Romeo und Julie* von Hector Berlioz," *Deutsche Musik-Zeitung* 1/19 (1860), 147.

35. Letter to Schubring of 25 February 1840, *Briefwechsel zwischen Felix Mendelssohn Bartholdy und Julius Schubring* (Leipzig: Duncker & Humblot, 1892), 160. Mendelssohn had, in fact, contributed another, purely occasional work, a *Festgesang* for male chorus, to be performed outdoors in the main square of Leipzig. By chance, this work has also managed to outlive its original occasion: in composing a new text for the second number of this piece, one Dr. W. H. Cummings ensured its immortality as "Hark, the Herald Angels Sing."

36. The role of this imagery of "darkness-to-light" in *Lobgesang* and a parallel view of Mendelssohn's own gradual "enlightenment" with regard to the role of this conceptual theme as the crux of his work are discussed by Douglass Seaton in "Darkness to Light: Emerging Revelation in the Content and Composition of Mendelssohn's *Lobgesang* (Symphony no. 2), Op. 52," paper delivered at the Annual Meeting of the American Musicological Society, Southern Chapter, Nashville, TN, 11 March 1988.

37. Mention of a "symphony in B♭" occurs in letters of 15 July and 17 August 1838 to Ferdinand Hiller and of 4 April 1839 to Ignaz Moscheles. The latter two letters clearly state that the symphony is in progress, and the Moscheles letter implies that it is well under way. The question of this projected symphony in B♭ and its relation to Op. 52 (*Lobgesang*), as well as some possible sketches pertaining to it are discussed in Seaton's dissertation, "A Study of a Collection of Mendelssohn's Sketches and Other Autograph Material, Deutsche Staatsbibliothek, Berlin, Mus. Ms. Autogr. Mendelssohn 19 (Ph.D. diss., Columbia University, 1977)," esp. pp. 107ff.

38. Seaton ("A Study of a Collection of Mendelssohn's Sketches") notes that the earliest sketch material preserved in the Berlin autograph collection (*Mendelssohn Nachlaß*, volume 19) does indeed correspond to the material of the present first movement *without* the vocal motto. This would seem to confirm the hypothesis that Mendelssohn grafted the motto-theme onto a symphonic allegro that had been at least partially conceived without it.

39. Radcliffe, *Mendelssohn*, 128.

40. "F. Mendelssohn-Bartholdy, *Lobgesang* [etc.], op. 52" (anon. review), *Neue Zeitschrift für Musik*, 16/47 (1842), 186.

41. One possible exception to this claim is the similarity of the agitated accompaniment figure of the B-section or modulating group (mm. 35ff.) to that heard across the beginning of the first chorus (no. 2. "Alles was Odem hat").

42. Gustav Schilling, Review of Mendelssohn's *Lobgesang*, Op. 52, in *Jahrbücher des deutschen National-Vereins für Musik und ihre Wissenschaft* 3 (1841), 281–84; Adolf Bernhard Marx, "Die Form der Symphonie-Cantate, auf Anlass von Beethoven's neunter Symphonie," *Allgemeine musikalische Zeitung* (hereafter AmZ), 49/29 (1847), cols. 496–98.

43. *Neue Zeitschrift für Musik* 16/47 (1842), 186.

44. "*Lobgesang*, eine Symphonie-Cantate . . ." (anon. review), *AmZ* 44/9 (1842), col. 209.

45. See Konold, *Die Symphonien*, 103. On the representation of social and aesthetic ideals in the early nineteenth-century music-festival culture in Germany, see Glenn Stanley, "Bach's *Erbe*: The Chorale in the German Oratorio of the Early Nineteenth Century," *19th-Century Music* 11/2 (Fall 1987), 121–49; Cecelia Hopkins Porter, "The New Public and the Reordering of the Musical Establishment: The Lower-Rhine Music Festivals, 1818–67," *19th-Century Music* 3/3 (March 1980), 211–24.

46. In choosing the major and minor modes of the same tonic (A) for these two symphonies, there is some sense that Mendelssohn could have understood them as a complementary pair of dark and light character, the one dominated by a misty, brooding tone and a feeling for the past, the other by clarity, light, and a joy in the present.

47. Felix Mendelssohn, *Reisebriefe aus den Jahren 1830–1832*, ed. Paul Mendelssohn Bartholdy (Leipzig: Hermann Mendelssohn, 1865), 126.

48. Ibid., 127.

49. Cited in John Michael Cooper, "'Aber eben dieser Zweifel': A New Look at Mendelssohn's 'Italian' Symphony," *19th-Century Music* 13/3 (1992), 171. See also pp. 170–72 for a fuller account of the correspondence relating to the genesis and first performance of the symphony. More extensive discussion may be found in John Michael Cooper, "Felix Mendelssohn Bartholdy and the *Italian* Symphony: Historical, Musical, and Extramusical Perspectives" (Ph.D. diss., Duke University, 1994).

50. The unpublished revisions to movements 2–4 of op. 90 and the evidence surrounding them are discussed in detail by Michael Cooper, "'Aber eben dieser Zweifel,'" pp. 176–86, and more extensively in his dissertation, "Felix Mendelssohn Bartholdy and the *Italian* Symphony."

51. See her letter responding to revisions in the slow movement, in Marcia J. Citron, *The Letters of Fanny Hensel to Felix Mendelssohn* (Stuyvesant, NY: Pendragon, 1987), 473.

52. Letter to his family of 8 February 1831; *Reisebriefe*, 119–23. The letter is cited in some older program notes on the symphony, such as those by Philip Hale (Boston Symphony) and Lawrence Gilman (*New York Tribune*) in connection with the "saltarello" finale. Given the rustic and southern Italian associations of the dance type evoked here (really more a tarantella), its connection to the urban carnival scene of 1830s Rome seems mistaken, even if one concedes the relevance of this image to the character of the symphony as a whole or to the first movement.

53. Interestingly, Mendelssohn seems to have contemplated at some stage of the work's genesis introducing the "new" development theme into the exposition, in the analogous position to its incursion here in the recapitulation, that is, at the end of the second group and before the closing material. (In the exposition this would have occurred in E minor.) This version is contained among the fragmentary materials for the first, third, and fourth movements in the Bodleian Library autograph Oxford MS. M. Deneke Mendelssohn b. 5 (fols. 136ʳ–46ʳ), which represent, John Michael Cooper argues, "a late reworking of the first complete version of the score." Some of these revisions were incorporated into the "first"

final version of 1833, but others (such as this passage in the exposition) were not. See Cooper, "'Aber eben dieser Zweifel,'" 176–81, and the second chapter of his dissertation cited in note 49 (pp. 67–163).

54. Letter to Abraham Mendelssohn Bartholdy of 15 February 1831, cited from *Felix Mendelssohn: A Life in Letters*, ed. Rudolf Elvers, trans. Craig Tomlinson (New York: Fromm International, 1986), 154.

55. D. F. Tovey, *Symphonies and Other Orchestral Music* (New York: Oxford University Press, 1989), 393.

56. Ibid.; Konold, *Die Symphonien*, 276.

57. Werner, *Mendelssohn: A New Image*, 268; Konold, *Die Symphonien*, 275. This resemblance supports a hypothesis that the movement—were it conceived as late as the time of Zelter's death in May 1832—may have been intended as a memorial to Mendelssohn's teacher.

58. A. W. Ambros, *Die Grenzen der Musik und Poesie* (Leipzig: Matthes, 1855), 176.

59. Ambros's reference to "Grotta Ferrata and old stations of the cross" suggests that he has in mind images familiar from landscape scenes produced by the numerous German painters active in Rome and its environs across the first half of the nineteenth century—painters such as Joseph Anton Koch, Ernst Fries, Karl Philipp Fohr, Friedrich Olivier, Franz Horny, Julius Schnorr von Carolsfeld, all of whom produced countless sketches, drawings, and paintings of such scenes in the Roman *campagna*.

60. Concert review in the *Rheinische Musikzeitung für Kunstfreunde und Künstler* 2 (1851–52), 566. The verb in the last clause here—*vorüberwallen*—specifically implies a passing pilgrims' procession. In an essay on "modern program music" from 1855, Richard Pohl (a member of the Liszt circle in Weimar) spoke of the A-major symphony as being "so aptly called the 'Italian' [Symphony] by the public" and asserted that "almost every listener today knows that [Mendelssohn] had in mind a musical depiction of a pilgrims' march" in the Andante con moto; see his "Moderne Programm-Musik," in *Hector Berlioz: Studien und Erinnerungen* (Leipzig: B. Schlicke, 1884), 89. Ignaz Moscheles seems to have suggested (on what authority is not clear) that the movement's melody had been inspired by a Bohemian (?) pilgrims' song; his assertion may simply reflect his own response to the stylistic association evoked here or to what he had heard others say about the movement. See W. A. Lampadius, *Felix Mendelssohn Bartholdy* (Leipzig: F. E. C. Leuckart, 1886), 190.

61. Konold, for one, writes: "Any programmatic attribution—beyond the alllusion to the Zelter song—must fail here; Mendelssohn was not concerned with musical 'depiction,' but with form-immanent plasticity and a harmonious, individual movement structure" (*Die Symphonien*, 282).

62. Mendelssohn remarked around this time (in a letter of 16 November 1830) that he was thinking of turning Goethe's poem, "Lilis Park," into a scherzo for a symphony (*Reisebriefe*, 60). The remark has been associated with the A-major symphony because of its chronological proximity; but a cursory glance at Goethe's fanciful poem, about a Circe-like "enchantress" who rules over a menagerie symbolizing her many amorous conquests, will show that, despite whatever potential the material might have for inspiring a musical scherzo, the present movement could hardly be the result.

63. *Rheinische Musikzeitung* 2 (1851–1852), 566.

64. Ambros, *Die Grenzen der Musik und Poesie*, 176.

65. Peter Rummenhöller, *Romantik in der Musik: Analysen, Portraits, Reflexionen* (Kassel: Bärenreiter, 1989), 124.

66. See, for example, Koch's painting *Winzerfest bei Olevano* (Neue Pinakothek, Munich), which depicts a wine harvest with figures dancing a "saltarello" in the background.

67. The "saltarello" to which Mendelssohn refers is distinct from the courtly dance-type of the Renaissance, which had since died out. In the eighteenth and nineteenth centuries the name was taken over by a lively folk dance in triple or compound meter that developed at first in the area around Rome, typically involving a strummed instrument and tambourine. The rhythmic-melodic ideas of Mendelssohn's movement may well have been inspired by dance music that he had encountered under that name, but they are essentially indistinguishable from the more common "tarantella" that one finds in a wide variety of virtuoso, salon, and ballet music and other contexts throughout the century.

68. Sebastian Hensel, *Die Familie Mendelssohn*, 1: 268.

69. Just how far Mendelssohn progressed with the symphony during the first period of its gestation, between 1829 and 1831, and how much was first conceived only later, when he returned to the symphony around 1840, is now almost impossible to determine. Douglass Seaton has discussed a page of single-line sketches, in one to four parts, for the exposition of the first movement ("A Draft for the Exposition of the First Movement of Mendelssohn's 'Scotch' Symphony," *Journal of the American Musicological Society* 30/1 [1977], 129–35). On the basis of the contents of the autograph miscellany in which the page is to be found, Seaton suggests a date of sometime later than 1834. If this is true, we would probably have to assume that during the original phase of its genesis the "Scottish" Symphony had scarcely progressed beyond ideas for the slow introduction or, at least, that any further ideas either had not yet been committed to paper or have since been lost.

70. Hans Christoph Worbs, *Felix Mendelssohn Bartholdy in Selbstzeugnissen und Bilddokumenten* (Reinbek bei Hamburg: Rowohlt, 1974), 99.

71. Anonymous review of the 3 March 1842 premiere in the Leipzig Gewandhaus, *AmZ* 44 (1842), col. 258; A[ugust] K[ahlert], "Felix Mendelssohn Bartholdy, Symphonie No. 3, Op. 56 [etc.]," *AmZ* 45 (1853), cols. 342–43; review of a Prague concert, *AmZ* 47 (1845), col. 562. References to a "ballad tone" in the modern literature include Worbs, *Felix Mendelssohn Bartholdy*, 98, and Carl Dahlhaus, *Nineteenth-Century Music* (Berkeley: University of California Press, 1989), 157.

72. Ambros, *Die Grenzen der Musik und Poesie*, 134.

73. Richard Wagner, "Das Judentum in der Musik" (1850), *Gesammelte Schriften und Dichtungen*, vol. 5 (Leipzig: Fritzsch, 1887), 79–80.

74. This character of a choral song of thanks or victory was clearly still palpable almost a century later for Erich Wolfgang Korngold, who used the music of this coda in setting just such a "victory chorus" (celebrating Duke Theseus's subjugation of the Amazon women and his bride, Hippolyta) in the score he concocted for Max Reinhardt's 1936 MGM film of Shakespeare's *Midsummer Night's Dream*.

75. Unpublished letter (New York Public Library), cited from R. Larry Todd, "Of Sea Gulls and Counterpoint: The Early Versions of Mendelssohn's *Hebrides* Overture," *19th-Century Music* 2/3 (1979), 203 (translation slightly amended).

76. See R. Larry Todd, *Mendelssohn: "The Hebrides" and Other Overtures* (Cambridge: Cambridge University Press, 1993), 26–27.

77. An intriguing, if probably fortuitous, parallel to the tonal design of Mendelssohn's exposition may be found in J. N. Hummel's overture to a musical "fairy play" entitled *The Ass's Skin, or the Blue Island (Die Eselshaut, oder die blaue Insel)*, which premiered in Vienna in 1814 and was revived in 1827. Hummel's overture begins with a slow introduction (Larghetto pastorale) in E major, followed by an allegro in *alla breve* time, E minor, with a scampering, stepwise accompaniment in staccato eighth notes in the strings. The major-mode bridge includes some (admittedly generic) horn-call motifs, but there seems to be no explicit attempt to evoke the titular animal here. A piano score of the overture is

reproduced in J. N. Hummel, *The Complete Works for Piano*, vol. 6, ed. Joel Sachs (New York and London: Garland, 1989).

78. Marx's account of his influence on the *Midsummer Night's Dream* overture can be found (in translation) in "From the Memoirs of Adolf Bernhard Marx," trans. Susan Gillespie, in *Mendelssohn and His World*, 216–17. Marx implies that, except for the chromatic idea from the second group (E–D♯–D♮–C♯), all the thematic material after the introductory chords and E-minor first group was newly invented in response to his demand for a more pointed characterization. Todd notes that an undated, incomplete autograph of the overture preserved in the Bodleian Library does, indeed, diverge from the final version with the first E major tutti at what is now m. 62 (*"The Hebrides" and other Overtures*, 13–14). See also Silber Ballan, "Marxian Programmatic Music," 149–54.

79. Letter of 15 February 1833 to Breitkopf and Härtel; translation (amended) from Todd, *"The Hebrides" and Other Overtures*, 72.

80. The parallel continues, for just as Titania appears next, with Bottom and the fairies, in act 4, so does the elfin music follow in the overture, as recapitulation. The versatile introductory chords perform here a scenic-musical elision (act 3 into act 4, development into reprise) so deft and "natural" that there is no hint of any imposed programmatic scenario. One might further note how, just as Bottom forms a comic, incongruous dissonance amid Titania and her fairy train, so Mendelssohn has introduced several incongruous, sustained tones in the bassoon, horn, and ophicleide (down to its lowest B) beneath the recapitulated elfin music.

81. In the later incidental music Mendelssohn confirmed a connection between the specific "hunting call" topic at the close of the exposition and the hunting party of Theseus and Hippolyta in act 4 (also confirmed in his letter to Breitkopf and Härtel), although the possible connotations of the sustained notes in the horns in the development remain open.

82. Along these same lines Franz Liszt likened the effect of the introductory chords to the "drooping eyelids" of the (imaginary) dreaming subject; if Shakespeare's play is itself the representation of a "dream," then the opening and closing chord-series portray the boundaries of that dreaming state. This conception is particularly apt for the musical rendition of the play (as overture), which necessarily takes place on an "interior" stage of the imagination, rather than before our empirical "waking" eyes. See Franz Liszt, *Sämtliche Schriften*, vol. 5, *Dramaturgische Blätter*, ed. Dorothea Redepenning and Britta Schilling (Wiesbaden: Breitkopf & Härtel, 1989), 25: "Die Akkorde der Bläser am Anfang und Schluß sind wie leise sinkende und wieder sich hebende Augenlider, und ist zwischen diesem Sinken und Heben eine anmuthige Traumwelt der lieblichsten Contraste gestellt."

83. See Silber Ballan, "Marxian Programmatic Music," 158–59.

84. For a more detailed discussion of Goethe's poems in relation to Mendelssohn's overture, see Lawrence Kramer, "*Felix culpa*: Goethe and the Image of Mendelssohn," in *Mendelssohn Studies*, ed. R. Larry Todd (Cambridge: Cambridge University Press, 1992), 68–76.

85. Todd describes this eight-page draft, preserved in the Bodleian collection of autograph materials, in *"The Hebrides" and Other Overtures*, 23–25. Though the manuscript is undated, the evidence certainly suggests that it dates from 1828, when the work was originally drafted.

86. Letter of 18 June 1828 from Fanny to Karl Klingemann, in Hensel, *Die Familie Mendelssohn*, 1: 220. "Er hat eine *Ouvertüre* mit *Introduction* vermeiden wollen und das Ganze in zwei nebeneinanderstehenden Bildern gemacht."

87. Todd, *"The Hebrides" and Other Overtures*, 47.

88. Ambros, *Die Grenzen der Musik und Poesie*, 86–87.

89. Todd, *"The Hebrides" and Other Overtures*, 77.

90. Ambros, who explicated the relationship between Goethe's verses and Mendelssohn's music at some length, details the implicit "events" of the coda as they supplement the more provisional closure of "Glückliche Fahrt" (*Die Grenzen*, 89). A reviewer of a late (1847) performance under Mendelssohn, cited by Todd, writes to the same effect about the coda (*"The Hebrides" and Other Overtures*, 77).

91. Kramer remarks of these closing measures, with reference to the allegorical implications of Goethe's poem, that "there could be no clearer suggestion that the dynamic process traced by the overture is cyclical and self-renewing" ("Goethe and the Image of Mendelssohn," 76).

92. A facsimile of the sketch, dated 7 August 1829, is given in Hensel, *Die Familie Mendelssohn*, 1: 281. A transcription can be found in Todd, *"The Hebrides" and Other Overtures*, 28–29, and in "Of Sea Gulls and Counterpoint," 199, where Mendelssohn's pen-and-ink drawing of "a view of the Hebrides and Morven" (likewise dated 7 August) is also reproduced (205).

93. Wulf Konold, *Felix Mendelssohn Bartholdy und seine Zeit* (Laaber: Laaber-Verlag, 1984), 181.

94. Letter of 7 April 1834 to Fanny Mendelssohn Hensel. Lady Wallace translates Mendelssohn's needling epithet for Fanny (literally, "you raven-sister") as "you wolf-sister," Tovey as "unnatural woman." See Felix Mendelssohn Bartholdy, *Letters from the Years 1833 to 1847*, trans. Lady Wallace (London: Longman, Roberts and Green, 1864), 32; Tovey, *Symphonies*, 395).

95. See Marcia Citron, ed., *The Letters of Fanny Hensel to Felix Mendelssohn* (Stuyvesant, NY: Pendragon, 1987), letter of ca. 27 February 1834 (no. 52).

96. See Werner, *Mendelssohn: Leben und Werk*, 311. (In a letter to Karl Klingemann from the end of 1835 Felix claims that he senses all too clearly that his "youth has ended with that day" [of his father's death] and that "I must now become serious for ever—my only wish is to become like my father, and to accomplish that which he expected from me.")

97. For instance, Eric Werner, *Mendelssohn: A New Image*, 271. Donald Mintz speaks of a "double" exposition and "combined reprise," which comes closer to describing the situation, although it is still important to recognize the independent and hence introductory quality of the opening F-major section. In comparing the final version with an earlier draft (which he submits may have been the version performed at the London premiere in 1834), Mintz notes that the overall formal outline of the work remained constant, even though the melodic-thematic detail underwent considerable changes: "*Melusina*: A Mendelssohn Draft," *The Musical Quarterly* 43 (1957), 480–99.

98. See the letter to Fanny Mendelssohn Hensel of 30 January 1836; *Letters 1833–1847*, 94–95.

99. "So umfuhr sie in der Luft das Schloß, indem sie aus der Höhe herunter ein entsetzliches Geschrei ausstieß, das so seltsam und unerhört klang, daß allen das Herz im Leibe bebte, und sie sich vor nichts so furchten, als diesen Ton noch einmal zu hören, so zerschmetternd und zerreissend klang es, so tiefbetrübt, als sollte nun gar die ganze Welt vergehen." See Ludwig Tieck, "Die sehr wunderbare Historie von der Melusina," in Tieck, *Schriften*, vol. 13 (Berlin: G. Reimer, 1829; rpt. 1966), 132–33.

100. Letter to Fanny Hensel of 7 April 1834; *Letters 1833–1847*, 32–33.

101. August Reissmann, *Felix Mendelssohn-Bartholdy: sein Leben und seine Werke* (Berlin: J. Guttentag, 1872), 49.

102. Eduard Devrient, *My Recollections of Felix Mendelssohn-Bartholdy and His Letters to Me*, trans. Natalia Macfarren (London: Richard Bentley, 1869), 22–23. Devrient

also claims that the nickname "Trumpet" overture was bestowed on the piece by himself along with the other members of the young composer's circle at this time (Mendelssohn perhaps included).

103. Mendelssohn, *Briefe aus den Jahren 1830 bis 1847*, ed. Paul Mendelssohn Bartholdy and Carl Mendelssohn Bartholdy (Leipzig: Hermann Mendelssohn, 1865), 190.

104. Tovey, *Symphonies*, 404.

105. "Aus Berlin," *Neue Zeitschrift für Musik* 24 (1846), 83–84.

106. H. Schellenberg, "F. Mendelssohn Bartholdy's Musik zu Racine's *Athalia*," *Neue Zeitschrift für Musik* 30/33 (23 April 1849), 184.

107. Eduard Devrient, *My Recollections of Felix Mendelssohn-Bartholdy*, 246–47.

108. Ibid., 247.

109. Friedhelm Krummacher, "'. . . fein und geistreich genug'—Versuch über Mendelssohns Musik zum *Sommernachtstraum*," in *Das Problem Mendelssohn*, ed. Carl Dahlhaus (Regensburg: Bosse, 1974), 112.

110. Ibid., 113–15.

111. Ibid., 111.

112. Tovey, *Symphonies*, 416.

113. The allegory of "Enlightenment" in Goethe's *Walpurgisnacht* and its significance for Mendelssohn are discussed by Leon Botstein in "The Aesthetics of Assimilation and Affirmation," 22–23, and by Lawrence Kramer in "*Felix culpa*: Goethe and the Image of Mendelssohn," 76–79. On this point and on the background of the composition as a whole, see also Douglass Seaton, "The Romantic Mendelssohn: The Composition of *Die erste Walpurgisnacht*," *The Musical Quarterly* 68 (1982), 398–410.

114. Mendelssohn already spoke about applying this term "symphony cantata" to the *Walpurgisnacht* setting, in revised form, in the letter to Karl Klingemann of 18 November 1840, where he first thanked his friend for suggesting this phrase as official generic designation for the *Lobgesang* (Klingemann, *Briefwechsel*, 251). In a letter to his mother of 28 November 1842 (two weeks before her death) Mendelssohn wrote: "I would like at last to turn the *Walpurgisnacht* into a Symphony-Cantata, as it was originally intended to be, but which it did not become due to a lack of courage on my part"; *Letters 1833–1847*, 312).

115. On the genesis, sources, and revisions of *Die erste Walpurgisnacht*, see Seaton, "The Romantic Mendelssohn," esp. 399–402, 410.

116. Letter to his family of 14 July 1831. One would at first assume that the "grand symphony" he contemplated here was something along the lines of the full-scale A-minor Allegro he eventually composed. However, in speaking later of the idea of a "symphony cantata" (comparable to the *Lobgesang*) in a letter to his mother of 28 November 1842, he added that this is how the work was "originally intended," although it "did not become so for want of courage on my part" (*Letters 1833–1847*, 312). This leaves open the possibility that even from the beginning Mendelssohn had contemplated including a number of instrumental movements in his setting of the *Walpurgisnacht*.

117. Seaton points out this series of motivic links in "The Romantic Mendelssohn," 408.

118. The autograph of this concerto is included among the other early autograph material (now much of it published) in the Mendelssohn-Archiv of the Staatsbibliothek zu Berlin Preußischer Kulturbesitz. The concert was first performed and recorded in the 1960s by Rena Kyriakou with the Vienna Pro Musica under Hans Swarowsky (Vox-Turnabout TV 34170S). On the origins of this work, as well as of the later published solo concertos, see Marian Wilson, "Felix Mendelssohn's Works for Solo Piano and Orchestra: Sources and Composition" (Ph.D. diss., The Florida State University, 1993), which also includes detailed analytical discussions of this whole corpus.

119. The two duo-piano concertos were rediscovered only after the Second World War, along with much else among Mendelssohn's juvenilia, and published in 1961.

120. Unlike the E-major double concerto, we have no direct evidence for a private performance. But considering that the autograph of the final movement bears the date 12 November 1824, it seems more than likely that Mendelssohn had pushed to complete the work in time for a performance on Fanny's birthday (14 November), the same occasion on which we know the E-major concerto to have been performed.

121. See the letter of 18 October 1831 to Abraham Mendelssohn. It is perhaps of interest, with regard to the new stance adopted toward conventional virtuosity in the design of this concerto, that in this same letter Mendelssohn voiced a new and very determined distaste for the practice of free improvisation at public concerts, a practice that remained an obligatory component of virtuoso concertizing well into the middle of the nineteenth century.

122. A review of Op. 25 in Ludwig Rellstab's *Iris im Gebiet der Tonkunst* remarks that the Presto finale is the most satisfying and original of the movements, "even though in character—though by no means in individual details—it is strongly reminiscent of [Carl] Maria von Weber." The same reviewer (presumably Rellstab himself), who had heard Mendelssohn perform the piece twice, also noted that the second-movement heading "Andante" should be taken to refer "more to the character of performance than to the actual tempo, which [the composer] takes much more slowly than is normally the case with an Andante"; "Concert für das Pianoforte . . . von Felix Mendelssohn Bartholdy, Op. 25," *Iris im Gebiet der Tonkunst* 4/34 (23 August 1833), 135.

123. Werner, *Mendelssohn: A New Image*, 358. "The concerto is justifiably forgotten today"; Werner adds, "It is hardly worthy of [the composer's] name." Abraham Veinus calls Op. 40 "a duller echo of the first [concerto]"; *The Concerto* (London, Toronto, and Melbourne: Cassel, 1948), 187. Mendelssohn's audiences, on the other hand, seem to have found the D-minor Concerto just as ambitious and "progressive" as the G-minor, and had every reason to do so (see n. 7).

124. "It is meant not merely as a bravura concerto and a showpiece for the pianist," this reviewer remarks, "but as a [genuine] piece of music, in which both orchestra and soloist are subordinated to the larger [compositional] idea, and only in this way are they ever subordinated to one another." *AmZ* 40/36 (1838) col. 589; see the complete translation of this review in the Historical Views and Documents that follow this Chapter.

125. For a recent appraisal of Cécile's character and critical speculation on the relation between this and the character of Felix's music, see Marian Wilson, "Mendelssohn's Wife: Love, Art, and Romantic Biography," *Nineteenth-Century Studies* 6 (1992), 1–18.

126. The sketched versions of the main theme, bridge, and second-key ideas are given by Hans Christoph Worbs in *Felix Mendelssohn Bartholdy*, 105–6.

127. Though see the discussion of these shorter concerted works for piano in Wilson, "Felix Mendelssohn's Works for Piano and Orchestra," pp. 47–103, 184–274, 385–449.

HISTORICAL VIEWS AND DOCUMENTS

REVIEW OF SYMPHONY NO. 5 IN D MAJOR ("REFORMATION")[1]

Hermann Deiters; translated by Thomas Grey

We have hesitated longer than usual to review this work, which is surely the most significant among the new series of Mendelssohn's posthumous works now appearing in print and likewise the one among all the posthumous works toward which we bring the greatest expectations. Nonetheless, our report does not seem to be too late, since to our knowledge this composition has as yet received relatively few public performances.

The work published in the present edition under the title "Reformation Symphony" was identified by Mendelssohn himself—as the catalog appended by J[ulius] Rietz to the published letters attests[2] (since this gives the authentic designation)—only as a "Symphony to Celebrate the Feast of the Reformation" [*Symphonie zur Feier des Reformationsfestes*], and we may perhaps be permitted to express our opinion that it would have been best to retain this title. For the two titles do not say exactly the same thing: the first suggests a much more intimate relation between the composition and the Reformation as an immediate object of representation [*Darstellungsobjekt*], thereby encouraging all sorts of murky speculations [*Grübeleien*] about motives and the interconnection of movements, in which the spiritual significance of this world-historical event is supposed to be reflected in the form of tonal images. The latter title, on the other hand ["Symphony to Celebrate the Feast of the Reformation"], emphasizes the sense of a musical glorification of a festal occasion, even if that occasion may carry a direct spiritual significance for its participants; and, of course, this does not preclude the possibility that the composer drew the impulses for his composition from the significance of this festival. Whoever finds this distinction meaningless or simply pedantic would recognize his or her error, upon closer examination of the matter, and have to concede that the name "Reformation Symphony" arouses certain expectations (in the reader of this title) that are not completely satisfied in the case of the listener, while the notion of a joyous and brilliant festal music—which one could not help associating with the object of that festival—would prove thoroughly justified here.

The symphony was composed, as the previously mentioned catalogue says, in the year 1830, to celebrate the feast of the Reformation [*sic*], and was performed in London and Berlin.[3] It thus belongs to the master's youth, though granted that even as a youth he had attained a level of complete artistic maturity and already left the unruly invention and unformed powers of the beginner's efforts far behind him. Mendelssohn's individual artistic personality is already revealed in its fully developed form in such works from this time as the *Hebrides* Overture, the A-major Symphony [no. 4], as well as the *Midsummer Night's Dream* Overture, written several years earlier. If we were to ask how this symphony compares, on the whole, with these contemporary works, we may confirm that this work, too, is distinguished by the same sureness and ease of invention and form, the same never-ending flow of thoughts, continuously enlivened by unexpected contrasts, the same fine touch in the treatment of technical (particularly instrumental) means—all of those virtues now intimately associated with the name of Mendelssohn. But at the same time, we would have to confess that the present symphony does not display quite the same degree of unexpected individuality [*Eigenthümlichkeit*] that so radically distinguishes those other early works from those of any other contemporary composer nor the same level of fine and delicate detail, by which Mendelssohn had achieved such magical and hitherto undreamed-of effects of harmony and instrumentation. Compared to those works, this one appears much simpler, conceived more in broad strokes [*mehr in grossen Zügen entworfen*]. Even in this, at least, it offers us happy testimony of Mendelssohn's facility in applying his artistry to the solution of any task he sets for himself and of the creative security and delight that always animate him, even if we do not place this alongside Mendelssohn's finest and most characteristic compositions of that [early] period. Although it has not been without some reservations that we have observed the rather extensive publication of posthumous works (many of them dating from his earliest youth) in recent times, none of these applies to the present symphony. Even if the master may have suppressed this work deliberately, we must express our thanks to the publisher for having finally made available to us another testament to the composer's powers, a formally rounded and complete work that is, at the same time, distinguished by its own particular mood and character.

The first movement of the symphony begins with an Andante (D major, $\frac{4}{4}$), in which tender, legato motives[4] rise up from the depths, the sonority and expression being gradually amplified by means of their imitative entries; these are twice answered by a short period for wind instruments, which, despite the slow tempo, already fully bespeaks a solemnity that is at once joyous and serious. Mixed into the continuation [*Anhänge*] of these motives, whose still more veiled tone-color gives an impression of longing and hope (only the lower strings play, without violins), is a new figure, *unisono*, speaking in a firm and powerful voice, as if prophesying something yet to come, in a manner reminiscent of old chorale singing:[5]

 etc.

The figure rapidly increases in volume and, as it continues, forms itself into a highly decisive gesture, suggesting some solemn call or invocation [*einem feierlichen Anrufe gleichenden Figur*]:

following which the whole string section enters at last, slowly ascending and sustaining a long fermata on the dominant the second time. Following directly upon that comes the main movement, *Allegro con fuoco* $\frac{2}{2}$ in D minor, whose main theme is derived from the calling figure of the introduction:

This theme's two-sided character of powerful exertion and restless dissatisfaction determines the nature of the whole first movement, which can be best expressed (if one is inclined to give metaphorical expression to musical compositions) as an image of battle and struggle; they are great powers that tirelessly exert themselves here, sometimes sinking back exhausted, sometimes grasping toward a ray of hope and rousing themselves once again into a state of the utmost restless passion. Following this first theme, which strides forth in a powerful tutti chord progression, comes a dotted rhythmic motion in the strings, punctuated by woodwind chords [mm. 53ff.], after which all the instruments advance forcefully together [mm. 65ff.], until this is rounded off by a brief pacifying gesture [m. 80]. Out of this arises a rapid upward eighth-note motion in the strings, *unisono*, against which the opening motive resounds in the wind instruments. The music gradually modulates to A minor, and once this key has been established (in a rather tumultuous manner), a second theme is heard, beginning in A minor and ending in A major, as if it were meant to express a sense of hope raising itself up from the darkness. To our mind, some intention along these lines is unmistakably expressed here, and rather too bluntly [*ein wenig zu deutlich ausgedrückt*]; aside from that, every listener will immediately identify this attractive and penetrating theme as "genuinely Mendelssohnian":

New motives extend this second theme melodically, gradually reintroducing the earlier feeling of unrest and introducing the emphatically marked closing section in A minor [mm. 182–99]. At this juncture we might call attention to the overall manner in which the movement has been handled so far. In the most animated passages the string instruments are treated almost exclusively in unison or octaves [*unisono*], in contrast to the wind instruments, which are handled as a unified [harmonic] mass; considering the general simplicity of the easily surveyed thematic composition, we clearly recognize here a conception realized in quick strokes, one that has been worked out equally fast, in accordance with first impulses. Overall, this character is also maintained in the second half of the movement, which follows directly upon the first part [i.e., the exposition] without any repeat. The closing chords are immediately followed by the opening dotted motive, lightly intoned in the winds; this ascends not to the perfect fifth (E♮) but, unexpectedly, to E♭, onto which are grafted quietly arpeggiated diminished-seventh chords in the strings; after a repetition of this brief period the color and mood are suddenly altered. At this point there begins a long and interesting alternating play of winds and strings; the winds give the signal for the restless eighth-note motion of the strings by enunciating the principal motive of the movement, which now entirely assumes the character of a repeated call to arms [*Anruf*]. While this figure in the woodwinds is expanded again into the familiar psalmodic figure of the introduction [see example on page 401], the texture and energetic, restless activity of the string parts also increase (this activity itself containing the seeds of the overall intensification); throughout all this we cannot fail to recognize [in Mendelssohn] the master of modulation, and finally the whole ensemble converges in a mighty B-minor statement [*Einsatz*; see mm. 269ff.]. This statement, the high point of the whole animated [development] passage, is repeated in several different keys at four-measure intervals. After a short imitative passage in eighth-note motion, accompanied by weighty half notes, the same energetic statement is repeated in shorter periods; we are presented with an image of a turbulent and active life that sweeps along everything in its path. The calming gesture that may be suggested by the wind instruments' attempts to begin the second theme is nonetheless driven back by the ceaseless movement of the strings. In introducing a new motive

into the fray here—against which the main theme is sounded in the winds, in closest succession—the composer succeeds in intensifying the activity still further. This motion leads at least into a condensation of the entire orchestral forces in the sustained note E [m. 367], from which the string parts descend *unisono*, giving way to conclusion on the dominant, which is given a nearly defiant tone by repetitions of that same [dominant] note. In total contrast to this and as a complete surprise, there appears here the quiet concluding phrase of the introduction, in D major [m. 381]; these measures sound like a gentle admonition at a point where, amid the raging storm of battle, one has nearly lost sight of the true goal. This also constitutes the transition to the reprise of the main theme. The first section [exposition] now repeats itself in a much abridged form; and what is more striking still, it is now kept very quiet, with none of the earlier agitation, even if one does not yet have a sense of actual tranquillity. The soft character of the second theme is played out in long phrases; then quiet, legato eighth-note figures indicate the original motion again; at first these appear individually; then they gradually gather together, *unisono*, and culminate once again in powerful chords (E flat as ninth of [V of] G minor).[6] An animated, powerful coda [*Schlusspartie*] is appended, in which earlier motives are touched on again and which provides a unifying conclusion to the whole. One can see from the preceding description of the second part of the movement[7] that the composer sought to make the form serve a distinct idea here. One might thus try to interpret just what the composer meant to represent by means of these various motives, by the highly original handling of the orchestra (in which the string *unisono* creates very much the impression of a collective force engaged in some strenuous conflict), or by the contrasts between the two halves of the movement, mediated by the interpolation of a few measures drawn from an entirely foreign context [i.e., the "Dresden Amen" of the introduction, recalled at m. 381]. For our part, our admiration of the composer is increased by observing how, for all the evident haste in which he sketched out the ground plan [*Grundriß*] of the piece and executed the drawing [*Zeichnung*] of it, so to speak, he was nonetheless able to produce a lively mood-picture as one continuous gesture [*Zug*]—even if we cannot look upon the all-too-prominent role of an idea, to the detriment of the form, without some reservations, and cannot advise anyone to emulate Mendelssohn in this particular regard.

Following the first movement there is a Scherzo, *Allegro vivace* (B♭ major, ³⁄₄), which is without a doubt the most immediately appealing movement of the symphony for the general listener; and even on closer acquaintance we believe that its freshness of invention and beauty of proportion combine to guarantee this movement pride of place. The composer begins by tossing at us an idea, first presented quietly in the woodwinds, that is distinguished by its liveliness and joyfully vigorous expression:

This theme returns in the full orchestra in the second part of the Scherzo [mm. 25ff.], following a contrasting section and a lively [retransitional] anacrusis. Yet more merry and pleasing motives are now appended to this theme, and the Scherzo section as a whole exudes a character of joyful confidence. Contrasting with this is a motive of great delicacy and mildness that begins the Trio (G major):

The embellishing trills of the accompaniment and even more the ensuing eighth-note figuration in the violins contribute to the typically Mendelssohnian character of delicacy and charm here. The melody as such, however, does not really rise above the ordinary.

It is just as difficult to determine wherein this overall movement exhibits any necessary inner relation to the idea of a "Reformation Symphony" as it is with the next movement, an Andante (G minor, $\frac{2}{4}$), which strikes a tone of soft, inward lament in a manner both simple and beautiful:

The melody might remind us somewhat of the aria "Ach, ich fühl's" from *Die Zauberflöte*, even if it does not, naturally, reach quite the same depth of expression. During a brief contrasting phrase, involving a modulation to E♭ major, the lament momentarily takes on accents of distress and despair and then quickly returns to the original motive; after the close of this phrase there occurs a significant allusion to the first movement: the opening measures of the second theme [mm. 50–52; cf. mvt. 1, mm. 138–39] are heard in a surge of deep yearning, leading to the close of the movement in G major. While the basses sustain the tonic note G with an air of expectancy, there sounds above, like a voice of consolation and encouragement, the melody of the chorale "Ein' feste Burg ist unser Gott" [A Mighty Fortress Is Our God], played by a solo flute. Other instruments begin to join with this, until the melody has been heard in its entirety in the chorus of woodwind instruments, entering one after another; violas and cellos are eventually added, and by the end even trumpets and trombones. This contrast with the preceding G-minor Andante surely sheds a meaningful light on that movement, too; and by the same token this reveals again a weakness [*Leichtigkeit*] in the conception of the work as a whole, for music possesses much deeper strains for expressing the inner lament of a congregation of believers and the encounter between such a lament and the promise of courage and faith as enunciated by a voice from above. After the chorale has faded away in the trills of the flutes there emerges in the strings, which now enter *en masse*, a lively, rushing motion in a syncopated figure of eighth and quarter notes (*Allegro vivace*, G major, $\frac{6}{8}$); this motion gradually accumulates force as it rises in register, and the main motive of the chorale is broken off and sounded alternately among the various wind instruments, conveying an increasing sense of urgency—as if eager to confirm the promise of salvation. This general crescendo [*Steigerung*] leads to powerful statements of the dominant-seventh chord. Basses and violins climb upward, and then the woodwind chorus (in repeated eighth notes) moves downward; so the whole orchestra unites in a headlong rush into the main theme of the last movement proper (*Allegro maestoso*, D major, $\frac{4}{4}$):

This theme continues in the same spirit, the expression of joyous celebration, a forceful consciousness of imminent victory in the familiar, *echt*-Mendelssohnian style. This general sense of motion is continued for some time, without any very distinct melodic idea emerging, until the following powerful and expressive idea is presented and subjected to polyphonic treatment:

In a similar vein the strongly marked motives of the wind instruments, in relation to the sixteenth notes of the strings, seem to portray a sense of advancing with an ironclad determination. The second theme, ushered in by the wind choir, can be identified according to its rhythm and expression as a triumphal march; the string instruments, which contribute some individual sustained notes and figures, then repeat the theme, powerfully preparing the close in A major. In the ensuing section [i.e., development, m. 166ff.] the chorale tune returns, and its individual phrases are presented against short, staccato chords in the strings, creating an attractive, songlike texture. As those chords gradually evolve into more coherent figures, the violins take up the melody of the chorale and continue it independently; and after a rapid phase of intensification we find ourselves once again within that headlong motion that had begun the [main section of the] movement. The previously cited motive [see the last example above] is subjected to a more extended fugato treatment here, against which the woodwind choir unexpectedly intones the chorale; the second theme follows without interruption. Truly, this music comes close to speech [*ist beinahe sprechend*]: the chorale clearly appears to be, if not exactly the cause, at least the motivating principle [*treibendes Element*] behind the sense of celebratory joy; or, perhaps better expressed: it forms an organic component of that joy. As an artist, Mendelssohn could not have handled it differently: a symbolic intertwining of this theme, conceived as the representation of an extramusical idea, which then generates the joyful mood (rather as we find later in Meyerbeer),[8] would not strike us as genuinely artistic; a true artist, on the other hand, could treat it as a musical idea only in its own right, combining it with the other motives of his composition and linking these together in organic fashion.

Whether those for whom this chorale melody possesses a deeply symbolic significance will be able to accept this kind of musical treatment (i.e., in a composition that by no means observes the strict and serious style but instead is predominantly expressive of a festive, joyful mood)—this is another question, which we cannot attempt to answer here. The most emphatic effect, in any case, is reserved for the end of the movement. The second theme is followed this time by some calmly flowing legato figuration in the lower instrumental parts, against an expressive cantilena line in the upper parts. After the figurational motion of the lower parts becomes amplified, rising up through the texture [mm. 264–305], the melody of the chorale is sounded by the full orchestra [m. 306], and the first two verses of the tune bring the movement to a conclusion of the greatest pomp.

Thus, this symphony (to return briefly to our original point) is, first and foremost, a brilliant example of the admirable facility and sureness with which Mendelssohn was able to approach musical form and instrumental technique in an effort to accomplish a particular aim, even at such an early age; we can only look with admiration and astonishment at the sureness of his powers of invention, even in the case of a work so rapidly conceived as this, and with what fine artistic sensitivity he was able to handle musical contrasts, to keep the motion going, and to avoid monotony. But in order to maintain the proper perspective for evaluating a piece such as this one, it is important to keep in mind that it is essentially an occasional work [*Gelegenheitswerk*]; neither is it so rich in new and original ideas as the A-major Symphony, nor is the handling of formal and instrumental detail in any way as fine and thoroughly nuanced as that which we admire in most of Mendelssohn's other orchestral works. Whatever interest may be lacking in this regard is, to some extent, compensated, as we have seen, by the distinct (sometimes palpably so) relation of the work to the external occasion that inspired it. By weaving the chorale tune "Ein' feste Burg" into the last movement, the composer has demonstrated that he had the significance of the [Reformation] festival in mind as he was composing this section; and we can easily infer that this inspiration extends to the other movements, as well. But surely we can assume, on the basis of the aesthetic principles articulated in his correspondence, that Mendelssohn would have strictly forbidden any attempt to clothe the content of the work in words or to specify that way some ideal progression [*einen sonstigen Fortschritt der Idee*]. There are no grounds, at any rate, to think of this as sacred, let alone specifically denominational [*konfessionell-tendenziöse*], music. If the Reformation may have had a deep emotional significance for Mendelssohn, he did not give expression to those feelings in this symphony. For the listener of whatever faith or denomination, it is quite irrelevant to know Mendelssohn's views on such matters, as the symphony itself requires no commentary but can be understood as a work of art quite on its own. It is simply a festive symphony [*Festsymphonie*], such as might provide a brilliant and cheerful conclusion to other, similarly serious festivities; it maintains straightforwardly its same character of jubilation and joyful optimism, with only occasional darker moments and without really striking any extremely serious chords, even if this jubilation does evolve, of course, out of earlier struggle and unrest. If it were not for the chorale and the short passage in the [first-movement] introduction, one would not for a moment guess that there was any deeper, let alone religious, meaning to the work, and such meanings as do surface here are a function of purely musical, rather than symbolic, import. It may be that just these points cited here—the distinctively "occasional" character of the work, conjoined with the danger of perhaps being misunderstood by those in search of deeper intentions—were determining factors in Mendelssohn's decision not to have the symphony published.

SCHUMANN ON MENDELSSOHN'S SYMPHONY NO. 3 IN A MINOR[9]

Translated by Thomas Grey

As for F. Mendelssohn-Bartholdy's new symphony (Opus 56, Breitkopf & Härtel), all those who have until now sympathetically followed the brilliant course of this rare musical star in the firmament of music have awaited it with the most eager anticipation. It has been regarded as the composer's first genuine essay in the symphonic genre: for what was in fact, his first symphony, in C minor, is a work of the composer's earliest youth; the second symphony, which he composed for the London Philharmonic Society, has not appeared in print[10]; and the "symphony-cantata" (entitled *Lobgesang*) cannot be regarded as a purely instrumental work. Thus, within the bountiful garland of the composer's oeuvre there still lacks, aside from the opera, only the symphony, while in all other genres he has proven himself quite fecund.

We know from thirdhand information that the present symphony was begun at an earlier period, when Mendelssohn was in Rome. However, the symphony was not actually completed until quite recently. This information is of much interest, indeed, with reference to an evaluation of the particular character of the piece. Just as when an old, yellowed page suddenly slips from an old and neglected volume, recalling to us times long past, and those times rise again [in our mind] in their full brilliance, so that we entirely forget the present moment—so might the imagination of this master have been flooded by happy memories when he happened upon those old melodies he had once sung while surrounded by the charms of Italy. So, perhaps, consciously or subconsciously, did this delicate tone-picture materialize, which might, like the Italian journey described in Jean Paul's *Titan*, make one forget for a moment the sorrow of never having been able to experience that blessed land for oneself, for it has already been observed how a distinctive popular tone [*ein eigenthümlicher Volkston*] infuses the whole symphony—indeed, one would have to be singularly deficient in imagination to overlook this aspect of it.[11] As with Franz Schubert's [C-major] symphony, the particularly delightful sense of color assures this Mendelssohn symphony its place in the symphonic canon. One does not encounter here that conventional brand of instrumental pathos or the massive expansiveness so common nowadays—there is nothing one would consider an attempt to outdo Beethoven. If anything, it resembles more the Schubert symphony, especially with regard to character, but with the exception that, where the latter work evokes the wild strains of gypsy life, Mendelssohn's symphony seems to transport us to Italian climes. This is also to say that the later composer possesses a pleasing and more decorous character [*ein anmuthig gesitteterer Charakter*] and that he speaks to us in accents less foreign [weniger fremdartig], while we must attribute other virtues to the Schubert work, especially its more richly developed powers of invention.

The overall plan [*Grundanlage*] of the Mendelssohn symphony is distinguished by the intimate relation of all four movements to one another. Even the melodic contour of the main themes of the four different movements is related; a cursory inspection of the thematic material will verify this. More than any other symphony, this one constitutes a tightly woven, complete whole: across the four movements, character, key, and rhythm are only slightly contrasted. As the composer himself has indicated in a prefatory note to this work, the four movements are to be performed one directly after the other, without any long pauses in between.

As regards the purely musical aspect of the work, there can be no doubts as to its high level of technical mastery. With respect to beauty and delicacy of structure—overall, as well as in the individual detail of connective material—it compares favorably with his overtures, and it is no less rich in delightful instrumental effects. Every page of the score attests to the finesse with which Mendelssohn is able to recall an earlier theme, how he is able to embellish a transition or a return so that the old material appears to us in an entirely new light, how full and interesting is the musical detail, yet without overloading [the texture] or [degenerating into ostentatious,] philistine displays of pedantic "learning" [*Gelehrtthuerei*].

The effect of this symphony on audiences will depend, to some extent, on the greater or lesser degree of virtuosity of the orchestra performing it. Of course, this is always the case, but all the more so here, where it is not so much the energy of the whole group that is paramount, but rather the delicacy of individual instrumental timbres. Above all, the piece calls for delicate handling of the woodwind instruments. Most irresistible is the Scherzo; a more genial movement of this kind has scarcely been written in recent times—the instruments speak here like real people.

The piano arrangement has been prepared by the composer himself and for that reason presents as true a reflection of the original score as one could hope for. Nonetheless, the arrangement can often suggest only by half all the charming [original] instrumental effects.

The conclusion of the symphony as a whole ["Finale: Maestoso," $\frac{6}{8}$] is sure to provoke conflicting opinions. Many will expect the symphony to conclude in the character of the last movement,[12] while instead, rounding out the whole in cyclic fashion [*das Ganze gleichsam kreisförmig abrundend*], [this final section] recalls something of the opening [introduction] of the first movement. We simply find this conclusion poetic; it is like an evening mood corresponding to a beautiful morning.

SCHUMANN ON THE OVERTURE TO "DIE SCHÖNE MELUSINE"[13]

Translated by Thomas Grey

There are not a few people who find themselves troubled by nothing so much as their inability to decide which of Mendelssohn's overtures is, in fact, the most beautiful or, indeed, the best. The problem was already severe enough in choosing among the earlier [three], but now a fourth has appeared. Thus, Florestan has identified the different factions as the Midsummer Night's Dreamers (by far the strongest), the Fingalists (by no means the slightest, especially among the fair sex [*beim anderen Geschlechte*]), and so on. The Melusinists are understandably still the smallest group, since the piece has not yet been heard anywhere in Germany outside Leipzig, and in England—where the Philharmonic Society gave the premiere of this work, to which they could claim the right of ownership—it is kept in reserve, only to be relied upon as a programming stopgap.

There are some works of such fine spiritual conception [*Geistesbau*] that coarse, bearlike criticism feels awkward and ashamed and finds itself humbly compelled to pay its compliments. Just as this was the case with the *Midsummer Night's Dream* overture (at least I can recall having read only poetic reviews of it, if that is not a contradiction in terms), so it seems to be again with that to "The Fairy-Tale of the Fair Melusina."

It seems to us that in order to understand this overture, there is no need to read the broadly discursive, if highly imaginative, story by Tieck, but only to know the following basic matters: that the charming Melusina was inflamed with a passionate love for the handsome knight Lusignan and let him wed her under the condition that he should leave her to herself on certain appointed days during the year. One day Lusignan broke this promise—[and discovered that] Melusina was, in fact, a mermaid, half fish, half woman. The material has been variously treated, in words as well as in music. But no more in this case than with the overture to *A Midsummer Night's Dream*, should one seek to follow some coarse narrative thread.[14] Mendelssohn always arrives at a purely poetic conception of things, and so here he portrays only the character of the man and the wife, of the proud, knightly Lusignan and the alluring, yielding Melusina; but it is as if the waves of the stream flooded their embraces, engulfed them, and separated them once more. Here each [listener] may well imagine coming to life all those jolly pictures over which the youthful imagination loves to dwell, those tales of life deep beneath the waves, full of darting fishes with golden scales, full of pearls lying in open seashells, full of sunken treasures that the ocean has stolen from men, full of emerald palaces towering one above the other, and so forth. This, it seems to us, distinguishes this overture from the earlier ones: it seems to narrate such things [*wie vor sich hin erzählt*] exactly in the manner of a fairy tale, rather than presenting them to us as a direct experience. In this way the surface may seem a bit cool to us at first, and mute: but how life transpires in the deep is something that music can express more distinctly than words, for which reason, too, the overture can do so (we admit) far better than this description.

What can be said about the musical composition [as such] after two hearings and a few random glances at the score is really limited to what is already self-evident: that it is written by a master in the handling of [musical] form and means. The whole thing begins and ends with a magical, wavelike figure that also resurfaces here and there in the course of the piece; and it has here [throughout the central portion of the work] the effect, as we have suggested already, of transposing one suddenly from the battlegrounds of human passions into that vast, all-encompassing liquid element, especially where the music modulates from A♭ through G to C [i.e., mm. 155–66, into the beginning of the development section]. The rhythm of the knight's theme in F minor would gain in prideful bearing and significance from a somewhat slower tempo.[15]   The melody in A♭ resounds delicately and caressingly, and we can detect the head of Melusina peeking out from behind it. Among individual instrumental effects we recall the lovely B♭ of the trumpets (toward the beginning), forming the seventh degree of the chord [m. 18]—a tone from ages past.

At first we believed the overture to be written in six-eight time, which had largely to do with the overly fast tempo of the first performance, where the composer was not present to conduct. The six-four meter that we subsequently discovered in the score has a more dispassionate, yet fantastic, appearance and encourages a more relaxed performance; all the same, it still seems to us [to imply something] too broad and measured. Many may think this an insignificant point, but it is based on an instinctive feeling that we cannot suppress, even if, in this case, we can offer it only as an opinion, without any genuine proof. However it is notated, the overture remains what it is.

REVIEW OF PIANO CONCERTO IN D MINOR, OP. 40[16]

Translated by Thomas Grey

There are, in general, two different genres among concertos, as among nearly all musical works, but with much greater justification in the case of concertos and bravura works of any kind when accompanied by a number of other instruments. In one case, the solo voice is regarded as the absolute sovereign,[17] to whom the orchestra or accompanying instruments act merely as servants, as support, proceeding alongside the soloist in abject obedience. In the other case, the orchestra is elevated to a fully independent role and given a significant voice [*ein gewichtiges Wort . . . mitzusprechen hat*] and is enabled to exercise a decisive influence on the shape of the whole; in this case, where both parts are closely bound together, one part can do little without the other, both interpenetrate each other without trying to gain the upper hand, and only in concert with one another do they form an integral whole. Concertos of this second kind have been composed, above all, by Mozart and Beethoven, as is generally recognized. The gulf between the one kind of concerto and the other is significant enough to allow for a considerable intermediate spectrum, approaching now one, now the other extreme, though without falling wholly into one or the other. If one were to argue over the precise boundaries demarcating these two approaches, it would generate only much pointless and acrimonious strife, as is nearly always the case in such arguments over boundaries. Just as the ruler must always remain in charge, if he or she is not to be ruler in name only, so must the solo instrument [*Bravour-instrument*] maintain a distinct advantage, even in the second type of concerto, in order to remain in control of things, to determine the principal motion, and to ensure that the brilliance of the ensemble serves the greater glory of this soloist. Otherwise, the monarchical element that must always reign within this form would be canceled and converted into a republican one, which would destroy the whole sense of this musical genre, principally attuned as it is to showcasing the brilliance of an outstanding talent. But just to what extent this absolute supremacy is actually justified and to what extent the orchestra should remain subjugated to it or, on the other hand, should take charge as a power in its own right, if without compromising its relationship to the leading power—on these matters opinion will remain divided as long as some people incline toward monarchy and others toward republicanism. If the [royal] figure we propose here strikes some people as too overweening, let them scale it down to the level of the well-to-do family; if these same people would be willing to recognize an analogy between the solo performer and the man of the house and, conversely, between the orchestra and the *Hausfrau*, then we would all still be of the same opinion. In saying this, we are reminded of Martial's desideratum regarding the wife: *Sit non doctissima conjux*.[18] But let us add this: nor should she be overly simple, but instead well educated in matters of mind and heart alike, merry and industrious—then in our estimation this relationship would be, in general, as sensibly regulated as one could hope for.

The concerto that we are concerned with here belongs to the second type; that is, it does not regard the orchestra as a mere servile group but instead grants it a power [*Gewalt*] comparable to that of the solo in terms of dignity and value. That is, it does not merely aim to be a brilliant bravura piece for the pianoforte player but aspires instead to the kind of work in which both soloist and orchestra obey a [larger] idea, and only on this basis does either one submit to the other. The [first movement] *All. appassionato* ($\frac{4}{4}$, D minor) conflates both powers from the outset and in such a way that they appear to engage in a conversation of brief, alternating phrases, after which (in the first principal solo section) these variously intersect, without compromising the brilliance of the solo part, but also without letting the latter dominate entirely. The movement turns just briefly to D major before closing with a tumultuous solo in D minor [mm. 282–320], powerfully supported by the orchestra. Then there enters, without pause, a simple transitional melody, whose harmonies alternate every two measures between C minor and D major[19]; when this series is repeated, the soloist takes part [m. 343], finally sustaining a dominant seventh chord on F by way of preparing the Adagio, $\frac{2}{4}$, in B♭ major. Even within this appendix to the movement [*Anhangsgedanken*] the notion of a divided sovereignty between solo instrument and orchestra is maintained. The same is true of the dignified second movement, where the melody as such is given a more individual physiognomy by virtue of its ingratiating way of blending with certain intermediate harmonies, while the piano itself serves to set off the simple melody with its arpeggiated figures. The final movement (Presto scherzando, $\frac{3}{4}$) is introduced by eight measures of tutti in G minor and four measures of $E\flat^6$, then D_4^6 (the key identified by the signature) in alternation with D minor, at which point the piano enters inquiringly [*wie anfragend*] in a brief exchange with the orchestra prior to breaking out into the extended first solo (*leggiero*), and so on. For the much of the remainder, then, the solo instrument dominates, as in the usual course of affairs, and the orchestra ends with a repeated cadence. One should really hear the work in live performance—it is always so difficult to convey an adequate impression of such works through words alone. This is all the more true considering that, despite the highly diverse taste presiding over today's concert life, one can note a general predilection for [virtuoso] performance and a readiness to pay most attention to this aspect of the work, which is so much an essential part of this genre. When the composer himself performed this work in Leipzig, it was received with tumultuous applause. There can be no doubt, then, that fine pianists will soon become acquainted with the piece, especially since it is not merely a "concert" work but a work of music as well, for which reason it is doubly deserving of the public's attention.

NOTES

1. Hermann Deiters, review of Felix Mendelssohn Bartholdy, Symphony no. 5 in D minor ("Reformation"), *Allgemeine musikalische Zeitung* 3 (1868), 349–50, 356–57.

2. See Felix Mendelssohn Bartholdy, *Briefe aus den Jahren 1833 bis 1847* (Nebst einem Verzeichnisse der sämmtlichen musikalischen Compositionen von Felix Mendelssohn Bartholdy, zusammengestellt von Dr. Julius Rietz), ed. Paul and Carl Mendelssohn Bartholdy (Leipzig: Hermann Mendelssohn, 1865), 519. Rietz's catalog includes, under "unpublished works, for orchestra," an entry for this work as "Sinfonie zur Feier des Reformationsfestes, D moll, 1830 (Aufgeführt in London und Berlin)."

3. The "Feast of the Reformation" is not quite accurate here (despite Rietz's catalog entry): that is a separate feast day in the Lutheran calendar (for which Bach composed his Cantata no. 80, "Ein' feste Burg"), while Mendelssohn's Symphony was conceived for the tercentennial celebration of the signing of the Augsburg Confession in 1530. Deiters is also wrong about a London performance, perhaps confusing this with the aborted attempt at a premiere in Paris in 1832. (Mendelssohn had contemplated a production of the work with the Philharmonic Society of London, but he seems to have given up the idea after its poor reception by the members of the Paris Conservatoire orchestra. Moscheles rehearsed the piece in London in 1855 but likewise decided against a public performance in the end.) Finally, Deiters's argument against the title *Reformationssymphonie* is still further undermined by the fact that Mendelssohn repeatedly referred to the work by just this name—in private correspondence, at least—in letters to his sister Fanny and others (see, e.g., the letters cited by Judith Silber in "Mendelssohn and his *Reformation* Symphony," *Journal of the American Musicological Society* 60 [1987], 310–36; see esp. 326–30). On the other hand, one of the earliest references to the work (a letter of 10 February 1830, to Carl Klingemann) does identify the project as a "Symphonie zum Reformationsfeste" (see p. 314 and n. 11).

4. "zarte und gebundene Motive." Deiters's wording may consciously allude to the use of suspensions (*stile legato, gebundene Styl*) to evoke a churchly *stile antico* in this introduction.

5. "welche an alte Choralweise erinnert." This evidently refers to old Roman Catholic chant or chorale—probably the practice of recitational psalmody or acclamations—rather than to the Lutheran chorale, as represented later on by "Ein' feste Burg," in the finale.

6. "*Es* als None zur G-moll." Deiters evidently means to identify the E flat as the upper member of the *dominant* ninth of G minor, heard here [mm. 477–81] in its third inversion.

7. Normally, the "second part" of the movement [*zweiter Theil*] would refer to development and recapitulation together. However, the following sentence makes it clear that the "second part" refers, in this case, specifically to the recapitulation.

8. Deiters is referring to Meyerbeer's use of "Ein' feste Burg" in the instrumental prelude to *Les Huguenots* (1836) and perhaps to the subsequent use of the chorale (as "Seigneur, rampart et seul soutien") as an identifying Protestant tag in the course of the opera itself. The difference between Meyerbeer's use of the chorale tune and Mendelssohn's is hardly so categorical as Deiters seems to imply.

9. Robert Schumann, from "Symphonies for Orchestra" (review-essay), *Neue Zeitschrift für Musik* 18/39 (1843), 155–56.

10. Schumann is referring to the posthumously published "Italian" Symphony (Op. 90), whose identity as such ("Italian") was clearly not known to Schumann at the time, as his further remarks here demonstrate. It is also evident that Schumann is unaware of the existence of the "Reformation" Symphony (also published posthumously, in 1868).

11. The (anonymous) review in the *Allgemeine musikalische Zeitung* of the symphony's first performance spoke of a "folk-like [*volkstümlich*] tone" characteristic of the whole symphony, and the review of the printed score, signed A. K. (August Kahlert?), spoke of a "song-like [*liedhaft*] tone" characteristic of the first-movement introduction and the work as a whole. See *Allgemeine musikalische Zeitung* 44 (1842), cols. 255–60, and 45 (1843), cols. 341–44.

12. It is unclear here whether Schumann's phrase "in the character of the last movement" [*im Charakter des letzten Satzes*] refers to some generalized character of finale movements or (more likely) to the character of the finale "proper" of this work (*Allegro guerriero*, A minor, $\frac{4}{4}$), which is followed here by the A-major coda or appendix, indicated in Mendelssohn's quasi-programmatic list of movements as "Finale: Maestoso."

13. Robert Schumann, "Overture to the 'Fairy-Tale of the Beautiful Melusina' by F. Mendelssohn-Bartholdy," *Neue Zeitschrift für Musik* 4/2 (5 January 1836), 6–7.

14. A person once asked Mendelssohn, out of curiosity, just what the overture to *Melusina* was actually about. Mendelssohn quickly responded: "Hm—a *mésalliance*." [Schumann's note]

15. It is not immediately clear whether by "slower tempo" Schumann means slower than whatever tempo is taken at the outset, slower than suggested by the marking "Allegro con moto," or slower than he heard it in performance. The latter meaning is clearly implied by the remarks in the last paragraph, but it would not exclude the former ones.

16. Anonymous review of Felix Mendelssohn-Bartholdy: Deuxième Concert pour le Pianoforte avec accomp. d'Orchestre. Oeuv. 40. *Allgemeine musikalische Zeitung* 40/36 (1838), cols. 588–90.

17. While the feminine construction of this phrase in the original German text (*als einzige Herrscherin*) is required by the gender of the noun "solo voice" (*Solostimme*), it is worth drawing attention to in light of the explicitly gendered figurative discourse that follows.

18. "Let one's wife not be too learned."

19. The effect of the harmonic juxtaposition described here (in mm. 333–44) is to imply a temporary tonicization of G minor as a transitional key between D minor and B♭, so that the D-major and C-minor harmonies function as V and iv of G minor, respectively.

8

On Mendelssohn's Compositional Style: Propositions Based on the Example of the String Quartets

Friedhelm Krummacher; translated by Douglass Seaton

I

To discuss music by Mendelssohn as if one were dealing with art of unquestionable quality would be a wasted effort. Just as one should not disregard all the injustice that befell Mendelssohn's personality, so one should not ignore the objections that in the past were leveled against his music. To complain of the denials of its worth has become the practice specifically of a body of literature that has concerned itself with justice. Mere complaints, however, remain fruitless, as long as one appeals only to changes of taste or anti-Semitic prejudices. What should be investigated, rather, is what—after disregarding that which stems from sheer ill will—objectively underlies the criticism of Mendelssohn.[1]

The doubts about Mendelssohn's music ought, therefore, to be countered by analysis rather than by strained apologetics. If one understands the divergent evaluations of his music as indications of objective difficulties, then it will become clear how much the contradictory opinions are grounded in Mendelssohn's manner of composition. Insofar, certainly, as criticism makes use of such terms as "shallow," "empty," "cold," and so on—as is generally the case—it evades refutation to the same extent that it gives up arguments. Criticism will become comprehensible, rather, where it bases itself on historical categories, and it can be discussed insofar as it directs itself toward criteria of compositional technique.[2]

In regard to their genre-historical and constructive assumptions, it does not have to be proven that the string quartets are especially suitable, as evidence of Mendelssohn's compositions, to be set against the current objections.[3] On one hand, these works hold a central position in Mendelssohn's oeuvre as do few other genres; on the other hand, they are—measured by the demands of the genre—especially open to conflicts of opinion.[4] Admittedly, one might object that questions of compositional technique would depend too much on analysis to be useful for a summary in the form of postulates. To be sure, a generalization would be risky, for it might increase the very tendency toward lump judgments that it would be intended to prevent. Thus, a "personal style" will not be defined in brief here. What will be attempted is only to outline a few of the main problems in Mendelssohn's composing. The point of departure is the model of the sonata movement, for which the opening movement of Op. 44 no. 2, will serve as a paradigm[5]; connected to that are several further considerations; at the end a couple of reservations will be pointed out.

II

1. The most familiar reproach against Mendelssohn's composing is that he merely adopted traditional forms and filled them up in a new way but at the same time also misunderstood and undermined them. It is undeniable that the sonata movements in particular express, in the succession of their parts and in their tonal layout, the formal scheme that was prescriptively formulated in Mendelssohn's lifetime and, moreover, by theorists within his circle.[6] Equally undeniably, they mostly lack the characteristics that one tends to expect from a proper sonata movement: terse motives and dualistic thematic styles, intensive working out and goal-oriented development, motivic fragmentation and contrasting diversion, dialectical process and dynamic energy. The question to what extent the current representation holds up against the multiplicity of Classic music is not at issue here. That the criticism of Mendelssohn's sonata-form movements proceeds from such expectations, however, can hardly be denied.[7] If it thereby reveals discoveries less than it exhibits its own failures, then it indicates a difficulty. When that is coupled with the observation that Mendelssohn's thematic style, which is lyrical and lacking in contrast, does not suit the filling out of the large-scale form, then the criticism implies—deliberately or not—the admissibility of departures from a predetermined norm. Evidently, the orientation to one ideal of form impedes the understanding of a construct that apparently follows the textbook model and yet differs from it. Precisely a type of criticism that sets up a historical conception of form as a standard easily behaves in an unhistorical and doctrinaire fashion. Such criticism might deserve to be described as "classicistic" more than does a piece of music that it rebukes as "classicism" because it does not satisfy Classic criteria. But if one were actually to concede to Mendelssohn alternative approaches to the construction of themes, then one might inquire into the consequences for the formal structure, rather than just deplore discrepancies between substance and framework. It would not be impossible, then, that the critic was documenting his or her own self-limiting bias rather than the unsuccessfulness of the object. If, therefore, Mendelssohn's thematic style were lacking in contrast, lyrical, or even static, then a problem with

his music would consist in how to resolve the contradiction between that style and the continuity of the formal process.

The first movement of Op. 44 no. 2 appears to be a model of clear organization: the course of the form is as regular as one could imagine. In the—repeated--exposition the principal area and the secondary area remain in tonic and relative major (E minor and G major), respectively; in the recapitulation they occur in the tonic and parallel key (E minor and E major) in turn; the closing group cites the principal theme in the relative major and tonic, respectively; between the theme groups are extensive, but nonthematic, transitions. The development section makes use of both themes as well as material from the transitions; the recapitulation shows no reorderings, and the coda presents—along with reference to the themes—a typical plan of intensification. The regularity of the form, the clarity of the caesuras, but also the absence of terse head motives, thematic contrasts, rhythmic drive, dramatic accents, and intensive working out make it understandable that the movement generally would be judged as an exemplary case of formalistic polish and classicistic convention.

2. As a rule it is true that the themes in Mendelssohn's sonata-form movements—and not only in these—show so little contrast that they correspond poorly with general expectations.[8] Even where the themes are not directly related, they can hardly be regarded as distinct from each other or in any sense as polar opposites. Unambiguous motivic relationships are not even decisive in this regard—though, to be sure, they also occur. In Op. 13, for example, the characteristic upbeat formula that separates the antecedent and consequent phrases in the principal theme returns again in the secondary area and closing group, thus permeating the entire movement. In Op. 44 no. 3 the upbeat sixteenth-note figure, which opens all the segments of the principal area, serves in chainlike repetition as the underpinning of the secondary area. (According to the autograph, it was also to support the closing group in the same way but was then eliminated and replaced by simple repeated notes, in order to avoid overuse. That was possible, however, only because this formula already functioned in the secondary area only as a means of embellishing repeated tones.) More significant than clear references to material, though, are those latent structural analogies that are determinants for the balance of the theme groups. Again in Op. 13 the themes divide up the structure by means of the previously noted upbeat formula into two analogous four- and two-measure groups, respectively, as well as the melodic gesture with upbeat leap and stepwise descent through the space of an octave in the first case and a fifth in the other. The same applies even more in the cases of Op. 12 and Op. 44 no. 2, where direct motivic relationships are avoided, but the themes are so alike in melodic, rhythmic, and metric characteristics that in Op. 12 their differences nearly blend away. One can hardly avoid thinking that the absence of thematic contrasts is no mere accident, that the thematic analogs much more reveal a deliberate calculation. Apparent exceptions are found most easily in Op. 44 no. 1 and Op. 80—besides the youthful quartet in E♭ major—and the observation requires modification for the Octet, Op. 20, and the First Quintet, Op. 18, (more, at any rate, than for the Second

Quintet, Op. 87, and the Trios, Opp. 49 and 66). In order to understand how these cases are to be classified, one must go beyond direct connections and take up the structural principle of the thematic formation.

In Op. 44 no. 2, too, the themes show no direct motivic relationship. It would probably be most convincing to explain the beginning of the secondary area as a concentration into a narrower range of the expansive opening of the principal area. Common to both themes, however, are metric and rhythmic characteristics: the upbeat quarter note is followed by even quarter-note motion, leading in the first case into suspensions of half and then quarter notes and then vice versa. This applies to the antecedent in each passage, while in each the consequent is constructed differently and more loosely. No one will maintain that the head motives are in any way distinguished as especially terse—rather the contrary. (That the first six notes of the principal theme state the theme of the finale of Mozart's G-minor Symphony turns out, on closer inspection, to serve as paradigm of their differences rather than of analogies.) The fact that both themes further resemble each other by the presence of a leading melodic voice and subordinate accompaniment, in periodic symmetry and the pattern of the lines and through varied repetitions and internal closure, already belongs to the structural principle of thematic construction.

3. Striking commonalities between themes reside not so much in motivic relationships and melodic resemblances but rather mainly in the principle of thematic construction. This becomes clearest if one compares the secondary themes to each other. They are almost always in the dominant or relative major (except in Op. 44 no. 1), and at least in the antecedent they rest on a pedal point (in some cases with figurational animation) and proceed throughout in uniformly relaxed motion (mostly in quarter notes); nearly always the upper voice dominates, generally in stepwise ascent or descent; the clearly profiled antecedent is followed by an oscillating or frankly stagnating consequent, after which both are repeated, although not without alternating. The principal themes are more strongly distinct from each other—ranging from explicitly cantabile melodic style in Op. 12 and Op. 44 no. 2, to the clustering of groups of motives in Op. 44 no. 3 and Op. 80, between which Op. 13 and Op. 44 no. 1 occupy something of a middle position. Even for the extreme cases, however, the observation applies that motivic fragments are structured into timbrally, rhythmically, and metrically closed blocks, which undergo expansion and consolidation in varied repetition. The standardization extends so as to raise the criticism that the music is cast from a mold.[9] The renunciation of exposition of motivic cells and antithetical measure-groups is, however, less obvious than it seems: further problems and consequences stem from it. The word "cantabile," as vague as it seems, might suggest itself, and one might be tempted to make it more precise by reference to Mendelssohn's Lieder.[10] But only one side of the situation will be grasped by that means, whereby it might suffice to speak of closed theme complexes, unitary melodic phases, and less contrary than stationary sections. Common to them are the following: one voice, usually the upper one, takes the lead; the accompaniment

arranges itself in chordal or figurational style underneath; the section is rhythmically unified; the periodization is strictly regular; antecedent and consequent are much less differentiated than they are simply successive melodic patterns; varied repetitions extend the themes to closed phases or areas; they are centered on a fundamental harmonic level with sparse modulation and either return to it or open themselves at the end by means of the dominant.

Op. 44 no. 2 can again serve as example. Beyond the rhythmic references the themes distribute the aforementioned structural characteristics in such a manner that they seem to be analogous song complexes. In both cases the melodic voice is chordally accompanied; in the principal theme the accompaniment is broken up in syncopations, while in the secondary theme it is tied to the pedal point. Antecedent and consequent are closely related to each other harmonically and rhythmically and form no contrasting segments, even though they are clearly divided into half sentences or half lines. The varied repetition in the principal area with the diversion toward the subdominant is followed by an addition of two analogous four-measure units, which connect via eighth notes to the transition (mm. 18–25). In the secondary theme the consequent, now in the cello, will be newly constructed at its repetition (mm. 65–68), in order to sustain the secondary dominant.

4. In Mendelssohn's case two notions stand in opposition to a thematic style that is only to a limited extent useful for motivic working out: on the one hand, that of the permeation of the movement by themes and, on the other hand, that of the constant mediation between the phases of the movement. From that there arises a particular function of those middle terms that, in spite of the length of the theme complexes, make up the major part of the exposition. Instead of mediating between contrary poles, they stand between analogous positions, and while the themes make up closed sections, the transitions supply dynamic and rhythmic contrasts by means of supplementary material. They achieve their significance less through thematic working out, which in the case of such a thematic style would be tricky as an anticipation of the development, but rather more by means of an independence that demands legitimation in their function. This applies primarily to the phase between the principal and secondary areas, secondarily also for the one that precedes the closing group (which, moreover, either reaches back to the principal area or at least forms some similar closed phase). This is not a matter of mere figurations of instability or of developmental motives, which would be introduced and let go freely and episodically.[11] It is precisely motivic terseness that is lacking these formulas, which, however, contravene extended caesuras and permeate the entire movement. They form figuration motives that remain diastematically flexible and rhythmically constant. From the outset they appear as new material after the principal thematic area, to which they counterpoise almost equal weight. But even so they contrast only to a limited extent, since connections also remain beyond the differences. To be sure, one also should not seek out relationships of material here, where they are not readily at hand. More important are essential relationships: exactly in cases where the principal thematic area cadences markedly on the tonic,

the transition impinges on it as a clearly new Gestalt, but it begins just as much in the tonic, becomes rhythmically unified, and in the succession of its formulas is extended to a similarly closed phase. By that means intensifications between the themes are then effected, which can now also partly take up the material of the themes.   The central function of the figurational motives first becomes understandable only at the conclusion of the movement: though they serve, first of all, for contrast and to stabilize longer expanses, they progressively become related to the thematic material and attached to it.

In contrast to the complicated process in Op. 44 no. 3, that of Op. 44 no. 2 is more representative. The first four-measure unit after the extension of the principal thematic area (mm. 25ff.) incorporates two motivic impulses: one (a) circumscribes the area of the tonic in unison sixteenth notes; the other one (b), with upbeat note repetitions and triadic descent in eighth notes, only later establishes the connection to the opening of the movement. In both cases—without employing the theme—the transition is filled out by intensification and exhaustive reduction up to the secondary thematic area. After that, its remnants join to motive a; the single insertion with reverse-dotted rhythm (m. 77) devolves, however, into motive b (mm. 78ff.), and from that is derived the accompaniment to the first citation of the principal thematic area, serving as closing group (mm. 84ff.), which in addition is imitated here in the cello.

5. The fact that Mendelssohn's developments do not primarily aim at intensive thematic working out would be open to objection if the themes were designed for that.   However much one might regret the absence of dialectic or drama, the avoidance of it is consistent. Criticism of the themes would be appropriate if their treatment strove toward the Classic model; but to the degree that they are governed by another thematic style, a textbook working out would be incongruous. One certainly can constitute model groups as usual and classify them according to techniques of setting, and it would be easy to show that the developments correspond in their layout with the expositions in such a way that the description "modified exposition" would not appear to be inappropriate. One who operates in that way may complain of the loss of the Classic standard.[12] But in that manner one would take as an assumption the very thing that needs to be discussed: the relationship between material and procedure. Obviously, the analogy of the parts of the form is just as much planned as is the avoidance of thematic contrast and intensive working out, for a thematic style that is built up less of pregnant head-motives than closed song lines permits motivic fragmentation and contrasting derivation only to a limited extent. Where, moreover, head motives are split off, there remain usable only formulas that little suit the process of development but that then become strung out like figurational motives into entire chains. On the other hand, though, the style of thematic melody rather suggests the repetition of lengthier melodic segments, which simultaneously, however, also necessitate techniques for varying them. The goal of the development is less to fragment themes, to develop and to liquidate them, than to vary them while preserving their integrity, to play out latent relationships, and to set up connections to the auxiliary

material. The development unfolds more richly the interconnections laid out in the exposition, without fundamentally altering them: from the unclassical structure of the themes it draws unclassical consequences. The fact that this takes place rather unpretentiously than ostentatiously may explain many misunderstandings of judgment. Naturally, the traditional techniques continue to persist, probably for the most part, in the weaker works, in which combinations that are not so compact succeed. In individual cases the procedures that express the principal themes are quite varied; in general, however, thematic working out subordinates itself to combinatorial connections; it recedes behind the repetition of theme segments in transposition, sequencing, and figurational variation, behind pairing of the themes with each other and with figurational motives.

If the development in Op. 44 no. 3 proceeds in exceptional fashion, though appropriately to its thematic structure, beginning by combining the themes in order then to dismantle them, then in Op. 44 no. 2, by contrast, a contraction of the antecedent and consequent of the main thematic area wanders cantus-firmus-like through the voices (mm. 103ff.). Only in passing does it undergo fragmentation; the syncopated accompaniment of the beginning becomes increasingly fleshed out, however, as in the closing group. In the second phase the opening of the theme and motive a are combined, at first inconspicuously in succession and then clearly simultaneously in imitative condensation (mm. 138ff.). In the third phase the opening of the principal thematic area connects to the citation of the secondary theme—the analogy of the themes is demonstrated directly (mm. 160ff.). As the main theme further undergoes diminution in free, apparently closer imitation, it then additionally serves in this form as accompaniment of the original form at the entrance of the recapitulation (mm. 173ff.). This represents not only a model case of economical retransition: this phase is much more the goal of the development and the center point of the movement. Secondary and principal thematic areas in succession reveal their connection, the principal theme is combined with itself, and the accompaniment formulas, like motive b, legitimate themselves at this point as derivative of the principal theme.

6. The fact that the recapitulation and coda can hardly function as "synthesis" is due to the status of the development. More especially, as a result, the recapitulation threatens to become a conventional repetition. It is likely to correspond to the exposition without reorganizations and irregularities—not, however, without differences. The most striking are the thoroughgoing abbreviations, which involve in particular the transition.[13] This might seem to suggest that the eliminated parts were so insignificant as to be expendable. The situation is not entirely so simple. Certainly, the omissions succeed in producing concision and reflect concern for monotony, but they are primarily based in the function of the parts involved. In the autographs, significantly enough, they are at first written out exactly, only thereafter being eliminated to the same extent that the course of the movement achieves its definitive contour. Their original purpose consisted in producing supplementary material, to bring in contrasts, to enter into combinations with the themes. This also motivates their now falling away: the

repetition would be illogical now that new impulses have been integrated, contrasts balanced, relationships unfolded. The abbreviations constitute precisely the interpretation of the course of the movement; at the same time the recapitulation continues the process of variation, relative now to complete parts of the form and not only to thematic details. Similarly, the coda does not form a mere appendage but rather a structural limb with its own importance. It corresponds broadly to the development, even though it does not achieve its scope, but it brings out additional, closely related combinations in greater concentration. Insofar as recapitulation and coda do not simply form abbreviated repetitions, they legitimate themselves by means of variation and concentration. The large-scale formal process corresponds to the principle of mediation of closed phases, which determines the resolution of the small groups.

The abbreviation of the recapitulations applies effectively to all Mendelssohn's mature sonata-form movements and further to all the movements that come to terms with the sonata scheme. In Op. 44 no. 2, after the shortened principal thematic area, all that remains of the first transition is the preparation of the secondary thematic area; for that purpose five measures of intensification are introduced, which are constructed from the extension of the principal thematic area (mm. 187–91). At the return of the secondary thematic area an interpolation is inserted, which spins out over a pedal point the motivic style analogous to b, relatable to the principal thematic area (mm. 212–20). After the closing group the consequent of the principal theme (in imitative combination with its beginning) is made use of for the first time and then intensified with a syncopated accompaniment (mm. 242ff.). In the coda the principal theme and motive a come together for the first time in the tonic, moreover in the outer voices (mm. 255ff.), after which group a (again for the first time) by itself undergoes an intensification in quasi-fragmented but de facto unison setting (mm. 259ff.). The sequence of secondary thematic area, principal theme, and their diminution is then comparable, with slight variation, to the central concluding limb of the development, but the principal theme links up here in a sonorous intensification as the closure to the movement (mm. 266ff., mm. 277ff.).

7. Mendelssohn's melodic style frequently encounters the reproach that it lacks profile, and undeniably there is a homogeneousness about it, which can upset its supporters. To be sure, criticism—here as elsewhere—also acknowledged according to the fashion a marked peculiarity, however variously one may value this. This principle-like plain homogeneity—where it genuinely occurs—is hardly identical with weakness or facility but rather has its function for Mendelssohn's composing. To understand it ought to be more important than the classification of typical turns of phrase, which then easily appear to be mere mannerisms.[14] In fact, the Classic principle of discontinuity of groups of motives and measures is largely given up, without, however, on that account renouncing thematic organization of the whole. The fact that such a lyrical melos—with which A. B. Marx already found fault[15]--enters into Classic formal structures has a significance that until now has hardly been correctly evaluated, for from this results that tendency to repetition of entire thematic segments in place of their motivic dismantling, which becomes

the opening for the idea of procedures of variation and combination. This happens, indeed, without constraint and also without strictness, yet the tendency is unmistakable. But should the movement be criticized for such melodic unity, then it could be assumed that the melodic style of the themes, first of all, looks neutral, just as it also does in Mendelssohn's variation-form works. In them, too, the themes might seem to be lacking in profile, if one took them out of context and judged them according to Classic standards. This melodic style contains not only possibilities for spinning out and unification in itself but also chances for construction of the often only associatively perceptible analogies and combinations for the purpose of linking otherwise isolated phases of the movements. Its dominance grows stronger in that the figurational motives subordinate themselves, so that, on one hand, they are magnified into areas of tone and, on the other hand, they can be combined with the theme segments. The contradiction between the structure of this melodic style and its function in the formal framework might be a ground for divergent judgments; then, too, it can also hardly be challenged that in weaker works there is the danger of pure disconnectedness.

How much all this applies to Op. 44 no. 2 hardly requires comment. The lyricism of the themes is as unmistakable as the initially limited profile of the figurational motives. The formulaic conduct of these motives is, at the same time, a prerequisite for its connection with the themes, to which they become associated as impulses of figural variation. Similarly, the congruence of the melodic style of the themes forms a basis for their connection at the end of the development and coda, to which, to be sure, metric and harmonic factors contribute, as well.

8. A concept of composition (i.e., Satzkonzept) that proceeds from themes with a uniformly dominant melodic voice may be directly questionable in the string quartet, for the relegation of three voices to mere background not only contradicts the idea of the obbligato accompaniment but, even more particularly, also contradicts the demand of the quartet for equal importance among the voices. It would rather seem to be more likely in orchestral music or chamber music with piano that groups of voices would be subordinated as filler or figuration. The frequent criticism that Mendelssohn's quartets suffer from a too orchestral setting bears witness to an ideal of pure chamber music that is compromised not only in the case of Mendelssohn.[16] Meanwhile, that which appears to be a vacuum of mere accompaniment to the presentation of themes also has its function here. Precisely because the alleged accompaniment scoring is primarily only like an undercoating, empty of expression and interchangeable with itself, it makes possible increasing alteration, consolidation, and likewise thematicization. It is not only an impulse of Romantic inclination but rather a prerequisite for the initiation of variation and combination of theme segments; it achieves its own structural significance the more that the thematic segments preserve their integrity instead of becoming broken up. The initial accompaniment function is therefore not simply an indicator of the song structure in the thematic formation but rather also an ingredient of a plan of scoring, which strives for the linking together of such song units. That which, measured by Classic procedures, rightly falls victim to criticism attains in this way

a triple justification. First of all, the figurative or chordal accompaniment belongs to the song scoring as a controlling point of departure. Second, its unprofiled flow gives incentive and latitude to the gradual development in the scoring. Finally, the accompaniment formulas legitimate themselves to the extent that they accumulate intensifying or motivic significance beyond their original role. The contradiction between appearance and function is once again constitutive: the melodic style that at the outset is self-contained has value not only for itself; and the accompaniment, which is at first subordinate, for its part attains comparable substance.

The fact that the principal thematic area in Op. 44 no. 2 is accompanied by syncopations in the middle voices and lengthier supporting tones in the cello certainly allows the melody part and its coherence to come out prominently but might still work poorly in terms of the scoring technique. As the principal thematic area returns in the closing group, however, formulas from motive-group b of the transition are added to it. The increasing penetration of the accompaniment with motive groups b and a, leading up to the contrapuntal treatment of the theme by means of its own abbreviation as a variant of b, marks the stages in the variative process of the development. By contrast, the secondary thematic area remains unaltered in its chordal structure, in order to couple itself with the citation of the principal theme toward the end of the development.

9. Lyrical melodic style and subordinate accompaniment are not easily compatible with the strict working out and thematic organization of sonata form. All the methods by which one might seek to solve this dilemma cannot be summarized in brief; they find a common denominator, however, in the abandonment of Classic usage: to measure Mendelssohn's procedure by the demands of Classic working out fails to the extent that his technique tries to dissociate itself from that approach. Moreover, the regularity of the formal shell is bound to be disappointing. Certainly, one also encounters motivic work and fragmentation everywhere; yet these arise more incidentally and neither especially artfully nor by logical consequence.[17] Hardly ever do they involve secondary thematic areas, which are cited only as wholes; and in their application to principal themes the danger persists that only gestures and formulas survive. It almost seems as if the preference for contrapuntal technique, which is just as often praised as criticized in Mendelssohn's music, serves as a compensation. If the stricter the counterpoint, the more it may be taken as an indicator of the restorative, then the simpler the triadically based thematic style, the more automatically one might make the accusation of false artifice. Yet Mendelssohn's procedures are not to be measured unqualifiedly by the yardstick of correct counterpoint; it would be much more sensible to ask how much they are able to free themselves from it. To be sure, passages of close imitation also turn up quite often in the quartets, but then they are introduced inconspicuously, and the not-altogether-rare canonic structures are either freely constructed or relegated to subordinate positions (as in Op. 44 no. 1). Fugati may also be found in mature works—unlike in the early oeuvre—less in sonata-form movements than in scherzi and rondo finales, where they become components of the artificial playing with contrasting elements of form. The single

quartet fugue (Op. 81 mvt. 4, 1827) and the fugal capriccio (Op. 81 mvt. 3, 1843) are—in opposite ways—textbook examples for extensive employment of traditional counterpoint—even using highly traditional thematic style. The repetition of transposed parts of themes, which fills long phases, can also have the same effect as cantus firmus-work, yet the countervoices do not form contrapuntal scorings but rather are parts in the process of variational combinations. It would be worth asking, finally, to what extent such instances anticipate the process of variational development that Brahms later deployed with incomparably richer motivic work. Yet here variation has not so much the sense of transformation of whole units [gestalten] but rather restricts itself more to figurational variation, associated with the chain of connections.

In Op. 44 no. 2 motivic fragmentation is found incidentally in the first phase of the development (cello, m. 110), subsidiary to the repetition of the theme model, and then at the end of the development in the combination of themes. One might demonstrate imitation in the second phase of the development; however, it really belongs to the category of theme repetitions, which here are directly motivated less by cantus-firmus work than by figurative variations. Fugati occur in the scherzo (mm. 77ff.) and finale (mm. 212ff.) of the work, not in the first movement. Instances of open work may be seen in the employment of the theme's beginning at the end of the development or in the scattering out of motive a in the coda (mm. 165ff., 259ff.). In one case it has to do, however, only with alternating distribution of the triadic formulas, and, in the other, with dismantled chains of unisons. The opening syncopated accompaniment, however, which is only hinted at unobtrusively in the beginning of the development, otherwise is withheld until the intensification group at the boundary between the recapitulation and coda (mm. 242ff.).

10. Mendelssohn's rhythmic idiom shares with almost all the components of his style of composition the fact that its problemlessness is not unproblematic. It would be tedious to go on in detail about its power, originality, or complexity. The details that come to mind most prominently include the steady flow in 6/8 (not only in barcarolles), the dotted rhythms (not only in marches), the evenness of relaxed quarter notes (not only in lyrical songs): a typification collectively that reaches across the borders of the genres.[18] An obvious example is the rhythmic resemblance of almost all the secondary themes, which the criticism challenges as undifferentiated mannerism. There are certainly contrary examples, again especially in scherzos and rondo finales, which, indeed, then fall subject themselves to the accusation of uniformity. Yet here, too, the facts of the matter appear to be more complicated. First of all, behind the facade of uniformity hides a profusion of differentiation, which—as is so often the case—is not recognizable at first glance. On the other hand, however, the apparent regularity has its function in the course of the movement and in Mendelssohn's composing as a whole. What the movement types have in common with regard to all rhythmic characteristics is a uniformity of its motion that probably marks most clearly the difference from the Classic style. The rhythmic style that lacks conflict, often restricted to relatively

simple formulas, primarily ensures the internal coherence of the larger segments of the music and, at the same time, their mutual linkage. If the avoidance of rhythmic contrasts and conflicts belongs straightforwardly to Mendelssohn's song setting, then rhythmic unification by means of figuration formulas above which the melodic voice expands also marks the analogous theme type. Insofar, then, as the steady stream of motion runs through entire phases of the movement, it also supports coherence in the case of changing diastematic substance; and where, on the other hand, the melodic style remains preserved, rhythmic formulas of one phase can be interspersed with, and mediatedly [*vermittelnd*] detached from, those of the following one. Above all, the rhythmic style (more than the diastematic) is decisive for the analogy of the themes, toward the relationship of which the movement plan is directed.

This even applies in a case of extreme rhythmic multiplicity such as Op. 44 no. 3, mvt. 1: the contrary rhythmic motives in the principal section become welded together in repeated statements, and as it goes on, they are less played out against each other than constantly set out in succession. In Op. 44 no. 2 the upbeat quality of the beginning of the theme determines the whole movement—with various nuances to be sure. The movement proceeds almost entirely with three kinds of motion: quarter notes in the themes, eighths and sixteenths in the figuration motives. It is characteristic how sparingly the syncopations of the theme's opening are introduced. The single surprise is the interpolation with dotted rhythm that points toward the closing group. Nevertheless, the exposition alone is a paradigm of rhythmic arrangement: quarter notes together with syncopations in the principal area, eighth notes in its extension, sixteenths and eighths in the transition, reduction to quarter notes in the secondary area, and so on. The principle of mediating combination depends as much on this as on the rhythmic analogy of the themes.

11.   While advanced harmonic style often serves as a yardstick of the Romantic or progressive, Mendelssohn's music is also confounded in those terms by the rebuke of simple convention. It would be difficult to demonstrate "pioneering innovations"—as Knepler demanded—directly in the harmonic style.[19] Lacking in harmonic functions and in contrast as opposed to the Classic, colorless and sparse in comparison to other Romantics, Mendelssohn's harmonic style is distinguished by slow changes of harmonic function, lingering on fundamental scale steps, and a narrow radius of mostly diatonic modulation; and where it makes use of chromatic coloring, these harmonies have the effect of being incidental and almost functionless. It would be easy to name a series of typical tendencies that his contemporaries already noted: the six-five and diminished seventh chord, the many pedal points and stereotypical suspensions, the raising of leading tones and secondary dominant evasions together with typical cadence formulas. Not only does the disposition of keys between the themes in the movements appear conventional, but it also does so between the movements in the cycle. In this aspect, however, not only are there exceptions and modifications, but directly in the early oeuvre one encounters unusual dissonances, key relations, and modulations. That does not change in the relatively simple harmonic style of the mature major

works, yet the evidence gives just as much to think about as the fact that immediately in first versions unexpected reversals and sharp dissonances often turn up, which are deleted or toned down only in the final revision. That fact indicates that such harmonies were not foreign to Mendelssohn, and just as it would be a hasty judgment to measure quality by harmonic daring, it would also not suffice to gloss over mere convention as economy. Nevertheless, that which deserves to be called economical in Mendelssohn's case is not only based on the ideal of polished euphony but should rather be explained on the basis of the function of the harmony. First of all, it is inherent in song texture that a diatonic framework should be presented unmistakably and undisturbed. Out of that, then, closed movement phases proceed, which are centered and thereby secured on a single scale degree. On the other hand, motivic and rhythmic caesuras can be bracketed in such a way that harmonic coherence is maintained across them. The fact that, finally, the simple course of the whole as background is only sparingly colored by chromaticism indeed supports the accusation of limited functional significance. Yet by that means the centering of the phases is strengthened, which compensates for the scope of the sometimes subtle nuancing.

The plainness of the harmonic disposition in Op. 44 no. 2 does not need to be elaborated. It is not limited only to the exposition but extends to the quite sparingly modulating development. The tonal centering of the units is especially clear, even in the transitional and development sections. In spite of that, the secondary area enters in an unexpected reversal after a rich preparation that is directed in another way (mm. 53–54), and the harmonic coloration of its repetition is as precisely meted out as that of the accompanying formulas to the principal thematic area. The insertion before the closing group finds harmonic accentuation also in the recapitulation (mm. 229ff.), and conversely, the junction of the principal thematic area and transition indicates how caesuras can be covered over by means of harmonic connection (mm. 24-25).

12. Hardly any peculiarity of Mendelssohn's has aroused so much criticism as the symmetry of "square" periodicity. Inseparable from that is the principle of persistent repetition of groups of measures: the two mutually reinforce each other. Again one can put forward exceptions, mostly in experimental early works and in mature scherzos, whose differentiated, partially even intricate metrical style is indisputable. But this alters only slightly the complete body of the major works, which in this regard can be measured neither against Mozartian variety nor against Brahmsian complexity. Besides the criticism that arose early on, however, the peculiar intertwining of regularly constructed measure groups was also remarked upon (a feature against which J. Chr. Lobe even thought it necessary to give a warning).[20] Irregularities, too, as one encounters them in the scherzi, result less from the lengths of the measure groups than from their intertwining and disparate contents. As far as this is concerned, the autographs can instruct the skeptic, too, that the regularity of the ordering of the periods has hardly anything to do with mere routine but rather forms throughout an object of constructive calculation. More productive than the search for irregularities (which, as far as possible, still

remain imperceptibly camouflaged) is the question of how the general regularity is to be understood. Obviously, the framework of measure groups and repetitions does not simply have the usual sense of patterning and confirmation. Probably it has that, too, but the repetition of such symmetrical structures does not concern discontinuous groups but rather closed units. Here they become problematic, because within the repeated groups change and contrasts are avoided or mitigated: what is repeated is what would anyway be intelligible and therefore can become monotonous. Three considerations are apparently determinative. The strict periodic structure is, first of all, like the plain harmonic style, a constitutive impetus of the lyrical organization of the lines; it furnishes the framework within the boundaries of which the movement is enclosed, in order to open itself up and gradually to unfold itself. Second, it serves for the stabilization and consolidation of the groups and phases, from the loosening of which the movement constitutes itself. Finally, it operates in the service of the mediation and connecting of such groups with their repetitions. In repetition the measure group undergoes confirmation, and if in the process variations are introduced, the impetus of the following group anticipated, then one is meshed with another. There is hardly a repetition without such variations, and departures from the rule can usually be accounted for. What is new here is not so much the principle as the consequence. The rigid framework is the prerequisite for continuous interweaving in consolidation and progress at the same time. This comes to fruition in the constant change of impulses, of which at least one remains preserved while the others change, in exchange for which the periodic style itself is only rarely disturbed. This framework is broken up for the first time only in the working-out and development phases, to be restabilized then at the quotations of the themes. Nowhere else, probably, can the categories that are determinative for Mendelssohn's art—those that may be identified by the catchwords economy and organicism, mediation and equilibrium, analogy and variation—to be pursued.

In Op. 44 no. 2 the themes themselves are entirely regular in their construction, but their repetitions are already model instances of variations in the functional sense. The same is true of the first four-measure group of the transition, the repetition of which exhibits concentrating variations. The link between principal area and transition introduces the first irregularity: a half measure is omitted (m. 25). In the transition, as in the development, the abbreviation takes place down to one- and half-measure groups, from which point the transition to the secondary area and the retransition to the recapitulation, respectively, link back to the earlier regularity. Like the metrical irregularities, literal repetitions appear in an outstanding position (so, e.g., the first combination of the principal theme and motive a at the beginning of the coda).

III

In conclusion, it is necessary to differentiate not only between genres but also within the quartets.[21] That the circumstances are modified in orchestral and keyboard works is clear, and that is especially the case for the vocal music, as fundamental as is the song-type. In the quartets the observations apply primarily to the sonata-form and also to the slow movements, which, beginning with Op. 44, come to grips with the "Lied ohne Worte." It seems to be otherwise, rather, with the scherzos—the supposed "elfen pieces": arranged from artificial play with formal types in ever-different hybridization, they are based on a thematic construction out of small building blocks, which come together in mosaic-like constellations to arouse constantly different expectations, which they then fulfill. With all the discrepancies, the same categories of mediation, economy, and equilibrium apply to them as to the final movements, which, as sonata rondos, take up impulses from sonata and song setting.

One must further modify in view of the stages of Mendelssohn's compositional progress, which the quartets document especially well. If in the early E♭-major Quartet—as in the youthful sinfonias—the discontinuity of the groups dominates, with all its consequences, then Op. 20 and Op. 18 announce the method of construction out of closed larger units, which certainly does not come from thematic analogies but rather from motivic intermeshing. As thoroughly as Op. 13 and still Op. 12 carry through formally as well as technically the coming to grips with Beethoven's late quartets, just as much does comparison with the models also reveal how directly in these exceptional works the process that is fundamental to Mendelssohn is tested. To that extent the encounter with Beethoven is—as paradoxical as it sounds—also a presupposition for the apparently "classicistic" quartets Op. 44. The theses that apply to them apply broadly to the adjacent works, such as Opp. 45, 49, 58, and 87, as well, but also probably to piano music, symphonies, and concertos of those years. The case is different for the late works, somewhat for Op. 66 with its concise motivic formulas and especially for Op. 80 with unmediated juxtapositions that contrast markedly. Decisive, however, is still the construction of closed phases as collision of variational and combinatorial technique.

A number of objections may arise. One might fail to grasp the analytic foundation and might be concerned that too much generalization has taken place here. Admittedly, it was emphasized—moreover, based on one emphatic example. However, in the case of the counterexample Op. 44 no. 3—by means of reversal of the premises—the applicability of the compositional principles sketched out here could be confirmed. The objection suggests itself that the fullness of relationships discussed earlier might be more an analytical construction. A confirmation can again be provided by the autographs, which—even for Op. 44—show how deliberately analogies, repetitions, and variants were worked out. The suspicion may remain that, when all is said and done, the material is too lacking in profile to support such relationships—even assuming their existence. With that the core question of Mendelssohn's music is certainly raised, but its intention is hardly removed from consideration by that means, however much it is also to be granted that qualitative problems and also differences between the works persist. One may find Mendelssohn's music too transparent, too weakly profiled, or too lacking in contrast—its technical standard, its personal individuality, and its historical influence, despite all differences in judgments of it, are nevertheless not to be ignored.

NOTES

This Chapter first appeared in German as "Zur Kompositionsart Mendelssohns: Thesen am Beispiel der Streichquartette," in *Das Problem Mendelssohn*, ed. Carl Dahlhaus, Studien zur Musikgeschichte des 19. Jahrhunderts 41 (Regensburg: Bosse, 1974), 169–84, and in *Felix Mendelssohn Bartholdy*, ed. Heinz-Klaus Metzger and Rainer Riehn, Musik-Konzepte: Die Reihe über Komposition 14/15 (Munich: Text + Kritik, 1980), 46–74.

1. Where a new interest in Mendelssohn is emerging at the present time, it is directed less toward the music than toward the circumstances of the biography and influence, based on untapped resources and letters. At least partially, this also goes for the important contributions that—among various examples—Eric Werner and Georg Knepler have produced. See Eric Werner, *Mendelssohn: A New Image of the Composer and His Age* (New York: Free Press of Glencoe, 1963), and "Mendelssohn," in *Die Musik in Geschichte und Gegenwart*, ed. Friedrich Blume (Kassel: Bärenreiter, 1961), 9: 59–98; Georg Knepler, *Musikgeschichte des 19. Jahrhunderts*, vol. 2 (Berlin: Hensche, 1961). But to the extent that Mendelssohn's music-historical significance is grounded in his oeuvre, the reservations toward, and prejudices against, his music may not be ignored.

2. The widespread objections to Mendelssohn's music are not laid out here in detail. In the following only a summary of the criticism, which runs throughout the entire German and English literature, mainly before the turn of the century, is extracted (even just the histories of music, dictionaries, and concert guides offer sufficient examples). A synopsis of the Mendelssohn reception is found in a study by the author in which the works mentioned here are also investigated more closely; see Friedhelm Krummacher, *Mendelssohn—der Komponist* (Munich: Wilhelm Fink, 1978).

3. What follows is directed primarily to the following works: String Quartets in E♭ major without opus number (1823); A minor, Op. 13 (1827); E♭ major, Op. 12 (1829); D major, E minor, E♭ major, Op. 44 nos. 1–3 (1837–1838), F minor, Op. 80 (1847); as well as the movements edited posthumously into Op. 81 (1–2, 1847; 3, 1843, 4, 1827); further the Octet in E♭ major, Op. 20 (1825, revised 1983); the String Quintets in A major, Op. 18 (1826; Intermezzo, 1832) and B♭ major Op. 87 (1845); together with the Piano Trios in D minor Op. 49 (1839) and C minor Op. 66 (1845), the Violin Sonata in F major without opus number (1838), and the Cello Sonatas in B♭ Op. 45 (1839) and D Op. 58 (1843). It is entirely intentional that the mature works thus advance into the foreground. However informative the youthful works that are still coming to light may be for Mendelssohn's early maturity and development, they are nevertheless quite uneven in quality. Mendelssohn's historical position, which brought about the unremitting conflict of opinions, is not based on them but rather on the later works.

4. Werner and Knepler, too, favored particular, emotionally effective works, especially Op. 13 and Op. 80, which, however, together form rather exceptional cases. Op. 80 stands at the end of the output—not without sharp differences from the rest of the oeuvre; and Op. 13 is so indebted to the late Beethoven that it may be pronounced epigonal, if one does not also try to grasp the fundamental—and not only qualitative—differences. Undoubtedly, however, the mature works that are condemned as "classicistic" are the most independent and historically most important.

5. This movement from Op. 44, no. 2, which is so especially regular, is chosen advisedly (the measure numbering in this case includes all the notated measures, inclusive of the second ending). The E♭ major Quartet, Op. 44 no. 3, realizes analogous principles to the E minor Quartet, which originated first, but with different thematic presuppositions, while Op. 44 no. 1, as the last of the three pieces, attempts to combine the experience of the two preceding ones with virtuoso brilliance. The quartets of Op. 44 hold an outstanding position in Mendelssohn's work in that they returned again to the problem of the Classic cycle after a somewhat lengthy hiatus. Since Op. 12, no chamber music had appeared (with the exception of the peripheral Konzertstücke Opp. 113–14 and the Intermezzo to Op. 18), and after the First Piano Concerto, Op. 25, works such as the "Scottish" and "Italian" Symphonies were only conceived but not definitively completed. This is probably connected to the crisis, testified to in many expressions in his letters, into which Mendelssohn fell after his years of travel.

6. Particularly by A. B. Marx, *Die Lehre von der musikalischen Komposition*, vol. 3 (Leipzig: Breitkopf & Härtel, 1845; 2d ed. 1848), 201ff., 255ff., and even earlier by H. Birnbach in the series of essays "Ueber die verschiedene Form größerer Instrumentalwerke aller Art und deren Bearbeitung," *Berliner allgemeine musikalische Zeitung* 4–5 (1827–1828), *passim.* Cf. also Fr. Ritzel, *Die Entwicklung der "Sonaten" im musiktheoretischen Schrifttum des 18.–19. Jahrhunderts*, Neue musikgeschichtlichen Forschungen 1 (Wiesbaden: Breitkopf & Härtel, 1968).

7. Cf. H. Mersmann, *Die Kammermusik (Führer durch den Konzertsaal*, pt. 3) vol. 3, *Deutsche Romantik* (Leipzig: Breitkopf & Härtel, 1930), 60ff.; K. H. Wörner, *Felix Mendelssohn-Bartholdy: Leben und Werk* (Leipzig and Wiesbaden: Breitkopf & Härtel, 1947), 76f., 84ff., 89; also Wilfrid Mellers, *Romanticism and the 20th Century*, Man and His Music 4 (Fair Lawn, NJ: Essential Books, 1957), 28–30.

8. This was the opinion, for example, of W. Altmann: Mendelssohn "frequently failed to contrast the themes of his sonata movement in the manner of the great classical masters"; "Mendelssohn," in Cobbett's *Cyclopedic Survey of Chamber Music* (London: Oxford University Press, 1929; 2d ed. 1963), 128.

9. J. Horton, *The Chamber Music of Mendelssohn* (London: Oxford University Press, 1946), 25, found, for example, that Mendelssohn's principal themes created only "a rule of pretty tunes." An exemplary collection of stereotypical objections may be found in H. Foss, "Felix Mendelssohn-Bartholdy," in *The Heritage of Music*, vol. 2 (London: Oxford University Press, 1934), 151–74.

10. Cf. the initial attempts by L. Leven, "Mendelssohn als Lyriker" (diss., University of Frankfurt am Main, 1926; Krefeld: B. Mahler, 1927). The studies by L. (Hochdorf) Tischler and H. Tischler, indeed, tried to style the "Lied ohne Worte" as the center of the oeuvre but primarily wanted to assign a "Lied-ohne-Worte style" to harmonic or melodic turns in the other works, without considering the structure of the song scoring as the compositional basis. See L. Hochdorf, "Mendelssohns 'Lieder ohne Worte' . . ." (diss., University of Vienna, 1938; typescript); L. H. and H. Tischler "Mendelssohn's Songs without Words," *The Musical Quarterly* 33 (1947), 1–16; "Mendelssohn's Style: The Songs without Words," *The Music Review* 8 (1947), 256–73.

11. Cf. the definition by K. von Fischer, *Die Beziehungen von Form und Motiv in Beethovens Instrumentalwerken*, Sammlung musikwissenschaftlicher Abhandlungen 30 (Straßburg: P. H. Heitz, 1948; 2d ed., Baden-Baden: Valentin Koerner, 1972), xvif. On the other hand, just such figuration was found fault with to a particular degree by criticism in Mendelssohn's case; see, for example, Th. Helm, *Beethovens Streichquartette* (Leipzig: Fritzsch, 1885), 314.

12. From the time that the study of form codified the Classic canon, Mendelssohn's procedure was also continuously reproached because it did not satisfy such a standard; see, for example, Fr. Brendel, *Geschichte der Musik in Italien, Deutschland und Frankreich*, 6th ed. (Leipzig: Heinrich Matthes, 1878), 479ff., or the work of Marx cited in note 16, 157f.

13. The fact that this abbreviation of the recapitulation belongs to Mendelssohn's fundamental trespasses against Classic formal structures was probably strongly emphasized only by W. Fischer; see "Felix Mendelssohn-Bartholdy: Zum 100. Todestag des Meisters deutscher Romantik," *Österreichische musikalische Zeitung* 2 (1947), 284–86.

14. K. Roeseling took such an approach in his study "Beiträge zur Untersuchung der Grundhaltung romantischer Melodik" (diss., University of Cologne, 1928; Oberkassel bei Bonn: J. Düppen, 1928), 84ff., 100ff.

15. A. B. Marx, *Die Musik des 19. Jahrhunderts und ihre Pflege: Methode der Musik* (Leipzig: Breitkopf & Härtel, 1855), 229.

16. Criticism of the orchestral scoring is found especially on the English-speaking side, for example, in the case of D. N. Ferguson, *Image and Structure in Chamber Music* (Minneapolis: University of Minnesota Press, 1964), 159; H. Ulrich, *Chamber Music: The Growth and Practice of an Intimate Art* (New York: Columbia University Press, 1948; 2d ed. 1953), 307f.; J. Horton, *The Chamber Music of Mendelssohn*, 23, 27, 45, and so on. On the other hand, P. H. Lang speaks of a "genuine feeling for ensemble work" in Mendelssohn's chamber music; *Music in Western Civilization* (New York: Norton, 1940), 822. On this topic see also L. Finscher, "Streichquartett," *MGG* (1963), 12: 1583f.

17. At any rate, in comparison with Beethoven. See, for example, the work of W. Broel, "Die Durchführungsgestaltung in Beethovens Sonatensätzen," *Neues Beethoven-Jahrbuch* 7 (1937), 37–90.

18. This may also motivate many of the formulations of G. Becking; see *Der musikalische Rhythmus als Erkenntnisquelle* (Augsburg: Filser, 1928; 2d ed. Stuttgart: Ichthys, 1958), 199ff.

19. Knepler, *Musikgeschichte*, 2: 273. That such colorations themselves could have been one of Mendelssohn's own contributions to "Romantic harmonic style" is hardly made entirely clear in E. Kurth, *Romantische Harmonik* . . . (Bern: Haupt, 1920), 185, 489.

20. J. Chr. Lobe, "Felix Mendelssohn Bartholdy: Eine biographische Skizze," in *Aus dem Leben eines Musikers* (Leipzig: Baumgärtner, 1859), 200–237, esp. 225f. Similarly, see also Ph. Spitta, "Niels W. Gade," in *Zur Musik* (Berlin: Breitkopf & Härtel, 1892), 355–83, particularly 372, as well as E. Bücken, *Die Musik des 19. Jahrhunderts bis zur Moderne* (Potsdam: Athenaion, 1932), 94.

21. It is the aim of the study cited in note 3 to identify more precisely such differentiation according to genre, form types, and types of setting, as well as by stages of Mendelssohn's compositional development.

HISTORICAL VIEWS AND DOCUMENTS

NOTES OF A MUSICAL TOURIST[1]

J. T.[2]

[The writer here reports on musical experiences within the Mendelssohn home in 1830, mentioning the presence and participation of some of the outstanding musicians who formed part of Mendelssohn's circle in those years—Adolf Bernhard Marx, the brothers Rietz, and Ferdinand David. The account demonstrates that these occasions were not simply for the performance of Mendelssohn's compositions but placed them in the context of chamber works by Haydn and Beethoven, including Beethoven's late quartets. Of considerable importance to the author is the claim that Mendelssohn worthily succeeds, and perhaps may even exceed, the classical composers in the field of chamber music.—Ed.]

During my stay at Berlin I enjoyed peculiar opportunities of becoming acquainted with the works of Felix Mendelssohn Bartholdy, the same gentleman who made so powerful an impression last season in London, at the Philharmonic and other concerts, by his Grand Symphony in C minor, and his Overture to "The Midsummer's Night Dream [*sic*]," as well as by his admirable performances on the piano-forte. You have already spoken in proper terms of both these noble compositions: I shall therefore merely add, that the symphony was written about three years ago, and the overture when he was only seventeen! By the time that he had attained his fourteenth year, Mr. M. had written many works of a high character. Of these I am in possession of three piano-forte quartetts, a comic opera, and two sonatas. These are the offspring of true genius: they bear the stamp of originality, and in every page one can perceive the hand of a master familiar with all the resources of his art. The quartetts are every way charming; their style is broad, free, and impassioned; they abound in exquisite traits of melody; and, what is rather remarkable, they are all in the minor key, to which, by the way, Mr. M. is very partial; for there is scarcely one of his great works in the major. They are upon the whole difficult of performance; but the study one must bestow in acquiring them is well repaid. I have had them tried very frequently, and I would not wish to listen to better music. The one in C minor, Op. 1, is of a very popular character, and a great favourite among us all here; but the other two, his op. 2 and 3, one dedicated to his master, Zelter, the other to Goethe, are more elaborate, and indeed altogether of a superior order: they require very nice and masterly performance. The following may give your readers some idea of what may be expected from the maturer years of one who could write thus at the tender age of fourteen.

Subject of the first Movement of Quartett in C Minor.

The Adagio of the Quartett in F Minor.

What vigor and fire in the finale of the same quartett!

Quartet in F Minor, finale theme.[3]

The scherzo of the Quartett in B minor is not less spirited, original, and extraordinary.

I trust that ere long these admirable compositions will be published in England.

. . .[4]

I was a regular attendant at the quartett parties, held twice a week, and sometimes oftener, in Mr. Mendelssohn's house. On these occasions, none were admitted but such as could appreciate and relish the classical works of Haydn, Mozart, and Beethoven. Mr. Marx,[5] the able editor of the Berlin Musical Gazette, a very agreeable and intelligent gentleman, was generally of the select few. The performers were Mr. Ritz,[6] an excellent and energetic performer, one of the best, I believe for chamber music, in the city; Mr. David Ritz,[7] a youth of about nineteen, often mentioned in your Foreign reports; a younger brother of the former[8]; and one or two others, whose uncouth patronymics it would be difficult for your *un-German* readers to pronounce. Mr. David, who was a concerto player at the age of twelve, possesses a brilliant tone, and performs with great execution and delightful expression. The younger Ritz, who played the violoncello, adds to a powerful tone a most vigorous bow. From long practice together, by which alone anything like unity of effect can be produced, they have acquired such proficiency as to render their performance quite satisfactory—a proficiency which even finer players, who seldom draw the bow together, must vainly hope to rival.

The selection of quartetts was principally from Haydn and Beethoven. Of the latter, the Op. 132, C major,[9] delighted me exceedingly. It is a remarkable specimen at once of the extravagance and power which characterize the later works of this master. It contains some wonderfully fine and novel effects, though, to speak impartially, as a whole it is unequal. The adagio, scherzo, and finale, are particularly charming. His Op. 127, in E♭, of a like arduous character, was also played with great animation and effect. Every one must admire the Siciliano movement.

Of Mr. Felix Mendelssohn's compositions, I was gratified with the performance of three, viz.: a quintett, a quartett, and a fugue in the strict style, à 4.[10] The quintett[11] is indeed a glorious work: it exhibits a more matured development of those features which I have already pointed out in speaking of his earlier instrumental writings. The quartett, however, is to my mind the finest by far of all Mr. M.'s compositions with which I am acquainted. It is in the key of A minor.[12] The ground-work of the whole piece is an exquisitely pathetic song, which I regret much that I cannot sufficiently remember, otherwise I might have presented it to your readers; and, certainly, the manner in which he has treated it throughout is eminently beautiful. The introduction is a stream of enchanting melody which is at length interrupted by a rapid passage of the tenor, imitated by the first violin thus[13]:

And then the allegro bursts in, and the following phrase is the one principally worked upon in the course of the movement:

The whole movement is of a wild and gloomy character, and though now and then relieved by some phrases of bewitching melody, yet there is a melancholy about even its lightest parts, that penetrates to the very heart.

The adagio which succeeds this energetic movement is of a religious character: it is solemn and impressive. Toward the middle of it, a very singular and original agitato episode breaks forth, which, after some curious and effective enharmonic changes, leads back to the first subject. I give you the commencement of the adagio.

The scherzo goes thus:

How playful and fanciful!

The finale is of the like lofty character as the first movement, and carries you along with it with the rapidity of thought. It is perhaps as fine a piece of writing as is to be found. On the whole, I have no hesitation in giving it as my most deliberate and decided opinion, that this quartett is, in every part of it, whether in the tender, the energetic, the solemn, or the gay, quite equal to any instrumental composition of Beethoven himself, with which I am acquainted; and I rather think that I know all his very best works. The fugue, though in the strict style, is very interesting, and from its quiet and flowing melody, tended much to soothe the excitation caused by the nervousness of the quartett.

Here, then, is a youth, who at the age of thirteen—an age when the faculties of most men are only about to appear—produced works in the highest classes of composition, instrumental and vocal, exhibiting the most original and felicitous conceptions, impassioned feeling, and scientific knowledge, not surpassed by any one in the prime of manhood:—who, before his sixteenth year, produced Grand Symphonies and Overtures, pronounced by competent judges to be worthy of a place beside those of the three greatest masters;—and who now (in his twenty-second year) is soaring into the regions of fancy with a strengthened wing, and even with a bolder flight. Is it too much, then to anticipate for him the proudest niche in the temple of Apollo? Haydn's early works have been lost, perhaps deservedly, in oblivion. With those of Mozart all are acquainted; but lovely though they be, it were ridiculous to put them forward as the germ of that genius which afterwards burst forth with so much splendour. And the opere prime of Beethoven were produced at a period of life much later than those of Mendelssohn. What, then, may not be expected from one who, in his first works, has not only surpassed those of the great names just mentioned, but in his later productions has equalled the elaborate compositions of their riper years. . . .

REVIEW OF MENDELSSOHN'S PIANO TRIO IN D MINOR, OP. 49[14]

Robert Schumann; translated by Douglass Seaton

[The excerpt translated here comes from a larger review of contemporary trios. Like Thomson in the preceding article, Schumann hopes to place Mendelssohn in historical context. Writing from a somewhat later perspective, Schumann regards Mendelssohn as the successor to the Romantic style of Beethoven and Schubert. He imagines him, however, to stand as Mozart to a yet-unknown future composer who would hold a position comparable to that of Beethoven; Schumann would, of course, find that later master in the young Johannes Brahms.—Ed.]

It only remains to say something about *Mendelssohn*'s Trio,—but only a little, since it is surely already in everyone's hands. It is the trio masterpiece of our time, as in their day were those of Beethoven in B♭ and D and that of Franz Schubert in E♭, a thoroughly beautiful composition, which in years to come will bring joy to grandchildren and great-grandchildren. The storm of recent years is gradually coming to an end and, we admit, has already cast up many pearls on the beach. Mendelssohn, although less tossed about by it than others, nevertheless also remains a child of his time, has also had to struggle, has often also had to hear some narrow-minded writers' idle chatter that "the true flowering of music is behind us," and has raised himself so high that we may well say that he is the Mozart of the nineteenth century, the most brilliant of musicians, who saw most clearly through the contradictions of the time and was first to resolve them. He will also not be the last artist. After Mozart came one Beethoven; the new Mozart will also be followed by a new Beethoven; indeed, he may already have been born. What more shall I say about this Trio that everyone who has heard it has not already said? Most fortunate, certainly, are those who have heard it played by its creator in person, for even if there are more dashing virtuosos, hardly any other knows how to perform Mendelssohn's works with such magical freshness as he himself. This should not make anyone afraid to play the Trio; in comparison to others, such as, for example, those of Schubert, it has fewer difficulties, but in first-rank works of art these always stand in proportion to its effect, for as the former increase, the latter increases correspondingly. Moreover, it need hardly be said that the Trio is not a piece just for the pianist; the other players also have to play their roles in lively fashion and can count on gaining satisfaction and appreciation. So may the new work be effective from all perspectives, as it should, and may it serve us as evidence of its creator's artistic power, which now appears to be near its full bloom.

MENDELSSOHN'S QUARTET IN F MINOR[15]

[By the middle of the nineteenth century the string quartet had become a symbol of Classicism and technical accomplishment. This effusive unsigned article invokes two powerful tenets of Romanticism to interpret Mendelssohn's String Quartet, Op. 80: the image of the composer as working under the force of pure inspiration and the necessity of approaching the work from an understanding of its persona—here, Mendelssohn grieving at the death of his sister Fanny. At its conclusion, the essay adopts an aesthetic position that Mendelssohn himself would have approved, suggesting that the definite, but verbally inexpressible, meaning of the music remains always precisely the same, for the hearer as well as for the composer-persona.—Ed.]

This Quartet, one of the most interesting, from circumstances no less than from beauty, of the enormous legacy of unpublished works that Mendelssohn left for his tardy executors to dole out to the world, with, to consider it at the best, the seeming indifference of ceaselessly lingering, uselessly protracted delay—this Quartet, that must be peculiarly dear to all who understand, and therefore necessarily love the music of Mendelssohn, since it is an epitome of whatever is most individual to, and therefore most fascinating in, the master—this Quartet is said to have been written at the time of the death of the composer's much-loved sister, a very few months before his own. All the spontaneity that is most eminently a characteristic of our author's music, all the passionate fervor in which no one that ever wrote has exceeded him, are evinced in this composition to an extent scarcely equalled in any of his other productions; while we see that the power of development, and the facility of construction, which essentially distinguish a master, in the beauty and originality of his ideas, prove his genius was exercised with that accustomed fluency which might be supposed to spring less from educational acquirement than from original instinct. The work presents every intrinsic evidence of being the result of impulse rather than of design, of having been written without premeditation or purpose, and because the ideas rather forced themselves upon the composer, and demanded of him expression, than were sought by him in fulfilment of a foregone intention. Such indication is corroborated by a story that prevails of the Quartet having been written with the electric velocity, that is proverbially called the speed of thought, but which is a speed that, practically, thought rarely attains,—namely, within some eight-and-forty hours; and it may therefore be regarded as the result of one of those sudden inspirations—no more material expression will compass my meaning—one of those inspirations by means of which a mind capable of great thought, with the means under control to mould such thought into form, even produces its greatest works the quickest. The complete unity of feeling that assimilates the several portions of the composition, the entire absence of research throughout the whole, the conciseness yet comprehensiveness of the plan of each movement,—these are among the characteristics to which I have referred, that give the work the character of being an improvisation; and it is this effect that most closely appeals to our sympathies, making us feel that the music is an unrestrained, unstudied outpouring from the innermost heart of one whose passion was as a fire intense and irresistible, igniting the sense of all whom it touches, and making us to burn with his emotion. In Italy, where modern art took its rise, Music was placed at the head of the sisterhood,—a supremacy that, however she be deprecated by such as cannot understand her, she more and more worthily asserts, especially as she is more and more successfully employed for the medium of expression of such subtleties of feeling as are without the scope of words, and, since they are not defined in our books, are beyond the power of graphic imitation. To this most exalted purpose is music, the chief of the fine arts, devoted in the work before us; in which the unsayable, the intangible, the invisible, the else-incommunicable, deepest emotions of the human heart are rendered, not with cold, severe nakedness of a metaphysical anatomy, but with the warm and truly genial glow of poetry, which, like the sunrise, beautifies all that it irradiates. The keenest anguish in every phase of our experience, from despair to resignation,—the two extremes of love that join in their mutual renewal—this is the train of emotion that the music we are now to hear embodies. It was written under the poignancy of the grief occasioned by a much-loved sister's loss; it is heard under the regret, which nothing but the brightness of his genius that evokes it can dissipate, for the loss of Mendelssohn; it may be strictly called her Monody; it must be felt to be his own. By the power of his genius the great musician stimulates, enforces our sympathies; our appreciation of this power defines their object; we cannot but feel all the beauty and all the pathos it embodies of his music; that we feel it and that we know it to be him who causes us to feel it, makes him the subject of the sorrow that it sings. Thus, let us believe that in listening to this Quartet we especially pay a tribute of feeling to the memory of the master; we heave a sigh on reading his epitaph—the epitaph of which himself is the author; in his own grief-accents let us acknowledge the tones of our regret, and our regret will wear the color of his beauty.

NOTES

1. Excerpted from a report in *The Harmonicon* 8/3 (March 1830), 97–101.

2. J. T. is presumably John Thomson (1805–1841), for whom Mendelssohn wrote a letter of introduction to his family on 30 July 1829. See Sebastian Hensel, *Die Familie Mendelssohn 1729 bis 1847 nach Briefen und Tagebüchern* (Berlin: Georg Reimer, 1918), 267; see also *The Mendelssohn Family (1729–1847) from Letters and Journals*, trans. Carl Klingemann and an American collaborator (New York: Harper, 1882), 197, where, however, Thomson's first initial is incorrectly given as *T.*, and both German and English versions insert the letter *p* after the *m* in his surname. Thomson later studied in Leipzig. He was named the first Reid Professor of Music at the University of Edinburgh in 1839. Thomson would also provide to the readers of *The Harmonicon* an arrangement of the third movement ("Intermezzo") of the Piano Quartet in F Minor, Op. 2, arranged for flute and piano. See *The Harmonicon* 8/6 (June 1830), 235–40.

3. Thomson's citation here is based on the piano repetition beginning in m. 13 rather than the opening string phrase.

4. The article continues with a report about *Die Hochzeit des Camacho* and Mendelssohn's songs, as well as some comments about Fanny, with whom Thomson was very impressed.

5. Adolf Bernhard Marx (1795–1866) edited the *Berliner allgemeine musikalische Zeitung* from 1824 to 1830.

6. Eduard Rietz (1802–1832) was a talented violinist and close friend of Mendelssohn.

7. This is an error. Thomson presumably meant to name here the violin prodigy Ferdinand David (1810–1873) who later became Mendelssohn's concertmaster with the Leipzig Gewandhaus Orchestra and the violin teacher at the Leipzig Conservatory.

8. Julius Rietz (1812–1877) was Eduard Rietz's brother and a fine cellist. He later taught composition at the Leipzig Conservatory, directed the Gewandhaus Orchestra after Mendelssohn's death, and, most importantly, served as editor for the collected edition of Mendelssohn's *Werke*.

9. Beethoven's String Quartet Op. 132 is, in fact, in the key of A minor. This seems a peculiar error, given Thomson's apparently good memory, manifested in his ability to recall themes from Mendelssohn's works in the following paragraphs.

10. It is not possible to identify the fugue. Mendelssohn had written a large number of fugues for quartet in early 1821, and it is not impossible that Thomson heard one of these. Perhaps a more likely candidate would be the fugue later published as Op. 81 no. 4, which had been composed in 1827.

11. Quintet in A major, Op. 18.

12. Op. 13.

13. Having put down this, as well as the other fragments of the quartett, from memory, some allowance must be made, should I have a wrong note or two. [Thomson's note]

14. Excerpted from the *Neue Zeitschrift für Musik* 13/50 (19 December 1840), 198.

15. From *Dwight's Journal of Music* 3/8 (28 May 1853), 61. Originally published in the London *Musical World*.

9

Piano Music Reformed: The Case of Felix Mendelssohn Bartholdy

R. Larry Todd

Mendelssohn is today generally not highly esteemed as a composer of piano music, yet the piano played a central role in his career. Some twenty-five years separate his earliest preserved efforts for the instrument (ca. 1820) from what were perhaps his final piano works, the *Lieder ohne Worte* Op. 102 nos. 3 and 5, composed in December 1845, less than two years before his death.[1] All told, the piano repertory comprises some 150 compositions. Of these, Mendelssohn released about seventy in seventeen opera; roughly twenty-five other works appeared posthumously during the nineteenth century in eleven additional opera.[2]

Whether composing for the piano or other instruments, Mendelssohn habitually used in his sketches a two-stave, treble-bass format, suggesting that if he did not work at the piano, the sound of the instrument was never far removed from the wellspring of his inspiration. Mendelssohn's powers as a keyboard performer and improviser—at the piano and organ alike—were widely celebrated and documented by such witnesses as Ferdinand Hiller, Ignaz Moscheles, Robert Schumann, Hector Berlioz, Joseph Joachim, and Goethe, among others.[3] His fastidious, elegant style of performance was especially highly prized. In an age of virtuosity, declared his early biographer, W. A. Lampadius,

Mendelssohn's skill as a virtuoso was no mere legerdemain, no enormous finger facility, that only aims to dazzle by trills, chromatic runs, and octave passages; it was that true, manly *virtus* from which the word virtuoso is derived; that steadfast energy which overcomes all mechanical hinderances, not to produce musical noise, but music, and not satisfied with any thing short of exhibiting the very spirit of productions written in every age of musical art. The characteristic features of his playing were a very elastic touch, a wonderful trill, elegance, roundness, firmness, perfect articulation, strength, and tenderness, each in its needed place. His chief excellence lay, as Goethe said, in his giving every piece, from the Bach epoch down, its own distinctive character.[4]

These encomia aside, Mendelssohn's own piano music has not withstood the test of time unscathed. For the most part, it impresses as comfortable (*gemütlich*), secure music for the salon. Its reliance on older models, for example, the music of J. S. Bach, and its generous applications of rigorous counterpoint were noticed by Robert Schumann for whom, to adopt Leon Plantinga's interpretation, Mendelssohn's piano music was somehow not "fully congruent with the expectations of present-day musical culture."[5] Mendelssohn's keyboard style also exudes a certain sentimental, even saccharine quality—regrettably reinforced after his death by numerous editions of the *Lieder ohne Worte* adorned with fanciful, unauthorized titles—that reflects the conservative temper of the *Restaurationszeit* in Germany and the Victorian period in England.

Occasionally, Mendelssohn himself expressed dissatisfaction with his piano music. After finishing the *Rondo brillant*, Op. 29, for piano and orchestra in 1834, he confessed to Ignaz Moscheles: "My own poverty in shaping new forms for the pianoforte once more struck me most forcibly whilst writing the Rondo. It is there I get into difficulties and have to toil and labor, and I am afraid you will notice that such was the case."[6] Later that year, in another letter to Moscheles: "You once said it was time I should write a quiet, sober piece for the pianoforte, after all those restless ones; and that advice is always running in my head and stops me at the outset, for as soon as I think of a pianoforte piece, away I career, and scarcely am I off when I remember, 'Moscheles said, etc.' and there's an end to the piece."[7] In 1835 Mendelssohn wrote to Ferdinand Hiller: "I have some new pianoforte things, and shall shortly publish some of them. I always think of you and your warning whenever an old-fashioned passage comes into my head, and hope to get rid of such ideas." Again in 1838, to Hiller: "Pianoforte pieces are not exactly the things which I write with the greatest pleasure, or even with real success; but I sometimes want a new thing to play, and then if something exactly suitable for the piano happens to come into my head, even if there are no regular passages in it, why should I be afraid of writing it down?"[8]

But if Mendelssohn judged his own piano music severely, he maintained a no less critical gaze toward the piano music of his own time. The music of Beethoven remained beyond reproach for him, and he also highly esteemed the piano works of his close friend (and senior by fifteen years) Moscheles and selected works by Weber (the sonatas, *Aufforderung zum Tanze*, and *Konzertstück*). Little else, however, elicited his critical approbation. Of Schubert's piano music, Mendelssohn knew relatively little,[9] and his opinions about Schumann's piano music have apparently not survived. As for Chopin and Liszt, he clearly admired their pianistic prowess and position as virtuosi of the highest order. On hearing in 1838 of the lionization of the pianist Theodor Döhler, Mendelssohn typically reacted, "What very different stuff Liszt and Chopin are made of! [Chopin] has more soul in his little finger than all Döhler has from top to toe."[10] Nevertheless, Chopin's—and especially Liszt's—music gave Mendelssohn pause. Thus to Moscheles he confided in 1835, "A book of Mazurkas by Chopin and a few new pieces of his are so mannered that they are hard to stand"; and, in 1837, "Chopin's new things, too, I don't quite like, and that is provoking."[11] In 1840, after Liszt's visit to Leipzig, Mendelssohn expressed himself at length about that phenomenon and the music of Liszt's *Glanzzeit*:

His playing, which is quite masterly, and his subtle musical feeling, that finds its way to the very tips of his fingers, truly delighted me. His rapidity and suppleness, above all, his playing at sight, his memory, and his thorough musical insight, are qualities quite unique in their way, and that I have never seen surpassed.[12] . . . The only thing that he seems to me to want is true talent for composition, I mean really original ideas. The things he played to me struck me as very incomplete, even when judged from his own point of view, which, to my mind, is not the right one. . . . Liszt's whole performance is as unpremeditated, as wild and impetuous, as you would expect of a genius; but then I miss those genuinely original ideas which I naturally expect from a genius.[13]

But Mendelssohn reserved his most scathing criticism for the dozens of second-rate virtuoso pianists who crisscrossed Europe pandering their glittery pianistic wares to the public. For Mendelssohn and for Schumann, they represented philistinism at its most pronounced in modern European culture. Thus, Friedrich Kalkbrenner, who had dared to claim Chopin as his pupil, Mendelssohn compared to a "little fish patty" or "indigestible sausage"; he saw little, if any, merit in Sigismond Thalberg's ostentatious fantasias; and, for Henri Herz, he reserved this withering rebuke:

Well, if he will only abstain from writing Variations for four hands, or. . . winding up with those Rondos that are so frightfully vulgar, . . . then . . . let him be made King of the Belgians,[14] or rather Semiquaver King. . . . He certainly is a characteristic figure of these times, of the year 1834; and as Art should be a mirror reflecting the character of the times,—as Hegel or some one else probably says somewhere,—he certainly does reflect most truly all salons and vanities, and a little yearning, and a deal of yawning, and kid gloves, and musk, a scent I abhor. If in his latter days he should take to the Romantic and write melancholy music, or to the Classical and give us fugues, . . . Berlioz can compose a new symphony on him, "De la Vie d'un Artiste," which I am sure will be better than the first.[15]

By 1837 Mendelssohn could only offer this pessimistic assessment: "For really the piano music of the present day is such that I cannot make up my mind to play it through more than once; it is so desperately empty and poor that I usually get tired of it on the first page."[16] Nevertheless, Mendelssohn continued to compose for the piano and to emulate, as in all his music, rigorously high, if traditional, artistic standards. We shall consider his piano oeuvre in four categories: (1) early student works from the 1820s; (2) the Songs without Words (*Lieder ohne Worte*), which occupied Mendelssohn's attention intermittently between the late 1820s and 1840s; (3) mature works of the 1830s and 1840s in large forms; and (4) mature works of the 1830s and 1840s in short forms.

EARLY WORKS: THE STUDENT PERIOD

Mendelssohn's earliest surviving piano works date from the early 1820s, when he was studying piano with Ludwig Berger and theory and composition with Karl Friedrich Zelter in Berlin and beginning to appear in the concert life of the city.[17] They include a *Recitativo* (which survives in a version with strings), several sonatas, variations, fugues, fantasias, etudes, and various other pieces. For the most part, these youthful efforts[18] reveal Mendelssohn's distinctly conservative bent and the marked influence of Zelter's traditional instruction, which led the impressionable student through figured bass, chorale, canon, and fugue. There are few signs here of the music of Beethoven, Weber, or other contemporaries; rather, Mendelssohn initially seemed intent on modeling his compositions on the eighteenth-century works of Haydn and Mozart and especially of J. S. Bach. Thus, a D-major set of variations set down probably in 1820 is based on a square-cut, eight-bar symmetrical theme that could almost pass for Haydn, followed by a contrasting theme in the minor that is suspiciously close to a theme from a Haydn sonata (Example 9.1a-b). The remainder of the composition oscillates between major and minor variations, a technique reminiscent of Haydn's variations in alternating modalities. Into each D-minor variation, however, Mendelssohn incorporates a canon, first at the octave, then at the third and fifth. This contrapuntal display can point only to his intense study of Bach's music.[19]

Considerably more ambitious in scope is the Piano Sonata in G minor, completed on 18 August 1821. Mendelssohn performed it before Hummel and likely before Goethe during the youth's first visit to Weimar in November of that year, but the sonata was published only posthumously in 1868 as Op. 105. It comprises two fast sonata-form movements that enclose a contrasting, cantabile Adagio. Especially noteworthy in the outer movements is their monothematic design; both movements are built up from short, concise motives, a procedure often encountered in the sonatas of Haydn and Clementi. Thus, Mendelssohn extracts the thematic material for the first movement from an initial half step, G–F#, which is immediately set against its mirror, D–E♭.[20] Subsequently, the half step reappears in a bass line that unfolds a chromatic descending fourth; this traditional figure, in addition to the liberal amount of counterpoint, imbues the movement with a distinctly eighteenth-century hue (Example 9.2). In much the same way, Mendelssohn's one-movement Sonata in B♭ minor of 1823 employs an essentially monothematic approach to sonata form; in addition, it begins with a slow introduction, which returns later in the movement, again bringing to mind similar experiments by Clementi and by Clementi's pupil and Mendelssohn's piano teacher Ludwig Berger.[21]

In February 1824 Zelter set his imprimatur on Mendelssohn's progress by declaring him a mature musician in the brotherhood of Sebastian Bach, Mozart, and Haydn.[22] Significantly, Zelter excluded Beethoven and other contemporary composers from his musical pantheon, though by this time his prize pupil was broadening the scope of his piano music beyond the eighteenth-century models he

Example 9.1a
Mendelssohn, Theme and Variations in D Major (ca. 1820), mm. 1–8, 17–21

had already essayed. For example, in June 1821, shortly after the premiere of *Der Freischütz* in Berlin, Mendelssohn heard Carl Maria von Weber introduce his *Konzertstück*. The performance deeply impressed the young composer, who adopted the telescoped form and other features of the *Konzertstück* in a number of works.[23] An especially striking example of the debt to Weber is the *Perpetuum mobile* in C major, which Mendelssohn composed for Moscheles's album during his Berlin sojourn of 1826[24] but left unpublished; it appeared posthumously in 1873 as Op. 119. In many ways Mendelssohn's piece is modeled on Weber's famous *Perpetuum mobile* finale from the Piano Sonata in C major, Op. 24, the same movement that Brahms later arranged as a study for the left hand. Example 9.3a-b offers two comparisons: the opening measures, which share rapid descending figuration in the treble supported by similar staccato harmonies in the bass, and fortissimo closing passages with bass octaves.

Example 9.1b
Haydn, Sonata in D Major (Hob. XVI:19), Third Movement, mm. 17–24

The keyboard idioms of other virtuosi, such as Johann Nepomuk Hummel and Ignaz Moscheles (who, when he gave Mendelssohn some finishing lessons in 1824, noted in his diary, "I am quite aware that I am sitting next to a master, not a pupil"[25]), also are evident in Mendelssohn's piano works of this time. Thus, a Capriccio in E♭ minor (ca. 1823) exhibits virtuoso figuration with wide leaps, and a Prestissimo in F minor (1824) and Vivace in C minor (1825) were conceived as etudes, Mendelssohn's response to "advances" in piano technique. On the other hand, Mendelssohn continued to explore the world of Bachian counterpoint. In 1824 he penned a double fugue in G minor, and in 1826, a lyrical Andante in D major that includes as a contrasting middle section a strict canon at the octave. Also in 1826, not long after finishing the *Midsummer Night's Dream* Overture, Mendelssohn conceived a deeply felt fugue in E♭ major; its subject quotes a passage from the *St. Matthew Passion*, which Mendelssohn first came to know in 1823 and then revived in performance in Berlin on 11 March 1829 (Examples 9.4a-b).[26]

But undoubtedly the major new influence, from around 1823, was the music of Beethoven. Numerous specific allusions to Beethoven's piano sonatas occur in Mendelssohn's piano music of the 1820s[27]; in addition, the debt extends to elements of tonal and structural planning. One example is the Piano Sonata in B♭ major, finished on 31 May 1827 but published posthumously in 1868 as Op. 106. The similarities of this work to Beethoven's magisterial Op. 106, the *Hammerklavier* Sonata, have been noted in the literature[28]; indeed, Mendelssohn

Example 9.2
Mendelssohn, Piano Sonata in G Minor, Op. 105, First Movement, mm. 1–3, 5–9

performed the *Hammerklavier* only a few months before finishing his Op. 106 sonata.[29] Both are in B♭ major, both begin with a rising figure that highlights the third scale degree, D, and both employ in their first movements a submediant relationship. Furthermore, as in the *Hammerklavier*, Mendelssohn's second movement is a minor-keyed Scherzo, albeit a Scherzo in 2/4 time, as if to recall the 2/4 Presto middle portion of Beethoven's Scherzo (mm. 81ff.). For the third movement Mendelssohn attempted a contemplative Andante in the distant key of E major, perhaps his response to Beethoven's extraordinary F♯-minor Adagio in the *Hammerklavier*. The lighthearted finale, strongly reminiscent of Weber, is linked to the slow movement by an extended transition that not only effects the necessary modulation (from E major to F major as dominant preparation) but also quotes the opening motive of the first movement. In addition, midway through the

Example 9.3a
Mendelssohn, *Perpetuum mobile* in C Major, Op. 119, mm. 1–4, 180–81

finale Mendelssohn recycles the material of the Scherzo, a technique clearly
derived from Beethoven's Fifth Symphony. These thematic recalls from the first
and second movements evidence Mendelssohn's growing interest at this time in the
use of cyclic techniques to strengthen the underlying sense of organic thematic
unity.[30]

Mendelssohn's piano music of the student period culminated in three
compositions: the Capriccio in F♯ minor, Op. 5, Sonata in E major, Op. 6, and
Sieben Charakterstücke (*Seven Characteristic Pieces*), Op. 7, which appeared in
Berlin between 1825 and 1827, the first piano works he released for publication.
Robert Schumann regarded the Capriccio as a "classic" masterpiece; upon hearing
it, Rossini was reminded of the sonatas of Domenico Scarlatti.[31] Its untoward
technical difficulties were duly noted in the *Allgemeine musikalische Zeitung*.[32]
Fittingly enough, in 1835 Mendelssohn designated the work as a birthday present
for the sixteen-year-old prodigy Clara Wieck.[33] Formally, the work consists of two
alternating sections, ABAB. The capricious character of the A section derives
from a series of treacherously expanding leaps and an early jolting turn to unstable
diminished-seventh harmonies. The B section, in contrast, is deliberately studied
in character: here Mendelssohn sets a sturdy, fuguelike subject against a rushing
countersubject in sixteenth notes. With characteristic zeal he indulges his
contrapuntal whim by systematically exploiting the subject, first in mirror inversion
and then in combination with the prime form.

Example 9.3b
Carl Maria von Weber, Piano Sonata in C Major, Op. 24, Finale, mm. 1–4, 326–28

Like the Piano Sonata Op. 106, Mendelssohn's Piano Sonata in E major, Op. 6, may be viewed as a response to Beethoven's late piano sonatas, though the influence of Weber is again clearly felt in a scintillating finale. In this work, according to Schumann, Mendelssohn touched "Beethoven with his right hand, while looking up to him as to a saint, and being guided at the other by Carl Maria von Weber (with whom it would be more possible to be on a human footing)."[34] Among the Beethovenian influences we may mention: (1) the singing, cantabile style of the first movement and its softly dampened sonorities (see the opening of Beethoven's Sonatas Opp. 101 and 109, and the second movement of Op. 90); (2) tonal relationships by step, as in the second movement, a Minuet in F♯ minor (see Beethoven's Op. 101); (3) experimentation with special pedal effects; (4) the use of widely spaced chords and broad registers; (5) the recall in the finale of material

Example 9.4a
Mendelssohn, Fugue in E♭ Major (1826), mm. 1–8

Example 9.4b
J. S. Bach, *St. Matthew Passion*, Recitative (no. 15), mm. 14–15

from the first movement (see Beethoven's Op. 101) and the device of linking movements; and (6) the use of a free recitative and fugato in the third movement.

The last cited owes its inspiration to the Adagio of Beethoven's Op. 101. Like Beethoven, Mendelssohn begins his slow movement with a first-inversion E-major harmony and then introduces a thematic idea sprung from a neighbor-note ornament encircling the pitch E (Example 9.5a-b). While Beethoven subsequently

Example 9.5a
Mendelssohn, Piano Sonata in E Major, Op. 6, Movements 2–3

subjects the motive to imitative counterpoint, Mendelssohn goes further and presents the motive in a full-fledged fugato with four descending entries.

Example 9.5b
Beethoven, Piano Sonata in A Major, Op. 101, Adagio, mm. 1–4, 9–12

Notwithstanding this strict, contrapuntal elaboration, Mendelssohn's opening unfolds as a fantasy-like recitative without regular bar lines (*Adagio e senza tempo*). Eventually, this gives way to an arioso-like Andante in F ♯ major ruled in triple time. A transition returns us to the recitative, which recommences on the dominant; the Andante then reenters a step lower, in B♭ major. Finally, in an extended transition, the dominant B♮ is clarified, and the music progresses through a gradual intensification of texture directly into the finale. The adventuresome tonal plan based on steps (E–F♯; B–B♭–B) may be attributed to Beethoven[35]; even so, the result is a highly effective and forward-looking approach to the problem of unifying the disparate movements of the sonata. Schumann prized Mendelssohn's Op. 6 as among the best piano sonatas of the time.

Mendelssohn broached a new direction in the *Sieben Charakterstücke*, a group of seven diverse pieces of varying lengths. Tonally, the group is unified through the use of sharp keys centered on E (Example 9.6a); in addition, the group obtains a certain programmatic shape by the inclusion of short, subjective titles that Mendelssohn added to suggest individual moods or characters. Some pieces reveal decidedly historicizing tendencies, as critics have noticed.[36] Thus, no. 1 offers thickly imitative, Bachian textures; no. 3 is a buoyant fugue in a Handelian vein; and no. 6 (titled *Sehnsuchtig*), in binary form, evokes the Baroque sarabande. No. 5 is a contrapuntal tour de force; it is a fugue filled with special devices, as "though the composer officially wished to demonstrate how diligently he had studied and mastered his subject through counterpoint."[37] Here, however, the model is neither Bach nor Handel but Beethoven; marked *Ernst, und mit steigender Lebhaftigkeit* (Seriously, and with rising energy), no. 5 presents an acceleration fugue that takes as a point of departure the fugal finale of Beethoven's Piano Sonata in A♭ major, Op. 110. Not only does Mendelssohn's subject bear a certain resemblance to Beethoven's sequential subject, but, like Beethoven, Mendelssohn applies erudite—for 1827, recherché—devices, as when he combines the mirror form of the subject in stretto against the prime form in augmentation (Example 9.6b).

The three remaining pieces of Op. 7 form a decided contrast. Nos. 2 and 4 are etudes (Mendelssohn treats the running sixteenth-note figuration of the latter in an opening fugal exposition); most progressive of all is the final piece, a lighthearted Scherzo punctuated by mischievous staccato work. Its title, *Leicht und luftig* (Light and airy), raises intriguing questions about Mendelssohn's programmatic purpose. Hermann Franck, a friend who reviewed Op. 7 in 1827,[38] attempted to describe its peculiar (*fremdartige*) character: "All flies past hastily, without rest, gathering together in colorful throngs, and then scattering in a puff. So this splendid piece impresses as a fleet-footed daughter of the air. Individual chords seem to sting before they resolve; again and again one is teased, as if in a foggy dream. All seems to resolve in a mild, limpid twilight, an indescribably lovely effect." Franck's interpretation brings to mind Mendelssohn's masterpiece of 1826, the *Midsummer Night's Dream* Overture, with which, in fact, Op. 7 no. 7 shares several stylistic features. Both are in E major, and both make use of descending tetrachords spanning the fourth E–B (Example 9.6c-d). What is more, the *Charakterstück* ends with an unexpected, though revealing, turn: broken arpeggiations in E minor well up from the depths of the piano. Significantly, the play on modality (major vs. minor) is the crucial device in the Overture by which

Example 9.6a
Mendelssohn, *Sieben Charakterstücke*, Op. 7, Key Plan

Example 9.6b
b. Mendelssohn, *Charakterstück*, Op. 7 no. 5, mm. 95–101

Example 9.6c
Mendelssohn, *Charakterstück*, Op. 7 no. 7, mm. 1–6

Example 9.6d
Mendelssohn, Overture to *A Midsummer Night's Dream*, Op. 21, mm. 8–11

Mendelssohn transports us from the ceremonial world of Theseus's court in Athens to the elfin world of Oberon and his train in the forest. Not surprisingly, for Schumann the *Charakterstück* represented a "forecast" of the Overture.

SONGS WITHOUT WORDS (*LIEDER OHNE WORTE*)

With the Songs without Words, most of which appeared during the 1830s and 1840s, Mendelssohn developed the musical genre to which his reputation as a composer of piano music became inseparably attached. Designed primarily for amateur domestic music making, these highly popular piano pieces struck resonant chords in respectable middle-class households throughout Europe, where the piano enjoyed increasing status as the preferred instrument. Attempts have been made to trace the origins of the Songs without Words to various character pieces of Schubert, Dussek, Tomasek, and Mendelssohn's teacher Ludwig Berger—thereby diminishing the scope of Mendelssohn's contribution—but with limited success.[39] The documentary evidence, though scanty, firmly indicates that the term and concept of *Lied ohne Worte* originated with Mendelssohn or his circle sometime during the late 1820s; indeed, from his talented sister Fanny Hensel, whose own piano Lieder began to appear in print toward the end of her life (in 1846 and 1847), we learn that the genre may have been inspired by a kind of musical game the siblings played as children.

In a little-known letter written to her brother in 1838, Fanny compared Mendelssohn's textless "piano songs" to the then-fashionable technique, popularized by Liszt and other virtuosi, of transcribing texted songs for keyboard performance:

Dear Felix, when text is removed from sung lieder so that they can be used as concert pieces, it is contrary to the experiment of adding a text to your instrumental lieder—the other half of the topsy-turvy world. I'm old enough to find many things utterly tasteless in the world at present: that may well fall into that category. But shouldn't a person think a lot of himself . . . when he sees how the jokes that we, as mere children, contrived to pass the time have now been adopted by the great talents and used as fodder for the public?[40]

This child's play aside, the new piano genre touched on a fundamental problem that confronted nineteenth-century aestheticians of music: in Friedhelm Krummacher's formulation, how to make instrumental music, now enjoying more and more autonomy from vocal music, comprehensible to the public.[41]

Understandably, the inherent contradiction in the title *Lieder ohne Worte* initially created confusion. Thus, the theorist Moritz Hauptmann, before he had an opportunity to examine the first book of Mendelssohn's new pieces, mistook them for a kind of vocal exercise: "What is it all about? Is he really in earnest? To be sure, in strictness, pure Lyric has no words, but that means no intelligence—no form, therefore no Art. . . . Still, Songs without Words must be uncanny, I think; I am not very fond of Crescentini's Solfeggios, because they seem to me to tax unduly the singer's power of expressing what he feels."[42]

Robert Schumann, who reviewed three volumes of Mendelssohn's Songs without Words, offered this conjecture about the origins of the pieces:

Who of us in the twilight hour has not sat at his upright piano (a grand piano would serve a statelier occasion), and in the midst of improvising has not unconsciously begun to sing a quiet melody? Should one happen to be able to *play* the cantilena along with the accompaniment, above all, should one happen to be a Mendelssohn, the loveliest "song without words" would result. Or, still easier: to choose a text and then, eliminating the words, give in this form one's compositions to the world.[43]

Inevitably, the interpretation of these compositions as songs with suppressed texts provoked further questions, and in 1842 Marc-André Souchay asked Mendelssohn about the specific meanings of some Songs without Words. Here are parts of Mendelssohn's celebrated reply:

People often complain that music is too ambiguous; that what they should think when they hear it is so unclear, whereas everyone understands words. With me it is exactly the reverse, and not only with regard to an entire speech, but also with individual words. These, too, seem to me so ambiguous, so vague, so easily misunderstood in comparison to genuine music, which fills the soul with a thousand things better than words. The thoughts which are expressed to me by music that I love are not too indefinite to be put into words, but on the contrary, too definite. . . . If you ask me what I was thinking of when I wrote it [the Song without Words], I would say: Just the song as it stands. And if I happen to have had certain words in mind for one or another of these songs, I would never want to tell them to anyone, because the same words never mean the same things to different people. Only the song can say the same thing, can arouse the same feelings in one person as in another, a feeling which is not expressed, however, by the same words.[44]

Thus, for Mendelssohn, music represented a higher form of language, one that communicated its meaning with a precision unmatched by the ambiguities of mere words.

With due deliberation, then, Mendelssohn left most of his Songs without Words untitled. Though they typically have clearly songlike qualities (e.g., lyrical treble melodies supported by an arpeggiated form of accompaniment) and are frequently cast in a ternary song form, suggesting again the trappings of the texted art song, for the large majority their poetic meanings or the types of poetic texts that they represent remain unknown. Of the thirty-six Lieder that Mendelssohn published, only five have titles he authorized. The three minor-keyed *Venetianische Gondellieder* (Venetian Gondola Songs), Op. 19 no. 6, Op. 30 no. 6, and Op. 62 no. 5, project the distinctive features of the barcarolle: in 6/8 time, they display melancholic treble melodies against a cross-current of undulating, arpeggiated accompaniments.[45] Op. 38 no. 6, titled Duetto, was written in 1836 at the time of Mendelssohn's engagement to Cécile Jeanrenaud. Throughout much of the Lied, the melodic material alternates between soprano and tenor registers; in the closing section the melody appears doubled at the octave in both voices. Op. 53 no. 5 is appropriately titled *Volkslied* (Folksong); with its open-spaced chords and strident introductory fifths (Example 9.7a), it captures something of the rough-hewn quality of the first movement of Mendelssohn's "Scottish" Symphony, Op. 56 and looks ahead to the A-minor episode of the finale to Brahms's Piano Sonata Op. 1.

A few other titles were evidently suppressed by Mendelssohn. For example, the autograph of Op. 53 no. 3 is titled *Gondellied*, and an autograph copy of Op. 53 no. 4 bears the heading *Abendlied* (Evening Song).[46] One piano Lied that Mendelssohn composed in 1844 but left unpublished is titled *Reiterlied* (Rider's Song); driven by an infectious staccato rhythm, this delightful piece contains an extended canonic passage, doubled at the octave, to convey the idea of a pursuit.[47] Finally, four other songs have titles attributed either to Mendelssohn or to his circle. Thus Op. 19 no. 3, which resounds with horn calls, is patently a *Jägerlied* (Hunters' Song) or *Jagdlied* (Hunting Song), a favorite topos of romantic music and poetry alike. Op. 62 no. 3 (Andante maestoso, 2/4 time) is a *Trauermarsch* (Funeral March); Op. 62 no. 6, with its delicate, harplike accompaniment, is the celebrated *Frühlingslied* (Spring Song); and Op. 67 no. 4, introduced by a swirling turnlike figure, is a *Spinnerlied* (Spinning Song).[48] But here the list ends, notwithstanding the superabundance of unauthorized, overtly sentimental titles ("Sweet Remembrance," "Consolation," and the like) that publishers saw fit to append after Mendelssohn's death.

Example 9.7a
Mendelssohn, *Lied ohne Worte (Volkslied)*, Op. 53 no. 5, mm. 1–2

The great majority of the Songs without Words fit into three categories; a few songs defy ready classification. The most frequent type, the solo Lied, is featured at the beginning of each set; other examples that display soprano melodies include Op. 38 nos. 2 and 3; Op. 53 nos. 2, 4, and 6; Op. 62 no. 6; Op. 67 no. 6; Op. 85 nos. 3, 4, and 6; and Op. 102 no. 4. Into a second category fall the duets, which have two treble melodic lines, typically doubled in thirds or sixths, as in the *Venetian Gondola Songs* Op. 19 no. 6 and Op. 62 no. 5; the *Duetto* Op. 38 no. 6 contraposes soprano and tenor melodic lines. A few Lieder suggest a hybrid between the solo and duet types. Thus, Op. 19 no. 2, Op. 30 no. 6 (the second *Venetian Gondola Song*), and Op. 67 no. 2 begin as solo Lieder but continue with passages displaying duetlike textures (Example 9.7b). In an extension of the duet, at least two Lieder, Op. 53 no. 3 and Op. 62 no. 2, suggest trio or quartet textures, with three or four treble melodic lines (Example 9.7c). The third category, the part-songs, are distinguished by homophonic textures; among these are Op. 19 nos. 3 and 4, Op. 30 no. 3, Op. 38 no. 4, Op. 53 no. 5 (*Volkslied*), Op. 62 no. 4, Op. 67 no. 5, Op. 85 no. 5, and Op. 102 no. 6. The third and fourth Lieder of Op. 19 stand in a special relationship: not only are they in A major, but they both make use of the same horn-call figure associated with the hunt. Indeed, Mendelssohn may have intended both as *Jägerlieder* or *Jagdlieder* (Example 9.7d).

This tripartite division of the *Lieder ohne Worte* into solo songs, duets, and part-songs mirrors a similar division in Mendelssohn's texted songs into solo Lieder, duets, and choral part-songs. What is more, among the texted Lieder we may find precisely those titles—*Frühlingslied* (Op. 34 no. 3, Op. 71 no. 2), *Volkslied* (Op. 63 no. 5), *Gondellied* (Op. 57 no. 5), and *Jagdlied* (Op. 59 no. 6, Op. 120 no. 1)—applied by Mendelssohn or his circle to some of the Songs without Words. In all likelihood, the inspiration for the Songs without Words lay in the wealth of German romantic lyric poetry, and the step from texted to textless song, from poem (whether an actual poem or abstract poetic type), to pure instrumental music was facilitated by the composer's ever-fertile imagination.

Example 9.7b
Mendelssohn, *Lied ohne Worte*, Op. 67 no. 2, mm. 4b–6, 28b–30

Example 9.7c
Mendelssohn, *Lied ohne Worte*, Op. 53 no. 3, mm. 9–12

Example 9.7d

Mendelssohn, *Lied ohne Worte (Jägerlied)*, Op. 19 no. 3, mm. 5b–9, and *Lied ohne Worte*, Op. 19 no. 4, mm. 5b–9

Mendelssohn evidently began to compose *Lieder ohne Worte* during the later 1820s for the albums of friends and family; a letter from his sister Fanny dated 8 December 1828 refers to a "*Lied ohne Worte*, of which he has composed several recently."[49] Not until 1832, however, did he contemplate the possibility of publishing a collection of these pieces. In July his first volume appeared as Op. 19 in London, Bonn, and Paris, followed in 1833 by a volume of songs with words, published as op. 19[a].[50] In preparing Op. 19, Mendelssohn drew upon some older piano pieces and created a few new ones to ensure a suitable balance between Lieder in major keys (nos. 1, 3, and 4) and minor keys (nos. 2, 5, and 6), between relatively short (no. 4) and longer Lieder (nos. 3 and 5), and among various types, including the solo Lied (no. 1), duet (no. 6), and part-song (nos. 3 and 4). Five additional volumes of *Lieder ohne Worte* appeared during Mendelssohn's lifetime: Opp. 30 (1835), 38 (1837), 53 (1841), 62 (1844), and 67 (1845), all with dedications to women, including, in the case of Op. 62, Clara Schumann. Then, after Mendelssohn's death, two additional volumes appeared, Opp. 85 (1850) and 102 (1868). These were assembled from miscellaneous pieces in the composer's *Nachlaß*, and among them figured some that he had rejected for inclusion in Op. 67, the sixth and last set published under his supervision. Though Opp. 85 and 102 may in no way be regarded as authentic opera, a manuscript source does survive that provides some clues about Mendelssohn's plans for a seventh volume of *Lieder ohne Worte*. Bearing an autograph title page dated 4 April 1846, the manuscript includes copies of Op. 85 nos. 1, 2, 3, and 5, the *Reiterlied*, and Op. 102 no. 2. Represented are the solo Lied (Op. 85 no. 1), the duet (Op. 102 no. 2), the part-song (Op. 85 no. 5), and the programmatic piece with title (*Reiterlied*), in accordance with the composer's usual procedure.

Mendelssohn's catalog of works includes several other pieces that, though not specifically titled, are essentially *Lieder ohne Worte*. Among these are the *Gondellied* in A major, a Duet without Words that appeared separately in 1838; and the six *Kinderstücke* (Children's Pieces), Op. 72, composed in London in 1842.[51] Nor was the *Lied-ohne-Worte* style limited to Mendelssohn's piano music. Mendelssohn titled at least one posthumous chamber work, for cello and piano, a *Romance sans paroles* (Op. 109), and the slow movements of the Piano Trios Opp. 49 and 66, String Quartets Op. 44, the Piano Concerto in D minor, Op. 40, and the Violin Concerto in E minor, Op. 64 are essentially further examples of the genre. What is more, many other composers emulated the *Lied-ohne-Worte* style. Several of Robert Schumann's *Phantasiestücke*, Op. 12, may be regarded as *Lieder ohne Worte*, as may the slow movements of Brahms's piano sonatas Opp. 1, 2, and 4;[52] related to them are the versions of Liszt's three *Petrarch Sonnets* for solo piano.[53] Spohr, Stephen Heller, Henry Litolff, Tchaikovsky, and Fauré composed songs without words. The young Richard Strauss produced one example for full orchestra in 1883 and later transformed Mendelssohn's *Gondellied* Op. 19 no. 6 into a *Wiegenlied* in the *Symphonia domestica* of 1903.[54] Finally, some measure of their enduring significance as a kind of topos in European culture is found in literature. The venerable Sherlock Holmes plays Mendelssohn's Lieder on request in the second chapter of *A Study in Scarlet* (1888) as a "testimony to his power on the violin." In Samuel Butler's scathing indictment of Victorian society, *The Way of All Flesh* (posthumously published in 1903), the protagonist Ernest Pontifex engages in a conversation about "modern music" with Miss Skinner and comes to the conclusion that he "never did like modern music"; "with his mind's ear" he seems to "hear Miss Skinner saying, as though it were an epitaph: STAY/I MAY PRESENTLY TAKE/A SIMPLE CHORD OF BEETHOVEN/OR A SMALL SEMIQUAVER/FROM ONE OF MENDELSSOHN'S SONGS WITHOUT WORDS." "Songs without Words" figure in the music-laden imagery of the Sirens episode in James Joyce's *Ulysses* (1922); and Aldous Huxley, in the fourth chapter of *After Many a Summer Dies the Swan* (1939), describes a "ridiculous Englishman with a face like a rabbit's and a voice like Songs without Words on the saxophone."

MATURE WORKS: THE LARGE FORMS

Mendelssohn produced only five mature piano works of ambitious scope. Three of these, the Fantasia in F♯ minor (*Scottish Sonata*), Op. 28, Six Preludes and Fugues, Op. 35, and *Variations sérieuses*, Op. 54, appeared in print during his lifetime; two additional variation sets were published posthumously as Opp. 82 and 83. The three-movement Fantasia, like the Schumann Fantasy, Op. 17, was conceived as a three-movement piano sonata; the Preludes and Fugues reflected Mendelssohn's desire to preserve the heritage of Bach's *Well-Tempered Clavier* and to renew the art of fugal writing; and the *Variations sérieuses* was Mendelssohn's contribution to a musical album in honor of Beethoven.

The origins of the Fantasia remain obscure. Its final version dates from 1833, though the original version, titled *Scottish Sonata* (*Sonate écossaise*), was probably composed as early as 1828.[55] The work thus belongs to a group of compositions inspired by Scottish subjects,[56] including the *Hebrides* Overture and the "Scottish" Symphony, though significantly, the Fantasia was drafted *before* and thus uninfluenced by Mendelssohn's celebrated Scottish sojourn in 1829. Whether or not a particular Scottish program for the Fantasia existed is not known; character-istically, Mendelssohn left no clues about its meaning when he suppressed the original title upon publishing the work in 1834. Still, certain features, notably in the first movement, betray the likelihood of some programmatic inspiration: the use of widely spaced harmonies and chords with open fifths, blurred, open pedal techniques, and dramatically spaced dissonant crescendos, all of which look ahead to similar special effects in Mendelssohn's later Scottish works.

The Fantasia comprises three movements, played without separation, in progressively faster tempos: Andante, Allegro, and Presto, the last a dramatic, full-length sonata movement that carries the structural weight of the composition. The probable source for this plan was Beethoven's *Sonata quasi Fantasia* (*Moonlight* Sonata, Op. 27 no. 2), which suggests, like Mendelssohn's Fantasia (*Sonate écossaise*), a mixture of genres. But the resemblance is primarily external, for Mendelssohn fills his Fantasia with distinctively original material. In the first movement, the brooding, melancholy Andante is prefaced by a series of rapid, hushed arpeggiations that rise from the depths of the piano. Out of this shadowy opening emerges a loose sonata form based on two melodious sections in the tonic minor and relative major; the arpeggiations of the opening return to provide a kind of connective tissue between the contrasting groups. In the center of the movement Mendelssohn works up the arpeggiations into a dramatic crescendo with rising chromatic scales in the bass. A recapitulation of the two principal themes follows; then, in the coda we are left with an open-pedal passage in which the first theme momentarily reappears, echolike, an effect not unlike the close of the *Hebrides* Overture (Example 9.8).

Mendelssohn's most substantial piano work, the Six Preludes and Fugues, appeared in 1837 as Op. 35. Combining freshly composed preludes with several earlier, independent fugues, he arranged the entire collection in a tonal plan based on alternating minor and major keys, with three sharp keys and three flat keys (E minor, D major, B minor, A♭ major, F minor, B♭ major). Several of the preludes have distinctly étudelike characters; in fact, Mendelssohn evidently viewed the work as a juxtaposition of technical and contrapuntal studies, for he first intended to title it "Six Études and Fugues."[57] The first prelude explores a technical device developed by Sigismond Thalberg during the 1830s and then exploited by Liszt and other pianists, the so-called three-hand technique. In this device melodic material

Example 9.8
Mendelssohn, Fantasia in F♯ Minor (*Sonate écossaise*), Op. 28, First Movement, Closing Measures

is entrusted primarily to the two thumbs in the middle register of the piano, and rapid figuration, often in some arpeggiated form, is executed above and below (Example 9.9). Mendelssohn used the technique in a variety of other piano works as well, including the Prelude in E minor (1842, without opus number), the Étude in B♭ minor, Op. 104b no. 1, and the Piano Concerto no. 2 in D minor. This last work's first movement displays arpeggio passages, through which, in Moscheles's words, "the melody seems to push its way."[58]

Other preludes feature a three-part texture with a treble melodic line supported by a running, sixteenth-note inner voice and walking bass (no. 2); a scherzolike arpeggiation study in staccato articulation (no. 3); a duetlike texture with two melodic lines in imitative counterpoint (no. 4); and *cantabile* soprano melodic lines supported by chordal accompaniments—pulsating, tremololike chords in no. 5 and arpeggiated block chords in no. 6. The conclusion of the fifth prelude is especially striking. The descending melody momentarily appears in an inner voice before reappearing in the soprano to pause on a diminished-seventh harmony. This dissonance resolves to a pulsating measure of the tonic F, but unexpectedly in the major mode, a striking historicism that alludes to the *tierce de Picardie* and the music of J. S. Bach (Example 9.10).

Example 9.9
Mendelssohn, Prelude in E Minor, Op. 35 no. 1, mm. 1–3

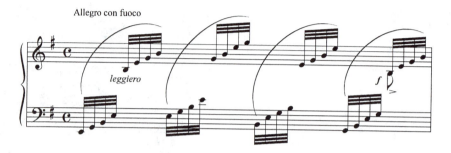

But it is the six fugues, of course, that reinvigorate the spirit of the *Well-Tempered Clavier.* Here is how Robert Schumann considered the question of Mendelssohn's debt to Bach:

In a word, these fugues have much of Sebastian and might deceive the sharp-sighted reviewer, were it not for the melody, the finer bloom, which we recognize as modern; and here and there those little touches peculiar to Mendelssohn, which identify him among a hundred other composers. Whether reviewers agree or not, it remains certain that the artist did not write them for pastime, but rather to call the attention of pianoforte players once more to this masterly old form and to accustom them to it again. That he has chosen the

Example 9.10
Mendelssohn, Prelude in F Minor, Op. 35 no. 5, mm. 68–73

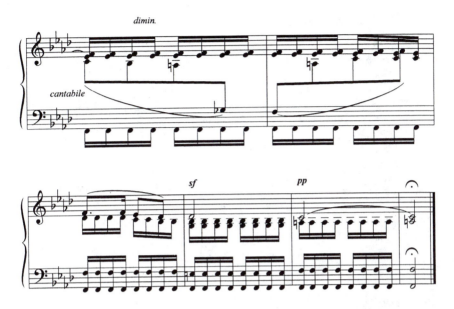

right means for succeeding in this—avoiding all useless imitations and small artificialities, allowing the melody of the cantilena to predominate while holding fast to the Bach form—is very much like him.[59]

In Schumann's view, then, Mendelssohn was attempting not necessarily to invoke the music of J. S. Bach directly but to explore in a modern keyboard idiom the style of fugal writing—more and more becoming, in 1837, an antiquated art.

Still, the fugues "have much of Sebastian." Thus, the subject of the second fugue (D major) offers what is clearly a rhythmically simplified version of the subject from Bach's D-major Fugue in the *Well-Tempered Clavier*, Book I (Example 9.11a-b). (Schumann was impressed enough by the lyricism of Mendelssohn's subject, however, to suggest that the fugue might be mistaken for a Song without Words.) To be sure, Mendelssohn's fugues do not lack those specialized "paper intricacies" for which Bach was celebrated. Thus, in the third fugue (B minor), Mendelssohn applies mirror inversion to his subject and later combines the two forms, first in stretto at the fourth and, at the conclusion of the fugue, in simultaneous contraposition. Similarly, in the first fugue (E minor), the winding, chromatic subject reappears in mirror inversion, though here, perhaps, this erudite procedure is overshadowed by those "touches peculiar to Mendelssohn." For one, the fugue culminates in a freely composed chorale in E major, with

Example 9.11a
Mendelssohn, Fugue in D Major, Op. 35 no. 2, mm. 1–8

Example 9.11b
J. S. Bach, Fugue in D Major, *Well-Tempered Clavier*, Book I, mm. 1–3

accompaniment in octaves, and concludes with a short andante postlude in the major; for another, it is designed as an acceleration fugue, perhaps in homage not to Bach but to the fugal finale of Beethoven's Piano Sonata Op. 110. In a similar way, the fourth fugue (a double fugue in A♭ major) draws its subject not from Bach but from Beethoven's Op. 110, also in A♭ major; here Beethoven's sequence of rising fourths is filled in with stepwise motion (Example 9.12a-b).

Opus 35 was one of three cycles in which Mendelssohn explored contrapuntal styles of writing. In 1837 he also released his Three Preludes and Fugues for Organ, Op. 37, and in 1844 and 1845, a period when he was editing selected organ works of Bach,[60] Mendelssohn composed the Six Organ Sonatas, Op. 65. Other

Example 9.12a
Mendelssohn, Fugue in A♭ Major, Op. 35 no. 4, mm. 1–9

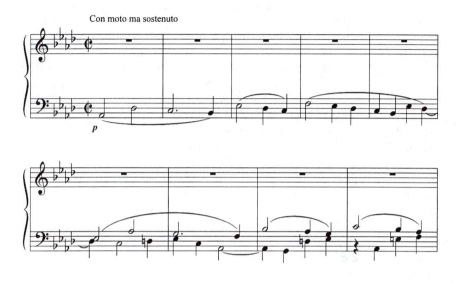

Example 9.12b
Beethoven, Piano Sonata in A♭ Major, Op. 110, Finale, mm. 27–30

composers around this time sought to renew their art through counterpoint: thus, Chopin studied the music of Bach during the 1840s, as did Clara and Robert Schumann, whose work culminated in Clara Schumann's Three Preludes and Fugues, Op. 16 and Robert Schumann's Six Fugues on BACH for Organ, Op. 60. But for Chopin and the Schumanns this study of counterpoint represented a relatively concentrated undertaking; for Mendelssohn, Opp. 35, 37, and 65 represented an ongoing commitment to the rejuvenation of modern music through traditional counterpoint.

Mendelssohn's three sets of piano variations, Opp. 54, 82, and 83, all date from the summer of 1841 (a piano duet arrangement of Op. 83 followed in 1844). Of these the *Variations sérieuses*, Op. 54, is often acknowledged as his masterpiece for the instrument, though the details of its creation are still not well known. In March 1841 the Viennese publisher Pietro Mechetti invited Mendelssohn to contribute a piano work to a Beethoven album, to be published in a limited edition whose sales would benefit efforts under way to erect a Beethoven monument in Bonn. The album appeared in December 1841 with Mendelssohn's variations and works by Chopin, Czerny, Liszt, Moscheles, and other pianists.

Mendelssohn's choice of "serious" variations was his response to the Beethoven tribute.[61] In fact, Op. 54 alludes to at least two Beethoven works, the *Thirty-Two Variations* in C minor for piano and, appropriately enough, the String Quartet Op. 95, which Beethoven labeled *Serioso*. As is well known, Beethoven's variations are constructed upon the traditional descending chromatic fourth, the chaconne bass pattern associated since the seventeenth century with the lament and other serious topics. Now, though this chromatic figure is not directly stated in Mendelssohn's theme, careful analytical prodding reveals that the two are not unrelated. First of all, embedded in Mendelssohn's theme and accompaniment are several descending scalelike lines (Example 9.13a). Thus, in the theme the initial a^1 descends to $g\sharp^1$; this pitch, though it literally skips by tritone to d^2 above, may also be heard to descend to the $g\natural^1$ in the contiguous tenor voice and from there to continue downward through f^1 and e^1. A complete octave descent, in fact, may be traced, beginning in the tenor (d^1–c^1–$b\natural$), then shifting to the alto ($b\flat^1$–$a1$–g^1) and concluding in the soprano (f^2–e^2–d^2). To be sure, these descents are not strictly chromatic and by themselves do not constitute invocations of the chaconne pattern. But convincing evidence is at hand: Mendelssohn's composing score of the *Variations sérieuses*, dated 4 June 1841,[62] contains several rejected variations, one of which clearly states the descending chromatic bass, reinforced at the octave with rapid figuration in the treble (Example 9.13b). Evidently, Mendelssohn did associate the chromatic bass with his theme.

Example 9.13a
Mendelssohn, *Variations sérieuses* in D Minor, Op. 54, Theme, mm. 1–4

Example 9.13b
Mendelssohn, *Variations sérieuses* in D Minor, Op. 54, Rejected Variation (Kraków, Biblioteca Jagiellońska, *Mendelssohn Nachlass* 35)

Mendelssohn's composing score of Op. 54 provides one other clue that links the work to Beethoven. The original version of the tenth variation, a fugato, resembled the fugal subject from the slow movement of the *Serioso* Quartet, a subject that unfolds another version of the descending chromatic figure (Examples 9.14a-b). The final version of Mendelssohn's tenth variation deviates clearly enough from the Beethoven, yet some telltale signs of the source remain, including rhythmic similarities and the use of the chromatic pitches B♭ and G♯ as auxiliary tones to the fifth scale degree A (Example 9.14a, m. 2; 14b, m. 42).

If the *Variations sérieuses* stand as a kind of homage to Beethoven, they also represent a major contribution to the nineteenth-century theme and variation. Mendelssohn devised the work as a theme with eighteen variations, in which the final variation functioned as an expanded coda. The first nine variations describe a course that gradually builds in intensity, through the use of increasingly faster rhythmic values and, in the fourth variation, the application of canon. Following the comparatively restrained tenth and eleventh variations, marked Moderato, the process of intensification resumes: in the twelfth and thirteenth, the theme is transferred from the soprano to the inner register; the thirteenth variation offers yet another example of the three-hand technique. The next two variations mark a

Example 9.14a
Mendelssohn, *Variations sérieuses* in D Minor, Op. 54, Fugato (Variation 10), mm. 1–5
and Rejected Version

Example 9.14b
Beethoven, String Quartet (*Serioso*), Op. 95, *Allegretto ma non troppo*

second structural pause. The fourteenth is a lovely major-key variation in which
the theme, still situated in an inner voice, is concealed by a lyrical soprano line
(Example 9.15). In the harshly dissonant fifteenth, marked *Poco a poco più
agitato*, the theme is finally disembodied and broken up among various registers
(Example 9.16). In the sixteenth and seventeenth variations, Mendelssohn
introduces brilliant virtuoso figuration that builds to a climax: the theme is
reintroduced intact over a dramatic dominant pedal point and finally, in the
culminating coda, presented in unrelenting syncopation. Near the end we hear an
arpeggiated flourish on a diminished-seventh harmony; then, a few quiet chords
outline the descending tonic minor triad.[63]

In his two other sets of variations, Mendelssohn chose themes of contrasting
characters: "sentimental" for Op. 82 and "gracious" for Op. 83.[64] Though

Example 9. 15
Mendelssohn, *Variations sérieuses* in D Minor, Op. 54, Variation 14, mm. 1–4

Example 9.16
Mendelssohn, *Variations sérieuses* in D Minor, Op. 54, Variation 15, mm. 1–4

meticulously crafted, these works do not measure up to the stature of Op. 54. In choosing a serious tone for Op. 54, Mendelssohn was indeed looking back at Beethoven's achievements, and that glance sufficed for him to create a worthy successor to Beethoven's C-minor Variations. In turn, Op. 54 influenced later works in that genre. Notable examples in the serious style include two by Brahms, the Variations in D major, Op. 21 no. 1, and, of course, the finale of the Fourth Symphony, based on a *rising* passacaglia figure. Example 9.17 gives one example of how Brahms alluded, consciously or unconsciously, to Mendelssohn's Op. 54. The tenth variation of Op. 21 no. 1—a variation in D minor—revives for a moment the eleventh variation of Mendelssohn's set. Mendelssohn's disjunct melodic configuration—a^1–g^1–d^2–$c\sharp^2$—may be traced in the same register in the Brahms. What is more, Mendelssohn's eighth-note turn figure (m. 3) resurfaces, and both examples are supported by a tonic pedal point. As had Mendelssohn, so did Brahms find inspiration in musical tradition.

Example 9.17a
Mendelssohn, *Variations sérieuses* in D Minor, Op. 54, Variation 11, mm. 1–4

Example 9.17b
Brahms, *Variations on a Theme by the Composer*, Op. 21 no. 1, Variation 10, mm. 1–4

MATURE WORKS: THE SHORT FORMS

The rest of Mendelssohn's piano music includes several short and intermediate-length compositions that fall conveniently into three groups: four works to which he assigned opus numbers (Opp. 14, 15, 16, and 33), six pieces he published separately in various albums and periodicals, and five works that appeared posthumously (Opp. 104a and b, 117, 118, and an Andante and Presto). Miscellaneous other pieces and fragments survive in manuscript and await further study.[65] A cluster of three works appeared in 1830 and 1831 as Opp. 14, 15, and 16, the *Rondo capriccioso*, *Fantasy on an Irish Song*, and *Three Fantasies or Caprices*. Precious little is known about the origins of Op. 15, a keyboard fantasy on the Irish song "The Last Rose," which was popularized during the nineteenth century in settings by such composers as Beethoven, Moscheles, and Flotow.

Considerably more is known about Opp. 14 and 16, which had their origins in 1828
and 1829.

The *Rondo capriccioso* was conceived in 1828 as an Étude in E minor; an
incomplete autograph of this version, which consisted of only the Presto, survives.
Some two years later Mendelssohn reworked the piece, apparently as a present for
the talented Munich pianist Delphine von Schauroth; on 13 June 1830 he dated his
second autograph, which now included the lyrical Andante introduction and
transition to the original Presto.[66] Mendelssohn himself frequently performed the
work, and it quickly entered the repertoire as a favorite virtuoso showpiece.
Analysis reveals how, when he added the Andante, he took pains to link it
thematically to the Presto: the two principal ideas describe descending forms of the
tonic major and minor triads, with several structural pitches embellished by
auxiliary tones (Example 9.18a-c). The device of joining slow and fast movements

Example 9.18a
Mendelssohn, *Rondo capriccioso*, Op. 14, mm. 4–8

was likely influenced by Carl Maria von Weber's *Konzertstück*; indeed, the *Rondo
capriccioso* is not unlike the condensed second and third movements of a concerto
and presages similar procedures Mendelssohn followed in his two three-movement
piano concertos, Opp. 25 and 40, and in two shorter works for piano and orchestra,
the *Capriccio brillant*, Op. 22, and *Serenade und Allegro giojoso*, Op. 43, which,
like Op. 14, have slow movements linked to fast finales.

Example 9.18b
Mendelssohn, *Rondo capriccioso*, Op. 14, mm. 27–30

Example 9.18c
Mendelssohn, *Rondo capriccioso*, Op. 14, Analytical Reduction

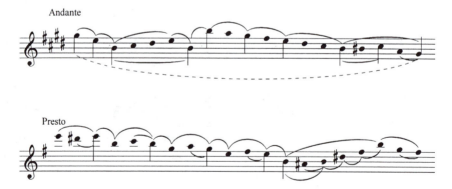

The three Fantasies, Op. 16, (also designated Caprices) were written during
Mendelssohn's visit to Wales in September 1829 as presents for the three daughters
of John Taylor, an Englishman who operated several lead mines. As a houseguest

at Taylor's summer residence at Coed Du, Mendelssohn sketched the scenery of the Welsh countryside during the day and improvised at the piano during the evening. The first piece, the opening of which brings to mind the opening of the Scottish Symphony (jotted down two months earlier), was inspired by the sight of carnations and roses. The rising diminished-seventh arpeggiations in the andante sections were evidently meant to suggest "the sweet scent of the flower rising up."[67] The second, a spirited Scherzo in E minor, was inspired by a creeping plant with trumpet-shaped flowers. Mendelssohn's Presto sought to capture the music that "the fairies might play on those trumpets."[68] With its gossamer textures, mock trumpet fanfares, and light staccato work in the high register, it effectively transports us to the world of the *Midsummer Night's Dream* Overture. As in the overture, Mendelssohn introduces a descending tetrachord figure in the minor (Example 9.19) and plays on the major versus minor modal duality by directing the Scherzo to conclude in a delicately scored passage in E major. The third fantasy, a gently undulating Andante, was Mendelssohn's representation of a rivulet; its original title, *Am Bach* (By the Brook), and thick, dark textures (e.g., mm. 50ff.) encourage comparisons with the celebrated slow movement of the same title in Beethoven's *Pastoral* Symphony. But despite all these extramusical elements, Mendelssohn suppressed the urge to provide special titles when he published Op. 16, allowing instead the (for him) superior language of absolute music and the listener's imagination to remain unencumbered.

The Three Caprices, Op. 33, in A minor, E major, and B♭ minor, were composed between 1833 and 1835 and published in 1836. Each begins with an introductory section that proceeds to a full-fledged movement in sonata form. The introductions range from a few measures of chords that hint at a thematic outline (no. 2), to more fully developed adagios that pause on the dominant (nos. 1 and 3). The opening Adagio of no. 1 presents a series of rising arpeggiations above a descending chromatic bass. Improvisatory in character, it recalls the tradition of the keyboard fantasia; indeed, the tempo marking *Adagio quasi fantasia* demonstrates, as does the title of Op. 16, that for Mendelssohn the distinction between the caprice and fantasy was not clearly drawn. As Carl Czerny attempted to explain, the essential character of the caprice resided more in its "singular or even eccentric ideas, than in the form."[69] The main bodies of the Caprices represent more or less straightforward sonata movements but suffer perhaps from their undue length and overworking of the thematic material. Still, Robert Schumann was favorably impressed by the second, which he compared, somewhat cryptically, to Walt's "cross-country summer flights" in Jean Paul's *Die Flegeljahre*.[70] At least one passage, marked by a gently syncopated figure in the treble, brings to mind a similar texture in Schumann's *Des Abends* from the first *Phantasiestück* of Op. 12, composed the following year in 1837 (Examples 9.20a-b).

Mendelssohn's six occasional piano pieces require only a brief comment here. Two appeared in contemporary music journals. The B-minor Scherzo, composed in London in June 1829, appeared that year in the *Berliner allgemeine musikalische Zeitung*, a Berlin music journal edited by the music theorist Adolf Bernhard Marx.

Example 9.19
Mendelssohn, Scherzo in E Minor, Op. 16 no. 2, mm. 1–8

The *Gondellied,* to which we have already referred, was published in Dresden in 1838 and then reprinted by Schumann in a supplement to the fourteenth volume of the *Neue Zeitschrift für Musik* in 1841. Four other pieces were solicited by publishers for special albums. The *Scherzo a capriccio* appeared in the *Album des pianistes* published by Schlesinger in Paris in 1836; the *Andante cantabile e presto* appeared in the *Musikalisches Album* from Breitkopf and Härtel in 1839; the Étude in F minor was written as an "étude de perfectionnement" for the *Méthode des méthodes de piano,* edited by Fétis and Moscheles for Schlesinger in 1840; and the Prelude and Fugue in E minor appeared in the album *Notre temps* from Schott in 1842 (for the occasion Mendelssohn joined a newly composed prelude, a kind of study in the three-hand technique, to a youthful fugue from 1827). Though rarely

Example 9.20a
Mendelssohn, Caprice in E Major, Op. 33 no. 2, mm. 37–39

Example 9.20b
Robert Schumann, *Phantasiestück* ("Des Abends"), Op. 12 no. 1, mm. 1–4

heard today, these pieces present the full range of Mendelssohn's favored pianistic styles: the capricious, lightly scored scherzo; the *Lied ohne Worte*; the two-movement concert piece with a lyrical slow movement linked to a fast finale; the piano study; and, finally, the fugue, the traditions of which influenced so much of his music.

A final group of five works appeared posthumously between 1860 and 1872. The *Andante* in B♭ and *Presto agitato* in G minor, joined together as *Zwei Clavierstücke*, were probably composed separately. The Andante suggests a *Lied ohne Worte*; the Presto is a short movement in sonata form. Two compositions in E minor were issued in 1872 as Opp. 117 and 118. The Allegro, Op. 117, a ternary-form movement with a contrasting middle section in the major, may have been written in 1836 for F. W. Benecke, the uncle of Mendelssohn's wife, Cécile.[71] The Capriccio in E minor, Op. 118, composed in 1837, begins with a lilting *Lied-*

ohne-Worte Andante in E major linked to a fast Allegro in E minor; the combination of slow and fast movements recalls the Op. 33 Caprices.

Of greater interest musically are the two sets of Preludes and Études, which appeared in 1868 as Opp. 104a and 104b. At least four of these pieces, Opp. 104a nos. 1–3 and 104b no. 1, were composed in 1836 and may have been intended for Mendelssohn's planned cycle of études and fugues, which ultimately appeared in 1837 as the Six Preludes and Fugues, Op. 35. The first étude of Op. 104b, in B♭ minor, offers a fine specimen of a study in the three-hand technique. What is more, the three "preludes" Op. 104a actually have the character of études. No. 1 is an octave study, while nos. 2 and 3 are built on running scalelike figures (designed for the left hand in no. 2 and broken between the left and right hands in no. 3). Also, the tonalities of Op. 104a—B♭ major, B minor, and D major—suggest that they may have been originally linked to three of the fugues from Op. 35 in the same keys, nos. 6, 3, and 2.

Mendelssohn's piano music marks few, if any, new stylistic departures in the distinguished nineteenth-century piano repertoire. Though impeccably crafted, his finely chiseled piano compositions are usually thought not to convey the depth and dramatic power of Beethoven's piano music, the lyrical warmth of Schubert's, the rich harmonic and tonal palette of Chopin's, or the bold, literary imagination of Schumann's, nor to rival in any way the formidable technical demands of Liszt's piano music or its challenging programmatic designs. Instead, Mendelssohn was content to preserve strong artistic ties to the past and to build cautiously on the foundations of earlier models. Almost certainly, his piano music was intended, in large part, as an antidote to what he regarded as the excesses and mediocrity of much contemporary piano music. His reform-minded efforts avoided the shifting sands of public taste in order to reembrace and reaffirm traditional compositional procedures. And if he relied heavily on exemplary historical models, that reliance was applauded in many quarters as a necessary corrective. Though twentieth-century criticism has not always received this repertoire kindly, the broader historical view may yet recognize Mendelssohn's substantial efforts on behalf of the piano.

NOTES

1. The six *Kinderstücke* (*Children's Pieces*), Op. 72, which appeared in London in 1847 shortly after Mendelssohn's death, were composed in 1842. See also n. 51.

2. A comprehensive catalog of Mendelssohn's music is still lacking. For the most current list of the piano music, see Chapter 12.

3. See Ferdinand Hiller, *Mendelssohn: Letters and Recollections*, trans. M. E. von Glehn (London: Macmillan, 1874; repr. New York: Vienna House, 1972), 5; Ignaz Moscheles, *Recent Music and Musicians*, trans. A. D. Coleridge (New York: H. Holt, 1873), *passim*; K. Mendelssohn-Bartholdy, *Goethe and Mendelssohn* (London: Macmillan, 1872), 11ff.; W. S. Rockstro, *Mendelssohn* (London: S. Low, Marston, Searle, and Rivington, 1884), 96, 112; H. F. Chorley, *Modern German Music*, 2 vols. (London: Smith, Elder and Co., 1854, rep. New York: Da Capo, 1973) 1: 49ff.; *Neue Zeitschrift für Musik* 13 (1840),

56; Sir George Grove's "Mendelssohn" article for *Grove's Dictionary of Music and Musicians*, repr. in 2d ed., ed. J. A. Fuller Maitland (London: Macmillan, 1904–1910), 3: 161–63.

4. W. A. Lampadius, *Life of Felix Mendelssohn Bartholdy*, trans. W. L. Gage (New York: F. Leypoldt, 1865; repr., Boston: Longwood, 1978), 175–76.

5. Leon Plantinga, "Schumann's Critical Reaction to Mendelssohn," in *Mendelssohn and Schumann: Essays on Their Music and Its Context*, ed. J. W. Finson and R. Larry Todd (Durham, NC: Duke University Press, 1984), 12.

6. Felix Mendelssohn, *Letters of Felix Mendelssohn to Ignaz and Charlotte Moscheles*, ed. F. Moscheles (Boston: Ticknor, 1888), 85.

7. Ibid., 121–22.

8. Hiller, *Mendelssohn: Letters and Recollections*, 43–44, 131.

9. In 1839 Diabelli brought out the first edition of Schubert's Piano Sonata in A minor D. 784, with an honorary dedication to Mendelssohn. Schumann may have introduced Mendelssohn to some of Schubert's other piano sonatas and pieces. Schumann's favorable perusal of the manuscript of the "Great" C-major Symphony in Vienna led Mendelssohn to perform a truncated version of that work in Leipzig in 1839.

10. Mendelssohn, *Letters to Ignaz and Charlotte Moscheles*, 170.

11. Ibid., 129, 156. For a more balanced account of Mendelssohn's view of Chopin, see Hiller. The mazurkas that provoked Mendelssohn were probably the Four Mazurkas, Op. 17, which appeared from Breitkopf and Härtel in 1835; the fourth mazurka, in A minor, an especially chromatic work, concludes with a celebrated "open-ended" cadence.

12. Ferdinand Hiller related Mendelssohn's observing Liszt, in 1832, flawlessly sight-read his Piano Concerto in G minor, Op. 25; Hiller, *Mendelssohn: Letters and Recollections*, 26–27.

13. Mendelssohn, *Letters to Ignaz and Charlotte Moscheles*, 203–4.

14. A reference to the Belgian Revolution, reportedly sparked by a performance of D.-F.-E Auber's *La muette de Portici* in Brussels in 1830.

15. Mendelssohn, *Letters to Ignaz and Charlotte Moscheles*, 112–13.

16. Ibid., 156.

17. Mendelssohn's first public performance as a pianist occurred on 28 October 1818 with the horn player Joseph Gugel; other early public performances took place on 31 March 1822 at the Schauspielhaus, where Mendelssohn participated in a performance of a double concerto by Dussek, and on 5 December 1822 at a concert of the soprano Anna Milder-Hauptmann. See Rudolf Elvers, "Ein Jugendbrief von Felix Mendelssohn," *Festschrift für Friedrich Smend* (Berlin: Merseburger, 1963), 95; *Allgemeine musikalische Zeitung* (hereafter *AmZ*) 24 (1822), 273, and 25 (1823), 55.

18. Several pieces are scattered in a workbook of composition exercises Mendelssohn undertook under Zelter's supervision; see Todd, 1983. Many others survive in manuscripts in the Mendelssohn Nachlaß of the Staatsbibliothek zu Berlin—Preußischer Kulturbesitz..

19. See R. Larry Todd, *Mendelssohn's Musical Education: A Study and Edition of His Exercises in Composition* (Cambridge: Cambridge University Press, 1983), 72–73.

20. Rearranged, the two half steps form the common Baroque fugal subject of a perfect fifth bordered by a diminished seventh: D–G–Eb–F♯.

21. An edition of the sonata is available (New York: C. F. Peters, 1981). See the first movements of Clementi's Op. 13 no. 6 and Op. 34 no. 2 and of Berger's Sonata in C minor. The latter is reprinted in *The London Pianoforte School*, ed. N. Temperley (New York: Garland, 1984), 15: 9–25.

22. The occasion was a rehearsal of Mendelssohn's Singspiel *Die beiden Neffen* on his fifteenth birthday (3 February 1824).

23. For example, the Piano Concertos Opp. 25 and 40, the *Capriccio brillant*, Op. 22, and, as we shall see later, the *Rondo capriccioso*, Op. 14.

24. London, British Library, Music Loan 95/2 (24 November 1826).

25. Mendelssohn, *Letters to Ignaz and Charlotte Moscheles*, 1.

26. For an edition of these compositions, see Mendelssohn, *Early Works for Piano*, ed. R. Larry Todd (Cambridge: Cambridge University Press, 1985). See also R. Larry Todd, "A Mendelssohn Miscellany," *Music and Letters* 71 (1990), 52–60; "From the Composer's Workshop: Two Little-Known Fugues by Mendelssohn," *The Musical Times* 131 (1990), 183–87.

27. See Todd, "A Mendelssohn Miscellany"; and Jocelyn Godwin, "Early Mendelssohn and Late Beethoven," *Music and Letters* 55 (1974), 272–85.

28. See William S. Newman, "Some 19th-Century Consequences of Beethoven's 'Hammerklavier' Sonata, Op. 106," *Piano Quarterly* 17 (1969), 12–18.

29. In February 1827 in Stettin. See *Berliner allgemeine musikalische Zeitung* (hereafter *BamZ*) 4 (1827), 83.

30. As in the finales of the Sextet, Op. 110 and the Octet, Op. 20.

31. See the foreword to Schumann's *Studies on Caprices of Paganini*, Op. 3 and Robert Schumann, *On Music and Musicians*, ed. Konrad Wolff, trans. Paul Rosenfeld (New York: Pantheon, 1946), 120; the Rossini anecdote is recorded in Hiller, 58.

32. *AmZ* 29 (1827), 688. For a translation of this short review, see the Historical Views and Documents section.

33. B. Litzmann, *Clara Schumann: Ein Künstlerleben*, 3 vols. (Leipzig: Breitkopf & Härtel, 1920), 1: 89.

34. Schumann, *On Music and Musicians*, 210.

35. Cf. the Arioso (*Klagender Gesang*) and concluding fugue of Op. 110, which modulate from A♭ minor/A♭ major to G minor/G major for the return of the arioso and the mirror inversion of the fugue.

36. Schumann, *On Music and Musicians*, 120–21; *BamZ* 4 (1827), 289; *AmZ* 30 (1828), 63.

37. *AmZ* 30 (1828), 63.

38. *BamZ* 4 (1827), 288.

39. See Willi Kahl, "Zu Mendelssohns Liedern ohne Worte," *Zeitschrift für Musikwissenschaft* 3 (1920–1921), 459–69; Dieter Siebenkäs, "Zur Vorgeschichte der Lieder ohne Worte von Mendelssohn," *Die Musikforschung* 15 (1962), 171–73; for a comparison of Mendelssohn's *Lieder ohne Worte* with Wilhelm Taubert's *Minnelieder*, see Elfriede Glusman, "Taubert and Mendelssohn: Opposing Attitudes toward Poetry and Music," *The Musical Quarterly* 57 (1971), 628–35. It should be stressed that the exact nature of Fanny Mendelssohn's role in the creation of the genre remains unclear.

40. Letter of 7 September 1838. Fanny Mendelssohn, *The Letters of Fanny Hensel to Felix Mendelssohn*, ed. and trans. M. J. Citron (New York: Pendragon, 1987), 261.

41. Friedhelm Krummacher, "Mendelssohn's Late Chamber Music: Some Autograph Sources Recovered," in *Mendelssohn and Schumann*, 73.

42. A. Schöne and F. Hiller, eds., *The Letters of a Leipzig Cantor*, trans. A. D. Coleridge, 2 vols. (London: Novello & Ewer, 1892), 1: 96–97.

43. Schumann, *On Music and Musicians*, 210. See also the Historical Views and Documents section for the complete review in another translation.

44. Letter of 15 October 1842. Felix Mendelssohn, *Letters*, ed. G. Selden-Goth (New York: Vienna House, 1947), 313–14. For Souchay's letter and a slightly different translation by John Michael Cooper of Mendelssohn's reply, see Oliver Strunk, ed., *Source Readings in Music History*, rev. ed., Leo Treitler, gen. ed., vol. 6, *The Nineteenth Century*, ed. Ruth Solie (New York: Norton, 1998), 156–59.

45. For one nineteenth-century discussion of these Venetian gondola songs, see the Historical Views and Documents sections.

46. Sächsische Landesbibliothek, Dresden; regarding Op. 53 no. 3, see Christa Jost, *Mendelssohns Lieder ohne Worte* (Tutzing: Schneider, 1988), 159ff.

47. The *Reiterlied* is available in Rudolf Elvers's critical edition of the *Lieder ohne Worte* (Munich: G. Henle, 1981).

48. A special case is the *Herbstlied*, a duet with words (Op. 63 no. 4) that Mendelssohn also notated as a *Lied ohne Worte*. The two versions were completed on 16 October 1836. See Jost, *Mendelssohns Lieder ohne Worte*, 127ff.

49. Sebastian Hensel, *Die Familie Mendelssohn 1729 bis 1847*, 2 vols., 15th ed. (Berlin: G. Reimer, 1911), 1: 222.

50. A facsimile of Mendelssohn's assignment of the copyright of Op. 19 to Novello is in Mendelssohn, *Letters to Ignaz and Charlotte Moscheles*, 67. The original English title for Op. 19 was *Melodies for the Pianoforte (alone)*.

51. The last opus that Mendelssohn prepared for the press, Op. 72, appeared with six of seven pieces written in June 1842 for the children of F. W. Benecke, whom Mendelssohn visited in England. The first English edition erroneously referred to these pieces as Christmas presents. See *The Musical Times* 32 (1891), 592. A modern, complete edition prepared by H. O. Hiekel is available (Munich: G. Henle, 1969).

52. See the study by George Bozarth, "Brahms's *Lieder ohne Worte*: The 'Poetic' Andantes of the Piano Sonatas," in *Brahms Studies: Papers Delivered at the International Brahms Conference, The Library of Congress, Washington, D.C., 5–8 May 1983*, ed. George Bozarth (Oxford: Clarendon, 1990), 345–78.

53. Among Liszt's transcriptions of Mendelssohn's texted Lieder for piano solo is a collection of seven arrangements from Opp. 19a, 34, and 47, which appeared in 1841 with a dedication to Mendelssohn's wife, Cécile; see Humphrey Searle, *The Music of Liszt* (London: Williams and Norgate, 1954), 547.

54. Further examples are cited in Jost, *Mendelssohns Lieder ohne Worte*, 20ff.

55. See Fanny's letters to Felix of 23 [May] and 4 June 1829 in Fanny Mendelssohn, *The Letters of Fanny Hensel to Felix Mendelssohn*, 41, 50.

56. See R. Larry Todd, "Mendelssohn's Ossianic Manner, with a New Source—On Lena's Gloomy Heath," in *Mendelssohn and Schumann*, 139–40.

57. See his correspondence with Breitkopf and Härtel in 1835, in Felix Mendelssohn Bartholdy, *Briefe an deutsche Verleger*, ed. Rudolf Elvers (Berlin: de Gruyter, 1968), 42, 45. Coincidentally, Carl Czerny's collection of preludes and fugues, *The School of Playing Fugues and of Performing Polyphonic Compositions and Their Particular Difficulties on the Piano in 24 Large Studies*, began to appear in 1837 as Op. 400, with a dedication to Mendelssohn.

58. Mendelssohn, *Letters to Ignaz and Charlotte Moscheles*, 168.

59. Schumann, *On Music and Musicians*, 214–15.

60. See Rudolf Elvers, "Verzeichnis der von Felix Mendelssohn Bartholdy herausgegebenen Werke Johann Sebastian Bachs," in *Gestalt und Glaube: Festschrift für Oskar Söhngen* (Witten: Luther-Verlag, 1960), 145–49.

61. The appeal for funds was announced in the *AmZ* in 1835, and the monument was unveiled in 1845 with a gala concert directed by Liszt.

62. Mendelssohn Nachlaß, vol. 35, Biblioteca Jagiellońska, Kraków.

63. Jack Werner attempted to link this cadence to one employed in traditional Jewish services for Passover. See "The Mendelssohnian Cadence," *The Musical Times* 97 (1956), 17–19.

64. Letter of 30 July 1841 to his sister Rebecka (New York Public Library, Mendelssohn Family Correspondence).

65. See the work list by John Michael Cooper in Chapter 12 in this volume. An edition of Mendelssohn's *Albumblatt* in A major for Ottilie von Goethe (1830) is now available (Wiesbaden: Breitkopf & Härtel, 1984).

66. Conservatoire Ms. 198, Bibliothèque nationale, Paris.

67. Letter of Anne Taylor in *Grove's Dictionary of Music and Musicians*, 2d ed., 3: 161–63.

68. Ibid.

69. Carl Czerny, *School of Practical Composition*, Op. 600, trans. J. Bishop, 3 vols. (London: R. Cocks, 1848, repr. New York: Da Capo, 1979), 1: 89.

70. Schumann, *On Music and Musicians*, 213.

71. See Margaret Crum, *Catalogue of the Mendelssohn Papers in the Bodleian Library, Oxford* (Tutzing: Schneider, 1983), 2: 6.

HISTORICAL VIEWS AND DOCUMENTS

REVIEW OF CAPRICCIO PER IL PIANOFORTE, COMP. DA FELIX MENDELSSOHN-BARTHOLDY. OP. 5. BERLINO PRESSO AD. MT. SCHLESINGER. Pr.17½ SGR.[1]

Translated by Douglass Seaton

[One of the earliest published reviews of Mendelssohn's music, this brief critique of the Capriccio Op. 5 establishes that the young composer was already well known beyond Berlin by the age of eighteen. The reviewer draws attention to both the originality of his musical ideas and the technical difficulty of his piano writing.—Ed.]

The young composer is already known from his great accomplishments, which, for the most part, have been so favorably received that one is prepared to indulge in the most beautiful hopes. The piece presently before us in no way disappoints these happy expectations. It is an imaginative piece of music, here and there somewhat strange, but well constructed, in F♯ minor, passing lavishly through all sorts of keys, often quickly and unexpectedly. Anyone who knows how to handle well, with appropriate velocity and precision, the many leaps at a prestissimo tempo and the not infrequent passages that are somewhat difficult and do not always fall comfortably under the fingers, in the right hand as well as the left, will both enjoy it and give enjoyment. It is thus a good piece of work for already skilled players and for those who, wanting to gain greater facility, will not shy away from the trouble of learning it. The Capriccio is to be recommended to them.

REVIEW OF FELIX MENDELSSOHN, SECHS LIEDER OHNE WORTE FÜR DAS PFTE. ZWEITES HEFT [OP. 30]. BONN, SIMROCK. PARIS, SCHLESINGER.[2]

Robert Schumann; translated by Douglass Seaton

Who has never sat at the spinet in the twilight hour (a grand piano would already be too grand in tone) and, while fantasizing, unconsciously begun to sing a soft melody along with it? If one could now casually unite the melody into the hands alone, and most of all if one were a Mendelssohn, then there would emerge the most beautiful songs without words. One would have a still easier time of it if one, first of all, set texts to music, then deleted the words and gave them to the world in that form, though that would not be the real thing but rather a sort of deception, for one would have to intend to pose thereby a test of musical clarity of feeling and induce the same poet whose words one had suppressed to underlay a new text to the composition of his song. If in the latter case he came right back to the old poem, then this would be a demonstration of the accuracy of the musical expression. On to our songs. They appear to be as clear as the sun. In purity and beauty the first almost matches the sentiment of the E-major one in the first volume; for there it flows still closer to the first sources. Florestan says that "whoever sang such a thing can expect a long lifetime yet, in this life just as after death; I believe it is my favorite." The initially double-voiced accompaniment in the middle [of the musical texture] later becomes at times one-voiced, which helps to prevent monotony; this last sounds almost like a self-contradiction.[3] In the second song Goethe's "Jägers Abendlied" comes to mind: "im Felde schleich' ich still und wild, gespannt mein Feuerrohr u.s.w."[4]; in its delicately hazy construction it achieves the same effect that the poet did. The third appears less significant to me and almost like a round sung in a La Fontaine-like family scene; nevertheless, it is genuine, unadulterated wine, which goes around the table, if not the most potent and rarest. The third [sic; should read "fourth"] I find exceptionally admirable, a little sad and introspective, but in the distance speak hope and homeland. In the French edition there are, as in all the pieces but especially in this one, significant differences from the German, which nonetheless do not appear to stem from Mendelssohn. The next has something indecisive in its character, even in its form and rhythm, and has a correspondingly indecisive effect. The last, a Venetian barcarolle, brings the whole to a soft and gentle ending. So plan to enjoy some new things from this noble spirit!

MENDELSSOHN'S VENETIAN GONDOLA SONGS WITHOUT WORDS[5]

[In this brief, unsigned essay is embodied the central paradox of Mendelssohn's song-without-words aesthetic. The writer recognizes in the opening sentences and again in the final sentence of the penultimate paragraph the fundamental fact that music expresses feeling in a way that is untranslatable and needs no mediation by words. At the same time, as Mendelssohn himself acknowledged, the listener's natural response to music is often a resort to language.—Ed.]

Without words, and without names even! It is music speaking for itself, or rather speaking for the human heart, disdaining any other interpreter. Each melody, with its accompaniment, is like a pure stream flowing through rich scenery. The stream is the soul's consciousness, the scenery is the work of mingled associations through which it flows, time's shadow on its surface. Sometimes however the accompaniment suggests unearthly scenery, enchanted regions, and the song is like the life of a soul disembodied, or translated where it knows no more the fretting bounds of time.

Several of these pieces however have a title, indicating merely their general character: there is one styled a "People's Song,"[6] and there are three "Venetian Gondola Songs." Let us look at these latter for the present. After being rocked by this music, till it haunts your thoughts, you feel that you know Venice, though you may never have been there.

"My soul is an enchanted boat,
Which like a sleeping swan doth float
Upon the silver waves of thy sweet singing."[7]

The atmosphere, the limpid coolness of the water, the rhythm of its motion, and the soft, sad, yet voluptuous coloring of all things; in short, the very volatile essence of all that life, is, as it were, caught and perpetuated in these subtle, accommodating forms of melody. What is the meaning of Venice in history, is a question which might perhaps be answered, if we could only tell what influence this music ministers to the mind. Hearing it and losing yourself in it, you inhabit an ideal Venice, the soul, as it were, of the real one, without its sins and infirmities, its horrible suicidal contrasts.

The first of the three (Number Six of the First Set [Op. 19b]) is a sustained Andante, in six-eight measure. The accompaniment, by a very simple figure, gives the rocking sensation of a gondola, while "the oars keep time." The gentle key, G minor, indicates soft moonlight or star-light; and presently the song floats off, in loving thirds and sixths, full of tenderness and musing sadness, which has more of longing in it than of regret for actual suffering. It rises higher and louder at times, but never breaks through the gentle spell, always sinks back into the dreaminess of the hour. The sentiment is so pure, that one might dream himself in heaven; only the sadness makes it human. Far off in the smooth stream, the boat for a time seems fixed, suspended, and the voice alone, amid its natural accompaniments, informs the distance. Again the motion is resumed, but fainter and more remote, and as the sounds die away in the smooth shining distance, how magical the effect of these soft high octaves, ever and anon twice struck, as if to assure us that beyond it is as beautiful as here; and finally all the harmonies converge into a single note, just as broad spaces on the farthest verge and boundary of sight are represented by a single fine line. At the introduction, after the rocking accompaniment, so soft and dreamy, has proceeded a few measures, you seem suddenly to touch the water and have a cold thrill of reality for a moment, as the harmonies brighten into the major of the key. The predominating expression of the Air, however, is more that of tranquil, childlike harmony and peace, than of any restless passion; as innocent delight just slightly tempered with the "still sad music of humanity." The coolness of the buoyant element allays all inward heat.

In the next one (Second Set [Op. 30], No. 6,) which is a quicker movement, marked *Allegretto tranquillo*, and in the key of F sharp minor, there is a more stirring and exquisite delight. It rises to a higher pitch of enthusiasm, as if the heart in its still joy overflowed. The beauty of nature seems almost too much for the soul, the harmony of all thing too complete. Fancy's images rise thicker than before. The hills, the clouds, the gleaming waters, seem more living than before, and the soul stretches out its arms to them. Listen to that long high trill, which seems to carry the thoughts up and afar, as if they had left the body to play with the fleecy, pearly clouds about the moon, while the boat glides on in its sleep unconsciously below; and then the rapture of that bold delicious cadence, with which the reverie is ended, as if the skies came down with us to earth! The memory of that aerial excursion haunts the following melodies; the song floats in the middle, between two accompaniments, the waves below, and a faint prolonged vibration of that same high note above, like a thin streak of skyey color in a picture.

The last one, which is No. 5 of the Fifth Set [Op. 62], is perhaps the most beautiful of the three. It is in A minor, *Andante con moto*, and still the same rocking six-eight measure. There is even more of the physical sensation of the water in this. Ever and anon the stillness is startled by a loud stroke of the key-note, answered by the fifth below, and sometimes in the lowest octave, which gives one an awed feeling of the depth of the dark element, as if a sounding line were dropped. And again the mingled gurgling and laughing of the water, as it runs off the boat's sides, seems literally imitated in those strange chromatic appogiaturas [*sic*], which now and then form a hurried introduction to the principal note. The whole tone and coloring of the picture is deeper than the others. It is a song of the *depth* of the waters. The chords are richer, and the modulations, climbing towards their climax, are more wild and awe-inspiring. But by degrees the motion grows more gentle, and the sea more smooth, and the strain melts away in a free liquid cadence, in the major of the key, like closing the eyes in full assurance of most perfect bliss.

You feel that no soul ever conversed more intimately with nature, than did Mendelssohn when he composed this music. And music only could reveal what is here revealed.

If you would know Mendelssohn truly, study him in these "Songs without Words." They are of his most genuine, most individual inspirations. They are quite various in character,—some thirty-six of them in all;—and there is scarcely a characteristic trait of the composer's style, developed in his larger works, which you will not find quite clearly pronounced in one of these little *Lieder*. In them you have the whole of Mendelssohn, that is of the innate, and not the acquired music of the man.

NOTES

    1. *Allgemeine musikalische Zeitung* 29 (1827), 688.

    2. From the *Neue Zeitschrift für Musik* 2/50 (23 June 1835), 202.

    3. Schumann appears to have in mind a play on the seeming contradiction between "one-voiced" (*einstimmig*) and "monotony" (*Monotonie*).

    4. "In the field I prowl, silent and fierce, with my flintlock cocked." The hunter goes on to envision his beloved and wonder whether she is thinking of him.

    5. From *Dwight's Journal of Music* 1/6 (15 May 1852), 45–46. The original title was simply "Mendelssohn's Songs without Words."

    6. The "Volkslied," Op. 53 no. 5.

    7. From Percy Bysshe Shelley, *Prometheus Unbound*, act 2, scene 5, lines 72–74.

10

The Organ Music

Robert C. Mann

The organ compositions of Felix Mendelssohn Bartholdy rescued both the instrument and its repertoire from the base level to which they had fallen by the early nineteenth century and provided a direction for both to follow through the remainder of the century and to the present day. Without doubt, Mendelssohn was the greatest organist of his time. His compositions were reflections of his celebrated improvisations, which had as a foundation the polyphonic traditions of the Baroque. The mature organ compositions went beyond a single style of music, however, and exhibited a skillful combination of Baroque and Romantic characteristics, masterfully integrated by his distinctive musical personality. His Six Sonatas for Organ, Op. 65, his last and finest compositions for the instrument, summarized the styles of the past and established a new direction for the future. These sonatas stand among the most innovative compositions for organ from any historic period and offer an unusual perspective on a composer not generally credited with innovation in his music.

When Mendelssohn came on the scene in the early nineteenth century, music in German Protestant churches was experiencing a decline that had started around 1730, twenty years before Johann Sebastian Bach's death. Previously, these Lutheran churches had enjoyed the best sacred music in Europe, and their organ music had been exemplary for its high quality and performance standards. The liturgy in these churches featured an extensive program of choral and organ music, which expressed eloquently the combination of orthodox and pietistic beliefs that flavored the time. Church musicians had been held in the highest esteem, and the respect that organists had for their instrument was reflected in the superior musical product that they created. This product was based on the organ as a polyphonic instrument, and the greatest examples of this style of organ composition came from the pen of Johann Sebastian Bach. The subsequent decline affected the quality of organ playing and organ compositions and greatly reduced the performance skills of organists throughout the first half of the nineteenth century. In the years following Bach's death his music fell into virtual oblivion, and it was unknown to nearly all but the master's students.

This decline came about because of Enlightenment philosophical ideas and the musical influence of both the *style galant* and the Enlightenment, which were antithetical to Baroque concepts and practices. The purpose of *galant* music was to entertain, and it did so in a simpler style, intended to please the ear. The Enlightenment philosophers questioned the need for liturgical worship and severed all ties with the Protestant liturgy. Endorsing a "natural" religion, they also challenged the need for music in the church. These philosophers maintained a general lack of interest in the church and were unable to see its music as a combined artistic and theological medium requiring high artistic standards and great integrity. Musical traditions disappeared, respect for church musicians was also lost, and the old, polyphonic forms of organ music were neglected. Church music was ultimately eclipsed by music of the theater and concert hall, where the Enlightenment composers directed their musical talents. Major composers of the Classic period had no interest in composing organ music, given the low esteem of the instrument and its function.

By the end of the eighteenth century the prestige of the organist's profession had deteriorated to the point that the organist's main job was outside the church, and the organ was played as an avocation. Craftsmanship in organ music was at a nadir, particularly where polyphonic styles from the past were concerned. Piano, vocal, orchestral, and string styles found their way into the organ music of this period, and the influence of the orchestra on organ construction affected organ music of the day.

During this interregnum in the history of organ music,[1] meager compositions for the organ replaced the pieces previously used in the liturgy. New was a pious character piece for the organ, frequently referred to as *religious adagio*, which emphasized extramusical ideas, frequently used a programmatic title ("Prayer," "Consolation," and so forth), and often took the ternary form of a piano character piece. Other primary qualities were homophonic texture, a clear, obvious melody supported by a predictable and lifeless chordal accompaniment, a slow tempo, and emotionalism. The end result was an ineffective, neutral style of composition intended to create a devotional mood, in which musical quality played little or no part. Such an "expressive" composition could be played at any point in the service, and the religious adagio soon became the most widely used organ piece in the early nineteenth-century Protestant Church.

Another type of organ music that was featured in the early nineteenth-century repertoire was the *postludium*, a short piece of no precise form that was frequently played at the end of the service. In addition, two forms of the fugue existed at the start of the nineteenth century: the *fughetta* and the "chromatic" fugue. The *fughetta* was short and is best illustrated in the numerous examples by Johann Ernst Rembt (1749–1810), a student of Johann Peter Kellner (1705–1772), who himself had studied with Bach. The "chromatic" fugue is a character piece that uses a subject that is more chromatic than diatonic in inflection.

By 1780 the chorale prelude had changed to a "romantic" tone painting—mood music—in which the composer was supposed to express the spirit of the text. Quoting the chorale *cantus firmus* was no longer essential, although composers sometimes used a fragment of the tune. Chorale preludes were still in evidence, though, as can be seen in the settings of Christian H. Rinck (1770–1846), a prolific composer of the period who juxtaposed homophonic style with polyphony. His rather pianistic chorale settings were published in *Der Choralfreund* (1832–1840) and in the second part of his *Practische Orgelschule*, Op. 55. M. G. Fischer (1773–1829), like Rinck a student of Johann Christian Kittel (who studied with Bach), composed more than 200 works in a similar dualistic style in an attempt to develop a new harmonic language. Non-chorale-based compositions such as pastorales and noels were also heard in the services.

Also in connection with the decline in organ playing must be mentioned the breakdown of the traditional method of organ instruction. The teacher-student method of learning to play the organ became a thing of the past. The new way to learn to play the organ was through an instruction book, a cosmopolitan educational tool of the Enlightenment. Instruction books of all kinds existed during the Enlightenment, and self-help organ manuals were abundant. Some well-known *Orgelschulen* were those of Abbé Georg Joseph Vogler (1797), Justin Heinrich Knecht (1795–1798), and Rinck (1820). *Der angehende praktische Organist* (1801–1808) by Kittel was a widely known, three-volume instruction book. All these methods were directed toward the less sophisticated talent and neglected the traditional intellectual skills (counterpoint) taught to organists of previous periods. They emphasized character pieces and chorale preludes in the styles of the day.

Another factor that influenced change in organ playing was the organ recital. Various secular organists traveled throughout Europe playing recitals that featured music unlike that traditionally heard in Protestant services. The most famous of the traveling virtuosi was Abbé Vogler (1749–1814), who played more than 2,000 organ recitals. Fascinated with organ construction, Vogler attempted to imitate orchestral sound (he was particularly fond of the crescendo practices of the Mannheim school) through unusual organ-building techniques. These ideas were ultimately represented in a portable organ that he invented, called the *orchestrion*, which he took on his tours. Although this instrument was an unsuccessful attempt to provide a replacement for the orchestra, the seeds had been planted for a multiplicity of musical and orchestral effects that found their way into the repertoires of many organists. Vogler composed more than 100 short preludes for the organ in the Sturm und Drang spirit, using spectacular, sensational effects and programmatic titles.

After the death of Bach in 1750 a small circle of pupils and musicians kept his compositions and teachings alive. Pupils including Kellner, Johann Tobias Krebs (1690–1762), Johann Philipp Kirnberger (1721–1783), and others continued Bach's teaching traditions through the late eighteenth century. Johann Nikolaus

Forkel (1749–1818) introduced Bach to the nineteenth century in his biography of Bach, written in 1802. Bach's last pupil, Johann Christian Kittel, lived until 1809 and was the nineteenth century's last direct link to the master.

Into this circle of Bach devotees the young Felix Mendelssohn Bartholdy was incorporated in 1819 at the age of ten years. Mendelssohn became a pupil of Karl Friedrich Zelter (1758–1832), who had studied with Kirnberger and was thoroughly grounded in appreciation for, and even adoration, of Bach's music and teachings. A friend of Goethe and director of the Berlin Singakademie, Zelter taught young Felix theory, counterpoint, and composition. A man of strong character and conservative thinking, Zelter was the strongest personality among Mendelssohn's teachers. He successfully controlled the youth's ego and created a disciplined and hardworking student, adding these virtues to the lad's exceptional talents. Zelter prepared Mendelssohn for his future by thoroughly grounding him in music fundamentals, Baroque polyphonic techniques, and musical forms.

Mendelssohn was introduced to the keyboard and church music of Johann Sebastian Bach by Zelter, who had personal copies and made them available to the young student. This introduction to Bach's music by such a devotee led Mendelssohn to a lifelong veneration of Bach and Bach's music. Next to Mendelssohn's father, Zelter was the most important figure in Mendelssohn's life until Zelter's death in 1832. Zelter provided the link to the historical past for Mendelssohn's musical and personal development.

Abraham Mendelssohn acknowledged the significance of Zelter's contribution to his son in the following letter, written on 10 March 1835:

I felt more strongly than ever what a great merit it was on Zelter's part to restore Bach to the Germans; for, between Forkel's day and his, very little was ever said about Bach, and even then principally with regard to his "wohltemperierte Clavier." He was the first person on whom the light of Bach clearly dawned . . . . His musical performances . . . were indeed a proof that no work begun in earnest, and followed up with quiet perseverance, can fail ultimately to command success. At all events, it is an undoubted fact, that without Zelter, your own musical tendencies would have been of a totally different nature.[2]

Another link to the past for young Felix was his study with a famous organ recitalist of the day, August Wilhelm Bach (1796–1869). A. W. Bach (who also studied with Zelter) served as organist at the Marienkirche in Berlin and, from 1832, as director of the Institute for Church Music. In addition to composing five volumes of music, Bach was an outstanding performer and teacher of the organ. He strongly supported both the Lutheran liturgical tradition and the music of Johann Sebastian Bach (no relation), and he was among the first musicians of his day to call for a reform in the quality of church music. His exceptional standards of church music and organ playing directly influenced Mendelssohn and generations of other organists (Richter, Schneider, Haupt, Ritter, Thiele, Todt).

Mendelssohn probably studied organ with A. W. Bach from late 1820 through most of 1823, age eleven through fourteen. During this time A. W. Bach was composing his first works for organ, preludes and fugues conceived in the Baroque polyphonic tradition that surely influenced Mendelssohn. Through A. W. Bach, Mendelssohn began to develop technical skills at the organ that were to develop fully at a later time (e.g., his prodigious pedal technique around the late 1830s).

Mendelssohn never became an organist in the traditional sense. He was never a regular church organist or a church musician, though playing the organ was very important to him, and he nurtured a genuine fascination for performing on the instrument and kept abreast of organ construction throughout his life. Although he apparently never considered himself to be a virtuoso organist, he was undoubtedly the finest German organist of his age. Sir George Grove made the following statement much later regarding Mendelssohn's love and attraction for the instrument: "He took extraordinary delight in the organ; some describe him as even more at home there than on the pianoforte, though this must be taken with caution. But it is certain that he loved the organ, and was always greatly excited when playing it."[3]

Family travels throughout Europe provided the young Mendelssohn with his first opportunities to discover and play organs of various qualities and sizes. Early accounts describe his playing on organs at the Church of St. George, Rotha (a two-manual and pedal Silbermann instrument built about 1718) and at the Sophienkirche, Dresden (a two-manual and pedal Silbermann, built in 1721). A family trip to Switzerland in 1822 introduced the young student to organs in small villages as well as the organ in the Bern Cathedral. His Italian tour in 1830–1831 acquainted him with more Swiss organs in Engelberg, Wallenstadt, Sargans, and Lindau.

An insight into Mendelssohn's keen desire to play and develop his technical skills on the organ can be gained from the following statement in a letter from Sargans, 3 September 1831: "happily an organ is always to be found in this country; they are certainly small, and the lower octave, both in the key-board and the pedal, imperfect, or as I call it, crippled; but still they are organs, and that is enough for me."[4]

Mendelssohn also mentioned practicing the D-major fugue subject from book 1 of the *Well-Tempered Clavier* on the organ *with his feet* as a means of improving his pedal technique:

I instantly attempted it, and I at least see that it is far from being impossible, and that I shall accomplish it. The subject went pretty well, so I practised passages from the D major fugue, for the organ, from the F major toccata, and the G minor fugue, all of which I knew by heart. If I find a tolerable organ in Munich, and not an imperfect one, I will certainly conquer these, and feel childish delight at the idea of playing such pieces on the organ. The F major toccata, with the modulation at the close, sounded as if the church were about to tumble down: what a giant that Cantor was![5]

Throughout his life, Mendelssohn sought out organs on which to practice. This was partly a means of developing his technical skills, but also he seems to have been intensely curious about the uniqueness of each organ. He frequently tried out recently built instruments in England when he traveled there.

Although Mendelssohn composed a substantial number of organ compositions, he published only two of them; those works were the only organ compositions to which he assigned opus numbers. Mendelssohn published his first organ work, Three Preludes and Fugues, Op. 37 (1837), at the age of twenty-eight. This collection formed a direct link with the past and also called attention to his association with English organists of the day. The other work, Six Sonatas for Organ, Op. 65, was published in 1845 and is a compilation of everything that he had learned through his life as an organ performer and composer. This work reflected both the past and the future.

The organ compositions of Mendelssohn were systematically preserved in the "Green Books" along with his other compositions, and very few of his known works for organ have been lost. Mendelssohn's complete works for the organ have been superbly edited in a five-volume set by the eminent scholar William A. Little,[6] and it is this collection that has been used in this study and to which musical references are made.

Five musical procedures or styles may be noted in analyzing the organ music of Mendelssohn: English Baroque voluntary style; chorale-based procedures; fugue or fugato; Baroque toccata; and melodic ornamentation practices. These varied stylistic characteristics appear often throughout the organ compositions.[7]

English organ music of the early nineteenth century was limited by its instrument, primarily the incomplete pedal division. The voluntary was the main organ composition played in English church services, and its musical style was not much more advanced than those voluntaries of William Walond (ca. 1725–1770) and John Stanley (1712–1786) from the eighteenth century. Mendelssohn's many trips to England and his association with English organists influenced him to improvise and compose in this style. He even considered calling the pieces of Op. 65 "voluntaries."

Mendelssohn's use of chorale-based procedures reflects the influence of the nineteenth-century chorale preludes of C. H. Rinck, whom Mendelssohn met in Darmstadt in 1822. The chorale preludes of J. S. Bach and other Baroque composers were also well known to the composer.

Fugue-style composition is a direct influence of Mendelssohn's early teachers, Zelter and A. W. Bach, and the study of the masterworks of J. S. Bach. Mendelssohn's counterpoint studies were extensive, and by the time he was thirteen he had established a reputation for improvising polyphonic organ compositions in public exceptionally well.

The Baroque toccata was also a legacy handed down from Mendelssohn's early instructors, and his knowledge of Baroque organ works by composers other than Bach was exemplary. Mendelssohn also knew the art of ornamenting melody lines, an art observed in his improvisations and described in his playing of Bach's music, when he would have memory slips and decorate Bach's melodies in the appropriate style.[8]

In addition to these procedures, three characteristics from the so-called interregnum or period of decadence are seen in Mendelssohn's organ music: improvisatory, quasi-virtuosic style; the desire for more varied tone color; and the character piece (religious adagio).[9] After Mendelssohn's juvenilia these qualities appeared more frequently in his organ music.

The first organ compositions of Mendelssohn date from the time he was a student of Zelter and A. W. Bach, from age eleven until he was nearly fifteen—1820 to 1823. Obviously, this was a formative time for the young composer, and the works show little originality. Instead, the organ styles of J. S. Bach, A. W. Bach, and C. H. Rinck dominate the music. These compositions are not necessarily significant as individual pieces, but they demonstrate Mendelssohn's development as an organist and illustrate how the young student perceived the organ as an instrument for making polyphonic music.

The young Mendelssohn's first organ composition is a Praeludium in D minor, composed on 28 November 1820 (Little V, I, 2). This piece is unlike the ones of this period that follow, in that it is not polyphonically conceived. The form is A (mm. 1–56), B (56–103), A (104–32). The work begins with a four-note theme over a pedal point and alternates between a thick chordal texture and a three-part texture for hands only. Not really suggestive of the influence of previously mentioned composers, the music primarily reflects the young composer's search for a style.

Three fugues in trio style are the next organ works among Mendelssohn's juvenilia—in D minor (composed 3 December 1820; Little V, II, 8), G minor (composed December 1820; Little V, III, 12), and D minor (composed 6 January 1821; Little V, IV, 15), respectively. These fugues were written as counterpoint exercises for Zelter and reflect the honing of Mendelssohn's skills in the Baroque polyphonic style, both as a composer and as a performer. The pedal lines clearly indicate the start of a formidable pedal technique.

The first composition in this group of youthful works that gives a hint of Mendelssohn's emerging talent, composed 9 May 1823 (D major; Little V, V, 20), is headed *Andante—sanft*. This piece is a religious adagio that emphasizes lyricism in the melodic lines. Three melodic fragments (mm. 1, 5, 13) are introduced and developed in this short work.

The [Passacaglia] *Volles Werk* (C minor), composed 10 May 1823 (Little V, VI, 24) is obviously modeled on Bach's Passacaglia in C minor, although Mendelssohn's work has no fugue. The basso ostinato is eight bars in length, like Bach's (see Example 10.1), and there are twenty-one variations. The first eleven variations quote the theme in the pedal, while the next five variations state it in the middle or upper register and in arpeggios. Eight bars of free material occur between the sixteenth and seventeenth variations, mm. 137 to 144. The closing variations are of a freer style, although the melody figures predominantly in the pedal line. The composition shows how well the fourteen-year-old composer knew Bach's Passacaglia.

Example 10.1a
J. S. Bach, Passacaglia in C Minor, mm. 1–8

Example 10.1b
Mendelssohn, Passacaglia in C minor, mm. 1–8

The influence of C. H. Rinck emerges in the chorale variations on "Wie gross ist des Allmächt'gen Gute," composed 30 July 1823 (Little V, VII, 35). This chorale partita consists of a four-voice harmonization of the chorale followed by three variations of the tune. The first variation suggests *Vorimitation* in the accompanying voices, with the *cantus firmus* stated in augmentation in the pedal; the second variation subjects the various chorale phrases to different canonic treatments; and the third variation introduces a series of detached chords in the hands over eighth-note figuration in the feet, which is taken by the hands immediately after it is introduced. The chorale partitas in volume 2 of Rinck's *Praktische Orgelschule* (1819–1821) influenced this type of composition.

Mendelssohn wrote only three pieces for the organ between the summer of 1823 and the publication of his Three Preludes and Fugues, Op. 37, in 1837, a fourteen-year period. They were the *Nachspiel* in D major, composed 8 March 1831 (Little V, VIII, 53); *Fuga pro organo pleno* in D minor, composed 29 March 1833 (Little V, IX, 60); and Andante con moto in G minor, composed 11 July 1833 (Little V, X, 66). These are somewhat inconspicuous pieces, although the *Nachspiel* is a lovely postlude of forty-five measures that concludes with a long-breathed, lyrical fugue. The work indicates some growth on the part of Mendelssohn as a composer, shows better control of his skills, and gives a hint of what was to come in the Sonatas. The latter two pieces were written for Vincent Novello. The Andante con moto is a lyrical miniature of only thirty-four measures.

It would be incorrect to assume that Mendelssohn had little or no interest in the organ during the fourteen-year period of relative inactivity as a composer of organ works (1823–1837). After all, he was only fourteen years old in 1823, and during much of this time he was completing his education and developing the wide area of cultural interests and activities required of a young man of his talent and station in life. He then began a career as a composer, conductor, and performer, and much of his time was taken with the demands of establishing such activities. A prolific correspondent, his time was increasingly occupied by letter-writing, and frequent travels throughout Germany and England were necessary to establish himself professionally.

The organ was never far from his thinking or his routine of activities, however, as his letters reveal. He kept up his organ practice wherever he traveled, playing frequently on whatever instrument was available, even bad ("crippled") instruments or instruments with limitations, in order to maintain and improve his technical skills. From Munich he wrote to his sister Fanny in a letter dated 6 October 1831,

> I also play on the organ every day for an hour, but unfortunately I cannot practise properly, as the pedal is short of five upper notes, so that I cannot play any of Sebastian Bach's passages on it; but the stops are wonderfully beautiful, by the aid of which you can vary chorals; so I dwell with delight on the celestial, liquid tone of the instrument.[10]

In 1829 Mendelssohn made the first of ten trips to England for the purposes of conducting and performing his music and to develop personal growth in the cultural and educational areas that were so important to his family background. During these visits he routinely practiced and performed on the best organs available, both rebuilt historical instruments and new instruments. Although he was not the first organist to play the music of Bach in England, he introduced major organ works of Bach that had not yet been played there.

The Londoners took to Mendelssohn as one of their own, a degree of recognition not awarded a foreign musician since Handel's time. Their adulation for him and his organ playing was profuse and sincere, and his organ-playing activities were adequately documented by organists and friends of the day. His first public performance in London as an organist was 10 June 1832, at St. Paul's Cathedral. In 1833 he returned to St. Paul's and played duets with the church organist, Thomas Attwood (1765–1838). On successive trips large numbers of English organists had opportunities to hear him. Mendelssohn played the organ for public or private audiences on five other trips before his death. He never gave up playing the organ, nor did he lose his celebrated performance skills.

The first organ compositions by Mendelssohn that reflect the growing friendship and affection that he maintained with English organists were the Two Fugues for the Organ [Duets] for Thomas Attwood, composed 11 January 1835. Attwood had been a distinguished student of Mozart and was a successful and prominent composer of church anthems. His friendship with Mendelssohn was the first of an ever-enlarging circle of organists and church musicians that was to include Samuel Wesley, Henry J. Gauntlett, and Vincent Novello.

The first fugue, in C minor (Little I, III.1, 12), would receive a great deal of attention from Mendelssohn over a period of years. The fugue subject was originally improvised by Mendelssohn in a performance for Attwood at St. Paul's in 1833.[11] The improvisation was written out a year later and, in January 1835, arranged for two players as a duet and dedicated to Attwood. Mendelssohn was to use the fugue again two years later in another revision as the first fugue of Op. 37, which was also dedicated to Attwood.

The idea of an organ duet probably came from a previous experience with Attwood, two years earlier, on 23 June 1833 at St. Paul's. On that occasion Mendelssohn performed with Attwood a four-hand version of one of Attwood's Coronation Anthems in an empty cathedral before a few friends and Mendelssohn's father, Abraham. The organ duet was a relatively new thing at this time, a fashionable spin-off from the popularity of the piano duet. It developed in Germany and continued to be popular during the remainder of the nineteenth century. Mendelssohn apparently enjoyed the experience of duetting with Attwood and commemorated the event by creating a four-hand composition two years later.

The first duet is a four-voice fugue in $\frac{12}{8}$ time, which has a subject that begins low in the *secondo* part and proceeds in a gently rocking movement of a relaxing nature. A pedal part is written for the *secondo* player, which often doubles the left-hand part. This doubling was necessitated by the limited ability of the pedal division on the St. Paul organ, a limitation typical of English organs, which made the playing of Baroque polyphonic styles very difficult.

The second fugue of the pair, in D major (Little I, III.2, 20), has similar linear characteristics as the first fugue, four-part imitative writing between the two players with *secondo* pedal doubled from the left hand. The mood of this second fugue is quieter, sustained, and lyrical, while the first is written to be played with the full principal division of the organ and with much more energy.

Mendelssohn's marriage in 1837 brought forth an abundance of creative energy, and during that year he completed and published his Three Preludes and Fugues for the Organ, Op. 37 (Little I, IV, I-III). This collection of compositions was dedicated to Attwood. From the standpoint of magnitude and quality, this was the best organ music composed by Mendelssohn up to this point.

These works have much in common with the Six Preludes and Fugues for Piano, Op. 35, which were composed in the years 1827–1837. In these piano compositions Mendelssohn came closer to liberating himself from stilted, Baroque, academic mannerisms, and he established a synthesis between the old polyphonic tradition and the new, free piano style. The writing of four-voice fugues for piano was a challenge for Mendelssohn that carried over to composing fugues for the organ.

In the Preludes and Fugues for Organ Mendelssohn was able to fuse together the past with the present in a sense of continuity that sounded "right," not a decadent reconstruction of antiquated procedures. Robert Schumann's comment about the Six Preludes and Fugues for Piano can also be used to describe Op. 37: "he . . . rather let the melodic nature of the *cantilena* dominate, while holding to the Bachian form."[12] This music opened the door for what was to come in the Six Sonatas, Op. 65.

The preludes of Op. 37 were written during Mendelssohn's honeymoon in Speyer in the upper Rhine Valley, 2–6 April 1837. The fugues had been written earlier, between 1833 and 1836. The music was well received by the public when it was published simultaneously by Novello and Breitkopf & Härtel in the spring of 1837 and has been a part of the organist's repertoire since that time.

Prelude I in C minor was composed on 2 April 1837. It is a monothematic movement that combines the imitative style of Johann Sebastian Bach with free, nineteenth-century development. The vigorous theme is introduced in the first four measures and recurs in imitation throughout the work. The prelude opens with a chord in the left hand and pedal, immediately followed by an octave leap and descending eighth-note scale pattern in the right hand (see Example 10.2). This

Example 10.2
Mendelssohn, Prelude I in C Minor, Op. 37 no. 1, mm. 1–10

beginning gives the work immediate energy and projection, which continue throughout the prelude. The first eighteen measures form an exposition, after which episodes, subject entries, and *stretti* alternate. The aggressive forward motion established at the start of the movement continues without interruption through 130 measures, after which the movement concludes with 6 measures of heavy chords, slowing the motion logically and with good musical effect. Mendelssohn would use this device frequently in the Six Sonatas.

The C-minor fugue (Little I, IV, I.2, 33) is the improvisation for Thomas Attwood at St. Paul's Cathedral in 1833 and later arranged for organ duet (1835). Mendelssohn now revised it a third time on 1 December 1836, to make it the initial fugue in his published collection of preludes and fugues for organ. The fugue obviously had a special appeal for Mendelssohn.

Although the fugue is in $^{12}_8$ meter, it is not representative of the giguelike style of fugues by Buxtehude and Bach in the same meter. The subject is a long, legato line that offers good harmonic possibilities. Two contrasting dynamic levels alternate throughout the fugue, identifying subject entries and episodes (forte for subject entries in mm. 1–23, 29–45, 51–65 and mezzo forte for episodes in mm. 24–29, 45–51). Although manual changes are not specified, these indications certainly encourage them.

Prelude II (Little I, IV, 2.1, 40), in the key of G major, was written on 4 April 1837. The tempo marking of Andante con moto, the dynamic level of mezzo piano, and the $^6_8$ meter combine to create a pastoral mood, a marked contrast to the first prelude of the collection. The composition is in ABA song form, with coda. The lovely, lyrical first theme appears in the top voice in the starting measure and is five bars long. It is immediately repeated in the tenor voice, followed by free material and a return of the theme in the dominant (section A, mm. 1–27). The middle section introduces a new theme in the soprano voice in D minor, which modulates quickly to B♭ major and then is treated in several related keys before returning to the home key (section B, mm. 27–56). The short recurrence of section A (mm. 56–68) is interesting because of its use of C♮ in the pedal line (mm. 60–63) for the first theme in a passage that suggests the dominant key (D major). The coda (mm. 68–88) quotes both themes. This is the most sensitive and delicate prelude of the three and shows more innovation on the part of the composer in style and harmony than do its companions.

Fugue II (Little I, IV, 2.2, 45) was composed on 1 December 1836 in Leipzig and is similar to the first fugue in polyphonic design. It has been described as "broad and dignified" by one writer[13] and "conventional throughout" and lacking "the spark of genius" by another.[14] The four-voice fugue is in $^4_2$ time. The craftsmanship of the counterpoint is of high quality, and the fugue contains a good deal of chromatic activity. The subject appears first in the pedal and, after the exposition (ending m. 10), appears in alternation with episodic and sequential material until the coda, m. 57. Within a five-measure portion of the brief coda, Mendelssohn incorporated the fugue subject three times in stretto.

Prelude III (Little I, IV, 3.1, 50) in D minor was composed on 6 April 1837, and one can imagine that it is reminiscent of Mendelssohn's organ improvisations. It is a grand, toccata-like work played Allegro and forte. Free material alternates with a polyphonic texture in which a subject and recurring countersubject are treated throughout. The composition begins with a twenty-three-measure introduction, which alternates cadential chords and freely played figuration. The subject is introduced in m. 24 and is followed by the countersubject in m. 27. After contrapuntal treatment of the two themes and episodes, there is a modulation to the key of F major (m. 60). The composer introduced a contrasting improvisatory figuration in a triplet rhythmic pattern in the right hand with chords in the left hand and pedal. This free material modulates through several minor keys before the subject is restated in the pedal (m. 79) with the triplet figuration continuing in the right hand. After a long episode in equal eighths using material from the countersubject, the triplet figuration again appears (m. 100) but soon accelerates into sixteenth-note figuration. This improvisatory section quotes the subject (m. 111) and concludes with a final statement of the subject in D minor at m. 121, followed by a long episode using familiar material. A coda (mm. 134–153) built on the subject continues after a cadence. The return here to quarter- and half-note rhythms creates a concluding deceleration.

Fugue III (Little I, IV, 3.2, 60) in D minor was originally composed on 29 March 1833 in Berlin [*Fuga pro Organo Pleno* for Vincent Novello]. The fugue in Op. 37 is a revised version of the earlier fugue: it is marked *Volles Werk* (full organ), and it uses a shorter version of the fugue subject than did the previous composition. The fugue is similar in structure to the other fugues in Op. 37. The subject first in the alto voice, followed by a countersubject that never figures prominently in the composition after its introduction. Following the exposition, the subject is treated in typical Baroque style among the four voices. This is the least interesting of the three fugues of the series.

The Three Preludes and Fugues for Organ constitute the best music for organ that had been written in a long time, and, in one sense, this music rescued German organ literature from the descending spiral in which it was moving. The dominating element in this music is the polyphonic Baroque style. It is in the preludes that innovation is seen. The use of Baroque polyphonic procedures in Preludes I and III, combined with the lyricism and harmonic ideas of the nineteenth century, produced music that offered "new wine" in "old skins."[15] All three preludes are improvisatory in general style, the first and last being in a grander, flamboyant manner. Each pair of preludes and fugues is unified according to spirit and mood. Mendelssohn's imaginative use of musical styles in this work anticipates Op. 65. Further, these examples resurrected the form of prelude and fugue and gave impetus for its use to such succeeding German composers as Hesse, Liszt, Merkel, and, later, Reger.

In spite of the successful publication of Op. 37 in 1837, Mendelssohn did not write other organ compositions for publication until Op. 65 in 1845. Mendelssohn completed his eighth visit to England in mid-July 1844 and returned to Germany to join his family for a holiday in the country in Soden, just outside Frankfurt. Three fine organ pieces from the work of that summer and late fall that were never to be included in Mendelssohn's later publications should be identified. These compositions were to remain isolated from the other organ pieces, one of them in total obscurity. Each is worthy of consideration as an example of Mendelssohn's developing style of organ composition.

The Andante in D major [with variations] (Little II, III, 9) was composed on 23 July 1844 in Soden. In addition to the original version, two manuscript copies of this piece exist, and the work was initially published by Novello in 1898. The piece is a quiet, gentle composition; a dynamic marking of piano is indicated at the start, and no additional markings are noted elsewhere in the score. The theme is sixteen bars long and is a tuneful, songlike melody similar to that of a simple character piece (see Example 10.3). The theme is played with hands only; pedal is used in all but one of the variations.

Example 10.3
Mendelssohn, Andante in D Major (1844), Theme

There are four variations, each flowing into the next in a unified, expressive progression. Variation 1 (mm. 16–32) quotes the melody in the left hand in quarter notes and in thirds, with an eighth-note figuration running in the right hand. Variation 2 (mm. 32–48) is written for manuals only and uses the soprano for the melody in quarter notes; the left hand has a triplet figuration of constantly moving notes. Variation 3 (mm. 48–69) has less movement, using quarter notes in both hands. The first three variations are performed without pause. Variation 3 concludes with a sustained cadence, and variation 4 (mm. 69–98) changes from common time to $\frac{6}{8}$ meter. The melody is in the right hand, moving in eighth notes, and is a variant of the theme. Sequence and repetition play important roles in this variation. The active rhythm of this variation gives more interest and helps to focus the forward direction of the whole composition. The piece concludes with a coda in the original meter (mm. 98–107), which brings back material from the first six measures of the composition with a closing in the home key.

The second independent composition from the summer of 1844, Allegro [Chorale and Fugue] in D minor/major (Little II, IV, 15), was composed 25 July 1844 in Soden. This composition is Mendelssohn's most extended organ work, comprising 198 measures, and has remained unavailable to organists until Professor Little's recent edition. It is a continuous work in three contrasting sections: Allegro (common time, D minor, forte); *più lento* (D major); and fugue (D major, in the tempo of the second section).

The long first section, Allegro (mm. 1-91), is an improvisatory tour-de-force that makes impressive technical demands on the player. A proud and grandly heroic theme introduced in the soprano (m. 2) dominates the section. It is repeated polyphonically throughout, with contrasting figuration of sixteenth notes as accompaniment or in episodes (see Example 10.4). Like the polyphonic preludes of Op. 37, this section of the piece shows a more rhapsodic and flamboyant direction than had generally appeared in Mendelssohn's organ music. A fiery chromatic passage in the hands and feet moves into a short, choralelike section, *più lento* (mm. 92–108). This thick harmonization of a hymnlike tune is played more slowly (and also notated in half notes) in D major. Following this brief contrast to the first section, a fugue begins simultaneously with the cadence of the chorale (m. 108). The subject of the long fugue (mm. 108–98) is dignified and strong, and its polyphonic treatment offers a sustained and powerful climax to balance the energy established in the opening Allegro.

The third independent composition from this period, Allegro in B♭ major (Little II, XIII, 69), was composed 31 December 1844. This composition is in the spirit of a rousing postludium, and it differs in compositional style from the organ works of Mendelssohn previously examined. At the beginning of the piece the melody is heard in the top voice, accompanied by staggered, repeated chords in both hands. The melody then shifts to a tenor range (m. 15) with continued accompaniment of chords in the right hand and bass. The composition never deviates from this style until the closing measures (127–35), when eighth-note descending figuration concludes the work.

After playing organ recitals in England for fifteen years, Mendelssohn enjoyed an exalted reputation among English organists. These organists, however, were unhappy that little of his organ music and extemporizations (they were especially astounded by his pedal technique) had made their way to the printed page. Popular demand prompted the publisher Charles Coventry to commission Mendelssohn to write a set of three voluntaries for the organ to be published by Coventry and

Example 10.4
Mendelssohn, Allegro (Chorale and Fugue) in D Minor/Major (1844), mm. 1–11

Hollier. The offer was extended just before Mendelssohn left London to return to Germany in July 1844, and Mendelssohn immediately accepted it. As soon as the composer returned to Germany, he began to work on the pieces.

By mid-August Mendelssohn had written seven movements,[16] and on 29 August 1844 he wrote to Charles Coventry about the possibility of changing the title from "voluntaries" to "sonatas."

I have also been very busy about the organ-pieces which you wanted me to write for you, and they are nearly finished. I should like to call them "3 *Sonatas* for the Organ," instead of *Voluntaries*. Tell me if you like this title as well; if not, I think the name of Voluntaries will suit the pieces also, the more so as I do not know what it means precisely.[17]

Coventry had evidently selected the original title himself, probably because of the English organist's familiarity with, and use of, voluntaries in the English service. As Mendelssohn completed these movements, he saw that he had gone considerably beyond the range of the English voluntary and needed flexibility to work with a variety of styles and forms that the voluntary did not offer. Moreover, the composer did not intend these pieces to be construed as sacred music and did not want their use limited to the church. The publisher apparently agreed to the change of title without reservations.

Of the seven movements composed by summer's end, only three were to find their way into the final version of Six Sonatas. Mendelssohn completed four more movements by September 1844. It was 19 December before he returned to the organ project, for which, by 27 January 1845, he had completed everything but the last movement of the Bb Sonata. He considered using his earlier Allegro in Bb major (Little II, XIII, 69) for the final movement but was unsure. Finally, Mendelssohn changed his mind about using that piece and, on 2 April 1845, completed the fugue in Bb (Little, III, VIII, 34) to replace it. Still unsatisfied, Mendelssohn rewrote the fugue again before the final publication.[18]

In the course of these months of work on what were to become the Six Sonatas, Mendelssohn wrote a number of individual movements that he hoped to incorporate into his sonatas. Some of these pieces were revised or rewritten entirely before he accepted a final version for publication. The Six Sonatas were completed by choosing from this collection of individual pieces those that he thought could be grouped into six separate sonatas. The definitive version was then put in manuscript in his own hand as Six Sonatas for Organ, Op. 65.[19]

A second manuscript was created by copyist Franz Xaver Gleichauf near the time of the original; it is not identical with the autograph. It shows certain changes from the first version and represents "an intermediate step between conception and publication, but not a consistently advanced stage of development over" Mendelssohn's autograph.[20]

The Six Sonatas for Organ were published on 15 September 1845, jointly by Coventry and Hollier in London, Breitkopf and Hartel in Leipzig, Giovanni Ricordi in Milan, and Maurice Schlesinger in Paris.[21] Coventry enlisted 190 subscribers for the first printing.[22] Mendelssohn dedicated Op. 65 to Dr. Fritz Schlemmer, a Frankfurt lawyer and good friend (who was also related to him by marriage).

An interesting aspect of the work is that Mendelssohn suggested the use of the title "Mendelssohn's School of Organ-Playing" in a letter to Coventry on 1 May 1845.[23] The composer evidently saw a didactic purpose in his Six Sonatas and had in mind educational goals for English organists. The publisher used this designation in first announcing the work, but Mendelssohn withdrew this title before its final publication.

A lengthy review of the work was published in the *Morning Chronicle* on 12 March 1846, in which Dr. Henry Gauntlett praised the composition.[24] Gauntlett was particularly taken with the Fourth Sonata. Robert Schumann praised the work in a letter to Mendelssohn written 22 October 1845:

Only the other day we became quite absorbed in your Organ Sonatas. . . . You are always striving to advance still more, and for this reason you will ever be an example to me. These intensely poetical new ideas--what a perfect picture they form in every sonata! . . . Above all, Nos. 5 and 6 seem to me splendid. It is really a fact, dear Mendelssohn, no one else writes such fine harmonies; and they keep on getting purer and more inspired.[25]

Mendelssohn apparently never played his Six Sonatas in public, although he played a private performance of the work for an English friend, W. S. Rockstro, in St. Catherine's Church, Frankfurt, in the spring of 1845. He played all six of the sonatas in one sitting, a feat, he later wrote Fanny on 20 April 1845, that he would not repeat: "I will play them to you at Ober-Liederbach, that is to say, by three at a time, for all six are too fatiguing, as I found out the other day when trying them."[26]

Mendelssohn's selection of the term *sonata* for his compositions did not mean that he intended to write these multimovement works according to the eighteenth-century Classic concept of sonata design. His primary concern regarding musical form in the sonatas was unity, that each movement have an appropriate relationship to the whole. Consequently, there is no conventional plan in the use of movements in these sonatas; Mendelssohn literally selected individual organ pieces that he had previously written and juxtaposed them accordingly in each sonata. Three of the sonatas are in four movements (nos. I, II, and IV), two sonatas are in three movements (nos. V and VI), and one sonata is in two movements (no. III).

Mendelssohn composed for the organ in much the same way that he improvised. He had great skill in combining polyphonic structures from the past with lyrical melodies of the present. Thus, a substantial number of the movements of the Six Sonatas follow Baroque polyphonic models, often using some form of fugue. Baroque and Classic instrumental forms such as theme and variation, binary, and ternary forms are contrasted with nineteenth-century character pieces (religious adagio or "song without words") and sonata-form movements to produce a new type of organ composition. Table 10.1 provides an overview of the sonatas according to keys, tempos, and formal structures.

Mendelssohn's ability to combine old with new forms and to use stylistic elements in an intimate and convincing way is a hallmark of his Six Sonatas. From

Table 10.1

Keys, Tempos, and Formal Structures of Movements in the Six Sonatas of Mendelssohn

	First movement	Second movement	Third movement	Fourth movement
		SONATA I		
Key	F minor	A♭ major	F minor	F major
Tempo	Allegro mode- rato e serioso	Adagio	Andante recitativo	Allegro assai vivace
Form/ style	Quasi-sonata	Ternary--ABA'	Free recitative	Toccata
		SONATA II		
Key	C minor	C minor	C major	C major
Tempo	Grave	Adagio	Allegro maes- toso e vivace	Allegro moderato
Form/ style	Prelude	Song without Words	Prelude	Fugue
		SONATA III		
Key	A major	A major		
Tempo	Con moto maestoso	Andante tranquillo		
Form/ style	Introduction/ Fugue/Coda	Binary--A|BA		
		SONATA IV		
Key	B♭ major	B♭ major	F major	B♭ major
Tempo	Allegro con brio	Andante religioso	Allegretto	Allegro maes- toso e vivace
Form/ style	Sonata	Ternary--ABA	Character piece --ABA	Introduction/ Fugue/Coda
		SONATA V		
Key	D major	B minor	D major	
Tempo	Andante	Andante con moto	Allegro maestoso	
Form/ style	"Chorale"	ABAB Coda	ABABA Coda	
		SONATA VI		
Key	D minor	D minor	D major	
Tempo	Andante sostenuto	Sostenuto e legato	Andante	
Form/ style	Variation	Fugue	Religious adagio	

*Robert C. Mann, "The Development of Form in the German Organ Sonata from Mendelssohn to Rheinberger" (D.M.A. diss., University of North Texas, 1978), 10-11.

The Baroque period, several compositional types are seen. Fugue writing or fughetta appears in every sonata except Sonata V. Sonata III contains a double fugue, the most brilliant of all Mendelssohn's organ fugues. The bravura toccata or prelude style occurs five times (I, 4; IV, 1, 4; V, 3; VI, 1). Chorales are used four times in the sonatas (I, 1; III, 1; V, 1; VI, 1). Variation form is used brilliantly in Sonata VI. The voluntary of the Anglican Church is reflected in Sonatas II, III, V, and VI.

Registration directions for Op. 65 are outlined in the composer's own preface to the work, and they follow Baroque concepts.[27] Mendelssohn thought it futile to identify precise registration for each sonata because of the diversity of organs and their stops. He therefore left the final selection of registration to the discretion of the player but gave suggested guidelines based on specific dynamic levels (a practice Josef Rheinberger [1839-1901] was to follow in his Sonatas for Organ at the end of the century):

ff = full organ [*organo pleno* plus reeds]
f = full organ without the loudest stops
p = several 8' stops
pp = one soft 8' stop

Pedal should use 16' and 8' stops with two exceptions: (1) in playing the first performance from manuscript of the Andante con moto from Sonata V, Mendelssohn used a single 8' stop for the pizzicato pedal line[28]; (2) in Sonata VI, variation 1, the composer specified in the score to use one 8' stop in the pedal.

Mendelssohn had Baroque tracker-action instruments in mind when he wrote his organ works, as those were the instruments that he was used to playing. Those instruments would not have had the combination pistons, crescendo pedal, and "orchestral" effects that appeared on organs later in the nineteenth century. The music he wrote for organ does not require any of these devices. It appears that he intended a Baroque *organo pleno* registration for his polyphonic toccata and fugal movements and the expressive and coloristic registrations of a nineteenth-century Romantic style for movements that were character pieces and religious adagios.

As already noted, the forms chosen for the Sonatas include sonata designs, binary forms, and character pieces. Sonata form is used twice (I, 1 and IV, 1), and several versions of binary form are seen (V, 2 and VI, 3). Five character pieces emphasizing cantilena melodies in "Romantic" harmonic idioms are found in the sonatas (I, 2; II, 2; III, 2; IV, 3; VI, 3). Also among the sonatas are movements requiring virtuoso, piano-type technique with arpeggiated figuration (I, 4; IV, 1; V, 3; VI, 1). Although Mendelssohn's harmonic style is classical in nature and largely predictable, he achieved dramatic results at times, with harmonic colors and juxtaposition of sonorities (e.g., in Sonata I, movement 1 the dramatic alternation of fugato passages with the chorale phrases).

Innovations in manual and pedal technique in the sonatas warrant discussion. As mentioned, a bravura, piano-style technique is demanded in several movements, for example, Sonata I, fourth movement, and Sonata VI, fourth variation. Arpeggios and scale passages using extensive ranges of the keyboard at fast speed increased technical demands on the players of that time. Arpeggiated figuration and lyrical, melodic passages were combined with hands and feet in Sonata IV, first movement, requiring even greater skills.

Mendelssohn's Six Sonatas required a pedal technique comparable to that demanded by Baroque organ music, in which the feet were called on to do everything that the hands were asked to do. These pieces featured pedal phrasings extensively marked by the composer, unusual in music of the first half of the nineteenth century. The organist of the Sonatas was required to play two-octave scale passages in the feet (I, 4), detached [staccato] notes (V, 2), legato and staccato articulation (VI, variation 2), and one pedal solo (III, 1). All of these innovative demands must have caused great difficulty for organists of the day because of the limited pedal divisions on English organs and the lack of contemporary music requiring such pedal skills.

Sonata I in F minor is a four-movement work and provides a good example of the grand style of improvisation for which Mendelssohn was known. The first movement, Allegro moderato e serioso (Little IV, I.1, 1), employs a very dramatic quasi-sonata design. After a ten-measure introduction, the first theme is introduced in the soprano voice (m. 11) and followed in imitation by the alto, tenor, and bass voices (through m. 20). At m. 21, a second exposition of the theme begins in the tenor voice and is imitated, in turn, in the soprano, alto, and bass (mm. 21–31). The first four notes of the theme provide development until m. 40, when the second theme is introduced. This new theme is played *mp* on a second keyboard (the first was *ff* on manual I) and consists of the first phrase of the chorale "Was mein Gott will das gescheh' allzeit." A dialogue ensues between the polyphonic theme and the chorale theme, with the fugato phrases juxtaposed dramatically at the beginning and end of each chorale phrase. The two melodies are joined for the first time in m. 54, and the development section begins in m. 60 when the first theme is inverted and imitated in the order alto, tenor, bass, soprano (mm. 60–70). After further development, the chorale reappears in m. 77, and the two themes alternate on separate keyboards as previously. A modified recapitulation begins in m. 91, which quotes the first theme in stretto and recalls the chorale theme in m. 93. The first theme is treated in stretto and inversion to build a thrilling climax, which cadences with a sustained German augmented sixth chord. After the cadence the chorale theme returns softly on the second keyboard. It is then answered by a fortissimo phrase played on the first keyboard, bringing the movement to a stirring conclusion.

The second movement, Adagio (Little IV, I.2, 8), is a ternary-form religious adagio, constructed as a dialogue between two manuals. The movement has a very simple melody, introduced in the soprano voice in the first measure. The divisions of the work are as follows: A, mm. 1–16; B, 16–40; A, 41–56; coda, 56–78.

A recitative-like free design is the structure for movement 3, Andante recitativo (Little IV, I.3, 11). In this movement Mendelssohn juxtaposed two radically different sonorities. The unaccompanied recitative begins *pp* in the first measure. It is answered (m. 4) by loud chords, sustained and hymnlike. This opposing dialogue continues in alternation throughout the movement. Two interesting elements are seen in this movement. First, the recitative section starts with one voice and adds new voices one by one in successive entrances. Second, chords are built by sustaining the notes of an arpeggio, creating an unusual sonorous effect (first seen in m. 29). The movement makes an effective prelude to the finale, into which it leads without pause.

Allegro assai vivace (Little IV, I.4, 14), movement 4 is a loud toccata in the grand pianistic idiom. The arpeggiated figuration at the opening uses tied notes in both hands and feet to sustain pitches and generate harmonic tension as well as to overwhelm the listener in a sea of sound. A heroic new melody is interjected in m. 68 that provides a new theme for the web of continuing arpeggiated sounds. The piece concludes with a wonderful stretto on the new theme (beginning on m. 112), more arpeggios, and two-octave scales in the pedal. This movement offers a wonderful example of what Mendelssohn's extempore use of pedal point must have been like.

Sonata II in C minor is the closest of Mendelssohn's sonatas to the English voluntary style. The English voluntary at the time of Mendelssohn followed a two-movement design—a slow movement and an allegro in fugato style. If Sonata II is considered in two movements (Grave-Adagio and Allegro maestoso e vivace-Fuga), it conforms to such a plan. The short first movement, Grave (Little IV, II.1, 21), is an introduction to the second movement, Adagio (Little IV, II.2, 22). The halting rhythm of the Grave section give the piece a peculiar charm, and the thick chords at the opening are reminiscent of the English voluntary. Of special interest are the linear and vertical styles of writing in the little fugato section (mm. 5–13) and the use of an inner-voice pedal point starting in m. 13.

The second movement, Adagio, is also in C minor and is an ornamented cantilena in the style of Mendelssohn's piano Songs without Words. A beautifully decorated melody, much like the melody of a Bach instrumental sonata, provides the foundation for the movement (see Example 10.5). The melody is restated numerous times in closely related keys. The accompaniment moves in continuously flowing sixteenth notes in two voices, while the pedal suggests a string bass pizzicato. This lovely movement is perhaps Mendelssohn's idea of a nineteenth-century trio sonata for organ.

The third movement of the sonata, which is in C major, is marked Allegro maestoso e vivace (Little IV, II.3, 25). This movement serves as a prelude to the fugue that follows it (without pause). This loud, bright work has an effusive theme, which is made memorable by the contrast of dotted notes with even rhythms in the melodic pattern. A coda begins in m. 51, which leads into the Fugue (Little IV, II.4, 28). This fugue is a reworked version of the C-major fugue composed by Mendelssohn in Frankfurt in 1839.[29] The new version manifests a higher level of

Example 10.5
Mendelssohn, Sonata II, Op. 65 no. 2, Second Movement, mm. 1–7

Adagio

craftmanship. Voice leadings are tighter, and measures have been deleted at the end of the work. The rather predictable subject has a surprise in the fifth measure, a chromatic F♯, giving the theme slight coloration. The work has two counter-subjects, of which the first is introduced in m. 6 and is used in the exposition of the fugue. The second countersubject appears at m. 39 (an eighth-note pattern) and continues to be used through the remainder of the piece.

Sonata III in A major is in two movements and was originally intended by Mendelssohn to be the first sonata in the series. He changed his mind at the time he returned proofs to Coventry and Hollier. The unusual two-movement form was probably an attempt on the composer's part to simulate the English voluntary, and it may have been at this time that he developed serious doubts as to continuing with the designation "voluntary." The opening of the first movement was probably written as his sister Fanny's wedding piece (October 1829), although the original copy of it has been lost.[30] The double fugue of the first movement is the most outstanding of all Mendelssohn's fugues for the organ.

The first movement (Little IV, III.1, 33) is a massive ternary (ABA) form. The central part, a double fugue over a chorale theme in the pedal, is preceded and concluded by a grand, marchlike melody set in stately, thick chords. The opening section, Con moto maestoso (see Example 10.6), is in A major and has a two-part design (mm. 1–8, mm. 8–24). The double fugue (mm. 24–112) is in A minor and

Example 10.6
Mendelssohn, Sonata III, Op. 65 no. 3, First Movement, mm. 1–8

begins with the first subject in m. 24, a very spirited and rhythmically active melody. Following the exposition of the first subject, the second subject appears in m. 58 for its exposition. While the expositions and developments of these two subjects are taking place, the pedal introduces the chorale "Aus tiefer Noth" (m. 40), whose phrases continue to form a foundation for the polyphonic activity in the hands. The agitation of the sixteenth-note second subject helps intensify the energy and tension in the work, which are sharpened in m. 80 when the first subject joins the second. After the final phrase of the chorale a long pedal point on the tonic gives way to a coda (beginning m. 99), in which both subjects are represented (see Example 10.7). The fugue ends with an exciting and impassioned pedal solo, which concludes with a two-octave descending scale. A free reprise of section A follows (mm. 113–27), succeeded by with a coda (mm. 127–35), which includes references to the first fugue subject.

Example 10.7
Mendelssohn, Sonata III, Op. 65 no. 3, First Movement, mm. 99–108

The second movement, Andante tranquillo, is a short (forty measures), lyrical, religious adagio in the style of the composer's Songs without Words. The form is ABA with coda, and the opening melody is one of Mendelssohn's most beautiful. It is not known why Mendelssohn ended Sonata III with this type of quiet movement. One writer suggests that Mendelssohn was unable to decide between a triumphal movement and a simple one.[31] Another writer declares that the sonata really ends with the first movement and that the slow movement may have been added to provide a quiet transition for an act of worship if the work were played as a voluntary in the worship service.[32]

Of all the Six Sonatas, it is possible that Sonata IV in B♭ comes closest to achieving Mendelssohn's goal of combining melodies that express his deep, personal feelings with the Classic forms that he loved. His unification of old forms and nineteenth-century musical language achieved a well-conceived balance in the four movements of this sonata.

The first movement, Allegro con brio (Little IV, IV.1, 44), comes closer to following Classic sonata form than any other movement in the sonatas. The movement is a pianistic toccata in which Mendelssohn joined melodies in a compact polyphonic style. The first theme of the exposition is introduced in m. 1 and is an arpeggiated passage of ascending and descending sixteenth notes that projects great energy. The second theme enters in m. 21 in the soprano voice and is contrasted by a jerky rhythmic pattern over strongly punctuated chords. The development section (mm. 44-62) unites both themes (m. 48), which are contrapuntally treated throughout the remainder of the movement. The recapitulation begins in m. 62 with the statement of both themes simultaneously in the tonic.

The second movement, Andante religioso (Little IV, IV.2,50), is a short (36 mm.), quiet (*mp*), and lyrical contrast to the robust and exciting opening movement. It is a character piece or religious adagio in three sections. The middle section (mm. 10–24) is a dialogue that alternates keyboards and quotes a fragment of the opening melody (for example, mm. 11–12, mm 13–14).

Movement 3, Allegretto (Little IV, IV.3, 52), is a pastorale movement in trio texture, in which the hands play on separate keyboards and the pedal provides foundational support in the manner of an instrumental trio. The flowing $\frac{6}{8}$ rhythm and sixteenth-note accompaniment figure create a Siciliano effect that combines nicely with the extended melody repeated throughout the piece at different pitch levels and in varied keys.

The Allegro maestoso e vivace (Little IV, IV.4, 57), movement 4, is in B♭ major and resembles in form the first movement of Sonata III in A major. Both are ternary-form movements dominated by fugues as their central sections. This movement begins with a martial theme in the hands (section A, mm. 1–22), which is supported by an ascending pedal theme. The long fugue subject (section B, mm. 22–26) is introduced in the pedals and is reminiscent of Bach. The fugal exposition (mm. 22–37) introduces the subject in the order bass, tenor, alto, soprano. Development of the fugue subject, featuring statements and inversions, continues through m. 83. In mm. 83–91 a brief recall of the opening chordal section (A) concludes the movement.

Sonata V in D major has similarities in form and style to the English voluntary. The work is in three movements, and the first movement, Andante (Little IV, V.1, 63), is in the style of a harmonized chorale. The tune is assumed to have been composed by Mendelssohn, as it cannot be matched with any known chorale tune (see Example 10.8). This short movement recalls the opening movement of Sonata II, which is also a prelude to the second movement of the sonata.

The second movement, Andante con moto (Little IV, V.2, 64) in B minor, suggests the mood of a scherzo in the form ABAB and coda. The main theme uses

Example 10.8
Mendelssohn, Sonata V, Op. 65 no. 5, "Original" Chorale Melody, First Movement, mm. 1–26

$^6_8$ meter to create a lilting melody, which is punctuated by a detached pedal line. Eight manual changes were suggested by the composer for this movement (identified in Little's edition). The second theme, a slowly moving chord progression over a "walking bass," enters in m. 16. The coda, which begins in m. 46, leads without pause into the final movement.

An Allegro maestoso (Little IV, V.3, 67) provides a rousing finale in D major, using two themes in the formal design ABABA and coda. This toccatalike movement is pianistic in technical demands, and the opening theme (mm. 1ff.) is a grand, heroic statement that features an octave jump, cascading descent, and chords. The second theme appears at m. 31 in the soprano voice, then moves to the left hand and to the pedals. It is stately and less active than the first and uses wide intervals in its design. This theme is accompanied by a busy triplet movement that creates an impassioned mood. The organization of this movement is A (mm. 1–30); B (mm. 31–63); A (mm. 63–79); B (mm. 80–112); A (mm. 112–33); coda (mm. 133–39). The coda uses slow-moving chords that recall the sonata's opening "chorale."

Sonata VI in D minor is a three-movement work in which all movements are closely connected to the German chorale "Vater unser in Himmelreich" (Our Father who art in heaven). In the first movement this familiar tune is used as the cantus firmus for a theme and four variations. (This type of composition, the chorale partita, was very popular in the Baroque period.) The opening chorale harmonization (Little IV, VI.1, 75), in five voices, is reminiscent of Bach's chorale settings and is especially noteworthy for its chromatic cadence over the tonic pedal point, which leads directly into the first variation (mm. 24-26). Variation 1 (mm. 26–55) is in trio texture with the unadorned *cantus firmus* in the soprano. A smoothly running sixteenth- note pattern in the left hand provides accompaniment, and a legato pedal line gives support. The quiet first variation leads directly into Variation 2 (mm. 55–71) in $\frac{12}{8}$ meter, which gently quotes the theme in a four-voice chordal treatment in the hands, while the pedal provides a soft, detached "walking-bass" foundation. After a cadence and brief silence Variation 3 (mm. 71–92) begins, using the tenor voice for the *cantus firmus*, above which parallel thirds and sixths form a rhythmic accompaniment supported by a detached pedal. Variation 4 (mm. 92–162), Allegro molto, is a brilliant toccata with an extended coda (mm. 163–81), which concludes with an unexpected pause followed by the first and last phrases of the chorale (mm. 182–90) in slow-moving, rich chords. The chorale tune is played throughout Variation 4 in various voices in augmentation, while the hands play bravura arpeggios occasionally punctuated by chords.

The movement proceeds without pause to the Fugue (Little IV, VI.2, 88), which may be considered a fifth variation of the previous movement because of its thematic relationship to "Vater unser." Evidence suggests that the practice of attaching a fugue to a series of chorale variations may have been a common procedure in Mendelssohn's improvisations.[33] This fugue subject has a definite melodic relationship to the chorale tune, and both it and the recurring countersubject offer relaxation and relief from the fourth variation. The subject is vocal in style, uses short phrases separated by rests, and does not express the tension and aggressive energy associated with many of Mendelssohn's imitative movements. The exposition presents the subject in the order tenor, alto, soprano, bass (mm. 1–29). Episodes and a variety of separate subject entries continue throughout the fugue. The fugue subject is repeated in the tonic in the soprano voice in the concluding statement (mm. 79–86). This movement is an excellent example of Mendelssohn's maturation in the blending of old forms with contemporary use of melody and mood.

The finale, Andante (Little IV, VI.3, 91), is a good example of the nineteenth-century character piece (religious adagio) in its style and form. This very quiet and sustained movement takes its spirit from the chorale and uses a melody based on the last four notes of the fugue (soprano voice) shifted to D major. This monothematic movement may be analyzed as follows: a (mm. 1–8, cadencing in F♯ minor), a' (mm. 9–16, cadencing in C♯ minor), extension (mm. 17–20, concluding on a C♯-major chord), a" (mm. 21–30), coda (mm. 31–36). The mood of this movement provides unification with the preceding movements, giving the entire work a strong feeling of cohesion.

The organ compositions of Mendelssohn yield a personal view of the composer because of the role the organ played in his life. Mendelssohn's experience of playing the organ was basically private and personal. He was moved to play the organ by a deep love for the instrument and an equally profound desire to make music on it. Mendelssohn no doubt saw his connection to the historical past best realized in organ repertoire from the Baroque (especially Bach) and in his own organ improvisations, in which he utilized forms from previous musical periods. He felt very comfortable in this kind of music-making because of his training under Zelter. The organ and the old polyphonic forms fitted together in ways that felt right to him.

Mendelssohn enjoyed playing the organ for small groups of friends, and many of his documented performances were for such groups. When he played the organ publicly, he did so with little intention of promoting his great fame or increasing his fortune, which he easily could have done because of his unequaled skills as an organist. Instead, he remained humble about his talents as an organist, continued to improve his skills, and sought the musical nourishment that it brought to him in practice until his untimely death. He seems never to have tried to make money from playing the organ, which suggests the almost spiritual role that it fulfilled in his life.

Mendelssohn's efforts at composing organ music must have been stimulated, at least in part, by a desire to educate English organists. English instruments were woefully inferior to German organs, and the playing skills of English organists, who held him in such high esteem, were also limited. In the first title to Op. 65, "Mendelssohn's School of Organ-Playing," he identified his intentions to improve the situation.

Mendelssohn introduced the organ music of Johann Sebastian Bach to the world, both in public performances and in published editions of Bach's organ music. In performing only his and Bach's organ music, he introduced a new repertoire for organists and caused organists and organ builders to reevaluate the organ as a musical medium and to examine the quality of the instrument in light of musical demands made on it. The demands of the organ repertoire established by Mendelssohn and those composers who followed him directly influenced the organ reform movement that swept Germany, France, and England in the latter half of the nineteenth century.

Because of the new repertoire and improved instruments on which to play it, a new standard of organ performance gradually developed that led to advanced technical skills on the part of organists. These skills were set in motion by Mendelssohn, establishing a standard for all organists to follow in his performances of extempore and composed music and in the exemplary quality of his own organ compositions, which challenged the organists who played and heard them.

Mendelssohn has been described as an "artist *sui generis*, a champion of old traditions rather than a sower of new seeds."[34] This may be true about much of his music, but in his Six Sonatas Op. 65 Mendelssohn created a new direction for organ music. In them he formed multimovement works for the organ that joined and tempered the technical and formal skills of the Baroque with the lyrical melodies, personal emotion, and drama of the nineteenth century. These grand, impassioned, and idiomatically conceived compositions brought innovation to organ repertoire and gave the instrument a new direction for the future.

The influence of Mendelssohn as a composer of organ sonatas is proved by the number of composers who wrote sonatas for the instrument after 1845. In Germany during the years 1845–1899, sixty-seven composers wrote 186 organ sonatas, 100 of these composed during the last two decades of the century.[35] Between 1845 and 1864 Christian Fink, Friedrich Kuhmstedt, Jan Albert Eyken, and Gustav Merkel composed large numbers of multimovement organ sonatas. One-movement sonatas were composed during this time period by August G. Ritter, Adolph Friedrich Hesse, Gustav H. G. Siebeck, and Friedrich Wilhelm Markull. From 1865 through the end of the century representative German composers of organ sonatas included Wilhelm V. Volkmar, Josef Rheinberger, Johann Georg Herzog, Samuel de Lange Jr., Wilhelm Rudnick, Max Reger, and others. French composers Alexandre Guilmant and Marie Joseph Erb also composed sonatas for the organ. Mendelssohn's sonatas were part of the repertoire of many French organists in the last half of the nineteenth century, and their influence resonates even in organ compositions in the symphonic style by Franck, Widor, and Dupré.

The success of his Six Sonatas would hardly be surprising to Mendelssohn himself, however, because at the time of their publication he wrote to Coventry, "I attach much importance to these Sonatas."[36] Organists have never failed to appreciate the Op. 65 sonatas, and these sonatas have been essential to the nineteenth-century repertoire of the instrument since their publication. They have been used as concert works, teaching pieces, contest requirements, and church music by organists of every level of talent and skill to the present day.

NOTES

1. This apposite term is used by Wm. A. Little in the preface to each volume of Felix Mendelssohn Bartholdy, *Complete Organ Works*, 5 vols. (London: Novello, 1987).

2. Felix Mendelssohn Bartholdy, *Letters from 1833 to 1847*, ed. Paul and Carl Mendelssohn Bartholdy, trans. Lady Grace Wallace, new ed. (London: Longmans, Green, 1890), 71.

3. Sir George Grove, "Mendelssohn," in *Grove's Dictionary of Music and Musicians*, ed. J. A. Fuller Maitland (Philadelphia: Presser, 1904), 3: 163.

4. Felix Mendelssohn Bartholdy, *Letters from Italy and Switzerland*, ed. Paul Mendelssohn Bartholdy, trans. Lady Grace Wallace (London: Longman, Green, Longman, Roberts, and Green, 1862), 280.

5. Ibid., 281.

6. See n. 1. Individual works in the following discussion are referred to by volume, number, and page in Little's edition.

7. Douglas L. Butler, "The Organ Works of Felix Mendelssohn Bartholdy" (D.M.A. diss., University of Oregon, 1973), 126.

8. Described by Dr. Henry Gauntlett in "Mendelssohn as an Organist," *The Musical World* (15 September 1837) and reprinted in Butler, 226–29. See the Historical Views and Documents accompanying this Chapter.

9. Butler, 14.

10. Mendelssohn, *Letters from Italy and Switzerland*, 294.

11. Little, Preface, 1: vi.

12. Robert Schumann, *Gesammelte Schriften über Musik und Musiker*, 3d ed. (Leipzig: Wigand, 1875), 252.

13. Joseph W. G. Hathaway, *An Analysis of Mendelssohn's Organ Works* (London: Wm. Reeves, 1898; repr. New York: AMS Press, 1978), 100.

14. Eric Werner, *Mendelssohn: A New Image of the Composer and His Age* (New York: Free Press of Glencoe, 1963), 365.

15. Butler, 81.

16. Little, 2: vi.

17. Edwards, 794; see Elise Polko, *Reminiscences of Felix Mendelssohn-Bartholdy: A Social and Artistic Biography*, trans. Lady Wallace (New York: Leypoldt & Holt, 1869; repr. Macomb, IL: Glenbridge, 1987), 216–17.

18. Little, 4: vi.

19. Volumes 2 and 3 of Professor Little's set contain the earlier versions of pieces used in Op. 65, as well as compositions that Mendelssohn did not use in the final version.

20. Little, 4: vi.

21. Because there were four different publishers of Op. 65, there were four sets of proofs for correction. This has caused numerous problems in modern editions of Mendelssohn's Sonatas, including identifying and correcting errors and selecting which phrasings and articulations to follow. Another significant problem is the metronome markings, which were hastily added by the composer at the last moment for publication. They are generally too fast and may have been entered by Mendelssohn from memory, without the aid of a metronome.

22. Edwards, 795.

23. Edwards, 795; see Polko, 218.

24. Review quoted in Edwards, 795.

25. Ibid., 796.

26. Sebastian Hensel, *The Mendelssohn Family (1729–1847): From Letters and Journals*, 2d rev. ed., trans. Carl Klingemann (1882; repr. New York: Haskell House, 1969), 2: 321.

27. These complete instructions are reprinted in Little, 4: ix.

28. W. S. Rockstro, *Mendelssohn* (New York: Scribner and Welford, 1884), 100, quoted in Edwards, 796.

29. The earlier version of this fugue can be found in Little, 3: 23.

30. Little, 4: xii.

31. François Sabatier, "Mendelssohn's Organ Works," *The American Organist* 16/1 (January 1982), 54.

32. Orlando A. Mansfield, "Some Characteristics and Peculiarities of Mendelssohn's Organ Works," *The Musical Quarterly* 3 (1917), 564.

33. Discussed in R. Larry Todd, "New Light on Mendelssohn's Freie Phantasie (1840," in *Literary and Musical Notes: A Festschrift for Wm. A. Little* (Bern: Peter Lang, 1995), 205–18.

34. Werner, viii.

35. Kremer, 159.

36. Letter of 26 May 1845, quoted in Edwards, 795; see Polko, 218.

HISTORICAL VIEWS AND DOCUMENTS

HENRY GAUNTLETT ON MENDELSSOHN AS AN ORGANIST[1]

On the organ the real artist, the musician, triumphs: there genius, however fascinating and extraordinary, invests itself with a loftiness and purity of sentiment—a luxuriance of fancy—a picturesque conception—a power as touching as it is extensive and irresistible. A grand instrument excites grand ideas, and nothing can be more interesting than to witness a highly gifted performer grapple with his thoughts when he sits down unpremeditatedly to a large organ, on which however astonishing his fertility of invention, unbounded his command of harmony, or dexterous and precise his finger, there is a clear and unincumbered [sic] arena for his display. As a pianist, M. Mendelssohn has been listened to with mingled emotions of delight and astonishment; as a composer he occupies a position of such acknowledged excellence as challenges and almost defies competition; the pupil of Zelter, the worshipper of Sebastian Bach, as an organist, becomes therefore an object of great and absorbing interest. During the present week he has twice touched the organ; on Sunday afternoon at St. Paul's Cathedral and on Tuesday morning at Christchurch Newgate Street. On both occasions the large auditories who assembled to listen to his efforts, testified how high they held in estimation the composer of the oratorio of "St. Paul." The first ten minutes is a trying situation for the popular organist, closely pressed on all sides, as he generally is, surrounded by persons not less excited than himself, by the promise of no ordinary intellectual gratification, and often by friends whose good opinions he is well assured he has had unreservedly surrendered to him. Genius, however mighty, is ever modest, and even the mind of a Mendelssohn does not instantaneously escape from the scene: hence his opening movements are distinguished for seriousness and solemnity: the perfect purity of his harmonies, the natural manner in which they follow each other, the rigid exclusion of every note not exclusively belonging to them, and their perfect unity one with the other, however, proclaim the refined and accomplished scholar, with whom art has become second nature; and as his thoughts thicken and the spirit retires to commune within itself, the themes break forth one by one, and a warmth and energy, a freedom and fluency diffuse a life, and spread a charm over his performance, that at once rivet the undivided attention of his auditors. Such was his first voluntary at St. Paul's: but his performance was interrupted ere he could give those memorable instances of his extraordinary abilities, by a ridiculous accident. He had played extemporaneously for some time, and had commenced the noble fugue in A minor, the first of the six grand pedal fugues of Sebastian Bach, when the gentlemen who walk about in bombazeen gowns and plated sticks, became annoyed at the want of respect displayed by the audience to their energetic injunctions. "Service is over," had been universally announced, followed by the command "you must go out, Sir." The party addressed moved away, but the crowd got no less; the star of Sebastian was in the ascendant. The virgers [*sic*] at St. Paul's are not without guile, and they possessed sufficient knowledge of organ performance to know that the bellows-blower was not the least important personage engaged in that interesting ceremony. Their blandishments conquered, and just as Mendelssohn had executed a storm of pedal passages with transcendant [*sic*] skill and energy, the blower was seduced from his post and a farther supply of wind forbidden, and the composer was left to exhibit the glorious ideas of Bach in all the dignity of dumb action. The entreaties of friends, the reproofs of minor canons, the outraged dignity of the organists, were of no avail; the vergers conquered, and all retired in dismay and disappointment. We had never previously heard Bach executed with such fire and energy--never witnessed a composition listened to with greater interest and gratification; and consoling ourselves with the hope that on Tuesday all might re-unite in a place where virgers are not, and under more fortunate auspices, we were hurried out of the cathedral.

Our hope was realized, and a scene of more unmingled delight we never participated in. The organ, through the spirited exertions of the parishioners, (their liberality joined to that of the Dean and Chapter of Westminster, and the Governors of St. Bartholemew's Hospital,) has been made a truly magnificent instrument, containing no fewer than ten diapasons and eight reed stops. M. Mendelssohn placed it before that in St. Paul's, and considered it the finest instrument he had yet played on in this country.[2]

It is the highest boast of genius, that its strains are not too high for the low and simple, nor yet too low for the wise and the learned. Many who were present on the Tuesday morning at Christchurch, were probably attracted there more by the desire to see the lion of the town, than from an earnest attachment to classical music: but all were charmed into the most unbroken silence, and at the conclusion only a sense of the sacred character of the building prevented a simultaneous burst of the most genuine applause. M. Mendelssohn performed six extempore fantasias, and the pedal fugue he was not allowed to go through with at St. Paul's. Those who know the wide range of passages for the pedals with which this fugue abounds, may conceive how perfectly cool and collected must have been the organist who could on a sudden emergency transpose them to suit the scale of an ordinary English pedal board. His mind has become so assimilated to Bach's compositions, that at one point in the prelude, either by accident or design, he amplified and extended the idea of the author, in a manner so in keeping and natural, that those unacquainted with its details could not by any possibility have discovered the departure from the text. His execution of Bach's music is transcendently great, and so easy, that we presume he has every feature of this author engraven in his memory. His touch is so even and firm, so delicate and *volant*, that no difficulties, however appalling either impede or disturb his equanimity.

His extempore playing is very diversified--the soft movements full of tenderness and expression, exquisitely beautiful and impassioned--and yet so regular and methodical, that they appear the productions of long thought and meditation, from the lovely and continued streams of melody which so uninterruptedly glide onwards in one calm and peaceful flow. In his loud preludes there are an endless variety of new ideas totally different from those usually in vogue; and the pedal passages so novel and independant [*sic*], so solemn and impressive, so grand and dignified, as to take his auditor quite by surprize [*sic*]. His last performance, on a subject given him at the moment, was the most extraordinary of his efforts. The theme was followed with an intenseness and ardour surpassing belief, but in the eagerness of pursuit was never deprived of its dignity or importance. There were no wild eccentricities, no excursive digressions, no ineffective displays of erudition: it was as if whilst anxiously untwisting the subtleties of counterpoint,--

"Something within would still be shadowing out
All possibilities: with thoughts unsought
His mind held dalliance, to which his hand
Gave substance and reality."

The enthusiasm, the fire and energy, with which the whole was carried on, was perfectly marvellous [*sic*]; he sat at the keys as one inspired, casting forth one gorgeous jewel after the other, sparking in all the radiance of light--throwing out a succession of bright passages, any one of which would have made the reputation of an ordinary performer. His invention never failed him for a moment; there was no return to any phrases or expressions used at an earlier part of his performance, and his genius appeared less unwearied and more boundless than during the first half hour.

Mr. Samuel Wesley, the father of English organists, was present and remained not the least gratified auditor, and expressed his delight in terms of unmeasured approbation. At the expressed desire of M. Mendelssohn, who wished that he could hereafter say he had heard Wesley play, the veteran took his seat at the instrument and extemporized with a purity and originality of thought for which he has rendered his name ever illustrious. The touch of the instrument, however, requires a strong and vigorous finger, and Mr. Wesley, who is at present an invalid, was unable to satisfy himself, although he could gratify those around him.

NOTES

1. Henry Gauntlett, "Mendelssohn as an Organist," *The Musical World* (15 September 1837), 8–10.

2. He was particularly pleased with the double diapason, in the swell, observing "how beautiful that *humming* is!" The *humming* of a double diapason is an effect, which when Wesley heard for the first time, he stopped playing and asked "pray who is that person who takes the liberty of humming behind my back all I do?" Oh! said the builder (Lincoln) I'll check that, and shut off the stop. The York organist dislikes a double diapason. When I attended (says he) morning service in a London church last December, we were reminded of the meagre and bad effect of which Burney complains on hearing "one solitary double

something *humming* an octave below, but 'which the organist very soon wisely [?] withdrew." (Dr. Camidge to J. Gray, Esq.) The younger Wesley uses the double diapason generally throughout the service. In the Exeter organ it runs throughout the great clavier, and forms the best feature of the instrument. [Gauntlett's note]

11

With Words: Mendelssohn's Vocal Songs

Douglass Seaton

INTRODUCTORY PERSPECTIVES

The Historical Position of Mendelssohn's Lieder

In order to understand Mendelssohn's historical position as a composer of songs, it is necessary to remember that his Lieder grew out of the tradition of the turn-of-the-century Berlin song school. Among the leading figures of this group were two of Mendelssohn's own teachers, Karl Friedrich Zelter (1752–1832), with whom Felix studied composition, and Ludwig Berger (1777–1839), his piano teacher. Also influential on the young Felix was the composer Bernhard Klein (1793–1832).

From the vantage point of history the Lieder of Schubert have become adopted as the ideal for Romanticism in the Lied of the decades of the 1810s and 1820s. The determining characteristic of his songs was the emphasis they placed on the position of the composer as reader, that is, as the interpreter of the poetry. This point of view later also applied to Schumann's songs.

An alternative song tradition to that of the Lied was the highly dramatic ballad, of which the principal exponent had been Johann Rudolf Zumsteeg (1760–1802). Its most important composer in the Berlin of Mendelssohn's youth was Johann Friedrich Reichardt (1752–1814), in such works as *Johanna Sebus*. The art-ballad undertook to support an extended narrative by means of free form and often an illustrative or evocative keyboard part. This genre had been explored early by Schubert and rejected by him or at least assimilated into the Lied type. Its leading exponent in the period of Mendelssohn's song-composing career was Carl Loewe (1796–1869) in Stettin (now Szczecin, on the Baltic coast at the German/Polish border).

Neither Schubert's nor Loewe's approach conformed to the ideal of the Berlin composers, however. The Berliners rather took the position that the principal interpreter of the song should be the singer. The composer's task consisted in giving singers a medium through which to render their own interpretations.

At the time, too, Schubert's Lieder were not widely known. Indeed, to get a fair perspective on the song repertoire of the 1830s and 1840s, one must realize that during this period Schubert's songs were less widely known and sung than those of Mendelssohn. Mendelssohn and Loewe, not Schubert (and certainly not Schumann), would have ranked as leading song composers in the 1830s.

Songs in Mendelssohn's Life and Career

Songs occupied Mendelssohn literally throughout his entire career as a composer. One of his first compositions appears to have been a song written for his father's birthday on 11 December 1819. His final efforts in the genre date from the month before his death; the Eichendorff *Nachtlied*, Op. 71 no. 6, and the Friedrich von Spee *Altdeutsches Frühlingslied*, Op. 86 no. 6, were composed in October 1847.

Some of the songs have notably intimate connections to occasions in Mendelssohn's personal life. This is naturally true of the birthday Lied for his father; and the late songs, especially those of Op. 71 and his last song, Op. 86 no. 6, express a sense of loss and deep sadness that reflects the death of his sister Fanny only a few months earlier. He discussed this with his friend the singer Livia Frege, one of his preferred singers of his songs, on 9 October 1847, only weeks before his own death.[1]

His songs formed a significant element of Mendelssohn's social life, providing the composer a means of relating to friends. Often they served as material to be entered into the albums of music-loving acquaintances or were given as gifts of respect or gratitude. The lullaby Op. 47 no. 6, for example, composed in June 1833, was a gift for Mendelssohn's godson Felix Moscheles, whose parents Ignaz and Charlotte were close friends of the composer. Mendelssohn gave Op. 71 no. 6 as a birthday gift on 1 October 1847 to his Leipzig friend Dr. Konrad Schleinitz, a member of the board of directors of the Gewandhaus concerts and among the founders of the Leipzig Conservatory.[2] In several cases the publications bore dedications to women of his circle: Op. 34 was dedicated to Julie Jeanrenaud, the composer's sister-in-law; Op. 47, to Konrad Schleinitz's wife Constanze; Op. 57, to Livia Frege.

Aesthetic Principles

The aesthetic under which Mendelssohn's songs operate is an especially interesting one.[3] As is well known, the composer took the position that the ideas and feelings expressed by music are stronger and more specific than those that can be stated in words:

[Words] seem to me so ambiguous, so vague, so easily misunderstood in comparison to a piece of genuine music, which fills one's soul with a thousand better things than words. What a piece of music that I love expresses to me are not thoughts that are too *vague* to be contained in words, but rather too *precise*. Thus I find in all attempts to express these thoughts something right but also in all of them something unsatisfactory, . . . because the word does not mean to one person what it means to another, because only the song says the same thing to one, arouses the same feeling in him, as in another--a feeling that does not, however, express itself by means of the same words.[4]

Mendelssohn made two important claims for music here. First, while words are unable to translate or interpret feeling, they constitute a natural response to it. Given that foundation, the relationship of words and music in a song becomes the reverse of that which is normally assumed. Rather than hearing the song as a text to which a melody and a background accompaniment are applied (i.e., in the way in which it is of necessity composed) or as a poem interpreted by music, the song is heard as a direct, unmediated expression of an idea in music, to which the words serve as one particular, voiced response.

The second tenet of Mendelssohn's aesthetic is that the emotion expressed in music is identical for every listener. That is, the feeling will be experienced directly by the auditor and thus, in the hearing, become his or her own. As a consequence, the hearer identifies the lyric persona in the music of the song as herself or himself. The words sung then become a response to the listener's own, musically determined emotion; thus, in an aesthetic sense, the listener becomes the fictive singer of the song.

This aesthetic position also applied to Mendelssohn's songs in two practical ways. For one thing, in belonging to the eighteenth-century north German Lied tradition, the songs were still intended for a public of amateur performers who would perform such pieces at home, rather than to be sung to a public of concertgoing listeners by a singer on a stage. The domestic Lied-singer and her or his audience of family and friends expected to select songs that were meaningful to express their own ideas. Only with the concert Lied performance tradition did the listener become more passive, encountering a selection of songs determined by the public singer (and, in a cycle, ordered by the composer) and presented as the expressions of an external, fictive persona. (The concert singer himself or herself would only rarely serve as the persona for the songs. Such a case might, perhaps, occur in encores where the song is chosen to express the singer's feelings to the audience, but otherwise it would smack of the maudlin.)

In addition, there were particular cases in which the songs were performed in circumstances where the actual singer(s) and/or listeners wished to appropriate them to establish themselves as the persona. The most striking of these is the case of Op. 71 no. 6, the *Nachtlied* on a text by Eichendorff, sung by Livia Frege at the memorial concert for Mendelssohn at the Leipzig Gewandhaus. In this instance, certainly, the song served to express the feelings of the audience—the fictive persona in that context must be understood to have been the actual bereaved friends and admirers of the composer.

WORDS IN MUSIC

By now, musicians and critics have learned from the immense success of Schubert's and Schumann's Lieder to think of the genre as a musical one, but that is not necessarily the only way to think of it. Indeed, in Sulzer's *Allgemeine Theorie der schönen Künste* the term "Lied" received two separate treatments, first as "Dichtkunst" and second as "Musik."[5] This outlook on the Lied still obtained when Mendelssohn began composing in the genre.

The poems that Mendelssohn chose for his songs represent a wide variety of types and styles, and they thus correspond to varied musical settings. Several came from amateur poets of the composer's own circle (as mentioned earlier). Others were by some of the leading Romantic poets of the late eighteenth and early nineteenth centuries. In addition, several texts came from older poets—including some dating back to the Middle Ages—and from folk poetry that Mendelssohn set to original music.

Songs from the Composer's Circle

In composing songs to texts by his friends and acquaintances, Mendelssohn participated in the convivial, social traditions of the genre. To a certain extent this portion of his song repertoire shows Mendelssohn making music more as an amateur than as a professional—not that this characterization reflects on the quality of the music. At the same time, the output of songs that resulted from these pairings of his friends' poetry with Mendelssohn's music demonstrates the impressive accomplishments of the circles in which the composer moved.

Among the most interesting song texts are two that were attributed to "H. Voss" when Mendelssohn published them in his Op. 9. These are *not* by the well-known poet Johann Heinrich Voss (1751–1826). They are sometimes credited to Johann Gustav Droysen,[6] who, indeed provided some other texts that Mendelssohn set, but it seems likely that, in fact, Mendelssohn wrote them himself. Mendelssohn's friend Adolf Bernhard Marx seems to have believed this to be the case: "E.g., the first poem is certainly not by H. Voss, but rather by the composer himself,"[7] and Mendelssohn's nephew Sebastian Hensel provides an explicit reference to Mendelssohn's having composed both text and music of Op. 9 no. 1: "At Whitsuntide [in 1827] he spent a few happy days at Sakrow, an estate near Potsdam belonging to the Magnus family, and there composed the words and music of a song which afterwards became the theme of the A minor quartet."[8] The text of this song, "Ist es wahr?," stands out among Mendelssohn's songs as a rare case of a setting of a nonrhyming and nonstrophic poem; indeed, the proselike song is correspondingly far from the norms of the Lied. The text of the other "H. Voss" song, Op. 9 no. 6, a barcarolle in which the protagonist sails away from the place of his youth over a placid tide, called forth again the bass figure that Mendelssohn had used at the opening of the *Meeresstille und glückliche Fahrt* Overture, as well as a lapping-water figuration that anticipates the composer's later Venetian gondola songs, with words (Op. 57 no. 5) and without.

Droysen, later a prominent historian, did contribute the texts of a number of Mendelssohn's early songs, including Op. 8 nos. 9 and 11; Op. 9 nos. 3, 4, 9, and 11; and, if Luise Leven was correct in her attribution based on the poetic style, Op. 84 no. 1.[9] The poem of Op. 9 no. 2 was written by the actor and singer Eduard Devrient, another of the young Mendelssohn's closest friends, for Devrient's fiancée.[10] Op. 8 no. 6, Op. 99 no. 3, and the unpublished "Mitleidsworte, Trostesgründe, neue Dornen diesem Herzen" have texts by Friederike Robert, a frequent visitor at the Mendelssohn home in Berlin during Mendelssohn's youth, wife of the poet and dramatist Ludwig Robert. The text of Op. 8 no. 6, adopts the manner of a folksong from Friederike Robert's native Swabia; its reference to birdsongs led Mendelssohn to a rare experiment in word-painting. Op. 99 no. 3, misattributed in the Rietz edition of Mendelssohn's works to the *Knaben Wunderhorn* collection, has been correctly attributed to Robert since 1936.[11] The poem—a typical one about the pain and value of love, symbolized by the pricking of a blue flower by a rose's thorn (a sort of synthesis of Goethe's texts "Ein Veilchen auf der Wiese stand" and *Heidenröslein*, although the music has a far more sincere sentiment than Mozart's or Schubert's to those comparable texts)—appeared in the journal *Chaos*, put out by the Goethe circle. Mendelssohn composed it in Weimar in 1830, at the beginning of his Grand Tour.[12] The cantata-like "Mitleidsworte, Trostesgründe" of 1825 bears the title *Glosse* in one manuscript[13]; it pursues a sort of free variations-on-a-theme design in both text and music.

By far the most prominent among Mendelssohn's amateur poet-acquaintances was Karl Klingemann, who established a close personal friendship with the composer in Berlin while Mendelssohn was still a teenager. Mendelssohn originally conceived his earliest setting of a Klingemann text, the *Romanze* Op. 8 no. 10, as an aria for *Die Hochzeit des Camacho*; the nineteenth-century standard edition of Mendelssohn's collected works, misdirectingly, labels the piece "Aus dem Spanischen." The song is quite unusual—not a Lied at all but a binary-form romance in the style of a sentimental Singspiel air.

Most of Klingemann's other texts belong to a more typical bourgeois-Romantic type. Several relate the experience of nature and the seasons to some sort of moral or to a message about emotional experience. Op. 9 no. 5, for example, connects the passing seasons to an observation about the fleeting quality of time when one experiences yearning: "Ach wie schnell die Tage fliehen, wo die Sehnsucht neu erwacht!" The *Frühlingslied* Op. 34 no. 3, by the contrast of an effervescent piano part and a simple chordal style, suggests that the feeling of joyful anticipation in springtime evokes the sense of a past dream. *Bei der Wiege*, Op. 47 no. 6, is a lullaby, but its moral message is that the spring serves as a symbol of future happiness to the child, whom it urges to have patience. A second *Frühlingslied*, Op. 71 no. 2, finds in the arrival of spring an encouragement to the languishing soul; the music is stirring and fanfarelike. Op. 84 no. 2, a *Herbstlied*, encourages the listener not to give way to the sadness symbolized by autumn but to rely on love, hope, and faith for strength—Mendelssohn responded conventionally by a shift of mode from minor to major for the refrainlike second half of each stanza. Op. 86 no. 1 is unusual among these texts in that it makes no explicit address to the listener; the poem merely describes the passing of the summer into autumn as inevitable, and one understands this as a metaphor for the passing of life. Mendelssohn also employed the shift of mode in this very early song (1826)—from major in the first two stanzas to minor in the final one.

The two remaining Klingemann songs do not fall into any particular category. The *Sonntagslied*, Op. 34 no. 5, depicts a lover left alone while everyone else celebrates a wedding. *Der Blumenstrauss*, Op. 47 no. 5, compares a gift of flowers as messengers of love to the much more expressive eyes of the lover.

Mendelssohn's attraction to Klingemann's poetry seems to have stemmed from his affinity with the values and sentiments that it embodied. Of course, when he read Klingemann's writing, he understood it in a personal, direct way, distinct from his readings of other poets, simply because he understood his friend from long and intimate acquaintance. Yet there are other reasons that Klingemann's poems appealed to Mendelssohn. By any standards, the spirit of these poems would have to be described as healthy and positive in comparison to much of contemporary Romantic poetry.[14] The composer must also have felt that in their unpretentious style Klingemann's poetry lent itself to the modest medium of the domestic Lied.

Mendelssohn's correspondence with Klingemann regarding song texts fortunately records some of his thoughts on the types of poems suitable for songs. The composer expressed his appreciation of Klingemann's work in several letters. On 1 January 1839 he thanked his friend for some new poems:

What joy you have given me with these songs; I don't know any whose verses appeared to me so to have flowed from the soul and which made me so warm and comfortable as yours do. My favorite is no. 5, *Herbstlied*; it seems to me to have been written from the heart, and I composed it straight off, but the poetry pleased me so much that I just do not know whether my music is as good or whether it only pleased me because I can sing it, so I am not sending it to you today. The second and third are such favorites of mine, too, but it is not so easy to get music for them—one can fall flat on one's face in trying to do so. But as a matter of fact I am fond of them all. They are the first new poems in a long time that satisfy me and have become my own. I've certainly been concerned in general to look for good poetry, but the new things one reads fade away as soon as one turns the page. Not your things; now I am happy for the song cycle you have in mind.[15]

The composer's criteria for a good song text are clear—the poems are sincere, they speak intimately to the reader, and they stay in the reader's mind.

From Rome in a letter of 26 December 1830–2 January 1831 Mendelssohn wrote,

You do not believe how much I want to compose something by you again, and yet you wrote to me that you were already reading old folk sayings in order to find the material. With your words I have the unique feeling that I do not have to *make* any music; it is as if I read it out of them and as if it stood before me. And if in the case of other poems, particularly Goethe,

the words resist music and want to stand alone on their own, yours, on the other hand, call out for tones, and in that case the right music cannot be lacking.[16]

The distinction between a text that demands to stand on its own and one that calls for music is important. For Mendelssohn, Goethe's poems resisted setting, probably because their sentiments seemed more complex, depending on a sophisticated reading of the poetic images and ideas. Klingemann's poetry, by contrast, appealed to the song composer because its feelings emerged more directly, and, as we have seen, for Mendelssohn feelings manifested themselves immanently in music.

Mendelssohn set texts by a few amateur poets with whom he was acquainted but who were not quite so intimately part of his personal circle of friends. Author of two of Mendelssohn's earlier songs was Albert von Schlippenbach (1800–1886), a city civil servant in Berlin. "Rausche leise grünes Dach" remains unpublished; "Die Sterne schau'n in stiller Nacht," Op. 99 no. 2, is a sentimental piece about filial love in the form of a dialogue between the stars and a daughter watching by her dying mother's beside. Egon Ebert (1801–1882), also a government official, was the poet of Op. 19 nos. 2 and 6, both songs of disappointment and separation.

The text of one of Mendelssohn's most popular songs, the *Volkslied* Op. 47 no. 4 ("Es ist bestimmt in Gottes Rath, dass man vom Liebsten, was man hat, muss scheiden"), was by a Viennese physician, Baron Ernst von Feuchtersleben (1806–1849). Mendelssohn responded to this comradely, yet moralizing, text with a setting that evokes the spirit of a students' choral song. The subsequent popularity of this song—it became almost a folk song—indicates how effectively he achieved the desired tone.

A single song, *Lieben und Schweigen*, was composed in 1840 or 1841 for the album of the Leipzig professor Konstantin Tischendorf (1815–1874), with a text by Tischendorf himself. Another occasional piece was the *Warnung vor dem Rhein* by Karl Simrock (1802–1876), a treatment of the Lorelei legend that Mendelssohn composed to fulfill a request—certainly not one of his most imaginative or successful pieces but effective in evoking in stylized fashion the popular style of a folk-legend song.

Songs of the Pre-Romantic and Romantic Poets

Not surprisingly, among Mendelssohn's earlier songs are several on texts by the poets who served as sources for the preceding generation of Berlin school composers. Ludwig Hölty (1748–1776), a member of the Göttinger Hainbund, authored two very different texts included in the Op. 8 collection. No. 1, *Minnelied im Mai*, is a simple, lilting nature/love song, in which the poet compares his happiness at his mistress's love to the blooming of the meadow in springtime. No. 8 is the fantastic *Hexenlied*, a small-scale, comic Walpurgisnacht with a brilliant piano part; it stands with the Octet as among the first instances of Mendelssohn's characteristic scherzo style. J. H. Voss, another Hainbund member, is also represented in Op. 8 by two songs, nos. 9 and 11. The former, *Abendlied* (setting only two of Voss's original seven stanzas), reflects on the day's end and suggests metaphorically the promise of a peaceful rest in death after a productive life. It features a flowing, obbligato-style line in the piano part. The latter is simply a poem of rejoicing at the arrival of spring; in setting it, Mendelssohn evoked the outdoors by galloping rhythms and hornlike figuration. The *Morgenlied* Op. 86 no. 2, also by Voss, is similarly full of enthusiasm for the beauty of nature, but in this case it is expressed in the praise of God.

Schiller is represented by a single romance, *Des Mädchens Klage*, taken from one of his plays, *Die Piccolomini*, the second of the trilogy *Wallenstein*, written in 1798–1799. This ballad-style text about a young woman who wishes to die of loss and despair was extremely popular with Mendelssohn's song-composer predecessors and had received three settings by Schubert.

Among the Romantic poets set by Mendelssohn are some of the leading literary figures of the movement. Foremost in Mendelssohn's biography, of course, is Goethe. The composer had known the poet from his childhood, when Zelter took him to Weimar in 1821. He later made several more visits, and the old poet and young composer became friends and mutual admirers. Given Mendelssohn's statement about the problem that he experienced in composing Goethe's texts, it comes as no surprise that only two of his completed songs are actually on poems written by Goethe (a setting of *Gretchen* was left incomplete). Both of these, *Die Liebende schreibt*, Op. 86 no. 3, and *Erster Verlust*, Op. 99 no. 1, treat lost love. Mendelssohn wrote to his sisters about *Die Liebende schreibt* in terms that recall his statement to Klingemann about the unsuitability of Goethe's words for music:

I am now composing [a song] which will not, I fear, be very good; but it will, at all events, please us three, for it is at least well intended. The words are Goethe's, but I don't say what they are; it is very daring in me to compose this poetry, and the words are by no means suitable for music, but I thought them so divinely beautiful, that I could not resist singing them to myself.[17]

Both Goethe settings come off as unusually dramatic, even overblown, among Mendelssohn's songs.

Three other songs attributed to Goethe, the two Suleika poems Op. 34 no. 4 and Op. 57 no. 3, together with the *Lied einer Freundin*, are actually by Marianne von Willemer, with whom the poet had an affair in 1814–1815. That Mendelssohn chose for Lied settings three songs that he apparently believed to be by Goethe but that, in fact, were not, suggests that his judgment of the difficulty of composing songs to Goethe texts was based on a genuine quality that he recognized instinctively in the words.

Mendelssohn may also have had external reasons for not composing more Goethe poems. While Mendelssohn indeed felt that Goethe's poems resisted lyric settings, this is surely not the case for all of them, as Mendelssohn's overgeneralization might suggest. In fact, Mendelssohn may have felt some reticence to place himself in comparison with his teacher and Goethe's favored Lied composer Zelter. Although he composed *Die Liebende schreibt* before Zelter's death, it was not published during Mendelssohn's lifetime. The other Goethe songs—including the ones by Marianne von Willemer—came only after both Goethe and Zelter had died.[18]

Among the early Romantic poets from whom Mendelssohn selected texts for Lieder were Ludwig Tieck (1773–1853), Johann Ludwig Uhland (1787–1862), and Joseph Freiherr von Eichendorff (1788–1857). The Tieck *Minnelied*, Op. 47 no. 1, praises the beauty of the poet's beloved as surpassing the beauties of nature. In addition to four Uhland settings, Mendelssohn left an incomplete *Reiselied*. Uhland's *Frühlingsglaube*, used for Op. 9 no. 8, is a moralizing text in which spring forms a metaphor for renewed hope; the music's animation expresses little but optimism, nothing of the melancholy it presumably will supersede. In the *Hirtenlied*, Op. 57 no. 2, a season-based love song—winter appearing as a time of separation and summer as the time of love fulfilled—Mendelssohn responded as one would expect, with a mode shift from minor to major. *Das Schifflein*, Op. 99 no. 4, tells a charming story about the power of music to create comradeship, as strangers traveling on a boat find fellowship in making music together; a barcarolle rhythm and horn-fifths representing the playing of the suntanned laborer who starts the music-making give the song its character. The *Wanderlied*, Op. 57 no. 6, is a model of the wanderlust poem, and Mendelssohn matched it with Schubert-like, lively and excited music. By contrast, Eichendorff's *Nachtlied*, Op. 71 no. 6, expresses the speaker's desire to find cheer as the tolling of the evening bell signals the dark and loneliness of night. Op. 99 no. 6, Mendelssohn's setting of "Es weiss und räth es doch keiner," treats this text entirely differently from Schumann's version in his Eichendorff cycle, Op. 39, including the third stanza, which Schumann omitted, and not recapitulating the first, so that the emotional progress from internal happiness to soaring joy becomes clearly embodied in the setting. Mendelssohn did not publish his version, perhaps deferring to Schumann's, which had already appeared. Two Eichendorff songs were published posthumously without opus numbers in the Mendelssohn collected works edition: *Das Waldschloss* (titled *Die Waldfrauen* in one manuscript[19]) is a Lorelei-type legend song, with hypnotic, magical, calling horns in Mendelssohn's setting; the *Pagenlied* suggests the amorous youth tiptoeing home from a nocturnal assignation.

Mendelssohn turned several times to texts by Hoffmann von Fallersleben (August Heinrich Hoffmann, 1798–1874), including the *Seemanns Scheidelied* (published posthumously in the *Werke* edition) and *Tröstung*, Op. 71 no. 1, in which one easily senses Mendelssohn himself searching for God's comfort after Fanny's death. Two unpublished songs also set Hoffmann von Fallersleben poems: the *Frühlingslied* "Ja, war's nicht aber Frühlingszeit" and "So schlaf in Ruh" (22 March 1838). Both are extant only in copies.

Nikolaus Lenau (1802–1850) supplied the words for the *Frühlingslied*, Op. 47 no. 3 ("Durch den Wald, den dunklen"), a passionate song that compares the beloved's glance to the warmth of spring after winter. It is not surprising to find that the melancholic Lenau also provided texts for three of the songs of separation in Op. 71: nos. 3, 4, and 5. Two songs are based on poems by Emanuel von Geibel (1815–1884): *Der Mond*, Op. 85 no. 5, which passionately compares the singer's beloved to the moon, and "Wenn sich zwei Herzen scheiden," Op. 99 no. 5, a restrained, almost churchly, song of the pain of parting.

Some of Mendelssohn's most successful songs take their texts from Heinrich Heine (1797-1856). Mendelssohn composed Heine's poetry effectively, despite its frequent complex and subtle ironies, and largely because he did not try too hard to double the problematic aspects of the words in the music. Instead, quite in keeping with Mendelssohn's song aesthetic, the music provides a characteristic, striking expression of feeling, which allows the text to respond with its own irony, believably motivated without becoming excessive.

The first of the Heine settings, the famous *Neue Liebe*, Op. 19a no. 4, employs Mendelssohn's "elfin scherzo" style to evoke the mysterious encounter with the elf-queen in the night forest. The following song, *Gruss*, simply asks the breeze to be the lover's envoy. The success of these two songs in Op. 19a must have encouraged Mendelssohn to include two more Heine Lieder in the next published set, Op. 34. No. 2 of this group is the composer's best-known song, "Auf Flügeln des Gesanges," setting two lovers in an exotic oriental garden. No. 6, the balladesque *Reiselied*, tells of the horseman's galloping through the night and of his self-deceptive dream of reaching his innamorata; for this Mendelssohn employed suitably rushing piano figuration. Op. 47 no. 2 presents a *Morgengruss* from a shepherd to his sleeping beloved, who does not awaken to acknowledge his greeting--he nevertheless convinces himself that she must still be dreaming of him. In another case of Mendelssohn's having set a Heine poem also set by Schumann, Op. 86 no. 4 is the well-known text "Allnächtlich in Traume seh ich dich." The beloved's forgotten word from the lover's dream is exquisitely suggested by the gap in the vocal line as the speaker tries to remember and by the failure of the accompaniment to reach a satisfactory conclusion. Again, Schumann's setting may have discouraged Mendelssohn from publishing his own, yet as an independent song it succeeds better than Schumann's would, were it extracted from *Dichterliebe*. Two unpublished Heine settings also survive, one titled *Im Kahn* or *Auf dem Wasser* ("Mein Liebchen, wir sassen beisammen") and the other *Erinnerung* ("Was will die einsame Thräne").

Two minor contributors to the Mendelssohn Lied corpus were Karl Immermann (1796–1840), the Intendant of the theater in Düsseldorf during Mendelssohn's period there, and Adolf Böttger (1815–1870), a young private teacher whom Mendelssohn knew in Leipzig. Immermann's *Todeslied der Bojaren* was not originally a proper Lied at all but a song for men's chorus, to be employed as incidental music in *Die Bojaren*, one play in Immermann's trilogy entitled *Alexis*. Böttger's "Ich hör' ein Vöglein" forms a sentimental Romantic lyric in which the speaker first describes the love duet of two birds among the flowers and then turns to notice a vague, questioning voice lost in the wind. Perhaps what appealed to Mendelssohn in this poem, judging by its treatment in the music, was the rather clichéd image followed by the undefined and open-ended continuation.

Three contemporary English Romantic writers also appear among Mendelssohn's songs. Among Mendelssohn's earliest songs—in styles as old-fashioned as Handel's or C.P.E. Bach's—he made settings in 1820 of the "Ave Maria" and "Raste Krieger, Krieg ist aus" from Sir Walter Scott's *The Lady of the Lake*.[20] During his visit to England in 1829 Mendelssohn composed, in the style of an English canzonetta, *The Garland*, to a poem by Thomas Moore ("By Celia's Arbor"). From Mendelssohn's maturity (1842) comes the *Venetianisches Gondellied*, adapted from Moore's *National Airs* by Mendelssohn's friend Ferdinand Freiligrath (1810–1876), an evocation of a nighttime tryst between Italian lovers, in which Mendelssohn took the opportunity to re-create in a vocal song the barcarolle style he had used so successfully in his Lieder ohne Worte. The two Byron songs "There Be None of Beauty's Daughters" and "Sun of the Sleepless" were composed with translations, respectively, by Klingemann and by Mendelssohn himself with consultation from the composer's sister Rebecca,[21] again in a style that suggests the English canzonetta rather than the *echtes* German Lied.

Songs from Historic and Folk Sources

In the mode of much of Romanticism, Mendelssohn drew on older poetry, as well as that of his contemporaries, including texts from the medieval German repertoire, the seventeenth century, and the folk-based tradition. Among his songs are three by thirteenth-century Minnesinger. Perhaps most striking in these texts is how they fit among the more modern poems; the juxtapositions of texts separated by six centuries reveal how the Romantic poets drew on the same lyric conceits as their medieval predecessors—nature and the seasons as settings for, parallels of, or contrasts to the lover's feelings. Op. 8 no. 7, the *Mailied* of Jakob von Wart, contrasts the beauty of the season to the unhappiness of the lonely poet. Mendelssohn's double-strophic setting leaves to the singer the responsibility to distinguish the change of mood for the fourth and final stanza. The *Frauendienst* of Ulrich von Liehtenstein (1198–1276) provided the text for Op. 19a no. l, a *Frühlingslied* that in two short stanzas simply likens the bloom of love in the singer's heart to the blooming of spring. The *Altdeutsches Lied* Op. 57 no. 1 is by one Heinrich Schreiber (presumably the Thuringian chancellor Henricus scriptor, fl. early thirteenth century). It compares the profession of love to the nightingale's song that goes unremarked in the forest and that thus ends only by expressing, but not communicating, love's pain.

Mendelssohn used texts by two seventeenth-century writers. The first of these, the *Pilgerspruch*, Op. 8 no. 5, is by Paul Fleming (1609–1640); it is a moralizing poem that urges patience and submission to God's will. Op. 86 no. 6, called *Altdeutsches Frühlingslied*, is an adaptation of a poem by the Jesuit Friedrich von Spee (1591–1635), but abridged and secularized by the change of the addressee from "Jesu" to "Liebste." The gist of the text, like that of the poem by Jakob von

Wart, contrasts the lover's sadness to the surrounding pleasure of springtime. This, Mendelssohn's last composition, belongs in spirit with the group that formed Op. 71—reflecting the loss of his beloved sister.

Mendelssohn drew several song texts from folk poetry traditions, including, like so many of his contemporary composers, *Des Knaben Wunderhorn*, from which three of his songs came. The earliest of the songs to stem from that source is Op. 8 no. 4, the *Erntelied*. This poem may, in fact, be largely or entirely by Clemens Brentano (1778–1842), in whose novel *Godwi* it had first appeared. Its message, like that of its immediate companion by Paul Fleming, is moralizing—in this case a reflection on Death the reaper, who mows all flowers, and on the expectation of their being transplanted to heaven—and it received an antique, choralelike setting. Also from *Des Knaben Wunderhorn* came Op. 34 no. 1, called *Minnelied* (or in one manuscript, *Mailied*[22]), which compares the beloved to the sun and the flowers and expresses the lover's patience in waiting for her. This was apparently a favorite song with Mendelssohn, who copied it and referred to it a number of times. The poem of Op. 86 no. 3, the *Jagdlied* from the *Wunderhorn* collection, speaks through the persona of a hunter trapping birds, that is, girls.

Several folktales come from other sources. Op. 57 no. 4 is modeled on a Rhenish folk text, apparently adapted for the collection *Deutsche Volkslieder mit ihren Original-Weisen* by Anton Zuccalmaglio, then revised by Mendelssohn and again by Klingemann.[23] The speaker praises the youthful beauty of his beloved and says that he would rather be with her than in heaven. From a Swedish ballad text comes Op. 19a no. 3, in which the singer adopts, for two stanzas each, the voices of a mother, a son who goes out into the winter storm to find his lost sister, and the narrator who tells of the youth's failure to return. Unpublished is the song *Mailied* or *Hüt du dich*, on the text "Ich weiss mir'n Mädchen hübsch und fein," taken from the 1777 *Eyn feyner kleyner Almanach*. The rather repetitious text (and music) warns the hearer against a lovely, blue-eyed maiden who will make a fool of him.

Summary

The types of texts that Mendelssohn used in his Lieder give a clear impression of the composer's idea of the functions of the song. Some represent explicitly moralizing poems, intended to promote virtues and values—even religious faith. Most, however, are love songs, and these belong generally to the venerable "seasonal" type, which either likens or contrasts the lover's experience to the experience of nature. A few come from the repertoire of folk and traditional poetry—the ballads, for example.

In addition, some of the songs reflect Mendelssohn himself. The songs on texts by Byron and Heine represent Mendelssohn's own reading of the Romantic poets and his personal taste in that poetry. Several text choices also clearly arose from Mendelssohn's life experience; obvious in this group would be the late songs of Op. 71, together with Op. 86 no. 6.

The music that underlies these texts manifests considerable expressive variety. These songs employ little direct word painting, in accordance with Mendelssohn's aesthetic principles. On the other hand, each text corresponds convincingly to its music. Mendelssohn met his task as he formulated it: to discover music that embodied a feeling to which the words of the poem seem a compelling response.

MUSICAL STYLE

Mendelssohn's songs represent what might appropriately be regarded as constituting a mature phase of the German mid-Romantic domestic Lied. If we set the Second Berlin School song style of Reichardt, Zelter, and Berger as markers for an early phase that belongs to the period up to about 1820 and the songs of Schumann launched by the Liederjahr of 1840 as a later and manneristic phase, then Mendelssohn's work in the genre occupies the position of a fully developed high style.

Vocal and Melodic Issues

In Mendelssohn's song style vocal lines tend to be lyrical and shapely. Even when evoking a folk style, the melodies have a sophisticated grace. Although the text underlay is mostly syllabic, the use of two-note slurs—usually descending—lends many of the melodic lines a notable softness or tenderness. On the other hand, genuinely aria-like attributes, such as elaborate melismas, appear only quite rarely, mostly in early songs that have some unusual kind of text—the extract from *Die Hochzeit des Camacho*, the Swabian song by Friederike Robert, or the Moore canzonetta "By Celia's Arbor." Moreover, there is little of the Schumannesque declamatory style (as can easily be shown by comparison of the *Dichterliebe* setting of "Allnächtlich im Traume" with Mendelssohn's Op. 86 no. 4—see Examples 11.1a and b). The finest accomplishment of the style is its achievement of balance between cantabile and prosody.

The intention that these songs belong to amateur singers manifests itself in the limited technical difficulty that their vocal lines pose for the performer. The expected vocal range runs generally from about d^1 to g^2 (very rarely a^2, with b^2 demanded only in songs that are not in Lied style at all), the upper notes of that range reserved for unusual climaxes, while the majority of a melody commonly lies in the tessitura from g^1 to d^2. Yet while they do not call for especially talented or professionally trained voices, the songs certainly expect better than mediocre singers. Mendelssohn must have had in mind a middle-class singer with good musicianship and some training—at least the equivalent of excellent choral experience, such as he might have found among the members of Zelter's Berlin Liedertafel or Schelble's Frankfurt Cäcilien-Verein.

Mendelssohn's setting of text accomplishes a fine suitability of vocal rhythm to the accentuation of his poetic texts, but unlike the earlier Berlin composers he managed this with considerable flexibility rather than mechanically adopting a

Example 11.1a
Robert Schumann, *Dichterliebe*, "Allnächtlich im Traume," mm. 1–8, Vocal Line

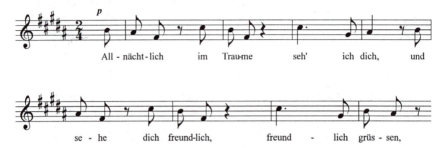

All - nächt-lich   im   Trau-me   seh'   ich dich,   und

se - he   dich freund-lich,   freund - lich grüs - sen,

Example 11.1b
Mendelssohn, "Allnächtlich im Traume," Op. 86 no. 4, mm. 6–20, Vocal Line

All - nächt - lich im Trau - me   seh'   ich dich   und
Du   siehst mich   an   weh - mü - thig - lich   und

seh' dich   freund-lich   grü - ssen, und   laut auf-wei-nend   stürz ich mich
schüt-telst das blon - de   Köpf - chen; aus   dei-nen Au-gen   schlei-chen sich

zu   dei - nen   sü - ssen   Fü -
die   Per - len - thrä - nen - tröpf -

ssen,   zu dei - nen   sü - ssen Fü - ssen.
chen,   die Per - len - thrä - nen - tröpf - chen.

consistent duration for each metric foot and placing stressed syllables regularly on strong beats.[24]   After his earliest songs he achieved flexibility, instead, by employing a variety of musical rhythmic levels to correspond to the metrical feet in the text, so that syllables can move sometimes more quickly and sometimes more slowly.   In addition, Mendelssohn often stretched syllables to create a suspension of the textual rhythm, most commonly late in a melody (Example 11.2 shows an admittedly somewhat extreme example). Occasionally, the declamation in the

Example 11.2
Mendelssohn, *Pilgerspruch*, Op. 8 no. 5, mm. 15–18, Vocal Line

songs, especially pitch accents, might be vulnerable to the criticism that weak syllables are unduly stressed; such stresses come about as the inevitable result of poets' flexible treatment of poetic meter in strophic poems. These few moments of compromise in word-accent for the sake of meter call for a singer to approach the performance sensitively,[25] but they never render an effective reading particularly difficult.

The melodies generally adopt arched designs, usually closing with a strong descent to the tonic, except when the text presents a question, when the close may take place on the third or fifth scale degree. Large leaps occur rarely, though sixths sometimes lend a melody a very characteristic quality, notably in "Auf Flügeln des Gesanges," Op. 34 no. 2. Chromaticism remains relatively restrained. Sometimes a rising chromatic line appears as an expression of rising emotion; the third stanza of Lenau's bitter *Auf der Wanderschaft*, Op. 71 no. 5 (mm. 14–18), provides an excellent example. The diminished fifth indicates sentimental feeling but not necessarily sadness, as Example 11.3, from Klingemann's *Frühlingslied*, Op. 34 no. 3, shows. The diminished seventh—heard only in Op. 71 no. 6 and Op. 99 no. 1—expresses profound anguish.[26]

Example 11.3
**Mendelssohn, *Frühlingslied*, "Es brechen in schallenden Reigen, Op. 34 no. 3, mm.
15–18, Vocal Line**

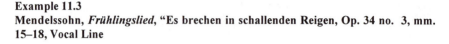

A particularly effective melodic device among Mendelssohn's songs is a kind
of melodic "overshot" that increases emotional charge. Examples may be found
in Op. 34 nos. 3 (m. 12) and 5 (m. 6). In both cases the "natural" version of the
phrase is heard first, and a variant with the "overshot" follows, raising the level of
excitement (see Examples 11.4a and b).

Word painting in the vocal parts of the Mendelssohn songs occurs only rarely.
In *Neue Liebe*, Op. 19a no. 4, the vocal melody tone-paints the "Hörner" and
"Glöcklein," and Luise Leven found in *Gruss*, Op. 19a no. 5, a vocal evocation of
"Geläute" or chiming.[27]   Likewise, the triadic-outline melody in Heine's
Morgengruss, Op. 47 no. 2, may suggest the shepherd's horn or pipe; certainly, the
leap of the octave at "ich schaue hinauf" depicts the upward gesture. In the
Jagdlied Op. 84 no. 3 the vocal line joins the piano in evoking the horn. Restraint
of melodic motion in the *Schilflied* Op. 71 no. 4—the melody hardly seems able to
escape the dominant $c\sharp^2$—indicates the calm of the pond.

The style of *Volkstümlichkeit*, mastered by the composers of the Second Berlin
School, served Mendelssohn merely as one option for expression, when it seemed
appropriate to the text. Perhaps the clearest example would be the Karl Simrock
Warnung vor dem Rhein, which explicitly models a legend-song. Other cases
would include "O Jugend, o schöne Rosenzeit!" Op. 57 no. 4, which perhaps hints
at the style of a children's play song; *Lieblingsplätzchen*, Op. 99 no. 3; *An die
Entfernte*, Op. 71 no. 3; and the *Morgenlied* Op. 86 no. 2.

Other singing styles are evoked, as well. Recitative, for example, occurs in
several songs. In *Das erste Veilchen*, Op. 19a no. 2, the arrival of the final line is
delayed by the repetition of the penultimate line in choppy recitative phrases. The
sentimental story of the girl watching by her mother's deathbed and talking to the
stars, "Die Sterne schau'n," Op. 99 no. 2, employs three contrasting styles: a
recitative-like narrative to set the scene, followed by a *Volkslied* style for the
daughter's address to the stars, and then a lyrical song style for the stars' response.
Böttger's "Ich hör' ein Vöglein locken" breaks into recitative to introduce the
concluding question, "Was mag die Stimme fragen, die in dem Wind verscholl?"
Two songs stand out as unusual in adopting the manner of a dramatic *scena*, and
both of these may have been influenced by Mozart. The very early *Der Verlassene*
(24 September 1821) resembles in tone Mozart's *Abendempfindung: An Laura*, K.

Example 11.4a
Mendelssohn, *Frühlingslied*, "Es brechen im schallenden Reigen," Op. 34 no. 3, mm. 11–14

523. The setting of Goethe's *Die Liebende schreibt*, Op. 86 no. 3, from ten years later, recalls Mozart's *Als Luise die Briefe ihres ungetreuen Liebhabers verbrannte*, K. 520.

Example 11.4b
Mendelssohn, *Sonntagslied*, Op. 34 no. 5, mm. 1–8

The Piano Parts—Texture and Harmony

Mendelssohn apparently fretted about what he regarded as his own lack of creativity in the invention of original piano figurations. In a letter to Ignaz and Charlotte Moscheles he mentioned his "poverty in inventing new figurations for the piano."[28] Given this, it seems remarkable how the piano part of each of his songs has its own distinctive and expressive pianistic pattern or patterns.

By comparison to the songs of Schubert and Schumann, but for different reasons in each case, those of Mendelssohn are often considered less interesting in the contribution of the piano to the meaning of the work. In the case of Schubert, this is because the piano parts of some of his best-known songs are so evidently pictorial, and this is not so obvious in the Mendelssohn songs, which came out of the Berlin tradition. In the case of Schumann, the difference lies in the relationship between the voice and the piano, for, whereas Schumann strongly favored the piano as the more expressive partner and concentrated the singer's role more on declaiming the text, Mendelssohn strove for a more equal balance, with greater emphasis on vocal melody.[29] Yet the expressive function of Mendelssohn's piano deserves more recognition.

Overall, Mendelssohn's song accompaniments can be grouped into two classifications: the simple chordal type and those that animate the harmonic support by some form of figuration.

The first published song, Op. 8 no. 1, best represents the first type (see Example 11.5). Other examples include Op. 9 no. 9, Droysen's *Ferne*; the

Example 11.5
Mendelssohn, *Minnelied*, "Holder klingt der Vogelsang," Op. 8 no. 1, mm. 1–4

Feuchtersleben *Volkslied* "Es ist bestimmt in Gottes Rath, dass man vom Liebsten, was man hat, muss scheiden"; and, to some extent, Friederike Robert's *Lieblingsplätzchen*, Op. 99 no. 3. This sort of piano writing evokes a *Chorlied* or social ensemble song. Of course, the piano allows for a free treatment of the texture, so that the actual number of voices represented ranges from three to as many as five. The *Maienlied* Op. 8 no. 7 is only a bit more complex in its piano part. Related to the *Chorlied* style is a type with organlike accompaniment, raising the image of a *Kirchenlied* for congregational singing with keyboard harmonization. The *Erntelied*, Op. 8 no. 4, with its choralelike melody, provides a clear example, as does Op. 9 no. 11, *Entsagung* by Droysen; for these texts the style seems particularly appropriate, for the former presents a moralizing song about death and the afterlife, while the latter is explicitly a prayer. The next song, Fleming's *Pilgerspruch*, incorporates both of these keyboard styles, along with some more independent keyboard writing, comprising repeated eighth-note chords and syncopated after-beat chords in the right-hand part. Sometimes the figuration actually becomes more countermelodic, as in the middle part of the Voss *Abendlied*, where the accompaniment to the choralelike melody creates something more like a chorale-prelude texture than a simple, chordally accompanied arrangement.

The figurational, more obviously keyboardistic accompaniment begins to become much more prominent beginning with the songs of Op. 19a, the first two of which offer typical examples. The archetype, of course, is "Auf Flügeln des Gesanges," Op. 34 no. 2, with its continuous rolled chords, which Thomas Stoner compares to the first prelude of the *Well Tempered Clavier*[30] (which might make "On Wings of Song" seem to be a prototype for Gounod's "Ave Maria"!). Similar is Op. 34 no. 4, the first of Marianne von Willemer's Suleika pieces (see Example 11.6).

Example 11.6
Mendelssohn, *Suleika*, "Ach, um deine feuchte Schwingen," Op. 34 no. 4, mm. 1–5

Not only arpeggiated chords but repeated chords belong in this group. The second Suleika song, Op. 57 no. 3, more or less a tremendously excited reinterpretation of the former one, demonstrates this alternative by its insistent sixteenth-note repeated chords (see Example 11.7). Less intense but still somewhat

Example 11.7
Mendelssohn, *Suleika*, "Was bedeutet die Bewegung?" Op. 57 no. 3, mm. 1–3

agitated is the syncopated treatment of the chord repetitions in *An die Entfernte*, Op. 71 no. 3, and *Der Mond*, Op. 86 no. 5. Between the broken- and the repeated-chord types stand the slightly animated, rocking chordal figurations of the two Klingemann songs *Der Blumenstrauss* and *Bei der Wiege*, Op. 47 nos. 5 and 6. Alternate figuration patterns include those of the Eichendorff *Wanderlied*, Op. 57 no. 6.

Such figures often permeate an entire song, giving unity and consistency of emotional expression. Of course, a single accompaniment style need not continue uniformly throughout a piece, and in quite a few of the songs changing moods in their texts correspond to changing figurations. This occurs most characteristically, as one would expect, at changes of scene and action—consequently of emotional position—in ballad-like songs, such as the Swedish *Winterlied*, Op. 19a no. 3, or the Heine *Reiselied*, Op. 34 no. 6.

Pictorial song accompaniments appear rarely in Mendelssohn's songs, as had also been the case in the works of his Berlin predecessors. He expressed his own misgivings about such an approach to music in mocking terms: "such a thing would always seem to me like a joke—something like the paintings in those children's primers, where they draw the roofs bright red, so that the children recognize that it is supposed to be a roof."[31] Yet there are examples of such accompaniments where, as is so common with Schubert, a figuration becomes a pictorial-expressive device. Mendelssohn's first experiment with this was the incomplete *Der Wasserfall* (probably dating from 1823), which tries to suggest the waterfall by torrential sixteenth-note arpeggiation.

Among the published songs pictorialisms already appeared in Op. 8. In no. 6, the Robert *Frühlingslied*, the piano obviously depicts twittering [*zwitschern*] birdsongs in the second stanza; Luise Leven points out that the postlude to this song, which consists of new material, allows the last word to go to a cuckoo in the forest—a bird not specifically named in the song text.[32] In the *Hexenlied* or *Andres Maienlied*, no. 8, roaring piano figuration depicts the rushing about of the witches.

One of the most common images evoked in the piano parts of Mendelssohn songs is that of the horn. Even when the texts do not explicitly refer to the instrument itself, the use of hornlike harmonies or figurations suggests nature or the forest. Examples include *Im Grünen*, Op. 8 no. 11; the Romanze *Wartend*, Op. 9 no. 3 (particularly the refrain); *Im Frühling*, Op. 9 no. 4 (mm. 18ff., 39ff.); the obvious elfin hunting party in *Neue Liebe*, Op. 19a no. 4; the introduction and postlude in *Gruss*, Op. 19a no. 5 (see Example 11.8); the fanfarelike melodic

Example 11.8
Mendelssohn, *Gruss*, Op. 19a no. 5, mm. 1–3

figures in Klingemann's *Frühlingslied*, Op. 34 no. 3; the mountain horns in the *Hirtenlied*, Op. 57 no. 2; the horn-fifths responding to the explicitly called-for "Hörnerklang" in Eichendorff's *Wanderlied*, Op. 57 no. 6; the "Jubelhorn" of the *Jagdlied*, Op. 84 no. 3; the horn in the party of musicians meeting on the boat in *Das Schifflein*, Op. 99 no. 4; and the balladesque Eichendorff *Das Waldschloss* (posthumous).

Other musical sounds are also evoked. The staccato chords that accompany the *Pagenlied* would be recognized as the singer's mandolin, even if the instrument were not referred to in the text. In Op. 19a no. 3, the *Winterlied* about the youth who goes vainly to search for his lost sister, the drone fifths in the interludes may evoke the balladeer's folk instrument. The drones in the *Sonntagslied*, Op. 34 no. 5, produce a similar scoring—instruments referred to in the poem include bells, organ, and shawm. Evening bells sound in the repeated offbeat B♭s in both the early *Abendlied*, Op. 8 no. 9, and the late *Nachtlied*, Op. 71 no. 6. The high, jingling rhythm of *Neue Liebe*, Op. 19a no. 4, suggests the elves' steeds' harness bells, even while the harmonies suggest horns (see Example 11.9).

Example 11.9
Mendelssohn, *Neue Liebe*, Op. 19a no. 4, mm. 1–12

Neue Liebe also illustrates another type of tone-painting—the galloping of the elfin riders. Expressively crucial to this song are the suspension of the galloping motion as the speaker arrives at the reflection "Galt das meiner neuen Liebe? Oder soll es Tod bedeuten?" and the resumption of the galloping rhythm pianissimo thereafter, as the elf-troop rides away. Another song that seems to employ the image of galloping is Op. 34 no. 3, Klingemann's *Frühlingslied*, though the text does not specifically refer to riding. Certainly, the repeated triplet eighth notes in Heine's *Reiselied*, Op. 34 no. 6, also suggest the galloping horseman.

The piano has an important role to play in several songs that refer to boats. The gondola song Op. 57 no. 5 comes to mind immediately, with its similarity to the pieces of the same genre among the Songs without Words. The essence of the figuration is the gently rocking compound-rhythm figuration, which makes for a seductively relaxing or even hypnotic effect. Also of this barcarolle type is *Scheidend*, Op. 9 no. 6 (see Example 11.10). Here the eighth-quarter rhythm in the

Example 11.10
Mendelssohn, *Scheidelied*, Op. 9 no. 6, mm. 5–8

bass is remarkable. As noted earlier, the opening left-hand motive echoes the opening of the concert overture *Meeresstille und glückliche Fahrt*. The close of Op. 99 no. 4, *Das Schifflein*, also briefly refers to this topos.

In a few songs Mendelssohn, like Schubert, took the poetic image of the motion of water or wind as the central image expressing the protagonist's emotional state. Luise Leven has identified this in the flowing sixteenth notes of the *Minnelied* Op. 47 no. 1 and in the *Schilflied*, Op. 71 no. 4, the latter actually expressing the pond's stillness rather than motion.[33] Thomas Stoner cites the sparkling triplets of the *Wanderlied* Op. 57 no. 6 and the right-hand, sixteenth-note motion of the *Altdeutsches Frühlingslied*, Op. 86 no. 6, as other examples of moving water images. He hears the right-hand arpeggiated figure in the *Winterlied* Op. 19a no. 3 as the sound of the spring breezes, but it might also evoke the rivulets of the melting snow.[34] There can hardly be any mistaking the stormy effect of the scene-setting and excitement-evoking presto rushing sixteenth notes in the Heine *Reiselied*, Op. 34 no. 6. In a more unusual instance of this sort of use of nature imagery for emotional expression, Mendelssohn's treatment of Byron's "Sun of the Sleepless" ("Schlafloser Augen Sonne," posthumous), the repeated high B octaves suggest the coldness of the moon's light and of lost joy.

The use of the accompaniment to suggest emotion, even without pictorial references to the images of the text, is very common, though more difficult to pin down. Not uncommonly, the rhythmic agitation in the piano part simply expresses a particular feeling of agitation in the speaker, the cause of which the text makes explicit. Stoner finds this agitation in several of the compound-meter songs, among which the Ebert *Reiselied*, Op. 19a no. 6, and the Schiller *Des Mädchens Klage* (posthumous) provide good examples.[35] In a duple meter the "concitato" repeated-sixteenth-note chords of the second *Suleika*, Op. 57 no. 3, embody the woman's excited mood (see Example 11.7). Syncopation can also convey increasing animation of the poet's spirit, as in "Ich hör ein Vöglein" (posthumous), where the piano introduces syncopation in the chordal accompaniment; this makes a good example of how the Mendelssohn song aesthetic works in practice, for clearly, here the voice comes in to give specificity to the emotion already being expressed in the piano part.

It is not unusual in Mendelssohn's Lieder for a shift of accompaniment style within a song to indicate a change of emotion. In *Das erste Veilchen*, Op. 19a no. 2, Stoner noted the change from hope to melancholy expressed in the shift of mode from major to minor and from sixteenth-note animation to more relaxed eighth-note motion.[36] In Op. 84 both of the first two songs, "Da lieg' ich unter den Bäumen" and *Herbstlied*, consist of dialogues between the poet and his own heart. The poet's sections of no. 1 are accompanied by a figuration that resembles the orchestral accompaniment in "Ich harrete des Herrn" in the *Lobgesang*, while the heart's stanzas feature a more intense alternating, syncopated rhythm between the hands in the piano part. In no. 2 the heart's worried questions correspond to the repeated chords and syncopated rhythm of the accompaniment, and the poet's reassurances come with rich, rolling broken chords. In Op. 99 no. 2, the story of the girl watching by her mother's deathbed, varied accompaniments indicate the various speakers and their positions: the narrator at the beginning gets a rather spare accompaniment, the stars' opening question a somewhat denser chordal one, the girl a simple, folklike treatment, and the stars' concluding stanza an enriched figurational setting. No. 6 of the same set, Eichendorff's "Es weiss und räth es doch Keiner," sets the secretive and intimate opening pair of stanzas in minor, andante, and $\frac{6}{8}$, and the closing pair, in which the speaker wishes to be a bird soaring to the heavens, in allegro vivace triplet broken chords in the parallel major. A shift of the motive from major in "Ich hör' ein Vöglein locken" (posthumous) to minor for "Ich hör' ein leises Klagen" obviously suits the poem; like the syncopation in this song, the change precedes the appearance of the corresponding text, which thus seems to express a response to emotion already present via the music.

Mendelssohn also found ways to let the omission of the piano in a song become an expressive effect. In two songs the piano has substantial passages in octaves, merely duplicating the vocal line without other accompaniment function: *Neue Liebe*, Op. 19a no. 4, and *Morgengruss*, Op. 47 no. 2, both incidentally by Heine. In Op. 71 no. 5, *Auf der Wanderschaft*, the piano drops out entirely to expose the bitter, empty feeling at "ist's nicht genug, dass du [Wind] mir auch entreissest ihren letzten Gruss?" A similar effect occurs in "Es lauschte das Laub," Op. 86 no. 1, at the end: "das Fenster im Laub ist leer und verlassen."

One of the most successful attributes of Mendelssohn's songwriting is the integration of the piano with the voice part so that the melodic material is shared in counterpoint or dialogue.[37] The use of contrapuntal texture serves principally to integrate the roles of the singer and instrument, so that the whole is perceived as the expression of a single mind. This occurs, for instance, in Op. 8 no. 7, Jakob von Wart's *Maienlied* (mm. 10–12, 20–22). *Gruss*, Op. 19a no. 5 (see Example 11.8), begins as a duet in parallel thirds between singer and the tenor voice of the

piano, but this dissolves after m. 8; a similar brief duet appears in mm. 15–17 of the
Klingemann *Frühlingslied*, Op. 34 no. 3. Another duetting song is Op. 84 no. 2,
Klingemann's *Herbstlied*, in which the duet occurs between voice and piano bass.

The *Pagenlied* (posthumous) continually turns over the melodic interest to the
instrument, while the singer sustains a note at the end of a phrase in such a way that
the instrument does not seem to be playing interludes but continuing the melody
until the singer rejoins it (see mm. 8ff., etc.). In Op. 86 no. 3, Goethe's *Die
Liebende schreibt*, the piano recalls phrases previously sung by the singer; in mm.
16–17 it takes up the singer's opening phrase, and in m. 37 it echoes the singer's
line from m. 36 ("dein freundlicher zu mir"). Then in m. 39 the piano seizes the
melodic role, leading the singer back into the music in the following measure. The
use of such a relationship for a special expressive effect occurs in *Morgengruss*,
Op. 47 no. 2, where the voice presents a melodic phrase that the piano then follows
but with the "melodic overshot" effect already encountered in some of the vocal
melodies (cf. the vocal line in mm. 15–16 and the piano in mm. 16–17); here the
device serves as an image of distance. In the Venetian gondola song, Op. 57 no.
5, the piano, otherwise confined to the characteristic accompaniment, plays a brief
echo just before the close of the song (mm. 64–65)—perhaps indicating a true
echo, perhaps an answer from the beloved Ninetta. A double echo sounds at the
ends of the first, second, and fourth stanzas in Op. 71 no. 3, *An die Entfernte*, as
first the bass and then the top line of the piano part reverberate the singer's closing
motive (in the first two stanzas the second echo breaks off incomplete). (Less
clearly motivated echoing effects occur in Op. 57 no. 4, "O Jugend, o schöne
Rosenzeit!"—see mm. 1–2, 3–4—and Op. 86, no. 5, *Der Mond*—see mm. 5–6 and
16–17.) In *Der Blumenstrauss*, Op. 47 no. 5, the piano presents two melodic
motives that are crucial to the feeling of the piece but that never appear in the vocal
line: the left-hand figure with a yearning appoggiatura, first appearing in mm. 1–2;
and a right-hand descending gesture that seems to express tenderness, introduced
in mm. 18–19.

A good example of how the piano can initiate an idea that becomes transferred
to the singer is the lullaby Op. 47 no. 6, in which the piano's opening motive is
finally taken up by the singer and given explicit words—"Bleibe nur fein
geduldig," the main point of the Lied. A similar, but less effective, such case may
be the treatment of "spie - - - len" and "stre - - ben" (mm. 14–15) in "Es lauschte
das Laub so dunkelgrün," Op. 86 no. 1; here the piano initiates a quasi-pictorial,
upward-leaping gesture that the voice then follows—though the result is a stress
on the weak syllable. When the same music returns for the word "Fenster," there
can be no justification except purely musical unity. In the ends of both of
Marianne von Willemer's Suleika songs, Op. 34 no. 4 and Op. 57 no. 3, the piano
relates to the vocal part in a similar way, but it provides the melodic climax that the
singer, resuming the vocal line of the earlier stanzas, does not reach (see Op. 34 no.
4 mm. 30–31, Op. 57 no. 3 mm. 34–35). Not surprisingly "Ich hör ein Vöglein"
(posthumous) also gives good examples of melodic material introduced first in the
piano (see mm. 11–14, 39–42).

Mendelssohn's use of harmony in the Lieder is similar to that in his other music. It does not strike the listener as unusually adventurous but as suave and subtly expressive. His modulations generally confine themselves to closely related keys; Luise Leven pointed out that they take place in subtly different ways.[38] Though the tonal ambience is always clear, tonality is often colored by the use of nonharmonic tones and chromaticism, producing what Stoner called "the characteristically Romantic ingredients of melancholy and yearning."[39] Contrast of major and minor modes is not uncommon, as has been noted in the discussion of several songs already; Stoner identified textually motivated shifts between the modes in nine of the seventy-three published songs.[40] In one special case the open fifth occurs to good purpose—the Romanze *Wartend*, Op. 9 no. 3, where the cadential harmony is often left open; at the very end of the song the chord is filled in to produce a "Picardy" third.

The diminished-seventh chord, which had not yet become so clichéd as it might appear to twentieth-century listeners, provided a common source of harmonic shading. Augmented-sixth chords are rare, as are augmented triads, and both occur only momentarily as products of chromatic passing motion.

Pedal points are quite common, especially in the early songs. In Op. 9 no. 11, *Entsagung*, the final close in the vocal melody is supported by an authentic cadence but followed by an archaic extension to a plagal conclusion; the "Amen" effect suits the text well. Pedals that serve as drones to create the image of folk instruments or styles have already been discussed. In some pieces pedal points also serve to generate harmonic tension; Stoner finds in Op. 19a no. 5, for example, that the pedal points "contribute to an understated inner disquiet," and that in the *Sonntagslied*, Op. 34 no. 5, the F♯ pedal (as the dominant of the supertonic) suggests the speaker's sadness.[41]

Forms

Mendelssohn's approach to form in his songs took as its point of departure the principles established by his Berlin predecessors. At the same time, his personal aesthetic justifies the results.

In the Berlin style, at the phrase/verse level, the musical design of the song depends closely on the construction of the poetic lines. Poetic meter and line-symmetry led to symmetrical musical phrasing based on two- and four-measure units. The prevalence in the texts of tetrameters (or alternating tetrameter and trimeter) and the frequent design of poems in couplets and quatrains made rather square musical forms the most natural framework for song stanzas. Structural articulation by end-stopping in the texts led to clear musical punctuations by cadences of various strengths at the ends of text lines/musical phrases and at stanza endings.

Yet Mendelssohn did not follow mechanically the meters, lineation, and punctuation of his poetry. As Luise Leven pointed out, he felt free to repeat words for the sake of musical form. A characteristic feature of Mendelssohn's melodies is that, while they generally are relatively syllabic and rhythmically continuous and do not repeat words and phrases, they manifest a tendency to grow elaborate as the end of the song or of the individual stanza approaches. This may be accomplished by repetition of the text of the closing line or lines, by extending single notes, or by an increasing ornamental expansion of the melody. An early and rather extreme example is Op. 8 no. 5, the *Pilgerspruch* by Paul Fleming; the first two of its short stanzas are expanded at their ends by word repetition and then by melodic elaboration, and the third stanza still further by the two-measure extension of the word "heißt." A more mature and rather more restrained case is provided by Op. 57 no. 1, Heinrich Schreiber's "Es ist in den Wald gesungen," in which the last four measures of the text and melody are simply repeated at the close of each stanza. Leven found Mendelssohn's treatment of "Es weiss und räth es doch Keiner," Op. 99 no. 6, a particularly egregious case; perhaps Mendelssohn's sensitivity to this partially accounts for his not having published the song.

Following in the Berlin tradition, Mendelssohn accepted the strophic design as the form of the Lied more or less by definition. This was not merely justified for him by reference to a desirable *Volkstümlichkeit*, however, but also by aesthetic principle. Hegel had argued that the strophic song was preferable to the through-composed type because in it music maintained its abstract integrity, not merely giving way to a slavish pursuit of the text.[42] This clearly ties in with Mendelssohn's own aesthetic position, according to which music holds the emotionally expressive role, and words provide only reflections of the emotion. Moreover, in this context, strophic form appears as inherently musical, in the sense that poetry is verbal text constructed musically, in which sense through-composed settings must be characterized as prosaic. Thus, the rooting of the Mendelssohn Lieder in strophic form must be understood not as unimaginatively tradition-bound but as a consequence of the integrity of the composer's philosophical position.

As might be expected, strictly strophic settings appear more frequently among the earlier songs than the later ones. According to Leven's count, in the songs composed before 1833, 60 percent are strophic; thereafter, most are in modified strophic forms.[43] Examples of the simple, strophic form include *Gruss*, Op. 19a no. 5. A text that must be regarded as a Lied in the sense of unsophisticated, popular song was especially likely to be treated in the simplest possible strophic manner; an example is the *Todeslied der Bojaren*, where the intention was to evoke the musical unsophistication of the characters singing the song in the drama. Other examples of consciously folklike strophic songs include Fallersleben's *Seemanns Scheidelied* and Simrock's *Warnung vor dem Rhein*.

In fact, absolutely strict, folklike, strophic construction is relatively unusual among Mendelssohn's Lieder,[44] for whereas the strophic setting must be regarded as more musical than the through-composed one that follows the word-meanings around by the nose, the mechanistically poetic setting can also be regarded as less than freely musical.

One way in which music emerges from the confinement of the form is by the addition of introductions, interludes, and postludes. The addition of the introduction—and likewise the emergence of the piano from the role of accompaniment between and after the sung phrases or stanzas—satisfies a function beyond merely establishing the singer's key or letting her or him rest. Within Mendelssohn's aesthetic, as already suggested, it embodies the emotional core of the song. To take just the most obvious example, the characteristic feeling of "Auf Flügeln des Gesanges" becomes clear in the first measure, before the melody and text enter. That feeling remains the expressive essence throughout the song; to some degree, as suggested earlier, the singer's part—text and melody—serves as a response to that underlying feeling. *Im Frühling*, Op. 9 no. 4, actually introduces the melody in the piano's introduction; consequently, when the voice enters in midphrase, the text has the effect of emerging from the flow of the speaker's feelings. In the J. H. Voss *Abendlied*, Op. 8 no. 9, the introduction/interlude/postlude has the effect of focusing the emotional emphasis on the expressive, contrapuntal, mid-strophe figuration in the song, not on depicting the sound of the evening bell with which the voice actually enters.

An alternative to a musical form that simply parallels all of the text stanzas is the construction of longer double-strophes. An example is Op. 47 no. 5, *Der Blumenstrauss*. With some modification Op. 19a no. 6, the Ebert *Reiselied*, and Op. 47 no. 1, Tieck's *Minnelied*, also provide instances. This approach works particularly well when a text has stanzas that, in some sense, alternate imagery, style, or point of view. This is the case in "Da lieg' ich unter den Bäumen," Op. 84 no. 1, where the stanzas alternate between the comforting speaker and his/her unhappy heart. The composer constructed double-length strophes, changing mode and piano figuration in the middle of each, as was noted earlier. "Auf Flügeln des Gesanges," in fact, employs double strophes for the first four of its five text stanzas, which describe the charms of the amorous Oriental setting; for the fifth, in which the lovers themselves appear on the scene, the music is compressed from phrases of both halves of the double stanzas, and a new conclusion is provided.

Also common as an alternative to strict strophic form is the modification of the stanzas using musical variation technique. This treatment, which integrates the principles of unity and variety, governs most of Mendelssohn's songs. Stoner identified strophic songs with variation for only the final stanza (A A . . . A^1) in nineteen cases among the seventy-three published songs and more or less continuous variation (A A^1 A^2) in sixteen.[45]

Some of the songs adopt a Bar-like form, wherein two opening stanzas are treated strophically, but the final stanza is set to new music. This generally requires a clear shift in textual content for the last stanza—as in Op. 86 no. 1, "Es lauschte das Laub," where the season changes from summer in the first two stanzas to autumn in the last, or in Op. 71 no. 6, where the first two stanzas reflect on the sadness of night and loneliness, and in the third the speaker becomes determined to continue to praise God through the night until the morning comes.

The close similarity of the A A A^1 type of modified strophic form to the "Bar" type is obvious. Leven, indeed, simply counted these pieces as modified strophic.[46] As has already been suggested, this may have only the musical purpose of rounding out the form by extending the conclusion, as in the *Pilgerspruch*, Op. 8 no. 5, or the romance Op. 9 no. 3. It also serves when a shift of viewpoint takes place in the final stanza of a text, but not a complete change of the situation. In the *Hexenlied*, Op. 8 no. 8, the change is one of mood from uncanny mystery to pure fun. In the first Suleika song, Op. 34 no. 4, this form reflects the change from the singer's longing for the beloved to her joyful thoughts of being with him.

A few genuinely nonstrophic songs do occur among Mendelssohn's oeuvre. While he certainly regarded the strophic plan as the natural form for the Lied, he obviously found reasons for abandoning it. Certain Lied poems present conditions that must be responded to by other forms. Furthermore, there are songs among this oeuvre that cannot be regarded as belonging to the genre of Lied, strictly defined, at all.

Binary-form songs are of two types. In the first type the text is such that the song must consist of two contrasting musical styles. The category includes Eichendorff's "Es weiss und räth es doch keiner," Op. 99 no. 6, where the four stanzas clearly group into pairs, with a reflective and intimate mood governing the first two and an ecstatic spirit the third and fourth. A particularly nice example, where the first two stanzas describe the setting and the third expresses the transition (minor to major) from the contemplation of the nighttime scene to the sweet thought of the beloved, is the Lenau *Schilflied*, Op. 71 no. 4.

In the second binary type the text is essentially strophic in two stanzas, and the composer found a reason to leave the first stanza open on or in the dominant. An early example is the Spanish romance, Op. 8 no. 10, which must be classified as an aria, rather than as a Lied, in any case. The setting of Schiller's Romanze *Des Mädchens Klage* belongs somewhat to the same model. Ulrich von Liehtenstein's *Frühlingslied*, Op. 19a no. l, presents a different kind of case, since it clearly belongs to the Lied genre; the choice of a binary, rather than strophic, setting undoubtedly originated in the slightly different structures of the two stanzas (placement of strong and weak syllables at line ends and abab cdcd rhyme scheme). Op. 9 no. 1, Mendelssohn's own *Frage*, is also binary; as the only completely irregular and unrhymed text among his songs, it is entirely different from any of its companions. *Morgengruss*, Op. 47 no. 2, for both metrical and textual reasons, justified a rounded binary form. The Thomas Moore *Venetianisches Gondellied*, Op. 57 no. 5, perhaps belonging to the English canzonetta tradition rather than the Lied genre, is probably best regarded as a closed (i.e., with the first part ending on the tonic) rounded binary form. This genre description certainly applies in the instance of Moore's *Der Blumenkranz* (The Garland, posthumous), composed in England on an English text, which is in clearly rounded binary form. The choice of rounded binary form for Byron's "Keine von der Erde Schönen" (There Be None of Beauty's Daughters, posthumous) may also stem from Mendelssohn's feeling that it should be treated as belonging to the English song genre.

Reprise-type songs are also represented. Mostly these are ternary (so-called first rondo) designs, possibly with variation of the reprise. Ebert's *Das erste Veilchen*, Op. 19a no. 2, is such a piece; the two stanzas contrast in both mood and poetic and musical design, but the final line is set to music freely derived from the beginning of the song. Goethe's *Die Liebende schreibt*, Op. 86 no. 3, is similar, but with two interior sections. Uniquely among Mendelssohn's songs, it is a sonnet. Each of its two quatrains and first tercet receives its own music, while the music for the closing tercet refers to that of the opening, creating an A B C A[1] design. A similar plan governs the narrative *Das Schifflein*, Op. 99 no. 4.

Genuinely through-composed structures are extremely rare. One song that employs this approach is Schlippenbach's "Die Sterne schau'n in stiller Nacht" (Op. 99 no. 2), which might qualify more as a sort of narrative *scena* than as a Lied.

Conspicuously absent from Mendelssohn's published songs are song cycles. In the first publication of Op. 9 the songs were grouped into two sets of six each, headed "Der Jüngling" and "Das Mädchen," respectively, so that two speakers or personae are implied, making the complete set appear to be a kind of quasi-dramatic Liederspiel. Thomas Stoner suggests that the songs from the two sets ought to be sung in alternation to create a dialogue.[47] Yet the twelve songs do not really produce any sort of through-line or plot; indeed, the speakers would not seem to be taking notice of each other.

While Mendelssohn did not construct his Lieder into cycles, he commonly composed them in groups, and from these he later selected certain individual pieces to make up an opus-numbered set and left others unpublished. As a result, it would be possible to reconstruct groups of songs that were conceived at the same time and study them as cycles.[48] One such set, which Mendelssohn abandoned entirely and which therefore was not scattered, is the set of four songs from 1830 contained in the manuscript miscellany that was added to the Mendelssohn Nachlaß in Berlin as volume 56: *Der Tag*, *Reiterlied*, *Abschied*, and *Der Bettler*. There is no indication of the author (or authors) of the poetry. In some ways, this group has the appearance of a cycle, as the texts seem to reflect moments in a speaker's life, there is a musical reminiscence of the first song in the last, and the keys provide some rounding or closure (A–C–B♭–a/A). Another possibility, especially considering the rather operatic vocal and orchestral piano style of these songs, is that they were intended for some dramatic context.

Mendelssohn wrote explicitly about the tonal design of a set of songs in a letter to Moscheles, describing his plan to publish a selection of the latter's songs:

The keys certainly follow in the maddest of ways—F major, B major, and so on anyhow; but I have always found that not a soul thanks you for the loveliest sequence in keys, and that it is rather a change from slow to fast, from serious to lively, that is particularly in demand. So pray excuse this fricassee of sharps and flats.[49]

Given this attitude, the sets of songs that Mendelssohn published as opus-numbered works certainly cannot be regarded as harmonically designed cycles in the sense in which the term is applied to the cycles of Schumann.[50] On the other hand, the stated intention to lay them out in such a way that a set presents a plan for contrast and variety at least strongly suggests the intention that they might be performed effectively as wholes.

One quasi-cyclic collection of songs deserves to be pointed out in particular, the set published as Op. 71. These songs have a common theme, that of the speaker suffering from, and coming to grips with, pain and loss. All of them date from relatively late in Mendelssohn's life, and he assembled the group in the few months remaining to him after his sister Fanny's death. The emotional content moves through various reactions to bereavement and grief, turning in no. 6, Eichendorff's "Nachtlied," toward a radical decision to join with Nature in praising God despite the darkness of the soul. The keys of the songs do not form a symmetrical plan, but they reflect the directions of the changing moods, with a radical move from B minor to E♭ major for the final song.[51]

CONCLUSIONS

Genre

Reflecting now on the relationships of the texts to the music of Mendelssohn's songs, it becomes clear that the poetic genres they incorporate affect the music in a variety of ways and make it possible to think of the songs as belonging to different types.

Relatively little represented among the songs are narrative poems. The ballad genre includes the Swedish *Winterlied*, Op. 19a no. 3, about the youth lost in the storm as he searches for his sister, and Heine's ironic reinterpretation of the ballad in the *Reiselied*, Op. 34 no. 6. Characteristics of these songs are freedom of form and variety in the piano part, reflecting the changing speakers, actions, or scenes. The same applies to the songs that belong to the genre of dramatic or narrative scena—for example, Goethe's *Die Liebende schreibt*, Op. 86 no. 3, or the scene of the maiden at her mother's death-bed, Op. 99 no. 2.

It was certainly part of Mendelssohn's conscious social program in music to compose songs that expressed the moral values of German bourgeois culture. Such songs attach to the tradition of the *Spruch* or proverb, sometimes with sacred overtones, and include several songs from Op. 8—the *Erntelied* (no. 4), the *Pilgerspruch* (no. 5), and the *Abendlied* (no. 9); from Op. 9—Droysen's *Ferne* (no. 9) and *Entsagung* (no. 11); and, of course, the famous *Volkslied*, Op. 47 no. 4. Characteristic features of the music of these songs are a rhythmically regular melody and a tendency to chordal accompaniment, both suggesting a chorale and giving the text a setting that bespeaks simplicity and truth.

Most of Mendelssohn's Lieder fall into the category of the confessional lyric, taking as their themes the emotional experience of either nature or love (or a combination of the two). These songs represent the new Romantic style of Lied. Nature as topos is likely to find its expression in a folklike melody and a pictorial accompaniment, often, as noted earlier, in evocations of horns, for example. Love lyrics generally produced a cantabile vocal line and a figurational accompaniment that embodies the emotional content of the song.

Performance

As was pointed out at the beginning of this Chapter, Mendelssohn's Lieder were principally intended to serve as material for domestic music-making in the German bourgeois drawing rooms of the *Vormärz*. The market for the songs was the cultivated commercial and professional class. The Mendelssohn household(s) represented the very best of this social stratum—the ideal to which German families might aspire. Of course, his songs were performed in the musical gatherings in his family home. From at least as early as 1822 the Sunday musicales in the Mendelssohns' Berlin salon included Lieder among their repertoire. The composer's younger sister, Rebecca, sang his songs there. According to Moscheles,[52] Mendelssohn's wife, Cécile, sang the *Minnelied* Op. 34 no. 1 in her own home in Leipzig.

Among the homes where we know Mendelssohn's songs were sung by amateurs was Buckingham Palace. Both Queen Victoria and Prince Albert sang the composer's songs from Op. 8 (as well as one by his sister Fanny) for him, when he visited there in 1842.[53]

Public performances of the songs by professional singers also took place, however. One of the leading singers of the period, Wilhelmine Schröder-Devrient, sang his popular farewell song "Es ist bestimmt in Gottes Rath, dass man vom Liebsten was man hat muss scheiden" at the last Gewandhaus concert before Mendelssohn's move to Berlin in 1841.[54] Livia Frege, who had retired from her professional career very young when she was married, not only sang his songs for Mendelssohn in private settings but sang Op. 71 no. 6, at the Gewandhaus memorial concert the week after his death.[55]

Such concert appearances were not only occasional. Most notably, Jenny Lind, a great favorite of Mendelssohn's, sang music from Op. 19a at her Leipzig debut on 5 December 1845, with Mendelssohn accompanying, and again at a benefit concert there slightly later. The following June she sang his songs at the Lower Rhine Music Festival at Aachen, including "Auf Flügeln des Gesanges."[56] Lind's affection for Mendelssohn was such that for some time after he died she was unable to sing his songs, but she did eventually return to singing them. Among other notable singers whose concert programs featured Mendelssohn's songs was the baritone Julius Stockhausen.[57] Clara Novello also sang Mendelssohn's Lieder on her concerts.

A rather remarkable instance in the performance history of Mendelssohn's Lieder was a program put on for him in Frankfurt in 1839, in which ten pieces of his music were performed together with *tableaux vivants*. Among the pieces staged were three songs—*Frage*, Op. 9 no. 1; the *Minnelied* "Leucht't heller als die Sonne," Op. 34 no. 1; and the first Suleika song, Op. 34 no. 3.[58]

That the musical public took Mendelssohn's songs to itself as expressions of its own spirit is clear from two performances for him of "Es ist bestimmt . . ." It was sung to him by an ensemble that serenaded him on his departure from Leipzig in 1841.[59] More impressively, it served as a farewell to the composer in Cologne in 1846—performed by a chorus of 2,000, most of whom sang the song from memory.[60]

Significance

Mendelssohn's songs reveal the composer himself as a person more intimately than do his works in any other genre. This is clear in the various ways in which the songs belonged to his personal life--in the use of poetry that expressed his own emotional life, in the choice of texts from his circle of friends and acquaintances, in the gifts and dedications of songs to those close to him, in the performances in which he collaborated with other musicians both professional and amateur.

In other, more abstract ways, the songs represent Mendelssohn's thinking about music. Intellectually, the songs manifested the aesthetic principles to which Mendelssohn subscribed, applying those principles to the genre in which they were, on the one hand, most tested and, on the other, most effectively revealed. In the way in which the text and music are interrelated, Mendelssohn found a position between music that slavishly "depicts" text, giving poetry the primary function in guiding the music, and music that merely offers a pleasant background or frame for the words. In his songs he met the challenge that his aesthetic stance demanded: to embody emotional content in the music and to set up the words as a verbal expression of that emotion.

Finally, the songs represent Mendelssohn's deeply held moral belief about music, embodying his commitment to composing for the domestic bourgeois consumer class, for his Lieder were not calculated to be imposing works of great art but to contribute the best that was possible in an intimate genre. At the same time, the songs hoped to make a contribution to the development of the moral and cultural life of the amateur singer and domestic listener. They had, in other words, a place in the cultural program to which, from the ground of his being, Mendelssohn always remained profoundly dedicated.

NOTES

1. See Wolfgang Stresemann, *Eine Lanze für Felix Mendelssohn* (Berlin: Stapp, 1984), 220; Eric Werner, *Mendelssohn: Leben und Werk in neuer Sicht* (Zurich: Atlantis, 1980), 515–16.

2. Sebastian Hensel, *Die Familie Mendelssohn 1792 bis 1847: Nach Briefen und Tagebüchern* (Berlin: Georg Reimer, 1918), 2: 451; *The Mendelssohn Family (1729–1847): From Letters and Journals*, 2d rev. ed. (New York: Harper, 1882; repr. New York: Haskell House, 1969), 2: 339.

3. See the author's "The Problem of the Lyric Persona in Mendelssohn's Songs," in *Felix Mendelssohn Bartholdy: Kongreß-Bericht Berlin 1994*, ed. Christian Martin Schmidt (Wiesbaden: Breitkopf & Härtel, 1997), 167–80.

4. Letter to Marc-André Souchay, 15 October 1842, in Felix Mendelssohn Bartholdy, *Briefe aus den Jahren 1830 bis 1847*, vol. 2, *Briefe aus den Jahren 1833 bis 1847*, ed. Paul and Carl Mendelssohn Bartholdy (Leipzig: Hermann Mendelssohn, 1875), 346–47:

[Wörter] scheinen mir so vieldeutig, so unbestimmt, so mißverständlich im Vergleich zu einer rechten Musik, die Einem die Seele erfüllt mit tausend besseren Dingen, als Worten. Das, was mir eine Musik ausspricht, die ich liebe, sind mir nicht zu *unbestimmte* Gedanken, um sie in Worte zu fassen, sondern zu *bestimmte*. So finde ich in allen Versuchen, diese Gedanken auszusprechen, etwas Richtiges, aber auch in allen etwas Ungenügendes, . . . weil nur das Lied dem Einen dasselbe sagen, dasselbe Gefühl in ihm erwecken kann, wie im Andern,—ein Gefühl, das sich aber nicht durch dieselben Worte ausspricht.

5. Johann Georg Sulzer, *Allgemeine Theorie der schönen Künste*, 2d ed., exp. (Leipzig: Weidmann, 1792; repr. Hildesheim: G. Olms, 1970), 3: 252–77, 277–82.

6. R. Larry Todd, work list, in Karl-Heinz Köhler and Eveline Bartlitz, "Felix Mendelssohn," *The New Grove Early Romantic Masters 2* (New York: Norton, 1985), 279.

7. Adolf Bernhard Marx, review of Felix Mendelssohn Bartholdy, *Zwölf Lieder mit Begleitung des Pforte*, in *Berliner allgemeine musikalische Zeitung* 7/27 (3 July 1830), 209: "z.B. das erste Gedicht ist gewiss nicht von H. Voss, eher von Komponisten selbst."

8. Hensel, *Die Familie Mendelssohn*, 1: 183; *The Mendelssohn Family*, 1: 133.

9. Luise Leven, "Mendelssohn als Lyriker: unter besonderer Berücksichtigung seiner Beziehungen zu Ludwig Berger, Bernhard Klein, und Ad. Bernh. Marx" (Ph.D. diss., University of Frankfurt am Main, 1926), 117.

10. See Therese Devrient, *Jugenderinnerungen* (Stuttgart: Carl Krabbe, 1908), 195.

11. Reinhard Fink, "Das 'Chaos' und seine Mitarbeiter," in *Otto Glauninq zum 60. Geburtstag: Festgabe aus Wissenschaft und Bibliothek*, ed. Heinrich Schreiber (Leipzig: Richard Hadl, 1936), 51.

12. Lily von Kretschman, "Felix Mendelssohn-Bartholdy in Weimar: Aus dem Nachlass der Baronin von Gustedt, geb. Pappenheim," *Deutsche Rundschau* 18/2, i.e., volume 69 (November 1891), 307.

13. Bodleian Library, Oxford, M. Deneke Mendelssohn collection, b.5 fol. 5–6.

14. One is reminded of Goethe's famous formulation "What is classic I call the healthy; and what is romantic, the unhealthy" (Das Klassische nenne ich das Gesunde, und das Romantische das Kranke); see Johann Peter Eckermann, *Gespräche mit Goethe in den letzten Jahren seines Lebens* (Stuttgart: J. G. Cotta, n.d.), 2: 56.

15. Karl Klingemann [Jr.], ed., *Felix Mendelssohn-Bartholdys Briefwechsel mit Legationsrat Karl Klingemann in London* (Essen: Baedeker, 1909), 234:

Wie hast Du mich mit diesen Liedern erfreut; ich kenne eben keinen, dessen Verse mir so aus der Seele geflossen schienen, und mir so gleich heimisch und warm machten, wie die Deinigen; mein Liebling ist no. 5. Herbstlied, das ist mir aus dem Herzen geschrieben, und ich habe es gleich komponiert, aber die Dichtung gefällt mir so sehr, dass ich noch gar nicht weiss, ob meine Musik auch gut ist, oder ob es nur mir gefällt, weil ich's singen kann; darum schicke ich sie Dir heut noch nicht. Auch das zweite und dritte sind mir solche Lieblinge, denen ist aber nicht leicht musikalisch beizukommen, man kann dabei auf die Nase fallen. Aber eigentlich sind sie alle meine Lieblinge; sind's doch seit langer Zeit die erste neuen Gedichte, die mich erfüllen und mein eigen geworden sind; ich lasse mir's sonst gewiss angelegen sein, nach guter Poesie zu suchen, aber was man neues liest, das verschwindet, indem man das Blatt umdreht. Deine Sachen nicht; nun freue ich mich auf die Liederkreise, die Du in petto behältst.

16. Ibid., 85–86:

Du glaubst nicht wie ich mich sehne, etwas von Dir wieder zu komponieren, und schriebst mir doch, dass du schon alte Volkssagen läsest, um den Stoff zu finden. Ich habe bei Deinen Worten das eigene Gefühl, dass ich keine Musik zu *machen* brauche, es ist als läse ich sie heraus und als stünde sie schon vor mir, und wenn bei anderen Gedichten, namentlich Goethe, die Worte sich von der Musik abwenden und sich allein behaupten wollen, so rufen Deine Gedichte nach dem Klang und da kann der wahre nicht fehlen.

17. Letter of 9 August 1831: "Jetzt mache ich eins, das nicht gut wird, fürchte ich; aber für uns Drei muß es schon angehen, denn es ist sehr gut gemeint; der Text ist von Goethe, aber ich sage nicht, was: es ist zu toll, gerade das zu componiren; es paßt auch gar nicht zur Musik; aber ich fand es so himmlisch schön, daß ich es mir singen mußte." Felix Mendelssohn Bartholdy, *Briefe aus den Jahren 1830 bis 1847*, vol. 2, *Reisebriefe aus den Jahren 1830 bis 1832*, ed. Paul Mendelssohn Bartholdy (Leipzig: Hermann Mendelssohn, 1882), 242. English translation from Felix Mendelssohn Bartholdy, *Letters from Italy and Switzerland*, trans. Lady Wallace, 2d ed. (London: Longman, Green, Longman, Roberts, and Green, 1862), 238.

18. Such hesitation did not necessarily apply to other genres. Two of Mendelssohn's most important larger works, the overture *Meerestille und glückliche Fahrt* and *Die erste Walpurgisnacht*, are based on Goethe. Mendelssohn began the latter in the knowledge that Zelter had attempted to set the text and failed, and Goethe, at least, was aware that Mendelssohn had started on it.

19. Darmstadt, Hessische Landes- und Hochschulbibliothek, Mus. ms. 1444b.

20. The "Ave Maria" comes from Canto III, stanza XXIX (lines 713ff.), there titled "Hymn to the Virgin." "Raste Krieger" is the "Song" at Canto I, stanza XXXI (lines 624ff.), beginning "Soldier, rest! thy warfare o'er."

21. The translation of "There Be None of Beauty's Daughters" is attributed to Klingemann in the appendix of Klingemann, ed., *Briefwechsel*; see p. 346. On the text of "Sun of the Sleepless," see Mendelssohn's letter to Rebecca of 23 November 1834, in *Briefe 1833–1847*, 68; *Letters 1833–1847*, 57.

22. Darmstadt, Hessische Landes- und Hochschulbibliothek, Mus. ms. 1444a.

23. See Thomas Stoner, "Mendelssohn's Published Songs" (Ph.D. diss., University of Maryland, 1972), 239, 352.

24. Cf. Leven, "Mendelssohn als Lyriker," 69; Stoner, "Mendelssohn's Published Songs," 62.

25. An observation aptly made by Thomas Stoner; see "Mendelssohn's Published Songs," 63.

26. Leven, "Mendelssohn als Lyriker," 71.

27. Ibid., 72.

28. "meine eigne Armuth an neuen Wendungen für's Klavier"; Felix Mendelssohn Bartholdy, *Briefe an Ignaz und Charlotte Moscheles*, ed. Felix Moscheles (Leipzig: Duncker & Humblot, 1888; repr. Walluf-Nendeln: Sändig, 1976), 74. The English translation reads, quite misleadingly, "my own poverty in shaping new forms [*sic*] for the pianoforte"; *Letters of Felix Mendelssohn Bartholdy to Ignaz and Charlotte Moscheles*, trans. and ed. Felix Moscheles (Boston: Ticknor, 1888), 85.

29. Erik Werba, "Der Lyriker Felix Mendelssohn-Bartholdy," *Oesterreichische Musikzeitschrift* 15 (1960), 18.

30. Stoner, "Mendelssohn's Published Songs," 199.

31. "so Etwas kömmt mir immer vor, wie ein Spaß, etwa wie die Malereien in den Kinderfiebeln, wo man die Dächer knallroth anstreicht, damit die Kinder merken, daß es ein Dach sein soll." Letter to Frau von Pereira, dated Genoa, July 1831; Mendelssohn, *Reisebriefe*, 206; cf. *Letters from Italy and Switzerland*, 198.

32. Leven, "Mendelssohn als Lyriker," 99–100; the first edition of the song contained a footnote saying, "The accompaniment for this song is actually written for a flute, a clarinet, two horns, and a cello."

33. Ibid., 93.

34. Stoner, "Mendelssohn's Published Songs," 245, 292, 159.

35. Ibid., 130, 295.

36. Ibid., 156.

37. Leven finds this rooted in the practice of Ludwig Berger; see "Mendelssohn als Lyriker," 94.

38. Ibid., 85.

39. Stoner, "Mendelssohn's Published Songs," 55.

40. Ibid.

41. Ibid., 168, 190.

42. Hegel's aesthetics is discussed in connection with Mendelssohn's music in Eric Werner, *Mendelssohn: A New Image of the Composer and His Age* (New York: Free Press of Glencoe, 1963), 124.

43. Leven, "Mendelssohn als Lyriker," 104–5.

44. Leven counted only 30 percent of Mendelssohn's songs (twenty-two of seventy-two) as strictly strophic or nearly so; ibid., 103.

45. Stoner, "Mendelssohn's Published Songs," 56–57.

46. Leven, "Mendelssohn als Lyriker," 103.

47. Stoner, "Mendelssohn's Published Songs," 325.

48. Cf. Richard Kramer's attempt to do this sort of thing for some cases in Schubert's oeuvre in *Distant Cycles: Schubert and the Conceiving of Song* (Chicago: University of Chicago Press, 1994).

49. Mendelssohn, *Letters to Ignaz and Charlotte Moscheles*, 56.

50. For two interesting approaches to harmonic unity within Schumann's song cycles, see Arthur Komar, "The Music of *Dichterliebe*: The Whole and Its Parts," in the Norton Critical Score edition of Robert Schumann, *Dichterliebe*, ed. Arthur Komar (New York: Norton, 1971), 63–94; Barbara Turchin, "Schumann's Song Cycles: The Cycle within the Song," *19th-Century Music* 8/3 (Spring 1985), 231–44.

51. I have discussed the cyclic character and structure of Op. 71 in greater detail in an essay originally presented at the festival conference "The Mendelssohns at the Millennium" held at Illinois Wesleyan University, Bloomington, IL, in March 1997.

52. Ignaz Moscheles, *Recent Music and Musicians: As Described in the Diaries and Correspondence of Ignatz Moscheles*, ed. Charlotte Moscheles, trans. A. D. Coleridge (New York: Henry Holt, 1874; repr. New York: Da Capo, 1970), 271.

53. See Mendelssohn's report of the occasion in his letter of 19 July 1842; Hensel, *Die Familie Mendelssohn*, 2: 223–30; *The Mendelssohn Family*, 2: 167–72.

54. Schumann reported this concert in the *Neue Zeitschrift für Musik* 14/29 (9 April 1841), 118.

55. See note 2; also Ferdinand Hiller, *Mendelssohn: Letters and Recollections*, trans. M. E. von Glehn (London: Macmillan, 1874), 217.

56. See Henry S. Holland and W. S. Rockstro, *Memoir of Madame Jenny Lind-Goldschmidt: Her Early Life and Dramatic Career, 1820–1851* (London: John Murray, 1891), 2: 327, 330, 411.

57. Julia Wirth, *Julius Stockhausen: Der Sänger des deutschen Liedes* (Frankfurt am Main: Englert & Schlosser, 1927), 494.

58. Mendelssohn described the amusing scenes in a letter to his mother of 3 July 1839; see Felix Mendelssohn Bartholdy, *Briefe 1833–1847*, 196–98; *Letters 1833–1847*, 165–66.

59. This is reported in Eduard Devrient, *Meine Erinnerungen an Felix Mendelssohn-Bartholdy und seine Briefe an mich* (Leipzig: J.J. Weber, 1869; 3d ed. 1891), 213; *My Recollections of Felix Mendelssohn-Bartholdy and His Letters to Me*, trans. Natalia MacFarren (London: Richard Bentley, 1869), 218.

60. Mendelssohn reported how touched he was by this in a letter of 27 June 1846 to Fanny; see Hensel, *Die Familie Mendelssohn*, 2: 441; *The Mendelssohn Family*, 2: 332.

HISTORICAL VIEWS AND DOCUMENTS

The following reviews demonstrate the way in which Mendelssohn's work was treated in the *Neue Zeitschrift für Musik* during the composer's lifetime and then shortly after his death. Neither takes an entirely positive or negative position, yet the clear sense in the first (from 1840) of Mendelssohn's mastery of the treatment of poetry in the genre of song gives way in the second (from 1848) to the depiction of him as a conservative formalist.

F. MENDELSSOHN-BARTHOLDY, SECHS LIEDER MIT BEGL. DES PFTE.—OP. 47—LEIPZIG, BREITKOPF U. HÄRTEL.—20GR.[1]

O[swald] L[orenz]; translated by Douglass Seaton

The most freshly and characteristically sung is unquestionably the *Morgengruß* (by Heine). In it a thorough understanding of the material unites with masterfully simple technique and naïveté of expression to produce a beautiful, well-rounded whole. For apt truth and the same charming naiveté the *Volkslied* hardly stands behind it, even if the necessary folk-style, which leads to a still greater simplicity, a certain artistic triviality, causes the latter to rank less high from the technical standpoint. This folksong, however, like his earlier ones, is a striking demonstration of the way that M. knows how to ensure the simplicity of a popular harmonization, by means of voice-leading and by means of his almost unnoticed artistic talent for uniformity, and always to give it a noble, delicate polish. This is reminiscent of the beautifying power of a good engraving, which can lend to an insignificant locale, a prosaically regular building such a bright, attractive appearance. The *Wiegenlied* seems to owe its existence to a less propitious hour. Despite interesting details and the overall smoothness of the form, the melody appears, on the whole, somewhat frigid and the entire impression, not effective. The *Minnelied* and *Der Blumenkranz* achieve their goal more securely, though we would not want to compare them to the first two songs mentioned earlier on the basis of their poetic core. Substance and form join hands in them, however, mutually elevating and supporting each other in intimate fellowship, assuring success. Only the singer must know how to disguise the fact that some passages of the first stanza work better than in the second, for example, at the words "Licht verdunkle" and so on. Meanwhile the *Frühlingslied* has the most active outdoor life, with a sturdy heart. Although the *Morgengruß* outdoes it in terms of characteristic coloring, by virtue of that quality [i.e., outdoorsiness] it might nevertheless turn out to be the most widely known of all.

F. MENDELSSOHN-BARTHOLDY, OP. 71.   SECHS LIEDER MIT BEGLEITUNG DES PIANOFORTE.—LEIPZIG, BREITKOPF U. HÖRTEL [*sic*]. PR. 25 NGR.[2]

Emanuel Klitzsch; translated by Douglass Seaton

In these songs the master shows us no new side; they are written in the same spirit that we already know from the earlier volumes. On the contrary, it would seem to us as if the sentiment has lost freshness, reflection plays too great a part, and formality, the tidy, harmonic decoration, the selectivity of the accompanying figures constitute the predominant element. The conception and the spirit of these songs are certainly noble throughout, yet not of such striking effect that the listener will be instantly moved. The two songs by Lenau, numbers 4 and 5, *Schilflied* and *Auf der Wanderschaft,* certainly aspire to high, poetic expression, yet the deep, melancholy tendency of the poet, the sentiment that for inward reasons is more inclined to submerge itself and only allows its protective outer covering to be gently shaken off, is only partially achieved by the musical expression. The last song, number 6, *Nachtlied* by Eichendorff, on the other hand, is of moving effect and immediate sentiment. A sense of apprehension pervades the whole. The song flows from a high devotion, a mood in which the truth of feeling speaks more powerfully. Mendelssohn remained, as always, within the formal; progress toward our point of the view did not make an impression on him. Repetitions appear everywhere, except in number 3, *An die Entfernte* by Lenau, a song that will win friends by virtue of its sensible, charming nature.

NOTES

1. *Neue Zeitschrift für Musik* 12/32 (17 April 1840), 126. Oswald Lorenz (1806–1889) was a regular reviewer of vocal music for the *Neue Zeitschrift* and other musical journals, as well as a song composer himself. He served briefly as the *Neue Zeitschrift*'s interim editor after Schumann gave up the position, to be succeeded by Franz Brendel.

2. *Neue Zeitschrift für Musik* 18/35 (29 April 1848), 213. Karl Emanuel Klitzsch (1812–1889) was educated in Leipzig and became a teacher at the Gynmasium in Zwickau, where he also worked as a church music director and choral conductor.

12

Mendelssohn's Works: Prolegomenon to a Comprehensive Inventory

John Michael Cooper

Among the most pressing desiderata facing Mendelssohn scholarship is a complete and reliable inventory of the composer's oeuvre, preferably in the form of a thematic catalog similar to Wolfgang Schmieder's Bach *Werkverzeichnis* or Franz Trenner's catalog of the works of Richard Strauss (which are problematic in many of the same regards as those of Mendelssohn). Several nineteenth-century efforts at such a listing survive; unfortunately, however, these inventories are also conspicuously incomplete.[1]

Among these early work lists, four deserve special attention. The composer himself prepared inventories of his compositions in 1836 and 1844, but these lists are by title only and in some instances provide erroneous information, as do three inventories published during the composer's lifetime.[2] In 1848 the Leipzig attorney Konrad Schleinitz (1802–1881), a close friend of Mendelssohn, prepared the first posthumous thematic catalog of the volumes present in the estate at that time for purposes of tax valuation; this inventory survives in at least two manuscript copies bearing supplemental annotations added between ca. 1849 and 1880.[3] The earliest posthumously published catalogs were prepared by the composer's longtime friend Julius Rietz (1812–1877), who published a thematic catalog in numerous editions under the auspices of Breitkopf and Härtel from 1853 onward and appended a "Verzeichnis der sämmtlichen musicalischen Compositionen von Felix Mendelssohn Bartholdy" to the edition of the composer's letters prepared by Paul and Carl Mendelssohn Bartholdy beginning in 1863. Finally, Schleinitz's inventory was copied and copiously annotated by that venerable grandfather of Mendelssohn scholarship Sir George Grove. Grove published the first useful nonthematic work list, along with information on various Mendelssohn manuscripts, in the entry for the composer in the early editions of his *Dictionary*, as well as several other articles.[4]

More modern contributions toward a summary overview of the Mendelssohn oeuvre include Eric Werner's list for *Die Musik in Geschichte und Gegenwart*; Philip Radcliffe's inventory in his biography of Mendelssohn, enlarged and corrected by Peter Ward Jones in 1990; Rainer Riehn's overview in the Mendelssohn volume of *Musik-Konzepte*; Eveline Bartlitz's work list for the *New Grove Dictionary*; and the enlarged and corrected counterpart of Bartlitz's list by R. Larry Todd in *The New Grove Early Romantic Masters 2*.[5] An important new contribution, provided in the 1997 volume of the Berlin *Mendelssohn-Studien*, is Hans-Günter Klein's inventory of the Mendelssohn autographs held in the Staatsbibliothek zu Berlin—Preußischer Kulturbesitz.[6] Although Klein's inventory addresses the challenges posed by the Berlin holdings with unprecedented success, scholars attempting to confront the Mendelssohn oeuvre as a whole still face a number of problems that both stem from the richness of the composer's musical legacy and account for the inadequacies of previous attempts to summarize it. The present Chapter offers an overview of these problems and a new listing of Mendelssohn's works, their editions, and their manuscript sources.

THE TASK

Any work list that attempts to summarize Mendelssohn's oeuvre according to traditional criteria must address a complex of issues seldom encountered collectively in the works of other composers. First of all, though Mendelssohn's prolificness and his constant self-criticism resulted in a substantial number of works left unpublished at his death, the approximately forty works published posthumously by his heirs bear, to most observers, no clear distinction in authority from that of the works he actually opted to publish. What is more, the posthumous publications often carry misleading titles and opus numbers. Thus, to the modern reader there is no indication that all works bearing opus numbers higher than 72 were published without (or rather, contrary to) the composer's permission: in the absence of a designation such as "Op. posth." the *Lauda Sion*, composed in 1846 and published in a seriously flawed edition in 1849 as Op. 73, might be taken to bear as much authority as *Elijah* (Op. 70) or the last works Mendelssohn saw through to press, the piano miniatures first published as Op. 72 late in 1847 (the so-called Christmas Pieces). *Tu es Petrus*, composed in 1827 but published in 1868 as Op. 111, might be taken as a document of Mendelssohn's late style, even though it belongs to a group of early sacred works that he consistently referred to as *Jugend-* or *Knabenarbeiten*. Still more problematic are the posthumously published symphonies. The works in this genre published as nos. 4 and 5 (Opp. 90 and 107) actually were composed between the First and Second Symphonies (opp. 11 and 52); yet most concertgoers naturally assume that the work presented to them as Mendelssohn's Fifth Symphony postdates that presented as his Fourth and that the Fourth Symphony postdates the Second and Third. In fact, the very opposite is true.

Second, because of Mendelssohn's penchant for revising his own works (reminiscent of the work patterns of his role model Goethe), some compositions are transmitted in numerous manuscripts, not all of them dated, that vary considerably from one to the other. Consequently, determining a definitive *Fassung letzter Hand* can be quite complicated, especially since manuscripts continue to come to light.

Third, there is the disposition of the manuscripts themselves. Mendelssohn himself periodically had many of his autographs bound, and after his death his family and friends began collecting the letters and musical autographs not included in the bound volumes already available. The heirs donated the majority of the music manuscripts to the Königliche-Preußische Bibliothek, Berlin,[7] in forty-four numbered, bound volumes in 1878, and this musical *Nachlaß* was subsequently augmented to comprise sixty-one volumes.[8] The circumstances of the musical *Nachlaß* are still not entirely sorted out: some volumes were demonstrably bound by the composer[9] while others are clearly posthumous assemblages[10] and others remain open to question. Most (vols. 1–5, 17–23, 25–31, 42, 45–50, and 56–60, as well as the organ part for vol. 51) are still held in the Staatsbibliothek zu Berlin; another seventeen (vols. 32–42, 44, 53–55, the score from vol. 51, and the unnumbered volume containing the Violin Concerto) are held in the Biblioteca Jagiellońska, Kraków; and four more (vols. 16, 24, 43, and 52) are otherwise dispersed.[11] In addition, some manuscripts were obtained by the composer's heirs, and, together with numerous autographs not obtained by them, these are now found around the globe, from Stockholm to Tokyo. A sizable number of these are in the Bodleian Library, Oxford, to which most of the composer's incoming correspondence and various other family papers have been donated by descendants and friends of the family.[12] Other collections exist in Darmstadt, Frankfurt am Main, Leipzig, London, New York, and Paris.[13]

Finally, classification of Mendelssohn's works is impeded by the composer's predilection for creating generic hybrids; traditional generic classifications are often ill suited for arranging his compositions in a fashion also consistent with the works' musical style. Setting aside Mendelssohn's two most important generic innovations, the *Lieder ohne Worte* and the programmatic concert overtures, the classic examples of this difficulty are the *Lobgesang* and *Die erste Walpurgisnacht*, Opp. 52 and 60. Musically and stylistically the two belong to same genre, although they are textually separated along the sacred/secular axis. Yet Op. 52 is designated a symphony-cantata and implicitly numbered between the C-minor and A-minor symphonies, while Op. 60 is generally considered a secular cantata, which places it in the company of, for example, the "Humboldt" cantata (1828), with which it shares few musical/stylistic links.

In short, because of these difficulties a work list of the present size and scope cannot provide a comprehensive inventory of the manuscripts for Mendelssohn's works. Rather, this inventory incorporates philological information within a framework oriented toward two more attainable goals: first, to provide an inventory of works that clearly distinguishes between works that the composer saw fit to publish and those that he withheld; and second, to identify, for the first time, numerous smaller compositions originally intended as constituent parts of larger works but ultimately suppressed.

To these ends, the work list is organized not according to the usual generic divisions but primarily around a division of sacred versus secular works, since for the increasingly secular nineteenth century this dichotomy is far less ambiguous than, for example, in Bach's oeuvre (where even secular works generally had considerable sacred connotations). Within these two broad categories the works are grouped according to their scoring and generic designation. Within each grouping, the works published by Mendelssohn are given in chronological order *according to date of publication*,[14] since the composer's decision to publish presumably indicates that the latest version of a work had achieved the status of more-or-less definitive authority in his estimation. These works are then followed by unpublished and posthumously published ones—arranged chronologically according to date of conception, since Mendelssohn granted no particular final authority to any single version by releasing it for publication. Undated works within a genre or grouping are listed alphabetically according to title at the end of each grouping. Mendelssohn's composition exercises, already cataloged elsewhere and of peripheral importance for this list, are not included here.[15]

While the history of Mendelssohn research and the nearly continual reemergence of sources previously unknown or considered lost clearly indicates that any work list dealing with sources will inevitably contain errors and incompletenesses,[16] gratitude is due to a number of Mendelssohn scholars whose additions, corrections, and suggestions have helped to make this work list as complete and accurate as possible. I wish to thank Hans-Günter Klein, Richard MacNutt, Douglass Seaton, Jeffrey Sposato, R. Larry Todd, Peter Ward Jones, and Ralf Wehner for their invaluable assistance in these matters. Although the perpetually changing state of Mendelssohn sources renders any comprehensive inventory provisional from the moment of its appearance, these scholars have gone to considerable pains to ensure that this list serves Mendelssohn scholarship optimally until it is superseded by another work list and/or the much-needed thematic catalog.

The following information is provided in the entries:

1. Title (as the work is generally known in the English-speaking world, with other common designations given in brackets);
2. Scoring;
3. Publication information (city, publisher, and date) for significant editions. Although complete publication histories are not possible in an inventory of the present size and scope, I have generally included: (1) the first German, English, and (in certain relevant cases) French editions, leading up to the work's publication in score; (2) the work's location in the so-called *Gesamtausgabe* edited by Julius Rietz and/or the more recent *Leipziger Ausgabe*; and (3) important subsequent editions. Except where otherwise indicated, "edn." refers to the simultaneous publication of score and/or parts and/or piano(-vocal) scores,

as relevant. Excerpts and arrangements published separately during Mendelssohn's lifetime (e.g., the many arrangements and editions of the "War March of the Priests" from *Athalie*) are identified only when they preceded publication of the complete work.

4. For most works, the principal manuscript sources, with locations identified according to international *RISM* sigla. Entries are provided in the following order: sketches—drafts—dated manuscripts (autographs and copyists' manuscripts, arranged according to the latest date given in each manuscript)—undated manuscripts. Manuscripts contained in the volumes of the *Mendelssohn Nachlaß* are identified by volume number (e.g., MN 1); in general, no attempt is made to distinguish the authority of the manuscript sources;
5. Principal facsimiles or facsimile editions;
6. Brief commentary on larger and more important works; and
7. Brief overview of some secondary literature pertaining to the work.

Abbreviations Used

Bibliographic abbreviations and abbreviations concerning instruments and instrumentation conform to those used in the *New Grove*. Libraries are identified according to international *RISM* sigla, and in most cases shelfmarks or other identifying information are included. For some of the leading collections the following specific abbreviations are employed:

D-B MN [x]: Staatsbibliothek zu Berlin—Preußischer Kulturbesitz, Mus.ms.autogr. F. Mendelssohn Bartholdy [x]. These manuscripts and volumes of manuscripts belonged to the former *Mendelssohn Nachlaß*. (Readers requesting the manuscripts should use the full modern shelfmark rather than the "MN" abbreviation.)

PL-Kj MN [x]: Volume of the former *Mendelssohn Nachlaß* held in the Biblioteca Jagiellońska in Kraków

MA: Item held in Mendelssohn-Archiv of Staatsbibliothek zu Berlin—Preußischer Kulturbesitz

MG: Item held in the deposits of the Mendelssohn-Gesellschaft in MA

GB: "Green books" collection of the Bodleian Library, Oxford

MDM: Item held in the M. Deneke Mendelssohn collection of the Bodleian Library, Oxford

Except where otherwise indicated, the sources listed are scores. Types of sources are identified by the following abbreviations:

R: Felix Mendelssohn Bartholdy, *Werke*, ed. Julius Rietz (Leipzig: Breitkopf & Härtel, 1874–1877)

L: *Leipziger Ausgabe der Werke Felix Mendelssohn Bartholdys*, ed. Internationale Felix-Mendelssohn-Gesellschaft (Leipzig: 1960–   )

A: autograph manuscript

C: contemporary copyist's manuscript[17]

C/A: contemporary copyist's manuscript with autograph entries, annotations, or corrections

FS: full score
PS: piano score or piano-vocal score
sk, skk: sketch, sketches
dr, drr: draft, drafts
inc: denotes a manuscript that begins at the beginning but breaks off before the end
frag: denotes a manuscript that evidently is removed from another one (i.e., begins somewhere other than at the beginning) of a work or movement

CONTENTS OF THE LIST

SECULAR WORKS

Stage Works Published by Mendelssohn

General literature: Eduard Devrient, *Meine Erinnerungen an Felix Mendelssohn-Bartholdy und seine Briefe an mich* (Leipzig: J. J. Weber, 1869); John Warrack, "Mendelssohn's Operas," in *Music and Theatre: Essays in Honour of Winton Dean*, ed. Nigel Fortune (Cambridge: Cambridge University Press, 1987), 263–97.

Die Hochzeit des Camacho, Op. 10 (opera in two acts). Libretto: F. Voigts, after Cervantes, *Don Quixote*. Edn: Berlin: Laue, [1828] (PS, arr. by Mendelssohn); R xv (FS). Mss: D-B MN 12 (A FS, 10 August 1825), D-B Mus.ms. 14310 (C/A FS; [1827]), D-B Mus.ms. 14310/5 (excerpts—C/A FS); GB-Ob MDM e.16 (libretto).

Remarks: Produced in Berlin, 29 April 1827. The authorship of the libretto has been the subject of considerable debate. Devrient refers only to "Klingemann," possibly meaning August Klingemann (not Mendelssohn's friend Carl), who authored the libretto for a Berlin production by the same title in 1811; more recently, Rudolf Elvers has shown that the author was the Hanover writer Friedrich Voigts.[18]

Literature: Rudolf Elvers, *"Nichts ist so schwer gut zu componiren als Strophen": Zur Entstehungsgeschichte des Librettos von Felix Mendelssohns Oper "Die Hochzeit des Camacho,"* mit dem Faksimile eines Briefes von Mendelssohn (Berlin: Mendelssohn-Gesellschaft, 1976).

Incidental Music to Sophocles's *Antigone*, Op. 55 (ch, orch). Edn: London: Ewer, [1843] (vocal parts and PS, choruses only); Leipzig: Kistner, [1843] (vocal parts and PS, choruses only), [1844] (PS, complete), [1851] (FS); R xv. Mss: D-B MN 19 (skk), D-B MN 20 (skk, misc. pages in score), GB-Ob MDM c.4 (choruses—A PS; 4 February 1842), D-B N.Mus.ms. 20 (C/A FS; 1843), D-B MN 56/2 (overture—A FS), D-B Depos. Berlin Ms. 4 (A PS 4 hands), D-B N.Mus.ms. 7 (C/A PS), GB-Ob GB XVI, 209c-d (dialogues).

Remarks: First produced in Potsdam, 28 October 1841.

Literature: A. M. Little, *Mendelssohn's Music to the Antigone of Sophocles* (Washington, DC: Gibson, 1893); Michael P. Steinberg, "The Incidental Politics to Mendelssohn's *Antigone*," in *Mendelssohn and His World*, ed. R. Larry Todd (Princeton: Princeton University Press, 1991), 138–57; Peter Andraschke, "Felix Mendelssohns *Antigone*," in *Felix Mendelssohn Bartholdy: Kongreß-Bericht Berlin 1994*, ed. Christian Martin Schmidt (Wiesbaden: Breitkopf & Härtel, 1997), 141–66.

Incidental Music to Shakespeare's *A Midsummer Night's Dream*, Op. 61 (solo vv, ch, orch). Edn: Leipzig: Breitkopf & Härtel, [1844] (PS 4 hands by Mendelssohn and PS—both excerpts only; words in German); London: Ewer,

[1844] (PS 4 hands by Mendelssohn; words in English) and [1845] (complete PS without texts); Leipzig: Breitkopf & Härtel, [1848] (FS); R xv. Mss: D-B MN 19 (skk), D-DS Mus.ms. 1002 (A PS; 1844), GB-Lbl Eg. 2955 (Scherzo, Notturno, Wedding March—A PS; 1844), PL-Kj MN 33 (A FS), location unknown (lacking Overture, Notturno, and Wedding March—C/A PS 4 hands; auctioned by Sotheby's on 6 December 1996), GB-Ob MDM c.57 (Intermezzo—C PS 4 hands), GB-Lbl MS eg 2955 (A PS 4 hands; Scherzo, Nocturne, Wedding March).

Remarks: Combined with concert overture, Op. 21 (see later). First produced in Potsdam, 14 October 1843.

Literature: Franz Liszt, "Über Mendelssohns Musik zum 'Sommernachtstraum,'" *Neue Zeitschrift für Musik* 40 (1854), 233–37; Friedhelm Krummacher, "'. . . fein und geistreich genug': Versuch über Mendelssohns Musik zum *Sommernachtstraum*," in *Das Problem Mendelssohn*, ed. Carl Dahlhaus (Regensburg: Bosse, 1974), 89–117; R. Larry Todd, *Mendelssohn: "The Hebrides" and Other Overtures* (Cambridge: Cambridge University Press, 1994).

Stage Works Unpublished or Posthumously Published

General literature: Devrient, *Erinnerungen*; Georg Schünemann, "Mendelssohns Jugendopern," *Zeitschrift für Musikwissenschaft* 5 (1923), 506–45; John Warrack, "Mendelssohn's Operas."

Quel bonheur pour mon coeur (dramatic scene for S and T, orch). Text: ? Ms: D-B MN 1[19] (A FS; [1820]).

Ich, J. Mendelssohn (Lustspiel in 3 scenes). Text: ? Ms: D-B MN 1 (A FS, inc; [1820]).

Remarks: Evidently never performed, though Schünemann ("Mendelssohns Jugendopern," 509) speculates that it may have been given on Abraham Mendelssohn's birthday.

Die Soldatenliebschaft (comic opera in 1 act). Libretto: J. L. Casper. Mss: D-B MN 7 (A FS; [30 November 1820)], GB-Ob MDM c.59, (C/A FS), GB-Ob MDM e.12 (libretto).

Remarks: Performed at the Mendelssohn home in Berlin with pf accompaniment on 11 December 1820, and with orchestra on 3 February 1821.

Literature: Karl-Heinz Köhler, "Zwei rekonstruierbare Singspiele von Felix Mendelssohn Bartholdy," *Beiträge zur Musikwissenschaft* 2 (1960), 86–93.

Die beiden Pädagogen (Singspiel in 1 act). Libretto: J. L. Casper, after Scribe, *Les deux précepteurs*. Edn: L v. Mss: D-B MN 8 (A FS; 24 January–14 March 1821), D-DÜh Ms. 53.79 (A PS 4-hands, Overture and duet "Ah, mich so zu kränken"), F-Pc Ms. 189 (terzetto—A; 1821), GB-Ob MDM b.7 (C/A FS; February 1821), GB-Ob MDM e.13/1 (libretto), GB-OB MDM e.13/2 (libretto, mostly in hand of Fanny Hensel).

Remarks: Performed in Berlin with piano accompaniment for Lea Mendelssohn Bartholdy's birthday on 15 March 1821, in April 1821, with string quintet accompaniment, and again in early 1822.

Literature: Köhler, "Zwei rekonstruierbare Singspiele."

Die wandernden Komödianten (comic opera in 1 act). Libretto: J. L. Casper. Mss: D-B MN 9 (A FS; 30 November 1821; Overture dated at end 9 December 1821), GB-Ob MDM e.14 (libretto).

Remarks: Rehearsed in Berlin, 8 March 1822.

Die beiden Neffen, oder der Onkel aus Boston (comic opera in 3 acts). Libretto: J. L. Casper. Mss: D-B MN 10–11 (A FS; 6 November 1823), GB-Ob MDM e.15 (libretto, acts 1 and 2 only).

Remarks: Rehearsed in Berlin, 3 February 1824.

Literature: Karl-Heinz Köhler, "Das Jugendwerk Felix Mendelssohns: Die vergessene Kindheitsentwicklung eines Genies," *Deutsches Jahrbuch der Musikwissenschaft* 7 (1962), 18–35.

[Die Heimkehr] aus der Fremde [Son and Stranger], Op. 89 (Liederspiel in 1 act). Libretto: Carl Klingemann. Edn: Leipzig: Breitkopf & Härtel [1851] (PS by Mendelssohn); London: Ewer, [1851] (PS, words by Henry F. Chorley); R xv. Mss: location unknown (auctioned by ?Drond, Paris, 8 April 1992—A FS; 12 December 1829), US-NYpm Lehman (A FS; 19 December 1829), US-NYp JOE 72-7 (aria "Wenn die Abendglocken läuten"—A PS; 31 December 1829), US-Wc (bass aria—C PS; based on 16 January 1833), US-NYpm Heineman Ms. 143 (A PS), D-DÜhi (overture—A PS), US-NYpm Heineman Ms. 143a (C/A PS), GB-Ob MDM c.44 (C/A), GB-Ob MDM b.6 (orchestra parts for overture and nos. 1–14, some in Mendelssohn's hand), US-Wc (libretto, with changes in Mendelssohn's hand).

Remarks: Performed in the Mendelssohn home in Berlin, 26 December 1829.

Literature: Thomas Krettenauer, *Felix Mendelssohn Bartholdys "Heimkehr aus der Fremde": Untersuchungen und Dokumente zum Liederspiel op. 89* (Augsburg: Wißner, 1994).

Incidental Music to Caldéron de la Barca's *The Steadfast Prince [Der standhafte Prinz]*. Mss: D-B MN 56/1 (A FS; 18 March 1833), D-B MN 42 (C FS).

Remarks: Still unpublished, this is the earliest known incidental music by a composer whose renown rests in no small part on his incidental music to *A Midsummer Night's Dream*, Op. 61. It was performed in Düsseldorf on 9 April 1833 to accompany Karl Immermann's translation/adaptation of Caldéron's play *El principe constante*, though only A. W. Schlegel's substantially different translation was at Mendelssohn's disposal during the work's composition.

Literature: Joseph Esser, "Felix Mendelssohn-Bartholdy und die Rheinlande" (Diss., University of Bonn, 1923).

Incidental Music to Victor Hugo's *Ruy Blas*. Edn: Leipzig: Kistner [1851](PS 4 hands and FS—overture only), [1853] (PS—Lied, Op. 77 no. 3); London:

Ewer, [1851] (PS 4 hands—overture only); R xviii. Mss: D-B MN 31 (Lied [chorus or 6–8 women's voices with string accompaniment] also published as Op. 77 no. 3—A FS; MN 31, 14 February 1839), D-B MN 31 (overture—A FS; 8 March 1839), US-NYpm Heineman MS 144a (Chor der Wäscherinnen—A PS).

Remarks: The overture was published separately by Leipzig: Kistner, and London: Ewer, [1851] (see Op. 95, later).

Incidental Music to Sophocles's *Oedipus at Colonos*, Op. 93. Edn: Leipzig: Breitkopf & Härtel, [1851] (PS and vocal parts), [1852] (FS and orch parts for overture); London: Ewer, [1851] (PS and vocal parts, words by W. Bartholomew); R xv. Mss: location unknown (25 February 1845), GB-Ob MDM c.96 (C/A ?PS, 2 August 1846), PL-Kj MN 40 (C PS), GB-Ob MDM b.6 (C, vocal parts), location unknown (auctioned by Sotheby's, 1985—C/A FS; "Zur rossprangenden Flur" only), I-R private possession (A PS, [December 1846]; "Zur rossprangenden Flur" and "Ach wär' ich, wo bald die Schaar der Feinde" only).

Remarks: Produced at Potsdam, 1 November 1845.

Incidental Music to Racine's *Athalie*, Op. 74. Edn: London: Ewer, [1848] (PS); Leipzig: Breitkopf & Härtel, [1848/49] (PS, PS 4 hands, parts for overture, and FS); R xv. Mss: D-B MN 19 (skk), PL-Kj MN 38[2] (choruses—A PS, May 1843), PL-Kj MN 39 (final chorus—A FS; 16 April 1844), PL-Kj MN 38[1] (A FS; 13 June 1844 [overture], final chorus [14 June 1844] with corrections dated 12 November 1845, text in French and German), D-B MA Ms. 4 (final chorus—A PS), GB-Ob MDM b.6 (vocal parts—C), location unknown (auctioned by Christie's London on 29 May 1986 FS and PS—C by Julius Rietz), GB-Ob MDM c.27 (libretto—C).

Remarks: Produced at Berlin-Charlottenburg, 1 December 1845.

Die Lorelei, Op. 98 (opera in 3 acts, frag). Libretto: E. Geibel. Edn: Leipzig: Breitkopf & Härtel [1852] (PS, PS without words, PS 4 hands without words); London: Ewer, [1852] (PS and PS 4 hands—finale to act 1 only; English texts by W. Bartholomew), [1868] (PS and PS 4 hands—"Ave Maria" and "Winzer-Chor" only, published individually); Leipzig: Rieter-Biederman (PS and PS 4 hands—"Ave Maria" and "Winzer-Chor" only, published individually); R xv. Mss: PL-Kj MN 44 (A FS [ca. August 1847]), GB-Ob MDM c.53 (no. 3, scene vii, and finale—C PS by Julius Rietz), GB-Ob GB XXVII, 97 (libretto—C/A).

Remarks: The Kraków autograph transmits some musical numbers not included in the Rietz edition.

Literature: Reinhold Sietz, "Die musikalische Gestaltung der Loreleysage bei Max Bruch, Felix Mendelssohn und Ferdinand Hiller," in *Max-Bruch-Studien: zum 50. Todestag des Komponisten*, ed. Dietrich Kämper (Cologne: Arno Volk, 1970), 14–45; R. Larry Todd, "On Mendelssohn's Operatic Destiny: *Die Lorelei* Reconsidered," in *Felix Mendelssohn Bartholdy:*

Kongreß-Bericht Berlin 1994, ed. Christian Martin Schmidt (Wiesbaden: Breitkopf & Härtel, 1997), 113–40.

Orchestral Works Published by Mendelssohn

General Literature: R. Larry Todd, "The Instrumental Music of Felix Mendelssohn-Bartholdy: Selected Studies Based on Primary Sources" (Ph.D. diss., Yale University, 1979); Wulf Konold, *Die Symphonien Felix Mendelssohn Bartholdys: Untersuchungen zu Werkgestalt und Formstruktur* (Laaber: Laaber Verlag, 1992); Bärbel Pelker, *Die deutsche Konzertouvertüre (1825–1865): Werkkatalog und Rezeptionsdokumente* (Frankfurt am Main: Peter Lang, 1993); William Lyle Pelto, "Musical Structure and Extramusical Meaning in the Concert Overtures of Mendelssohn" (Ph.D. diss., University of Texas at Austin, 1993); R. Larry Todd, "The Symphonies and Overtures of Mendelssohn," in *The Nineteenth-Century Symphony*, ed. D. Kern Holoman (New York: Schirmer, 1997); Thomas Christian Schmidt, *Die ästhetischen Grundlagen der Instrumentalmusik Felix Mendelssohn Bartholdys* (Stuttgart: M & P Verlag für Wissenschaft und Forschung, 1996); Wolfram Steinbeck, "'Der klärende Wendepunkt in Felix' Leben': Zu Mendelssohns Konzertouvertüren," in *Felix Mendelssohn Bartholdy: Kongreß-Bericht Berlin 1994*, ed. Christian Martin Schmidt (Wiesbaden: Breitkopf & Härtel, 1997), 232–56.

Symphony no. 1 in C minor, Op. 11 (orch). Edn: London: Cramer, Addison, & Beale, [1830] (PS 4 hands with vn, vc ad lib); Berlin: Schlesinger, [1834] (parts and PS 4 hands, and PS of Allegro only), [1847/48] (FS); R i. Mss: US-Wc ML 30.8j Op. 11 (A PS 4 hands with parts for vn, vc ad lib; 1829), GB-Lbl RPS MS.289 (A FS), GB-Ob MDM d.57 (C FS [probably originally MN 24]), GB-Lbl g.703 (arr. of scherzo from Octet Op. 20—C FS; after 1857).

Remarks: First performed in Berlin in 1824, this first-published of Mendelssohn's mature symphonies was widely acclaimed in its day and was one of the first works to establish him as a composer of international standing. Mendelssohn revised the 1824 version for his trip to England in 1829, in the process substituting an orchestrated version of the Scherzo from the String Octet, Op. 20, for the original Minuet (which itself was adapted from the C-minor Viola Sonata of 1824). The manuscript sources of the full score include both Minuet and Scherzo. The first English edition (1830) included only the Scherzo, while the 1834 Schlesinger edition included only the Minuet; subsequent editions have included only the Minuet.

Literature: Wulf Konold, "Opus 11 und Opus 107: Analytische Bemerkungen zu zwei unbekannten Sinfonien Felix Mendelssohn Bartholdys," in *Felix Mendelssohn Bartholdy*, ed. Heinz-Klaus Metzger and Rainer Riehn, *Musik-Konzepte* 14/15 (Munich: text+kritik, 1980), 8–28; Greg Vitercik, *The Early Works of Felix Mendelssohn: A Study in the Romantic Sonata Style* (Philadelphia: Gordon and Breach, 1992).

Overture to *A Midsummer Night's Dream*, Op. 21 [*Ein Sommernachtstraum*] (orch). Edn: London: Cramer, Addison, & Beale, [1832](PS 4 hands by Mendelssohn and parts); Leipzig: Breitkopf & Härtel, [1832] (PS 4 hands by Mendelssohn and parts), [1833/34] (PS),[1835] (FS); R ii. Mss: PL-Kj MN 32 (A FS; 6 August 1826), US-Ws MS 6256 (A PS 4 hands; 10 July [1832]), GB-Ob MDM b.5 (A FS, inc.), D-LEst Nr. 6705, Bestand "Breitkopf & Härtel" (C/A PS).

Remarks: In 1843 Mendelssohn drew upon the overture in writing the incidental music for a Potsdam performance of Shakespeare's play (see Op. 61 under "Stage Works," earlier). Mendelssohn intended this overture to be published with *The Hebrides* and *Calm Sea and Prosperous Voyage* under a single opus number.

Literature: George Grove, "Mendelssohn's Overture to 'A Midsummer Night's Dream,'" *The Musical Times* 44 (1903), 728–38; Heinrich Wirth, "Natur und Märchen in Webers 'Oberon,' Mendelssohns 'Ein Sommernachtstraum' und Nicolais `Die lustigen Weiber von Windsor,'" in *Syntagma Musicologicum: Festschrift Friedrich Blume zum 70. Geburtstag*, ed. Martin Ruhnke and Anna Amalie Abert (Kassel: Bärenreiter, 1963), 389–97; Todd, *"The Hebrides" and Other Overtures*.

Capriccio brillant, Op. 22 (pf, orch). Edn: Leipzig: Breitkopf & Härtel, London: Mori & Lavenue [1832] (parts and PS serving as pf solo arr.), Leipzig: Breitkopf & Härtel, [1843] (PS 4 hands), idem [1862] (FS); R viii. Mss: F-Pc Ms. 195 (pf only—A; 18 September 1831), D-DS Mus.Ms. 1000 (A FS, 18 May 1832).

Remarks: The Paris manuscript for this work reveals that it was conceived as a composition for piano solo. The work was also known as "Rondo brillante" in many early editions.

Literature: Marian Wilson, "Felix Mendelssohn's Works for Solo Piano and Orchestra: Sources and Composition" (Ph.D. diss., Florida State University, 1993); Stephan D. Lindeman, "Structural Novelty and Tradition in the Early Romantic Piano Concerto" (Ph.D. diss., Rutgers University, 1995).

Concerto no. 1 in G minor for Piano and Orchestra, Op. 25 (pf, orch). Edn: London: Mori & Lavenue, [1832], and Leipzig: Breitkopf & Härtel, [1833] (parts); idem, [1862] (FS); R viii. Mss: D-B MN 18 (sk), US-NY private collection of Lillian Kallir (orchestra only—A FS), GB-Ob MDM c.57 (parts for vn 1 and vc/cb only—C, probably from Munich premiere).

Literature: Wilson, "Piano and Orchestra."

The Hebrides Overture, Op. 26 [*Die Hebriden*] (orch). Edn: Leipzig: Breitkopf & Härtel, London: Mori & Lavenue, [1833] (PS 4 hands by Mendelssohn), [1834] (parts and PS), idem [1835] (FS); R ii. Mss: US-NYp *MNY (sk in letter of 7–11 August 1829), GB-Ob MDM c.47 (skk for recapitulation and coda; ca. October–November 1830), US-NYpm Lehman (A FS; 16 December 1830; complete facsimile—Hugo von Mendelssohn Bartholdy, ed., *Felix*

Mendelssohn Bartholdy, Die Hebriden: First Version of the Concert-Overture [Basel: Amerbach, 1947]), D-Dl Mus. 5543-N-507 (C FS of first version by Eduard Rietz, [December 1830–January 1831]), GB-Ob MS. Horsley b.1 (A PS 4 hands; 19 June 1832), private possession (A FS; 20 June 1832), GB-Lbl RPS Ms. Loan 4.778 (C FS; ca. 1832), GB-Ob MDM d.58 (C/A FS), US-NYpm (C FS).

Remarks: First performed in London on 14 May 1832. The Overture exists in numerous versions and with numerous titles, including "Ouvertüre zur einsamen Insel," "Die Hebriden," "The Isles of Fingal," and "Fingal's Cave." Mendelssohn intended it to be published with the *Midsummer Night's Dream* and *Calm Sea and Prosperous Voyage* Overtures under a single opus number.

Literature: Gerald Abraham, "The Scores of Mendelssohn's 'Hebrides,'" *Monthly Musical Record* 78 (1948), 172–76; Ernest Walker, "Mendelssohn's 'Die einsame Insel,'" *Music and Letters* 26 (1954), 148–50; R. Larry Todd, "Of Seagulls and Counterpoint: The Early Versions of Mendelssohn's *Hebrides* Overture," *19th-Century Music* 2 (1979), 197–213; Todd, *The "Hebrides" and Other Overtures*; Peter Ward Jones, "Mendelssohn Scores in the Library of the Royal Philharmonic Society," in *Felix Mendelssohn Bartholdy: Kongreß-Bericht Berlin 1994*, ed. Christian Martin Schmidt (Wiesbaden: Breitkopf & Härtel, 1997), 64–75.

Calm Sea and Prosperous Voyage Overture [*Meeresstille und glückliche Fahrt*] (orch), Op. 27. Edn: Leipzig: Breitkopf & Härtel, and London: Mori & Lavenue [1835] (PS, PS 4 hands, parts, and score); R ii. Mss: GB-Ob MDM b.5 (sk), GB-Ob MDM b.5 (A FS, inc), D-AMms 6/1 (parts—C, 1838), US-NYpm Cary 62 (A FS), US-NYpm Cary 75 (A FS), D-LEsm (FS proofs with extensive autograph corrections and changes), location unknown (auctioned by J. A. Stargardt, 1981—A FS frag), CH-E 37,8 (C FS).

Remarks: First performed in Berlin, 8 June 1828. Based on two poems by Goethe, this overture was revised in 1834 for planned inclusion with the *Midsummer Night's Dream* and *Hebrides* Overtures as a trilogy of concert overtures published under a single opus number.

Literature: Todd, *The "Hebrides" and Other Overtures*; Lawrence Kramer, "*Felix culpa*: Mendelssohn, Goethe, and the Social Force of Musical Expression," in *Classical Music and Postmodern Knowledge* (Berkeley: University of California Press, 1995), 122–42.

Rondo brillant in E♭ major, Op. 29 (pf, orch). Edn: London: Mori & Lavenue, [1834] (parts); Leipzig: Breitkopf & Härtel, [1834/35] (parts), [1835] (PS 4 hands), [1865] (FS); R viii. Mss: D-B MN 28 (A FS, 29 January 1834), D-DS Mus.ms. 1003 (C/A FS; ca. 14 March 1834).

Literature: Wulf Konold, "Felix Mendelssohn Bartholdys *Rondo brillant* op. 29: Ein Beitrag zur Geschichte des einsätzigen Konzertstücks im 19. Jahrhundert," *Die Musikforschung* 38 (1985), 169–83; Wilson, "Piano and Orchestra."

The Fair Melusine Overture, Op. 32 [*Ouvertüre zum Mährchen der schönen Melusine*] (orch). Edn: Leipzig, Breitkopf & Härtel, [1836]; R ii. Mss: D-B MN 50 (A FS; 14 November 1833), US-NY private collection of Broude Brothers (A FS; 17 November 1835), GB-Lbl RPS MS. 4.779 (first version—C/A FS), A-Wn PhA 744 (C/A FS; 17 November 1835—second version), GB-Lbl (A PS; 21 January 1836), GB-Lbl (Breitkopf & Härtel edn of PS 4 hands, with autograph changes, dated 21 January 1836), A-Wgm A 198 (A PS 4 hands).

Remarks: Peter Ward Jones has recently shown that this work, not the *Calm Sea and Prosperous Voyage* Overture (as has previously been assumed), was probably the second of the two overtures offered by Mendelssohn to the Philharmonic Society of London on 27 April 1833.

Literature: Donald Mintz, "Melusine: A Mendelssohn Draft," *The Musical Quarterly* 43 (1957), 480–99; Peter Ward Jones, "Mendelssohn Scores in the Library of the Royal Philharmonic Society," 64–75.

Piano Concerto no. 2 in D minor, Op. 40 (pf, orch). Edn: London: Novello, [1838] (pf and string parts); Leipzig: Breitkopf & Härtel [1838] (pf and string parts), [1862] (FS); R viii. Mss: D-B MN 19 (skk), D-B MA Ms.3 (dr for first mvt), D-B MN 29 (piano only—A; 26 July 1837), D-B MN 29 (orchestra only—A FS, 5 August 1837), US-Wc (A correction sheets), US-NHbm (A PS), US-NYpm Koch (A pf part, serving as pf solo arr.)

Remarks: Composed during Mendelssohn's honeymoon trip in the summer of 1837, the D-minor Concerto was premiered in Birmingham on 21 September 1837, with the composer as soloist. The work remained quite popular for some time, especially in London (where it received some seventeen performances between 1838 and 1878); it has since lost ground to the G-minor Concerto, Op. 25. The complex source situation is indicative of the work's difficult compositional history.

Literature: Wilson, "Piano and Orchestra."

Serenade and Allegro giojoso, Op. 43 (pf, orch). Edn: London: Novello, [1839] (orch parts and pf part serving as pf solo arr.); Bonn: Simrock, [1839], [1860] (FS); R viii. Mss: D-B MN 19 (skk), D-B MN 30 (A FS; 1 April 1838), S-Smf (serenade only—A PS).

Literature: Wilson, "Piano and Orchestra."

Overture in C major for Wind Instruments, Op. 24 (wind insts/winds and perc). Edn: London: Cramer, Addison & Beale, [1839] (parts, PS, and PS 4 hands by C. Czerny); Bonn: Simrock, [1839] (parts, PS, and PS 4 hands by C. Czerny), [1852] (FS); R vii. Mss: D-B N.Mus.ms. 96 (first version for 11 winds—A FS; 27 June 1826), GB-Ob MDM c.24 (A PS 4 hands; Christmas 1838), S-Smf (A PS 4-hands).

Remarks: The version of 1824/1826 differs from the 1838 version primarily in length and orchestration. The former is scored for fl, 2 cl, 2 ob, 2 bn, 2 hn, tpt, and basshorn; the latter, for picc, fl, 4 cl, 2 ob, corno di bassetto, 2 bn, contrabassoon and basshorn, 4 hn, 2 tpt, 3 tbn, and perc.

Literature: David F. Reed, "The Original Version of the *Overture for Wind Band* of Felix Mendelssohn-Bartholdy," *Journal of Band Research* 18 (1982), 3–10.

[Symphony no. 2]. See *Lobgesang, eine Symphonie-Kantate nach Worten der heiligen Schrift*, Op. 52, under "Accompanied Secular Choral," later.

Symphony no. 3 in A minor, Op. 56 ("Scottish"). Edn: London: Ewer, [1842] (PS 4 hands, arr. by Mendelssohn); Leipzig: Breitkopf & Härtel [1842] (PS 4 hands, arr. by Mendelssohn), [1843] (score and parts); R i. Mss: D-B N.Mus.ms. 111 (sk; 30 July 1829), D-B MN 19 (skk), PL-Kj MN 36 (A FS; 20 January 1842), D-DS Mus.ms.1001 (A PS 4 hands; 1842), GB-Lbl Loan 4.291 (C FS; 1842—Royal Philharmonic Society), GB-Ob MDM c.22 (first movement—A FS, frag), US-Wc (FS proof sheets for first German edn, with changes and corrections in Mendelssohn's hand).

Remarks: The work's genesis, spanning some fourteen years from the well-known initial idea that befell the composer during his trip to Scotland in 1829 until publication in 1842, in many ways typifies Mendelssohn's compositional process: there are large-scale structural reworkings, refinements of motivic and thematic detail that enhance the sense of overall unity, and changes that clearly reflect the programmatic underpinnings.

Literature: Douglass Seaton, "A Draft for the Exposition of the First Movement of Mendelssohn's 'Scotch' Symphony," *Journal of the American Musicological Society* 30 (1977), 129–35; Rey M. Longyear, "Cyclic Form and Tonal Relationships in Mendelssohn's 'Scottish' Symphony," *In Theory Only* 4 (1979), 38–48; Peter Mercer-Taylor, "Mendelssohn's 'Scottish' Symphony and the Music of German Memory," *19th-Century Music* 19 (1995), 68–82.

Violin Concerto in E minor, Op. 64 (vn, orch). Edn: Leipzig: Breitkopf & Härtel, Milan: Ricordi [1845] (parts and PS with vn), [1851] (PS 4 hands), [1862] (score); R iv. Mss: D-B MN 19 (skk), GB-Ob MDM b.5 (skk), PL-Kj MN [unnumbered] (A; 16 September 1844; facsimile ed. H. C. Robbins Landon, Luigi Alberto Bianchi, and Franco Sciannameo [New York: Garland, 1991]), PL-Kj MN 39 (C FS by Henschke, with autograph corrections by Mendelssohn reflecting the revisions of the winter of 1844/1845).

Remarks: Closely related to an unfinished piano concerto in E minor drafted ca. 1842–1844 (see later). The Violin Concerto has enjoyed virtually uninterrupted popularity since its premiere in the Leipzig Gewandhaus on 13 March 1845.

Literature: George Grove, "Mendelssohn's Violin Concerto," *The Musical Times* 47 (1906), 611–15; Reinhard Gerlach, "Mendelssohns Kompositions-weise: Vergleich zwischen Skizzen und Letztfassung des Violinkonzerts op. 64," *Archiv für Musikwissenschaft* 28 (1971), 119–33; idem, "Mendelssohns schöpferische Erinnerung der 'Jugendzeit': die Beziehungen zwischen dem Violinkonzert, op. 64, und dem Oktett für Streicher, op. 20," *Die Musikforschung* 25 (1972), 142–52; idem, "Mendelssohns Kompositionsweise

(II): Weitere Vergleiche zwischen den Skizzen und der Letztfassung des Violinkonzerts op. 64," in *Das Problem Mendelssohn*, ed. Carl Dahlhaus (Regensburg: Bosse, 1974), 149–67; Douglass Seaton, "A Study of a Collection of Mendelssohn's Sketches and Other Autograph Material, Deutsche Staatsbibliothek Berlin *Mus. ms. autogr. Mendelssohn 19*" (Ph.D. diss., Columbia University, 1977); R. Larry Todd, "The Instrumental Music."

Orchestral Works Unpublished or Posthumously Published

General Literature: Helmut Christian Wolff, "Zur Erstausgabe von Mendelssohns Jugendsinfonien," *Deutsches Jahrbuch der Musikwissenschaft* 12 (1968), 96–115; Albert James Filosa Jr., "The Early Symphonies and Chamber Music of Felix Mendelssohn Bartholdy" (Ph.D. diss., Yale University, 1970).

[Concerto movement] ("Rezitativo—Allegro") in D minor (pf/str). Mss: D-B MN 1 (A pf part and FS; 7 March 1820), GB-Ob MDM b. 5 (string parts except for vn 1—A; 12 April 1820).

> Remarks: Pf part contains cues for strings, and the score's designation of "viole" and "bassi," as well as the indication of *divisi* violas in the GB-Ob part, suggest an orchestral work. (Previous work lists have identified the piece simply as a "Recitativo" for piano and strings and grouped it with Mendelssohn's chamber music.) There are discrepancies between the piano part and the string parts.

> Literature: R. Larry Todd, "The Instrumental Music."

Sinfonia no. 1 in C major (str). Edn: L i. Ms: D-B MN 3 (A FS; [before 5 September 1821]).

Sinfonia no. 2 in D major (str). Edn: L i. Ms: D-B MN 3 (A FS; [before 5 September 1821]).

Sinfonia no. 3 in E minor (str). Edn: L i. Mss: D-B MN 3 (A FS; [before 5 September 1821]), US-NYpm Lehman (A FS; 24 December 1821).

Sinfonia no. 4 in C minor (str). Edn: L i. Ms: D-B MN 3 (A FS; 5 September 1821).

Sinfonia no. 5 in B♭ major (str). Edn: L i. Ms: D-B MN 3 (A FS; 15 September 1821).

Sinfonia no. 6 in E♭ major (str). Edn: L I. Ms: D-B MN 3 (A FS; ?autumn 1821).

Sinfonia no. 7 in D minor (str). Ed.: L i. Ms: D-B MN 4 (A FS; ?1821–1822).

Sinfonia no. 8 in D major (str/orch). Edn: L i. Mss: D-B MN 2 (str only—A FS; 6–27 November 1822), D-B MN 6 (version for orch, 4th mvt inc—A FS; 30 November 1822), D-B N.Mus.ms. 25 (A FS—4th mvt, frag [missing portion of preceding item]).

> Remarks: Sinfonia no. 8 exists in two versions. The first is for strings only; the second, for strings plus double winds.

Violin Concerto in D minor (vn, str). Edn: Yehudi Menuhin (New York: Peters, 1952) (PS); L ii (FS). Mss: GB-L private collection of Yehudi Menuhin (A FS; 1822), D-B MN 3 (A FS; [1822]).

Piano Concerto in A minor (pf, str). Edn: L ii. Ms: D-B MN 3 (A FS; [1822]).

Remarks: Dinglinger has suggested that this Concerto is closely related to the A-minor Piano Concerto of J. N. Hummel.

Literature: Wolfgang Dinglinger, "Felix Mendelssohn Bartholdys Klavierkonzert a-moll: Umgang mit einer Modellkomposition," *Mendelssohn-Studien* 8 (1993), 105–29; Wilson, "Piano and Orchestra"; Lindeman, "Structural Novelty and Tradition."

Sinfonia no. 9 in C major (str). Edn: L i. Mss: D-B MN 6 (A FS; 12 March 1823), US-STu (A FS; 26 December 1823; published in facsimile [Los Angeles: University of California Library, 1951].

Double Concerto in D minor (pf, vn, str). Edn: L ii. Mss: D-B MN 4 (A FS; 6 May 1823), GB-Ob MDM b.5 (wind and timpani parts in score—A).

Sinfonia no. 10 in B minor (str). Edn: L i. Ms: D-B MN 13 (A FS; 13 May 1823–18 May 1823).

Sinfonia no. 11 in F minor (str). Edn: L i. Ms: D-B MN 6 (A FS; 14 June–12 July 1823).

Sinfonia no. 12 in G minor (str). Edn: L i. Ms: D-B MN 13 (A FS; 27 August–17 September 1823).

Concerto in E Major for Two Pianos (2 pf, orch). Edn: L ii. Ms: D-B MN 15 (A FS; 17 October 1823).

Remarks: First performed by Felix and Fanny on 14 November 1824; a second performance was given on 13 July 1829, during Mendelssohn's first visit to England, with the composer and Ignaz Moscheles as soloists.

Literature: Eric Werner, "Two Unpublished Mendelssohn Concertos," *Music and Letters* 36 (1955), 126–38; Köhler, "Das Jugendwerk"; Peter John Roennfeldt, "The Double Piano Concertos of Felix Mendelssohn" (D.M.A. diss., University of Cincinnati, 1985).

Sinfonia no. 13 in C minor (1 movement only) (str). Edn: L i. Ms: D-B MN 13 (A FS, 29 December [1823]).

Concerto in A♭ for Two Pianos (2 pf, orch). Edn: L ii. Mss: D-B MN 14 (A FS; 5 September–12 November 1824), GB-Ob MDM c.57 (parts for pf and str—C).

Remarks: First performed on 22 November 1824; performed by Mendelssohn and Carl Loewe in Stettin on 20 February 1827.

Literature: Eric Werner, "Two Unpublished Mendelssohn Concertos," *Music and Letters* 36 (1955), 126–38; Roennfeldt, "The Double Piano Concertos."

[Three Marches for Harmonie Musik in E♭] (ww). Ms: GB-Ob (C FS; ?ca. 1833–1834).

Symphony in D minor, Op. 107 ("Reformation") (orch). Edn: Bonn: Simrock, and London: Novello, Ewer & Co., [1868] (parts, PS, PS 4 hands, FS); R i. Mss: D-B MN 26 (A FS; 12 May 1830, rev. 11 November 1832), US-Wc (A FS, frag), location unknown (C FS—*Stichvorlage* for first edn; auctioned by Phillips on 14 June 1989).

Remarks: This symphony—actually the second of Mendelssohn's mature works in the genre—was posthumously published as the Fifth in 1868; Mendelssohn, however, rejected the work outright, stating (after an 1837 performance conducted by Julius Rietz in Düsseldorf) that of all his compositions it was the one he would most like to see burned.

Literature: A. Heuss, "Das 'Dresdener Amen' im ersten Satz von Mendelssohns Reformationssinfonie," *Signale für die musikalische Welt* 62 (1904), 281–84, 305–6; Judith Karen Silber, "Mendelssohn and the *Reformation* Symphony: A Critical and Historical Study" (Ph.D. diss., Yale University, 1987); idem, "Mendelssohn and His *Reformation* Symphony," *Journal of the American Musicological Society* 40 (1987), 310–36; Konold, *Die Symphonien*; Vitercik, *The Early Works*; Todd, "The Symphonies and Overstures"; Ulrich Wüster, "'Ein gewisser Geist': Zu Mendelssohns Reformations-Symphonie," *Die Musikforschung* 44 (1991), 311-30.

Concert Piece in F [Op. 113] (cl, bassett-horn, orch). Edn: Christian Rudolf Riedel (Wiesbaden: Breitkopf & Härtel, 1989). Ms: F-Pc Ms. 209 (A FS; 6 January 1833).

Remarks: For PS version, see under Chamber Music, later.

Overture in C major, Op. 101 ("Trumpet") (orch). Edn: Leipzig: Breitkopf & Härtel, [1867] (PS, PS 4 hands, FS); R i. Mss: GB-Ob MDM b.5 (skk), F-Pc Ms. 206 (A FS without trombones; 4 March 1826, rev. 10 April 1833), GB-Lbl RPS MS. 777 (C FS with A tbn parts).

Literature: Todd, "The Instrumental Music."

Symphony in A major, Op. 90 ("Italian") (orch). Edn: Leipzig: Breitkopf & Härtel, and London: Ewer, [1851] (parts, PS, PS 4 hands, FS); R i. MS: D-B MN 27 (A FS, 13 March 1833), D-B MN 28 (last three movements only—A FS; [June 1834]), GB-Lbl Ms. Loan 4.290 (C, [1848]), GB-Ob MDM b.5 (A FS, frags for first, third, and fourth movements).

Remarks: The 1833 version was published as Mendelssohn's Fourth Symphony, Op. 90, in 1851. The 1834 reworking of the last three movements, which Mendelssohn decidedly preferred to the familiar version, remains unpublished. Ludwig-Reichert-Verlag (Wiesbaden) has published facsimiles of all the extant autographs, as well as an edition of the 1834 revision (1998).

Literature: Wulf Konold, *Felix Mendelssohn Bartholdy, Symphonie Nr. 4 A-dur Op. 90 ("Italienische")* (Munich: Fink 1987); John Michael Cooper, "'Aber eben dieser Zweifel": A New Look at Mendelssohn's 'Italian' Symphony," *19th-Century Music* 15 (Spring 1992), 169–87; Konold, *Die Symphonien*; Vitercik, *The Early Works*; John Michael Cooper, "Felix Mendelssohn Bartholdy and the *Italian* Symphony: Historical, Musical, and Extramusical Perspectives" (Ph.D. diss., Duke University, 1994).

Fantasie und Variationen über [Carl Maria von Webers] Preziosa (2 pf, orch). Ms: RUS-SPk (A FS, [May 1833]).

Remarks: Composed with Ignaz Moscheles between Mendelssohn's arrival in London on 25 April and the performance on 2 May. Moscheles published a version for two pianos without orchestra in 1834 as his Op. 87b, evidently with reworkings and additions that Mendelssohn's sisters found displeasing (see Marcia J. Citron, ed. and trans., *The Letters of Fanny Hensel to Felix Mendelssohn* [Stuyvesant, New York]: Pendragon Press, 1987, 124–26]). The original 1833 version with orchestra has only recently come to light.

Trauermarsch, Op. 103 (orch). Edn: Leipzig: Rieter-Biedermann, [1868] (parts, PS, PS 4 hands, FS); R vii. Ms: D-B N.Mus.ms. 105 (A; ca. 8 May 1836).

Remarks: Written for the funeral of Norbert Burgmüller (1810–1836), whom Mendelssohn had befriended in London in 1833 and whose works had figured in his Düsseldorf concert programs.

[Symphony in B♭] (orch). Mss: D-B MN 19 (skk, ca. 1838–1839), US private collection of David C. Huntington (A FS, inc).

Remarks: Adapted for use as opening Sinfonia of the *Lobgesang*, Op. 52.

Literature: Seaton, "A Study"; Eric Werner, "Mendelssohniana, dem Andenken Wilhelm Fischers," *Die Musikforschung* 28 (1975), 19–33.

Ruy Blas Overture, Op. 95 (orch). Ms: D-B MN 31 (A FS; 8 March 1831).

Remarks: See also Incidental Music to Victor Hugo's *Ruy Blas*, earlier.

Marsch [in D] componirt zur Feyer der Anwesenheit des Malers Cornelius in Dresden, April 1841, Op. 108. Edn: Leipzig: Rieter-Biedermann, [1868] (parts, PS, PS 4 hands, FS); R iii. Ms: D-B MN 18 (C/A).

Piano Concerto in E minor (pf, orch). Ms: GB-Ob MDM b.5 (A FS, inc; ca. 1842–1844).

Literature: R. Larry Todd, "An Unfinished Piano Concerto by Mendelssohn," *The Musical Quarterly* 68 (1982), 80–101.

Symphony in C major (orch). Ms: GB-Ob MDM b.5 (A FS, inc; ca. 1844–1845).

Remarks: Reproduced in condensed-score transcription in the Mendelssohn article in the early editions of George Grove's *Dictionary of Music and Musicians*.

Literature: R. Larry Todd, "An Unfinished Symphony by Mendelssohn," *Music and Letters* 61 (1980), 293–309.

[Orchestral movement in G minor/C major] (orch). Ms: location unknown (A; auctioned by Hans Schneider, 1978).

Accompanied Secular Choral Works Published by Mendelssohn

Lobgesang: eine Symphonie-Cantate nach Worten der heiligen Schrift/ Hymn of Praise, Op. 52. Edn: Leipzig: Breitkopf & Härtel, London: Novello, [1841] (parts, PS, FS); R xiv; Douglass Seaton, ed. (Stuttgart: Carus, 1989); Wulf Konold, ed. (Wiesbaden: Breitkopf & Härtel, 1998). Mss: D-B MN 19 (skk), GB-Ob MDM c.93 (C/A FS—first version, for performances of July–September 1840), PL-Kj MN 34 (A FS; 27 November 1840—revised version), GB-Ob MDM c.22 (no. 7—A FS, frag).

Remarks: For the *Lobgesang* Mendelssohn drew upon an already-sketched symphony in B♭ (see earlier), joining to it a nine-movement cantata based on texts chosen mostly from the Bible. To unify the whole he employed a recurring trombone call.[20] The work was thus designated a "symphony-cantata" at its publication (though it was implicitly numbered as the Second Symphony).

Literature: Rudolf Werner, "Felix Mendelssohn Bartholdy als Kirchenmusiker" (Frankfurt am Main, 1930), 89–97; Stephen Town, "Mendelssohn's 'Lobgesang': A Fusion of Forms and Textures," *Choral Journal* 33 (1992), 19–26.

Die erste Walpurgisnacht, Op. 60. Text: Goethe. Edn: Leipzig: Kistner, and London: Ewer, [1844] (parts, PS, FS); R xv. Mss: D-B MN 18 (skk, ca. 1832), D-B MN 19 (skk, ca. 1842), GB-Ob MDM c.22 (skk, ca. 1842), GB-Ob MDM c.47 (skk), D-Lm PM 143 (A FS; Milan, 15 July 1831, Paris, 13 February 1832, Leipzig, December 1842, Leipzig, 15 July 1843—includes appended score for piccolo, 3 trombones, bass drum, and cymbals for Nos. 5–7), PL-Kj MN 37 (A FS; 15 July 1831/13 February 1832), D-B MN 56/3 (A FS; frag), F-Pc Ms. 207 (A FS, frag), D-B MN 49 (A PS 4 hands—frag), US-NYpm (C PS), US-NYpm (A, album leaf), location unknown (A frag; auctioned by Hans Schneider in 1978; facsimile of first page in Katalog Nr. 225, no. 125), location unknown (A tenor part; facsimile in Carl Baldamus, *Autographa berühmter Tonkünstler* [Berlin: n.p., 1853], vol. 3), US-NH SC Ma21/M522/Er87 (A tenor part with bass line, ca. 1832).

Remarks: Like the *Lobgesang*, the *Walpurgisnacht* is a generic hybrid, a combination of symphony and cantata—in this case, on an avowedly secular subject (a ballad by Goethe). Unlike its sacred counterpart, however, Op. 60 is the product of a long and tormented compositional history. Begun during Mendelssohn's Grand Tour of 1830–1831, the first version of the work was premiered shortly after Goethe's death, during Mendelssohn's benefit concerts in the winter of 1831–1832; publication, however, became possible only after an extensive reworking in the early 1840s. The work's complex compositional history and the nature of the reworkings clearly document the Romantic side of Mendelssohn's compositional personality.

Literature: Reinhard Szeskus, "*Die erste Walpurgisnacht*, op. 60, von Felix Mendelssohn Bartholdy," *Beiträge zur Musikwissenschaft* 17 (1975), 171–80; Carl Dahlhaus, "'Hoch symbolisch intoniert': zu Mendelssohns *Erster Walpurgisnacht*," *Österreichische Musikzeitschrift* 36 (1981), 290–97; Douglass Seaton, "The Romantic Mendelssohn: The Composition of *Die erste Walpurgisnacht*," *The Musical Quarterly* 68 (1982), 398–410; Lawrence Kramer, "*Felix culpa*: Mendelssohn, Goethe, and the Social Force of Musical Expression"; Christoph Hellmundt, "Mendelssohns Arbeit an seiner Kantate *Die erste Walpurgisnacht*: Zu einer bisher wenig beachteten Quelle," in *Felix Mendelssohn Bartholdy: Kongreß-Bericht Berlin 1994*, ed. Christian Martin Schmidt (Wiesbaden: Breitkopf & Härtel, 1997), 76–112.

An die Künstler (Festgesang), Op. 68 (male vv, brass). Text: Schiller. Edn: Bonn: Simrock, and London: Ewer, [1846] (parts, PS, FS); R xv. Mss: PL-Kj MN 41 (A FS; 19 April 1846), D-B N.Mus.ms. 406 (C/A FS [*Stichvorlage* for first edn], with horn and organ parts in an attached score—C).

    Literature: M. Rasmussen, "The First Performance of Mendelssohn's *Festgesang* An die Künstler op. 68," *Brass Quarterly* 4 (1961), 151–55.

Accompanied Secular Choral Works Unpublished or Posthumously Published

In rührend feierlichen Tönen (wedding cantata) (SATB solos, ch, pf). Text: ? Ms: D-B MN 2 (A FS; 13 June 1820 [*recte* 1821]).

Große Festmusik zum Dürerfest (solo vv, ch, orch). Text: Levetzow. Edn: In Kent Eutgene Hatteberg, "Gloria (1822) and Große Festmusik zum Dürerfest (1828): Urtext Editions of Two Unpublished Choral-Orchestral Works by Felix Mendelssohn, with Background and Commentary" (D.M.A. diss., University of Iowa, 1995). Mss: D-B MN 17 (A FS; 1828), US-Wc (text, 2 copies).

    Remarks: Performed in Berlin, 18 April 1828.

Begrüßung ("Humboldt Cantata") (solo vv, ch, orch). Ms: D-B MN 48 (A FS; 12 September 1828).

    Literature: Karl Schönewolf, "Mendelssohns Humboldt-Kantate," *Musik und Gesellschaft* 9 (1959), 408–11.

Festgesang ("Möge das Siegeszeichen") (ch, pf). Edn: Christoph Hellmundt (Leipzig: Breitkopf & Härtel, [1997]). Ms: RUS-SPsc Ms. NeM F XII 35 (A; 30 March 1838).

    Remarks: In his preface to the first edition of this occasional work commissioned by Anton Christanell (1801–1882) of Schwaz, Christoph Hellmundt points out that the Festgesang reveals strong thematic ties to the symphony-cantata *Lobgesang* (see earlier).

Festgesang ("Gutenberg" cantata) (male ch, orch). Edn: Leipzig: Breitkopf & Härtel, [1840] (PS); London: Ewer & Co., [1844] (version for mixed chorus—PS); R xv. Mss: D-B N.Mus.ms. 531 (nos. 1, 3, and 4—PS, arr. SATB), D-F Mus. Hs. 560 (version for male ch—C).

    Remarks: Published in 1840 for male chorus and orchestra, the work also is transmitted in the Berlin autograph for mixed chorus. In 1847 this version was published as a piano-vocal score by Ewer & Co. in London and Breitkopf & Härtel in Leipzig. No. 2 was adapted by W. H. Cummings in 1856 as "Hark! The Herald Angels Sing."

    Literature: Peter Mercer-Taylor, "Mendelssohn's 'Scottish' Symphony and the Music of German Memory," *19th-Century Music* 19 (1995), 68–82.

Gott segne Sachsenland ("Lied zur Feier der Enthüllung der Statue Friedrich August von Sachsen") (double male ch, brass). Edn: Reinhard Kapp, in *Richard Wagner: Sämtliche Werke*, vol. 16, *Chorwerke mit einer*

Dokumentation zum Thema Wagner und der Chor und zu den Chorwerken Wagners (Mainz: Schott, 1993), 219–23. Mss: D-B MN 19 (sk), PL-Kj MN 38² (A FS; 2 June 1843).

Remarks: The main theme is familiar as "My Country, 'Tis of Thee" or "God Save the King/Queen."

Concert Arias (All Unpublished or Posthumously Published)

Che vuoi mio cor?/Was ist, mein Herz? (A FS, str). Text: Italian text ?; German text by W. Osterwald. Edn: Berlin, [n.p.], Milan, Lucca, [1880] (PS by A. Matthias). Mss: D-B MN 6 (C FS; ?1823), GB-Ob MDM c.50/1 (C FS), location unknown (auctioned by Christie's London on 29 May 1986; C FS by Julius Rietz).

Remarks: Performed by the Royal Philharmonic Society on 9 March 1882.

Ch'io t'abbandono (bar, pf). Text: Metastasio. Ms: US-NYpm Heineman MS 1444A (A FS 5 September 1825).

Tutto è silenzio (S, orch). Text: ? Ms: US-Wc Whittall ML30.8j T9 (A FS, inc; 23 February 1829).

Infelice!/Ah, ritorna, età dell' oro (S, orch). Text: Metastasio. Mss: D-B MN 28 (A FS; 3 April 1834), GB-Lam Ms. 171 (parts—C/A, [1834]), GB-Lam Ms. 172 (parts).

Remarks: Long assumed to be an early version of the concert aria posthumously published as Op. 94, this work, in fact, bears little resemblance to its published counterpart, which Mendelssohn in 1843 described as a "new" concert aria written for Sophie Schloss. Aside from the introductory recitative and the words "Ah, ritorna" the texts are substantially different, and aside from the principal theme of the Andante the music bears little resemblance.

Infelice!/Ah, ritorna, età felice/Unglücksel'ge!/ Kehret wieder, gold'ne Tage, Op. 94 (S, orch). Text: Metastasio. Edn: Leipzig: Breitkopf & Härtel [1851 (words in Italian and German)] (parts, PS, FS); London: Ewer, [1851 (words in Italian and English)] (parts, PS, FS). Ms: PL-Kj MN 38² (A FS; 15 January 1843).

On Lena's Gloomy Heath (bar, orch). Text: Ossian [J. Macpherson]. Mss: GB-Ob MDM c.50/2 (C FS), GB-Lbl Ms. Add. 48597 C FS), GB-Lbl RPS Loan 349 (C FS); I-BGc Legato Piatti-Lochis 8869.

Remarks: Composed ca. September 1846; performed in London, 15 March 1847. The Italian manuscript is in the hand of Alfredo Piatti, a cellist who played under Mendelssohn in London.

Literature: R. Larry Todd, "Mendelssohn's Ossianic Manner, with a New Source: *On Lena's Gloomy Heath*," in *Mendelssohn and Schumann: Essays on Their Music and Its Context*, ed. Jon R. Finson and R. Larry Todd (Durham, NC: Duke University Press, 1984), 137–60.

O lasst mich einen Augenblick noch hier (B, orch). Text: Goethe. Mss: D-DS Mus.ms. 1446 (A FS, inc), PL-Kj MN 44 (A FS, inc).

Remarks: The two versions, though quite different, both break off at exactly the same point in the text.

Choral Songs Published by Mendelssohn

Songs are identified first by text incipit, then by title(s).

General Literature: Lars Ulrich Abraham, "Mendelssohns Chorlieder und ihre musikgeschichtliche Stellung," in *Das Problem Mendelssohn*, ed. Carl Dahlhaus (Regensburg: Bosse, 1974), 79–87.

Six Songs for Four-Part Mixed Chorus, to Be Sung Outdoors [Sechs vierstimmige Lieder . . . im Freien zu Singen], [vol. 1], Op. 41 (SATB). Edn: Leipzig: Breitkopf & Härtel, [1838], and London: Ewer, [1844 (PS with English texts)]; R xvi.

No. 1. Ihr Vögel in den Zweigen schwank ("Im Walde"). Text: Platen. Ms: GB-Ob MDM c.16 (A; January 1838).

Nos. 2–4 "Drei Volkslieder," "Liebesgeschichte," "Drei rheinische Volkslieder," in F-Pc Ms. 201 (A), and D-DÜhi (C with A title).

No. 2. Entflieh mit mir. Text: Heine. Mss: D-B MN 28 (A; [22 January 1834]), F-Pc Ms. 200 (A), F-Pc Ms. 201 (A; 22 May 1835), D-DÜh (C/A).

No. 3. Es fiel ein Reif. Text: Heine. Mss: D-B MN 28 (A; [22 January 1834]), F-Pc Ms. 201 (A; 22 May 1835), F-Pc Ms. 200 (A), D-DÜh (C/A).

No. 4. Auf ihrem Grab. Text: Heine. Mss: D-B MN 28 (A; 22 January 1834), F-Pc Ms. 201 (A; 22 May 1835), F-Pc Ms. 200 (A), D-DÜhi (C/A).

No. 5. Der Schnee zerrinnt ("Mailied"). Text: Hölty. Mss: F-Pc Ms. 197 (A; 23 November 1837), D-B N.Mus.ms. 116 (A inc; mm. 1–23 of ms continued in GB-Ob MDM c.16), GB-Ob MDM c.16 (A frag; completion of D-B N.Mus.ms. 116), RUS-SPsc Ms. HeM F XII 100 (A).

No. 6. Und frische Nahrung ("Auf dem See"). Text: Goethe. Mss: D-B N.Mus.ms. 116 (A; 1839), D-B N.Mus.ms. 109 (parts for S,A, and B—A and C by Cécile Mendelssohn Bartholdy, inc), F-Pc Ms. 197 (A inc), US-Wc (A, frag).

Six Songs for Four-Part Mixed Chorus, to Be Sung Outdoors [Sechs vierstimmige Lieder . . . im Freien zu Singen], vol. 2, Op. 48 (SATB). Edn: Leipzig: Breitkopf & Härtel, [1840], and London: Ewer [1844 (PS with English texts)]; R xvi.

Nos. 1–3 "Der erste Frühlingstag"

No. 1. O sanfter süsser Hauch ("Frühlingsahnung," "Am ersten Frühlingstag"). Text: Uhland. Ms: D-B MN 31 (A; 5 July 1839).

No. 2. Liebliche Blume ("Die Primel"). Text: Lenau. Ms: D-B MN 31 (A; [1839]).

No. 3. Süsser, goldner Frühlingstag ("Frühlingsfeier"). Text: Uhland. Ms: D-B MN 31 (A; 28 December 1839).

No. 4. Wie lieblicher Klang ("Lerchengesang," "Canon"). Text: ? Mss: D-B MN 31 (A; 15 June 1839), D-B N.Mus.ms. 16 (A; 19 June 1839; facsimile in Max Schneider, ed., *Felix Mendelssohn Bartholdy: Denkmal in Wort und Bild* [Basel: Amerbach, 1947], appendix).

No. 5. O wunderbares tiefes Schweigen ("Morgengebet"). Text: Eichendorff. Ms: D-B MN 31 (A; 18 November 1839).

No. 6. Holder Lenz, du bist dahin ("Herbstlied," "Herbstklage"). Text: Lenau. Ms: D-B MN 31 (A; 26 December 1839).

Lieblich mundet der Becher Wein ("Ersatz für Unbestand") (male vv). Text: Rückert. Edn: In *Deutscher Musenalmanach* (Leipzig: Kistner, [1839]) and independently by Leipzig: Kistner, [1840]; R xvii. Ms: D-B MN 31 (A; 22 November 1839).

Six Songs for Four-part Male Chorus [Sechs Lieder für vierstimmigen Männerchor], Op. 50 (4 male vv). Edn: Leipzig: Kistner, [1840], and London: Ewer, [1844 (words in English by W. Bartholomew)]; R xvii. Ms: location unknown; formerly in Koch collection.

No. 1. Setze mir nicht, du Grobian ("Türkisches Schenkenlied," "Türkisches Trinklied"). Text: Goethe. Ms: D-B MN 30 (A; [1838]).

No. 2. Wer hat dich, du schöner Wald ("Der Jäger Abschied," "Der deutsche Wald"). Text: Eichendorff. Ms: PL-Kj MN 34 (A; 6 January 1840).

Remarks: With optional accompaniment for four horns and bass trombone in 1840 edn.

No. 3. Wie Feld und Au' so blinkend im Thau ("Sommerlied"). Text: Goethe. Mss: D-B MN 29 (A; [1837]), D-B N.Mus.ms. 109 (parts—A and C by Cécile Mendelssohn Bartholdy), GB private collection (A).

No. 4. Am fernen Horizonte ("Wasserfahrt"). Text: Heine. Mss: D-B MN 29 (A; [ca. February 1837]), RUS-SPsc Ms. HeM F XII 100 (A), GB private collection (A).

No. 5. Was quälte dir dein armes Herz? Liebesschmerz. ("Liebe und Wein," "Vin à tout prix"). Text: ? Ms: D-B MN 31 (A; 7 December 1839; in this ms the response to the opening question is "Dein banges Herz").

No. 6. Vom Grund bis zu den Gipfeln ("Wanderlied"). Text: Eichendorff. Ms: PL-Kj MN 34 (A; 6 January 1840).

Six Songs for Four-Part Mixed Chorus, to Be Sung Outdoors [Sechs vierstimmigen Lieder . . . im Freien zu Singen], vol. 3, Op. 59 (SATB). Edn: Leipzig: Breitkopf & Härtel, [1843], and London: Ewer, [1843 (words in English by W. Bartholomew)]; R xvi.

No. 1. Im Grün erwacht der frische Muth ("Im Grünen"). Text: Chézy. Mss: D-B MN 31 (A; 23 November 1837), D-B N.Mus.ms. 109 (parts—A and C by Cécile Mendelssohn Bartholdy; 1839–1840), location unknown (with Op. 100 no. 4, Op. 59 no. 3, Op. 88 no. 6, and Op. 59 no. 5, and Op. 59 no. 6—A; [ca. March 1843]; auctioned by Hans Schneider, 1995).

No. 2. Tage der Wonne, kommt ihr so bald ("Frühzeitiger Frühling"). Text: Goethe. Ms: PL-Kj MN 38^2 (A; 17 June 1843).

No. 3. O Thäler weit, o Höhen ("Abschied vom Wald"). Text: Eichendorff. Mss: PL-Kj MN 38² (A; 3 March 1843), location unknown (with Op. 59 no. 1, Op. 100 no. 4, Op. 88 no. 6, Op. 59 no. 5, and Op. 59 no. 6—A; 4 March 1843; auctioned by Hans Schneider, 1995).

No. 4. Die Nachtigall, sie war entfernt ("Die Nachtigall," "Canon"). Text: Goethe. Mss: PL-Kj MN 38² (A; 19 June 1843), location unknown (A; 12 July 1845; facsimile in Ernst Wolff, *Felix Mendelssohn Bartholdy* [Berlin: Harmonie, 1906; enlarged 2d edn 1909], facing p. 168).

No. 5. Wann im letzten Abendstrahl ("Ruhethal"). Text: Uhland. Mss: PL-Kj MN 38² (A; 4 March 1843), location unknown (with Op. 59 no. 1, Op. 100 no. 4, Op. 59 no. 3, Op. 88 no. 6, and Op. 59 no. 6—A; [ca. March 1843]; auctioned by Hans Schneider, 1995).

No. 6. Durch schwankende Wipfel ("Jagdlied," "Vorüber"). Text: Eichendorff. Mss: PL-Kj MN 38² (A; 5 March 1843), location unknown (with Op. 59 no. 1, Op. 100 no. 4, Op. 59 no. 3, Op. 88 no. 6, and Op. 59 no. 5—A; auctioned by Hans Schneider, 1995).

Choral Songs Unpublished or Posthumously Published

Einst ins Schlaraffenland zogen (4 male vv). Ms: D-B MN 1 (A; [1820]).

Lieb und Hoffnung (4 male vv). Ms: D-B MN 2 (A; [1820]).

Kein bess're Lust in dieser Zeit ("Jägerlied") (4 male vv). Text: Uhland. Ms: D-B MN 2 (A; 20 April 1822).

Seht, Freunde, die Gläser ("Lob des Weins") (solo male vv, male ch). Ms: D-B MN 2 (A; [1822]).

Wenn der Abendwind durch die Wipfel zieht (SAT). Ms: location unknown (auctioned by J. A. Stargardt, 19 March 1997—A; 23 August 1828).

Lasset heut am edlen Ort (SATB). Text: Goethe. Mss: D-DÜk (A; 25 December 1828; facsimile in *Festlied zu Zelters siebzigstem Geburtstag am 11. Dezember 1828* [Leipzig: Bibliographisches Institut, (1928)]), D-F Mus. Hs. 360 (C).

Remarks: Although Zelter's birthday fell on 11 December, the autograph in DÜk, given as a gift to Johann Heinrich Daniel Stümer (who would sing the role of the Evangelist in Mendelssohn's 1829 performances of the *St. Matthew Passion*), is clearly inscribed: "Herrn Stümer hochachtungsvoll von Felix Mendelssohn Bartholdy am Weihnachtsabend 1828."

Der weise Diogenes (canon, 4 male vv). Text: R. Reinick. Mss: D-B MN 28 (in G major—A; 11 February 1833; facsimile in supplement to *Die Musik* 8/2 [1908–1909]), D-B N.Mus.ms. 100 (in A major—A; with added *Nachgesang* ["Wie hehr im Glase blinket"]), D-B N.Mus.ms. 110 (A), GB-Ob MDM c.54 (C).

Seht doch diese Fiedlerbänden ("Musikantenprügelei") (4 male vv). Text: R. Reinick. Edn: In Albert Kopfermann, "Zwei musikalische Scherze Felix

Mendelssohns," *Die Musik* 8/2 (1908–1909), 179–80. Ms: D-B MN 28 (A; 23 April 1833).

Worauf kommt es überall an ("Dreistigkeit") (4 male vv). Ms: D-B MN 29 (A; 23 February 1837), GB private collection (A).

Trunken müssen wir alle sein ("Lob der Trunkenheit") (4 male vv). Text: Goethe. Ms: D-B MN 30 (A; [1838]).

Wozu der Vöglein Chöre belauschen ("Lied aus *Ruy Blas*"). See Incidental Music to Victor Hugo's *Ruy Blas*, earlier, and Op. 77, later.

Schlummernd an des Vaters Brust ("Nachtgesang") (4 male vv). Edn: In *Repertorium für deutschen Männergesang* ii (Leipzig: Kahnt, [1856]); R xvii. Ms: location unknown (A; 15 January 1842).

Auf, Freunde, laßt das Jahr uns singen ("Die Stiftungsfeier," "Lied für die Stiftungsfeier der Gesellschaft der Freunde der Musik in Berlin"). Edn: In *Repertorium für deutschen Männergesang* iii (Leipzig: Kahnt, [1859]); R xvii. Ms: D-B MN 20 (A; 15 January 1842).

Wohl perlet im Glase der purpurne Wein ("Die Frauen und die Sänger") (SATB). Text: Schiller. Ms: PL-Kj MN 40 (Er kommt aus dem kindlichen Alter der Welt—A frag; 25 January 1846), D-B MA Ms. 10 (A), US-Wc (A).

Six Songs for Four-part Male Chorus [Sechs Lieder für vierstimmigen Männerchor], vol. 2, Op. 75 (4 male vv). Edn: Leipzig: Kistner, [1849], and London: Ewer, [1849 (words in English)]; R xvii.

No. 1. Wem Gott will rechte Gunst erweisen ("Der frohe Wandersmann"). Text: Eichendorff. Mss: PL-Kj MN 39 (A; 8 February 1844), F-Pc Ms. 188 (A; 24 November 1844).

No. 2. Schlafe, Liebchen, weil's auf Erden ("Abendständchen," "Ständchen"). Text: Eichendorff. Ms: PL-Kj MN 34 (A; 14 November 1839).

No. 3. So lang man nüchtern ist ("Trinklied," "Trinklied aus dem Divan"). Text: Goethe. Mss: D-B MN 29 (A; ca. February 1837), GB private collection (A).

No. 4. So rückt denn in die Runde ("Abschiedstafel"). Text: Eichendorff. Mss: US-Cn (C, 12 February ?1838), PL-Kj MN 39 (A; two versions, dated 26 January 1844 and 29 August 1844), GB-OB MDM b.5 (A; [?ca. May–June 1844]), F-Pc Ms. 188 (A, 24 November 1844), US private collection of Walter Benjamin (A), D-B MA Ms. 131 (C/A).

Four Songs for Four-part Male Chorus [Vier Lieder für vierstimmigen Männerchor], vol. 3, Op. 76 (4 male vv). Edn: London: Ewer, [1849 (words in English)], and Leipzig: Breitkopf & Härtel, [1850]; R xvii.

No. 1. Gaben mir Rath und gute Lehren ("Das Lied vom braven Mann"). Text: Heine. Mss: D-B MN 29 (A; [1837]), PL-Kj MN 34 (A).

No. 2. Wo solch' ein Feuer noch gedeiht ("Rheinweinlied"). Text: Herwegh. Ms: PL-Kj MN 39 (A; 9 February 1844).

No. 3. Was uns einst als deutsche Brüder ("Lied für die Deutschen in Lyon"). Text: Stoltze. Ms: PL-Kj MN 41 (A; 8 October 1846).

No. 4. Nun zu guter Letzt ("Comitat"). Text: von Fallersleben. Mss: PL-Kj MN 44 (A; 14 September 1847), US-Bm (A).

Six Songs for Four-part Mixed Chorus [Sechs vierstimmige Lieder], vol. 4, Op. 88 (SATB). Edn: London: Ewer, [1850/51 (words in English by W. Bartholomew)], and Leipzig: Breitkopf & Härtel, [1850/51]; R xvi.

No. 1. Mit der Freude zieht der Schmerz ("Neujahrslied"). Text: Hebel. Mss: PL-Kj MN 39 (A; 8 August 1844), D-B N.Mus.ms. 161 (A; 1 October 1845), D-B MA Ms. 10 (A).

No. 2. Ich hab' ein Liebchen ("Der Glückliche"). Text: Eichendorff. Ms: PL-Kj MN 38^2 (frag and A; 20 June 1843).

No. 3. O Winter, schlimmer Winter ("Hirtenlied"). Text: Uhland. Mss: D-B MN 31 (A; two versions, one dated 14 June 1839, the other not dated), D-B N.Mus.ms. 16 (A; 19 June 1839; facsimile in Max Schneider, ed., *Felix Mendelssohn Bartholdy: Denkmal in Wort und Bild* [Basel: Amerbach, 1947], appendix).

Remarks: See also Op. 57, no. 2, later.

No. 4. Kommt, lasst uns geh'n spazieren ("Die Waldvöglein"). Text: Schütz. Ms: PL-Kj MN 38^2 (A; 19 June 1843).

No. 5. Durch tiefe Nacht ein Brausen zieht ("Deutschland"). Text: Geibel. Ms: PL-Kj MN 44 (A).

No. 6. Durch Feld und Buchenhallen ("Der wandernde Musikant"). Text: Eichendorff. Mss: PL-Kj MN 34 (A; 10 March 1840), location unknown (with Op. 59 no. 1, Op. 100 no. 4, Op. 59 no. 3, Op. 59 no. 5, and Op. 59 no. 6—A; [ca. March 1843]; auctioned by Hans Schneider, 1995).

Four Songs for Four-part Mixed Chorus [Vier vierstimmige Lieder], vol. 5, Op. 100 (SATB). Edn: Leipzig: Breitkopf & Härtel, [1852], and London: Ewer, [1852 (words in English)]; R xvi.

No. 1. Die Bäume grünen überall ("Andenken"). Text: Hoffmann von Fallersleben. Mss: PL-Kj MN 39 (A; 8 August 1844), D-B N.Mus.ms. 161 (A; 1 October 1845).

No. 2. Saatengrün, Veilchenduft ("Lob des Frühlings"). Text: Uhland. Ms: PL-Kj MN 38^2 (A; 20 June 1843).

No. 3. Berg und Thal will ich durchstreifen ("Frühlingslied"). Text: ? Ms: location unknown (?1843–1844).

No. 4. O Wald, du kühlender Bronnen ("Im Wald," "Waldlust"). Text: ? Mss: D-B MN 31 (A; 14 June 1839), D-B N.Mus.ms. 16 (A; 19 June 1839; facsimile in Max Schneider, ed., *Felix Mendelssohn Bartholdy: Denkmal in Wort und Bild* [Basel: Amerbach, 1947], appendix), location unknown (with Op. 59 no. 1, Op. 59 no. 3, Op. 88 no. 6, Op. 59 no. 5, and Op. 59 no. 6—A; [ca. March 1843]; auctioned by Hans Schneider, 1995), GB-Ob MDM b.5 (A).

Four Songs for Four-part male chorus, [Vier Lieder für vierstimmigen Männerchor], Op. 120 (4 male vv). Edn: Leipzig: Breitkopf & Härtel, 1874; R xvii.

No. 1. Auf, ihr Herrn und Damen schön ("Jagdlied," "Jagdgesang"). Text: after W. Scott. Mss: D-B MN 29 (A; 27 November 1837), US-Wc (A), location unknown (tenor part only—A; auctioned by J. A. Stargardt, 1974); location unknown (bass part only—A; auctioned by Sotheby's on 21 November 1990).

No. 2. Seid gegrüßet, traute Brüder ("Morgengruß des thüringischen Sängerbundes"). Text: ? Ms: PL-Kj MN 44 (A; 20 February 1847).

No. 3. Süsse Düfte, milde Lüfte ("Im Süden"). Text: ? Ms: F-Pc Ms. 197 (A; 24 November 1837).

No. 4. Im Nebelgeriesel, im tiefen Schnee ("Zigeunerlied"). Text: Goethe.

Sahst du ihn herniederschweben [Trauergesang], Op. 116 (mixed vv). Text: F. Aulenbach. Ed.: Leipzig: J. Rieter-Biedermann, [1869]; R xiv; Wm. A. Little (Stuttgart: Carus, 1998). Ms: PL-Kj MN 40 (A, 8 July 1845).

Not dated:

In Frankfurt auf der Zeile, da steht ein junger Mann (2 male vv). Ms: D-F Mus. Hs. 2467 (A).

Songs and Vocal Duets Published by Mendelssohn

Songs are identified first by text incipit, then by title(s).

General literature: Luise Leven, "Mendelssohn als Lyriker, unter besonderer Berücksichtigung seiner Beziehungen zu Ludwig Berger, Bernhard Klein und Adolph Bernhard Marx" (Ph.D.diss., Universität Frankfurt am Main, 1926); Thomas Stoner, "Mendelssohn's Published Songs" (Ph.D. diss., University of Maryland, 1972); Francis Lewis Woodward, "The Solo Songs of Felix Mendelssohn" (D.M.A. thesis, University of Texas at Austin, 1972); Lawrence Kramer, "The Lied as Cultural Practice: Tutelage, Gender, and Desire in Mendelssohn's Goethe Songs," in *Classical Music and Postmodern Knowledge* (Berkeley and Los Angeles: University of California Press, 1995), 143–73; Douglass Seaton, "The Problem of the Lyric Persona in Mendelssohn's Songs," in *Felix Mendelssohn Bartholdy: Kongreß-Bericht Berlin 1994*, ed. Christian Martin Schmidt (Wiesbaden: Breitkopf & Härtel, 1997), 167–86.

Twelve Songs [Zwölf Gesänge], Op. 8. Edn: Berlin: Schlesinger, [ca. 1827], and London: Ewer, [1845 (nos. 1–11 only—words in English and German; English texts by W. Bartholomew)]; R xix.

1. Holder klingt der Vogelsang ("Minnelied"). Text: Hölty.

4. Es ist ein Schnitter, der heisst Tod ("Erntelied"). Text: from *Des Knaben Wunderhorn*. Ms: location unknown (auctioned by J. A. Stargardt, 19 March 1997—A; 24 January 1824).

5. Lass dich nur nichts nicht dauern ("Pilgerspruch"). Text: P. Flemming.
      Remarks: Published with English text in *Apollo's Gift, or the Musical Souvenir* (London: S. Chappell, 1829).

6. Jetzt kommt der Frühling ("Frühlingslied, in schwäbischer Mundart"). Text: Robert. Ms: D-B MN 49 (arr. S, fl, cl, 2 hn, vc—A; 2 April 1824).

Remarks: Also published as "Maid of the Valley" (text by W. E. Attfield) in *The Musical Gem: A Souvenir for 1834* (London: Mori & Lavenu, [1833]). See also under Unpublished Chamber Music, later.

7. Man soll hören süsses Singen ("Maienlied"). Text: Jakob von der Warte.

8. Die Schwalbe flügt ("Andres Maienlied," "Hexenlied"). Text: Hölty.

9. Das Tagewerk ist abgethan ("Abendlied"). Text: J. H. Voss.

10. Einmal aus seinen Blicken ("Romanze, aus dem Spanischen"). Text: F. Voigts? Ms: D-F Mus. Hs. 1975 (C).

11. Willkommen im Grünen ("Im Grünen"). Text: J. H. Voss.

Composed by Fanny Mendelssohn and published in Op. 8:

2. Was ist's, das mir den Athem hemmet ("Das Heimweh"). Text: F. Robert.

3. Schöner und schöner schmückt sich der Plan ("Italien"). Text: F. Grillparzer.[21]

12. Duet: An des lust'gen Brunnens Rand ("Suleika und Hatem"). Text: Goethe (Marianne von Willmer?). Edn: R xviii, xix. Ms: D-F (C).[22]

Twelve Songs [Zwölf Lieder], Op. 9. Edn: Berlin: Schlesinger, [1830], and London: Ewer, [1845] (words in English and German; English texts by W. Bartholomew); R xix.

1. Ist es wahr? ("Frage"). Text: "H. Voss."[23] Mss: D-DS Mus.ms.1444c (C), GB-Ob MS. Horsley b.1 (C).

Remarks: The melody of this song also appears in the slow movement of the A-major String Quartet, Op. 13, composed in 1827 and published in 1830. In addition, the song was published with the title "Is It True?" (text by Walter Thornton) in *The Musical Gem: A Souvenir for 1834* (London: Mori & Lavenue, [1833]).

2. Kennst du nicht das Gluthverlangen ("Geständnis," "Frage"). Text: ? Mss: D-LEm (A; 3 December 1831), GB-Ob MS. Horsley b.1 (C).

3. Sie trug einen Falken auf ihrer Hand ("Wartend: Romanze"). Text: Droysen. Mss: D-B MN 20 (A; 3 April 1829), D-DS Mus.ms. 1459 (C, inc).

4. Ihr frühlingstrunknen Blumen ("Im Frühling"). Text: Droysen. Mss: F-Pc Ms. 193 (A; 27 January 1830), GB-Ob MDM c.16 (A; [January 1831]), location unknown (auctioned by Christie's London, 19 May 1993—A; 6 December 1845).

5. Ach, wie schnell die Tage fliehen ("Im Herbst"). Text: K. Klingemann. Mss: D-B N.Mus.ms. 8 (A; 6 August 1830), location unknown (auctioned by J. A. Stargardt, 1983—A; 21 November 1843).

6. Wie so gelinde die Fluth bewegt ("Scheidend," "Auf der Fahrt"). Text: "H. Voss." Mss: F-Pc Ms. 193 (A; 13 January 1830), D-F (A; August 1830).

Remarks: The opening measures are alluded to in the *Meeresstille und glückliche Fahrt* Overture, Op. 27 (see earlier).

8. Die linden Lüfte sind erwacht ("Frühlingsglaube"). Text: Uhland. Mss: D-B MN 49 (A; 19 January 1830), F-Pc Ms. 193 (A; 27 January 1830).

9. In weite Ferne will ich träumen ("Ferne"). Text: Droysen. Ms: D-DS Mus.ms. 1459 (C).

11. Herr, zu dir will ich mich retten ("Entsagung"). Text: Droysen. Ms: D-DS Mus.ms. (C; based on 30 May 1832).

Composed by Fanny Mendelssohn and published in Op. 9:

7. Fern und ferner schallt der Reigen ("Sehnsucht"). Text: Droysen.[24]

10. Und wüssten's die Blumen ("Verlust"). Text: Heine.[25]

12. Im stillen Klostergarten ("Die Nonne"). Text: Uhland.[26]

Far from the moveless dark bright eye ("Charlotte und Werther"). Edn: as "Charlotte and Werther" in *Apollo's Gift, or the Musical Souvenir for 1831* (London: S. Chappell, [1830]). Ms: D-B MN 18 (with English as well as inc German text ["Lang ist her"]—A; 1829).

Remarks: The 1830 publication is titled "Charlotte to Werter" and uses a text by W. F. Collard. The music of this song was reused for "Es freut sich Alles weit und breit" ("Seemans Scheidelied,") text by Hoffmann von Fallersleben, published in 1850. Mendelssohn had nothing to do with this *Umdichtung*, however, or with the others published by Hoffmann von Fallersleben in the 1850s.

Leg in den Sarg mir mein grünes Gewand ("Todeslied der Bojaren") (male vv, pf). Edn: In K. Immermann, *Alexis* (Düsseldorf: Schaub, 1832); R xix. Mss: D-B N.Mus.ms. 73 (C/A; 13 October 1841), D-B MN 59 (A), location unknown (version for male vv, 2 fl, 2 ob, 2 cl, 2 bn; auctioned by Hans Schneider, 1977),GB-Ob MDM c.50/2 (C, English translation).

Remarks: Composed in 1831 (letter from Karl Immermann to Hermann Immermann, 12 December 1831).

Trala. A frischer Bua bin i (TT). Edn: In K. Immermann, *Andreas Hofer* (Düsseldorf: Schaub, 1834). Ms: D-B MN 20 (A; 9 December 1833).

Six Songs [Sechs Gesänge], Op. 19[a] (S, pf). Edn: Leipzig: Breitkopf & Härtel, [1833], and London: Ewer [1845] (words in English and German; English texts by William Bartholomew); R xix. Ms: US-NYpm Cary (A).

1. In dem Walde süße Töne ("Frühlingslied"). Text: Ulrich von Lichtenstein. Ms: D-B MN 49 (A; 21 February 1830), US-Wc (A; 24 February 1830).

2. Als ich das erste Veilchen erblickt ("Das erste Veilchen," "Der ersten Liebe Verlust," "Der erste Verlust"). Text: E. Ebert. Mss: D-DS Mus.ms. 1459 (in F—C; based on 24 September 1831), D-DS Mus.ms. 1459 (in E♭—C; based on 4 July 1832), RUS-SPsc Ms. Pазноɞ₃ F XII 33 (A), RUS-SPsc Ms. HeM F XII 100 (A).

3. Mein Sohn, wo willst du hin so spät? ("Winterlied, aus dem Schwedischen," "Volkslied"). Text: folk song. Mss: D-DS Mus.ms.1444c (A), location unknown (A; auctioned by Sotheby's on 17 May 1990).

4. In dem Mondenschein im Walde ("Neue Liebe"). Text: Heine.

5. Leise zieht durch mein Gemüth ("Gruß," "Frühlingslied"). Text: Heine. Mss: D-DS (C; based on 19 September 1832), location unknown (A; 22

December 1836; auctioned by J. A. Stargardt on 28 June 1990), location unknown (A; auctioned by Sotheby's on 17 May 1990).

Remarks: Rudolf Elvers has remarked that at least fourteen *Albumblätter* transmit this Lied in whole or in part; see Rudolf Elvers, "Auf den Spuren der Autographen Felix Mendelssohn Bartholdys," in *Beiträge zur Musikdokumentation: Franz Grasberger zum 60. Geburtstag*, ed. Günter Brosche (Tutzing: Hans Schneider, 1975), 85.

6. Bringet des treusten Herzens Grüsse ("Reiselied," "In die Ferne"). Text: Ebert. Mss: D-B MN 18 (A; 16 October 1830), GB-Ob MDM c.16 (A; January 1831), D-DS Mus.ms. 1459 (in E—C), D-DS Mus.ms. 1459 (in D♭—C, text inc).

[Two Eichendorff Lieder]. Edn: Supplement to *Neue Zeitschrift für Musik* 8 (1838), and Elberfeld: Arnold, [1850/51]; R xix.

1. Und wo noch kein Wandrer gegangen ("Das Waldschloß," "Die Waldfrauen"). Text: Eichendorff. Mss: D-B MN 20 (A; 17 August 1835), D-DS Mus.ms.1444b (A).

2. Wenn die Sonne lieblich schiene ("Pagenlied," "Auf der Reise," "Der wandernde Musikant," "Der Zitherspieler"). Text: Eichendorff. Mss: D-B N.Mus.ms. 98 (A; 25 December 1832), location unknown (auctioned by Sotheby's, 1984—A; 16 July 1833), location unknown (auctioned by J. A. Stargardt, 1993—A; 1 October 1835, with Op. 34, no. 2).

Six Songs [Sechs Gesänge], Op. 34. Edn: Leipzig: Breitkopf & Härtel, [1837], and London: Ewer, [1845/46 (words in English and German; English texts by W. Bartholomew)]; R xix.

1. Leucht heller als die Sonne ("Minnelied," "Mailied"). Text: from *Des Knaben Wunderhorn*. Mss: D-B MN 20 (A; 11 May 1834), GB-Ob MDM c.21 (A; 22 December 1836; facsimile in Ernst Wolff, *Felix Mendelssohn Bartholdy* [Berlin: Harmonie, 1906; enlarged 2d edn, 1909], facing p. 129), D-B MA Depos. MG 9 (A, inc), D-DS Mus.ms.1444a (A), formerly private collection of Hugo von Mendelssohn Bartholdy, Basel (A—with "Auf Flügeln des Gesanges"; facsimile in Max Schneider, ed., *Felix Mendelssohn Bartholdy: Denkmal in Wort und Bild* [Basel: Amerbach, 1947], 82), D-B MA Ms. 12 (C), D-DS Mus.ms. 1459 (C).

2. Auf Flügeln des Gesanges ("Abendlied"). Text: Heine. Mss: D-B MN 20 (melody line and text only—A; ca. August–December 1835), location unknown (auctioned by J. A. Stargardt, 1993—A; 1 October 1835, with "Wenn die Sonne lieblich schiene"; facsimile in Ernst Wolff, *Felix Mendelssohn Bartholdy* [Berlin: Harmonie, 1906; enlarged 2d edn, 1909], facing p. 92), formerly private collection of Hugo von Mendelssohn Bartholdy, Basel (A; with "Leucht heller als die Sonne"; facsimile in Max Schneider, ed., *Felix Mendelssohn Bartholdy: Denkmal in Wort und Bild* [Basel: Amerbach, 1947], 81–82), D-DS Mus.ms. 1459 (in F—C).

3. Es brechen im schallenden Reigen ("Frühlingslied"). Text: K. Klingemann. Ms: GB-Ob MDM c.21 (A).

4. Ach, um deine feuchten Schwingen ("Suleika"). Text: Goethe (i.e.,
Marianne von Willemer). Ms: CH-B private collection (A).
Remarks: See also under unpublished songs, later.

5. Ringsum erschallt in Wald und Flur ("Sonntags," "Sonntagslied"). Text:
K. Klingemann. Mss: D-B MN 28 (A; 28 December 1834), location
unknown (A; 31 January 1836; auctioned by Erasmushaus on 8 October
1994; in letter to Klingemann—facsimile in Ernst Wolff, *Felix
Mendelssohn Bartholdy* [Berlin: Harmonie, 1906; enlarged 2d edn, 1909],
facing p. 127), D-DÜhi Ms. 60.348 (A, ca. 1837), D-DS Mus.ms.1444b
(A), US-Wc (A).

6. Der Herbstwind rüttelt die Bäume ("Reiselied"). Text: Heine.

Two Byron Romances. Edn: *Album Musical auf das Jahr 1837* (Leipzig: Breitkopf
& Härtel, 1836), and independently (Leipzig: Breitkopf & Härtel, [1837]); R
xix.

1. There Be None of Beauty's Daughters ("Keiner von der Erde Schönen").
Mss: D-B N.Mus.ms. 79 (A; 3 August 1833), GB-Ob MS. Horsley b.1
(C).
Remarks: Both manuscripts bear only the English text.

2. Sun of the Sleepless ("Schlafloser Augen," "Erinnerung"). Mss: D-B MN
28 (A; 31 December 1834 [German text]), D-DS Mus.ms.1444b (A inc;
[ca. 1835] [German text]), F-Pbn Ms. 202 (A [English text with German
translation added in Mendelssohn's hand]).
Literature: Monika Hennemann, "Mendelssohn and Byron: Two Songs
almost without Words," *Mendelssohn-Studien* 10 (1997), 131–56.

Six Songs [Sechs Lieder], Op. 47 (S, pf). Edn: Leipzig: Breitkopf & Härtel,
[1839], and London: Ewer, [1846 (words in English and German; English
texts by W. Bartholomew)]; R xix.

1. Wie der Quell so lieblich klinget ("Minnelied," "Im Walde"). Text: L.
Tieck. Mss: GB-Ob MDM c.47 (A; 15 August 1838), location unknown
(A; in songbook written for Cécile Mendelssohn Bartholdy, Christmas
1845; auctioned by Sotheby's, 1959).

2. Über die Berge steigt schon die Sonne ("Morgengruß"). Text: Heine. Ms:
location unknown (A; in songbook written for Cécile Mendelssohn
Bartholdy, Christmas 1845; auctioned by Sotheby's, 1959).

3. Durch den Wald, den dunklen ("Frühlingslied"). Text: Lenau. Mss: D-B
MN 31 (A; 17 April 1839), location unknown (A; in songbook written for
Cécile Mendelssohn Bartholdy, Christmas 1845; auctioned by Sotheby's,
1959).

4. Es ist bestimmt in Gottes Rath ("Volkslied"). Text: E. von Feuchtersleben.
Mss: D-B MN 31 (A; 18 April 1839), location unknown (formerly Koch
collection—A; 18 April 1839).

5. Sie wandelt im Blumengarten ("Der Blumenstrauß"). Text: Klingemann.
Mss: US-Wc ML 30.8j Op. 47 (A; 5 May 1832), GB-Ob MS. Horsley b.1
(A; 28 February 1839), location unknown (A; in songbook written for

Cécile Mendelssohn Bartholdy, Christmas 1845; auctioned by Sotheby's, 1959).

6. Schlummre und träume ("Bei der Wiege," "Wiegenlied"). Text: Klingemann. Mss: GB-Ob MDM b.5 (A; 15 August 1833), D-B MN 31 (A, [?ca. April 1839]), D-B N.Mus.ms. 571 (A), D-DS Mus.ms 1444a (A), US-Wc (A).

Remarks: Composed in 1833 for Felix Moscheles.

Wozu der Vöglein Chöre belauschen ("Lied aus *Ruy Blas*") (2 vv, pf). Text: Hugo. Edn: In A. Schmidt, ed., *Orpheus: musikalisches Taschenbuch auf das Jahr 1840* (Leipzig and Vienna: F. Riedl, 1839). See Incidental music to Victor Hugo's *Ruy Blas*, earlier, and Op. 77 no. 3, later.

Three Duets [Drei zweistimmige Volkslieder] (2 vv, pf). Edn: first published individually, and then together by Schlesinger in [1857]; R xviii.

1. Wie kann ich froh und lustig sein. Text: P. Kaufmann. Edn: In *Album neuer Original-Compositionen für Gesang und Piano* [. . .] (Berlin: Schlesinger, [1837]). Ms: US-NYp JOB 82-10 (A; 3 September 1837).

2. Wenn ich auf dem Lager liege ("Abendlied"). Text: Heine. Edn: In *Album neuer Original-Compositionen für Gesang und Piano* [. . .] (Berlin: Schlesinger, [1838]). Mss: US-NYp JOB 82-10 (A; 3 September 1837), GB-Ob MDM b.5 (A; 19 January 1840).

3. Ich stand gelehnet an den Mast ("Wasserfahrt"). Text: Heine. Edn: In *Album neuer Original-Compositionen für Gesang und Piano* [. . .] (Berlin: Schlesinger, [1838/39]). Ms: location unknown (A, in presentation copy presumably for Eduard Devrient, with Op. 63 no. 1 and Op. 77 no. 1; auctioned by Richard MacNutt Ltd. in 1994).

By Celia's Arbour All the Night/[An Celias Baum in stiller Nacht] ("The Garland"/"Der Blumenkranz"). Text: T. Moore. Edn: London: Ewer, and Braunschweig: Spehr, [1841]; R xix. Mss: D-B MN 20 (A; 24 May 1829—with English and German text), D-B N.Mus.ms. 99 (A; 6 February 1841—German text only, for Sophie Schloß; facsimile in Max Schneider, ed., *Felix Mendelssohn Bartholdy: Denkmal in Wort und Bild* [Basel: Amerbach, 1947], 129–30), D-B N.Mus.ms. 162 (C/A [*Stichvorlage*]—English and German text).

Six Songs [Sechs Lieder], Op. 57 (S, pf). Edn: Leipzig: Breitkopf & Härtel, [1842/43], London: Wessel & Stapleton, [?1843 (words in English and German; English texts by W. Bartholomew)], and Paris: Grus [1843 (with French texts by L. Delâtre)]; R xix.

1. Es ist in den Wald gesungen ("Altdeutsches Lied"). Text: Heinrich Schreiber. Mss: F-Pbn (A; 26 July 1839), US-STu (A; 4 January 1841), location unknown (A; in songbook written for Cécile Mendelssohn Bartholdy, Christmas 1845; auctioned by Sotheby's, 1959), location unknown (with Op. 57, nos. 2 and 4—A; auctioned by Sotheby's, 1959), US-Wc (A).

2. O Winter, schlimmer Winter ("Hirtenlied," "Des Hirten Winterlied"). Text: Uhland. Mss: D-B MN 31 (A; 20 April 1839), D-B N.Mus.ms. 102 (A; 12 January 1840), US-NYpm Heineman (A; 18 November 1840, in letter to Charlotte Moscheles; facsimile in Felix Moscheles, ed., *Felix Mendelssohn Bartholdys Briefe an Ignaz und Charlotte Moscheles*, [Leipzig: Dunker & Humblot, 1888], 203), US-Wc (A), location unknown (with Op. 57, nos. 1 and 4—A; auctioned by Sotheby's, 1959).
   Remarks: See also the choral version, Op. 88 no. 3, earlier.

3. Was bedeutet die Bewegung? ("Suleika"). Text: Goethe (i.e., Marianne von Willemer). Mss: D-B MN 31 (A inc; [1839]), US-NH Speck Collection (A; 7 June 1841), location unknown (A; 28 June 1841; auctioned by Sotheby's, 1959), location unknown (A; in songbook written for Cécile Mendelssohn Bartholdy, Christmas 1845; auctioned by Sotheby's, 1959), US-Wc (A), US-Wc (A), RUS-SPsc Ms. Pазноʁ₃ F XII 33 (A).

4. Von allen schönen Kindern auf der Welt ("O Jugend, o schöne Rosenzeit," "Rheinisches Volkslied"). Text: Zuccalmaglio. Mss: D-DÜst (A; 9 January 1841; facsimile in Sabine Zahn, *Das Niederrheinische Musikfest 1818–1958: eine Dokumentation* [Cologne, 1984]), location unknown (A; in songbook written for Cécile Mendelssohn Bartholdy, Christmas 1845; auctioned by Sotheby's, 1959), US-Wc (A), F-Pc Ms. 205 (A), location unknown (with Op. 57, nos. 1 and 2—A; auctioned by Sotheby's, 1959).

5. Wenn durch die Piazzetta die Abendluft weht ("Venetianisches Gondellied," "Rendez-vous"). Text: after Thomas Moore. Mss: D-B MN 20 (A; 17 October 1842), location unknown (A; in songbook written for Cécile Mendelssohn Bartholdy, Christmas 1845; auctioned by Sotheby's, 1959), PL-Kj MN 38^2 (A), D-B N.Mus.ms. 101 (A).

6. Laue Luft kommt blau geflossen ("Wanderlied," "Frische Fahrt"). Text: Eichendorff. Mss: PL-Kj MN 35 (A; 29 April 1841), location unknown (A; 19 May 1843; auctioned by J. A. Stargardt, 1979), D-B N.Mus.ms. 95 (A).

Six Duets [Sechs zweistimmige Lieder], Op. 63 (SS, pf). Edn: Leipzig: Kistner, [1844], and London: Ewer, [1844 (words in English and German)]; R xviii.

1. Ich wollt' meine Lieb'. Text: Heine. Mss: GB-Lbl (sk), US-NYpm (A; 22 December 1836), location unknown (with Op. 77 no. 1 and "Ich stand gelehnet an den Mast"; auctioned by J. A. Stargardt on 28 June 1990); location unknown (A, in presentation copy presumably for Eduard Devrient, together with Op. 77 no. 1 and the "Wasserfahrt" of the *Drei zweistimmige Volkslieder* [Berlin: Schlesinger, 1836–1838]; auctioned by Richard MacNutt Ltd. in 1994; facsimile in *Richard MacNutt Ltd., Catalogue 116* [1994]); GB-Lbl MS Zweig 50 (C with note of presentation by Marianne von Willemer).

2. Wie war so schön doch Wald und Feld ("Abschiedslied der Zugvögel," "Herbstlied"). Text: Hoffmann von Fallersleben. Ms: US-Wc (A; 20 May 1844).

3. Wohin ich geh' und schaue ("Gruß"). Text: Eichendorff. Mss: US-NYpm Heineman (A; ca. December 1836), US-NYp JOF 72-16 (A; 26 March 1844).

4. Ach, wie so bald verhallet der Reigen ("Herbstlied"). Text: Klingemann. Mss: PL-Kj MN 39 (A; [1844]), GB private collection (A).

   Remarks: The manuscript version of this Lied bears a different text ("Ach, wie so schnell bist du entschwunden"), possibly not by Klingemann. The piece also exists as a *Lied ohne Worte* in D-B MN 18 (A; 16 October 1836); see unpublished piano solo, later.

   Literature: R. Larry Todd, "'Gerade das Lied wie es dasteht': On Text and Meaning in Mendelssohn's *Lieder ohne Worte*," in *Musical Humanism and Its Legacy: Essays in Honor of Claude V. Palisca*, ed. Nancy Kovaleff Baker and Barbara Russano Hanning (Stuyvesant, NY: Pendragon, 1992), 355–79.

5. O säh ich auf der Heide dort ("Volkslied"). Text: after R. Burns. Mss: D-B MN 20 (A; 17 October 1842), location unknown (arr. 1 v—A; in songbook written for Cécile Mendelssohn Bartholdy, Christmas 1845; auctioned by Sotheby's, 1959), PL-Kj MN 39 (A).

6. Maiglöckchen läutet in dem Thal ("Maiglöckchen und die Blümelein"). Text: Hoffmann von Fallersleben. Ms: PL-Kj MN 39 (A; 23 January 1844), US-NYpm Heineman (A; 22 December 1836), US-Wc (A).

Six Songs [Sechs Lieder], Op. 71 (S, pf). Edn: Leipzig: Breitkopf & Härtel, [1847], and London: Ewer, [1847 (words in English and German)]; R xix.

1. Werde heiter, mein Gemüthe ("Tröstung"). Text: Hoffmann von Fallersleben. Mss: PL-Kj MN 40 (A; 22 December 1845), location unknown (A; in songbook written for Cécile Mendelssohn Bartholdy, Christmas 1845; auctioned by Sotheby's, 1959), US-Bm Richards Collection (A; 11 January 1846), location unknown (auctioned by Christie's, London, 1976—A; 13 January 1846), D-B N.Mus.ms. 80 (A; 13 February 1846), location unknown (A; 30 August 1846; auctioned by J. A. Stargardt on 8–9 April 1987; facsimile on p. 243 of catalog), D-B MA Ep. 98 (A; 20 January 1847, in letter to A. Lindblad; facsimile in *Bref till Adolf Fredrik Lindblad, från Mendelssohn, Dohrn, Almquist, Atlerbom, Geiger, Frederika Bremer, C. W. Böttiger och andra* [Stockholm: Bonnier, 1913], after p. 52), US-Wc (A), US-Wc (A).

2. Der Frühling naht mit Brausen ("Frühlingslied," "Frühling"). Text: Klingemann. Mss: location unknown (A; in songbook written for Cécile Mendelssohn Bartholdy, Christmas 1845; auctioned by Sotheby's, 1959), PL-Kj MN 40 (A; 3 April 1845), location unknown (with Op. 86, no. 5—A; 21 March 1846; auctioned by Sotheby's, 1959); US-Wc (A), D-B MA Ms. 14 (C/A).

3. Diese Rose pflück' ich hier ("An die Entfernte"). Text: Lenau. Ms: PL-Kj, originally in MN 44 (A; 22 Sep. 1847, missing by 1882).
4. Auf dem Teich, dem regungslosen ("Schilflied," "Die Nacht"). Text: Lenau. Mss: D-B MN 20 (A; 3 November 1842), GB private collection (A; 24 March 1845 [photocopy in US-NYp]).
5. Ich wandere fort ins ferne Land ("Auf der Wanderschaft"). Text: Lenau. Mss: location unknown (A; in songbook written for Cécile Mendelssohn Bartholdy, Christmas 1845; auctioned by Sotheby's, 1959), PL-Kj MN 44 (A; 27 July 1847).
6. Vergangen ist der lichte Tag ("Nachtlied"). Text: Eichendorff. Mss: location unknown (A; in songbook written for Cécile Mendelssohn Bartholdy, Christmas 1845; auctioned by Sotheby's, 1959), location unknown (A; 1 October 1847), RUS-SPsc Ms. Разное₃ F XII 33 (A).

Songs and Vocal Duets Unpublished or Posthumously Published

General Literature: Luise W. Leven, "Mendelssohn's Unpublished Songs," *Monthly Musical Record* 88 (1958), 206–11; Thomas Stoner, "Mendelssohn's Lieder Not Included in the *Werke*," *Fontes Artis Musicae* 26 (1979), 258–66.

Ihr Töne schwingt euch ("Lied zum Geburtstag meines guten Vaters") (S, pf). Ms: GB-Ob MDM c.21 (A; 11 December 1819; facsimile in Ernst Wolff, *Felix Mendelssohn Bartholdy* [Berlin: Harmonie, 1906; enlarged 2d edn, 1909], facing p. 13).

Duet in D major (ST, orch). Ms: D-B MN 1 (A): see Quel bonheur, earlier.

Ave Maria (S, pf). Text: W. Scott. Ms: D-B MN 1 (A; [1820]).

Pauvre Jeanette (S, pf). Edn: In R. Larry Todd, *Mendelssohn's Musical Education* (Cambridge: Cambridge University Press, 1983), 148. Ms: GB-Ob MDM c.43 (A; [1820]).

Raste Krieger, Krieg ist aus (S, pf). Text: after Sir Walter Scott. Edn: In Leven, "Mendelssohn als Lyriker." Ms: D-B MN 1 (A; [1820]).

Da ging ich hin ("Die Nachtigall") (S, pf). Ms: D-B MN 2 (A; ca. 1821).

Nacht ist um mich her ("Der Verlassene") (S, pf). Edn: In Leven, "Mendelssohn als Lyriker." Mss: D-B MN 2 (A; 24 September 1821), D-B MA Depos. MG 17 (A; facsimile in Max Schneider, ed., *Felix Mendelssohn Bartholdy: Denkmal in Wort und Bild* [Basel: Amerbach, 1947], 49–50).

Ein Tag sagt es dem andern (S, A, "cembalo"). Ms: D-B MN 2 (A; [ca. 1822].

Von allen deinen zarten Gaben (S, pf). Edn: In Leven, "Mendelssohn als Lyriker." Ms: D-B MN 2 (A; 18 September 1822).

Schlummre sanft und milde ("Wiegenlied") (S, pf). Edn: In Leven, "Mendelssohn als Lyriker." Mss: D-B MN 2 (A; 18 September 1822), GB-Ob MDM c.54 (C).

Sanft weh'n im Hauch der Abendluft (S, pf). Text: Matthison. Mss: D-B MN 2 (A; 28 December 1822), GB-Ob MDM c.54 (C).

Rieselt hernieder ("Der Wasserfall") (S, pf). Text: Klingemann. Edn: In Leven, "Mendelssohn als Lyriker." Mss: D-B MN 2 (A, inc; ca. 1823), GB-Ob MDM c.54 (C).

Er ist zerbrochen ("Faunenklage") (S, pf). Ms: GB-Ob MDM b.5 (A; 8 June 1823).

Sicheln schallen (S, pf). Text: Hölty. Ms: GB-Ob MDM b.5 (A; ca. June 1823).

Tanzt dem schönen Mai entgegen (S, pf). Text: ? Ms: GB-Ob MDM b.5 (A; ca. June 1823).

Am Seegestad (S, pf). Text: Matthison. Ms: GB-Ob MDM c.47 (A; 26 September 1823).

Durch Fichten (S, pf). Text: Matthison. Ms: GB-Ob MDM c.47 (A; ca. September 1823).

Ich denke dein (S, pf). Text: Matthisson. Ms: GB-Ob MDM c.47 (A; 1 October [?1823]).

Rausche leise, grünes Dach (S, pf). Text: A. von Schlippenbach. Mss: F-Pc Ms. 192 (A; ?December 1824), GB-Ob MDM c.22 (C), GB-Ob MDM c.50/2 (C).

Mitleidsworte, Trostesgründe, neue Dornen diesem Herzen ("Glosse") (S, pf). Text: F. Robert. Mss: D-DS Mus.ms. 1459 (C; based on 1 [or 7?] June 1825), GB-Ob MDM b.5 (A).

Es rauscht der Wald (S, pf). Ms: D-B MN 20 (A; ca. 1827).

[Four Songs] (S, pf). Text: ? Ms: D-B MN 56/5 (A; 1 May 1830).

    1. Sanft entschwanden mir ("Der Tag")

    2. Immer fort ("Reiterlied")

    3. Leb wohl mein Lieb' ("Abschied")

    4. Ich danke Gott ("Der Bettler")

    Remarks: Arguably the most important of Mendelssohn's unpublished songs, since they constitute his only apparently explicit song cycle: there are thematic links among the songs, and the last clearly repeats thematic material from the first. The poet remains unknown, as does the occasion for the songs' composition.

Von schlechtem Lebenswandel (?1830) [lost].

    Remarks: See the composer's letter to his family of 30 November 1830, from Rome.

Weiter, rastlos, atemlos vorüber ("An Marie") (S, pf). Text: ? Edn: Carl Reinecke (Munich: Aibl, [1882]). Ms: D-B MN 49 (A; ca. 1830).

    Remarks: Published with "Erwartung," "An ihrem Grabe," and "Warum ich weine." Edn gives text in German and French.

Wisst ihr wo ich gerne weil' ("Lieblingsplätzchen") (?June 1830). See Op. 99 no. 3, later.

Ich reit' ins finstre Land hinein ("Reiselied"). Text: Uhland. Ms: US-NYpm Lehman (A, inc; 1830).

Ein Blick von deinen Augen ("Die Liebende schreibt") (10 August 1831). See Op. 86 no. 3, later.

Da lieg' ich unter den Bäumen ("Verschwunden") (5 December 1831). See Op. 84 no. 1, later.

Auf, schicke dich recht feierlich ("Weihnachtslied"). Text: C. F. Gellert. Edn: Hans Gerber, *Albert Baur: Ein Lebensbild aus der Zeit deutsches musikalischen, religiösen und politischen Aufbruchs im 19. Jahrhundert* (Freiburg im Breisgau: Waldkircher, 1971). Mss: D-B N.Mus.ms. 98 (A; 19 December 1832), D-B Mus. ep. F. Mendelssohn-Bartholdy 39 (A, 20 Dec. 1832 [in letter to A. Baur]).

Warum sind denn die Rosen so blaß? (S, pf). Text: Heine. Ms: D-B MN 20 (inc; ?May 1834).

Ich weiß mir'n Mädchen ("Mailied," "Andres Mailied," "Hüt du dich") (S, pf). Text: from *Des Knaben Wunderhorn.* Mss: D-B MN 20 (A; 14 May 1834), D-DS Mus.ms.1444a (A).

Mit Lust thät ich ausreiten ("Jagdlied") (25 May 1834). See Op. 84 no. 3, later.

Erwacht in neuer Stärke ("Morgenlied") (?3 December 1836). See Op. 86 no. 2, later.

Das ist der Tag des Herrn ("Sonntagsmorgen") (3 December 1836). See Op. 77 no. 1, later.

Was will die einsame Thräne? ("Erinnerung") (S, pf). Text: Heine. Mss: D-B MN 18 (C/A), GB-Ob MDM c.50/1 (C, inc).

Zarter Blumen leicht Gewinde ("Lied der Freundin," "Die Freundin") (S, pf). Text: Goethe (i.e., Marianne von Willemer). Ms: D-DÜk (A; 13 July 1837; facsimile edited by Max Schneider [Düsseldorf: Goethe-Museum and Internationale Felix-Mendelssohn-Gesellschaft, 1960]), GB-Ob MDM e.6 (A).

Mein Liebchen, wir sassen beisammen ("Im Kahn," "Auf dem Wasser," "Wasserfahrt") (S, pf). Text: Heine. Mss: location unknown (A; 12 December 1837; facsimile in Felix Moscheles, ed., *Felix Mendelssohn Bartholdys Briefe an Ignaz und Charlotte Moscheles,* [Leipzig: Dunker & Humblot, 1888], 148), location unknown (auctioned by Drouot, Paris, 1974—A; 16 June 1840), GB-Ob MDM b.5 (A; 16 April 1841), location unknown (A; 1842—given by Mendelssohn to Mary Wood, later the wife of W. Sterndale Bennett), location unknown (A; in songbook written for Cécile Mendelssohn Bartholdy, Christmas 1845; auctioned by Sotheby's, 1959), D-DÜhi (A; January 1846), GB-Ob MDM c.50/2 (C), D-B MA Ms. 142 (C by Cécile Mendelssohn Bartholdy; 21 November 1847), US-STu (C by Ignaz Moscheles).

So schlaf in Ruh'. Text: Hoffmann von Fallersleben. Ms: GB-Ob MDM c.50/2 (C; based on 22 March 1838).

O könnt' ich zu dir fliegen. Mss: D-B MN 30 (A; 15 August 1838), GB-Ob MDM c.22 (C), GB-Ob MDM c.50/2 (C), D-F Mus. HS 1976 (C).

Im Walde rauschen dürre Blätter ("Herbstlied") (26 February 1839). See Op. 84 no. 2, later.

Nun mußt du mich auch recht verstehn ("Auf Wiedersehn") (S, pf). Ms: location unknown (A; 25 January 1840; auctioned by J. A. Stargardt on 6 March 1985).

An den Rhein, zieh nicht an den Rhein ("Warnung vor dem Rhein") (S, pf). Text: C. Simrock. Edn: Bonn: Simrock, [1849]; R xix. Ms: location unknown (ca. 25 February 1840).

Ich hör ein Vöglein ("Im Frühling") (S, pf). Text: A. Böttger. Edn: in A. Böttger, *Gedichte*, 2d edn (Leipzig: Klemm, 1846). Mss: PL-Kj MN 35 (A; 20 April 1841, US-SM (A; 21 April 1841), D-B N.Mus.ms. 4 (C/A; 8 July 1841), US-Wc (A).

Ein Schifflein ziehet leise ("Das Schifflein") (6 June 1841). See Op. 99 no. 4, later.

Ach, wer bringt die schönen Tage ("Erster Verlust") (9 August 1841). See Op. 99 no. 1, later.

Es weiß und rät es doch Keiner (September 1842). See Op. 99 no. 6, later.

Mein Vater ist ein Appenzeller. Text: Folksong. Ms: location unknown (A; 29 September 1842; auctioned by J. A. Stargardt, 1974)

Der Geissbub bin ich auch noch da. Text: Swiss folk song Ms: CH private collection (A; 29 September 1842).

> Remarks: Mendelssohn had jotted down the melody on an earlier trip through Switzerland in 1831, titling it "Auf dem Vierwaldstätter See"; see GB-Ob MDM g.3.

> Literature: Rudolf Grumbacher and Albi Rosenthal, "'Dieses einzige Stückchen Welt . . .': Über ein Albumblatt von Mendelssohn Bartholdy," *Mendelssohn-Studien* 5 (1982), 123–30 [includes facsimile].

Und über dich wohl stimmt (9 July 1844). Ms: location unknown.

Wenn sich zwei Herzen scheiden (22 December 1845). See Op. 99 no. 5, later.

Der trübe Winter ist vorbei ("Altdeutsches Frühlingslied") (7 October 1847). See Op. 86 no. 6, later.

Three Duets [Drei zweistimmige Lieder], Op. 77 (2 vv, pf). Edn: Leipzig: Kistner, [1848/49], and London: Ewer, [1849 (words in English and German)]; R xviii.

   1.   Das ist der Tag des Herrn ("Sonntagsmorgen," "Sonntagslied," "Morgenlied"). Text: Uhland. Mss: D-B MN 20 (A; 3 December 1836; facsimile in Max Schneider, ed., *Felix Mendelssohn Bartholdy: Denkmal in Wort und Bild* [Basel: Amerbach, 1947], 113), location unknown (auctioned by J. A. Stargardt, 1981—A; 7 March 1840), location unknown (A—auctioned by Richard MacNutt Ltd. in 1994).

   2.   Ein Leben war's im Aehrenfeld ("Das Aehrenfeld"). Text: Hoffmann von Fallersleben. Ms: PL-Kj MN 44 (A; 18 January 1847).

   3.   Wozu der Vöglein Chöre belauschen ("Lied aus *Ruy Blas*"). See Incidental Music to Victor Hugo's *Ruy Blas*, earlier; see also under song title in Songs and Vocal Duets Published by Mendelssohn.

Three Songs [Drei Gesänge], Op. 84 (low v, pf). Edn: Leipzig: Breitkopf & Härtel, [1850/51], and London: Ewer, [1850 (words in English and German)]; R xix.

   1. Da lieg' ich unter den Bäumen ("Verschwunden"). Text: Klingemann. Mss: D-B MN 18 (A; 5 December 1831), location unknown (A; 12

October 1844; auctioned by Sotheby's on 18 November 1988), PL-Kj MN 39 (A).

2. Im Walde rauschen dürre Blätter ("Herbstlied"). Text: Klingemann. Ms: D-B MN 31 (A; 26 February 1839).

3. Mit Lust thät ich ausreiten ("Jagdlied"). Text: from *Des Knaben Wunderhorn*. Ms: D-B MN 20 (A; 25 May 1834).

Six Songs [Sechs Gesänge], Op. 86 (v, pf). Edn: London: Ewer, [1850 (words English and German)], and Leipzig: Breitkopf & Härtel, [1850/1851]; R xix.

1. Es lauschte das Laub. Text: Klingemann. Mss: location unknown (A; ca. 1826), US-Wc (A).

2. Erwacht in neuer Stärke ("Morgenlied"). Text: J. H. Voss. Mss: location unkwown (A; 3 December 1836), location unknown (A; in songbook written for Cécile Mendelssohn Bartholdy, Christmas 1845; auctioned by Sotheby's, 1959), F-Pc Ms. 203 (A; 12 May 1846).

3. Ein Blick von deinen Augen ("Die Liebende schreibt"). Text: Goethe. Mss: US-NYpm Lehman (A; 10 August 1831), D-DS Mus.ms. 1459 (C; based on 25 November 1831), RUS-SPsc Ms. Pазhoʁ₃ F XII 33 (A).

4. Allnächtlich im Traume seh' ich dich. Text: Heine. Mss: D-DÜhi Ms. 60.348 (A; ca. 1837), RUS-SPsc Ms. Pазhoʁ₃ F XII 33 (A).

5. Mein Herz ist wie die dunkle Nacht ("Der Mond"). Text: Geibel. Mss: location unknown (A; in songbook written for Cécile Mendelssohn Bartholdy, Christmas 1845; auctioned by Sotheby's, 1959), location unknown (with Op. 71, no. 2—A; 21 March 1846; auctioned by Sotheby's, 1959), F-Pc Ms. 210 (A), US-Wc (A).

6. Der trübe Winter ist vorbei ("Altdeutsches Frühlingslied"). Text: F. von Spee. Ms: GB-Ob MDM b.5 (A, 7 October 1847; possibly originally contained in MN 44, as identified by Schleinitz in 1848).

Six Songs [Sechs Gesänge], Op. 99. Edn: Leipzig: Breitkopf & Härtel, [1852], and London: Ewer, [1852 (words in English and German)]; R xix.

1. Ach, wer bringt die schönen Tage ("Erster Verlust"). Text: Goethe. Mss: PL-Kj MN 35 (A; 9 August 1841), US-NYpm Lehman (A), US-Wc (A).

2. Die Sterne schau'n. Text: A. von Schlippenbach. Ms: F-Pc Ms. 192 (A).

3. Wisst ihr wo ich gerne weil' ("Lieblingsplätzchen"). Text: Friederike Robert. Ms: D-B MN 49 (A; ca. June 1830).

4. Ein Schifflein ziehet leise ("Das Schifflein"). Text: Uhland. Ms: PL-Kj MN 35 (A; 6 June 1841).

5. Wenn sich zwei Herzen scheiden ("Fahrwohl"). Text: Geibel. Mss: PL-Kj MN 40 (A; 22 December 1845), location unknown (A; in songbook written for Cécile Mendelssohn Bartholdy, Christmas 1845; auctioned by Sotheby's, 1959), F-Pc Ms. 210 (A).

6. Es weiß und rät es doch keiner. Text: Eichendorff. Mss: PL-Kj MN 38² (A; [September 1842]), RUS-SPsc Ms. Pазhoʁ₃ F XII 33 (A).

Not dated:

Bist auf ewig du gegangen ("Erwartung") (S, pf). Edn: Carl Reinecke (Munich: Aibl, [1882], words in German and French). Ms: D-LEs Gewandhaus Nr. 46 (C).

    Remarks: Published with "An Marie," "An ihrem Grabe," and "Warum ich weine."

Der Eichwald brauset ("Des Mädchens Klage") (S, pf). Text: Schiller. Edn: London: Ewer, and Leipzig: Schuberth, [1866]; R xix. Ms: location unknown (facsimile in *Emil Naumanns Illustrierte Musikgeschichte* [6th edn, n.d.], before page 537).

Catina belina ("Canzonetta Veneziana") (S, pf). Ms: GB-Ob MDM c.50/1 (C). Possibly not by Mendelssohn.

Ein Mädchen wohnt (S, pf). Ms: GB-Ob MDM c.50/1 (C). Possibly not by Mendelssohn.

Ich flocht ein Kränzlein schöner Lieder ("Lieben und Schweigen") (S, pf). Text: Konstantin von Tischendorf. Edn: In *Die musikalische Welt* (1872). Ms: D-LEs Gewandhaus Nr. 46 (C).

    Literature: Paul Losse, "Ein bisher ungedrucktes Lied von Mendelssohn," *Musik und Gesellschaft* 9 (1959), 68–71.

Ich soll bei Tage und bei Nacht (S, pf). Ms: GB-Ob MDM c.50/1 (C). Possibly not by Mendelssohn.

Ja, wär's nicht aber Frühlingszeit (v, pf). Text: Hoffmann von Fallersleben. Ms: GB-Ob MDM c.50/1 (C). Possibly not by Mendelssohn.

Meine Ruh ist hin ("Gretchen") (v, pf). Text: Goethe. Ms: D-LEm PM 144 (A inc).

Vier trübe Monden sind entflohn ("An ihrem Grabe") (v, pf). Edn: Carl Reinecke (Munich: Aibl, [1882], words in German and French). Ms: D-LE Stadtarchiv Gewandhaus Nr. 46 (C).

    Remarks: Published with "An Marie," "Erwartung," and "Warum ich weine."

Weinend seh ich in die Nacht ("Warum ich weine!") (S, pf). Edn: Carl Reinecke (Munich: Aibl, [1882], words in German and French). Ms: GB-Ob MDM c.50/2 (C).

    Remarks: Published with "An Marie," "Erwartung," and "An ihrem Grabe."

Wie die Blumen (S, pf). Ms: GB-Ob MDM c.50/1 (C). Possibly not by Mendelssohn.

Auch um deine feuchten Schwingen ("Suleika"). Ms: location unknown (A; auctioned by Sotheby's, 1959).

    Remarks: Auctioned in 1959, this song is described in the Sotheby's as "[a]n entirely different setting from Op. 34, no. 4.—Unpublished."

Es weh'n die Wolken über Meer ("Abschied") (S, pf). Ms: location unknown (C/A; auctioned by Sotheby's on 17 May 1990).

Chamber Music Published by Mendelssohn

General Literature: Friedhelm Krummacher, "Zur Kompositionsart Mendelssohns: Thesen am Beispiel der Streichquartette," in *Das Problem Mendelssohn*, ed. Carl Dahlhaus (Regensburg: Bosse, 1974), 169–84, repr. in *Felix Mendelssohn Bartholdy*, ed. Heinz-Klaus Metzger and Rainer Riehn, Musik-Konzepte 14/15 (Munich: Text+Kritik, 1980), 46–74, and translated in the present volume; idem, *Mendelssohn—Der Komponist: Studien zur Kammermusik für Streicher* (Munich: Wilhelm Fink, 1978); R. Larry Todd, "The Instrumental Music of Felix Mendelssohn-Bartholdy: Selected Studies Based on Primary Sources" (Ph.D. diss., Yale University, 1979).

Piano Quartet no. 1 in C minor, Op. 1 (vn, va, vc, pf). Edn: Paris: Maurice Schlesinger, Berlin: Schlesinger [1823] (parts); [1839] (arr. pf 4 hands by F. Mockwitz), [1856] (parts and FS); R ix.   Mss: D-B MN 2 (A; 20 September–October 1822), GB-Lbl 47858 (C).

Remarks: Though the C-minor Piano Quartet is, of course, not Mendelssohn's first composition or even his first in the genre,[27] it is historically significant as Mendelssohn's first published work—published when he was only fourteen.

Literature: Peter Ward Jones, "Mendelssohn's Opus 1: Bibliographical Problems of the C Minor Piano Quartet," in *Sundry Sorts of Music Books: Essays on the British Library Collections, Presented to O. W. Neighbour on His 70th Birthday*, ed. Chris Banks, Arthur Searle, and Malcolm Turner (London: The British Library, 1993), 264–73.

Piano Quartet no. 2 in F minor, Op. 2 (vn, va, vc, pf). Edn: Berlin: Schlesinger, [1824] (parts), [1843] (PS 4 hands by F. Mockwitz), and [1856] (parts and FS); R ix. Mss: D-B MN 13 (A inc; 9 November–3 December 1823), GB-Lbl 47858 (C).

Remarks: The third movement was published as "Intermezzo," arranged for flute and piano by John Thompson, in *The Harmonicon* 8 (1830), 236–40.

Violin Sonata in F minor, Op. 4. Edn: Berlin: Laue, [1824] (parts); Leipzig: Hofmeister, [1833] (parts—new edn), [1850] (parts and FS); London: Ewer, [1850] (parts and FS); R ix. Mss: location unknown—formerly MN 13 (A FS; 3 June 1823), GB-Ob MDM c.57 (vn part only—C).

Piano Quartet no. 3 in B minor, Op. 3 (vn, va, vc, pf). Berlin: Laue, [1825] (parts); Paris: Richault [1827] (parts; "nouvelle édition avec changements et corrections par l'Auteur"); Leipzig: Hofmeister, [1833] (parts—new edn.), [1861] (parts and FS); R ix. Ms: D-B MN 13 (A FS; 7 October 1824–18 January 1825).

String Quartet no. 1 in E♭ major, Op. 12 (2 vn, va, vc). Edn: Paris: Richault, [1830] (parts); Leipzig: Hofmeister,[1830] (parts), [1836] (PS 4 hands) [1841] (FS); Berlin: Schlesinger, [1839] (PS 4 hands); R vi. Ms: F-Pc Ms. 191 (A FS; 14 September 1829).

String Quartet no. 2 in A minor, Op. 13 (2 vn, va, vc). Edn: Leipzig: Breitkopf & Härtel, and Paris: Richault, [1830] (parts and PS 4 hands by Mendelssohn); Leipzig: Breitkopf & Härtel, and London: Ewer, [1843] (FS and new edn of PS 4 hands); R vi; L iii. Mss: D-B MN 25 (A FS; 26 October 1827), GB-Ob MDM c.21 (Intermezzo—C FS; based on 2 January 1832), GB-Lbl Add. 32179 (C/A FS).

Variations concertantes in D major for Cello and Piano, Op. 17 (vc, pf). Edn: London: Cramer, Addison, & Beale, [1830], and Vienna: Mechetti, [1830/31]; R ix. Ms: GB-Ob MDM c.8 (A; 30 January 1829).

The Evening Bell. See under Unpublished or Posthumously Published, later).

String Quintet no. 1 in A major, Op. 18. Edn: Bonn: Simrock, and Paris: Richault, [1833] (parts); Bonn: Simrock, [1838] (PS 4 hands), [1849] (FS); R v. Mss: GB-Ob MDM c.22 (dr), US-NYpm Lehman (A FS; 31 March 1826 [at end of first movement—17 April]), F-Pc (C FS; based on 21 May 1826), D-B MN 23 (Intermezzo only—A FS; 23 February 1832), F-Pc (parts for first version, va2 missing—A), D private collection (final version—A FS), D-B N.Mus.ms. 169 (parts from 1st Simrock edn. with A changes and collettes).

   Remarks: Like the *Midsummer Night's Dream Overture* and the Octet for Strings, the familiar version of Op. 18 is the product of a substantial reworking in the early 1830s; most important among these are the removal of a canonic minuet and its replacement by the Intermezzo written in memory of Eduard Rietz, Mendelssohn's childhood friend who died in early 1832.

Octet for Strings, Op. 20 (4 vn, 2 va, 2 vc). Edn: Leipzig: Breitkopf & Härtel, [1833] (parts and PS 4 hands), [1848] (FS); R v. Mss: D-B MN 18 (skk), US-Wc ML30.8j Op. 20 (A; 15 October 1825; facsimile ed. Jon Newsom [Washington, DC: Library of Congress, 1976]). See also the remarks earlier regarding the Symphony no. 1 in C minor, Op. 11.

   Remarks: With the *Midsummer Night's Dream Overture*, Op. 21, the first of Mendelssohn's mature masterpieces. Like Op. 21, the Octet was written around the composer's sixteenth birthday and performed successfully but published only after extensive revision in the early 1830s.

   Literature: Todd, "The Instrumental Music"; Vitercik, *The Early Mendelssohn*.

Cello Sonata no. 1 in B♭ major, Op. 45 (vc, pf). Edn: Leipzig: Kistner, and London: Novello, [1839]; R ix. Mss: location unknown (A; 13 October 1838), GB-Ob MDM c.45 (pf part only—C/A).

   Remarks: Also published arr. for violin and piano, with the violin part prepared by Ferdinand David (Leipzig: Kistner, [1839]).

Three String Quartets, Op. 44 (2 vn, va, vc). Edns (all published separately): Leipzig: Breitkopf & Härtel, [1839] (parts), [1839/40] (PS 4 hands by F. Mockwitz, rev. by Mendelssohn), [1840] (FS); R vi; L iii.

   No. 1 in D major. Mss: D-B N.Mus.ms. 9 (A FS; 24 July 1838), D-B N.Mus.ms. 108 (first movement only—A FS).

   No. 2 in E minor. Ms: D-B MN 29 (A FS; 18 June 1837).

No. 3 in E♭ major. Ms: D-B MN 30 (A FS; 6 February 1838).

Remarks: Among Mendelssohn's most influential chamber works, these quartets also inspired Robert Schumann's series of string quartets, which were dedicated to Mendelssohn in 1843. For observations concerning performance practices of these works suggested by Ferdinand David's heavily annotated violin part, see Clive Brown, "Bowing Styles, Vibrato and Portamento in Nineteenth-Century Violin Playing," *Journal of the Royal Musical Association* 113 (1988), 97–128.

Literature: Gerhard Schuhmacher, "Zwischen Autograph und Erstveröffentlichung: Zu Mendelssohns Kompositionsweise, dargestellt an den Streichquartetten op. 44," *Beiträge zur Musikwissenschaft* 15 (1973), 253–61; Friedhelm Krummacher, "Zur Kompositionsart Mendelssohns: Thesen am Beispiel der Streichquartette" (see Chapter 8 of this volume).

Piano Trio no. 1 in D minor, Op. 49. Edn: Leipzig: Breitkopf & Härtel, and London: Ewer, [1840] (parts and FS); R ix. Mss: D-B MN 19 (skk), D-B MN 31 (A FS; 18 July 1839), D-LEs—Archiv Breitkopf & Härtel Nr. 1646 (pf part only—A; ?23 September 1839).

Cello Sonata no. 2 in D major, Op. 58. Edn: Leipzig: Kistner, and London: Ewer, [1843]; R ix. Ms: location unknown (A; ca. June 1843).

Remarks: Also published in an arrangement for violin and piano, with the violin part prepared by Ferdinand David (Leipzig: Kistner, [1844]).

Piano Trio no. 2 in C minor, Op. 66. Edn: Leipzig: Breitkopf & Härtel, London: Ewer, and Paris: Schlesinger, [1846] (parts and FS); R ix. Mss: D-B N.Mus.ms. 537 (A FS; 30 April 1845), GB-Ob MDM c.57 (vn and vc parts only—C/A).

Chamber Music Unpublished or Posthumously Published

Trio in C Minor (vn, va, pf). Edn: In J. A. McDonald, "The Chamber Music of Felix Mendelssohn-Bartholdy" (Ph.D. diss., Northwestern University, 1972). Ms: D-B MN 1 (A FS; 9 May 1820).

Fuga, Largo in D minor (vn, pf). Edn: In R. Larry Todd, *Education*, 161–63 Ms: GB-Ob MDM c.43 (A; ca. 12 May 1820).

Andante and Fugue in D minor (vn, pf). Ms: D-B MN 1 (A, ca. July 1820).

Violin Sonata in F major (vn, pf). Edn: Renate Unger (Leipzig: Deutscher Verlag für Musik, 1977). Ms: D-B MN 1 (A; [1820]).

Remarks: The sonata's Andante and Presto are separated in the manuscript from the opening Allegro.

Prelude ("Andante") and Fugue in D minor, G minor (vn, pf). Edn: In R. Larry Todd, *Education*, 179–80. Mss: GB-Ob MDM c.43 (without tempo indication—A; ca. 1820), D-B MN 1 (A, ca. 1820).

Theme and Variations in C major (vn, pf). Edn: In Todd, *Education*, 181–85. Ms: GB-Ob MDM c.43 (A; ca. 1820).

Andante in G minor (vn, pf). Edn: In Todd, *Education*, 189–90. Ms: GB-Ob
   MDM c.43 (A; ca. 1820).
Fugue in G minor (vn, pf). Edn: In Todd, *Education*, 191–93. Ms: GB-Ob MDM
   c.43 (A; ca. December 1820).
   Remarks: Exists in a version for organ, as well; see later.
Movement in G minor/major (vn, pf). Edn: In Todd, *Education*, 199–96. Ms: GB-
   Ob MDM c.43 (A; ca. 1820).
Prelude in D major (vn, pf). Edn: In Todd, *Education*, 199–201. Ms: GB-Ob
   MDM c.43 (A; ca. 1820).
Fugue in D major (vn, pf). Edn: In Todd, *Education*, 202–03. Ms: GB-Ob MDM
   c.43 (A; ca. 1820).
Fugue in D minor (vn, pf). Edn: In Todd, *Education*, 204–05, 208–10, 211–12.
   Ms: GB-Ob MDM c.43 (A; ca. 1820).
   Remarks: The manuscript contains three versions of this fugue.
Fugue in D major (vn, pf). Edn: In Todd, *Education*, 206–07. Ms: GB-Ob MDM
   c.43 (A; ca. 1820).
Fugue in D minor (vn, pf). Edn: In Todd, *Education*, 213–15. Ms: GB-Ob MDM
   c.43 (A; ca. December 1820).
   Remarks: Exists also in a version for organ, dated 3 December; see later.
Andante in D minor (vn, pf). Edn: In Todd, *Education*, 215–19. Ms: GB-Ob
   MDM c. 43 (A; ca. 1820).
Fugue in D minor (vn, pf). Edn: In Todd, *Education*, 224–26. Ms: GB-Ob MDM
   c.43 (A; ca. 1820).
Allegro in C major (vn, pf). Edn: In Todd, *Education*, 229–32. Ms: GB-Ob MDM
   c.43 (A; ca. 1820).
Fugue in C major (vn, pf). Edn: In Todd, *Education*, 233–36. Ms: GB-Ob MDM
   c.43 (A; ca. 1820).
Fugue in D minor (vn, pf). Edn: In Todd, *Education*, 238–40. Ms: GB-Ob MDM
   c.43 (A; ca. 1820–1821).
   Remarks: Exists also in a version for organ, dated 5 January; see later.
Fugue in A minor (vn, pf). Edn: In Todd, *Education*, 240–43. Ms: GB-Ob MDM
   c.43 (A; ca. 1820–1821).
Fugue in C major (vn, pf). Edn: In Todd, *Education*. 243–45. Ms: GB-Ob MDM
   c.43 (A; ca. 1820–1821).
Fugue in C major (vn, pf). Edn: In Todd, *Education*, 246–48. Ms: GB-Ob MDM
   c.43 (A; 17 January 1820 [?*recte* 1821]).
Fugue in C minor (vn, pf). Edn: In Todd, *Education*, 249. Ms: GB-Ob MDM c.43
   (A; ca. 1820–1821).
Fugue in C major (vn, pf). Edn: In Todd, *Education*, 250–52. Ms: GB-Ob MDM
   c.43 (A; 20 January 1820 [?*recte* 1821]).
Fugue in C minor (vn, pf). Edn: In Todd, *Education*, 253–54, 255–57. Ms: GB-
   Ob MDM c.43 (A; 24 January 1820 [?*recte* 1821]).
   Remarks: The source includes a sketch for this fugue and a second
   complete version dated 28 [January 1821].

Minuet in G major (vn, pf). Ms: D-B MN 2 (A; [ca. 1820–1821]).

Violin Sonata in D minor (vn, pf). Ms: D-B MN 2 (A inc; [1821]).

[Twelve Fugues] (str qt). Ms: D-B MN 2 (A FS; 1821).

> [No. 1] in D minor (24 March 1821).
>
> [No. 2] in C major (28 March 1821).
>
> [No. 3] in D minor (4 April [1821]).
>
> [No. 4] in D minor (7 April 1821).
>
> [No. 5] in C minor (11 April 1821).
>
> [No. 6] in D minor (18 April 1821).
>
> [No. 7] in C minor (27 April 1821).
>
> [No. 8] in E♭ major (2 May [1821]).
>
>> Remarks: Uses "O Haupt voll Blut und Wunden" as *cantus firmus.*
>
> [Fugue in C major] (inc)
>
> [Fugue in G minor] (inc)
>
> [No. 9] in G minor (4 May 1821).
>
>> Remarks: Uses "Herzliebster Jesu" as *cantus firmus.*
>
> [No. 10] in F major.
>
>> Remarks: Uses "Wie schön leuchtet der Morgenstern" as *cantus firmus.*
>
> [Fugue in G minor] (inc)
>
> [No. 11] in A major.
>
>> Remarks: Uses "Vom Himmel hoch da komm ich her" as *cantus firmus.*
>
> [Fugue in G major] (inc)
>
> [Fugue in F major] (inc)
>
> [No. 12] in C major.
>
>> Remarks: Uses a *cantus firmus* that is evidently original.

Piano Quartet in D minor (vn, va, vc, pf). Edn: In McDonald, "The Chamber Music." Ms: D-B MN 3 (A FS; [1822]).

String Quartet in E♭ major. Ms: GB-Lbl Add. 30900 (A, 5–30 March 1823. Facsimile (Berlin: Hermann Erler, 1879, and London: Neumeyer, [1880]).

> Remarks: The ms reproduced in facsimile is not in Mendelssohn's hand; see *Catalogue III*, p. 175.

Violin Sonata in D minor (vn, pf). Ms: D-B MN 20 (A inc; ca. June 1823).

Viola Sonata in C minor (vla, pf). Edn: Leipzig: VEB Deutscher Verlag fur Musik, 1966; New York: Belwin Mills, [n.d.]. Ms: D-B MN 4 (A; 23 November 1823–14 February 1824).

> Remarks: The Minuet of this sonata was later adapted for use in the C-minor Symphony, Op. 11 (see earlier).
>
> Literature: Köhler, "Der unbekannte."

Clarinet Sonata in E♭ major (cl, pf). Edn: Eric Simon and Felix Guenther (New York: Sprague-Coleman, 1941—based on C in D-B MN 42); Gerhard Allroggen (Wiesbaden: Breitkopf & Härtel, 1987—based on A in US-NYpm). Mss: US-NYpm Cary (A; 17 April [1824]), D-B MN 42 (C; based on 17 April [1824]).

Sextet in D major, Op. 110 (vn, 2 va, vc, cb, pf). Edn: Leipzig: Kistner, [1868] (parts and FS), [1869] (PS 4 hands); R ix. Ms: D-B MN 4 (A FS; 10 May 1824).

Fugue in E♭ major for String Quartet, Op. 81 no. 4. Edn: Leipzig: Breitkopf & Härtel, [1850] (parts), [1851] (FS); R vi. Ms: D-B MN 18 (A FS; 1 November 1827).

> Remarks: Published with Op. 81 no. 1–3 under the title *Andante, Scherzo, Capriccio, & Fugue.*

The Evening Bell (hp, pf). Edn: London: Chappell, 1876 (parts and pf arrangement). Mss: D-B MN 18 (C; based on November 1829), location unknown (arr. pf duet—C/A; arr. by G. Attwood, M.A. Cantab).

> Remarks: The erroneous statement, given in the *New Grove* work list and elsewhere, that this work was first published in a volume titled *Musical Haunts in London* stems from a misunderstanding. George Grove made the association of the two titles in his original *Dictionary*, but in fact *Musical Haunts in London* is the title of an 1895 book by F. G. Edwards (author of important monographs on the Mendelssohn oratorios, among other things), in which the compositional history of *The Evening Bell* is related.

Concert Piece in F major, Op. 113 (cl, basset-hn, pf). Edn: Offenbach: André, [1869] (PS and parts); R vii. Ms: US-Wc (A; 30 December 1832). See also posthumously published orchestral works, earlier.

Concert Piece in D Minor, Op. 114 (cl, bassett-hn, pf). Edn: Offenbach: André, [1869] (PS and parts); R vii. Ms: S-Smf (A; 19 January 1833).

Piano Trio in A major (vn, vc, pf). Mss: GB-Ob MDM b.5 (A inc; ?ca. 1834), location unknown (A inc.; auctioned by J. A. Stargardt on 5 October 1989).

String Quartet Movement in F major (2 vn, va, vc). Ms: D-B MN 19 (A inc; ?ca. 1834).

> Literature: Seaton, "A Study," 132.

Assai tranquillo in B minor (vc, pf). Ms: DÜhi (A; 25 July 1835; facsimile in Reinhold Sietz, "Das Stammbuch von Julius Rietz," *Studien zur Musikgeschichte des Rheinlandes* 52 [1962], 222–23).

Violin Sonata in F major (vn, pf). Edn: Yehudi Menuhin (Leipzig: Peters, 1953). Mss: D-B MN 30 (A; 15 June 1838), D-B MN 30 (C/A).

Capriccio in E minor for String Quartet, Op. 81 no. 3. Edn: Leipzig: Breitkopf & Härtel, [1850] (parts), [1851] (FS); R vi. Mss: PL-Kj MN 38² (A; 5 July 1843), F-Pc (A; 11 August 1843).

> Remarks: Published with Op. 81 nos. 1–2 and 4 under the title *Andante, Scherzo, Capriccio u. Fuge.*

String Quintet in B♭ major, Op. 87. Edn: Leipzig: Breitkopf & Härtel, and London: Ewer, [1850] (parts), [1850/51] (FS); R v. Ms: GB-Ob MDM b.5 (skk, ?FS frag), PL-Kj MN 40 (A FS; 8 July 1845).

> Remarks: Friedhelm Krummacher, characterizing this work as "the abandoned attempt" in Mendelssohn's search for a new path in his late chamber works, also demonstrates that the published version of the work

represents seriously flawed editorial procedure in the finale; the autograph transmits a substantial revision that demonstrably reflects Mendelssohn's latest thoughts but has not yet been incorporated into any published editions.

Literature: Friedhelm Krummacher, "Mendelssohn's Late Chamber Music: Some Autograph Sources Recovered," in *Mendelssohn and Schumann: Essays on Their Music and Its Context*, ed. Jon W. Finson and R. Larry Todd (Durham, NC: Duke University Press, 1984), 71–84.

Lied ohne Worte in D major, Op. 109 (vc, pf). Edn: Leipzig: Senff, and London: Novello, Ewer & Co., [1868]; R ix. Ms: PL-Kj MN 44 (A; ca. October 1845).

Andante in E major for String Quartet, Op. 81 no. 1. Edn: Leipzig: Breitkopf & Härtel, [1850] (parts), [1851] (FS); R vi. Mss: PL-Kj MN 44 (sk), PL-Kj MN 44 (A FS; ca. August 1847).

Remarks: Published with Op. 81 nos. 2–4 under the title *Andante, Scherzo, Capriccio u. Fuge*.

Scherzo in A minor for String Quartet, Op. 81 no. 2. Edn: Leipzig: Breitkopf & Härtel, [1850] (parts), [1851] (FS); R vi. Ms: PL-Kj MN 44 (A FS; ca. August 1847).

Remarks: Published with Op. 81 nos. 1 and 3–4 under the title *Andante, Scherzo, Capriccio u. Fuge*.

String Quartet in F minor, Op. 80. Edn: Leipzig: Breitkopf & Härtel, and London: Ewer, [1850] (parts and PS 4 hands), [1851] (FS); R vi. Mss: PL-Kj MN 44 (A FS; September 1847), GB-Ob MDM g.10 (sk).

Literature: Hans-Günter Klein, "Korrekturen im Autograph von Mendelssohns Streichquartett Op. 80: Überlegungen zur Kompositionstechnik und Kompositionsvorgang," *Mendelssohn-Studien* 5 (1982), 113–22; Krummacher, "Mendelssohn's Late Chamber Music"; Rainer Cadenbach, "Zum gattungsgeschichtlichen Ort von Mendelssohns letztem Streichquartett," in *Felix Mendelssohn Bartholdy: Kongreß-Bericht Berlin 1994*, ed. Christian Martin Schmidt (Wiesbaden: Breitkopf & Härtel, 1997), 209–31.

Not dated:

Duet in D minor (2 vn). Ms: GB-Ob MDM b.5 (A).

Theme in A major for variation (str qt). Ms: GB-Ob MDM b.5 (A).

Allegretto in E major (vc, fl, cl, 2 hn). Ms: GB-Ob MDM b.5 (A).

Remarks: Instrumentation of "Frühlingslied," Op. 8 no. 6.

Works for Piano Alone Published by Mendelssohn

General Literature: Karl Gustav Fellerer, "Mendelssohn in der Klaviermusik seiner Zeit," in *Das Problem Mendelssohn*, ed. Carl Dahlhaus (Regensburg: Bosse, 1974), 195–200; Christa Jost, *Mendelssohns Lieder ohne Worte* (Tutzing: Hans Schneider, 1988); R. Larry Todd, "Piano Music Reformed: The Case of Felix Mendelssohn Bartholdy," in *Nineteenth-Century Piano Music*, ed. R. Larry Todd (New York: Schirmer, 1990), 178–220, rev. repr. in the present volume.

Capriccio in F♯ minor, Op. 5 (pf). Edn: Berlin: Schlesinger, [1825], London: Clementi, Collard & Collard, [?1828], Leipzig: Hofmeister, and London: Ewer, [1843]; R xi. Ms: D-B MN 13 (A; 23 July 1825).

Sonata in E major, Op. 6 (pf). Edn: Berlin: Laue, [1826]; R xi. Mss: GB-Ob MDM b.5 (skk), GB-Ob MDM c.8 (A; 22 March 1826).

Fugue in E minor (pf). Edn: *Notre temps* 7 (Mainz: Schott, 1842); R xi. Ms: D-B MN 42 (C; based on 16 June 1827).

>   Remarks: Published with fugue of 13 July 1841; see later.

Sieben Characterstücke, Op. 7 (pf). Edn: Berlin, Laue, [1827], and Leipzig: Hofmeister, [1833] (new edn.); R xi.

>   No. 1 in E minor. Mss: GB-Ob MDM c.8 (A; 6 June 1826), US location unknown (A; 18 October 1828).[28]

>   No. 2 in B minor. Mss: GB-Ob MDM c.8 (A; 17 July 1824), US-NYpm (A).

>   No. 3 in D major.

>   No. 4 in A major. Mss: GB-Ob MDM c.8 (A; 4 June 1826).

>   No. 5 in A major.

>   No. 6 in E minor.

>   No. 7 in E major.

>   Literature: Todd, "The Instrumental Music"; Wolfgang Dinglinger, "Sieben Characterstücke op. 7 von Felix Mendelssohn Bartholdy," *Mendelssohn-Studien* 10 (1997), 101–30.

Scherzo in B minor (pf). Edn: *Berliner allgemeine musikalische Zeitung* 6 (1829), and in *Album du pianiste* [no. 1] (Berlin: Schlesinger, [1838]; R xi. Ms: D-B N.Mus.ms. 23 (A; 12 June 1829).

Introduction and Rondo Capriccioso, Op. 14 (pf). Edn: London: Cramer, Addison & Beale, [1830/31], and Vienna: Mechetti, and Paris: Richault, [1831]; R xi. Mss: D-B MA Depos. MG 44 (A frag; [?1822]), US-NYpm Lehman (A; 4 January 1828), F-Pc Ms. 198 (A; 13 June 1830), location unknown (A; 19 September 1831), D-DS (C; based on 19 September 1831).

>   Remarks: The ms in US-NYpm is headed "Etude" and transmits only the "rondo" of Op. 14.

Fantasia on "The Last Rose of Summer," Op. 15 (pf). Edn: London: Cramer, Addison & Beale, [1830/1831], and Vienna: Mechetti, [1831]; R xi. Ms: location unknown (?1827).

Trois fantaisies ou caprices, Op. 16 (pf). Edn: London: Cramer, Addison, & Beale, and Vienna: Mechetti, [1831] (published individually); R xi.

>   No. 1 in A minor. Mss: D-B MN 20 (titled "Nelken u. Rosen in Menge"—A; 4 September 1829), US private collection of Louis Krasner (A; 4 September 1829), D-B MN 49 (A), GB-Ob MDM c.50/1 (C).

>   No. 2 in E minor. Mss: location unknown (A; 13 November 1829), US private collection of John Bass (A; 22 February 1835), D-B MN 49 (A).

>   No. 3 in E major (originally titled "Am Bach"). Mss: US-R (A; 4 September 1829), D-B MN 20 (C; based on 5 September 1829), D-B MN 49 (C; based on 5 September 1829).

Two musical sketches [Zwei Clavierstücke]. Edn: In *The Musical Gem: A Souvenir for 1834* (London: Mori & Lavenue, [1833]); (Leipzig: Senff, [1859/60]); R xi.

No. 1 in B♭.

No. 2 in G minor.

Songs without Words, vol. 1, Op. 19[b] (pf). Edn: London: Novello ("Original Melodies for the Pianoforte"), [1832], and Bonn: Simrock, [1833]; R xi; Rudolf Elvers and Ernst Herttrich (Munich: Henle, [1981]. Ms: US-SM (A; 20 July 1832).

No. 1 in E major (August–September 1831). Mss: location unknown (auctioned by L'Augnec, Paris, 1986—A; 4 April 1832), D-DS (C; based on a ms dated 19 April 1832).

No. 2 in A minor. Ms: US-NH (A; 11 December 1830).

No. 3 in A major ("Jägerlied").

No. 4 in A major. Mss: US-NYpm (A; 14 September 1829), GB-Ob MDM c.50/1 (C).

No. 5 in F♯ minor.

No. 6 in G minor ("Venetianisches Gondellied," "Auf einer Gondel") Mss: D-B MN 18 (A; 16 October 1830), GB-LEbc (A; 1 June 1831).

Fantasia in F♯ minor ("Sonate écossaise"), Op. 28 (pf). Edn: Bonn: Simrock, [1834]; R xi. Mss: D-B N.Mus.ms. 103 (A; 29 January 1833), S-Smf (A).

Songs without Words, vol. 2, Op. 30 (pf). Edn: Bonn: Simrock, and London: Novello, [1835]; R xi; Rudolf Elvers and Ernst Herttrich (Munich: Henle, [1981]. Ms: US-NYpm Lehman (A; facsimile in Max Schneider, ed., *Felix Mendelssohn Bartholdy: Denkmal in Wort und Bild* [Basel: Amerbach, 1947], appendix).

No. 1 in E♭ major.

No. 2 in B♭ minor. Mss: US-NY private collection (A; in letter to Fanny Hensel dated 26 June 1830), D-DS Mus.ms.1459 (A; 30 September 1830), D-B MN 18 (dr; facsimile in Jost, *Mendelssohns Lieder ohne Worte*, 31).

No. 3 in E major.

No. 4 in B minor. Ms: MN 28 (A; 30 January 1834).

No. 5 in D major. Mss: D-B MN 28 (A; 12 December 1833), D-B MA Ms. 12 (C).

No. 6 in F♯ minor ("Venetianisches Gondellied").

Three Caprices, Op. 33 (pf). Edn: Leipzig: Breitkopf & Härtel, and London: Mori & Lavenue, [1836]; R xi.

No. 1 in A minor. Mss: D-B MN 28 (A; 9 April 1834), S-Smf (A), D-B MA Ms.5 (C/A).

No. 2 in E major. Mss: D-B MN 28 (A; 12 September 1835), S-Smf (A).

No. 3 in B♭ minor. Mss: D-B MA Ms.5 (C/A), location unknown (A frag; auctioned by Hans Schneider, 1992).

Scherzo a capriccio in F♯ minor (pf). Edn: In *L'album des pianistes* (Paris: Schlesinger, 1836), and independently by Bonn: Simrock, and London: Cramer, Addison & Beale, [1836]; R xi. Ms: F-Pbn Ms. 199 (29 October 1835).

Six Preludes and Fugues, Op. 35 (pf). Edn: Leipzig: Breitkopf & Härtel, and London: Mori & Lavenue, [1837]; R xi.

> No. 1 in E minor. Mss: location unknown (fugue—A, 16 June 1827; auctioned by Christie's, 10 May 1977), D-B MA Ms.2 (fugue—A, 21 November 1831), D-B MN 23 (prelude—A]), J-Tm (prelude—A; ca. June 1836), US-Wc (fugue—A).

> No. 2 in D major. Mss: D-B MA Ms.6 (fugue, arranged for org 4 hands—A; 11 January 1835, D-B MN 28 (prelude—A; 6 December 1836), D-B MN 29 ("Fughetta"—A; arr. for organ), D-B MN 56/4 (fugue—A).
>
> Remarks: See also "Fughetta in D major" under Two Fugues for Organ Duet, later).

> No. 3 in B minor. Mss: location unknown (fugue—A; 21 September 1832; auctioned by J. A. Stargardt, 1962), D-B MN 28 (prelude—A; 8 December 1836), D-B MN 23 (prelude and fugue—A).

> No. 4 in A♭ major. Mss: D-B MN 19 (sk), D-B MN 28 (fugue—A; 6 January 1835), GB-Ob MS Horsley b.1 (prelude—A; 7 October 1836), D-B MN 23 (prelude—A), D-B MN 28 (fugue—A inc).

> No. 5 in F minor. Mss: D-B MN 28 (fugue—A; 3 December 1834), D-Dlb (fugue—A; 30 December 1835), D-B MN 28 (prelude—A; 19 November 1836), D-B MN 56/4 (fugue—A).

> No. 6 in B♭ major. Mss: D-B MN 28 (fugue—A; 27 November 1836), D-B MN 28 (prelude—A; 3 January 1837).
>
> Literature: R. Larry Todd, "'Me voilà perruqué': Mendelssohn's Preludes and Fugues Op. 35," in *Mendelssohn Studies*, ed. R. Larry Todd (Cambridge: Cambridge University Press, 1993), 162–99.

Songs without Words, vol. 3, Op. 38 (pf). Edn: Bonn: Simrock, and London: Novello, [1837]; R xi; Rudolf Elvers and Ernst Herttrich (Munich: Henle, [1981]. Ms: US-NY private collection of Rudolf Kallir (A).

> No. 1 in E♭ major. Ms: GB-Ob MS. Horsley b.1 (A).

> No. 2 in C minor. Ms: US-Wc ML 30.8b M46 Op. 85 no. 3 (A; 29 March 1836; facsimile in Jost, *Mendelssohns Lieder ohne Worte*, 142).

> No. 3 in E major. Ms: D-DÜhi (A; 2 January 1835).

> No. 4 in A major. Ms: location unknown (A; auctioned by Sotheby's on 18 November 1988).

> No. 5 in A minor. Ms: D-B MN 29 (A; 5 April 1837).

> No. 6 in A♭ major ("Duetto"). Mss: D-B MN 18 (A—27 June 1836), GB-Ob MDM c.21 (A; 27 June 1836).

Gondellied ("Barcarole") in A major (pf). Edn: supplement to *Neue Zeitschrift für Musik* 14 (1841); London: Ewer, [1841]; R xi. Mss: D-B MN 20 (C [Lea Mendelssohn Bartholdy]/A; 5 February 1837; titled "Lied auf einer Gondel"), location unknown (auctioned by Christie's, London, 1981—A; 5 February 1837).

Andante cantabile and Presto agitato in B major (pf). Edn: In *Musikalisches Album auf das Jahr 1839* (Leipzig: Breitkopf & Härtel, [1838]); Leipzig: Breitkopf & Härtel, [1838/1839]; R xi. Mss: D-B MA Depos. MG 18 (A; ca. 25 January 1833—presto agitato differs from published version), D-B MN 30 (A; 22 June 1838).

Etude in F minor (pf). Edn: I. Moscheles and F. J. Fétis, *Méthode des méthodes de piano* (Paris, [ca. 1840]); Berlin: Schlesinger, [1841/42]. Ms: location unknown (A; 13 March 1836).

Songs without Words, vol. 4, Op. 53 (pf). Edn: Bonn: Simrock, and London: Ewer, [1841]; R xi; Rudolf Elvers and Ernst Herttrich (Munich: Henle, [1981]).

No. 1 in A♭ major. Mss: GB-Ob MS. Horsley b.1 (A; 28 February 1839), D-B MN 31 (A frag).

No. 2 in E♭ major. Ms: GB-Ob MDM c.1 (A; 24 February 1835; facsimile in Jost, *Mendelssohns Lieder ohne Worte*, 52).

No. 3 in G minor ("Gondellied"). Ms: D-B MN 31 (A; 14 March 1839; facsimile in Jost, *Mendelssohns Lieder ohne Worte*, 160).

No. 4 in F major ("Abendlied"). Ms: D-Dlb (A; 1 May 1841).

No. 5 in A minor ("Volkslied"). Ms: PL-Kj MN 35 (A; 30 April 1841).

No. 6 in A major. Ms: PL-Kj MN 35 (A; 1 May 1841).

Prelude and Fugue in E minor (pf). Edn: Prelude published with fugue of 16 June 1827 (see earlier) in *Notre temps* 7 (Mainz: Schott, 1842); London: Ewer, [1842]; R xi. Mss: PL-Kj MN 35 (prelude—A; two versions, the first dated 13 July 1841), D-B MN 42 (A).

Variations sérieuses in D minor, Op. 54 (pf). Edn: in *Album-Beethoven* (Vienna: Mechetti, [1841]); London: Ewer, [1841], and Vienna: Mechetti, [1842]; R xi. Mss: PL-Kj MN 35 (A; 4 June 1841), GB-Lbl 47860 (A).

Literature: Christa Jost, "In Mutual Reflection: Historical, Biographical, and Structural Aspects of Mendelssohn's *Variations sérieuses*," in *Mendelssohn Studies*, ed. R. Larry Todd (Cambridge: Cambridge University Press, 1992), 33–63.

Songs without Words, vol. 5, Op. 62 (pf). Edn: Bonn: Simrock, and London: Ewer, [1844]; R xi; Rudolf Elvers and Ernst Herttrich (Munich: Henle, [1981]). Mss: D-B MA Dep. MG 3 (C/A; 31 January 1844), GB-Lbl (arrangement for pf 4 hands—A; 9 June 1844 [ed. Robin Langley (Kassel: Bärenreiter, 1982)]).

No. 1 in G major. Mss: PL-Kj MN 39 (A, 6 January 1844), PL-Kj MN 39 (A; 12 January 1844).

No. 2 in B♭ major. Mss: PL-Kj MN 38² (A; 29 July 1843), US-NY private collection of Rudolf Kallir (A; 13 September 1843).

No. 3 in E minor ("Trauermarsch"). Mss: S-Smf (A; 19 January 1843), PL-Kj MN 38² (A; 16 March 1843; facsimile in Jost, *Mendelssohns Lieder ohne Worte*, 178), US-NY private collection of Rudolf Kallir (A; 13 September 1843), US-Wc (A).

No. 4 in G major. Mss: PL-Kj MN 38^2 (A), US-NYpm Cary (A).

No. 5 in A minor ("Venetianisches Gondellied"). Mss: location unknown (auctioned by Hans Schneider, 1993—A; 24 January 1841; facsimile in Wehner, [see Literature], 55), location unknown (A; 11 October 1842; auctioned by Sotheby's on 21 November 1990; facsimile in Wehner, [see Literature], 56), US-NYpm Lehman (A—*Stichvorlage*), US-Wc (A).

    Literature: Ralf Wehner, "'. . . ich zeigte Mendelssohns Albumblatt vor und Alles war gut.'": Zur Bedeutung der Stammbucheintragungen und Albumblätter von Felix Mendelssohn Bartholdy," in *Felix Mendelssohn Bartholdy: Kongreß-Bericht Berlin 1994*, ed. Christian Martin Schmidt (Wiesbaden: Breitkopf & Härtel, 1997), 37–63.

No. 6 in A major ("Frühlingslied"). Mss: D-B MN 20 (A; 1 June 1842), US-NYpm Lehman (A), US-NY private collection of Rudolf Kallir (A; 12 November 1843), CH-G Biblioteca Bodmeriana (C; based on 1 June and September 1842).

Songs without Words, vol. 6, Op. 67 (pf). Edn: Bonn: Simrock, and London: Ewer, [1845]; R xi; Rudolf Elvers and Ernst Herttrich (Munich: Henle, [1981]). Mss: D-B MA Ms. 1 (C/A), D-B N.Mus.ms. 27 (arranged for pf 4 hands by Czerny, with autograph changes by Mendelssohn).

No. 1 in E♭ major. Mss: PL-Kj MN 38^2 (A; 29 July 1843), [D-LEm location presently unknown] (A; 7 April 1844; facsimile in Hermann Heyer, ed., *Felix Mendelssohn Bartholdy: Zum Gedenken an die 100. Wiederkehr seines Todestages* [Leipzig: Rat der Stadt, 1947], Tafel II), GB-Ob MDM b.5 (A; ?ca. May–June 1844), GB-Lbl (arrangement for pf 4 hands—A; 9 June 1844 [ed. Robin Langley (Kassel: Bärenreiter, 1982)]), GB-Ob MDM c.47 (C/A; 24 December 1844), D-B N.Mus.ms. 38 (C/A; 13 January 1845), PL-Kj MN 39 (A).

No. 2 in F♯ minor. Mss: PL-Kj MN 40 (A; 3 May 1845), CH-B private collection (A; 25 May 1845).

No. 3 in B♭ major. Mss: CH-B private collection (A; 25 May 1845), PL-Kj MN 40 (A; [May 1845]), D-B MN 20 (A; 23 November [1845]).

No. 4 in C major ("Spinnerlied"). Mss: PL-Kj MN 40 (A; 5 May 1845), CH-B private collection (A; 25 May 1845), PL-Kj MN 38^2 (A).

No. 5 in B minor. Mss: PL-Kj MN 39 (A; 5 January 1844), GB-Ob MDM b.5 (A; ca. May–June 1844), GB-Ob MDM c.47 (C/A, 24 December 1844), D-B N.Mus.ms. 38 (C/A, 13 January 1845).

No. 6 in E major. Mss: GB-Ob MDM c.47 (C/A, 24 December 1844), D-B N.Mus.ms. 38 (C/A; 13 January 1845).

Six Pieces for the Piano-forte, composed as a Christmas Present for His Young Friends by Felix Mendelssohn Bartholdy [Christmas Pieces, Kinderstücke], Op. 72 (pf). Edn: London: Ewer, [1847], and Leipzig: Breitkopf & Härtel,

[1848]; R xi. Mss: PL-Kj MN 40 (A), GB-OB MDM c.47 (C/A), GB-Ob MDM c.23 (C/A).

No. 1 in G major. Ms: GB-Ob MDM d.56/2 (A; 24 June 1842).

No. 2 in E♭ major. Mss: GB-Ob MDM d.56/2 (A), GB-Ob MDM d.59 (C).

No. 3 in G major. Ms: GB-Ob MDM d.56/1 (A, 21 June 1842).

No. 4 in D major. Mss: GB-Ob MDM d.56/2 (A), GB-Ob MDM d.59 (C).

No. 5 in G minor. Ms: GB-Ob MDM d.56/1 (A).

No. 6 in F major. Mss: GB-Ob MDM d.56/2 (A), GB-Ob MDM d.59 (C).

Remarks: See also "Andante and Variations, B♭ Major" and "Sostenuto in F" under unpublished or posthumously published works for piano alone, later.

Works for Piano Alone, Unpublished or Posthumously Published

Sonata in D major (2 pf). Ms: GB-Ob MDM b.5 (A; [ca. October 1819])
Remarks: Peter Ward Jones has recently shown that this is probably Mendelssohn's earliest surviving composition.

[Allegro] in G minor (2 pf). Ms: GB-Ob MDM b.4 (A; 21 February [1820]).

Lento—Vivace in G minor (pf 4 hands). Ms: D-B MN 1 (A; 1820).

[Four Little Pieces] (pf). Edn: In Todd, *Education*. Ms: GB-Ob MDM c.43 (A; ca. 1820).

No. 1 in G major.

No. 2 in G minor (canon).

No. 3 in G major.

No. 4 in G minor (canon).

Theme and Variations in D major (pf). Edn: In Todd, *Education*, 220–23. Ms: GB-Ob MDM c.43 (A; ca. 1820).

[Six Little Pieces] (pf). Ms: D-B MN 1 (A; [1820]).

No. 1. Allegro in C major. Ms: US-NYpm Lehman (A).

No. 2. [Allegro] in G minor.

No. 3. Andante in A major.

No. 4. Allegro molto in B minor. Mss: US-NYpm Lehman (A), GB-Ob MDM c.43 (A).

Nos. 5 and 6 are found separately substantially later in the volume but are evidently numbered as part of this series of pieces:

[No.] 5. [Piece in E minor].

No. 6. [Piece in A minor].

Andante in F major (pf). Ms: D-B MN 1 (A; [1820]).

Piece in D major/D minor (no tempo-Adagio) (pf). Ms: D-B MN 1 (A; 11 May 1820).

Sonata in A minor (pf). Ms: D-B MN 1 (A; 12 May 1820 [date at end of first mvt]).

Largo in D minor (pf). Ms: D-B MN 1 (A; [1820]).

[Piece in F minor] (pf). Ms: D-B MN 1 (A; [1820]).

Recitativo (Allegro) in E minor (pf). Ms: D-B MN 1 (A; [1820]).
   Remarks: Crossed out.
[Piece in E minor] (pf). Ms: D-B MN 1 (A; [1820]).
   Remarks: Crossed out.
Largo–Allegro in C minor (pf). Ms: D-B MN 1 (A; [1820]).
Andante in C major (pf). Ms: D-B MN 1 (A; [1820]).
   Remarks: Crossed out.
Adagio in D major (pf). Ms: D-B MN 1 (A; [1820]).
Presto in C minor (pf). Ms: D-B MN 1 (A; 1 July 1820).
Sonata in E minor (pf). Ms: D-B MN 1 (A; 13 July 1820).
Sonata in F minor (pf). Mss: D-B MN 1 (first mvt only—A; [1820]), D-B MN 2
   (second and third mvts—A; [1820]).
Sonata in F major (pf). Ms: D-B MN 1 (A inc; [1820])
Andante and Presto in C major (pf 4 hands). Ms: D-B MN 2 (A; [1820]).
Etude in D minor (pf). Ms: D-B MN 2 (A; 28 [?December 1820]).
Etude in A minor (pf). Ms: D-B MN 2 (A; 28 December 1820).
Allegro in A minor (pf). Ms: D-B MN 2 (A; 5 January 1821).
Etude in C major (pf). Ms: D-B MN 2 (A; 30 March [1821]).
Sonata in G minor, Op. 105 (pf). Edn: London: Novello, Ewer & Co., and Leipzig:
   Rieter-Biedermann, [1868]; R xi. Ms: D-B MN 2 (A; 18 August 1821).
Largo–Allegro di molto in C minor/major (pf). Ms: D-B MN 2 (C; based on
   [1821]).
Sonatina in E major (pf). Ms: D-B MA Ms. 142 (A; 13 December 1821; facsimile
   in Hans-Günter Klein, "'. . . dieses allerliebste Buch': Fanny Hensels Noten-
   Album," *Mendelssohn-Studien* 8 [1993], between pp. 152 and 153).
   Remarks: Entered in Fanny's music album.
[Three Fugues] (pf). Ms: D-B MN 2 (A; [1822]).
   No. 1 in D minor.
   No. 2 in D minor.
   No. 3 in B minor.
Fantasia in C minor (pf). Ms: D-B MN 2 (A; ca. 1823).
Allegro in D minor (pf). Ms: D-B MN 2 (A; 19 February 1823).
Sonata in B♭ minor (pf). Edn: R. Larry Todd (New York: Peters, 1981). MS: GB-
   LEbc (A; 27 November 1823).
Capriccio in E♭ major (pf). Ms: GB-Ob MDM c.8 (A; ca. 1823–1824).
Fantasia in D minor (pf 4 hands). Ms: D-B MN 4 (A; 15 March 1824).
Prestissimo in F minor (pf). Ms: GB-Ob MDM c.8 (A; 19 August 1824).
Fugue in G minor (pf). Ms: GB-Ob MDM c.8 (A; 11 September 1824).
Vivace in C minor (pf). Ms: GB-Ob MDM c.8 (A; 29 January 1825).
Fugue in C♯ minor (pf). Ms: D-B MN 13 (A; 5 January 1826).
Andante and Canon in D major (pf). Mss: GB-Ob MDM b.5 (sk), GB-Ob MDM
   c.22 (sk), GB-Ob MDM c.8 (Andante—A inc; ca. January 1826), US-NYpm
   Lehman (A; ca. January 1826).
Fugue in E♭ major (pf). Ms: GB-Ob MDM c.8 (A; 11 September 1826).

Perpetuum mobile in C, Op. 119 (pf). Ed. Leipzig: Kistner, [1873], and London: Novello, Ewer & Co., [1874]; R xi. Mss: GB-Lbl Ms. Loan 95,2 (A; 24 November 1826, in album of Ignaz Moscheles), D-B N.Mus.ms. 117 (A; ca. June 1829), US-Wc (A, "Scherzo").

Fugue in E minor (pf). Ms: D-B MN 42 (C/A; 16 January 1827).

Sonata in B♭ major, Op. 106 (pf). Edn: London: Novello, Ewer & Co., and Leipzig: Rieter-Biedermann, [1868]; R xi. Ms: D-B MN 20 (A; 31 May 1827).

Lied [ohne Worte] in E♭ major (pf). Ms: D-B MA Ms. 142 (A; 14 November 1828; facsimile in Hans-Günter Klein, "...dieses allerliebste Buch": Fanny Hensels Noten-Album," *Mendelssohn-Studien* 8 [1993], after p. 152).
    Remarks: entered in Fanny's music album.

Scherzo in B minor (pf). Ms: D-B N.Mus.ms. 23 (A; 12 June 1829).

Andante con moto in A major (pf). Edn: J. Draheim, ed. (Wiesbaden: Breitkopf & Härtel, 1984). Mss: D-DÜk (A; 21 May–3 June 1830), GB-Ob MDM c.22 (C; based on 21 May–3 June 1830).
    Remarks: Written for Ottilie von Goethe.

Lied [ohne Worte] in A major (pf). Mss: D-B MN 18 (A; 13 June 1830; facsimile in Jost, *Mendelssohns Lieder ohne Worte*, 31), GB-Ob MDM d.28 (A; in letter to Fanny Hensel dated 14 June 1830).

Con moto in A major (pf). Ms: US-NYpm Morgan MA 2616 (A; 3 November 1831).

Presto agitato in B minor (pf). Ms: D-B MA Depos. MG 18 (A; 25 March 1833).
    Remarks: Preceded in autograph by "Andante" of "Andante and presto agitato" published in 1838 (see earlier).

Study in F major (pf) (21 April 1834). See Op. 104b no. 2, later.

Study in B♭ minor (pf) (9 June 1836). See Op. 104b no. 1, later.

Prelude in B minor (pf) (12 October 1836). See Op. 104a no. 2, later.

Lied [ohne Worte] in F♯ minor (pf). Ms: D-B MN 18 (A; 16 October 1836; facsimile in Jost, *Mendelssohns Lieder ohne Worte*, 128).
    Remarks: Published in texted form as vocal duet, Op. 63 no. 4.
    Literature: R. Larry Todd, "'Gerade das Lied wie es dasteht.'"

Prelude in F minor (pf). Ms: D-B MN 28 (A; 13 November 1836).

Prelude in D (pf) (27 November 1836). See Op. 104a no. 3, later.

Prelude in B♭ (pf) (9 December 1836). See Op. 104a no. 1, later.

Con moto in B♭ minor (pf). Ms: D-B MN 18 (A inc; [?ca. 1836–1837]).

[Allegretto] in A (pf). Edn: Leopold Hirschberg, in *Jede Woche Musik* [Berlin], 19 October 1927. Mss: D-B MN 29 (A; 22 April 1837; facsimile in Jacques Petitpierre, *The Romance of the Mendelssohns* [London: Roy, 1947], 122–23), GB-Ob MDM e.6 (A; facsimile in Peter Ward Jones, *The Mendelssohns on Honeymoon* [Oxford: Oxford University Press, 1997], 20).

Capriccio in E, Op. 118 (pf). Edn: Breitkopf & Härtel, 1872. Ms: D-B MN 29 (A; 11 July 1[837]).

Allegro in E minor ("Albumblatt: Lied ohne Worte"), Op. 117 (pf). Edn: London: Ewer, and Leipzig: Leede, [1859]; first assigned Opus no. 117 in London: Novello, [1870], and Leipzig: Kistner, [1872]. Mss: GB-Ob MDM b.5 (C; ca. 1836), GB-Ob MDM Don. c.44 (A).

Study in A minor (pf) (ca. 1838). See Op. 104b no. 3, later.

Sonata in G major (pf). Ms: GB-Ob MDM b.5 (A inc.; ca. 1839–1841).

　　　　Literature: R. Larry Todd, "The Unfinished Mendelssohn," in *Mendelssohn and His World*, ed. R. Larry Todd (Princeton: Princeton University Press, 1991), 158–84 [includes facsimile].

Allegro brillant in A major, Op. 92 (pf duet). Edn: Leipzig: Breitkopf & Härtel, and London: Ewer, [1851]; R x. Mss: D-B MN 19 (sk), F-Pc Ms. 208 (A; 23 March 1841).

Lied ohne Worte in F♯ minor (pf). Ms: D-B MN 31 (A; 5 April 1839).

Lied ohne Worte in F major (pf). Ms: location unknown (A; ca. 1841; facsimile in *Die Musik* 16/11 [August 1924]).

Variations in E♭ major, Op. 82 (pf). Edn: Leipzig: Breitkopf & Härtel, and London: Ewer, [1850]; R xi. Mss: PL-Kj MN 35 (dr and A; 25 July 1841), US-Wc (A).

Variations in B♭ major, Op. 83 (pf). Edn: Breitkopf & Härtel, [1850]; R xi. Ms: D-B MN 20 (A; ca. 1842),

Andante and Variations in B♭ major, Op. 83a (pf 4 hands). Edn: Breitkopf & Härtel, and London: Ewer, [1850]. Mss: GB-Ob MDM d.56/1 (A; ca. June 1842), D-B N.Mus.ms. 241 (A; 10 February 1844), GB-Ob MDM c.47 (C).
　　　　Remarks: Originally part of Op. 72.

Sostenuto in F major (pf). Ms: GB-Ob MDM d.56/1 (A; ca. June 1842).
　　　　Remarks: Originally part of Op. 72.

Lied [ohne Worte] in D major (pf). Ms: S-Smf (A inc; ca. 19 Jan 1843).

Lied [ohne Worte] in D major (pf). Ms: PL-Kj MN 38[2] (A; 18 March 1843).

[Piece in B♭ major] (pf). Ms: location unknown (A frag; 5 January 1843; auctioned by Hudson Rogue Co., 1990)

Lied ohne Worte in D minor ("Allegro marcato alla marcia," "Reiterlied") (pf). Edn: Ernst Walker (London: Novello, 1947); Rudolf Elvers and Ernst Herttrich (Munich: Henle, [1981]). Mss: PL-Kj MN 40 (A; 12 December 1844), GB-Ob MDM c.47 (C with A title; 24 December 1844), US-STu (A; 4 April 1846), US-STu (C; based on ms of 4 April 1846), D-B N.Mus.ms. 1 (A; 18 December 1846), GB-Ob MDM d.60 (C by Klingemann, Christmas 1848), GB-Ob MDM c.50/2 (C).

Presto in F♯ minor (pf). Ms: F-Pc Ms. 199 (A; 29 October 1845).

Piece in F major ("Auf fröhliches Wiedersehn") (pf). Ms: F-Pc Ms. 212 (A; 4 April 1847).

Lieder ohne Worte, vol. 6, Op. 85 (pf). Edn: London: Ewer, [1850], and Bonn: Simrock, [1850/1851]; R xi; Rudolf Elvers and Ernst Herttrich (Munich: Henle, [1981]).

No. 1 in F major. Mss: GB-Ob MDM c.47 (C with A title; 24 December 1844), D-B N.Mus.ms. 38 (C/A; 13 January 1845), US-STu (C; based on 4 April 1846), GB-Ob MDM d.60 (C by Klingemann; Christmas 1848),

No. 2 in A minor. Mss: D-B MN 20 (A; 9 June 1834; facsimile in Jost, *Mendelssohns Lieder ohne Worte*, 151), GB-Ob MDM c.47 (C with A title; 24 December 1844), D-B N.Mus.ms. 38 (C/A; 13 January 1845), US-STu (C; based on 4 April 1846).

No. 3 in E♭ major. Mss: D-B MN 20 (A; ca. August 1835), US-Wc ML30.8b M46 Op. 85 no. 3 (A; 29 March 1836), US-STu (C; based on 4 April 1846), GB private collection (A; 2 September 1846), GB-Ob MDM d.60 (C by Klingemann; Christmas 1848).

No. 4 in D major. Mss: PL-Kj MN 40 (A; 3 May 1845), PL-Kj MN 40 (A; 6 May 1845), US-STu (C; based on 4 April 1846), D-B private collection (A).

No. 5 in A major. Ms: PL-Kj MN 40 (A; 7 May 1845).

No. 6 in B♭ major. Mss: PL-Kj MN 35 (A; 1 May 1841), GB-Ob MDM d.60 (C by Klingemann; Christmas 1848), PL-Kj MN 38^2 (A).

Lieder ohne Worte, vol. 8, Op. 102 (pf). Edn: London: Novello, Ewer, & Co., [1867], and Bonn: Simrock, [1868]; R xi; Rudolf Elvers and Ernst Herttrich (Munich: Henle, [1981]).

No. 1 in E minor. Mss: D-B MN 19 (sk), D-B MN 20 (A; 1 June 1842).

No. 2 in D major. Mss: PL-Kj MN 40 (A; 11 May 1845), US-STu (C, 4 April 1846), CH-B private collection (A), GB-Ob MDM c.50/2 (C).

No. 3 in C major ("Kinderstück"). Ms: PL-Kj MN 40 (A; 12 December 1845).

No. 4 in G minor. Ms: GB-Ob MDM c.50/1 (C by N. Simrock; 19 October 1865, based on ms dated 4 February 1841).

No. 5 in A major ("Kinderstück"). Ms: PL-Kj MN 40 (A; 12 December 1845).

No. 6 in C major. Ms: GB private possession (A; 5 July 1842).

Three Preludes, Op. 104[a] (pf). Edn: London: Novello, Ewer & Co., and Leipzig: Senff, [1868]; R xi.

No. 1 in B♭ major. Ms: D-B MN 28 (A; 9 December 1836).

No. 2 in B minor. Ms: D-B MN 28 (A; 12 October 1836).

No. 3 in D major. Ms: D-B MN 28 (A; 27 November 1836).

Three Studies, Op. 104[b] (pf). Edn: Leipzig: Senff, [1868]; R xi.

No. 1 in B♭ minor. Ms: D-B MN 20 (A; 9 June 1836).

No. 2 F major. Ms: D-B MN 28 (A; 21 April 1834).

No. 3 in A minor.

Not dated:

Allegro vivace in F minor (pf). Ms: D-B MN 42 (A inc).

Andante in G minor (pf 4 hands). Ms: GB-Ob MDM b.5 (A).

Sonata in A major (pf) (possibly not by Mendelssohn). Ms: GB-Ob MDM b.5 (C).

Lied [ohne Worte] in E♭ major (pf). Mss: GB-Ob MDM c.22 (dr, inc), D-B MA
Ms. 142 (A inc).

Organ Works Published by Mendelssohn

General Literature: Susanna Vendrey, "Die Orgelwerke von Felix
Mendelssohn Bartholdy" (Ph.D. diss., University of Vienna, 1965); François
Sabatier, "Mendelssohn's Organ Works," trans. J. Christopher O'Malley, *American
Organist* 16 (1982), 46–56.

Three Preludes and Fugues, Op. 37 (org). Edn: London: Novello, [1837], and
Leipzig: Breitkopf & Härtel, [1837/1838]; R xii; Wm. A. Little, ed., *Felix
Mendelssohn Bartholdy: Complete Organ Works*, vol. 1 (London: Novello,
1990).

No. 1 in C minor. Mss: D-DS Mus.ms. 1445a (fugue—A; 30 July 1834), D-B
MA Ms. 6 (fugue, arranged for org 4 hands—A; 11 January 1835 [see
also under Two Fugues for Organ Duet in Organ Works Unpublished or
Posthumously Published, later]), D-B MN 29 (prelude—A; 2 April 1837),
I-Rsc ms. A 134 (A; 8 September 1840), D-B MN 29 (fugue—A).

No. 2 in G major. Mss: D-B MN 29 (fugue—A; 1 December 1836), D-B MN
29 (prelude—A; 4 April 1837), I-Rbc (A; 8 September 1840), GB-Ob
MDM c.50/1 (prelude—C/A).

No. 3 in D minor. Mss: US-Wc (fugue—A; 29 March 1833), GB-Lbl MS
add. 14396 (C; based on 29 March 1833), D-B MN 29 (prelude—A; 6
April 1837), I-Rbc (A; 8 September 1840).

Literature: Pietro Zappalà, "I *Preludi* dei 'Präludien und Fugen' op. 37 di
Felix Mendelssohn Bartholdy," in *La Critica del testo musicale: metodi e
problemi della filologia musicale*, ed. Maria Caraci Vela (Milan: Libreria
Musicale Italiana, [1995]), 287–318.

Fughetta in A. Edn: Carl Geißler, *Neues vollständiges Museum für die Orgel* 8
(1840–1841); Little, *Complete Organ Works*, vol. 1. Ms: location unknown.

Remarks: Sharply cut version of Op. 7 no. 5; arrangement may have been
prepared by Carl Geißler, a friend of Mendelssohn and editor of the *Museum*.

Six Sonatas, Op. 65 (org). Edn: London: Coventry & Hollier, Leipzig: Breitkopf
& Härtel, [1845]; R xii; Little, *Complete Organ Works*, vols. 2–4.

No. 1 in F minor/F major. Mss: PL-Kj MN 39 (movement 4—A; 18 August
1844), PL-Kj MN 39 (movement 2—A; 19 December 1844), PL-Kj MN
40 (movement 1—A; 28 December 1844), GB-Ob MDM c.48 (A and
C/A bound in same vol.; ?Spring 1845).

No. 2 in C minor/C major. Mss: D-B MN 31 (fugue—A; 14 July 1839), PL-
Kj MN 40 (movements 1–3—A; 21 December 1844), GB-Ob MDM c.48
(movements 3–4—A; ?Spring 1845), PL-Kj MN 39 (movement 4—A),
GB-Ob MDM c.48 (complete sonata—C/A).

Remarks: See Postlude in D major, later, for an earlier version of movement 3. See Fugue in C major dated 14 July 1839, later, for the original version of movement 4.

No. 3 in A major. Mss: GB-Ob MDM g.1 (drr; [1829]), PL-Kj MN 39 (movement 1—A; 9 August 1844), PL-Kj MN 39 (movement 2—A; 17 August 1844); GB-Ob MDM c.48 (C and C/A bound in one volume; ca. 1845).

No. 4 in B♭ major. Mss: PL-Kj MN 40 (movements 1 and 2—A; 2 January 1845), PL-Kj MN 40 (movement 4—A; 2 April 1845), GB-Ob MDM c.48 (A and C/A bound in one volume; ?Spring 1845).

No. 5 in D major. Mss: PL-Kj MN 39 (movements 2–3—A; 9 September 1844), PL-Kj MN 39 (movement 1—A; [December 1844]), GB-Ob MDM c.48 (A and C/A bound in one volume; ?Spring 1845).

Remarks: For earlier versions of the first two movements, see the Chorale and Fugue in D major of 25 July 1844 and the Chorale in D major of ca. December 1844, later.

No. 6 in D minor/D major. Mss: PL-Kj MN 40 (A; 27 January 1845), GB-Ob MDM c.48 (A and C/A bound in one volume; ?Spring 1845).

Literature: Susanna Großmann-Vendrey, "Stilprobleme in Mendelssohns Orgelsonaten op. 65," in *Das Problem Mendelssohn*, ed. Carl Dahlhaus (Regensburg: Bosse, 1974), 185–94; Robert C. Mann, "The Development of Form in the German Organ Sonata from Mendelssohn to Rheinberger" (D.M.A. diss., University of North Texas, 1978); Gerd Zacher, "Die riskanten Beziehungen zwischen Sonate und Kirchenlied: Mendelssohns Orgelsonaten op. 65, Nr. 1 und 6," in *Felix Mendelssohn Bartholdy*, ed. Heinz-Klaus Metzger and Rainer Riehn, Musik-Konzepte 14/15, 34–45 (Munich: Text + Kritik, 1980).

Organ Works Unpublished or Posthumously Published

Prelude in D minor. Edn: Little, *Complete Organ Works*, vol. 5. Ms: D-B MN 2 (A; 28 November 1820).

Fugue in D minor. Edn: Little, *Complete Organ Works*, vol. 5. Ms: D-B MN 2 (A; 3 December 1820).

Fugue in G minor. Edn: Little, *Complete Organ Works*, vol. 5. Ms: D-B MN 2 (A; December 1820).

[Toccata] in D minor. Edn: Little, *Complete Organ Works*, vol. 5. Ms: D-B MN 2 (A inc; late 1820–early 1821).

Fugue in D minor. Edn: Little, *Complete Organ Works*, vol. 5. Ms: D-B MN 2 (A; 6 January 1821). [This piece may have been intended for violin and piano.—Ed.]

Remarks: See also under Chamber Music Unpublished or Posthumously Published, earlier.

Andante in D major. Edn: Little, *Complete Organ Works*, vol. 5. Mss: D-B MN
2 (A; 9 May 1823), GB-Ob MDM c.54 (C; based on 9 May 1823).

[Passacaglia] in C minor. Edn: Little, *Complete Organ Works*, vol. 5. Mss: D-B
MN 2 (A; 10 May 1823), GB-Ob MDM c.54 (C).

"Wie groß ist des Allmächt'gen Güte" (chorale and variations). Edn: Little,
Complete Organ Works, vol. 5. Ms: D-B MN 5 (A; 30 July–2 August 1823).

Remarks: See also under unpublished or posthumously published sacred
works, later.

Postlude in D major. Edn: Little, *Complete Organ Works*, vol. 5. Ms: GB-Ob
MDM c.51/2.9 (C made in 1853, based on 8 March 1831).

Remarks: In a later version in C as Op. 65 no. 2, third movement; see
earlier.

[Piece in E major]. Ms: D-B MN 5 (A inc; [ca. 1823]).

Fuga pro Organo pleno in D minor. Edn: Little, *Complete Organ Works*, vol. 5.
Ms: GB-Lbl MS add. 14396 (A; 29 March 1833—cf. Op. 37, no. 3, earlier).

Andante con moto in G minor. Edn: Little, *Complete Organ Works*, vol. 5. Ms:
GB private possession (A; 11 July [1833]).

Fantasie and Fugue in G minor. Edn: Little, *Complete Organ Works*, vol. 5. Ms:
D-B MN 5 (A inc; ca. mid-1823).

Fughetta in D major. Edn: Little, *Complete Organ Works*, vol. 1. Ms: D-B MN
29 (A; ?July 1834).

Remarks: Organ version of piano fugue, Op. 35 no. 2.

Two Fugues for Organ Duet. Edn: Little, *Complete Organ Works*, vol. 1. Ms: D-
B MA Ms. 6 (A; 11 January 1835).

No. 1 in C minor. Arrangement of Op. 37 no. 1, fugue.

No. 2 in D major. Arrangement of Op. 35 no. 2, fugue.

Fugue in E minor. Edn: Little, *Complete Organ Works*, vol. 1. Ms: D-B MN 31
(A; 13 July 1839).

Fugue in F minor. Edn: Little, *Complete Organ Works*, vol. 1. Mss: D-B MN 31
(A; 18 July 1839), GB-Ob MDM c.48 (A; ca. 1844).

Fantasia [on O Haupt voll Blut und Wunden]. Edn: R. Larry Todd, Appendix to
Felix Mendelssohn Bartholdy, O Haupt voll Blut und Wunden (Madison, WI:
A-R, 1981); also Todd, "New Light" (see Literature). Ms: GB-Ob MDM b.5
(A inc; ?ca. August 1840).

Remarks: Probably used to raise funds for the Leipzig Bach monument,
6 August 1840.

Literature: R. Larry Todd, "New Light on Mendelssohn's *Freie Fantasie*
(1840)," in *Literary and Musical Notes: A Festschrift for Wm. A. Little*, ed.
Geoffrey C. Orth (Bern: Peter Lang, 1995), 205–18.

Prelude in C minor. Edn: Little, *Complete Organ Works*, vol. 1. Ms: location
unknown (A; 9 July 1841; facsimile in *Exeter Hall* 1 [1868]).

Andante in F major. Edn: Little, *Complete Organ Works*, vol. 2. Ms: PL-Kj MN
39 (A; 21 July 1844).

Allegretto in D minor. Edn: Little, *Complete Organ Works*, vol. 2. Ms: PL-Kj MN
39 (A; 22 July 1844).

Remarks: A version of Op. 65 no. 5, movement 2, in D minor rather than
the B minor of the final version.

Andante and Variations in D major. Edn: London: Novello, Ewer, & Co., 1898;
Little, *Complete Organ Works*, vol. 2. Mss: PL-Kj MN 39 (A; 23 July 1844),
GB-Ob MDM c.48 (A inc), D-LSta (C/A).

Remarks: The 1898 Ewer edition was coupled with the Allegro in B♭ (see
later).

Allegro, Chorale, and Fugue in D major. Edn: Little, *Complete Organ Works*, vol.
2. Ms: PL-Kj MN 39 (A; 25 July 1844).

Con moto maestoso in A major. Edn: Little, *Complete Organ Works*, vol. 2. Ms:
PL-Kj MN 39 (A; 9 August 1844).

Remarks: Cf. Op. 65 no. 3, movement 1.

Andante and Con moto in A major. Edn: Little, *Complete Organ Works*, vol. 2.
Ms: PL-Kj MN 39 (A; 17 August 1844).

Remarks: Cf. Op. 65 no. 3, movement 2.

Allegro in D major. Edn: Little, *Complete Organ Works*, vol. 2. Ms: PL-Kj MN
39 (A; 9 September 1844).

Remarks: Cf. Op. 65 no. 5, movement 3.

Andante in B minor. Edn: Little, *Complete Organ Works*, vol. 2. Ms: PL-Kj MN
39 (A; 9 September 1844).

Remarks: Cf. Op. 65 no. 5, movement 2.

Chorale in A♭ major. Edn: Little, *Complete Organ Works*, vol. 2. Ms: PL-Kj MN
39 (A; 10 September 1844).

Adagio in A♭ major. Edn: Little, *Complete Organ Works*, vol. 2. Ms: PL-Kj MN
39 (A; 19 December 1844).

Remarks: Cf. Op. 65 no. 1, movement 2.

Grave and Andante con moto in C minor. Edn: Little, *Complete Organ Works*, vol.
3. Ms: PL-Kj MN 40 (A; 21 December 1844).

Remarks: Cf. Op. 65 no. 2, movements 1 and 2.

Allegro moderato e grave in F minor. Edn: Little, *Complete Organ Works*, vol. 3.
Ms: PL-Kj MN 40 (A; 28 December 1844).

Allegro in B♭ major. Edn: London: Novello, Ewer, & Co., 1898; Little, *Complete
Organ Works*, vol. 2. Ms: PL-Kj MN 39 (A; 31 December [1844]).

Remarks: The 1898 Ewer edition was coupled with the Andante and
Variations in D major (see earlier).

Chorale in D major. Edn: Little, *Complete Organ Works*, vol. 2. Ms: PL-Kj MN
39 (A; ca. December 1844).

Remarks: Cf. Op. 65 no. 5, movement 1.

Allegro con brio in B♭ major. Edn: Little, *Complete Organ Works*, vol. 3. Ms:
PL-Kj MN 40 (A; 2 January 1845).

Remarks: Cf. Op. 65 no. 4, movement 1.

Andante alla Marcia in B♭ major. Edn: Little, *Complete Organ Works*, vol. 3.
Ms: PL-Kj MN 40 (A; 2 January 1845).
Remarks: Cf. Op. 65 no. 4, movement 2.
Chorale [and variations] in D minor. Edn: Little, *Complete Organ Works*, vol. 3.
Ms: PL-Kj MN 40 (A; 26 January 1845).
Remarks: Cf. Op. 65 no. 6, movement 1.
Finale (Andante sostenuto) in D major. Edn: Little, *Complete Organ Works*, vol.
3. Ms: PL-Kj MN 40 (A; 26 January 1845).
Remarks: Cf. Op. 65 no. 6.
Fugue in D minor. Edn: Little, *Complete Organ Works*, vol. 3. Ms: PL-Kj MN 40
(A; 27 January [1845]).
Remarks: For Op. 65 no. 6.
Moderato in C major. Edn: Little, *Complete Organ Works*, vol. 3. Ms: PL-Kj MN
40 (A; [?ca. January 1845]).
Remarks: Cf. Op. 65 no. 2, movement 3.
Allegro moderato maestoso in C major. Edn: Little, *Complete Organ Works*, vol.
3. Ms: PL-Kj MN 40 (A; ca. 1845).
Fugue in B♭ major. Edn: Little, *Complete Organ Works*, vol. 3. Ms: PL-Kj MN
40 (A; 2 April 1845).
Remarks: Cf. Op. 65 no. 4, movement 4.
Allegro assai in C major. Edn: Little, *Complete Organ Works*, vol. 3. Ms: PL-Kj
MN 40 (A inc; ca. January 1845).

SACRED WORKS

General Literature: Rudolf Werner, "Felix Mendelssohn Bartholdy als
Kirchenmusiker" (Diss., University of Frankfurt am Main, 1930); Annemarie
Clostermann, *Mendelssohn Bartholdys kirchenmusikalisches Schaffen: Neue
Untersuchungen zu Geschichte, Form und Inhalt* (Mainz: Schott, 1989); Ralf
Wehner, *Studien zum geistlichen Chorschaffen des jungen Felix Mendelssohn
Bartholdy*, Musik und Musikanschauung im 19. Jahrhundert: Studien und Quellen,
Bd. 4 (Leipzig: Studio, 1996).

Oratorios Published by Mendelssohn

General Literature: Arntrud Kurzhals-Reuter, *Die Oratorien Felix
Mendelssohn Bartholdys: Untersuchungen zur Quellenlage, Entstehung,
Gestaltung und Überlieferung* (Tutzing: Hans Schneider, 1978).
St. Paul [*Paulus*], Op. 36 (solo vv, ch, orch). Edn: London: Novello, [1836] (PS
by Mendelssohn; overture for pf 4 hands; words in English by Wm. Ball);
Bonn: Simrock, [1836] (choral parts and PS by Mendelssohn; overture for pf
4 hands)], [1837] (score, orchestra parts, and PS 4 hands of overture only); R
xiii; ed. R. Larry Todd (Stuttgart: Carus, 1997). Mss: GB-Ob MDM d.53
(libretto drr), D-B MN 19 (skk), PL-Kj MN 53–54 (A FS; 1835–1836), PL-Kj

MN 55 (A PS), GB-Ob MDM c.52 (vocal parts in Italian—C; based on 28 June 1846), location unknown (corrections or insertions for organ part—A; auctioned by J. A. Stargardt, 1970); GB-Lbl MS Add. 33571 (C—overture only).

Remarks: Originally the product of a commission from Johann Schelble and the Frankfurt *Cäcilienverein*, *Paulus* was premiered in Düsseldorf at the 1836 Niederrheinisches Musikfest. See also "Pieces for *St. Paul*" under Other Accompanied Sacred Works Unpublished or Posthumously Published, later.

Literature: Gottfried Wilhelm Fink, "Paulus," *Allgemeine musikalische Zeitung* 34 (1837), cols. 497–506, 513–30; Otto Jahn, *Über Felix Mendelssohn Bartholdys Oratorium Paulus* (Kiel, 1842; repr. in his *Gesammelte Aufsätze über Musik* [Leipzig: Breitkopf & Härtel, 1866], 13–39); F. G. Edwards, "First Performances: I. Mendelssohn's *St. Paul*," *The Musical Times* 32 (1891), 137–38.

Elijah [Elias], Op. 70. Edn: Bonn: Simrock, and London: Ewer, [1847] (PS, choral parts, and solo parts), [1848] (orchestral parts and FS); R xiii; ed. Paul Horn (Stuttgart: Carus, 1978 [No. 28 only]; ed. R. Larry Todd (Stuttgart: Carus, 1994). Mss: D-B MN 22 (skk), PL-Kj MN 51 (A FS), D-B MN 51 (A organ part), D-B MN 57 ("Denn er hat seinen Engeln befohlen"—A choral score, a cappella; with C of letter from Mendelssohn to King Friedrich Wilhelm IV of Prussia dated 15 August 1844), D-B N.Mus.ms. 654 ("Was hast du an mir getan"—dr), D-B N.Mus.ms. 653 ("Was hast du an mir getan"—A, frag), GB-Ob MDM c.39 (A PS, inc), GB-Ob MDM c.51 ("Is not His word like a fire"—C/A), GB-Ob MDM c.51 ("Be not afraid"—A frag), GB-Ob MDM c.51 (organ part—C), GB-Ob MDM c.57 (chorus parts for S, A, and T—C/A), GB-Ob MDM c.94 (vn part for performance in Birmingham, 26 August 1846—C/A), GB-Ob MDM c.95 (organ part for performance in London, 16 April 1847—C/A), GB-Bp Ms. 1721 (FS used by organist for performance in Birmingham, 26 August 1846—C/A; contains metronome markings and biblical citations in Mendelssohn's hand), US-Wc ("Höre, Israel"—A PS), US-Wc (Introduction and Overture arranged for pf 4 hands—A), GB-Ob MDM g.10 (A frag and corrections), GB-Lbl 47859 A and B (correspondence and musical notation related to performance in Birmingham 26 August 1846). Additional sources: GB-Ob Deneke 265 (printed, but not published, chorus parts for first performance), GB-Lbl Add. MS 47859B (printed, but not published, chorus parts for the first performance).

Remarks: In almost every sense a successor and counterpart to *Paulus*, *Elias* exists in two more or less chronologically discrete versions. It was premiered in Birmingham on 26 August 1846 and underwent substantial revisions between that performance and the premiere of the familiar version in April 1847. The English translations were prepared by William Bartholomew, who was also responsible for the English versions of several other major Mendelssohn works (including Psalm 115 and *St. Paul*).

Literature: Otto Jahn, "Über Felix Mendelssohn Bartholdy's Oratorium Elias," *Allgemeine musikalische Zeitung* 50 (1848), cols. 113–22, 137–43; F. G. Edwards, *The History of Mendelssohn's Oratorio "Elijah"* (London: Novello, Ewer & Co., 1896); Donald Mintz, "Mendelssohn's *Elijah* Reconsidered," *Studies in Romanticism* 3 (1963), 1–9; Jack Werner, *Mendelssohn's "Elijah"* (London: Chappell, 1965); Arno Forchert, "Textanlage und Darstellungsprinzipien in Mendelssohns *Elias*," in *Das Problem Mendelssohn*, ed. Carl Dahlhaus (Regensburg: Bosse, 1974), 61–77; Ross Wesley Ellison, "Mendelssohn's *Elijah*: Dramatic Climax of a Creative Career," *American Choral Review* 22 (1980), 3–9; Martin Staehelin, "*Elijah*, Johann Sebastian Bach, and the New Covenant: On the Aria 'Es ist genug' in Felix Mendelssohn Bartholdy's Oratorio *Elijah*," in *Mendelssohn and His World*, ed. R. Larry Todd (Princeton: Princeton University Press, 1991), 121–36; Martin Geck, "Religiöse Musik 'im Geist der gebildeten Gesellschaft': Mendelssohn und sein *Elias*," in *Von Beethoven bis Mahler: Leben und Werk der großen Komponisten des 19. Jahrhunderts* (Reinbeck bei Hamburg: Rowohlt, 2000), 256–79.

Oratorio Posthumously Published

[*Christus*], Op. 97. Edn: Leipzig: Breitkopf & Härtel, [1852] (PS, PS without words, and FS); London: Ewer, [1852] (PS, with English text by W. Bartholomew), [1860] (score); R xiii; R. Larry Todd (Stuttgart: Carus, 1994). Mss: GB-Ob MDM b.5 (skk), PL-Kj MN 44 (A).

Remarks: The title of this incomplete oratorio stems exclusively from the composer's friend Ignaz Moscheles.

Chorale Cantatas (All Posthumously Published)

General Literature: Brian W. Pritchard, "Mendelssohn's Chorale Cantatas: An Appraisal," *The Musical Quarterly* 62 (1976), 1–24 [does not include *Wer nur den lieben Gott läßt walten*]; Pietro Zappalà, *Le "Choralkantaten" die Felix Mendelssohn-Bartholdy* (Venice: Fondazione Levi, 1991); Ulrich Wüster, *Mendelssohns Choralkantaten: Gestalt und Idee—Versuch einer historisch-kritischen Interpretation* (Frankfurt am Main: Peter Lang, 1996).

Christe, du Lamm Gottes (ch, str). Edn: Oswald Bill (Neuhausen-Stuttgart: Hänssler, 1977). Mss: MN 21 (C FS; based on Christmas 1827), D-DS Mus.ms. 1519a (C FS), GB-LEbc (C/A FS; 11 November 1829, for Thomas Attwood).

Jesu, meine Freude (ch, str). Edn: Brian W. Pritchard (Hilversum: Harmonia, 1972); Günter Graulich (Stuttgart: Carus, 1979). Ms: US-Cn Case MS VM 2.1 M537j (A FS; 22 January 1828; facsimile ed. O. Jonas [Chicago: Newberry Library, 1966].

Wer nur den lieben Gott läßt walten (S, ch, str). Edn: Oswald Bill (Kassel: Bärenreiter, 1976); Thomas Christian Schmidt (Stuttgart: Carus, 1996). Mss: D-DS Mus.ms. 1519b (C FS; ca. April–July 1829), location unknown (C FS; title page contains note from Charles Neate indicating that he received the ms from Mendelssohn in June 1829; facsimile of p. 3 in Maggs Bros. Catalog No. 512 [1928], 178).

O Haupt voll Blut und Wunden (Bar, ch, orch). Edn: Martin Lutz (PS) (Wiesbaden: Breitkopf & Härtel, 1973); Oswald Bill (Stuttgart: Carus, 1980—based on A in D-DS and C in D-F); R. Larry Todd (Madison: A-R, 1981). Mss: location unknown (A FS; 12 September 1830; auctioned by Hans Schneider, 1971), D-B N.Mus.ms. 119 (C/A FS; 12 [?recte 13] September 1830), D-DS Mus.ms. 1447 (A FS; 13–14 September 1830); D-F Mus. Hs. 194 (C), GB-Lbl MS Add. 65422 (C by Vincent Novello, [1832]—chorale only).

Vom Himmel hoch, da komm' ich her (S, Bar, ch, orch). Edn: Karen Lehmann (Stuttgart: Carus, 1984). Mss: D-B MN 21 (A FS; 28 January 1831), GB-Ob MDM c. 57 (C of bass part in hand of R. Dirichlet).

Wir glauben all' an einen Gott (ch, orch). Edn: Günter Graulich (Stuttgart: Carus, 1980). Mss: location unknown (A FS; ca. March 1831—formerly in MN 23), GB-Ob MDM c.51 (C FS by A. Schirmer; before 1853), GB-Ob MDM c.51 (C FS by W. Bartholomew; ca. 1853), D-F Mus.Hs. 194 (C FS).

Remarks: Mendelssohn's autograph title etiquette on MN 23 indicates that an autograph for this cantata was included in the volume when it was bound, and the incipit is also provided in the inventory prepared by Conrad Schleinitz; today, however, the autograph is missing.

Ach Gott, vom Himmel sieh darein (Bar, ch, orch). Edn: Brian W. Pritchard (Hilversum: Harmonia, 1972); Günter Graulich (Stuttgart: Carus, 1980). Mss: D-F Mus.Hs. 197 (A FS; 5 April 1832), D-B MN 21 (C/A FS; January 1832 [?sic]), D private collection (C FS; January 1832).

Psalm Settings Published by Mendelssohn

General Literature: Wolfgang Dinglinger, *Studien zu den Psalmen mit Orchester von Felix Mendelssohn Bartholdy* (Cologne: Studio, 1993).

Non nobis Domine [Nicht unserm Namen, Herr] (Psalm 115), Op. 31 (S, ch, orch). Edn: Bonn: Simrock, [1835] (FS, PS, and parts); London: Hedgley, [?1845] (PS, with English text by W. Bartholomew); R. Larry Todd (Stuttgart: Carus, 1994). Mss: D-B MN 23 (A FS; 15 November 1830), D-B N.Mus.ms. 97 (A FS and A PS; 19 May 1835), GB-Ob MDM c.47 (sk), D-F Mus.Hs. 194 (C FS—contains only Latin text).

Wie der Hirsch schreit (Psalm 42), Op. 42. Edn: Leipzig: Breitkopf & Härtel, [1838] (choral parts and PS by Mendelssohn), [1839] (FS and orchestral parts); London: Novello, [1838] (PS by Mendelssohn; words in English); R xiv; Günter Graulich (Stuttgart: Carus, 1980). Mss: D-B MN 19 (skk), D-B

MN 29 (A FS; 22 December 1837), D-B N.Mus.ms. 106 (nos. 1–6—A FS), D-B MA MG 1 (nos. 6—A PS), D-F Mus.Hs. 2404/7 (C FS).

Literature: Douglass Seaton, "A Study of a Collection of Mendelssohn's Sketches and Other Autograph Material Deutsche Staatsbibliothek Berlin *Mus.ms. Autogr. Mendelssohn 19*" (Ph.D. diss., Columbia University, 1977), 136–79.

Defend me, Lord (Psalm 31) (ch). Edn: *The National Psalmodist* (London: Coventry & Hollier, 1839). Mss: D-B MN 31 (A; 27 February 1839), GB-Ob MDM c.54 (C), US-Wc (inc).

Da Israel aus Aegypten zog (Psalm 114), Op. 51 (8 vv, orch). Edn: Leipzig: Breitkopf & Härtel,[1840/41] (parts and PS [by Mendelssohn]), London: Novello, [1841] (PS by Mendelssohn; words in English), [1841] (score); R xiv; Oswald Bill (Stuttgart: Carus, 1982). Mss: D-B MN 31 (A FS; 9 August 1839), D-B MA Ms. 7 (A PS), GB-Ob MDM b.5 (organ part—A; evidently used for first English performance, 23 September 1840), GB-Ob MDM c.93 (C/A [English translation by Mendelssohn; score used for first English performance, 23 September 1840]), US-Wc (A PS).

Kommt, laßt uns anbeten (Psalm 95), Op. 46 (T, ch, orch). Edn: Leipzig: Kistner, [1842] (FS, PS, and parts); London: Novello, [1842] (PS with words in English); R xiv; R. Larry Todd (Stuttgart: Carus, 1990). Mss: D-B MN 19 (sk), D-B MN 30 (A; inc), D-B MN 30 (A; 6 April 1838), D-B MN 31 (no. 4—A; 11 April 1839), PL-Kj MN 35 (A; 3 July 1841), D-B MA Ms. 11 (A PS), US-Wc ML 30.8j P8 (no. 2—A), GB-Ob MDM c.46 (A frag—6 pages of PS and one page of score), ?D private collection, US private collection of Mrs. Eugene Allen Noble (frag; 5 December 1844).

Literature: Wolfgang Dinglinger, "Felix Mendelssohn Bartholdy: Der 95. Psalm op. 46—'. . . von dem nur ein Stück mir ans Herz gewachsen war,'" *Mendelssohn-Studien* 7 (1990), 269–86.

Psalm Settings Unpublished or Posthumously Published

General Literature: Pietro Zappalà, "I salmi di Felix Mendelssohn Bartholdy" (Ph.D. diss., Università di Pavia, 1992); Ralf Wehner, *Studien zum geistlichen Chorschaffen des jungen Felix Mendelssohn Bartholdy* (Leipzig: Studio, 1996).

Gott du bist unsre Zuversicht (Psalm 19) (5 vv). Ms: D-B MN 2 (A; ca. June 1821).

Die Himmel erzählen (Psalm 19) (2S,A,T,B). Ms: D-B MN 2 (A; 16 June 1820 [?*recte* 1821]—two versions, on pp. 107–12, 113–19; "Das Gesetz des Herrn" on pp. 145–46).

Literature: Wehner, *Studien*.

Ich weiche nicht von deinen Rechten (Psalm 119: 102) (4 vv). Edn: Pietro Zappalà, "Di alcuni motetti giovanili di Felix Mendelssohn Bartholdy," in *Ottocento e oltre: Scritti in onore di Raoul Meloncelli*, ed. Francesco Izzo and

Johannes Streicher (Rome: Editoriale Pantheon, 1993), 203–33. Ms: GB-Ob MDM b.5 (A; ?1823).

Deine Rede präge ich meinem Herzen (Psalm 119:11) (4 vv). Edn: Pietro Zappalà, "Di alcuni motetti giovanili di Felix Mendelssohn Bartholdy," in *Ottocento e oltre: Scritti in onore di Raoul Meloncelli*, ed. Francesco Izzo and Johannes Streicher (Rome: Editoriale Pantheon, 1993), 203–33. Ms: GB-Ob MDM b.5 (A; ?1823).

Jauchzet Gott alle Lande (Psalm 66: 1, 2, 20) (SSA solos, SSA double choir, bc). Ms: D-B MN 2 (A; 8 March 1822).

Lord, hear the voice (Psalm 5) (male ch). Mss: D-B MN 31 (A; 26 February 1839), GB-Ob MDM c.54 (C).

[Seven psalm melodies and harmonizations] (ch). Ms: PL-Kj MN 38² (A; 13 November 1843).

    Dem Herrn der Erdkreis (Psalm 24).

    Warum toben die Heiden (Psalm 2).

    Gott als ein König gewaltlich regirt (Psalm 93).

    Nun singt ein neues Lied dem Herrn (Psalm 98).

    Ihr Völker auf der Erde (Psalm 100).

    Auf dich setz' ich Herr mein Vertrauen (Psalm 31).

    Wer in des allerhöchsten (Psalm 91).

Warum toben die Heiden (Psalm 2) (solo vv, ch) (15 December 1843). See Op. 78, later.

Richte mich Gott (Psalm 43) (8 vv) (3 January 1844). See Op. 78, later.

Mein Gott, mein Gott, warum hast du mich verlassen (Psalm 22) (solo vv, ch) (1844). See Op. 78, later.

Why, O Lord, Delay/Hymne: Lass, o Herr, mich Hülfe finden (Psalm 13), Op. 96 (A, ch, org). Edn: organ version: movements 1–3 only (without opening number) as *Anthem for a mezzo soprano, with chorus* (London: Cramer, Addison, & Beale, [1841]) and as *Drei Geistliche Lieder* (Bonn: Simrock, [1841]); the added movement 4 was published as a supplement, London: Cramer et al., [1843]; orchestral version: posthumously published as *Hymne*, Op. 96 (Bonn: Simrock, [1852]; PS London: Novello, [1852]); Günter Graulich (Stuttgart: Carus, 1978), David Brodbeck (Stuttgart: Carus, 1998). Mss: PL-Kj MN 34 (A; 12 December 1840), D-B N.Mus.ms. 308 (C/A—score and four vocal parts), GB-Lbl Add. 31801 (C/A, 14 December 1840 [*Stichvorlage* for Cramer]), PL-Kj MN 38² (A; 5 January 1843), GB-Lbl Add. 31801 (C/A, ca. 16 January 1843).

    Remarks: Publication of the orchestral version, originally planned by Cramer in London and Simrock in Bonn, did not occur in Mendelssohn's lifetime. To date, all editions of this version have been based on the original orchestral score and have not incorporated the substantial revisions (including articulations, dynamics, and new instrumental doublings) that the composer entered into the copyist's score sent to London on 16 January 1843.

Literature: David Brodbeck, "Some Notes on an Anthem by Mendelssohn," in *Mendelssohn and His World*, ed. R. Larry Todd (Princeton: Princeton University Press, 1991), 43–64.

Singet dem Herrn ein neues Lied (Psalm 98), Op. 91 (dbl ch, orch, org). Edn: Leipzig: Kistner, [1851] (parts, PS, FS), London: Ewer, [1851 (PS with English words by W. Bartholomew)]; R xiv; R. Larry Todd (Stuttgart: Carus, 1990). Mss: PL-Kj MN 38² (A FS; 27 December 1843), location unknown (auctioned by Phillips on 14 June 1989—C FS by W. Bartholomew with English text—January 1851).

Literature: Wolfgang Dinglinger, "Ein neues Lied: Der preußische Generalmusikdirektor und eine königliche Auftragskomposition," *Mendelssohn-Studien* 5 (1982), 99–111.

Jauchzet dem Herrn alle Welt (Psalm 100) (SATB). Edn: *Musica sacra* 8 (Berlin: Bote & Bock, 1863); R xiv/C. Ms: PL-Kj MN 39 (A; 1 January 1844).

Three Psalms, Op. 78 (8 vv). Edn: Leipzig: Breitkopf & Härtel, and London: Ewer, [1849] (the three pieces published individually); R xiv; David Brodbeck (Stuttgart: Carus, n.d.).

Warum toben die Heiden (Psalm 2) (solo vv, ch). Edn: Stuttgart: Carus, 1967. Mss: PL-Kj MN 38² (A; ca. 15 December 1843), PL-Kj MN 40 (A).

Richte mich Gott (Psalm 43) (8 vv). Edn: Stuttgart: Carus, 1990. Mss: PL-Kj MN 39 (A; 3 January 1844), PL-Kj MN 40 (A).

Mein Gott, mein Gott, warum hast du mich verlassen (Psalm 22) (solo vv, ch). Edn: Stuttgart: Stuttgart, 1968. Ms: PL-Kj MN 39 (A; [1844]).

Literature: David Brodbeck, "A Winter of Discontent: Mendelssohn and the *Berliner Domchor*," in *Mendelssohn Studies*, ed. R. Larry Todd (Cambridge: Cambridge University Press, 1992), 1–32.

Denn er hat seinen Engeln befohlen (Psalm 91) (dbl ch). Edn: Berlin: H. Moser, in *Volksliederbuch für gemischten Chor* (Leipzig: C. F. Peters, 1915), 122–27; Stuttgart: Carus, 1997. Ms: D-B MN 57 (A; with copy of letter to King Friedrich Wilhelm IV of Prussia dated 15 August 1844).

Remarks: Reused (orchestrated) in *Elijah*, Op. 70. According to Rudolf Werner, the piece was published shortly after it was presented to the Berlin Domchor; this edition, however, dates from 1911.

Other Accompanied Sacred Works Published by Mendelssohn

Three Sacred Pieces, Op. 23 [Kirchen-Musik] (ch, org/orch). Edn: Bonn: Simrock, [1832] (parts and vocal score with figured basso continuo), and Bonn: Simrock, [1838] (FS for No. 2, parts only for nos. 1 and 3); R xiv. Ms: D-F Mus.Hs. 195(C).

No. 1. Aus tiefer Noth (T, ch, org). Edn: Günter Graulich (Stuttgart: Carus, 1979). Mss: GB-Ob MDM c.47 (skk), GB-Ob MDM c.47 (A; 18–19 October 1830).

No. 2. Ave Maria (T, dbl ch, org/orch). Edn: Günter Graulich (Stuttgart: Carus, 1977). Mss: D-B N.Mus.ms. 104 (A; 30 September–16 October 1830 [*Stichvorlage* for first edn.]), D-F Mus.Hs. 2501 (organ part—A), D-F Mus.Hs. 195 (A; 17 November 1831 [arr. 8 vv]).

No. 3. Mitten wir im Leben sind (2S 2A 2T 2B). Ms: D-B N.Mus.ms. 22 (A frag).

Literature: Ulrich Wüster, "'Aber dann ist es schon durch die innerste Wahrheit und durch den Gegenstand, den es vorstellt, Kirchenmusik ...': Beobachtungen an Mendelssohns *Kirchen-Musik* op. 23," in *Felix Mendelssohn Bartholdy: Kongreß-Bericht Berlin 1994*, ed. Christian Martin Schmidt (Wiesbaden: Breitkopf & Härtel, 1997), 187–208.

Three Motets, Op. 39 (female ch, org or pf). Edn: Bonn: Simrock, and London: Novello, [1838] (published individually); R xiv; Günter Graulich (Stuttgart: Carus, 1977).

1. Hear My Prayer, O Lord/Veni, Domine (SSA, org). Mss: D-B MN 49 (A; 31 December 1830), S-Smf (A), D-F Mus.Hs. 194 (C).

2. O Praise the Lord/Laudate pueri (SSA, org). Mss: F-Pc Ms. 196 (A inc; 14 August 1837), location unknown (auctioned by Sotheby's, 1984—A; [ca. 1830?])

3. O Lord, Thou Hast Searched Me Out/Surrexit Pastor (SSAA, org). Ms: D-B MN 49 (A—frag; 30 December 1830).

Te Deum, Morning Service ("We Praise Thee O God") (A major) (SSATB solos, chor, org). Edn: London: Ewer, [1846]; R xiv. Mss: D-B MN 23 (A), D-B N.Mus.ms. 234 (A).

Verleih' uns Frieden (ch, orch). Edn: Leipzig: Breitkopf & Härtel, [1839] (FS and PS; words in German and Latin); London: Novello, [1839] (PS, with title "Da pacem Domine: Motett/Grant Us Thy Peace: Prayer"; words in English and German); R xiv; Günter Graulich (Stuttgart: Carus, 1980). Mss: D-B MN 23 (A FS; 10 February 1831), D-B N.Mus.ms. 243 (C/A FS), US-NYpm (C/A PS), D-F Mus.Hs. 194 (C PS), GB-Ob MDM c.57 (orchestral parts—C), F-Pc Ms. 211 (A PS), location unknown (A FS; facsimile in supplement to *Allgemeine musikalische Zeitung* 51 [1839]).

Lord Have Mercy upon Us (ch, org). Edn: London: Ewer, [1842], and *Album für Gesang* (Leipzig: Bösenberg, 1842); Günter Graulich (Stuttgart: Carus, 1992). Ms: D-B MN 28 (A; 24 March 1833).

Remarks: As Peter Ward Jones kindly pointed out in a personal communication, the title "For the Evening Service," which appeared on the first edition in the *Album für Gesang* for 1842, is a misnomer for the chorus "Lord Have Mercy upon Us" and may have resulted from the composer's lack of familiarity with the English liturgy. More appropriate is the title of the first Ewer edition (ca. 1842): "Responses to the Commandments."

Hear My Prayer (Hör mein Bitten) (S, ch, org or orch). Text: W. Bartholomew (paraphrase of Ps. 55). Edn: Berlin: Bote & Bock, [1845] (version with org acc, and arrangement for S and pf); London: Ewer, [1845] (version with org acc); London: Novello, Ewer & Co., [1880] (version with orch); R xiv; R. Larry Todd (Stuttgart: Carus, 1985). Mss: PL-Kj MN 39 (A; 25 January 1844), GB-Ob MDM c.37 (orchestral arrangement without voices—A FS; February 1847), GB-Lva (A—organ version), GB-Lbl Add. MS 46347 (C FS of orchestral arrangement).

Remarks: Until Mendelssohn's orchestral arrangement was published ca. 1880, the work was also known in an orchestral arrangement prepared by the composer's friend Ferdinand Hiller and published by Bote & Bote in Berlin.

Literature: Friedhelm Krummacher, "Composition as Accommodation? On Mendelssohn's Music in Relation to England," in *Mendelssohn Studies*, ed. R. Larry Todd (Cambridge: Cambridge University Press, 1992), 80–105.

Drei Motetten, Op. 69 (SATB, org). Edn: (London: Ewer, [1847], and) Leipzig: Breitkopf & Härtel, 1848. Mss: PL-Kj MN 44 (A), US-Wc (A).

Jubilate Deo (O Be Joyful in the Lord) (5 April 1847). Ms: GB-Ob MDM c.22 (C). Edn: London: Ewer, [1847] (without opus no., as second part of the *Te Deum*, which had already been published independently in 1846; see earlier).

Magnificat and Nunc dimittis published together as *Magnificat and Nunc dimittis*, Op. 69 (London: Ewer, [1847]):

Evening Service [Magnificat] (My Soul Doth Magnify the Lord) (12 June 1847).

Benedictus [i.e., Nunc dimittis] (Lord Now Lettest Thou Thy People) (13 June 1847). Edn: Günter Graulich (Stuttgart: Carus, 1976). Mss: GB-Ob MDM b.5 (dr for "Denn er hat die Niedrigkeit seiner Magd"), GB-Ob MDM c.22 (C).

Other Accompanied Sacred Works Unpublished or Posthumously Published

Gloria in E♭ (2SATB, ch, orch). Edn: In Kent Eugene Hatteberg, "*Gloria* (1822) and *Große Festmusik zum Dürerfest* (1828): Urtext Editions of Two Unpublished Choral-Orchestral Works by Felix Mendelssohn, with Background and Commentary" (D.M.A. diss., University of Iowa, 1995); Pietro Zappalà (Stuttgart: Carus, 1998). Ms: D-B MN 45 (A FS; [ca. March 1822]).

Magnificat in D (SATB, ch, orch). Edn: Pietro Zappalà (Stuttgart: Carus, 1997). Ms: D-B MN 45 (A FS; 19 March–31 May 1822).

Jesus, meine Zuversicht (motet) (2SATB, ch, pf). Edn: Günther Graulich (Stuttgart: Carus, 1991). Ms: D-B MN 4 (A; 9 June 1824).

Salve regina, E♭ (S, str). Edn: Werner, *Felix Mendelssohn Bartholdy als Kirchenmusiker*; Günter Graulich (Stuttgart: Carus, 1980). Ms: D-B MN 49 (A FS; 9 April [?1824]).

Kyrie in D minor (ch, orch). Edn: Ralph Leavis (Oxford: Oxford University Press, 1964) (PS); R. Larry Todd (Stuttgart: Carus, 1986). Ms: GB-Ob MDM c.20 (A; 6 May 1825).

> Literature: Wehner, *Studien*, 155-87.

Te Deum in D major (2S 2A 2T 2B, dbl ch, bc). Edn: L vi/1 (1966; rev. edn. 1988); Werner Burkhardt (Stuttgart: Carus, 1976); Barbara Mohn (Stuttgart: Carus, 1996). Ms: D-B MN 46 (A; 5 December 1826).

> Literature: Robert Madison Campbell, "Mendelssohn's *Te Deum in D*: Influences and the Development of Style" (Ph.D. diss., Stanford University, 1985); idem, "Mendelssohn's *Te Deum in D*," *American Choral Review* 28/2 (April 1986), 2–16.

Salvum fac populum tuum (soloists, ch, orch). Ms: D-B MN 46 (A FS; 18 July [?1827 or 1828]—inserted into A for *Te Deum*, after original "Salvum fac").

> Literature: Werner, *Felix Mendelssohn Bartholdy als Kirchenmusiker*, 36–38; Campbell, "Mendelssohn's *Te Deum*," 92–96; Wehner, *Studien*, 139–42.

Tu es Petrus, Op. 111 (ch, orch). Edn: Bonn: Simrock, and London: Novello, Ewer & Co., [1868] (PS); R xiv; Brian W. Pritchard (Hilversum: Harmonia, 1976); John Michael Cooper (Stuttgart: Carus, 1996). Mss: D-B MN 47 (A FS; 14 November 1827), A-Wgm Ms. A. 199a (C/A FS; 18 November 1829), D-B MA Ms. 53 (A FS; based on A in MN 47), D-LEs Gewandhaus Mr. 49 (C FS), D-F Mus. Hs. 196(C FS).

> Literature: Wehner, *Studien*, 188-99.

Was mein Gott will (ch). Ms: D-B MN 5 (A; 29 April 1827—text omitted).

Ave maris stella (S, orch). Edn: Hans Ryschawy (Stuttgart: Carus, 1993). Ms: D-B MN 58 (A FS; 5 July 1828).

Hora est (bar, 16 vv, org). Edn: M. Hützel (Stuttgart: Carus, 1981). Mss: location unknown (A; 14 November 1828, for Fanny Hensel), S-Smf (A; 6 December 1828), A-Wgm H. 27170 (C), D-LE Stadtarchiv Gewandhaus Nr. 50 (C—based on A of 14 November 1828).

O beata et benedicta ("Zum Feste der Dreieinigkeit") (motet) (2S A, org). Edn: Paul Horn (Stuttgart: Carus, 1978). Mss: D-B MN 49 [originally in MN 18] (A; 30 December 1830), D-B MN 18 (C).

Responsorium and Hymnus ("Vespergesang") Op. 121 (T, male ch, vcl, org). Edn: Leipzig: Leuckart, [1873]; R xiv; Günter Graulich (Stuttgart: Carus, 1979). Ms: D-B N.Mus.ms. 15 (A; 5 February 1833).

[Pieces for *St. Paul* (Op. 36)] (solo vv, ch, orch).

> No. 2 Chorale, "Ach bleib mit deiner Gnade" (4 vv, orch). Ms: D-B MN 28 (A FS; ca. 1834–1835).

> No. 3 Recit., "Die Menge der Gläubigen" (S, str). Ms: D-B MN 28 (A FS; ca. 1834–1835).

> No. 13 Chorus, "Herr Gott, dess' die Rache ist, erscheine" (B, male vv, orch). Ms: D-B MN 28 (A FS; ca. 1834–1835).

"Lobt ihn mit Pfeifen" (SATB solos, ch, orch). Ms: D-B MN 28 (A FS; ca. 1834–1835).

Recitative and Women's Chorus, "Danket dem Gott/Danket dem Herrn, dem freundlichen Gott" (T, female vv, orch). Ms: D-B MN 28 (A FS; ca. 1834–1835).

No. 32 Chorus: "Danket den Göttern" (female vv, orch). Ms: D-B MN 28 (A FS; ca. 1834–1835).

Duet, "Gelobet sey Gott" (T B, orch). Ms: D-B MN 28 (A FS; ca. 1834–1835).

Chorale, "O treuer Heiland Jesu Christ" (ch, orch colla parte). Ms: D-B MN 28 (A choral score; ca. 1834–1835).

Recit. "Paulus sandte hin" (STB, orch). Ms: D-B MN 28 (A FS; ca. 1834–1835).

No. 28 Recit. and chorale, "Mit unser Macht ist nichts getan" (B, ch, orch). Ms: D-B MN 28 (A inc; ca. 1834–1835).

No. 16 Arioso, "Doch der Herr, er leitet die Irrenden recht," (S, pf). Edn: as no. 1 of *Zwei geistliche Lieder*, Op. 112 (Bonn: Simrock, [1868]); R xiv; Günter Graulich (Stuttgart: Carus, 1978). Ms: PL-Kj MN 55 (A PS; ca. 1835), D-DS Mus.ms.1445b (A PS), D-B MN 20 (C/A PS).

Aria, "Der du die Menschen lässest sterben," (S, pf). Edn: as no. 2 of *Zwei geistliche Lieder*, Op. 112 (Bonn: Simrock, [1868]); R xiv; Günter Graulich (Stuttgart: Carus, 1978). Mss: GB-Ob MDM c.23 (C PS), PL-Kj MN 54 (A PS), S-Smf (C PS), GB-Lbl Hirsch M.1349 (C PS), D-B N.Mus.ms. 14308/5 (C/A—version with orchestra).

No. 42 Chorale, "Erhebe dich, o meine Seel." Mss: PL-Kj MN 54 (A FS), PL-Kj MN 55 (A PS).

No. 43 Chorus, "Des Herrn Will gescheh." Mss: PL-Kj MN 54 (A FS), PL-Kj MN 55 (A PS).

Remarks: The relationship of these numbers to the final version of the oratorio as well as a thorough exploration of them in intrinsically musical terms remain to be investigated. With the exception of the arioso "Doch der Herr" and the aria "Der du die Menschen lässest sterben," which were published by Simrock in 1868, the numbers remain unpublished. The aria "Ich habe den Heiden," later replaced by the duet "Denn also hat uns der Herr geboten," is extant only in fragmentary form (the last page of what was evidently an autograph fair copy is given on page 10 of D-B MN 19); the other numbers are transmitted in complete or virtually complete form in D-B MN 28. A performance of the latter group was given in Chemnitz in October 1995, but they remain unpublished.

Literature: Kurzhals-Reuter, *Die Oratorien*; George Grove, "Mendelssohn's Oratorio 'St Paul,'" *The Musical Times* 50 (1909), 92–94.

Herr Gott, dich loben wir ("Lied zur Feier des tausendjährigen Bestehens von Deutschland") (solo vv, dbl ch, orch, org). Edn: R. Larry Todd (Stuttgart: Carus, 1997). Ms: PL-Kj MN 38^2 (A FS; 16 January 1843).

[Three chorale harmonizations] (ch, ww, br).
> 1. Allein Gott in der Höh'. Edn: Günter Graulich (Stuttgart: Carus, 1985). Ms: PL-Kj MN 38^2 (A; [December 1843]).
> 2. Vom Himmel hoch da komm ich her. Ms: PL-Kj MN 38^2 (A; 15 December 1843).
> 3. Wachet auf.

Lauda Sion, Op. 73 (solo vv, ch, orch). Edn: London: Ewer, [1848] (PS; words in English and Latin), and Mainz: Schott, [1849] (PS and FS; two printings: one with words in Latin and German, the other with words in Latin, German, and English); R xiv; R. Larry Todd (Stuttgart: Carus, 1996). Mss: GB-Ob MDM b.5 (sk), PL-Kj MN 41 (A FS; 10 February 1846), GB-Lbl 41571 (C PS), B-Bc (C frag).
> Remarks: Performed in Liège, 11 June 1846.
> Literature: Albert van der Linden, "Un Fragment inédit du 'Lauda Sion' de F. Mendelssohn," *Acta musicologica* 26 (1954), 48–64; idem, "A propos du 'Lauda Sion' de Mendelssohn," *Revue Belge de musicologie* 17 (1963), 124–25.

Er wird öffnen die Augen der Blinden (ch, orch). Ms: PL-Kj MN 41 (A FS; [1846]).
> Remarks: Intended for *Elijah*.

A Cappella Sacred Works Unpublished or Posthumously Published

In secula seculorum amen (vocal fugue) (4 vv). Ms: GB-Ob MDM c.43 (A; ?1821).
> Literature: Wehner, *Studien*, 98–100.

Ich will den Herrn nach seiner Gerechtigkeit preisen (motet) (4 vv). Ms: D-B MN 2 (A; [1821]).

Tag für Tag sei Gott gepriesen (motet) (5 vv). Ms: D-B MN 2 (A; [1821]).

Jube dom'ne (SATB, dbl ch). Edn: Günter Graulich (Stuttgart: Carus, 1980—based on C/A in D-F; see later); Ralf Wehner (Leipzig: Deutscher Verlag für Musik, 1993—based on ms in D-B MN 45 and parts in GB-Ob MDM b.5). MS: D-B MN 45 (A; 23–25 October 1822), GB-Ob MDM b.5 (parts for S1, A1, and T1—A), D-F Mus.Hs. 161 Nr. 1 (C/A; 4 November 1822).
> Literature: Wehner, *Studien*, 57–66.

Kyrie in C minor (SAATB, dbl ch). Edn: Günther Graulich (Stuttgart: Carus, 1980—based on ms in D-F); Ralf Wehner (Leipzig: Deutscher Verlag für Musik, 1993). Mss: D-B MN 6 (A; 12 November 1823), D-F Mus.Hs. 161 Nr. 2 (C/A).

Two sacred pieces (ch). Ms: D-B MN 5 (A).
> 1. [Wie groß ist des Allmächt'gen Güte] ([July 1823]—no text; see also unpublished or posthumously published organ works, earlier).

2. Allein Gott in der Höh' sey Ehr (10 September 1824—two versions, pp. 17 and 19).

Two sacred choruses, Op. 115 (male ch). Edn: Leipzig: Rieter-Biedermann, [1868] (PS), [1869] (score); R xiv; Günter Graulich (Stuttgart: Carus, 1980). Ms: location unknown (ca. 1833–1834).

   1. Beati mortui.

   2. Periti autem.

Und ob du mich züchtigest (canon, 5 vv). Ms: D-B MN 20 (A; 24 December 1835), D-B N. Mus. ms. 5120 (A). See also under Canons, later.

Pater peccavi, Canone a 3 (3 vv). Ms: US-Wc (A; 7 August 1841, for F. Kistner). See also under Canons, later.

Venez et chantez ("Cantique pour l'Eglise wallone de Francfort") (4 vv). Ms: PL-Kj MN 41 (A; [1846]).

Die deutsche Liturgie (8vv). Edn: (nos. 1–3) *Musica sacra* 7 (Berlin: Bote & Bock, 1855); R xiv; Judith Silber (Stuttgart: Carus, 1997). Ms: PL-Kj MN 41 (A; 28 October 1846).

   Kyrie. Edn: Günter Graulich (Stuttgart: Carus, 1975).

   Heilig. Edn: Günter Graulich (Stuttgart: Carus, 1975).

   Ehre sei Gott in der Höhe. Edn: Günter Graulich (Stuttgart, 1975).

   [Unpublished:]

   Responses.

   Amens.

Ehre sei dem Vater (dbl ch). Mss: GB-Ob MDM b.5 (dr; ?1844), PL-Kj MN 40 (A; 17 January 1844), PL-Kj MN 40 (A; 2 March 1845), PL-Kj MN 40 (A; 5 March 1845), PL-Kj MN 40 (A [undated fair copy headed "Gloria patri (in canone)"]).

   Literature: David Brodbeck, "*Eine kleine Kirchenmusik*: A New Canon, A Revised Cadence, and an Obscure 'Coda' by Mendelssohn," *Journal of Musicology* 12 (1994), 179–205.

Six Anthems, Op. 79 [Sechs Sprüche] (dbl ch). Edn: Leipzig: Breitkopf & Härtel, [1849 (score and choral parts)], and London: Ewer, [1849 (score with piano reduction; words in English)]; R xiv/C.

   Rejoice, O Ye People [Frohlocket ihr Völker] ("Weihnachten"). Mss: PL-Kj MN 38² (A; 15 December 1843), PL-Kj MN 40 (A), location unknown (C—formerly MN 43).

   Thou, Lord, Our Refuge Hast Been [Herr Gott du bist unsre Zuflucht] ("Am Neujahrstage"). Mss: PL-Kj MN 38² (A; 25 December 1843), location unknown (C—formerly MN 43).

   Above All Praises [Erhaben o Herr über alles Lob] ("Am Himmelfahrtstage"). Mss: PL-Kj MN 41 (A; 9 October 1846), location unknown (C; based on 9 October 1846—formerly MN 43).

   Lord, on Our Offences [Herr gedenke nicht unsrer Uebelthaten] ("In der Passionszeit"). Mss: PL-Kj MN 39 (A; 14 February 1844), PL-Kj MN 40 (A), location unknown (C—formerly MN 43).

Let Our Hearts Be Joyful [Lasset uns frohlocken] ("Im Advent"). Mss: Pl-Kj MN 41 (A; 5 October 1846), location unknown (C; based on October 1846—formerly MN 43).

For Our Offenses [Um unsrer Sünden willen] ("Am Charfreitag"). Mss: PL-Kj MN 39 (A; 18 February 1844), location unknown (C—formerly MN 43).

Literature: David Brodbeck, "A Winter of Discontent: Mendelssohn and the *Berliner Domchor*," in *Mendelssohn Studies*, ed. R. Larry Todd (Cambridge: Cambridge University Press, 1992), 1–32.

Gott fürchten ist die Weisheit (canon for 4 vv). Ms: D-B N.Mus.ms. 341 (A; 24 January 1847). See also under Canons, later.

Undated:

In secula seculorem amen. Ms: GB-Ob MDM c.43 (A).

Literature: Wehner, *Studien*.

ARRANGEMENTS AND EDITIONS OF OTHER COMPOSERS' WORKS

General Literature: Rudolf Elvers, "Verzeichnis der von Felix Mendelssohn Bartholdy herausgegebenen Werke Johann Sebastian Bachs," in *Gestalt und Glaube: Festschrift für Vizepräsident Professor Dr. Oskar Söhngen zum 60. Geburtstag am 5. Dezember 1960* (Witten: Luther-Verlag, 1960), 145–49.

Bayerischer Walzer aus Bamberg (pf). Ms: location unknown (A; ca. 1830—auctioned by Hans Schneider, 1979).

Sechs Schottische National-Lieder, gesungen von Mad. Alfred Shaw in den Concerten zu Leipzig (S, pf). Edn: Leipzig: Kistner, 1839; repr. with commentary by Rudolf Elvers, Leipzig: Deutscher Verlag für Musik, 1977. Ms: location unknown.

Works by J. S. Bach:

Partita no. 3 in E major for unaccompanied violin, BWV 1006: Preludio. Ms: D-Bh (vn, pf).

Partita no. 2 in D minor for unaccompanied violin, BWV 1004: Chaconne. Edn: London: Ewer, 1847 (vn, pf).

Literature: John Michael Cooper, "Felix Mendelssohn Bartholdy, Ferdinand David und Sebastian Bach: Mendelssohns Bach-Auffassung im Spiegel der Wiederentdeckung der 'Chaconne,'" *Mendelssohn-Studien* 10 (1997), 157–80.

Orchestral Suite no. 3 in D major, BWV 1068 (orch). Edn: Leipzig: B. Senff, and London: Ewer, [1866?] (edition of BWV 1068 by Ferdinand David, "die Clarinetten und die drei Trompeten arrangirt von Felix Mendelssohn Bartholdy"). Ms: GB-Ob MDM c.22 (wind parts—A).

Gottes Zeit ist die allerbeste Zeit, BWV 106. Ms: US-Wc Whittall (parts for cl, bsn—A).

St. Matthew Passion, BWV 244. Ms: GB-Ob MDM c.68 (C by Eduard Rietz, with cuts, annotations, and alterations by Mendelssohn; [1829]), GB-Ob

MDM b.8 (parts for strings and choruses—C/A; [1829]), GB-Ob MDM b.9 (parts—C/A; [1829]), GB-Ob Mus. d.210 (parts—C/A; [1829]), location unknown ("Blute nur du liebes Herz," "Aus Liebe will mein Heiland sterben," "Erbarme dich mein Gott"—A; Palm Sunday 1841; auctioned by Sotheby's, 1959).

Literature: For a detailed description of the manuscripts documenting Mendelssohn's arrangement of BWV 244 for the Berlin 1829 performances, see Margaret Crum, *Catalogue of the Mendelssohn Papers in the Bodleian Library, Oxford, Vol. II: Music and Papers* (Tutzing: Hans Schneider, 1983), 30–32. See also Martin Geck, *Die Wiederentdeckung der Matthäuspassion im 19. Jahrhunderts: Die zeitgenossischen Dokumente und ihre ideengeschichtliche Deutung* (Regensburg: Bosse, 1967); Barbara David Wright, "Johann Sebastian Bach's 'Matthäus-Passion': A Performance History 1829–1854 (Ph.D. diss., University of Michigan, 1983); Michael Marissen, "Religious Aims in Mendelssohn's 1829 Berlin-Singakademie Performances of Bach's *St. Matthew Passion*," *The Musical Quarterly* 77 ((1993), 718–26.

Work by Ludwig van Beethoven[29]:

Piano Sonata in A♭, Op. 26:, third movement (*Marcia funebre*)." Ms: F-Pc Ms. 194 (orch—A inc).

Work by Luigi Cherubini:

Overture to *Les deux journées* [*Der Wasserträger*] (orch). Ms: GB-Ob MDM c.51 (pf 4 hands—A; 9 January 1837).

Work by Domenico Cimarosa:

Terzetto ("Le faccio un inchino") from *Il matrimonio segreto* (orch). Ms: PL-Kj 42 (A).

Remarks: Orchestrated for the Leipzig Gewandhaus Orchestra; performed in second "Historisches Konzert" of 1846–1847 season (see Alfred Dörffel, *Geschichte der Gewandhausconcerte zu Leipzig von 25. November 1781 bis 25. November 1881* [Leipzig: Gewandhaus, 1884], 115).

Works by George Frideric Handel:

Solomon. Ms: D-B MN 28 (organ part).

Literature: Karl Gustav Fellerer, "Mendelssohns Orgelstimmen zu Händelschen Werken," *Händel-Jahrbuch* 4 (1931), 79–97.

Israel in Egypt. Mss: D-B MN 28 (organ part), D-B MA Ms. 8 (organ part), D-DÜhi MS 69.2082 (timpani part, used in September 1833), US-NYp JOB 72-13 [DREXEL] (organ part for "The Lord Is a Man of War"—A), GB-Ob Deneke 72 (org part for part 1—A, and complete organ part—C/A), GB-Ob Deneke 3 (Arnold edn., with A additions and changes, "bezeichnet zur Aufführung in der Pauliner Kirche zu Leipzig, 7 Nov. 1836").

Dettingen Te Deum. Mss: D-B N.Mus.ms. 9035 (formerly MN 52), GB-Ob MDM b.5 (organ part—C/A).

Messiah [Messias]. Ms: PL-Kj MN 38² (organ part for "For unto Us" and "Hallelujah" chorus).

Work by Ignaz Moscheles:

   Septet in D major, Op. 88 (vn, va, cl/vn, hn/va, vc, db, pf). Ms: D-B MA Ms. 9 (pf 4 hands—A; August 1833).

Works by Wolfgang Amadeus Mozart:

   Concerto in E♭ for Two Pianos, K. 265, cadenza. Ms: location unknown (auctioned by Christie's, London, 1977—A; 1 June 1832).

   Symphony no. 41 in C major, K. 551 ("Jupiter"), first movement. Ms: D-B MN 2 (pf 4 hands—A).

CANONS

General literature: Ralf Wehner, "'. . . ich zeigte Mendelssohns Albumblatt vor und Alles war gut": Zur Bedeutung der Stammbucheintragungen und Albumblätter von Felix Mendelssohn Bartholdy," in *Felix Mendelssohn Bartholdy: Kongreß-Bericht Berlin 1994*, ed. Christian Martin Schmidt (Wiesbaden: Breitkopf & Härtel, 1997), 37–63.

Canon on theme from Mozart's Symphony no. 41 in C major, K. 551 ("Jupiter"), fourth movement. Ms: US-NYp (A; 4 November 1821, for Eduard Rietz in letter to Mendelssohn's family).

Canon in A (3 pts). Ms: D-B private collection (A; 13 May 1825, for Sigismund Neukomm).

Canon (3 pts). Ms: D-B MA Ms. 63 (A; 16 September 1826).

Kurzgefasste Übersicht des canonischen Rechts (3 vn). Ms: location unknown (A; 6 February 1827, for Heinrich Romberg; sold at auction on 10–11 June 1927 by Leo Liepmannssohn, Berlin).

Canon in B minor (3 pts with bass). Mss: D-KN Stadtarchiv (A; 27 September 1827, for Ferdinand Hiller; facsimile in Reinhold Sietz, "Beiträge zur rheinischen Musikgeschichte des 19. Jahrhunderts, III: Felix Mendelssohn und Ferdinand Hiller," *Jahrbuch des Kölnischen Gesschichtsvereins* 41 [1967], facing p. 100), D-Zsch Ms. 4414-A1 (A; 19 May 1830), A-Wst MH 4691 (A; 13 September 1830), A-Wst (A; 3 November 1831), D private collection (A; 22 March 1832), location unknown (A; 16 April 1832, for F. Chopin; facsimile in L. L. Binental, *Chopin: Dokumente und Erinnerungen aus seiner Heimatstadt* [Leipzig: Breitkopf & Härtel, 1932]), GB-Lbl Add. ms. 35.026 (A; 7 September 1837, for Eliza Wesley; facsimile in Suppl. to *The Musical Standard* 22 March 1902), D-B N.Mus.ms. 147 (A; 7 September 1839, for Bernhard Müller), D-B MN 60 (A; 8 September 1839—bass omitted), location unknown (A; 8 July 1844).

Canon (3 pts). Ms: location unknown (A; 9 April 1829, for Henriette Sontag; sold at auction on 6–7 June 1978 by J. A. Stargardt, Marburg).

Canon in C minor on theme from Beethoven, Piano Concerto no. 3, first movement (3 pts and bass). Mss: D-B MN 20 (A; [1830–1831]), D-Dlb (A; 28 February 1837, for O. Böhme—2 canonic parts and bass), D-B MA Ms. 94 (A).

Canon in G (2 va). Ms: GB-Ob MDM c.22 [4ʳ] (A; ca. 1830).

Canon in E♭ (2 va). Mss: GB-Ob MDM c.22 [4ʳ] (A; ca. 1830), US-NYpm Morgan (A; 26 June 1831, in letter to Sir George Smart).

"Wohl ihm" (4 vv). Ms: location unknown (A; 30 May 1832, for Ignaz Moscheles).

"Der weise Diogenes," Canon (TTBB). Mss: D-B MN 28 (in G major—A; 11 February 1833; facsimile in supplement to *Die Musik* 8/2 [1908–1909]), D-B N.Mus.ms. 100 (in A major—A). See also under part-songs, earlier.

"Denn ach sie sind Philister." Ms: D-B MA Nachl. 7; 30, 1 [no. 14], 50–54 (A; in letter to Franz Hauser).

  Literature: See Wehner, "'. . . ich zeigte Mendelssohns Albumblatt," 36.

Canon (3 pts) [text by Gustav Nauenberg]. Mss: F-Pc Ms. 216 (A; 11 April 1833), location unknown (A; 11 April 1833, for Gustav Nauenberg; sold at auction 29 May 1911 by Charavay, Paris—see Rudolf Elvers, "Verlorengegangene Selbstverständlichkeiten: zum Mendelssohn-Artikel in *The New Grove*," in *Festschrift Heinz Becker zum 60. Geburtstag*, ed. Jürgen Schlader and Reinhold Quandt [Laaber: Laaber, 1982], 420).

Canon in B minor (3 pts). Mss: location unknown (A; 16 December 1835, for Carl Künzel), location unknown (A; 2 February 1836; facsimile in Emil Michelman, *Carl Künzel: Ein Sammler-Genie aus dem Schwabenland* [Stuttgart: Cotta, 1938], Tafel XIII), D-B MA Ep. 110 (A; P.S. from Mendelssohn in letter from Cécile Mendelssohn Bartholdy to Fanny Hensel; Fanny's solution in letter to Mendelssohn dated 31 July 1837, reprinted in Citron, *The Letters*, 534–35), D-B N.Mus.ms. 44 (A; 17 September 1837, for Charles Wooloton), location unknown (A; 14 January 1842—auctioned by Sotheby's on 17 May 1990), location unknown (A; 11 July 1842, for Charlotte Moscheles; offered at auction 15 May 1960 by J. A. Stargardt, Marpurg; facsimile in Felix Moscheles, ed., *Letters of Felix Mendelssohn to Ignaz and Charlotte Moscheles* [Boston: Ticknor, 1888], 225), I-Mt Ms. Mus. 197 (A; 20 April 1846; facsimile and solution in Pietro Zappalà, "Autografi mendelssohniani a Milano," in *Musica e Cultura* 2 [1988], 98).

"Und ob du mich züchtigst, Herr" (canon for 5 vv). Mss: D-B MN 20 (A; 24 December 1835), D-B N.Mus.ms. 5120 (A). See also under a cappella sacred works unpublished or posthumously published, earlier.

Canon (3 pts). Ms: D-HVst Sammlung Harrys Sign. 4045 (A; 19 April 1836).

Canon (3 pts). Ms: GB private collection of heirs of William Sterndale Bennett (A; May 1836, under portrait by Theodor Hildebrand).

Canon. Ms: GB-LEmg (A; supplement to letter of 19 January 1837 to Ferdinand David).

Canon in C major (2 pts). Mss: GB-Ob MDM b.5 (skk), D-B MA Ep. 110 (A; 24 July 1837; 2nd P.S. by Mendelssohn in letter from Cécile Mendelssohn

Bartholdy to Fanny Hensel; Fanny's solution in letter to Mendelssohn dated 31 July 1837, reprinted in Citron, *The Letters*, 534–35), F-P Musée A. Mickiewicz Ms. 982 (A; 18 April 1846; facsimile in Józef Mirski, comp., *Maria Szymanowska (1789-1831) Album: Materialy biograficzne, sztambuchy, wybor kompozycji* [Kraków: Polskie Wydawn. muzyczne, 1953], 93).

Canon in B minor (2 pts). Mss: GB-Ob MDM g.4 fol. 40^v (A; 24 September 1837), GB-Ob MDM e.6 fol. 79 (A; 24 September [1837]), D-B MN 30 (A; 24 September 1837), D-B Album of Ferdinand Möhring, Mus.ms.autogr. S2 (A; 14 February 1840, solution by F. Möhring), GB-LEbc (A; 6 January 1841, pasted into score of *St. Paul*), US-Wc (C by W. T. Freemantle; 6 January 1841), location unknown (A; 25 January 1841, for Arthur Lutze, auctioned by J. A. Stargardt, 8 September 1982), D-B N.Mus.ms. 380 (A; 7 April 1841, for R. Lepsius [see Louise W. Leven, "An Unpublished Mendelssohn Manuscript," *The Musical Times* 89 [1948], 361–63]), D-LEmg (A, with solution in foreign hand; facsimile in Claudius Böhm and Sven-W. Staps, *Das Leipziger Stadt- und Gewandhaus Orchester: Dokumente einer 250jährigen Geschichte* [Leipzig: Verlag Kunst und Touristik Leipzig, 1993], 103), D-B (C, based on a score dated 23 December 1841), D-L Internationale Mendelssohn Stiftung (A; 4 July 1844; facsimile in *Top-Magazin Leipzig* 5 [1995], 22), I private collection (A; 8 July 1844, for Alfredo Piatti), A Salzburger Liedertafel (A; 5 September 1845, in Stammbuch Alois Taux; facsimile in Rudolf Angermüller, "Die Autographensammlung des Alois Taux," *Mitteilungen der Internationalen Stiftung Mozarteum* 37 [1989], 177–85), GB-Lbl MS Loan 79,4 (A, frag; 10 January 1846), US-STu no. 715 (A; 5 February 1846), location unknown (A; 19 January 1846—formerly Freemantle Collection), location unknown (A; 26 August 1846; facsimile in *The Autographic Mirror* 2 [1865], 179), location unknown (A; [late August] 1846; facsimile in *The Musical World* [19 August 1848], p. 534), GB-Ob MDM c.22 fol. 3^r (A).

Double Canon (4 pts). Mss: GB-Ob b.5 (sk, 3 pts), D-B MN 30 (A; ?ca. 1837–1838 [ed., solved by C. Hartford Lloyd, *Musical News*, 16 September 1892]), GB-Ob c.50 (C [MS of solution by C. Hartford Lloyd]), D-B MN 31 (A; ?ca. March–April 1839), F-Pc W. 8 (A; 4 December 1839, for A. Hesse), CH private collection (A; 29 July 1846, for Adolph Hesse).

Canon in C minor (2 pts with bass). Mss: D-B MN 19 (A dr), D-B MN 30 (A; January 1838), F-Pbc Ms. 213 (A; 10 February 1839), location unknown (A; 9 July 1839, for "Herrn Boyer"; see Sotheby's 29–30 April 1980, lot 399 [with date incorrectly given as 9 July 1829]), DK-KK (A; 11 November 1840, for Hans Christian Andersen), D-LE Gewandhaus Stammbuch C. Kuhlau (A; 16 April 1846), location unknown (A, for painter Kietz; facsimile in V. A. Heck-Katalog XXVI [Vienna, 1925], Tafel II).

"Ich danke Ihnen ergebenst" (canon, 2 pts). Ms: US-NYp *ZBT 164 (A; 8 March 1839, as note of thanks to F. Whistling).

"Wie lieblicher Klang" ("Lerchengesang"), Canon (4vv). Text: ? Mss: D-B MN
    31 (A; 15 June 1839), D-B N.Mus.ms. 16 (A; 19 June 1839; facsimile in Max
    Schneider, ed., *Felix Mendelssohn Bartholdy: Denkmal in Wort und Bild*
    [Basel: Amerbach, 1947], appendix).
          Remarks: Published as Op. 48 no. 4 (see earlier).
Canon. Ms: US-Wc (A; 11 December 1839, for A. Heyse).
Canon in B minor (3 pts and bass). Ms: D-DÜk (A; 26 May 1840).
Canon (2 pts). Ms: location unknown (A; 25 September 1840—see Maggs Bros.
    Kat. [January/February 1913], Nr. 500).
Canon in E♭. Ms: location unknown (A; 28 March 1841).
Canon in A minor (2 pts, for pf). Mss: PL-Kj MN 35 (A; 22 April 1841,
    composition score of canon intended for Victor Carus), location unknown (A;
    22 April 1841, [for Victor Carus] "zu freundlicher Erinnerung am
    Passionsmusiken, Hymnen an die Freude, Schlachtgesänge . . ."; auctioned by
    J. A. Stargardt on 29–30 November 1966), F-Pc Ms. 214 (A; 30 June 1846).
Canon. Ms: location unknown (A; 19 May 1841, ?for Julius Stern).
"Pater peccavi," (Canon, 3 vv). Ms: US-Wc (A; 7 August 1841, for F. Kistner).
    See also under A Cappella Sacred Works Unpublished or Posthumously
    Published, earlier.
Canon (2 pts). Mss: location unknown; formerly private collection of Eusebius
    Mandyczewski (A; 23 December 1841, for Leon Herz), D-B (C).
Canon in F♯ minor (2 pts). Mss: GB-Ob MDM b.5 fol. 32ʳ (A; 7 June 1842),
    location unknown (A; 25 September 1844; auctioned by J. A. Stargardt on
    23–24 May 1967; fascimile in Moscheles, 237), D-LEu (A; 2 November 1844,
    for Louise Lallemant; facsimile in Felix Mendelssohn Bartholdy, *Briefe aus
    Leipziger Archiven*, ed. H.-J. Rothe and R. Szeskus [Leipzig: Deutscher
    Verlag für Musik, 1972]), GB-Lbl Ms. Egerton 2955 (A; 6 May 1847).
Canon. Ms: location unknown (A; 7 July 1843).
Canon in B minor (3 pts). Ms: GB-Ob MDM c.22 [6ᵛ] (A; ?ca. 1844).
Etude pour I Violon ou Canon pour II Violons. Mss: GB-Ob MDM c.22 [6ᵛ] (A;
    ?ca. 1844), J-T Documentation Center of Modern Japanese Music (A; 11
    March 1844, for Joseph Joachim; facsimile in Otto Erich Deutsch, ed., *St.
    Cecilia's Album* [Cambridge: W. Heffer, 1944]).
Scherzo osia canone a 4. Ms: US private collection (A; 8 July 1844, possibly for
    Ignaz Moscheles).
Canon in E major. Ms: US-AUS (A; 9 July 1844).
"Die Nachtigall, sie war entfernt" ("Die Nachtigall"), Canon (4 vv). Ms: location
    unknown (A; 12 July 1845, for Frau A. von Woringen; facsimile in Ernst
    Wolff, *Felix Mendelssohn Bartholdy* [Berlin: Harmonie, 1906], facing p. 168).
    See Op. 59 no. 4, earlier.
Canon (3 pts). Ms: I-M Museo della Scala Ms. Mus. 197 (A; 20 April 1846;
    facsimile and solution in Zappalà, *Autografi*, 27ff., 98).
Canon (2 pts). Ms: location unknown (A; 29 April 1846).

Canon (2 pts). Ms: location unknown (A; 26 August 1846; facsimile in *The Autographic Mirror* [London and New York: Cassell, Petter, and Galpin, 1864], vol. 2).

Canon (2 pts). Ms: US-Wc (A; 2 September 1846, for A. de Chene de Vere).

"Gott fürchten ist die Weisheit" (canon for 4 vv). Ms: D-B N.Mus.ms. 341 (A; 24 January 1847). See also under a cappella sacred works unpublished or posthumously published, earlier.

Undated:

"Ach liebe Fanny verzeih, verzeih, daß ich so lang geschwiegen." Ms: CH private collection (A; in letter to Fanny, undated but probably from the 1820s).

 Literature: See Wehner, "'. . . ich zeigte Mendelssohns Albumblatt," 36.

Canon in F major (6 pts). Ms: D-B MA Depos. Berlin Ms. 5.

NOTES

 1. Most obvious here, of course, are the inventories published during the composer's lifetime, such as Adoph Julius Becher's "Vollständiges Verzeichniss der Compositionen von Dr. F. Mendelssohn-Bartholdy," *Orpheus-Almanach* 3 (1842), iii–viii.

 2. For example, around 1834 Mendelssohn prepared an inventory of published and unpublished works for Ignaz Moscheles, in which several erroneous opus numbers are given; for a facsimile, see Eckart Kleßmann, *Die Mendelssohns: Bilder aus einer deutschen Familie* (Zurich: Artemis, 1990), 121. The 1844 inventory is described in detail in Rudolf Elvers, "Felix Mendelssohn Bartholdys Nachlaß," in *Das Problem Mendelssohn*, ed. Carl Dahlhaus (Regensburg: Bosse, 1974), 42–43, and the "Musikalien" portion of this inventory is transcribed in Peter Ward Jones, *Catalogue of the Mendelssohn Papers in the Bodleian Library, Oxford*, vol. 3, *Printed Music and Books* (Tutzing: Hans Schneider, 1989), 283–302. For the published inventories, see the [Leipzig] *Allgemeine musikalische Zeitung* 34 (1837), 845ff.; Becher, "Vollständiges Verzeichniss"" (see n. 1); and the Breitkopf & Härtel *Verzeichnis im Druck erschienener Compositionen* (Leipzig, 1841).

 3. The first of these copies is held in the Mendelssohn-Archiv of the Staatsbibliothek zu Berlin—Preußischer Kulturbesitz, and the second, evidently later exemplar survives in the Bodleian Library, Oxford.

 4. George Grove, "Mendelssohn," in *Grove's Dictionary of Music and Musicians*, 1st ed. (London: Macmillan, 1887), ii: 253–310; rpt. with modifications in subsequent editions and in Grove, *Beethoven, Schubert and Mendelssohn* (London: Macmillan, 1951), 253–394; see also George Grove, "Mendelssohn's Oratorio 'St Paul,'" *The Musical Times* 50 (1909), 92–94; and the Preface to Sebastian Hensel, *The Mendelssohn Family*, trans. Karl Klingemann, 2d ed. (New York: Harper, 1882).

 5. Eric Werner, "Mendelssohn, Jakob Ludwig Felix," *Die Musik in Geschichte und Gegenwart*, ed. Friedrich Blume (Kassel: Bärenreiter, 1961), 9: cols. 59–98; Philip Radcliffe, *Mendelssohn* (London: J. M. Dent, 1954), 3d edn. rev. Peter Ward Jones, 1990); Rainer Riehn, "Werkverzeichnis," in *Felix Mendelssohn Bartholdy*, ed. Heinz-Klaus Metzger and Rainer Riehn, Musik-Konzepte 14/15 (Munich: text + kritik, 1980), 147–52; Eveline Bartlitz, work list in *The New Grove Dictionary of Music and Musicians*, ed. Stanley Sadie (London: Macmillan, 1980), 12: 152–56, rev. by R. Larry Todd in *The New Grove Early Romantic Masters 2*, ed. Stanley Sadie (New York: Macmillan, 1985), 270–83.

6. Hans-Günter Klein, "Verzeichnis der im Autograph überlieferten Werke Felix Mendelssohn Bartholdys im Besitz der Staatsbibliothek zu Berlin," *Mendelssohn-Studien* 10 (1997), 181–215.

7. Until 1992, the Deutsche Staatsbibliothek, East Berlin; now Haus 2 of the Staatsbibliothek zu Berlin—Preußischer Kulturbesitz (the former Staatsbibliothek Preußischer Kulturbesitz is now Haus 1). Since the holdings of the two branches have now been consolidated in the East Berlin branch of the library, this list refers to the branches under their single *RISM* siglum (D-B) or as the Berlin Staatsbibliothek.

8. For a personal communication conveniently summarizing the dispositions of the volumes on 31 March 1993, I am indebted to Dr. Hans-Günter Klein, Director of the Mendelssohn-Archiv of the Berlin Staatsbibliothek. Further information concerning the problems of the manuscripts is given in Rudolf Elvers, "Felix Mendelssohn Bartholdys Nachlaß," in Dahlhaus, *Das Problem Mendelssohn*, 35–46. See also Elvers, "Auf den Spuren der Autographen von Felix Mendelssohn Bartholdy," in *Beiträge zur Musikdokumentation: Festschrift Franz Grasberger zum 60. Geburtstag*, ed. Günter Brosche (Tutzing: Hans Schneider, 1975), 83–91.

9. These manuscripts, most of which are bound in green covers, are most easily recognized by the autograph contents inventories on their outer front covers or, as in volume 20, autograph title pages written on blank sheets of paper and inserted before groups of materials all dealing with a single work or a group of related compositions. In addition, the majority are accounted for in Mendelssohn's 1844 inventory of his *Musikalien* (see Peter Ward Jones, *Catalogue* [Tutzing: Hans Schneider, 1989], 283–302, esp. 291–93).

10. Most obvious among these are those volumes whose outer front cover bears a gilded Prussian eagle (the old seal of the former Royal Prussian Library); these volumes were obviously assembled at the time the volumes were being prepared for donation to the library.

11. Volume 16 (containing the *Meeresstille und glückliche Fahrt* Overture and the Overture to *Die Hochzeit des Camacho*) was never among the volumes contributed to the library; volume 24 (the C-minor Symphony, Op. 11) is today in GB-Ob MDM d.57; volume 43 was disassembled before 1877 and is represented in various individual autographs; and volume 52 (the arrangement of Handel's *Dettingen Te Deum* for Zelter and the Singakademie) now carries the shelfmark Mus.ms. 9035 in the Berlin Staatsbibliothek.

12. See the preface to Margaret Crum, *Catalogue of the Mendelssohn Papers in the Bodleian Library*, vol. 2, *Music and Papers* (Tutzing: Hans Schneider, 1980).

13. For descriptions of some of these collections, see Oswald Bill, "Unbekannte Mendelssohn-Handschriften in der Hessischen Landes- und Hochschulbibliothek Darmstadt," *Die Musikforschung* 26 (1973), 345–49; Peter Krause, *Autographen, Erstausgaben und Frühdrucke der Werke von Felix Mendelssohn Bartholdy in Leipziger Bibliotheken und Archiven* (Leipzig: Musikbibliothek der Stadt Leipzig, 1972); J. Rigbie Turner, *Music Manuscripts in the Pierpont Morgan Library: A Catalogue* (New York: Pierpont Morgan Library, 1988).

14. The customary ordering of published works according to date of conception is problematic in Mendelssohn's case because of the often far-reaching differences between the initial versions and those by which the works are known.

15. For the composition exercises, see R. Larry Todd, *Mendelssohn's Musical Education: A Study and Edition of His Exercises in Composition* (Cambridge: Cambridge University Press, 1983).

16. This is particularly true of *Albumblätter*. For example, although Rudolf Elvers was able to state in 1985 that there were fourteen such autographs for the Lied "Leise zieht durch mein Gemüt" (Op. 19[a], no. 5), most of these are not included in this list. See Rudolf Elvers, "Auf den Spuren der Autographen von Felix Mendelssohn Bartholdy," in *Beiträge zur Musikdokumentation: Festschrift Franz Grasberger zum 60. Geburtstag*, ed. Günter Brosche (Tutzing: Hans Schneider, 1975), 85.

17. For purposes of identification and correlation, when copies bear the date of the original autograph from which they were made, that date is given here in the entry for the copy as well as that of the autograph. When more precise information is available as to the date at which the copy was made, that information is provided as well.

18. See Rudolf Elvers, *"Nichts ist so schwer gut zu componiren als Strophen": Zur Entstehungsgeschichte des Librettos von Felix Mendelssohns Oper "Die Hochzeit des Camacho,"* mit dem Faksimile eines Briefes von Mendelssohn (Berlin: Mendelssohn-Gesellschaft, 1976), 12–15.

19. The pieces in the earliest volumes of the original *Mendelssohn Nachlaß* seldom carry specific dates. Since the etiquette on the front cover of MN 2 bears the autograph inscription "ang[efangen] Dec. 3. 1820," however, and since the compositions in the preceding volume that are dated were written in 1820, a date of [1820] has been ascribed to all works in the first volume.

20. Peter Ward Jones has perceptively suggested that this invocation might be an allusion to the horn motive that introduces and unifies the Schubert "Great" C-major Symphony, which Mendelssohn premiered in Leipzig in 1839. See Peter Ward Jones, review of R. Larry Todd, *Mendelssohn and His World* (Princeton: Princeton University Press, 1991); *Music and Letters* 74 (1993), 97–99. More recently, Christoph Hellmundt has pointed out that some material of the *Lobgesang* was adapted from the *Festgesang* ("Möge das Siegeszeichen") of 1838; see later.

21. Autograph in Staatsbibliothek zu Berlin—Preußischer Kulturbesitz (shelfmark MA Ms. 3), dated 24 August 1825. See Klein, *Die Kompositionen Fanny Hensels in Autographen und Abschriften aus dem Besitz der Staatsbibliothek zu Berlin—Preussischer Kulturbesitz* (Tutzing: Hans Schneider, 1995), 54.

22. Autograph held in the Mendelssohn-Archiv of the Berlin Staatsbibliothek (shelfmark MA Ms. 35) and dated 28 April [1825].

23. The pseudonym "H. Voss" may refer either to Mendelssohn himself or to Johann Gustav Droysen. Sebastian Hensel reports unequivocally that Mendelssohn wrote the text and music for Op. 9 no. 1; see *The Mendelssohn Family*, 133. Gustav Droysen claims that his father was the author of this text as well as several others in Op. 9; see "Johann Gustav Droysen and Felix Mendelssohn-Bartholdy," *Deutsche Rundschau* 111 (1902), 194–95. Rudolf Elvers concurs with Droysen in his article "Verlorengegangene Selbstverständlichkeiten: Zum Mendelssohn-Artikel in *The New Grove*," in *Festschrift Heinz Becker zum 60. Geburtstag am 26. Juni 1982*, ed. Jürgen Schläder and Reinhold Quandt (Laaber: Laaber, 1982), 417–21.

24. The autograph is contained in D-B MS. MA Depos. Lohs 2,1 and dated 24 July 1828.

25. The autograph is contained in D-B MA Depos. Lohs 2,14 and dated 28 December 1827.

26. The autograph is held in D-B MA (Ms. 32) and is dated 22 August [1822].

27. Earlier in the same year Mendelssohn had composed the Piano Quartet in D minor (see unpublished and posthumously published chamber works, later).

28. Facsimile of copy given by Thérèse Devrient in A. J. Hipkins, ed., *The International Exhibition for Music and the Drama* (Vienna: M. Perles, 1893), 119.

29. See also under Canons, later.

Index

About the Contributors

LEON BOTSTEIN is President of Bard College, Musical Director of the American Symphony Orchestra, and Editor of *The Musical Qaurterly*.

JOHN MICHAEL COOPER is Assistant Professor of Music at the University of North Texas.

GEORG FEDER was the director of the Joseph Haydn-Institut, Cologne, Germany, from 1960 to 1990.

THOMAS GREY is Associate Professor and Chairman of the Music Department at Stanford University.

MARIAN WILSON KIMBER is Associate Professor of Music at the University of Southern Mississippi.

FRIEDHELM KRUMMACHER holds the Chair of Musicology at the Christian-Albrechts-Universität in Kiel, Germany.

ROBERT C. MANN is Professor of Music at Stephen F. Austin State University in Texas.

DONALD MINTZ is Professor of Music at Montclair State University in New Jersey.

DOUGLASS SEATON is Professor of Music History and Musicology at The Florida State University.

R. LARRY TODD is Professor and Chair of the Music Department, Duke University.